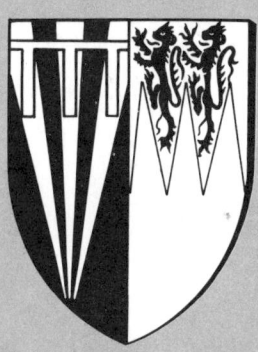

eagles, are often borne in pairs. *Gules, three eagle's wings or,* is the coat ascribed to Sir WALTER BAND in the *Roll* of EDWARD II. (Their frequent use in German crests will be referred to later on.) When the wings are thus conjoined they are often termed a *vol,* and when the points are turned downwards this is styled *un vol abaissé,* or the wings are said to be *conjoined in lure* (that is, after the fashion of the instrument used by falconers to lure the hawk back after its flight). The coat of the SEYMOURS, Dukes of SOMERSET is: *Gules, two wings conjoined in lure, the tips downward,* or *(de Gueules, à un vol abaissé d'or).* Plate XXV., fig. 5. A single wing is often termed a *demi-vol. Gules, a demi-vol abaissé argent,* is the coat of the Princes of BEVILACQUA of Italy. (*See* USENBERG, p. 490.) *Argent, two demi-vols addorsed sable,* is borne by the Prussian Barons von KÖNIG.

Per chevron argent and gules, three demi-vols erect counter-changed, was used by the important family of the Counts von ORTENBURG in Carinthia.

EAGLE'S LEGS are also borne, couped, or erased at the thigh. Of these a single example may suffice:—the Marquis d'ARCHIAC in France, bore: *Or, two eagle's legs couped at the thigh in pale gules.* (SEGOING, *Armorial Universel:* planche 24. Paris, 1679.)

Among the curiosities of Heraldry we may number the coat of the Danish family of STIXEN, now extinct, which was: *Azure, an eagle displayed, without a head or.* The family of SCHAD in Wurtemberg bore: *Or, an eagle displayed, without feet, and having a ribbon tied about its neck or.* The STÄHLIN VON STORKSBURG, in Bavaria carried: *Azure, an eagle displayed or, its head concealed by a tilting helm argent.*

The Norman family of SACQUEVILLE, or SACQUINVILLE, used, *d'Hermine, à l'aigle pamée de gueules,* that is, with drooping wings and head and open beak. The *Wappenrolle von Zürich* gives (No. 503) a curious example

supra) differenced this coat by charging the cross with *five escallops argent*. (*See* Chapter XIV., p. 452.)

When two or more eagles are borne in a shield they are sometimes, but quite needlessly, blazoned *eaglets;* but even the heraldic purists who insist on this distinction admit that it need not be made when the birds are separated by an Ordinary. Thus: *Azure, a pale between two eagles displayed argent*, is the coat of WOODWARD, of Warwickshire and the neighbouring counties. *Argent, a saltire gules between four eagles displayed azure*, is used by HOBART, Earls of BUCKINGHAMSHIRE. The great Italian house of the GONZAGAS, Dukes of MANTUA, bore: *Argent, a cross patée-throughout gules, between four eagles displayed sable* (*vide* p. 535).

Except as a crest, or supporter, the eagle of heraldry seldom appears in any other attitude than *displayed*. An eagle *volant, i.e.*, flying bendways across the shield, occurs in the armorials as the coat of STAYLTON or STALTON;—*Sable, an eagle volant argent*, but I do not remember any other example.

An eagle *rising*, that is in the act of taking flight (in French *essorant*), is almost equally rare. The French family of SAFFRES, bear the canting coat; *de Gueules, à cinq saffres, ou aigles de mer, essorants d'argent*, 2, 1, 2.

The founder of the French Empire deviated from the mediæval idea of the imperial bird, in favour of the pre-heraldic and classical type. The arms of the Napoleonic Empire are:—*Azure, an eagle rising* (its head turned to the sinister); *grasping in both claws a thunderbolt or*. (Plate XXV., fig. 3.) The official blazon of this coat was simply: *d'Azur, à l'aigle d'or, empiétant un foudre du même*. (SIMON, *l'Armorial Général de l'Empire Français*, tome i., page 1. Paris, 1812.)

Parts of eagles occur not unfrequently in armory; MONRO of Foulis bears: *Or, an eagle's head erased gules*. (Plate XXV., fig. 4.) WINGS, presumed to be those of

coat is often borne by the chief line *en surtout* above the quartered coats of 1. ANJOU-NAPLES; 2. SICILY; 3. LAVAL; 4. BOURBON-CONDÉ; as representing CHARLOTTE of ARRAGON, wife of GUY, Comte de LAVAL (*vide infra*, p. 452).] The famous CHARLOTTE DE LA TRÉMOILLE, Countess of DERBY (d. 1664), was daughter of CLAUDE, Prince de TALMONT, etc., by CHARLOTTE, daughter of WILLIAM, Prince of ORANGE (*v. i.,* p. 466). In Scotland the eagle displayed occurs at an early date. The RAMSAYS bore: *Argent, an eagle displayed sable, beaked and membered gules.* The CARNEGIES, now Earls of SOUTHESK, used: *Or, an eagle displayed azure, beaked and membered gules* now *charged on the breast with a covered cup of the field.* But early seals of this family show the eagle standing on a barrel, which was allusive to their tenure of the estate of KINNAIRD "for the serwise of the kepeing of the Kyngis ale sellar within the Schirefdome of Forfar" (STODART, *Scottish Arms*,ii.,pp. 137-138). *Argent, three eagles displayed gules, crowned or,* is the coat of the DE COURCYS, Barons of KINGSALE, in Ireland.

The *allerion* (in French *alérion*), originally synonymous with an eagle, was in the hands of some fanciful heralds, deprived of its legs and beak, as in the arms of the House of LORRAINE still quartered by the Emperors of AUSTRIA:— *Or, on a bend gules three allerions argent.* The myth which refers the origin of this coat to a fowling exploit in Crusading days is too absurd for further quotation. The charges are really anagrams (alerion) of the name LORAINE (*see* PLANCHÉ, *Pursuivant*, pp. 86-91).

The coat of the great French family DE MONTMORENCY is still blazoned with *allerions* instead of the original four eagles: *d'Or, à la croix de gueules cantonné de seize alérions d'azur.* The MONTMORENCY-LAVAL (*vide*

the great Scottish house of LINDSAY, Earls of CRAWFORD, etc., derives its origin, bore: *Gules, an eagle displayed or*, which was also the bearing of the families of RYE, Marquess de VARAMBON; VIENNE; FERRONAY (banneret of Touraine), etc. *Or, an eagle displayed azure*, the coat of the PRIGNANI, was borne by Pope URBAN VI.

The French family of COLIGNY (Ducs de CHÂTILLION, Marquesses d'ANDELOT, etc.), used: *Gules, an eagle displayed argent, crowned or.* In England in early times the eagle was only borne by a very few families of distinction. RALPH DE MONTHERMER, Earl of GLOUCESTER in right of his wife, bore (as in Plate XXV., fig. 1), *Or, an eagle displayed vert*, arms which were afterwards quartered with those of MONTACUTE in the shields of the Earls of SALISBURY and WARWICK. The notorious PIERS GAVESTON, created Earl of CORNWALL by EDWARD II., bore: *Vert, six eagles displayed or.*

The Eagle appears in the coat of QUEEN'S COLLEGE, OXFORD, which are those of its founder ROBERT DE EFLESFELD, confessor to PHILIPPA, Queen of EDWARD III.:—*Argent, three eagles displayed gules armed or.* It will be seen from the foregoing examples that the heraldic eagle has usually its beak and claws (sometimes the beak, legs, and claws) of a different tincture from the rest of its body. In the first case it is sufficient to use the phrase *armed*, which includes beak as well as claws: in the latter case the term employed is usually *beaked and membered* (in French *becquée et membrée*), the legs including the claws. In the Armory of Germany and the Low Countries the whole unfeathered part of the leg is intended when the term *armed* is used.

The arms of the great French family DE LA TRÉMOILLE (Vicomtes and Ducs de THOUARS, Ducs de la TRÉMOILLE, Princes de TALMONT, et de TARENTE, etc.), are: *d'Or, au chevron de gueules accompagné de trois aigles d'azur, becquées et membrées du second.* [This

The arms of the Markgravate of MAHREN, or MORAVIA, in the Austrian *Écu complet* are: *Azure, an eagle displayed chequy argent and gules crowned or* (p. 496). The Duchy of WESTPHALIA (one of the Saxon and Anhalt quarterings) bears: *Azure, an eagle displayed, crowned or;* and the same coat (but often with the crown omitted) is used for the Palatinate of SAXONY. *Azure, an eagle displayed argent,* is the coat of the Counties of ARENSBERG, and MÜHLINGEN ; and, with a golden crown, of the House of ESTE, from which our own Royal Family derives its descent, and of which the Dukes of MODENA are the chief representatives (p. 508). The arms of the Duchy of CARNIOLA, or CRAYN, are given at p. 495, *infra*. The famous Genoese family of DORIA bore : *Per fess or and argent, an eagle displayed sable.*

The Princes of LOBKOWITZ quartered with their own arms (*Per fess gules and argent,* the coat of the house of ZEROTIN): *Argent, an eagle displayed in bend sable, crowned or, and charged on the breast with an eagle of the field.* A parallel coat to this curious blazon is recorded in the *Wappenrolle von Zürich*, No. 115, where *Argent, an eagle displayed in bend gules* is the coat of SCHÖNEN. The Marquises of FAGNANI in Italy also bear : *Azure, an eagle in bend argent.*

The Counts of SAARWERDEN used : *Sable, a double-headed eagle displayed argent;* a coat which appears in the escucheon of the Dukes of NASSAU.

Gules, an eagle displayed chequy sable and or, is the coat borne by Popes INNOCENT III., GREGORY IX., and ALEXANDER IV. of the family of SIGNIA at Agnani.

Per bend argent and gules, an eagle counter-changed, is the coat of the Italian family of SECCANO ; and, with the tinctures *azure* and *argent,* of the Venetian LOMBARDI.

The family of DE LIMESAY in Normandy, from which

eagle. Later on, since the union of Lithuania to Poland in 1385, the arms were quartered with the following coat: *Gules, a knight mounted on a white horse, and bearing on his buckler azure a cross patriarchal or*, for LITHUANIA.

The arms of the imperial city of FRANKFURT are identical with those of POLAND.

The arms of the Markgravate of BRANDENBURG, which was given in pledge by the Emperor SIGISMUND to FREDERICH of HOHENZOLLERN, Burg-grave of Nürnberg in 1417, and which became the foundation of the splendid fortunes of the present Imperial German dynasty, were: *Argent, an eagle displayed gules with "klee stengeln" on its wings or, and armed of the last.* (In silbernem Felde ein aus gebreiteter rother Adler mit goldenem Schnabel, und goldenen Füssen. Die beiden Flügel des Adlers sind jeder mit einem goldenen Kleestengel belegt.) (For *Klee-Stengel*, see note, p. 344.)

As might be expected, both the *sable* single-headed eagle of the German kingdom, and the double-headed eagle of the Holy Roman Empire, enter with great frequency into the armorial bearings of the Princes, provinces, and cities of the Empire. A large and interesting volume might easily be written which should deal exclusively with the Heraldry of the Eagle. It is not possible in our limited space to do more than allude to a few of the most important examples.

The coat of the Duchy of SILESIA is: *Or, an eagle displayed sable, crowned (and often armed) of the field; on its breast and wings a crescent with a cross between its horns argent.* The Dukes of GLOGAU bore the same without the cross. (Plate XLVI.)

The County of TIROL bears: *Argent, an eagle displayed gules crowned, armed, and with " klee-stengeln " or.* (Im silbernem Felde ein rother ausgebreiteter gekrönter Adler mit goldenem Schnabel und Füssen, und goldenen Klee-stengeln auf den Flügeln.)

in a lozenge, upon the seal of ISABEL DE ST. VRAIN in 1262. (DEMAY, *Le Costume d'après les Sceaux*, p. 229.) On the magnificent encaustic pavement of the church of Saint Pierre de Dive, in Calvados, which is probably of the early part of the thirteenth century, the double-headed eagle displayed occurs with very great frequency. (This pavement is engraved in DE CAUMONT, *Abécédaire d'Archéologie*, pp. 384-386.) *Argent, a double-headed eagle displayed sable, over all a cotice gules*, was the coat worn by the celebrated BERTRAND DU GUESCLIN, Constable of France (d. 1380). The Marechal de BOUCIQUAUT bore a like eagle, though his arms are differently tinctured; they are:—*d'Argent, à l'aigle éployée de gueules, armée d'or* (See the *Armorial de l'Héraut Gelre*). The double-headed eagle occasionally occurs in English Heraldry, as in the coat of SPEKE, of Jordans, *Barry of eight argent and azure, a double-headed eagle displayed gules* (Plate XXV., fig. 2).

The consideration of the use of the Imperial Eagle as an augmentation may be fitly deferred to the special Chapter on AUGMENTATIONS.

The Eagle now borne for the German Empire is single-headed, of *sable*, armed and langued *gules*. Over its head is placed the crown of CHARLEMAGNE (fig. 97, p. 617). Upon its breast is an escucheon which contains the personal arms of the Emperor, viz., the Royal Arms of PRUSSIA :—*Argent, an eagle displayed sable crowned, and with* klee-stengel *or, armed gules, holding in its dexter claw the Royal sceptre, and in the sinister the Royal Orb, on its breast a small escucheon of the arms of the House of* HOHENZOLLERN, viz., *Quarterly argent and sable* (Ein von Silber und Schwartz quadrirter Schild).

The arms of the Kingdom of POLAND are : *Gules, an eagle displayed argent crowned or.* This appears as early as the year 1255, on the seal of King BOLESLAS, where the shield borne by the royal knight is charged with the

Heiligenscheine. (The double-headed eagle, thus adorned, also appears on the counter seal with an inscription allusive to EZEKIEL xvii. 3 and 7. See ROEMER BÜCHNER, *Siegel,* etc., No. 73.)

After the adoption of the double-headed eagle as the arms of the Empire, the single-headed eagle displayed became the distinctive possession of the King of the Romans; the second head being added on his attainment of the Imperial Crown. See among other examples the fine counter-seal of MAXIMILIAN, as King of the Romans, in VRÉE, *Die Seghelen der Graven van Vlaendren,* plate xlvi., Bruges, 1640. Here the single-headed eagle with the *Heiligenscheine* is the charge of his shield, and bears on its breast a small escucheon of AUSTRIA, impaling BURGUNDY-ancient (apparently *sans bordure*). But on MAXIMILIAN'S signet (*Ibid.,* No. 56) after his attainment of the Imperial dignity the eagle (which bears the correct impalement) is double-headed.

On the *Aurea Bulla* of CHARLES VI. (1711-1740) the *Heiligenscheine* is converted into a flat circular plate. It is only on the seal of CHARLES VII. (1740-1745) that the sword and sceptre both appear in the dexter claw, and the orb in the sinister, of the Imperial eagle.

The first instance of a Great Seal in which the Imperial Eagle is represented bearing on its breast the escucheon of the personal bearings of the Emperor, is that of CHARLES V. (ROEMER BÜCHNER, *Die Siegel,* etc., No. 88); on this the arms of the Spanish kingdoms are represented crowned. Many of CHARLES'S seals have this escucheon uncrowned (*See* VRÉE, *Die Seghelen de Graven van Vlaendren,* plates lxii., etc.). On one Seal, as Duke of BURGUNDY, Plate lxii., his escucheon is of AUSTRIA-modern only. The coats of CASTILE impaling LEON are sometimes similarly used alone.

As a heraldic charge, apart from any connection with the Empire, we find the double-headed eagle displayed

PARIS, *circa* 1250, now preserved in the British Museum, this eagle occurs unmistakably for the Emperor of Germany. In the *Roll of Arms of the Thirteenth Century*, probably written about 1280, its first and third entries are:—I. L'Empereur d'Almaine ; d'or a ung aigle espany ove des deux têtes sable. III. Le Roy d'Almaine, d'or un egle displaye sable. (*Archæologia*, xxxix., p. 378.) In the *Wappenrolle von Zürich*, if No. 12 be (as seems pretty certain), the shield of the Empire, the eagle is still single-headed.

The earliest use of the double-headed eagle on an Imperial seal with which I am acquainted is afforded by a counter-seal of the Emperor WENZESLAUS (King of BOHEMIA, elected King of the Romans, and crowned at Aachen in 1376, but deposed in 1400). On this counter-seal the double-headed eagle bears on its breast a round escucheon charged with the Bohemian lion. But on this Dr ROEMER BÜCHNER makes the following remark :—

"Irrig ist es wenn dieses Contrasiegel als doppelter Reichsadler angesehen wird, schon als böhmischer König führte er solches, daher kein Reichswappen, wahrscheinlich sind die Adler von Brandenburg und Schlesien hier vereint." (*Die Siegel der deutschen Kaiser*, etc., No. 64 Frankfurt am Main, 1851.) On the Great Seal itself of WENZESLAUS the Emperor is seated between two shields, the dexter one charged with the single eagle displayed, the arms of the King of the Romans ; the sinister bearing the double-tailed lion of BOHEMIA. If this view be correct, as an undoubted emblem of the Holy Roman Empire the double-headed eagle first occurs (so far as seals are concerned) on that of the Emperor SIGISMUND (son of CHARLES IV., King of HUNGARY and BOHEMIA, crowned at Aachen in 1414, and as Emperor at Rome in 1434, died in 1437). Here, for the first time, the armorial shield is charged with the double-headed eagle, of which the heads are "diademed" or surrounded by the golden

STANTINE XIV. It appears first on a seal appended to a charter of 1497. (*See* KOEHNE, *Notice sur les Sceaux et Armoiries de la Russie*, pp. 8, 9, Berlin, 1861.) STEPHEN NÉMANJA, Czar of SERVIA and BOSNIA, had long previously assumed the double eagle of Byzantium (but silver instead of gold, on a shield *gules*); and used it, crowned with an eastern crown, as the crest of his crowned helm. (See the account of *The Book of Arms of the Nobility of Bosnia, or Illyria, and Servia,* etc., in the year 1340, given in EVANS' tour *Through Bosnia and the Herzegovina, in* 1875, pp. 214-225.)

The double-headed eagle displayed was borne, with variations of tincture and accessories, by several of the great Byzantian families: KORESSIOS bore: *Sable, beneath the Imperial crown proper, a double-headed eagle displayed or, holding in each of its claws a sword paleways argent.* VATATZES used: *Vert, the double eagle displayed or, above each of its heads an estoile argent.* LASCARIS bore: *Or, a double-headed eagle displayed sable armed gules, beneath an Eastern crown of three points of the last.*

Although, as we have seen, the assumption of the double-headed eagle displayed as the arms of the Holy Roman Empire has been commonly attributed to the Emperor SIGISMUND, it is quite clear that it had been in use at an earlier date. It appears, I think not for the first time, on the coins of the Emperor LOUIS THE BAVARIAN in 1314. The seals of his sons, Duke WILLIAM of BAVARIA, Count of OSTREVANT, and ALBERT, Count PALATINE of the RHINE, *circa* 1350, bear the shield of their arms (Quarterly, 1 and 4, BAVARIA; 2 and 3, FLANDERS quartering HOLLAND, *vide* p. 462), upon the breast of a double-headed eagle displayed. (VRÉE, *Généalogie des Comtes de Flandres*, plate lix.) Earlier instances still are afforded by a shield in one of the windows of York minster, *circa* 1307; and in a MS. copy of MATTHEW

modern days as a quartering in the shield of the Dukes of MANTUA to denote their pretensions to the Eastern Empire, derived from the Marquesses of MONTFERRAT. But DUCANGE very properly remarks that—" hæ recentiores conjecturæ ingenii potius acumine quam ipsa nituntur rei veritate, cum biceps aquila longe recentior videatur præsertim apud Byzantinos ; ut pote quæ *uniceps* in insignibus gentilitiis Palæologorum Montferratensium descripta sit qua Imperium Constantinopolitanum designatur ; deinde in effigie Constantini Palæologi (1041-2), Michaelis imperatoris filii (quam initio hujus dissertationis describimus) pallium aquilis cum unico capite inspersum conspiciatur." So also on the coins of THEODORUS LASCARIS, MICHAEL, and ANDRONICUS PALÆOLOGUS, the eagle is single-headed.

The eagles on a coin of THEODORUS LASCARIS in 1251 are double-headed : and the letter of DEMETRIUS PALÆOLOGUS to CHARLES VII. of France, *circa* 1400, has a seal of blue wax (according to Imperial custom), charged with the double-headed eagle. MENÊTRIER thinks that the use of the double-headed eagle by the Emperors of the East arose in the same manner as that of the double cross which appears on their coins.

He says that as the cross was used as a sceptre, and when two Emperors were co-regnant it was represented with a double traverse and held by both ; so on their seals and coins they united two eagles into one. But it appears more likely that the Byzantine princes borrowed the double-headed eagle from the Turkish dynasty of the Seljooks. This emblem still remains carved over the principal entrance of the Turkish fort of Kara Hisar in Anatolia. The double-headed eagle, which is the charge of the Imperial Arms of Russia, was assumed by the Grand Duke IVAN BASILOVITZ of Moscow, who, in 1472, married SOPHIA, daughter of THOMAS PALEOLOGUS, and niece of the last Emperor of Byzantium, CON-

East, especially by SIGISMUND who joined both the eagles together with their heads separate, to show the sovereignties of the two empires conjoined in his person : which practice was continued by his successors " (*System of Heraldry*, i., 337-338). The Imperial eagle was " not one eagle with two heads, but two eagles, the one laid upon the other, and their heads separate, looking different ways, which represent the two heads of the Empire after it was divided into East and West."

"Non emin biceps est aquila" subdit Cuspianus "ut imperitum vulgus credit, sed duæ simul quarum altera alteram expansis alis obtegit," etc.

NISBET, however, seems to be mistaken when he adds to the passage above given from Cuspidion (as he calls him) the assertion that this was also the opinion of BELLARMINE, as will be seen from the following quotation:—"Sed hanc sententiam cui adstipulatur Flaccus Illyricus, jure exagitat cardinalis Bellarminus, qui non duas aquilas in insignibus imperatores gerere, sed unum divisum in dua capita, ejusque rei causam esse quod Imperium esset inter duos principes, quorum alter in Occidente, alter in Oriente, sedem habebat.

"Cui quidem Bellarmini sententiæ consentanea sunt quæ habet Ioannes Georgius Trissinus, poeta Italicus (lib. 2, *de Italia a Gothis liberata*):—

> " ' Il grande imperio ch'era un corpo solo
> Avea due capi ; un nel'antica Roma ;
> Che regeva i paesi occidentali,
> E l'altra nella nova, che dal volgo
> S'appella la citta di Constantino.
> Onde l'aquila d'oro in Campo rosso
> Insegna imperial, poi si dipinse
> E si dipinge con due teste ancora.' "

The double-headed eagle of gold on a red field, here referred to as borne by the Emperors of the East, was indeed used by them in later times, and appears in more

The eagle properly displayed as a heraldic charge upon a shield is shown on a somewhat smaller seal of the Emperor GUNTHER VON SCHWARZBURG, elected King of the Romans in 1349 (No. 58, of ROEMER BÜCHNER). On the Great Seal of the Emperor CHARLES IV. (King of Bohemia), elected King of the Romans in 1308, crowned at Rome in 1312, this throned effigy is placed between two shields, one of the single eagle; the other bearing the lion of BOHEMIA. (ROEMER BÜCHNER, *Siegel der Deutschen Kaiser*, No. 59, etc.)

An Imperial dalmatic of the fourteenth century bears golden roundles charged with the single-headed eagle (BOCK, *Kleinodien*, taf. xi., 14).

THE DOUBLE-HEADED EAGLE.—The origin of the double-headed eagle displayed is a matter of some uncertainty.

DUCANGE (vol. vii., *Dissertatio de Inferioris Ævi Numismatibus*, p. 151) writes:—

"Quædam Germanos bicipitem aquilam sibi adrogasse existimant ex quo in clade Variana signa Romanorum et aquilæ duæ in eorum venere potestatem; tertia a signifero priusquam in manus hostium veniret, in cruenta palude, ut ait Florus, quas quidem binas aquilas diis patriis in lucis ii suspenderint.

Ulricus Huttenus:—

"Vindice ut Arminio, ceteris prope rura Visurgis
Romanas acies miro Germano motu
Quintiliumque ducem conciderit, unde birostræ
Contigerint aquilæ, traducti insignia regni
Excussumque jugum non tantum hæc tempora nossent."

NISBET thinks that it originated in the arms of the Emperors of the East, who, he says, when the throne was occupied by two co-regnant princes, placed two eagles, one above the other in one shield on their seals and coins; and that it was adopted in Germany "by the Emperors of the Western Empire, upon the decline of that of the

> " Now were also the surcoats
> Of each King the same.
> Albert the Imperial Prince
> On a rich yellow cloth
> Many a black eagle
> Distributed according to his wish
> The same *he* also had,—
> Surcoat and housings,—
> Nassau the arrogant
> The surcoat was observed
> Woven, and worked
> In the same colour and form."

SPENER (*Opus Heraldicum*, pars. spec., pp. 66-67, quoting from FUGGER, *Spiegel der Ehren des Hauses Oesterreich*) says that, as Emperor, ALBERT bore, on the breast of the single-headed eagle of the Empire, his arms—*Quarterly*; 1. AUSTRIA; 2. STYRIA; 3. CARNIOLA; 4. HAPSBURG.

On the Great Seal of the Emperor LOUIS IV. (Duke of Bavaria, elected King of the Romans in 1314, crowned as Emperor at Rome in 1328) the throne is borne by eagles, and the eagle displayed surmounts the cross on the Imperial sceptre.

This is the first Imperial Great Seal to which a counter-seal is attached; this bears without a shield a standing eagle turned to the sinister, but with its head regardant to the dexter. (ROEMER-BÜCHNER, *Die Siegel der Deutschen Kaiser*, etc., No. 55.)

On the *secretum* of MARGARET, Sovereign Countess of HOLLAND, second wife of the Emperor LOUIS, the single eagle is represented; and on others of her seals it bears a lozenge shield charged with four lions: two of HOLLAND, and as many of FLANDERS: the red lions of HOLLAND in chief and base; the sable lions of FLANDERS in the flanks. (VRÉE, *Gen. Com. Flandr.*, p. 58.) The pourfilar lines which would have made the lozenge *quartered per saltire* are omitted, as they are also in the quartered escucheon of Queen PHILIPPA of HAINAULT in Westminster Abbey. (*See* pp. 462, 463.)

of the Romans" in *The Gentleman's Magazine*, vol. ccviii., pp. 1-13, which also contains coloured plates of the encaustic tiles to which reference is here made. It is curious that, at least in England, RICHARD does not seem ever to have used the German eagle as his arms, but at Great Malvern the eagle (which is there doubleheaded) is surrounded by the *bordure bezantée*. At Warblington in Hampshire the rampant lion is borne in an escucheon without the bordure on the breast of a double-headed eagle. It must be noted, however, that in many cases the glass and tiles are probably of a later date, and we cannot safely appeal to them as affording evidence of RICHARD'S own use.

The coins of ADOLF OF NASSAU, elected King of the Romans in 1291, bear the single eagle displayed; and in 1298 the surcoats and housings used at the battle of Gellheim by ADOLF and his rival competitor for the Imperial Crown—ALBERT of AUSTRIA, son of the Emperor RODOLPH,—were of yellow cloth charged with the same figure.

We learn this from the rhythmical chronicle of a contemporary poet, OTTACAR VON STEYERMARCK, from which the following lines are quoted in a paper in the *Cornhill Magazine*, 1865, from which I also borrow the appended translation.

" Nu warn auch die Wappen-Klayt
Yetweders Kunigs geleich
Albert der Furst Reich
Auf ain reiches Tuch gel
Mangen Swarczen Adaler
Hies wurcheusz nach Seiner Pet.
Dieselben *er* hat—
Wappen Rokh und Degkh—
Von Nazzau der kech ;
Des Wappen-Klayt man markht
Geweben, und gewarcht
In derselben Vart und Gestalt."

charged with the eagle. OTTO was thus armed at the battle of BOUVINES :—

> " Quar il porte, ce n'est pas fable,
> L'escut d'or à l'aigle de sable."
> (PHILL. MONSKES, MS. *Historia Francorum.*)

From BOCK'S *Kleinodien*, etc., we see that OTTO'S imperial mantle was powdered with single eagles displayed, and with lions rampant. (Taf. x., 13.)

In his letters FREDERICK II. (elected King of the Romans at the age of three years; and crowned as Emperor at Rome by Pope HONORIUS in 1220) often speaks of his victorious eagle banners. A boldly sculptured escucheon of this Emperor, with the single-headed eagle displayed, is still extant in the north aisle of the choir of Westminster Abbey (fig. 62, p. 242).

The *secretum* of FLORENT V., Count of HOLLAND (son of WILLIAM, Count of HOLLAND, who was elected King of the Romans in 1247, crowned at Aachen 1248, and slain in 1256), bears the lion of HOLLAND in a shield placed upon the breast of a single-headed eagle displayed (VRÉE, *de Seghelen der Graven van Vlaendren*, pl. lxxix.). This eagle is also one of the charges on the seal of WILLIAM'S sister ALICE, wife of JEAN D'AVESNES, and on the counter-seal it is curiously dimidiated with the lion rampant (Plate XXXVII., fig. 6).

The seal of RICHARD, Earl of CORNWALL, and POICTOU, brother of our King HENRY III., and elected King of the Romans in 1257, bears, *circa* 1260, his arms (*Argent, a lion rampant gules, within a bordure sable charged with bezants*) supported by the eagle displayed; and his son EDMUND used the same arrangement.

These arms remain in the painted glass, or appear on the encaustic pavement, in many of the churches in England with which he was connected. A list of these churches will be found in an article on " RICHARD King

government, or defence of its provinces. It was thus borne, for example, by the Counts of SAVOY, as Marquesses, or Markgraves, of the Empire in Italy, a title which constantly recurs upon their seals. (*See* also p. 535.)

The single-headed eagle displayed of the Empire was also borne as the supporter of the escucheon of Savoy. See the gold "*Doppel Doppia*" of CHARLES EMANUEL, King of SARDINIA, 1746 ; and it has not yet been disused by the Kings of Italy. (It thus appears, for instance, on the centre of the reverse of the Cross of the Order of the Crown of Italy.)

Under FREDERICK I. BARBAROSSA (Duke of Swabia, elected King of the Romans in 1152 ; crowned as Emperor, at Rome, in 1155), the eagle had become the recognised standard of the Holy Roman Empire.

"At quæ Cæsareæ, signum latiale cohortis
Regia fulget avis, magnorum densa virorum
Agmina ceu magni glomeravit viscera regni."

(Quoted from GUNTHERUS, by DUCANGE, tom. vii., sectio xviii.).

The eagle is embroidered with the *Heiligenscheine*, or "glory" round its head, upon the gloves which formed part of the Imperial coronation robes in the twelfth century (*See* BOCK'S splendid work ; *Die Kleinodien des Heil. Römischen Reiches*, etc., taf. viii., Wien, 1864); and the head of the eagle is for the first time thus encircled (*diademed*) on the Imperial seals, by ALFONSO of CASTILE, elected King of the Romans in 1257. (ROEMER-BÜCHNER, *Die Siegel*, etc., No. 48 ; VRÉE, *Genealogia Comitum Flandriæ*, pl. xvi. ; OETTER, *Wappenbelustigung*, i., 50.)

The eagle appears on the coins of the Emperor OTTO IV., 1208, and on those of several of his successors. The Emperor is represented on horseback bearing a shield

Vienna. (*See* LABARTE, *Handbook of the Arts of the Middle Ages*, fig. 50, p. 114, 1855.)

The Imperial seal upon which the eagle first appears in any shape is that of the Emperor HENRY III. (1039-1056) in which the sceptre carried by the prince is surmounted by a single-headed eagle. (*See* Dr ROEMER BÜCHNER'S *Die Siegel der Deutschen Kaiser*, No. 26, p. 24, whose note is worth transcribing. "Die römischen Consuln hatten einen elfenbeinern Stab, mit darauf geschnitztem Adler, wie viele Münzen, und diptycha consularia beurkunden. Sollte nicht von denselben HEINRICH III. dieses uralte Zeichen der Herrschaft angenommen haben, und hierdurch der Adler, als Reichsadler aufgenommen worden sein?")

At the battle of Mölsen on the Elster, in 1080, GODFREY DE BOUILLON, afterwards the first Christian King of JERUSALEM, is said to have borne the banner of the Emperor HENRY, which was charged with the eagle — " dux cum aquila præcedens Imperatorem" (WILLIAM OF TYRE, *Historia Belli Sacri*, p. 150). HENRY'S rival, RODOLPH of SWABIA, who fell in the same battle, used, after his coronation in 1077, a Great Seal on which he is represented holding in his right hand a very short sceptre or staff surmounted by an eagle with close wings. (GLAFEY, *Specimen decadem Sigillorum*, table iv., p. 25 ; Leipsic, 1749 ; and ROEMER BÜCHNER, *Die Siegel*, etc., p. 26.)

The earliest appearance of the eagle as a heraldic charge, which has come under my notice, is afforded by the Great Seal of the Markgrave LEOPOLD of Austria in 1136; on it the mounted figure of the Markgrave bears a shield charged with the eagle displayed. (HERGOTT, *Monumenta Austriæ*, tom. i., tab. 1.) From about this time it was borne not only by the Emperor, and the King of the Romans, but by the princes who, as Vicars of the Empire, or Lords of its Marches, were charged with the

Fig. 62.—The Eagle of Germany.

CHAPTER VIII.

ANIMATE CHARGES. III.
A. THE EAGLE.—B. OTHER BIRDS.

SECTION A.

THE EAGLE.—In the eagle as a heraldic bearing we have a point of contact between ancient Mythology or symbolism, and mediæval Heraldry. The bird of Jove, King of gods and men, adopted as the standard of the Roman Emperors in heathen times, continued in use after Rome had become Christian.

After the coronation of CHARLEMAGNE in Rome, on Christmas Day in the year 800, that prince, claiming to be the successor of the old Roman Emperors, is said to have adopted the eagle as his ensign, and placed it conspicuously on his palace at Aachen.

The eagle of the Holy Roman Empire was borne by the German Emperors in the attitude known as "displayed;" that is with the body upright, the wings on either side raised to the level of the head, and the legs extended beneath them. The eagle thus displayed is enamelled on the hilt of the Sword of CHARLEMAGNE, still preserved in the Imperial Treasury in the Burg at

companion of man, which appears frequently in armory, both at home and abroad; the talbot (a species of mastiff) and the greyhound are the most frequently used.

Argent, a talbot passant gules (in chief a crescent for difference), is the coat of Viscount WOLSELEY (Plate XXIV., fig. 9); *Argent, a greyhound courant sable*, is that of MORETON. *Azure, a greyhound (saliant) argent collared gules*, is borne by the Austrian Counts BLOME; and with the collar *or* by the French Counts NICOLAY.

Vert, a greyhound passant argent collared gules buckled or, is ascribed to the Byzantine house of SCYLITZES; *Azure, a talbot statant argent*, to the Silesian Barons HUNDT.

Three greyhounds courant fessways in pale, argent, was borne with the field *gules*, or *sable*, by various families of MAULEVRIER; and *Azure, three greyhounds pursuing a stag argent, all bendways and "at random,"* is the coat of YARDLEY. *Argent, a chevron gules between three talbots passant sable*, was used by TALBOT of Norfolk. *Azure, a chevron or between three greyhounds courant argent*, is the coat of GRIMMINCK of the Netherlands; and, with the hounds also *Or*, of DE HONDT of Flanders.

a nut, are, with trifling variations, those of several families of NUTSHALL, and SQUIRE. *Argent, a chevron azure between three squirrels gules* (with or without nuts), is the coat of LOVELL.

FOUQUET, the celebrated Finance Minister of LOUIS XIV., bore: *d'Argent, un écureuil rampant de gueules* (often augmented thus: *à la bordure de gueules semée de fleurs-de-lis d'or*); with the ambitious motto: "*Quo non ascendam?*" *Or, a squirrel on a mount proper*, is the coat of STUMPF of Bavaria; and of SICHTERMANN in the Netherlands. *Or, three squirrels gules*, is borne by SQUIRE, and ASHWEED; also by the Danish ALKE-VEDERS. *Or, three squirrels sable*, is a coat of DU BOIS.

THE APE as a charge is more frequently met with abroad than in British Heraldry, but there are nevertheless a few examples of its use. *Vert, an ape sejant, banded and chained to the sinister side of the shield argent*, is the coat of APPLEGH. *Sable, a chevron or between three apes argent chained gold*, are the arms of LOBLEY. *Argent, an ape gules, holding an apple or*, is the canting coat of AFFENSTEIN (*Zürich Wappenrolle*, No. 412). Without the apple this is borne by PASCAL-COLOMBIER of France. Apes are used as supporters by the FITZ-GERALDS, Dukes of LEINSTER; and by the MAXWELLS of Pollok, as far back as the reign of ROBERT III.

RATS.—I do not remember any instance in which rats occur as a British charge, but they are found in some foreign coats. The arms of the See of ARRAS are: *Or, a rat sable in the centre point between two pastoral staves paleways addorsed proper, the whole within an orle of ten rats of the second*. *D'Or, à trois rats de gueules*, is the coat of the Breton family of DE LA BEN-NERAYE. *Argent, a rat rampant sable*, was the coat of the Bavarian BILLICHS now extinct. Rats support the arms of RENAUD DE VELORT, in 1449.

DOGS.—I have left until the last the Dog, the faithful

the charges *gules* is that of FULLERTON. It is also the charge in the arms of the Styrian FISCHL, *Gules, on a bend an otter holding in its mouth two fish proper.*

THE BEAVER is borne as canting arms by the Swiss family of BIBER, *Or, a beaver rampant sable* (*Wappenrolle von Zürich*, No. 294) and also, but sometimes *gules*, by the Barons BIBRA.

THE BADGER is naturally the charge in the coats of the English families of BROCK (*Argent, a badger passant sable*); and BADGER (the same but the field *or*); as well as in those of the Swiss DACHS, *Gules, a badger rampant or*, and of the Bavarian Counts von DACHSBERG (the same but with the charge *argent*).

THE HEDGEHOG, called anciently an Urchin, appears in the allusive coats of HÉRISSON and HERRIES (Plate XXIV., fig. 10), *Argent, three urchins sable;* and in the French coats of LE HÉRISSÉ: *d'Or, à trois hérissons d'azur;* and *d'Argent, au chevron de gueules accosté de trois hérissons de sable.* JEZ, of Poland, *Gules, a hedgehog or.*

The kindred PORCUPINE is the canting coat of the French family of MAUPEOU (*mal peau*), Comtes d'ABLEIGES, Marquises de MAUPEOU. SIMON EYRE, Lord Mayor of LONDON in 1445, bore: *Gules, a porcupine erect argent, armed, collared, and chained or* (probably, as sometimes blazoned, an *urchin* in allusion to his name). It is the dexter supporter of the DE LISLES.

MOLES are borne by the MITFORDS (Lords REDESDALE), *Argent, a fess between three moles passant sable;* and by the Polish TRZYKRETI: *Argent, three moles fessways in pale sable. D'Or, à trois taupes de sable,* are the arms of FAYDIDE DE CHALANDRAS. MOLL in Holland uses: *Or, on a mount in base vert a mole sable;* another Dutch family of MOLLE bears: *Vert, on a chief or a mole sable.*

THE SQUIRREL occurs in some English coats, usually as an allusive charge. *Or, a squirrel sejant gules,* are the arms of SQUIRE. *Argent, a squirrel sejant gules, cracking*

of that Ilk (Plate XXIV., fig. 7). *Azure, a hare saliant with a hunting horn vert, garnished gules, pendent at its neck;* and as the canting coat of several German and Netherland families of HAAS, etc. HAAS of Bavaria bears, *Gules, a hare leaping argent. Vert, on a mount a hare sejant proper,* is borne by VAN NOORT.

THE RABBIT occurs somewhat more frequently still. *Argent, a chevron between three conies sable,* is the coat of STRODE of Devonshire. *Vert, three rabbits argent,* is borne by VAN DEN SANTHEUVEL of Holland.

The family of AYDIE, Marquises de RIBÉRAC in France, bore *de Gueules, à quatre lapins d'argent,* 2 et 2. *Gueules, au chevron d'or accosté de trois têtes de lapin d'argent,* is the coat of DUMONT DE BOSTAQUET, in Normandy. *Or, a lion rampant gules on a bordure azure seven rabbits argent spotted sable,* are the *armes parlantes* of the Portuguese family of COELHO; sometimes the lion is charged with *three bars chequy or and azure.* (Em campo de ouro hum Leaõ de purpura faxado de tres faxas, empequetado de ouro e azul, armado de vermelho; bordadura azul com sete coelhos de prata malhados de prato.)

King MANUEL granted to NICOLAO COELHO, a companion of VASCO DA GAMA, a special coat: *Gules, between two columns argent (each on a mount in base vert, and bearing a shield azure charged with the* "Quinas" *of* PORTUGAL) *in chief a lion rampant or, and in base a ship upon the sea proper.*

SEALS are borne by the BENNS of Holland: *Gules, three seals argent fessways in pale the middle one contourné;* and by DE WULF: *Vert, two seals rampant addorsed or.*

OTTERS and OTTER'S HEADS, are occasionally found in Scottish Armory. The coat of MELDRUM is: *Argent, a demi-otter issuant from a bar wavy sable* (Plate XXIV., fig. 8). *Argent, a chevron between three otter's heads erased sable,* is the old coat of BALFOUR; and the same with

in a very conventional manner (*see Glossary of English Terms*); its chief use in British Armory is as a supporter. Plate XXIV., fig. 5, is an instance of its employment as a charge; *Per pale argent and gules an antelope passant counter-changed*, the coat of DIGHTON of Lincolnshire.

THE HORSE alone, as distinct from its use in conjunction with a mounted knight, is scarcely so frequent a charge as we might have expected.

The escucheon of WESTPHALIA, *Gules, a horse courant argent* (Plate XXIV., fig. 6), formed part of the arms of the Electors of HANNOVER, and so was borne by the four GEORGES, and by WILLIAM IV., as a part of the Royal Arms of GREAT BRITAIN. *Gules, a demi-horse argent hoofed and maned or, issuing out of water* (either *proper*, or in its conventional representation *barry wavy argent and azure*) is the coat of TREVELYAN. *Gules, on a base vert, a horse passant argent,* cingled *sable;* is borne by the Counts BYSTRZONOWSKI.

One chief use of the horse is as an allusive coat. *Gules, a horse argent*, are the arms of the Roman CAVALLI, and *salient* of the French CHIVALETS, and CHEVALERIE; *Or, a horse rampant gules* are those of RENNER; *Argent, a horse sable, saddled gules*, those of POULAIN; *Argent, a horse proper* of RÖSSLER. *Argent, a fess between three colts courant sable*, is the arms of COLT (Baronet). *Gules, a mule passant argent*, is the canting coat of MOYLE. The humble ass is the charge of the family of ESEL (*Sable, an ass argent, a chief of the same*); and *Or, an ass issuant from the base sable*, is the coat of VAN DER EESE of Holland; *Azure, an ass passant sable* (? *proper*) is borne by LOVARI of Udine. *Sable, a fess (or) between three asses argent*, are the canting arms of AYSCOUGH.

The Bavarian family of FRUMBESEL, now extinct, used to bear ; *Argent, an ass rampant gules.*

We have the HARE in the Scottish coat of CLELAND

PLATE XXIV.

1. Bull.
Bevill.

2. Bull's Head.
Turnbull.

3. Goats.
Thorold.

4. Paschal Lamb.
Pascal.

5. Antelope.
Dighton.

6. Horse.
Westphalia.

7. Hare.
Cleland.

8. Otter.
Meldrum.

9. Talbot.
Wolseley.

10. Herrison.
Herries.

11. Mole.
Mitford.

12. Ermine spots.
Henderson.

The sheep which is borne on an *azure* field by the Counts ALESSANDRI of Florence has two heads.

The Barons von WIEDERHOLD of Bavaria use: *Per pale or and azure, over all a ram salient argent.* *Gules, a ram passant argent,* is the coat of the Franconian Counts VOIGT DE RIENECK ; and, with the ram *salient,* is also borne by the Barons BOJANOWSKI. In the *Wappenrolle von Zürich, Or, on a mount vert a ram passant sable,* is the canting coat of RAMENSPERG (No. 72). *Or, three lambs sable,* is borne by LAMMENS of Holland.

Vert, three rams argent, is borne by BELIN ; and by PASTUREAU. *Azure, a chevron between three rams or,* is the coat of RAMSEY.

THE PASCHAL LAMB.—A lamb bearing on its shoulder a flag, or banner, *argent charged with a cross gules,* and having its head adorned with the saintly glory similarly charged, occurs not unfrequently in German Armory. *Gules, a paschal lamb argent, on a terrace vert,* is the coat of the Bavarian WÜLFER (and, without the terrace), of LAMPOINS of Holland. Plate XXIV., fig. 4. *Azure, a paschal lamb argent,* is borne by PASCAL of France, PETIT, and WOLTHERS of Holland. A curious use of this charge as a symbol of the Resurrection, and as a canting coat, is found in the arms of the families of OSTERTAG in Bavaria and Suabia : *Azure, on a mount in base, a Paschal lamb argent.* (OSTERHAUSEN, OSTERHAMMER, and OSTERRIETH, also have the Paschal Lamb among their charges, and see the arms of PERTH, Chap. XXI., p. 632.)

The late LYON granted to the honourable family of LAMB of Brechin, of which ancient city one was Provost, the following arms : *Azure, a Paschal Lamb proper, on a chief argent three hawk's heads erased, also proper.* The crest is a Paschal Lamb proper, and the motto, *Virtus sine macula.*

THE ANTELOPE of Heraldry is generally represented

by the Kings of NAVARRE. The French term for *belled* is *clarinée*. (On the original arms of STYRIA, *v.* p. 499.)

The family of VAQUER of Majorca bear: *Azure, on a terrace a cow with her calf all argent.*

The calf is frequently used as a canting charge. *Azure, a calf passant or;* and the same *on a mount vert*, are both borne by the families of KALFF of Holland. *Argent, three calves passant sable;* are the arms of MEDCALFE, or METCALFE. *Argent, on a bend sable three calves or*, are those of VEALE.

The *Heads of bulls, oxen*, etc., may like those of stags, etc., be borne either caboshed, or in profile; they are drawn in profile unless the other form is prescribed in the blazon. *Argent, a bull's head erased sable*, Plate XXIV., fig. 2, is the older coat of the Scottish family of TURNBULL; in later times three heads were substituted for the single one. (*See* BUFFLE, in *French Glossary*.)

GOATS and GOAT'S HEADS are found occasionally as heraldic charges. The family of THOROLD of Lincoln bears: *Sable, three goats salient argent* (Plate XXIV., fig. 3). *Sable* (or *vert*), *three goats passant argent*, is borne by the families of STANSFELD, or STANSFIELD, of Yorkshire; MARSTON of Lincolnshire uses: *Sable, three goats salient argent* (Plate XXIV., fig. 3), as does THOROLD. CABRERA, in Spain, bears: *Argent, a goat rampant sable within a bordure of rocks proper;* a very curious example (PIFERRER, *Nobiliario . . . de España*, No. 537).

SHEEP, both rams and lambs, are frequently found as allusive charges. The coat of LAMBTON, Earl of DURHAM, is: *Sable, a fess between three lambs trippant argent.* *Vert, a lamb argent*, is the coat of LAMBERT of Ireland; VAN BUTEN; LAMMENS; and ADRIANI. LAMBRECHT of Flanders bears the same with the field *azure*. *Azure, a sheep argent*, is borne by SCHAEP of Holland; and *rampant* by the Marquis AGNELLI.

really only applied to the attire and the piece of the skull connecting the horns, as in the coat of COCKS, Earl SOMERS; *Sable, a chevron between three stag's attires argent (de Sable, au chevron d'or, accompagné de trois massacres de cerf d'argent)*; and single antlers also occur as in the Scottish coat of BOYLE of KELBURNE (the paternal coat of the Earl of GLASGOW), *Or, three hart's horns erect gules two and one* (Plate XXIII., fig. 12).

In the quartered coat of the Dukes of BRUNSWICK two quarters are each charged with a single stag's horn, *Argent, a stag's horn gules* is used for the County of REGENSTEIN; *Argent, a stag's horn sable* for that of BLANKENBERG.

BULLS, OXEN, COWS and CALVES.—When bulls or cows, etc., occur in Heraldry they are said to be *armed* of their horns, and *unguled* of their hoofs, as in the coat of BEVILL of Gwarnack, Plate XXIV., fig. 1. *Argent, a bull passant gules armed and unguled or;* this is also the coat of the Margravate of NIEDER LAUSITZ (*v.* p. 500). ASTLEY, Earl of SHAFTESBURY bears: *Argent, three bulls passant sable armed and unguled or.* *Gules, on a mount in base vert an auroch, or wild ox argent*, were the original arms of the AUERSPERGS, Princes of AUERSPERG, Dukes of MUNSTERBERG in Silesia, etc. *Argent, on a mount vert, a young bull statant gules* is the coat of the Princes PONIATOWSKI, and the Counts ZALEWSKI, and KOMOROWSKI of Poland, of the clan CIOLEK; it is also borne by the WAIDER of Tirol. *Argent, a bull rampant gules*, is the coat of TORÀ in Spain. *Or, a bull passant sable horned or*, is borne by the Barons PLESSEN; *de Gueules, à une vache d'argent*, is borne as a canting coat by LA VACHE DE LA TOUCHE of Brittany. The PUGET, Marquises de BARBENTANE, bear: *d'Argent, à une vache passante de gueules surmontée d'un estoile entre les cornes.* *Or, a cow sable*, is borne by VACHER of Cambray. *Or, two cows passant in pale gules, collared, armed and belled azure*, were the arms of the Counts of BÉARN, and borne

it also appears on the seal of the ABBEY of HOLYROOD HOUSE in commemoration of a legend regarding the foundation of the religious house which is at least as old as the first half of the fifteenth century being told in the old Ritual Book of the Abbey (*Bannatyne Club Miscellany*, ii., 11) dating about the time of the captivity of JAMES I. in England. King DAVID I., according to BELLENDEN'S narration, coming to visit the Castle of Edinburgh on the Festival of the Elevation of the Holy Cross, when the country all round was "ane great forest, full of hartes, hyndes, toddis, and siclik manner of beistes," joined, contrary to the admonition of his confessor, a hunting party of his nobles, and had a miraculous escape from an enraged stag by the intervention in some shape of the Cross, and as an atonement for his having profaned this holy day and in thankfulness for his deliverance, he founded the Abbey of Holyrood House: Sir GREGAN CRAWFORD is said to have aided in some way in the King's preservation, and thence acquired the coat alluded to, *Argent, a stag's head erased gules.* The favourite position however of the stag's head is *cabossed* (or *caboshed*), that is, full-faced with no part of the neck visible. LEGGE, Earl of DARTMOUTH bears: *Azure, a buck's head cabossed argent. Sable, three buck's heads cabossed argent* belongs to the family of CAVENDISH, Dukes of DEVONSHIRE. *Argent, on a bend azure three buck's heads cabossed or*, to that of STANLEY. *Barry of six argent and azure over all three stag's heads cabossed or,* is, with many variants, a coat of WOODWARD of Gloucestershire, and the neighbouring counties. In Scotland the stag's head cabossed, known as the *Caberfae,* is most associated with the family of MACKENZIE, whose arms are, *Azure, a stag's head cabossed or* (sometimes with *a star or* between the tynes). The French term of blazon for this bearing is "*un rencontre.*" BOUTON uses the term *massacre,* which is

require separate explanation. The antlers of stags, being regarded as ornaments, rather than as weapons, are known as *attires*, and their branches are called *tynes* (*cors* in French), and the beast is said to be *attired*, (*ramé* in French). As in the case of bulls, unicorns, and other cloven-footed animals, the stag is said to be *unguled* (*onglé*) when its hoofs are of a different tincture from its body. A stag in the walking attitude is said to be *trippant*. Plate XXIII., fig. 7, *Azure, a stag trippant or, attired and unguled gules*, is the coat of STRACHAN of Glenkindy, in Aberdeenshire. *Azure, three bucks trippant or*, is borne by GREENE. When standing still and full-faced, it is described as *at gaze*. The Barons von HIRSCHBERG bear, *Argent, a stag at gaze gules*. (Plate XXIII., fig. 8) *Vert, a stag at gaze or*, is borne by SOMERFORD of Stafford. The family of RAE of Pitsindie in Perthshire bore: *Argent, three roebucks courant gules* (Plate XXIII., fig. 9). A stag reposing is said to be *lodged*, or *couchant*: — *Sable, a stag lodged argent* (Plate XXIII., fig. 10), is the coat of DOWNES of Chester. *Vert, three bucks lodged or*, is a coat of ANDERSON. In the attitude of a lion saliant it is described as *springing; d'Azur, à trois cerfs elancés d'or*, is the coat of the Counts BORLUUT DE HOOG-STRATEN of Holland. *Or, three bucks rampant sable, unguled or, their attires wreathed of the tinctures*, is borne by the German Counts of WALMODEN. Another family of WALMODEN bears: *Or, three bouquetins, or chamois, sable.*

The REINDEER is borne by the HIRSCHMANNS of Franconia: tinctured *gules* it is used as a supporter by the Marquis of DOWNSHIRE, Viscount HEREFORD, the Lords KENSINGTON, etc. (see *English Glossary, s.v.*).

MOOSE-DEER are the supporters of the Lords CARLINGFORD and CLERMONT.

In Scotland the stag's head erased in profile, is borne by several branches of the family of CRAWFURD; and

azure field by the Russian and German Barons le FORT, and it is thus represented in the insignia of the Chief Order of Knighthood of Denmark; and in the arms of the STERCKS of Brussels, but in this last it is of *sable, armed gules, in a field argent*, and the tower bears *three armed men*. The French family of DE BARRY bears: *Azure, three elephants or ; the two in chief affrontés*. As supporters the elephant is used by the Prussian Counts von GOTTSTEIN; the Danish families of AHLEFELD, DANESKIOLD, etc.; and the English Earls of POWIS.

The ELEPHANT'S HEAD alone, is the charge of the arms of the Dutch family of DERX, who bear : *Or, an elephant's head in profile proper*. *Sable, on a fess between three elephant's heads argent as many mullets of the field*, is the coat of PRATT, Marquis of CAMDEN. Its tusks are borne by the Counts AVOGLI of Ferrara : *Azure, three elephant's tusks issuing from the dexter flank argent*.

THE CAMEL (or DROMEDARY), is used in British Armory as an allusive charge by the families of CAMEL who bore *Azure* (or *sable*) *a camel argent;* and *Or, three camels sable*. *Vert, a camel argent* (or *or*) is borne by FALLOWES of Chester. The French CALMELS D'ARTENSAC use: *d'Argent, à trois chameaux arretés statant d'azur*. Its hump makes the camel an appropriate coat for the Italian GOBBI : *Azure, on a terrace vert a camel argent*. KRÖCHER of Prussia bore anciently, *Or, a camel passant sable;* the more modern coat is, *Azure, a camel argent*. Camel's heads are borne by KEMELS in Flanders, *Azure, a chevron between three camel's heads or:* and by DIEK of Holland. Camels support the arms of the Counts of ROMRÉE.

STAGS (BUCKS, HARTS, HINDS, DOES) are frequent in British and German heraldry; much less so in that of the southern countries.

The terms of blazon used in regard to them differ somewhat from those applied to beasts of prey, and

or, is the coat of the BARINGS, Earls of NORTHBROOK, etc.

FOX.—The Fox is an animal seldom met in British Heraldry. *Gules, a fox or*, is assigned to the family of GAVENOR. *Argent, two foxes counter salient in saltire gules*, the sinister surmounting the dexter (Plate XXIII., fig. 6), is the coat given for CADRODHARD, a British prince of the tenth century who certainly never bore it. It is, however, quartered in memory of their descent, by the family of WILLIAMS-WYNNE of Wynnstay. *Argent, three foxes passant* (or *courant*), *gules* (or *sable*), is borne by TREGOZ of Cornwall.

Abroad, it is somewhat more frequently found. *Or, on a mount, a fox proper*, is the canting coat of the Dutch Counts van VOS; other families of the name bear the *fox passant, or rampant, gules*. *Or, a fox rampant sable*, is the coat of the Venetian BALBI; *Vert, a fox rampant argent*, is borne by the Barons von REINECK; *Argent, a fox rampant gules*, are the *armes parlantes* of the Tirolese Counts FUCHSS, whose supporters are two foxes *gules*, mantled ermine. *Per fess argent and azure* (sometimes *azure and argent*) *a fox rampant counter-changed*, is the coat of the ZANI of Venice. The French families of RENARD, and RENAUD, bear the fox passant *or*; the first on a field *gules*, the other on a field *azure*. *Azure, three foxes rampant gules*, is the coat of VON DER HEIM, and of RODENBERG in Holland.

THE ELEPHANT is but little used in Heraldry; and in British Armory is seldom found except as an allusive charge. *Gules, an elephant passant argent* (*armed or*), is assigned to the English ELPHINSTONES. *Gules, an elephant argent on a mount in base or*, is the canting coat of the Counts von HELFENSTEIN of Suabia, and appears very quaintly drawn in the *Wappenrolle von Zürich*, taf. ii., fig. 40. In its conventional representation, *Argent, with a castle on its back proper*, it is borne in an

The wolf's head appears frequently as a charge, especially in Scottish coats. The arms of ROBERTSON of Strowan (Plate XXIII., fig. 3), are: *Gules, three wolf's heads erased argent.* In representing the head of the wolf it is usual to have a portion of the neck depicted ; and in the older representations of the boar's head, both at home and in Germany, the same was the case.

BEAR.—The Bear is not an animal frequently represented in its entirety in British coats. When borne it is usually in reference to the name, and is drawn with a muzzle, and often with a collar and chain. *Argent, a bear rampant sable muzzled or*, is the coat of BERNARD, or BARNARD, and, with the addition of a collar and chain, of the BERESFORDS. *Argent* (or *Or*), *a bear passant sable*, are the arms of FITZ URSE. In Foreign Heraldry, as might be expected, its use is somewhat more frequent ; and it is generally drawn without collar, muzzle, or chain. *Or, a bear rampant sable*, is the coat of OELPER in Bavaria. *Argent, a bear passant sable*, of the Prussian families of BEHR, and ROCHOW. *Argent, a bear statant sable*, appears in the *Wappenrolle von Zürich* for BÄRENSTEIN ; muzzled and collared the same is borne by BEHR of Prussia ; and BIORN of Denmark. The well known arms of the Swiss Canton of BERNE are : *Gules, on a bend or a bear passant sable.* *Argent, a bear erect sable*, is the coat of the Swiss Abbey of ST. GALL (Plate XXIII., fig. 4).

The white POLAR BEAR is certainly intended in the coat of WOHNSFLETH of Holstein : *Azure, a white bear rampant contourné collared gules ;* and the same animal is very probably represented in the arms of ARESEN of Denmark ; *Azure, a bear passant argent.*

The BEAR'S HEAD frequently figures as a charge, and is usually drawn muzzled. *Azure, three bear's heads argent, muzzled gules* (Plate XXIII., fig. 5) are the well known arms of the family of FORBES in Scotland. *Azure, a fess or, in chief a bear's head proper, muzzled and ringed*

PLATE XXIII.

1. Boar. *Baird.*
2. Boars' Heads. *Elphinstone.* 
3. Wolves' Heads. *Robertson.* 
4. Bear. *St. Gall.* 
5. Bears' Heads. *Forbes.* 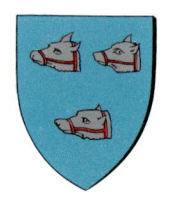
6. Foxes countersalient. *Williams.* 
7. Stag trippant. *Strachan.* 
8. Stag at gaze. *Somerford.* 
9. Stags courant. *Rae.* 
10. Stag lodged. *Downes.* 
11. Stag's Head cabossed. *Mackenzie.* 
12. Stags' Horns. *Boyle.*

Argent, à chevron between three "porcs" sable appears in the *Rolls of Arms* for SWYNETHWAYTE.

Among the curiosities of Heraldry we may place the canting arms of HAM of Holland: *Gules, five hams proper*, 2, 1, 2. The VERHAMMES also bear: *Or, three hams sable*. These commonplace charges assume almost a poetical savour when placed beside the very matter-of-fact coat of the family of BACQUERE: *d'Azur, à un ecusson d'or en abîme, accompagné de trois groins de porc d'argent;* and that of the WURSTERS of Switzerland; *Or, two sausages gules on a gridiron sable, the handle in chief*.

WOLVES.—The wolf occurs in a good many coats in British Armory and is usually drawn *salient*, or leaping forward as if to seize its prey. It is however sometimes represented *passant*, as in the canting coat of LOWE, *Gules, a wolf passant argent*. *Vert, a wolf sejant argent*, is borne by the Dutch family DE WOLF. *Or, a wolf passant sable*, is the coat of the old Counts of WOLFFS-THAL. *D'Or, au loup rampant d'azur armé*, etc., *de gueules* are the arms of the French Marquises d'AGOULT. *Gules, a wolf rampant argent*, was the *armes parlantes* of the Counts of WEISSENWOLFF. *Gules, a wolf saliant or*, is the coat of the Marquis d'ALBERTAS.

In Spanish Heraldry the wolf is the most common of animals. It is there very often represented as *ravissant*, *i.e.*, carrying the body of a lamb in its mouth and across its back. *Or, a wolf saliant regardant sable ravishing a dog proper*, is the coat of the Austrian Barons von KALITSCH.

The she-wolf occurs in several foreign coats: the French family of LOPPIN bear: *d'Argent, à deux louves rampantes et affrontées de sable*. The SÉGURS bear *Azure*, and the same charges *argent*. *Gules, on a mount vert, a she-wolf couchant and suckling her young or*, is the coat of the LUPARELLA family at Rome. *Gules, a she-wolf suckling two children proper*, is the allusive coat of the Bavarian family of ROMUL.

BOAR.—The boar, *i.e.*, the wild boar, or *sanglier*, is represented in profile, and in British armory is usually *passant*. Like the lion it is often described as *armed and langued*, but this is needless when tusks and tongue are of the natural colour. The French armorists call the tusks of the wild boar its *défenses*, and the beast instead of being termed *armed* is said to be *défendu*. *Gules, a boar passant or* (Plate XXIII., fig. 1) belongs to the family of BAIRD of Auchmedden in Banffshire. *Argent, a boar rampant sable*, is the coat of the Counts von BASSEWITZ; the Barons von EBERSPERG bear: *Argent, on a mount vert a boar passant sable.*

The head of the wild boar (*hure*) is of frequent occurrence as a heraldic charge; and is often described as *armed;* thus, Plate XXIII., fig. 2 is the coat of ELPHINSTONE: *Argent, a chevron sable between three boar's heads erased gules armed argent* (*d'Argent, au chevron de sable, accompagné de trois hures de sanglier de gueules aux défenses d'argent*). *Azure, three boar's heads couped or* is the well known coat of the great Scottish family of GORDON; and *Or, three boar's heads erased gules, armed and langued azure*, is borne by URQUHART. Sometimes the heads are borne erect, muzzle upwards; *Argent, three boar's heads erased erect sable*, is the coat of BOOTH (originally that of BARTON, see NISBET, ii. 49).

The domestic PIG, as distinct from the savage wild boar, finds a place in Heraldry, usually as the charge of a canting coat; as for instance:—*Azure, three boars passant in pale argent*, is the coat of BACON. *Sable, three boars argent*, is the coat of SWYNEHOWE. Similarly in France the DES PORCELLETS (Marquises de MAILLANE) bore originally *d'Or, à un porcelet passant de sable*. Other less important branches of the house blazon the beast as a *sanglier*. The Marquises de HOUDETOT bore anciently, *d'Or, à six porcs de sable;* and the blazon of the Norman HAUTOTS is *d'Or, à sept porceaux de sable.*

engravings show, the charge may have been developed out of a variation in the drawing of the *fleurs-de-lis Sable, three leopard's heads reversed jessant de lis*, are the arms of WOODFORD. *Sable, three leopard's heads or, jessant de lis argent*, are those of MORLEY. *Gules, three leopard's heads or, jessant de lis azure, over all a bend of the last*, are the arms of TENNYSON, and probably are only a variation of the similar arms of DENYS, or DENNIS. Lord TENNYSON, the poet-laureate, has a grant of the following coat: *Gules, on a bend nebulé between three leopard's heads jessant de lis or, a laurel wreath in chief proper.*

With the Heraldic leopard we may couple the LYNX, the PANTHER, and the WILD CAT, or CATAMOUNT, which appears in some Scottish crests.

The domestic cat, dignified by the old Heralds with the title of *musion*, occurs in the canting arms of KEATE, or KEATS (*Argent, three cats in pale sable*). The COMPTONS of Catton, in allusion to their place of residence, bore: *Sable, three cats passant gardant argent collared and belled or.* The cats in the arms of the Scotch family of SCHIVES, or SEEVES: *Sable, three cats passant in pale argent*, are said to be civet cats, and are thus allusive to the name. There are several Foreign coats which bear a panther, but in the Armory of Britain the heraldic panther is only met as a supporter; as thus borne by the Duke of BEAUFORT it is a leopard-like beast, inflamed at the ears and mouth, and *semé* of roundles of various colours.

Per fess argent and gules, in chief a demi-panther issuant argent inflamed proper, is borne by the Princes of STARHEMBERG. The Tirolese FICHTERS bear: *Per fess argent and gules, a heraldic panther counter-changed. Argent, a panther rampant azure*, is the coat of HOCHART of Würtemberg. *Azure, a panther rampant argent crowned or*, is the coat of the Pomeranian JATSKOW.

so greatly afflicted with vanity that she could be robbed of her whelps if a mirror were placed in her path, the depredators finding it easy to carry off their prey while the mother was contemplating her personal charms! (*See* GUILLIM, *Display of Heraldry*, pp. 188, 189.) *Argent, a tiger or, regardant at a mirror on the ground proper*, was the coat of SIBELL of Kent.

THE LEOPARD.—The leopard of natural history, as distinct from the lion, is not a frequent charge in British Armory, and it is quite probable that in most ancient instances in which it is found, the lion was really intended. *Gules, a leopard passant gardant or, spotted sable*, is the coat of ARLOTT, and the charge is clearly canting on the leopard of natural history (*v.* p. 210). The leopard also occurs occasionally as a supporter. The leopard's head, however, is a frequent heraldic charge: it is represented full-faced, and no part of the neck appears. Plate XXII., fig. 12, is the coat of POLE, Duke of SUFFOLK: *Azure, a fess between three leopard's faces or*. (*See* DALMATIA, p. 494.)

The Marquises de BARBANÇOIS in France bore: *de Sable, à trois têtes de léopard d'or arrachés et lampassés de gueules*.

A curious combination of the leopard's head (often reversed) with the *fleur-de-lis* occurs in several old English coats. *Gules, three leopard's heads jessant de lis or*, appears to have been borne by the family of CANTE-LUPE in the thirteenth century. Of this family was THOMAS DE CANTELUPE, Bishop of HEREFORD, 1275-1282, and the arms since borne for that see (Plate XXII., fig. 11) are the arms of that prelate only differenced by the leopard's heads being reversed. Mr PLANCHÉ, in his *Pursuivant of Arms*, pp. 103, 104, shows that the original arms of the CANTELUPES were the *fleurs-de-lis* alone; and though it is quite possible that the leopard's heads were added intentionally to mark an alliance or sub-infeudation, it yet appears probable that, as his

the coat of the HERBERTS, Earls of PEMBROKE and MONTGOMERY; it is also borne by VAUGHAN. *Sable, three lions passant in pale argent*, is the coat of ENGLISH. *Quarterly or and gules four lions passant gardant counterchanged* was borne by LLEWELLYN AP GRIFFITH, Prince of NORTH WALES; and is still used at times as the Arms of the Principality of WALES. *Azure, six lions rampant or*, is the coat of WILLIAM LONGESPÉE, Earl of SALISBURY; and LEYBURNE bears: *Or, six lions rampant sable*, in several ancient *Rolls of Arms*.

II. OTHER BEASTS.

THE TIGER.—The tiger of real life is but rare as an armorial charge, and it is used in armory mainly as a crest, and for supporters granted to persons for service in India. Thus the supporters granted to OUTRAM (baronet) are two tigers, rampant gardant, wreathed with laurels and crowned with Eastern crowns, all proper.

A very modern coat, granted to BRADBURY in 1874, is: *Argent, on a mount in base a tiger passant proper, on a chief vert two other tigers dormant, also proper.*

The Tiger is as infrequently found in Foreign Heraldry, and I have only on record three instances of its use. The modern blazon of the Italian FIRENZUOLA is: *Argent, a tiger rampant proper girt round the body or, and holding a reaping hook proper*, but I think the old blazon was a wild cat.

The HERALDIC TIGER found in a few English coats, and sometimes used as a supporter, bears but little resemblance to the real animal. As drawn it has the body of a lion but the head nearly resembles that of a wolf (Plate XXII., fig. 10). *Or, a tiger passant gules*, is the coat of LUTWYCHE. In one or two old English coats the tiger is drawn in combination with a mirror. One of the old beliefs regarding the tigress was that she was

(305) WILDENVELS: *Per pale argent and sable, in the first a demi-lion statant-gardant gules issuant from the dividing line.*

(408) TANNENVELS: *Azure, a lion rampant or, queué argent.*

(489) RINACH: *Or, a lion rampant gules headed azure.*

A curious use of the lion as a charge occurs in several ancient coats of the Low Countries, *e.g.* in that of TRASEGNIES, whose arms are: *Bandé d'or et d'azur; à l'ombre du lion brochant sur le tout, à la bordure engrêlée d'or.* Here the *ombre du lion* is properly represented by a darker shade of the tincture (either of *or* or of *azure*), but often the artist contents himself with simply drawing the outline of the animal in a neutral tint.

Among other curiosities of the use of the lion are the following foreign coats.

BOISSIEU in France, bears: *de Gueules, semé de lions d'argent.*

MINUTOLI of Naples: *Gules, a lion rampant vair, the head and feet or.*

LOEN of Holland: *Azure, a decapitated lion rampant argent, three jets of blood spurting from the neck proper.*

PAPACODA of Naples: *Sable, a lion rampant or, its tail turned over its head and held by its teeth.*

The Counts REINACH of Franconia: *Or, a lion rampant gules, hooded and masked azure* (*see* above).

Of coats in which several lions appear the following are examples.

Argent, three lions rampant gules, crowned azure is the coat of BARBANÇON. *Argent, three lions rampant sable,* is used by CHEVERELL in England, and with the lions *crowned or,* by HALEWIJN of Flanders (*Armorial de Gueldre*). *Gules, three lions rampant or,* was the coat of Prince TALLEYRAND-PÉRIGORD.

Or, three lions passant in pale sable, is borne by CAREW. *Per pale azure and gules three lions rampant argent,* is

PLATE XXII.

1. Lions Combatant.
Wycombe.

2. Counterpassant.
Glegg.

3. Issuant.
Markham.

4. Issuant.
Chalmers.

5. Naissant.
Esme.

6. Lions' Heads.
Scott.

7. Lion's Gambs.
Newdegate.

8. Lion's Paws.
Usher.

9. Lions' Tails.
Corke.

10. Tiger.
Lutwyche.

11. Lions' Heads reversed
and Jessant de lis.
See of Hereford.

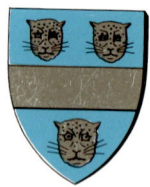

12. Leopard's Face.
Pole, Duke of Suffolk.

bezant, is the coat of the BENNETS, Earls of TANKERVILLE.

Parts of a lion are not unfrequent as charges, particularly the head, either erased or coupéd. *Argent, three lion's heads erased gules* (Plate XXII., fig. 6) is the coat of SCOTT of Balweary. *De Sinople, à trois têtes de lion arrachées d'or* is borne by BERTHELAY QUESQUERTIN, of France.

A *lion's gamb* is the whole fore-leg, in the walking attitude unless otherwise specified, as in Plate XXII., fig. 7, the coat of NEWDEGATE, which is *Gules, three lion's gambs, erased argent*. *Two lion's gambs, issuant from the flanks of the shield and conjoined in chevron*, is the bearing of several English families, *e.g., Azure, two lion's gambs chevronways argent, supporting a cinquefoil or*, is a coat of CHIPPENDALE.

A *lion's paw* is cut off at the middle joint, and is usually drawn erect, as in fig. 8, the coat of USHER OF FEATHERSTONE: *Argent, three lion's paws couped and erect sable.*

Lion's tails are occasionally found as heraldic charges; as in the Cornish coat of CORKE: *Sable, three lion's tails erect erased argent* (fig. 9). They also occur as the canting coat of TAYLARD: *Or, on a mount gules in base three lion's tails erect of the second curved towards the sinister.*

Only a single example of the use of the *lioness* as a heraldic charge is known to me. The family of COING in Lorraine bears: *d'Azur, à une lionne arrêtée d'or.*

The following fourteenth century examples of the use of the lion as a heraldic charge are taken from the oft quoted *Wappenrolle von Zürich*, and should be of interest to the student of early armory.

(51) END: *Azure, a lion rampant-gardant argent, its feet or.*

(186) MARTDORF: *Argent, a lion statant-gardant gules.*

(284) CASTELN: *Per pale or and argent, a lion statant-gardant gules.*

crest; and very occasionally is used as a heraldic charge, either *issuant* or *naissant*, terms which, though often confounded, should be carefully distinguished. The latter term is only used when the charge is represented as rising out of the *middle* of an Ordinary, or other charge (*quasi nunc esset in nascendo*). Thus in Plate XXII., fig. 5, is the coat of Sir HENRY EAM, or ESME, K.G., temp. EDWARD III.: *Or, a demi-lion rampant gules naissant from a fess sable.* Whereas fig. 4, the coat of CHALMERS of Balnacraig, is blazoned: *Argent, a demi-lion rampant sable issuing out of a fess gules; in base a fleur-de-lis of the last.* Fig. 3 is the coat of MARKHAM: *Azure, on a chief or a demi-lion rampant issuant gules.* It should be noticed that this distinction between *naissant* and *issuant* is not observed by modern French Heralds, who apply both terms indifferently to a *demi-lion*. So far as my observation goes, if there is any distinction it is this:— that an animal rising from the base line of the shield, or of an Ordinary, is generally said to be *issuant (issant)*, while an animal rising out of the midst of it is usually blazoned as *naissant*. *D'Azur, au lion naissant d'or*, is the coat of CLAIRAMBAULT, Marquis de VENDEUIL; with the lion crowned this is also the coat of the Barons ERATH of Nassau. *D'Azur, semé de fleurs-de-lis d'or, au lion naissant d'argent* was borne by the old French crusading family of MOREUIL. (*Salle des Croisés*, 1202.)

Per fess, or, and wavy azure and argent; in chief a lion rampant issuant gules (*Von Gold über Blau quer getheilt, im oberen goldenen Felde ein wachsender rother Löwe, im untern blauen zwei silberne wellenförmig gezogene Querbalken*) are the arms of the County of RÖTELN, or RÖTELEN, quartered in the full shield of the Grand-Dukes of BADEN (*v.* p. 491). *Argent, three demi-lions rampant gules* is the coat of STURMY. *Or, three demi-lions rampant gules* is borne by TOURNAI, Comtes d'OISI. *Gules, three demi-lions rampant argent, in the centre point a*

are required to face the sinister they are said to be *contournés*. But in Germany this is a matter which is treated as of no importance. The German heraldic artist who arranges a series of shields for decorative purposes has no hesitation about turning the charges to the sinister if it seem desirable; and in the case of quartered or impaled coats in which several lions appear, it is quite usual to make the lions turn so as to face each other, or to look towards the central line of the shield. Thus in the arms of WALLENSTEIN, Duke of FRIEDLAND, the arms are *Quarterly, 1 and 4, Or, a lion rampant azure, crowned of the field; 2 and 3, Azure, a lion rampant crowned or.* Over all, en surtout, as an augmentation, *the Imperial arms: Or, a double-headed eagle displayed sable.* Here the lions in the first and third quarters are drawn *contournés*, so as to face those in the second and fourth (*cf.* pp. 473, 490). The German heralds arrange helmets and crests on the same principle of symmetry. (*See* Chapter XIX.)

In British Heraldry two lions rampant placed face to face are said to be *counter-rampant*, or *combatant*.

When back to back they are said to be *addorsed* (*addossés*).

Or, two lions combatant gules, is the coat of WYCOMBE. (Plate XXII., fig. 1.) *Per pale argent and or, two lions combatant, the dexter gules the sinister argent*, is borne by the Barons STEIN DE BRAUNSDORF. *Gules, two lions rampant addorsed argent*, is a coat of ROGERS.

When two or more lions *passant* in pale face in opposite directions they are said to be *counter-passant*, as in Plate XXII., fig. 2 ; the arms of GLEGG : *Sable, two lions counter-passant in pale argent.* Or, three lions counter-passant sable, is the coat of TESTU, Marquis de BALINCOURT.

A demi-lion rampant, that is, the upper half of a lion rampant, with a portion of the tail, often occurs as a

KERBESCAT, KERANGUEN, etc. It is styled *diffamed* when without a tail, and *eviré* when represented without indications of sex. Other leonine monsters are occasionally found, *e.g.*, two-headed lions, and lions bi-corporate and tri-corporate. Examples of the last are afforded by the seal of EDMUND CROUCHBACK, 1st Earl of LEICESTER; and in the coat assigned to the family of NASH;—*Or, a tricorporate lion rampant azure the bodies issuing from the dexter and sinister chief points and from the base, all uniting in one head gardant in the fess point* (Plate XXI., fig. 10).

The Arms of the Republic of VENICE are the Evangelistic Symbol of its Patron Saint, ST. MARK. *Azure, a winged lion couchant or, holding between its fore-paws an open book thereon the words* PAX TIBI, MARCE, EVANGELISTA (MEUS) *proper* (Plate XXI., fig. 11).

By an utterly unnecessary refinement the name of *lioncels* is often given to a number of lions represented in the same field, or to lions charged upon an Ordinary, and therefore of smaller size. Thus, the coat of WILLIAM LONGESPEÉ, Earl of SALISBURY (Plate XXI., fig. 12), is often blazoned:—*Azure, six lioncels three, two, one, or.* The family of DE BEAUVAU in France thus blazons its coat:—*d'Argent, à quatre lionceaux de gueules armés et couronnés d'or* (these lions are represented 2 and 2). The French family of MONTGOMMERY bears; *de Gueules, au chevron d'hermine accompagné de trois lionceaux léopardés d'or.*

We often find instances in which the lion is borne not of one tincture but barry, or bendy, or chequy, or otherwise divided. The arms of the Grand Dukes of HESSE are:—*Azure, a lion barry argent and gules crowned or.* The Spanish MENDEZ bear *Argent, on a lion gules three bends or.*

Lions and other animals ordinarily face to the dexter side of the shield, unless otherwise blazoned; when they

fig. 8), an allusive coat to an old orthography of the name "mautelent," or mutilated. Allusion has already been made to the representation of the lion with a double tail (*queue fourchée*), and to the fact that this, which has in process of time become a real difference or distinction in the case of some important coats, arose simply from the exuberance of the painter's fancy in treating the swelling, or central enlargement, of the tail of the conventional mediæval lion.

The coat of the kingdom of BOHEMIA is now, *Gules, a lion rampant, queue fourchée argent, crowned or.* (In the 14th century *Zürich Wappenrolle* the tail is thus treated.) In the historical Heraldry of ENGLAND we have other examples: *Gules, a lion rampant queue fourchée argent* is the coat of SIMON DE MONTFORT, Earl of LEICESTER (Plate XXI., fig. 9); and *Or, a lion rampant queue fourchée vert* was borne by the SUTTONS, Barons DUDLEY. *Azure, a lion rampant queue fourchée or* appears in the old *Rolls of Arms* for STAPLETON. In many important historic coats the lion is represented crowned (in some cases the crown is a much later addition to the original arms). In many coats especially in Foreign Armory the lion grasps some object with its paws; thus *Azure, a lion rampant or holding a quince of the last, slipped vert,* are the arms of the Italian SFORZA. *Azure, on a mount in base vert, a lion rampant crowned or, and holding a sabre argent,* is borne by the Princes of KOHARY in Hungary. At times it is collared (with or without a chain), or gorged with a coronet or antique crown. A lion is said to be *morné* in the very rare examples in which it is deprived of its natural weapons the teeth and claws. A lion *morné* appears as a canting charge in the coat of the old French family of DE MORNAY:—*Fascé d'argent, et de gueules, au lion morné de sable couronné d'or brochant sur le tout.* I have noticed that the lion *morné* occurs in the arms of several old Breton families, KERBOURIOU,

léopardés de gueules regardants; with the addition of the special augmentation of a Duke of the French Empire: *a chief gules semé of étoiles* (drawn as mullets) *argent* (*à un chef de gueules semé d'étoiles d'argent*).

An attitude slightly differing from *rampant*, is that known as *salient*, in which the animal is represented in the act of springing upon its prey, both its hind legs being on the ground and its fore-paws elevated and extended, as in No. 7, the arms of the DALLINGTONS: *Gules, a lion salient or. Or, a lion salient sable,* is the coat of FELBRIDGE. (This is an attitude seldom, or never, met with in Foreign blazon.)

A few other attitudes are enumerated by heralds, but though sometimes used for crests, are rarely if ever found in arms; such is *statant*, in which the lion stands with all four legs upon the ground. In French blazon this is described as *posé*. *Azure, a lion statant or*, are the arms assigned to EDMUND BROMFIELD, Bishop of LLANDAFF, in 1389. A lion in the same attitude but presenting his full face to the spectator, is said to be *statant-gardant*. This is the attitude in which the lion now appears in the Royal Crest of England. In some modern blazons the word *statant* is omitted.

The lion *couchant* is represented lying down; and *dormant*, as sleeping with its head resting on its fore-paws. *Sable, a lion or, couchant upon a terrace azure* is the coat of the family of HEIN of Lorraine. *Sejant* is the term applied to a lion sitting;—*sejant-gardant*, when in this attitude the full face is shown;—*sejant-rampant* when though still seated the fore-paws are raised in the air, as in the coat of HOHENHÄUSER of Suabia; *Argent, a lion sejant-rampant sable*;—and *sejant-affronté* when, as in the Royal Crest of SCOTLAND, the seated lion is shown with its whole body facing the spectator.

Or, a lion rampant dismembered, or *couped at all its joints, gules,* is the coat of the MAITLANDS (Plate XXI.,

towards the spectator as in No. 2, the coat of SHERBURNE of Stonyhurst in Lancashire, *Argent, a lion rampant vert*. *Azure, fleury, a lion rampant-gardant argent* is the original coat of the HOLANDS, or HOLLANDS, Earls of KENT, and Dukes of SURREY (*v.* p. 215); *Gules, a lion rampant-gardant argent* was the coat of MARNEY. *Gules, a lion rampant-gardant or*, is borne by the Counts and Princes of SAYN.

When the lion is *rampant-regardant* the general attitude is the same but the head looks backward and is accordingly seen in profile, as in No. 3, the coat of PRYSE of Goggerdan in Wales, *Or, a lion rampant-regardant sable*. *Or, a lion rampant-regardant gules*, was borne by GUTHRIE of Halkertoun in Scotland.

When *passant* (in French blazon, *un lion léopardé*) the beast is depicted in a walking attitude the dexter forepaw elevated, the other three resting on the ground, the head in profile and the tail curved over the back, as in the English coat of GIFFARD (No. 4). *Gules, three lions passant argent* (*de Gueules, à trois lions léopardés d'argent*). The position termed *passant-gardant*, the attitude of the Royal lions of ENGLAND, is the same, but the animals are front or full-faced, as in No. 5, the coat of LESTRANGE, *Gules, two lions passant-gardant argent* (*de Gueules, à deux léopards d'argent*). *Argent, a lion passant-gardant gules, crowned with an imperial crown, and gorged with an open one, both proper*, are the arms of OGILVY, Earls of AIRLY. The same position with the head in profile and looking backward is known as *passant-regardant*, as in (No. 6) the Irish coat of MACMAHON: *Argent, three lions passant-regardant in pale gules*. This coat is also borne by the Marquises of MACMAHON in France, the family to which belongs the late President of the French Republic, Le Maréchal MARIE EDMÉ PATRICE MACMAHON, Duc de MAGENTA, who bears the same arms: *d'Argent, à trois lions*

occupied by the lion in British and Foreign Heraldry it may suffice to add here a few other examples in which the royal beast figures in important coats.

The MARSHALLS, Earls of PEMBROKE bore : *Per pale Or and vert, a lion rampant sable*. The TALBOT coat is, *Gules, a lion rampant within a bordure engrailed or;* the GRAYS of Howick bore the same, but with the charges *argent* (*v.* p. 435).

The Counts of POICTOU ; the GOYONS, Ducs of VALENTINOIS ; the Dukes of COURLAND ; the Counts of SUSENBERG, etc., all bore: *Argent, a lion rampant gules crowned or*.

Azure, billetty a lion rampant or, are the well known arms of the Counts of NASSAU (*v.* pp. 404 and 466). A similar coat : *Argent, billetty* (couchés) *azure, a lion rampant gules*, was borne by the Counts of GEROLDSECK (*v.* p. 490).

Azure, fleury and a lion rampant argent is the coat of HOLLAND of England ; and, with the charges *or*, of BEAUMONT, both in England and in France. *Azure, crusily a lion rampant or*, was borne by the BRAOSES, BREUS, or BREWES (*v. ante* BRUCE, p. 144); the LOVELLS bore the reverse.

The tressured lion of SCOTLAND is treated separately (pp. 177, etc.), but *Argent, a lion rampant azure within the Royal tressure gules*, is the coat of LYON, Earl of STRATHMORE (*v.* p. 349).

In Plate XXI., are exhibited the attitudes of lions in later heraldry, some of which are applicable to other animals. In the examples which were given above, all are in the original and most frequent attitude known as *rampant*, the left foot alone supporting the body, the head in profile, the tail elevated and curved, as in fig. 1, the arms of PERCY, or LOUVAIN. In the position known as *rampant-gardant* (the "*léopard lionné*" of French blazon) the attitude of body, legs, and tail is the same but the head is front faced, *i.e.* the full face is turned

ZÄHRINGEN ; of the Vicomtes de GOYON ; of the MAULÉONS, and LAUTRECS, crusaders in 1224; of the MONTLEONS, bannerets of Touraine ; MONTBAZON, SOISSONS, ROSTAING, SABRAN, VERTHAMONT, etc. *Or, a lion rampant azure* (Plate XXI., fig. 1), the arms of LOUVAIN, is the well known coat of PERCY, Earls of Northumberland; and of RIVERS, Earls of DEVON, etc. It was also borne by the Counts of ZUTPHEN, in Holland ; by the Counts, afterwards Princes of SOLMS ; by the GRAMONTS (Ducs de CADEROUSSE, GUICHE, and GRAMONT, in France) ; by the Neapolitan ACQUAVIVA, Dukes of ASTI, etc.

Sable, a lion rampant argent (de Sable, au lion d'argent), is the coat of CROMWELL ; VERDON ; SEGRAVE ; (later *crowned or*) in England ; of the Duchy of AOSTA ; of the Norman Counts of MEULLENT ; of the Barons of QUERNFURTH ; and the Counts of GONDRECOURT.

Sable, a lion rampant or (de Sable, au lion d'or) are the arms of the Duchy of BRABANT ; of the CAPECI of Naples; the Marquesses of NYDEGGEN ; the CHAUVIGNY, Comtes de BLOT, etc.

Vert, a lion rampant argent (de Sinople, au lion d'argent), is borne by the Barons BOLEBEC in England, the HUMES or HOMES of Scotland, the DIAZ of Spain, etc. A list at least as extensive might easily be given in which the like arms are borne with the simple differences of the addition of a crown,—as in the coat of the Lordship of GALLOWAY: *Azure, a lion rampant argent, crowned or,* also borne by the Counts of GLEICHEN ; and of EBERSTEIN (one of the BRUNSWICK quarterings),—or of the lion's tail being *fourchée* (originally a mere freak of the artist's brush, afterwards converted into a real mark of difference) thus : *Argent, a lion rampant queue fourchée gules,* is the coat of VALKENBURG ; and in England was borne by MOUNTFORD ; HAVERING ; ST. PAUL ; and BREWSE.

With the above indications of the important position

Argent, a lion rampant gules (d'Argent, au lion de gueules) is borne by the Counts of ARMAGNAC in France; the Barons of WARTENBERG (*Wappenrolle von Zürich,* No. 191), the Counts von ALTDORF; the PREISSACS, Ducs de FIMARCON, and D'ESCLIGNAC in France; and by the family of FEZENSAC (*Salle des Croisés,* 1097).

Argent, a lion rampant sable (d'Argent, au lion de sable), are the arms of STAPLETON, and FITZ ROGER in England, the Welsh families of LLOYD; MORGAN; WYNN, etc., the Counts BARBARANI, and LOREDAN of Venice, the Barons BERSTETT of Austria, the French families of FIENNES, and POLASTRON (both in the *Salle des Croisés,* thirteenth century), etc.

Azure, a lion rampant argent (d'Azur, au lion d'argent) is borne in England by the MONTALTS, and CREWES; in Scotland by LAMONT, M'DOUGALL, and M'NEILL (quartered with other coats, *v.* p. 512). In Italy it was carried by the BELLUOMI, and the Venetian ROSSI, etc.

Azure, a lion rampant or (d'Azur, au lion d'or), is a coat of frequent occurrence both in Britain and on the Continent. At home it is an early coat of NEVILE; BRAOSE or BREWYS; and was borne by HUGHES; MEREDITH; and LLOYD in Wales; in France by SAULX, Duc et Pair de TAVANNES; the families of LA NOË, PIEDEFER, GRAÇAY, MUSY, etc.

Gules, a lion rampant argent (de Gueules, au lion d'argent) are the arms of the English MOWBRAYS, quartered by the Duke of NORFOLK; and of the Scottish WALLACES. Abroad it is borne by the PONTEVEZ, Ducs de SABRAN (*Salle des Croisés,* 1096); the Neapolitan Counts D'ARIANO; the MANTELLI of Italy, the LÖVENSCHILDS of Denmark; the ANTOINGS, VAN NOORDENS, VAN SANDWYKS, etc., of the Low Countries, etc.

Gules, a lion rampant or (de Gueules, au lion d'or), the arms of FITZ ALAN of Arundel, is also a coat borne with great frequency. It is the old coat of the Dukes of

PLATE XXI.

1. Lion Rampant.
   Louvain.

2. Lion Rampant gardant.
   Sherburn.

3. Lion Rampant regardant.
   Pryse.

4. Lions Passant.
   Gifford.

5. Lions Passant, gardant.
   Le Strange.

6. Lions Passant, regardant.
   M'Mahon.

7. Lion salient.
   Dillington.

8. Lion dismembered.
   Maitland.

9. Lion Queue fourchée.
   Montfort, Earl of Leicester.

10. Tricorporate Lion.
    Nashe.

11. Winged Lion.
    Venice.

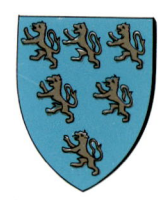

12. Lioncels.
    Longespee, Earl of Salisbury.

standing with regard to the blazons of the Heralds' College in modern times; but in the heraldry of Scotland this usage, though introduced, has not been at all times so clearly admitted.

In Foreign Armory a lion is understood to be represented rampant unless some other position be expressed, and it may be noticed that the royal beast is only very exceptionally borne *proper*, that is of its natural colours. Of the multitude of coats charged with lions only a few ancient examples can be recorded here.

Or, a lion rampant sable (d'Or, au lion de sable) is the well known coat of the Counts of FLANDERS (pp. 483); of the Duchy of JULIERS (quartered by the Counts PALATINE OF THE RHINE, and in the Royal Escucheon of PRUSSIA); by the Lords of KÖNIGSTEIN; and of MAHLBERG, the latter quartered by the Princes of NASSAU, and the Grand Dukes of BADEN. It was borne by the Counts of LYONNAIS ET FOREZ, and the families of GRASSE, and LEON (*Salle des Croisés*, 1096). In Britain it was used by the families of WELLES; GRIFFITHS, Princes of CARDIGAN and GWENT; and by their kinsmen the MATHEWS.

Or, a lion rampant gules (d'Or, au lion de gueules) is the blazon of the Counts of HOLLAND, and the original coat of the Counts of HAPSBURG, now Emperors of AUSTRIA. It was also early borne in France by the families of FOUCAULD; and DU PUY; in Germany by the Counts UNRUH; RECKHEIM; and ROUCY; in Britain by the CHARLETONS, and other descendants of the Princes of POWYS; in Scotland by FARQUHARSON, MACDONALD, and MACINTOSH; and by the DUFFS, Earls, now Dukes, of FIFE.

Argent, a lion rampant azure (d'Argent, au lion d'azur) is the coat of the CRICHTONS of Frendraught; of the BRUCES, and FAUCONBERGES, or FALCONBRIDGES; and of the Counts MENSDORFF-POUILLY of Austria.

lion and the leopard is still preserved. The *lion* is our lion rampant. The *léopard* is the same beast but passant-gardant; while the names *lion-léopardé* and *léopard-lionné* are respectively given to our lion passant, and rampant-gardant.

The knowledge of natural history possessed by the early heralds, or wearers of coat-armour, was limited. Most of them had never seen a lion; but the graphic and spirited character of the drawing made up for its want of realism. Mr RUSKIN (*Modern Painters*, iv., 106) contrasting the true, or mediæval, griffin with its false or *renaissance* counterpart, remarks that the Lombard workman did really see a griffin in his imagination and carved it from the life. The mediæval herald had in like manner so truly beheld with his immortal eyes a creature possessed of the power and majesty of the lion, that he delineated it as he had seen it. The lions of the fourteenth century are perhaps the best. Towards the sixteenth their grotesque character becomes somewhat exaggerated; but they still convey the idea of strength and kingly dignity; and are vastly superior to the utterly un-idealised lion of more modern heraldry.

Before enumerating the different attitudes of lions in later heraldry, the terms *armed* and *langued*, as applied to them and to other beasts of prey, have to be explained. The former term applies to the claws and teeth, the latter to the tongue. When a lion, or other animal, is described as *armed argent and langued gules*, it is meant that the claws and teeth are *argent*, and the tongue *gules*. In English heraldry it is presumed that, unless otherwise blazoned, the lion is armed and langued *gules*, and there is therefore no occasion to mention the fact. In the case, however, of either the lion, or the field which is charged with it, being *gules*, the lion is represented armed and langued *azure*, unless otherwise described. This is the general under-

The earliest trace which we have of the arms of any member of the English royal house is on the shield of King JOHN as prince, on whose seal are two lions passant, or *léopards-lionnés*. These become three on his seal as king, in 1290. On the other hand the earliest Great Seal of RICHARD I. (*c.* 1189), where we have also the earliest representation of the arms of any actual monarch, exhibits a lion rampant ; but as the convex shield presents but half its surface, Mr PLANCHÉ (following HENRY SPELMAN in his *Aspilogia*) considers that the complete device had been two lions rampant-combatant. (*See* the *Catalogue of Seals in the British Museum*, vol. i., Nos. 80 and 91.) He finds corroboration of this view in the words of the contemporary poet WILLIAM DE BARR, who says of RICHARD, "rictus agnosco leonum illius in clypeo;" and in the description in GEOFFREY VINESAUF'S Chronicle of his interview with FREDERICK BARBAROSSA, in the Isle of Cyprus, where the English King's saddle is described as having behind "two small lions of gold turned towards each other with their mouths open and each stretching out his forelegs as if to attack and devour the other." It may be remarked that VINESAUF'S evidence would be stronger if he had alluded to the lions as the coat-armour of RICHARD ; his description rather implies that they were embroidered on his saddle. In any case, however, after a universal and authoritative recognition of four hundred years' standing of the English royal animals as lions, they can hardly again be degraded on doubtful antiquarian grounds into leopards. The idea that sprang up in the middle ages that the leopard was the issue of the pard and lioness, helped to bring that heraldic animal into disrepute, and accounts for the anxiety of the early English armorial writers to adopt or revert to the designation of lions.

In French blazon the old distinction between the

occasion of the marriage of the same King's daughter, the Princess MARGARET, with King ALEXANDER III. of Scotland, a robe was made for the King, of purple sarcenet with three leopards in front and three behind; and these little leopards were also placed on the violet brocade robe made for the Queen (*Close Roll*, 1252). The designation of leopards continued to be generally adhered to throughout the reigns of the three EDWARDS, though the identity of the animals was occasionally disputed; and NICOLAS SERBY was "*Leopard*" Herald in the reign of HENRY V. But by the end of the fifteenth century it seems to have been decided by competent authority that the three beasts in the royal coat were lions; and the early armorialists, JOHN of Guildford, NICHOLAS UPTON, and the rest, protest strongly against their being called anything else.

Mr PLANCHÉ considers that, from a historical point of view, these writers and their successors are in the right, and his reasoning is somewhat as follows. In the early days of coat-armour, more especially in England, the animals most usually met with were lions and leopards, which in the rude drawing of the day were distinguishable only by their respective attitudes. The lion's normal position was rampant; the "ramping and roaring lion" of the Psalmist, erect and showing but one eye and one ear; that of a leopard was what came to be defined as "passant-gardant," walking along but showing both eyes and ears. As the necessity for varying the attitude of either animal arose out of the multiplication of coats, the terms came into use of *lion léopardé* for what we call a lion rampant-gardant, and *léopard lionné* for a lion passant. Now, when a lion came to be repeated more than once in a coat of arms, and space did not admit of its being placed in the rampant attitude, it was very apt to assume the position of a leopard *lionné*, or even of a leopard simply.

CHAPTER VII.

ANIMATE CHARGES :—II. BEASTS.

I. THE LION. — No animal has anything like so prominent a position in early, and even in later heraldry, as that which is held by the Lion. The earliest known example of it is on the seal of PHILIP I., Count of FLANDERS, appended to a document of 1164; and before long it became the ensign of the Princes of NORWAY, DENMARK, SCOTLAND, and (according to most writers on the subject) ENGLAND, of the Counts of HOLLAND, in fact of most of the leading potentates of Europe, with the important exception of the German Emperors and Kings of FRANCE. In England in the reign of HENRY III. it was borne by so many of the principal nobles, that no idea can have existed that sovereign houses had an exclusive right to it. In Foreign Armory the coats in which the lion appears as the principal, most frequently as the sole charge, may be numbered by thousands.

The English lions which appear first on the seals of RICHARD I., 1195, 1198 (DEMAY, *Le Costume d'après les Sceaux*, p. 144) were, in the reign of HENRY III. and for two centuries afterwards, more generally designated leopards, and that not only (as has been said) in derision by the French but by the English themselves. In token of their being his armorial insignia, three leopards were sent to HENRY III. by the Emperor FREDERICK II. GLOVER'S *Roll, c.* 1250, which gives lions to six of the English Earls, begins with "*Le roy d'Angleterre porte, Goules trois lupards d'or.*" On the

interesting as an example of a heraldic charge evolved out of ancient symbolism. As borne in comparatively modern times it is blazoned as: *Gules, three legs in armour embowed and conjoined at the thighs proper, spurred and garnished or.* An early example of this coat is engraved in Mr PLANCHÉ'S *Pursuivant*, p. 112, with the legs encased in the banded chain mail of the thirteenth century, and without spurs. This coat has been quartered as "Arms of Pretension" by various English families; and still appears among the quarterings borne by the Earls of DERBY; and the Dukes of ATHOLE; and M'LEOD. It is also borne for the name of AUFFRECK. The legs would in foreign blazon be described as "conjoined in pairle:" and the coat is thus borne on the Continent by the Franconian family of RABENSTEINER; and by DROGOMIR in Poland.

A remarkable Spanish coat is that borne by the family of BONES COMBES: *Or, two legs issuing from the flanks of the shield, the feet immersed in water in base all proper.* (*Escudo de oro, y dos piernas en ademan de bañarse.* PIFERRER, *Nobiliario de los Reinos y Señorios de España*, vol i., No. 279, Madrid, 1857-1860.) The MALAGAMBAS bear: *Azure, a human leg proper, shod, and pierced by an arrow in bend argent, distilling blood. On a chief of the second three estoiles of the first.*

FEET alone occur in the *Armes parlantes* of VOET and SNEEVOET of Flanders; *Azure, three human feet argent.* A family of VOET in Holland bears: *Gules, a human foot argent;* and one of the same name in Flanders bears: *Azure, three human feet, the soles alone appearing, proper.*

D'Azur, à une Foi d'or were the arms of FOI DE ST. MAURICE. This bearing occurs in a very few instances in English Heraldry. *Sable, two arms issuing from the flanks and embowed in fess argent, the hands conjoined, between three crescents of the second*, is recorded in CAMDEN'S *Visitation of Huntingdonshire* in 1613 (Camden Society), p. 55 for CRESPIN, or CRISPIN. *Gules, two arms issuing from the flanks, the hands conjoined argent between three hearts or;* are the *armes parlantes* of PUREFOY, Bishop of HEREFORD (1554-1557). Another coat borne by a family of the same name is: *Sable, six armed hands embracing in pairs argent two and one. Gules, two hands issuing from the sinister base and grasping a broken two-handed sword in bend-sinister proper*, is the coat of KEMP, in Scotland. *Sable, two arms issuing from the flanks in base, conjoined in chevron and grasping a human heart or*, is the allusive coat of DE LA FOY.

Gules, three dexter arms vambraced fessways in pale argent, the hands proper, is the coat of ARMSTRONG.

Gules, three dexter arms conjoined at the shoulders, and flexed in pairle or, the fists clenched proper; is borne by the family of TREMAYNE (Plate XX., fig. 10).

HUMAN RIB BONES appear in the canting coats of COSTANZO of Naples, DE LA COSTE DU VIVIER, etc.

The arms of the Portuguese DA COSTA are: *Gules, six human ribs argent, ranged 2, 2, 2, fessways in pale.*

HUMAN LEGS AND FEET occur with some frequency as Heraldic charges (Plate XX., fig. 8). *Argent, a man's leg erased at the thigh in pale sable*, is borne by the family of PRIME in Sussex.

The well known insignia of the ISLAND and KINGDOM OF MAN (Plate XX., fig. 9) is at least as ancient as the middle of the thirteenth century. This was the ancient symbol of Trinacria (Sicily), afterwards adopted as the arms of that kingdom under MURAT, and it is

Gules, a fess between four hands (argent or *or)* is the coat of the QUATERMAINES.

An arm is often represented as issuing from the edge of the shield. In some University arms it issues from the chief, as in those of the UNIVERSITY OF PARIS, which are: *Azure, three fleurs-de-lis or, a hand and arm issuing from clouds in chief and holding a book proper.* In French blazon an arm is called *a dextrochère,* or *a senestrochère* according as it is represented a right or a left hand. (RIETSTAP says, but wrongly, according as it issues from the dexter or sinister flank.) If the elbow is not shown the term is *un avant bras.*

Or, a right hand and arm issuing from a cloud in sinister flank and holding a sword proper in pale, was borne by the Princes POTEMKIN in Russia. The arms of the County of SCHWERIN as quartered by the Princes of MECKLENBURGH, are; *Gules, an arm in armour to the wrist embowed, issuing from clouds on the sinister side, and holding a gem ring, all proper, round the arm a scarf azure.* (The *clouds* were originally only the puffings at the top of the sleeve!)

Or, a chief azure, thereon a hand and arm proper vested ermine, the maniple (sleeve or *fanon) ermine extending over the field in pale;* is the coat of VILLIERS DE L'ISLE ADAM, Grand Master of the Knights of the Hospital of St. John. Similar to this the coat of MOHUN: *Gules, a dexter arm proper in a maunch ermine, the hand holding a fleur-de-lis or (cf.* p. 458).

Several of the Highland Chieftains have a quartering in which a hand issues from the flank and holds a cross-crosslet (*see* Plate XLIII., figs. 4, 5, 6, and pp. 512, 513).

In French Armory two arms are sometimes represented as issuing from the flanks, the hands being clasped in the centre of the escucheon; this bearing is known as a *Foi.* The Counts COUSIN DE LA TOUR-FONDUE bear: *d'Azur, à une Foi d'argent.*

between two horns per fess, the dexter *or* and *sable;* the sinister *sable* and *argent*).

In the coat of the family of DE LA SABLONNIÈRE of the Netherlands two human skeletons *sable* hold a sieve *gules* in an *argent* field. The family of LEICHNAM, in Hesse, bear: *Gules, a corpse enshrouded on a bier proper*, as canting arms.

In British Armory the HUMAN ARM is very frequently employed as a crest, often *embowed* and *vambraced*, that is in armour; sometimes couped at the elbow, and upright (a *cubit arm*), and holding a variety of weapons, etc.: *Argent, a hand appaumé* (*i.e.*, open, showing the palm) *couped gules*, are the arms of O'NEILL, Earl of TYRONE; the sinister hand is known as the "Badge of ULSTER," and is the distinguishing mark of the dignity of all Baronets except those of Scotland and Nova Scotia.

Azure, a hand appaumé argent are the canting arms of MAGNE, in France, and are also those of the family of WAROQUIER, or VAROQUIER; whence arose the French proverbial "*Je te donnerai les armes de* VAROQUIER!" a threat of a box on the ear! A BLESSING HAND is one of which the thumb and two first fingers are alone extended, as in the act of Episcopal benediction.

Such a hand occurs occasionally as in the arms of BENOIT: *Azure, a chevron or between three hands blessing argent*. In Scottish Heraldry it is the crest of the MILLARS.

Azure, three hands (sometimes dexter, sometimes sinister) *argent* are the *armes parlantes* of MALMAYNS; and *Or, three clenched fists proper*, those of POIGNET.

Argent, a chevron azure between three sinister hands appaumés gules is borne by the Lords MAYNARD (Plate XX., fig. 7), while the French Counts MAYNARD DE ST. MICHEL are content to use *d'Azur, à une main dextre appaumée d'or*.

pierced by two darts or. The VANNS of Holland use *Or, two human hearts gules inflamed or, the dexter projecting over the sinister.* The arms of the Counts COLLEONI of Milan are, in modern times, blazoned as: *Per pale argent and gules, three hearts reversed counterchanged.* In ancient, and less delicate, times the bearings had a different significance as *armes parlantes.*

Or, six beards sable, are the arms of the Venetian BARBANI; and *Or, a beard sable,* of the BARBONIANI.

The TONGUE appears as a charge in the coat of LINGUET: *Azure, two pens in saltire argent, on a chief of the last three tongues gules.*

The LIPS (and TEETH) are used in the canting coat of LIPPE of Switzerland: *Argent, two upper lips each above a row of teeth fesseways in pale proper, all within a bordure azure.*

The TEETH alone: *Argent, three molars gules* are borne by CAIXAL of Spain; *Or, on a fess gules three double teeth argent,* is the coat of the Dutch KIES.

The JAW BONE appears in the coat of the Spanish QUEXADA: *Argent, five jaw bones gules 2, 1, 2;* while QUIJADA bears: *Argent, four lower jaws, 2, 2, azure.*

The whole SKULL, either alone, or in conjunction with the piratical crossbones, is occasionally used as a heraldic charge: as by DIDIER DE MORTAL: *de Sable, à trois têtes de mort d'argent; au chef d'azur chargé d'un cheval issuant du sécond* (note the *"pale horse"* of death, REV. vi. 8, in the chief). VAN GORCUM in Holland bears: *Per pale* (a) *Gules, two crossbones supporting a skull argent;* (b) *Azure, two swords in saltire proper.* The Dalmatian family of MORTE is even more funereal: *Sable, two crossbones in saltire supporting a skull argent.*

The whole SKELETON is used as supporters by the PELETS; and as a crest by the VAN SCHOONHOVENS of Ghent (holding an arrow and between two wings *or*), and by TOD VON LEWENTHAL (holding bow and arrow and

In the coat of the French family of DENIS the eyes are weeping, *de Gueules, à deux yeux larmoyants au naturel, les larmes d'argent en chef, et une rose d'or en point.* The BELLEVOIRS carry the matter further; their coat is: *Sable, two human eyes in chief proper, the base of the shield semé de larmes argent.* One more example will suffice—the FORMANOIRS bear: *Or, fretty sable, the claire-voies charged with human eyes proper.*

Of the HUMAN HEART in Armory, not perhaps the oldest but the most famous example occurs in the DOUGLAS coat to which the heart was added (at first uncrowned) by the first Earl of DOUGLAS, in commemoration of his uncle the good Sir JAMES having set out to Palestine bearing the heart of his royal master, in order that it might be deposited in the soil of the Holy Land: a journey frustrated by his falling in an encounter with the Moors in Spain (*See* LOCKHART'S *Spanish Ballads*). *Or, a heart gules* is borne by CORTI. *Argent, three hearts gules* (*d'Argent, à trois cœurs de gueules*), is the canting coat of CŒURET, Marquis de NESLE; and *d'Argent, three green hearts* (*d'Argent, à trois cœurs de sinople*) that of CŒURVERT. *Or, three hearts sable the points in pairle* are the arms of the Counts of DERNBACH.

In many coats additions of a sentimental character are found. *Azure, a heart inflamed or,* is borne by ST. HILAIRE; *Or, a heart gules, a pansy issuant therefrom, azure* (*or vert*); is the coat of CHAILOUS, or CHAYLAU; *Azure, a heart or winged argent* is that of GENESTET. But even a more distinctively "Valentine" character is found at times. The GOESHEN, or GÖSCHEN, family bear: *Argent, a heart gules, inflamed and pierced by an arrow or, the point and feathers azure.* The GUJANS of Chür bear: *Azure, a heart gules, pierced by two arrows in saltire argent,* the flame has developed into *a surmounting estoile.* The family of RHODIUS of Brabant bear: *Gules, a heart inflamed,*

coat of the TRIVULZI of Milan, *d'Or, à un tête de Gérion de carnation, couronné d'or, avec les barbes et cheveux grises.* Here the *tre volti*, triple faces, are two in profile towards the flanks; the third is *affronté*.

The head of JANUS with its double face, occurs in the arms of several families, *e.g.*, JANER in Spain bears, *Or, the head of Janus crowned with an antique crown proper.*

The head of ARGUS is the charge of the arms of the French family of SANTEUIL:—*d'Azur, à une tête d'Argus d'or,* the head being plentifully covered with an indefinite number of eyes—of course these are *armes parlantes*="*cent œuil.*"

Other heads are occasionally met with; the heads of BOREAS, ÆOLUS, MIDAS, and of ST. JOHN THE BAPTIST, and ST. DENIS, have all of them come under my observation, and some of them in more than one instance.

The conventional representation of a CHERUB—the angelic head surrounded by six wings—appears in the arms of the Italian family of BUOCAFOCO, or BUCCAFOCO;—*Gules, a seraph or.* Three such cherubs are the coat of the French CHÉRINS; *d'Or, à trois cherubins de gueules;* and the Counts TRIANGI naturally bear: *Gules, a chevron ployé argent between three cherubs proper, their wings or.* The Italian house of MALATESTA of Rimini, bore: *Vert, three human heads affrontés proper;* and the GRYNS of Cologne chose as their heraldic property the coat: *Sable, three human heads affrontés, grinning, or grimacing, proper* (*!*) *and crowned or.*

The HUMAN EYE appears as a charge (usually in *armes parlantes*) in more coats than might have been expected. The coat of the HESHUYSENS of Amsterdam is: *Azure, two human eyes in fess proper* (Plate XX., fig. 11). The Catalan GRANULLAS bear: *Or, two human eyes in chief proper.*

The FINIELS of Languedoc have no less than nine; *d'Azur, à neuf yeux ouverts d'argent,* 3, 3, 3.

LLOYDS, Lords MOSTYN; the PRICES; and WYNNS; it is: *Gules, a Saracen's head erased at the neck proper, wreathed about the temples sable and argent.* This is also the coat of the BRUUNS of Denmark. It should be remarked that "Moor's heads" are generally drawn as those of "blackamoors," or negroes, as in Plate XX., fig. 6 which represents the arms of SARDINIA: *Argent, a cross gules between four Moor's heads couped sable, banded of the first.* A single Moor's head proper, on a chief *argent* (as the "arms of CORSICA") was granted as an augmentation to the arms of ELLIOTT, Earl of MINTO, and is still borne in their escucheon. It is also the coat of the Florentine PUCCI; of VAN DER ELST and of GENDRON in HOLLAND. *Or, a Moor's head and bust proper, wreathed sable and or,* is the canting coat of the Tirolese Counts MOHR DE TARANTSBERG; and a similar coat is borne by MAIR of Bavaria. *Argent, three negro's heads in profile sable wreathed of the colours* is borne by the CANNINGS.

The long continued struggle between the Turks and Hungarians accounts for the introduction of the head of a dead Turk with his single long lock of hair into several important Hungarian and Transylvanian coats. The Austrian Counts and Princes of SCHWARZENBERG impale, or use as a quartering, with their own arms of SEINSHEIM (*Paly of eight argent and azure*) the following concession:—*Or, a raven sable, collared of the field, perched on the head of a dead Turk, and picking out his eye;* no doubt an agreeable memorial of a hard fought fight!

A singular coat Plate XX., fig. 5 belongs to the Scottish family of MORISONS of Dairsie in Fife. *Azure, three Saracen's heads erased, conjoined in one neck, and wreathed with laurel all proper, the faces respectively turned towards the chief and flanks of the shield.* In Foreign Heraldry a somewhat similar arrangement is known as a "*Tête de Gérion,*" and is borne as the canting

times *a staff raguly*, at others) *a tree eradicated, all proper*.

The coat ascribed to DRUMMOND of Kildies is: *Or, three bars undy gules, over all a naked man in motion brandishing a sword proper*.

In Foreign Heraldry kings, queens, bishops, priests, mounted or dismounted knights, pilgrims, miners, and men of other occupations, appear properly habited in great variety; in our own Armory they occur only occasionally. Plate XX., fig. 3, is the coat of the Irish MAGUIRES—*Vert, a mounted knight armed cap-à-pie and holding in his hand a sword all proper*.

The arms of LITHUANIA (which were quartered with the arms of POLAND, *Gules, an eagle displayed argent* in the shield of that kingdom) were: *Gules, a knight armed cap-à-pie mounted on a white horse, brandishing his sword all proper, and bearing an oval buckler Azure thereon a cross patriarchal or* (*vide post*, p. 486).

A volume would be required for the full description of all the curious instances of the use of the human figure in Continental Armory, here it will suffice to mention but one more instance. The Spanish family of PALACIO in the Asturias, bears, *on a green field two couples of both sexes* performing the national dance of the *fandango!*

When we come to the consideration of the HUMAN BODY in its several parts as a Heraldic charge the abundance of examples is even more embarrassing.

HUMAN HEADS are borne in profile, or *affrontés*, and either couped or erased, that is either cut cleanly off at the neck, or having a ragged edge of pieces of skin. The *Savage's head* is usually wreathed with foliage; while the *Saracen's head* is usually banded, or wreathed about the temples, and wears earrings, as in the arms of GLEDSTANES (Plate XVII., fig. 9). Plate XX., fig. 4 gives us the arms of MARCHYDD, or MERGETH, AP CYNAN, a Welsh chieftain, still borne by his descendants the

PLATE XX.

1. Man.
Dalzell.

2. Savage.
Emlyn.

3. Horseman.
Maguire.

4. Saracen's Head.
Lloyd.

5. Heads conjoined.
Morison.

6. Moors' Heads.
Sardinia.

7. Sinister Hand.
Maynard.

8. Leg.
Prime.

9. Legs.
Isle of Man.

10. Arms.
Tremayne.

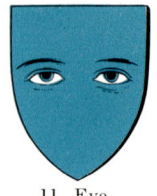

11. Eye.
Heshuysen.

12. Heart.
Douglas.

empoignant de ses deux mains la queue du renard et s'en frottant le corps," all proper!

Azure, a naked boy pointing to a star in the dexter chief, all proper, is the coat recorded for the Scottish family of OSWALD, in PONT'S MS. (*vide infra*).

A naked boy shooting (not *Cupid*) is one of the charges of the Bolognese ARFETTI; and the SCHEUCHENSTUEL DE RHAIN in Bavaria, a family now extinct, bore: *Gules, on a mount in base sable a naked boy with extended legs, and arms akimbo.*

I have a good many similar examples in which the motive for the adoption of the charge is hard to find. This, however, is not the case in the canting coat of the family of BESSON, who bear: *d'Or, à deux enfans* (jumeaux, *en patois* bessons) *de carnation, affrontés, se tenant d'une main et portant de l'autre chacun un rameau.*

The Barons GEMELL, and the Sicilian GEMELLI, have arms of which the *motif* is the same. Two nude children are the supporters of the family of NICEY in Champagne; and two naked virgins with dishevelled hair those of the Counts des ULMES.

A SAVAGE, or wild man, usually represented naked but wreathed about the head and loins with verdure, and holding a rough bough of a tree as a club, occurs frequently both at home and abroad, but with us is more common as a crest or supporter than as a charge of the escucheon. (The charge in the coat of OSWALD is often thus drawn.)

In Germany still, and among ourselves before the sixteenth century these savages are often not wreathed but are drawn covered with hair, and in aspect "*affenartig*," as a German writer terms them. An English example of the savage man is afforded by the arms of the families of EMELIE, EMLAY, or EMLINE, of Northamptonshire, and elsewhere (Plate XX., fig. 2). They bear: *Sable, a wild man standing wreathed, and holding* (some-

Azure, Hercules proper, combating a lion rampant or, appears as the coat of WILL at Augsburg; rending a tree in the arms of FAURE; and slaying the hydra in the canting coat of HERKLOTS.

The personification of FORTUNE is a favourite, both as a crest and as a charge, in German armory. Usually she is represented, as in the arms of ANTONELLI, naked, standing on a globe (sometimes floating on waves), and holding a veil, or sail, above her head.

Besides such instances as have been already referred to, the naked human figure is a not unfrequent charge abroad, though we have not many instances of it at home. The shield of the Scottish family of DALZIEL of that Ilk (Plate XX., fig. 1), which goes back at least to the fourteenth century, is *Argent, a naked man proper.* Occasionally in early examples the arms are drawn extended, and in some representations, though not in the earliest, the body is swinging from a gibbet. This is an allusion to a probably not very ancient legend, in which the founder of the family is said to have recovered the body of King KENNETH III., who had been hanged by the Picts.

All such legends in connection with Heraldic bearings must be received with the utmost incredulity. In ninety-nine cases out of a hundred the story has been invented to account for the arms; not the arms assumed as a historical hieroglyphic.

The coat of the VEGNUDINI of Bologna is *Argent, on a terrace a naked woman standing between two vine shoots, and holding in her right hand a pruning-hook, all proper, on a chief azure three mullets or.*

The Pomeranian family of PIRCH have a very remarkable coat: *Per pale* (a) *Azure, a fish haurient in pale argent;* (b) *Gules, on a terrace a naked woman affrontée, a fox running between her legs from right to left and holding in his mouth a quantity of hay*—" la dite femme

as holding the apple in one hand, and the serpent wriggling in the other. On the other hand the Spanish family of EVA apparently consider there is a sufficiently transparent allusion to their own name, and to the mother of mankind, in the simple bearings: *Or, on a mount in base an apple tree vert fruited of the field, and encircled by a serpent of the second.*

The family of ABEL in Bavaria make the patriarch in the attitude of prayer to serve as their crest; while the coat itself is: *Sable, on a square altar argent, a lamb lying surrounded by fire and smoke proper.*

SAMSON slaying the lion is the subject of the arms of the VESENTINA family of Verona. The field is *gules*, and on a terrace in base *vert* the strong man naked bestrides a golden lion and forces its jaws apart. The Polish family of SAMSON naturally use the same device, but the field is *Azure* and the patriarch is decently habited. The STARCKENS of the Island of OESEL also use the like as *armes parlantes;* the field in this case is *Or*. After these we are hardly surprised to find that Daniel in the lions' den is the subject of the arms of the Rhenish family of DANIELS, granted late in the eighteenth century; the field is *Azure*. The Bolognese DANIELI are content to make a less evident allusion to the prophet; their arms are: *Per fess azure and vert, in chief* "the lion of the tribe of Judah" *naissant or, holding an open book with the words* "LIBRI APERTI SUNT." (DANIEL vii. 10.)

The Archangel St. MICHAEL in full armour, as conventionally represented, treading beneath his feet the great adversary, *sable*, is the charge on an *azure* field of the VAN SCHOREL of Antwerp; and he also appears in the arms of the city of BRUSSELS.

Heathen mythology has been laid under contribution even more frequently than Holy Writ. NEPTUNE is to be found in the arms of NOLTHENIUS of Guelderland.

The bearings which appear in some of the Post-Reformation Sees are derived from representations of the Blessed Trinity, or of the Saints to whom the Cathedrals were dedicated, which appeared on the ancient seals.

The figure of the Blessed Virgin bearing the Divine Child which appears, on an *azure* field, in the arms of the See of Salisbury had a similar origin. These are identical with the arms of the PHOUSKARNAKI (or FOUSKARNAKI) of Greece. As *armes parlantes* the curiously designated Breton family of LENFANT-DIEU use *d'Azur, à un enfant* JÉSUS, *les mains jointes d'argent, naissant d'un croissant d'or, surmonté d'un soleil du même, et accosté de deux étoiles d'or*. The family of LORETTE use also as *armes parlantes* the following coat: *Per pale azure and or, the figure of* NÔTRE DAME DE LORETTE *holding in her arms the Holy Child.*

The families who bear the names of saints, such as ST. ANDREW, ST. GEORGE, ST. MICHAEL, have (perhaps not unnaturally) included in their arms representations of their family patrons.

The Bavarian family of REIDER include in their shield the mounted effigy of the good knight ST. MARTIN dividing his cloak with a beggar (date of diploma 1760). The figure of the great Apostle of the Gentiles appears in the arms of the VON PAULI. JOERG, and JÖRGER, of Austria, similarly make use of St. GEORGE.

Continental Heraldry affords not a few examples of the use of the personages of Holy Writ. The ADAMOLI of Lombardy bear: *Azure, the Tree of Life entwined with the Serpent, and accosted with our first parents, all proper* (*i.e.*, in a state of nature). The addition of a *chief of the Empire* to this coat makes it somewhat incongruous.

The family of ADAM in Bavaria improve on Sacred History by eliminating EVE, and by representing ADAM

CHAPTER VI.

ANIMATE CHARGES:—I. THE HUMAN FIGURE.

NEXT to geometrical figures, the most prominent charges in armorial bearings are those derived from the animal and vegetable creation; and of these those which represent man its lord, may be supposed to claim precedence in our consideration.

The entire human figure, naked or clothed, appears occasionally in our own Armory, but is still more frequently met with in the wider range of Foreign Heraldry; this contains many very curious examples, only a few of which can find description within the narrow limits of the present work.

The figure of the BLESSED SAVIOUR seated in majesty (as represented in REVELATION, i. 16—ii. 12—xix. 15) is the charge, derived from ancient seals, of the arms of the See of CHICHESTER. The utter ignorance of many of the old heraldic writers (if we can in courtesy confine it only to those of far back times) could scarcely be better exemplified than by the treatment which the noblest of all charges has undergone at their hands. The figure of the "Lord of Life and Glory" has become according to them "*Azure, a* PRESTER JOHN *sitting on a tombstone, in his left hand a mound, his right hand extended, all or; on his head a linen mitre, and in his mouth a sword ppr.*" (FOSTER'S *Peerage.*) Where the whole bearing was thus travestied it is no wonder that the details have become ridiculous! "The rainbow throne of light" has been degraded into a tombstone, and the sword issuing from the mouth into a skewer passing through it!

de-lis sable, is that of TOMLIN. *Or, three hurts, on each a mullet argent*, is borne by MONTCHAL, of France. When roundles are parted, or counterchanged, they retain in English the name of *roundles;* thus in Plate XIX., fig. 4, *Per bend argent and sable, three roundles within a bordure engrailed all counterchanged*, are the arms of PUNCHYON of Essex.

In French Blazon a roundle composed of metal and colour is called a *besant-tourteau*, or a *tourteau-besant*, according as the *field* on which it is placed is of colour, or of metal.

A curious instance of the bearing of *besants-tourteaux* is afforded by the Spanish coat of FUENSALDA: *de Gueules, à six besants tourteaux d'argent et de sable posés 2, 2, 2, les 1 et 3 à dextre, et le 2 à senestre, coupés; les trois autres partis.*

Roundles *barry wavy of six argent and azure* (the conventional representation of water), are called *Fountains*, or *Sykes*, as in the canting coat of WELLS; *Azure, three fountains;* and in that given on Plate XIX., fig. 5, *Sable, a bend or between three fountains*, the arms of STOURTON; *Argent, a chevron sable between three sykes*, is the canting coat of SYKES. Akin to this last bearing is the *Gorge* or *Gurges*, or *Whirlpool*, a spiral line of *azure* commencing in the fess point of a field of *argent*, and occupying the whole shield; it is figured in Plate XIX., fig. 6, and was borne, in the reign of HENRY III., as *armes parlantes*, by the Wiltshire family of GORGES. In GLOVER'S *Roll of Arms*, No. 188, this bearing takes an unusual form: being, *Argent, four concentric annulets azure*, the exterior one is cut by the outline of the shield. It is there given thus: "Rauf de Gorges Roele dArgent & dazur" (*sic*).

PLATE XIX.

1. Billet.
Callendar.

2. Bezants.
Zouche.

3. Torteaux.
Courtenay.

4. Roundles.
Punchyon.

5. Fountains.
Stourton.

6. Gurges.
Gorges.

7. Rainbow.
Hacke.

8. Annulet.
Lowther.

9. Annulet Stoned.
Eglinton.

10. Vires.
Virieu.

11. Fret.
Harrington.

12. Escutcheon.
Hay.

The BANDINI of Florence bear: *Gules, three plates*, but these roundles are *balls* in the coat of HOFREITER DE DACHAU. Plate XIX., fig. 3, *Or, three torteaux*, is the well known coat of COURTENEY, and of the Counts of BOULOGNE; and was also quartered for the County of GRONSFELD by the Counts of BRONCKHORST, of the Holy Roman Empire. *Barry of six argent and azure in chief three torteaux*, was the arms of GREY; with *a label ermine* this was the coat of the unhappy Lady JANE GREY, proclaimed Queen of England, and executed in 1554.

Another well known British coat, that of ZOUCHE (Plate XIX., fig. 2), bears: *Gules, ten bezants*, 4, 3, 2, 1. *Argent, six hurts*, 2, 2, 2, are the arms of DE CASTRO in Spain. *Argent, a chevron gules between three hurts*, appears in early *Rolls of Arms* for BASKERVILLE.

Perhaps the most important Foreign instance of the use of roundles is afforded by the coat of the Florentine MEDICI, Grand Dukes of TUSCANY, which was originally, *Or, six balls gules*. (NOTE, *not torteaux* as very often wrongly blazoned by English writers, but *palle, i.e.* balls, possibly pills!) These were borne sometimes seven, or eight in number; but six, in orle, is the most usual arrangement. The uppermost one was changed into a ball bearing the Arms of France, as an augmentation by LOUIS XI. of France, in 1465. (*See* the grant in Mrs PALLISER'S *Historic Devices*, etc., p. 171.) This is sometimes wrongly depicted. While the *palle* are properly drawn as balls, the one in chief is wrongly represented as a flat plate of *azure*. In Florence itself, however, the French augmentation is properly shown as a ball, like the others in shape; these are often in very high relief, as in the MEDICI chapel in the church of San Lorenzo.

Roundles are often charged, thus: *Ermine, three pomlis, each charged with a cross or*, is the coat of HEATHCOTE, Lord AVELAND; and *Gules, three plates, on each a fleur-*

aucune etymologie claire, et ne sont point intelligibles."—(*La Science Héroique*, cxv.)

This nomenclature is not found in the early *Rolls of Arms;* where, as in the Armory of the Continent, all roundles of metals are *besants*, and all those of colour *torteaux*. In Scotland the English use as to roundles of colour has been adopted, but the practice of calling those of metal *Bezants or*, and *Bezants argent* has never gone out of use.

A few examples of the use of roundles, at home and abroad, may now be given.

Azure, a bezant, is ascribed to BASSINGFORD, and to BISSET. *Gules, a bezant* to BURLAY, and GOSPATRIC. RANDLE HOLME gives, *Or, a hurt*, as the canting coat of HURTLE; and, similarly, *Argent, a torteau* to TORTOX (probably a family of his own invention).

In the *Zürich Wappenrolle* (14th century) *Or, a ball sable*, is the coat of TÜFEL; *Sable, a plate*, is that of SCHMID, according to SIEBMACHER, *Wappenbuch*, iii., 115.

Azure, a chevron or between three bezants are the well known arms of HOPE.

MONTESQUIOU, Marquis de FEZENSAC, bears: *d'Or, à deux tourteaux de gueules, l'un sur l'autre, en pal*. With the *tourteaux of sable* this is the coat of BELLY in France. *Azure, two plates in pale*, is borne by VERDUZAN. *Azure, three plates*, two and one, is the coat of the Princes of MONTLÉART. *Gules, three bezants*, was borne in England by DENHAM; LA TOUCHE; and others ;—the same, but with the bezants (sometimes plates) *figured*, by GAMIN of France. I suspect the roundles in the coat of BOULENGER of Holland to be balls, and not bezants: *d'Azur, au chevron d'or, accompagné de trois bezans du même;* and in that of BOULA DE MAREUIL, *d'Azur, à trois besans d'or*. *Gules, three balls in fess or*, is the coat of CLOOT of Brabant.

PLATE XVIII.

1. Canton.
(*Noel.*)

2. Canton.
(*Kingscote.*)

3. Canton and fess.
(*Woodville.*)

4. Gyron.
(*De Cluseau.*)

5. Gyrons.
(*Mortimer.*)

6. Flanches.
(*Hobart.*)

7. Lozenge.
(*Hyde.*)

8. Mascle.
(*Fawkes.*)

9. Lozenges conjoined.
(*Montacute.*)

10. Mascles conjoined.
(*De Quinci.*)

11. Fusil.
(*Champney.*)

12. Fusils conjoined.
(*Percy.*)

Spanish *plata*, silver). (Coins as heraldic charges are noted hereafter in Chapter XIII., p. 389.) The French call both bezants and plates by the general name of *besans*, affixing thereto the designation of the metal, *e.g. besans d'or, besans d'argent*, etc. The Roundles of colour, or of fur, are similarly called by the general term of *tourteaux*, and their colour is specified. In German Heraldry the roundles are nearly always globes. In British Armory by a *Torteau* is meant only a flat, round plate *gules*. The difference between those of the roundles which are globular and those which are flat should be noted ; and in drawing duly expressed by shading. A Roundle *azure* is called a *Hurt;* this is probably globular, and the name derived from the English *hurt*, or whortleberry, not, as GERARD LEGH contends, from a hurt, or bruise, received in war! The French call it a *tourteau d'azur*. Roundles of *sable* are called *Ogresses, Pellets*, and *Gunstones ;* and are evidently intended to be globular. Their most usual name—*Pellets*—is thought by some to be derived from the Spanish *peletta*, the leaden knob of a bird-bolt or blunt-arrow. *Pomeis*, or *pomeys* is the name given to roundles of a green colour, obviously from *pomme*, an apple. (A recent authority, the writer of the article on "Heraldry" in the *Encyclopædia Britannica*, 9th Ed., vol. xi., p. 697, tells us that this is called a "*Pompey*"!) Roundles of *purpure* are not often met with, but are called *golpes*, or wounds ; these, I suppose, should not be globular in shape, as are the still rarer *Oranges*, of *tenné;* and *Guzes*, of *sanguine* (eyeballs according to GERARD LEGH!). Roundles of fur are flat.

This confusing English nomenclature is the subject of the just disapproval of Foreign Armorists, particularly of DE LA COLOMBIÈRE, who says :—" De vouloir pratiquer ponctuellement tous ces differens termes c'est plutost obscurcir la science que l'eclaircir ; c'est pourquoy je ne sçaurois approuver ces noms bizearres qui n'ont

labels argent, respectively of five, four, and three points in pale; and (with the labels *or*) this is the coat of EFFEREN VON STOLBERG in Prussia; and of the Florentine BUONACORSI, now extinct.

On early seals the number of the points of the label varies considerably. On that of GUILLAUME D'ASPRE-MONT, one of the *Chevaliers Bannerets* of Touraine in 1213, his shield bears (*gules*) a lion rampant (*or*) crowned (*azure*), and debruised by a label of ten points. (See *La Touraine*, par BOURASSÉ, p. 371, folio, Tours, 1855, while at p. 347 the number of points is *seven.*) Seven is also the number borne by DE RAMEFORT, another *Chevalier Banneret* of Touraine :—*Fusillé or and azure, a label of seven points gules.*

There are many other curious points connected with the use of the label into which we have not space now to enter. Besides those which are charged, some of which will be noticed in a future chapter, I have notes of some which are bordered, engrailed, etc.; but I conclude this sub-section with two curious examples. *Or, a file (i.e.,* label) *of three points gules from each a bell pendent azure the clapper sable.* This is the canting coat of BELFILE.

TOMKOWITZ, in Poland, bears: *Vert, a label of three points in fess argent, a ball of the same affixed to the bottom of the centre point.*

XIII. ROUNDLES.—We may include the ROUNDLES among the Sub-Ordinaries. These are balls, or circular discs, of metal or colour, and have, very needlessly, special names given to them in respect of their tinctures. Unless distinctly described as a *ball*, a roundle of gold is called a *Bezant*, a name probably derived from the gold coins of BYSANTIUM in use among the Crusaders; usually it is a small flat plate of gold, but is sometimes *figured* as a coin,—when this is so it must be expressed. A similar disc of silver is called a *Plate* (from the

Very rarely we meet with the label as a sole charge in British Armory. *Argent, a label of five points azure,* is ascribed to HENLINGTON : and *Azure, a label of five points or* to SABBEN. Occasionally the label occupies an unusual position. GUILLIM says that *Argent, a label of five points in bend sable* was the coat of one MORIEN, buried in St. Mary's Church at Oxford. *Argent, a label of five points in bend gules* is an Irish coat of GOFFE. In the coat of DE LA ROCHE DE BEAUSAINT: *Per pale gules and ermine over all a bend wavy argent; a label azure* is placed bendways upon the Ordinary. In the arms of the Dutch BARESTIJNS: *Argent, a wolf passant gules,* a label of the same is beneath the wolf's feet. The Frisian family of ROORDA bears: *Argent, two roses in chief gules, in base a label sable.*

AURELLE DE LA FREDIÈRE in Auvergne, bears : *Or, a chevron azure in chief, a label reversed gules.*

In the coat of OHA DE ROCOURT in Belgium : *Argent, a barbel in pale gules,* a semi-circular label of five points *azure* surmounts the head of the fish.

It is rare to meet with a label with less than three points, though I have found a few examples. The Spanish family of BERENGUER has (as its 1st and 4th quarters) *Or, a label of one point azure.*

In HARL. MSS., 1441 and 5866, there is recorded a coat of FITZ SIMONS : *Sable, three crescents argent, in chief a label of two points, in fess one of a single point of the second.* The coat of DE LA VERGNE in Brittany is *Gules, in chief a label of two points or.*

LALANDE bears : *d'Or, à deux lambels de trois pendants, le premier de gueules, l'autre de sable posés l'un sur l'autre.*

The Barons von der LIPPE of Courland use : *Argent, two labels, each of four points, in pale sable.*

The Barons HOENS in Flanders have : *Azure, three*

times only) in the coat of DE LA BÉDOYERE : *d'Azur, à six billettes percées d'argent.*

A billet with four equal sides is called a *delve*, and represents a divot, or spade-full of turf, or earth, thus delved out. *Argent, five square billets, or delves,* 3 and 2, *gules,* is the coat of the Piedmontese MASSON. *Argent, a chevron between three delves gules,* is the coat of WOODWARD of Kent.

XII. THE LABEL (OR FILE).—This figure is sometimes numbered under the SUB-ORDINARIES. Its use as a *brisure,* or mark of difference, will be considered in the Chapters on CADENCY or DIFFERENCE. Here it will be treated of as a common charge. We do not know with certainty what it was at first assumed to represent. It is apparently a narrow ribbon or bar, "*filum*," "*lambel,*" stretching across the shield, from one side to the other, and having other narrow ribbons, varying in number, dependent from it at right angles. In modern times these *points* are usually three in number; and they are often drawn slightly *patées,* or broader at the lower ends. The modern form of the cadency label is as unsightly as it is without authority.

I have already printed in BOUTELL'S *Heraldry, Historical and Popular,* p. 469, a number of interesting examples of the use of this bearing as a sole charge, etc.

LE CORNUT DE ST. LÉONARD (Liège) bears: *Gules, a label of three points argent;* DU ROZON (Brittany), TROGOFF, LARDIER, and CHARDOIGNE (France): *de Gueules, au lambel d'or.*

BLANDIN (Brittany): *Argent, a label of five points sable;* DE KERSBEKE the same, but the label of *gules.*

GROBBENDONCK (Brabant): *Quarterly,* 1 and 4. *Sable, a label argent:* 2 and 3. *Or, a fess embattled counter-embattled gules;* VAN OOSTENWOLDE, and DU PONT, *Or, a label azure;* MONFRAIN, the reverse.

Earls of MORLEY, use: *Sable, a stag's head caboshed, between two flaunches argent*. *Gules, two leopard's faces between as many flaunches or* is the coat of FRERE. When the flaunches are smaller in size they are sometimes blazoned as *flasques*, or *voiders*. The HAMILTONS of Colquot in Scotland are said to bear: *Gules, three cinquefoils between two flasques argent*.

XI. THE BILLET (AND DELVE).—BILLETS are small oblong rectangular figures, regarding which it has been disputed whether their name is derived from letters or logs of wood. In British Armory they are usually borne in a perpendicular position, abroad they are often *couchées*. BILLY in France bears: *de Gueules, à trois billettes, d'argent*. Plate XIX., fig. 1, *Sable, a bend between six billets or*, is a coat of CALLENDAR in Scotland; and of ANVIN in Picardy (which goes back to the Second Crusade). A similar coat, but with the bend engrailed, both it and the billets being *argent*, was borne by the Lords ALINGTON.

Gules, a bend between six billets or (*de Gueules, à la bande d'or accompagnée de six billettes du même, rangées en orle*) is the coat of the French Marquises de SAVEUSE.

Azure, a bend between seven billets or (four in chief and three in base) was borne by the Marquises de CHASTELLUX. *D'Azur, à onze billettes d'argent*, 4, 3, 4 is the coat of BEAUMANOIR, Marquis de LAVARDIN.

Gules, three billets in pairle sable, are the *armes parlantes* of the Silesian family DIE SCHINDEL. *Argent, three billets couchées gules* is borne by the WOESTWYNCKELE of Flanders. *Argent, six billets couchées sable*, are the coat of the Dutch family of VAN VEEN. *Gules, four billets couchées in pale argent* that of ABILLON. Occasionally the billet is borne *voided; d'Azur, à dix billettes vidées argent*, was borne by the Marquis de ST. PERN.

More rarely still they are pierced circular, as (some-

COURRAN, and the Vicomte de PLÉDRAN in Brittany bore the same but differently arranged—3, 3, 1.

The great house of DE ROHAN (Ducs de ROHAN, BOUILLON, and MONTBAZON, Princes de LEON, MONTAUBAN, SOUBISE, etc.), bore: *de Gueules, à neuf mâcles d'or* (3, 3, 3) *accolées et aboutées.*

The same coat but with the field *azure* is that of LE SÉNÉCHAL, Barons de QUÉLEN, Marquis de PONTECROIX.

Thirteen mascles conjoined or (4, 4, 4, 1) *in a field gules* is borne by TIGNIVILLE. *Azure, a fess between three mascles or,* is the coat of BETHUNE, or BEATON (the family to which Cardinal BEATON belonged). *Sable, a fess between three mascles or,* is borne by the Scottish MICHELLS or MITCHELLS.

RUSTRE.—A Lozenge pierced with a circular opening is called a *Rustre (ruste)*. *Or, a rustre sable,* is borne by CUSTANCE. The Irish PERYS have *Or, three rustres sable.* SOUMERET D'ESSENAU, in Flanders, uses the reverse. *De Gueules, à trois rustes d'argent,* is the coat of SCHESNAYE. The Belgian family of AAVAILLE, bear: *Or, a fess gules between three rustres azure.*

The fields LOZENGY, FUSILLY, MASCALLY, have been already noticed in Chapter III.; and are probably more ancient than these charges which have been derived from them.

X. THE FLAUNCHE (FLASQUE, AND VOIDER).— The FLAUNCHE borne only in pairs, is a projection from each side or flank of the shield, bounded by the segment of a circle. In French blazon the shield is said to be *flanqué en rond*. *De Sable, flanque en rond d'argent,* is the coat of the Spanish family of MARTINET. The HOBARTS, Earls of BUCKINGHAMSHIRE bear: *Sable, a star of eight points or, between two flaunches ermine* (*de Sable, à une étoile rayonnante d'or, flanqué en rond d'hermine*) (Plate XVIII., fig. 6). The PARKERS,

(*fusee*) from the French *fuseau*. The family of CHAMPNEYS, county Devon, bear: *Argent, two fusils in fess gules*, as Plate XVIII., fig. 11. *Azure, three fusils conjoined in fess argent*, is borne by the Austrian Counts von EGGER, and by FRIBERG (*Wappenrolle von Zürich*, No. 153). *Azure, three fusils in fess or*, is the canting coat of FUSÉE DE VOISENON in France (*d'Azur, à trois fusées d'or accolées en fasce*); and LE FUSELIER in Cambray, bears: *d'Or, à cinq fusées d'azur rangées en bande*.

Perhaps the best known English example is that afforded by the coat of PERCY, Earls and Dukes of NORTHUMBERLAND: *Azure, five fusils conjoined in fess or* (Plate XVIII., fig. 12). In early *Rolls* these were called "mill pecks," and are probably *armes parlantes*.

A Lozenge *voided*, that is deprived of its middle, only a border being left, is called a *Mascle,* from *macula*, the mesh of a net. (It may be noted that in some early *Rolls of Arms* this term is applied to a lozenge.) Plate XVIII., fig. 8, *Ermine, a mascle sable*, is the coat of FAWKES of Yorkshire. The Mascle is frequently found in Low Country and Breton coats. *Argent, a mascle sable*, is borne by LOHÉAC DE TRÉVOASEC; and (with the charge azure) by TRÉANNA. *Argent, three mascles azure*, is the coat of MERSEMAN of Flanders; of MAES and DE GOYER of Holland; *Argent, three mascles sable*, of PANHUYS; MADOETS; WAES; and GOVAERTS, all also of the Netherlands.

Gules, three mascles argent, was borne by LE BASCLE, Comte ARGENTEUIL; and by VERRUSALEM, one of the seven patrician families of LOUVAIN.

Mascles are most frequently borne combined, thus the great family of DE QUINCY, Earls of WINCHESTER, bore: *Gules, seven mascles conjoined*, 3, 3, 1 *or* (Plate XVIII., fig. 10). FERRERS bore the same.

Or, seven mascles conjoined azure, 3, 1, 3, is the coat of

(183)

on a lozenge-throughout or, a trefoil vert is the coat of the French family of BENTOUX.

In the Armory of England and of the Low Countries the Lozenge is a frequent charge : either detached, or conjoined with others. Plate XVIII., fig. 7 is the coat of HYDE, Earl of CLARENDON : *Azure, a chevron between three lozenges or. Gules, three lozenges argent* is a coat of GREYSTOCK. *Or, three lozenges gules,* is borne on the Continent by the Dutch families of WOERDEN ; HOOLA ; VAN GEESDORP ; VAN VLIET ; by TROISDORFF in Westphalia, and GAUTHIER DE GOURAVAL in France. *Or, three lozenges sable* is the coat of DE LINDT ; JANSDAM ; and KEMP in the Netherlands.

Frequently the lozenges are borne touching each other at the points in fess, in pale, or in bend. *Argent, three lozenges conjoined in fess gules* is the well known coat of MONTAGU, or MONTACUTE, Earls of SALISBURY (Plate XVIII., fig. 9). *Sable, three lozenges conjoined in fess ermine,* are the arms of GIFFARD. *Argent, three lozenges conjoined in bend sable* is borne by the Austrian Barons von SEUSENEGG ; the same in pale is borne by HOUCHIN, Marquis de LONGASTRE. *Ermines, three lozenges ermine in triangle, meeting at the fess point ;* is the coat ascribed to HALLOFTE or HOLLOFTE. These lozenges in French would be blazoned "*en pairle* ;" thus the Counts BRAUN VON WARTENBERG bear (for BRAUN), *d'Argent, à trois losenges de gueules appointées en pairle.*

Five lozenges are often borne conjoined in pale, fess, bend, or in cross. In the Low Countries there are a very considerable number of coats containing eight, nine, and especially ten, lozenges conjoined. The last are usually arranged 3, 3, 3, 1 ; thus HAUDION, Count de WYNEGHEM bears : *Argent, ten lozenges conjoined azure* 3, 3, 3, 1 ; and the Barons CARTIER D'YVES do the same.

An elongated lozenge, each of whose sides is much longer than its horizontal diameter, is called a *fusil*

TOLLEMACHES, whose arms were : *Argent, a fret sable ;* the ETCHINGHAMS, whose coat is : *Azure, a fret argent,* and other families who now bear a single fret, are found recorded as originally bearing *Fretty* in the ancient *Rolls of Arms.*

A *Fret,* like a saltire or cross, is also (though infrequently) borne, singly or in combination with others, as a minor charge, and is then of smaller size and couped. The coat of OYRY is : *Azure, three lucies hauriant argent, two and one ; and as many frets or, one and two.*

IX. THE LOZENGE (and its variations, the FUSIL, MASCLE, and RUSTRE).—The LOZENGE is a four side figure (*rhombus*) of which the angles at the top and bottom are acute, and those at the flanks obtuse. As a single charge, or uncharged Sub-Ordinary, it is seldom found in British Armory. *Gules, on a lozenge or a chevron azure* is the coat of BROCKE. *Per fess or and gules a lozenge counter-changed* is that of KIRKE, or KYRKE. It is more frequently found in Foreign blazons, where it is commonly drawn as a lozenge *throughout, i.e.* its points touch the borders of the escucheon. This is also blazoned as *vêtu,* or *chapé-chaussé.* The EUBINGS of Bavaria bore : *de Gueules, le champ vêtu d'argent.*

Gules, a lozenge argent (*de Gueules, à une losange d'argent*) is the coat of the extinct family of RORDORF in Bavaria and of the Counts von GRAVENECK or GRAFENEGG (of the Holy Roman Empire). The reverse is borne by the Swedish and Prussian Counts of SCHWERIN ; and is the same as that of EUBING above.

Gules, a lozenge-throughout per pale or and sable is the curious coat of FIDELER (SIEBMACHER, *Wappenbuch,* ii., 153).

Per fess argent and azure, a lozenge-throughout counter-changed; are the arms of CORRER, or CORRARO, of Venice. This coat is also sometimes blazoned : *Coupé d'azur, sur argent, chapé-chaussé de l'un en l'autre.* *Gules,*

Earl of ROSEBERY, in 1823, this heraldic anomaly is done away, and the blazon is now: *Vert, three primroses within a double tressure flory-counter-flory or.* (*See* STODART, *Scottish Arms*, vol. i., pp. 262-263, where mention is also made of an older use of the Royal Tressure, *or*, by "Sir ARCHIBALD PRIMROSE of Dalmenie, knight and baronet, be his Majesty CHARLES ye ii. create, *Vert, three primroses within a double tressure flowered counterflowered or.*")

There are in Foreign Heraldry a few coats in which the Tressure appears. *Or, a tressure azure*, is the coat of TROMENEC in Brittany.

Or, a double tressure flory-counter-flory vert, over all a cross gules (*d'Or, au double trescheur fleuré, contrefleuré de sinople à la croix de gueules brochante sur le tout*) is borne by ROCQUENGHIEN of Cambray; and BAULANDE of Hainault. BOSSUT of Liège bears the same but with a *saltire gules brochant* over all; ESCORNAIX (otherwise VAN SCHORISSE) bears the same, but with a *chevron gules brochant* over all. (*See* MAURICE, *Toison d'Or*, p. 91.) In the cut of the arms of DES CORNAIS in MENÊTRIER'S *Méthode du Blazon* (opposite p. 154, No. 8) the *chevron gules* does not pass the inner edge of the tressure; and there is the addition of an *escucheon en surtout, Azure a bend or.* In the other cases, and in the next example, the Ordinary *en surtout* comes to the edge of the shield, *v.* p. 178.

Vert, a double tressure flory-counter-flory or, over all a chevron azure, is attributed to ALLOIS of Belgium.

VIII. THE FRET.—This Sub-Ordinary at an early period originated in the still earlier fretty coats (*vide* pp. 96-97); as a charge it is peculiar to British Armory. It is produced by the interlacing of the bendlet and bendlet-sinister with a large mascle of equal width. Plate XIX., fig. 11, is the coat of the HARRINGTONS, *Sable, a fret argent* (and is probably a canting coat derived from a herring net). The MALTRAVERS, who bore: *Sable, a fret or;* the VERDONS, who bore: *Or, a fret gules;* the

gested a doubt of the genuineness of this instrument on the ground of an obvious error in the date of it, King JAMES not having been at Fala until the month of October. It appears however that the discrepancy is simply due to a clerical error (*See* NAPIER'S *Partition of the Lennox*, pp. 217-226; and RIDDELL'S reply in *Additional Remarks on the Lennox Representation*, pp. 79-87).

When the Royal Tressure is granted to the bearer of a quartered coat it is usually placed upon a bordure surrounding the quartered shield, as in the case of the arms of the Marquess of QUEENSBERRY, to whom, in 1682, the Royal Tressure was granted upon a *bordure or*. A like arrangement is borne by the Earl of EGLINTON, and is found upon a seal of Earl HUGH, appended to a charter of 1598.

The Royal Tressure has at least twice been granted as an augmentation to the arms of foreigners. JAMES V. granted it to NICOLAS CANIVET of Dieppe, secretary to JOHN, Duke of ALBANY (*Reg. Mag. Sig.*, xxiv., 263, Oct. 24, 1529). JAMES VI. gave it to Sir JACOB VAN EIDEN, a Dutchman on whom he conferred the honour of knighthood.

In a few exceptional and later cases the floriation of the Tressure has been somewhat varied. The Tressure (Plate XVII., fig. 12) granted to CHARLES, Earl of ABOYNE, third son of the second Marquess of HUNTLY, is adorned with crescents without, and demi-fleurs-de-lis within ; and the Tressure borne by the Earl of ABERDEEN, another member of the GORDON family, bears thistles, roses, and fleurs-de-lis alternately. On 12th March 1762, a Royal Warrant was granted directing LYON to add a "double tressure counterflowered as in the Royal Arms of Scotland," to the arms of ARCHIBALD, Viscount PRIMROSE. Here the Tressure was *gules*, as in the Royal arms, although the field on which it was placed was *vert*. In a new record of the arms of ARCHIBALD,

or of ANGUS ; or to those of the DOUGLASES of Morton; the LINDSAYS, Earls of CRAWFORD; and the KEITHS, who were genealogically equally entitled to it. The families of MURRAY of Touchadam; CHARTERIS of Kinfauns ; and MURRAY of Tullibardine (*Scottish Seals*, ii., No. 771) all had the Royal Tressure in their arms before the sixteenth century. The towns of ABERDEEN and PERTH also obtained early the right of honouring their arms with the addition of the Royal Tressure. It appears on the still existing matrix of the Burgh seal of ABERDEEN which was engraved in 1430. It was at a rather later date that it appears in the arms of the BUCHANANS and MAITLANDS. It is not easy to explain the motive of an Act of Parliament of JAMES III. of the date 1471, which, however, was never carried into effect, that there should in future be no tressure about the lion in the Royal Coat:—" In tyme to cum thar suld be na double tresor about his armys, but that he suld ber hale armys of the lyoun without ony mar." In later times the Royal Tressure was occasionally borne by virtue of Royal Warrants, several of which are recorded in the Lyon Register ; and it must be presumed to have been so granted in various cases in which the warrant is no longer extant. It has been held to be *ultra vires* of LYON to allow it (except by a special warrant from the Sovereign) to any family which could not prove descent from an ancestor entitled to bear it. JAMES V. in 1542 granted a warrant to LYON to surround the arms of JOHN SCOT, of Thirlstane, with the Royal Tressure, in respect of his ready services at Soutra Edge with three score and ten lances on horseback, when other nobles refused to follow their Sovereign. The grant was put on record by the grantee's descendant PATRICK, Lord NAPIER ; and is the tressured coat borne in the second and third quarters of the NAPIER arms. (It may be mentioned that the late Mr RIDDELL sug-

pendent within the Royal Tressure gules; the tressure being an addition to his paternal coat (Plate XXXIII., fig. 9). No tressure, however, was borne by the CAMPBELLS, or the Earls of MAR, who were equally descended from sisters of King ROBERT. As early as the middle of the fourteenth century we find several families of mark bearing the tressure without having any near connection with the Royal House. Thus the FLEMINGS of Biggar bore: *Gules, a chevron within a double tressure flory-counter-flory argent* (Plate XVII., fig. 10). It will be noticed that the chevron, or other Ordinary, in Scottish coats is not prolonged beyond the inner edge of the tressure ; in a few foreign coats hereafter to be given (p. 181) this rule is not observed. MALCOLM FLEMING, on whose seal in 1357 the tressure occurs (LAING, *Scottish Seals*, ii. No. 366), probably obtained that armorial distinction in reward for his devoted service to the cause both of ROBERT BRUCE and his son. It was two generations later that Sir MALCOLM FLEMING, of Biggar and Cumbernauld, allied himself to the Royal House by marriage with a daughter of ROBERT, Duke of ALBANY. The Royal Tressure also occurs on the seal of WILLIAM LIVINGSTON as early as 1357 (LAING, *Scottish Seals*, ii., No. 650), and with these two families may be classed a house of more mark—that of the SETONS, whose representative Sir ALEXANDER SETON bore the tressure in 1337 (*Scottish Seals*, ii., No. 891); certainly not (as has been sometimes represented) in virtue of descent from King ROBERT'S sister CHRISTIAN, whose husband, Sir CHRISTOPHER SETON, was only collaterally (if at all) related to the head of the Scottish house of SETON.

Of the descendants of the daughters of ROBERT II. and ROBERT III., the Lords of the ISLES ; the KENNEDYS ; the LYONS ; the GRAHAMS of Garvock ; and the EDMONSTONES, all bore the Tressure ; but no such addition was made to the arms of the Earls of DOUGLAS,

coming a defence to the lion of Scotland. It is easier to laugh at the transparent absurdity of this fable than to account for the first introduction of the Fleurs-de-lis into the Royal Coat of Scotland. Historically no alliance between SCOTLAND and FRANCE can be found earlier than the reign of ROBERT BRUCE.

On the seal of ALEXANDER II. the lion is the sole charge. On the Great Seal of ALEXANDER III. (1249-1286) the lion rampant appears alone upon the shield borne by the monarch, but the caparisons of this charger have the lion surrounded by a bordure; this is charged with small crosslets but the inner edge has a border of *demi-fleurs-de-lis*. (VRÉE, *Généalogie des Comtes de Flandre*, Plate xv.) A portion of this seal is engraved in LAING'S *Scottish Seals*, vol. ii., Plate ii., fig. 1, and I am inclined to think not so accurately as in VRÉE'S example, where the whole seal is given, and the *crosslets* distinctly shown on the bordure. To this bordure I believe we must trace the origin of the tressure flory-counter-flory, which had no direct connection with any French alliance connubial or political.

In the *Roll of Arms of the Thirteenth Century*, to which the date 1272 is assigned, we find what is, so far as I can trace, the first blazon of the Scottish Arms, No. 11. "Le Roy d'Escoce, d'or un lion rampant et un borde florette de gulez." This may correspond sufficiently with the bordure upon the seal of ALEXANDER III. referred to above, but it assuredly is not the tressure flory-counter-flory as borne in later times. This was certainly held in honour in Scotland in the fourteenth and fifteenth centuries, and occasionally bestowed as an augmentation of their arms on persons descended maternally from the Royal House; and upon others who were thought to have deserved well of their King and country. THOMAS RANDOLPH, Earl of MORAY, whose mother was ISOBEL, sister of King ROBERT BRUCE, bore: *Argent, three cushions*

Among the curiosities of Heraldry is the coat of BENEWITZ of Bavaria, who bear: *The arms of the EMPIRE within a circular orle nebuly azure.*

The Barons von SCHAWENBURG use: *Argent, a* (plain) *bordure nebuly of or upon azure, over all a saltire gules.*

VII. THE TRESSURE.—This bearing is almost peculiar to Scotland, and is very familiar in consequence of its position in the Royal Arms of that country. A plain tressure is a diminutive of the orle, and is depicted half its thickness; it is never borne alone. There are a very few instances here given in which a triple tressure is used. *Azure, three concentric orles or,* is a coat ascribed to LANDELLS; *Gules, three such orles argent,* is attributed to Sir JOHN CHIDIOK in the *Roll* of 1308. In foreign coats the plain tressure, or orle, is sometimes repeated. The Breton family of BAIGNEAU bear: *Or, four concentric orles* (or *plain tressures*) *sable.*

But in Scotland the tressure is always double, and almost always flory-counter-flory of fleurs-de-lis, to the number of eight at least. In the well known case of the Royal Arms of Scotland the tressure is often inaccurately depicted, all the heads of the fleurs-de-lis being turned outwards in spite of (or rather in ignorance of the meaning of) the blazon.

When properly drawn the fleurs-de-lis are cut horizontally into two parts; and the upper and lower portions project alternately from the outer edge of the outer tressure, and from the inner edge of the inner one. No portion of the fleur-de-lis now appears upon the thin strip of the field which is shown between the two tressures. (*See* Plates XXXVI., XXXVII., XXXVIII., etc.)

Popular belief long associated this bearing in the Arms of Scotland with a supposed alliance between one ACHAIUS, King of the Dalriadic Scots, and CHARLEMAGNE; and declared that it commemorated the agreement that the French lilies should be for all time

shire family of LANDALE of that Ilk, which has long been borne *en surtout* by their heirs-general, the Earls of HOME, is: *Or, an orle azure.*

In very early English blazons the Orle is sometimes described as "*un faux ecusson.*" (*See* the *Falkirk Roll* of 1298, and the still earlier *Rolls* of 1240 and 1256; MS. 414 in the Heralds' College; and HARL. MS. 6589.)

The ORLE is seldom found charged, or formed by any other than the line following the outline of the escucheon in which it is borne. But KNOX, Earl of RANFURLY in Ireland, bears: *Gules, a falcon volant or within an orle wavy argent;* ULSTER'S *Register* also has recorded a coat granted in 1693 to a cadet of this family, which has the orle waved on the outer, but engrailed on the inner, side; and a coat of LANDEL, presumably differenced from that already given, has the orle engrailed on the inner edge; and there is another in which the inner edge is indented. PONT'S MS. gives as the coat of NORIE: *Per pale argent and sable an orle engrailed on both sides, and charged with four quatrefoils, within a bordure all counterchanged.*

The family of CHADWICK bears: *Or, on an orle gules, the outer edge engrailed, eight martlets argent, all within an orle of eight crosslets sable.*

Six, eight, or more minor charges, such as bezants, martlets, crosslets, etc., placed round the shield as they would be arranged if there were a bordure charged with them, are said to be "*in orle*" as in the coat of GLEDSTANES, now GLADSTONE (Plate XVII., fig. 9): *Argent, a savage's head couped, distilling drops of blood, wreathed with bay and holly leaves all proper, within an orle of eight martlets sable.*

The coat of CONSIDINE also has an unusual orle: *Argent, an orle gules flory and counter-flory on the outer edge only vert; in the centre a dagger in pale azure, the hilt or.*

The coat of Lord GRAY, although to appearance a differenced coat—*Gules, a lion rampant within a bordure engrailed argent,* seems to belong to the same category of principal arms; just as in English Armory the TALBOTS, Earls of SHREWSBURY, bore: *Gules, a lion rampant within a bordure engrailed or,* in which coat the bordure appears to be not a brisure denoting cadency from an ancestor who bore simply *Gules, a lion rampant or,* but rather a difference originally assumed to distinguish the family of TALBOT from other families who bore the common charge of *a lion or on a field gules.* (My MS. *Ordinary* contains the names of over a hundred families to whom this coat is attributed.)

In Spanish coats the bordure is sometimes found of the same tincture as the field, only separated from it by the pourfilar line; thus the Andalucian family of CANIZARES bears: *Gules plain, a bordure of the same charged with eight saltires couped* (flanchis) *or.* ESCORNA similarly bears: *Argent, an ox statant gules, on a bordure of the field eight bells azure.* (On Spanish bordures see my "Heraldry of Spain and Portugal," and pp. 440, 475, *infra.*)

In England the use of the bordure as a principal charge is not unfrequent, and in such cases it is itself generally charged with eight repetitions of a minor charge, bezants, escallops, roses, etc.

The different families of ERPINGHAM bore: *Argent,* with bordures of various tinctures for difference, *azure, vert, gules,* and *sable,* charged with martlets *argent,* or *or.* We cannot say which was the original or principal coat. The various D'ARCY coats afford like examples.

VI. THE ORLE is a narrow bordure detached from the edge of the shield. *Gules, an orle argent* (Plate XVII., fig. 8), was the coat of JOHN BALLIOL, the vassal King of SCOTLAND. The coat of the Berwick-

King of the ROMANS, second son of King JOHN of ENGLAND, bore : *Argent, a lion rampant gules crowned or, within a bordure sable, charged with bezants,* varying in number. (Plate XVII., fig. 1.) *Quarterly or and azure, a bordure counter-changed* is used by AUBER in France, and (with *sable* instead of *azure*) by ADALBERT. Occasionally a double bordure is found in the Heraldry of the Peninsula. Of this one example may suffice. The Portuguese ORTINS bear ; Em campo azul hum Sol de ouro, e duas bordaduras, a primiera de prata cheya de rosas verdes ; a segunda composta de prata e vermelho. (*Azure, a sun in splendour within two bordures, the first argent charged with roses, vert; the second compony argent and gules.*)

There are some coats in which the effect of several bordures is produced, and which require skill and attention in blazoning. For example: the Counts de THIERMES bear : *Or, a bordure azure,* and *en surtout an escucheon argent thereon a lion rampant gules crowned or within a bordure azure.* Here the effect is the same as if the *argent* shield bore a triple bordure, *azure, or,* and *azure.*

A CIRCULAR BORDURE is found in the coat of the Scottish family of KILGOUR. *Argent, a dragon volant in pale wings displayed within* a circular bordure *sable thereon three crescents of the field (see* STODART, *Scottish Arms,* ii., plate lv.). The French blazon of this bordure would be *Vêtu en rond.* The German family of LEO bear : *d'Or, au lion de sable, le champ vêtu en rond du mème.* The Florentine BELLINCIONI use the same, the field of *argent,* the lion and bordure *gules,* and the Swiss RHEINAU, *Azure, a lion rampant or, a bordure circular gules.*

Of this bearing *Vêtu en ovale* is a variation. *Or, six mule shoes azure nailed argent, the field* vêtu en ovale *ermine,* is the coat of FERRIÉRE DE TESSÉ.

PLATE XVII.

1. Bordure.
(*Earl of Cornwall.*)

2. Bordure.
(*Maule.*)

3. Bordure.
(*Dunbar.*)

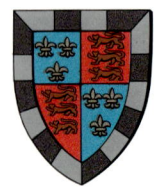

4. Bordure compony.
(*Duke of Gloucester.*)

5. Bordure counter compony.
(*Oliphant of Condie.*)

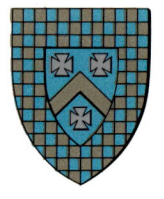

6. Bordure checquy.
(*Barclay of Touch.*)

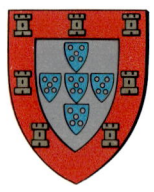

7. Bordure of Castile.
(*Portugal.*)

8. Orle.
(*Baliol.*)

9. Orle of martlets.
(*Gledstanes.*)

10. Tressure flory counter flory.
(*Fleming.*)

11. Tressure.
(*Howard.*)

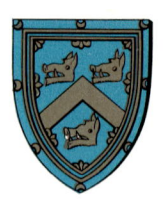

12. Tressure.
(*Earl of Aboyne.*)

pons, are often charged. A bordure *counter-componé* differs from the bordure-*goboné* in having two rows of pieces. It is, in fact, Chequy of two rows. Such a bordure appears in the coat of OLIPHANT of Condie (Plate XVII., fig. 5). *Gules, three crescents argent, a bordure counter-compony of the tinctures. Barry of six or and sable, a bordure counter-compony of the same* is the coat of the Barons SAVA of Italy and Provence. A curious Italian bordure counter-compone is that of the RIZZOLETTI of Padua—the outer panes are alternately *sable* and *argent*, while the inner row is of *gules* and *argent*. A similar example is found in the coat of the Galician Counts of STADNICKI. There the outer *compons* are of *azure* and *argent*, the inner ones of *argent* and *gules*. In bordures goboné, and counter-componé the pieces, or panes, follow the outline of the shield and the lines which divide them are usually drawn as if radiating from the centre point. But in a bordure chequy, these are not only three rows of panes or chequers but the dividing lines do not follow the outline; the chequers are all rectangular, and the bordure as a whole is treated as if it were itself cut out of a chequered field; as in Plate XVII., fig. 6. BARCLAY of Touch bears: *Azure, a chevron or between three crosses patée argent ; a bordure chequy of the second and first*. When a bordure is blazoned flory, crusily, bezanté, or billetty: it is understood to be charged with *eight* fleurs-de-lis, crosslets, bezants, billets, etc.

The expressions a "*bordure of* ENGLAND" or a "*bordure of* FRANCE" are used to imply in the one case, a bordure *gules* charged with eight golden lions passant gardant ; and in the other, a bordure *azure* charged with eight fleurs-de-lis *or*. Similarly, a "*bordure of* CASTILE" (now borne in the Royal Arms of PORTUGAL), is of *gules* charged with the golden castles of CASTILE. (Plate XVII., fig. 7.) RICHARD, Earl of CORNWALL, elected

and its use for this purpose will be more fitly considered in the chapter on DIFFERENCES. (Chapter XIV., p. 437.)

But there are a few examples in Scottish Armory in which the bordure is used as a principal figure. Plate XVII., fig. 2, is the coat of the MAULES, Earls of PANMURE, it is *Per pale argent and gules, a bordure charged with eight escallops, all counter-changed.* These number six only in Sir DAVID LINDESAY'S MS. and on the seal of Sir DAVID MAULE, in 1320. (*See* the *Registrum de Panmure*, I., clxiv., edited by JOHN STUART, LL.D., privately printed in 1874.) Fig. 3 of the same plate is the coat of the old Earls of DUNBAR and MARCH, unquestionably the chiefs of their family. It appears on the seal of Earl PATRICK as early as 1292; and the bordure is there charged with eight roses; this is the usual number, though it varies in the seals of his descendants, and occasionally the bordure appears to be uncharged.

The *Bordure* may of course be formed of any of the compound partition lines; as in the coats of BARNEWALL and KNIGHT above given where the bordure is engrailed. The HAMILTONS of Neilsland difference with a bordure-quarterly, *engrailed argent*, and *invecked azure*. It may further be parted per pale, or per fess, or be borne quarterly. It may also be compony, or gobony, that is divided into pieces of alternate metal and colour. The Spanish family of IRRIBERI, bear: *Or plain, within a bordure componé of eighteen pieces of azure* and the field. Such bordures are frequently used, as will hereafter be shown, as marks of cadency; and only one is therefore given here. HUMPHREY, Duke of GLOUCESTER, fourth son of HENRY IV., bore the Quartered coat of FRANCE and ENGLAND, *within a bordure componé sable* (sometimes *azure*) *and argent* as in Plate XVII., fig. 4.

In *goboné*, or *componé*, bordures, the *pieces* or *com*-

CHENSY (*Rolls* of 1277 and 1296). *Gules, three escucheons argent*, is the coat of JOHN FITZSIMON (*Roll temp.* HENRY III.); and its reverse (Plate XIX., fig. 12) is the well known bearing of the Scottish family of HAY. PLANCHÉ suggests that did we know the paternity of EVA, wife of WILLIAM DE HAYA, who was living in 1174, we might probably be able to account for the adoption of these arms without going back, as the preposterous legend does, to the times of the Danish invasion of Scotland.

The same coat: *Argent, three escucheons gules*, is the bearing of the Counts de RIBEAUPIERRE, or RAPPOLSTEIN, of Alsace (MORICE, *Chevaliers de la Toison d'Or*, No. 144); of RABENSTEIN in the *Wappenrolle von Zürich* (No. 385); of the ancient Dukes of SPOLETO; of the French families of ABBEVILLE DALENONCOURT; LA MOTTE, etc.; of LE BRUYN of Holland; and of the English D'AVILLIERS (*temp.* EDWARD I.). *Or, three escucheons vair*, was borne by DE FONTAINE in 1203 at the Third Crusade (*Salles des Croisés* at Versailles).

V. THE BORDURE (*bordure*).—The BORDURE is, as its name denotes, a border surrounding the shield. According to French usage it should occupy one-fifth of it; but in practice its size depends on whether it is borne charged or plain. The confusion in ancient blazons between coats in which this or an escucheon is the sole charge has been already noted. *Chequy or and azure a border gules*, was the coat of the Counts de DREUX, created Earls of RICHMOND in England. *Ermine, a bordure gules* appears in the *Roll* of 1286 as the arms of HUNDESCOTE. *Ermine, a bordure engrailed gules* is the coat of BARNEWALL, Lords TRIMLESTOWN, in Ireland, etc. *Or, a bordure engrailed sable* is borne by KNIGHT. Its chief use, especially in Scotland, has been as a *brisure;* that is, as a mode of differencing the younger branches of families from the parent stock;

The coat blazoned above is that drawn in the MS. *Armorial du Héraut* "BERRY," *circa* 1450, No. 716.

> "D'or et d'azur, au pié party,
> Au chef pallé, fessé, contre-fessé,
> À deux quantons gironnés
> Et un escu d'argent par my (*i.e.*, 'en abîme')
> Sont les armes de Pressigny."

There are slight variations, but MENÊTRIER (or his editor), for once goes all wrong in *La Nouvelle Méthode du Blason*, 1718, p. 263. A good modern French blazon, given in RIETSTAP'S *Armorial Général* under MARANS, is : *Fascé-contre-fascé d'or et d'azur de six pièces, à un écusson d'argent en abîme ; au chef tiercé en pal* (a) *tranché d'or et d'azur ;* (b) *parti d'azur et d'or;* (c) *taillé d'azur et d'or*, but the tinctures are repeated (four times) in a way which would have been very shocking to an English Herald of the old school.

IV. THE INESCUCHEON, OR ESCUCHEON (*écusson*).— The former name is applied only when, as in the MORTIMER coat above recorded, there is but one such charge ; when there is more than one they are called escucheons. This is however a modern refinement which does not get universal acceptance.

Argent, an inescucheon ermine is said to be the coat of BAZIN, or BASING ; and its reverse that of BLANKFRONT. It is not always easy to determine whether a coat should be blazoned as charged with an escucheon, or with a bordure ; for instance in GLOVER'S *Ordinary* the coat of GWYN is said to be both : *Vair, an escucheon or ;* and *Or, a bordure vair.* *Azure, an escucheon argent* (*d'Azur, à l'écusson d'argent*) is the coat of WAVRIN, as borne in 1191 (Third Crusade) ; and still by the Counts of WAVRIN in Belgium (See *Armorial de Gueldre*, No. 154). *Or, an escucheon gules,* is the coat of the Lordship of BITSCH, quartered by the Counts of HANAU. *Or, three escucheons barry of six vair and gules,* is borne by MONT-

yielded his own horse to ALPHONSO VI., whose charger had been killed under him; and in order to secure the return of the horse to him, he cut off with his sword a *giron*, or gusset-shaped piece, from his surcoat, that so he might be recognised by the king at the close of the combat. (*See* MENÊTRIER, *Traité de l'Origine des Armoiries*, Paris 1680.) The GIRON arms are: *Or, three points, or girons, moving from the base of the shield gules; and a bordure chequy of the same tinctures.* The Dukes of OSSUNA bear: *Per fess* (a) *in chief,* CASTILE *impaling* LEON; (b) *in base, Or, three girons accosted, issuing from the base gules;* for GIRON *the whole within a bordure chequy gules and or, thereon five escucheons azure, on each as many plates in Saltire,*—"*las Quinas Reales*" of PORTUGAL. (*Vide infra*, p. 441.)

In the remarkable coat of MORTIMER, Earl of MARCH, Plate XVIII.,fig. 5, a small *gyron* (sometimes called a "*bast esquierre*") occurs at each end of the chief. The arms are blazoned: *Barry of six or and azure, on a chief of the first two pallets between two gyrons of the second, over all an inescucheon argent.* Otherwise: *Azure, three bars or, on a chief of the last two pallets of the first, the corners gyroned of the first and second, an inescucheon argent.* (*See* the seal of EDMUND MORTIMER, *infra;* and also the chapter on DIFFERENCES, *infra* p. 448.)

The curious arms of the French family of PRESSIGNY resemble those of MORTIMER; and the coat was one which was thought so difficult to describe clearly and succinctly as to be a test of a man's knowledge of French blazon. It is: *Per pale or and azure three bars counterchanged; a chief also per pale and of the same tinctures, thereon two pallets between as many girons all counterchanged. In the centre point of the whole shield an escucheon argent.* These were the arms of RENAUD DE PRESSIGNY, Maréchal de FRANCE, in 1270.

of Knights made at the Siege of Calais in 1348 (HARL. MS. 6589, printed in *Notes and Queries*, 5th. S., vol. iv. p. 324), is the coat of Sir WILLIAM DE LA ZOUCHE, *Gules, bezantée, a canton indented in the bottom*. *Or, a canton indented at the bottom gules* was the coat of BESYNGBURGH. *Azure, a chevron engrailed, and a canton indented at the bottom*, was borne by DEDNAM.

Instances of the use of the *Quarter* and *Canton* as "DIFFERENCES:" as "AUGMENTATIONS:" and as "MARKS OF ILLEGITIMACY:" will be found respectively in the subsequent Chapters which treat of those subjects.

A *Canton*, and *Fess* (or *bar*), are sometimes conjoined in one bearing without any dividing line; as in Plate XVIII., fig. 3 which is the coat of WOODVILLE or WIDVILLE: *Argent, a fess and canton conjoined gules*, borne by Queen ELIZABETH WOODVILE, wife of EDWARD IV. *Or, a fess and canton sable*, are the coat of GEOFFREY RIDEL, Bishop of ELY (1174-1189). *Chequy or and gules, a canton barry argent and of the second*, are the arms of TREDERN in Brittany. *Ermine, on a canton gules an escucheon voided argent*, is the coat of SURTEES of Durham.

III. Next to the QUARTER or CANTON, we may place the GYRON (*giron*) which is the lower half of a *Quarter*, formed by a diagonal line; or we may define it as the piece included by half the partition line *per bend*, and half the partition line *per fess* meeting in the fess point.

There is, I believe, only one instance in British Armory in which a single *Giron* occurs as a charge; it is in the coat of CHIVERS: *Argent, a giron azure, and three cinquefoils gules*. Plate XVIII., fig. 4, is the coat of DE CLUSEAU in LIMOUSIN, *d'Argent, au giron de gueules*. Girons appear in the arms of the GIRON, Duke of OSSUNA, Marquis of PENAFIEL in Spain. The name is said by BARNABÉ MORENO DE VARGAS to have been assumed by RODRIGUE GONSALEZ DE CISNEROS who

of the last an eagle displayed argent. Only two of the cinquefoils are here visible; the third is hidden by the quarter, but is supposed to be still existing under that addition or augmentation. (*Vide post*, p. 427.)

II. THE CANTON (*Franc-canton*).—This as stated above is a diminutive of the *Quarter*. It occupies the ninth part of the shield (or the space either on the dexter or the sinister in the upper portion of the escucheon if the shield were supposed to be charged with a plain cross drawn of the correct proportions). Both the quarter and canton are, theoretically, additions to the original coat; and if occasion require it are considered exempt from the ordinary rule which forbids colour on colour, or metal on metal. Plate XVIII., fig. 2, is the coat of KINGSCOTE, *Argent, ten escallops, four, three, two, and one sable; on a canton gules a pierced mullet or.* In all such cases the number of charges named is that of what is assumed to be the original coat, including those "absconded" or hidden by the canton, as in the similar case of the quarter. Usually the canton used is the dexter one, but in a few cases the sinister canton is employed. *Chequy or and gules a sinister canton argent*, are the arms of SLEICH. *Sable, a sinister canton argent* is in SIEBMACHER'S *Wappenbuch*, for EYTZENRIET.

Per fess argent and or, on a canton gules the lion of St. Mark, is the coat of the Venetian FOSCARI. A rather remarkable coat is that of SCHATZ of Bavaria; *Per bend sinister argent and gules a canton of the last.* This is, however, rather a case of a German *parted* coat.

The *Canton* has been sometimes thought to indicate the square banner of a knight-banneret. It may have done so very occasionally. I remember three coats in which the lower edge of the charge is indented, as if it had been intended to give the idea of a banner (though not necessarily that of a banneret, which was simply square). In the Second *Calais Roll, i.e.*, the *Roll*

CHAPTER V.

THE SUB-ORDINARIES.

THE charges known by this name are as follows:—the QUARTER; the CANTON; the GYRON; the INESCUCHEON; the BORDURE; the ORLE; the TRESSURE; the FRET; the LOZENGE; the FLAUNCHE and FLASQUE; the BILLET; the LABEL; and ROUNDLES of various colours.

I. THE QUARTER (*franc-quartier*).—As its name denotes this bearing occupied originally the quarter of the shield, *i.e.*, the first fourth part of the field cut off by the palar and fess lines meeting in the fess point. It is found drawn of this size in early English blazons. In modern ones it has undergone some diminution and cannot now be practically distinguished in most cases from its former diminutive, the *Canton*, except when, as in the instances now given, it is the sole charge. *Argent, a quarter sable* is the coat of SUTTON, Lord LEXINGTON; *Gules, a quarter argent* is the old coat of BLENCOWE. SHIRLEY, Earl FERRERS, uses: *Paly of six or and azure a quarter ermine. Counter-vair a quarter ermine*, is borne by SALPERWICK, Marquis de GRIGNY: the Président LAMOIGNON bore: *Losangé de sable et d'argent au franc-quartier d'hermine.* GENDRON uses *d'Azur, au franc-quartier d'or;* DUBUISSON, *d'Argent, au franc-quartier de gueules;* and DASBOURG of Luxemburg, *Or, a quarter sable. Gules, fretty or, on a canton of the same a lion passant sable* is the old coat of DE RIBAUMONT who took part in the First Crusade. In the *Armorial de Gueldre* the arms of the Sire de LEEFDAEL are: *Or, three cinquefoils gules, on a quarter*

The Norman family of BRÉZÉ, Comtes de MAULEVRIER, bore : *d'Azur, à un écusson d'argent bordé d'or en abîme ; accompagné de huit croisettes d'or en orle.* These arms appear on the handsome monument by GOUJON, erected in the Cathedral of Rouen by DIANE DE POITIERS (mistress of HENRI II.) to the memory of her husband the Duc de BRÉZÉ.

47. Passion.   48. Greek.   49. Calvary.

50. Patriarchal.   51. Potent.   52. Lorraine.

53. Patty.   54. Patty-fitchy.   55. Maltese

56. Patonce.   57. Fleur-de-lisée.   58. Flory.

59. Fourchy.   60. Aiguisée.   61. Tau.

is as a subordinate charge. Thus: *Azure, a bend between six crosses-crosslet-fitchy or*, is the coat of the Earldom of MAR. The CHEYNES bear the same but with the charges *argent.* The Scotch family of SPALDING bears : *Or, on a cross azure five crosses-crosslet of the first.*

Gules, a fess between six crosses-crosslet or is the well known coat of the BEAUCHAMPS, Earls of WARWICK. (Plate XV., fig. 4.) *Argent* (and *Or*), *a fess dancetty between three crosses-crosslet-fitchy gules*, are coats of SANDYS of England (sometimes the crosslets are *botonné*, or *treflé*, in these coats). *Gules, a fess between three crosses-crosslet-fitchy or*, is borne by GORE, Earl of ARRAN in Ireland.

Azure, a fess engrailed between six crosses-crosslet or, was the coat of WILLIAM CAMDEN, the Antiquary. *Gules, a fess chequy* (or *counter-compony*) *argent and sable, between six crosses-crosslet of the second* was the coat of BOTELER, or BUTLER in England. *Argent, a chevron gules between three crosses-crosslet-fitchy sable, within the Royal Tressure of Scotland*, is the coat of the KENNEDYS, Earls of CASSILIS, and Marquesses of AILSA. *Azure, a fess argent between six crosses-crosslet-fitchy or*, is the arms of the old Scottish house of RATTRAY (Plate XV., fig. 5). The LONGUEVILLES of Huntingdon, bore : *Gules, a fess dancetty ermine between six crosses-crosslet-fitchy argent.* The CRAVENS, Earls of CRAVEN, use *Argent, a fess between six crosses-crosslet-fitchy gules.*

Argent, six crosses-crosslet-fitchy sable, on a chief azure two mullets or, is the coat of CLINTON, Duke of NEWCASTLE. *Argent, on a fess gules three crosses-crosslet of the field* was borne by CORSANT, a family who were engaged in the First Crusade. (*Salle des Croisés* at Versailles.)

Vert, a saltire between twelve crosslets or is the coat of the Lordship of MEHRENBERG, quartered by the House of NASSAU. (Notice these are crosslets proper, *i.e.*, small plain equal armed crosses.)

heads curved outwards. (*See* Plate XV., fig. 6, the Arms of MONTFORT.) The Barons von UFFELE in Flanders use: *Argent, a cross guivrée azure* (over all *Argent, three fess-de-moulin sable*). *Gules, a cross gringolée argent*, is borne for MERCKELBACH. *Argent, a cross gringolée gules*, are the arms of HAGEN, and OTHEGRAVEN.

A CROSS URDÉE is one in which the arms are spread at the end into a lozenge shape. In Plate XIV., fig. 12 the Cross of the MANFREDI (there called a cross *retranchée*) is of this shape, but is also pommetty.

THE CROSS AVELLANE is one of which the arms take the conventional form of a filbert. It is but rarely met with except as the cross which adorns the Orb of Sovereignty in the British Regalia.

THE CROSS AÌGUÌSÉE is simply one of which the points are sharpened into the shape of a chevron. (Page 164, fig. 60.)

CROSSLETS.

These are properly only little crosses; but the word is often used as an abbreviation for the fuller term *Cross-Crosslet*, or *Crossed Crosslet*. In these latter each arm of the cross is recrossed by a small piece at right angles. In the *Cross-Crosslet-fitchy* the lower arm is pointed, and the traverse thereon is usually omitted. Crosslets are usually borne in groups; sometimes as powderings of the field (see *Semé*, or *Crusily*, p. 112). There are, however, instances in which both the Cross-Crosslet and the Cross-Crosslet-fitchy are found in arms as a sole charge. *Argent, a cross-crosslet gules*, is a coat of BRIERLEY; of CROSSLEY; and of DUNNING in Scotland, *Ermine a cross-crosslet sable* is the coat of CARROLL. *Argent, a cross-crosslet-fitchée sable* is borne by the Kentish SCOTTS. *Gules, a cross-crosslet-fitchée argent*, is a coat of ROUSSET in France. *Sable, a cross-crosslet argent*, is used by DURRANT, or DURANT.

But, as has been said, the chief use of the cross-crosslet

of WASSELEY, WASTERLEY, or WESTLEY, sometimes blazoned as:—

THE CROSS CLECHÉE, is not a common form in British Armory. In it each arm of the cross expands into a kind of curvated lozenge shape, voided like the handle of a mediæval key, and having a small knob at each angle (Plate XV., fig. 7). *De Gueules, à la croix clechée et pommettée d'or*, were the arms of the Counts of TOULOUSE; a circumstance from which this cross derives its ordinary Heraldic name of "*a cross of Toulouse.*" In the seal of RAYMOND VII., Count of TOULOUSE in 1228, the "voiding" is only a plain cross. *D'Azur, à la croix de Toulouse d'or*, is the coat of VENASQUE in France. *Azure, a cross of Toulouse argent*, is borne by BOFFIN D'ARGENÇON in France. *Or, a cross of Toulouse gules* are the arms of LUPIA in Spain. The same coat is borne by the Italian MOZZI (Plate XV., fig. 7); and by ST. GILLES, ROUSSET, LAUTREC, and L'ISLE JOURDAIN in France.

A CROSS FOURCHÉE, OR FOURCHETTÉ, is one in which each arm of the cross forks like a **V**. *Or, a cross fourchetté sable* is the coat of TRUCHSESS DE KULENTHAL in Germany; the reverse is used by VAN VIERACKER. (Page 164, fig. 59.)

THE CROSS TAU is in the shape of a broad letter **T**. *Or, a cross Tau azure*, were the arms of the Order of ST. ANTHONY (probably originally the cross, or crutch-head, of a pilgrim's staff). With the field *argent* this forms the first and fourth quarters of the coat of the Barons HANNET in Prussia. *Argent, a cross Tau gules*, is borne by VAN GENT of Utrecht; and, with the cross in bend, by the Counts von ROTHALL (SIEBMACHER, *Wappenbuch*, iii., 14). *Azure, a cross Tau or*, is used by the VROOMBAUTS of Flanders. (Page 164, fig. 61.)

THE CROSS GUIVRÉ, or GRINGOLÉE, is a plain cross couped; at the extremity of each arm are two serpent's

Per pale argent and azure, a cross moline counter changed, is borne by LIGNIÈRES.

Gules, a cross moline or, is borne by VILLEHARDOUIN. *Sable, a cross moline argent* is the coat of UPTON in England; UITENHAGE in Holland; DEYN in Guelders, etc. The UPTONS, Viscounts TEMPLETOWN, make the charge *or*.

THE CROSS SARCELLY, or RECERCELLÉE, is simply a variety of the cross *ancrée*, or *moline;* only differing from the latter in having the hooks at the end drawn larger so as to admit of another convolution. The cross of the BECS, or BEKES, referred to above, is often drawn after this fashion. *Argent, a cross sarcelly voided or*, is the coat of BASING.

In Plate XV., fig. 13 gives us the arms of KNOWLES, or KNOLLYS, formerly Earls of BANBURY: *Azure, crusily and a cross-moline disjoined, or voided throughout, or*.

THE CROSS BOTONNY (or BOTONNÉE) (*treflé*) is represented on Plate XIV., fig. 11, the arms of WINWOOD, *Argent, a cross botonny-sable*, in it each arm of the cross terminates in a trefoil. *Argent, a cross botonny gules*, borne by BRYERLEGH; *Azure, a cross botonny argent*, by GOLDISBURGH; and *Or* by WADE of Kent. *Gules, a cross botonny or* was used by JOHN BOKINGHAM, Bishop of LINCOLN (1362-1398). *Quarterly gules and azure over all a cross botonny or* is the coat of PIERREFEU, and THOMAS DE LA VALETTE, in France. *Gules, a cross between four crosslets botonny argent* are the arms of DE CLAIRON, Comtes de HAUSSONVILLE in France. The Cross botonny is occasionally met with *fitchy* at the foot.

THE CROSS POMMETTY (POMMETTÉE), or POMMELLY, is one of which the arms end in a ball, or globe. It is sometimes called a *croix bourdonnée*, from the round ball by which the tops of the *bourdons*, or pilgrim's staves, were surmounted. *Argent, a cross pommetty sable* are the arms

shaped. It must however be noticed that this is rather a modern refinement, and that the cross moline of the *Rolls of Arms* is not thus pierced. *Argent, a cross moline sable* is the coat of COLVILLE. The COLVILLES of Ochiltree bear the same *square-pierced*, as in Plate XIV., fig. 6. These two are NISBET'S instances (i., p. 115), and it will be noticed that here the piercing is duly expressed. In my view the cross *moline* and the cross *ancrée* are practically the same thing; and if there be a piercing it should be, as in French blazon, distinctly expressed. *D'Or, à la croix ancrée de gueules* is the coat of the AUBUSSONS, Comtes de la FEUILLADE; Ducs de la ROANNAIS. *Argent, a cross ancrée sable* is borne by the Marquises and Comtes de MONTALEMBERT in France (Plate XV., fig. 2). *Gules, a cross moline or, in chief two mullets argent* is borne by the Marquises de COURVOL. The Dutch family of BENTINCK, now Dukes of PORTLAND in England, use: *Azure, a cross moline argent*; the Marquises de SALVERT in France use the same. This coat is also attributed to MOLINEUX; but the MOLYNEUX family, Earls of SEFTON, etc., usually bore the charge *Or*, and often square, or even quarter, pierced (*cf.* Plate XV., fig. 1). (The difference between quarter piercing and square piercing is, that the former is much larger than the latter, taking up the whole square at the point of intersection of the arms of the cross.) *Gules, a cross moline argent* (sometimes *ermine*) are the arms of BEC, or BEKE. They are also those of the Principality of RATZEBURG (quartered by Mecklenburg), and of the Principality of CAMIN (quartered in the full coat of Prussia). Both of these Principalities are Bishoprics seized and secularised at the "Reformation." *Or, a cross moline*, and in the *dexter canton* a *rose gules* is borne by SYMENS in Brabant. *Per fess or and azure, over all a cross moline argent*, is the coat of the County of GRADISCA.

(158)

de-lis, as in Mr BURNETT'S sketch, Plate XIV., fig. 9, or perhaps better in my own on page 164, fig. 58. *Sable, a cross flory between four escallops argent*, is borne by FLETCHER of Saltoun. Or, *a cross flory sable*, the coat of LAMPLOWE, or LAMPLUGH. RADA in Spain bears *Or, a cross flory sable*, often drawn as a *Cross of Calatrava*. *Argent, a cross flory sable*, is the coat of SWINNERTON. The Cross *fleuretté* or *flurty*, or *fleur-de-lisée* (fig. 57), is again often confounded with the preceding one. But correctly drawn it should be a plain cross couped having a demi-fleur-de-lis attached to the extremity of each arm ; it is represented in Plate XIV., fig. 10, the arms of PEREIRA. This is known abroad as the *Cross of Calatrava* from the Cross which appears in the arms of that famous Spanish Order. (The badge of the Order was different in shape, being more like the *cross flory*.) The *Cross of Calatrava* figures in many important Spanish coats, and is often drawn and blazoned *voided*, *i.e.*, the body of the cross is in outline, allowing the field to be visible in the intermediate space. The Spanish VILLA-GOMEZ use : *Or, a Cross of Calatrava gules between four cauldrons sable*. The PANTOJAS of Estremadura bear : *Azure, a cross florencée gules bordered or, within a bordure of sixteen panes gules and argent*. In English blazon this would be, *Azure, a cross fleur-de-lisée or*, voided *gules*, etc. The French VILLEQUIERS bear : *Gules, a cross fleur-de-lisée between twelve billets or* (NISBET wrongly makes the field azure).

THE CROSS ANCRÉE, and the CROSS MOLINE.— The cross *ancrée* has its extremities terminating in two curved pieces like the hooks of a grapnell (as on Plate XV., fig. 2). It resembles the cross *moline* (which is so called from its being similar in shape to the iron cross in the centre of a mill stone) except that the latter is now borne pierced in the centre, in French *ajourée ;* the piercing is usually square, but may be round, or lozenge-

THE CROSS PATONCE. — *The cross patonce* is at the same time one of the most frequent, and beautiful of the forms of the Cross used in British Armory. It has foliated ends and expands slightly by curved lines from the centre. It is given *voided* on Plate XIV., fig. 8; the arms of PILKINGTON, *Argent, a cross patonce voided gules*, but is better represented in its usual form on page 164, fig. 56.

Argent, a cross patonce gules, is the coat of COLVILLE, and CARLYLE. With the charge *sable* it is borne by BANESTRE, or BANESTER; and *azure*, by the Barons of MALPAS. *Barry of eight argent and gules, over all a cross patonce sable*, is the coat of GOWER (one of the principal charges in the coat of the Dukes of SUTHERLAND); others of the name have borne *Ermine, a cross patonce gules*, which is also the coat of GRINDALL and INGHAM. *Gules, a cross patonce argent* (or more frequently *or*) is the coat of LATIMER (often blazoned *flory, See* p. 153). *Or, a cross patonce gules*, is borne by FREVILLE. *Sable, a cross patonce or*, is used by LASCELLES and, within a bordure, by the Earls of HAREWOOD of that name. *Azure, a cross patonce or*, is borne by the WARDS, Viscounts BANGOR. *Azure, a cross patonce between five martlets or*, is the coat assigned by later Heralds to EDGAR ATHELING, and other Saxon princes. It is used as the Arms of UNIVERSITY COLLEGE, OXFORD. Its employment by the Plantagenet Sovereigns as a coat of Augmentation is referred to elsewhere in this volume (Chapter XVI.).

There is often some confusion between the *Cross Patonce* and THE CROSS FLORY or FLEURY. The distinction is supposed to consist in this; that, while the arms of the *cross patonce* gradually expand, those of the *cross flory* are of equal width very nearly to the end. But I agree with NISBET and GIBBON in thinking the true *cross flory* to be one of which the end terminates in fleurs-

times *engrailed*) *between three crosses patty-fitchy sable*, is the coat of FYNDERNE or FINDERNE.

THE CROSS POTENT (*potencée*) is a plain Greek cross, having at the end a piece of equal width placed at right angles, so that the cross appears to be formed of four T's, or *potents* (fig. 51).

Gules, a cross potent or, is the coat of CHATTERTON; *Azure, a cross potent* (sometimes *engrailed*) *or*, that of BRANCHELEY; *Sable, a cross potent or*, that of ALLEYN. The arms of the Duchy of CALABRIA are *Argent, a cross potent sable*—often quartered in the 2nd and 3rd, with ARRAGON in the 1st and 4th. *Azure, a saltire between four crosses potent or*, is borne by VIALART in France (*d'Azur, au sautoir d'or cantonné de quatre croix potencées du même*).

The *cross potent* is occasionally found *fitchy*. Such a coat was assigned by the Heralds of later time to ETHELRED, King of WESSEX.

THE CROSS OF JERUSALEM.—This is the name given to the cross potent with its accompanying crosslets which appear in the arms of JERUSALEM (*see* Plate IX., fig. 1). Many attempts have been made to account for its adoption. The most probable, perhaps, is that which sees in the middle cross the initials H and I of Hierusalem, or of the Blessed Saviour IHESVS, and in the whole bearings the hieroglyphic of the five Sacred Wounds. The charge has been adopted by several foreign families. *Argent, the Cross of Jerusalem gules*, is used by LIBOTTON of Liège; the reverse by CABELLIC, and CROUSNILHON, and LEZERGUE of Brittany. *Sable, the Cross of Jerusalem or*, is the coat of the Barons BERNARD DE FAUCONVAL. The Swiss DIETRICHS use *Azure*, the same cross *or*.

A coat somewhat resembling the coat of JERUSALEM has already been given for LICHFIELD (Plate XIV., fig, 7).

between three crosses patty argent, with many differences. *Azure, three crosses patty argent*, is the coat of DUGUID; with the field gules, of DAWSON. *Or, a fess between three crosses forming vert*, is borne by RILEY; *d'Or, au chevron accompagné de trois croix patées d'azur*, is borne by DANES of France. In French Armory the *cross patée* appears most frequently in Breton coats: *Argent, a cross patty between four mascles gules* is borne by the Breton KERGROAS; and *de Gueules, à trois croix patées d'hermine* is the coat of JOUSSEAUME, Marquis de la BRETESCHE. The Poitevin family of BARLOT bear: *Sable, three crosses patty argent*. This shield is often borne *en bannière* (*vide ante*, p. 57). The *cross patty* is occasionally formed by a compound line. *Or, a cross patty engrailed* is ascribed to PESHALL.

In common English parlance, the *cross patty* is often, but quite erroneously, termed a *Maltese Cross*, which is a bearing quite different in shape (as will be seen by a reference to page 164; figs. 53 and 55, where the two crosses are drawn in close proximity). This is a mistake which is sometimes made by people who ought to be better informed. The badge of the "Order of Valour," the highly-esteemed VICTORIA CROSS, is actually a *cross patty*, but in the Royal Warrant of its institution it is declared that the badge "shall consist of a *Maltese* Cross of bronze," etc.

THE CROSS PATTY-FITCHY (*patée fichée*) (fig. 54).—The *cross patty-fitchy* consists of the three upper portions of the *cross patty*, but the fourth is a point or spike—a cross "fixibyll," sharpened so as to be driven into the ground. This is a pretty common charge in British Armory. *Gules, a cross patty-fitchy or*, are the arms of HEYTON; *Or, a cross patty-fitchy gules* are those of SCUDAMORE. *Gules, a fess counter-compony argent and sable, between three crosses patty-fitchy argent*, was the coat of BOTELERS, Lords SUDELEY. *Argent, a chevron* (some-

Plate XIV., fig. 5, the coat of LAWLEY. That this was the original bearing of the Counts of COMMINGES, or COMMENGES, is shown by the seal of Count BERNARD V. in 1226. Here the shield and caparisons of his horse are charged with a narrow cross which expands rapidly at the ends ; and in fact these form a continuous bordure to the escucheon. This fact is especially worthy of remark, because the origin of the present coat, and the meaning of its charges, have been a source of discussion and perplexity to several writers. It is blazoned now as: *de Gueules, à quatre otelles d'argent.* The *otelle* is a charge which occurs but seldom ; and it has been taken variously to be the blade of a spear ; a *cicatrised wound*, or a *peeled almond!* (The latter two even in MENÊTRIER, *Méthode du Blason*, p. 24, Lyons, 1718;—and *l'Art du Blason Justifié*, p. 130, Lyons, 1661.) Such are the far-fetched *fantaisies* of the old Armorists ! Really the *otelles* were nothing more than the pieces of the field which appeared within the arms of the cross-*patée-throughout*: but ignorance turned the charge into the field, and the field into the charge; and then, to account for the result, indulged in such speculations as to its origin as those I have above recorded. *Or, a cross patty sable, fimbriated (i.e.,* bordered) *gules;* otherwise blazoned (or *gules voided sable*) is the coat of the Counts RAOUSSET DE BOULBON. *Per saltire or and argent, over all a cross patty azure* was used by the celebrated HUGH PUDSEY, Bishop of DURHAM (1153-1195). (The charge of VOLZ already given is a long cross *patée* at the ends.) The Cross given on Plate XIV., fig. 5, is a cross *patée-throughout, i.e.,* its extremities reach the edges of the shield.

Gules, a chevron between ten crosses patty argent is the well known coat of BERKELEY, Earls of that place. (Their original coat was the simple chevron.) The Scottish families of BARCLAYS bore : *Azure, a chevron*

disposed so that the second and longer traverse is placed as near to the base of the upright as the smaller one is to its summit (fig. 52). This bearing derives its name from the fact that it was used as their badge by the family of the Dukes of LORRAINE. It does not appear in their coat of arms, but depends by a chain from the necks of their eagle supporters. *Azure, a cross-of-Lorraine argent*, is the coat of EESEN and SWIENEZIC ; and *Argent, a cross-of-Lorraine sable*, is that of the French MARCELS. *Per pale or and azure a cross-of-Lorraine counter-changed*, is borne by FURSTENHAUER. The family of ARNOLET DE LOCHEFONTAINE, Marquises de BUSSY D'AMBOISE used: *Azure, a cross-of-Lorraine or, within a bordure nebulée-fleur-delisée of the same* : a noteworthy form of the bordure.

The Cross, having four equal arms known as the GREEK CROSS (fig. 48), also called a *cross couped;* and a *cross hummetty* (in French *une croix alésée*), appears in the arms of the modern Kingdom of GREECE—*Azure, a Greek cross argent*, and is also borne by the Marquises of ST. GELAIS, in France. *Gules, a cross couped argent* is the coat of SWITZERLAND. *Or, a cross couped azure* is borne by YVOR of France, and its reverse by SOLVI of Spain and GLAVENAS of France. XAINTRAILLES of GASCONY uses : *d'Argent, à la croix alésée de gueules.*

The CROSS PATTY (*patée*) in old writers is called sometimes FORMY, or PATLE FORMÉE (fig. 53). It is a cross of equal arms which are flattened out ; the lines which spring from the centre being usually slightly curved, or concave. *Argent, a cross patty sable* is the early coat of BANASTRE : *Azure, a cross patty or*, is borne by WARD ; *Gules, a cross patty argent*, by ATTON ; *Gules, a cross patty or* (perhaps *patonce* is intended) by LATIMER. The CROSS-PATTY is sometimes borne, not as a *cross couped*, but as a *cross patty-throughout, i.e.*, its bounding lines are produced to meet the edges of the shield, as in

charges which were so frequently placed in the cantons, or spaces around the arms, of the cross.

The true Latin cross, the *Cross of the Passion* or *Long Cross* (fig. 47) is accordingly seldom met with. In this case the arms do not touch the borders of the shield, and the vertical piece is much longer than the traverse. An instance of its use is afforded by the coat used for the See of DUNKELD, which is: *Argent, a passion cross sable between two passion nails gules.* I assume that this is also the bearing in the coat of ANWICKE: *Argent, a holy cross sable.* It is so, certainly, in the coat of AUSTIN of Norfolk: *Gules, a chevron between three long crosses or.* In French blazon it is sometimes termed a cross *haussée*. *Sable, a Latin cross patée or,* is borne by the Bavarian family of VOLZ. When the "long Cross" is represented upon three *steps, degrees* or *grices,* it is called a *Cross-Calvary* (fig. 49). *Argent, a Cross-Calvary on three degrees gules,* is the Scottish coat of LEGAT (the steps need not be named as the title alone suffices). *Argent, a cross "graded of three" sable*—the coat of WYNTWORTH—is the same charge. *Argent, a Cross-Calvary gules, on a chief azure five besants,* was the coat of Bishop WESTON of Exeter (1721-1742); the cross being added as a difference to the Weston coat.

A CROSS PATRIARCHAL is the long, or Latin-Cross with a double traverse (fig. 50). *Sable, a Cross-Patriarchal argent,* was the coat borne in the twelfth century by several English prelates named TURBINE: RALPH, Archbishop of CANTERBURY (1114-1122); his brother SEFFRID, Bishop of CHICHESTER (1125-1143), and their nephew JOHN, of ROCHESTER (1125-1137). HESME in France uses the reverse. VESEY, Viscount de VESCI bears: *Or, on a cross sable a cross-patriarchal of the field.* In the Cross-Patriarchal both traverses are situated above the centre of the perpendicular beam; but the CROSS OF LORRAINE has the traverses

or pairle; *i.e.*, the Ordinary is drawn as touching the edges of the shield. It is now, however, depicted differently; being couped and pointed at its extremities as in Plate XVI., fig. 12, *Argent, a shake-fork sable.* From a supposed identification with the hay-fork, it is commonly known as a "*Shake-fork*" in Scotland. The Breton family of CONIGAN, Barons de ROZ, bear: *Quarterly* 1 and 4; *Argent a pairle sable.* 2 and 3: *Or, three buckles azure.*

Only one example is known to me in which the pairle is bounded by any line but the straight one; it is that of the family of BUGGE in Denmark, whose coat is; *Argent, a pairle engrailed vert.*

THE CROSS.

The use of the CROSS as an Ordinary has been referred to in page 141. But it was most natural that the symbol of salvation should be in use also as a favourite armorial charge; and that it should be represented, as is the case, in a great variety of ways. A few only of these can here be brought under the notice of the student, for Dame JULIANA BERNERS in the *Boke of St. Albans* writes that "crossis innumerabull are borne dayli," and BERRY'S *Encyclopædia Heraldica* enumerates three hundred and eighty-five varieties! The Cross of the Passion itself, with the long vertical arm, and the shorter horizontal one, is that which was probably intended when the charge was first assumed. On the long shields of the crusaders it would be the natural form; but as the shield became shorter in proportion to its width it was represented in the form in which it now appears as an Ordinary, having the *traverse*, or horizontal bar, placed across the centre of the shield; so making the four arms of nearly equal size, and extending to the borders of the shield. This alteration was moreover convenient as affording space for the

Mr STODART'S *Scottish Arms*, p. 215, that the seal of WILLIAM YOUNG bears the piles and a chief charged with escallops.

IX. THE PALL (*Pairle*).—This is a **Y**-shaped figure produced by the union of the upper half of a saltire with the lower half of a pale.

The French name appears to be derived from the Latin *pergula*, or Italian *pergola*, a forked stick or prop. It is of very infrequent use in British Armory. Its English name has been derived from its supposed identity with the Archiepiscopal *Pallium* borne in the arms of the See of CANTERBURY (Plate XVI., fig. 11) and some other Ecclesiastical coats, and which will be noticed in its proper place as a charge, and not as an Ordinary (*vide post*, Chapter XIII.).

In Foreign Heraldry the Ordinary is only occasionally found. *Or, a pairle sable* is the coat of the Barons von RÜPPELIN in Würtemburg; Plate XVI., fig. 10, *d'Azur, au pairle d'or*, is that of PEPIN in Brittany; *d'Azur, au pairle d'argent* is borne by COLLET. The town of ISSOUDUN or YSSOUDUN bears *d'Azur, au pairle d'or, accompagné de trois fleurs-de-lis, mal-ordonnées du même*, the pairle being intended to recall the initial of its name. (The phrase *mal-ordonnées* is used by French armorists when instead of three charges being arranged in the usual way two and one, they are, as in the present case, placed one above two.) *Azure, a pairle argent* is borne by the French family of COLLET, *Gules, a pairle argent* is the coat of the Bavarian DEICHSLERS. *Gules, a pairle ermine* is the coat of TAFFIN. *Gules, a pall-reversed ermine*, is an almost unique example in British Armory, and is borne by the family of KELDON, or KELVERDON, in Essex. The Barons KFELLER DE SACHSENGRUN, in Austria, use, *Gules, a pairle-reversed argent*.

In many old representations of the arms of the CUNNINGHAM family in Scotland the charge is the pall,

Before passing from the subject we may note that an ingenious attempt has been made by a modern writer to trace the piles, especially when borne three in number, to the tails, or ends, of the pennons borne in mediæval wars. The paper referred to is by Mr G. J. FRENCH; it was read before the Archæological Association in 1857, and was reprinted for private circulation. Mr FRENCH argues that, as the pile is often borne *wavy*, or *engrailed*, the idea that it was derived (as some writers assert) from the piles driven into the ground as foundations for a building, is utterly untenable. On the other hand the wavy piles would very fairly represent such pennons or tails of standards as the soldiers bore in the Crusades, etc. He points out that the early kite-shaped shield admitted the displayal of these rays in a perpendicular direction (as in the coat of ANSTRUTHER, Plate XVI., fig. 2), but that the smaller heater-shaped shield of a later period made it more convenient to gather the points in the base (as in the coat of BRECHIN, fig. 3). He refers to the MS. of Sir DAVID LINDSAY, in which both arrangements appear in the Arms of the same family: " On the shield of Erskyn lord of Brechine " the piles converge to the base; and on that of the " lord of Brechane of *auld* " (*i.e.*, as anciently borne), "the piles are placed perpendicularly." Another instance he finds in the coat: *Argent, three piles sable, on a chief of the first as many annulets of the second*, borne by Sir JOHN YOUNG, who in 1541, married MARGARET SCRYMGEOUR, of the family who were hereditary standard-bearers to the Kings of Scotland, and afterwards, Earls of DUNDEE. Mr FRENCH thinks the piles were assumed by YOUNG in memory " of the standard borne by her ancestors as the charge on his armorial shield "! The SCRYMGEOURS, however, really bore: *Gules, a lion rampant or, holding a scimetar argent;* and in 1521, *i.e.*, twenty years before the match referred to, we find in

tures. (Plate XVI., fig. 6.) In the coat of ISHAM, as borne in modern times, the piles are found of small size in the chief of the shield; *Gules, a fess, and in chief three piles wavy argent* (Plate XVI., fig. 4); but originally the piles were of the ordinary size, and were debruised by the fess; as in GLOVER'S *Ordinary of Arms*, HARL. MS., 1392. Three piles wavy issuant from the base are frequent in French Armory, and are often blazoned as flames. *Or, three piles wavy issuing from the base azure*, is the coat of the Marques de FUMEZ. The HENDERSONS of Fordel (Plate XVI., fig. 5) have the piles issuant from the sinister side of the shield: *Gules, three piles issuant from the sinister flank argent; on a chief of the last a crescent azure* (*vert* in WORKMAN'S MS.) *between two ermine spots sable*. (But see STODART, *Scottish Arms*, i., 308.)

In Foreign blazon when piles thus issue from the flank they are called an *émanche;* or the shield is said to be *Émanché*. Plate XVI., fig. 8, is the coat of VON RIGEL, in Bavaria; *d'Argent, à une émanche de trois pièces de gueules mouvante du flanc dextre*. (The piles here are shorter than our English ones.) The family of HOTMAN, originally from the Duchy of Cleves, bear: *Parti emanché d'argent et de gueules*. The family of AQUIN in Dauphiné bear: "*d'Azur, à quatre piles renversées d'argent, appointées vers le chef en chevron;* c'étoient anciennement cinq A à l'antique liez qui faisoient un A quint." MENÊTRIER, *Méthode du Blason*, pp. 132-133.

It should be noticed that the Ordinary in its proper English form of a wedge issuing from the chief, is, I believe, absolutely unknown to French Armory. The pile-reversed issuing from the base is, however, not rare, and is called a *pointe*.

If this *pointe* is gradually curved upwards the shield is blazoned *enté en pointe*. Plate XVI., fig. 9, is the coat of LERNOUT in Flanders, and is: *d'Or, à la pointe entée de sable chargée d'un fleur-de-lis du champ*.

Plate XVI., fig. 2, contains the coat of ANSTRUTHER of that Ilk: *Argent, three piles sable.* When the piles are three in number a somewhat fanciful connection has been traced between them and *passion nails*, by which designation they are sometimes blazoned. They are often represented *in point* as in the coat of HOLLIS above given, and are not then conjoined where they leave the chief. *Or, three piles in point azure*, is the early coat of BRYAN; and *Sable, three piles in point argent*, that of HALKETT. *Or, three piles in point gules*, are the arms of the Lordship of BRECHIN (See *Roll* of 1256), originally borne by David, Earl of HUNTINGDON, brother of King WILLIAM THE LION (Plate XVI., fig. 3). This coat has often been erroneously tinctured; *Argent* being substituted for the field *Or*. The arms have thus been made identical with those of the family of WISHART, who have been described as "WISHARTS, Lords of BRECHIN!" There were no such persons. The right tincture of the field is the ancient one of *Or*, whether it appear in the quarterings of the MAULES, Lords PANMURE, and Earls of DALHOUSIE; or in the arms of the City, or in those borne by custom for the See of BRECHIN. In all these cases the arms of the territorial Lords of BRECHIN are intended, and not those of the comparatively insignificant family of WISHART. The same coat is also borne for BASSETT; and, piercing a human heart, for the family of LOGAN in Scotland.

Where three piles are used, a common arrangement is that two issue from the chief, and one (reversed) from the base. Three *sable* piles thus arranged in a silver field are the coat of HULSE (Plate XVI., fig. 7). In several English coats the piles are *flory, i.e.*, the point of each terminates in a little fleur-de-lis; for example, *Or, three piles issuing bendways from the dexter chief, and flory, at the points sable*, are the arms of NORTON. Those of WROTON have the piles issuant from the sinister base, and are of the same tinc-

PLATE XVI.

1. Pile.
(*Chandos.*)

2. Three piles.
(*Anstruther.*)

3. Piles in point.
(*Brechin.*)

4. Piles in chief.
(*Isham.*)

5. Piles from sinister.
(*Henderson.*)

6. Piles from sinister base.
(*Wroton.*)

7. Pile reversed.
(*Hulse.*)

8. Emanche.
(*Rigel.*)

9. Pointe entée.
(*Lernout.*)

10. Pall.
(*Pépin.*)

11. Pall.
(*Canterbury.*)

12. Shakefork.
(*Cunningham.*)

of the Lordship of BREDA; *Gules, three saltires argent,* which was quartered in the shield of the Princes of ORANGE, and has from it come into the escucheon of the Prussian monarchy.

Azure, three saltires argent, on a chief or as many of the field (*d'Azur, à trois flanchis d'argent, un chef d'or chargé de trois flanchis du champ*) is the coat of BALZAC, Marquis d'ENTRAGUES in France.

Or, six saltires gules (three, two, one), are the arms of PAPENBROEK in Holland; and those of the city of AMSTERDAM are: *Gules, on a pale cousu sable three saltires argent.*

VIII. THE PILE.—The Pile is a triangular wedge-shaped figure, issuing (unless it be otherwise specified) from the Chief, of which if it be borne alone it occupies a little more than the third part.

Argent, a pile gules (*d'Argent, à une pile de gueules*) (Plate XVI., fig. 1) is the old coat of the family of CHANDOS. The Lords CHANDOS bore the field *or*. *Or, a pile engrailed sable*, is borne by WATERHOUSE; and *Argent, a pile wavy gules*, by DELAHAY. *Azure, a pile wavy issuant from the dexter corner of the escucheon or*, are the arms of ALDAM of Kent. *Ermine, on a pile gules three lions of* ENGLAND, was the coat granted in 1663 by CHARLES II. to his natural son JAMES CROFTS, afterwards Duke of MONMOUTH; it was quartered with *Or, an escucheon of* FRANCE, *within the double tressure flory and counter-flory* of SCOTLAND. *Argent, two piles sable* (and the reverse) are the arms of HULLES. *Ermine, two piles in point sable* (that is issuing from the dexter and sinister angles of the escucheon and meeting, or nearly meeting, in the base are the arms of HOLLIS, Earl of CLARE (1624). The coat of D'ESTAMPES (already given in Plate X., fig. 4) contains two such piles in chevron issuant from the base. *Or, two piles issuant from the base gules*, is the coat of the Barons d'OMPHAL of Holland.

JOHNSTON bore: *Argent, a saltire sable, on a chief gules three cushions or.* TWEEDIE: *Argent, a saltire engrailed gules, a chief azure.* JARDINE: *Argent, a saltire and a chief gules, on the last three mullets of the first.* MOFFAT, of that Ilk: *Sable, a saltire and chief argent;* otherwise, *Argent, a saltire azure and chief gules.* (PONT'S MS.) TENNENT: *Argent, a saltire and chief gules.*

The Saltire, in Foreign Armory is subject to some of the variations incidental to the cross, thus: *Or, a saltire couped and flory azure,* is the coat of LE BARBU. *Or, a saltire and ancred, or moline, azure (d'Or, à la croix ancrée en sautoir d'azur)* is borne by the Ducs de BROGLIE of France, who came originally from Piedmont. *Argent, a saltire pommetty azure* is the coat of FIOLO of Venice. *Argent, a saltire échanchré (v. p. 76) gules, in chief a crown or,* are the arms of VAN HUCHTENBROEK in Holland. Saltire may also be borne in greater numbers than one; or may be one of several charges in a coat. In this case, according to general usage in Scotland and England, the arms of the saltire are usually, though not invariably, couped horizontally; and not, as in Dutch Armory, at right angles to the several limbs. Plate XV., fig. 12, is the coat of GLANVILLE of England; *Azure, three saltires or;* and of BOYSLEVÉ, Marquis d'HAROUÉ; and MOLEN, Marquis de ST. PONCY, in Brittany. For the Saltire thus used as a charge the French name is *flanchis.* There are many instances of its use in the Armory of the Netherlands: *Sable, three saltires or;* and *Or, three saltires gules;* are both coats borne by Dutch families named ALMOND. *Argent, three saltires gules,* are the arms of the Counts van der DILFT DE BORGHVLOET; of BESOYEN; and FAVELETTE. *Azure, three saltires argent (d'Azur, à trois flanchis d'argent)* is the coat of BEVERWIJCK; BEAUMONT; VAN DEN HEUVEL, etc.

Perhaps the best known instance is that of the Arms

PLATE XV.

1. Cross moline.
(*Molyneux.*)

2. Cross ancrée.
(*Montalembert.*)

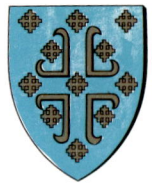

3. Cross moline voided.
(*Knowles.*)

4. Cross crosslets.
(*Beauchamp.*)

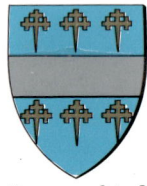

5. Cross crosslets fitchée.
(*Rattray.*)

6. Cross gringolée.
(*Montfort.*)

7. Cross of Toulouse.
(*Mozzi.*)

8. Saltire.
(*St. Andrew's Cross.*)

9. Saltire.
(*Dalrymple.*)

10. Saltire and chief.
(*Bruce of Annandale.*)

11. Saltire ancrée.
(*Broglie.*)

12. Saltire couped.
(*Glanville.*)

old coat of the house of LENNOX is *Argent, a saltire between two roses gules ; (d'Argent, au sautoir de gueules accompagné de quatre roses du champ)*. They later bore the saltire *engrailed*; a coat which is also that of the NAPIERS, and MACFARLANES.

When a saltire is charged, it is the rule in Scotland that the charges should slope with its limbs, the central charge, if any, being upright, thus in Plate XV., fig. 9 the DALRYMPLE coat is *Or, on a saltire azure nine lozenges of the field.*

The old rule was that the width of the arms of the saltire if uncharged was one fifth of the field, but if charged one third. The latter part of the rule was not observed in the old examples which remain to us. In Scottish Heraldry the saltire is often used in combination with the chief, this of course does not encroach upon, or cover any part of, the saltire, which is accommodated to the diminished space of the field. The Arms of the ANNANDS, the old Lords of ANNANDALE: *Or* (sometimes *argent*), *a saltire and a chief gules* (Plate XV., fig. 10), were adopted by the BRUCES when that lordship was acquired; apparently first by the fourth Lord of ANNANDALE, the father of ROBERT BRUCE the competitor for the throne; whose son charged the chief with *a lion passant gardant or*, perhaps as a souvenir of the original arms of BRUCE. The BRUCE coat was differenced, both chief and saltire being made *wavy*, by the BRUCES of Balcaskie and Kinross.

The combined saltire and chief of the ANNANDS were not only adopted by the different branches of the family of BRUCE, but by the KIRKPATRICKS; JOHNSTONS; JARDINES; MOFFATS; and other families feudally connected with the Lords of ANNANDALE, or belonging to that district.

The KIRKPATRICK coat was: *Argent, a saltire and chief azure, the last charged with three cushions or.*

enclosures were formed, and that the upper angle formed a convenient place for the foot of one who desired to leap the barrier. The tradition that the apostle ST. ANDREW suffered martyrdom upon a cross of that shape led to the prevalence of the saltire as a heraldic charge in Scotland, Burgundy, and other countries where ST. ANDREW is a popular saint; more particularly in Scotland, where the adoption of ST. ANDREW as the national patron goes back to a date before the introduction of armorial bearings. ST. ANDREW was as stated above also the patron saint of Burgundy; and in Spain the capture of Baeza from the Moors, on St. Andrew's Day in 1227, gave an impulse to the adoption of the saltire by some of the families who figured thereat ("Heraldry of Spain and Portugal," p. 5.) The CROSS OF ST. ANDREW, of silver on an azure field, the banner of Scotland, is represented on Plate XV., fig. 8. The cross known as that of ST. PATRICK is *Argent, a saltire gules.* It occurs as the arms of the FITZGERALDS, Dukes of LEINSTER, Earls of TYRCONNEL, KILDARE, etc.; but I am not aware of its appearance in any way as a national ensign until it was made part of the insignia of the Order of ST. PATRICK upon its foundation in 1783. *Gules, a saltire argent (de Gueules, au sautoir d'argent),* is the coat of the great house of NEVILLE, Earls of WAR- WICK, WESTMORELAND, etc. It was also borne by VANDER AA, in Flanders; VAN EYCK; VAN JUTPHAAS; BORGHARTS; OULTRE, and other Low Country families. The reverse is the coat of GERARD, and WINDSOR in England; of FLEMAL; BENTHEM; OOSTDIJK; GOHAING; VAN DEN EECKHOUT; and others in the Netherlands. LA GUICHE in France bears: *Vert, a saltire or (de Sinople au sautoir d'or).* The family of MAXWELL in Scotland bears: *Argent, a saltire sable;* and the same coat, but with the Ordinary *engrailed (d'Argent, au sautoir engrêlé)* is the coat of the COLQUHOUNS. The

CARLYLES, Lords TORTHORWALD, in Scotland (Plate XLII., fig. 5).

A large number of families bear the cross formed by the varying partition lines. *Argent, a cross engrailed sable (d'Argent, à la croix engrêlée de sable)*, belongs to the SINCLAIRS, Earls of ROSSLYN. (*See*, too, the arms of the Earls of CAITHNESS, etc., in Plate XLIII., figs. 1, 2.) It was also the coat of the family of MOHUN, and FITZ-HENRY in England; DU GUÉ, Vicomtes de MÉJUS-SUAUME in Brittany; FEUQUERAY, etc.

Argent, a cross embattled sable, is the bearing of BALMANNO; and AUCHINLECK in Scotland; with the cross *gules* it was borne in early times by DALINGRIDGE; DRAYTON; and GOURNEY (or GURNEY); DE LA LYNDE; and TIPTOT, in England; by CROVILLE; LANCY; and the Cardinal de LENONCOURT, in France. *Argent, a cross raguly sable (d'Argent, à la croix écotée de sable)*, was the coat of SANDYS. *Gules, a cross engrailed argent*, was borne by the INGLETHORPES of Norfolk, of whom one was Bishop of ROCHESTER 1283-1291; and the reverse is the coat of LAWRENCE. *Or, a cross engrailed gules* were the arms of the family of DE LA HACHE; and of several families in the Low Countries, *e.g.* HAYNIN; WARCOING; WAMBRECHIES; VAN DUDZEELE, etc. *Or, a cross engrailed vert*, is borne as a differenced coat for HUSSEY, the original coat being the plain cross. *Sable, a cross engrailed or*, is the well known bearing of the Suffolk family of D'UFFORD (or D'OFFORD) of which JOHN was Archbishop of CANTERBURY, in 1348.

VII. THE SALTIRE (*Sautoir*).—This Ordinary takes up the space occupied by a bend and a bend-sinister combined in the form of the letter **X**. Its name is of uncertain etymology, but it seems to be derived in some way from the verb *sauter*, to leap. My own idea is that it may have originated in the strengthening stays of a palisade, such as that by which the lists and their

renversés d'or, au chef d'argent, chargé de trois étoiles d'argent.

VI. THE CROSS.—The CROSS as an Ordinary occupies the space of a pale and a fess united. Its many varieties as a heraldic charge will find separate treatment in a supplement to this Chapter, page 151. In this place we shall only deal with the plain Cross as an Ordinary.

As might be expected, this form is frequently found as a sole charge. *Argent, a cross gules* (Plate XIV., fig. 1) is the "CROSS OF ST. GEORGE," and forms the ancient banner of ENGLAND; is also borne as the Arms of the ORDER OF THE GARTER; and of the Republic of GENOA, of which ST. GEORGE was the patron saint; by the Prince-Archbishops, Electors of TRIER, or TREVES; by the City of PADUA; and by some families named ST. GEORGES in France, of whom one family bore the title of Marquises de VÉRAC. The families of IBANEZ DE SEGOVIA in Spain; of the Florentine POPOLESCHI; of BIÖRNSEN in Denmark; of VAN BOUCHOUT in the Netherlands; all used the same. The reverse (*Gules, a cross argent*) is the arms of the great ORDER OF THE KNIGHTS HOSPITALLERS OF ST. JOHN OF JERUSALEM, Sovereigns of RHODES and MALTA; of the Dukes of SAVOY; of the Lordship of ASPREMONT; and of the cities of VICENZA and TOURNAY, etc.

Argent, a cross sable (*d'Argent, à la croix de sable*) was the coat of the Prince-Archbishops, Electors of COLOGNE.

Azure, a cross argent, was the coat of the Byzantine family of DUCAS; with the cross *or*, of LA CROIX, Duc de CASTRIES; of the city of VERONA; of the families of TEIXEIRA in Portugal; and OLUJA in Spain. *Or, a cross gules*, is the coat of DE BURGH, Earl of ULSTER; of BIGOT; of the principality of ANTIOCH; of FABERT (*Maréchal de France*); of the Barons ANDLAU; the Counts of RECHTEREN; and the Barons HEECKEREN, etc. It is also borne (for CORSBY) *en surtout* by the

PLATE XIV.

1. Cross.
(*St. George.*)

2. Cross raguly.
(*Laurence.*)

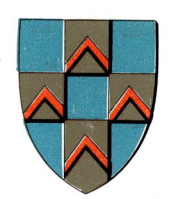

3. Cross quarter pierced.
(*Whitgreave.*)

4. Cross wavy voided.
(*Duckinfield.*)

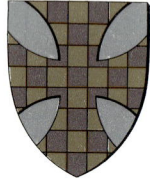

5. Cross patée checquy.
(*Lawley.*)

6. Cross moline square pierced.
(*Colvile.*)

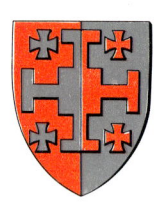

7. Cross potent quadrat.
(*Lichfield.*)

8. Cross patonce voided.
(*Pilkington.*)

9. Cross flory.
(*Lamplowe.*)

10. Cross fleur de lisé.
(*Pereira.*)

11. Cross botonnée.
(*Winwood.*)

12. Cross retranchée and pommettée.
(*Manfredi.*)

is the coat of Sir WALTER DE MANNY (founder of the Charterhouse); of the LEVIS, Ducs de MIREPOIX and DE VENTADOUR in France; the Barons van HAERSOLTE; and MULERT; the ARMELLINI of Italy; VAN ALKMAAR of Holland, etc.

Argent, three chevrons gules, is the coat of the family of DU PLESSIS RICHELIEU, of which the great Cardinal Duc de RICHELIEU was a member; of the Marquis de BASSOMPIERRE; of the County of RAVENSBERG (now quartered in the Royal Arms of Prussia); it was borne also by PHILIPPE DE BELESME, Comte d'ALENÇON (First Crusade); by the families of CHÂTEAU-GONTIER; BOIS-YVON; DE GORTERE *dit* SOMBEKE; and by that of SETTIMO, Princes de FILIOLA in Sicily.

The reverse (*Gules, three chevrons argent*) is borne by JESTYN AP GWRGANT (one of the ancient Welsh princes); BANESTER; MANCICOURT (who also bore the reverse); FAVERGES, etc. GALLOT in France has a rather peculiar coat—*Ermine, three chevrons, the centre one gules, the others sable* (*d'Hermine, à trois chevrons, le premier et le dernier de sable, le second de gueules*).

The Chevron, like the pale and the fess, is not infrequently borne coticed, and even double coticed though rarely; the diminutive chevrons employed for this purpose are called "couplecloses," but are not used singly. Three chevronels are borne "interlaced" or "braced" in base, in a few English coats. *Argent, three chevrons braced sable* are the coat of HEDWORTH; and BRACKENBURY; *Azure, three chevrons braced or,* is that of FITZHUGH. [Most frequently this bearing is found in combination with a chief as in the arms of WYVILL: *Or, three chevronels braced vair, a chief gules* (Plate XIII., fig. 12.)] The French coat of LA GRENÉE in Picardy, is: *de Gueules, à deux chevrons entrelacés, l'un de l'argent renversé et mouvant du chef, l'autre d'or.*
The GANNAY in Berry bore: *de Gueules, à trois chevrons*

solitary example of a chevron thus treated is the Scottish coat of JOHN ALEXANDER of Kinglassie, *Per pale argent and sable a chevron brisé at the summit; and in base a crescent, all counter-changed.* In a chevron *rompu*, or *failli*, there is a lack of continuity in one of the limbs, and the position of the failure must be specified; thus the Provençal family of MAYNIER, Barons d'OPPEDE, bears: *d'Azur, à deux chevrons d'argent, l'une failli à dextre, l'autre à senestre.* In the coat of BEAUMONT in Maine (Plate XIII., fig. 11) five chevrons are thus *faillis*, or *rompus*, alternately: "*d'Argent, à cinq chevrons de gueules rompus, les* 1, 2, 3, *à dextre, les autres à senestre.*"

In the last two examples more than one chevron occurs in the field; when this is the case English heraldic writers often call them "chevronels," as if they were diminutives of the chevron. French blazon knows no such distinction; and it is one for which there is no reason but the desire to complicate matters.

Argent, two chevrons azure, is a coat of BAGOT, and TYRREL in England; of RENNEBURG, or RAIMBERT in Westphalia; of LINDENPALM in Denmark. The Counts de PERCHE, in the First Crusade (1100), bore: *Argent, two chevrons gules;* BELESME; KENDENICH; BREITENBACH, etc., do the same. *Argent, two chevrons sable,* is the coat of the family of M'LAREN; *Azure, two chevrons or,* is borne by CHAWORTH in England; SARTIGES in France; TOLLENS in Holland, etc.

Three chevrons appear in several coats of great families *Or, three chevrons gules (d'Or, à trois chevrons de gueules)* are the arms of the DE CLARES, Earls of GLOUCESTER, etc.; and were also borne by the Counts of HANAU (Holy Roman Empire); the Barons VOORST, or VOERST; by CRÈVECŒUR; and *wavy gules* by the VAN DER RYTS of Flanders. The Counts of MERAVIGLIA bore them *azure.*

Or, three chevrons sable (d'Or, à trois chevrons de sable)

springing not from the base but from one of the sides of the escucheon (in which case it is said to be *couché*) or from the chief, when it is blazoned as "reversed." *Gules, a chevron reversed argent*, is the coat of the Bavarian Barons RUMLINGEN DE BERG; and of the Tyrolese family of MALGÖL; and Plate XIII., fig. 5, shows the arms of the Tuscan Counts BULGARINI: *Gules, a cross argent surmounted by a chevron reversed gules. Or, a chevron couched azure*, is the coat of DOUBLET.

The chevron is often borne engrailed, embattled, wavy, indented, etc. When its top is blunted it is said in French blazon to be borne *éciné*. In the arms of LA ROCHE-FOUCAULD, Plate XIII., fig. 9, the uppermost chevron is thus treated. *Barry of ten argent and azure three chevronels gules, the first éciné (Burelé d'argent et d'azur à trois chevrons de gueules brochants sur le tout le premier éciné).*

In the coat of the family of ZUR SUNNEN in Basel (given in the *Zürich Wappenrolle*, No. 548) the chevron *or* is terminated by a fleur-de-lis *argent*—the field is *gules*. A rare example of a chevron invecked (*cannelé*) is that of VAN HEYLBROUCK of Flanders: *d'Argent, au chevron cannelé de sable*.

The chevron occasionally appears in chief; thus the arms of the Earls of STRATHERN were those of STUART (*Or, a fess chequy azure and argent*) with *in chief a chevron gules*. (*Or, two chevrons gules*, STRATHERNE ancient.) Similar coats are those of the English families of KIRTON, who bear: *Argent, a fess, and in chief a chevron gules ;* STRELLS, the same but with the charges sable ; and SPRINGHOSE, *Gules, a fess and in chief a chevron argent*.

The chevron is "broken" or "fracted," *brisé*, when each limb is broken across, as in Plate XIII., fig. 10, which is the coat of the Counts de LINAGE in France (*d'Azur, au chevron brisé d'or, accompagné de trois roses d'argent*). A

and NETTANCOURT : SPARRE, Barons de CRONENBURG ; the families of MONTAUBAN ; SWART ; and VAN VEEN, (Holland) ; HARELBEKE (Flanders) ; HERBESTEIN, etc. *Sable, a chevron ermine* is borne by BAYNARD ; and *Gules, a chevron vair* by BLAKET.

When the chevron is of fur, the spots and panes do not follow the lines of the Ordinary, but are placed paleways ; a chevron chequy follows the same rule, as in Plate XIII., fig. 2, the coat of the Lords SEMPILL: *Argent, a chevron chequy gules and of the field, between three hunting horns sable garnished and stringed of the second* (*d'Argent, au chevron échiqueté de gueules et d'argent, accompagné de trois cors de chasse de sable liés de gueules*). In like manner when a chevron is charged the charges are placed paleways, unless it is specified that they are to follow the direction of the chevron, thus in Plate XIII., fig. 3, the arms of PRINGLE are : *Azure, on a chevron argent three escallops of the field.* In the coat of HEPBURN : *Gules, on a chevron argent a rose between two lions combatant of the first :* the lions of necessity follow the lines of the chevron.

In foreign coats the chevron is often drawn *ployé*, *i.e.*, with its limbs curved inwards. I believe this has arisen simply, as in the analogous case of the fess *voutée* (page 125), from the surface of the escucheon having been convex ; but in course of time, it has become the ordinary use of some families, even when the escucheon affords a plane surface, and it is accordingly so specified in many foreign blazons. Thus, *Argent, a chevron* ployé *gules* (*d'Argent, au chevron ployé de gueules*) is the coat of the Danish AUGUSTINS or OWSTINS; the reverse is that of the RODENEGGS, Counts WOLKENSTEIN. The Barons von NEYDECK bear : *Or, a chevron ployé gules.* Plate XIII., fig. 4 gives the coat of VON MOLL in Tirol : *Azure, a chevron ployé between three estoiles or.*

This Ordinary sometimes assumes an abnormal position,

PLATE XIII.

1. Chevron.
(*Stafford.*)

2. Chevron checquy.
(*Sempill.*)

3. Charges on a chevron.
(*Pringle.*)

4. Chevron ployé.
(*Moll.*)

5. Chevron reversed.
(*Bulgarini.*)

6. Fess between chevrons.
(*Fitzwalter.*)

7. Chevronels.
(*Clare.*)

8. Chevron cotised.
(*Clutton.*)

9. Chevron écimé.
(*La Rochefoucauld.*)

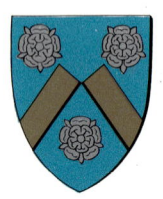

10. Chevron fracted.
(*Rozier de Linage.*)

11. Chevron rompu.
(*Beaumont.*)

12. Chevrons interlaced.
(*Wyvill.*)

Argent, a chevron azure, is borne by the Venetian Counts CANALI; the Barons von POLLNITZ; the Danish ERIKSENS; the families of METSCH; BEAUREPAIRE; BROUILLART; ASBACH, etc.: its reverse is used by the English families of LADBROOKE (or LODBROKE); GURWOOD; STANGATE, etc.; and by those of BRÜHL; MALMONT; LA PORTE; COLOMBIER; CIOLI, etc., abroad. *Argent, a chevron sable* is borne by the TRELAWNEYS, and PRIDEAUX (in the latter case the *label gules,* originally borne for difference, has become a regular portion of the charges). HOLBEACH bears the same, but with the chevron engrailed.

Azure, a chevron or, is in England borne by the Norman D'ABERNONS; in France, by the family of GORREVOD, Ducs de PONT DE VAUX, Princes of the Holy Roman Empire, etc. It is borne by the VENDELINI of Venice; by DUIVEN or DUINEN; and by VERREYCHEN, Counts de SART, in the Low Countries; by MONTCLAR; HERAUT; CHAMPSDIVERS; and others in France; by the Counts GÖTTER of Prussia and as canting arms by the families of SPARRE in Sweden; and MYPONT in Burgundy. With the field *billetty or* it is the coat of the Counts de CRUYCKENBERG; with the field *flory argent,* by BLANCHAERT in the Netherlands; and with the field *bezantée,* by DU CHESNEAU. *Azure, a chevron per pale or and argent* is the coat of the SALIGNONS in France.

The families of TOUCHET, Lords AUDLEY; KYNASTON; VAN DRIESCHE in Holland, etc., bear *Ermine, a chevron gules.* *Gules, a chevron argent* was the original coat of the great House of BERKELEY; and is also borne by the Counts of HERBESTEIN; and the Prussian Barons LEDEBUR. *Gules, a chevron argent* (often *ermine*) is the coat of the great family of GHISTELLES in Flanders; *Gules, a chevron or* is the coat of the CHAMPERNONS, and COBHAMS; HERZEELE, Marquises of FAULQUEZ;

The Burgundian Heralds naturally followed the German use, which still prevails. In it charges, animate and inanimate, are freely turned to the sinister whenever symmetry or artistic effect appear to require it, and this without conveying to the intelligent observer the smallest suggestion of illegitimate descent. (For Bendy-sinister, *v.* p. 95.)

For fuller treatment of this subject, and an explanation of the use of the Bendlet, Baton, etc., as marks of bastardy, see the Chapter on ILLEGITIMACY.

V. THE CHEVRON.—The *Chevron* or *Cheveron* (a word said to be derived from an old name for the barge-couples of the gable of a house), is a figure composed of two bands issuing from the dexter and sinister base of the shield, and conjoined at or about the honour point.

This Ordinary is probably the one most in use in English Armory; and is certainly that which, interposed between three other charges, is employed most largely in the Armory of France. In German Heraldry it is not of frequent occurrence, and it is extremely rare in that of the Peninsula. (*See* my paper on the "Heraldry of Spain and Portugal.") In French Armory the limbs of the chevron are for the most part drawn so as to meet at a more acute angle than among ourselves, and the point is somewhat higher in the field; indeed, sometimes it is drawn so as actually to touch the top line of the escucheon. But the necessity of finding room for charges above and below the chevron has caused it to be not only diminished in bulk but drawn with a very obtuse angle. By far the best and most elegant examples are those in which the angle does not at most *exceed* a right angle.

A Chevron occurs as *armes parlantes* for the families of TEYES, and TEYEYES (*Argent, a chevron gules*) in the letter of the Barons to the Pope in 1301 : *Or, a chevron gules* (*d'Or, au chevron de gueules*) is the coat of STAFFORD, Duke of BUCKINGHAM (Plate XIII., fig. 1).

of LA TANIÈRE of Cambray; of RAPPACH ; etc. *Azure, a bend-sinister embattled or,* is the coat of RONCHIVECCHI in Tuscany ; *Azure, a bend sinister or,* that of FETZER (SIEBMACHER, *Wappenbuch,* ii., 164, and many others). *Azure, a bend-sinister vairé gules and argent,* is borne by HUNNENWEILER. *Per fess gules and or, a bend-sinister vair,* by BERN. *Ermine, a bend-sinister gules* (*d'Hermine, à la barre de gueules*) were the canting arms of BARRE in France. *Gules, a bend-sinister argent,* are the arms of RAUCH in Württemberg. *Sable, a bend-sinister or,* is borne by HERWEGH ; and, with the charge *argent,* by SULMETINGEN. To this list, large additions might be made, but these are quite sufficient to prove that the use of the bend-sinister has no necessary connection with illegitimacy, or dishonour. France was the original birth-place of an idea which was altogether erroneous: it was thought, quite without reason, that illegitimacy was denoted if the charges (for instance a lion rampant) faced to the sinister, whereas it was customary in early times for the escucheons on monuments, etc., in churches to have the arms so painted as that the charges faced to the High Altar. (Thus, in the Chapel of the CHEVALIERS DE LA TOISON D'OR at Dijon, the arms of the Knights whose stalls were on the north side are all arranged in this way.) FAVYN, who describes them, in the *Theâtre d'Honneur et de Chevalerie,* pp. 956-959, says " Le peintre ignorant a faict tous les Tymbres tournez à gauche pour regarder le Grand Autel, et mesmes quelques Armes, *ce qui est bastardise.*" He was of course utterly wrong in the last assertion. In our own Chapel of ST. GEORGE at Windsor, the stall-plates of the early Knights of the GARTER have the helmets and shields of those on the north side, thus arranged. So are also the coats emblazoned on the stalls upon the north side of the Choir in the Cathedral at Haarlem, which I have described in *Notes and Queries,* 5th Series, vol. ix., pp. 61, 101, etc.

VILLEPROUVÉE in France bears : *de Gueules, à la bande d'argent accostée de deux cotices d'or ;* a coat borne in the early *Rolls of Arms* for COUE, or COWE ; and for DAWTREY. The cotices are often borne engrailed, indented, wavy, etc., while the bend is plain ; or *vice versa.* Azure, *a bend engrailed argent plain coticed or,* is the coat of the Earls FORTESCUE. *Sable, a bend ermine between two cotices flory counterflory or* is the coat of KECK, or KELK.

A single example of the *cotice* as a sole charge occurs to me in the rather remarkable coat of the family of DES BAILLETS, who bore—*Argent, a cotice purpure.* Another curious coat is that of DIAZ in Spain :—*Argent, two cotices, the upper one sable, the lower one vert.*

The bend is sometimes borne doubly coticed ; *Ermine, a bend doubly coticed gules* is the coat of CELLES in Belgium ; *Argent, a bend engrailed between four cotices gules* is borne by LAYFORTH (GLOVER'S *Ordinary*). *Gules, a bend vair between four cotices or,* is the coat of GARDNER.

A still narrower diminutive, the riband or fillet, has been already represented in Plate IX., fig. 6 as debruising the lion of the arms of ABERNETHY.

The BEND-SINISTER (*Barre*) differs from the Bend only by its position. It runs from the sinister chief to the dexter base. Examples of its use formerly existed in Britain ; but in most cases the charge has come to be turned into the Bend (dexter), from an idea that in its original form it suggested illegitimacy. This is a popular error. No such association originally attached to it, and in many countries none such attaches to it still. Plate XII., fig. 11, is the coat of the family of LOREYN in the Netherlands ; *Or, on a bend sinister azure three stars of the field (d'Or, à la barre d'azur chargée de trois étoiles du champ).* The BENIGNI of Rome bear : *Argent, a bend-sinister sable.* *Argent, a bend-sinister gules,* were the arms of BISSET ; they are those of ZERRES in Bavaria ; of the Barons HASENBERG ; of HERDA in Westphalia ;

wavy sable. *Or, two bendlets gules* (*d'Or, à deux bandes de gueules*), are the arms of D'OYLY; GUALTERI (Italy); WOUTERS; and VAN MORSLEDE (Netherlands). *Argent, two bends azure* is borne by the Marquises SPOLVERINI. *Argent, two bendlets wavy azure* (*d'Argent, à une jumelle ondée d'azur en bande*); is the coat of the Italian CAETANI, or GAETANI, to which Pope BONIFACE VIII. belonged. In Plate XII., fig. 7, is the coat of WILBRAHAM. The arms of DELAMERE in Cheshire, are: *Argent, three bends wavy azure*. *Or, three bendlets ermine*, are the arms of the Spanish family of GUEVARA. *Or, three bendlets azure*, are those of the CONTARINI of Venice, etc.; ADHÉMAR DE MONTEIL, Comte de GRIGNAN, in France bears: *d'Or, à trois bandes d'azur*. (The letters of Mme. DE SEVIGNÉ were addressed to her daughter, the Comtesse de GRIGNAN.)

What appears to have been the original coat of BIRON viz., *Argent, three bendlets gules*, is now borne with the bendlets enhanced (Fr. *haussés*) *i.e.* placed higher in the shield, as in the arms of the poet, Lord BYRON. (Plate XII., fig. 8.) *Gules, three bendlets enhanced or*, are the coat of DE GREILLY, Lords of Manchester; and now figure in the arms of that city. The coat of KNATCHBULL (Plate XII., fig. 9), *Azure, three crosslets fitchées bendways between two bendlets or*, may be compared with that of NORTHCOTE (Plate IX., fig. 10), to exemplify the difference between " in bend " and " bendways."

The Cotice (*cotice*) is the name applied by the French to bendlets when more than four are placed in the shield; it is also the name given to the bendlets which often accompany a bend, as the endorses do a pale (*v. ante* p. 123). Thus Plate XII., fig. 10 is the coat of HARLEY, Earl of OXFORD :—*Or, a bend cotised sable* (*d'Or, à la bande de sable accompagnée de deux cotices du même*). *D'Argent à la bande de sable, accostée de deux cotices du même* is the coat of the French Marquises de CUSTINE.

ermine, that of SOMERY ; and *Argent, a bend counter-flory gules*, that of BROMFIELD.

Two foreign varieties of the bend deserve notice. In the bend *engoulée*, a characteristic bearing of Spain, each extremity of it issues from the mouth of a dragon, lion, or leopard. Thus in Plate XII., fig. 5, SANCHEZ, *Argent, a bend vert*, engoulée of *dragon's heads or*. (*See* my paper on the "Heraldry of Spain" in the *Genealogist*, vol. v.) The other is that arched and modified bend called in Germany the *Rauten Kranz* (Kränzlein), or "crown of rue." This forms the charge upon the barry coat of SAXONY ; *Barry of ten sable and or, over all a crancelin vert*. It is given in Plate XII., fig. 6, and is already familiar to us both as quartered with the Royal Arms of the United Kingdom by the late Prince Consort, and as borne *en surtout* by H.R.H. the PRINCE OF WALES, and his other descendants. The French call this bearing a *Crancelin*, and blazon Saxony thus :—*Burelé de sable et d'or de dix pièces; au crancelin de sinople*. The origin of this bearing is still somewhat a matter of doubt ; the legend usually put forth to account for it has no probability at all. The *Crancelin* though usually borne *vert* is not so always. RÜDICKHEIM uses *Or, a crancelin in bend gules*. FANCHON of Liège bears the arms of Saxony, but with the crancelin *gules*.

Like other Ordinaries the Bend has its diminutives ; the Bendlet, the Cotice, and the Riband. The bendlet is seldom borne singly. The French call the charge by the name of *bande* up to the number of four.

Argent, two bendlets sable (*d'Argent, à deux bandes de sable*), is the coat of BRADSHAW ; of the Barons STEIN ZU LEIBENSTEIN ; and of PEPPENBERG (*Zürich Wappenrolle*, No. 332), etc. The same with the bendlets engrailed is borne by RADCLYFFE ; with the bendlets nebuly by STAPLETON. A curious coat is that assigned to WIGMUR in Scotland, *Argent, two bendlets*, the *inner sides alone*

PLATE XII.

1. Bend. (*Scrope.*)
2. Bend ermine. (*Ward.*) 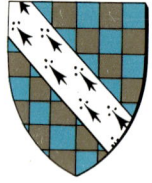
3. Charges on a bend. (*Bunbury.*) 
4. Charges on a bend. (*Savile.*) 
5. Bend engoulée. (*Sanchez.*) 
6. Rauten-kranz. (*Saxony.*) 
7. Bendlets wavy. (*Wilbraham.*) 
8. Bendlets enhanced. (*Byron.*) 
9. Bendways. (*Knatchbull.*) 
10. Bend cotised. (*Harley.*) 
11. Bend sinister. (*Loreyn.*) 
12. Baton sinister. (*Duke of Grafton.*)

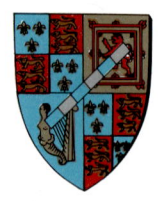

Or, a bend sable is borne by MAWLEY (or DE MALOLACU); SANDOVAL; and SO, of Spain; GONNELIEU; COMPAGNI (Tuscany); and GERARD DE BRIORDE (First Crusade, 1112).

The original coat of the family of DENNISTOUN of that Ilk in Scotland was *Argent, a bend sable*, which is also borne by several Barons STEIN, or STAIN; the Counts HEERDT in Holland, etc.

The WARDS of Bexley bore: *Chequy, or and azure*, a *bend ermine* (Plate XII., fig. 2), the ermine spots on a bend are placed bendways, as is also the case with the panes of chequy and vair. Thus, the arms of MENTEITH in Scotland are: *Or, a bend chequy azure and sable (d'Or, à la bande échiqueté d'argent et de sable)*. Here the three rows of the chequy are arranged to follow the direction of the bend.

Considerations of space seem to have established the rule regarding the position of charges placed upon a bend; if their height is greater than their breadth they follow the line of the bend, if not the charges are placed in the bend paleways. This will be understood by the examples given in Plate XII., figs. 3 and 4. BUNBURY bears: *Argent, on a bend sable* three *chessrooks of the field;* and SAVILE, Earl of MEXBOROUGH; *Argent, on a bend sable three owls of the field.* Coats Tierced in bend, or in bend-sinister, are given on p. 87.

Like the other Ordinaries the bend is varied by indenting, engrailing, etc., a few examples will suffice.

Azure, a bend engrailed or, is the coat of BERMINGHAM. That of BATURLE DU CASTEL, in Lorraine, is *d'Azur, à la bande cannelée d'argent.* The poet SCARRON bore: *Azure, a bend counter-embattled or (d'Azur, à la bande bretessée d'or). Azure, a bend wavy or*, is the coat of ALDAM; *Gules, a bend flory counter-flory or*, is borne by GOLDINGTON; and in another coat for the same name the tinctures are changed to *or* and *azure*. *Sable, a bend raguly*, is the coat of MASTON; *Vert, a bend dancetty*

fess wavy between two gemels sable. With regard to "tiercing," as in the case of the Pale so is it with the Fess. A shield divided per fess and also charged with a fess, is commonly blazoned *Tiercé,* or *Tierced per fess;* a third part of the field being occupied by each tincture. Of this simple bearing, particularly in Germany, examples are very numerous, and many are given in the section on " Parted Coats " (*See* pp. 86, 87).

IV. THE BEND (*Bande*) is a piece crossing the shield diagonally from the dexter chief to the sinister base. For it, as for the preceding Ordinaries, the old heralds claimed the third part of the shield ; but, even if charged, it seldom covers more than the fourth part of the field in modern usage.

In Plate XII., fig. 1, *Azure, a bend or,* is the simple coat which formed the subject of the memorable controversy between the families of SCROPE and GROSVENOR (*See* Chapter XIV.), and which was adjudged to the former. It is also borne by the Counts THUN DE HOHENSTEIN (Bohemia) ; CASSAGNET, Marquis de FIMARCON ; the Marquis de LENTILHAC (*Salle des Croisés,* 1248), the families of HUMIÈRES ; HÉRIPONT (Belgium) ; DURFORT ; BIRON ; DE MOLAY ; ZOTRA, etc. Its reverse, *d'Or, à la bande d'azur* was borne by GUILLAUME DE TRIE in 1147 (Second Crusade), and by the English family of TRYE, of Leckhampton in Gloucestershire ; as also by LA BAUME, Counts de ST. AMOUR ; and the Venetian family of MOROSINI.

Or, a bend gules, are the arms of the Grand-duchy of BADEN ; of the Principality of LIGNE ; of DE SALINS (First Crusade) ; of CLÉMENT (Maréchal de France in 1248), etc. Its reverse : *Gules, a bend or,* is the coat of CHALON (1096, in First Crusade, quartered by the Princes of ORANGE); HENNIN, Comte de BOSSU ; of NOAILLES (Ducs de NOAILLES, Ducs de MOUCHY, Princes de FOIX, etc.) ; of DE SALINS ; TONNERRE ; LA RODE ; etc.

the reverse by MUSCHAMP; GROUCHES, Marquises of CHEPY and GRIBAUVAL; the Barons HEINBURG; LÖBENSTEIN (*dit* VÖLKEL), etc.; CORDOVA of Spain; and the BONACOLSI of Italy (who also use *Or, three bars gules*). *Gules, three bars vair* was the coat of GHERARDINI of Venice, and MERCŒUR of France. The DE COMBAUT, Ducs de COISLIN, in France, used *Gules, three bars chequy argent and azure.*

Or, three bars wavy gules (Plate XI., fig. 10) are the arms of DRUMMOND in Scotland, and BASSET in England.

Argent, three bars wavy azure are borne by PARDAILLAN (1270, last Crusade); GALEOTTI (Naples); FERRERA; TOLEDO (Spain); PODENAS, Princes de CANTALUPO; SIX; and VAN LUCHTENBURG, or LUYTENBURG, of Holland.

Argent, four bars azure, were the arms of Sir JOHN HORBURY (temp. EDW. I.), and are borne by MAILLART (Liège); and MOLEMBAIS (France); and *wavy* by VAN SABBINGEN (Zealand); and FIEFVET (Artois). *Ermine, four bars gules*, was the coat of Sir JOHN SULBY, or SULLY, K.G., ob. 1338.

Barrulets are often borne in pairs, and are then called BARS-GEMELS (French *jumelles*) as in the coat of HUNTERCOMBE (Plate XI., fig. 11), *Ermine, two bars-gemels gules* (sometimes *sable*). *Gules, two bars-gemels or*, are the coat of RICHMOND; and the reverse that of FITZ-ALURED.

As in the case of the bend, hereafter referred to, the fess is "coticed," thus, in Plate XI., fig. 12, HARLESTON of Essex bears: *Argent, a fess ermine coticed sable.* BADLESMERE in England, summoned to Parliament as Baron, 3rd. EDW. II.; and MONESTAY in France bear: *Argent, a fess between two bars-gemels gules*. By ELIOT, Earl of ST. GERMAN'S the same coat is borne, except that the gemels are *wavy azure*. FINCHFIELD, again, bears the fess wavy and the gemels straight:—*Argent, a*

Princes of OLDENBURG; MAUVOISIN and ROSNY in France; VALLGORNERA in Spain; WALLONCAPELLE, or WAELSCAPPEL, VAN SCHOONVELT, and WESTCAPPEL in the Low Countries.

Sable, two bars argent, was the coat of Admiral de RUYTER, and *engrailed* of ROUSE of Norfolk.

Vert, two bars dancetty argent, are the arms of the Barons SPIEGEL.

Or, two bars counter-embattled sable, is borne by VAN BRONKHORST, in the Netherlands.

Argent, two bars dancetty sable, by the Counts REEDE (Guelders), and the REEDE-GINKELS, Earls of ATHLONE.

As a pendant to the CARMICHAEL coat, referred to above, we may give the arms of WAYE of Devon; *Sable, two bars wreathed argent and gules.*

A curious example is the coat of MONTCONIS in Burgundy: *Gules, two bars, that in chief wavy or, the one in base plain argent.* (In later times the field is azure.)

Plate XI., fig. 9, *Argent, two bars battled counter-embattled gules (d'Argent, à deux fasces bretessées et contre bretessées de gueules)*, are the arms of ARKEL.

Of coats with three bars there are a greater number still.

Argent three bars gules, are the arms of CAMERON; of MULTON; of the Counts BOULAINVILLIERS; of the great family of CROY (Comtes de CHIMAY, Marquises d'ARSCHOT, Princes de CHIMAY and de CROY of the Holy Roman Empire, Grandees of Spain); of FROISSART; VAN BEERVELT; CHÂTEAU MELIAND (Bannerets of Touraine); of LEITOENS of Portugal; etc., etc.

Argent, three bars sable (d'Argent, à trois fasces de sable) is the coat of AFFLECK or AUCHENLECK; HOUGHTON; ST. AMAND in France, etc.

Gules, three bars or, is carried by BEAUMONT; MASCARENHAS (Portugal); LÖVENICH (Westphalia); and

French, *divise*) with further diminutions known as the "closet," and the "barrulet." In English Armory the bar is never borne singly (the "*bar sinister*" is an ignorant vulgarism, and an entire misnomer for something totally different, as will be shown hereafter). In France under the title of *Fasce en divise*, abbreviated into *divise*, the bar is occasionally seen (two coats in which it appears in chief have been already blazoned on p. 120). M. GUIZOT, the eminent French statesman, bore : *d'Azur, à la divise d'argent*. The Prince of Poets, DANTE ALIGHIERI bore : *Per pale or and sable, over all a fess diminished, or bar, argent* (*Parti d'or et de sable à la divise d'argent brochante sur le tout*).

Plate XI., fig. 8, *Gules, two bars or* (*de Gueules, à deux fasces d'or*) is the coat of the ancient family of HARCOURT, both in England and in France; in the latter country they attained the ducal title in 1700.

Ermine, two bars gules, are the arms of the Irish family of NUGENT, Marquises of WESTMEATH. A branch of this family has reached the highest dignities of the Austrian Empire with the title of Prince.

Argent, two bars gules, is the coat of the Barons DERVAL (Brittany); LORENZ; and MASSOW in Saxony; NEIMANS in Bavaria; VON BRAUNBERG; the Counts von ROTENBURG; the Lordships of ISENBURG (quartered by the Princes von WIED); and of BREUBURG (quartered by the Counts of LÖWENSTEIN and ERBACH); and of many other noble families.

Argent, two bars sable, are the arms of the house of ISENBURG, Princes and Counts of the Holy Roman Empire; LE BARBIER, Marquises de KERJAN in Brittany.

Gules, two bars. argent, are the arms of MARTIN; SERVATI of Genoa; the Counts ARNIM of Prussia; the Barons von ERTHAL in Franconia, and OCHSENSTEIN in Rhenish Prussia. *Or, two bars gules*, is ·the coat of the Counts of BERLO (Prussia), and FÜRSTENBURG; the

quartered by EGMONT, p. 99, and the Glossary of English Terms.)

Plate XI., fig. 5, is the well-known coat of STEWART, or STUART, in Scotland : *Or, a fess chequy azure and argent.* (It may here be remarked parenthetically that three is the proper number of rows of "panes" on a fess, bend, chief, or other Ordinary blazoned as "chequy.") Mr ELLIS combats the popular idea that this coat was allusive to the office of Steward, and represented the chequers formerly used in keeping accounts. The cognate family of BOTELER descended from CHRISTIAN, grand-daughter and heir of WALTER FITZALAN, elder brother of the first Steward of Scotland, certainly bore the same fess chequy between six crosslets. CHRISTIAN'S father and grandfather, however, seem to have borne a different coat; and in any case there is no evidence of a descent which has been suggested from the early bearers of a chequy field—the WARRENS, and the House of VERMANDOIS, who bore *Chequy or and azure. Or, a fess chequy argent and gules* is the coat of the Westphalian Counts de la MARCK, now borne in the *Écu Complet* of the Kingdom of PRUSSIA.

A curious variety of the fess is shown in the coat of CARMICHAEL : *Argent, a fess wreathed (câblée, or tortillée) azure and gules* (Plate XI., fig. 6). *Sable, a fess wreathed or and azure, between three crescents argent,* is a coat of WILKIE. In Italian coats the fess seems often *voutée,* or curved upwards; and less frequently downwards (*affaissée*). Plate XI., fig. 7, are the arms of the Venetian family of BALBI-PORTO : *Gules, a fess arched, per pale or and azure* (*de Gueules, à la fasce voutée d'or et d'azur*); but in most cases this arises simply from the fashion of painting the arms on the convex surface of a shield, or cartouche. The convexity of the surface gives the fess an arched appearance.

The diminutive of the Fess is called a "bar" (in

PLATE XI.

1. Fess.
(*Beauchamp.*)

2. Fess dancettée.
(*West.*)

3. Fess dancettée.
(*Plowden.*)

4. Fess embattled.
(*Aberbury.*)

5. Fess checquy.
(*Stewart.*)

6. Fess tortillé.
(*Carmichael.*)

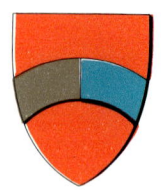

7. Fess arched.
(*Balbi-Porto.*)

8. Bars.
(*Harcourt.*)

9. Bars counter-embattled.
(*Arkel.*)

10. Bars wavy.
(*Drummond.*)

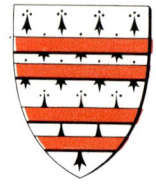

11. Bars gemelles.
(*Huntercombe.*)

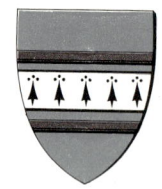

12. Fess cotised.
(*Harleston.*)

ST. MAUR, Ducs de MONTAUSIER, Pairs de France, 1664; the Ducs de SAN SEVERINO, and the Counts de MARSI of Naples; VAN DE WERF, and the Barons TAETS D'AMERONGEN in the Netherlands. A D'AUBIGNY bore it in the Crusade of 1205.

Gules, a fess engrailed argent, is used by the Counts von NESSELRODE; and was the original coat in England of the family of DAUBIGNY or DAUBENEY, who afterwards (as in other instances) enlarged the engrailment into a fess of fusils conjoined. *Gules, a fess ermine*, are the arms of CRAWFURD.

Argent, a fess dancetté sable, belongs to the WESTS, Earls of DELAWARR (Plate XI., fig. 2). The fess *dancetté* has three points only. A somewhat unusual form of it is borne by the PLOWDENS of Shropshire (the family to which EDMUND PLOWDEN, the distinguished lawyer of the 16th century belonged); it is given on Plate XI., fig 3, and is *Azure, a fess dancetté, the two upper points flory* (terminating in fleurs-de-lis) *or*. The like coat, but with the field sable, is borne by DORAND, Yorkshire. Somewhat analogous to this are the coats of CAVILL, *Argent, a fess flory counter-flory gules;* and *Argent, a fess sable flory counter-flory gules*, DUSSEAUX.

Of other variations the following are examples:—
Azure, a fess indented ermine (d'Azur, à la fasce endenté d'hermine); the same but *nebulée* is borne for ALLEN. *Gules, a fess wavy argent* is the coat of DRYLAND.

When a fess is blazoned as "embattled" (*crénelé*), only the upper line is cut into battlements (Plate XI., fig. 4). ABERBURY or ADDERBURY bears: *Or, a fess embattled sable*. If both lines are embattled with the battlements opposite each other, the fess is known as *bretessé;* if the battlements on the one side correspond to the indentations of the other, it is styled "embattled counter-embattled." (*See* hereafter, page 127; the arms of ARKEL

ROGIER ; *Argent, three pallets wavy gules* by VALOINES (DE VALONIIS), a coat quartered in Scotland by the MAULES, Earls of DALHOUSIE, etc. *Gules, five pallets raguly argent* is a coat of SOMERVILL.

A narrower diminutive of the pale is the *endorse* (in French *vergette*). A pale placed between two of them is said to be *endorsed*. The family of BELASYSE, Earls of FAUCONBERG, bore: *Argent, a pale engrailed, endorsed sable* (Plate X., fig. 11).

In accordance with its supposed derivation from a piece of palisading, the pale (with its diminutives) is sometimes found pointed (*aiguisé*, or *fitché*) at its lower end; if it is cut short it is said to be *coupé*, or *hummetty*. *Or, three pallets couped and pointed gules* is the coat of the Counts de BRIEY (Plate X., fig. 12). Occasionally the pales or pallets are cut short before reaching half-way down the shield; they are then said to be *pals retraits* (*v. ante.* p. 121). The arms of VAN HAMBROEK are: *Or, three pallets sable, retraits en chef.* VAN EYCK bears the same coat, but with the field *argent*.

III. THE FESS (in French *fasce*) is a horizontal bar stretching across the centre of the shield; like the pale it theoretically (only) contains the third part thereof. A multitude of coats have this as their sole charge. *Gules, a fess argent*, are the well known arms of the House of AUSTRIA; the Ducs de BOUILLON; the Counts of VIANDEN, etc. Plate XI., fig. 1, *Gules, a fess or* is the old coat of BEAUCHAMP. *Argent, a fess azure* (*d'Argent, à la fasce de sable*) are the arms of the Canton of ZUG, in Switzerland; BAROZZI, in Venice; the Dukes of LEUCHTENBERG in Russia; of CHARTERS in Scotland; and, with the fess wavy, of BELLAFILLA of Spain.

Argent, a fess gules is the coat of several illustrious houses, those of BÉTHUNE, Ducs de SULLY, 1606; the Counts von MANTEUFFEL in Prussia and Russia; the

DAGUET DE BEAUVOIR; and is the same as *Tiercé en pal de sable, d'azur, et de vair*. *Tierced in pale gules, argent, and azure* is the coat of RAINIER: and, with the colours inverted, of VON PONDORFFER.

The English blazon only allows one pale in the shield; though of its diminutive the pallet several may be borne. French blazon has no distinctive name for this diminutive.

The coat borne by ELEANOR of PROVENCE, Queen of HENRY III. of England, given on Plate X., fig. 9, *Or, four pallets gules (d'Or, à quatre pals de gueules)*, are the arms of PROVENCE, and of the Counts of BARCELONA, and Kings of ARRAGON. At the time of their assumption the *barras longas* made a fitting coat; canting or allusive to the name of BARCELONA. *Argent, on a chief or three pallets gules*, are the arms of the KEITHS, Earls MARISCHAL of Scotland. (Plate X., fig. 10.) A family of the name settled in Prussia, bore the same but with the field *vert*. *Argent, two pallets sable (d'Argent, à deux pals de sable);* are the coat of the Counts von WITTGENSTEIN, and of the English family of HARLEY. *Sable, two pallets wavy ermine*, are the arms of CLARKE of Kent.

A coat charged with three pallets is a frequent bearing both at home and abroad. *Or, three pallets gules*, are the well known arms of the Counts of FOIX (later they quartered therewith those of the County of BÉARN; *Or, two cows in pale gules, collared, horned, and belled azure*). *Gules, three pallets or*, were borne by the FAUCIGNY, Princes de LUCINGE. *Argent* (also *gules*), *three pallets ermine*, is a coat of QUESADA in Spain; *Vair, three pallets gules*, was borne by AMUNDEVILLE in England; and by the family of YVE in Flanders, Counts de RUYSBROEK, and Barons d'OSTICHE, etc. *Argent, three pallets vert*, is the coat of ZAVALA in Spain. *Or, three pallets wavy azure* is borne by

Azure, a pale argent (*d'Azur, au pal d'argent*) is the coat of the family of LEYEN, Counts and Princes of the Holy Roman Empire; and of the Florentine ABBATI. The following families (among others), bear: *Gules, a pale argent* (*de Gueules, au pal d'argent*); the Venetian VIARO; CANALI; CANABRI; the Counts HAAG; Barons FRAUNBERG; and FRAUNHOFEN; the family of BÜLOW in Denmark; and the Barons MITTROWSKI in Austrian Silesia.

The Ducs des CARS, Princes de CARENCY; and the Italian PITTI, both bear, *Gules, a pale vair*.

Gules, a pale or, were the arms of the family of GRANT-MESNIL, Lord High Steward of England temp. HENRY I. *Or, a pale azure*, is borne by SCHÖNSTEIN of Bavaria; *Or, a pale gules*, by BIEDMA of Spain; *Sable, a pale or*, by VON DER ALM.

The Pale has the usual variations; being also formed with the external lines indented, engrailed, etc. *Argent* (sometimes *Or*), *a pale dancetty* (sometimes *indented*) *gules*, is the coat of STRANSHAM, or STRAYNSHAM, of Kent. *Argent, a pale wavy sable*, is borne by BOTON. *Azure, a pale rayonné or*, by LIGHTFORD. This last bearing (which is very rarely seen) is also used by the Irish O'HARAS, Lords TYRAWLEY; *Vert, on a pale radiant or, a lion rampant sable* (Plate X., fig. 8). The "*chef-pal*" has already been noticed on p. 120, *ante*. Occasionally the pale, or rather a portion of it, is combined with another Ordinary. KETHEL in Holland uses, *Azure, a pale retrait in chief* (*i.e.*, a *demi-pal*) *soutenu by a chevron between three cauldrons or*. (*See* also p. 123, *infra*.)

If there be given to the Pale its stated size of one-third of the field the following coats may be blazoned either "Per pale . . . and . . . a pale . . . ;" or (which avoids any mistake) "Tierced in pale" (*vide* pp. 86-87 for "TIERCED COATS").

Per pale sable and azure, a pale vair; is borne by

a barrulet *haussé*, or elevated, above its ordinary position. The arms of DE POISIEU in Dauphiné are: *Gules, two chevrons argent, in chief a divise of the last (de Gueules, à deux chevrons d'argent, sommés d'une divise du même)*. Sometimes the *divise* is placed immediately beneath a chief, which is then said to be "supported" (*soutenu*) thereby, as in the case of the arms of the ORSINI family in Rome, who bore: *Bendy of six argent and gules, on a chief of the first supported by a divise or, a rose of the second (Bandé d'argent et de gueules, de six pieces, au chef d'argent chargé d'une rose de gueules et soutenu d'une divise d'or)*. Of this family were the French DES URSINS, Marquises of TRAINEL, etc. The Roman family charge the divise with an *eel (une anguille naiante or ondoyante) azure* for ANGUILLARA. (Plate X., fig. 6.)

A Chief is sometimes used united to another Ordinary; Thus, FAHRBECK in Bavaria bears: *Argent, a chief-pale sable;* that is, the charge is a chief and pale united. ESQUIROU DE PARIEU, in France, bore: *Sable, a pairle and chief argent*. Occasionally the chief is formed by a concave line, and is then called a *chef vouté*; as in the coat of DIENHEIM in Bavaria: *Gules, a lion rampant argent crowned or, a chief vouté of the second*. (Plate X., fig. 5.)

II. THE PALE (French *pal*) is a vertical band in the middle of the shield; its capacity was fixed by old writers at one-third of the field, but it is usually somewhat smaller, even when charged.

Argent, a pale sable (d'Argent, au pal de sable), are the well known arms of the ERSKINES, Earls of MAR (Plate X., fig. 7). The same coat is borne by the Counts KREYTSEN in Prussia; the Barons SKRBENSKY DE HRZISTIC (Silesia); the Danish family of ANDERSEN; RICHTERSWYL (*Zürich Wappenrolle*, No. 259); SPANOFFSKY DE LISSAU; VON KETTENHEIM; etc., etc. The Swedish family of BRAHE bears the reverse.

The Ordinary of the Chief has been very generally used as an "Augmentation," or addition granted by a Sovereign as a reward for services (*See* Chapter XVI.); and it was also customary for Cardinals, and other members of Ecclesiastical Regular Orders ; as well as the members of certain Military and Religious Orders, *e.g.*, ST. JOHN OF JERUSALEM, ST. STEFANO in Tuscany, etc., to place the arms of the Order to which they belonged, on a chief above their personal arms, which might also possibly themselves contain a chief among charges.

In Plate X., fig. 4, are the arms of the Chevalier d'ESTAMPES, Bailli de VALENCE in the ORDER OF ST. JOHN, who bears his paternal coat: *Azure, two girons chevronways or ; on a chief argent, three ducal coronets gules ;* the whole *abaissé* under a chief of the arms of the ORDER OF ST. JOHN, *Gules, a cross argent.*

There are a few instances in Continental Heraldry in which for other reasons two chiefs are borne in the same coat, one *abaissé* beneath the other.

The "chiefs" assumed respectively by the partisans of the Guelphic and Ghibbeline factions in Italy were sometimes carried in coats which already had a chief. Thus the BONVICINI of Bologna used: *Gules, a tree eradicated argent, on a chief cousu azure three letters* **B** *of the second ;* the chief *abaissé* beneath the Guelphic chief: *Or, an eagle displayed sable crowned or.* The Marquises RANGONI bear : *Barry argent and azure, on a chief gules and escallop argent ;* the chief *abaissé* under another *argent, thereon an eagle displayed gules crowned or.* The Barons von HAEFTEN bear : *Gules, three pallets vair, a chief or, charged with a label sable, and abaissé under another chief or, thereon a crane sable.*

Some writers assign to the chief a diminutive called a "fillet." Of this charge there are few, if any, certain examples in English Armory. The charge in French Armory is called a *divise*, and should rather be regarded as

PLATE X.

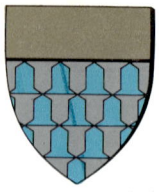

1. Chief. (*Tichborne.*)
2. Chief indented. (*Estcourt.*) 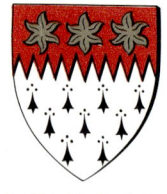
3. Napoleonic Ducal Chief. (*Soult.*) 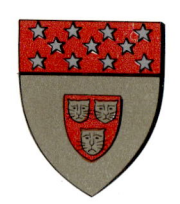
4. Knight of St. John. (*Estampes.*) 
5. Chief arched. (*Von Dienheim.*) 
6. Divise. (*Orsini or Ursins.*) 
7. Pale. (*Erskine.*) 
8. Pale rayonné. (*O'Hara.*) 
9. Pallets. (*Arragon.*) 
10. Pallets. (*Keith.*) 
11. Pale cotised. (*Belasyse.*) 
12. Pallets humetty and fitché. (*Briey.*)

of the shield. This may be the case when the chief is itself charged ; but, practically, the rule has never been strictly observed either with regard to this or the theoretical allotments of space in the case of other Ordinaries. It is much more frequently depicted as including about a fourth part of the shield.

The following examples of early coats bearing chiefs as the sole charge are from the *Salle des Croisés* at Versailles.

(2) EUSTACHE D'AGRAIN, Prince of SIDON and CÆSAREA (1100) *Azure, a chief or (d'Azur, au chef d'or).*

(10) GARNIER, Comte de GRAY (1100) and (77), BAUDOIN DE GAND, Seigneur d'ALOST (1096) *Sable, a chief argent (de Sable, au chef d'argent.*

(95) RAYMOND II., Comte de SUBSTANTION et de MELGUEIL (1109) *Argent, a chief sable (d'Argent, au chef de sable).*

(157) GUILLAUME D'AUNOY (1204) *Or, a chief gules (d'Or, au chef de gueules).*

Argent, a chief gules, is the coat of the Duchy of MONTFERRAT, and of the families of D'AVAUGOUR ; SOLIGNAC ; CHAUMONT (Burgundy) ; MENZIES in Scotland ; and WORSLEY in England. *Argent, a chief azure* was borne by the Marquises of GAMACHES in France ; and SALUCES (Piedmont), as well as by the families of FITZALAN ; CLUN ; VAN DE WEERDE, etc.

In Plate X., fig. 1, *Vair, a chief or (de Vair, au chef d'or)* is the coat of the TICHBORNE family ; while fig. 2 is an example of a chief formed by a different partition line and charged. *Ermine, on a chief indented gules three estoiles or (d'hermine, au chef endenté de gueules, chargé de trois étoiles d'or);* the arms of the family of ESTCOURT. *Argent, a chief indented* (or *dancetty*), *sable* was borne by JEAN DE ST. SIMON in the Third Crusade, and by the families of HARSICK and LE POER. *Or, a chief indented azure,* is the well known coat of the great Irish family of BUTLER.

FUSIL, MASCLE, and RUSTRE); the FLAUNCH and FLASQUE; the BILLET; and the LABEL.

Various explanations are given of the origin of the Ordinaries, by heraldic writers. LOWER is inclined to derive them from the stripes, and bands or belts, of military costume. PLANCHÉ, with greater probability, traces them to the various bands of wood, or metal, by which the shield was strengthened. This derivation would seem to me almost certain did we not remember that, as a matter of fact, these Ordinaries do not figure to any very great extent in early Heraldry; certainly they are not so frequently found as we should expect to be the case if they had taken their rise from the bands and borders which appeared on so many of the early shields before the rise of systematic heraldry. We should expect, then, that a multitude, perhaps the majority, of the earliest coats would bear a fess, or bordure, a cross, or bars, or pales. Yet an examination of a list of early arms, for example those given in the earliest *Rolls of Arms*, or exposed in the *Salle des Croisades* at Versailles, will show how far this is from being the case. The Ordinaries are there, indeed; but there is no preponderance of them over other charges, animate or inanimate. The preponderance is all in the other direction.

Some have sought the origin of the Ordinaries in the strips of wood of which the barriers, or lists, for tournaments were composed. The Cross is really the only Ordinary of whose origin we can be quite certain.

I propose now to take these Ordinaries singly; premising that each of them may be formed not only by the right line but by any of the varying lines which have been described and figured under PARTITIONS.

All the Ordinaries are frequently charged; and two or more may be combined in a coat of arms.

I. THE CHIEF (CHEF) is a charge formed by a horizontal line, which includes in theory the upper third part

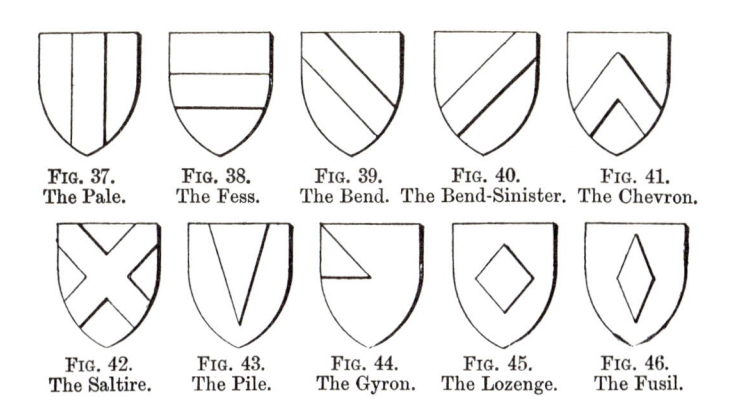

FIG. 37. The Pale.   FIG. 38. The Fess.   FIG. 39. The Bend.   FIG. 40. The Bend-Sinister.   FIG. 41. The Chevron.

FIG. 42. The Saltire.   FIG. 43. The Pile.   FIG. 44. The Gyron.   FIG. 45. The Lozenge.   FIG. 46. The Fusil.

CHAPTER IV.

ORDINARIES.

ARMORIAL writers, as has been already said, divide the conventional figures of Heraldry into two classes, HONOURABLE ORDINARIES; and SUBORDINATE ORDINARIES, or SUB-ORDINARIES, though they are not at all agreed as to whether some of them should be placed in the first, or in the second class; their arrangement in the one or the other is a matter of no practical consequence. The Chief, and the Quarter, or Canton, may seem to be respectively entitled to some precedence over others of their class, as being those which have been most frequently used for the reception of Honourable Augmentations to the shield; but beyond this there is really no order of precedency, and their arrangement and classification is simply a matter of taste and convenience.

The Honourable Ordinaries are: I. The CHIEF; II. The PALE; III. The FESS; IV. The BEND (and BEND-SINISTER); V. The CHEVRON; VI. The CROSS; VII. The SALTIRE; VIII. The PILE; and IX. The PALL or PAIRLE; some of these are figured above. Several of these have diminutives of the same shape.

The Sub-Ordinaries are the QUARTER (now generally of a smaller size and called a CANTON); the GYRON; the INESCUCHEON; the BORDURE; the ORLE; the TRESSURE; the FRET; the LOZENGE (with its variations the

An example of early English diaper is to be found on the shield of the sepulchral effigy in the Temple Church, which was for so long a time erroneously attributed to GEOFFREY DE MAGNAVILLE, Earl of ESSEX ; and to which allusion has already been made at p. 45.

In a few foreign coats diaper was so constantly and uniformly used that in process of time it has become a regular charge, and appears as an integral part of the blazon.

is said to be *goutté*, or gutty; in French blazon *goutté d'argent, d'azur*, etc.; but the usual pedantry of English heralds has invented a specific name for the drops of each metal or tincture, except gold, which remains *goutté d'or*. Accordingly *semé of drops argent* has become *goutté d'eau*; of *gules, goutté de sang*; of *azure, goutté de larmes*; of *sable, goutté de poix*; and of *vert, goutté de l'huile*! *Sable, goutté d'eau, on a fess argent three Cornish choughs proper* (Plate VIII., fig. 12) was the canting coat of the Marquesses of CORNWALLIS. The choughs are legitimate enough as charges of *armes parlantes*, but the tears, or wails, are surely far-fetched!

DIAPERING is a mode of ornamenting the surface of the field and its "Ordinaries" with arabesque patterns, and was early practised. Many beautiful and tasteful examples of it remain on early glass, sculptures, and enamels. There are some fine instances of it in Westminster Abbey, among the most remarkable of which is the enamelled shield of WILLIAM DE VALENCE, Earl of PEMBROKE (which, reduced in size, forms the frontispiece to BOUTELL'S *Heraldry, Historical and Popular*); and the monument of EDMUND "Crouchback," Earl of LANCASTER. Early specimens of diaper are also to be seen at Beverley Minster and at Hatfield. Diaper was largely used in the armorial glass of Germany in the fourteenth and later centuries. Often the patterns, which are usually indicated by lighter or darker shades of the tincture employed, are exceedingly tasteful and artistic.

In the tasteless times of the 18th century, German Heraldic engravings suffered much from a profusion of diaper, which obscured the actual bearings. The coats added in the later editions of SIEBMACHER'S great *Wappenbuch* will show the decadence of true artistic feeling in this respect, as well as in the general treatment of the escucheons and of the charges delineated.

In Foreign Armory charges not so employed in British Heraldry are frequently met with as powderings.

The Spanish family of CLAVER bears the canting coat, *Or, semé of keys azure.* The Florentine FORABOSCHI use, *Sable, semé of balls argent.* The French GODEFROI bear, *Azure, semé of acorns or;* and GUILLOU DE LA LARDAIS, *Argent, semé of sage leaves vert.* *Or, treflé vert,* is the coat of HOETIMA. Sometimes the field is *semé* with more than one charge. Thus the arms of the French Marquises de SIMIANE (Plate VIII., fig. 10) are *Or, semé alternately of castles and fleurs-de-lis azure;* and those of ANGLURE, Counts de BOURLEMONT and ESTOGES, Princes d'AMBLISE, Ducs d'ABRY, etc.: are, *Or, semé of hawk's bells, each supported by a crescent gules (d'Or, semé de grelots d'argent, soutenus chacun d'un croissant de gueules).* These crescents were originally "*angles.*" [*See* an account of these arms in the paper on "Les Saladins d'Anglure," which is appended to the valuable *Armorial* of GILLES LE BOUVIER, dit "BERRY," Roi d'Armes de France de CHARLES VII., published by M. VALLET (DE VIRIVILLE), Paris, 1866.] Usually a field *semé* of small charges also bears a more important one. *Or, semé of hearts gules, over all three lions passant gardant in pale azure, crowned of the field,* are the arms of DENMARK (Plate VIII., fig. 9). The coat of the Duchy of LÜNEBURG, which forms the second quartering in the arms of our Hanoverian Sovereigns, has a similar *semé* field, but it is charged with *a lion rampant azure, crowned gold.* Plate VIII., fig. 11, is the coat of the House of NASSAU, Princes of ORANGE, which appeared *en surtout* on the Royal Escucheon during the reigns of WILLIAM III. and MARY II.; it is, *Azure, billetty and a lion rampant or.* A field *semé*, or bestrewed with an indefinite number of drops, or "*gouttes,*"

complicated coats of Grand Quarterings, letters of the alphabet are often employed instead of, or in addition to, the numerals he recommends.

SEMÉ.

When the field is strewed with an indefinite number of small charges (fleurs-de-lis, crosslets, hearts, and cinquefoils being the most commonly used for this purpose) it is said to be *semé*, or powdered, with the charge. Small charges, as will be shown elsewhere, were thus used in early times as a mode of "gerating," or "differencing," the arms of persons of the same family.

A field thus *semé* appears as if it were cut out of a larger surface, as the external rows of the charges are divided by the outline of the escucheon.

In some ancient coats there is no other charge in the escucheon but those with which the field is *semé*. Azure, *semé of fleurs-de-lis or* is the early form of the Royal Arms of FRANCE; and is blazoned as "FRANCE-ANCIENT." The term *Fleury*, or *flory*, is often used instead of *Semé of fleurs-de-lis*. Thus, Azure, *fleury argent*, is the coat of HARLEWIN; of MALAPERT DE NEUFVILLE; of HERVILLY DE MALAPERT; MONTAUBAN, etc. *Argent, fleury gules*, was borne by MONTJOY in England; the Barons de HAUTPENNE; and the Low Country families of OUPEY, and KERCKEM, Barons de WIJER. *Or, fleury azure*, was used in England by MORTIMER. *Gules, fleury or*, are the arms of CHÂTEAUBRIAND; and are the original coat of ALÈGRE, Marquis de TOURZEL.

Billetty and *crusily* are, similarly, terms used for *semé* of billets or cross-crosslets. *Or, billetty azure*, is found for the coat of GASCELIN; and *Gules billetty or*, for that of COWDREY, in early *Rolls of Arms;* so also, *Or, crusily azure*, is borne by PETMORE; and *Gules, crusily or*, by FERNLAND.

in Mr NICHOLS'S practice always follows the tincture of the field, and this is also the case in the blazons of this book.]

Exception.—A comma (not otherwise required) may be occasionally requisite after the metal "or," if there is any danger of its being mistaken for the conjunction.

4. The metals and tinctures may be either printed at length ; or abbreviated, as arg., az., sa., etc., being equally clear either way if not encumbered with commas.

5. Print always "three *wolf's* heads, three *lion's* jambs, three *palmer's* staves," etc., not "three *wolves'* heads, three *lions'* jambs, and three *palmers'* staves ; " the charges being each the head of one wolf, the jamb of one lion, the staff of one palmer, etc. ; and it is grammatically sufficient that the nominative cases "heads," etc., should agree with the numeral three.

6. For 3, 2, 1 ; 2 and 1 ; etc., use the words three, two, one, as the figures may produce confusion with the numbering of quarterings.

7. Where there are complicated quarterings, clearness may sometimes be produced where two coats only are quartered by the expression Quarterly; as, "Quarterly of FRANCE and ENGLAND," "of HASTINGS and VALENCE," etc., or, "Quarterly of 1 and 4 *Azure, a bend or*, SCROPE;" and 2 and 3, *Or, a chevron gules*, STAFFORD. Otherwise the term "Grand Quarterings" is sometimes employed, and then numerals of different characters may be used to distinguish the grand and the subordinate quarterings, as thus :—

Quarterly of four Grand Quarters :—

    I. *Quarterly :* 1 and 4, *Or, a pale gules.*
                2 and 3, *Azure, a cross argent.*
    II. *Ermine, a pale vert.*
    III. *Per pale :* (a) *Gules a chief ermine.*
               (b) *Vert, a lion rampant or.*
    IV. *Azure, three bars argent.*

To this rule of Mr NICHOLS we may add that, in very

ANDER coats given above, the French say, *l'un à l'autre*, or *de l'un en l'autre*. In very many of the French coats which I have used as examples in the pages following I have thought it might be useful to the student who wishes to extend his studies beyond the Heraldry of his own country, to find here the French blazon of the coat cited; by attention to these, and with the aid of a Glossary of French terms of blazon hereafter to be given in these pages, I think the student will have no difficulty in acquiring such a knowledge of French blazon as will enable him to use with facility the many valuable Armorials and Heraldic treatises which exist in the French language.

There used to be much looseness, variety, and unskilfulness in the printing and punctuation of English armorial blazon. Some writers loaded it with unnecessary commas and semicolons, some left out points altogether, and there was often an embarrassing mixture of Roman and Italic characters, and no rule was observed as to where figures and where letters should be used. In 1863 the late Mr J. GOUGH NICHOLS in Vol. I. of the *Herald and Genealogist* laid down, after much consideration of the subject, the following rules, whose excellence is so patent that they have since come into very general use. They are here reproduced almost in his words:—

1. Begin the blazon of every coat or quartering with a capital letter.

2. Use no other capitals except on the occasional occurrence of a proper name (we mean such as a Katharine wheel, a Moor's head or Turkey cock, though some of these may be reduced at will, to moors or turkeys, etc., as the French and Germans do with all adjectival proper names).

3. Introduce no more points than are absolutely necessary, and seldom any stronger than a comma, unless in very long and complicated coats. [A comma

The arms of NEILSON are: *Argent, three sinister hands bend-sinisterways couped at the wrist gules.* Here each hand is placed diagonally in the direction of a bend-sinister; while, agreeably to the rule as understood, they are ranged 2 and 1, in the shield.

The expression "counter-changed," of frequent use in blazon, requires explanation. When the field is of a metal and colour separated by any partition line, the charge or charges are said to be counter-changed when the charge or portion of a charge which lies on the metal is of the colour, and *vice versa*. Thus in Plate IX., fig. 11, for ALEXANDER, Earl of STIRLING, *Per pale argent and sable, a chevron, and in base a crescent, all counter-changed.* Here on the *argent* the charges are *sable*; on the *sable* they are *argent*.

Again in Plate IX., fig. 12, CHETWODE bears: *Quarterly argent and gules four crosses patée counter-changed.*

The French blazon of these coats is, of ALEXANDER, *Parti d'argent et de sable, au chevron accompagné en pointe d'un croissant, le tout de l'un en l'autre;* and of CHETWODE, *Ecartelé d'argent et de gueules, à quatre croisettes pattées de l'un à l'autre.*

It will be seen by the examples just given that French blazon differs in some prominent respects from our own. The preposition *de* is prefixed to the tincture, or tinctures of the field, while the preposition *à* as invariably precedes the charges. Where we should say that an Ordinary is "between" such and such charges, the French say that it is accompanied by them; "*accompagné de*," etc. (But see the Glossary of French terms for the distinction between *accompagné* and *accosté*.) *Brochant sur le tout* is the French equivalent for our "over all." *Posé en pal* or *en sautoir*, etc., stand for "paleways" or "saltireways;" *rangés en pal, rangés en sautoir*, etc., are the equivalents for our "in pale," "in saltire," etc.

For counter-changed, as in the CHETWODE and ALEX-

PLATE IX.

1. Jerusalem.

2. De Vere.

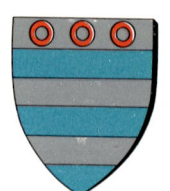

3. De Grey.

4. Wilmot.

5. Haig.

6. Abernethy.

7. Fairfax.

8. Russell.

9. Babington.

10. Northcote.

11. Alexander.

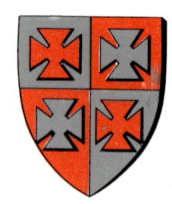

12. Chetwode.

it is understood, that, unless otherwise specified, the two charges are placed in pale; *i.e.* one above the other;—thus DE MONTESQUIOU bears : *Or, two torteaux.* Here we should understand, what the French blazon expresses, "*d'Or, à deux torteaux de gueules, l'un sur l'autre en pal.*"

Or again, in the case of three repetitions of the same charge, either with or without an Ordinary interposed, it is understood that, unless otherwise expressed, two are placed in the upper part of the shield, and one in the lower part. (If the number be six they will usually be arranged 3, 2, 1.)

In other cases the disposition of the charges requires specification; they may be "in chief," "in pale," "in bend," or "in cross," "saltire," "orle," etc. Thus BABINGTON (Plate IX., fig. 9) bears: *Argent ten torteaux;* but it is desirable to add that they are arranged 4, 3, 2, 1.

In connection with this subject it is needful to point out the difference between the expressions "paleways," "fessways," bendways," etc.; and the expressions "in pale," "in fess," "in bend;"—phrases sometimes used loosely as synonymous with them.

"Paleways," "bendways," etc. mean that the charge or charges are individually placed in the direction of a pale, bend, etc. Thus a sword erect is "a sword paleways." Three such erect swords would still be "paleways" if they were placed two and one; or in fess; in bend, etc.; these latter words only explain the relation in which two or more charges stand to each other.

The three lions passant-gardant in the arms of ENGLAND are blazoned "in pale;" else they might be arranged two and one. On Plate IX., fig. 10, is the coat of NORTHCOTE, Lord IDDESLEIGH : *Argent, three crosses botonné* (or *treflé*) *in bend sable.* Here the three crosses are *relatively to each other* "in bend," though each is paleways, or upright, if correctly drawn.

The words "over all" are sometimes used to express the fact that a charge is placed upon other charges. As in Plate IX., fig. 7 FAIRFAX bears: *Argent, three bars gemels gules, over all a lion rampant sable crowned or.*

IV. If the coat also contain a chief, canton, or bordure, it with its charges should be mentioned last. In some overloaded coats, most of which are posterior to the times of HENRY VII., the term "charged with" is sometimes applied to the Ordinary, instead of the charges being blazoned as "on" it.

In Plate IX., fig. 8 RUSSELL, Duke of BEDFORD, bears; *Argent, a lion rampant gules, on a chief sable three escallops of the field.* Here the last three words exemplify that avoidance of needless repetition and tautology which is a characteristic feature of the language of blazon.

It is a rule that the same tincture should not be twice named in the description of a coat. To avoid this the phrases "of the field," "of the same," "of the second," "of the third," "of the last," are made use of; while, as has been already pointed out, the name of a tincture coming after several charges applies to all. So also, as in the above blazoned coat of WILMOT, the use of the expression "as many" obviates the repetition of the name of the same number. It must, however, never be forgotten that, while succinctness in blazon is to be aimed at, and tautology to be avoided, it is far better to err on the safe side. The avoidance of ambiguity is far more important than the avoidance of tautology. Many a young (and for that matter, many an old) herald might say in the familiar words of the Latin accidence, *Brevis esse laboro, fio obscurus.* Foreign heralds are more sensible than our pedants in this respect.

There are, however, many things practically taken for granted in modern blazon. For instance; when the coat contains two or three repetitions of the same charge

in the blazon of Plate IX., fig. 5, the coat of HAIG of Bemersyde, *Azure, a saltire between two stars in chief and base and as many crescents in flanks argent.*

An exception to the rule above stated as to an Ordinary being first mentioned after the field, occurs when that Ordinary debruises, or surmounts (*i.e.*, is placed upon), another charge, as in the Scottish coat of ABERNETHY (Plate IX., fig. 6), *Or, a lion rampant gules, debruised by a ribbon, or bendlet, sable.*

III. If the Ordinary itself be charged, its charges are named next.

Thus in Plate IX., fig. 4, the arms of WILMOT, Earl of ROCHESTER, are thus blazoned:—*Argent, on a fess gules between three eagle's heads erased sable, as many escallops or.*

(Here, according to the previous rules, we name—1st, the field; 2nd, the charges, beginning with the ordinary; then 3rd, the charges placed upon the ordinary. The French custom is a little different: the charges upon the ordinary are named before those on the field. Thus the arms of the poet CORNEILLE are: —*d'Azur, à la fasce d'or, chargée de trois têtes de lion de gueules, et accompagnée de trois étoiles d'argent, posées deux en chef et une en pointe.*)

In both the British examples it will be noticed that the words "as many" are used to avoid the repetition of the number two.

In the HAIG coat the blazon also illustrates the usage by which when two or more charges of the same tincture are named consecutively, the tincture applying to them all is only named once. The terms used to denote the position of a charge in chief, base, or flanks, are also here to be observed. It is scarcely needful to point out the distinction between "in chief," and "on *a* chief."

or tacked on, to the original coat. (The term *cousu*, however, is sometimes employed by French heralds when there is no apparent violation of the law.)

As a general rule metal is laid upon colour, colour upon metal. The furs are ordinarily used with colour; their use with metal is comparatively so rare as to be exceptional. But there are cases in which metals alone, colours alone, and furs alone, are employed; and instances will be recorded of each as we proceed.

To "blazon" a Coat of Arms is to describe it in heraldic phraseology so exactly that any one acquainted with the language of armory may be able accurately to depict it from its concise description. The probable derivation of the word "blazon" is from the German *blasen*, to blow a horn. A flourish of trumpets was used to attract the attention of the bystanders when before a tournament a formal announcement was made of the armorial coat of each combatant. Glossaries of the technical terms of British and of French Armory are contained in Chapters towards the close of this present work.

It is desirable at this stage to lay down with more precision than has yet been done the principal rules of blazon.

RULES OF BLAZON.

I. The field should be first named, whether it be of one tincture, or a composite one (either by reason of the division of the field, or by being *semé* or strewn with small charges).

II. After the field the charges follow, beginning with those of most importance, or occupying the centre of the field. If the charge is an ordinary or its diminutive (unless it be a chief, bordure, or canton), it usually claims precedence over other charges in the field; as

There are recognised exceptions to the general rule: when the "field" is a composite one, of metal (or fur) and colour, it is not considered an infraction of the law if the charge is of either metal, or colour, or fur. For instance, the old arms of the Counts of VENDÔME are: *Gules, a chief argent, over all a lion rampant azure crowned or.* (See *L'Armorial de Geldre;* and PLANCHÉ'S *Roll.* The later coat was: *Argent, a chief gules,* etc.) Here, though the greater part of the *azure* lion appears on the red field, the fact that the field is a composite one of metal and of colour saves it from the imputation of violating the law.

Again, the rule does not apply to the mere accessories of a charge. For instance, in the arms of MARIA THERESA on Plate XL., the red lion rampant in the quarter of LEON is *crowned or,* a golden crown upon a silver ground, without this being considered any violation of the law. So also when teeth, tongue, claws, etc., are specified to be of another tincture than the animal to which they belong, it is no breach of the law if, for example, the lion's red tongue is projected on an azure field.

Again, bordures (which are used by way of difference) and the other marks of cadency, are legitimate exceptions to the rule. Thus, the Ducs d'ANJOU differenced by placing a bordure *gules* around the arms of FRANCE (*Azure, three fleurs-de-lis or*) and, though the red colour impinges on the blue, the law is not considered to be broken thereby.

There are also many instances in which chiefs, cantons, etc., have been added to a coat by way of augmentation, as in the cases referred to later in the Chapters on MARSHALLING and AUGMENTATIONS. These are also counted lawful exceptions. A chief of this description is by no means infrequent in Foreign Heraldry; and is known in French blazon as a "*chef cousu,*" sewed,

OF JERUSALEM (Plate IX., fig. 1), which are: *Argent, a cross potent between four crosses or*, are the best known instance (sometimes even it is asserted the *only* instance) of a permitted violation of the rule. In this, and a few other cases, the arms are styled *arma inquirenda* or *armes pour enquérir*, and it is asserted that they were originally composed for the express purpose of causing the beholder to enquire the reason of such an infraction of heraldic usage, and so to stamp them on his memory. When a limited view is taken of Heraldry, and the investigation is confined to the Armory of a single country, such assertions seem capable of easy justification. In our own country, for instance, distinct violations of the law in question are of great rarity. But when the student extends his view over the much larger field of Continental Heraldry he finds such assertions are quite unwarrantable. The general law, indeed, remains in force; but the exceptions which the present writer has collected may be counted by the hundred rather than by the dozen; and, in the great majority of these cases, the idea that they were intended as *armes pour enquérir* is one which cannot be entertained. The families are often of no very special note, and the arms do not commemorate any special circumstance as is the case in the Arms of JERUSALEM. They are simply coats assumed either anterior to the formulation of the law, or in disregard of it when formulated. A sufficient number of such coats will be noted as we proceed, or be placed in the Appendix.

There are some coats in which an apparent violation of the law has arisen from the fact that the metals employed in depicting them have become tarnished. What was supposed to be fine gold has become dim. *Or* has become *purpure;* and *argent* deteriorated into *sable!* Errors have thus arisen, and have been perpetuated by the ignorance of painters, although the cases I have referred to above are not so to be accounted for.

lower and sinister sides of an "Ordinary," or other charge. Charges are of two kinds :—I. Those of simple outline and geometrical form, which have predominated since the earliest ages of coat-armour, and in the oldest coats are often the only charge on the shield. These are called by the French—*Pièces héraldiques ;* and are subdivided by us into "ORDINARIES" and "SUB-ORDINARIES." II. COMMON CHARGES, which are the representations of objects of all kinds, including animals, flowers, and the whole range of things natural or artificial.

These charges, whether Ordinaries or Common Charges, may be depicted of any of the recognised metals, colours, or fur. COMMON CHARGES, such as birds, beasts, and fishes, flowers, trees, and many other things, are frequently depicted of their natural colours, and are then blazoned "proper." The blazon, "*a fir tree proper;*" or "*a salmon naiant proper,*" would imply that the fir tree, or the salmon were to be depicted, not merely by the heraldic colours, but by those which belong to them in nature. In the case of roses which might be red or white, and yet "proper," it is usual to specify the tincture, in order that ambiguity may be avoided. The ORDINARIES (and even the COMMON CHARGES to some extent) may be composed and divided by partition lines of the same kind as those which are used to divide the field.

It is a primary fundamental canon of Heraldry that metal is not to be placed upon metal, or colour on colour. This is the one heraldic rule with which all persons seem to be acquainted, and which has become almost a proverbial saying :—" Metal on metal is false heraldry," etc. This rule no doubt originated in the necessity for securing distinctness in the days when arms were actually borne on the military shield, surcoat, and banner ; and when it was of the utmost importance that they should be easily distinguishable from afar off. But the interdiction is far from absolute. The arms of the KINGDOM

respectively of lines in pale intersecting lines in bend; and of lines in fess intersecting those in bend.

Paly-bendy or and azure (Plate VII., fig. 12) is the coat of BUCK, Baronets of Lincolnshire.

With this section we may group the French *Trianglé*, in which the field is divided by three series of parallel lines into triangles. Plate VIII., fig. 1 represents the coat of the family of GISE in Gloucestershire; which is blazoned *Lozengy couped in fess argent and sable* (otherwise *Barry of six indented*). The Counts SCHIZZI, of Cremona, bear *Trianglé de gueules et d'argent*. The Swedish family of CARLSSON bear *Trianglé azure and or;* the shield being divided by two lines fessways, and by three in bend and bend-sinister. In the coat of VON TÖLNZ, which is also given as an example by RIETSTAP, the partition is made by two horizontal, two palar, and five diagonal lines, so that, as he observes, the coat might be blazoned: *Chequy of nine panes, each per bend sable and argent*.

Barry-pily is the name given to the field when it is divided by long, narrow, pile-shaped indentations lying horizontally, or barwise, across it. It does not greatly differ from the French *émanché en pal*. Plate VIII., fig. 2 is the coat of HOLLAND of Lincoln, *Barry-pily of eight gules and or*.

The French *émanche* is formed by two or three triangular or wedge-shaped pieces united at their base and issuing from one or other of the flanks of the shield. The number of its points requires to be specified, as well as its position issuing from the dexter or the sinister flank.

DIFFERENT KINDS OF CHARGES.
RULES OF BLAZON, ETC.

Armorial Charges are supposed to stand out somewhat in relief upon the field, and so to cast a slight shadow upon it. It is therefore usual, particularly in uncoloured drawings, to make the outline a little thicker on the

PLATE VIII.

1. Lozengy couped. (*Gise.*)
2. Barry pily. (*Holland.*) 
3. "Mit linker stufe." (*Aurberg.*) 
4. "Schneckenweise." (*Megenzer.*) 
5. Fretty. (*Willoughby.*) 
6. Papelonné. (*Monti.*) 
7. Plumeté. (*Tenremonde.*) 
8. Semé of fleurs de lis. (*France, ancient.*) 
9. Semé of hearts. (*Denmark.*) 
10. Semé. (*Simiane.*) 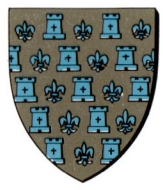
11. Billetty. (*Nassau.*) 
12. Gutté d'eau. (*Cornwallis.*)

In Spanish Heraldry *Chequy of fifteen panes* (arranged in five horizontal and three vertical rows) is often met with. Plate VII., fig. 7, is the coat of PORTOCARRERO, *Chequy of fifteen or and azure*. ALVAREZ DE TOLEDO, Duke of ALVA, so celebrated in the history of the Netherlands, bore : *Chequy of fifteen, azure and argent*.

The arms of the Portuguese discoverer VASCO DA GAMA were : *Chequy of fifteen, Or and gules, on each point of the last two bars gemels argent*. On an escucheon *en surtout* the Royal Arms of PORTUGAL, as an augmentation.

LOZENGY (*losangé*). If the field is divided into panes of a diamond shape by lines in bend and bend-sinister, it is said to be *Lozengy* (an early term in the *Rolls of Arms* was *Masculy*, now used for *semé* of Mascles).

Plate VII., fig. 9., *Lozengy argent and gules* belongs to the FITZWILLIAMS, Earls of SOUTHAMPTON and FITZWILLIAM ; and to the family of DU BEC-CRÊPIN ; as well as to the SALAMONI of Venice, and the Neapolitan family of LATRI.

A considerable number of foreign families bear *Lozengy*. *Lozengy gules and or* is the coat of CENTELLES in Spain ; and the reverse was the coat of CRAON in France.

(In blazoning begin with the tincture of the first whole lozenge.)

FUSILLY (*fuselé*). When the lozenges are elongated, the term used is *Fusilly*. *Fusilly argent and gules* is the coat of the GRIMALDI, Sovereign Princes of MONACO, and Dukes of VALENTINOIS in France. (Plate VII., fig. 10.)

The arms of BAVARIA are generally drawn as *Fusilly in bend argent and azure*, though they are often blazoned *Lozengy in bend*. It will be seen from Plate VII., fig. 11, that the lozenges, or fusils, do not stand vertically over each other but are in bend.

Analogous to this coat are the variations known as *Paly-bendy* and *Barry-bendy*, these are composed

with the Count of Horn by order of the Duke of Alva, are as follows :—

Quarterly ; I. and IV. *Per pale* (*a*) Egmond, as above : (*b*) *Argent, two bars embattled - counter - embattled gules* (Arkel).

II. and III. Duchy of Guelders. *Per pale* (*a*) *Azure, a lion rampant contourné* (*i.e.* facing to the sinister) *crowned or* (Guelders): (*b*) *Or, a lion rampant sable* (County of Juliers).

Over all an escucheon en surtout, Quarterly 1 and 4. *Argent, a lion rampant sable* (Fiennes) ; 2 and 3. *Gules an estoile of eight rays argent* (Baux).

Chequy (*Echiqueté*).—When the field is divided by horizontal and perpendicular lines into at least twenty square or oblong pieces the bearing is known as *chequy ;* if there are fewer *panes* or *points* the number must be expressed.

Plate VII., fig. 6 is the ancient coat of the Warrens, Earls of Surrey (still quartered by the Dukes of Norfolk), *Chequy or and azure.* The adoption of the chequy coat at a very early period by cognate families in England and in France, some generations removed from a supposed common ancestor, is much founded on by Mr Ellis in support of his contention that hereditary armorial bearings are of greater antiquity than we have been able to assign to them.

Chequy of nine panes only, occurs in some important foreign coats, as in that of Van den Hecke (Plate VII., fig. 8) which is thus blazoned, *de Cinq points de gueules équipollés à quatre d'hermine* (sometimes *azure* and *ermine*). The Counts of Geneva bore : *Cinq points d'or équipollés à quatre d'azur.* Saint Priest bore the same.

Cinq points d'argent équipollés à quatre de gueules, was the coat of the Portuguese navigator Magalhaens ; and the Venetian Cetracini. The same, but of *Or* and *sable,* is the coat of the Italian Grifoni.

"Did you ever see a fret thus formed before (I mean nayled)? To correct your blazon learne by this: Hee beareth Sable, a Musion Or, oppressed with a Troillis G. cloué dargent; for this which you call a fret, is a lattice, a thing well known to poor prisoners," etc. (The passage is given at length in LOWER'S *Curiosities of Heraldry*, pages 254, 255.)

A *grillage* in which the interlacements are composed of pallets and barrulets, in other words of vertical and horizontal pieces, may occasionally be met with, as in the coat of the Lombard family of the GENICEI, who use: *Gules, a grille, or lattice, composed of four vertical pieces interlaced with as many horizontal ones, argent.*

CHEVRONNY (*Chevronné*), that is the field divided into equal portions by lines in the direction of a chevron, occurs but rarely in Armory of Britain.

Chevronny of four argent and gules is attributed to WHITHORSE, and is I believe a solitary instance of this division. The reverse is borne by VON WERDENSTEIN (*Wappenbuch*, i., 111), and VON SPARNECK (*ibid.*, i., 105). *Chevronny of four azure and or* is the coat of GRIESEN-BERG (in the *Wappenrolle von Zürich*, No. 144); the reverse was borne by the Barons von BUSSNANG. The coat is rarely seen reversed so that the points of the chevrons are to the base, but I know of one example, the coat of the Barons von WITZLEBEN. This is *Chevronné renversé de quatre pièces d'argent et de gueules*. *Chevronny of six argent and gules* are the arms of the Counts of EPPSTEIN (now quartered by the Counts zu STOLBERG), and are borne also by the Genoese family of FORNARA. *Chevronny of six or and sable* is the early coat of the Counts of HAINAULT.

Chevronny of twelve pieces, or and gules (Plate VII., fig. 5) is the coat of the Counts of EGMOND, or EGMONT, in the Netherlands.

The full arms of LAMORAL, Count EGMOND, executed

ermine is a coat of GIFFARD and of VALOYNES ; and *Azure, fretty of eight pieces raguly or*, is borne by BROAD-HURST.

In Continental Armory the number of pieces of which the fretty is composed is usually limited to six ; three in bend, as many in bend-sinister. The intermediate spaces, through which the field appears, are called *claire-voies*, and these are frequently charged, so that the field is both *semé* and *fretty*.

Gules, fretty and flory or, is the coat of HAMELYN in England ; and of ALZON in Auvergne. *Sable, fretty and fleury argent (de Sable, fretty d'argent, les clairevoies semées de fleurs-de-lis du même)* are the arms of DE LA CHAPELLE in Belgium. Occasionally the fretty itself is found charged, usually with roundles ; of these the best known example is the coat of TRUSSELL, *Argent, fretty gules besanty :* here the besants are placed at the intersection of the pieces of the *fretty*. A similar coat, *Or, fretty gules platy*, is an old coat of VERDON ; and *Or, fretty sable platy* is the canting coat of PLATT.

These coats should be carefully distinguished from those which have the analogous bearing of a trellis.

A Trellis (*treillis*) is properly composed of bendlets dexter and sinister which are not interlaced, but are usually nailed (*cloués*) at the crossings. In these cases the head of the nail is very much smaller than the bezant, or plate, which appears in the coats blazoned above.

In Sir JOHN FERNE'S *Blason of Gentrie*, there is an amusing passage in which the distinction between a *fret* and a *trellis* is pointed out ; and of which Sir WALTER SCOTT makes use in *Quentin Durward*. The coat is *Sable, a musion (i.e.* a mouser, or domestic cat) *or*, oppressed *with a trellis gules nailed argent ;* which has been wrongly described by one of the interlocutors as a *fret*. (The comic man of the company describes it as "a cat in the dairy window.") But the Herald inquires

tional case in which it is correct. The French family of BORSAN bear *Bendy of nine*, but it is composed of three tinctures *or, gules*, and *argent*, each three times repeated.

BENDY OF TEN (*Coticé*).

Bendy of ten or and azure was the coat of the MONTFORTS, or MOUNTFORDS; *or and gules* was borne by the Vicomtes de TURENNE (*Salle des Croisés*, 1096) When the coat is divided by a palar line, the bends on either side are counter-changed and the coat is blazoned, *Bendy per pale counter-changed;* as in the coat of KORBLER of Styria: *Parti et contre-bandé de gueules et d'or.*

When the field is covered by an interlacement of small bendlets and bendlets-sinister, it is said to be *fretty*. The fretwork is supposed to be in relief on the field, not a mere painted pattern, and it is shaded accordingly. *Or, fretty azure* (Plate VIII., fig. 5) is the coat of the family of WILLOUGHBY in England; and of LA MOUSSAYE, Vicomtes de ST. DENOUAL in France.

Azure, fretty argent is borne by CAVE; and ETCHINGHAM (or ICHINGHAM) in early *Rolls of Arms;* as canting arms by FRESTEL. FRETEL of Normandy also bore: *d'Argent fretté de gueules;* which is the coat of SANCOURT; St. DIDIER, DOMAIGNÉ; and MARCHALCK VON BIBERSTEIN. *Argent, fretty sable* is an old coat of TOLLEMACHE in England; and of HUMIÈRES in France. *Sable, fretty or* is borne by BELLEW; BRACKENBURY; and MALTRAVERS; LINIÈRES DE MOTTEROUGE; PONTON; SAILLY, etc. *Gules, fretty vair*, is the coat of SURGÈRES, and MAINGOT in France. *Gules, fretty or*, is the well known coat of AUDELEY; and its reverse, *Or, fretty gules*, is borne by the Counts of DAUN; by VILLA in Italy; MONTJEAN, and NEUFVILLE in France; as well as by VERDON in England; with a *canton ermine* it is the coat of NOEL, Earls of GAINSBOROUGH, etc. The fretty is rarely formed by a compound line, but *Gules, fretty engrailed*

von LANDAU. The Princes of CALERGI in Greece bear: *Bendy of four azure and argent;* the Italian ALAMANI, the reverse.

Bendy (of six) is much more common. *Bendy of six or and azure* is the coat of ST. PHILIBERT in England; of the Tuscan BIANCHETTI; of the Genoese FIESCHI, and the Marquises BONELLI. Plate VII., fig. 4, is the arms of PLAYTER of Suffolk, *Bendy wavy of six argent and azure.*

Bandé d'argent et de gueules is borne by BERG, Counts von SCHELKLINGEN; and by the family of COËTQUEN (Counts d'UZEL, and COMBOURG; Marquises de ROISIN, and DE COËTQUEN). *Bendy wavy gules and argent* is the coat of the Venetian SALONISI.

Bandé d'or et de gueules is used by the Lombard Counts MILLESIMO; MIOLANS (the Neapolitan family of AQUINO, Ducs de CASOLI, quarter with it: *Per fess gules and argent, a lion rampant counter-changed*). The LONGUEVAL, Princes de BUCQUOY, use *Bendy of six vair and gules.*

Bendy-sinister of six is occasionally found. *Bendy-sinister argent and gules*, was used by DAMIGLIA of Italy; the same of *azure and argent*, by the Austrian Barons BARRÉ DE BAREY, where it is of course an instance of *armes parlantes;* as also by the family of BARRUEL DE ST. VINCENT (*Barré d'or et d'azur*).

Bendy of seven occurs once; the family of ESCHELBACH in Bavaria bears it: *azure, argent, gules, argent, gules, argent, azure.*

Bendy-sinister of eight gules and argent was the coat of VON SEUBERSDORFF (SIEBMACHER, *Wappenbuch*, i., 82). The bends are now usually dexter.

Bendy of eight azure and argent is used by the Venetian family of ZENO; and is also borne by the ATAIDES of Portugal.

Usually *Bendy of nine* would not be a proper blazon for a field charged with four bendlets, but there is an excep-

de MORTAGNE; FLECHIN, Marquis de WAMIN; VANDER AA. *Fascé d'or et de sinople* is the coat of CRUSSOL, Duc d'USEZ. (NOTE.—*Barry of seven* does not exist; being blazoned as a field charged with three bars.) *Barry of eight* is not nearly as frequently found as *Barry of six*. *Barry of eight or and sable* is the coat of the GONZAGAS, Dukes of MANTUA. *Barry of eight or and gules* that of FITZ ALAN; and POYNTZ; the Comtes de GRANDPRÉ; the Roman RINALDI; the Counts of REINECK, etc. *Barry of nine* only exists exceptionally, the proper blazon being a field charged with four bars; but the coat of DE BART of France is properly :—*Barry of nine or, azure, and argent*; each tincture being thrice repeated. *Barry of ten* or more pieces (French *burelé*) is occasionally found. *Burelé d'argent et de sable*, VAUDEMONT (*Salle des Croisés*, 1147), CLERAMBAULT; WARNBACH, etc. The following use *Burelé d'or et de sable*, THYNNE, Marquess of BATH; BOTVILLE; Counts von BALLENSTEDT (*i.e.*, BALCKENSTADT, *armes parlantes*). *Burelé argent and azure* is carried sometimes by DE VALENCE and LUSIGNAN; of *argent and gules* by ESTOUTEVILLE, or STUTEVILLE, etc. *Burelé or and gules* is the coat of TOMASI of Naples. Sometimes this coat is varied by counterchanging, the field being divided by a palar line; *Barry per pale counter-changed or and gules*.

BENDY (*Bandé*). This is similarly formed, but by diagonal lines from the dexter chief to the sinister base, dividing the shield into (usually) six bends, or pieces of equal width. If the number be six it need not be expressed. *Bendy of four* is a not uncommon Continental bearing. *Bandé de gueules et d'argent de quatre pièces* is the coat of the Venetian family of EMO; EGBRET (*Zürich Wappenrolle*, No. 390); the Austrian Princes of SCHÖNBURG; the families of SCHLEGEL; and VAN WYL. The reverse is borne by Barons von AUTENRIED; and by the Counts

buch, ii., 12), the Barons von LAHER in Austria; the families of ALTSTETEN (*Zürich Wappenrolle*, 276); VILLIERS; CASTANEDA; LANVAON; VAUDETAR; MICHELI; GRIENENSTEIN, etc., etc.

Barry wavy of six argent and azure was one of the BASSETT coats; and was also used by SANDFORD and BROWNING, at home; and abroad by BOROLLA, LE GAL, etc. (this coat was often drawn *nebuly* in early *Rolls of Arms*). *Barry of six argent and gules* were the arms of the BARRYS, Earls of BARRYMORE in Ireland; the Counts von ARNSTEIN; the Counts von BEUCHLINGEN; the Princes of POLIGNAC; the Counts of BOULAINVILLIERS, the families of BARONCELLI; ASLOWSKI (Poland), BOUDOYER; YOENS; MALEMORT (*Salle des Croisés*, 1096); the ARMANES, Marquises of BLACONS; MIZOU, etc.

Barry nebuly of six argent and gules (*Fascé nebulé d'argent et de gueules*) is the coat of BASSET, BLOUNT, and D'AMORI, in England; of the ROCHECHOUART, Ducs de MORTEMAR, in France (early coats are *Fascé ondé*). *Barry nebuly of or and sable* (Plate VII., fig. 3) is the coat of BLOUNT, Earl of DEVON. *Barry of six argent and sable* is borne by RÜDBERG (*Zürich Wappenrolle*, No. 316), PALLANDT; and RAAPHORST, of the Netherlands; AMIRATO of Florence; LOUVILLE; ORTELART of France. *Barry of six ermine and gules* is the coat of HUSSEY. *Barry of six or and azure* was borne by the CONSTABLES of England; the Counts of SLAWATA (Poland); GREYSPACH; REINFELDEN; RODEMACHER; and CHAMBON, Marquis d'ARBOUVILLE. *Barry of six or and gules*, by the Princes of LOOS-CORSWAREN; TURRETINI of Lucca; CAMPORELLS; and AMPURIAS of Spain; ODENKIRCHEN; RUFFELAERT; KERLECH, etc. *Barry nebuly or and gules* was another BASSET coat. *Barry or and sable* (*Fascé d'or et de sable*) is the coat of PEMBRIDGE; the Barons CEVA (Piedmont); COËTIVY, Princes

GOTSCHEN, or GÖSCHEN, in Silesia (SIEBMACHER, *Wappenbuch,* i., 161), and of WALLENSTEIN of Hesse. If in addition to the pales the shield is cut by a line *per fess,* or *per bend,* the tinctures are so arranged that in the lower part of the shield the metal corresponds with the tincture in the upper, and the coat is then said to be: *Paly per fess counterchanged* (*Palé contre-palé*). ROSENBERG in Franconia bears: *Palé contre-palé de gueules et d'argent de six pièces;* DE REVEST in France, *Palé contre-palé d'argent et d'azur de huit pièces.*

BARRY (*Fascé*). This is the term used when the field is divided by horizontal lines into an even number of equal portions, as in the coat of the "Sires" or Sieurs de COUCY (Plate VII., fig. 2), *Barry of six vair and gules; Fascé de vair et de gueules.* To this family belonged Queen MARIE (DE COUCY), second wife of King ALEXANDER II. She was the daughter of INGELRAM DE COUCY, who died in 1242. The old boastful motto of the family is well known:—*Je ne suis roi ni duc ni compte aussi; Je suis le Sire de Coucy.* (French heralds, as in the corresponding case of *Paly,* do not express the number if the bars are six.) The *Barry* may be formed of compound lines. *Barry of four* is not often seen in English or French blazons, but is not unusual in Germany. *Barry of four, vert and argent,* is the coat of the Counts MANIAGO of Venice; *Or and gules,* of SIGINOLFI of Sicily. *Barry of four or and azure* was borne by the Counts von SPITZENBERG in Austria.

Barry of six is one of the most common of parted coats, being found, both with straight and compound lines, in the armory of all countries, and is borne by many great houses.

Barry of six argent and azure is the coat of the GREYS, Earls of STAMFORD. It was also the coat of the Counts von TRUHENDIN (SIEBMACHER, *Wappen-*

Argent and azure, by VON BERCHOLTSHOFEN of Bavaria; and the reverse by GUNDRICHING of Tirol.

(NOTE.—*Paly of five, argent and sable*, is the same as *Argent, two pallets sable;* but would be thought a shockingly incorrect blazon by heraldic purists, whose extreme attention to these trivialities often has to stand them instead of a real knowledge of the subject.)

Paly of six is a frequent bearing at home and abroad.

Paly of six, argent and azure, was the original coat of ANNESLEY (now borne with *a bend gules over all*); it was the coat of the Marquises of ROSMADEC, and of BERTRAND; ESTISSAC; FONTENAI; and others.

Paly of six or and gules, was the coat of AMBOISE; of FAUCIGNY, Princes de LUCINGE; of BRIQUEVILLE, in the First Crusade; of BEAUMONT, and ST. BRICE, etc.

Paly of six ermine and vair, is the canting coat of PALVERT in France (notice that there is fur only in this coat, as an exception to the rule stated on p. 78).

The city of RENNES bears: *Paly of six argent and sable*, but adds thereto a chief of BRETAGNE; *Ermine plain.*

Paly of six or and vert is now borne by ERQUERRER of Spain, and by the Italian TRIVULZI (originally these bore *Or, three pallets vert*).

Occasionally the paly is formed by compound (*i.e.*, not straight) lines. *Paly wavy of six argent and gules*, is one form of the coat of VALOINES (DE VALONIIS). *Palé ondé d'or et de gueules* is that of MOULINS.

(NOTE.—*Paly of seven* is incorrect; the coat would be a field charged with three pallets.)

Paly of eight is not a frequent bearing. *Paly of eight argent and azure* is, however, borne by the Princes of SCHWARZENBERG, in Austria. *Paly of eight or and gules* is used by LIMA of Portugal; and of *azure and argent* by JUYÀ of Spain. *Paly of eight gules and argent* is the coat of VON

PLATE VII.

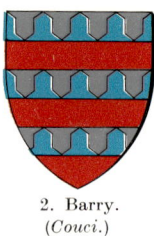

1. Paly.
(*Athole.*)

2. Barry.
(*Couci.*)

3. Barry nebuly.
(*Blount.*)

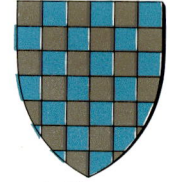

4. Bendy wavy.
(*Playter.*)

5. Chevronny.
(*Egmond.*)

6. Checquy.
(*Warren.*)

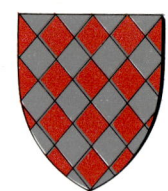

7. Checquy.
(*Portocarrero.*)

8. Equipollé.
(*Van den Hecke.*)

9. Lozengy.
(*Fitzwilliam.*)

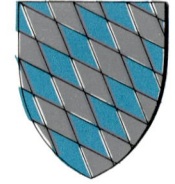

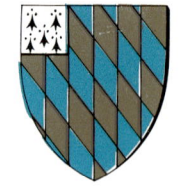

10. Fusilly.
(*Grimaldi.*)

11. Fusilly in bend.
(*Bavaria.*)

12. Paly bendy.
(*Buck.*)

zontal instead of in a vertical direction (that is when the apex of the pile is on either the dexter or the sinister flank of the escucheon) the field is said to be *embrassé* (*à dextre,* or *à senestre*). Thus the VON VÖLCKER of Frankfurt bear: *Argent, a rose gules, the field* embrassé à senestre *of the second.* We should blazon this: *Gules, a pile throughout issuing from the dexter flank, charged with a rose of the field.* Exceptionally the *embrassé* is formed by a compound line, thus the Austrian Barons von RUCHSTEIN bear: *de Gueules, embrassé-vivré à dextre d'argent.* (Plate VI., fig. 12.)

A large class of parted fields, often classed by French writers under the general term of *Rebattements,* consist of regular divisions of alternate tinctures formed by parallel lines, either arranged to follow one direction only; or intersecting another set parallel in another direction.

PALY (*pallé* or *palé*) is the term used when the field is divided into an even number of equal stripes by palar, or perpendicular lines. If the number of divisions is not specified it is understood to be of six pieces, but it is better to specify the number. Plate VII., fig. 1 is the feudal coat of the Earldom of ATHOLE, and would be blazoned: *Paly or and sable; Palé d'or et de sable;* or *Paly of six or and sable.*

Paly of four is seldom met with in English Armory, but is more frequent in Germany. *Paly of four or and vert* is the coat of MARSHALL; and *Paly of four argent and vair* was borne by WILLIAM DE LONGCHAMP, Bishop of ELY (1189–1197).

Paly of four sable and argent was the coat of the old Counts von CAPLENDORF (SIEBMACHER, *Wappenbuch* ii., 22), of VOIT of Nuremburg; MEPPEN (Prussia), and STÜBNER of Austria (sometimes *or and sable*).

Paly of four gules and argent, was borne by the Barons von STARCKENBERG (*Wappenbuch,* ii., 32); of

tinctures are sometimes employed; the field being of one, and each of the side pieces of the *enchaussure*, or mantel, being of another.

The Danish family of MOST bore: *Argent, chapé of sable to the dexter, and of gules to the sinister;* and in Plate VI., fig. 10 the coat of the Franconian VON ABSPERG is, *d'Argent, chapé-ployé à dextre de gueules, et à senestre d'azur.*

Chaperonné is the term applied to a reduced form of *chapé*, which does not extend below the fess line.

When both *chapé* and *chaussé* are found in one field the size of each is somewhat restricted; and the shield, of which the four corners are cut off by diagonal lines, has the appearance of being charged with a lozenge throughout (*i.e.* one whose points touch the borders of the escucheon) as in the coat of SCHWEREN (Plate VI., fig. 11). The French equivalent for *chapé-chaussé* is *vêtu.* (*See* page 182, where the same coat with other tinctures, that of the Venetian CORRARO, is blazoned by both terms.) *Gules, vêtu argent,* is the coat of EUBING. The Spanish ABARIA bear: *Argent, a letter* B *sable, the field vêtu gules.*

The coat of the Sicilian family of SANTAPAU, Princes de BUTERA, *Gules, three bars argent, chapé and chaussé d'or,* is, however, drawn differently in MORICE, *Le Blason des Chevaliers de la Toison d'Or,* No. CCLXXIX., here as none of the pieces of the *chapé* or *chaussé* come into contact with each other the central space of the field is not a lozenge-throughout but a lozenge truncated. A single *enchaussure* is very rare. VON ROSDORFF bears: *Lozengy argent and gules, an enchaussure to the sinister or.* There are a few German coats in which this *enchaussure* is conjoined with a large fleur de lis in bend, or in bend-sinister. The Augsburg VON SCHROTT bear: *Sable, a fleur de lis conjoined with an enchaussure or.* When the *chapé,* or *chaussé,* is placed in a hori-

Bavarian coat of AURBERG. This is blasoned by DE LA COLOMBIERE: "*Coupé à senestre parti en cœur et recoupé à dextre, tout d'un trait d'argent.*" By RIETSTAP the same coat is thus blazoned: *Mi-coupé failli en partant, et récoupe vers senestre d'argent sur sable.*

Another tripartite division is made in the form of the letter **Y**, or the same reversed; this is known as *Tiercé en pairle*, or *Tiercé en pairle renversée;* examples of both are given in Plate VI. Fig. 6 is the coat of the Saxon family of VON BRIÈSEN, *Tierced in pairle sable, argent, and gules.* Fig. 7 is that of the VON HALDERMANSTETEN: *Tierced in pairle reversed, argent, or, and azure.*

There are also certain other bipartite, or tripartite, divisions used in Continental heraldry in which the field is described as "mantled" (*mantelé*) "coped" (*chapé*) or "shod" (*chaussé*).

These are "partitions" not "charges;" but they differ from other parted-fields in this respect, that any charges which appear on the field are confined to it; and do not usually extend beyond its unmantled, or unshod, portion.

Mantelé nearly corresponds to our partition: *Parti per chevron.* The Venetian GHISI bear: *Argent, mantelé gules.* The field is according to rule, named first, the *mantelé*, which descends from the chief, follows.

Chapé is formed by two lines which start from the centre of the top line of the shield and descend to the dexter and sinister base. We might blazon it "per pile reversed throughout." Plate VI., fig. 8, *d'Argent, chapé de pourpre,* is the coat of the Burgundian family DE HAUTEN. Another Burgundian family, DE MONTBAR, bears: *Quarterly argent and gules chapé counterchanged. Chaussé* is the reverse of *chapé.* When the *chapé*, or *chaussé*, is formed by arched or concave lines it is said to be *ployé*, as in the Bavarian coat of VON SCHLEICH (Plate VI., fig. 9); *de Gueules chaussé-ployé d'argent.*

When a shield is *chaussé-ployé*, or *mantelé*, three

the reverse. *Tierced in fess, gules, sable, and argent*, is borne by the Counts von SCHWEIDNITZ in Prussia ; of *argent, gules, and sable*, by the Counts von ZEDWITZ of Bohemia. *Tierced in fess, sable, argent, and gules*, is the coat of ELTERSHOFEN ; *Or, argent, and gules* of RECHT-HALER ; *Sable, azure, and or*, of the Counts von WESTER-REICH ; *Or, gules, and argent* of SATTELBOGEN.

Tierced in bend or, gules, and azure, are the canting arms of the family of NOMPAR in Guyenne ; here the arms are allusive to the name the divisions being *non pair*, unequal in number. The Italian family of AMICI bear : *Tierced in bend, or, gules, and argent* (*tiercé en bande d'or, de gueules, et d'argent*). (Plate VI., fig. 5.) The GIUDICI have the same coat but tinctured *azure, argent, and gules ;* while the Barons von DORNBERG reverse these tinctures. UCKERMAN uses : *Tiercé en bande d'argent, d'azur, et d'or*. By the German family of TÜRLING is borne the coat : *Tierced in bend* (*sinister*), *or, sable, and argent*. (*Tiercé en barre d'or, de sable, et d'argent*.) MENDEL bears the same, but the tinctures are *vert, or, and sable :* (a family of the same name bears : *Tierced in bend, argent, vert, and sable*).

A very curious German partition is that of *Tierced in gyron gyronnant ;* in it the whole field is occupied by three spiral girons ; VON MEGENZER bears this *gules, sable,* and *argent*. (Plate VIII., fig. 4.) A variation of the same is, *Tierced in pale gironnant ;* which (with the same tinctures) is borne by the VON TEUFEL.

Parted coats are much more varied among the Germans than among ourselves.

Other German partitions are unknown to British or French Armory, and, though formed by straight lines, are difficult to blazon succinctly in the heraldic phraseology of either country. One is the partition per fess with a right or left step ("*mit einer rechten stufe*, or *mit einer lincken stufe* "). In Plate VIII., fig. 3 represents the

A variation of the ordinary gyronny of eight is that of BÉRANGER which is: *Gironné en croix d'or et de gueules* (the four girons of gules taking the form of a cross, patée-throughout.) MAZINGHEM has the same, but of or and azure. The seal of JEANNE, Dame de CAROUGES, of the twelfth century, has a shield with this bearing. (ELLIS, *Antiquities of Heraldry*, Plate XV., p. 189.) D'ENGHIEN bears, *Gyronny of ten argent and sable, each piece of the last charged with three crosslets fitchées of the first.*

The BASSINGBURNE coat (Plate VI., fig. 2) is *Gyronny of twelve, vair and gules.*

Gyronny is sometimes composed of more than two tinctures, thus a branch of the Milanese family of ORIGO bears: *Gyronny, sable, argent, vert, sable, argent, vert, sable, vert.* This is an arrangement which appears more curious than commendable.

A curious form of gyrons is found in German Armory, in it the gyrons are formed, not by straight lines but by curves. The family VON ALDENBURG bear: *Gyronny-curved of eight, sable and argent (Gironné de sable et d'argent de huit pièces gironnantes);* and the family of ROCHAUSEN have a similar coat of six pieces gules and argent (*Mal-gironné de six pièces gironnantes de gueules et d'argent*).

In Continental Heraldry, and especially in that of Germany and Italy, we frequently meet with a tripartite division of the shield. This is most commonly effected by two horizontal lines; but very frequently by two lines in pale, or in bend, or bend-sinister. In these cases the shield is said to be Tierced (*tiercé*) in fess, pale, bend, or bend-sinister, as the case may be. In Plate VI., fig. 4 is the coat of the Venetian family of FRANCHI: *Tierced in fess vert, argent, and gules.* The VENDRAMINI bear this of *azure, or, and gules.* The POLANI, also of Venice, bear *Tiercé en fasce d'or, d'azur, et d'argent.* PFUHLINGEN bears

this as a "mistake which has unfortunately been made." And in the text above the note he indicates his opinion thus:—"The gyron upon which the tinctures ought to begin is the uppermost on the dexter side, *i.e.*, the first of the four triangles above the horizontal line which crosses the fess point of the escucheon." On the other hand the opinion of the late LYON, who made the sketch for Plate VI., is sufficiently indicated by it. In that opinion I most unreservedly agree; and I am fortified in my adhesion by the fact that the French and German Heralds are unanimous in counting the first *giron* to be that which occupies the first and most honourable position, depending from the dexter half of the uppermost edge of the shield, and bounded by it, by the upper half of the palar line, and the upper half of the bend.

The CAMPBELLS, Earls of LOUDOUN, bore: *Gyronny ermine and gules*, and in this case the ermine should occupy that which we have indicated as the first giron of the shield. (Compare STODART, *Scottish Arms*, vol. ii., plate 5.)

The coat of the French DE BELLEVILLES is: *Gyronny of six gules and vair (Gironné de gueules et de vair de six pièces)*.

The MAUGIRONS of Dauphiny bear: *Gyronny of six argent and sable (Gironné d'argent et de sable de six pièces)*. These are *armes parlantes* inasmuch as being of only six pieces, instead of eight, the coat is *mal-gironné;* and, moreover, in this coat the division is made by the palar line, and by two diagonal lines which do not start as in the preceding instance from the extremities of the top line of the shield, but commence some way lower down (Plate VI., fig. 3).

A similar instance of a coat *mal-gironné* is afforded by the arms of the MONTANGONS which are: *Mal-gironné d'or et d'azur*. In the coat of MUDERSBACH the dividing lines are indented:—*Gironné-denché de gueules et d'argent*.

PLATE VI.

1. Gyronny of eight. (*Campbell.*)
2. Gyronny of twelve. (*Bassingbourne.*) 
3. Gyronny of six. (*Maugiron.*) 
4. Tierced in fess. (*Franchi.*) 
5. Tierced in bend. (*Amici.*) 
6. Tierced in pairle. (*Briesen.*) 
7. Tierced in pairle reversed. (*Haldermansteten.*) 
8. Chapé. (*Hautin.*) 
9. Chaussé-ployé. (*Schleich.*) 
10. Chapé-ployé. (*Absperg.*) 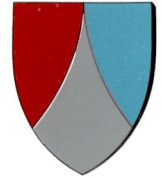
11. Vêtu. (*Schwerin.*) 
12. Embrassé. (*Ruchstein.*)

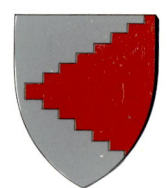

both of the Duke of ARGYLL and of the Earl of BREAD-ALBANE, as *Gyronny sable and or.* A reference to STODART'S *Scottish Arms*, vol. ii., will show that WORKMAN'S MS., *circa* 1565, is said to give the tinctures of the Earl of ARGYLL'S coat as *sable and argent*, though *or* is added in a later hand (p. 102); while LINDSAY II. gives *sable and or* for the arms of CAMPBELL of Strachur (p. 332).

I imagine that in all these and other cases in which the tincture precedes the metal, the blazon has been made to fit the idea entertained by the writer as to the answer which should be given to the enquiry suggested above:—Which is the first giron of the shield; or which is the one in which the metal should first appear?—Sir DAVID LINDSAY'S MS., plate 40 *c*, places the metal in that giron which is formed by the dexter half of the top line of the shield. It is tinctured *argent*, not *or;* and it also appears thus on the ceiling of St. Machar's in Aberdeen. (See *The Heraldic Ceiling of the Cathedral of St. Machar, Old Aberdeen*, No. 28, p. 114. New Spalding Club, 1888. LINDSAY II. gives: *Gyronny of eight argent and sable*, for CAMPBELL of Glenorchy. See STODART, *Scottish Arms*, ii., 286, 323. WORKMAN'S blazon has been already noticed.) I have already referred to the discrepancy which exists in NISBET'S plates, but in both of his volumes the greater number of examples show the metal in the position which it occupies in our plate. FOSTER in his *Peerage* adopts the same disposition in the cuts of the arms of three CAMPBELL peers; BREADALBANE, CAWDOR, and STRATHEDEN. In the ARGYLL arms he takes the other course. In his *Baronetage* the CAMPBELL coats are drawn, some in one way, some in the other. Particular attention is due to the opinion expressed by SETON in *The Law and Practice of Heraldry in Scotland*. At pages 96 and 105 the coat is drawn as in our example; but in a note at page 453 he speaks of

GYRONNY.

When the field is divided into eight sections by a vertical, a horizontal, and the two diagonal lines (the bend, and the bend-sinister) all intersecting in the fess point, the coat is blazoned *Gyronny* (*gironné*); because each of the eight pieces has the form of the Sub-Ordinary known as a *gyron*, or *giron* (*see* page 167). We sometimes meet with coats in which the girons number six, ten, twelve, or sixteen, equal pieces. In such cases, *i.e.* when the number is not eight, it must be specified of how many pieces the *Gyronny* consists.

The well known coat of the Clan CAMPBELL (whose chief is the Duke of ARGYLL) is represented on Plate VI., fig. 1. It is blazoned: *Gyronny or and sable*. Well known as this coat is, and one than which it would seem few could be easier to draw correctly, it is surprising to find how frequently it is inaccurately represented, and how great a diversity of opinion exists among Heraldic authorities as to which is its correct form. The question is,—Which is to be accounted *the first giron?*—or, the coat being drawn in outline, which is the first segment to be coloured *or*, that which is partly formed by the dexter half of the top line of the shield; or that which lies immediately below it, and is formed by the upper half of the bend, and the dexter half of the fess line? This is a point on which in Scotland itself there is no general consensus of opinion. The plates in NISBET'S *Heraldry* show the coat sometimes after one fashion, sometimes after the other. In FOSTER'S *Peerage and Baronetage*, and other similar works, there is the same diversity of treatment. Perhaps it may be useful to point out the authorities for each of the modes.

It may be first of all mentioned that though the common blazon is that already given (*Gyronny or and sable*), yet CRAUFURD in his *Peerage* blazons the arms,

LUCIANO in Italy; and the Counts WORACZICSKY-BISINGEN in Bohemia, all bear: *Quarterly argent and azur* (*d'Argent, écartelé d'azur*). The Marquises de SÉVIGNÉ used *Quarterly sable and argent*.

As an example in which the quartering is effected both by a straight line, and in combination with one of the more complicated ones, we may take the arms of the family of SANDFORD, which are (Plate V., fig. 10) *Quarterly per fess indented azure and ermine*. *Quarterly per pale dovetail gules and or*, are the arms of BROMLEY, Barons MONTFORD. *Quarterly indented* (both lines) *argent and sable; argent and gules; gules and ermine;* are all FITZ-WARINE coats. *Quarterly wavy or and sable* is the coat of SANDON.

A shield divided into four by the intersection of the two diagonal lines (the bend, and the bend-sinister) is said to be: *Quarterly per saltire*, but the first word is usually omitted in English Blazon (*Ecartelé en sautoir*). *Per saltire or and azure*, is borne by the families REDINGHURST; of HERSTRATEN in the Netherlands; BALNEO, or BAIGNI, in Italy. *Per saltire gules and argent*, is the coat of VON PAULSDORF, and of VON ESENDORF, and BENSTEDT. So also the VON HARTZHEIM in Westphalia, bear: *Per saltire gules and or* (Plate V., fig. 12); while the coat of the GANGALANDI in Tuscany, and LANGEN in Westphalia, is *Per saltire argent and sable* (*Ecartelé en sautoir d'argent et de sable*). *Per saltire wavy gules and argent* is borne by ELTERSHOFEN.

Continental Heraldry has other modes of quartering unknown to English blazon. Of these one of the most curious is shown in Plate V., fig. 11. It is the coat of VON TALE in Brunswick. Here each piece takes the form of the mystic *fylfot*, or *gammadion*. This coat is blazoned by the French Heralds: *Ecartelé en équerre de gueules et d'argent;* because the shape of the pieces suggests the carpenter's square.

coat of the Counts von KÜNIGL in Tirol is given in Plate V., fig. 7, *Per bend-sinister argent and gules, the gules* fitchée *in the argent (Taillé d'argent sur gueules le gueules fiché sur l'argent).* In modern blazons this coat is as frequently drawn per bend, as per bend-sinister.

If the field is divided into two parts by two diagonal lines, drawn from near the dexter and sinister base, and meeting like a gable in the fess point, or in the honour point of the escucheon, it is said to be *Parted per chevron (Divisé en chevron).* Thus ASTON bears: *Per chevron sable and argent (Divisé en chevron de sable et d'argent),* Plate V., fig. 8. *Per chevron nebuly gules and argent* is the coat of COVERDALE. This is not a common partition abroad. The French *Chapé,* though somewhat similar, is not the same (*see* that word, p. 88).

A coat divided by two lines, the one *per pale,* and the other *per fess,* is blazoned *Quarterly (Ecartelé).* The STANHOPES, Earls of CHESTERFIELD, bear: *Quarterly ermine and gules (Ecartelé d'hermine et de gueules),* Plate V., fig. 9. *Quarterly vert and or* is the coat of the OMODEI of Italy. *Quarterly or and sable* are the arms of BOVILE ; *Quarterly or and vert* those of BERNERS. The families of CALDORA of Naples ; MANFREDI of Faenza ; the Counts de MONTREVEL ; and the Marquises de CANDOLLE in France, all bear: *Quarterly or and azure (Ecartelé d'or et d'azur).* The house of HOHENZOLLERN bears, *Quarterly argent and sable (Ecartelé d'argent et de sable).* The arms of the Princes of COLLALTO, and of the Lords HOO, are the reverse. GONTAUT, Duc de BIRON in France ; and the Lords SAY in England (by descent from the MANDEVILLES, Earls of ESSEX), bear : *Quarterly or and gules.* The same coat is that of the Counts WALDERSEE in Prussia, and of LE BOUTEILLER DE SENLIS. The families of CREVANT, Marquis d'HUMIÈRES in France ; the families of COURCELLES in France ;

PLATE V.

1. Per pale.
(*Waldegrave.*)

2. Per pale indented.
(*Hickman.*)

3. Per fess.
(*Giusto* or *Zusto.*)

4. Per bend embattled.
(*Boyle.*)

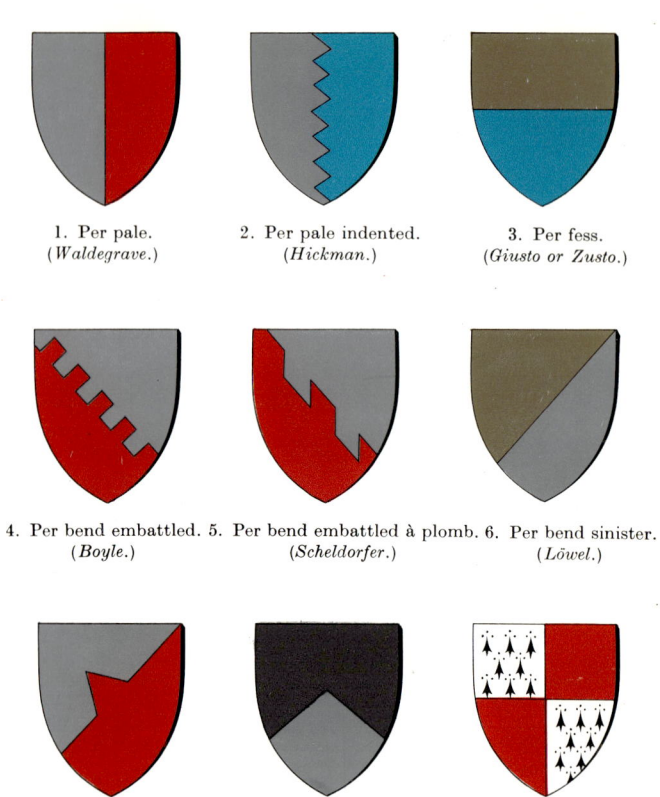

5. Per bend embattled à plomb.
(*Scheldorfer.*)

6. Per bend sinister.
(*Löwel.*)

7. Per bend sinister fitchée.
(*Künigl.*)

8. Per chevron.
(*Aston.*)

9. Quarterly.
(*Stanhope.*)

10. Quarterly per fess indented.
(*Sandford.*)

11. Quarterly en équerre.
(*Tale.*)

12. Per saltire.
(*Hartzheim.*)

When the partition is made by a line drawn from the dexter point in chief to the sinister base, the shield is said to be divided *Per bend* (for which the French equivalent is *Tranché*. *Per bend Or and azure* (*Tranché d'or et d'azur*) are the arms of CRANE; *Per bend Or and vert*, those of HAWLE or HAWLEY. The Venetian family of NANI bear: *Per bend Or and gules* (*Tranché d'or et de gueules;* otherwise, *d'Or tranché de gueules;* or *Tranché d'or sur gueules*). The Florentine CAPPONI use: *Per bend sable and argent* (*Tranché de sable sur argent*).

In Plate V., figs. 4 and 5 are instances where the dividing line is not the straight one. Fig. 4, *Per bend embattled argent and gules* (in French, *Tranché enclavé d'argent sur gueules*) are the arms of the Irish family of BOYLE. Here the sides of the embattlements are drawn at right angles to the line of partition. In Foreign Heraldry they are often drawn parallel to the sides of the escucheon (*à plomb*); thus the VON SCHELDORFER of Bavaria bear: *Per bend embattled à plomb argent and gules* (*Tranché enclavé à plomb de deux pièces d'argent sur gueules*) (Plate V., fig. 5).

The Piedmontese GUASCHI; and the English families of GOSNOLD, MARKINGTON, and WHISTLEFORD bear: *Per bend indented azure and or* (*Tranché endenté d'or et d'azur*).

If the partition line run from the sinister chief to the dexter base the division is known as *Per bend-sinister*, in French blazon *Taillé*. *Per bend-sinister or and argent* (*Taillé d'or sur argent*), are the arms of LÖWEL in Bavaria (Plate V., fig. 6); while the GRIFFONI of Rome bear the reverse: *Per bend-sinister argent and or*. These last are examples of coats which are exceptional as being composed of metal only (*vide* p. 78) no colour being employed. The arms of the Swiss canton of ZÜRICH are: *Taillé d'argent et d'azur*. The curious coats are those of the Counts VON WRATISLAW (Bohemia), *Per pale gules and sable;* and CHANAC, *Parti de gueules et d'azur.* So are those of BONVILLE, *Per pale argent and or;* and FORTIGUIERRE, *Parti d'or et de vair* (a combination of metal and fur which is not frequent).

The division of the shield may be composed of any of the lines of partition described above, but instances of their use in this manner are much less frequently found abroad than among ourselves. *Per pale indented argent and azure* (Plate V., fig. 2) is the coat of the HICKMANS, Earls of PLYMOUTH; and *Per pale dancetty argent and gules,* that of AMAURI D'EVREUX, Earl of GLOUCESTER, temp. HENRY III.

When the dividing line is horizontal the shield is said to be *Parted per fess (i.e.* in the direction of the ordinary called a *fess).* This division is known in French blazon by the single word *Coupé.* Plate V., fig. 3 is the coat of the Venetian familes of GIUSTI, and TROTTI: *Per fess or and azure (Coupé d'or et d'azur;* or *d'Or coupé d'azur).* The families of DONATI at Florence; FRANCHI at Genoa; LANFRANCHI at Pisa; POPEL in Bohemia; and the Duchy, formerly Bishopric, of MAGDEBURG; all bear: *Per fess gules and argent (de Gueules coupé d'argent).* The County of SCHWERIN (which is the *surtout* of the arms of the Princes of MECKLENBURG); the Counts of STOCKAU; the Counts of MUNTZENBERG; and the LOMELLINI, at Genoa; bear: *Per fess gules and or (Coupé de gueules et d'or).* It will be noticed that the tincture first mentioned is that which stands in the chief, or upper, part of the shield.

Per fess indented ermine and gules are the arms of BROME (*Coupé endenté d'hermine sur gueules*); *Per fess wavy or and gules,* those of DRUMMOND of Concraig, and *Per fess embattled gules and argent,* those of VON PREYSING (the Barons of the name bear *or and azure*).

simple uncharged coats whose simplicity is usually an indication of their antiquity. As the nomenclature of this part of the subject is, particularly in English blazon, greatly connected with some of the charges which are known as the "ORDINARIES" and "SUB-ORDINARIES" it is desirable that the student should have such a knowledge of these as may be needful for his understanding of what a *pale, bend, fess, chevron,* etc., are, which will be fully explained in the succeeding chapter, and are set out in the accompanying figure.

The simplest forms of partition are those in which the field is divided into two equal parts by a perpendicular, horizontal, or diagonal line. Usually one of these parts is occupied by a metal or fur, the other by a colour; though there are exceptional cases (*vide infra*). When the dividing line is perpendicular the field is said to be *Parted per pale;* or more succinctly, *Per pale.* The French denote this by the one word *Parti.* The tincture first named is that on the dexter side of the shield. The families of WALDEGRAVE (Plate V., fig. 1); the Counts RANTZAU in Denmark; the Principality, formerly Bishopric, of HALBERSTADT; the Counts VON JULBACH, and ROCKENHAUS in Germany all bear; *Per pale argent and gules. (Parti d'argent et de gueules.)* The like coat, but with reversed tinctures, is borne for the Bishopric, now Principality, of HILDESHEIM; by the Barons von URBACH; the families of WANGELIN of Mecklenburg, and BONI of Venice. *Per pale or and sable* is borne by the English family of SERLE; and the reverse by the Counts von ROST of Tirol, and the baronial families of WATZDORFF in Saxony; and STECKBORN. The ancient family of BAILLEUL in France bears: *Parti d'hermine et de gueules.* The Venetian family of NANI: *Per pale argent and vert. Per pale argent and sable* is the coat of the Counts of TRAUN; *Per pale or and gules* is that of the Barons DORNBERG DE HERTZBERG. Exceptional

POTENTÉ (*potencé*), in the form of potences, crutches, or of the *panes* in the fur *potent* (Plate IV., fig. 11). (Fig. 25.)

DOVETAILED (*mortaisé*), requires no explanation. (Fig. 26.)

URDY (*palissé*), is very rarely seen. In French blazon the pieces are taller, like palisades, and there is no indentation at the bottom. (Fig. 27.)

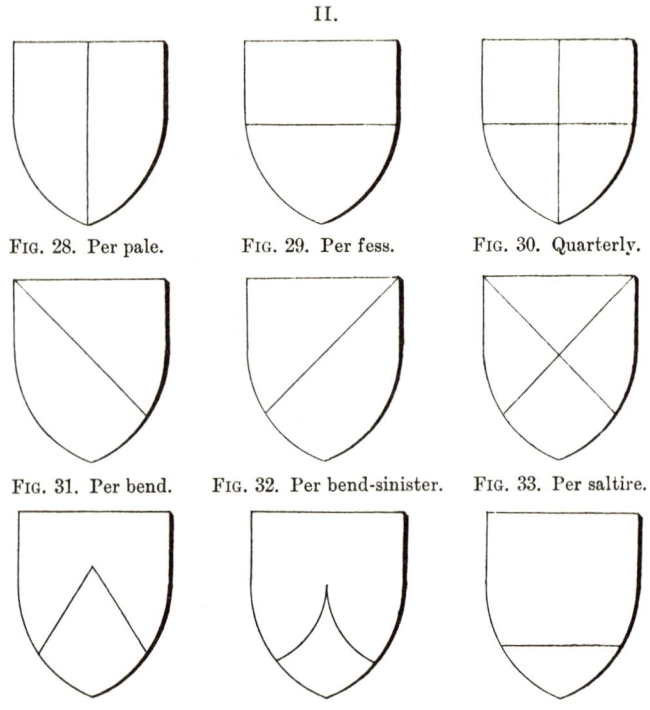

II.

FIG. 28. Per pale.   FIG. 29. Per fess.   FIG. 30. Quarterly.

FIG. 31. Per bend.   FIG. 32. Per bend-sinister.   FIG. 33. Per saltire.

FIG. 34. Per chevron.   FIG. 35. Enté en point.   FIG. 36. Champagne.

MODES OF PARTITION; OR DIVISIONS OF THE SHIELD.

THE MODES OF PARTITION.

The modes of partition fall next to be considered, and will be best understood by reference to the examples given. These are taken by preference from the class of

the term *échancré* to denote a larger form of engrailure consisting of only three or four concave indentations.) (Fig. 17.)

EMBATTLED ; having the form of rectangular embattlements. For this term the French have two equivalents ; *crénelé* and *bretessé*. *Crénelé* is used when the upper, *bretessé* when the lower, edge of an ordinary is embattled. (Fig. 18.)

INDENTED (*dentelé, danché, denché,* or *endenté*) with regular indentations like the teeth of a saw. (Fig. 19.) Some French Armorists, such as PALLIOT, make the teeth shorter and smaller for *dentelé* than for *endenté*, in which they are longer and more acute. There is really no such distinction practically employed in modern blazons.

INVECKED (*cannelé*) is the converse of *engrailed*, the only difference being that the convex part of the indentation is turned outwards. (Fig. 20.)

WAVY, UNDY ; (*ondé*) formed by a wavy line. (Fig. 21.)

NEBULY (*nebulée* or *nuagé*). The wavy conventional representation of clouds. (The old *nebuly* was like the second line of No. 5. In French this is known as *enté*.) (Fig. 22.)

DANCETTY (*vivré*). This is similar in character to *indented*, but there is a real distinction between them as the teeth in *dancetty* are much broader, much less acute, and are usually not more than three in number. BOUTELL (in his *Heraldry, Historical and Popular*, p. 80), indeed says : "*Dancettée*:—deeply indented," but this definition is not in accord with his cut on p. 18. (Fig. 23.)

RAGULY (*écoté*), with inclined battlements or crenelures ; now regular in form but originally suggestive of the trunk of a tree from which the branches had been lopped off. (Fig. 24.)

(*see* p. 116). The straight line is of course that most commonly employed, but of the other forms of line, *engrailed*, *indented*, and *wavy*, are the most in use, as well as the oldest; the others, the last four of which are seldom seen, belong to the later developments of armory. (*See* the Glossary of English Terms, *infra*.)

I.

ENGRAILED.	Fig. 17.	
EMBATTLED.	Fig. 18.	
INDENTED.	Fig. 19.	
INVECKED.	Fig. 20.	
WAVY, or UNDY.	Fig. 21.	
NEBULY.	Fig. 22.	
DANCETTY.	Fig. 23.	
RAGULY.	Fig. 24.	
POTENTÉ.	Fig. 25.	
DOVETAILED.	Fig. 26.	
URDY.	Fig. 27.	

PARTITION LINES.

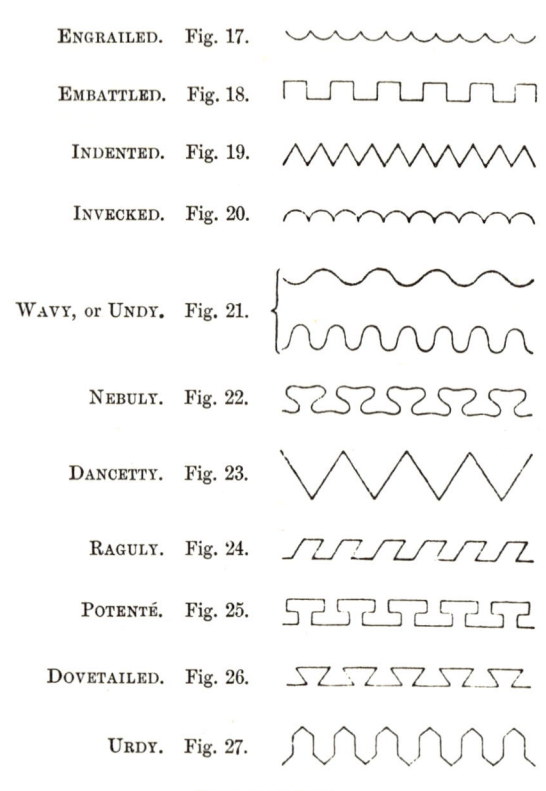

PARTITION LINES.

ENGRAILED (*engrêlé*); this line is formed by a row of small semi-circles, or concave indentations, the points being turned outwards. (The French use

of STÖRCK VON PLANCKENBERG in Styria is, *Fur au naturel, a pale gules*. This is almost *papelonné* in appearance. The Franconian family of JARSDORFF bears: *Quarterly*, 1 and 4, *Fur au naturel* in the form of scales (vair-shaped pieces); and 2 and 3, *gules plain*. *Vert, an ox skin stretched out, paleways proper* is the coat of DE LA NAYE of Liège; and SCHEURLER of the Hague bears *Gules*, a similar skin *or* (sometimes, but mistakenly, blazoned an *escucheon or*).

Furs are common in the Armory of England, Normandy, and naturally in Brittany, *Ermine plain* being the arms of the ancient Sovereigns of that land. Contrary to ordinary expectation the furs are not used with any frequency in the arms of the more northern nations of Europe; on the contrary, they are there seldom met with. For example, I do not remember a single instance in the Heraldry of Poland, while on the other hand they are frequently found in the blazons of Spain and Italy.

PARTED COATS, ETC.

Having now seen what colours and furs are employed in Armory, the next matter which requires our consideration is the division of the shield by partition lines. Under the subject of the division of a field by partition lines there falls to be considered:—

1. *The Species of Partition Line;* which is either (*a*) straight; or (*b*) composed of curves, or indentations.
2. *The Mode of Partition, i.e.*, the various directions in which the field is divided by these partition lines. The chief forms of these lines whose names form part of the technicology of Heraldry are shown in the accompanying cut, and it will be shown later by examples (Chap. IV.) that these lines have a further use as the boundaries of the class of charges which are known as the Ordinaries

about way of saying *Or, a bend argent, bordered and papelonné sable.*

The ALBERICI of Bologna bear: *Papelonné of seven rows, four of argent, three of or;* but the ALBERGHI of the same city, *Papelonné of six rows, three of argent, as many of gules.* The connection with *vairé* is much clearer in the latter than in the former. CAMBI (called FIGLIAMBUCHI), at Florence, carried *d'Argent, papelonné de gueules;* MONTI of Florence and Sicily, and RONQUEROLLES of France the reverse.

No one who is familiar with the licence given to themselves by armorial painters and sculptors in Italy, who were often quite ignorant of the meaning of the blazons they depicted, will doubt for a moment the statement that *Papelonné* is simply ill drawn *Vair.*

The seal of MICHAEL DE CANTELU, *circa* 1200, is an ancient example in which *Vair* is represented in the manner now known as *Papelonné.* (ELLIS, *Antiquities of Heraldry,* plate xvii. from *Archæologia Cantiana,* vi., 216.)

Besides the conventional representations of the fur of animals, their actual fur, or skin, is occasionally found represented in the wide range of Continental Armory, though such examples are of the greatest rarity.

One of the most interesting of these examples is afforded by the Arms of BREGENZ. In the fourteenth century MS. the *Wappenrolle von Zürich,* No. 127, the coat is evidently *Vair, a pale ermine,* both being *au naturel;* but in a modern German blazon of the Austrian arms it is said that the quarter "enthält im blauen, mit einem goldenen Gilter bedeckten Felde einen Pfahl von Hermelin mit drei übereinander stehenden schwarzen Hermelinflammen—wegen der Graffschaft Bregenz." (SCHMIDT, *Die Wappen aller Fürsten und Staaten,* 1869.) This writer was evidently ignorant of the fact that the whole bearings are of fur.

In SIEBMACHER'S *Wappenbuch,* ii., plate 44, the Coat

In *Plumeté* the field is apparently covered with feathers. *Plumeté d'argent et d'azur*, is the coat of CEBA (note that these are the tinctures of *Vair*). SOLDONIERI of Udine, *Plumeté au naturel* (but the SOLDONIERI of Florence bore: *Vairé argent and sable* with *a bordure chequy or and azure*), TENREMONDE of Brabant: *Plumeté or and sable*. (Plate VIII., fig. 7.) In the arms of the SCALTENIGHI of Padua; the BENZONI of Milan; the GIOLFINI, CATANEI, and NUVOLONI of Verona, each feather of the *plumeté* is said to be charged with an ermine spot sable.

The bearing *Papelonné* is more frequently found; and I have collected a good many French and Italian examples, of which a few are here blazoned.

In it the field is covered with what appear to be scales; the heraldic term *papelonné* is derived from a supposed resemblance of these scales to the wings of butterflies. Plate VIII., fig. 6 is the coat of MONTI, *Gules, papelonné argent*.

DONZEL at Besançon bears: *Papelonné d'or et de sable*. (It is worthy of note that DONZÉ of Lorraine used: *Gules, three bars wavy or*. The two families, in fact, both bore variations of *Vair*, or *Vairé*.) The FRANCONIS of Lausanne are said to bear *de Gueules papelonné d'argent*, and on *a chief of the last a rose of the first*, but the coat is otherwise blazoned: *Vairé gules and or*, etc. The coat of ARQUINVILLIERS, or HARGENVILLERS, in Picardy is *d'Hermine papelonné de gueules* (not being understood, this has been blazoned "*semé of caltraps*"). So also the coat of CHEMILLÉ appears in French books of Blazon indifferently as: *d'Or papelonné de gueules;* and *d'Or semé de chaussetrapes de gueules*. GUÉTTEVILLE DE GUÉNONVILLE is said to bear: *d'Argent semé de chaussetrapes de sable*, which I believe to be simply *d'Argent papelonné de sable*). The BARISONI of Padua bear: *Or, a bend of scales, bendways argent, on each scale an ermine spot sable, the bend bordered sable;* this is only a round-

1297, the arms of No. 8, ROBERT DE BRUIS, Baron of Brecknock, are: *Barry of six, Vairé ermine and gules, and azure.* Here the *vair* is *potent;* so is it also in No. 19, where the coat of INGELRAM DE GHISNES, or GYNES, is: *Gules, a chief vair.* The same coat is thus drawn in the *Second Nobility Roll,* 1299, No. 57.

POTENT (-counter-potent) does not occur with great frequency in modern British Armory. Like its original *Vair,* it is always of *argent* and *azure,* unless other tinctures are specified in the blazon. (The true counter-potent, if ever used, is drawn as in Plate IV., fig. 12.)

A considerable number of British and foreign families bear *Vair* only; such are VARANO, Dukes de CAMERINO; VAIRE, and VAIRIÈRE, in France; VERET, in Switzerland; GOUVIS, FRESNAY (Brittany); DE VERA, in Spain; LOHEAC (Brittany); VARENCHON (Savoy); SOLDANI-ERI (Florence). *Counter vair* is borne by LOFFREDO of Naples; by BOUCHAGE, DU PLESSIS ANGERS, and BROTIN, of France. HELLEMMES of Tourney uses: *de Contre vair, à la cotice de gueules brochante sur le tout.*

When the panes of vair are not of argent and azure but of different tinctures the fur is known as *Verry, vairy,* or *vairé* of such colours, as in the arms of DE BEAUFFREMONT, and MIGNIANELLI, given above, p. 70. Plate IV., fig. 13, *Vairé Or and gules* is the canting coat in England of FERRERS, Earls of Derby; and by connection with them, *Vairé gules and ermine* was borne by GRESLEY; and *Vairé argent and sable* by MEYNELL. Abroad: *Vairy or and azure* was the coat of the Counts of GUINES; of BONNIÈRES, Ducs de GUINES; of ROCHEFORT (*Salle des Croisés*). *Vairé d'argent et de pourpre* is borne by GRUTEL; *Vairé d'or et de sable* by DE LA JARDINE of Provence.

Two curious forms of *Vair* occasionally met with in Italian or French coats are known as "*Plumeté*" and "*Papelonné.*"

BELSCHES and BELCHER use *Vair* as part of their arms (*Paly of six or and gules, a chief vair*). The great family of the Ducs de BEAUFFREMONT in France use *Vairé d'or et de gueules* for a like reason. When the *Vair* is so arranged that in two horizontal rows taken together, either the points or the bases of two panes of the same tincture are in apposition, the fur is known as COUNTER VAIR (*Contre Vair*), Plate IV., fig. 8. Another variation, but an infrequent one, is known as VAIR IN PALE (*Vair appointé*, or *Vair en pal*; but if of other colours than the usual ones *Vairé en pal*). In this all panes of the same colour are arranged in vertical, or palar, rows (Plate IV., fig. 9). VAIR IN BEND (or in bend-sinister) is occasionally met with in foreign coats; thus MIGNIANELLI in Italy bears: *Vairé d'or et d'azur en bande;* while *Vairé en barre* (that is, in bend sinister) *d'or et de sable* is the coat of PICHON of Geneva.

POTENT, and its less common variant COUNTER POTENT, are usually ranked in British Heraldic works as separate furs. This has arisen from the writers being ignorant that in early times *Vair* was frequently depicted in the form now known as *Potent*. (By many heraldic writers *Potent* is styled *Potent-counter-potent;* but in my opinion tautologically. When drawn in the ordinary way, as in Plate IV., fig. 11, *Potent* alone suffices.) An example of *Vair* in the form now known as *Potent* (or, as above, *Potent-counter-potent*) is afforded by the seal of JEANNE DE FLANDRE, wife of ENGUERRAND IV. DE COUCY; here the well-known arms of COUCY, *Barry of six vair and gules*, are depicted as if the bars of vair were composed of a row of *potent*. (VRÉE, *Généalogie des Comtes de Flandre*, plate 112.) In the *Roll of Arms of the time of* EDWARD I. the *Vair* resembles *Potent* (-counter-potent), which Dr PERCEVAL erroneously terms an "invention of later date." (See *Archæologia*, xxxix., p. 390.) In the *First Nobility Roll* of the year

cups, or panes, of argent and azure, arranged in horizontal rows (as in Plate IV., fig. 7). In early Heraldry the panes were formed by undulating lines, as in Plate IV., fig. 6, and *Vair* is usually thus represented in our early *Rolls of Arms*. (It is usual to describe this form as *Vair ancient*. The *Vair* in the *Wappenrolle von Zürich* of the fourteenth century, is thus drawn.) This form is still occasionally met with in foreign Heraldry, where it is blazoned as *Vair ondé* or *Vair ancien*. The family of MARGENS in Spain bears: *Vair ondé, on a bend gules three griffons or ;* and TARRAGONE of Spain : *Vairé ondé, or and gules.*

In modern times the white panes are generally depicted as of silver, not of white fur. The verbal blazon nearly always commences with the metal, but in the arrangement of the panes there is a difference between French and English usage. In the former the white panes are generally (and I think more correctly) represented as forming the first, or upper, line ; in British Heraldry the reverse is the case. The *Vair* of Heraldry, as of commerce, was formerly of three sizes, and the distinction is continued in foreign armory. The middle, or ordinary size, is known as *Vair ;* a smaller size as *Menu-vair* (whence our word miniver) ; the largest as *Beffroi*, a term derived from the bell-shaped cups, or panes. In French Armory, *Beffroi* should consist of three horizontal rows ; *Vair*, of four ; *Menu-vair*, of six ; this rule is not strictly observed, but in French blazon if the rows are more than four it is usual to specify the number ; thus VARROUX bears, *de Vair de cinq traits*. *Menu-vair* is still the blazon of some families ; BANVILLE DE TRUTEMNE bears : *de Menu-vair de six tires ;* the Barons van HOUTHEM bore : *de Menu-vair, au franc quartier de gueules chargé de trois maillets d'or.*

In British Armory *Vair* is only of one size, but from the bell-shaped cups or panes the English families of

Besides the two furs ermine and vair, and their variations, we may notice that not only is the ermine spot, or tail, used as an independent charge, either alone or in specified numbers, but that in Foreign Heraldry it is also used of various tinctures, and on various fields.

ERMINE *plain* (*d'Hermine*) is not, I think, the coat of any family of Great Britain or Ireland. It was borne on the Continent by the Dukes of BRITTANY, and by the families of BOURGHIELLES, LE BRET, COIGNE, GUILLAND, PIERREFORT, ST. MARTIN, QUINSON, etc.

Ermines plain (*Contre-hermine*) is borne in France by LAVAL, ROUX, MAUBLANC, and ROUSSELET.

Of the use of *Erminois* (*d'Or semé de mouchetures d'hermine de sable*), without a charge, I only remember one instance, that of VANDER EZE of Guelders.

Other variations are :—

Gules, semé of ermine spots or, the arms of VAN LEEFVELT.

Gules, semé of ermine spots argent, with a fleur de lis of the same, are those of BEUVILLE.

Azure, semé of ermine spots or, over all a lion argent, is the coat of SCHLEIDEN, in Prussia. LE RÉVÉREND DU MESNIL bears *Ecartelé*, aux 1 and 4 ; *de Sinople, à trois mouchetures d'hermine d'or;* au 2 and 3 ; *de Gueules.* (*Vert, three ermine spots or; quartering Gules plain.*)

Ermine spots are not unfrequently borne as distinct charges, thus :—

Argent, a single spot of ermine (*d'Argent, à une moucheture d'hermine*) is borne by the families of BŒUVRES, BOIS, CHAI, DRUAYS, etc.

Argent, three ermine spots sable, by FIRMAS, BARTELLE-LA MOIGNON, and the Barons DUROY ; *d'Argent, au chevron d'azur, accompagné de trois mouchetures d'hermine de sable,* are the arms of COLLONGUE.

Gules, six ermine spots or, is the coat of BAYSSE.

VAIR is usually represented as composed of alternate

There is another use of a plain red shield which must not be omitted. In the full quartered coat of some high sovereign princes of Germany—SAXONY (duchies), BRANDENBURG (PRUSSIA), BAVARIA, ANHALT—appears a plain red quartering ; this is known as the *Blut Fahne*, or *Regalien* quarter, and is indicative of royal prerogatives. It usually occupies the base of the shield, and is often diapered.

The sombre *Sable* shield (*de Sable plein*) is borne, not only by the "unknown knight" of the mediæval tales of chivalry, but by the families of DESGABETS D'OMBALE, and by a branch of the Norman and English house of GOURNAY.

The French families of BARBOTTE, PUPELLIN, and TRIBLE, all bear *de Sinople plein ;* and even the comparatively rarely used tincture *Purpure* is also the plain coat of the French AUBERTS.

I venture to affirm that there is no subject on which so many books have been published with so little original research as Heraldry ; and I may be allowed to express a hope that the list above given, which is much more complete than any which has appeared in preceding Heraldic treatises, and which (with other portions of this book) will hardly escape the hands of future freebooting "compilers," may be useful as saving them from writing nonsense as to coats of a single metal or colour being "almost unknown." If to the forty, or thereby, coats of plain metal or colour given above there be added the many coats in which a single fur (*ermine* or *vair*, with their variations) is the sole charge, there will be I dare to say at least a hundred examples of a use, which is certainly curious and infrequent, but which is not of such extreme rarity as is often ignorantly asserted. A parallel, but even worse case, is that of "*armes fausses*," metal on metal, and colour on colour (*see* Appendix, *infra*).

bearing of the shield. A plain golden coat (*d'Or plein*) is borne in France by the families of BISE, BORDEAUX, DE PUY-PAULIN, and PAERNON ; in Spain by MENESEZ of Andalucia ; in Germany and Switzerland by BOSSENSTEIN (if we may credit SIEBMACHER, *Wappenbuch*, iii. 118 ; *Or, an eagle displayed gules*, being the more usual coat); and by VON LAHR of Rhenish Prussia. It is also the coat of the Italian family of BANDINELLI, to which Pope ALEXANDER III. belonged. In this case (as upon his monument in the church of St. John Lateran at Rome) I have noticed that the plain gold field is diapered. Other coats hereafter blazoned were similarly treated. (*See Diaper*, pp. 114, 115.)

D'Argent plein :—The plain silver shield which we have been accustomed to think of as an *écu d'attente*, borne by the youthful esquire who had as yet performed no deeds of valour entitling him to the knightly rank and emblazoned shield, turns out to be the ordinary bearing of the French families of MAIGRET, or MEGRET ; of BOCQUET, or BOQUET ; of PELLEZAY ; and of the Polish ZGRAIA.

The plain coat of *Azure* (*d'Azur plein*) is attributed to BERINGTON of Chester, in HARL. MS., 1535 ; to DE LA BARGE DE VILLE, in Lorraine ; to FIZEAUX of France and Holland ; to the Swiss family of MAIENTHAL ; and to the CONTRIZAKIS of Greece.

Plain *Gules* (*de Gueules plein*) occurs more frequently ; it is the well-known coat of the house of D'ALBRET, of the Kings of NAVARRE ; and of the Ducs de NARBONNE. It was borne as a canting coat by BONVINO, and by the Florentine ROSSI, and RUBEI; by the French SARRANTE ; DU VIVIER DE LANSAC ; and the MARCHANDS of Liège. The FORTUNATI of Trieste (possibly as a canting reminiscence of "*rouge et noir*"?), and the German Counts von HERTENSTEIN, XIMENEZ in Spain, and CZERWNIA of Poland, all bore *de Gueules plein*.

needful to give here the respective synonyms of the different metals and colours.

Tinctures.	Princes.	Peers.
Or.	Sol.	Topaz.
Argent.	Luna.	Pearl.
Gules.	Mars.	Ruby.
Azure.	Jupiter.	Sapphire.
Sable.	Saturn.	Diamond.
Vert.	Venus.	Emerald.
Purpure.	Mercury.	Amethyst.
Sanguine.	Dragon's head.	Jacinth.
Tenné.	Dragon's tail.	Sardonyx.

It has been said generally that a coat of arms consists of a charge or charges, placed upon a field; but while this is the general rule there are numerous exceptions; there are coats which consist only of a field; a single metal, tincture, or fur being alone employed. These are comparatively rarely met with, though in foreign Heraldry their frequency has been much underrated by previous writers; and there is a very large number of coats, both at home and abroad, in which, while the field is divided by partition lines into surfaces of two or more colours, there is nothing which can technically be called a charge. Many of these simple coats are of great antiquity.

FIELDS OF A SINGLE METAL, TINCTURE, OR FUR.

I have been able, in the course of a good many years' study, to collect examples in which each of the heraldic tinctures, furs, and metals has been used as the sole

giving very imperfect information regarding the coat which they were designed to represent; and in the seventeenth century it first occurred to heralds that by an arrangement of lines and points, it might be possible, even without the use of colour, to indicate heraldic tinctures in sculpture or engraving.

The first system of this kind appears to have been that of FRANCQUART, in Belgium, c. 1623. It was succeeded by those of BUTKENS, 1626; PETRA SANCTA, 1638; LOBKOWITZ, 1639; GELENIUS; and DE ROUCK, 1645; but all these systems differed from each other, and were for a time the cause of confusion, and not of order. Eventually, however, the system of PETRA SANCTA (the author of *Tesseræ Gentilitiæ*) superseded all the others, and has remained in use up to the present time.

By it, *Or* is represented in engravings by dots; *argent* is left plain; *gules* is denoted by perpendicular; *azure* by horizontal lines; *sable* by the conjunction of both. *Vert* is indicated by diagonal lines from the dexter to the sinister; *purpure* by diagonal lines from the sinister to the dexter.

By the side of each metal and colour in Plate III. is placed its representation by lines and points.

Another device for indicating the tinctures in engravings and sketches was that called "tricking;" in it letters and abbreviations were used to mark the tinctures, and a numeral the repetition of a charge.

The arms in SIEBMACHER'S *Wappenbuch*, Nürnberg (1st edition in 1605, later edition 1734), are thus tricked, as are those in MAGNENEY'S *Recueil des Armes*, Paris, 1633.

One of the absurd pedantries affected by English armorialists was the substitution of planets for the ordinary names of the tinctures in the blazons of Sovereign Princes; and of precious stones in those of peers. As this mode of blazoning, though now happily discarded, was adhered to by writers as late in date as GUILLIM, it is

assigned to them by various heralds, on the ground that the tinctures of the arms of the Sovereign must be the most honourable. According to this reasoning *azure* would hold the first place in France, and *gules* in England.

The only furs in use in the early days of heraldry were *ermine* and *vair*. The former, of white with black spots of special shape, was supposed to represent the white skin and the black tail of the animal so called. *Ermine* is often thus represented, as was originally always the case, by a white field with black spots. But in the middle ages the field was often of silver (*argent*). The *ermine* on the "*Stall plates*" of the Knights of the Garter in St. George's Chapel at Windsor, has the field of silver, not of white. (*See* Mr HOPE'S paper on these " *Stall plates*," read before the Society of Antiquaries of London, *Archæologia*, vol. li.) *Vair* is said to represent the fur of a species of squirrel, much used for lining cloaks and mantles according to the sumptuary laws of olden times. As the number of coats of arms increased several varieties of these furs were introduced. *Ermines, Erminois*, and *Pean*, are really only variations of *ermine ;* and have no more right to be separately enumerated as furs than have the varieties of *ermine* and *vair* hereafter to be noticed. A black fur with white spots, the reverse of *ermine*, is known as *ermines* (in French, *contre-hermine*). In *erminois* the fur is gold colour with black spots, or tails ; *Pean* is the reverse, black with gold spots. These latter are not known by a special name in foreign heraldry, but the field is said to be of such or such a colour *semé d'hermines*. Thus, *erminois* would be in French blazon ;— *d'Or, semé d'hermines de sable ; Pean* would be *de Sable, semé d'hermines d'or*. Other variations are noted further on in this Chapter ; and *see* Plate IV.

Drawings, engravings, and sculptures in which colour was unattainable, laboured under the disadvantage of

PLATE IV.

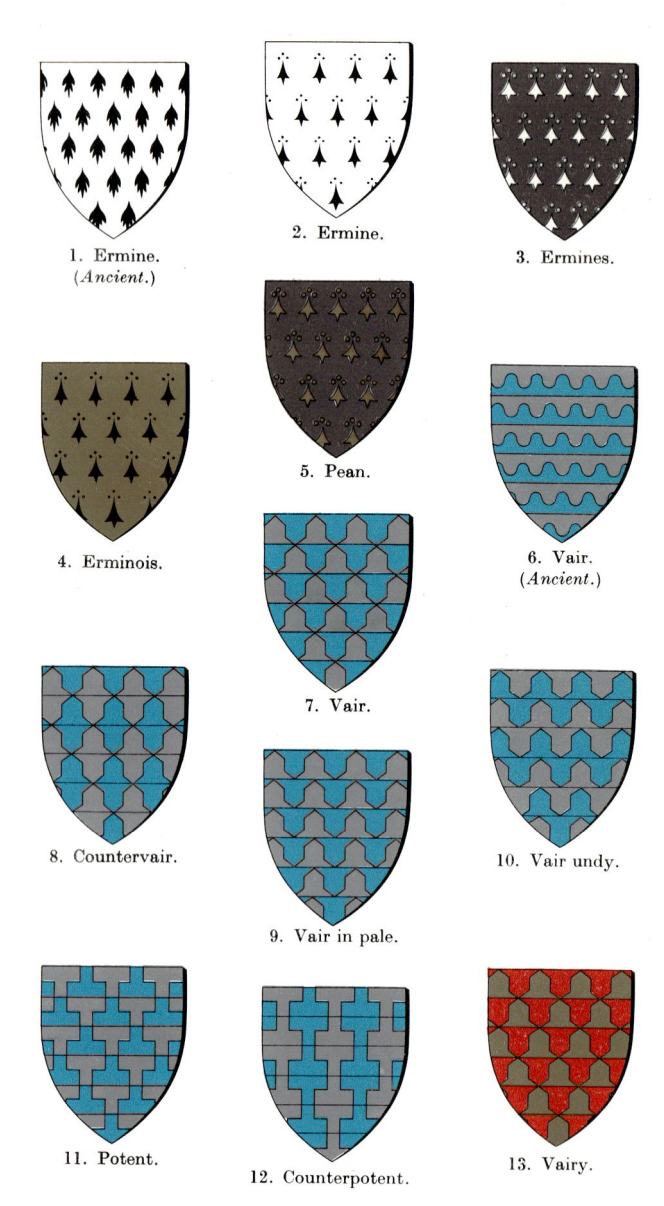

1. Ermine. (*Ancient.*)
2. Ermine.
3. Ermines.
4. Erminois.
5. Pean.
6. Vair. (*Ancient.*)
7. Vair.
8. Countervair.
9. Vair in pale.
10. Vair undy.
11. Potent.
12. Counterpotent.
13. Vairy.

which the blazon is too lengthy for insertion in this place) which was granted to a Bohemian knight in 1701.

The use of the term "*proper*" of course covers every shade which can be found in an artist's palette; it is indicated in German *hachures* by indented lines in the direction of *purpure;* but *Eisen-farbe* seems to have an independent existence in some modern coats.

Carnation is the technical French term for the colour of naked flesh, and is often employed in blazon.

Of the regular tinctures *purpure* is much less used in British Armory than any other. In France it was disputed as to whether it was a separate tincture at all. The lion of LEON is often blazoned *purpure*, but was not intended to be of a tincture distinct from *gules*. (*See* my paper in *Notes and Queries*, iii. series, vol. i. p. 471; and another in the *Genealogist*, vol. v., p. 49, on "The Heraldry of Spain and Portugal.")

The old armorists covered their ignorance of the history of the subject on which they wrote, and filled their treatises, by assigning to each metal and colour special attributes, not only when these were used alone, but varying according to their combinations with others. Into these absurdities we need not enter; they were quite incompatible with the long prevalent system of differencing the coats of members of the same family by change of tincture; and as a matter of fact at no time, and in no country, were the moral qualities of the bearer indicated by the tinctures or charges of the shield. Tinctures which were supposed appropriate to represent the moral qualities of one member of a family would obviously often have been quite inappropriate to indicate those of his brothers, or of his sons. Still, an idea prevails that one colour or metal is more honourable than another, as gold is a more precious metal than silver; and the colours have usually been ranked in the order in which they are here placed. *Gules* and *azure* have each the first place

notice will be found under that word. Practically these abatements ("*Sottises anglaises*" is the severe, but not unjust estimate of the learned French writer on blazon, le Père MENÊTRIER) were never in use, and the colours were, therefore, not needed. There is, however, in the Lyon Register, one instance only of the use of *sanguine* as the tincture employed in an honourable coat. The arms of the family of CLAYHILLS of Invergowrie, are :— *Per bend sanguine and vert, two greyhounds courant bendways argent.* I have also met with a few foreign instances of the use of *tenné*; the Prussian Counts of BOSE bear as their first quarter, *Azure, a Latin cross patée alésée tenny.*

Besides the metals, tinctures, and furs which have been already described, other tinctures are occasionally found in the Heraldry of Continental nations; but are comparatively of such rarity as that they may be counted among the curiosities of Blazon; which would require a separate volume. That of which I have collected most instances is *Cendrée*, or ash colour; which is borne by (among others) the Bavarian family of ASCHAU as its *armes parlantes:—Cendrée, a mount of three coupeaux in base, or.*

Brunâtre, a brown colour, is even more rare as a tincture of the field; the MIEROSZEWSKY in Silesia, bear, *de Brunâtre, a cross patée argent supporting a raven rising sable, and holding in its beak a horse-shoe proper, its points towards the chief.*

Bleu-céleste, or *bleu du ciel*, appears occasionally, apart from what we may term "landscape coats." That it differs from, and is a much lighter colour than, azure is shown by the following example. The Florentine CINTI (now CINI), bear a coat which would be numbered among the *armes fausses*, or *à enquérir:—Per pale azure and bleu-celeste an estoile counter changed.*

Amaranth, or *Columbine*, is the field of a coat (of

PLATE III.

1. Or.

2. Argent.

3. Gules.

4. Azure.

5. Sable.

6. Vert.

7. Purpure.

8. Tenny.

9. Sanguine.

the chief of the shield; H C I, its base; D F H the dexter flank; E G I, the sinister flank; and in each case the centre letter marks the "point" of that particular region.

TINCTURES.

Armorial insignia consist for the most part of one or more objects called "charges," depicted on a *field, i.e.* the escutcheon which represents the knightly shield, and whose points have been already explained. One coat of arms differs from another, not by the differences of the charges only, but by differences of colour; or, more correctly speaking, of tincture, both in the charges and in the field. The field may be of one, or of more than one tincture, divided by the partition lines hereafter to be explained, which are represented on page 75. The tinctures used in British Heraldry are nine in number; and comprise two metals, five colours, and two furs. Of these furs there are several variations to be noted presently.

The metals are *Or*, that is gold, Plate III., fig. 1; and *Argent*, that is silver, fig. 2; in painting these are often represented by the colours yellow and white; but they are more properly represented by the actual metals.

The colours are red, known as *gules;* blue, known as *azure;* black, as *sable;* green, as *vert;* purple, as *purpure.* The French equivalents are, *d'azur, de gueules, de sable, de sinople, de purpure.*

Besides these are two other colours mentioned in old heraldic treatises—orange, known as *tenny* or *tenné*, and blood colour, termed *sanguine.* These last occur so rarely in British Heraldry as to be scarcely worthy of enumeration with the other five. They were intended by the old heralds to be used in the system of "abatements" which they had invented, and of which some

SYLVANUS MORGAN derives it from EVE'S spindle; just as, according to his fancy, the tasteless form of the shield affected in his time was a reminiscence of ADAM'S spade!

POINTS OF THE ESCUCHEON.

To facilitate the description, or, as it is technically called,

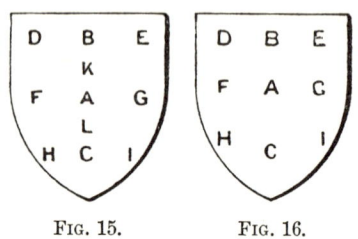

FIG. 15.   FIG. 16.

"blazoning" of arms, the surface or "field" of the escucheon has been mapped out into nine, or sometimes (and more conveniently), into eleven points, represented in the woodcuts above, each point being known by its special name.

	ENGLISH.	FRENCH.
A.	Fess point,	le centre (abîme); "en cœur."
B.	Middle chief,	le point du chef.
C.	Middle base,	la pointe de l'écu.
D.	Dexter chief,	le canton dextre du chef.
E.	Sinister chief,	le canton sénestre du chef.
F.	Dexter flank,	le flanc dextre.
G.	Sinister flank,	le flanc sénestre.
H.	Dexter base,	le canton dextre de la pointe.
I.	Sinister base,	le canton sénestre de la pointe.
K.	Honour point,	le point d'honneur.
L.	Nombril point	le nombril de l'écu.

It will be observed that the dexter and sinister sides of the shield are so called from their position in relation to the right or left side of the supposed bearer of the shield, and not to the eye of the spectator. D B E is

base, the quartered coat of HAINAULT and HOLLAND, without a pourfilar line. (These coats are blazoned in the chapter on MARSHALLING.) Two seals of ALFONZO of SPAIN in 1324, 1325, have the arms on an *écu en bannière*. The ancient but very inconvenient custom still prevails by which the arms of an unmarried lady, or a widow, are placed upon a lozenge-shaped shield. On the Continent, and especially for widows, this usage has many exceptions; and an oval shield, which obviates the mutilations so frequently necessitated by the adoption of the lozenge, is increasingly in use. The employment of the *Écu en lozange* goes back to the thirteenth century. An early instance is engraved by DEMAY (Fig. 283), it is of the date 1262, and in it ISABELLE DE SAINT VRAIN bears in a lozenge her arms, a double-headed eagle displayed. But in these early times, the lozenge was occasionally, if rarely, used by men also. PIERRE DE LA FAUCHE thus sealed in 1270; and JEAN, Comte d'ARMAGNAC, in 1369. In the last named year JEANNE DE BRETAGNE, wife of CHARLES DE BLOIS, thus bore her arms (DEMAY, *Le Costume d'après les Sceaux*, p. 229).

In VRÉE, *Généalogie des Comtes de Flandre*, plate 58, are engraved two seals of MARGARET, Countess of HAINAULT, HOLLAND, etc., wife of the Emperor LOUIS (of Bavaria), in which her arms are borne in a lozenge on the breast of the Imperial eagle (single-headed). The shield is not quartered according to modern usage, but bears four lions rampant, 1, 2, 1. The two in chief and base are the red lion of HOLLAND; the two in flanks, the black lion of FLANDERS. As in the coat of her granddaughter MARGUERITE DE BAVIÈRE, described above, there is no division of the quarters by a pourfilar line (these coats are referred to below in the Chapter on MARSHALLING). The lozenge has been used in Britain for unmarried ladies since the fourteenth century.

There are a few early examples of shields of circular shape. [*See* the seal of JEAN, Duc de BERRY, 1408, (Plate of Seals, No. 1, *infra*); and that of MARIE D'ANJOU, Queen of CHARLES VII.] A monumental slab at Chetwynd in Shropshire has a circular shield charged with arms, GOUGH, *Monuments*, vol. i., p. cviii. (quoted in BOUTELL, *Christian Monuments*, note on p. 74). The arms of Savoy were often borne on a circular escucheon on the breast of an eagle (*vide post*. Chap. VIII., p. 243-244). The *Écu en bannière*, a shield of a square shape, has from very early times been used by Knights Bannerets; and in France it is still employed by certain families, which descend from persons who have held the dignity of Chevaliers Bannerets. Thus the Poitevin family of BARLOT bear: *de Sable, à trois croix patées d'argent. L'écu en bannière.* The BEAUMANOIRS, Marquises de LAVARDIN, whose arms are: *d'Azur, à onze billettes d'argent*, 4, 3, 4; do the same. The arms of the ARCHAMBAULTS, who descend from the first House of BOURBON, are often borne *en bannière*, they are: *d'Or, au lion de gueules, accompagné de huit coquilles d'azur, rangées en orle.*

But in the fourteenth, and commencement of the fifteenth centuries the *écu en bannière* was not unfrequently used by great ladies. M. DEMAY, in his *Costume d'après les Sceaux*, engraves (Fig. 284) an instance; in it the arms of JEANNE, Dame de PLASNES, are impaled with those of her husband. In VRÉE, *Généalogie des Comtes de Flandre*, plate 60 contains the seal of MARGUERITE DE BAVIÈRE, wife of JEAN SANS-PEUR. She was the daughter of ALBERT DE BAVIÈRE, Count of HAINAULT, HOLLAND, etc., son of the Emperor LOUIS. On her seal the *écu en bannière* appears to be quarterly, but really it is impaled:—*Per pale:* 1. *Per fess,* (*a*) *in chief* BURGUNDY-modern; (*b*) *in base* BURGUNDY-ancient. 2. Also *Per fess;* (*a*) *in chief* BAVARIA; (*b*) *in*

of the Counts of Foix, Béarn, Toulouse, etc. (*See* DEMAY, *Le Costume, etc.*, p. 228.) An oval shield was also in use in southern countries, especially in Italy, where it is still greatly employed; and it is the form almost invariably used there, and elsewhere, for the Arms of Ecclesiastics. On the seals of ENGUERRAN DE COUCY, in 1380, and of OLIVIER DE CLISSON, Constable of France, in 1397, the oval shield has the notch *à bouche* which converts it into the *Écu en palette* (DEMAY, *Le Costume, etc.*, p. 230). The prevailing forms became more florid in the sixteenth century, particularly in Germany (*see* figs. 12, 13, and 14).

What may be called the "vair-shaped" shield was much in vogue in Britain in the eighteenth, and early part of the present century; as were other still more untasteful forms; but within the last fifty years there has been, along with a revived knowledge of, and taste for, Art, a reversion to the earlier and simpler types of the shield. The "heater-shaped" shield is now very generally employed for single coats; while for those which contain quarterings, or small charges, the shield with straight top and sides and ogee curves in base, which finds favour in France; or the Spanish shield (which is the same, except that the base is formed by a segment of a circle) are much used. (*See* p. 53, fig. 10.)

In Great Britain the Royal Arms are very generally represented (or misrepresented) in an oval, sometimes even in a circular shield. This has arisen from the circumstance that the shield is encircled by the Garter which forms the principal ensign of the Most Noble Order of that name. In imitation of this, oval shields, which are surrounded by the collars, or by garters or bands bearing the mottos of the Orders, are often, but without any necessity, employed by the Knights of the THISTLE, BATH, etc. (On the use of the oval shield abroad, *see* page 58.)

top and the sides, were beginning to lose something of their convexity, though the top angles were still rounded off. (*See* also the seal and *secretum* of ROBERT II., Comte de DREUX, *circa* 1202, in VRÉE, *Généalogie des Comtes de Flandre*, plate 7.) A little later the shield becomes slightly elongated, and all its lines flatter; the top line joins the side ones at a distinct angle, instead of being rounded off as formerly. Both types occur on the seal and the *secretum* of PIERRE DE DREUX, son of ROBERT II., and husband of ALICE, Duchess of BRETAGNE, *c.* 1212. On his seal the shield borne by the Count was of the elongated triangular shape; the heart-shaped shield appears on the *secretum*. (VRÉE, *Généalogie des Comtes de Flandre*, plate 8.)

To this type succeeded the regular "heater-shaped" shield; flat on the top, with the sides gently curved and meeting at a point, which prevailed in the thirteenth and fourteenth centuries. Later, especially after the introduction of the custom of quartering arms, there was an increasing tendency to give greater width to the base of the shield. About the middle of the fourteenth century we find the shield *penché* or *couché* (that is placed at an angle instead of being *droit*, or in a vertical position), and supporting on its upper angle the crested helm, with its mantling or lambrequins. In this form the shield was suspended above the pavilions at the tournaments. (*See* the Plates from the *Armorial de Geldre;* and the *Zürich Wappenrolle*.) Towards the end of the fifteenth century appeared such forms as those represented in Fig. 8, p. 53. This shield is said to be *à bouche*, and the notch at the angle was contrived as a rest for the lance of the wearer.

In southern countries, especially in Spain, the shield assumed a distinctly rounded shape in the base, which has been retained in the Peninsula to the present day, and of which examples are found in the mediæval seals

PLATE II.

EXPLANATION OF FIGURES.
1. 13th Century Maire de Soissons (*Demay*). 2. Adam de Hereford (*Morice*, XIV.). 3. From Champlevé enamel of Geoffrey Plantagenet, 1157, at Le Mans. 4. Abbey of St. Victor, Marseilles, 12th Century (*Demay*). 5. Robert d'Artois, 1237 (*Demay*).

against these was provided for by a shield of large dimensions, sufficient to cover the whole of the body. On the Bayeux Tapestry this appears of a kite-shaped form, but, as is evident from our plates, it was really curved round the warrior's body, and was adorned and strengthened by a metal border and intersecting bands, or by a boss with a projecting spike and floriations, which afterwards became the foundation of the heraldic charge known as the escarbuncle (Plates I. and II.). The latest instances of the use of this boss are probably afforded by the seals of RICHARD CŒUR DE LION; and of RICHARD DE VERNON, in 1195. (DEMAY, *Le Costume d'après les Sceaux*, p. 141.)

As the texture of the coat of mail became closer, and the pieces of which it was composed more continuous, its powers of resistance were greatly increased, and the large, heavy, cumbersome shield was no longer needed. Accordingly the shield, though still somewhat curved, and sufficiently large to protect the vital organs, underwent a considerable diminution in size, as well as a modification in shape (Plate II., fig. 5). Upon the early seals where the warrior is represented on horseback, bearing his shield, the curvature of the shield often prevents us from having a full view of the bearings depicted upon it; but on the counter-seal, or *secretum*, which contained only, or chiefly, the representation of the owner's shield of arms, this is represented flat, or with only a slight incurvation. The form given to it varied considerably at various times. On the earliest armorial seals the shield is of a heart shape, with round top and sides as in the seal of HENRY DE FERRIÈRES in 1205 (*cf.* the *secretum* of EUSTACIA DE CHÂTILLON, 1218; VRÉE, *Gen. Com. Fland.*, plate vi.; DEMAY, *Le Costume d'après les Sceaux*, fig. 205, 1205). The *secretum* of PHILIPPE DE MALDEGHEM in 1207 (VRÉE, *Généalogie des Comtes de Flandre*, plate 4), shows that the lines of the shield, both at the

Fig. 7.   Fig. 8.   Fig. 9.   Fig. 10.

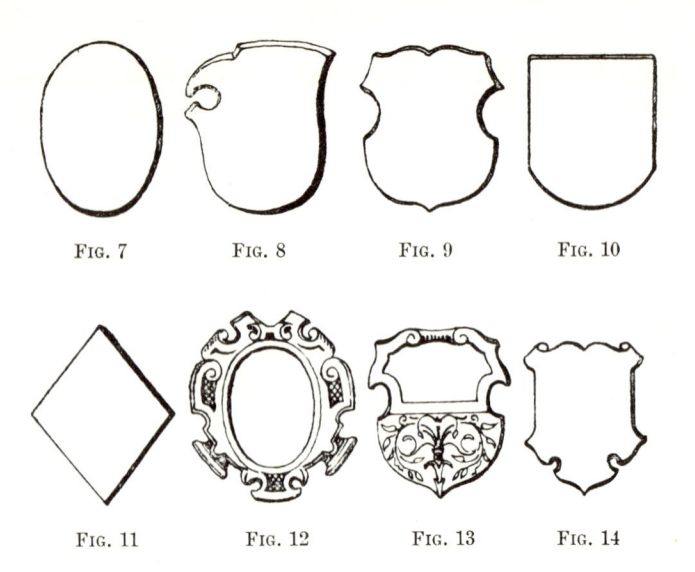

Fig. 11.   Fig. 12.   Fig. 13.   Fig. 14.

CHAPTER III.

As the primary use of Armorial Ensigns was to distinguish warriors by the devices on their shields, so when these bearings came to be depicted on seals, or monuments, or in *Rolls of Arms*, they continued to be represented upon a shield or escucheon. This varied in form at different times, following the modifications which took place in the equipment of the warrior; the size and shape of the shield being materially affected by the quality of the armour.

At the time of the Norman Conquest this was composed of links interlaced; or of scales, rings, and other small pieces of steel, sewn upon the linen or leather hauberk, which was usually quilted in diamond-shaped spaces. While this rude armour, which is depicted in the Bayeux Tapestry (*see* also Plate II., fig. 1), was usually sufficient to turn an arrow shot from a distance, it was utterly inadequate to resist the thrusts of a spear, or sword, at close quarters; and the defence of the warrior

fleurs de lis; AYMAR ALLEMAN, a griffon passant; ODO ALLEMAN, a single fleur de lis. GUI ALLEMAN in 1307 bore four fleurs de lis and a label. The branch of this family at Uriage bore an eagle, and that at Arbent in Bresse, a lion. Finally, SIBOUD ALLEMAN, Bishop of GRENOBLE, in the year 1455, having assembled in his Episcopal Palace all his relations of the name, to the number of twenty-three, they resolved that for the future all should bear exclusively the arms of the ALLEMANS of Vaubonnois, namely: *Gules fleury or, over all a cotice argent.* (MENÊTRIER, *De l'Origine des Armoiries et du Blason*, pp. 88, 89.) MENÊTRIER declares that he had himself seen the formal document drawn up on this occasion; and he adds, "Je pourrois alleguer cent autres exemples semblables de diverses maisons de Normandie, de Champagne, de Bourgogne, et des Pays Bas."

In our own country mutations of arms were by no means infrequent, as in the case of the FERRERS, Earls of DERBY; and a noble marrying a lady of higher position, or greater possessions, usually assumed her arms. (Further allusion to this will be found hereafter in the chapter on MARSHALLING.)

In Spain the introduction of Hereditary Arms does not appear to have been earlier than the commencement of the thirteenth century. In Italy the case was the same. JOVIUS, Bishop of NOCERA, in 1556, writes:—"Al tempo di Friderico Barbarossa vennero in uso l'insegne delle Famiglie, chiamate da noi 'Arme,' donate de principi, per merito dell' honorate imprese fatte in guerra, ad effeto di nobilitare i vallorosi Cavallieri, ne nacquero bizarrisime inventioni ne' cimieri et pitture ne gli scudi."

In Sweden the earliest known example of an armorial shield is of the year 1219. (*See* HILDEBRAND, *Det Svenska Riksvapnet;* in the *Antiqvarisk Tidskrift för Sverige;* 1883.) The shield is engraved on p. 326.

third *Azure, three garbs or* for CRAIGMYLE, were borne by the BURNETTS of Kemnay; and, with the difference of a mullet *sable* in the fess point of the quartered coat, by the late GEORGE BURNETT, LL.D., Lyon King of Arms, and joint author of the present work, a younger brother of BURNETT of Kemnay, in Aberdeenshire.

The seal of WILLIAM LINDSAY, Lord of ERCILDOUN and CRAWFORD, in 1170, is not armorial; that of SIMON of LINDSAY of the same date has an eagle displayed—the heraldic charge of the Norman family of the LIMESAYS—which in 1345 becomes the (single) heraldic supporter of the family arms (*Gu. a fess chequy arg. and az.*) upon the seal of Sir DAVID LINDSAY, Lord of CRAWFORD (LAING, *Scottish Seals*, i., Nos. 503, 504, 509, and ii., 629, 630. See also *Lives of the Lindsays*, vol. i., pp. 3-5 and 440).

BUTKENS in his *Trophées de Brabant* (Lib. 4., cap. 3), attributes the rise of Armorial bearings in the Low Countries to about the middle of the twelfth century. He says:—"Certes il nous seroit bien difficile de trouver quelles armoiries les Princes mesmes portoient en ce temps là,—puisque dans leurs Sceaux l'on ne trouve aucune marque ou Blason; et véritablement le port des armes n'est si ancien, n'y les armes si héréditaires, comme on les imagine maintenant, et ou ce qu'on peut juger des Sceaux, le Blason en nos quartiers n'a esté en usage que peu devant l'an MCLX."

Even in the thirteenth century arms had not become definitely hereditary. In 1223 AYMAR DE SASSENAGE bore a bend. In 1251 GUILLAUME DE SASSENAGE bore two swans accostés by two cotices fretty. In 1249 GUILLAUME, Seigneur de BEAUVOIR, bore Quarterly, and a cotice in bend; in 1279 a GUILLAUME DE BEAUVOIR (who MENÊTRIER thinks may have been the same person) bore a lion. EUDES ALLEMAN, Seigneur des CHAMPS, in 1265, bore a bend between six

DE ROSOY in 1201 bears three. (DEMAY, *loc. cit.*, pp. 193-194.)

A like process went on elsewhere; the seal of JOHN DE MUNDEGUMBRI of Eagleshame, about 1170, bears a single fleur de lis (LAING, *Scottish Seals*, i., No. 590); and three fleurs de lis became later the arms of the family of MONTGOMERY. The seal of WILLIAM DE INAYS, appended to the instrument of fealty by which certain Scottish magnates did homage to EDWARD I. in 1296, bears only a single six-pointed mullet, or star (heraldic bearings at that time not having become generally adopted in Scotland); in later times the INNES coat was charged with three mullets (*Ane Account of the Familie of Innes*. Spalding Club, 1864, page 56). Similarly, the seal of RICHARD FALCONER of Hawkerston, in 1170 bears a fleur de lis supporting two falcons (LAING, i. 323). In the same year the seals of ROBERT, PATRICK, and WALTER CORBET (*Ibid.*, i., 201-3) have corbies perched upon the branches of a tree; while, in 1292, GILBERT and WILLIAM CONNISBURGH have on their seals (*Ibid.*, i., 199-200) conies in the midst of foliage. In all these cases, as in many others, the device assumed in reference to the name became the foundation of the regular heraldic bearings of the family.

Mr STODART says (*Scottish Arms*, ii., 291):—" The seal of ODO BURNARD, attached to a charter relating to Arlesey, 1200, has a leaf, or perhaps a flower of seven leaves on a short stalk; another seal of the same person, a little later, has three leaves on a shield. The leaves have been called burnet (pimpernel) leaves, but all the Scottish blazons have holly. One leaf appears on the seal, 1252, of RICHARD BURNARD of Faringdon in Roxburghshire." Hence came the arms borne by the BURNETTS of Leys, etc.: *Argent three holly leaves in chief vert, and a hunting horn in base sable, garnished and stringed gules.* These arms, quartering in the second and

in 1180 and 1186 are represented as bearing the plain shield with its ornamented boss; but before 1197 HENRI II. had assumed the coticed bend. ROTROU III. Count of PERCHE, in 1190 uses no arms; but in 1197 his son GEOFFROI bears the shield with the three chevrons (DEMAY, *Le Costume*, etc., pp. 189-192). So also in Scotland the seal of ALAN STEWART in 1170 had apparently no arms upon the shield borne by his mounted effigies; but in 1190 the shield of the same ALAN bears for the first time the fess chequy (LAING, *Scottish Seals*, i., 772-773).

We need not however suppose, and M. DEMAY warns us against so doing, that "le blason fait son apparition dans les dernières années du douzième siècle, brusquement, sans transition." On the contrary he adduces some interesting examples of earlier date which enable us to see how the transition was effected. Passing by for the present the development of the fleur de lis in the arms of France, which will be referred to in another section, we may cite the following instances. On a seal of ENGUERRAN, Count de ST. POL, anterior to the year 1150, the mounted knight bears a long uncharged shield, but the base of the seal is *semé* with garbs. These garbs later became true heraldic charges; and, to the number of five, were the blazon of the family of the CANDAVÈNE, to which ENGUERRAN belonged. The seal of HELLIN DE WAVRIN, in 1177, bears an eagle volant holding a serpent in its claws; in 1193 the eagle displayed appears as the charge of the seal of ROBERT DE WAVRIN, Seneschal of Flanders. In 1195, the seal of ROGER DE MEULAN has a lion passant; two years later the lion, but rampant, is enclosed in a shield on the seal of JEAN DE MEULAN; and ROGER DE MEULAN is represented holding this escutcheon on his seal of 1204. JULIENNE, Dame de ROSOY, is represented in 1195 between two roses; in 1201 the roses have become heraldic, and the shield of ROGER

rencontre le lion pour la première fois dans le type de Philippe d'Alsace, en 1170. Le sceau de 1164" (an authentic seal, not the one referred to above) "du même comte, n'en fait pas mention.[1] On le chercherait en vain sur les sceaux des prédécesseurs de Philippe" (*Le Costume d'après les Sceaux*, p. 189, Paris, 1880). We have then here the first certainly authentic use of arms upon a seal towards the close of the twelfth century. Other seals which M. DEMAY adduces corroborate very strikingly the generally received idea that it was only after the middle of the twelfth century that regular armorial bearings came into general use. This evidence is here given in a condensed form. The seal of MATHIEU I. DE MONTMORENCY, in 1160, has no arms; that of MATHIEU II., in 1177, bears a shield with the older form of the Montmorency coat, a cross between four alerions. No arms are visible on the seal of CONON, Count of SOISSONS in 1172, but in 1178 and 1180 his shield bears a lion passant. MATHIEU II., Count of BEAMOUNT SUR OISE, in 1173 has no arms, but his successor MATHIEU III. in 1177 seals with a shield charged with a lion rampant. The COUCY seal in 1150 has no armorial bearings, but the well-known coat: *Barry of six vair and gules*, appears on the seal of 1190. The lion borne by the family of GARLANDE does not appear on the seal of GUI DE GARLAND in 1170, but is engraved on that used in 1192. In 1185 GERARD DE ST. AUBERT bears no arms; but in 1194 his buckler is charged with *Chevronny and a bordure*. On the seal of BALDWIN THE BRAVE, Count of HAINAULT, of the date of 1182, the well-known arms: *Chevronné of six, or and sable* do not appear, but they are represented on his counter-seal in 1282. The Counts of CHAMPAGNE

[1] On further consideration I think the matter is explicable otherwise, as I see M. DEMAY, fig. 92, ascribes the disputed seal of PHILIPPE D'ALSACE to about 1181.

was simply developed out of the constructional boss of the older shields. The seal of THIERRY II., Count of BAR and MONTBELIARD, appended to a deed dated 1093, is said to bear two barbel addorsed, as in the later arms. HUGH II., Duke of BURGUNDY, in 1102, bears on his seal a shield, Bendy of six within a bordure, the well known arms of Burgundy-ancient. RAOUL DE BEAUGENCY, a follower of GODFREY DE BOUILLON in the First Crusade, in a deed dated 1104, seals with a shield: Chequy and a fess. In the same year a seal of SIMON DE BROYES has a shield bearing the canting arms of the *broyes* which later formed part of the coat of JOINVILLE, or DE GENEVILLE. The seal of GUIRAND DE SIMIANE in 1113, and later, bears the ram which is the charge of the coat of that family.

The earliest seal of a Count of Flanders given by VRÉE, in his work *De Seghelen der Graven van Vlaendren*, which bears a shield charged with the lion of Flanders is that of Count ROBERT on plate 4, attached to a charter of 1072. But of this MABILLON has demonstrated the falsity; and on that ground, and not (as Mr ELLIS rather unworthily suspects) because it "conflicts with a cherished theory," Mr PLANCHÉ passes it over entirely in his *Heraldry Founded on Facts;* and says of the seal of PHILIP I. Count of FLANDERS in 1164 (?) that it is the earliest unquestionable example in the collection of UREDIUS (*i.e.* WREE, or VRÉE, as afore mentioned) on which the lion appears as a heraldic bearing. But I am pretty sure that Sir CHARLES MEYRICK also expressed a doubt as to the authenticity of this seal, not because the use of the arms "conflicts with a cherished theory," but on account of some peculiarities of the armour. I gather also that DEMAY, the great French authority on Sigillography, agrees with him, since he passes over this particular seal, and says :—"On

relief, which passes over the charges.[1] (See Mr. J. GOUGH NICHOLS'S valuable, and most interesting paper on this effigy in the *Herald and Genealogist*, vol. iii., pp. 97-112.)

EYSENBACH, in his *Histoire du Blason* gives a list of very early seals upon which armorial bearings appear, but which are, in my opinion, of very doubtful authenticity. To the contract of marriage of SANCHO, Infant of CASTILLE, with GUILLEL-MINE, daughter of CENTULUS GASTON II., Viscount of BEARN, of the year 1000, are appended seven seals of which two remain entire; one has a shield charged with a greyhound, the other has a shield bendy. The former is supposed to have been that used by GARCIA ARNAUD, Comte d'ANCE et de MAGUSAC, who lived at the time, and whose descendants bore a greyhound as their armorial charge. But I believe this whole document to be a fabrication of a much later date. A like doubt attaches to two seals of ADELBERT OF LORRAINE affixed to charters of the years 1030, 1037, which have on them shields charged with an eagle *au vol abaissé*. A charter of RAYMOND DE ST. GILLES, dated 1088, is said to bear a seal on which is the cross which formed the bearing of the Counts of TOULOUSE, and was called by their name, the cross *vidée, clechée, et pommettée* (*vide infra*, p. 161), and which I believe

[1] Similarly the seal of EON DE PONTCHASTEAU in 1200, is charged with three crescents and a chief, over all the floriated boss. Even as late as 1231 the seal of EON *fils le comte* has a shield with an escarbuncle which is evidently constructional. (*See* MORICE, *Mémoires pour servir de Preuves à l'Histoire Ecclésiastique et Civile de Bretagne*, Paris 1742, tome i., seals xxviii., xxi.) From the same work are taken the shields engraved on Plate I., fig. 5, of ROBERT DE VITRÉ, 1172, whose long *pavoise* has an escarbuncle of fourteen rays, and that of ADAM D'HEREFORD (Plate II., fig, 2) on which the shield has a boss, and is strengthened with a bordure, and bands in cross and saltire. The shield Plate I., fig. 11 is from DEMMIN, *Weapons of War*, page 174.

chapter of this work.) On these the effigy of the owner was represented as in life; clad in the armour of the period, with shield and sword or lance. Sometimes, indeed, as upon the seals of the early Counts of Flanders (*See* VRÉE, *de Seghelen*, plates 5, 6, 7), only the inside of the large curved shield is seen upon very early instances; but on the later seals the shield is so turned that if any armorial bearings had been depicted they would have been visible. When we remember that the very object of the adoption of armorial bearings was to distinguish the bearer in war from other persons, we may be quite sure that had the user of the seal possessed such armorial bearings, such clear indications of the personality of the proprietor would not have been omitted from the seal which authenticated his charters and formal documents. Let us then see what light comes to us from these contemporary witnesses. Some early shields are represented in Plate I., these bear no heraldic devices; the long curved oval shield is often strengthened by a border; by bands of metal nailed upon the wood; and, most frequently, by a metal floriated boss, the arms of which extended to the edges of the shield; and from which in later times some varieties of the Cross, and the heraldic charge known as the escarbuncle, may have been derived. That this latter was not originally a heraldic distinction may be proved *inter alia* by the fact that on the shield of GEOFFREY PLANTAGENET, alluded to in the preceding page, the floriated boss appears, irrespective of the rampant lions which formed his armorial bearings. (Plate II., fig. 3.)

So also on the recumbent effigy on the floor of the Temple Church so long, but erroneously, attributed to GEOFFREY DE MAGNAVILLE, Earl of ESSEX, and which may possibly date from about the close of the twelfth century, the shield, which bears three bars dancetty, is strengthened by an escarbuncle, or floriated cross, in

PLATE I.

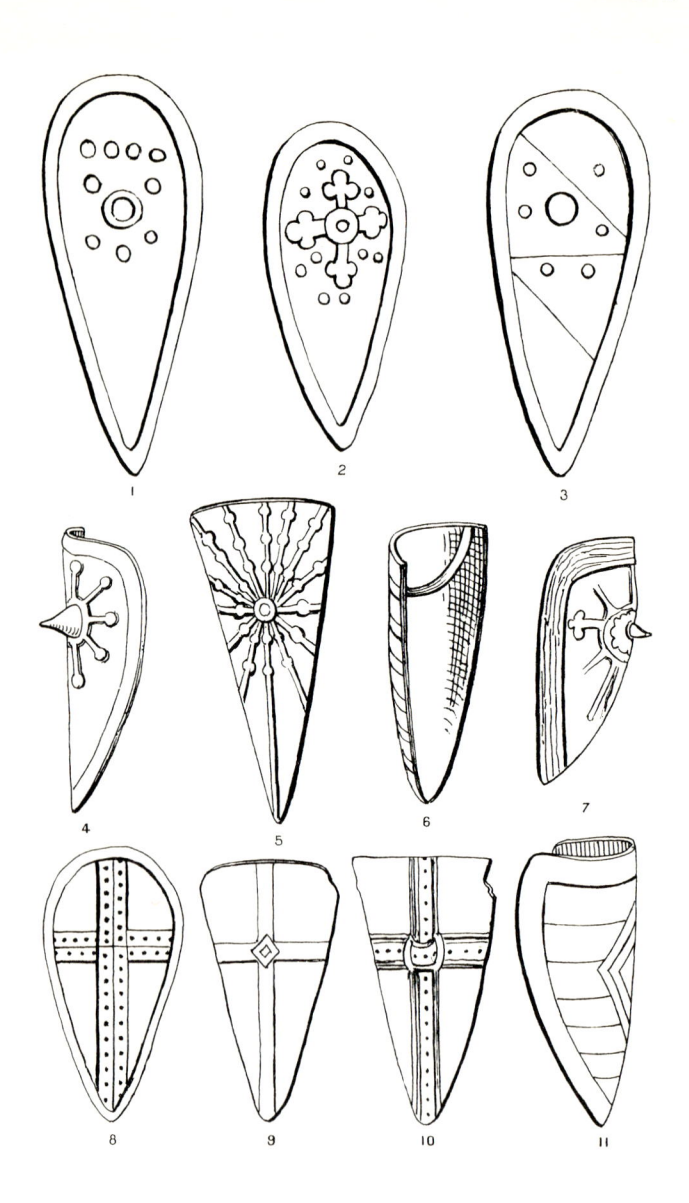

EXPLANATION OF FIGURES.

1, 2, 3. Bayeux Tapestry. 4. Jourdain de Tesson, 12th Century. 5. Vitré (*Morice*). 6. 11th Century (*Demmin*, p. 290). 7. Berchfold IV. Von Zähringen, 1177. 8, 9, 10. 12th Century Chessmen. 11. From *Demmin*, pp. 174 and 291.

and was father of our HENRY II., is preserved in the Museum at Le-Mans, and is one of the earliest examples of armorial bearings upon a monumental memorial which exist. I have engraved the shield on Plate II., fig. 3. I do not know of any sepulchral monument in England which has armorial bearings of an earlier date than the thirteenth century. One of the earliest is the slab of Sir WILLIAM DE STAUNTON at Staunton, Notts, of the date 1226; which bears his arms (*arg.*) *two chevrons (sable) within a bordure* (BOUTELL, *Christian Monuments*, p. 140). The slab of ETHELMAR DE VALENCE, Bishop of Winchester, 1261, bears the barruly shield of VALENCE (BOUTELL, *ibid.*, p. 118). Other early instances are afforded by the incised slab of JOHN, Baron of GREY-STOCK, summoned to Parliament by writ in 1295, which remains at Greystock, though in a mutilated condition (BOUTELL, *ibid.*, p. 75). The slab of Sir RICHARD DE BOSELYNGTHORPE, *c.* 1280, bears a small shield charged with a chevron (*ibid.*, p. 146).

Armorial bearings are still less ancient upon coins. MENÊTRIER tells us that the earliest French coins upon which they appear are the *deniers d'or* of PHILIPPE DE VALOIS struck in 1336. It was not until the reign of HENRY VIII., that arms appeared on our own silver coins. Mr ELLIS indeed finds arms in the unheraldic device of a plain cross between four radiating doves, which appears on a coin of EDWARD THE CONFESSOR, and out of which the Heralds evolved the coat of arms (*Azure, a cross flory between five martlets or*) which was at a much later date, in the thirteenth century, attributed to that prince. (*See* Chapter IV., p. 157.)

But I quite agree with Mr SETON (*Law and Practice of Heraldry in Scotland*, p. 189), in considering that seals form the most authentic, as well as the earliest, record of heraldic bearings. (The rise and development of the use of seals is the subject of fuller treatment in another

man gleichwol alle die Alte vom Adel, so auf jedem Thurnier erschienen, sollte so fleissig zusammen geschrieben haben, indem es auch kaum zu thun möglich gewesen wäre, weil man vor HENRICI IV. Zeiten, nicht einmal die Fürsten, Hertzogen, Grafen, und Herren mit ihren Zunamen, in den alten Diplomatibus aufgezeichnet finde, und nicht eigentlich gewust, wie sie geheissen haben ; wie vielweniger hälte man solches also von der Ritterschafft wissen konnen."

Having thus disposed of Mr ELLIS'S *cheval de bataille*, we may proceed to consider the evidence which is trustworthy with regard to the date at which armorial bearings were adopted into general use, and finally became hereditary ensigns of noble descent.

This evidence we should expect to find on sepulchral monuments ; on coins, and seals ; and in any lists, or documents descriptive of events in the course of which armorial bearings would be likely to be borne. MENÊTRIER (in his *Traité de l'Origine des Armoiries*, p. 54) assures us that there is no tomb of an earlier date than the eleventh century on which armorial insignia are depicted. MENÊTRIER seems to me to have understated the matter by at least a century. CLEMENT IV., who reigned 1265-8, is the first of the Popes on whose tomb, at Viterbo, armorial bearings are depicted.

The tombstone of WILLIAM, Count of FLANDERS, who died in 1127, bears his effigy [WREE, *de Seghelen der Graven van Vlaendren*, plate 9. Te Brugghe (Bruges), 1640] ; the long oval shield which covers the greater part of the body has no armorial bearings, but is ornamented and strengthened by the usual floriated boss, or "escarbuncle" of the period.

The splendid plaque in champlevé enamel which was formerly an ornament of the tomb of GEOFFROI PLANTAGENET, Count d'ANJOU, who died in 1151,

Teutschen Adels, 1688, of which the following passage as given in RUDOLPHI, *Heraldica Curiosa*, p. 16 (Nürnberg, 1698), is a summary. "Wiewol diese Meinung schon etliche Anstösse leiden müssen, indem einige dem Rixner in seinen Thurnier-Buch, wo er diesen Thurnier, und alle damals anwesende Personen beschrieben und genennet, wenig trauen wollen, sowol, weil solches bey keinen andern Scribenten zu finden ist, als auch, weil er selbsten zu seiner Beglaubigung nichtanders vorbringt als dasz er solches bey einem Pfarrer in Sachsen in einem geschriebenen Buch gelesen, und abgeschrieben habe, welches dem Goldasto *in Rational, ad lib. der Reichs-Satz*, pag. 305, gar verdächtig ist, weilen er hinzu setzt, es habe gedachter Pfarrer gleich nach solcher Abschrifft sein Manuscript verbrennt; da doch solches zu gründlichern Beweiss hätte billig sollen aufbewahret werden. Ferner können sie das reine Teutsche in der Thurnier Ordnung, welche Rixner dem HENRICO AUCUPI zuschreibt, mit der damaligen Redens-Art nicht zusammen reimen, wie ingleichen, wan er sagt, dass diese Thurnier-Ordnung, mit Zuziehung der '*vier Reichs Herzogen,*' nahmlich Pfaltzgraf Conrad bey Rhein; Herman, Hertzog in Schwaben; Bernhard, Hertzog in Bayern; und Conrad, Herzog in Francken, etc., gemacht worden; da doch damalen der Hertzog in Francken und Pfaltzgraf eins gewesen; wozu noch kommen die unnöthige Wiederholungen in den meisten Articuln, und die Unterschrifft welche einige Dignitäten bemerckt, woran doch zu zweiffeln, ob sie damals schon gewesen; wie auch der iibelangebrachte Titel, *der Edlen*, als welcher in denselbigen Zeiten nicht den Rittern, sondern Fürsten und Herren gebühret habe; von dem IX. und XI. Articul, wollen sie ebenfalls zweiffeln, ob sie sich zu besagten Zeiten schicken. Endlich will ihnen auch unglaublich scheinen, dass, da man vor Zeiten die Bischöffe in Teutschland nicht einmal ordentlich aufgezeichnet hat,

p. 283) The date of the tourney at Göttingen, which I find quoted from the *Braunschweiger Chronicle*, as 1119, is probably a mistake for 1129, as LOTHAIR was only elected King of the Romans at Mainz in the year 1125.

It is pretty clear, both from the entire lack of outside corroboration, and from internal evidence hereafter noticed, that RÜXNER'S *Thurnier Buch* was not derived from any ancient MS., but is an elaborate fiction, so far as it relates to the tourneys which he asserts were held antecedently to the twelfth or thirteenth centuries; and that no credence whatever is to be attached to the long lists of members of later noble families who are said to have taken part in the tourneys; or to their blazons; or to those *Leges Hastiludiales*, which, by requiring four generations of noble descent from those who participated in these sports, would have carried back systematic and hereditary armory at least a century beyond their supposed promulgation by HENRY THE FOWLER in 937.

Even with regard to tournaments which we know with certainty really took place, RÜXNER'S list is seriously inaccurate. He omits any mention of that which was held at Neuss in 1175; and which was worthy of remembrance since in it forty-two knights and their esquires lost their lives in the *melée*.

According to the *Chronicum Belgicum Magnum* there was held near Cologne, in the year 1240, a tourney in which sixty knights and esquires were slain. Neither of this, nor of the one held at Nürnberg in 1433 does RÜXNER make any mention. With regard to the *Thurnier-Ordnung* it can be shown that, instead of dating from the tenth century, they were first drawn up at Heidelberg in 1481, and Heilbronn in 1484. Some other respects in which RÜXNER trips, are set forth, and the whole matter is well summed up, in Dr MICHAEL PRAUN'S treatise *Von dem Adelichen Europa, und denen Heerschilden des*

Pruliaco, *qui torneamenta invenit,* apud Andegavum occiditur." A similar entry appears in the *Chronicon S. Martini Turon :*—" fuit proditio apud Andegavum, ubi Gaufridus de Pruliaco, et alii Barones, occisi sunt. *Hic Gaufridus de Pruliaco torneamentum invenit.*" These entries probably only mean that GEOFFREY DE PREUILLY was the first who formulated the rules under which these military exercises were to be held. DU CANGE (VI. *Dissertation sur l'histoire de S. Louis, par de Joinville*) remarks, that tourneys are considered by the writers of the middle ages as sports essentially French: and MATTHEW PARIS in 1179 calls them "joûtes françaises "—" *conflictus gallici.*" There is abundant evidence that these tourneys were no child's play. In 1186 GEOFFREY PLANTAGENET, Duke of BRITTANY, son of HENRY II. of England, was slain in a tourney at Paris. JOHN, Markgrave of BRANDENBURG, thus lost his life in 1269. FREDERICK II., Count Palatine, fractured his spine by a fall from his horse in one of these encounters. In the twelfth century the Popes INNOCENT II., EUGENIUS III., and ALEXANDER III., fulminated their bulls against them, as later did INNOCENT III., and other popes. PHILIPPE LE BEL and PHILIPPE LE LONG issued *Ordonnances* against them (*v.* DU CANGE), but it was only the unfortunate death in 1559 of HENRI II. of France, who was killed in a tourney by a splinter from the lance of DE MONTMORENCY, which caused their discontinuance.

We may reasonably conclude that the tournaments which probably originated in Germany were introduced into England from the neighbouring kingdom of France; in which kingdom they were first systematised and regulated. The earliest regular tournament of which we can find a record in the old German chroniclers appears to be that which was held at Nürnberg in 1127, under the Emperor LOTHAIR (BRUNNER, *Annales Boici,* tom. iii.,

from others in the work, that the writer from whom are borrowed the above eloquent sentences, attached a larger amount of credence than would generally be conceded at the present day, or at all events by the present writer, to the stories which account for many existing armorial bearings, by declaring that they were special rewards for special prowess in the Crusades; or that the Saracen's heads, crescents, crosses, escallop shells, and other charges which figure in them, had direct reference to the part the ancestors of the present bearers played in those stirring events. Still, there is no doubt that, as stated above, the Crusades had an appreciable effect in the extension, consolidation, and systematising of Heraldry which the student must not overlook, or altogether ignore.

The tournaments, which became general in the thirteenth and following centuries, had probably a very much larger influence in these respects than can be attributed to the Crusades; and they certainly contributed very greatly to the conversion of personal into hereditary insignia.

Military exercises and sham fights may be traced back to classical times with much greater probability than hereditary insignia (*see* VIRGIL, lib. vii.), but it would be difficult to say whether tournaments, in the usual sense of the term, originated in Germany or in France. Under the Carlovingian kings military exercises, analogous to the jousts of later times, certainly took place. The historian NITHARD gives some details of a joust which was held on the occasion of the interview between the brother princes, LOUIS THE GERMAN, and CHARLES THE BALD in 842. DU CANGE attributes the origin of tourneys to the French; and quotes the *Chronicon Turonense* which thus records the death in 1066 of GEOFFREY DE PREUILLY (of the family of the Counts de VENDÔME). "Gaufridus de

les croisades que les armoiries devinrent héréditaires. On conçoit aisément que les fils de ceux qui s'etaient approprié des symboles pour ces pieuses expéditions,[1] se firent un point de religion et d'honneur de transmettre à leurs descendants l'écu de leurs pères comme un monument de leur valeur et de leur piété. Au retour de la croisade, en effet, cette enseigne qui avait été plantée sur la brèche d'Antioche, ou de Jérusalem, qui avait été bênite par le légat du pape sur le tombeau de Jesus Christ, était révérée comme une sainte relique et précieusement gardée comme une gloire de famille.

"Flottant sur le plus haut des tours du manoir, elle signalait au loin la demeure d'un champion et peut-être d'un confesseur de la foi. Bien plus, les signes qu'on y voyait étaient reproduits par l'armurier sur le bouclier du croisé ; par le peintre sur les vitraux de la chapelle seigneuriale ; par l'imagier sur le chêne des portes du château ; par la châtelaine elle même sur la nappe de l'autel, où étaient déposées les saintes reliques que le croisé avait pieusement enlevées de quelque église schismatique de l'Orient (!) . . . Ces enseignes et ces symboles durent naturellement passer, je le répète, comme la plus précieuse partie de l'héritage, au fils ainé du défunt, qui en adoptait les emblèmes sans y rien changer, les transmettait à son tour à ses enfants comme une signe de suprématie, de commandement ; comme la preuve de leur descendance d'un homme illustre, en un mot, comme une marque de noblesse,"—*Histoire du Blason, et Science des Armoiries*, pp. 70, 71, Tours, 1848.

It may be suspected, not only from this passage, but

[1] "Dans ces expeditions de la Terre Sainte, ceux qui avoient deja de ces Symboles se les rendirent plus propres ; et ceux qui n'en avoient, en choisirent, tant pour se faire remarquer, dans les combats (leur armure de tête empechant qu'on ne connût leur visage) que pour être distinguez des autres."—MEZERAY, *l'Abrégé Chronologique de l'Histoire de France*, tom. ii., p. 515.

Comte de FLANDERS), the conical helmet (which had already become cylindrical with a domed covering) was replaced by the cylindrical helm with a flattened top; to which a few years later was added the plate which completely covered the face with the exception of two small slits (*œillières*) to enable the wearer to see, and still smaller holes through which he breathed. (Plate II., fig. 5).

On two seals of RICHARD CŒUR DE LION the prince is represented; on that of the date 1189 (*British Museum Catalogue*, No. 80) he is shown as wearing the old conical Norman helmet, but on that of 1198 (No. 87) the helmet has the flat top, and this is the case on the seal of King JOHN in the following year (*Brit. Mus. Cat.*, No. 91).

The flat-topped helmet worn by RICHARD I. on his second great seal (of 1198) is remarkable as being the most ancient helmet bearing a crest with which we are acquainted; it bears the lion of England in the centre of a fan-shaped crest. The next known example is that of MATHIEU II. DE MONTMORENCY, Constable of France, in 1224, on which the head and neck of a peacock rise from the flat-topped helm. (DEMAY, p. 138, also engraved in VRÉE, *Sigilla Com. Flandr.*, plate 10.)

The Crusades must also have had considerable effect in causing arms, which had previously been assumed and changed at pleasure, to become hereditary. The descendants of a knight who had fought with distinction under certain ensigns in the Holy Wars, would feel a very natural pride in preserving and handing down to posterity the banner or the shield with the blazonings which recalled their ancestor's prowess. On this point EYSENBACH says, on the whole with justice:—" Les croisades rendirent l'usage des armoiries plus général et leur pratique invariable; elles les régularisèrent tout à fait, puisqu'elles devinrent dès lors des récompenses accordées aux chevaliers et aux villes qui s'étaient distingués dans les guerres saintes. Ce fut aussi depuis

proclamation from HENRY V. forbidding all persons who had not borne arms at Agincourt to assume them, except in virtue of inheritance or of a grant from the crown. [G. B.]

SECTION B. (BY J. W.)

It has been seen that the works of the old armorialists will not afford us help in tracing the origin and development of armory. But we are not without the needful materials, in seals, monuments, painted windows, and (more especially in England) in *Rolls of Arms*.

The influence exerted by the Crusades upon the adoption of heraldic insignia appears to me to have been exaggerated by some writers, but we need not deny that the influence was considerable. In armies composed of people of diverse languages the use of banners with definite and familiar devices, under which the members of different followings might rally; and of some distinctive insignia by which the leaders might be easily recognised, appears a matter of necessity; a necessity probably greater in the time of the Third Crusade (1189-1192) when the hosts of England, France, and Germany were combined, than at any other; and a period which coincides remarkably with the general adoption of armorial bearings.

The substitution which took place at this period of the cylindrical helmet (which covered the whole visage of the wearer, leaving him only small apertures through which to see and breathe), for the old open Norman conical helmet, with its nasal guard, must have had a very considerable effect in the same direction. (*See* Plate II.) On its adoption it became no longer possible for soldiers to recognise their leader by his face. The date of the commencement of this substitution is about 1180, at which time (as we see by the seal of PHILIPPE D'ALSACE,

hound coat was first used by them, and then abandoned for a coat resembling that of the other SINCLAIRS?

While the right of property in arms and their inherently hereditary character was thus fully recognised, there are some curious exceptional instances, also in the fourteenth century, of arms being granted by feudal lords to their vassals or retainers, and being transferred by gift and devised by will. On 26th February 1356-7 WILLIAM, Baron of GREYSTOCK, granted a coat-armorial to ADAM OF BLENCOWE, who is said to have been his standard-bearer at Cressy and Poitiers. FROISSART tells us of Lord AUDLEY immediately after the victory of Poitiers dividing among his four esquires a gift bestowed on him by the Black Prince, and giving them at the same time leave to bear his own arms with a difference. In 1391 THOMAS GRENDALL of Fentoun, cousin and heir of JOHN BEAUMEYS, sometime of Sautray, in respect that the said arms with their appurtenances are escheated to him as next heir, granted the said arms with their appurtenances to Sir WILLIAM MOIGNE, Knight, which arms are *Argent, on a cross azure five garbs or*. CAMDEN gives other instances of gifts and assignations of arms in the reigns of HENRY IV. and HENRY VI., but it is doubtful if these would have been sustained as legal in later times. (*See* Appendix.)

The military character which then attached to arms is shown by the deposition of a witness in 1408, to the effect that, though descended of noble blood, he had no armorial bearings because neither he nor his ancestors had ever been engaged in war. Even in the beginning of the fifteenth century there was probably a good deal of assumption of arms *proprio motu*, and the *Boke of St. Alban's* contains the rather startling dictum that any one might assume arms at his own hand, provided they had been borne by no one else. In the year 1419, the increase in the unlicensed use of arms had called forth a

remisit et relaxavit, et omnino de se et heredibus suis in perpetuum prædicta arma cum toto triumpho honore et victoria ore tenus in audientia nostra. Quare nos in solio nostro, tribunali regali Sancti Patris (?) cum magnatibus et dominio [dominis] regni nostri personaliter sedentes, adjudicavimus, et finaliter decretum dederimus per præsentes, quod prædictus Hugo Harding et heraedes sui de cætero in perpetuum habeant et teneant gaudeant et portent prædicta arma integraliter, absque calumpnia, perturbatione, contradictione, reclamatione, prædicti Willielmi, seu heredum suorum. In cujus rei testimonium has literas nostras fieri fecimus patentes apud dictum villam nostram de Perthe secundo die Aprilis anno regni nostri septimo anno de Domini 1312."

Making allowance for the transcriber's errors in extending a few words, and regarding "Sancti Patris" as a misreading for some other word, the technical phraseology of the document is so exactly what prevailed in Scotland at that date, that it is difficult to doubt its genuineness. Like other Englishmen (then in the partial occupation of Scotland, and gradually giving way in the struggles of 1312), HARDING would look on Scotland as an integral portion of EDWARD'S dominions; and thus presumably consider it an offence for any Scotchman to bear the arms which he bore. But his acceptance of ROBERT BRUCE as arbiter of the duel, and of his letters patent as King of Scots is somewhat remarkable. SIN-CLAIR (SAINTCLARE in the writing of that date) might readily be misread "SAINTELOWE." We know from the evidence of seals that the SINCLAIRS of Roslin bore the engrailed cross (probably as in later times *sable*) as far back as the thirteenth century, also from the *Armorial de Gelre* that the SINCLAIRS of Herdmanstoun, who are not known to have been of kin to them, bore in the reign of DAVID II. the same cross engrailed but of *azure* for a difference. Is it possible that the grey-

obviated by restraining the bearers' fancy, and regulating the number, position, and colour of the charges, and the attitudes of such animals as were represented on the shields; and in the course of time Sovereigns found it necessary to interfere with the unrestricted assumption of arms within their respective realms, and to regulate the bearing of them. It became an established rule that no two families in the same kingdom were to bear the same arms; and the right to bear a particular coat sometimes became matter of hot dispute. Before the establishment of the Court of Chivalry (of which in a future Chapter) the question who had the preferable right was in England as elsewhere generally decided by the ordeal of combat. Sir EDWARD BYSSHE in his notes on NICOLAS UPTON *De Studio Militari* gives some instances of such armorial combats in England, also of one of which the scene was in Scotland, the particulars of which are rather curious. According to the document which he gives at length, in the year 1312 HUGH HARDING, an Englishman, and WILLIAM DE SEINTE-LOWE (?) a Scotsman, each claimed the right to the coat *Gules, three greyhounds courant or, collared azure*. The combat which was to decide between them took place at Perth in the presence of King ROBERT BRUCE, when the Englishman was the victor, and the following letters were (according to BYSSHE) granted by the King of Scots, declaring the Englishman's superior right:—
" Robertus Dei Gratia rex Scotiæ [Scotorum?] Omnibus ad quos presentes literæ pervenerint salutem. Cum nos accepimus duellum apud nostram villam de Perthe die confectionis presentium inter Hugonem Harding, Anglicum, appellantem, de Armis de Goules tribus leporariis de auro currentibus colloree de B, et Willielmum de Seintlowe (?) Scotum, appellatum, eisdem armis sine differentia indutos: Quo quidem duello percusso, prædictus Willielmus se finaliter reddidit devictum, et prædicto Hugoni

Between the Second Crusade and the Third, we can point to the already noticed seal of PHILIP I. of FLANDERS. Among English royal personages the first on whose seal an armorial design occurs is King JOHN, and that before he was king; he bore *vita patris* two lions passant. RICHARD CŒUR DE LION had also two armorial seals (afterwards to be described) one in use before, the other after the Third Crusade (1189). The glorious but fruitless expedition alluded to, in which the Sovereigns, Nobles, and Knights of France, Germany, and England, were brought into intimate contact, had doubtless considerable influence in extending over Christendom a custom, whose practical utility in distinguishing one knight from another had been its first recommendation. The fashion of tournaments also helped, and before long the ownership of a distinctive shield of arms (not necessarily granted by the Sovereign, but often assumed *proprio motu*), became essential to the idea of a baron, knight, or gentleman.

We may therefore regard the latter half of the twelfth century as the earliest period to which we can trace the use of arms in the proper sense. Early in the thirteenth century the practice began of embroidering the family ensigns on the surcoat worn over the hauberk or coat of mail, whence originated the expression "coat of arms." Arms were similarly embroidered on the jupon, cyclas, and tabard, which succeeded the surcoat; and displayed on the banners and pennons of knights, or floating from the shafts of their lances; they were also enamelled or otherwise represented on furniture, personal ornaments, and weapons.

In the infancy of arms great latitude was allowed in representing the charge fixed on or inherited. It was used singly, or repeated, or in any attitude which the bearer chose, or which the form of his shield suggested. But as coats of arms multiplied, confusion could only be

crosses of different forms, and spots. (Plate I., figs. 2, 3.) On one hand it requires little imagination to find the cross *patée* and the cross *botonnée* of heraldry prefigured on two of these shields. But there are several fatal objections to regarding these figures as incipient *armory*, namely, that while the most prominent persons of the time are depicted, most of them repeatedly, none of these is ever represented twice as bearing the same device, nor is there one instance of any resemblance in the rude designs described to the bearings actually used by the descendants of the persons in question. If a personage so important and so often depicted as the Conqueror had borne arms, they could not fail to have had a place in a nearly contemporary work, and more especially if it proceeded from the needle of his wife.

[See LOWER'S acute remark as to the absence from the shields of the simple heraldic figures known as the *Ordinaries*. "Nothing but disappointment awaits the curious armorist who seeks in this venerable memorial the pale, the bend, and other early elements of arms. As these would have been much more easily imitated with the needle than the grotesque figures before alluded to, we may safely conclude that personal arms had not yet been introduced."—*Curiosities of Heraldry*, p. 19.—J. W.]

The Second Crusade took place in 1147; and in MONTFAUCON'S plates of the no longer extant windows of the Abbey of St. Denis, representing that historical episode, there is not a trace of an armorial ensign on any of the shields. That window was probably executed at a date when the memory of that event was fresh; but in MONTFAUCON'S time, the beginning of the eighteenth century, the *Science héroïque* was matter of such moment in France that it is not to be believed that the armorial figures on the shields, had there been any, would have been left out.

has been discovered between the length of the tapestry and the inner circumference of the nave of the Cathedral greatly favours this supposition. This remarkable work of art, as carefully drawn on colour in 1818 by Mr C. STOTHARD, is reproduced in the sixth volume of the *Vetusta Monumenta;* and more recently an excellent copy of it from autotype plates has been published by the Arundel Society. Each of its scenes is accompanied by a Latin description, the whole uniting into a graphic history of the event commemorated. We see HAROLD taking leaving of EDWARD THE CONFESSOR; riding to Bosham with his hawk and hounds; embarking for France; landing there and being captured by the Count of Ponthieu; redeemed by WILLIAM of Normandy, and in the midst of his Court aiding him against CONAN, Count of BRETAGNE; swearing on the sacred relics to recognise WILLIAM'S claim of succession to the English throne, and then re-embarking for England. On his return, we have him recounting the incidents of his journey to EDWARD THE CONFESSOR, to whose funeral obsequies we are next introduced. Then we have HAROLD receiving the crown from the English people, and ascending the throne; and WILLIAM, apprised of what had taken place, consulting with his half-brother ODO about invading England. The war preparations of the Normans, their embarkation, their landing, their march to Hastings, and formation of a camp there, form the subjects of successive scenes; and finally we have the battle of Hastings, with the death of HAROLD and the flight of the English. In this remarkable piece of work we have figures of more than six hundred persons, and seven hundred animals, besides thirty-seven buildings, and forty-one ships or boats. There are of course also numerous shields of warriors, of which some are round, others kite-shaped, and on some of the latter are rude figures, of dragons or other imaginary animals as well as

the Jewish twelve tribes are a familiar case. ÆSCHYLUS and EURIPIDES describe the devices on the shields of their heroes, there being however no correspondence between the two enumerations. TACITUS alludes to figures of animals on the shields of Celtic tribes; and PLUTARCH to those of the savage hordes of Denmark, Norway, and North Germany. But the omission of all such devices on what representations and descriptions have been handed down to us of the shields of the early middle ages, shows that the bulls, boars, wolves, and horses of TACITUS, and the more conventional symbols of the cohort ensigns, if any traditional memory of them had been assured, played no prominent part in the life of these ages, and certainly had no hereditary character. As little can we trace any connection between the language of arms and the mysterious symbols found sculptured on stone in Wales, Norway, Denmark, and more extensively in Scotland, of whose significance archæologists have as yet been unable to give a plausible explanation. (*See* Dr STUART'S splendid work on the *Sculptured Stones of Scotland*, published by the Spalding Club.)

The evidence afforded by the famous tapestry preserved in the public library of Bayeux, a series of views in sewed work representing the invasion and conquest of England by WILLIAM the Norman, has been appealed to on both sides of this controversy, and has certainly an important bearing on the question of the antiquity of coat-armour. This panorama of seventy-two scenes is on probable grounds believed to have been the work of the Conqueror's Queen MATILDA and her maidens; though the French historian THIERRY and others ascribe it to the Empress MAUD, daughter of HENRY III. The latest authorities suggest the likelihood of its having been wrought as a decoration for the Cathedral of Bayeux, when rebuilt by WILLIAM'S uterine brother ODO, Bishop of that See, in 1077. The exact correspondence which

articles and concludes with the alternative "aut nobilitatis famæ insignium gentilitiorum denique amissionem incurrat." (ELLIS, *Antiquities of Heraldry*, pp. 149-150.)

Mr ELLIS considers that these *Leges Hastiludiales* quite outweigh the negative evidence against the introduction of hereditary arms which Mr PLANCHÉ and others found in their absence from seals, and sepulchral monuments before the eleventh or twelfth century. But if we have some hesitation about accepting all Mr ELLIS'S conclusions he has at least brought to light two facts of importance. *First*—That the figures of mediæval heraldry contain in some instances, elements suggested by those of earlier ages. Even Mr PLANCHÉ while giving a general denial to this proposition seems to make an exception in the case of the origin of the three legs in the shield of the Kingdom of Man, which he is willing to admit may have been derived from the classical symbol of Trinacria (Sicily). *Second*—That we have instances too many to be accounted for by accident, of arms more or less similar both in their colours and charges, being borne in the beginning of the thirteenth century by cognate families whose common descent was from an ancestor who lived before the Norman Conquest, a fact of which in the present state of our knowledge the adoption through collateral consanguinity seems a more satisfactory explanation than the hypothesis that a common ancestor bore arms at a time when no tangible evidence is producible of the existence of hereditary insignia.

Admitting the ingenuity of much of Mr ELLIS'S argument, a full consideration of the whole evidence has led the present writer to take up a position more nearly approaching that of Mr PLANCHÉ. Instances certainly occur in remote times of nations, tribes, and individuals distinguishing themselves by particular emblems or ensigns, more especially in war, as these ensigns afforded rallying points in the field of battle. The standards of

legs conjoined in pairle as in the well-known arms of the Isle of Man. (Figs. 1, 2, 3, and 4, p. 18.)

The lines in the seventh book of the *Æneid* of VIRGIL (655-658)

> "Post hos insignem palmâ per gramina currum
> Victoresque ostentat equos, satus Hercule pulchro
> Pulcher Aventinus; clypeoque *insigne paternum*,
> *Centum angues*, cinctamque gerit serpentibus hydram."

are relied on as evidence of the hereditary character of classic symbols.

The Roman cohort ensigns which appear on TRAJAN'S column at Rome, devices which occasionally bear a resemblance perhaps not always accidental to the designs of later ages, are assumed to be the family insignia of the commander of the cohort, and with other devices of tribes and clans are considered by Mr ELLIS to have descended through the dark ages until they appeared in the eleventh century as hereditary coat-armour. (*See* Figs. 5 and 6, p. 19.)

But the argument on which the ingenious author most relies is the recognition of hereditary ensigns as not only being, but having been for generations, the badge of gentility, in the *Leges Hastiludiales* of HENRY THE FOWLER, of the date 938. These laws contain not only specific directions regulating the use of "insignia gentilitia" and of their registration by the heralds, but regard them as the exclusive privilege of the nobly born and exclude from participation in the tournaments all whose ancestors had not borne them for at least four generations. Cap. XII. *De hominibus novis*.

"Quisquis recentioris et notæ nobilis et non talis ut a stirpe nobilitatem suam et origine quatuor saltem generis auctorum proximorum gentilibus insignibus probare possit is quoque ludis his exesto."

Article XIII. imposes penalties for the breach of other

the shields and banners verbally described and pictorially represented in the centuries preceding the twelfth. For example, ANNA COMNENA in her biography of her father the Greek Emperor ALEXIUS I., written in the beginning of the twelfth century, gives a minute account of the convex shields of the French knights of that date, with a surface of highly polished metal and a boss in the centre ; and in a Spanish manuscript of the year 1109 in the British Museum, we have circular shields ornamented as well as plain, but destitute of any approach to an armorial device. While, from the date of the Norman Conquest of England onwards, sealing became a necessary form for the validity of writs, and the arms on a seal are the most important evidence of the bearing of the owner, the earliest authentic instance of an armorial shield on a seal is on that of PHILIP I. Count of Flanders, appended to a charter of date 1164.

The chief representative of an opposite position is Mr W. G. ELLIS, who in his *Antiquities of Heraldry* (1869) has collected a mass of interesting matter relating to what he calls the heraldry of ancient times, and of all nations of the world, and he certainly succeeds in showing to how great an extent pictorial symbols, which had originally a meaning, have been in use among all nations of mankind, civilised and savage. His plates are curious as showing the occasional occurrence among these manifold devices of some resembling modern figures of blazon. The crescent, the mullet, the lozenge, the quatrefoil, and the fleur de lis are traced by him to counterparts existing among Egyptian, Chinese, Indian and Japanese emblems, and among the figures on Etruscan vases he shows us what in heraldic language would be called a bull's head caboshed and a not unheraldic looking demi-boar. We have also on the Greek vases two dolphins naiant in pale, a demi-wolf, and three

The levelling principles of the French Revolution were naturally hostile to the study of Armory, but long before that event the conceits of the old heralds had helped to bring into disrepute what had once been an essential branch of a liberal education. Armorial art, too, had declined with the general decline of the arts: the symbols had lost their beauty, and it was but natural that the philosophers of the eighteenth century, who could see nothing but folly in the life of the ages that had gone before them, held heraldry in little respect.

It is now more than fifty years since a revival of interest began in heraldry and in the kindred subject of genealogy. The value of heraldry to the historical student began to be recognised, and its true origin and history to be made the subject of serious criticism. Mr J. A. MONTAGU'S *Guide to the Study of Heraldry* (1840), and Mr M. A. LOWER'S *Curiosities of Heraldry* (1845), are works of real value, and at least equally so, a work called *The Pursuivant of Arms* by the late Mr PLANCHÉ, *Somerset Herald*, first published in 1851. Mr PLANCHÉ'S conclusions have been very much acquiesced in by most later writers on the subject. Two of these as expressed in the author's own words are—
" 1. That heraldry appears as a science at the commencement of the thirteenth century; and that, although armorial bearings had then been in existence undoubtedly for some time previous, no precise date has yet been discovered for their first assumption. 2. That in their assumption the object of the assumer was not, as it has been generally asserted and believed, to symbolise any virtue or qualification but simply to distinguish their persons and properties, to display their pretensions to certain honours or estates, attest their alliances, or acknowledge their feudal tenures." In support of his views Mr PLANCHÉ appealed to the entire absence of any indication of the existence of armorial bearings in

regarded as a standard authority on Scottish Armory. By and by a few enlightened armorialists began to remark the absence of armorial bearings from early seals and monuments, and to doubt if their introduction was not the invention of a much later age. Among these was the learned French Jesuit Père MENESTRIER who flourished towards the close of the seventeenth century and whose heraldic works are of the highest interest and of great authority.

[His *Origine des Armoiries* appeared in 1680, and his opinion as briefly summed up (and one which he had already expressed in his rare little duodecimo volume *Abrégé Méthodique des Principes Héraldiques; ou du Véritable Art du Blason*, published in 1661, and of which there are several later editions some of great rarity) is that hereditary arms originated in tournaments and are consequently of German origin. This is an opinion with which I shall deal later on.—J. W.]

The earliest instance MENESTRIER could find of a coat of arms on a sepulchral monument in France, Germany, Italy, or the Low Countries, was on the tomb of a Count VON WASSERBURG in the church of St. Emmeran at Ratisbon bearing the date 1010, and the learned father expressed his conviction that the arms themselves could not be of so early a date, and that they had been added on some subsequent occasion when the monument had undergone a restoration.

EDMONSON in his *Complete Body of Heraldry* (1780) a work in which he was greatly aided by Sir JOSEPH AYLOFFE, had a glimpse of the truth in this matter, but more erudition is displayed in the *Inquiry into the Origin and Progress of Heraldry in England*, by the Rev. JAMES DALLAWAY, who, rejecting the mythological theory, still clung to the idea that the coins of the Anglo-Saxon Kings bore heraldic devices.

the common story that "if a man stricken of a scorpion shall sit upon an asse with his face to the taile of the ass, his pain shall pass out of him into the asse. He that believes this," he adds, " is the creature that must be ridden upon." GUILLIM has gone through a number of editions, and is still in deserved favour with students of heraldry.

In 1661, fifty years later than the first edition of GUILLIM, SYLVANUS MORGAN produced his *Sphere of Gentry* and *Armilogia*, treatises vying in absurdity with those of any of GUILLIM'S predecessors. Adam's *original escutcheon*, whose form corresponded with his spade, was, according to MORGAN, a plain red shield; Eve's, of the lozenge shape indicating her spindle, was of argent, and Adam in virtue of his wife being an heiress (!) bore *Gules an inescutcheon argent!* Abel bore *Quarterly argent and gules*, in front of a pastoral staff to indicate that he was a shepherd. We also see suspended from a fruit tree Adam's shield, as borne after his fall, of the pattern which we would now call *Gyronny of eight.* "Joseph's Coat," to which one division of the work is devoted, is not "of many colours" as we would expect, but *Chequy sable and argent.* The armes of each of Jacob's sons are given, and the standards set up in the camp of Israel are adduced as evidence that regular heraldry was then in use. (LOWER, *Curiosities of Heraldry*, pp. 5 and 6.)

DE LA COLOMBIÈRE in his *Science Héroique* published in 1699 expresses a like belief in the primeval antiquity of Heraldry. From that time, however, various writers abroad and in our own country began to be less credulous, and were content to deduce the origin of armorial insignia from ancient mythology, or the usages of classical times. Among these may be numbered the learned Scottish Herald NISBET, who traces arms to the Roman *Jus imaginum*, and whose elaborate work is still

the matter, ye shall perceive the beringe of armes and armory are much more auncient."

Sir JOHN FERNE'S work, *The Blazon of Gentrie*, in 1586, has a fund of information regarding antediluvian Heraldry. The use of furs in heraldry is deduced from the "coats of skins" of our first parents, and arms are assigned not only to Adam (innocent and fallen), but to Jabal, Jubal, Naamah, and Tubal Cain. (LOWER, *Curiosities of Heraldry*, pp. 4 and 5.)

GUILLIM'S *Display of Heraldrie*, which was first published in 1611, is a work of much higher order than the former productions. In the short introduction to the history of Heraldry, along with indications of a half belief in the speculations of previous writers, there occurs the remark, " the antiquity of gentilicial arms in Britain will prove of far later date than many of our gentry would willingly be thought to have borne them." In GUILLIM'S work we have in fact for the first time a methodical and intelligent treatise on the usage of arms in England, giving examples of a large number of the charges as borne in actually existent coats. Conceits, doubtless, we have which recall those of his predecessors. It is firm matter of faith with him as with them that each tincture, ordinary, and charge denote some special virtue or quality in the original bearer of the coat.

Considerable credulity is shown in his excursions into the field of Natural History. There is scarcely a bird, beast, or fish described as a heraldic charge with regard to which he does not favour us with some strange piece of folk lore, no doubt the ordinary belief of the people of his time. For instance, he tells us that " the milk of the seal or sea calf is very wholesome against the falling sickness, but she sucketh it out and spitteth it lest it should profit any other." While we are told that the hair of women will, under certain conditions, turn into very venomous serpents, we are to refuse credence to

and pincers in saltire; 15. *Sable, the box of alabaster;* 16. *Argent, the orb of sovereignty azure, banded and crossed or;* 17. *Azure, the three dice* (1 and 2) *proper;* 18 and 19 together. *Gules, the handkerchief of S.* VERONICA *with the impress of the Sacred Face;* 20. *Or, three passion-nails in pile gules.* The 6, 7, 10 and 11 quarters form a separate arrangement ; 6 and 10 are *or;* 7 and 11 *azure;* in 6 and 7 are *the Sacred Hands wounded ;* in 10 and 12 *the Sacred Feet also wounded.* Over these last four is an escucheon *en surtout argent charged with the Sacred Heart.* Thus the "five wounds" occupy the centre of the whole escucheon. This is also surmounted in German fashion by three crowned or coroneted helms, which bear as crests :— 1 (centre) *A banner gules charged with a cross argent, between the reed and sponge, and the lance ;* 2 (to the dexter) *The cross and ladder;* 3 (to the sinister) *The pillar, scourge, and whip.*—J. W.]

GERARD LEGH, in answer to the question when began armes, whether at the siege of Troy or not, says :—" At the siege of Troy there was a certain perfectness of it, determined amongst princes, as in our days now we do perfect things that were but rudely done of auncient tyme. Some things also be imperfect that were done of our forefathers. I mean herein of no other thing but of armes also, and in armorye, whose lawes were before the siege of Troy, as appeareth in Deuteronomion, which hath had since then so many addicions, that few here-haughtis know the lawe of armes, nor yet many civilians." In the course of the argument are blazoned the coats of the nine worthies " Duke Josua, Hector, David, Alexander, Judas Machabeus, Julius Cæsar, King Arthur, Charlemagne, and Sir Guy Erl of Warwike," and the conclusion arrived at is that " although the siege of Troye be of aunciente 2751 years past, yet, if ye waye

stones, where Lucifer with mylionys of aungelis owt of hevyn fell into hell and odyr places, and ben holdyn ther in bondage ; and all " (the remaining angels) " were erected in hevyn of gentille nature."
" Criste," says the same authority " was a gentylman of his moder's behalue, and bare cotarmure of aunseturis. The iiij euangelists berith wittnesse of Cristis workys in the gospell with all thappostilles. They were Jewys and of gentylmen come by the right lyne of that worthy conqueroure Judas Machabeus, but that by succession of tyme the kynrade fell to pouerty, after the destruction of Judas Machabeus and then they fell to laboris and ware calde no gentilmen, and the iiij doctores of holi church Seynt Jerom Ambrose Augustyn and Gregori war gentilmen of blode and of cot armures." (*See* LOWER, *Curiosities of Heraldry*, pp. 2, 249.)

[At a much later date arms were assigned to the Blessed Saviour that He might not appear at a disadvantage in those Chapters of the Continent where, as at Mayence, the members had to prove their sixteen quarters.

An escucheon thus put up in the Cathedral at Mayence is still extant, and is described and figured in the *Gentleman's Magazine*, vol. ccix. It is a shield of twenty quarters in five vertical rows each of four quarters, which are charged with the instruments of the passion, and other bearings : 1. *Argent, the cock that warned* S. PETER ; 2. *Azure, one of the water pots of Cana argent ;* 3. *Gules, the thirty pieces of silver in three piles each of ten pieces ;* 4. *Azure, the Passover chalice argent ;* 5. *Gules, a label in bend bearing the letters* I.N.R.I. ; 8. *Argent, the hand that smote Him and dried up, in bend sable ;* 9. *Argent, the seamless coat gules ;* 12. *Sable, the lantern argent ;* 13. *Or, the crown of thorns traversed by the reed and hyssop in bend ;* 14. *Argent, the hammer*

FIG. 5.   FIG. 6.
COHORT ENSIGNS, *Vide* p. 27.

CHAPTER II.

SECTION A. (BY G. B.)

WHEN, and how, did the bearing of armorial insignia originate? Before entering on the investigation here suggested, let us see, briefly, what the old armorial writers had to say upon the subject.

Except a short treatise of the fourteenth century by BARTOLO DI SASSOFERRATO, *De Armis et Insiginis ;* and another by JOHANNES ROTHE of Eisenach ; the earliest work extant on Heraldry is that of NICHOLAS UPTON, *De Studio Militari,* written early in the fifteenth century, and edited by Sir EDWARD BYSSHE, in 1654. Lady JULIANA BERNERS' *Boke of St. Alban's,* which appeared in 1486, was in a great degree borrowed from UPTON'S treatise. The first edition of GERARD LEGH'S *Accedens of Armory* was published in 1562, and Sir JOHN FERNE'S *Blazon of Gentrie,* in 1586.

Only a few specimens can be given of the speculations in which these authors indulge regarding the antiquity of coat-armour, and its mystical or symbolical meaning.

Some of them go beyond Adam in their search for the origin of armorial bearings. " At hevyn," says the author of the *Boke of St. Alban's,* " I will begin, where were V. orderis of aungelis, and now stand but IV. in cote armoris of knawlege encrowned ful hye with precious

her favour after a long abeyance), that lady at the same time assuming the DE ROS as surname of herself and family. Perhaps the most absurd example from its tautology was when Sir JOHN FLEMING LEICESTER, Bart., of Tabley in Cheshire, was raised to the peerage as Lord DE TABLEY, of Tabley House.

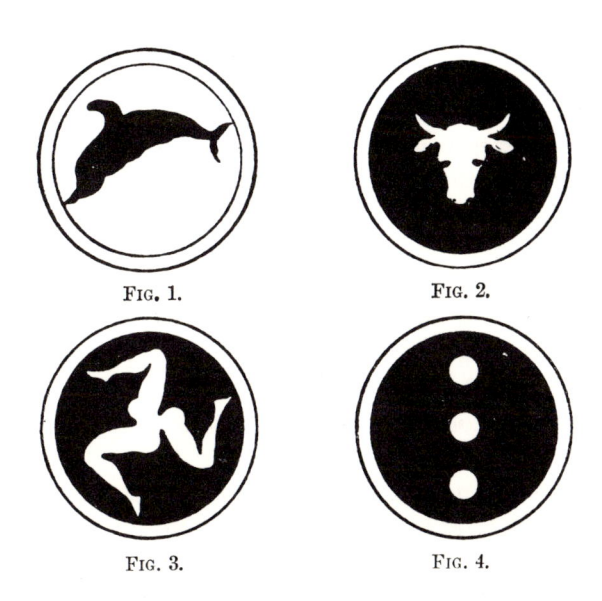

FIG. 1.

FIG. 2.

FIG. 3.

FIG. 4.

From **ETRUSCAN VASES**, *Vide* p. 26.

tional cases it was retained for the sake of euphony, or from coalescing with the initial vowel, as in DE LA BÈCHE, DEATH (D'ATH), DELAMERE, DELAWARR, DEVEREUX (D'EVEREUX), DANVERS (D'ANVERS), DANGERFIELD (D'ANGERVILLE). Even these names were sometimes translated into the vernacular. In the *Restoration of Edward IV.* we read of "Sir MARTYN OF THE SEA" (DELAMERE); and in FABYAN'S *Chronicle* of "Syr EDMUND OF THE BECHE." In the fifteenth and sixteenth century the Lords DELAWARR were frequently called LA WARR, though the title passed to America in the form of DELAWARE.

As a rule, however, the old historical surnames in England never were preceded by the prefix in question; and the writer of this is greatly disposed to deprecate the foolish fashion which began about a century ago, and has gone on to a considerable extent both in England and Ireland, of assuming (by royal licence) a De before the surname, under, no doubt, an erroneous impression that in feudal and chivalric times the name was thus used. One of the earliest instances was in 1752 when Lord CLANRICARDE and other BOURKES were transmuted into DE BURGHS. Since then other BOURKES have followed suit, and POWERS, VESEYS, CLIFFORDS, GREYS, COURCYS, TRAFFORDS, and MULLINSES, have been transformed into DE LA POERS, DE VESEYS, DE CLIFFORDS, DE COURCYS, DE TRAFFORDS, and DE MOLEYNS; and the example set by families of consideration has been followed by persons whose surnames possess no historic associations. The extensive introduction of the French particles into peerage titles is also matter of regret. The barony now styled DE ROS used to have the English form of ROOS when held by the families of CECIL, MANNERS, and VILLIERS; the present modification of it was adopted in 1806, by Lady HENRY FITZGERALD (when the barony was revived in

bourgeois descent, since he used a prefix which seemed equivalent to their familiar *von*. In Holland the prefix *van* or *vander* is no sign of nobility. In Flanders, *De* at the commencement of the name is only the equivalent of the French *Le*, and, like it, is no mark of noble descent. DETIMMERMAN is only the equivalent of Le CHARPENTIER; DEHANTCHOUMAKER of Le GANTIER; DEMEULENAER of Le MEUNIER, and so forth. In Austria since the middle of the eighteenth century the diplomas of persons ennobled run after this fashion " . . . Item uti particula *de*, vel *a*, si voluerit." So is it generally in Belgium.

The *particule nobiliaire* is but little in use in Italy and Spain. The princes COLONNA, BORGHESE, GABRIELI, etc.; and such families as DORIA, DONATO, BALBI, MACHIAVELLI, would not think of using it. Nevertheless, when a member of such a family settles in France the common usage begins to prevail, and the Commendatore STROZZI, becomes gradually DE STROZZI. Sometimes the name of the family is translated, FIESCHI becomes DE FIESQUE; and CASANOVA, DE MAISONNEUVE.—J. W.]

Turning to England, the Norman adventurers with whom surnames began, took their names for the most part from their paternal fiefs, or sometimes from their places of birth or residence, and they thus naturally used the *de*. Their younger sons, and others, applied the *de* to estates awarded them as their portion of the conquered country, calling themselves DE HASTINGS, DE WINTON, a form of their name probably never in vernacular use, and completely discarded with the disappearance of Norman-French, by either being dropped altogether, or passing into "of." In a very few excep-

than his tailor grandfather, but who scouted the idea that it indicated noble descent:—

> "Hé quoi, j'apprends que l'on critique
> Le *de* qui précède mon nom.
> 'Etes vous de noblesse antique?'
> Moi, noble! oh vraiment,
> Messieurs, non!
> "Non, d'aucune chevalerie
> Je n'ai le brevet sur vélin.
> Je ne sais qu'aimer ma patrie,
> Je suis vilain, et très vilain,
> Je suis vilain,
> Vilain, vilain."

Under the First Empire many titles were granted without the *de*. CAMBACÉRES was "le Duc CAMBACÉRES;" PASQUIER, "le Duc PASQUIER." Under the Second Empire, in 1858, the Code Pénal was revised and the assumption of names and titles stringently forbidden. Applications for change of name, and for the addition of the particle, or for its separation from a name with which it had become incorporated, required to be made to the Garde des Sceaux, and were often granted.

At the present day when a German is ennobled, or, as we should say, made a gentleman of coatarmour, he acquires the right to use the territorial prefix *von*, in some shape. Sometimes the preposition is affixed to his previously plebeian name, and SCHNEIDER becomes VON SCHNEIDER. But in cases like to this, in which the surname is obviously unterritorial, it is often retained unaltered and the *von* is inserted before the name of some territorial possession, real or imaginary, the newly ennobled becoming MÜLLER VON MÜLLERSHAUSEN, and the like. The Viennese gentry could hardly be persuaded that LUDWIG VAN BEETHOVEN was only of

that on some of its expressions was founded the claim advanced in Lorraine in 1750, that "à la quatrième génération, un anobli, devenu gentilhomme selon les règles héraldiques, acquérait le droit de transmettre la particule de sa fief à son nom.")

In 1699 LOUIS XIV. published a declaration for Franche Comté that "les anoblis et tous autres (que les nobles de race) ne peuvent prendre le *de* devant leurs noms." This article, which made the particule "forbidden fruit" to all but "*nobles de race*," naturally increased the number of those who desired to make use of it; and moreover in consequence of the edict, the *de* appeared in the dictionaries as a sign of nobility. "Cet article *de* marque le génitif, et se met devant les noms de famille qui viennent de seigneuries, M. DE CHÂTEAUNEUF ; M. DE GRAMMONT" (RICHELET, *Dictionnaire*, 1707). The Duc de ST. SIMON, in his *Mémoires*, speaks of its wholesale usurpation: "Le *de* s'usurpait aussi par qui voulait depuis quelque temps." However, the *de* continued to be the subject of legal grants; and, after the Restoration, HOZIER was authorised to insert the particule in the official certificates before the name of the person ennobled.

In 1822, LOUIS XVIII. asked a person to whom he was giving audience how he could reward the devotion he had evinced, and was met by a request for permission to use the *de*. "'Prenez-en deux!' dit le Roi, en fredonnant le vers d'Horace :—

    . . . . 'Gaudent prænomine molles
    Auriculæ . . . .'"

Almost in our own time there was the poet PIERRE JEAN DE BÉRANGER, who may have fairly inherited the particule from remoter progenitors

le nom de plusieurs procureurs" (VIAN, *La Particule Nobiliaire*). The procureur du Roi in the bailliage de Dijon, about the same time, declared, "l'âme et la raison de la loi trouve que tous nos roturiers en général qui changent leur nom en un autre gentilhommesque, ou lesquels y adioustent un article, sont sujets à la peine de faux, car ils usurpent *une qualité de noble* qui tient espèce de rang signalé en France."

On the other hand, a decision was given by the Parliament of Toulouse in 1566, at the instance of a certain procureur, "de rétablir sur le tableau le nom de cet officier et, *comme signe de noblesse*, la particule que l'on y avait à tort omise."

JEAN LOIR, Commissary-general of Artillery, etc., obtained from HENRI IV. in 1596, permission to prefix the *de* to his name; and similar licences, which were understood to convey nobility, were granted in later reigns. Before the *Ordonnance* of 1579 (which provided the contrary) the possession of a noble fief acquired by purchase, even by a "roturier," conferred nobility on its possessor, who, of course, assumed its designation; and LOUIS XIV. in 1696 "permettait aux possesseurs de biens en roture dans les *directes* du Roi d'en prendre le nom."

In 1585, CHARLES III., Duke of LORRAINE, perceiving that many of his subjects assumed the particule and so attributed to themselves nobility in order to avoid certain imposts, published an *Ordonnance*, which strictly prohibited "aux Anoblis et issus de Nobles qu'ils n'aient à soi par adjonction vocale *le, la, du* ou *de*, et semblables mots, qui ne servent que pour obscurcir la famille dont ils sont sortis;" but the edicts had little effect. (The edict is printed in full in the appendix, and it is probable

of the Duc de GÈVRES, the Marquis de GRIGNON, and the Seigneur de NOVION ; NOMPAR, the original appellation of the Ducs de la FORCE. The families of POT, MIRON, MILON, PHILIPPEAUX, AMELOT, RUSÉ, BRULART, FOUQUET, and many other marquises and counts, never used 'the *de*. M. LAINÉ gives the following list of eminent families who never used the particule, or only assumed it in modern times : —DAMAS,—CHABOT,—BERMOND, Seigneur d'ANDUSE—MALVOISIN ou MANVOISIN— PRUNELÉ,—FOUCAUD,—OSMOND,—MORETON,— QUATREBARBES, — GOYON, — BEAUPOIL,—VISDELOU,—SÉGUIER,—DAVID,—LASTEYRIE,—FAYDIT, —GASCQ, — GUISCARD, — YSARN, — COUSTIN, — AUTHIER,—MAINGOT,—BRACHET (*v. Les Salles des Croisades*, par le Comte de DELLEY de BLANCMESNIL, p. 265, Paris, 1866). JACQUES TEZART, Seigneur des ESSARTS, Baron de TOURNEBU, was highly offended at the unauthorised addition of the *de* to his ancient and illustrious name.

Still, the fact that by the many the *de* was associated with the possession of nobility caused it to be coveted and assumed by many who had no right at all to use it. In 1474, LOUIS XI. authorised a notary named DECAUMONT to separate the first syllable from the rest, and to become DE CAUMONT. An *Ordonnance*, given at Amboise, March 26, 1555, and registered at Rouen, interdicted the use of any name but the legal patronymic, and enjoined even gentlemen to sign legal documents by their family names, to the exclusion of the appellations of their seigneuries. This was confirmed in 1560, by article 110 of the *Ordonnance* d'Orléans. The Parliament of Toulouse, in 1566, gave a decision, "ordonnant d'enlever la particule mise dans le tableau, *comme signe de noblesse*, devant

from one another, also served to increase the use of the *de*. But the earliest known use of the particule to indicate the possession of a fief dates from the reign of PHILIP I. (about 1062).

HUGH THE GREAT, Duke of France and Count of Paris, had the surname of CAPET, but used no territorial *de*. Later the possession of a fief afforded an easy and natural means of forming a distinctive surname; thus the Lords of Montmorency, who had generally borne the ordinary name of BOUCHARD, became BOUCHARD DE MONTMORENCY.

The family of MONTMORENCY bore the seemingly proud title of *Premier Baron Chrétien;* which, however, like many other things, was not really so great as it appeared to be. Its origin appears to have faded out of remembrance, but a little research shows that it simply meant that the Baron de Montmorency was the first of the four Vassal Barons, or Chevaliers Bannerets, of the *Chrétienté*, or possessions of the bishop, in the Ile de France. The other three were: le Vicomte de MEAUX, le Vicomte de MELUN, and le Sire de l'ILE ADAM.

But persons of much lower grade, having no pretensions to nobility, assumed as a distinctive surname the name of the town or district whence they came. In "*La Vie de St. Louis*," by the confessor of Queen MARGARET, we find the name of "JEAN DE CROY, mason, townsman of Compiègne." Even serfs leaving their own village, where a Christian name had sufficed, added its name with the *de* to their own. As late as the elections in 1789, the serfs in the Jura Mountains had no surnames.

On the other hand many of the noblest families of France never used the "*particule*." FOUCAULD, Seigneur de la ROCHE, became indeed much later, "le Duc de la ROCHEFOUCAULD." POTIER was the name

his father had borne, as had been done long before by the Jews, and by both Greeks and Romans. This was, of course, the origin of the many British and Scandinavian surnames which end in the syllable "son"; ROBERTSON, JOHNSON, etc.; and of the Sclavonic surnames terminating in "ski," "off," "vitch," etc. In the Latin Cartularies, the formula is usually "ODO filius ISAMBARDI"; "PETRUS filius ALBERTI," etc. The *Cartulary of St. Pére, de Chartres*, in 1119, has the briefer form "ANSOLDUS ROGERII," "ALCHERIUS ADALONIS," etc. In the *Grand Capitulaire* of Champagne a deed of 1261 mentions GULIELMUS RAIMUNDI ; others allude to BERNARDUS ANFREDI, GULIELMUS GIRAUDI, etc. When these names were translated into the vernacular they naturally became, PIERRE D'ALBERT, ANSOLDE DE ROGIER, GUILLAUME DE RAIMOND, GUILLAUME DE GIRAULD, etc. (*La Particule Nobiliaire*, par LOUIS VIAN, Paris, n.d.).

In this way the "*particule*" originated, and some of the most ancient families in France, such as the DE GUILLAUME, Seigneurs de Montpellier ; the DE PIERRE, Seigneurs de Ganges ; the D'ANDRÉ, Seigneurs de Montfort ; the DE JEAN, the DE BARTHÉLEMY, and others who bear apparently Christian names employed as surnames, trace the origin of the fact back to those early times. "Dans le onzième, et dans le douzième siècle, et quelque fois dans le troizième siècle, chaque personnage ne portait que son prénom ou nom de baptême, remplacé quelque fois par une designation personelle, un sur nom ou un sobriquet."—BLANCMESNIL, *Les Salles des Croisades*, xxiii. The Conquest of England, the Crusades, and other military expeditions, which made it needful to adopt surnames to distinguish persons of the same Christian name

noblesse and gentry of Britain has been a cause of much of the foreign confusion of ideas with regard to the nobility of our untitled families, which has been already adverted to.

[A historical investigation into the origin of the *Particule Nobiliaire* will show conclusively that it is not, and never has been, a *titre de noblesse;* an infallible mark of gentle descent; but we must recognise the fact that in later times it has so generally been found in connection with the names of families of noble descent as to have become in many countries of the Continent one of its distinguishing marks. On the introduction of Christianity into Europe its preachers strenuously endeavoured to substitute, at baptism, the Christian name of a saint or martyr for the pagan name, often full of undesirable associations, of the neophyte. This was not done without a severe struggle. SS. CHRYSOSTOM (Homily xiii., *Epistle to the Corinthians*) and GREGORY THE GREAT allude to this repugnance, and enforce the substitution. An examination of the "Personen Register" in the *Urkundenbuch der Abtei Sanct Gallen* (vol. i., A.D. 700-840, Zürich, 1863) will show how little success had attended the attempt. The number of Scriptural or saintly names is absolutely insignificant as compared with the host that are neither the one nor the other. But even where the effort was successful the list of holy names was a limited one, and it was necessary to adopt surnames as an additional means of distinguishing individuals when, as at Bayeux in 1171, there were a hundred and ten knights, besides those of lower grade, who all bore the name of GUILLAUME. The commonest and readiest way of distinguishing persons who bore the same appellation was that of adding to the son's name that which

armigeri natalitii. 3. Esquires created by the King's letters patent, and their eldest sons. 4. Esquires in virtue of their offices; justices of the peace, and others, who bear any office under the crown." "To these," continues BLACKSTONE, "may be added the esquires of Knights of the Bath, each of whom constitutes three at his installation, and all foreign, nay Irish peers." BLACKSTONE'S mention of Irish peers is accounted for by the fact that before the Union of 1801 peers of Ireland were in law foreigners. CAMDEN'S third class of esquires no longer exists, creation by letters patent or investiture having long ceased. CHRISTIAN, in his *Notes to Blackstone*, would limit the official title of esquire to holders of offices of trust under the crown who are styled esquires in their commissions; and he remarks on BLACKSTONE'S omission of barristers, who have been decided by the Court of King's Bench to be esquires by office. No Esquires of the Bath have been appointed since 1812, and by the statutes of the Order in 1847, these Knights have no longer the power to nominate any. In the common usage of this country, at the present day, the designation "esquire" is habitually placed after the names of all persons supposed to be in comfortable circumstances; and its use is considered almost essential in addressing a letter to anyone who, in the looser sense of the word, would be called a "gentleman."

In connection with the same subject some remarks may not be inappropriate on the use of the preposition *de* in French, or *von* in German, the presence or absence of which as a prefix to the surname is often supposed by foreigners to be an absolute test as to whether a person is, or is not, "noble" in the Continental sense, *i.e.*, as having, or not having, the right to use armorial bearings. The absence of the "*Particule Nobiliaire*" from the surnames of the majority of the

sense to any one whose education, profession, perhaps whose income, raises him above ordinary trade or menial service ; or to a man of polite and refined manners and ideas.

A cognate word to gentleman, whose popular acceptation has come to differ much from its original meaning, is esquire. It originally meant the armour-bearer or shield-bearer of a knight.

["L'Écuyer était dans le principe le serviteur Noble qui assistait le Chevalier et portait son Écu ou ses armes quand il allait à la guerre ; plus tard, le droit de porter un Écu peint des armoiries et de devises fut le droit particulier à ceux qui étaient Nobles de race ancienne, de là l'origine du nom d'Écuyer (armiger) qualification que prirent tous les gentilshommes dans la suite des temps. Un arrêt du Parlement de Paris du 30 Octobre 1554, avait proclamé le titre d'Écuyer : 'Caractéristique de la Noblesse, jusqu'à preuve du contraire.' Noble et Écuyer sont deux expressions qui marchaient toujours ensemble dans le langage légal d'autre fois."—*Le Héraut d'Armes*, p. 111, Paris, 1863.— J. W.]

A knight fully equipped in the days of chivalry was attended by two esquires, whose spurs were not of gold, like the knight's, but of silver. An esquire was created by the king by placing spurs on his heels and a collar about his neck. It is difficult to say who in strict law is now entitled to be designed an esquire. Every gentleman of coat-armour is not an esquire. BLACKSTONE quotes with approval CAMDEN'S definition of four classes of esquires. These are : " 1. The eldest sons of knights, and their eldest sons in perpetual succession. 2. The eldest sons of the younger sons of peers, and their eldest sons in perpetual succession ; both which species of esquires Sir HENRY SPELMAN entitles

signa damus et concedamus." As further English examples of the Sovereign conferring rank by a personal act, we need hardly allude to the accolade in knighthood, and the creation of an esquire by the imposition of a collar of livery.

Out of Great Britain the term "noble" is still habitually used in its original sense, and the prerogative of raising persons to noble rank is continually exercised by Continental Sovereigns. The practice which has gradually established itself in England of restricting the words "noble" and "nobility" to members of the Peerage, has perhaps been partly brought about by the devolution by the Sovereign of his right to concede armorial ensigns to the Kings of Arms ; the Sovereign's prerogative being only directly exercised in creating Peerages, in advancing to the rank of Baronet, in conferring simple Knighthood (which has fallen into disuse on the Continent), and in nominating to the several chivalric orders. The difference of usage in this matter between Britain and the Continent has not unfrequently been the source of a strange confusion of ideas on the other side of the Channel, particularly at the minor courts of Germany, where we have heard of a member of the British aristocracy, of the most ancient and distinguished lineage, in respect that he was not himself a peer, or "noble" in the popular English acceptation, having to give the *pas* to a "Baron" or "Herr Von," who had newly received his patent of nobility along with his commission in the army.

While the stricter meaning of the word is retained to the present day in the expression "gentleman by birth," it has often come to be difficult for one who is not a genealogical expert to know who is, or who is not, a gentleman of coat-armour, the less abrupt gradation of ranks and the courtesy of society having caused the word gentleman to be applied in a somewhat loose

known, or *nobilis.* "A plebeian had no blazonry on his shield, because he was *ignobilis,* or unworthy of notice. . . . Hence arms are the criterion of nobility. Every nobleman must have a shield of arms. Whoever has a shield of arms is a nobleman. In every country in Europe without exception a grant of arms or letters of nobility is conferred on all the descendants."

[LE ROQUE, in his *Traité de Noblesse* (4to, Rouen, 1734), says:—"Le Roy par ses lettres patentes concernant les Armoiries, les a non seulement confirmées dans la non-dérogeance: il annoblit tacitement ceux qui ne sont pas nobles, puisqu'il leur accorde ou confirme des armoiries."

At page 59 he adds:—"Quand un souverain permet par ses lettres à un non noble d'avoir des armoiries il l'annoblit tacitement, pourvu que la concession n'ait point quelque cause contraire; car puisqu'on ne peut porter des armoiries nobles sans être noble ou anobli, le prince donnant pouvoir à quelqu'un d'en porter, il lui accorde en même temps la Noblesse, puisque sans cela la concession serait inutile: *Concesso uno conceduntur omnia, sine quibus explicari non potest.*"—J. W.]

As illustrating the usage of letters of nobility existing in our own country reference may be made to two examples of the reign of HENRY VI. (printed from the *Excerpta Historica* in the *Herald and Genealogist,* i., p. 135), one to NICHOLAS CLOOS, the other to ROGER KEYS, clerk, and THOMAS his brother. CLOOS had been engaged in the works of King's College, Cambridge, and KEYS in those of Eton College; and in reward for their services each had a grant of nobility containing the express words "nobilitamus nobilemque facimus et creamus," these being followed by others showing that armorial ensigns were regarded the usual tokens of nobility: "in signum hujus nobilitatis arma et armorum

at the courts of their superiors similar to those by which the latter held their lands from the Sovereign. By a constitution of this kind, but with variations in detail, society was held together in the different parts of Europe. The landholder was the nobleman or gentleman; and the smallest tenant of land held by military tenure participated in the privileges of nobility. The gentry of England had many privileges recognised by law. If a churl, or peasant, defamed the honour of a gentleman, the latter had his remedy in law; but if one gentleman defamed another the combat was allowed. For similar offences a gentleman was punishable with less severity than a churl, unless the crime was heresy, treason, or excessive contumacy. A gentleman, in his examination, was not subjected to torture; and, if condemned to death, he was beheaded and not ignominiously hanged. A churl might not challenge a gentleman to combat, "*quia conditiones impares.*"

Side by side with feudalism grew up the use of distinctive devices, by which on banner or shield the performers of military service were distinguished. Like the *jus imaginum* of classic times, the right to bear *iusignia gentilitia* became in the later middle ages the distinctive privilege of the nobly born. "Nobiles," says Sir EDWARD COKE, "sunt qui arma gentilitia antecessorum suorum proferre possunt." To use the words of CAMDEN, "Nobiles dividuntur in minores et majores. Nobiles minores sunt equites aurati, armigeri, et qui vulgo generosi et *gentlemen* vocantur." Or in the language of Sir JAMES LAWRENCE (*Nobility of the British Gentry*, p. 3, 4th edition, London, 1840), "Any individual who distinguishes himself may be said to ennoble himself." A prince judging an individual worthy of notice gave him patent letters of nobility. In these letters were blazoned the arms which were to distinguish his shield. By this shield he was to be

ou du Véritable Art du Blason, appeared in 1661; and *La Pratique des Armoiries* in 1671. In later books the designation is usually "*la Science du Blason*," etc. The great German authority, SPENER, entitles his work *Opus Heraldicum*, whence RUDOLPHUS took the title *Heraldica Curiosa*.—J. W.]

Before entering on the consideration of armorial distinctions, it may be advisable to make a few preliminary observations on a subject intimately connected with them: differences of social rank, and surnames.

At all times, and in all countries, the condition of society has been one of inequality. In the heroic days of Greece we have a glimpse of families or races of larger, stronger, more vigorous men, ruling over the rest of the community. In ancient Rome there were two great classes, corresponding with the new settlers, and the ancient inhabitants of the country who had to make way for them. In old Celtic times, when cattle were the synonym of wealth, the unequal distribution of this wealth, which had its origin in the natural diversities of character, led to a gradation of rank which is recognised in the Brehon laws. The broadly marked difference between the nobleman or gentleman, and the rest of the community, is one of the most prominent features of mediæval life; and the source from which the less abrupt gradations of rank in modern society have been gradually developed. According to feudal ideas the whole land was, in the first instance, the property of the Sovereign, from whom it was held under the obligation of rendering stated military service; with or without the further obligation of attendance at his court and council. The immediate vassals of the Crown, who were in the first instance called Barons (as emphatically the King's *men*), enjoyed in some cases the office of *Comes*, or *Dux*, and had vassals who held their lands from them by a like military tenure; and with obligations of attendance

The "science" or rather art, which teaches us the language, and instructs us in the origin and development, of these symbols, should with greater propriety be termed Armory. This is the designation applied to it by the earliest writers on the subject, both in England and in France, but it is one which for more than two and a half centuries, has greatly fallen into disuse; and the better understood name of Heraldry consequently appears in the title of the present work. The term Armory is used by GERARD LEGH, *Accidence of Armory*, 1568; BOSSEWELL, *Armorie of Honor*, WYRLEY, *True Use of Armorie*, 1592; BOLTON, *Elements of Armorie*, 1610. GUILLIM (or the writer who used his name) led the more modern fashion by calling his work, first published in 1610, *A Display of Heraldry*. Sir GEORGE MACKENZIE'S treatise on the *Science of Heraldry, treated as a part of the Civil Law and Law of Nations*, was published in 1680. Though one of NISBET'S earlier books was, in 1716, entitled *An Essay on the Ancient and Modern use of Armory*, his later and principal work, printed in 1722, was called *A System of Heraldry*.

[On the other side of the Channel, JEAN LE FERON in 1544 calls his work *Le Grand Blason d'Armoiries*, a term also employed by BARA in 1581 and following years. GELIOT'S work, published in 1635, is *La Vraie et Perfect Science des Armoiries;* DE LA COLOMBIÈRE in 1644 uses the term "La Science Héroïque;" but three years later appeared FAURE'S *Abrégé Méthodique de la Science Héraldique*. SEGOING, who printed his *Mercure Armorial* in 1648, calls its later editions *Le Trésor Héraldique*. The many small, but most valuable, treatises of the learned Jesuit PÈRE MENÉTRIER have similarly varying titles, *e.g.*, *l'Abrégé Méthodique des Principales Héraldiques;*

A

TREATISE ON HERALDRY,
BRITISH AND FOREIGN.

CHAPTER I.

ETYMOLOGICALLY a treatise on Heraldry should be an explanation of the duties of a Herald. Though an analogy has been drawn between the Greek κῆρυξ, or Latin *fecialis*, and the herald of later times, the latter was essentially a mediæval officer whose name seems to be derived from *Heer*, a host, and *Held*, a champion.

He was in the first place the messenger of war or peace between sovereigns; and of courtesy or defiance between knights. His functions further included the superintendence of trials by battle, jousts, tournaments, and public ceremonies generally. When the bearing of hereditary armorial insignia became an established usage its supervision was in most European countries added to the other duties of the herald. The office survives in our own, and in some other countries, but with duties greatly curtailed; and with this narrowing of his functions the term "Heraldry" has come to signify, not a knowledge of the multifarious duties of a herald of former times, but chiefly the study of that part of them which relates to family and national insignia, including also subsidiarily such kindred topics as precedence, hereditary and personal titles and dignities, and the insignia which are attached to them.

Fig.			Page
84.	,,	Adolphus, Duke of Cambridge	421
85.	,,	Princess Royal	421
86.	,,	Princess Augusta	421
87.	,,	,, Elizabeth	421
88.	,,	,, Mary	421
89.	,,	,, Sophia	421
90.	Escucheon of Henri de Ferrières		453
91.	The "Écu-Complet" of the Austrian Empire		497
92.	Daubeny Achievement		599
93.	Helmet of Sovereign		602
94.	,, Peers		602
95.	,, Baronets and Knights		602

Fig.		Page
96.	,, Gentlemen	602
97.	Crown of Charlemagne	617
98.	Arms, etc., of Prince Putbus	627
99.	Seal of Louis, Count of Flanders	648
100.	Banner of Percy	649
101.	,, from Bayeux Tapestry	649
102.	,, ,, ,, ,,	649
103.	,, ,, ,, ,,	649
104.	,, ,, ,, ,,	649
105.	,, of Maurice de Berkeley	651
106.	Tabard or Coat of Arms	674

LIST OF FIGURES

Fig.		Page
1.	From Etruscan Vases	18
2.	,, ,,	18
3.	,, ,,	18
4.	,, ,,	18
5.	Cohort Ensigns	19
6.	,, ,,	19
7.	Shield, Oval	53
8.	,, à bouche	53
9.	,,	53
10.	,, Spanish	53
11.	,, Lozenge	53
12.	,, 16th Century	53
13.	,, ,, ,,	53
14.	,, ,, ,,	53
15.	English Points of Escucheon	59
16.	French ,, ,,	59
17.	Line, Engrailed	75
18.	,, Embattled	75
19.	,, Indented	75
20.	,, Invecked	75
21.	,, Wavy or Undy	75
22.	,, Nebuly	75
23.	,, Dancetty	75
24.	,, Raguly	75
25.	,, Potenté	75
26.	,, Dovetailed	75
27.	,, Urdy	75
28.	Per Pale	77
29.	,, Fess	77
30.	Quarterly	77
31.	Per Bend	77
32.	,, Bend-Sinister	77
33.	,, Saltire	77
34.	,, Chevron	77
35.	Enté en point	77
36.	Champagne	77
37.	The Pale	116
38.	,, Fess	116
39.	,, Bend	116
40.	,, Bend-Sinister	116
41.	,, Chevron	116
42.	,, Saltire	116
43.	,, Pile	116
44.	,, Gyron	116
45.	,, Lozenge	116
46.	,, Fusil	116
47.	Cross, Passion	164
48.	,, Greek	164
49.	,, Calvary	164
50.	,, Patriarchal	164

Fig.		Page
51.	,, Potent	164
52.	,, Lorraine	164
53.	,, Patty	164
54.	,, Patty-Fitchy	164
55.	,, Maltese	164
56.	,, Patonce	164
57.	,, Fleur-de-lisée	164
58.	,, Flory	164
59.	,, Fourchy	164
60.	,, Aiguisée	164
61.	,, Tau	164
62.	Eagle of Germany	242
63.	Fleur-de-lis, from Tomb of Count d'Euat, St. Hilaire	315
64.	Fleur-de-lis, from Portrait in Sauvageot Collection	315
65.	Fleur-de-lis, from stained glass in Depaulis Collection	315
66.	Fleur-de-lis, from Rey, Plate IV., Fig. 31	315
67.	Fleur-de-lis, from Seal of Falaise	315
68.	Fleur-de-lis, from Seal of the Châtelet of Paris	315
69.	Fleur-de-lis, from Rey, Plate XVII., Fig. 210	315
70.	Fleur-de-lis, in time of latest Bourbon Kings	315
71.	Early Swedish Coat, from HILDEBRAND, *Det Svenska Riks Vapnet*	326
72.	Arms of Créquy	344
73.	Helmet from Worsaac, Nordiske Oldsager	345
74.	Helmet from Worsaac, Nordiske Oldsager	345
75.	Lymphad	366
76.	,,	366
77.	Helmet	395
78.	,,	395
79.	,,	395
80.	*Label* of PRINCE OF WALES	421
81.	,, WILLIAM, Duke of CLARENCE	421
82.	,, EDWARD, Duke of KENT	421
83.	,, LEOPOLD, Duke of ALBANY	421

(xxxvi)

PLATE			
XXX.	Emblazoned, Arms containing Flowers, Fleur-de-lis, Thistle, Chaplet, Pomegranate, Rye, and Garb	*facing page*	332
XXXI.	,, Arms containing Sword, Spear, Battle-axe, Helmet, Bow, Arrow, Pheon, Battering-Ram, Caltrap, Chains, and Water-Budget	,,	346
XXXII.	,, Arms containing Barnacle, Stirrup, Castle, Tower, Column, Ladder, Stair, and Lymphad	,,	358
XXXIII.	,, Arms containing Maunch, Buckle, Crown, Key, Cup, Cushion, Caldron, Horn, Clarion, and Words	,,	376
XXXIV.	Banners, Sail with Arms, etc.	,,	388
XXXV.	*Seals*		416
XXXVI.	*Arms* of JEAN, Duc d'ALBANY	,,	446
XXXVII.	*Seals*	,,	448
XXXVIII.	Emblazoned, Marshalling, Dimidiation, etc.	,,	464
XXXIX.	,, Marshalling	,,	482
XL.	,, *Achievement* of MARIA THERESA	,,	494
XLI.	,, Marshalling	,,	510
XLII.	,, Marshalling	,,	512
XLIII.	,, Marshalling	,,	522
XLIV.	,, Armorial du Héraut Gueldre	,,	538
XLV.	,, Wappenrolle von Zürich	,,	540
XLVI.	,, Wappenrolle von Zürich	,,	546
XLVII.	,, Illegitimacy	,,	574
XLVIII.	,, Illegitimacy	,,	576
XLIX.	Crests	,,	606
L.	Crowns and Coronets	,,	624
LI.	Emblazoned, Royal Arms of England, etc.	,,	661
LII.	,, Royal Arms of Great Britain, etc.	,,	662
LIII.	,, National Arms	,,	664
LIV.	,, National Arms	,,	666
LV.	,, Partitions, etc.	,,	668
LVI.	,, Partitions, etc.	,,	670

LIST OF PLATES

Plate				
I.	Shields		facing page	44
II.	Examples of Shields and Armour		,,	54
III.	Emblazoned, *Tinctures*		,,	60
IV.	,,	*Furs*	,,	62
V.	,,	Modes of Partition	,,	80
VI.	,,	Modes of Partition	,,	84
VII.	,,	Modes of Partition	,,	90
VIII.	,,	Modes of Partition	,,	100
IX.	,,	Rules of Blazon	,,	108
X.	,,	Arms containing *Chief* and *Pale*	,,	118
XI.	,,	Arms containing *Fess*	,,	124
XII.	,,	Arms containing *Bend*	,,	130
XIII.	,,	Arms containing *Chevron*	,,	136
XIV.	,,	Arms containing *Cross*	,,	140
XV.	,,	Arms containing *Cross* and *Saltire*	,,	144
XVI.	,,	Arms containing *Pile* and *Pall*	,,	146
XVII.	,,	Arms containing *Bordure*, *Orle*, and *Tressure*	,,	172
XVIII.	,,	Arms containing *Canton*, *Gyron*, *Flanche*, *Lozenge*, *Mascle*, and *Fusil*	,,	190
XIX.	,,	Arms containing *Billet*, *Roundles*, *Gurges*, *Rainbow*, *Annulet*, *Vires*, *Fret*, and *Escutcheon*	,,	192
XX.	,,	Arms containing Human Figure and parts thereof	,,	198
XXI.	,,	Arms containing Lions	,,	212
XXII.	,,	Arms containing Lions and parts of Lions, and also Tiger and Leopard	,,	222
XXIII.	,,	Arms containing Boar, Wolf, Bear, Fox, and Stag	,,	228
XXIV.	,,	Arms containing Bull, Goat, Lamb, Antelope, Horse, Hare, Otter, Talbot, Herrison, Mole, and Ermine	,,	236
XXV.	,,	Arms containing Eagle, Falcon, Owl, Swan, Stork, Pelican	,,	260
XXVI.	,,	Arms containing Chough, Papingoes, Cock, Martlet, Bream, Salmon, Dolphin, Barbel, Trout, Stockfish, Escallops	,,	266
XXVII.	,,	Arms containing Snake, Serpent, Griffin, Dragon, Wyvern, Cockatrice, Unicorn, Seahorse, and Mermaid	,,	288
XXVIII.	,,	Arms containing Sun, Crescent Star, Estoile, Mullet, Mount, Hill, River, and Hedge	,,	308
XXIX.	,,	Arms containing Trees, Forest, and Leaves	,,	318

Surgeon Major G. B. Stuart, 7 Carlton Street, Edinburgh.
W. G. Taunton, Esq., New Club, Jersey, Channel Islands.
Achilles Taylor, Esq., Midland Educational Co., Birmingham.
The Right Hon. Lady Jane Taylor, 16 Eaton Place, London, S.W.
Mr James Thin, Bookseller, 55 South Bridge, Edinburgh (3 Copies).
Messrs Thomson Brothers, Booksellers, 74 George Street, Edinburgh.
John A. Trail, Esq., LL.B., W.S., 30 Drummond Place, Edinburgh.
Messrs H. & C. Treacher, Booksellers, 1 North Street, Brighton.
Alexander Ure, Esq., Advocate, 26 Heriot Row, Edinburgh.
George Seton Veitch, Esq., Friarshall, Paisley (*per* Mr A. Gardner, Bookseller, Paisley).
William Wardlaw Waddell, Esq., 1 Royal Gardens, Stirling.
Mr Gilbert G. Walmsley, Bookseller, 50 Lord Street, Liverpool.
John Watson, Esq., Glasgow (*per* Mr H. Hopkins, Bookseller, Glasgow).
Lieut.-Col. Gould Hunter-Weston, F.S.A., Hunterston, West Kilbride.
T. W. Wightman, Esq., Parkend Villa, Ferry Road, Edinburgh (*per* Mr J. R. M'Intosh, Bookseller, Edinburgh).
Mr Alfred Wilson, Bookseller, 18 Gracechurch Street, London, E.C.
Sir Albert W. Woods, Garter, College of Arms, Queen Victoria Street, London, E.C.
Rev. John Woodward, Rector of St. Mary's Church, Montrose (2 Copies).
Messrs D. Wyllie & Son, Booksellers, 247 Union Street, Aberdeen.
Harold Edgar Young, Esq., 6 Arundel Avenue, Liverpool (2 Copies).
William Laurence Young, Esq., Belvidere, Auchterarder.

(xxxii)

David Murray, Esq., LL.D., Glasgow (*per* Mr H. Hopkins, Bookseller, Glasgow).
George Neilson, Esq., Glasgow (*per* Mr H. Hopkins, Bookseller, Glasgow).
W. Neish, Esq., The Laws, Dundee.
E. Carrington Ouvry, Esq., East Acton, London, W.
Messrs Palmer & Howe, Booksellers, 73 Princess Street, Manchester.
J. Balfour Paul, Esq., Lyon King of Arms, 32 Great King Street, Edinburgh.
Mr Y. J. Pentland, Bookseller, 11 Teviot Place, Edinburgh.
Messrs E. A. Petherick & Co., 33 Paternoster Row, London, E.C. (6 Copies).
Mr G. Petrie, Bookseller, 52 Nethergate, Dundee.
Moro Phillips, Esq., West St. House, Chichester.
Mr William Potter, Bookseller, Exchange St. East, Liverpool.
Messrs George Robertson & Co., Booksellers, Melbourne.
Mr H. Robinson, Bookseller, 48 Fishergate, Preston.
J. Brooking-Rowe, Esq., Castle Barbican, Plympton, S. Devon.
S. G. Stopford Sackville, Esq., Drayton House, Thrapston.
Arthur Sanderson, Esq., 5 Carlton Terrace, Edinburgh (*per* Mr J. R. M'Intosh, Bookseller, 7 North Bank Street, Edinburgh).
Fred. R. Sanderson, Esq., 1 Regent Terrace, Edinburgh (*per* Mr J. R. M'Intosh, Bookseller, 7 North Bank Street, Edinburgh).
Signet Library, Parliament Square, Edinburgh.
Sir Walter G. Simpson, Bart., of Balabraes, Ayton.
David Smith, Esq., 20 Cardin Place, Aberdeen (*per* Messrs D. Wyllie & Son, Booksellers, Aberdeen).
Messrs J. Smith & Son, Booksellers, 129 West George Street, Glasgow.
Bellingham A. Somerville, Esq., Friars Hill House, Wicklow.
The Right Hon. Earl of Southesk, K.T., Kinnaird Castle, Brechin (*per* Mr Matthew Welsh, Bookseller, Montrose).
The New Spalding Club, Aberdeen.
S.S.C. Library, Edinburgh (*per* Messrs Bell & Bradfute, Booksellers, Edinburgh).
Captain Stansfield of Duninald, Duninald Castle, Montrose (*per* Mr Matthew Welsh, Bookseller, Montrose).
Mr Thomas G. Stevenson, Bookseller, 22 Frederick Street, Edinburgh (2 Copies).
Mr James Stillie, Bookseller, 19*a* George Street, Edinburgh.
Stockport Free Library Committee.
The Right Hon. Earl of Strathmore and Kinghorne, Glamis Castle, Forfar.

Mons. C. Klincksieck, Paris (*per* Messrs Longmans & Co, Publishers, London).
Mr Alderman Stuart Knill, Fresh Wharf, London Bridge, E.C.
Perceval Landon, Esq., Hertford College, Oxford.
James Lang, Esq., 9 Crown Gardens, Dowanhill, Glasgow.
Edward B. Lees, Esq., Thurland Castle, Kirkby Lonsdale.
Mrs Thomas Leslie, Woodend House, Banchory.
Alex. Littlejohn, Esq., Invercharron House, Ardgay.
The Right Hon. Earl of Lonsdale, The Castle, Whitehaven.
The Most Noble the Marquess of Lothian, K.T., Monteviot, Jedburgh.
George Lowson, Esq., High School of Stirling.
Messrs Lupton Bros., Booksellers, 16 Market Hall, Burnley (2 Copies).
Messrs M'Corquodale & Co., Limited, St. Thomas Street, Southwark, London.
P. M. MacIntyre, Esq., Advocate, 12 India Street, Edinburgh.
Rev. G. S. Mackay, Doune (*per* Messrs Macniven & Wallace, Booksellers, Edinburgh).
Alexander Mackenzie, Esq., Saint Catherine's, Paisley (*per* Mr A. Gardner, Bookseller, Paisley).
J. Maclauchlan, Esq., Chief Librarian, Free Library, Dundee.
Messrs James MacLehose & Sons, Booksellers, 61 St. Vincent Street, Glasgow.
Messrs Macniven & Wallace, Booksellers, 138 Princes Street, Edinburgh (2 Copies).
James Mann, Esq., Glasgow (*per* Mr H. Hopkins, Bookseller, Glasgow).
F. J. Martin, Esq., W.S., 9 Glencairn Crescent, Edinburgh (*per* Messrs Macniven & Wallace, Booksellers, Edinburgh).
Thomas A. Mathieson, Esq., 3 Grosvenor Terrace, Glasgow.
The Right Hon. Viscount Melville, Melville Castle, Lasswade.
Messrs Melville, Mullen & Slade, Booksellers, Melbourne (2 Copies).
Messrs J. Menzies & Co., Booksellers, 12 Hanover Street, Edinburgh.
John Millar, Esq., Seagrove House, Seafield (*per* Mr Andrew Elliot, Bookseller, Edinburgh).
James William Mitchell, Esq., Lyon Clerk, Colinton Mains, Colinton.
Alex. Moffatt, Esq., 23 Abercromby Place, Edinburgh.
Arthur D. Morice, Esq., Eastbank, Aberdeen (*per* Messrs D. Wyllie & Son, Booksellers, Aberdeen).
Mr Alex. Moring, First Avenue Hotel Buildings, High Holborn, London, W.C. (2 Copies).
J. Gardiner Muir, Esq., Hillcrest, Market Harborough.

(xxx)

L. Morgan Grenville, Esq., Maids Moreton Lodge, Buckingham.
Hartwell D. Grissell, Esq., M.A., Chamberlain to His Holiness Pope Leo XIII., Brasenose College, Oxford.
Robert Guy, Esq.,. Glasgow (*per* Mr H. Hopkins, Bookseller, Glasgow).
His Grace the Duke of Hamilton and Brandon, Easton Park, Wickham Market.
The Right Hon. Lord Hamilton of Dalzell, Motherwell.
Messrs Harrison & Sons, Publishers, 59 Pall Mall, London, S.W.
Simeon Hayes, Esq., 94 Ashdell Road, Sheffield.
C. E. H. Chadwyck Healey, Esq., Q.C., 119 Harley Street, London, W.
Rev. H. Grosett Heaven (of Lundy), 26 Sion Hill, Clifton, Bristol.
Mr John Heywood, Bookseller, Deansgate, Manchester.
James Hilton, Esq., F.S.A., 60 Montagu Square, London.
Charles Hindley, Esq., 41 Holywell Street, London, W.C.
Mr John Hitchman, 51 Cherry Street, Birmingham.
Messrs Hodges, Figgis & Co., Publishers, 104 Grafton Street, Dublin (3 Copies).
Messrs W. & R. Holmes, Booksellers, 3 Dunlop Street, Glasgow.
H. Hopkins, Esq., 85 Renfield Street, Glasgow.
Admiral G. Phipps Hornby, Lordington, Emsworth.
Captain H. R. Howard, Verulam Road, St. Albans (*per* Civil Service Supply Association, London).
James C. Howden, Esq., M.D., Sunnyside, Montrose (*per* Mr Matthew Welsh, Bookseller, Montrose).
Col. Hunter of Plâs Côch, Anglesea.
The Right Hon. Lord Iveagh, 5 Grosvenor Place, London.
Richard Dickson Jackson, Esq., London (*per* Mr H. Hopkins, Bookseller, Glasgow).
Robert Jeffrey, Esq., Crosslie (*per* Mr H. Hopkins, Bookseller, Glasgow).
Mr George P. Johnston, Bookseller, 33 George Street, Edinburgh.
William Johnston, Esq., Glasgow (*per* Mr H. Hopkins, Bookseller, Glasgow).
Messrs. Jones & Evans, 77 Queen Street, London, E.C.
Mr William Jones, Bookseller, 6 Duke Street, Cardiff.
William F. Kay, Esq., Trinity, Edinburgh (*per* Mr J. R. M'Intosh, Bookseller, 7 North Bank Street, Edinburgh).
The Right Hon. Lord R. Kerr, District Lodge, Curragh Camp, Ireland.

Edward Cox, Esq., of Cardean, Meigle, N.B.
R. J. Blair Cunynghame, Esq., M.D., 18 Rothesay Place, Edinburgh.
William Ogilvy Dalgleish, Esq., Errol Park, Errol, Perthshire.
Hugh Davidson, Esq., Lanark (*per* Messrs Macniven & Wallace, Booksellers, Edinburgh).
Col. G. R. Dease, Celbridge Abbey, Celbridge, Ireland.
Messrs A. & F. Denny, Booksellers, 304 Strand, London, W.C.
C. Wriothesly Digby, Esq., Meriden Hall, Coventry, Warwickshire.
Messrs Douglas & Foulis, Booksellers, 9 Castle Street, Edinburgh (6 Copies).
Archibald H. Dunbar, Esq., Northfield, Bournemouth.
Mr Henry S. Eland, Bookseller, 236 High Street, Exeter.
Mr Andrew Elliot, Bookseller, 17 Princes Street, Edinburgh (2 Copies).
T. Leonard Ellis, Esq., Coatbridge (*per* Mr H. Hopkins, Bookseller, Glasgow).
Reginald S. Faber, Esq., 10 Oppidans Road, Primrose Hill, London, N.W.
R. S. Ferguson, Esq., F.S.A., Chancellor of Carlisle, Lowther Street, Carlisle.
Henry Forrester, Esq., Glasgow (*per* Mr H. Hopkins, Bookseller, Glasgow).
Miss Foster, Moor Park, Ludlow, Shropshire (2 Copies).
Mrs W. E. Franklin, Bookseller, 42 Moseley Street, Newcastle-on-Tyne.
A. D. Weld French, Esq., Boston, Massachusetts, U.S.A. (*per* Mr George P. Johnston, Bookseller, Edinburgh).
Principal Geddes, University of Aberdeen, Chanonry Lodge, Old Aberdeen.
Messrs Georges' Sons, Booksellers, 89 Park Street, Bristol.
George More-Gordon, Esq., of Charleton, Montrose (*per* Mr Matthew Welsh, Bookseller, Montrose).
George Graham, Esq., Glasgow (*per* Mr H. Hopkins, Bookseller, Glasgow).
F. J. Grant, Esq., W.S., Carrick Pursuivant, 42 Ann Street, Edinburgh.
Mr John Grant, Bookseller, 25 George IV. Bridge, Edinburgh.
Messrs R. Grant & Son, Booksellers, 107 Princes Street, Edinburgh.
George Gray, Esq., Glasgow (*per* Mr H. Hopkins, Bookseller, Glasgow).
Everard Green, Esq., Reform Club, London.
Messrs William Green & Sons, Booksellers, 18 St. Giles Street, Edinburgh.

Messrs Bickers & Son, Publishers, 1 Leicester Square, London W.C.
Alexander Blair, Esq., Sheriff of the Lothians & Peebles, 35 Moray Place.
The Right Hon. Lord Bolton, Bolton Hall, Wensley, Yorkshire.
W. L. Bradbury, Esq., 10 Bouverie Street, London, E.C.
James Bromley, Esq., The Homestead, Lathom, Ormskirk.
Messrs Brook & Chrystal, Booksellers, 11 Market Street, Manchester.
William Broughton, Esq., 3 Florence Villas, Woodford.
Mr William Brown, Publisher, 26 Princes Street, Edinburgh (8 Copies).
Messrs D. Bryce & Son, Publishers, 129 Buchanan Street, Glasgow.
William Buchan, Esq., Town Clerk, Peebles.
Charles A. Buckler, Esq., Surrey Herald, 6 Hereford Square, South Kensington, London.
Mr John Bumpus, Bookseller, 350 Oxford Street, London, W.
Lieut.-Col. W. St. George Burke, Auberies, Sudbury, Suffolk.
John William Burns, Esq., Kilmahew (*per* Mr H. Hopkins, Bookseller, Glasgow).
James W. Carlile, Esq., Gayhurst House, Newport Pagnell, Bucks (2 Copies).
The Right Hon. Lord William Cecil, Burghley House, Stamford.
His Honour Judge Chalmers, 12 Union Road, Leamington.
Alexander M. Chance, Esq., Lawnside, Edgbaston.
Messrs Clarke & Hodgson, Booksellers, 5 Gallowtree Gate, Leicester.
Mr William F. Clay, Bookseller, 2 Teviot Place, Edinburgh (3 Copies).
H. J. B. Clements, Esq., Killadoon, Celbridge, Ireland (*per* Messrs Hodges, Figgis & Co., Publishers, Dublin).
Mr Edward Clulow, The Library, Derby.
G. E. Cokayne, Esq., Norroy King of Arms, Exeter House, Roehampton, S.W.
Messrs A. J. Combridge & Co., 31 Newgate Street, London, E.C.
Messrs Cornish Brothers, Publishers, 37 New Street, Birmingham.
Mr J. E. Cornish, Publisher, 16 St. Ann's Square, Manchester.
J. A. Crawford, Esq., Northfield, Annan (*per* Mr Andrew Elliot, Bookseller, Edinburgh).
Sir Claude Champion de Crespigny, Bart., Champion Lodge, Maldon.

LIST OF SUBSCRIBERS

Aberdeen Public Library (*per* Messrs D. Wyllie & Son, Booksellers, Aberdeen).
Aberdeen University Library.
Sir Charles Adam, Bart., of Blairadam, Kinross-shire.
William Adams, Esq., 5 Shandwick Place, Edinburgh (*per* Mr George Wilson, Bookseller, Edinburgh).
Advocates' Library, Edinburgh, c/o J. T. Clark, Esq., Librarian.
James H. Aitken, Esq., Gartcows, Falkirk (*per* Mr George P. Johnston, Bookseller, Edinburgh).
Mr E. G. Allen, Bookseller, 28 Henrietta Street, Covent Garden, London, W.C.
Archibald Anderson, Esq., 30 Oxford Square, London, W.
Messrs J. T. Anderson & Co., Stationers and Heraldic Artists, 62 King Street, Manchester.
The Right Rev. the Bishop of Argyle and the Isles (*per* Messrs R. Grant & Son, Booksellers, Edinburgh).
Army and Navy Co-operative Society, Limited, Victoria Street, London, S.W.
Messrs Asher & Co., Publishers, 13 Bedford Street, London, W.C.
Miss Ashton, 6 Osborne Terrace, Edinburgh.
B. Bagnall, Esq., Ellerslie, Eaton Gardens, Hove, Sussex.
J. Bagnall, Esq., Water Orton, near Birmingham.
Mr James Bain, Bookseller, 1 Haymarket, London, S.W.
Charles B. Balfour, Esq., Newton Don, Kelso.
Richard Barnwell, Esq., Glasgow (*per* Mr H. Hopkins, Bookseller, Glasgow).
Thomas Bate, Esq., Kelsterton, Flint.
W. A. C. à Beckett, Esq., Penleigh House, Westbury, Wilts.
James Bell, Esq., Glasgow (*per* Mr H. Hopkins, Bookseller, Glasgow).
Joseph Bell, Esq., M.D., 2 Melville Crescent, Edinburgh.
Alfred Bevan, Esq., 39 Queen's Gate, London, S.W. (*per* Mr E. Stanford, Publisher, London).
Joseph Bewley, Esq., Dublin (*per* Messrs Hodges, Figgis, & Co., Publishers, Dublin).

of love ") of GEORGE HARVEY JOHNSTON, Esq., who is himself an enthusiastic and well-instructed student of Heraldry, and for whose intelligent and sustained interest in the work I am delighted to make my sincere and grateful acknowledgments.

My critics will, I trust, be of the mind of HORACE:—

". . . . non ego paucis
Offendar maculis, quas aut incuria fudit,
Aut humana parum cavit natura."
De Arte Poetica, l. 351-3.

JOHN WOODWARD.

MONTROSE, 1891.

of the differences referred to above. Specimens of blazon in Spanish, German, and Portuguese are included in the work, and the instances adduced in illustration are drawn for the first time from the Armory of every European state. In the choice of these I have been mainly guided by the desire to justify a position which I take up as regards *armes parlantes*, and to which allusion is made in the last Chapter of the book.

The first volume will be the more useful to the beginner; the second will, I hope and think, be of equal use and interest to those who have already mastered the general principles of the Science.

My object has been, then, to set forth historical facts; there is no dearth of treatises which will enable the student who has acquired a knowledge of these "dry bones," to clothe them with any desired amount of poetic and graceful fiction.

With regard to the illustrations I should say that the plate of *fac-similes* from the *Armorial de Gelre* is only entitled so to be described as far as its general outlines are concerned. The splendid edition of this work, published in *fac-simile* by M. VICTOR BOUTON, had not come under my notice at the time my drawing was made, and the colouring is what I conceived should be there, rather than the (often erroneous or unheraldic) tinctures employed in the MS. itself. I must also guard myself against the supposition that I endorse the authenticity of all the coats which appear in the *Salle des Croisés* at Versailles to which I have often referred. Some coats which appear there may be open to serious doubts; but these do not, I think, exist in regard to any of the examples quoted in the present work.

The utility of such a book as this largely depends upon its having a good Index. Both the reader and the writer are to be congratulated that in the present case the Index has been the careful work (I think a "labour

in this country is one of the causes why a Scotchman can rarely speak and write on any of these subjects without being exposed to the charge of using a language he does not understand."—(*Scotland in the Middle Ages*, p. 302.)

These remarks were equally applicable to persons of other nationalities besides that to which the Professor referred, but in all civilised countries many more persons are now interested in Heraldry than was the case when those words were written, and when a knowledge of the subject almost required of its possessor an apology for having wasted his time on a study deemed by the ignorant frivolous and unprofitable.

No doubt what was called the "jargon of heraldry," and, even more, the undue importance attached by its professors to the petty *minutiæ* of blazon, had the natural effect of deterring many from it as a serious study. Heraldry has indeed in each country a language of its own, intended to express facts clearly and distinctly. That in use in Britain is a mixture of English and Norman-French, which assumed nearly its present shape in the thirteenth century. In the Heraldry of France, though some of the terms are the same as, or similar to, those in use among us, there are considerable differences in others, and still greater differences in modes of blazon.

As the student who wishes to take a wider view of an interesting subject than is to be obtained from works describing the uses of his own country, will have at the outset to make the acquaintance of many of the most useful treatises which are written in the French language, I have endeavoured to facilitate his progress by adding to the work a French, as well as an English, Glossary; and by printing so many blazons in the French language as should be sufficient to give a person of moderate intelligence a fair idea of the phraseology employed, and

facts. Nor will the reader find herein any allusion (except occasionally by way of warning) to the many fables which have been so often repeated in our heraldic works as now frequently to be taken for approved facts, such as those which profess to account for the origin of the arms of many illustrious families by legends which will not endure examination by the light of history.

These legends are often poetical and interesting; nevertheless Heraldry has suffered in public estimation as much by the continuous repetition of stories which an elementary knowledge of history proves to be fictitious, as by an entirely needless association with a multitude of absurdities in natural history, with which many of the old professed treatises on Heraldry were padded, and which are only of interest to us as affording a gauge of our ancestors' ignorance and credulity.

Of late years there has been as great a revival of interest in Heraldry as in other archæological matters. Its value is becoming increasingly recognised, not only as an interesting link between the present and the past, but as an important auxiliary, which those who are concerned in historical or artistic studies cannot afford to neglect.

Forty years ago the late Professor COSMO INNES, one of the leading historical antiquaries of the time, wrote on this subject as follows:—

" I hope it will not alarm any one if I venture merely to allude to the science of heraldry, a study which of old engaged the attention of all that were gentle born— which is now left to the tender mercies of the lapidary and the coach-painter—*Requiescat!* I might indeed suggest the great importance of some knowledge of heraldry to the student of historical antiquities. For the pursuit of family history, of topographical and territorial learning, of ecclesiology, of architecture, it is altogether indispensable; and its total and contemptuous neglect

position and long continued historical research enabled him to speak with a knowledge and authority to which I could not pretend.

I have, therefore, not only had the pleasure to comply with a very proper condition that Dr BURNETT'S name should appear in conjunction with my own upon the cover and title-page of the book, but I have also printed *in extenso*, and clearly marked with his initials, both in the text and in the synopsis, those valuable portions of the work to which allusion is made in the preceding paragraph.

The portion of Chapter I. which relates to the use of the *particule nobiliare* is a condensation of a paper previously written by me at Dr BURNETT'S request; and I must also add, in fairness to myself, that I had communicated to him the general result of a rather laborious examination I had undertaken into the authenticity of RÜXNER'S *Thurnier Buch* and the *Leges Hastiludiales*.[1]

The extension of the scope of the work has necessitated its growth from one volume to two; and even so I have been obliged to somewhat curtail the Chapters on *Marshalling*, *External Ornaments*, and *Marks of Illegitimacy*, which are condensations from my much more extensive collections; and I am fully aware that the work might have been made more entertaining to the general reader had it been practicable to include chapters on several collateral subjects, as well as to bring under notice more of the many Curiosities of Heraldry.

The object I have had in view, however, is not to furnish amusement to the general reader, but to make the work one of real utility to the student. Fine writing and the graces of composition have therefore had to give place to what is often a very bald and bare statement of

[1] This general result is stated much too broadly in some posthumous articles on Heraldry printed in the *Edinburgh Encyclopædia* over his initials.

INTRODUCTION

THE present work was undertaken, and considerable progress made in its execution, by my late friend Dr GEORGE BURNETT, who so long and so worthily, filled the office of *Lyon* King of Arms. At his much regretted decease, in 1889, his MS. was placed in my hands with the request that I would see through the press the work, then supposed by his friends to be nearly complete. An examination of the MS., however, proved that this was very far indeed from being the case. It consisted only of 230 pages, scarcely equal to 150 of the present work; and, with every desire to be helpful, I could at that time only decline the task of completing a book of which three-fourths remained to be written, and the majority of the illustrations to be drawn.

It was, however, thought by others who were interested a pity that Dr BURNETT'S labour (which included the preparations for thirty-two of the plates) should be altogether lost; and I eventually accepted a proposition by which, upon certain conditions, the MS. and plates in preparation were to be handed over to me to be utilised in any way which I might think desirable.

In the exercise of my judgment I determined to rewrite the book; mainly in order that I might be able to give it a far wider application than Dr BURNETT had intended, and convert it into an Introduction to general European Heraldry. But I decided to print in full those portions of his work which seemed to me the most interesting and valuable; and especially those relating to Scottish matters, with regard to which his official

publication unfortunately out of print, but which should not be neglected by anyone who likes his learning leavened by humour.

John Woodward was the son of Charles Woodward and was born at Bristol on 17 January 1837. He was educated at Edinburgh University, and was ordained a deacon in the Church of England in 1861 and priest in 1862, both ordinations being conferred by the Bishop of Chichester. He was assistant master at St John's College, Hurstpierpoint; senior assistant master of St Saviour's Grammar School, New Shoreham, 1862–66. He became in 1866 Rector of St Mary's (Episcopal) Church, Montrose, until his death. He was FSA Scot, and an Acting CF; Chaplain to the Order of St John of Jerusalem, 1868; Precentor and Conductor of the Association of Church Choirs, Dundee, 1874. He was given the hon LL D of Aberdeen in 1892, and died on 4 June 1898. His writings were: *The Heraldry of Bristol Cathedral*, 1867; *Notes on the Arms of the Episcopates of Great Britain and Ireland*, 1868; *Leaves from the Diary of a Holiday Tour in France, Switzerland, and Italy*, 1871; a *Supplement to Bedford's Blazon of Episcopacy*, 1873; *The Heraldry of Spain and Portugal*, 1888; *A Treatise on Heraldry*, 2 vols, 1891 (1892) and 1896; and *Ecclesiastical Heraldry*, 1894. He had also written a booklet about St Mary's Church, Montrose.

L. G. Pine

(xviii)

Certainly from the sixteenth-century treatises onward a fantastic natural history, derived from book-bound medieval science, competed with ignorance of the true origins of heraldry to present it as a mystery which the ordinary man could not follow.

It was not until the later nineteenth century that antiquaries working in the spirit and with the methods of modern scholarship began to study heraldry. The subject has now been firmly based and there is no longer any excuse for heraldic ignorance. There are still, it is true, many places, popular television and radio programmes, and newspapers having pre-eminence, in which gross heraldic errors are perpetuated, but the sources of correction are available.

To make one such source more readily available is the object of the present reprint. Woodward's work has two important qualities. It goes right behind the books on heraldry and gives original evidences derived from representations of arms which exist in rolls of arms, in windows or in carvings. Secondly, its information is not limited to England or Scotland, but is liberal in heraldic instances taken throughout Europe. There is no other publication at present in English which gives such detail on Continental heraldry.

George Burnett's part in the present edition was not large, and he died before its appearance. He was a very learned scholar who bore his erudition lightly and who could write with humour. The details of his career are: born 1822, died 1890; called to Scottish bar, 1845; Lyon Depute, 1864; Lord Lyon King of Arms, 1866 until his death; LL D Edinburgh, 1884. His chief work was an edition of the Exchequer Rolls, 1264–1507. He had also written anonymously a pamphlet entitled *Popular Genealogists, or the Art of Pedigree Making* (1865). This little work is out of print but readers of Burnett's contributions to the *Treatise* should try to obtain a copy, for the rich enjoyment it can afford. There is a notice of it in Vol iv of *The Ancestor*, another

INTRODUCTION TO THE NEW EDITION

No less an heraldic authority than Oswald Barron wrote of the present work, 'Dr. Woodward's *Treatise on Heraldry, British and Foreign*, ... must be counted the only scholarly book in English upon a matter which has engaged so many pens'. This opinion, written in 1911 and repeated in later editions of the *Encyclopædia Britannica,* in Barron's article on Heraldry, is strikingly endorsed in the account of the same subject in *Chambers's Encyclopædia* (1964). There, D. L. Galbreath, writing on continental heraldry, observes: 'The only scholarly work covering the heraldry of the Continent is John Woodward, *Treatise on Heraldry*'. In the same work, the present Garter King of Arms said that Woodward and Burnett's *Treatise* condenses a mass of information. It has been mentioned by some writers that errors occur in Woodward's work, because he relied upon unchecked material, but in general it may fairly be said that Woodward's *Treatise* is the best learned guide to the subject. It is intended for a reader already conversant with the rudiments of heraldry, and for whom the terms used have lost the mystery associated with an old foreign tongue.

Heraldry in its origins was intended for use in warfare; the safety and the lives of soldiers depended upon swift recognition of devices. There was no more room in medieval warfare for the conceits of some later overburdened coats of arms than there would have been in the 1939-45 war for confusion in aircraft recognition. Such confusion in both medieval and modern times spelt disaster. Yet almost from the beginnings of writing on heraldry there has been abundance of quaint and indeed absurd ideas on the subject.

CHAPTER XXII.

FLAGS—BANNERS—STANDARDS. (J. W.)

Banners of the Bayeux Tapestry—Banners and Bannerets—*Bacheleries*—Fiefs *en bannière*—*Ecuyer-banneret*—A banneret, how made—Arms on Sails of Ships—Standards—Variations of—*Pennoncelles*—*Guidons*—National Flags—Battle of the Standard—The *Carroccio* in Italy—English flags—The "*Union Jack*"—The *Oriflamme*—*Vexilla*—*Le Drapeau blanc*—The *tricolor* of France—Imperial Standard of Germany

pp. 649—660

CHAPTER XXIII.

MISCELLANEOUS (J. W.).

Royal Arms of ENGLAND—National Arms—Partitions and Curious Coats—*Armes Parlantes*—Scandinavian Names assumed from Arms—Conclusion . . . . . pp. 661—674

REFERENCE MATERIALS

ENGLISH GLOSSARY . . . . . . pp. 676—708
GLOSSARY OF FRENCH TERMS OF BLAZON . pp. 709—747
APPENDICES . . . . pp. 748—755
INDEX . . . . pp. 756—859

crests—Lambrequins—Wreaths—The *calotte* and *capeline*—Feather lambrequins—Tinctures of mantlings—*Contoise*—The Crest-Coronet—Mantles, pavilions, etc.. . pp. 599—616

CHAPTER XX.

EXTERNAL ORNAMENTS.

II. CROWNS AND CORONETS. (J. W.)

The Iron Crown—*Il Sacro Chiodo*—Crown of CHARLEMAGNE—Early English Crowns—Development of Crowns—Coronet of Prince of WALES—Crown of SCOTLAND—Closed-crowns—French crowns, and coronets—Crowns of Emperors—The *Szent Korona*—Russian Crowns at Moscow—Royal Prussian Crown—Archducal coronet—Princely Crowns—Crown of Doge of VENICE—*Coronets*, licence in use of—Ducal coronet—Used by Marshals of France, and Spanish Grandees—Coronets of Marquesses, Earls, Counts, Barons, etc.—*Mortiers*—Coronets of Dutch Admirals—British ignorance—The *Toques* of the French Empire . . . . . pp. 617—626

CHAPTER XXI.

EXTERNAL ORNAMENTS.

III. SUPPORTERS. (J. W.)

Supports, Tenans, Soutiens—Origin of Supporters—Evidence of early seals—Single supporters—the Unicorn of SCOTLAND—The Apostolic Eagle—Double Supporters—Breton use—Supporters mantled—Crested Supporters—Triple Supporters—French Royal Supporters—Free use of Supporters abroad—*Ordonnances des Pays Bas*—Unnecessary restrictions—Pedantic attention to minutiæ—Supporters with banners—Use of Supporters in Spain and Italy—Slavonic and other uses—The "beast"—Compartments—British absurdities—Inanimate Supporters (Orders of ST. JOHN, etc.)—Badges of Office, in Britain, France, Italy, Holland, and Spain—The *Cordelière*, *Lacs d'Amour*—Palms, etc.—Motto bands—The use of Supporters, to whom limited—Choice of new Supporters—More British absurdities . . . . . . pp. 627—648

(xiii)

The Canton—Arms on a bend—The bordure of the legitimated Plantagenets—Arms of Royal bastards—Bastards of noble families—Venality of the old heralds—The *bordure-wavy*—Marks of bastardy in Scotland—The *bordure-goboné*—The *bordure-wavy*, a Scotch mark of legitimate cadency—Marks of illegitimacy in France—Royal bastards—Burgundy and the Low Countries—Interesting series of brisures—Spanish and Portuguese bastards — Italian, German, and Scandinavian examples—The bend-sinister no certain mark of illegitimacy in Continental Armory . . . . . pp. 548—582

CHAPTER XVIII.

BADGES. (J. W.)

Early heraldic devices—The badge the earliest form—General use of for all decorative purposes—Knots and other devices—Royal Badges—The *planta genista*—The White and Red Roses—The Swan—White Hart—The Falcon and Fetterlock, etc.—The Ostrich Feather badge—Royal badges—Livery Collars—Collar of SS. . . . . . . pp. 583—598

CHAPTER XIX.

EXTERNAL ORNAMENTS.

I. HELM AND CREST—WREATH—CREST-CORONET—LAMBREQUINS. (J. W.)

Crests assumed later than Arms—Early crests—The "fan-shaped" crest, or *écran*—Crested helm—In England of minor importance—Crests not hereditary—Used to denote cadency—German helms—*Armoiries timbrées* in France—Limitation of use—Materials and position of helm—The Stall Plates and Crests at Windsor—Use of several crested helms in Germany—Use in Scandinavia—In France—Spain—Portugal—Ecclesiastics, right of, to use Crests—Reasons for choice of Crest—Buffalo horns—Wings—*Vol-banneret*—*Trompes d'Éléphant*—Composed crests—Penaches, hats, the *plumail*—The mitre, and mitred crests—German anomalies—English anomalies—"Our *crest!*"—Differenced crests—Use of more than one—Absurd

German usages—Arms of MARIA THERESA—*Écu Complet* of Austrian Empire—French and Spanish Marshalling—Italian—Swedish—Quarterings separated by a Cross or other Ordinary —The *Dannebrog* . . . . . . pp. 453—512

(SECTION II., BY G. B. AND J. W.)

Heraldry in the Highlands—The Escucheon *en surtout*—DOUGLAS quartered coats—Scottish bordures—Arms of feudal dignities *en surtout*—Augmentations (G. B.)—Arms of the heiress of a mother, but not of a father—Issue of Morganatic marriages—Official arms of Ecclesiastics, etc.—Arms of Kings of Arms—Electors of the Holy Roman Empire—Grand Masters, etc., of Orders of ST. JOHN; ST. STEPHEN; the TEUTONIC ORDER, etc. (J. W.) . . . . pp. 512—527

CHAPTER XVI.

AUGMENTATIONS. (J. W.)

Arms of EDWARD *the Confessor*—HOWARD augmentation—Sir JOHN CLERK, and the DUC DE LONGUEVILLE—DUNOIS—RUTLAND—Augmentations granted by HENRY VIII. to his wives—Grants by JAMES I., and by CHARLES II.—Later Military and Naval Grants—Scottish concessions—Imperial Augmentations — Guelphic and Ghibbeline Chiefs — French concessions—Papal grants—Russian Augmentations—Arms of SUWOROFF, MENSCHIKOFF, etc.—Prussian grants—The IRON CROSS—Arms of BLUCHER, MOLTKE, BISMARCK, etc.—Swedish concessions—Spanish grants—Arms of COLUMBUS, CORTEZ, and VASCO DA GAMA . . . pp. 528—547

CHAPTER XVII.

HERALDIC MARKS OF ILLEGITIMACY. (J. W.)

Coat armour evidence of nobility—Actual status of bastards in the Middle Ages—The bendlet-sinister, an early and general brisure for illegitimacy—Vulgar error—A *bar* sinister an impossibility —The *filet en barre*, or *baton péri en barre*—*Coûtume de Lorraine* — Low Country *Ordonnances* — The *faux escu* —Mistake of NISBET and SETON with regard to it.

Candlestick — Censers — The *Gonfanon* — Bell — Scourges — Ecclesiastical Hat—*Pallium*—Pilgrims' Scrips and Staves.

DOMESTIC.—Maunch—Buckles—Cushions—Crowns, etc.—Cups—Musical Instruments — Harp of IRELAND — Horns — The Clarion, or Rest — Dice — Cards — Chess-rook — Money — Cauldron—Eatables—Mirrors—Combs—Wearing Apparel—Agricultural Instruments—Mallets—Letters and Words
pp. 345—395

CHAPTER XIV.

CADENCY OR DIFFERENCING. (J. W. AND G. B.)

Obligation of Cadets to difference arms—Effects of the *Wars of the Roses* in England—Permanency of old families in Scotland—Sub-infeudation — Rise of Surnames—Few names and original coats in Scotland.

Modes of Differencing—Change of tincture—Addition of charges—The Label—Royal Cadency in England—Arms of Prince Consort—Canton—Quarter—Escucheon—Change of Ordinary—Changes of Charges—Augmentations—Ecclesiastical differences—The Bordure—Bordures of Plantagenet Princes, etc.—French Royal Cadency—Spanish bordures—Use of Bordure in Scotland—The Marks of Cadency—Difference by Quartering—The Escucheon *en surtout*—Mortimer Coats—Low-Country families — CROY and LANNOY — MONTMORENCY differences . . . . pp. 396—452

CHAPTER XV.

MARSHALLING. (SECTION I., BY J. W.)

Adoption of wife's arms—Early seals—Composed coats—Impalement by Dimidiation—Arms of Cinque Ports—Abbey of St. Etienne at Caen—Polish dimidiated coats—Simple Impalement—*Cheminée* of the *Palais de Justice* at Bruges—LEUCHTENBERG—Spanish *parti* coats—DACRE tomb at Lanercost—Dimidiation *per bend*, and *per bend-sinister* — Arms of expectation.

Quartering—Grand-quarters—PERCY arms—Quartering *per saltire*—*Jus expectationis* — *Erb-verbrüderung* — Escucheon *en surtout* — Low-Country usages—Arms of an elected sovereign—

strueux—Wyverns—The Cockatrice and Basilisk—Architectural Monsters — The Salamander — *L'Amphiptère* — The Sphinx, Harpy, and Hydra—The Unicorn—The Sea-Unicorn—The Phœnix—The Pegasus—The Centaur—*Le Centaur Sagittaire*—The Sea-Horse—The Sea-Stag—The Cock-Fish—The Sea-Lion—The Sea-Dog—The Mermaid or Siren—The Faun, Devil, and Cerberus . . pp. 286—304

CHAPTER XI.

INANIMATE CHARGES.—I. ASTRONOMICAL.

The Sun—The Moon—Crescents—The Star, Estoile, and Mullet—Constellations—Comets—Rainbows—Thunderbolts—Storms—The Wind—*Champagne*—Mount—Terrace—Water—River—Volcanoes—Fire—Flames . . . . pp. 305—314

CHAPTER XII.

INANIMATE CHARGES.—II. THE VEGETABLE KINGDOM.

I. TREES, and FLOWERS.—Groves—Forests—Trees—Branches—The *Créquier*—Palms—Leaves—The Trefoil—The Nenuphar Leaf—Quatrefoils—Cinquefoils—Fraises—The Rose of ENGLAND—The Fleur-de-lis of FRANCE—The Natural Lily—The Thistle of SCOTLAND—Wreaths and Chaplets—Other Flowers Tobacco.

II. FRUITS. — Pomegranates — Grapes — Oranges — Garbs—Vegetables—*Klee-stengeln* . . . . pp. 315—344

CHAPTER XIII.

INANIMATE CHARGES.—III. MISCELLANEOUS.

MILITARY.—Sword—Spears—Cronels—Helmets—Axes—Bows—Arrows—Scythes (Polish)—Shields—Banners—Beacons—Battering-Rams—Caltraps—Chains (NAVARRE)—Water-Budgets—Horse-shoes—Polish Coats—Breys—Barnacles—Stirrups—Castles—Towers—Bridges—*Brog*—Columns—Ladders—Slings—Portcullis—Cannon—Needle-gun.
NAUTICAL.—Ships—Lymphads—Boats—Anchor—Noah's Ark.
ECCLESIASTICAL CHARGES.—Keys—Crozier—Tiara—Chalice—

Domestic economy in arms—Wolves—*Ravissant*—The Bear—
The Polar Bear—The Bear's Head—The Fox—The Elephant
—The Camel—Deer, etc.—Moose-deer—Holyrood Abbey—
Bulls—Calves—Heads—Goats and Goat's Heads—Sheep—
The Paschal Lamb—The Antelope—The Horse and Ass—The
Hare—Seals—Otters—Beavers—Urchins—Moles—Squirrels
—Apes—Rats—Dogs, etc. . . . . pp. 208—241

CHAPTER VIII.

ANIMATE CHARGES.—III. BIRDS.

I. THE EAGLE.—The Eagle of the Holy Roman Empire—Its origin
and development—The single-headed Eagle—The double-
headed Eagle—The *Heiligenscheine*—The Eagle in other
princely and Royal coats—The Eagle of the German Empire
—The Allerion—The Eagle of the French Empire—Parts of
the Eagle.
II. OTHER BIRDS.—The Vulture—The Falcon—Owls—The Swan
—Heron—Stork—Crane and Heron—Ostrich and Pelican—
Ravens and Choughs—The Popinjay—Cocks and Hens—
Swallows and Martins—Peacocks, and Birds of Paradise—
Other birds . . . . pp. 242—267

CHAPTER IX.

ANIMATE CHARGES.—IV. FISH, REPTILES, INSECTS.

I. FISH.—The Dolphin—The DAUPHINS of FRANCE—The Barbel
—The Salmon and Pike—The Whale—The Eel—Shell-fish.
II. REPTILES.—Serpents—Lizards—Crocodiles—Scorpions—Tor-
toises—Frogs and Toads—*Johnnie Crapaud*—Leeches,
Worms, and Snails.
III. INSECTS—The Butterfly—The House-fly—Wasps—The Bees
of the French Empire—Ants—Grasshoppers—Wood-lice—
Fleas . . . . pp. 268—285

CHAPTER X.

ANIMATE CHARGES.—V. MONSTERS.

The Griffin—The Sea-Griffin—The Dragon—*Le Dragon Mon-*

The Giron—Arms of the GIRONS, MORTIMERS, and PRESSIGNY.
The Inescucheon, or Escucheon.
The Bordure—A Bordure circular—*Vêtu en rond, et en ovale*—The Orle—*Un faux écusson*.
THE TRESSURE—The Royal Tressure of SCOTLAND—Its origin—Its early use—As an Augmentation—Grant of to Foreigners—Variously floriated—Foreign use of the Tressure.
The Fret—The Lozenge—The Lozenge-througnout.
The Fusil—Mascle—Rustre.
The Flaunche—*Flanqué en rond*—Flasque—Voider—The Billet, and Delve.
The Label—Labels of unusual number of points—Labels in unusual positions—Curious Labels—Roundles—*Noms bizarres*—The Arms of the MEDICI—Roundles charged—*Besans-tourteaux*, and *Tourteaux-besans*—Fountains, and Gurges
pp. 165—193

CHAPTER VI.

ANIMATE CHARGES.—I. THE HUMAN FIGURE.

Arms of See of Chichester, and other ecclesiastical foundations—Saints—Biblical personages—Mythological—Nude figures—Savages—Knights—Dancers—Parts of the human body—Moor's heads—Hungarian memorials of Turkish fights—Heads of GERION, JANUS, ARGUS, BOREAS, MIDAS, etc.—Cherubim and Seraphim—The human eye—The heart—Valentine coats—Beards, lips, teeth—Piratical coats—The skeleton—Arms and hands—University of Paris—*Dextrochères*, etc.—The *Foi*—Human legs and feet . . . . pp. 194—207

CHAPTER VII.

ANIMATE CHARGES.—II. BEASTS.

I.—THE LION—The Lions of ENGLAND—Leopards in French and English blazon—Different attitudes—Parts of the Lion—Early and curious examples of the Lion in Arms—*L'Ombre du Lion*.
II.—OTHER BEASTS.—The Tiger—Its vanity!—The Leopard—Leopard's heads—*Jessant de lis*—The ferocious Musion—The Panther—The Catamount—The wild Boar—The domestic Pig—

CHAPTER IV.

ORDINARIES.

Classification simply for convenience—Origin of the Ordinaries—The CHIEF—Double Chiefs—*Chefs abaissés*—Guelphic and Ghibelline Chiefs—The fillet—The *divise*—The Chief-pale—The Pale—Tierced in pale—Pallets—*Endorse*—Pallets—*Retraits*.
The FESS—The STUART arms—The Bar—Bars gemels—Tierced in fess.
The BEND—The bend *Engoulée*—The *Kräntzlein*, or *Crancelin*—Bendlets—Bendlets enhanced—The Cotice.
The BEND-SINISTER—No certain mark of illegitimacy—Arrangement of arms in Churches—The Chapel of the Golden Fleece at Dijon—The Cathedral at Haarlem—St. George's Chapel, Windsor.
The CHEVRON—Different usages of—Chevron *ployé*—Chevron *ecimé*—Chevrons *rompus*, *brisés*, *faillis*—Chevronels—Couple closes.
The CROSS as an Ordinary—The SALTIRE—The Saltire and Chief —*Flanchis*—The PILE—*Emanche*—*Pointe*—Mediæval pennons —The *Pairle* . . . . pp. 116—151
The CROSS as a Charge—Varieties of—The Passion, or Long Cross —Cross Calvary—Cross Patriarchal—Cross of LORRAINE—Greek Cross, or Cross Couped—Cross Patty, or Formy—The *Otelle*—The Maltese Cross—The VICTORIA Cross—The Cross Patty-fitchy—The Cross Potent—The Cross Potent-fitchy—The Cross of JERUSALEM—The Cross Patonce—The Cross Flory, or Fleury — The Cross Floretty, or *Fleur-de-lisée* — The Cross of CALATRAVA—The Cross *Ancrée*, or Moline—The Cross Sarcelly, or *Recercelée*—The Cross Botonny—The Cross Pommetty—The Cross *Clechée*—The Cross of TOULOUSE—The Cross Tau—The Cross *Guivré*, or *Gringolée*—The Cross *Urdée*—The Cross Avellane—The Cross *Aiguisée* —Crosslets . . . . pp. 151—164

CHAPTER V.

THE SUB-ORDINARIES.

The Quarter—The Canton—The Canton-indented—The Canton and Fess.

(vi)

—Restrained by Sovereign—Right to Arms disputed—Grants and assignations of Arms — Military character of.—(G.B.) pp. 19—36

B.—Origin and development of Coat-Armour—Materials for inquiry—Influence of the Crusades—Change in armour still more influential — Tournaments and jousts — Origin of — Dangerous sport—Originated in Germany—Regulated and systematised in France—RÜXNER'S *Thurnier Buch*, an elaborate fiction—The *Leges Hastiludiales* of late origin—The negative evidence of seals, coins, tombs—Arms of the Popes—Early tombs with arms in Britain—Shields without arms—Early seals—Transition of personal devices into hereditary Arms— Use of Arms in Scotland, the Low Countries, France, Spain, Italy, Sweden—My conclusion as to date.—(J. W.) pp. 36—52

CHAPTER III.

SHAPE OF SHIELD—TINCTURES—PARTED COATS.

Primary use of Armorial Insignia—The shield—Shape and size affected by character of armour—The Bayeux Tapestry armour and shield—Type at commencement of 13th century —Later forms—The Spanish shield—Oval shields—*à bouche*— *Écu en palette*—*Écu en bannière*—Circular escucheons—*Écu en lozange*—Points of the Escucheon—Tinctures—Metals—Furs —Exceptional use of other colours—*Cendrée*—*Brunâtre*— *Bleu-celeste*—*Amaranthe*—*Eisen farbe*—*Carnation*—*Proper*— Purpure—Nonsensical ideas as to arms being indicative of moral qualities—Furs—Ermine—Vair—Modes of indicating colours by *hachures*—Fields of a single metal, tincture, or fur —The *Blut-fahne* or *Regalien* quarter—Varieties of Ermine— Varieties of Vair—*Beffroi*—*Menu-vair*—*Potent*—*Vairé*, or Verrey—*Plumeté*—*Papelonné*—Fur *au naturel*—Arms of BREGENZ—Parted Coats—Partition lines—Modes of partition —*Ecartelé en equerre*—*Gyronny*—The CAMPBELL coat— German and other Continental partitions—*Chapé*—*Chaussé* —*Chaperonné*—Paly—Barry—Bendy—Fretty—Chevronny— Chequy—Lozengy—Rules of Blazon—*Armes Fausses*—*Semé* —Diaper . . . . pp. 53—115

SYNOPSIS

INTRODUCTION TO THE NEW EDITION	xvii
INTRODUCTION	xxi
LIST OF SUBSCRIBERS	xxvii
LIST OF PLATES	xxxv
LIST OF FIGURES	xxxvii

CHAPTER I.

INTRODUCTORY.

The duties of a Herald—Definition of Heraldry, or Armory—Social rank in feudal times—*Insignia Gentilitia*—Who are "noble"?—Letters of nobility, Grants of Arms—Continental practice—Gentleman—Esquire—[The *Particule Nobiliare*—Christian names—Formation of Surnames—"*Le Premier Baron Chrétien*"—Surnames not used even in 18th Century—Noble families not using the *particule*—Legislation about the *particule* in France, and in Lorraine — BÉRANGER — The German *von*—Use of the *particule* in Holland, Italy, Spain, etc.—(J. W.)] In England—Silly modern assumptions.—(G. B.)
pp. 1—18

CHAPTER II.

ORIGIN AND DEVELOPMENT OF COAT-ARMOUR.

A.—Origin of Armorial insignia—Ancient treatises—*Boke of St. Alban's*—*Seize Quartiers* of our Saviour at Mentz (J. W.)— Coats ascribed to the patriarchs—Earliest tomb with Armorial shield—PLANCHÉ'S conclusions—Earliest Armorial Seal— ELLIS's theory—Etruscan and Greek vases—Roman cohort ensigns—The *Leges Hastiludiales* ascribed to HENRY the FOWLER—Early standards and shields bearing charges had no hereditary character—The Bayeux Tapestry; its evidence against the use of personal arms (J. W.)—The Second Crusade —Mr BURNETT'S conclusion as to date of arms—Arms assumed

Representatives
Continental Europe: BOXERBOOKS, INC., *Zurich*
Canada: M. G. HURTIG LTD., *Edmonton*

Published by the Charles E. Tuttle Company, Inc.
of Rutland, Vermont & Tokyo, Japan
with editorial offices at
Suido 1-chome, 2–6, Bunkyo-ku, Tokyo, Japan

© 1969 by Charles E. Tuttle Co., Inc.

All rights reserved

Library of Congress Catalog Card No. 70-77120

Standard Book No. 8048 0694-2

First Tuttle edition published 1969

PRINTED IN JAPAN

HOFSTRA UNIVERSITY
LIBRARY

WOODWARD'S
A TREATISE ON
Heraldry
BRITISH AND FOREIGN
WITH ENGLISH AND FRENCH GLOSSARIES

BY

JOHN WOODWARD, F.S.A.scot., etc.
(RECTOR OF ST. MARY'S CHURCH, MONTROSE)

AND

GEORGE BURNETT, LL.D., etc.
(LYON KING OF ARMS)

NEW INTRODUCTION BY
L. G. PINE

CHARLES E. TUTTLE CO.: PUBLISHERS
RUTLAND, VERMONT

WOODWARD'S

A TREATISE ON HERALDRY

PLATE XXV.

1. Eagle displayed.
   Monthermer.

2. Two-headed Eagle.
   Speke.

3. Imperial Eagle.
   France.

4. Eagle's Head.
   Munro.

5. Wings.
   Seymour.

6. Goshawk.
   Weele.

7. Falcon rising.
   Price.

8. Hawks' Bells.
   Bellchamber.

9. Owls.
   Prescott.

10. Swans.
    Wolryche.

11. Stork.
    Oglander.

12. Pelican.
    Chantrell.

of the eagle displayed in an unusual position: *Or, an eagle displayed sable, armed gules; its body fessways with the head to the dexter flank.* This coat is attributed to EPTINGEN, of Basel. (*See* also EGGENBERG, Plate liv., fig. 5.)

SECTION B.—OTHER BIRDS.

THE VULTURE.—The Vulture appears but rarely in armory, but there are some examples of it. *Azure, a vulture rising argent; on a chief or, an estoile gules,* is the coat of the Dutch family of BUSC, settled at Berbice. *Or, on a mount vert, a vulture rising gules,* is used by GEYER of Bavaria; *Gules, a vulture rising argent,* by GEYER of Strasburg; other families of the name have similar bearings with different tinctures.

THE FALCON is generally represented *close;* that is, in a sitting posture with its wings closed on the body; an attitude presumed with regard to other birds when the contrary is not expressed in the blazon. The falcon is distinguished from the eagle by being also *jessed and belled, i.e.,* having globular bells attached to its legs by small thongs or *jesses.* These jesses are sometimes drawn flotant from the leg, and with vervels, or rings, at the ends.

Armorists sometimes profess to distinguish the large goshawk, or falcon, from the smaller sparrow-hawk; but practically they are hardly recognisable from each other in heraldic drawings. When the beaks, claws, jesses, bells, etc., are of a different tincture from the bird the fact requires to be specified in the blazon.

Plate XXV., fig. 6, is the coat of WEELE of Staverton (*Visitation of Devonshire,* 1620): *Sable, a goshawk, perched on a stock issuant from the base, armed, jessed, and belled or.*

Or, a falcon rising azure, is borne by PRICE of Plas Cadrant in Anglesey (Plate XXV., fig. 7). *Azure, a falcon belled argent,* is the canting coat of FALCOZ DE LA

BLACHE, Comtes d'ANJOU (*d'Azur, au faucon d'argent grilleté du même*).

The family LE TONNELIER, Comtes de BRETEUIL, Marquises de FONTENAY, carried : *d'Azur, à un epervier essorant d'or, longé et grilleté* (lined and belled) *du même.* HAWKER of Wiltshire bears : *Sable, a hawk on its perch argent, beaked and legged or* NOBELAER of Holland uses : *Or, a falcon sable hooded, and standing on its perch in base, gules.* DE WEERT of the same country bears : *Argent, a falcon sable, hooded, lined, and membered or.*

In several coats the falcon is represented seizing on its prey (*trussing* is the English phrase, *empiétant* the French). *D'Azur, à un faucon d'or, grilleté d'argent empiétant une perdrix du second, becquée et onglée de gueules,* is the coat of TARLET. *Sable, a hawk or, trussing a duck proper, on a chief of the second a cross botonny gules,* is borne by MADAN, or MADDEN, in England and Ireland. *Or, three falcon's heads erased gules,* was the coat of NICOLSON, baronets.

In Armory OWLS are represented full-faced, as in the arms of PRESCOTT, baronets : *Sable, a chevron between three owls or* (Plate XXV., fig. 9).

THE SWAN besides being the device of the great family of BOHUN (*vide infra,* p. 589), is a favourite bird in the old heraldry both of England and of the Continent. WOLRYCHE bears : *Azure, a chevron between three swans argent* (Plate XXV., fig. 10). *Gules, a swan contourné argent, beaked sable, membered or,* is the coat of the Lombard Counts PARAVICINI. *Or, a swan gules, beaked and membered sable,* was used by the old Westphalian Counts von STEINFURT. *Gules, a swan argent, beaked and membered sable, gorged with a crown or,* is the coat of STORMARN in the Royal Arms of Denmark.

The head and neck of the swan, frequently used as a crest (Plate XLV., fig. 2); also occurs as a heraldic charge : *Azure, three swan's heads erased argent, gorged with ducal coronets or,* is carried by BAKER of Gloucestershire. *Gules, three swan's heads and necks conjoined in pairle argent,* is the curious coat of the Counts PRZICHOWITZ of Poland.

THE HERON, STORK, and CRANE are seldom distinguishable in heraldic drawings. Plate XXV., fig. 11 is the coat of OGLANDER: *Azure, a stork between three crosslets fitchées or.* The Barons DOBRZENSKY bear: *Azure, a stork proper. Gules, three cranes argent,* were the arms of the Scottish Lords CRANSTOUN.

THE CRANE is usually represented standing on one leg holding in the claw of the other bent one a stone called its "*vigilance,*" from a fable that this was so held that the noise of its fall might awaken the bird if it fell asleep! This makes it a fitting canting charge for the name of WACHTER! Several baronial families of this name bear: *Argent, a crane sable with its vigilance on a mount vert.*

SIEBMACHER (*Wappenbuch,* i., 131) ascribes to the Rhenish family of WEILER, the coat following: *Azure, a double-headed stork argent. Argent, a heron volant in fess azure, membered or,* are the *armes parlantes* of HERONDON; while families of HERON use, *Gules, a heron argent; Argent, a heron sable;* and the reverse. This bird is the chief charge in several coats of the Spanish GARCIAS.

THE OSTRICH is usually depicted in early Heraldic drawings with a horse-shoe, key, or nail in its beak. This arose from the mediæval idea, not altogether extinct even now, that the bird had the capacity to digest any substance however hard, and especially iron.

The MACMAHONS of Ireland carried: *Argent, an ostrich sable, in its beak a horse-shoe or.* MATTHEWS of Cornwall, used simply, *Sable, an ostrich argent. Gules, an ostrich argent, in its beak a horse-shoe azure,* are the *armes parlantes* of the Bavarian family of STRAUSS. Other families of the name vary the tinctures.

OSTRICH FEATHERS are often borne for Crests and

Badges; the best known instance is afforded by the Badge (often erroneously called the Crest) of the Prince of WALES (on which *see* Chapter XVIII.).

THE PELICAN is represented in both British and Foreign Armory with a bowed neck *vulning* (*i.e.* wounding) her breast; from an old belief that she was accustomed to feed her young with her blood. When thus occupied, standing in her nest, and surrounded by her little ones, she is said to be *in her piety*, as in Plate XXV., fig. 12, the coat of CHANTRELL of Berkshire: *Azure, a pelican in her piety, argent.* Bishop FOX of Winchester, who founded Corpus Christi College at Oxford bore: *Azure, a pelican or, vulned gules;* which still forms part of the coat armorial of the college. (*Tierced in pale:*—1. FOX; 2. The See of WINCHESTER; 3. The arms of Bishop OLDHAM.) *Azure, three pelicans argent, vulned proper*, is the coat of PELHAM. *Argent, three pelicans in piety or, their nests vert*, was borne by the Scottish family of PATTERSON.

THE RAVEN occurs early in British Armory as a canting charge. In GLOVER'S *Roll*, THOMAS CORBET bears: *Or, two crows* (or *corbies*) *sable.* *Argent* (and *or*), *a raven proper* (*i.e. sable*), are the coats of several families of this name, as well as of RAVENTHORPE.

Or, three crows (or *ravens*) *sable*, is borne by CORNEILLE, and by the Counts de CORNEILLAN, and the families of CORBOLI of Tuscany, RAVESCHOOT of Flanders, RAVEN and DE ROECK of Holland, CRAYEN of Prussia and Saxony, etc. The *Cornish Chough* of Heraldry is a crow of purplish-black colour, with red beak and legs. We have it in Plate XXVI., fig. 1; the coat of ONSLOW: *Argent, a fess gules between six Cornish choughs proper.*

Three such choughs in a field *argent* are said to be the bearings of THOMAS À BECKET, Archbishop of CANTERBURY; as well as of CORNWALLIS. *Argent, a cross sable* between four Cornish choughs proper, is the coat of the Lords AYLMER.

THE PARROT (*Papingoe*, or *Popinjay*), occurs in GLOVER'S *Roll* as the coat of MARMADUKE DE THWENG or TWENGE, "*d'Argent, à trois papegayes de vert ung fece de goules.*" In Scotland its most familiar use is as the coat of PEPDIE: *Argent, three papingoes vert, beaked and membered gules* (Plate XXVI., fig. 2), a coat which is quartered by the HUME, or HOME, family in most of its different branches. It is also the coat of SORIN in France.

The same coat, but with the field *Or*, is borne in France by the Counts GUIOT DE PONTEIL, and the Marquesses GUIOT DE DOIGNON (*d'Or, à trois perroquets de sinople, bequés et membrés de gueules*).

A single popinjay appears in the coat of the French family of PARIZOT (*d'Azur, à un perroquet d'or*). In the *Zürich Wappenrolle* of the 14th century No. 527 is, *Gules, a parrot azure legged or, holding in its beak a horse-shoe argent*, a coat attributed to HEIDEGK.

COCKS occur frequently in Armory. *Argent, three cocks gules, armed, crested, and jelloped* (the term applied to its gills) *sable*, is the coat of COKAYNE (Plate XXVI., fig. 3): *Argent, three cocks gules*, is with similar allusive intent the bearing of the COCKBURNS of Scotland. *Argent, a cock gules, armed, crested, and jelloped or*, is used by the Counts HAHN, of Mecklenburg ; and *Argent, a cock sable, armed and crested gules*, by LE COCQ, Counts de HUMBEKE in Brabant. The Marquises de VOGUÉ bear *Azure, a cock or. Gules, a cock argent, having pendent from its neck a shield azure charged with a fleur-de-lis or*, is the coat of the Marquises de l'HÔPITAL DE VITRY.

Or, on a mount in base vert, a hen sable crested gules, was borne by the princely Counts of HENNEBERG, and appears in the full coat of the arms of PRUSSIA ; as well as in those of the Saxon Duchies.

Azure, three hens or, is the coat of the Dutch family of

KIP ; while LE CAUDRELIER of Artois uses: *Azure, a hen sheltering her chickens or* (*d'Azur, à une poule d'or, couvante des poussins du même*). *Argent, three hens sable*, are the arms of the Counts VON MOLTKE (Denmark, etc., see p. 544).

SWALLOWS (*Hirondelles*) were allusively borne by the ARUNDELS of Sussex, whose coat, *Sable, six swallows argent*, 3, 2, 1, is found upon a seal of the twelfth century. The Martin, or swift, a species of swallow, is the origin of the martlet, one of the best known charges of Heraldry. There are early examples of the martlet properly furnished with legs, but about the close of the thirteenth century the custom arose by which the bird is represented without feet, and sometimes without a beak. It was early in use as a charge for differencing coats, but was employed in a manner quite different from its use as a mark of cadency in modern Heraldry.

THE MERLETTE in Foreign Armory is drawn somewhat differently from the British martlet; it is without the long cleft tail, and in fact only differs from the *canette* (or duckling) by being represented without beak, or feet. The coat of FENWICK is: *Per fess gules and argent, six martlets counterchanged* (Plate XXVI., fig. 4). *D'Argent, à la fasce de sable, accompagnée de trois merlettes du même, rangées en chef*, was borne by the French Marquises de BEAUHARNAIS, to which belonged the Empress JOSEPHINE. The Duc de MORNY, who was conspicuously associated with the Second French Empire, bore: *Argent, three martlets sable within a bordure compony alternately of the arms of Dauphiny and of those of the French Empire* (*vide infra*, Chapter XVII.). *Or, three martlets in fess gules*, is the coat of the Counts of VELEN in Westphalia. (On arms of EDWARD *the Confessor*, see p. 528.)

THE PEACOCK occurs in a few instances, and mostly as an allusive bearing ; it is borne either with its wings

PLATE XXVI.

1. Cornish Chough.
   Onslow.

2. Papingoes.
   Pepdie.

3. Cocks.
   Cokayne.

4. Martlets.
   Fenwick.

5. Bream Naiant.
   Breame.

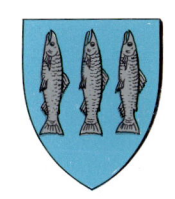

6. Salmon hauriant.
   Way.

7. Dolphin.
   Dauphin of France.

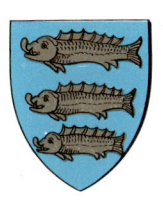

8. Dolphins.
   Dolfini.

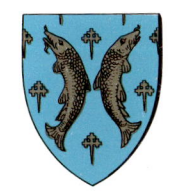

9. Barbel.
   Bar.

10. Trout.
    Troutbeck.

11. Stockfish.
    Iceland.

12. Escallops.
    Dacre.

close, or with its tail expanded, in the latter case it is blazoned as *in its pride*.

Or, on a mount vert, a peacock in its pride, is the canting coat of DE PAEUW of Holland, and is sometimes borne without the mount. *Or, four bendlets gules, over all a peacock* (close) *proper*, is borne by the Princes of WIED.

In the *Wappenrolle von Zürich*, No. 476 is a coat attributed to HURUS. In it the head and neck of a peacock *azure* rises from a small *champagne gules;* and the whole of the rest of the field is occupied by the feathers of the expanded tail *proper*. The French family of PONNAT use: *d'Or, à trois têtes de paon d'azur*, and have peacocks (close) as supporters.

Sable, three peacocks close argent, is the canting coat of PEACOCK. Another family of the name in Scotland uses: *Argent, three peacocks in pride proper*, which is also borne allusively by PAWNE.

DUCKS, GEESE, PHEASANTS, MOOR-FOWL, PLOVERS, FINCHES, DOVES, and other birds, occasionally appear both in British and Foreign Armory, and then usually with an allusion to the name of the bearer; there is nothing in their use which makes it needful to enlarge this chapter with examples, but the BIRD OF PARADISE requires a special mention as a foreign charge. *D'Argent, à trois oiseaux de paradis sable*, is borne naturally enough by the French family of PARADIS DE PAULHAC. The Russian families of RJEVSKI; and YEROPKIN, use: *Argent, on a terrace vert, a cannon mounted or, supporting a bird of paradise proper;* this is also the coat of the Princes WIASEMSKI of Livonia. (*See* KLINGSPOR, *Baltisches Wappenbuch.*) The arms of the family of FINCKE-NAUGEN in Courland are: *Or, three finches' eyes proper*. (*Ibid.*, plate xxxiii.)

The mythical PHŒNIX, represented as an eagle amid flames, comes more properly under the head of Chimerical, or Mythological Figures (*vide infra*, Chapter X.).

CHAPTER IX.

ANIMATE CHARGES.   III.—FISH,—REPTILES,—INSECTS.

FISH.—The Heraldry of Fish is the subject of a very interesting and beautifully illustrated monograph by Mr THOMAS MOULE, published in 1842. Under this category are recognised various animals which in modern zoology would not be so designed, such are the Whale, Dolphin, etc. The kind of fish which forms a heraldic charge is often unspecified, though an acquaintance with local phraseology would often enable us to determine the exact species of the fish intended. Thus the blazon of the coat of GARVINE in Scotland is simply: *Azure, three fishes naiant argent*, but we know at once that these fish are "garvies," or sprats. *Vert, three fishes or, spotted gules* is borne by DOGGE, and we see that the Dog-fish is certainly intended. In the early *Rolls of Arms*, however, we have the Luce, or Pike; the Herring, Salmon, etc. borne allusively by the families of LUCY (*Gules, three luces hauriant argent*); HERINGAUD (*Gules, three herrings hauriant argent*); SALMON (*Sable, three salmons hauriant argent*), etc. *Hauriant* is the term employed when the fish are represented paleways, rising to the surface for air; *naiant* describing them when swimming fesseways.

Azure, three bream naiant or, are the arms of the family of BREAME of Essex (Plate XXVI., fig. 5). *Azure, three salmon hauriant argent:* is the coat of WAY of Buckinghamshire (Plate XXVI., fig. 6).

The DOLPHIN is in Heraldry considered the King of fish, as the lion is of beasts, or the eagle of birds. Its form, borrowed from classical mythology, resembles but faintly that of the dolphin of zoology. Whether blazoned *naiant* or *hauriant*, the dolphin is most frequently depicted as *embowed*, or in a curved attitude.

Dauphin was a title given in France in ancient times to certain feudal seigneurs, and was adopted from the charge borne in their shields of arms. The old romance of GERARD DE ROUSSILLON mentions "dauphins," in an enumeration of feudal titles along with "comtes, bers (barons), and bannerets." The chiefs who bore this title were the Dauphin de VIENNOIS, and the Dauphin d'AUVERGNE.

In 1343 King PHILIP of France purchased the domains of HUMBERT III., Dauphin de VIENNOIS. The common story that it was a special condition of the purchase that the title and arms of the Dauphin should be always borne by the *eldest* son of the King of France seems to be without solid foundation. ("Le titre de *dauphin* fut spécialement affecté au fils du roi qui reçut cette province en appanage. Ce fut d'abord le second fils du roi qui porta le titre du *dauphin ;* mais dans la suite ce nom fut réservé au fils aîné, héritier présomptif de la couronne." CHÉRUEL, *Dictionnaire Historique des Institutions, etc., de la France*, tome i, p. 260, Paris, 1855.)

The Dauphins of VIENNOIS bore: *d'Or, au dauphin d'azur, crêté, oreillé et barbé de gueules* (Plate XXVI., fig. 7). This coat was quartered in the second and third quarters by the Dauphins of FRANCE, with the plain coat of FRANCE in the first and fourth; the addition of the quartering of DAUPHINY being a sufficient brisure. The *fleur-de-lisé* coronet of the Dauphin was arched in with four golden dolphins (Plate L., fig. 18).

The family of LA TOUR DU PIN, who claimed descent from the Dauphins d'AUVERGNE, also quartered their arms, but the French Heralds make this difference that in this latter case the dolphin is borne *pamé*, *i.e.* lifeless, with gaping mouth and closed eye, and of the one colour only. The normal position of a heraldic dolphin is that which it assumes in these coats, viz., *embowed*, with the head and tail towards the dexter side of the escucheon. If the dolphin be blazoned as *naiant*, it is still, if borne singly, represented as *embowed*, but when as in the case of the Venetian DOLFINI (Plate XXVI., fig. 8) three dolphins are borne *naiant* in pale (of *or* on an *azure* field in this case) the bodies are more nearly straight; and the same is the case when three dolphins are blazoned *hauriant*), as in the arms of VANDEPUT (*Or, three dolphins hauriant azure*).

The Scottish family of MONYPENNY bears: *Argent, a dolphin naiant azure.* Two dolphins *hauriant addorsed* form the charge of several English coats, *e.g., Argent, on a field vert*, HAMNER: *Sable, on a field argent*, COLSTON; *Or, on a field gules*, ELLEY, etc.; and are used as supporters by the TREVELYANS, BURNABYS, etc.

THE BARBEL, or BAR, is in favour in French Heraldry, the fish being borne in pairs *adossés*, their backs curving towards each other; as in the arms of the powerful Counts and Dukes of BAR (BAR LE DUC), whose territories lay on the Meuse west of Lorraine, they bore: *d'Azur, semé de croix recroisettées, au pied fiché, d'or, à deux bars adossés de même* (Plate XXVI., fig. 9 and p. 496). It is said that the seal of THIERRY II., 1093-1104, bears the barbel, and that the field was made *crusily* by RENAUD I., d. 1149. CLERMONT-NESLE, bore a similar coat but with the field *de gueules treflé*. DE ROUVILLE carried: *d'Azur, semé de billettes d'or, à deux bars adossés d'argent.* The Counts LAVAULX-VRÉCOURT bore: *d'Azur, à deux bars adossés d'argent, accompagnés de quatre croisettes d'or.* The Counts of BARBY, whose arms are included in the Saxon quarterings, used, *Azure, two barbel addorsed between four roses or.* *Gules, two barbel addorsed or*, is the coat of the Counts of MUMPELGARD, or MONT-

BEILLARD, and of the Counts of PFIRDT, or FERRETTE. (Plate XLV., fig. 1.)

SALMON are sometimes represented in the same attitude as by the Princes of SALM who carry: *Gules, two salmon addorsed between four crosslets argent. Argent, two salmon addorsed gules,* is the coat of the Counts von WERNIGERODE of Prussia.

PIKE were known as lucies, or geds. Under the latter term they form the charge of the GEDDES arms: *Azure, three geds hauriant argent. Azure, a pike in bend argent,* is borne by GIEDE, of Denmark.

A curious Dutch coat is that of the Viscounts JAN DE LA HAMELINAYE, etc. :—*Sable, two pike affrontés in bend, biting an eel ondoyant in bend sinister, argent.*

In Foreign Armory three fishes are occasionally found in pairle (arranged in the form of the letter Y), thus KIPPENHEIM and BERNBACH both bore: *Gules, three barbels in pairle or, their tails to the centre.* So also DORNHEIM, *Gules, three fish in pairle heads inward argent:* DIE HINDER bore, *Gules, three fish conjoined in pairle with one head argent. Azure, three fish in pairle argent,* is the coat of KRECHWITZ. An unusual but rather tasteful arrangement is shown in the arms of TROUTBECK, as shown in Plate XXVI., fig. 10. *Azure three trout fretted tête à la queue argent.*

A salmon with a ring in its mouth is one of the charges of the arms used for the City of GLASGOW; and two such salmon are employed as supporters of its shield. It is here connected with a local legend of ST. MUNGO, or KENTIGERN, though Mr MOULE (*Heraldry of Fish,* p. 126) reminds us that it occurs in the tale of POLYCRATES, related by HERODOTUS a thousand years before ST. MUNGO lived; as well as in the Koran.

Gules, three salmon hauriant each with a ring in its mouth argent, are the arms of SPROTTIE.

The arms of ICELAND; *Gules, a stockfish* (or dried cod),

argent crowned with an open crown, or, is borne among the quarterings of the Kingdom of Denmark (Plate XXVI., fig. 11).

THE WHALE.—Only two or three examples of the use of the whale as a heraldic charge have come under my notice. The arms of the Dutch family of DOLL are: *Azure, a whale argent, naiant upon the upper part of a fess wavy of the same*, but this seems to be only a variation of the coat borne by the DOLKS which was: *Argent, a dolphin sable crowned or, its tail curved in the air disporting itself above the base of the shield barry of four azure and argent*. *Azure, a whale argent finned and tailed gules;* is the coat of WAHLEN. (See *Fierté*, in the *Glossary of French Terms*.)

Gules, three whales hauriant each having in its mouth a crozier or, were the arms of WHALLEY ABBEY. *Argent, three whale's heads erased sable* is the coat of WHALLEY.

In French Blazon the head of a fish (like that of a wild-boar) is termed a *hure*. *D'Azur, à la fleur-de-lis d'or, accompagné de trois hures de saumon d'argent*, is the coat of LE BRIS DE HOUARÉE. LE BOURG of Brittany bears: *de Sable, au sautoir d'argent cantonné de quatre hures de saumon du même*.

The Polish family of BYDANT bear: *Gules, two fish jaws argent affrontés in pale ;* a like coat is borne by LUZYANSKI.

THE EEL occurs not unfrequently in Armory. It is represented *ondoyant, i.e.*, with a wavy outline (*See* ANGUILLARA, p. 120). *Argent, two eels ondoyants, and affrontés in pale between as many estoiles gules :* is said to be borne by a Scottish family of ARNEEL. *Or, three eels gules without heads paleways*, 2 and 1, is the very curious coat of VERGEYLL of Holland. (For eels in Spanish coats *vide infra*, p. 390, *sub voce* "CAULDRON.")

Of SHELL-FISH, or what pertains to them, the most prominent and important bearing is the shell of the scallop, or escallop. *Argent, on a bend azure three escallops of the field*, is borne by the BERNARDS, Earls of BANDON, in Ireland. This charge was associated with the ancient pilgrims, of whose equipment the scallop-shell, probably as a convenient drinking vessel, usually formed a part. (*Vide infra*, p. 375.) The banner of ROBERT DE SCALES at the siege of CARLAVEROCK was of *Gules, charged with six escallop shells argent*. An even better known example is afforded by the coat of the great family of DACRE: *Gules, three escallops argent*. (Plate XXVI., fig. 12.) This is also the coat of the KEPPELS, Earls of ALBEMARLE. *Azure, three escallops or*, was borne by the PRINGLES, whose name was supposed to be a corruption of pilgrim. *Or, on a chief sable three escallops argent* is the coat of GRAHAM, Duke of MONTROSE; and *Argent, a chevron between three escallops sable*, is borne by LITTLETON, Viscounts COBHAM. *Argent, on a bend gules coticed vert three escallops or*, was the coat of DARWIN, the naturalist. When the inside of the escallop shell is shown it is called a *vannet*, and is often drawn without the *oreilles* :—the little projecting pieces at the junction of the shell. The French VANNELATS bore: *Azure, a vannet or*.

CRABS, LOBSTERS, CRAYFISH, PRAWNS and SHRIMPS, all are found in the armorial menagerie. *Azure, a chevron argent between two fleurs-de-lis in chief and a crab in base or*, is the coat of CRAB of Robslaw. *Or, a lobster in pale gules*, is the coat which is blazoned on the tomb of Cardinal NICOLAS DE CUSA in the church of S. Pietro in Vincoli at Rome. THIARD, Marquis de BISSY, bears: *d'Or, à trois écrevisses de gueules, posés en pals* 2 and 1.

REPTILES.

Reptiles of all kinds, serpents, adders, crocodiles,

lizards, scorpions, tortoises, down to frogs and toads, are found occasionally in British Armory, and still more frequently are to be met with in the heraldry of Continental States.

Serpents or snakes may be represented *erect*, or *erect-wavy* (*ondoyants en pal*), or *gliding* forward in a horizontal line: or *nowed*, that is tied in a knot, or, in the form by which the ancients symbolised eternity, in a circular form with the tail in the mouth. Three such serpents *argent* on an *azure* field were borne by the French family of LAUZON.

Argent, two serpents erect addorsed sable, are given as the arms of LONGSHARE; and *Gules, an adder nowed or,* the coat of NATHELEY, is represented in Plate XXVII., fig. 1.

Gules, three snakes nowed in triangle argent (Plate XXVII., fig. 2), is said to have been the coat of EDNOWAIN, Lord of Llys Bradwen in North Wales, and is still borne by several Welsh families who claim him as their progenitor.

The coat of VAUGHAN of Talgarth (Plate XXVII., fig. 3), is, *Azure, three boy's heads argent, having serpents encircling their necks proper.*

The most famous instance in which a serpent is used in Continental Armory is afforded by the arms of the family of VISCONTI, which afterwards became from them the recognised coat of the Duchy of MILAN:—*Argent, a serpent ondoyant in pale azure crowned with a ducal crown or, and vorant a child gules.* (Plate XXVII., fig. 4, and p. 495.) An absurd fable is of course extant to account for the origin of this remarkable coat, but when we find it, as we do, among the series of escucheons adorning the splendid tomb of JEAN GALEAZZO VISCONTI in the Certosa at Pavia, and accompanied by the name of the lordship ANGLERIA or ANGUIVARIA, for which it was borne, we see that we have here only another instance of the adoption of *armes parlantes*. (*See* MENÊTRIER, *Origine des Armoiries*, p. 105.—DANTE refers to "*la Vipera*," *Purgatorio*, viii., 81.)

In the coats borne by the several families of the GUZMANS of Spain, of which one is engraved on Plate XXXIII., fig. 8, the caldron, or cooking pot, which was the peculiar ensign of the *ricos hombres*, is accompanied by a number of serpents issuing from it. This has been thought to indicate some legend of African campaigns, but I have elsewhere said ("The Heraldry of Spain and Portugal") that they have a more prosaic origin, and are simply the eels which would find a natural place in the *caldera* (*vide post*, pp. 389, 390).

The serpent represented, as in the arms of MILAN, *ondoyant in pal*, is termed in French blazon *une couleuvre*.

The celebrated COLBERT, Marquis de SEIGNELAY, Ministre des Finances of LOUIS XIV., bore: *d'Or, à une couleuvre ondoyante en pal d'azur;* and the same coat was used by the COLBERTS, Marquises de TORCY, de SABLÉ, de MAULEVRIER, de ST. PONANGE, and de COLBERT-CHABANNAIS.

The Roman family of BICHI, or BISSI, used: *Gules, a column argent, its capital and base Or, encircled by a serpent azure vorant a child vert*(*!*) *Argent, a couleuvre vorant a smaller one proper,* is one of the quarters (formerly the crest) of the Italian CIPRIANI. Several Polish houses originating in, or affiliated to, the families of WONZ, bear the *couleuvre*. WONZ I.—*Azure, a couleuvre ondoyant in pale or.* WONZ II.—*Gules, a like couleuvre sable, in its mouth a slip of orange fruited proper.* WONZ III.—The same, but *crowned and holding a globe or in its mouth.* WONZ IV.—*Gules, a couleuvre crowned Or.* WONZ V.—Like VISCONTI, but *the infant proper.* WONZ VI.—*Gules, two couleuvres ondoyants and affrontés en pale, each crowned or.*

Argent, two bars gules, over all as many serpents

affrontés paleways azure, is the coat of the well known Breton family DU REFUGE.

In a good many foreign coats the serpent is represented entwined around the stem of a tree (sometimes holding in its mouth the forbidden fruit) as in the coat of the Austrian SCHRECKS, the Dutch CRULLS, etc. (*See* also Chapter VI., pp. 195, 196.) Under the system adopted in the French Empire by which the dignity or office of an individual was indicated by an addition to the charges of the shield, *A canton azure, on it an antique mirror in pale or, wreathed with a serpent argent;* was the distinguishing badge of a "Count Senator." (*See L'Armorial Général de l'Empire Français*, tome i., planche xv., etc.)

The Polish family of DZIULI bear: *Or, three serpents ondoyants fessways in pale azure.*

Vert, three asps paleways or, is the canting coat of ASPENELL.

The *Heads of serpents*, apart from their bodies, are sometimes met with as heraldic charges.

The Castilian GARCINI bear: *Or, on a bend gules three serpent's heads vert.* But as there is a French family of GARCIN to which the Spanish house probably belongs, and which bears the same arms, but with the substitution of monstrous or chimerical heads for those of the snake, it is pretty clear that the latter was not the original bearing. In the coat of the Castilian BEJARANO we have, however, undoubted serpent's heads, *Argent, five serpent's heads or, langued gules.* (This coat may be put among the examples of *armes fausses;—armes pour enquérir*, etc.) Another family of the name in Estremadura bears: *Gules, a lion rampant proper, between the heads of four serpents vert* (or proper) *issuing towards the lion from the angles of the shield.* A cross couped and ornamented at its extremities with serpent's heads is termed a cross *gringolée* (*See* p. 161, Plate XV., fig. 6).

LIZARDS.—*Azure, three lizards or,* is borne by the Irish COTTERS.

The French family of LE TELLIER, Marquis de LOUVOIS bore a doubly canting coat: *d'Azur, à trois lézards d'argent, posés en pals, rangés en fasce ; au chef cousu de gueules chargé de trois étoiles d'or.* Here notice the *chef* blazoned *cousu,* or tacked on to the field, to avoid the reproach of false heraldry ; the three lizards (*stelliones*) and the three etoiles (*stellæ*) as canting charges. *Or, three lizards vert,* is the coat of ROSVERN in Brittany; and of VAN DER HELCK in Holland. *Azure, on a plain in base a chameleon proper, in chief the sun in splendour,* is a coat assigned to ORY.

The CROCODILE, or ALLIGATOR, appears as the charge of a few coats. *Gules, a chevron argent between three alligators proper,* is the coat of HITCHCOCK. DUCLAU, Barons of the French Empire, bore in their first quarter : *Or, three grenades sable, inflamed proper,* 2 and 1, *in base a crocodile azure.* The DALBIACS bear : *Or, an olive tree eradicated vert, on a chief gules a crocodile· issuant from the sinister proper.* (This family is of French origin and the coat is often blazoned *Per fess gules and or,* etc.)

Sable, a crocodile or, is borne by AUTROCHE of France.

A crocodile is the crest, and is also the dexter Supporter granted as an Augmentation to SPEKE, the discoverer of the sources of the Nile (*v.* Appendix).

The city of NÎMES has for its arms (derived from a medal of Nemausus) : *Gules, a crocodile vert chained in front of a palm tree rising from a terrace vert.* On either side are the letters COL and NEM (for *Colonia Nemausensis*), founded for the veterans of Africa after the battle of Actium.

SCORPIONS.—*Argent, a chevron between three scorpions sable,* is the coat of COLE. Other varieties exist ; sometimes the chevron, sometimes the scorpions, are tinctured *gules.* *Argent, a scorpion sable in pale,* is the coat of the CAPRINI of Verona; one of the quarterings of SCORPIONE of Milan; and is also borne by the GUINANDS of Neufchâtel. *Argent, a chevron sable between three scorpions fessways gules*, is borne by BELLERO in Belgium.

TORTOISE.—The tortoise is borne as the charge in the arms of several English families of GAWDEY, either *passant*, or *erect*: *i.e.* displayed like the heraldic eagle. *Vert, a tortoise passant argent*, is the coat most frequently seen. It has been adopted also as a charge in the coat of the Scottish family of GOUDIE: *Argent, a chevron between two trefoils slipped in chief vert, and a tortoise passant in base gules*. The French CHAUTONS bear: *d'Azur, au chevron d'or, accompagné de trois tortues du même*. HENRION, Barons de PANSEY, bear: *Or, a chevron azure between three tortoises erect, sable*.

Vert, three tortoises erect, is the coat of HARPENY or HALPENY. The French ROSSELS use: *d'Azur, à trois tortues d'or*.

FROGS AND TOADS.—These reptiles occur as Heraldic Charges with considerable frequency, and are often allusive in some way to the name. The best known family in Britain which bears them is probably that of the BOTREAUX of Cumberland: *Argent, three toads erect sable*. *Argent, a chevron between three powets* (or tadpoles) *sable*, is a coat of some Scottish families of RUSSELL (the chevron is sometimes *gules*), and the tadpoles are often blazoned as *gouttes* reversed.

We may pass over the old fable that the French *fleurs-de-lis* were derived from an earlier coat (borne by PHARAMOND!!), *Azure, three toads or;* a legend from which our neighbours across the Channel have perhaps (though by no means certainly) derived the *sobriquet* of "*Johnnie Crapaud.*" Rather it seems probable that this appellation is of Flemish origin. PHILIP VON ARTEVELDE perhaps had it in his mind when he declared that the French soldiers could not pass the river Lys to attack him "à moins qu'il ne fussent crapauds," a conviction which cost him dear; but thenceforth "*crapauds franchos*" appears to have been the *sobriquet* attached to the victorious French. (*See* REY, *Histoire du Drapeau, etc., de la Monarchie Française,* tome ii., p. 32. Paris, 1837.)

As a canting charge the frog is found in the arms of the German families of FROSCH (*Sable, on a bend wavy or, three frogs proper*), FROSCHAMMER, FROSCHAUER, FRÖSCHL, etc. Of the latter name two families in Bavaria use: *Gules, a frog paleways proper;* and *Sable, a frog or.* Similarly the Spanish family of GRANOLLACHS use: *Azure, two bends or, on each three frogs vert.* *Argent, three frogs vert,* is borne by DE LA RUELLE in Belgium, and by a Breton family, GAZET DE BRANDAY. *D'Or, à trois crapauds de gueules,* is the coat of COISPEL. The Saxon family of LOSS, Counts of the Empire, carry: *Gules, a frog bendways within a circular wreath of laurel vert.* *Vert, three frogs seated or,* are the arms of the Netherland families VAN RYCKEVORSEL. Frogs were used as supporters by Lord SOMERVILLE, *c.* 1570-1580 (STODART, *Scottish Arms,* i., 309).

The zoology of Armory makes no pretensions to scientific accuracy, and we may therefore include in this Chapter LEECHES. Of these PREEDE in Shropshire bears three in a field *argent.* The IGELSTRÖMS of Livonia and Esthonia use: *Gules, a river in bend wavy argent, thereon five leeches sable.* EGLOF DE SCHÖNAU in Swabia: *Azure, on a bend argent three leeches sable.* The French family of DOULLÉ bears: *d'Argent, à trois sangsues de sable posées en pals* 2 and 1.

The ordinary *Earth worm* appears in the coat of the RÉVÉRONI: *de Gueules, à un ver tortillé d'argent en fasce; au chef d'azur chargé d'un soleil naissant d'or.* The Barons von FECHENBACH of Franconia use: *Argent, a worm embowed in pale sable.* The DU VERNEY of Lyons use: *Vert, three silk-worms bendways, 2 and 1, and charge the chief (? or) with as many mulberry leaves proper.* The Breton SOUEFF bear: *Barry azure and or, semé of silkworms counter-changed.*

SNAILS are borne by ALESSO, Marquis d'ERAQUY in Italy, etc. (*d'Azur, au sautoir d'or accompagné de quatre limaçons d'argent*).

INSECTS.

BUTTERFLIES.—This insect is more frequently found as a heraldic charge in French Armory than in our own. The PAPILLON, Vicomtes de BRAITEAU, use *d'Or, a trois papillons de gueules.* A family of the same name settled in England bear: *Azure, a chevron between three butterflies argent. Sable, a butterfly volant argent* is the coat of BOLLORD. The Breton family of BARIN (from which came the Marquises of BOIS-GEFFROY; LA GRANDE GUERCHE, and DE LA GALISSONIÈRE) bear: *Azure, three butterflies or,* as did also the English MUSCHAMPS. The AVAZZI of Bologna used: *Azure, on a pale argent two butterflies (proper* or *or*). DROUALLEN, in Brittany, carries: *Argent, three butterflies sable. Argent, a fess embattled sable between three butterflies gules,* is an English coat for KERFORD. *Gules, a chevron between three butterflies argent,* is the coat of JAGOU, and (but with the chevron *or*) of ALLAIRE in France, and the Channel Islands.

FLIES.—The ordinary House Fly is borne as a canting charge in the coat of the Venetian family of FIERAMOSCA: *Paly gules and argent, over all on a bend or, three flies sable.* The family of VLIEGE in Flanders used: *Azure, a cross argent between four flies or.* (This coat is now borne by a family of GHISELIN, who have assumed the name and arms of VLIEGE.) *Argent, a chevron between three flies sable,* is the coat of DE THOU, Comte de MESLAY; and *Azure, a chevron between three flies or*, that of MOUCHARD, Comte de CHABAN, both of France. The Florentine VESPUCCI bear: *Gules, a bend azure semé of flies or.* In Santa Maria Novella at Florence this VESPUCCI coat appears, with, in the sinister chief, a pot of lilies, on the tomb of ANTONIO STROZZI. (*See* also LITTA, *Celebri Famiglie Italiane.*) *Per pale gules and azure* (or *azure and gules*) *three flies* (sometimes blazoned *gad-flies*, sometimes *bees*) *or*, are coats used by several English families named DORE, DAWRE, or DOORE.

Next to FLIES naturally come SPIDERS, of which there are some rather curious examples. *Or, three spiders azure*, is the coat of the English CHETTLES. The Russian family of RUKOFF bears: *Tierced in bend-sinister*, 1. *Vert, a spider in its web proper;* 2. *Azure, a dragon sable winged gules;* 3. *Lozengy argent and azure, a dragon, as in* 2. The extinct family of RAGNINA at Ragusa, used the canting coat: *Gules, a bar argent, in chief three spiders sable, in base as many bends of the second.*

BEES are often used in Armory as an emblem of industry and perseverance, as well as in allusion to the name of the bearer. *Azure, three bees volant or*, is used in England for BYE; and, with a chevron of the same, for BEE, and BEEBEE. The flies of MUSCHAMP (*vide supra*) are sometimes blazoned as bees. *Argent, a bend between six bees sable*, is the canting coat of BEESTON.

The Emperor NAPOLEON replaced the proscribed *fleurs-de-lis* by golden bees, which he used as decorations for his coronation robes, and also employed in the heraldic augmentations hereafter to be described. The origin of the assumption of the bee by NAPOLEON as an Imperial badge is curious. In the year 1653 there was discovered at Tournay a tomb supposed to be that of CHILDERIC (*d.* 480), father of CLOVIS. Among the precious articles enclosed therein, or found in proximity to it, were about three hundred small objects of gold and fine stones, which somewhat resembled in shape an insect, and to which the name of "bees" was given. These, and the other contents of the tomb were presented by the Archbishop of Mentz to LOUIS XIV., and were long preserved in the Bibliothéque Royale at Paris. These so-called bees were stolen in 1832, and only two remain at the present day. One of them is figured in the separate plate opposite p. 21 of the *Histoire de l'Orfévrerie-Joaillerie*, by MM. LA CROIX et SERÉ; Paris, 1860.

Among those who were present at the discovery, or whose attention was immediately directed to it, was JEAN JACQUES CHIFFLET, at that time physician to the Archduke LEOPOLD, Governor of the Netherlands, and afterwards chamberlain of PHILIP IV. (He is best known, perhaps, as the author of the *Insignia Gentilitia Equitum Ordinis Velleris Aurei*, printed at Antwerp in 1632; and containing a catalogue of the Knights of the Order of the Golden Fleece, with the blazon of their arms, etc., in Latin and French.)

CHIFFLET was charged by the Archduke to write an account of the discovery; and in his opinion these golden insects had been employed as the decorations of the royal mantle, which very possibly was the case. But CHIFFLET went further, and declared that in these insects was to be found the origin of the *fleur-de-lis*. This statement occasioned a great literary controversy with regard to which it will be sufficient to say here that CHIFFLET'S assertion was very hotly contested by TRISTAN DE ST. AMAND (*Traité du Lis*, 1656); and later by the celebrated antiquary MONTFAUCON in his great work, *Les Monumens de la Monarchie Française*. (*See* the *Histoire du Drapeau, etc., de la Monarchie Française;* par. M. REY, tome. ii., p. 27, Paris, 1837.) The Emperor NAPOLEON, whose ambition it was to pose in some sort as the successor of Princes anterior to the line of CAPET, assumed these bees as the badge of his new Empire; and, as has been stated, caused them to be largely employed among its heraldic insignia.

Not only his coronation mantle, and that of the Empress JOSEPHINE were thus *semés;* but the mantling surrounding the Imperial arms was similarly decorated; as were those of the "Princes-Grands-Dignitaires" of the Empire, to whose armorial bearings there was also added, as indicative of their high office, a *chef d'azur semé d'abeilles d'or* (SIMON, *l'Armorial Général de l'Empire Français*, tome. i., p. v., planches 5, 7, 8). The *chief azure charged with three fleur-de-lis or*, which had figured in the arms of Paris, and of so many of the cities of the French Monarchy, was replaced by a *chief gules charged with three golden bees*. This chief also figured for a time in the escucheons of Aachen, Amsterdam, Antwerp, Bremen, Brussels, Cologne, Dijon, Florence, Genoa, Ghent, Hamburg, Lyon, and Parma. Under the "Second Empire" the Napoleonic bee naturally came again into favour; but, so far as my observation extends, did not succeed in ousting the restored *fleurs-de-lis* from the armorial insignia of French cities, and corporate bodies.

The Low Country family of NOUST bears: *Argent, three bees vert; Or, a bee azure*, is the coat of the Castilian PECHA. The coat of Sir ROBERT PEEL, Bart. (Prime Minister, 1834-1835; 1841-1846) was: *Argent, three sheaves of as many arrows proper banded gules, on a chief a bee volant or.* *Sable, a chevron between three bees argent*, is used by SEWELL, and GERLINGTON; with the field *Azure* this was the old coat of BYRES (*see* STODART, *Scottish Arms*, i., 329).

The Swiss HUMMELS use: *Azure, a bee in pale or winged argent, its legs sable;* a family of the same name in Bavaria, uses the curious coat: *Argent, on a bend or three bees of the first, their heads downwards.* (This is a curious coat, being what would be styled "false heraldry," as composed of metal on metal. The *lambrequins* of the helmet are similarly of *argent* and *or;* whatever may be its cause the infraction of the general rule is certainly deliberate.) The French FREPPELS bear: *Azure, a bee or.* *Gules, semé of bees volant or*, is the coat attributed to the Byzantine house of SCLEROS. The French family of GUESPEREAU has as its *armes parlantes, Azure, three wasps or.* Beehives with bees flying around them occur in some very modern coats, and, though improperly, as crests.

ANTS.—The family of BIGOT, Counts de ST. QUINTIN in France, have the curious coat *d'Azur, à trois fourmis d'or posees en fasces l'une sur l'autre.* (The curiosity of this coat consists in the fact that whereas the vast majority of heraldic charges are necessarily represented much smaller than in nature, the escucheon must be of a very miniature character in which these charges are not drawn on a highly magnified scale.) Another family of the name BIGOT DE LA CHAUMIÈRE has the coat: *Argent, a chevron gules between three ants sable.* As *armes parlantes* the CASSANTS of Piedmont bear: *Bendy or and vert, each piece of the first charged with an ant sable; a chief or, thereon an eagle displayed sable.* A most singular coat is that of the family of ALQUERIA DE BOIGUES, in Catalonia: *Or, eight ants in pale,* 2, 2, 2, 2, *sable, each enveloped in a flame or.* (*See* PIFERRER, *Nobiliario de los Reinos y Señorios de España*, iv., No. 1742, Madrid, 1857-1860.) *Argent, six ants,* 3, 2, 1, *gules,* is assigned to an English family of TREGENT; and *Argent, a bend azure between three emmets sable,* to MASSY; I think I have met with no other instances in our own Armory.

GRASSHOPPERS and CRICKETS may be not unfitly joined together here. Both are used as *armes parlantes.* The Genoese family of GRILLO (Marquises d'ESTOUBLON in France) carry: *Gules, on a bend or a cricket sable.* The GRIONI of Venice used: *Azure, on a bend or three grasshoppers sable.* *D'Argent, à une cigale de sable*, is the canting coat of the SEGALAS of France. The WOODWARDS of Kent bear: *Argent, a chevron between three grasshoppers vert;* but the most familiar example of the use of this insect in British Armory is afforded by the crest of the GRESHAMS; a golden grasshopper (usually on a mount *vert*), which forms the vane of the Royal Exchange in London.

Even the unattractive WOODLOUSE has its representatives in the Armory of the Continent, the arms of the French family of MAÇON being: *d'Argent, à un chevron accompagné de trois cloportes de sable.*

Perhaps of all insect coats the most singular is that of the PULLICI of Verona: *Or, semé of fleas sable, two bends gules, over all two bends sinister of the same.* This may remind us of the jest of HENRY VIII., who affected to take the ermine spots in the arms of WISE—(*Sable, three chevrons ermine*)—for even more ignoble insects, as charges "becoming an old coat." The old Heralds, who pretended to find in Armorial charges the hieroglyphic of the moral character of the bearer, would no doubt have discovered in the PULLICI charges the symbols of restless activity and relentless bloodthirstiness!

CHAPTER X.

ANIMATE CHARGES.—V. MONSTERS.

IT has been seen that the conceptions of the old heraldic writers with regard to many actual animals partook largely of the fantastical. But creatures altogether imaginary also figure largely in Armory, though perhaps not to so large an extent in our own as in that of the Continent. A large number of the Supporters of our Peers are, however, of this character. The monster of most frequent occurrence in English Heraldry is the GRIFFIN, or GRYPHON.

We find the original idea of this creature in classical sculpture (probably derived from Assyria), and in Teutonic legend :—a creature supposed to have been originally generated between the lion and the eagle, having the body and hind-legs of the former; the head, wings, and fore-legs being derived from the latter. In mediæval times the existence of such a creature was no matter of doubt. The "veracious" Sir JOHN MAUNDEVILLE tells us in his *Travels* that they abound in "Bacharia." "Sum men seyn that thei han the body upward as an egle, and benethe as a lyoun; and treuly thei seyn sothe that thei ben of that schapp. But o Griffoun hathe the body more gret and more strong than 8 lyouns of such lyouns as ben o' this half (of the world) and more gret and stronger than an 100 egles such as we han amonges us . . ."

"Griffin's claws," probably the horns of a species of ibex, were to be found not only in cabinets of antiquities but in the treasuries of cathedrals and other religious foundations. The *grypishey*, or "Griffin's egg," probably that of an ostrich, was often mounted as a drinking cup, and esteemed a treasure of the greatest rarity. (See *Report of Historical MSS. Commission*, I., p. 66.) I am inclined to think that griffins, and other monsters afterwards noticed, may have found their way into Armory from the Lombardic style of architecture, in which they are continually employed.

DE CAUMONT (*Abécédaire d'Archéologie*, iii., 184) says, "Le basilic, l'aspic, le dragon, et autres figures symboliques du demon, méritent d'être attentivement étudiées dans les églises romanes où elles se trouvent."

These grotesque figures were denounced by ST. BERNARD in a letter written to WILLIAM, Abbot of ST. THIERRY, about the year 1125 (*i.e.*, just about the time of the rise of Hereditary Heraldry). He says: "À quoi bon tous ces monstres grotesques en peinture et en sculpture? . . . À quoi sert une telle difformité, ou cette beauté difforme? Que signifient . . . ces centaurs monstrueux . . . ces quadrupèdes à queues de serpent . . ." etc. (Quoted by DE CAUMONT from MABILLON, *inter opera Sti. Bernardi*.)

In one of the earliest Heraldic MSS. in the College of Arms (L. 14), the arms of SIMON DE MONTACUTE are represented. The shield contains a Griffin statant; but the usual attitude in British Armory, and the all but invariable attitude of the creature in Foreign Heraldry, is *segreant* (the equivalent phrase for *rampant*); this charge was afterwards adopted by others of the name of MONTACUTE, and was, I suppose, the origin of its use as Supporter by the Dukes of MANCHESTER.

Or, a griffin passant gules, is the canting coat of GRIB in Denmark. (The arms of STYRIA are at p. 495.)

Mr PLANCHÉ, in his *Pursuivant of Arms*, gives four examples of its use from a *Roll* temp. EDWARD III. "Monsire de GRIFFIN" is there said to have borne, as *armes parlantes*, "*Sable, à une griffin d'argent beke et pieds d'or.*" Plate XXVII., fig. 5 is the coat of TRAFFORD, of Trafford, County Lancaster: *Argent, a griffin segreant gules.* This coat was also borne by the Neapolitan family of GRIFFA; and occurs in the *Wappenrolle von Zürich* (No. 352) for BERNSTEIN. The Russian Princes LAPOUKHIN bear a shield *Per fess, in chief* the arms of the Russian Empire; *in base* the coat just blazoned. The Supporters of the Austrian Imperial Arms are *Two griffins or, the wings and plumage of the breast sable.* As a supporter the griffin appears frequently in British Armory. It is thus used by the Dukes of CLEVELAND and MANCHESTER, the Viscounts BARRINGTON, Earls of CAITHNESS, Lords DELAMERE, and by the Earls of MAR.

Or, a griffin segreant sable, is attributed to IVAN AP CADIFOR VAWR, a Welsh prince; and is still borne by several families of MORGAN. *Argent, a griffin segreant azure, diademed or,* is the coat of the Italian FRANCIOTI. The PERALTAS of Spain bear: *Gules, a griffin within a chain in orle or.*

The Griffin occurs with considerable frequency in the arms of the Baltic Provinces; and forms, consequently, the charge of several quarterings in the arms of MECKLENBURG, and in the full shield of the Prussian Monarchy; thus, *Azure, a griffin segreant gules, crowned or,* are the arms of the Duchy of STETTIN; *Azure, a griffin segreant or,* are those of the Lordship of ROSTOCK. *Argent, a griffin segreant barry* (or *bendy sinister*), *gules and vert,* is borne for the Duchy of WENDEN. *Argent, a griffin segreant gules* (*crowned or*), is carried for POMERANIA. Without the crown these arms are used for MONTEPULCIANO.

The great princely family of the ESTERHAZY-GALANTHA in Hungary use: *Azure, a griffin segreant crowned and standing upon a crown or, holding in its right claw a drawn sword, and in its left a rose branch proper.* *Azure, a griffin segreant or,* is the coat of the Portuguese

PLATE XXVII.

1. Adder nowed. *Natheley.*
2. Snakes. *Ednouain.* 
3. Snake entwined. *Vaughan.* 
4. Serpent Vorant. *Visconti.* 
5. Griffin Segreant. *Trafford.* 
6. Griffins' Heads. *Toke.* 
7. Dragon. *Dauney.* 
8. Wyvern. *Drake.* 
9. Cockatrice. *Langley.* 
10. Unicorns' Heads. *Preston.* 
11. Seahorse. *Tucker.* 
12. Mermaid. *Prestwich.*

ROBALOS, or REVALDOS; the Italian RIVARI, and AFFAITATI; of GRATET (Count de BOUCHAGE, and Marquis de DOLOMIEU in France), etc.

Gules, a griffin segreant argent, are the arms of English families of BRENT, and SWILLINGTON, and of the Polish *herba*, or clan of GRYF; as such they are borne by SZCEPANOWSKI; OSTROWSKI; ODORSKI; and the Counts KONARSKI.

The Silesian GREIFFN (SIEBMACHER, *Wappenbuch*, i., 67), and the Barons von GREIFFENSTEIN, bear: *Sable, a griffin segreant argent;* and the Sicilian ACCORAMBONI: *Per fess, gules and or, a griffin counterchanged.* In the *Wappenrolle von Zürich*, No. 74, is the coat of GRIFFENSTEIN: *Or, on a conventional mount vert (isolated and of four coupeaux) a griffin statant sable, the beak and forelegs gules;* and WILDENBERG, No. 134, bears: *Or, a griffin segreant sable, the beak and foreclaws gules.*

Although the griffin is usually found singly in Armory there are a considerable number of instances in which more than one is depicted in the shield. In the *Roll* of EDWARD III., referred to on a preceding page, JOHN DE MEUX is said to bear: " d'azure, a vi. griffins d'or," which was double the number which sufficed his contemporary OLIVER DE WITH.

In British Armory when three griffins appear they are usually represented passant, as in the later arms of WITH or WYTHE (with the same tinctures as above). *Argent, a chevron between three griffins passant sable*, is the coat of FINCH, Earl of AYLESFORD. *Argent, a chevron gules between three griffins segreant vert*, is a coat of FORSYTH, in Scotland. *Azure, two griffins segreant and combatant argent*, is the coat of CASTELAIN in French Flanders.

The head of the griffin is represented in armory with prominent ears; a feature which requires attention, inasmuch as it is this which distinguishes the griffin's heads, borne as separate charges, from the heads of eagles similarly used. Plate XXVII., fig. 6 is the coat of TOKE in Kent; *Per chevron sable and argent, three griffin's heads counterchanged.* The DRAKELOWS of Essex, and the Counts d'HANE DE STEENHUYSE in Belgium bear: *Argent, a chevron gules between three griffin's heads erased sable. Per pale or and azure, on a chevron between three griffin's heads erased, four fleurs-de-lis, all counterchanged*, are the arms of POPE, Earl of DOWNE, and are attributed to the poet of that name.

A variety of the GRIFFIN is found in the *Gryphon-mariné*, or Sea-Griffin. In it the fore part of the creature is that of the eagle, but the wings are sometimes omitted; and the lower half of the animal is that of a fish, or rather of a mermaid. Such a creature is the charge in the arms of the Silesian family of MESTICH; *Argent, a sea-griffin proper.* (SIEBMACHER, *Wappenbuch*, i., 69). *Azure, a (winged) sea-griffin per fess gules and argent crowned or*, is the coat of the Barons von PUTTKAMMER. One or two other Pomeranian families have the like charge without wings. GORCKEN bears: *Or, a sea-griffin per fess sable and gules*, and PAULSDORF: *Gules, a sea-griffin per fess or and argent.* GORKE used: *Argent, a sea-griffin azure, its tail gules.*

THE DRAGON.—Before the beginnings of Heraldry the winged and four-legged monster known as the DRAGON was familiar in legend; and it is hardly yet a settled question whether the Armorial monster, which also figures in so many early romances, may not be the traditional representation of the last survivors of real animals now extinct. As now depicted it has a head resembling that of the griffin, a scaled body with four legs with claws, bat wings, and a long barbed tail and tongue. A monster somewhat of this kind (but with two legs only) is found upon some of the shields borne by the Normans in the Bayeux Tapestry, and in more than one instance appears with its head transfixed by the Saxon spears. By some these have been considered regular banners, but if so they are unique, as no other mediæval examples are known of standards cut out to the shape of an animal. Standards of this shape, however, are represented as borne by the Dacians in the sculptures on TRAJAN'S Column, and on the Arch of TITUS at Rome, and a possible exception is noted below.

Mr FRENCH in an interesting pamphlet, *On the Banners of the Bayeux Tapestry*, etc. (reprinted from the *Journal of the Archæological Association*, in 1857), very plausibly suggests that, as the figures on the Saxon spears correspond exactly with those nailed upon the Norman shields, they were those which had been torn off by the spears of the Saxon warriors from the shields of their invaders. We may here remark that the term "*dracones*" which is occasionally applied to standards in mediæval chronicles has no reference at all to standards of this kind. "*Draco*" was a general term for a serpent; and the long snake or whip-like pennons were so called (*vide infra*, p. 657).

In *Excerpta Historica*, p. 404, there is printed, however, a mandate of King HENRY III. in 1244, directing "a dragon to be made in fashion of a standard, of red silk sparkling all over with gold, the tongue of which should be made to resemble burning fire, and appear to be continually moving, and the eyes of sapphires or other suitable stones, and to place it in the Church of St. Peter, Westminster, against the King's coming."

The Dragon is not a frequent charge in British Armory, but is more often met with as a supporter, or as a crest.

The Arms of the City of LONDON are supported by *two dragons rampant argent, the inside of their wings charged with a cross gules.* The Red Dragon is the badge of the Principality of WALES. It was used as a Supporter of the Royal Arms by all our Tudor Sovereigns, and also appears on the Standards of HENRY VII. and HENRY VIII. (*Excerpta Historica*, pp. 56, 57.) *Two dragons sable, ducally gorged and chained or*, are the supporters of the arms of the Baroness NORTH.

The English family of DAUNEY bears: *Argent, a dragon rampant sable* (Plate XXVII., fig. 7); and the family of RAYNOR is said to use: *Argent, a dragon volant in bend sable*. The Irish O'NEYLANS have: *Gules, a dragon statant proper*.

The Imperial yellow Dragon of China (*gorged with a mural crown and chained sable*), is the sinister supporter of the arms of Viscount GOUGH.

The DRAGON of Foreign Heraldry corresponds with the WYVERN of British Armory, having only two legs, and being usually represented with its tail nowed in a circle. The arms of DRAKE of Devonshire are blazoned, *Argent*, a wyvern, *its wings displayed, and the tail nowed gules;* but these are obviously *armes parlantes*, and the charge is the *dragon* of foreign armory (Plate XXVII., fig. 8). *Gules, a dragon winged argent, inflamed* (*i.e.* with fire issuing from its mouth) *proper*, was borne by the Barons von DRACHENFELS. A like coat, but with the dragon *or*, belongs to DRAGE of Denmark. *Argent, a dragon sable crowned or, holding in its mouth a flaming brand proper*, is the coat of Austrian Counts von WURMBRAND. The Genoese house of DRAGHO used, *Azure, a dragon argent;* and the DE DRAGO of Rome, *Argent, a dragon vert*. The BORGHESE family, to which Pope PAUL V. (1605-1621) belonged, used, *Azure, a dragon or* (often with a chief of the Empire). In the Low Countries the Barons de DRAECK carry: *Azure, a dragon or;* which is also the coat of DE DRAGON DE RAMILLIES in Artois. The Florentine DRAGOMANNI have, *Or, a dragon gules* (*d'Or, à un dragon ailé à deux pattes de gueules les ailes levées*). *Two wyverns gules* are the supporters of the arms of the Duke of MARLBOROUGH.

The Dalmatian GAZZARI bear: *Argent, two dragons affrontés their tails nowed in saltire rampant against a covered cup or, surmounted by a fleur-de-lis of the same.* The dragons in the arms of the Italian families of POZZO (Princes DELLA CISTERNA, etc.) correspond to our wyverns:—*Or, a well gules accosted by two dragons affrontés vert, their tails nowed in saltire beneath the well.*

A dragon with a human face is known in French blazon as a *dragon monstreux*. The family of ANCEZUNE, Ducs de CADEROUSSE, bear: *Gules, two such dragons affrontés or* (each holds with one claw its beard of snakes, and the tails and each claw of the feet are also serpentine).

Sometimes only a portion of the dragon is represented. The Princes BUONCOMPAGNI bear: *Gules, a dragon naissant or* (issuant from the base); to this family belonged Pope GREGORY XII. (1572-1585).

Two wyverns inflamed proper, are the supporters of the arms of the Earls of EGLINTON.

THE COCKATRICE only appears to differ from the Wyvern in possessing a cock's head and wattles, with a barbed tongue. It occurs in the coat of LANGLEY, *Argent, a cockatrice sable beaked, wattled, and membered gules* (Plate XXVII., fig. 9). This creature was, I believe, identical with the BASILISK; it was assumed to possess the same deadly powers, and to have been produced in a very remarkable way, viz., from an egg laid by a patriarchal cock and hatched by a toad! " Le basilic a par devant la forme d'un coq, par derrière celle d'un serpent;—'habet caudam ut coluber, residuum vero corporis ut gallus,' selon le texte de Vincent de Beauvais. C'est ainsi qu'il était représenté sur un église des environs de Lyon." The cut given by DE CAUMONT in illustration of this passage, from the Lombardic sculpture at Lyon, has the name BASILICUS engraved above the creature (*Abécédaire d'Archéologie*, iii., 183, 184. See also the "Account of the Basilisk" in J. ROMILLY ALLEN, *Christian Symbolism*, p. 390). *Or, a basilisk vert*, is the coat of the Spanish family of BAS: with the charge *sable* it is that of TRAPPEQUIERS in Flanders. *A cockatrice or, winged azure*, is one of the Supporters used by the Earls DELAWARR.

THE SALAMANDER, — the well known device of FRANCIS I. of France, which occurs with such frequency in the chateaux of Fontainebleau, Blois, Chambord, etc. —is the charge of the Italian family of CENNINO: *Azure, a salamander or in flames proper*. Tinctured *vert*, and in flames, it is the crest of DOUGLAS, Earl of ANGUS. The family of BRACCHE has such salamanders as supporters.

THE AMPHIPTÈRE is simply a winged serpent. *Azure, an amphiptère or, rising between two mountains argent*, are the arms of CAMOENS the Portuguese poet. *Azure, a bendlet purpure* (probably originally *argent* but discoloured) *between two amphiptères or*, was borne by POTIER of France. These were used as supporters by the POTIERS, Ducs de TRESMES, and DE GEVRES, who, however, used quite different arms: *Azure, three dexter hands or, over all a canton chequy argent and azure*.

THE CHIMÆRA is a monster of rare occurrence abroad, and does not occur in our own Heraldic menagerie. It is depicted as possessing the head and breast of a woman, the forepaws of a lion, the body of a goat, the hind legs of a griffin and the tail of a serpent. A simpler prescription for its composition consists of the fore parts of a lion, the body of a goat, and the tail of a dragon. The Chimæra on the mosaic pavement at Aosta is thus represented. (*See* DIDRON, *Annales Archéologiques*, xvii., p. 389.) The family of FADA of Verona have their own peculiar recipe: *Gules, a winged chimæra argent, the head and breasts carnation* (or proper) *the feet those of an eagle.*

THE SPHYNX resembles the preceding in having the head and breasts of a woman; as usually drawn the rest of the body is that of a lion, though according to some writers, it should possess the paws of a lion, the body of a dog, and the tail of a dragon. It occasionally appears in Foreign Heraldry as a convenient hieroglyphic to commemorate some service in Egypt, and is the crest of the British families of ASGILL, Baronets LAMBERT, GOATLEY, etc. The GILLARTS of Brittany bear: *Azure, a sphynx couchant, winged or, on a chief argent three ermine spots sable.* The SAVALLETTES of Paris use: *Azure, a sphynx, and in chief an estoile or.* The Austrian Counts PROKESCH D'OSTEN carry: *Azure, a sphynx couché on a pedestal or, on a chief indented argent a cross of Jerusalem gules;* and have sphynxes as supporters.

The arms of the families of VRANX D'AMELIN; HOLBERG; OSTERBECH; etc., have the same supporters. The old family of FRIES in Austria, has its arms charged with a creature which can differ but little from a sphynx: *Per fess sable and or, a lion rampant counterchanged, the head being that of a girl.*

THE HARPY is somewhat more frequently found in Armory. It has a human female head, the body of an eagle, and in British Heraldry is, I think, used only as a crest (*e.g.* by TRIMNELL, ASHLEY, etc.) and as the supporters of the arms of the extinct Lords HOO. On the Continent there are several examples of it in arms. Probably the most important is the coat borne by the extinct RIETBERGS, Princes of OST-FRIESLAND: *Sable, a harpy crowned, and with wings displayed all proper; between four stars, two in chief as many in base, or.* The family of RITTBERG in Ost-Frisia, probably connected with the preceding, bear: *Or, a harpy proper crowned of the field.* The Harpy of the Danish REIGS-DORPS (or RIGSTRUPS), has a human body and arms, as well as the ordinary female head. The body is habited *gules*, and the head is crowned *or ;* but the rest of the charge has the usual *sable* feathers. The extinct family of KNOB in Denmark used: *Azure, a harpy proper habited or, the arms akimbo.* Another Danish family, that of KALF, has a coat only varying from this in its tinctures; the field is *Or*, and the body is habited *azure.* *Azure, a harpy or, the head proper*, is the coat of LAMI in France; and *Or, a harpy gules*, is that of BAUDRAC of the same country. The City of NÜRNBERG bears: *Azure, a harpy displayed armed, crined, and crowned or.*

Another classical monster is the HYDRA, a dragon with seven heads. *D'Argent, à un hydre de sinople*, is borne by GARRAULT of France. The Marquises de BELSUNCE, in Navarre, use the same coat, but one of the creature's heads is nearly severed and jets forth blood. The Comtes de JOYEUSE used: *Azure, three pallets or, on a chief cousu gules three hydras of the second.*

THE UNICORN.—Of fabulous creatures none is more famous than the Unicorn, mentioned by Greek and Roman authors as a native of India. It is represented as a horse furnished with a single long and twisted horn, and having a goat's beard, and cloven hoofs. The supporter of the Royal Arms of SCOTLAND for about a century antecedent to the union of the crowns, it became at that time one of the Supporters of the arms of the United Kingdom, and in that function is familiar to all. Its use as a charge in British Heraldry is comparatively modern. *Sable, a unicorn passant argent*, is the coat of STEAD. In Scotland the coat of the PRESTONS of that Ilk, afterwards of Craigmillar, *Argent, three unicorn's heads couped sable, armed or* (Plate XXVII., fig. 10) is at least as old as the fifteenth century. *Gules, a fess vair between three unicorns passant argent* (or *or*), is borne by several families of WILKINSON on both sides of the border.

The Unicorn is somewhat frequently used by British Peers as a supporter. A unicorn *argent*, armed, maned, and unguled (hoofed) *or*, is the dexter supporter of the Arms of the Duke of RICHMOND. A like creature, but gorged with a collar per pale *azure* and *or* and chained of the last, is the dexter supporter used by the Duke of SOMERSET. Two unicorns *argent* support the arms of the Duke of RUTLAND. The supporters used by the Earls of STAMFORD are spotted *ermine*. The Barons of KINGSALE use two unicorns *azure* each maned, armed, gorged with the coronet of an English prince, and chained *or*. There is no more real incongruity in a blue unicorn than there is in a red lion ; but the unicorn is so generally used of a white colour that this example seems strangely exceptional. It is not, however, quite unique ; Unicorns are frequently found as supporters in Foreign Armory, and those used by the Livonian Barons de BRUININGK are green with golden horns. (KLINGSPOR, *Baltisches Wappenbuch*, plate xix.) A unicorn was one of the supporters of COLBERT, Minister of Finance to LOUIS XIV. (LA POINTE, *Chevaliers de l'Ordre du St. Esprit*, planches 128, and *s*). As a charge the unicorn occurs on the armory of Germany with considerable frequency. *Per bend sable and or, a unicorn rampant counter-changed* is used by KENTZ of Nürnberg. *Azure, a unicorn salient argent* is borne by the Silesian Barons von PARCHWITZ, and the Bavarian Barons von WALDENFELS. *Or, a unicorn salient gules*, is the coat of DE WITH of Holland. *Argent, three unicorns sable*, is borne by CLAIRAUNAY of France.

A SEA UNICORN, that is a unicorn whose body ends in a fish's tail, is borne by the Prussian DIE NIEMPTSCHER : *Per fess argent and gules, a sea unicorn counter-changed* (SIEBMACHER, *Wappenbuch*, i., 69).

THE PHŒNIX is represented as an eagle displayed issuing from flames. The modern coat of the family of SAMUELSON, created baronet in 1884, is: *Sable, three piles wavy two issuing from the chief, the third from the base, argent, on each a phœnix in flames proper.* The Phœnix issuing from a ducal coronet is the well known crest of the SEYMOURS, Dukes of SOMERSET. It was one of the very numerous devices of Queen MARY STUART, and also of her rival Queen ELIZABETH.

THE PEGASUS, the winged horse of APOLLO, is a charge somewhat analogous to the unicorn. It is best remembered as appearing in the coat granted to MICHAEL DRAYTON, the poet: *Azure, gutty d'argent a Pegasus of the second. Gules, on a mount of three coupeaux in base vert, a Pegasus salient argent,* is borne by WYSS in Switzerland. *D'Azur, à un Pégase d'argent, ailé d'or* are the arms of POLLIA in Bresse. The Bavarian family of HABERSTOCK, now extinct, bore, *Gules, on a mount in base argent, a Pegasus statant of the last.* There is a canting allusion to the name in the arms borne by the Prussian HOCHREUTERS: *Argent, a Pegasus salient sable. Sable, a Pegasus salient argent between seven flames or,* are the original arms of SEEBACH. Two Pegasi are the supporters of the arms of the Viscounts MOLESWORTH, the dexter is *Argent, winged or;* the sinister *Gules, semé of crosses crosslet or.* A Pegasus *argent* is the sinister supporter of the arms of Lord MOUNT-TEMPLE. Two winged stags were the supporters of JAMES ELPHINSTONE, Lord COUPER, in 1620 (LAING ii., p. 58). (See also the French Royal supporters, *infra,* p. 636).

THE CENTAUR, a monster, half man, half horse, is but seldom met with in Heraldry. *Gules, a female centaur passant without arms argent, the hair plaited en queue,* is the singular coat of the KRAUTERS of Nürnberg. The DE BROUILLI, Marquises de PIÉNNE, used as supporters *two centaurs gules holding clubs or* (as represented in LA POINTE, *Chevaliers de l'Ordre du St. Esprit*, planche 57, these have no fore legs but this is, I conjecture, an error of the artist. It must, however, be noted that this is the earliest type of the centaur, as is evident from the *bassi relievi* at Olympia). When represented discharging an arrow from the bow the technical term employed is *centaur-sagittaire*. *Vert, a centaur-sagittaire or,* is borne by the Counts REILLE ; and *Per fess or and azure, a centaur-sagittary counter-changed,* is the coat of the Roman SATURNINI. Such a figure is sculptured on a column in the Romanesque cloister of ST. AUBIN at Angers. (DE CAUMONT, *Abécédaire d'Archéologie*, iii., 185; *cf.* DANTE, *Divina Commedia; Inferno*, xii., 56, 60.)

THE SEA-HORSE. — The sea-horse is found in the Scottish coat of ECKFOORD ; *Argent, in a sea vert, a sea-horse rampant issuant proper.* *Per chevron gules and or, three sea-horses crowned, counter-changed,* is borne by ESTON of Eston in Devon ; and *Azure, a chevron between three sea-horses or,* or *argent,* is the coat of the TUCKERS (Plate XXVII., fig. 11).

THE SEA-STAG was borne by the family of LINDENBERG in Prussia, now extinct : *Argent, a sea-stag gules. Gules, a sea-stag or, its tail curved to the dexter,* is the coat of the Silesian POGORSKI (correct MOULE, *Heraldry of Fish*, p. 209).

THE COCK-FISH is a still more curious compound ; it is used as the charge in the arms of the Bavarian family of GEYSS : *Or, a cock sable, beaked of the first, crested and armed gules, its body ending in that of a fish curved upwards proper.*

THE SEA-LION. — This creation occurs in the " Mediæval Bestiaries," under the name of the " *Serra,*" it is there usually winged. Without wings it appears in the arms granted to Sir ROBERT HARLAND, Baronet : *Or, on a bend wavy between two sea-lions sable, three buck's heads caboshed argent.* The crest is a sea-lion holding an anchor in pale. The sea-lion is also the crest of the Earls of THANET and of HOWTH; of azure and supporting a tower in flames it is that of the DUCK-WORTHS, Baronets. Two sea-lions *argent, guttées de larmes*, were the supporters granted to Admiral BOS-CAWEN, and his descendants, Viscounts FALMOUTH. A sea-lion and a mermaid are the supporters of the arms of the ST. LAWRENCES, Earls of HOWTH: *Gules, two swords in saltire proper between four roses argent, barbed vert.*

THE SEA-DOG is a supporter of the arms of the Lords MOWBRAY and STOURTON. Mr MOULE, *Heraldry of Fish*, p. 149, says:—"The sea dog of heraldry is no other than the male or dog-otter, being a four-footed animal, but is drawn, according to heraldic fancy, with a broad fin continued down the back from the head to the tail; the feet webbed, and its whole body, legs, and tail covered with scales." This statement may be correct; the otter may be the original of the heraldic creature known as the sea-dog, but it is quite clear that, as represented, the latter finds a fitting place among armorial monsters. The otter, of whose use in armory *The Heraldry of Fish* contains a sufficient number of instances both as a charge and as a supporter, is usually drawn *proper*, and is thus very unlike the heraldic sea-dog.

THE MERMAID, or SYREN (*Sirène*), is represented with the head, body, and arms of a beautiful girl, but with the tail of a fish.

"Desinat in piscem mulier formosa superne."
HORACE, *de Arte Poetica*, l. 4.

Such were, perhaps, the syrens of Cape Pelorus who failed to lure to destruction ULYSSES and his companions; HOMER, *Odyssey*, xii., 39, 166; but OVID (*Metamorphoses*, v., 552) represents them as having wings. (On the

Syren, see the chapter on the "Mediæval Bestiaries" in *Christian Symbolism in Great Britain and Ireland*, by J. ROMILLY ALLEN, 1887, being the "Rhind Lectures on Archæology for 1885.")

In British and French Armory the mermaid usually carries in her hands a comb and a mirror. *Gules, a mermaid argent crined or, holding a mirror and comb of the third*, is the coat of PRESTWICK, formerly Baronets (Plate XXVII., fig. 12). *Argent, a mermaid gules* (or *proper*) is borne by two families of ELLIS. The seal of Sir WILLIAM BRUWERE, or BRUERE (temp. RICHARD I.), is one of the earliest instances of the use of this bearing in British Armory; in it the right hand rests on the hip; the left touches the head, possibly has the traditional comb. (MOULE, *Heraldry of Fish*, p. 214.) *Vert, three mermaids, two and one, each with comb and mirror or*, is the coat of WOLLSTONECROFT. *Gules, three winged syrens argent*, is borne by BASFORD (*see* p. 303).

Few of the monsters of Heraldry have so ancient a pedigree as the mermaid. Mr MOULE says (*Heraldry of Fish*, p. 211): "The relation of a being, half-fish and half-human, is of the earliest antiquity." It was thus that the Philistine idol Dagon was represented. In Babylonia a similar idol was worshipped. The mermaid is depicted on the ancient Greek Vases; and occurs frequently in Norman and Lombardic Church Architecture (See the Sculptures of the crypt of the church at Parize-le-Châtel, figured by DE CAUMONT, *Abécédaire d'Archéologie*, tome iii., p. 189.)

In it the syren is usually represented holding in each hand the long tresses of her luxuriant hair, sometimes she bears a comb; at others a fish. Often in ancient sculpture, as still frequently in German Armory, the mermaid is represented with a double tail, held up in either hand, a tail replacing each leg; and this I believe to be the more correct mode of delineation, though it is not, I think, known to British Armory, except as the crest of WALLOP.

Such a mermaid appears in the arms of the Bavarian family of BAIBEL (*Gules, a mermaid with two tails which she holds in her hands all proper*). The Bavarian BENDERS use: *Azure, a mermaid proper, holding her two tails sable;* and the Augsburg family of FEND carry: *Gules, a syren proper holding in her hands her two tails or.* Such a syren (proper) is the crest of the great Roman house of COLONNA. The DIE RIETTER of Nürnberg bear: *Per fess, sable and or, a mermaid holding her tails proper, vested gules and crowned or.* The BERBERICH of Würzburg, have as arms: *Gules, a syren with two tails, crowned and holding in each hand a fish all proper. Or, a syren proper holding her two tails vert in her hands, crowned with an antique crown or,* is the coat of the Counts DA SCHIO. *Azure, a syren with comb and glass argent within a bordure indented gules,* were the arms of the family of POISSONIER, in Burgundy. The heiress having married into the ancient house of BERBISSY, the latter assumed the syren as a *tenant* (or supporter), to its own punning arms: *d'Azur, à une brebis d'argent, sur une terasse de sinople,* as appears in the stained glass of Notre Dame at Dijon (*See* MOULE, *Heraldry of Fish,* pp. 212, 213). The mermaid, or syren, is frequently used in Britain and in France as a crest, and as a supporter to the shield. The Viscounts BOYNE thus employ two mermaids each holding a mirror proper. The shield of the Viscounts HOOD is supported by a merman and a mermaid; the former holds a trident, the latter a mirror, all proper. (The supporters of the Earl of HOWTH have already been mentioned, p. 299.) The dexter supporter used by the Earl of SANDWICH is a merman (or triton) holding a trident, and crowned with an Eastern crown. The SCOTS of Harden had mermaid supporters (*see* STODART, *Scottish Arms,* i., 383); and one is still used in this capacity by Lord POLWARTH; as the dexter supporter it was employed by Sir WALTER SCOTT ("the Wizard of the North"). A triton and a mermaid were the supporters of the CAMPBELLS of Ardkinlas. Mermaids are the supporters of the arms of PIERRE, Duc de BOURBON in 1352 (DEMAY). They were early the supporters and badge of the great family of the BERKELEYS (*see* my *Heraldry of Bristol Cathedral*).

The French THOLOSANI bear: *Azure, a siren with two tails, and upraised hands proper.* The supporters are two mermaids with double tails, each holding a banner of the arms. The crest is a demi-mermaid, holding in each hand a banner *argent.* The SERENELLI of Verona use: *Azure, a mermaid proper habited gules, holding her two tails argent.* The Dutch Barons MEERMAN bear: *Sable, a merman in armour, holding a sabre, and a circular buckler argent.*

In France the family DU BEC, Marquises de VARDES, etc., had their arms (*Fuzilly argent and gules*) supported by two mermaids. The like supporters of ST. GEORGES, Marquises de VERAC, hold mirrors. (In LA POINTE, *Les Chevaliers du St. Esprit*, planches 40, 149, the mermaids in both instances are drawn so as to indicate a division of the tail into two.) The latter family also used as a crest a syren in a tub, holding a mirror. This is the famous MELUSINE, used as crest and supporters by the house of LUSIGNAN, in memory of ISABEL, the betrothed of HUGH DE LUSIGNAN, Count de la MARCHE, who was Queen of King JOHN of England, and afterwards wife of HUGH DE LUSIGNAN. The same supporters (without mirrors) and crest, were used by DE CASTILLE, Marquis de CHENOISE; these, and the supporters of the GIBELLINI, also have bat-wings. Mermaids support the arms of MONTROSE.

DEVILS.—As some of the monsters described in this

chapter were taken to be the hieroglyphics of the Evil One, we may not unfitly add here a few examples in which his personality is represented without the interposition of any veil.

The German family of TEUFEL naturally bear: *Or, a devil gules.* The TROLLES of Denmark, with equal propriety, carry the same personage in a less mischievous form: *Or, a devil in profile decapitated gules, his right hand raised, his left clutching his tail; his head full-faced resting against his breast.* The HÖEGKS, Barons of HOEGHOLM, use the same but omit the head. The KUGLERS of Württemberg bear: *Or, a devil standing on a ball, and holding another in each hand, all sable.* The demon of the SISSINKS of Groningen is a personage of more elaborate construction: *Or, a horned devil having six paws, the body terminating in the tail of a fish, all gules.*

The classical FAUN, out of which the modern conception of the form of the devil appears to have been developed, appears as a supporter of the arms of SWEERTS, YSEMBART, and other Low-Country families.

The Bavarian Counts von FROHBERG have their arms supported by creatures which partake of the nature of a faun:—savages whose legs adjacent to the shield are replaced by those of a deer, or goat (TYROFF, *Wappenbuch des Adels des Königreichs Baiern*, Erster band, Taf. 39).

In the Armory of Germany the grotesque element has very much more play than in our own; and an account of its curiosities would contain many examples of monstrous beings as wonderful as those which have been described above; but as for the most part they occur in single instances only, I have not thought it needful to swell this chapter by descriptions of them. I conclude with one more classical example. The family of MEDICO DAL SALE in Verona bear: *Or, a Cerberus sable, collared gules, sejant on a terrace vert.*

CHAPTER XI.

INANIMATE CHARGES.—I. ASTRONOMICAL.

BEFORE treating of the large and important class of armorial charges which are taken from the vegetable kingdom, it will conduce to clearness if we advert to those Heraldic Charges which may be termed "Astronomical," consisting for the most part of conventional representations of the heavenly bodies, and also of certain representations of what used to be called "the elements," some of which impart a semi-pictorial character to heraldic shields.

THE SUN, surrounded by rays, is described in British Armory as being *in his splendour*. In all but the earliest heraldry our great luminary is depicted as a globe of gold with the lineaments of a human face, surrounded by rays, alternately waved and straight. French Armorists tell us that when the sun is depicted of any other tincture than *or* or *argent*, it is only the *ombre du soleil*, or the sun in eclipse. Nevertheless in the earliest English example, the coat of JEAN DE LA HAYE, in the *Roll of Arms* known as ST. GEORGE'S ROLL, the blazon is: *Argent, the sun in his splendour gules,* and the human lineaments are not expressed. *Azure, the sun in splendour or,* is borne as a coat of Augmentation for the Marquisate of LOTHIAN, being quartered with: *Gules, on a chevron argent, three mullets of the field* for KER, Lords of JEDBURGH. It is used by the Austrian Barons DIETRICH DE DIEDEN; and as *armes parlantes* by the French family of SOLAGES, and by ZON (or VAN SON) in the Netherlands. It is similarly borne by the Counts de SONNBERG in Austria, and the families of

SONNEBERG (who however sometimes difference by making the sun *argent*, or bearing it of *gules* in a silver field). In the coat of the Counts von SONNEBERG (Plate XXVIII., fig. 1.) the sun is clear of the mountain, the blazon being *Azure, the sun or, in base a mount of the same;* sometimes the mount is *sable*, and the Swiss family of the name bear: *Argent, a sun gules, in base a mount of three coupeaux vert.*

The Spanish family of BILQUES DE ORCION substitute the quartered arms of CASTILE and LEON for the human face; and some English families of DYSON have as their charge *the sun half eclipsed, i.e. per pale sable and or.*

Gules, a sun or, is the coat of SONNEMAER.

Azure, the sun rising from behind a hill or, is the coat of the Scottish family of HILL; and the same with the mount *argent* is used by the Bavarian family of ANNS.

There are other coats in which two, or three, suns appear. *Gules, three suns argent,* is the coat of CHALANGE in France. *D'Azur, à trois soleils d'or,* is the canting coat of the Breton TRÉSÉOLS, and of VAN SON in Holland. *Sable, two demi-suns accosted,* are the curious arms of HAEHNEL of Bavaria.

THE MOON is represented by a crescent (*croissant*) one of the prevalent figures in Heraldry, both as a difference and as a charge; and one which, perhaps with more reason than in other cases, is associated with crusading times. Its ordinary position in Armory is *montant*, or with both horns upward, a position which is only expressed in French armory when a crescent thus depicted is found in conjunction with others not so situated. *Azure, a crescent argent,* was borne as an allusive coat by LUCY, by VERNON, Marquis de BONNEUIL, by TOGORES of Spain, and by other families.

When the horns of the crescent are turned to the dexter side of the shield it is called a *crescent-increscent*, (*croissant-tourné*); when to the sinister its appellation is a *crescent-decrescent (croissant-contourné)*; and when reversed *croissant-versé*.

We have an example of these three less frequent positions of the crescent in the shield of the Austrian family of PUCHBERG. (Plate XXVIII., fig. 3.) *Azure, three crescents, those in chief addorsed, that in base reversed or.* BANNES, Marquis de PUYGIRON, bears a similar coat, but the crescents are of *argent*, and the single one is in *chief.* The LUNELS of Languedoc, bore: *Azure, a crescent versé argent;* and the great Arragonese house of LUNA: *Chequy or and sable, on a chief argent, a crescent versé, chequy as the field.* (For LUNELS, see *French Glossary.*)

In Scotland the coat of the OLIPHANTS (Plate XXVIII., fig. 2), is *Gules, three crescents argent; Or, three crescents gules,* that of the EDMONSTONS ; and, *Gules, three crescents within the Royal tressure or,* that of the SETONS.

Gules, three crescents argent, is the coat of the ancient family of VAN WASSENAER in the Netherlands ; often quartered with those of the Burg-gravate of LEYDEN : *Azure, a fess or.*

The Princes PICCOLOMINI of Siena bear : *Argent, on a cross azure five crescents or.* To this family belonged Popes PIUS II. and PIUS III.

The combination of the crescent and cross in the shield of CATHCART, Plate XXVIII., fig. 4, *Azure, three crosslets fitchées rising from as many crescents argent,* has a pleasing effect. The coat of MINSHULL combines the crescent and star, *Azure, an estoile issuing from a crescent argent;* these are the arms of the town of PORTSMOUTH.

Sable, a crescent between two stars in pale argent is the coat of the East Anglian family of JERMYN, Earls of ST. ALBANS, 1660-1683.

Some confusion exists in the language of blazon between the armorial representation of the stars as heavenly bodies, and a very different object, the mullet (*molette*) or rowel of a spur. Mr PLANCHÉ, *Lancaster Herald*, lays it down as a rule that an estoile or star should always have six points, to distinguish it from a mullet, which has five, and that these points should not be wavy unless the star be said to be *rayonnant*.

In most European countries, however, the *estoile* has five straight rays (a single one uppermost, otherwise it is blazoned in French *renversée*) and the *molette* six. I should be inclined to make the distinction consist solely in the charge being pierced or unpierced; in the one case a molette, or spur rowel, is obviously intended; in the other a star. In the case of stars of more than five points the number should be specified. *Gules, a star of eight* (sometimes of twelve) *points argent* is the coat of BAUX, Duc d'ANDRÉE, quartered by Queen ELIZABETH WIDVILLE, wife of EDWARD IV.; of six points it is used by the Counts von STERNENBERG. *Azure, a star of six points within a bordure argent* was the arms of GOETHE. The Princes of WALDECK bear: *Or, an estoile of eight points sable* (Plate XLI.). *Per fess gules and argent, three estoiles of six points counterchanged*, is the coat of the Counts of ERPACH, who quarter *Argent, two bars gules* for BREUBERG.

The English coat of DE VERE (Plate IX., fig. 2) is usually blazoned *Quarterly, gules and or, in the first quarter a mullet argent*. But the charge in this coat is really a star. A beautifully diapered example of this shield exists at Hatfield, Broad Oak, Essex, of the date 1298, a period when the rowelled spur was not in general use.

Plate XXVIII., fig. 5, is the Scottish coat of SUTHERLAND: *Gules, three stars or*. The MURRAYS bore: *Azure, three stars argent;* and the BAILLIES of Lamington: *Azure, nine stars, 3, 3, 2, 1 argent*. The existence of the 13th century MURRAY seals is sufficient evidence

PLATE XXVIII.

1. Sun.
Sonnenberg.

2. Crescents.
Oliphant.

3. Increscent, Decrescent, etc.
Puchberg.

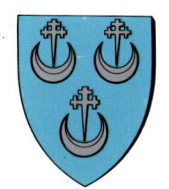

4. Cross and Crescent.
Cathcart.

5. Stars.
Sutherland.

6. Estoile.
Ingleby.

7. Mullets.
Wollaston.

8. Mount.
Watson.

9. Hill.
Hinsberg.

10. Burning Mount.
M'Leod.

11. River.
Lauterbach.

12. Hedge.
Yare.

that, as in the case of DE VERE, the bearings were stars, not mullets.

The Portuguese ROJAS (whence came the Spanish Dukes of LERMA) bear: *Gules, five stars of six points or.*

When minutely drawn or sculptured, the star is not depicted as a plane figure but with each ray raised to a central ridge. This point is much more attended to in French Armory than in our own.

The coat of INGLEBY: *Sable, an estoile argent* (Plate XXVIII., fig. 6) is given as an example of the ordinary English estoile or star, and in Plate XXVIII., fig. 7, the coat of WOLLASTON: *Argent, three mullets pierced sable,* is given as indicating the distinction referred to above.

Azure, the sun and moon in chief, and the seven stars in base or, is the coat said to have been borne by JOHN DE FONTIBUS, Bishop of ELY (1219-1225). (PARKER'S *Glossary of Heraldry* places the stars in orle, and the other charges in pale.)

The PLANETS and even CONSTELLATIONS are occasionally found in modern coats. The astronomer LAPLACE, created a Count by NAPOLEON I., bore: *d'Azur, à deux planètes de Jupiter et de Saturne, avec leur satellites et anneaux placés en ordre naturel, posées en fasce, d'argent ; à un fleur à cinq branches d'or en chef.*

The constellation of the *Great Bear* appears as one of the many charges in the landscape which is called the *arms* of the STOFFELLA of Austria ; and in the coat of ADLERSTJERNA of Finland.

Azure, the stars composing the constellation of the Great Bear arranged in bend argent, is a much better coat from a heraldic point of view, and is borne by BAR of Hannover. The same constellation also figures in the arms of the Scottish DICKSONS, now settled at Gothenberg, etc., in Sweden. (*Cf.* the arms of MADRID, p. 313.)

In Swedish Armory occasional use is made of the astronomical planetary signs ; and the symbol for MARS,

♂ appears in several coats granted to distinguished military officers. In British Heraldry the azure chief in the unheraldic coat granted to Sir JOHN HERSCHEL, the astronomer, is charged with the planetary symbol of Uranus ♀ irradiated *Or*. The rest of the shield is *argent* charged with a pictorial representation of the "forty-feet reflecting telescope," with all its apparatus of ladders, gallery, elevators, and observer's house,—a sad specimen of the degraded state of heraldic taste at the period of the grant.

The arms of THOYTS in Essex are: *Azure, on a fess between three six-pointed mullets or, two astronomical symbols of the planet Venus.*

A COMET, or blazing-star, occurs in several foreign and in one or two British coats. *Azure, a comet in the dexter chief, its rays in bend or,* is borne by CARTWRIGHT in Scotland; and by the Roman MELIORATI. The same coat, but with the charge in pale, is borne by one of the Spanish families of DIAZ; and identical with the last, but with the field *gules*, are the arms of the Sicilian ROSSI, Princes of CERAMI. The Norman family of PIGACHE DE LAMBERVILLE bear: *Argent, three comets gules.*

The arms of the present Pope, LEO XIII., of the Counts PECCI, are: *Azure, on a mount in base a pine tree proper, in sinister chief a comet its tail in bend sinister, and in base two fleurs-de-lis or, over all a fess argent.*

RAINBOWS are found in a good many foreign coats; they are conventionally represented as of four bands, *or, gules, vert,* and *argent;* unless their tinctures are specified, as in the coat of the Barons HACKE, who bear: *Argent, two rainbows addorsed, moving from the flanks each of three bands, gules, or, and the external one azure.* Occasionally the rainbow is borne *proper* as by the Barons PFULL: *Azure, three rainbows in pale proper.*

CLOUDS AND LIGHTNING are also heraldically

represented. The family of LEESON, Earls of MILTOWN in Ireland bear : *Gules, a chief argent in the base thereof a cloud proper, and issuant therefrom rays of light paleways or.*

A more conventional coat is that of DONNERSPERG : *Sable, three thunderbolts or issuing from a chief nebuly argent; in base a mount of three coupeaux of the second.* This conventional THUNDERBOLT, of arrow-headed rays conjoined with wings, was the canting coat of the Danish family of BLIX : the field *azure*, the thunderbolt *argent*. Two thunderbolts appear in the elaborate shield of the family of the Russian Marshal SUWAROFF, Prince ITALISKY.

The family of CLAPS in Flanders have a landscape in a thunderstorm! The Italian TEMPESTA bear a storm represented more conventionally : *Gules, eleven hailstones argent* (3, 2, 3, 2, 1).

The conventional representation of the north wind, the head of BOREAS, is borne as *armes parlantes* in the escucheon of the BORIAS of Spain ; and also appears in that of the BRASCHI, Dukes of NEMI. Pope PIUS VI. (1775-1800) was of this family. The arms are : *Gules, a garden lily slipped proper in dexter chief, the conventional symbol of the wind blowing on and bending down the lily; on a chief argent three estoiles or.*

From the heavens above we descend to the earth beneath. Examples already given have shown how the earth is represented : (*a*) by a *champagne*, a piece in base cut off by a straight horizontal line, corresponding to a chief, and often counted as an Ordinary by French Heralds: (*b*) by a *terrace*, which is a *champagne* represented more naturally with a less regular outline and usually green in colour ; (*c*) by a *mount* (as in Plate XXVIII., fig. 8); this is simply a piece of a roughly semicircular shape in the point of the shield, but is usually blazoned conventionally with three or more *coupeaux* (in

French a *tertre*) one above two, as in Plate XXVIII., figs. 1 and 9. A considerable number of German and Swiss coats bear the *mount-in-base*, after this fashion.

The conventional representation of WATER is by a base or *champagne*, *Barry-wavy argent and azure*, as in the well known coats of the cities of OXFORD, BRISTOL, etc., is frequent in Spanish Armory (Plate XXXIX., fig. 1). But later the sea is represented rather as in nature, at times still, at times *un mer agité*, and a semi-pictorial character is given to the bearings employed.

In the earliest times of heraldry, the charges depicted on the shield were separate and independent, and were more or less conventional even when the objects, such as birds or beasts, might have been represented naturally. The best and most artistic heraldry retains this conventional character to the present day.

A less severe style seems to have been introduced upon the Continent at an earlier date than among ourselves. Still there are a few pretty old Welsh and other coats, of a more pictorial character, usually connected with a legendary history. But while our own Armory was severe in character that of some of the states of the Continent aimed not unfrequently at more pictorial effect. For instance, as I have shown in greater detail elsewhere, many Spanish coats effloresced into the landscape style. Castles rise out of the waves, or are placed upon a mount; armed men appear upon their battlements, and beasts of prey ramp against their sides or issue from their doors. In the coats granted to COLUMBUS and CORTEZ, towns with spires and belfries; and seas strown with palm-clad isles; replace the conventional and more artistic charges which had amply sufficed for earlier times (Plate XXXIX., fig. 1).

A tree upon a mount in base occurs with great frequency, birds perch upon it, beasts of prey ramp against its trunk (*v.* p. 317), or are represented passant in front of or behind it. The arms of the city of MADRID are, *Argent, on a mount in base a tree with a bear rampant against its trunk proper, the whole within a bordure azure, charged with seven stars of the first.* In Italy and Germany the same tendency is not so pronounced, at least in mediæval coats, for later the degraded and debased style which characterised English Heraldry in the seventeenth and eighteenth centuries finds too many counterparts in the Heraldry of Germany of the same period.

It will be sufficient to cite here one or two instances in which the tendency to depart from earlier simplicity becomes manifest. Plate XXVIII., fig. 11 is the coat of LAUTERBACH : *Gules, a river flowing in bend sinister;* here the river, represented with the outline of a bend sinister wavy, has lost something of its conventionality. Its surface is slightly flecked, sometimes even fishes disport themselves therein. In Plate XXXII., fig. 8, the arms of the ARIGONIO family of Rome are represented as, *Argent, a lion passant along the tops of three columns gules, on a chief azure, an eagle displayed or.* The Silesian coat of BUSCH (Plate XXIX., fig. 5) shows the commencement of the landscape style. *Azure, a lion passant or, issuant from, and half concealed by a forest proper.*

THE MOUNT IN BASE, which nearly corresponds to the French *terrasse* is not unknown in Scottish Heraldry. The coat of WATSON of Saughton (Plate XXVIII., fig. 8) is ; *Argent, an oak tree growing out of a mount in base proper, surmounted by a fess azure;* the WOODS of Balbegno bore, *Azure, an oak tree issuing from a mount in base or; pendent from one of the boughs by straps gules two keys of the second* (as Thanes of Fettercairn).

The conversion of the devices which appeared on the Burgh Seals into armorial coats assisted the spread of a less pure style of heraldry. Instances of the semi-pictorial style will be found in Plates XLII., and XLIII., in the arms of the Highland chiefs; we have there the rock in the sea; the castle on its mount, the burning mountain (as it appears also in Plate XXVIII., fig. 10), the coat of M'LEOD of Lewis, *Or, a mountain azure inflamed proper.* It will be noted that here the mountain is not, as is usual in Continental heraldry, in the base of the shield, but is detached from it. *Argent, a volcano proper* is borne by CHAUMONT in France. The Barons GYLDENHOFF, of Sweden and Livonia, have as the second quarter of their arms; *Argent, two volcanoes in action accostés proper.* With these exceptions, we have left untouched the element of fire, but it will be sufficient to say that the conventional representation of it by wavy piles, *gules* or *or,* issuing from the edges of the shield, degenerated into flames *au naturel. D'Or, à trois flammes de gueules* is the coat of AROUET DE VOLTAIRE; *d'Azur, à trois flammes d'or ombrées de gueules,* that of BRANDT, Counts de MARCONNÉ. *Or, on a chief gules three flames of the field,* is used by CHAUMELLS in France; and *Sable, on a fess argent three flames gules,* is borne by DEEGHBROODT (or DEYBROOT), of Flanders. *Argent, a fire-brand in bend azure inflamed proper,* is the coat of BRANDIS in Bavaria. The Polish clan of BRANT I. has the same charge *sable* on a field *or;* and the Barons BRANDT, of Baden, use *Or, three fire-brands paleways sable each inflamed at the top, and in three places on either side, proper.*

Fig. 63.   Fig. 64.   Fig. 65.   Fig. 66.

Fig. 67.   Fig. 68.   Fig. 69.   Fig. 70.

CHAPTER XII.

INANIMATE CHARGES.—II. THE VEGETABLE KINGDOM.

TREES, FLOWERS, FRUITS, ETC. — The vegetable kingdom has largely contributed to Armorial blazonry. Entire trees though not found in early examples became fairly common by the fourteenth or fifteenth centuries. Though sometimes drawn "eradicated," that is, showing the branches of the root, they are for the most part represented on a mount in base, which in German Heraldry is often replaced by the conventional symbol of a hill with three rounded tops or *coupeaux*. Oaks are the trees most common in British Armory.

Argent, on a mount in base a grove of (fir) trees proper, appears in the Scottish Registers for the family of WALKINSHAW of that ILK. The same coat, with the species of tree undefined, is used as canting arms by FORREST, and by BUSH.

In France a family in the Lyonnais, named DUBOIS, naturally uses: *d'Argent, à un forêt de sinople ;* others of the name in Lorraine are more simply contented with : *d'Azur, à une arbre d'or.* The family DE LA FORESTIE DES AUBAS bears : *Or, a forest vert, on a chief azure three mullets of the first;* resembling which is a Picard coat: *Argent, three trees vert, on a chief azure as many mullets of the field;* DE LA FOREST places these trees on a mount, and charges the chief with the three *fleurs-de-lis* of France. In Holland the VAN DEN BOGAERT use: *Argent, on a terrace five trees vert.* The coat of the Viscounts O'CALLAGHAN of Ireland is : *Argent, a mount in base on the sinister side thereof a "hurst" of oak trees, therefrom a wolf issuant all proper.* With this we may fitly compare the coat given in Plate XXIX., fig. 5 for the Silesian family of BUSCH : *Azure, on a mount in base vert, a lion passant or, issuant from a grove of trees in the sinister flank of the second.* The DE BUISSONS of Geneva use: *Or, three bushes vert,* two and one. The French BUISSONS (Marquises d'AUSSONNE, and DE BOURNAZEL), bear: *Or, on a mount in base a bush proper, on a chief argent a lion issuant sable.*

The family of WOOD of Hareston in Devon bore at the Visitation of 1620, *Argent, on a mount in base an oak tree proper fruited or* (Plate XXIX., fig. 1). (*Vide ante,* p. 313, for WOOD of Balbegno, and WATSON of Scotland.) *Argent, on a mount in base a tree, the trunk surmounted by a salmon holding in its mouth a ring; from the dexter branch a bell* (that of ST. KENTIGERN) *pendent, and on the top of the tree a robin all proper,* are the arms of the SEE, also assumed for the City of GLASGOW. The salmon and robin refer to miracles attributed to ST. MUNGO, or KENTIGERN. An interesting historical coat is that granted to the PENDERELLS, who hid CHARLES II. in an oak tree after the defeat of Worcester: *Argent, an oak tree proper fructed or; surmounted by a fess sable, thereon three Royal crowns.* (*Vide infra,* Chapter on AUGMENTATIONS.) *Argent, an oak tree vert*, is the coat of the O'CONOR-DON of Ireland.

Azure, on a mount an apple tree fruited proper, are the *armes parlantes* of the Dutch APPELBOOMS, and of the Barons APFALTRER. The coat of M'GREGOR, called M'GREGOR of AULD in a sixteenth century MS., is: *Argent, a fir tree eradicated in bend sinister surmounted by a sword proper, supporting on its point an antique crown gules* (sometimes *or*) (Plate XXIX., fig. 2). *Argent, a pine tree eradicated vert, fruited or*, is borne by the Marquises CHATON DE MORANDAIS in France. *Azure, a palm tree eradicated or*, is the coat of TAGLIAVIA of Sicily (Plate XXIX., fig. 3); *Or, a palm tree on a mount vert*, are the *armes parlantes* of PALM in Austria. *Or, an olive tree vert*, is borne by the families of VIEDMA, AMBOIX, CHARLES and OLIVER. *Gules, an olive tree proper, eradicated argent and fruited or*, is the canting coat of OLIVIERA in Portugal; and the OLIVIERS, of which name there are many families in France and the Low Countries, nearly all use the olive in some form or other as the charge of their arms. *Ermine, an olive branch vert*, is borne by the Barons ZANGIACOMI. *Argent, three cypress trees eradicated vert, on a chief gules as many besants*, was used by TARDY, Comte de MONTRAVEL; *Or, three laurels vert, on a chief azure as many thunderbolts argent*, by the LAURÈS of France (*cf.* PLINY on the laurel).

In the Heraldry of Spain, Portugal, etc., a tree on a mount in base is a frequent charge, and it is very generally supported by one or two animals rampant against the trunk of the tree; or passant in front of, or behind it. *Gules, a pine tree vert, eradicated argent between two lions rampant against it or*, is the Portuguese coat of MATOS. *Or, a palm tree vert, supported by two lions rampant azure*, is borne by LANARIO of Naples. *Or, a tree eradicated vert, supported by two lions rampant gules*, is attributed to the Byzantine house of CANTACUZENE.

The wild cherry tree, in French *créquier*, is depicted in the ancient conventional manner in the arms of the French Ducs de CRÉQUY (Plate XXIX., fig. 4; and, better, on p. 344, fig. 72). *D'Azur, au créquier d'or*, is the coat of ANAUT. *Argent, a nut tree eradicated vert*, is borne by NOZIER, and NOGARET in France, and by FACCHINETTI in Italy. To the last named family belonged Pope INNOCENT IX. (1591-1592.) *Or, a willow proper*, is the coat of the Counts de SALIS.

Occasionally we find a dead tree used as a charge. *Argent, on a mount vert a dry tree*, is the coat of the Barons MÜHL of Brunswick. The KORNKOOPERS of Holland use: *Argent, a dry tree sable*. The stocks, or stems of trees eradicated, with or without branches sprouting from them; or the branches alone, are frequent Armorial charges. *Or, the stem of a tree couped in bend sable*, is borne by the Counts von SCHÖNFELD of Austria. *Or, two trunks of trees erect in pale sable*, is the coat of DORGELO of Northern Germany; which seems a corruption of D'ARGELO in France, a family which has the same bearings. The Portuguese TRONCOSO have the *armes parlantes* of *Azure, two tree trunks in saltire or*. *Argent, three tree trunks couped sable*, is similarly the coat of BLACKSTOCK in Scotland; and *Vert, three trunks of trees raguly and erased argent*, is that of the English STOCKTONS.

Equally conventional in its drawing with the coat of CRÉQUY given above, is the linden branch which forms the charge of the arms of the Counts von SECKENDORFF, knotted into a form somewhat resembling the figure **8** (Plate XXIX., fig. 6). The Italian family DELLA ROVERE, Dukes of URBINO bore: *Azure, an oak tree eradicated or, its four branches knotted saltireways*. These were the arms of Pope SIXTUS IV. (1461-1484), and were also

PLATE XXIX.

1. Oak Tree. *Wood.*
2. Fir Tree. *M'Gregor.* 
3. Palm Tree. *Tagliavia.* 
4. Crequier. *Crequy.* 
5. Forest. *Busch.* 
6. Lime Branch. *Seckendorf.* 
7. Hazel Leaves. *Hazlerigg.* 
8. Laurel Leaves. *Foulis.* 
9. Lime Leaves adossés. *Ortlieb.* 
10. Trefoil. *Hervey.* 
11. Treflé. *Hilinger.* 
12. Quatrefoil. *Vincent.*

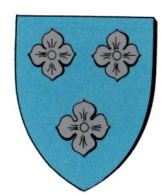

quartered in the first and fourth by ALEXANDER VII., with his personal arms of CHIGI (*Gules, in base a mount of six coupeaux, and in chief an estoile or*), in the second and third places.

Argent, on a mount in base three hop-poles with the vines all proper, is the coat of the English HOUBLONS, or HOBILLIONS (originally refugees from France at the revocation of the Edict of Nantes).

Palm branches are a frequent armorial charge: *Azure, two palms in saltire between four estoiles or*, is the coat of RICHARDOT, Comte de GAMARAGE, Prince de STEEN-HUYSEN. *Azure, three palm branches or*, is the coat of the PALMIERI.

Argent, two vines interlaced, issuing from a mount of six coupeaux in base all proper, is borne by the Princes RUSPOLI; and *Gules, two vine shoots addorsed, each bearing a bunch of grapes proper*, is used by the Austrian Counts and Princes LICHNOWSKI.

Leaves of plants are common in Armory both at home and abroad. The family of HAZELRIGG have: *Argent, a chevron between three hazel leaves slipped vert* (Plate XXIX., fig. 7). *Argent, three laurel leaves vert*, is used by FOULIS (Plate XXIX., fig. 8) canting, of course on the French "*feuilles*." *Azure, three laurel leaves or*, is quartered by the Dukes of SUTHERLAND for LEVESON.

Argent, three holly leaves vert, is the coat of QUÉLEN (Ducs de la VAUGUYON, Princes de CARENCY), of France, and by TERBRUGGEN, and VAN DER HULST, of Holland, LE MASSON, and IRVINE of Scotland.

Vert, three holly leaves or, and the same coat with *mulberry leaves*, are attributed to two families of WOODWARD.

Allusion has been already made (page 50) to the arms of BURNETT; and the Scottish coat of IRVINE of Drum:— *Argent, three bunches of holly leaves each consisting of as many leaves, slipped vert, banded gules*, is both ancient and well known.

The English family of MALLERBY used *Or* (sometimes *Argent*), *a bunch of nettles vert*, canting on *mal herbe*. It is somewhat strange that the French MALHERBES resisted a like temptation, and preferred, *Ermine, six roses gules*.

A curious use of the linden leaf as a portion of a partition line is shown in Plate XXIX., fig. 9, the arms of ORTLIEB of Nürnburg. The FIGUEROAS of Spain use: *Or, five fig leaves in saltire vert;* while the FIGUEIREDOS of Portugal use the same on a field *gules* (the stalks are usually in chief).

A single leaf is not often found as a heraldic charge, but *Argent, a linden leaf vert*, occurs in the *Zürich Wappenrolle*, No. 273, for REGROLTZWILE (REYNOLDSWYLE); and the like coat, but, with the charge in bend, and with the stem in base, is the coat of the Austrian Barons DEBSCHÜTZ DE SCHADEWALDE. *Argent, an aspen leaf proper*, appears in the Armorials for ASPINALL; and the German family of EWIG are content with a single *oak leaf argent on a field gules*. The Dutch VAN HULSTS also bear: *Or, a holly leaf in bend gules*. The coat of the Counts von BISMARK, to which family Prince BISMARK, the late great Chancellor of the German Empire, belongs, are: *Azure, a trefoil without a stalk or, in each of the spaces between the foils an oak leaf argent* (See p. 545).

The TREFOIL is usually blazoned *slipped* (*i.e.* stalked), *Gules, on a bend argent three trefoils slipped vert* (Plate XXIX., fig. 10), is the coat of the HERVEYS, Marquesses of BRISTOL, and was borne by JOHN HERVEY (apparently their ancestor) before 1407, as is apparent from the proceedings in the GREY and HASTINGS controversy.

The Irish national badge of the shamrock, is identical with the trefoil. A curious example of the trefoil in conjunction with a partition line may here be given as a pendant to the somewhat similar coat of ORTLIEB already referred to. It is that of the extinct family of HILINGER of Bavaria, and is given on Plate XXIX., fig. 11. (On *Klee-Stengel*, see note at end of chapter.)

The rue leaves of the *Crançelin*, or *Rauten-kranz*, to which allusion has been already made, p. 131, are undistinguishable from trefoils.

In French Armory the trefoil is especially frequent as a charge in Breton coats. It is also often met with in Low Country arms, but is seldom found in those of other countries.

In German Heraldry a charge known as the *nenuphar* leaf, which resembles a trefoil without a stalk, occurs in the charge of some important coats. This leaf, which is that of an aquatic plant, has given rise to some curious divergences of blazon. It is sometimes found described as a "heart;" as the bouterol of a sword; and even as the horns of a species of beetle,—*Schröterhörner!* These variations have been the result of the ignorance of artists who gave themselves licence in depicting a charge of whose true meaning they were in doubt.

The coat of the Duchy of ENGERN, or ANGRIA: *Argent, three (such charges) gules* (sometimes the field is *gules* and the charges *or*), which appears in the coat of the Princes of ANHALT; in the *Écu Complet* of PRUSSIA, and in the escucheons of the Saxon Duchies, for the County of BREHNA, is blazoned in all the ways referred to above. (*See* SPENER, *Opus Heraldicum*, pars. spec., p. 26, etc., who leaves the question of the real meaning of the charge in an uncertainty which I shall not pretend to remove.) The nenuphar leaf as now borne is usually slipped. *Gules, two leaves of nenuphar their stalks twisted in saltire argent*, is the coat of the Austrian Princes von KAUNITZ. *Azure, three leaves of nenuphar slipped or*, is borne by the Swedish Barons KOSKÜLL;

Argent, three nenuphar leaves slipped vert, is the coat of the Dutch VAN DER MEER, and DE JONG. In German coats linden leaves are often found in *pairle,* the points of the leaves directed to the two upper corners and the base of the shield. *Argent, three linden leaves in pairle gules issuing from a ball in the centre or,* is used by the Barons ROMBERG.

The flowers called QUATREFOILS, and CINQUEFOILS, are of very frequent use as heraldic charges. (In these names the syllable *foil* imports petal, not leaf, in the botanic sense.) Neither of these charges is furnished with a stalk. *Azure, three quatrefoils argent,* is the coat of the VINCENT family (Plate XXIX., fig. 12), sometimes with the addition of two bars of the same between the charges. *Per fess azure and argent, two quatrefoils in pale counter-changed,* are the arms of the MOCENIGO family of Venice: the Barons BIEDERMANN of Austria and Saxony use, *Per pale sable and argent, two quatrefoils* (otherwise *roses*) *counter-changed.* *Azure, three quatrefoils or,* appears in early English *Rolls* for BARDOLF. *Per bend dancetty azure and argent, four quatrefoils counterchanged,* is used by the Yorkshire family of CHAYTOR, Barts.

Cinquefoils appear at an early date as an Armorial charge, and they are usually, though by no means invariably, drawn *pierced, i.e.* having a small central circular aperture. A cinquefoil *ermine* appears on the seal of ROBERT DE BELLOMONTE (or BEAUMONT) Earl of LEICESTER, in the earliest days of Heraldry, and even in the thirteenth century cinquefoils were used in the arms of several families related to, or feudally connected with, the Earls of LEICESTER (who bore the *ermine* cinquefoil on a field *gules.* *Azure, a cinquefoil ermine,* is the coat of the Lords ASTLEY (temp. EDWARD I.). *Gules, crusily, a cinquefoil or,* was borne by GILBERT DE UMFRAVILL, Earl of ANGUS in 1290 (his seal *see* LAING, *Scottish Seals,* i., No. 87, has ten crosses in orle).

Gules, three cinquefoils ermine, often argent (Plate XXX., fig. 1) is the coat of the great family of HAMILTON in Scotland, whose alleged descent from the Earls of LEICESTER is, however, doubtful. *Argent, three cinquefoils sable* are the coat of the Lords BORTHWICK. *Gules, three "narcissuses" argent, pierced of the field (or cinquefoils)*, are the arms of LAMBART, Earl of CAVAN. In Foreign Armory the cinquefoil, like the trefoil, is found chiefly in Breton and Low Country coats.

A charge resembling the cinquefoil is the FRAISE, or strawberry flower, which in Scottish Armory is recognised as a distinct bearing: the difference in representation is that the foils are somewhat less widely separated, as in Plate XXX., fig. 2, the arms of FRASER: *Azure, three fraises argent*, a coat in use in the thirteenth century, but with this difference that the number of charges is more frequently six (borne three, two, one), than the present number.

In the earliest Heraldry, cinquefoils, sexfoils, and roses, are hardly distinguishable from each other, thus in the *Wappenrolle von Zürich*, No. 343, is the coat of ROSENBERG, *Argent, a rose gules seeded or*. There are no barbs and it might as well be blazoned a *cinquefoil pierced* did we not know from the name of the bearer the flower intended. The heraldic history of the rose has been in later times quite distinct from that of the other charges.

Azure, crusily, three cinquefoils argent, is one of several D'ARCY coats, varying only in tincture for difference, but the charge is often drawn as a sexfoil in early *Rolls of Arms*.

THE ROSE.—The Rose, which is now esteemed the national floral emblem of England, appears to have been first used as a badge by EDWARD I., who probably inherited it from his mother, ELEANOR of PROVENCE, or assumed it in memory of his descent from her. The Rose of Provence was, according to tradition, introduced into that country by THIBAULT IV. and the returning Crusaders.

On a Great Seal of EDWARD III. in 1340, small roses appear between the words of the inscription. Under RICHARD II. in 1377, the garters prepared for the King and the Earl of DERBY had roses thereon (BELTZ; *History of the Order of the Garter*, p. 244), and there are other instances of its use; but it was not, it seems, one of the prominent Royal Badges until the "*Wars of the Roses;*" these derived their names from the Red and White Roses which formed the respective badges of the rival houses of LANCASTER and YORK.

It is not at all clear under what circumstances the roses were assumed as the emblems of the rival factions. The red rose has been thought to be a badge of the Lancastrian honour of RICHMOND. With perhaps greater probability, the use of the white rose has been traced to RICHARD of CONINGSBURGH, Earl of CAMBRIDGE, second son of EDWARD III. He married, as his second wife, MAUD, daughter of Lord CLIFFORD, whose family are said to have assumed the white rose as a badge in memory of "*Fair Rosamond*" CLIFFORD. (*See* Chapter on BADGES *infra*.)

As a heraldic bearing the rose seldom appears as a sole charge in English Armory; but abroad it was used by several important families. *Argent, a rose gules, barbed and seeded proper*, was borne by the old Counts, now Princes, of LIPPE. It is quartered in the Saxon Arms for the Burg-gravate of ALTENBURG; and was the *armes parlantes* of the Barons, Counts, and Princes of ROSENBERG. These are also the bearings of the ancient Royal Burgh of MONTROSE.

Azure, a rose or, is the coat of COSSINGTON; *Ermine, a rose gules, barbed and seeded proper*, is borne by BOSCAWEN, Earls of FALMOUTH, and was the original coat of NIGHTINGALE. *Or, a rose sable*, is the coat of the

Lordship of WILDENFELS quartered by the Counts ZU SOLMS.

As early as the thirteenth century roses (possibly then not clearly distinguished from cinquefoils) were borne by the Earls of LENNOX; and at a comparatively early date by other families feudally connected, or allied, with them, *e.g.* the NAPIERS, and MACFARLANES; besides WEDDER-BURNS, and BLACKADDERS in Berwickshire. Plate XXX., fig. 3, is the coat of LENNOX: *Argent, a saltire between four roses gules.* The conventional representation of a rose, has five (occasionally six), fully opened petals, between which are barbs to represent the calix; and stamina, or seeds, in a small circular centre. Thus borne, it is not represented as *slipped* or leaved, unless these facts be expressed in the blazon. When a rose is said, as above, to be *barbed and seeded proper*, it is meant that the barbs are green; and the stamens, or seeds, of yellow. The colour of the rose always requires specification. In the *Wappenrolle von Zürich* the arms are twice given (Nos. 142, 213) of the family of GÜTINGEN: *Argent, a rose gules, barbed, seeded and slipped proper* (at the latter place the seeding seems to be *argent*). No. 265 of the same MS. is the coat of ROSENECK: *Or, a fess azure between six roses gules, stalked proper.* No. 33, the arms of BUCHEG is: *Gules, on a pale or three roses of the first slipped and seeded proper.*

In the early Heraldry of England the rose is not generally slipped. The arms granted in 1450, to KING'S COLLEGE, CAMBRIDGE, by HENRY VI. are: *Sable, three roses argent; a chief per pale azure and gules, in the first a fleur-de-lis, in the second a lion passant gardant or;* but in later grants, as in the coat granted to WILLIAM COPE, cofferer to HENRY VII., *Argent, on a chevron azure between three roses gules, as many fleurs-de-lis or* (Plate XXX., fig. 4), the roses are slipped.

THE FLEUR-DE-LIS.—Of all the floral devices used in Heraldry the most famous is the *fleur-de-lis*, now generally identified with the iris. Its floral character has been altogether denied by some writers who have professed to trace its origin to the head of a lance, spear, or sceptre, to an architectural finial; to a frog, a bee, a sacred mono-

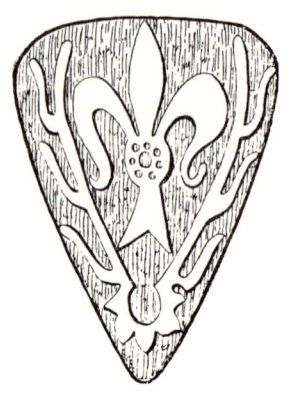

FIG. 71.—EARLY SWEDISH COAT
(FROM HILDEBRAND, *Det Svenska Riks Vapnet*).

gram, etc. (The student who is interested will find all these suggestions stated, and refuted, in the excellent work of M. REY; *Histoire du Drapeau, des Couleurs, et des Insignes de la Monarchie Française*, 2 vols. 8vo., Paris, 1837, and can hardly fail to be surprised at the prodigious number of treatises which have been published on the subject.)

It is at first sight so difficult to explain the reason why, when other great potentates were assuming for their armorial emblems the lion, the eagle, etc., the sovereigns of France should have preferred the apparently humble iris-flower, that we are hardly surprised to find the fact accounted for by the tradition that it was brought from heaven itself by an angel to CLOVIS, King of the Franks, on the occasion of his baptism, as a special mark of favour on the part of the BLESSED VIRGIN, whose peculiar symbol the lily has always been. The tradition has many variations of place and circumstance. It is, however, somewhat surprising to find that the French Bishops at the Council of Trent, when disputing for the precedence of their Sovereign, fortified their claim by alleging that the King of FRANCE had received the *fleurs-de-lis* direct from heaven: "Gall(or)um regem unctum esse et lilia divinitus accepisse!" (DE LA ROQUE; *Traité singulier du Blason*, p. 47, as quoted in REY, ii., 17.)

The most probable explanation of the origin of the *fleur-de-lis* as the device of the Kings of France is that put forth by M. REY, which has received the approval also of Mr PLANCHÉ, "that the Fleur de lys, or Flower de Luce was merely a rebus signifying Fleur de Louis." Up to the time of LOUIS VII. the kings of that name (identical with CLOVIS) called themselves, and signed themselves, LOÏS or LOYS. Even after the name had settled into its present form, "Loys" was still the signature of the Kings of France up to the time of LOUIS XIII. (REY, *loc. cit.*, ii., 44). LOYS, or LOUIS, VII. received from his father the surname of "FLORUS."

The coins of LOUIS VI. and LOUIS VII. are the earliest on which the *fleur-de-lis* appears. But it also appears at that time on the coins of FLORENCE (a city which was the mint of many European sovereigns, and whence the designation of *florin* is derived). M. REY, in view of these facts, inquires:—"Ne peut-on pas dire alors que cette coincidence du surnom de Florus avec le nom de Loys ou lis, de celui de Florence avec celui de fleur de lis, et enfin de tous ces noms et surnoms entre eux, a donné lieu à la formation du nom de notre illustre insigne?"

M. REY traces the *fleur-de-lis* as an artistic ornament to very early times; centuries antecedent to its adoption as an armorial ensign. (It is curious that on a coin of

HADRIAN, Gaul is personified by a woman bearing in her hand a lily: the legend is *Restitutori Galliæ.*) On a medal of GALBA the *fleur-de-lis* forms the head of the sceptre. MONTFAUCON gives an example from an ancient diptych in which the crown of the Empress PLACIDIA (daughter of THEODOSIUS THE GREAT), who died in 450, is ensigned with a *fleur-de-lis*. These, and a multitude of other early instances, are given in his plates by M. REY, to whose work I again refer the curious reader.

In France, as in many other countries, the sceptre borne by the prince was, at a very early date, ornamented by a floral emblem, varying in details but bearing a general resemblance to the *fleur-de-lis* of later times.

The seals of the Emperors HENRY I. (*d.* 1024) and CONRAD II. (*d.* 1039) afford early illustrations of the custom. (*See* GLAFEY, *Specimen decadem Sigillorum*, etc., tab. iv., Lipsiæ 1749; and ROEMER-BÜCHNER, *Die Siegel der deutschen Kaiser*, etc., pp. 22, 23, Frankfurt am Mayn, 1851.) In France the germ of the armorial *fleur-de-lis* may thus be traced to the *fleurons* which adorn the sceptres and the crowns of HENRI I., PHILIPPE I., and LOUIS VI. A signet of LOUIS VII. bears a *fleur-de-lis florençée*, but the charge first takes a definite heraldic shape on the seals of PHILIP AUGUSTUS (*d.* 1223); whose Great Seal represents him crowned with an open crown of *fleurons* and holding in his right hand a *fleur-de-lis* (several of his successors are similarly represented), in his left a sceptre surmounted by a lozenge charged with the like emblem. On his counter-seal is engraved in an oval a *fleur-de-lis* entirely of the heraldic shape. (M. DEMAY, in his book so often cited in previous pages, points out, pp. 194-196, the analogy which exists between the *fleurons*, held in the hand, or surmounting the sceptre as well as adorning the crown, of the effigies of the BLESSED VIRGIN depicted on the seal of the chapter of Notre-Dame at Paris in 1146, and on that of the Abbey of Faremoutiers in 1197, with those borne by ST. LOUIS IX. in 1226.) On the occasion of the coronation of his son PHILIP (in his own lifetime), the king, LOUIS VII., regulated the details of the ceremony, and among other things prescribed that the prince should wear "ses chausses appelées sandales ou bottines de soye, couleur bleu azuré semée en moult endroits de fleurs de lys d'or, puis aussi sa dalmatique de même couleur et œuvre" (GOURDON DE GENOUILLAC, *L'Art Héraldique*, p. 224).

On the counter-seal of LOUIS VIII. (1223-1226) there is a heart-shaped escucheon *semé de fleurs-de-lis* (Plate XXXVII., fig. 5). The counter-seal of ST. LOUIS IX. bears a single *fleur-de-lis*. The shield and caparisons of the horse of his brother CHARLES, Comte d'ANJOU (afterwards King of SICILY), as borne on his Great Seal, have FRANCE-ANCIENT (*i.e. semé de fleurs-de-lis*) *within a bordure of* CASTILE, derived from his mother BLANCHE, daughter of ALFONSO VIII. of CASTILE. On her seal of vesica shape Queen BLANCHE is represented holding a *fleur-de-lis* in her hand, and the space between the legend and her effigy is occupied by two *fleurs-de-lis*. On her circular counter-seal the field is occupied by a large castle for CASTILE, having on either side a small *fleur-de-lis* (*see* Plate XXXVII., fig. 6), and a third *fleur-de-lis* surmounts the castle on the inscription band which bears the words "BLACHA FILIA REGIS CASTELLE" (VRÉE, *Généalogie des Comtes de Flandres*, plate xxxix.). By an edict, dated 1376, CHARLES V. reduced the number of *fleurs-de-lis* in his shield to three "pour symboliser la Sainte-Trinité." On the counter-seals of LOUIS XII. and FRANCIS I., the escucheon is surmounted by an open crown of *fleurs-de-lis*, is supported by two kneeling angels, and the point rests in the petals of a garden lily, slipped and budded proper. (Plate XXXVII., fig. 1.)

On the first Great Seal of EDWARD III. (Jan.-Oct. 1327) a small *fleur-de-lis* is placed above each of the castles which had appeared on either side of the throne in the Great Seal of his father EDWARD II. (The same matrix had served for EDWARD I. and EDWARD II. with slight additions.) On his second Great Seal (1327-1336) a *fleur-de-lis* alone appears on either side of the throne.

The fourth Great Seal (Feb.-June 1340) is the first on which his arms appear: *Quarterly*, 1 and 4, FRANCE; 2 and 3, ENGLAND. The shields upon the canopy of the obverse have but three *fleurs-de-lis;* but on the reverse the shield surcoat and housings have the French quarter *semé de fleurs-de-lis*. On the second Great Seal of HENRY IV., in 1411, the *fleurs-de-lis* in the quarters of FRANCE, are reduced to three (Plate XXX., fig. 5). The French quarter was only removed from the arms of the Kings of ENGLAND in 1801. (*See* the *Catalogue of Seals* in the Department of MSS., British Museum, Vol. i., Nos. 160, 161, 182, 259.)

In Scotland, Queen MARY, in 1564, has on her counter-seal the shield charged with the arms of FRANCE (dimidiated), and SCOTLAND (entire) (LAING, *Scottish Seals*, i., No. 64).

At the head of this Chapter are indicated several of the many forms in which the beautiful bearing of the *fleur-de-lis* has been represented in the arms of FRANCE, up to the close of the Monarchy.

The arms of FLORENCE are: *Argent, a fleur-de-lis florencée gules*, as in Plate XXX., fig. 7.

The family of CHÂTEAUBRIAND, who used originally the arms: *de Gueules, semé de pommes de pin d'or*, are said to have received permission from ST. LOUIS IX. to substitute for them *de Gueules, semé de fleurs-de-lis d'or*, in reward for the valour displayed by GEOFFREY DE

CHÂTEAUBRIAND at the battle of Mansourah in 1250, with the proud motto, "*Mon sang teint les bannières de France.*"

The letters of nobility granted by CHARLES VII. in December 1429 to the brothers of LA PUCELLE, JEANNE D'ARC, with the surname of DU LIS, are: *Azure, between two fleurs-de-lis of France, a sword in pale proper, hilted, and supporting on its point an open crown, Or.*

The *Fleur-de-lis* appears early, but not frequently, in British Armory, in which somewhat later it was to become a favourite charge. Allusion has already been made to its adoption by the MONTGOMERIES (*ante* p. 50).

In the *Roll of Arms* known as GLOVER'S *Roll*, said to be of the time of HENRY III., WILLIAM DE CANTELOWE (CANTELUPE) bears: *Gules, three fleurs-de-lis or* (*vide ante*, p. 225); and ROBERT AGULON, *Gules, a fleur-de-lis argent*. Others of this name bore: *Azure, a fleur-de-lis argent,* afterwards the coat of the DIGBYS, Earls of BRISTOL. *Or, a fleur-de-lis azure,* are the arms of PORTMAN. *Or, a fleur-de-lis sable,* is the coat of TILLY, Marquis de BLARU in France. *Per pale azure and or, two fleurs-de-lis accostés counterchanged,* are the arms of the FUGGERS, the merchants and bankers of Augsburg; Counts in 1507, and in 1803 Princes of the Holy Roman Empire. *Gules, three fleurs-de-lis or,* was also borne by the family of BROWN of Colstoun.

Azure, fleury (or *semé de fleurs-de-lis*) *argent,* is an old coat of MORTIMER; and was also borne by BAZENTIN, and the MALAPERTS, Barons de NEUFVILLE. Some important Low Country families bear: *Argent, fleury gules, e.g.* the Barons d'HAULTEPENNE; KERCKEM, Barons de WYER; and OUPEY. (In the *Armorial de Gelre,* the arms of the last-named family are drawn as,

Argent, six fleurs-de-lis gules.) *Azure, six fleurs-de-lis and a chief or*, was borne by the Princes of PORTIA, of the Holy Roman Empire.

Several ancient families in the Low Countries bore *fleurs-de-lis* dimidiated by a horizontal line, *i.e.* with the lower half of the flower wanting. In the thirteenth century MS. just quoted (*L'Armorial du Héraut Gelre*, or *Gueldre*), the arms of " Le Sire de LINTRE" are: *d'Argent, à trois fleurs-de-lis au pied coupé de sable.* The Sires de WESEMAEL bore the same, *Gules* and *argent*, and those of BERGEN OP ZOOM, *Or*, the flowers *gules*. The French DE VIGNACOURTS, of whom were two Grand Masters of the Knights of St. John, ALOF DE VIGNACOURT (1601-1612), and ADRIAN (1690-1697), bore: *Argent, three fleurs-de-lis dimidiated gules.*

The Barons VENNINGEN bear (Plate XXX., fig. 6) *Argent, two staves or sceptres, ending in fleurs-de-lis gules.* A similar coat is that of the DELBENE of France who bear: *Azure, two fleurs-de-lis in saltire, each of the long stalks ending in three roots argent.* The Veronese DEL BENE bear: *Azure, two garden lilies in saltire argent*, so these are only varieties of drawing the same coat.

The *fleur-de-lis* has been represented in a hundred different ways, as may be seen in the plates of REY'S work already referred to, *l'Histoire du Drapeau, des Couleurs, et des Insignes de la Monarchie Française.*

From these most of the characteristic examples engraved in the woodcut at the head of this chapter are taken.

No. 1 is from the demolished church of ST. HILAIRE at Poitiers; and also appears on the tombs of the Comtes d'EU, at that place. (REY, Plate ii., fig. 12).

No. 2 is from a portrait in panel in the Sauvageot Collection, dating from the close of the fifteenth century (REY, Plate ii., fig. 85).

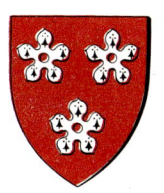

PLATE XXX.

1. Cinquefoils. *Hamilton.*
2. Fraises. *Fraser.* 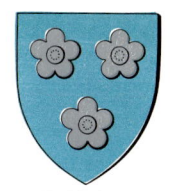
3. Roses. *Lennox.* 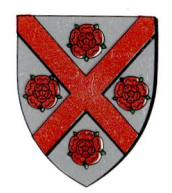
4. Roses slipped. *Cope.* 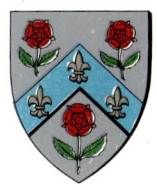
5. Fleurs de lis. *France.* 
6. Fleur-de-lisé. *Venningen.* 
7. Fleur de lis florencée. *Florence.* 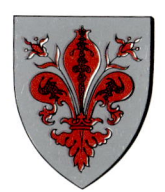
8. Thistle. *Leven.* 
9. Chaplet. *Lascelles.* 
10. Pomegranate. *Granada.* 
11. Rye. *Riddell.* 
12. Garb. *Grosvenor.*

No. 3 is from stained glass in the Depaulis Collection (REY, Plate iv., fig. 16).

No. 4 (REY, Plate iv., fig. 31).

No. 5 is from the seal of Falaise (REY, Plate iv., fig. 33).

No. 6 appears on the seal of the Châtelet of Paris in 1337 (REY, Plate i., fig. 8).

No. 7 (REY, Plate xvii., fig. 210).

No. 8 is the bulging and ungraceful form affected under the latest Bourbon Kings.

The association of the *fleur-de-lis* with a leopard's (or lion's) face in the arms of the CANTELUPES, and of the See of HEREFORD is alluded to elsewhere (p. 225).

The *fleur-de-lis* in early examples was often drawn with a globular centre, as in fig. 65, and Mr PLANCHÉ (in the *Pursuivant of Arms*, p. 103) suggests that this may have originated the bearings just referred to, the globular space being filled up with the leopard's head to denote some family alliance.

Argent, on a chief azure, two fleurs-de-lis or, was borne by CLINTON of Baddesley. *Azure, a cross argent between four fleurs-de-lis or*, is the coat of SEVASTOS of Byzantium. *Gules, a chevron between three fleurs-de-lis or*, is the coat of BROUN or BROWN of Scotland (*cf.* p. 331).

The earliest known armorial shield in Sweden bears a *fleur-de-lis* between two stag's attires, connected by the *crane*, or scull plate in base (*vide* fig. 71, p. 326, and p. 52, *ante*). *Sable, a chevron between three fleurs-de-lis argent*, is borne by several important Welsh families (VAUGHAN, Earls of LISBURNE; WYNN, POWELL, EVANS, WILLIAMS, GRIFFITHS, etc., who claim descent from EDNOWAIN AP BLEDDYN). *Sable, a fess between six fleurs-de-lis or*, is borne by the Barons de la MOTTE FOUQUÉ.

With the *fleur-de-lis* in its conventional form we may fitly couple its prototypes the iris and garden lily. In their botanical forms both are occasionally found as heraldic charges. The Picard family of LIHONS bears : *Azure, two garden lilies argent.* The Marquises of ANJORRANT in France, now extinct, used : *Azure, three garden lilies argent, slipped and leaved vert.* HENRY VI. in 1440, granted to the COLLEGE of ST. MARY at ETON, the coat : *Sable, three garden lilies argent, on a chief per pale azure and gules, a fleur-de-lis of France, and a lion of England.* *Sable, three lilies proper,* are the arms attributed to WINCHESTER COLLEGE. *Azure, three lilies argent,* is the canting coat borne by LILLIE of Scotland.

The arms of the City of DUNDEE are : *Azure, a pot of three lilies proper.*

The natural lily supports the shield of France in the counter-seals of LOUIS XII. and FRANCIS I. (*vide supra*, p. 329 ; and Plate XXXVII., fig. 1).

THE THISTLE, now the national emblem of SCOTLAND, has no place in the early Armory of that country. It was unknown as the badge of Scotland prior to the reign of JAMES III., 1460-88 when, in 1474, it appears first on the groats in the silver coinage. In an inventory of the effects of that prince made at his death in 1488, a coverlet "of variand purper tartar browden with thrisselis" is one of the items. On the altar diptych preserved at Holyrood, which contains the portraits of JAMES III., and his Queen, MARGARET of Denmark, the arras behind the kneeling figure of the Queen is powdered with thistles. The picture, or at least this portion of it, was probably painted by MABUSE about 1485. (*See* Dr LAING'S *Historical Description of the Altarpiece*, Edinburgh, 1857. This should be read with the *Athenæum* criticism on the picture, then exhibited at the STUART Exhibition in London, No. 3199, Feb. 16, 1890.) The thistle only appears on the gold coins of Scotland in 1525.

THE ORDER OF THE THISTLE was instituted by

JAMES V. in 1540. On the counter-seal of Queen MARY, 1542-1567, the shield of the Royal Arms of Scotland is surrounded by the collar of the Order; and behind each of the supporters is a badge of the crowned thistle. (LAING, *Scottish Seals*, i., 59.) The signet of Queen MARY (No. 66) similarly has the collar of the Order of the Thistle around the shield. It need hardly be said here that the legend attributing the date of the foundation of the Order of the Thistle to the year 809 is as mythical as the person, King ACHAIUS, who is said to have been its founder.

The reader may gauge the real ignorance which exists as to the reason for the assumption of the thistle as the badge of Scotland by consulting the articles on the subject stored in that most useful of all periodicals or magazines, *Notes and Queries*. In it the question has been raised, over and over again, but we never get one step further than the well-worn story that at the battle of Largs one of the Danish invaders trod with bare foot on the prickly flower, and that his cry of pain caused the failure of the attempted surprise!

After the thistle had become the national badge we naturally find it often introduced into new coats of arms, and augmentations granted to old ones. It was usually slipped and leaved, as in the coat of concession granted to the first Earl of LEVEN (Plate XXX., fig. 8), *Azure, a thistle ensigned with an Imperial Crown, all proper;* and its use is pretty frequent in the somewhat debased heraldry of the close of the last century and the beginning of the present. *Or, three thistles vert flowered gules*, is the coat of the Scottish family of ROMANES.

The thistle is found also as a charge in Foreign Heraldry, and, usually, as an allusive one. For example, *Gules (or Azure), three thistles or* (often with a chief of the Empire), is the coat of the CARDONAS of Spain. (Plates XI. and XLI.) *Or, three thistles vert flowered gules*, is borne by CARDON and DIBBITS in Flanders, CHARDON DU HAVET in France. *Argent, three thistles proper* is the coat of the French DONODEI and TRICARDS (*d'Argent, à trois chardons au naturel*). FOURNILLON uses: *Gules, on a bend or three thistles proper.*

DAISIES, OR MARGUERITES; ASTERS.—*Argent, three daisies gules stalked and leaved vert*, is attributed as *armes parlantes* to DAISIE, or DEISIE, of Scotland. The Marquises de MARGUERIE in France similarly use: *d'Azur, à trois marguerites, tigées et feuillées d'argent.* MARGUERIT in Franche Comté uses: *Vert, three marguerites or.* The Dutch MATELIEFS bear: *Azure, on a mound in base vert three daisies proper.* The Bavarian SPRÜNERS have used since 1571, *Per fess azure and or, in base three marguerites argent slipped vert.*

The Bavarian HORNUNGS had a grant in 1589 of *Gules, on a mount in base vert three asters azure, slipped proper.*

WREATHS, or CHAPLETS OF LEAVES or FLOWERS, or of both combined, are found both in British and Foreign Heraldry. *Argent, three chaplets gules* (Plate XXX., fig. 9) is borne by LASCELLES; and by HILTON, in early *Rolls of Arms.*

Argent, three chaplets of roses gules leaved vert, is the coat of the Irish HEARNES, and of HOEDE in Flanders. A well known coat of this class is that borne by FITZWILLIAM, and the Barons of GREYSTOCK: *Barry* (of six, eight, or more) *argent and azure, three chaplets of roses gules (leaved vert)*. *Gules, three chaplets argent*, are the canting arms of GARLAND. SCHIECK of Hesse, uses *Or, three chaplets of roses gules.* *Gules, a wreath of white roses leaved proper*, is the coat of the German GRANTZ, or KRANTZ (SIEBMACHER, *Wappenbuch*, ii., 75).

The Counts WREDE in Germany use: *Or, a laurel wreath set with five roses gules (on a canton azure a sword in pale proper).* *Azure, three laurel wreaths*, is borne in France by MILLY. *Or, a chaplet of oak leaves proper banded gules,* is the surtout of the arms of the Princes CAROLATH-BEUTHEN (of the Holy Roman Empire) by whom it was borne for the Barony of SCHÖNAICH. *Azure, three oak-wreaths or,* is the coat of CHAMPREDONDE. *Sable, three chaplets argent,* is the coat attributed to VAN ARTEVELDE of Flanders.

Or, a crown of thorns sable (quartering in the 2nd and 3rd *Azure, three bezants*) are the arms of BUROSSE of Gascony. *Argent, five crowns of thorns sable,* 2, 2, and 1, was borne by the Vicomtes de MEAUX. (*Salle des Croisés,* à Versailles, 1248.)

GILLYFLOWERS, PINKS, ETC.—*Argent, three gillyflowers slipped gules within a Royal tressure vert,* was the coat of the LIVINGSTONES, Viscounts KILSYTH. *Argent, three carnations gules, slipped vert,* is borne by NOYCE. The Earls of ROSEBERY now bear: *Quarterly,* 1 and 4. *Vert, three primroses within a double tressure flory counterflory or* (for PRIMROSE) (*v.* p. 180); 2 and 3. *Azure, a lion rampant double queued sable* (for CRESSY).

CORNFLOWERS, ETC.—*Argent, a chevron gules between three* "blue bottles" *slipped proper,* is borne by BOTHELL; with the *chevron azure* this is also the coat of BOTHELIER in France.

TULIPS.—As might be reasonably expected a considerable number of families, and especially in Holland, have this flower as a heraldic charge. VAN GENNEP uses, *Or, on a terrace vert a tulip gules, slipped proper and crowned of the first;* LOKE in Zealand has: *Argent, on a terrace vert a tulip or, slipped and leaved proper.* The coat of D'ARRIPE of Amsterdam is, *Or, a chevron azure between three tulips proper.* BLUMERT of Nürnberg, and ISNARD in Provence bear: *Azure, three tulips slipped and leaved or;* and THUMERY: *Or, a cross engrailed sable between four tulips gules slipped and leaved vert.*

THE PANSY AND VIOLET.—These flowers which are

almost, if not entirely, unknown in our own Armory, are not very scarce as Continental charges. *Gules, three violets slipped argent,* is the canting coat of VILLY in France. VAULTIER (*dit* BEAUREGARD) of Brabant uses: *Sable, a chevron argent between in chief two violets slipped and leaved, and in base an anchor, all or.* VAN GROENENDYK has: *Or, a chevron between three violets gules, slipped proper.* VERGNIES of Holland bears: *Azure, a chevron between three pansies or.* The Barons de LEUZE, in the Low Countries have for arms: *Argent, a chevron gules, between three pansies slipped and leaved proper.*

SUNFLOWER AND MARIGOLD.—The arms of the Dutch family of BLOM are: *Argent, on a terrace a sunflower proper;* and of VAN BLOMMESTEIN: *Sable, three marigolds slipped and leaved or.* The DADVISARDS, Marquises de TALAIRAN bore: *Azure, a sunflower on a terrace; and turning towards a sun in dexter chief, all or.* The Marquises d'ESPAGNET in Provence use: *Azure, three marigolds on one stalk leaved or; on a chief gules a sun in splendour.* The Counts de MAISTRE use: *Azure, three marigolds or* (XAVIER DE MAISTRE was of this family); another Dutch family of BLOM use the same.

Many other flowers are found as heraldic charges, especially when they can be employed as *armes parlantes; e.g.* the arms of the family of GIACINTO are: *Gules, a hyacinth proper.* The Dutch VLASBLOMS have: *Argent, on a terrace a flax plant with three flowers all proper.* The cotton plant is the charge of the arms of COTONER of Majorca; *Or, a cotton plant of five shoots vert, each flowered argent;* to this family RAFAEL and NICOLAS COTONER, Grand Masters of the Knights of ST. JOHN (1660-1680), belonged. The Counts JACQUEMINOT bear: *Or, an orange branch vert, flowered argent and fruited proper.*

I have only noted two or three examples of the use of the tobacco plant, which appears to me somewhat ungrateful on the part of *nouveaux riches* who have made a fortune by its sale. As an honourable exception I may quote the arms of CARDOZO : *Sable, five bezants in saltire, on a chief indented argent three tobacco plants vert.* Baron MÜLLER, the great Australian botanist, had a grant of the following appropriate coat : *Or, two branches of the eucalyptus accosted, the feet interlaced proper.*

This section may be fitly closed with the coat of RAMÉRA of Spain : *Or, a bouquet proper, tied with ribbons gules.*

FRUITS.—Various fruits appear in the Armory of our own and Foreign nations. *Argent, a pomegranate gules* (originally *vert*), *seeded and slipped proper*, are the well-known *armes parlantes* of the Kingdom of GRENADA (Plate XXX., fig. 10), and the escucheon of the Spanish Royal Arms is usually *enté en point* of this quartering. *Gules, a pomegranate or*, is used in England by families of GRANGE and GRANGER. *Or, a fess indented ermine between three pomegranates leaved proper*, is the coat of BARR. *Azure, three pomegranates or*, is borne in France by GRANDIN ; and, with a *fess argent*, by VILLERS. *Argent, three pomegranates proper*, is the coat of GRENIER, and GRANIER, another family of the same name (GRANIER DE CASSAGNAC) uses : *Gules, three pomegranates slipped and leaved or, seeded of the field.* The Sicilian family of GRANATA bears : *Azure, a pomegranate or, seeded gules.*

BUNCHES OF GRAPES are of frequent occurrence.

Argent, a bunch of grapes pendent stalked and leaved proper, was the coat of VINEY ; and the same *between two flaunches sable, on each a boar's head argent* (for EVANS), was borne by Viscountess BEACONSFIELD (1868-1872), wife of BENJAMIN DISRAELI, Prime Minister of the United Kingdom. *Gules, two vine shoots addorsed each bearing a bunch of grapes, leaved proper*, are the arms of the Princes LICHNOWSKI in Silesia. *Or, a fess gules between three bunches of grapes azure*, is used by the Dutch UYTREDERS.

ORANGES are occasionally found, mostly as canting charges, but not often in British Armory. The Breton family, ORENGES DE LIMÉROU uses: *Palé d'argent et de gueules, à la bordure de sable, chargée de huit oranges d'or.* (Another French family D'ORANGE DE LA FEILLÉE bears this coat slightly differenced : *Argent, three pallets gules, and the bordure with five oranges.*) *Azure, three oranges or, leaved vert,* is the coat of WICHERS of Holland. To LIVINGSTONE, Viscount TEVIOT, there was granted as an augmentation to be borne in the 1st and 4th quarters of his arms : *Azure, three oranges slipped proper within an orle of thistles or.* *Vert, three lemons or,* is the coat of LIMOS of Spain ; and with the field *azure* of LIMOJON of France. The *bezants* of MELUN are melons (?).

APPLES and PEARS.—These fruits appear in a considerable number of coats at home and abroad. *Argent, a fess between three apples gules* is borne by APPLETON (many families of this name bear the same coat with variations of the tinctures). *Argent, three apples slipped gules,* is the coat of APPLEGARTH. In France, POMEREU, Marquis de RICEYS, bears : *Azure, a chevron argent between three apples slipped and leaved, the stalks in chief, or.* The Venetian MEMMI used : *Per fess or and azure six apples counter-changed* (three and three). PERROTT bears : *Gules, three pears or, on a chief argent a demi-lion issuant sable.* *D'Azur, à trois poires d'or feuillées du même* is the coat of POIRIER in France. Two curious examples of the manner in which charges were converted into *armes parlantes* are the following :—CRESTIENNOT in Paris bears : *Argent, a chevron between three "*bon chrétien*" pears azure;* and WARDEN in Scotland : *Argent, a chevron gules between three warden pears leaved proper.*

ACORNS occur not unfrequently. *Argent, three acorns slipped vert,* is the coat of AIKENHEAD of that Ilk. *Azure, three acorns or,* was used by PORET, Marquis de BLOSSEVILLE; VAN EYCK ; and DU CHESNE ; and, with the addition of stalk and leaves, by Barons von GREINDL; VAN AELST; and with the field *argent* by Barons CLOEPS DE HEERNESSE in Belgium, etc. *Azure, a chevron between three acorns or*, is the coat of VERREYCKEN, and with *the cups vert* is borne by IFELD or IFIELD. *Sable, on a fess between six acorns or, three oak leaves proper*, is the coat of OKE, and OKEDEN.

PINE APPLES are often not distinguishable in Armory from FIR CONES which are a pretty common bearing. *Argent, three pine apples vert, stalked or* is a coat of APPLETON. *Argent, three pine cones vert*, is that of KEROULLÉ in Brittany. *Gules, three pine apples or*, was borne by the French Marquises de PINS, and by ARGENSOLA of Spain. *Or, three pine apples vert* is used by the Spanish PINOS. *Azure, three pine cones or* is the coat of the Counts and Princes von WALDBURG. The original coat of the CHÂTEAUBRIANDS has been referred to already on p. 330.

Instances appear in Armory of the use of many other fruits. Walnuts, cherries, strawberries, ananas, elderberries, melons, pepper-pods, etc. are all found as charges at home or abroad.

Ears of rye and of barley appear in very early English coats; one for the name of RYE, *Gules, on a bend argent three rye stalks sable;* the other for GRANDORGE, *Azure, three ears of barley or*. The Scottish family of RIDDELL uses, *Argent, a chevron gules between three ears of rye slipped and bladed proper* (Plate XXX., fig. 11).

GARBS, or WHEAT SHEAVES, belong to the earliest class of English bearings; they appear first on the seal of RANULF BLUNDEVILLE, Earl of CHESTER, who died in 1232. The garbs thus becoming the arms of the Earls of CHESTER were largely assumed as charges by families related to, or feudally dependent on them. In 1389, when the SCROPE and GROSVENOR controversy was decided, the GROSVENORS being found not legally entitled to the disputed coat (*Azure, a bend or*) assumed in its stead; *Azure, a garb or* (Plate XXX., fig. 12) as suggesting a descent from the Earls of CHESTER. This coat is still quartered by the GROSVENORS, Dukes of WESTMINSTER. It was also the coat of the family of the Counts de ST. PAUL, who fought in the First Crusade (*Salle des Croisés* à Versailles), and, with a bee volant in chief gold, of the Polish Counts KAMAROWSKI. Among the families referred to above as feudally connected with the Earls of CHESTER were the CHOLMONDELEYS of Vale Royal, who bear: *Gules, a garb, in chief two helmets or* (Plate XXXI., fig. 4) (Marquises CHOLMONDELEY; Barons DELAMERE). The Earldom of CHESTER is now one of the dignities of the Prince of WALES.

Azure, a garb, and in chief two mullets or, is the coat of WAUCHOPE of Niddry in Scotland.

The garb in Heraldry is often *banded* of another tincture, thus the COMINS, or COMYNS, of Yorkshire bore: *Argent, three garbs gules, banded or*. The arms of the ancient family of COMYN (Earls of BUCHAN, etc.), of such note and so ramified in Scotland in the thirteenth century, is *Azure, three garbs or;* the sheaves were originally of cummin, and borne allusively to the name, but they have long been understood and blazoned as *garbs*, or sheaves of wheat. Similarly the PEVERELLS bore: *Azure, three garbs argent*, which were originally sheaves of pepper (*vide infra*, Chapter on BADGES, p. 586). *Sable, three garbs argent*, was borne by M'MURROUGH, King of LEINSTER in Ireland, as well as by the old families of SEGRAVE, and DELAFIELD; these are also the arms of the County of BÜCHHEIM in Germany now quartered by the Counts von SCHÖNBORN.

The Vicomtes de BROSSE, *dit* DE BRETAGNE, chevaliers bannerets of Touraine, afterwards Comtes de PENTHIÈVRE, and Ducs d'ETAMPES bore, *Azure, three garbs or, banded gules* (quartering 2 and 3, BRETAGNE, *Ermine plain*).

Argent, a chevron between three garbs gules, is the coat of SHEFFIELD, Duke of BUCKINGHAM, in 1703; and *Azure, a chevron between three garbs or,* is that of the HATTONS of Cheshire (Earls of WINCHELSEA).

Gules, a chevron between three handfuls of wheat (glanes) *or,* are the *armes parlantes* of the French GLANNES, Barons de VILLERS-FARLAY.

The coat of the family of LE SERGEANT DE MARSIGNY in Artois is worthy of note because in it (*d'Azur, à trois gerbes mal-ordonnés d'or*) the charges are arranged one and two, instead of in the almost invariable fashion two and one.

VEGETABLES, the humbler but more important fruits of the earth, are only very occasionally met with in British Armory; but in Continental Heraldry their use is much more frequent. The humble cabbage and turnip and others are employed, usually indeed in the manner of which we have already seen such a multitude of instances, as allusive to the name of the bearer.

COOLE, or COELEN, in Brabant uses only *Argent, three cabbage leaves vert;* but another family DE COOLE, in Holland, bears: *Azure, three cabbages or,* a coat which is borne by the Russian family of KATCHENEVSKI with the addition of *a chief of the last thereon a harp gules.* The Dutch COOLMANS have as arms: *Gules, three cabbages argent. Argent, three cabbages vert,* is borne by KUMPSTHOFF of Rhenish Prussia.

THE TURNIP, AND BEETROOT, are more frequently used than the preceding. The Italian RAPACCIOLI and RAVANI, and RAEPSAET in Flanders use, *Azure, a turnip argent leafed vert.* RAPE or RASPÉ, of Tournay, the same on a field *gules.*

BEANS, AND BEAN CODS are found in British Armory. *Azure, three beans or,* is assigned to MERTON, while *Argent, three bean cods fessways in pale vert,* is borne by HARDBEANE. *Azure, a chevron between three bean pods paleways argent*, is used by LE FEVERE DE MANEGHEM of Flanders; and *Or, three bean pods azure*, by FAVIÈRES.

I have in my collection instances of the use of Maize, Lettuce, Fennel, Sage, Artichokes, Truffels, Celery, Carrots, Peas, Cucumbers, etc., but it would lengthen out this chapter unreasonably were I to give instances of all. One more, however, ought not to be passed over, the MUSHROOM, as being about the last bearing which we would fancy a *novus homo* would be likely to assume, yet I have seven or eight instances. The Count de LESSEPS bears, *Argent, on a terrace two vine shoots fruited, and at their base as many mushrooms vert; in the sinister chief a radiant sun proper.* LAUNAY DU VALAY bears: *Gules, six mushrooms argent;* and GUYOT D'ANFREVILLE: *Azure, a chevron argent between three mushrooms or.*

NOTE.—The *Klee-Stengeln* which appear on each of the wings of the eagles displayed of PRUSSIA, BRANDENBURG, etc., in the form of a golden trefoil with a long curved stalk reaching to the breast, appear to be only the development of some simple lines which are found in early examples of the 13th century to indicate the anatomical construction of the eagle's wings (*See* Plate XXXVIII., fig. 1, and HILDEBRAND'S *Heraldisches Musterbuch*, Plate xxviii., fig. 9).

FIG. 72.—ARMS OF CRÉQUY.

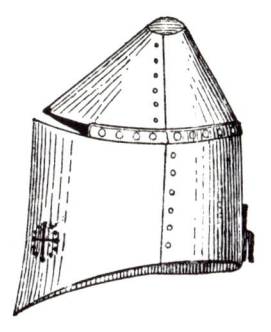

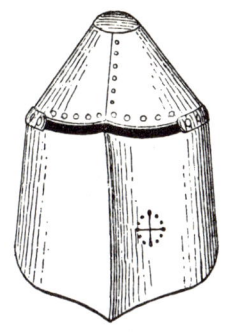

FIG. 73.   FIG. 74.
(HELMETS FROM WORSAAE, *Nordiske Oldsager*, fig. 570.)

CHAPTER XIII.

INANIMATE CHARGES.—III. MISCELLANEOUS.

MILITARY CHARGES.—Heraldry being military in its origin, and connected in its early development either with military expeditions, or with the jousts which were preparatory for them, it is natural that the implements of warfare, and other objects connected therewith, should find an important place among its emblems.

First of these naturally comes the knightly sword. As a heraldic charge this has a long straight blade with a cross handle; its hilt and its pommel are often of a separate tincture, usually *or*, or gold. *Or, a two-handled sword in pale azure*, is a coat of the Scottish SPALDINGS.

The family of KILPEC, of Kilpec in Herefordshire, bear: *Argent, a sword in bend sable* (Plate XXXI., fig. 1). The heiress of this family married PHILIP MARMION, Baron of SCRIVELSBY, temp. HENRY III., Hereditary-Grand Champion of England. From this family the Championship passed to the DYMOCKS, who bore: *Sable, a sword in pale argent, hilted or*, as their official coat, quartered with their personal arms: *Sable, two lions passant in pale argent crowned or.* It seems probable that the MARMYONS had similarly used the coat in combination with their personal arms: *Vair, a fess gules.*

The ERSKINES of Dun quartered in the 2nd and 3rd places: *Gules, a sword in pale argent, hilted and pommelled or*, with the well known ERSKINE coat: *Argent, a pale sable*, in the 1st and 4th. In British Armory, if the contrary be not expressed, the point of the sword is in chief. *Azure, a sword argent*, is the coat of the Genoese FERRI; and the same, but hilted *or* and with the point in base, of GOUDELIN, Vicomtes de PLÉHÉDEL in Brittany. The arms granted to JEANNE D'ARC have been already noticed at p. 331, *ante*. The arms borne by Maréchal LANNES, Duc de MONTEBELLO, were: *Vert, a sword in pale or*, and a chief with the insignia of a duke of the French Empire (*vide ante*, Plate X., fig. 3).

Gules, an antique sword in bend, point in base proper, is the coat of VILLENEUVE (*Salle des Croisés* at Versailles).

The Arms of the City of LONDON are: *Argent, a cross gules; in the first canton a sword* (often called a *dagger*) *of the second*. It is often said that this "dagger" commemorates the despatch of the rebel JACK CADE, by Sir WILLIAM WALWORTH, then Lord Mayor. Like too many heraldic legends this story is without foundation in fact. The sword is simply the well known emblem of ST. PAUL, patron saint of the city; and *Gules, two swords in saltire argent, hilted and pommelled or*, are still the arms of the See of LONDON. They are also borne by HITROF of Russia. *Azure, two swords in saltire argent hilted or*, are the ancient arms of BONAR of Kimmerghame in Scotland; and, with the points in chief, are borne by the family of SPADA of Lucca.

Per fess sable and argent, over all two swords in saltire gules, are the arms of the Arch-Marshalship of the Holy Roman Empire, held by the Electors, now Kings, of Saxony. (Hence came the two red swords so

PLATE XXXI.

1. Sword.
Kilpec.

2. Spear.
Shakespeare.

3. Battle Axe.
Congreve.

4. Helmet.
Cholmondeley.

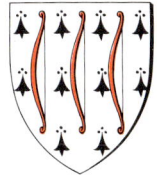

5. Bow.
Bowes.

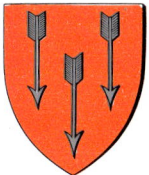

6. Arrow.
Hales.

7. Pheon.
Sydney.

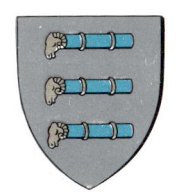

8. Battering Rams.
Bertie.

9. Caltrap.
Trapper.

10. Chains.
Navarre.

11. Chains.
Cadenat.

12. Water Budget.
De Ros.

familiar to all collectors of Dresden china.) *Azure, three swords in pile argent (hilts in chief)*, is the coat of MINIBERTI of Italy, and ODET of Brittany. *Sable, three swords in pile, points in base argent, hilts and pommels or*, is the coat of PAULET, or POWLETT, Marquess of WINCHESTER.

When swords are borne *barwise, i.e. fessways in pale*, the blazon must specify to which side of the escucheon the points are directed. CHUTE uses: *Gules, three swords barwise, points to the dexter, proper, hilted or*. *Gules, three swords barwise argent, hilted or, the centre one pointing to the sinister*, is a coat of O'SHEA ; another has the swords *two in saltire, points downwards, surmounted by a third in pale its point in chief*. The Roman SPADAS bear: *Gules, three swords bendways in pale argent, the hilts to the chief or; on a chief azure three fleurs-de-lis or*.

Of SPEARS and LANCES we find a good example in the canting coat granted to our great dramatic poet WILLIAM SHAKESPEARE ; *Or, on a bend sable a spear of the first, steeled* (or *pointed*), *argent* (Plate XXXI., fig. 2). *Azure, a lance or*, is the coat of the Italian SOLDATI ; the same, *enfiled at its point by an annulet argent*, is borne by DANBY of France.

Argent, a broken spear bendways between two pierced mullets (or *spur-rowels*) *of six points all azure*, is the coat of AUCHMUTY of that Ilk. *Gules, three tilting spears, erect in fess the points argent*, is borne by AMHERST, Earls AMHERST.

Gules, three tilting spears or, armed argent, two in saltire the third reversed in pale; are the arms of the *herba*, or clan, of JELITA in Poland, as such they are borne by the Counts BIELSKI ; and ZAMOISKY, etc.

CRONELS, which are the blunted ends of lances used in jousts and tournaments, are found in the coat of

WISEMAN, *Sable, a chevron ermine between three cronels argent.*

JOGHEMS of Holland bears : *Gules, three cronels argent,* (*vide infra,* p. 388, under CHESS-ROOK.)

Or, a pike head in bend sable, is the coat of the Counts von REICHENSTEIN ; with the field *argent* it is found in the *Wappenrolle von Zürich,* No. 490, for MAZINGEN ; *Gules, a lance head bendways argent,* is the coat of the Counts LAINCEL in France. *Sable, three spear heads argent gutty de sang,* is the coat of APREECE, or PRICE, and is also borne with the addition of *a chevron argent* by other Welsh families of PRICE, WILLIAMS, REES, WATKINS, JONES ; the Squire of the Black Prince, Sir DAVID GAM, bore the same.

Sable, a battle axe or, headed argent, is the coat of OLDMIXON. *Gules, a Lochaber axe between three boar's heads erased argent,* is borne by RANKEN of Scotland.

Azure, an axe argent in bend sinister, is the coat of the Barons BIEL of Mecklenburg. *Gules, a broad axe argent, the handle or* (the blade turned to the sinister), are the arms of the Polish *herba* of TOPOR, and as such are borne by the Counts OSSOLIN-OSSOLINSKI ; TARLO ; MORSKI ; and ZABIELLO. The Polish Counts OKSZA-GRABOWSKI, and the family of OKULICZ in Russia, bear the like ; but the blade is turned to the dexter, and the handle is *sable.*

Argent, two halberts in saltire azure, was used by ECCLES of Kildonan. *Gules, two halberts addorsed or,* is borne by the Marquises ACHEY DE THORAISE in France. *Argent, three doloires, or broad axes, gules, those in chief addorsed,* is the coat of RENTY in Artois ; quartered from early times with *Argent, three bars gules,* by the great house of CROY, Princes de CHIMAY (MAURICE, *Toison d'Or,* planches xv., xxii., etc., and *v. infra,* p. 549).

CONGREVE of Congreve bore: *Sable, a chevron between three battle-axes argent* (Plate XXXI., fig. 3).

HELMETS, as external appendages to Armorial Coats, will be dealt with elsewhere (Chapter XIX). Plate XXXI., fig. 4, are the arms of CHOLMONDELEY already blazoned on page 342. *Gules, a close helmet argent*, is ascribed to ROBERTOUN in PONT'S MS., and in MACKENZIE'S *Science of Heraldry*, p. 66. *Argent, three morions sable banded gules*, are the arms of the Barons KETELHODT. *Azure, three helmets argent*, is the coat of the ANTELMI of Venice, and GUIBERT of France. *Sable, three tilting helms argent*, is an old coat of DAUBENY.

Of BOWS we have an example in Plate XXXI., fig. 5. *Ermine, three bows bent and stringed paleways in fess sable*, the *armes parlantes* of BOWES, Lords BOWES of Clonlyon in Ireland. With the bows *gules* this coat is quartered by the Earls of STRATHMORE, for BOWES of Streatham in Northumberland. These are long-bows, but the crossbow is also used in British Heraldry, and is that which most generally appears in the Armory of Continental nations; as an exception we find, *Or, three long bows fessways in pale azure, stringed sable*, the coat of the Bavarian Counts d'ARCO. (TYROFF, *Wappenbuch des Adels des Königreichs Baiern*, Erster Band, Plate xiv., Nürnberg, 1818.)

Gules, a crossbow or, is used by BALISTE of France, and by ZMODSKI of Poland. *Ermine, a crossbow bent in pale gules*, is the coat of ALBASTER in England, a curious corruption of the original ARBALESTIER. The ARBALESTES, Vicomtes de MELUN, bore: *d'Or, au sautoir engrêlé de sable cantonné de quatre arbalètes tendues de gueules*.

ARROWS, if not otherwise blazoned, are borne paleways with the points downwards, and are said to be *barbed* of the tincture of the points, and *feathered*, or *flighted*, of that of the feathers. In Plate XXXI., fig. 6 is the coat of HALES of Norfolk: *Gules, three arrows or, feathered and barbed argent*. *Vert, an arrow argent, the point upward*, is said to be the ancient coat of M'ADAM ; but the coat registered is, *Vert, three arrows argent.*

Argent, an arrow in bend-sinister or, winged sable, is the curious coat of ALF, in Denmark. Several baronial families DE HEUSCH in Limburg use : *Or, an arrow in bend gules the point in chief.* *Azure, two arrows in saltire or*, is the coat of PILLERA, and BULING, both of the Netherlands. *Azure, three arrows argent*, is the canting coat of ARREAU, in France ; the same, but with the charges *or*, is that of the English ARCHERS. *Gules, three arrows or, feathered and headed argent*, is the coat of HALES.

ARROWS IN BUNDLES (usually of three only) are called sheaves, and are said to be *banded.*

BIRD-BOLTS, or QUARRELS, are names given to the shorter arrows used with the crossbow : *Azure, three bird-bolts or*, are the *armes parlantes* of BOLTON (the bird-bolts have blunted heads). *Argent, three bird-bolts gules*, appears in CHARLES'S *Roll* for RALPH DE BOZON.

A BROAD ARROW and a PHEON are represented similarly, except that the Pheon has its inner edges jagged, or engrailed. In English Heraldry the Pheon is represented with the point downwards, as in Plate XXXI., fig. 7, the arms of SYDNEY, Earl of LEICESTER : *Or, a pheon azure.* In French Armory the pheon is drawn with the point uppermost. The Breton Counts WALSH, originally from Ireland, use : *Argent, a chevron gules between three pheons sable.*

SCYTHES.—The scythe-blades, which appear in the coats of several great Polish houses, would scarcely seem to be of military origin, and fitly to claim a place in this section. This is however the case. The scythe-blade fixed vertically at the end of a long pole, was the *arme blanche* of the Polish peasantry ; and those who have read the history of their attempts to regain national independence will hardly need to be reminded how very efficient a weapon this proved itself to be at close quarters, and especially against cavalry, in many a sanguinary conflict. The Counts ALEXANDROWICZ, bear: *Gules, two scythe-blades in saltire between two broken swords in pale, the hilt of the one in chief, that of the other in base proper.* The families which compose the house, or *herba* of ROLA, bear: *Gules, three scythe-blades in pairle, issuing from a rose in the centre point, all argent.* This coat is borne by the Counts ROLA-WOLSKI. Another great Polish house, that of PRUSS II., has the coat: *Gules, two scythe-blades in oval, the points crossing each other argent, and the ends in base tied together or, the whole surmounted in chief by a cross patriarchal-patée, of which the lower arm on the sinister side is wanting.* These are the arms of the Counts JEZIERSKI.

SHIELDS differing in shape from the Sub-Ordinary already referred to as the *Escucheon* (Chapter V., p. 169), are sometimes found in Continental Heraldry.

The Polish clan of JANINA bore: *Or* (often *gules*), *an oval buckler of bronze* (or *purpure*), the coat used by SOBIESKI.

Gules, a round (or oval) target, with pointed centre argent in bend-sinister, is the *surtout* of the Barons ROTHSCHILD, now Lords ROTHSCHILD in the Peerage of the United Kingdom.

Gules, a round target between three antique crowns or, is the coat of GRANT, of Ballindalloch.

TENTS. — *Sable, three tents argent,* is borne by SABCOTT of Northamptonshire; and TENTENIER of Holland uses: *Azure, on a terrace vert, a tent argent, surmounted by a weather cock or.* *Sable, a chevron between three tents argent,* is borne by TENTON, and *Azure, three tents or,* by the French family DE LA CHASTRE.

MILITARY BANNERS occur chiefly in comparatively recent heraldry in Great Britain, as in the present coat of BANNERMAN: *Gules, a banner displayed argent, thereon a canton azure charged with a saltire of the second*, which seems to have superseded in the 17th century the insignia formerly borne by that family (STODART, *Scottish Arms*, ii., 396). The coat of the English GARBETTS is said to date from 1486; it is: *Gules, on a knightly banner flowing to the dexter argent, an Imperial eagle sable.* The Counts and Dukes of WÜRTTEMBERG, since 1336, quartered with their arms the official insignia of Great Standard Bearer of the Empire: *Azure, the Imperial banner* (charged with a single-headed eagle displayed) *in bend proper.* The Portuguese family of BANDEIRA use: *Gules, on a banner argent, its lance and fringe or, a lion rampant sable.* *Gules, a banner gathered round the splintered staff in bend or,* is borne by the Austrian Counts CETTNER, and by PRZEROWA of Poland. KINGDOM in England bears: *Azure, three banners bendways in pale, to the sinister, or.* *Azure, three pennons argent in pale and saltire,* are the arms of STANDAERTS in Belgium. (For GONFANONS, *v.* p. 372.)

BATTERING RAMS appear in the coat of the family of BERTIE, of which were the Earls of ABINGDON, the Dukes of ANCASTER and KESTEVEN, and the Earls of LINDSEY in England; they are: *Argent, three battering rams fessways in pale proper, armed and garnished or* (otherwise and more correctly *azure*). (Plate XXXI., fig. 8.)

BEACONS, used to convey intelligence of the approach of an enemy, or to muster troops, appear in two or three British coats. *Sable, three beacons inflamed proper, with ladders or,* are the arms of DAUNT; and the like coat, but with the field *azure*, is that of GERVIS.

The CALTRAP, or CHEVAL TRAP (*chausse-trape*), was a military instrument of iron, with four sharp points so arranged that however it lay one point was uppermost. It was placed to defend a post against the approach of cavalry. The family of TRAPPE (whose arms are recorded in the *Visitation of London* in 1563) bore: *Argent, three caltraps sable* (Plate XXXI., fig. 9). *Or, three caltraps gules,* is a coat granted to HORSEMAN in 1590. The French family of GUETTEVILLE DE GUÉNONVILLE bore: *d'Argent, semé de chausse-trapes de sable.*

CHAINS as a Heraldic Charge are directly associated with military affairs. They are mostly found in the armory of the southern countries of Europe, especially in the Peninsula. The most illustrious example of their use occurs in the arms of the Kingdom of NAVARRE (Plate XXXI., fig. 10), *Gules, a cross, saltire, and double orle of chains, linked together or,* the coat which according to tradition was assumed by SANCHO "*the Strong*" in memory of a successful attack in 1212 on the camp of the Moorish army under MIRAMOMELIN, which was defended by a strong barricade of chains through which SANCHO and his followers cut their way. MENÊTRIER points out that this coat is an allusive one to the name of NAVARRE; *una varra,* or *'na varra,* in the Basque *patois* being the name of a chain. Notwithstanding this I have elsewhere ("The Heraldry of Spain and Portugal," p. 2) given my reasons for the opinion that this story is not lightly to be relegated to the ordinary limbo of heraldic myths. In any case, the chain was assumed into the coat of many of the noble families who were said to have been present with SANCHO on this occasion. (*See* ARGOTE DE MOLINA, *Nobleza del Andaluzia,* i., cap. 46.)

The MENDOZAS bore: *Gules, a bend vert bordered or, over all an orle and saltire of chains of the last.* ZUÑIGA adopted *a chain in orle or* over the plain coat, *Argent, a bend sable;* and MENESEZ assumed, *Or, a chain in bend azure.* Among the other families using chains as charges are PERALTA, SOTO, URBINA, TELLEZ, etc. Many others bore it as a charge on a bordure, *e.g.,* BERMUDEZ, MUÑOZ, FERNANDEZ, IRIARTE, YRUSTA,

VARELA, etc. (*See* PIFERRER, *Nobiliario* . . . . *de España*.)

On the counter-seals of Kings LOUIS V., PHILIP V., and CHARLES IV., of France, the shield of FRANCE-ANCIENT is placed within an 8 foil upon a device of the chains of NAVARRE, in memory of their mother, JEANNE, wife of PHILIP IV. (*le Bel*) and daughter and heiress of HENRY I., King of NAVARRE. (*See* VRÉE, *Généalogie des Comtes de Flandre*, Plates xli., xlii.) In later times, as by LOUIS XIV., the arms of NAVARRE were not quartered with those of FRANCE, but were borne on a separate escucheon, the two shields being *accolés*, under one helmet and crown. (The dalmatic worn by the sinister supporter, and the banner borne by it, are alike charged with the arms of NAVARRE. *See* a good contemporary example in DE LA POINTE, *Chevaliers de l'Ordre du St. Esprit*, planche i., Paris, 1689.)

The chains of NAVARRE came in time to be confounded, by some ill-informed heraldic writers, with a carbuncle or escarbuncle, and we accordingly find them sometimes so blazoned. (I have in an earlier chapter pointed out that this heraldic charge originated in the metal boss and bars with which an ancient shield was strengthened, and was no portion of its heraldic bearings, though in some cases it afterwards became an integral part of them, as in the case of the arms of the Dukes of CLEVES, *Gules, an escucheon argent, over all an escarbuncle or*. Possibly the name of the bearing may have originated in a precious stone set as an ornament in the central boss of the shield.) FERRET of France uses: *Azure, a chain bendways or*. Chains are borne in the English coat of ANDERTON ; *Sable, three chains argent*. The coat of the French CADENETS : *Azure, three chains bendways or*, is given in Plate XXXI., fig. 11. *Argent, two chains in saltire gules* (or *azure*), is borne by ZANCHINI of Tuscany; and *Azure, two chains in saltire, attached to an amulet in the centre-point argent,* is the well known coat of the ALBERTI. *Sable, a chain, of two links and as many half links, in pale argent,* were the arms of the Barons von NEUHOFF (or NEUENHOF), to which belonged the unfortunate adventurer, THEODORE, King of CORSICA.

THE WATER BUDGET (*bouse*), is a conventional representation of the leather bags in which water was carried ; and probably dates from crusading times when such vessels were employed in the marches across the deserts. It was depicted with considerable variety of form in the early *Rolls of Arms.* It is very seldom met with except in English Heraldry, where its primary use appears to have been as a canting coat. The TRUSBUTS, Barons of WARTRE in Holderness, bore, *d'Argent, à trois boutz d'eau de gulez,* and thereby symbolised both their family name, and their baronial estate. ROSA, heiress of the TRUSBUTS, married EVERARD DE ROS ; and, as was usual in the case of great heiresses, her arms were assumed by her descendants, and were borne with variations of tincture by several families of DE ROS, or DE ROOS, of these an example is given on Plate XXXI., fig. 12. The water budget is found as a charge in a few Scottish coats mostly of modern date, in which as in several modern English coats, borne by families of the name of ROSE, it was probably assumed without any other connection as associated with the name of DE ROS.

The Lords ROSS bore : *Or, a chevron chequy sable and argent between three water bougets of the second.* The ROSES of Kilravock bear, *Or, a boar's head couped gules between three water bougets sable.*

Of the equipment of a knight the shoes of his horse formed a very important part and we may therefore include them in this section. A horseshoe being the badge of the MARSHALLS (*See* PLANCHÉ, *Pursuivant,* p. 114) horseshoes were assumed as *armes parlantes* by their descendants the FERRERS who appear to have borne, *Sable, six horseshoes argent*. (Sometimes the colours are reversed.) Later they bore (as Earls of DERBY) *Vairé or and gules, on a bordure azure six horseshoes argent*. *Or, three horseshoes sable*, is the coat of STAEL and VAN DER HOVEN in Holland; it is also that of FERRIER in Scotland, and forms the foundation of several modern grants in that country.

The early coat of HENRI DE FERRIÈRES appears on his seal in 1205 (DEMAY, p. 205). It bears an escucheon with a bordure charged with six horseshoes. I have engraved it page 453, fig. 90. *Azure, a horseshoe argent*, is the coat of the Counts, and Princes, von TRAUTSON. *D'Argent, à trois fers de cheval de gueules cloués d'or*, is the coat of LA FERRIÈRE. FERRAGUT in Spain bears, *Gules, a horseshoe and in base a passion nail paleways or*.

It is perhaps in the Armory of the great houses of Poland that the horseshoe occupies the most prominent place. The family of the Counts DOLENGA bear: *Azure, a horseshoe argent ensigned at the top with a small cross patée or; and between the branches of the shoe, an arrow in pale of the second flighted of the third, point in base*. (Plate LVI., fig. 12.) The Counts GUTAKOWSKI bear: *Azure, between three estoiles, a horseshoe argent, surmounted by a plume of three ostrich feathers proper*. The Counts de RYTWIANY-ZBOROWSKI, of the great family of JASTRE-ZEMBIEÇ, bore: *Azure, a horseshoe reversed* (that is with the points in chief) *between its branches a small cross pattée en abîme*. (It must be noticed that French Armory differs from our own with regard to the position of the horseshoe; in *our* blazon the horseshoe is borne with the semicircular curve towards the chief, but in French blazon this is *un fer de cheval versé*.)

The family of POBOG, bears: *Azure, a horseshoe argent, ensigned in chief with a small cross patée or;* to this house belong the Counts ZAPOL-ZAPOLSKI. The family of KRZYWDA bear the same coat, except that the cross patée on the horseshoe lacks its sinister arm, and that another gold cross patée is placed *en abîme*.

BREYS, or BARNACLES, a twitch to curb horses, occur in the arms of DE GENEVILLE, or JOINVILLE, Seigneurs de BROYES; and this coat appears in several early English *Rolls of Arms*.

Azure, three breys or, on a chief argent a lion issuant gules. These are said to be the chief arms of the family (to which DE JOINVILLE the chronicler of the Crusades belonged). But in GLOVER'S *Roll*, No. 103, and *Second Nobility Roll* of EDWARD III., No. 77, this coat with a chief ermine is attributed to GEOFFREY DE GENEVILL. The Lords GENEVILE in Ireland appear to have borne the same, and in the *Armorial de Geldre* the chief is distinctly ermine. So also in PLANCHÉ'S *Roll*, and in the *Rolls* of the Thirteenth Century, and CHARLES'S *Roll*. SIMON DE GENEVILLE (No. 102 in GLOVER'S *Roll*) bears the coat first given, but differenced with the field sable. *Gules, a barnacle argent*, is borne by WYATT (Plate XXXII., fig. 1). *Argent, a barnacle sable*, is the coat of BARNAKE, and of POYLE; the first named also bore, *Argent, three horse barnacles sable*. *Per fess gules and azure* (one or) *three barnacles argent*, was another coat of WYATT, or WYOT.

STIRRUPS are generally borne attached to a leather thong and buckle, as in the coat of SCUDAMORE, Plate XXXII., fig. 2. *Gules, three stirrups leathered and buckled or*, borne by the Viscounts SCUDAMORE in Ireland. The GIFFORDS used the same but on an *azure* field. *Gules, three stirrups leathered argent*, are the arms of the Barons d'HEMPTINES in Belgium.

Gules, a stirrup (without a leather) *argent*, is the coat of the *herba* of STRZEMIE in Poland, borne by the JANISZEWSKI, etc., and (*within a bordure or*) by the Counts BRZOSTOWSKI.

CASTLES.—This may be as convenient a place as any

in which to speak of Castles and other buildings, many of which were of course military in their nature; and are frequent Heraldic charges. The Castle is generally represented by an isolated wall, above which appear towers usually, though not invariably, three in number, and this fact requires specification in the blazon.

The best known example is afforded by the *armes parlantes* of the kingdom of CASTILE, now and for many generations back occupying the first and fourth quarters in the shield of the Spanish Monarchy. They are represented on Plate XXXII., fig. 3, and are, *Gules, a castle triple-towered or.* Later refinement has specified that the gate, or port, is *azure*. By modern rules we find that the colour of the masoning, or marks of mortar between the stones, should also be indicated; this is almost invariably *sable*, and as its mention is by no means general, I do not advise the student to cumber his blazon therewith; though I give the example of *Gules, a castle triple-towered argent masoned sable*, which is the blazon of a quartering of LINDSAY for the feudal title of LINDORES. Occasionally the field is thus masoned as in the coat of PEREZ, of Portugal, *Argent, masoned sable a fess gules.* (*Vide* p. 362.)

Gules, a castle argent, is one of the quarterings of M'LEOD. This was the coat of the Marquises of CASTILLON, and was also the bearing of the CASTILLES, Marquises de CHENOISE; and of DE CASTELLANE. It was also that of SALVIAC (First Crusade). *Gules, a castle with two towers argent, the port and windows sable*, are the coat of the Lordship of HOMBURG, quartered by the Counts of SAYN.

The Yorkshire family of RAWSON bears: *Gules, rising out of water in base azure a square castle in perspective, having at each angle a tower and cupola argent.* · If the cupolas of towers are surmounted by a vane they are said to be *girouettés* of such a tincture.

PLATE XXXII.

1. Barnacle.
   Wyatt.

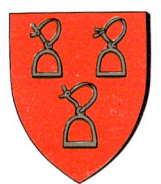

2. Stirrup.
   Scudamore.

3. Castle.
   Castille.

4. Tower.
   Towers.

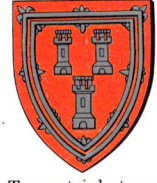

5. Tower triple towered.
   Aberdeen.

6. Castle.
   Châtelain.

7. Column.
   Colonna.

8. Columns.
   Arigonio.

9. Ladder.
   Scala.

10. Stair.
    Gradenigo.

11. Lymphad with Fire.
    Lorn.

12. Lymphad under Sail.
    Earl of Caithness.

The French nobles used these vanes, generally banner-shaped and gilded and painted, or pierced, to represent their family arms, as a sign of their *noblesse* ; DU VIEUX-CHÂTEL DE KERLEORET in Brittany, bears : *d'Azur, à un château d'argent girouetté d'or.* The CHÂTELAINS of France use : *Azure, a chateau of three towers girouettés azure,* as in Plate XXXII., fig. 6.

In many old representations the Heraldic Castle stretches across the whole field from one edge of the shield to the other, as still in the arms of the great Polish *herba* of GRZYMALA. (*See* NIESIECKI, *Korona Polska,* Warsaw, 1728-1743.) *Or, a castle triple-towered gules, the port open, the portcullis sable* (now borne, but not originally, *on a terrace vert*). These arms with slight variations are borne by the Counts GRZYMALA (DE GRUDNA-GRUDZINSKI); the Counts JABLONOWSKI; and the Count POTULITZ-POTULICKI. (Some add a knight in armour at the gate.) The Castle is thus borne in several City arms (*e.g.* those of Prague and Cracow) and in the bearings adopted for several of the Tuscan *Compartimenti* (See *Le Armi dei Municipj Toscani,* Firenze, 1864).

TOWERS are frequent in Armory ; and, like castles, are often placed upon a mount in base, or rise out of water, treated either naturally, or conventionally, *i.e. Barry argent and azure.* Or, *a castle gules, in base the sea argent,* is the coat of BROUCHIER of Provence ; and the same, but with *the base wavy azure and argent,* is borne by FERNANDES DE CASTILLO of Spain. The Tower is, however, often represented as an isolated charge, as in Plate XXXII., fig. 4, the coat of TOWERS : *Azure, a tower or.* If the tower be surmounted with turrets, as is often the case, the fact is mentioned. *Or, a tower triple-towered azure,* is a coat of BLUNT, or BLOUNT. In modern blazon the castle and tower are not so distinctly defined as in earlier instances. I subjoin examples of both bearings. *Azure, fleury or, over all a castle argent*, was borne by LA TOUR D'AUVERGNE (Vicomtes de TURENNE, Comtes d'AUVERGNE, Ducs de BOUILLON, Princes de SEDAN).

Gules, on a mount or, a tower argent, roofed azure, is the coat of the Bavarian Barons HARSDORF.

Vert, a tower argent, is the coat of LESVAL in Flanders; and *with a chain of the last bendways over all* of the Spanish CATENAS (*vide ante*, p. 353). The French Marquises D'APCHIER, bore: *Or, a castle triple-towered gules, from each of the exterior towers a battle-axe issuant azure, the edge of each turned to the flanks of the shield.* This may have been the model for the Irish coat of HICKS: *Argent, a tower sable, issuant from the top four axes two turned to the dexter, as many to the sinister azure.*

Argent, a tower gules, in front of two sceptres in saltire azure, is the coat of the Princes von THURN.

Azure, a tower or, is borne by CANO, Barons de MEGHEM; and by the Spanish CASTELLETS; also (with a naked woman issuing therefrom and holding a flower azure) by the Bavarian Barons von FÜRSTENWÄRTER. *Azure, on a rock a castle triple-towered argent*, is the coat of Prince POZZO DI BORGO. The arms of the city of EDINBURGH are: *Argent, on a rock proper, a castle triple-towered sable, masoned of the first, topped with vanes gules; the windows and portcullis closed of the last.* In the blazon of these arms in the last edition of BURKE'S *General Armory* (which had, if I mistake not, the supervision of the late Mr STODART, *Lyon Clerk-Depute*, so far as Scottish coats is concerned) the blazon is as above, except that the towers are said to be "*topped with three* fans *gules*"! I have ventured to turn these into *vanes;* but I have a strong suspicion that the "fans" of the official blazon are really only the red pointed roofs of the three towers, which as drawn would have somewhat the shape of an inverted fan. The arms of the city of ABERDEEN as confirmed by Sir CHARLES ERSKINE, LYON, in 1674 are: *Gules, three towers triple-towered, within a double tressure flory-counter-flory argent* (Plate XXXII., fig. 5).

In some Irish and Spanish coats the castle is borne supported by two lions or other animals rampant. The arms borne by the O'KELLYS are: *Gules, on a mount vert a tower supported by two lions rampant argent.* A family of GONZALÈS bear: *Azure, on a mound in base, a castle argent, supported by two lions or, a bordure engrailed of the last.* The Portuguese CAMARA use: *Sable, on a terrace in base vert, a tower supported by two greyhounds argent;* a variation is: *Sable, out of the sea in base a tower argent supported by two seals proper.*

In the *Wappenrolle von Zürich* there is given the curious coat of WILL: *Or, on a rocky base bendways gules a castle azure.* (No. 326.)

It need hardly be mentioned that castles entered largely into the so-called arms of cities. These arms were usually derived from the Common Seal of the Burgh, on which a castle was naturally the prominent figure.

The arms of HAMBURG are: *Argent, on a terrace vert a castle triple-towered gules, the port open.* Those of the city and Marquisate of ANTWERP are: *Gules, three towers in triangle connected by walls argent: in chief two human right hands couped, in bend and bend sinister.* To this was often added a chief of the Empire.

The arms of the City of DUBLIN are: *Azure, three towers argent inflamed proper.* *Gules, three towers triple-towered argent,* is the coat of COUDENBERG, one of the seven patrician families of Brussels. *Or, three castles azure,* is used by TORELLES of Spain. *Or, five castles in saltire sable, within a bordure gules thereon nine saltires or,* is borne by the PEÑERANDAS of Spain. *Azure, three towers argent,* is the coat of the Marquise de POMPADOUR.

The Vicomtes von DAM in Flanders use: *Per fess gules and sable three towers argent mal ordonnés* (*i.e.* one in chief and two in base).

THE CASTLE or TOWER sometimes occurs in conjunction with other buildings, or with a projecting wall. In the *Armorial de Geldre*, the arms of TURPIN DE VINAY are represented with "*un pan de mur*" stretching towards the sinister flank of the shield. In the later Supplement which follows M. VALLET'S edition of the *Armorial de Berry*, the coat of VIGNAY or LA TOUR DE VINAY is blazoned: *de Gueules, à une tour d'argent, et un avant-mur crénelé du même* (No. 1950, p. 198). *Azure, a bridge argent supporting a castle or*, is borne by PONTAUT; this resembles the eighteenth century English coat of TROWBRIDGE, Bart. *Or, over water in base a bridge of three arches embattled thereon a tower proper, its flag flying azure charged with a cross potent of the field ; on a canton of the third two keys in saltire gold.*

Of bridges without castles there are a good many instances. The Scottish family of BRIDGE naturally bears: *Gules, a bridge of one arch argent, streams transfluent proper*. *Azure, a bridge argent*, is a coat of PIERREPONT, and (with square arches) PONTBRIANT. *Gules, a bridge of two arches or*, is borne by the Marquises of PONTEVÈS in France. *Or, a bridge of three arches sable*, is used by the Prussian BRÜCKNERS. The Venetian Counts da PONTE carried *Azure, a bridge of one arch with steps* (? the Rialto) *or*. In the coat of REYNELL of Devon the whole field is *Argent, masoned sable, with a chief of the second* (*vide ante*, p. 358).

WALLS are occasionally found alone without towers thus, *Argent, a wall gules*, is the coat of the Danish Counts REVENTLOW. *Azure, in base a wall embattled or*, is the coat of the Markgravate of OBER-LAUSITZ, quartered in the arms of the Saxon Duchies. *Or, a broken wall in fess proper, on a chief sable three escallops of the first, and in base a rose gules*, was borne by GRAHAM of Inchbrakie. Of other buildings there is a great variety borne usually with some canting reference. *Azure, a house argent*, is the coat of CASANOVA; *Gules, a portal or*, appears for LA PORTE; *Or, a palace azure* for DESPALAU of Spain; PALAU has *Or, a palace vert, a bordure compony of the colours. Gules, a church argent*, for KIRCHNER; *Azure, a chapel or*, for LA CHAPELLE. *Gules, three single arches or*, is a coat of ARCHER. *Sable, three dove cotes argent*, appears for SAPCOTE in the *Visitation of Huntingdon* by CAMDEN in 1613. We have one or two instances in which a whole town is represented. The arms of the Spanish Kingdom of VALENCIA are: *Gules, a city argent*. One of the quarterings granted to CORTEZ was: *Azure, rising from a champagne barry wavy azure and argent*, a representation of the city of MEXICO proper. The escucheon of PIZARRO contains two such coats; one *Sable, a town rising out of waves argent;* the other *Sable, a town on an island, the spire of the church crowned with an Imperial crown proper.*

In contrast with these almost the slightest shelter possible, a mere roof supported on four posts, called in Polish by the name of *Brog*, appears in the arms of the illustrious Polish family of LESZCZYC; *Gules, a square roof or, on four posts argent*, borne by the Counts LESZCZYC DE RADOLIN-RADOLINSKI, and by the Counts SUMIN-SUMINSKI.

COLUMNS and PILLARS, are not of frequent occurrence as heraldic charges, but there are a few instances in British armory and more abroad.

In Plate XXXII., fig. 7, are the arms of the great Roman family of COLONNA, Princes of PALESTRINA, Dukes of PALIANO, etc.; *Gules, a column argent, its base and capital or, surmounted by a crown of the last.* This coat is also used by the COLONNA, Counts WALEWSKI of Poland. *Or, a pillar sable enwrapped with an adder argent*, is an English coat for MYNTER. *Gules, a column crowned or, round it a serpent twined azure engoulé of the first,* is the coat of BISCIA of Rome. The same, but the snake replaced by a vine shoot, is borne by BAISNE of Provence. *Azure, three pillars or,* is used by the GASTINELS of Normandy, and *Sable, three pillars, the centre one crowned or,* by EZEL of Silesia. *Or, a column gules between three Cornish choughs proper,* is used by KYNDER. A Scottish coat, that of EDWARD, is, *Azure, a fess argent, surmounted of a pillar gules issuing from the base wavy azure.* The Cornish TREMENHEERES bear: *Sable, three columns paleways in fess argent.* The MAJORS of Suffolk use, *Azure, three Corinthian columns each surmounted by a ball, two and one, argent.*

A curious Italian coat that of ARIGONIO of Rome; *Argent, three columns paleways in fess supporting a lion passant gules, on a chief azure, an eagle displayed or,* Plate XXXII., fig. 8.

LADDERS in British Armory are invariably scaling ladders having hooks at the top of the perpendiculars. *Argent, three scaling ladders bendways gules,* is a coat of KILLINGWORTH; *Or, three scaling ladders bendways throughout gules* (that is they touch the edges of the shield) is borne by CHEPSTOW, otherwise SCHIPSTOW. The ordinary ladder without hooks appears as a canting charge in the coat of the Princes della SCALA, of Verona. Anciently they bore: *Gules, a ladder of four steps in pale argent.* The more modern coat is that given in Plate XXXII., fig. 9; *Gules, a ladder of five steps in pale, supported by two greyhounds rampant argent, langued, collared and crowned or.*

The SCALIGERS, who pretended descent from the SCALA Princes, used: *Or, an eagle displayed sable, holding in its claws a ladder of three steps gules.* The Florentine SCALI bore: *Azure, a ladder in pale or,* and another SCALA family used the reverse.

In the *Zürich Wappenrolle* there is an early instance of the use of a ladder as a charge; No. 430, the coat of WERIANT, is, *Argent, a mount in base of three coupeaux vert supporting a ladder of four steps in pale gules.* Or, *a scaling ladder in bend sable,* is used by the Barons von LÜTZOW; *Argent, a scaling ladder gules barred or,* is the coat of the Counts BREDOW. *Gules, a ladder in bend or,* was borne by MAYA (GOUSSENCOURT, *Le Martyrologe des Chevaliers de S. Jean,* ii., 12).

The Barons von DONOP bear, *a scaling ladder gules* consisting of a single pole hooked at the top, and with traverses as steps, *on a field argent.* The GRADENIGHI of Venice appear to have borne originally, *Gules, a ladder in bend argent,* but in process of time the ladder has been converted into a regular stair, filled up *azure;* as in Plate XXXII., fig. 10, the coat of the Counts GRADENIGO. In the *Wappenrolle von Zürich* No. 322, is the canting coat of LAITERBERG, *Argent, two ladders in saltire gules.*

THE CATAPULT, or BALISTA is known in Armory by the old name of a *swepe.* I am only acquainted with one instance of its use. MAGNALL bears: *Argent, a swepe azure, charged with a stone or.*

THE SLING, which was in effect a catapult on a small scale, occurs in the British coat of CARDEN: *Sable, a sling between two pheons argent;* and in a very few foreign coats. CHARBONNEAU in France bears: *de Gueules, à une fronde tortillée en triple sautoir d'or, mise en pal, chargée d'un caillou d'argent; et accostée de deux autres de même.*

THE PORTCULLIS or HERSE (*herse sarasine*), so well known as a Tudor badge (*v.* post 596) occurs not very frequently as an armorial charge. *Argent, a portcullis sable, chained proper,* is a coat of REYNOLDS in England; and in Scotland is recorded in WORKMAN'S MS. as the *armes parlantes* of WINDYGATE (!) more generally borne as *Gules, a portcullis or*, which is also the coat of APEL-VOISIN in France (*de Gueules, à une herse sarasine d'or*).

In CARR'S MS., printed as an appendix to TONGE'S *Visitation of the County of Durham* (Surtees Society) is the coat of ROBERT LEWEN, Sheriff of Newcastle: *Argent, a bend bretessé gules, over all a portcullis in chief azure.* Here the portcullis is not an isolated charge, but it occupies the whole chief with its two horizontal and five vertical bars, the latter ending in spikes.

In later times CANNON, and other fire-arms, have found their way into the list of Armorial charges. *Argent, a culverin in fess sable*, is the coat of LEIGH. LEVERSAGE bears: *Gules, three lion's heads erased argent, in the centre a matchlock or.* MARCHAL DE SAINCY uses: *Azure, on a mound argent flory vert, a cannon mounted proper.* *Gules, three cannon fessways in pale argent*, is the coat of GUNNING. *Gules, six cannon mounted* aculés 2, 2, 2, *argent*, are the arms assigned to the Province of GUIPUSCOA in Spain.

The coat of arms granted in 1864 to JOHAN NICOLAS DREYSE, inventor of the needle gun, is interesting though not a good specimen of heraldic skill: *Gules, two needle guns in saltire proper, surmounted by an escucheon of the Prussian arms. In base an old-fashioned musket proper. On a chief azure the rising sun irradiated or.*

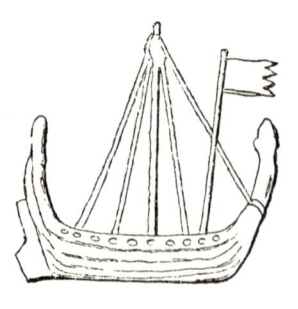

FIG. 75. 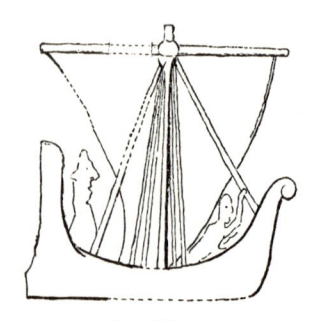   FIG. 76.

SHIPS occur in Armory first on the semi-heraldic seals of maritime burghs. In early examples they are usually of the fishing boat type, with a single mast carrying a large square sail, either furled or set. The *Lymphad*, or ancient galley, thus equipped, and also furnished with oars, is a characteristic and important bearing in the early heraldry of Scotland, especially in the arms of the families of the Hebrides and Western coast. It is frequently carved on the crosses and memorial slabs of Iona and the Western coast (See Figs. 75 and 76 from *Sculptured Monuments of Iona and the West Highlands*, by JAMES DRUMMOND, R.S.A., Plates XVII., XXV., XXXV., XXXVI., etc.).

In all these examples the boat is of one type, single masted, apparently undecked, and having the high prow and stern characteristic of the Viking age. (See the Bayeux Tapestry, and the engravings of the chapter on War Ships in DU CHAILLU'S *Viking Age*, vol. ii.)

On a seal of ANGUS OF THE ISLES of the year 1292, appended to a Homage Deed in the Chapter House at Westminster, the lymphad, or galley with furled sail, appears, but is not included in a shield (LAING, *Scottish Seals*, i., No. 79). The seal of ALEXANDER, Lord of the ISLES and Earl of ROSS, in 1338 has a shield borne on the breast of an eagle displayed, and charged 1st and 4th with a galley under sail; 2 and 3 with the arms of the Earldom of ROSS (*Gules, three lions rampant argent*). (LAING, ii., No. 537.) On the handsome seal of ALEXANDER, Lord of the ISLES and Earl of ROSS, the shield is thus charged: 1. A galley surmounted by an eagle displayed (Lordship of the ISLES); 2. ROSS, as above; 3. *Azure, three garbs or* (BUCHAN); 4. *On a bend between six crosslets, three buckles* for LESLIE, all the quarters within a Royal Tressure (LAING, i., No. 451, Plate XII., fig. 6). In the seal of JOHN, Lord of the ISLES and Earl of ROSS in 1454, ROSS and the ISLES are quartered within the Tressure, precedence being given to the Earldom (LAING, ii., No. 452, Plate XII., fig. 4). On a later seal of the same person in 1476, after his resignation of the Earldom of ROSS, the galley alone appears and is surmounted by an eagle displayed, all within the tressure. In no later representation of the galley of LORN, or of the Lord of the ISLES is it represented under sail. It is often drawn with sail furled, and oars in action; but sometimes as at anchor, with the oars in saltire across the mast; sometimes with no visible oars, and with flames in the crow's nest at the top of the mast. (This is sometimes, but without any reason at all, called "*St. Anthony's fire*," probably it was only the beacon intended to mark out the position of the chief's galley.) This is represented in Plate XXXII., fig. 11, a coat of LORN. The Lords of LORN claimed seniority to the Lords of the ISLES in descent from SOMERLED; and their arms (generally considered feudal rather than arms of descent) are quartered by the families of ARGYLL and BREADALBANE in the simpler form, *i.e.*, the galley alone without the eagle displayed. The Earls of ATHOLE and of ARGYLL have borne the coat somewhat differently; ATHOLE had *Argent* (or more generally *Or*), *a lymphad sable with fire at the top of the mast;* ARGYLL bore more generally, *Argent, a lymphad, sails furled and oars in action sable, flags flying gules.*

A similar coat to the last was quartered by the HAMILTONS as the feudal arms of ARRAN after they became Earls of that island. The old feudal coats of the Earldoms of ORKNEY and CAITHNESS also consisted of a ship, or lymphad, of different tinctures, which we find marshalled in different ways in the coat of the SINCLAIRS after they came into possession of the latter Earldom and resigned the former.

On the seal of JOHN, Earl of CAITHNESS in 1292, the galley is represented without a sail, and is surrounded by the Royal Tressure. (LAING, *Scottish Seals*, i., No. 149.) On that of HENRY SINCLAIR, Earl of ORKNEY, 1407, the shield is: Quarterly 1st and 4th (*Argent*) *a cross engrailed* (*sable*) for SINCLAIR; 2nd and 3rd (*Azure*) *a galley with sails furled* (*or*) *no tressure*, for ORKNEY (LAING, i., No. 745). The coat of CAITHNESS: *Azure, a lymphad or, under sail argent*, is given in Plate XXXII., fig. 12. The seal of AGNES, Countess of BOTH-WELL, daughter of HENRY, Lord SINCLAIR, in 1564, bore: Quarterly 1st and 4th *a galley within the Royal Tressure*; 2nd and 3rd *a galley under sail;* over all, in an escucheon *en surtout*, the engrailed cross of SINCLAIR (LAING, ii., 907). The seal of Bishop THOMAS MURRAY of CAITHNESS (1348-1360) has on it a shield containing a lymphad within a tressure (LAING, ii., 1094). The modern arms of the Earls of CAITHNESS combine both the coats given above: *Quarterly*, 1, *the galley at rest, oars in saltire, within the tressure;* 2 and 3, *Or, a lion rampant gules*, SPAR; 4, *the galley under sail*. The quarters are divided by the engrailed cross *sable* of SINCLAIR (*vide infra*, Chap. XV., page 511, and Plate XLIII.).

On the seal of EDWARD PLANTAGENET, Earl of RUTLAND, Admiral of ENGLAND, 1395, the ship, of one mast, bears a sail charged with his arms: *Per pale* (*a*) the arms of EDWARD THE CONFESSOR differenced by a label of three points; (*b*) FRANCE ANCIENT quartering ENGLAND, differenced by a label of five points (*vide* p. 474). I have engraved the ship from DEMAY on Plate XXXIV., fig. 4. The Arms of the City of PARIS are *Gules, a galley under sail argent, on a chief azure three fleurs-de-lis or.*

Boats, and ships fully rigged, with three masts, occur in late coats. *Argent, a three-masted galley, sails furled sable*, is the coat of MEARES; and *Azure, a three-masted galley, sails furled or, flags gules*, that of JOWETT.

Argent, a boat sable, with two paddles or, occurs in the

Wappenrolle von Zürich, No. 435, for OBERREIDERN. The Danish families of BOTH and BOTHMER bear: *Argent, a boat,* the former *gules,* the latter *sable;* but the coat of the Counts BOTHMAR in Germany is: *Azure, a boat argent.* Gules, *a boat or* is borne by the Polish *herba* of LODZIA, of which are the Counts LODZIA, the Counts SZOLDRSKI, and the Princes PONIN-PONINSKI. The Princes GIOVANELLI in Austria use: *Gules, on a sea in base azure a boat argent, therein two young rowers ppr.* *Gules, on a sea azure a ship with three sails argent, on each a cross of the field,* is the coat of the Counts HENNIN of Baden. The Danish Counts STRUENSEE bore: *Argent, on the sea a ship proper flying Danish flags, all within a bordure or.* *Or, three boats in pale sable* (sometimes manned) is a coat of BAAD in Denmark, and the French ALLEMANDS bore: *Azure, three ships or, rigged, etc., argent.*

THE ANCHOR, though frequently found as an armorial charge in British Heraldry, is not remarkably more frequent in it than in the coats of other nations, some of which have no sea-board.

Azure, an anchor argent, is borne by OFFER in Scotland, by LANGLOIS in Bavaria, OESTERREICH in Pomerania, and PIOT in Dauphiny. The Barons von LUDERITZ of Prussia use: *Argent, an anchor bendways gules, the flukes in chief.* *Or, an anchor sable,* is the coat of CHAPPELL in England, of CROELS in Brabant, of GROONENDYCK and POLANEN of Holland, and the Barons van der HOOP (the last of course is a canting coat on the anchor as the emblem of Hope). *Argent, two anchors in saltire sable, on a chief azure three mullets or,* was borne by the Comtes de ST. CRICQ in France. *Or, three anchors in pairle sable* (without rings), is the Dutch coat of BON.

Azure, on a bend argent three anchors sable, is used by LANSER of Luxemburg. *Sable, a chevron between three anchors or*, are the *armes parlantes* of ANCRAM. *Argent, a fess wavy between three anchors azure*, is a coat of JAMIESON. The Greek family of ZALLONI bear: *Or, a Greek cross gules between four anchors sable.* We ought not to pass from things nautical without recording that Noah's Ark is found as the charge of several foreign coats. *Azure, on waves in base Noah's Ark, surmounted by the dove volant bearing an olive leaf proper* is the coat of the French family of L'ARCHEL. The Sicilian family of BONO have a coat which shows the charge under other circumstances; *Azure, on a mount in base the Ark of Noah or, surmounted by a rainbow or, gules, vert, azure, and argent.* The Polish clan of KORAB bear: *Gules, the Ark of Noah, prow and poop ending in lion's heads, the ark having also a tower(!)*, as such it is borne by OSTROWSKI, BOGUSLAWSKI, FALEBOWSKI, etc.

Of the use of things ECCLESIASTICAL as heraldic charges, the best examples are found in the arms used for Episcopal Sees, and other ecclesiastical foundations. In them naturally the *pallium*, the mitre, the pastoral-staff, or crozier, the sword of St. Paul, the keys of St. Peter, occur with considerable frequency. The Arms of the See of LONDON have already been given (p. 346 *ante*); those of the See of EXETER: *Gules, the keys of St. Peter in saltire or, wards in chief, surmounted by the sword of St. Paul in pale proper, hilted gold*, are depicted in Plate XXXIII., fig. 6.

But these ecclesiastical charges appear also in personal arms. *Argent, a crozier*, or pastoral staff, *in pale sable*, is the coat of the Scottish M'LAURINS, who claim descent from an Abbot of Achtow, in Balquidder. (*See* SKENE, *Celtic Scotland*, iii., 343-4.) BENOIT in Dauphiny bears, *Gules, a pastoral staff argent.* The Breton DES AUBRAIS, use *Gules, three croziers or.* As a canting charge the crozier appears naturally in several Swiss and German coats of families of BISCHOFF, *e.g.*, those of Basel use:

Azure, a crozier or; a family of this name from the same city now settled in England uses, *Argent, on a pile sable a crozier or* (this coat is often found blazoned: *Sable, a crozier or, the field chapé-ployé argent* (vide ante, p. 88).

The Dutch family of PABST bear: *Gules, the papal tiara proper.* Another in Germany uses the same, but with the field *sable.* The VAN DER HELLEN have a coat which we should be inclined to pronounce decidedly that of some ecclesiastical foundation:—*Azure, a chevron between three chalices or, each surmounted by the Sacred wafer.* The Kingdom of GALICIA, in SPAIN, has as its *armes parlantes:*—*Azure, crusily* (or between six crosslets) *a monstrance* (originally a covered chalice) *or.*

The family of ARRAS uses: *Gules, a church candlestick or.* GISSEY in France bears: *Gules, three such candlesticks, each surmounted by an estoile, or. Or, three candlesticks sable,* is the Scottish coat of KYLE, but whether these are ecclesiastical or secular I have no means of determining. *Gules, a lighted candle proper, guttering on the sinister side,* is the coat of BERNALEZ in Spain.

The family of LE SENS, Marquises de MORSAN in Normandy, naturally use: *Gules, a chevron between three censers or.*

There is one charge of considerable importance in Foreign Heraldry which is ecclesiastical in its origin, viz., the GONFANON, or church banner. This is a square or oblong piece of stuff with triple pendants. Unlike the military banner, which was simply a square flag nailed by one of its sides to a lance or staff, the gonfanon, or church banner, was furnished with rings sewn on its upper edge, and was suspended from a cross beam.

It appears generally in the arms of families who were the *avoués*, or *advocati*, of bishoprics and other ecclesiastical foundations, who administered civil justice, and led to war the military contingent which under the feudal system these foundations had to provide. The

Wappenrolle von Zürich of the 14th century (the most important of continental armorials) gives five examples of the use of this bearing on Plate VI., Nos. 128-132. WERDENBERG: *Argent, a gonfanon sable, fringed or.* VELKIERCH (FELDKIRCH), and CHÜR, both: *Or, a gonfanon gules.* TETNANG: *Argent, a gonfanon gules;* and ASPERG: *Gules, a gonfanon or.* (I have figured the charge on Plate XLV., fig. 3, from the *Zürich Roll.*)

The best known example of this charge is found in the coat borne by the Counts of AUVERGNE, of whom ROBERT V. became Count of BOLOGNE or BOUILLON in 1260, in right of his mother ALICE, who was daughter of HENRY I., Duke of BRABANT, by MATHILDE DE BOULOGNE. They bore: *Or, a gonfanon ringed gules, fringed vert* (*Salle des Croisés* at Versailles). (In the *Armorial de Geldre*, the horizontal piece is reduced to a mere strip from which hang three broad pendants.) A legend, which appears to be entirely without foundation, ascribes the origin of this bearing in the arms of the Counts of BOULOGNE to a consecrated banner which was said to have been sent by the Pope to a brother of GODFREY DE BOUILLON. The true origin is that already suggested above.

Azure, a gonfanon or, is the coat assigned in SIEBMACHER, *Wappenbuch,* iii., 12 to the Counts of HERRENBERG. *Argent, a gonfanon gules, its rings or,* were the arms of the Counts of MONTFORT of the Holy Roman Empire. (MONTFORT and FELDKIRCH are coupled together under this blazon in the modern *écu complet* of the Austrian Empire. *See* p. 499.)

BELLS.—The bells which appear as heraldic charges are supposed to have an ecclesiastical origin; and, indeed, are usually blazoned "Church-bells," to distinguish them from the *grelots*, or hawk-bells, to which allusion has already been made. *Argent, three bells azure,* is the family coat of the poet WORDSWORTH.

Sable, three church-bells argent (sometimes with a canton ermine), is borne by several families named PORTER. BELL in Scotland; BRÜMMER of Esthonia; BELS of Flanders; HAMING, and DE BEYER of Holland; all use *Azure, three bells or*. *Or, three bells sable*, is the coat attributed to the Byzantian COMNENI. *Per fess azure and or three bells counter-changed*, are the *armes parlantes* of the Bavarian KLÖCKEL. *Sable, a chevron ermine between three church-bells argent*, is the coat of BELL in England.

In Continental Armory the clapper of the bell is very often of a different tincture. In French blazon the term employed to denote this is *bataillé*. The Comtes de BELLEGARSE bore : *d'Azur, à la cloche d'argent, bataillée de sable*. *Argent, a bell azure, the clapper of the field*, is the canting coat of CLOCK, in Holland.

SCOURGES.—The BATTUTI of Bologna have as *armes parlantes* the following bearings, which may, I suppose, be included among ecclesiastical charges:—*Argent, a bend azure between two scourges gules, each of four cords ending in little spiked balls, or*.

CARDINAL'S HAT.—*Argent, a cardinal's hat, its strings nowed gules*, is the coat formerly assigned to SCLAVONIA, or the WINDISCHE-MARK ; as now borne in the Austrian *Écu Complet* it is not a cardinal's hat properly so called, *i.e.*, one entirely of red ; but a flat ecclesiastical hat of black, edged and tied with crimson. The Dutch VAN GOGH use ; *Argent, three cardinal's hats gules;* and the Belgian DE BORMANS have the same on a field *or*. The Florentine CAPPELLI bear, *Or, a cardinal's hat gules*. *Argent, a flat hat gules, its strings twisted of the same and or* is borne by NAIMER, and NEUMAYER, in Bavaria, and is I suppose intended as the cardinal's hat. *Argent, three flat hats stringed in pale gules*, is the coat of HÖLTSLER.

THE PALLIUM, or PALL, an ecclesiastical vestment,

the use of which is almost entirely confined to Archbishops, appears in the arms of the Sees of CANTERBURY (Plate XVI., fig. 11), ARMAGH, and DUBLIN; and in those of the French See of EMBRUN. Formerly it was also the principal charge of the See of YORK.

PILGRIM'S STAVES and SCRIPS may be considered to come under the category of ecclesiastical charges. *Argent, three bourdons, or pilgrim's staves, gules* (often *in pile*) appear in early *Rolls of Arms* (*e.g.*, in HARL. MS., 6589, JENYN'S collection) for BURDON. *Azure, three pilgrim's staves or*, is another coat of this name; and is also the canting coat of PILGRIM.

The French family of BOURDON DU PLESSIS, uses: *Sable, three pilgrim's staves paleways, two and one, or.* The connection with the name is pretty clear in the coat of TROTTIER of France; *Azure, three pilgrim's staves or, attached to each an escallop gules.* The Low Country family of STEPS also bears another BOURDON coat: *Gules, three bourdons or.*

As to the PILGRIM'S SCRIP, or WALLET, this is used by ROMIEU; *Or, a pilgrim's scrip azure, thereon an escallop argent;* and the English family of PALMER carries: *Argent, a chevron between three palmer's scrips sable, garnished or.* Another family of this name unites both staves and scrips; *Argent, a chevron vert between three palmer's scrips and staves sable garnished or,* is the coat of the Irish PALMERS (Baronets).

The multitude of articles used in domestic life which appear in our own Armory, and the still wider range taken in Foreign Heraldry, will permit of only a few being mentioned in a work of this limited magnitude; and a selection must therefore be made of such as appear to have some special claim to notice. Nearly every culinary or domestic vessel, for instance, appears in one or other foreign or British coat; usually, of course, these charges have been adopted as *armes par-*

lantes, when even a remote connection could be traced between their names and the designation of the bearers.

First of all we will take articles of dress.

Plate XXXIII., fig. 1, is the coat of HASTINGS, Earls of HUNTINGDON, *Argent, a maunch sable; Azure, a maunch or*, is that of CONYERS. This bearing is known in French blazon as *une manche mal-taillée*, it is really only the long hanging sleeve of a mediæval female robe, and *mal-taillée* is only a synonym for old-fashioned. There is a good deal of latitude in the way in which maunches are represented; but, as Mr. PLANCHÉ remarks, "this charge, however extravagantly drawn, cannot exceed the absurdity of the fashion it commemorates." *Or, a maunch gules*, is also a HASTINGS coat and was borne by the Earls of PEMBROKE. HENRY DE HASTINGS, No. 146, in GLOVER'S *Roll*, also bears this in *Roll of Arms of Antiquarian Society*, No. 77; and RAUF THONEY, No. 79, with the field *argent*. WILLIAM DE MOHUN : *Gules, a maunch argent and label azure*, is No. 156 of ST. GEORGE'S *Roll*. Other HASTINGS bore : *Argent, a fess gules between three maunches sable. Argent, a chevron between three maunches sable*, is the coat of MANSEL. (For MOHUN *see* under MARSHALLING, p. 458 *infra*.) *Sable, a maunch argent*, was borne by THOMAS WHARTON, Governor of Carlisle, created Lord WHARTON in 1544 by HENRY VIII., who also gave him, as an armorial augmentation, a *bordure or charged with eight pairs of lion's paws saltire-ways erased gules* (the paws of the Scottish lion!) in memory of his bravery and skill against the Scottish forces at Solway Moss.

This charge is very rarely found except in British Armory, where it appears as early as the 13th century; I have, however, noted a few foreign examples. The Poitevin family DE LA COSTE uses : *de Gueules, à la manche mal-taillée d'or*. CONDÉ DE COERNEY in Champagne, bears : *Or, three maunches gules*.

PLATE XXXIII.

1. Maunch.
   Hastings.

2. Buckles.
   Leslie.

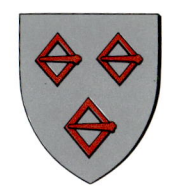

3. Buckles, Lozenge-shaped.
   Jerningham.

4. Dúcal Crowns.
   See of Ely.

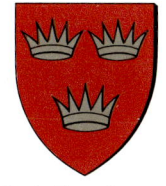

5. Antique Crowns.
   Grant.

6. Keys.
   See of Exeter.

7. Covered Cups.
   Schaw.

8. Caldrons.
   Guzman.

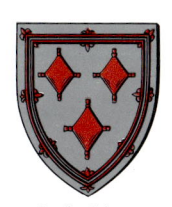

9. Cushions.
   Randolph.

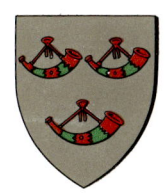

10. Hunting-horn.
    Hunter.

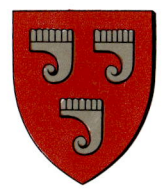

11. Clarion.
    Granville.

12. Words.
    Mendosa.

BUCKLES (*fermaux*) occur in England as early as CHARLES'S *Roll*, and are supposed to have a military as well as a civil significance. There is some diversity in the mode of drawing this charge; the best known is that in which they are borne in the Scottish coats of LESLIE and STIRLING: *Argent, on a bend azure three buckles or*, Plate XXXIII., fig. 2. (*See* also Plate XLII., fig. 4.) The buckles in the arms of JERNINGHAM are lozenge-shaped, and are depicted in Plate XXXIII., fig. 3: *Argent, three lozenge-shaped arming-buckles gules.* The buckles in Continental Armory are generally of the lozenge shape. *Sable, a lozenge-shaped buckle argent,* is the coat of Baron von SCHMIDBURG in Bohemia. The Prussian Counts WALLENRODT use: *Gules, a lozenge-shaped buckle argent, the tongue broken in the middle.* A similar coat, but with the lower part of the charge curved into a semi-circle, is also borne by several families of ZEDLITZ, Barons and Counts in Austria and Prussia.

One of the best known instances of the buckle as a heraldic charge is afforded by the arms of PELHAM: *Gules, two half-belts palewise in fess, the buckles in chief argent.* This coat was assumed by Sir JOHN DE PELHAM to commemorate his share in the capture of King JOHN of France, in the battle of Poitiers. It was also used as a badge by the PELHAMS, Earls of CHICHESTER, etc. *Gules, three round buckles argent,* are the early arms of ROCELINE or ROSSELYN (*temp.* EDWARD I.).

The buckle is used in several Scottish coats as a difference to indicate a LESLIE or STIRLING connection. The STIRLINGS bore *Argent, on a bend (engrailed) sable (or azure) three buckles or:* in 1292 the buckles were borne on a chief. Sir JOHN DE STRYVELIN in 1342 bore: *Argent, on a chief gules three buckles or* (See *The Stirlings of Keir;* priv. print, 1858; and STODART, *Scottish Arms,* ii., pp. 80, 81).

CUSHIONS have become important in the Heraldry of Scotland from having been, as far back as the thirteenth century, the bearings in the coat of the family of RANDOLPH (more correctly RANULF) who became Earls of MORAY in 1312. In the earliest RANULF seal, *circa* 1280 (LAING, *Scottish Seals*, i., No. 688), the cushions are of a square shape, with a point uppermost and without tassels, and may therefore be better designated pillows, or *oreillers*, as FROISSART terms them, and as they are styled in CHARLES'S *Roll*. BRUCE'S famous comrade in arms, and nephew, got the Royal Tressure as an honourable addition to his coat; and these bearings: *Argent, three cushions lozengeways within a double tressure flory-counter-flory gules*, which appear on the seal of THOMAS Earl of MORAY in 1314 (*Scottish Seals*, i., 690) (Plate XXXIII., fig. 9), were inherited by the DUNBARS, Earls of MORAY (*Scottish Seals*, i., 196, 297), the heirs of line of the RANULPH family; and continued to be borne by the descendants (illegitimately) of those Earls, the DUNBARS of Westfield, sometimes to the exclusion of their ancestral coat of DUNBAR. (*See* STODART, *Scottish Arms*, ii., 9-12.) Earls of MORAY of a later and distant lineage have since borne the cushions within the tressure as the feudal arms of their Earldom; but in later times with the field *Or* instead of *Argent*.

Cushions appear in the arms of other noble Scottish families including those of the JOHNSTONS, who bear the ANNANDALE saltire and chief, the latter charged with three cushions (not however placed lozengeways) in respect of their supposed connection, feudally or otherwise, with the RANDOLPHS (*vide ante*, p. 145).

Gules, three square cushions argent (afterwards *tasselled or*), were the arms of GREYSTOCK, Barons of GREYSTOCK, 1306. PLANCHÉ, *Pursuivant*, thinks that these cushions (*carreaux*) came from the family of CARRO, RANULPH DE GREYSTOCK having purchased from the King the wardship and marriage of the heiress. "*De goules à trois horeillers d'or* is in GLOVER'S *Roll* for REDMAIN; and in CHARLES'S *Roll, Argent, three pillows gules,* is the coat of WUNHALE.

CROWNS and CORONETS, as ensigns of dignity and external ornaments of the escucheon, fall to be noticed in a subsequent chapter. The kind which appears most frequently as an armorial charge is the mediæval open-crown; a circlet of gold with four foliations (three of which are visible, an entire one in the centre, two others in profile, or only half visible, one on either side of it), these foliations are vulgarly called "strawberry leaves," and the crown itself is often styled "a ducal coronet," though erroneously, since there is in it no reference to ducal or other titular rank.

Three such crowns appear in the arms of the See of ELY, *Gules, three open crowns or,* the mythical coat of ST. ETHELREDA (Plate XXXIII., fig. 4). And these bearings are used by ESSCHEDE of Holland, and JAGENSDORFF of Bavaria. A curious coat is that of DU FAURE, in France; *Azure, three open crowns enfiling a bend of the field.* *Argent, three open crowns gules,* is borne by KONINCK of the Netherlands, and in the arms of the kingdom of SWEDEN: *Azure, three open crowns or,* where they are often, but mistakenly, asserted to indicate the former union of the three Scandinavian kingdoms, SWEDEN, NORWAY, and DENMARK. (On this see SCHEFFER, *de Antiquis verisque Regni Sueciæ Insignibus;* Holmiæ, 1678; and HILDEBRAND: *Det Svenska Riksvapnet,* 1883.) *Sable, three open crowns in pale or,* are the arms of the See of BRISTOL. *Per pale or and gules, two open crowns counterchanged,* is the coat of CEPEDES of Spain.

The EASTERN, or ANTIQUE, CROWN, is drawn like the *corona radiata* of classic times, usually with eight pointed rays (of which five are visible) proceeding from a golden circlet (Plate L., fig. 13). The Scottish family of GRANT, now represented by the Earl of SEAFIELD, bears: *Gules, three antique crowns or* (Plate XXXIII., fig. 5).

Azure, an antique crown of five rays (*i.e.* of five visible rays) *or*, is the coat of MALCHUS, Counts of MARIEN-RODE in Württemberg.

A ROYAL CROWN, that is a floriated circle closed by bands of gold gemmed and surmounted by an orb and cross, appears occasionally as an armorial charge. The arms of the Spanish kingdom of TOLEDO are, *Azure, a royal crown or*, the cap is *gules*. These are also the *armes parlantes* of KÖNIG in Bavaria. *Gules, an Imperial crown proper*, is borne by LANDESCRON, and *Gules, the crown of* CHARLEMAGNE (fig. 97, p. 617) *proper*, by KAISER. This coat was also borne *en surtout* by the Electors of HANNOVER for their dignity of Arch-Treasurer of the Holy Roman Empire: as such it appears in the Royal Arms of the United Kingdom as used by the five Sovereigns of the House of HANNOVER. KEYSER bears the same but the field is *azure*. *Azure, a coronet enfiling a sceptre proper*, is the coat of the Barons KÖNIG of Württemberg.

SCEPTRES.—*Azure, two sceptres in saltire or*, was borne by the Princes of HOHENZOLLERN *en surtout*, as the ensign of their office of *Arch-Chamberlain of the Holy Roman Empire*. The same coat forms the first and fourth quarters of the arms of the Barons von SONDERNDORFF, and is also borne by the WESTHOFENS of Lübeck.

The Princes of THURN and TAXIS have *en surtout*, for the first of their principalities, the following coat: *Argent, two sceptres in saltire azure, over all a tower gules, the port of the second.*

THE ORB OF SOVEREIGNTY, *Or*, on a field *gules*, was the badge of the Electoral dignity attached to the PALATINATE of the RHINE. *Azure, an orb argent*, *banded and surmounted by the cross or*, is the coat of the Marquises de MUN. *Or, an orb azure ensigned of the field*, was used by QUAEDBACH of Liège: the family of VERSCHOW bear the curious coat: *Argent, an orb reversed azure, ensigned or.*

STAVES.—The Irish USHERS use: *Azure, a chevron ermine between three batons or rods or.* The ULSTER King of Arms of that name, in 1588, appears to have borne: *Gules, three batons paleways or.*

CUPS.—As allusive to their name and office the BUTLERS of ORMONDE, etc., quartered with their personal arms (*Or, a chief indented azure*) the coat: *Gules, three covered cups or.* A Portuguese family of BOTILHER, combines these bearings. It uses: *Gules, two covered cups or, and a chief per fess indented or and azure.* A German descent is attributed to it (but I think it is clear from the arms erroneously), in the rare work *La Nobiliarchia Portugueza* of M. A. MONTEIRO DE CAMPOS, 1754, p. 248. "BOTILHER, Saõ Alemães e por allusaõ ao appelido, trazem por armas em campo vermelho duas copas de ouro cubertas, e hũ chefe endentado de ouro, e azul." Bishop BUTLER of BRISTOL, and of DURHAM, the author of the *Analogy*, bore: *Argent, three covered cups in bend sable between two cotices engrailed gules.* The BUTLERS, Earls of LANESBOROUGH, make all the charges *sable*. *Gules, three covered cups argent*, was the ancient coat of D'ARGENTINE; and the SCHAWS, or SHAWS, of Sauchie bore: *Azure, three covered cups or*, Plate XXXIII., fig. 7. The LAURIES of Maxwelltown used: *Sable, a cup argent, issuing therefrom a garland between two laurel branches all proper.* This seems to be derived from an older coat given by PONT and PORTEOUS, *Sable, a garland with an open cup resting on the upper part of it argent* (*See* STODART, *Scottish Arms*, ii., pp. 198, 403). The Neapolitan Princes PIGNATELLI (to which house Pope INNOCENT XII. belonged) bear:

Or, three pots with handles sable (those in chief *affrontés*). These are *pignates*, and, of course, allusive to the name. The CANNEGIETER of Holland bear a similar coat, but the *pignates* are *gules*. Analogous to these is the canting coat of the BICCHIERI of Verona who use: *Argent, a fess gules between three drinking glasses half-filled with red wine proper*. The Vicomtes CROESEN of Flanders bear: *Sable, three chevrons between as many goblets argent*, but the family of CROESEN of Holland uses: *Azure, a chevron between three goblets* bottoms upward. (Are these punning coats from the French *griser?*) The Marquises FIASCHI naturally bear: *Gules, a flask argent*.

MUSICAL INSTRUMENTS have, indeed, no direct relation to the preceding charges, yet there may be some appropriateness in including them here. Not a few of them are found represented in both British and Foreign Armory. The Violin "the Queen of musical instruments," is borne allusively by the English SWEETINGS: *Gules, three violins transposed (i.e. head downwards) argent, stringed sable*. This is also the coat of the Dutch Barons von SWIETEN. The Barons von der HOUVEN in Rhenish Prussia bear: *Argent, three violins necks upwards or*—(notice *les armes fausses*)—as a variation from the ordinary family of the same name who bear: *Argent, three violins sable, stringed or, necks in base*. To the Italian family of VIOLA is attributed the following coat: *Azure, a violin or, crossed by its bow in bend sinister proper*. In the *Wappenrolle von Zürich* No. 212 is the coat of the old family of WILDENFINGEN: *Argent, three viols transposed gules, corded sable* (the viols have very short necks after the fashion of the time—fourteenth century). The Scottish family of SUTTIE of Inveresk use: *Azure, three viols transposed argent, stringed sable*.

THE LUTE naturally figures in *armes parlantes*, being borne by LUETTE in Brittany: *d'Azur, à un luth d'or, posé en bande, accompagné de deux mains d'argent*. A modern family of LAUTZ in Silesia has had a grant of *Azure, a lyre argent in bend, stringed or, all within a bordure of the last.*

The Bolognese LIRONI use: *Azure, a violoncello in bend-sinister, crossed by its bow in pale; in chief three mullets, all or.* The Swiss family VON STAIN bears: *Gules, a mandoline transposed in bend argent.* In France, GUITTARDI, and GUITTON, both use: *Gules, a guitar or.*

DRUMS.—The family of BUBNA in Bohemia (Counts since 1644) had as their ancestral coat a cymbal, but now bear: *Gules, a drum bendways proper;* while the French TABOUROTS use: *Sable, a chevron between three drums fessways argent.* THIMUS of Liège has: *Gules, a tambourine or.*

CYMBALS (or SHAWMS) are the natural armorial property of SCHAUMANN of Prussia. *Gules, a cymbal of bronze, supported by an iron leg proper.* (This is a very modern invention.)

HARPS.—The best known example of the use of this instrument in British Armory is, of course, the coat now borne in the Royal Arms of the United Kingdom for IRELAND. *Azure, a harp or, stringed argent.* There has been some little uncertainty as to the exact time, and the reason, of the adoption of this coat as the National arms. RICHARD II. granted to ROBERT DE VERE, Marquess of DUBLIN, and Duke of IRELAND, as an augmentation to his arms a coat *Azure, three crowns or, (within a bordure argent).* The three crowns in pale appear on the Irish coins of HENRY V. and his successors; and, without the bordure, were the well known arms assigned by early Heralds to ST. EDMUND of Wessex; and it is not clear why the bearings were considered appropriate to IRELAND. But it is certain that previous to this date Ireland had no other well determined armorial ensign, otherwise it, and not this coat, would naturally have been assigned to the royal favourite.

HENRY VIII. substituted the present harp for the crowns upon his coinage, probably in consequence of his having received from the Pope a harp said to be that of BRIAN BOROIHME: but he did not use the harp in his armorial bearings. In 1552, EDWARD VI. created a King of Arms for Ireland, by the title of ULSTER; and the harp formed one of the charges in the arms and badge assigned to the new official. None of the Tudor sovereigns quartered any arms for IRELAND, though all used the harp on their Irish coins. The Irish harp crowned, appears as a badge on ELIZABETH'S second Great Seal (1586-1603). (*British Museum Catalogue of Seals*, vol. i., No. 990.) On her silver coinage for Ireland the escucheon contains *three* harps, perhaps for the three districts of LEINSTER, MUNSTER, and CONNAUGHT, but at her funeral there was carried the Banner of Ireland, *Azure, a harp, crowned with an open crown or, and stringed argent.* JAMES I. adopted this, but without the crown, as a quartering for IRELAND; and continued the use of the crowned harp as the badge of that kingdom. (I have been indebted to the notes of "GARTER" LEAKE for some of the above information).

Sable, a harp argent stringed or, is the 17th century coat of HARPHAM; and, with the inversion of the two first tinctures, is borne by HARPSFIELD of England, and HARPEN of Prussia. *Gules, a harp or,* is the coat of LA HARPE in Switzerland, and of the Duc D'ARPAJON in France. *Gules, a harp argent stringed or,* is the first quarter in the arms of the Russian Princes BAGRATION.

A curious use of the harp as an allusive charge is found in the arms borne by several families named DAVID, in France, Burgundy, Moravia, Flanders, etc.

HORNS AND TRUMPETS.—Of these the *hunting horn*, bent into a nearly semi-circular shape occurs most frequently in Armory. It is often *garnished* with mouthpiece and bands of a different tincture (*enguiché et virollé*) and stringed (*lié*). In Scottish Heraldry it is the invariable practice to represent the hunting-horn with its mouthpiece on the dexter side of the escucheon. In England, and on the Continent, the reverse is the case. Besides its use as a charge canting on the name it occasionally has reference to some right of forestry. The coat of the FORRESTERS of Carden in Scotland, is *Azure, three hunting-horns sable, garnished gules*. The Lords FORRESTER of Corstorphine use: *Argent, a fess gules between three hunting-horns sable, garnished or, stringed of the second*. The old coat, recently revived, of HUNTER of Hunterston is given Plate XXXIII., fig. 10. *Or, three hunting-horns vert, garnished and stringed gules*. The PENNYCOOKS (or PENICUIKS) of that Ilk, bore: *Argent, a bend azure between three hunting-horns, stringed sable*. This coat has reference to the tenure of the lands of Penicuick, the *reddendo* of which was the blowing six blasts of the horn at the King's hunt.

Argent, a bugle-horn stringed sable, was borne by KINGSLEY of KINGSLEY at a very early date, as hereditary Forester of Delamere. The arms of the Princes of ORANGE were: *Or, a hunting-horn azure, banded gules*, and appear *en surtout* in the escucheon of the Princes of NASSAU. *Azure, a hunting-horn argent, virolled gules*, is the coat of the Counts of MANDELSLOH. *Or, a hunting-horn turned to the dexter and set on a mount gules*, was borne by the Barons HORNECK DE HORNBERG in Bavaria.

In the *Wappenrolle von Zürich*, No. 93 is the old coat of HORENBERG: *Or, out of a mount in base vert two hunting-horns paleways sable stringed gules*. Here the horns are but slightly curved towards the flanks of the shield; but in ancient coats the horns are sometimes represented as straight. A well known instance occurs in the arms of TRUMPINGTON: *Azure, crusily and two horns in pile or.* This is also the coat of PYPE.

Azure, three bugle-horns or, is the coat of CORNET, and of the Barons TRICORNET.

The important *herba* of TROMBY I. in Poland has as its arms, *Argent, three hunting-horns in pairle sable, stringed and garnished or,* which are accordingly borne by the Princes RADZIWILL. *Or, three hunting-horns gules, garnished argent,* is the coat of the Counts and Princes of HORN in the Netherlands. The Florentine GUICCIARDINI bore: *Azure, three hunting-horns argent, the mouth-pieces and viroles or, banded gules.*

Gules, three trumpets fessways in pale argent, is the canting coat of CALL (Baronets).

In Plate XXXIII., fig. 11, is represented the old coat of GRANVILLE (afterwards Earls of Bath) which is blazoned as: *Gules, three clarions or;* sometimes as *rests,* or *organ-rests,* otherwise as *sufflues* or *clarichords,* etc. Some have supposed it was a *rest* to support the end of the lance carried by a mounted knight. But that no such contrivance was ever in use is shown by the evidence of seals, monuments, etc. PLANCHÉ in his *Pursuivant* has an interesting passage on this charge, which he conceives to have been a clarion, a canting badge of the CLARES, Earls of GLOUCESTER, under whom the GRANVILLES held the lordship of Neath. He suggests that the ancient *clarion* which, as usually drawn, bears little resemblance to a trumpet, may really have been that classical instrument the Pan's pipe or mouth organ. The CLARES were Lords of GLAM*organ*. PLANCHÉ gives a drawing of the charge from Sir CHRISTOPHER BARKER'S *Heraldic Collections* (HARL. MS., 4632) in which it is clearly an organ. (*See* also the *Journal of the British Archæological Association,* vol. iv.)

Azure, two organ-pipes in saltire between four crosses patée argent, was the coat of Lord WILLIAMS of Thame, 1554.

The family of DE BLASERE in Flanders bears : *Or, a whistle in pale gules*. *Gules, on a bend or, a flute, or shepherd's pipe, of the first*, appears to be the original coat of the Border family of ELLIOT. *Sable, three pipes argent*, is the coat of PIPER.

I may here mention that a musical stave with notes occurs in the arms of VAN NOOTEN in Holland; and that in those of ROLAND DE LATTRE, better known as ORLANDO DI LASSO (ennobled, in 1570, by the Emperor MAXIMILIAN II.), the musical characters known as a "sharp," "flat," and "natural" appear as armorial charges.

DICE, CARDS, AND OTHER INSTRUMENTS OF AMUSEMENT.—*Gules, three dice in perspective argent marked* (for six in front, three on the sinister side, two on the top) *sable*, is the coat of MATHIAS in England; of a family of the same name in France, and of QUINTANA in Spain. For the former families the allusion is clear to the "lot" cast by which ST. MATTHIAS was chosen to the office of the Apostolate. MACIAS, in Spain, similarly bears : *Gules, six dice (two, two, and two) all marked for sixes sable* (PIFERRER, *Nobiliario de España*, vol. ii., No. 1113). The English families of AMBESACE bear varying coats of the like origin, of which one example will suffice : *Or, on each of three dice sable an ace point argent*. *Azure, three pair of playing tables* (backgammon-boards) *open proper, edged or*, is a coat of PEGRIZ. The Dutch family of CAARTEN use : *Gules, a playing card argent charged with the ace of spades sable*.

CHESS PIECES are also borne. The *rook* (*roc d'échiquier*) is a somewhat favourite bearing in Continental coats usually in *armes parlantes*. In early English *Rolls*, however, it appears apart from this. *Gules, three chess-rooks ermine*, is the coat of FITZSYMON in the *Roll of Arms* of 1277 (HARL. MS., 6137); and *Gules, three chess-rooks argent*, was borne by Sir EDWARD WALSINGHAM in the time of EDWARD I.

Families of ROKEWOOD, in the eastern counties of England, used: *Argent, six chess-rooks three, two, one sable; and Argent, three chess-rooks and a chief sable.* *Azure, three chess-rooks argent*, is the coat of the Breton Barons BONNEFOUX, and the Vicomtes de GUITON, as well as of the Marquis d'AUX, and the Ducs de ROQUELAURE. *Azure, a fess between three chess-rooks or*, is borne by BODENHAM. The chess-rook is also borne in the arms of numerous families of ROCA, ROCCHI, DE LA ROQUE, ROQUES, ROQUEMAUREL, ROQUETTE, etc. It must however be stated that, in at least some of these cases, as certainly in that of the family of DE LA ROQUE D'ESTUER, the bearing is probably rather the *cronel*, or blunted end, of a tilting lance, than the chess-rook. This was called a *roquet*, or *roc*, from its resemblance to the chess-rook. MENÊTRIER says, "*Roc* est le fer morné d'une lance de tournoi, recourbé à la manière des croix ancrées" (cited in C. VON MAYER'S *Heraldisches A b c-Buch; see* also JOUFFROY D'ESCHAVANNES' *Traité Complet du Blason*, p. 158 ; and the whole matter is treated in an interesting way in HILDEBRAND'S treatise, *det Svenska Riks Vapnet*, pp. 45-48 ; where are given the above quotation and a reference to VIOLLET LE DUC'S *Dictionnaire raisonné du Mobilier*).

The Spanish family of ROCABRUNA bear: *Gules, semé of chess-rooks or;* and the Catalonian ROCABERTI bore: *Or, three pallets gules between twelve chess-rooks sable.*

I have met also with examples of other chess pieces, *e.g.*, ROHRMANN in Germany uses: *Gules, a chess knight or;* KONING of Holland, *Azure, a chess king or.*

A great number of families in Holland named ZUYLEN bear charges known as *zuylen* (often blazoned as *columns*) which are, in all probability, nothing more than the familiar chess-rook.

PLAYING TOPS appear as charges in the *armes parlantes* of TOPCLIFFE : *Argent, a chevron between three*

PLATE XXXIV.

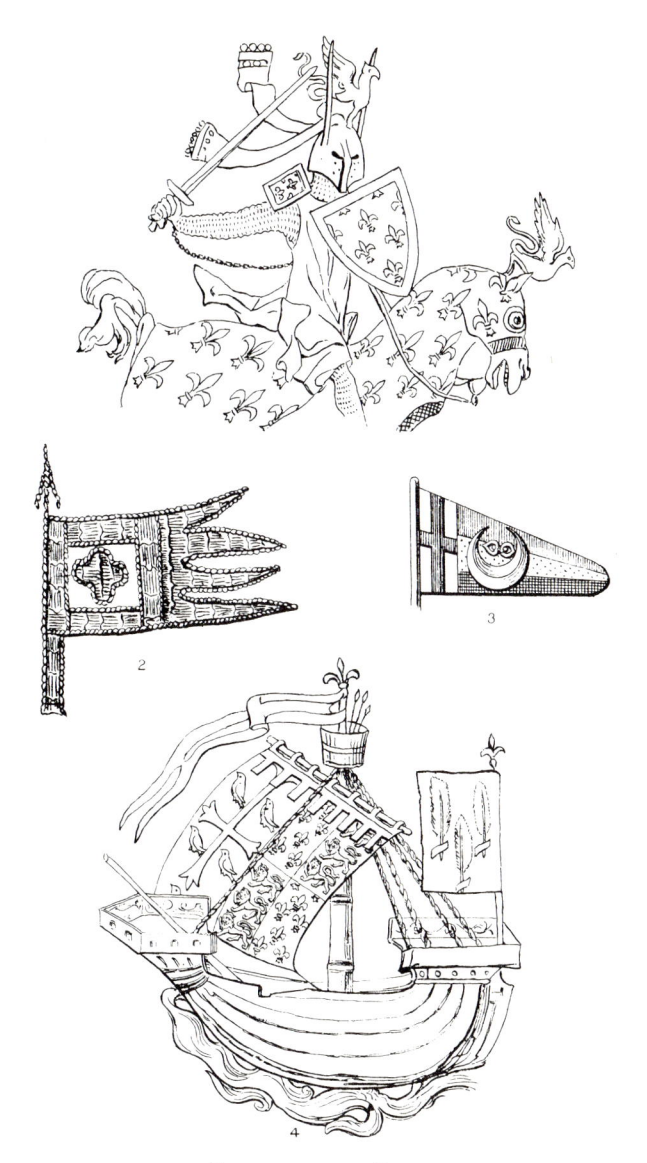

EXPLANATION OF FIGURES.
1. From Seal of Philippe Comte de Valois, 1327 (*Demay*). 2. Banner from Bayeux Tapestry. 3. Pennoncelle of Percy (Archæologia Æliana). 4. From Seal of Earl of Rutland, Admiral of England, 1395 (*Demay*).

playing tops sable; and *Azure, a top or, the peg argent,* is used by TOLLENAER of Holland.

MONEY.—Under Roundles (p. 191) we have alluded to the fact that figured *bezants,* gold coins in fact, are found as armorial charges ; we have now to give a few instances of the use of these and other coins. The Sires de MONNET, who were Vicomtes de SALINS, bore at a very early date : *Azure, nine plates,* 3, 3, 2, 1. The Counts von SCHILLING have the curious coat : *Gules, a fess sable thereon twelve plates* = shillings (notice *les armes fausses*). The DUYSENTDAELDERS of Amsterdam bear : *Gules, in chief the figure* 1, *and in base three thalers argent.* The MICHELI of Venice have a coat which is said to be historical : *Barry of six azure and argent, charged with twenty-one roundles* (6, 5, 4, 3, 2, 1) *of or on the azure bars, and azure on those of argent.* [Another variation is : *Barry of six azure and argent, the azure bars charged with eleven bezants* (5, 4, and 2) *and a twelfth on the last piece of argent.*] This coat is said to commemorate the fact that the Doge DOMENICO MICHELI, the Crusader, finding himself short of cash for the payment of his troops, distributed to them circular pieces of leather, afterwards to be redeemed for golden coin. If this be true the earliest bank notes were not of paper.

When we turn to DOMESTIC CHARGES we find some curious instances. The CAULDRON, or COOKING-POT, which appears in the coats of arms of so many great Spanish families, ought perhaps rather to be counted among the military charges. The *Pendon y Caldera* were presented by the Sovereign to the newly created *Ricos hombres,* or Knights Bannerets, — the banner denoting authority to levy and lead troops, the cauldron the ability to feed them. " Las insignias de los Ricos hombres eran un pendon con divisa, y una caldera, que les davan los Reyes, despues de haver velado una noche en la y glesia que mas devocion tenian. Con el pendon les concedian la facultad de hazer gente para la guerra; la caldera significava eran ponderosos para la sustentar y mantener." (*Origen de las dignidades seglares de Castilla y Leon*, lib. i., cap. ix.) Out of these cauldrons often issue a number of eels, which are often blazoned as serpents, as in the arms of GUZMAN, Dukes of MEDINA-SIDONIA, etc. *Azure, two cauldrons in pale chequy or and gules, the handles and five serpents issuing at the junction of the handles with the cauldron all compony of the second and third.* The whole within a bordure-compony of the arms of CASTILE, and LEON. Plate XXXIII., fig. 8. The GUZMANS, Counts of TEBA, bore: *Per saltire, azure and argent in chief and base a cauldron, as in the coat above, but with the serpents vert; in each flank five ermine spots (2, 1, 2) sable.* To this family belonged the Empress EUGÉNIE, wife of NAPOLEON III. The original GUZMAN coat appears to have been: *Azure, two cauldrons in pale or; a bordure gules thereon eight cauldrons of the second.* HERRERA bears: *Gules, two cauldrons in pale or, a bordure of the first thereon twelve cauldrons of the second* (PIFERRER, *Nobiliario de los Reinos y Señorios de España*, No. 511).

In some important coats, especially in the northern provinces of Germany, a triangular *crémaillière*, or pothook with a ratchet, for supporting a cauldron over the fire, is frequently found as a charge. *Or, a crémaillière gules*, is the canting coat of KETTLER, Duke of COURLAND. *Argent, a crémaillière sable*, was borne by the Counts van der DECKEN, and by the family of GRUBEN, both of Hannover. The Barons HADELN use: *Gules, three crémaillières in fess argent.*

THE SCOPULI of Mantua bear; *Gules, a besom argent in pale, the handle in chief or;* while the ESCOBARS of Estremadura have *Or, three ozier besoms vert, banded gules, the handles in base.* The Castilian PADILLAS carry *Azure, three frying pans paleways in fess, each between as* many crescents argent, one in base, another to the left hand, and the third above, the hollows of all being turned towards the instrument. (These charges have a preposterous legend, the simple reason of their use, viz. as canting charges, being too prosaic for some minds.)

EATABLES, which we would hardly expect to find in armorial coats, nevertheless occur there occasionally, not merely in the figurative coat borne by the Dutch PAIN ET VIN, *Azure, a wheat ear and a bunch of white grapes leaved proper;* but in a much less conventional way. The extinct family of REICHBROD bore: *Quarterly,* 1 and 4, *Argent, an eagle displayed sable;* 2, *Azure; and* 3, *Gules; in each of these last quarters five white loaves arranged in cross.* A family (not the great one) of MONCADA in Arragon, bears: *Argent, seven flat loaves proper* (2, 2, 2, 1). Two families of FRANGIPANI have *armes parlantes;* the one bears, *Gules, two lions rampant affrontés holding (and breaking) a round loaf proper;* the other uses, *Azure, two hands argent which hold a broken loaf or.*

Gules, an egg argent, is the coat of BUSCH. The German DOMEYERS bear: *Sable, a chevron ployé between three eggs argent;* while the Silesian JAWORSKI use: *Gules, ten eggs* 4, 4, 2, *argent.* (*See* also p. 228, *ante,* the arms of WURSTER, etc.)

MIRRORS are frequently found in German coats for the name of SPIEGEL, and its compounds. The Counts SPIEGEL ZUM DESENBERG bear: *Gules, three round mirrors argent in square frames or.*

THE COMBS which appear in several coats are for the most part either those used for carding wool, as in the coat of TUNSTALL, *Sable, three wool-combs argent;* or curry combs, as in the arms of the Belgian Marquises MAILLEN D'OHEY—*d'Or, à trois peignes de chevaux de gueules. Gules, a chevron between three wool-combs argent,* is the well-known coat of PONSONBY, Earl of BESSBOROUGH. The Swedish family of ANREP bear: *Or, a comb in fess, its teeth upwards azure;* those of the name in Esthonia and Prussia pierce the comb at one end with a circular aperture. The family in Livonia bear: *Or, a comb in bend, teeth downwards sable;* and the Russian Counts ANREP-ELMPT use: *Or, a comb in bend azure, the teeth downwards* (See KLINGSPOR, *Baltisches Wappenbuch*).

THE JUNGINGENS of Suabia have: *Azure, a pair of scissors open, blades upwards, argent,* a coat which goes back at least to the fourteenth century, when it appears in the *Wappenrolle von Zürich,* No. 290.

WEARING APPAREL is represented chiefly by Hats.

Per fess argent and azure, a hat counterchanged stringed gules, is the coat of CAPELLO of Venice. *Argent, three caps sable, banded or,* is borne by the English CAPPERS. *Argent, a chevron gules between three caps of maintenance azure,* appears to have been the original coat of the BRUDENELLS, Earls of CARDIGAN; though they are now generally blazoned as *morions* or steel caps.

GLOVES occur in the old coat of WANCY or WAUNCY: *Gules, three dexter gloves, fingers downwards, argent;* another coat of the name is, *Gules, six gloves argent.*

SHOES.—ZAPATA of Spain uses: *Gules, five shoes chequy or and sable; on a bordure of the field eight escucheons of or a bend sable* (sometimes *azure*).

Gules, two slippers in pale or, is the coat of ABARCA in Spain; *Or, three boots sable,* is a coat of HUSSEY; and *Argent, three shambrogues sable,* is that of COKER. *Argent, three skates fessways in pale gules;* and *Azure, three like skates or,* are both canting coats of Dutch PATYNS. The Barons de RAET bore: *Gules, three skates or paleways* 2 and 1.

THE MAUNCH has been already noticed on page 376 *supra,* but there are one or two instances of other articles of wearing apparel. COTTEBLANCHE bears: *d'Azur, à trois cottes d'argent;* and the ABBENBROEKS of Holland use: *Gules* (or *azure*), *a pair of linen breeches argent.*

AGRICULTURAL AND INDUSTRIAL IMPLEMENTS.—Ploughshares, pickaxes, shovels, rakes, fire-pans, eel-spears, fish-hooks, hammers, mill-sails, gates, and many others appear in Armory as occasional charges but do not need more than an allusion here. But the mallet, or hammer, appears so early as a charge, and in such important coats, that we must make an exception in its favour.

MAILLY bears, *Or, three mallets vert*, the principal arms of the family (See *L'Armorial de Geldre*, No. 83, and the *Salle des Croisés* at Versailles, No. 160). Branches of this family differenced by change of tincture, the mallets being *gules*, or *azure*. The branch in Picardy, and that settled in Burgundy bore: *Gules, three mallets or*, which was also the coat of DE MONCHY (*Salle des Croisés*, No. 75) and D'HAMERE-ROLLAINCOURT used, *d'Argent, à trois mallets de gueules*. In these Low Country coats the mallet is of a peculiar shape, like the apex of a chevron, with a short handle. The mallets are also sometimes drawn *penchés*, or inclined bendways (they are so in the above coat of DE MONCHY). *Vert, on a chief argent three mallets penchés gules*, is the coat of GIELIS, one of the seven patrician families of Louvain. *Sable, on a chief argent three mallets penchés of the field*, is borne by the Counts von STEEN. *Azure, on a chief or three mallets penchés gules*, is used by QUAREBBE; and *Gules, on a chief argent three mallets penchés sable*, is the coat of the VAN DER LINDENS, Barons d'HOOG-VOORST. (*Vide* Plate XL.).

DE BACQUEVILLE, also an ancient family, bears: *Or, three hammers gules*. (In the *Armorial de Berry* the blazon is, *d'Or, à trois maillets de gueules*, but I think wrongly.) In the *Rolls of Arms of the Thirteenth Century* the coat, *Sable, three hammers argent*, is ascribed both to JOHN and RICHARD MARTELL; and WILLIAM MARTELL bears: *Gules, three hammers argent*. (In the *Armorial de Berry* this coat appears for "LE SEIGNEUR DE MARTIAU," No. 557.) In the same *Roll*, WILLIAM DE HURSTHELVE bears: *Azure, three hatchets argent*.

LETTERS OF THE ALPHABET, WORDS, AND ARITHMETICAL FIGURES, are found in a good many foreign coats; but in only a few English ones. Among these we find one very instructive example in the old coat of VAVASSOUR. On the seal of MALGERUS, or MAUGER, LE VAVASSEUR the charge is a capital **M** with widely spread legs, which also of course contains the letter **V**, and was practically a monogram of the wearer's names. This was the origin of the *fess dancetty*, which, of *Sable, on a field or*, is the charge of the family arms to the present day (*See* PLANCHÉ, *Pursuivant of Arms*, p. 125). *Argent, a chevron between three old English T's sable*, is the coat of TOFTE; *Gules, three S's or* that of KEKITMORE, both English examples.

Gules, on a fess argent the letter A sable, is the coat of the Barons ALTHANN. *Sable, a fess between three A's or*, is borne by DE FIZE of Liège. The family of VAN DER EE uses, *Or, a chevron azure between three E's gules*. Every letter of the alphabet is similarly employed.

The Italian ABICI bear: *Azure, the letters* **A B** *in chief and* **C** *in base gules (note)*. The ORSENIGHI use: *Argent, a lion rampant gules over its neck a label argent charged with the letters,* **A B C D E F**. The Sicilian QUARANTA have, *Azure, on a fess argent* **X X X X** *sable*. PESC in Holland, bears: *Gules, three* **S***'s argent*. The extinct family of ZACHREISS in Bavaria used: *Sable, on a fess argent the word* Lich. The MAGALOTTI of Florence bear: *Barry of six or and sable on a chief gules the word* LIBERTAS (or LIBERTÀ) *or*. This word LIBERTAS appears also in the arms of several cities, *e.g.* LUCCA, bears: *Azure, between two bendlets the word* LIBERTAS.

The Duchy of RAGUSA bears: *Argent, three bends azure, over all the word* LIBERTAS *in fess or.* The city of ROME still uses the well known letters, **S P Q R,** preceded by a cross, all *argent, in bend on a field gules (vide ante,* p. 229).

Many Spanish families bear their motto in a bordure around the shield, and sometimes introduce it into the shield itself. Plate XXXIII., fig. 12, is the coat of MENDOZA, Duke of INFANTADGO: *Per saltire vert and or, the chief and base charged with a bend gules bordered of the second; the flanks with the words* AVE MARIA *on the dexter, and* GRATIA PLENA *on the sinister, all azure.*

JOVE uses: *Per saltire vert and or, the first charged with two bends of the second; the flanks with the words,* AVE, *and* MARIA. (PIFERRER, *Nobiliario, etc.,* No. 790.)

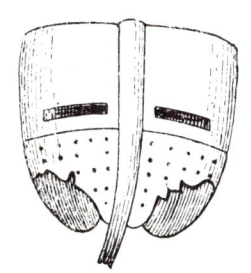

FIG. 77.

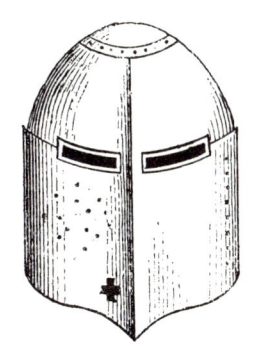

FIG. 78. 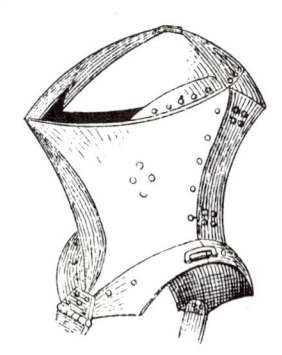   FIG. 79.

CHAPTER XIV.

CADENCY, OR DIFFERENCING. (J. W.; AND G. B.)

BEFORE armorial bearings had been for a century in general use it was found necessary to distinguish by their variations, not only different families but different members, or branches of the same family. It came to be understood that the head of the house could alone use the pure unaltered coat. Even the heir apparent, or heir presumptive, had no right to use the ancestral coat without some variation; in common with the other cadets he had to bear it with a *difference*, or *brisure*. This was early an unwritten but generally accepted law. The obligation of cadet lines to difference their arms was recognised over nearly the whole of civilised Europe in the fourteenth century; and when, later, the obligation seemed in danger of being forgotten it was made the subject of direct legislation.

In the treatise of ZYPŒUS, *de Notitia juris Belgici*, lib. xii., quoted also in MENÊTRIER, *Recherches du Blazon*, p. 218, we find the following :—

"Ut secundo et ulterius geniti, quin imo primogeniti vivo patre, integra insignia non gerant, sed aliqua nota distincta, ut perpetuo lineæ dignosci possint, et ex quâ quique descendant, donec anteriores defecerint. Exceptis Luxemburgis et Gueldris, quibus non sunt ii mores." (The exception is curious. I have printed the Regulations in force in Portugal in the Appendix to this book.)

The choice of these *brisures* was, however, left to the persons concerned; and there is, consequently, a great variety of these ancient modes of difference which it is the object of this chapter to set forth in detail.

In England, where great stringency of regulation has prevailed with regard to some armorial matters of small importance, it has (as is often the case) been accompanied with extreme laxity as regards other, and more important, ones.

The old system of differencing was practically abandoned in the sixteenth century, and was replaced by the present unsatisfactory "Marks of Cadency," consisting of minute charges intended to denote the order of birth of a series of brothers, and themselves to be charged in a second generation by a still minuter series. Even to this limited extent the system has been found unworkable, and beyond a second generation there is not even the semblance of provision for indicating cadency.

In the remarks on DIFFERENCES printed in the Appendix to LOWER'S *Curiosities of Heraldry* from an essay by Sir EDWARD DERING, *circa* 1630, occur the following just remarks :—

"These minute differences, as they were antiently dangerous and insufficient, so in manner as they are now used they were then unknown ; neither is there art enough by any of our heralds' rules, though much refined of late, to guide one so as to know which of the crescent-bearers was the uncle, or which the nephew, and for crescent upon crescent, mullet upon mullet, etc., in a pedigree of no great largeness, perspective glasses and spectacles cannot help you ; but you must have Lyncean eyes, or his that could write Homer's *Iliads*, and fold them into a nutshell."

As in England so on the Continent generally *brisures* have gone greatly into disuse. It is in Scotland alone that the old system of differencing has never ceased to be *in viridi observantia*. In fact the most striking peculiarity of Scottish Heraldry is the importance which it has always attached to distinguishing the arms of the cadets of a family from those which pertain to its chief. It must, however, be confessed that circumstances, presently to be referred to, have made this an easier matter than it has been elsewhere.

Anyone who has given attention to the different economic conditions of England and Scotland will have little difficulty in apprehending the reasons which have made differencing at once easier and more important in North Britain than in the southern kingdom. These are the permanency of the old families; and the closeness of the family and feudal tie. At an early period the leading families of England began to wane, not merely out of power but out of existence. Great baronial houses continually ended in heiresses and co-heiresses who often divided estates, and carried them to meaner men. The great struggle between the Houses of York and Lancaster known as the *Wars of the Roses*, swept whole families of both the greater and lesser nobility off the face of the earth. Of the twenty-five barons appointed to enforce the observance of Magna Charta, who must have been chief among the magnates of England, there is not a male descendant surviving in its present peerage. It is not intended to imply that the present nobility of the British Empire is inferior in point of ancient lineage, or in any other respect, to the existing *noblesse* of any other European country. The foreigner, who looks simply to the date of the Peerage dignity of one of our nobles, is very liable to form an entirely false idea with regard to this matter. He does not know, probably he has no means of knowing, that a person called to the House of Lords, *Imperante Victoria*, may be the head, or still more probably the cadet, of a family of untitled gentlemen who can trace their descent in the male line, if they care so to do, to a companion of the Norman Conqueror. Sir BERNARD BURKE tells us that "WROTTESLEY, a Baron of Queen VICTORIA'S reign, can establish what no other member of the House of Lords can —a male line of descent from a FOUNDER KNIGHT OF THE GARTER," although "Vernon is sprung from Richard, Baron of Shipbroke recorded in *Domesday Book;* . . . . and Bagot is the head of a race of gentlemen traceable back to the Conquest, from a junior branch of which sprang the celebrated house of Stafford, ducal under the title of Buckingham." (*The Rise of Great Families*, p. 33, 1873.) Still there has been a great extinction of once noble names. A large proportion of the surnames borne by knightly and noble families in the fourteenth, and earlier centuries, have utterly passed away from common ken. We find them recorded, with the ensigns which their owners bore, in our Heraldic *Ordinaries* and *Rolls of Arms*, but a large proportion of them would sound unfamiliar in the ears of modern Englishmen.

On the other hand, the Scoto-Norman Barons were remarkable for their numerous progeny; a physical fact for which the intermixture of Celtic blood has been suggested as a cause. Sub-infeudation, which in England had been prohibited from the time of the Plantagenet kings, was largely practised in Scotland. The great baron, owner of an extensive but thinly peopled domain, could provide each of his sons with a fief to be held from him for rent, or military service. Each son divided his fief among his children; and this sub-infeudation went on till every powerful family could count a large array of cadets; many of them, no doubt, in comparatively obscure positions, but the tie of blood, carefully cherished on both sides, imparted a patriarchal character to the relation of superior and vassal.

The student can hardly fail to notice the striking

difference between England and Scotland in the matter of the number and variety of surnames, and arms attaching to them. Whole districts of Scotland have their predominating names, which are generally those of the old feudal families. Argyllshire is peopled with CAMPBELLS; Inverness-shire with MACDONALDS; Aberdeenshire with GORDONS, and FORBESES; and the southern counties with SCOTTS, KERS, ELLIOTS, JOHNSTONES and MAXWELLS.

Surnames were for a long time after their introduction, used only by the gentry; and when they began to be assumed by the lower orders, the clansman almost invariably took the name of his chief, considering himself a member of his family, at least by adoption, if not by a closer tie the remembrance of which tradition had preserved. In England it was far otherwise. New men emerged, and founded new families; it was easier to adopt new arms than (even for those who might possibly have succeeded in doing so had they tried) to trace a connection with those who had passed away.

Hence it comes to pass that while in England the multitude of entirely distinct coats of arms is enormous, in Scotland the number of original coats is small; but the distinct and well defined insignia of the chief of the family are differenced in such a manner as to show forth, more or less clearly, his relation to the head of the house, and to other cadets; and in many cases also to suggest his maternal descent. I have Dr BURNETT'S authority for stating that :—" In the Official Register of Arms from 1672 up to 1888 the entries for members of the families of CAMPBELL, HAMILTON, STEWART, and SCOTT, compose about a ninth of the whole; and if we add the MURRAYS, DOUGLASES, HAYS, GRAHAMS, MACKENZIES, DRUMMONDS, GRANTS, FORBESES, CUNNINGHAMS and FRASERS, we have exhausted a fourth of the existing record of arms. In the case of the most numerous family, the CAMPBELLS—for whom more than a hundred coats are registered—by far the larger number have been assigned to persons either certainly having, or with a high degree of probability claiming, a connection with the head of the house." One of the principal duties imposed on LYON by the Scottish Parliament in 1592, is the assigning of proper differences to cadets, and the bearing of arms without such differences was made penal, by the statutes of 1662, and 1672.

In most English heraldic books this important subject of *differencing* is only adverted to very briefly; and this almost entirely with reference to the little regarded practice of modern times. One bright exception is the excellent work by my late friend the Rev. C. BOUTELL, *Heraldry, Historical and Popular;* in which there is a most valuable and interesting Chapter on "Cadency and Differencing," the materials for which are mainly extracted from the English *Rolls of Arms.*

The Scottish Herald NISBET treats the subject much more fully than his English contemporaries, in a separate work on *Marks of Cadency,* as well as in his *System of Heraldry;* one of the causes of the popularity of the latter being, I imagine, the fact that in it a larger number of the differenced arms of cadets were there made accessible to the reader than could be found elsewhere (out of the Lyon Register), before the publication of BURKE'S *General Armory.* But NISBET was not in possession of historical materials which are now easy of access; and his work chiefly relates to the differencing of comparatively modern times. Though in Scotland *Rolls of Arms* do not exist of the early date of those which we possess in England (many of which have been printed within the last quarter of a century), the two volumes of *Scottish Seals,* edited by Mr H. LAING, supply us with materials equally ancient ; and are in later times supplemented by the illuminated manuscripts of the sixteenth century by Sir DAVID LINDSAY ; and by the collections of WORKMAN, and others, which have been made accessible to the student and general reader in the late Mr STODART'S volumes of *Scottish Arms.*

With regard to continental modes of differencing contemporary information more than sufficient for our purpose is at hand in the admirable collections of seals contained in the works of VRÉE, and DEMAY (from which I have already derived materials for the earlier portions of this work); in the Armorials of the Heralds "GUELDRE," and GILES BOUVIER, "BERRY" Roi d'Armes ; in the works of SPENER and SIEBMACHER ; and the several treatises of MENÊTRIER, and LA ROQUE ; as well as in MAURICE'S *Blazon des Armoiries de tous les Chevaliers de l'Ordre de la Toison d'Or;* and the *Martyrologe des Chevaliers de l'Ordre de S. Jean de Jerusalem,* by GOUSSANCOURT.

We will now proceed to detail the principal modes by which Cadency was denoted.

The principal modes of differencing hereafter to be described are the following :—

1. Change of Tincture (p. 403).
2. The addition of Small Charges to the Field ; or charging an Ordinary with Minor Charges (p. 406).
3. The addition of the Label (p. 414).
4. The addition of a Canton or Quarter (p. 425).
5. The addition of an Escucheon, not *en surtout* (p. 427).
6. The addition (or change) of an Ordinary (p. 428).
7. Changing the boundary lines of an Ordinary (p. 432).
8. Diminishing the number of Charges (p. 434).
9. Change of Minor Charges (p. 434).

10. The use of the Bordure (p. 437).
11. The use of the "Marks of Cadency" (p. 444).
12. The addition of Quarters (p. 446).
13. Augmentations, and Official Arms (p. 448).
14. The Escucheon *en surtout* (p. 448).
15. Examples of Cadency combining the preceding (p. 448).

The differences used to denote Illegitimacy are treated separately in Chapter XVII., p. 530.

I. DIFFERENCE BY CHANGE OF TINCTURE.—One of the earliest modes of difference was to preserve the figures, but vary the tinctures. Two families of CHANDOS bore a *pile gules;* the Herefordshire branch on a field *or;* the Derbyshire branch (to which belonged Sir JOHN CHANDOS, K.G., d. 1369) bore it on a field *argent.* In the reign of HENRY III. the LOTERELS bore: *Or, a bend between six martlets sable,* of which a differenced coat in the *Roll* of EDWARD II. is that borne by Sir GEOFFREY LOTEREL: *Azure, a bend between six martlets argent.* The FURNIVALS, who held lands under the LOTERELS, assumed the same bearings, but varied the tinctures. In the *Roll of the Thirteenth Century,* WALTER DE FURNIVAL bears: "*d'Argent, un bend et six merloz gules;*" and the same coat is ascribed to GERARD DE FURNIVAL in ST. GEORGE'S *Roll,* No. 210; which also contains another coat borne by THOMAS FURNIVAL (No. 208): *Or, a bend between six martlets gules.* The same charges, but with different tinctures, were used by other feudal allies of the FURNIVALS and LUTTERELS. The ECCLESHALLS bore: *Sable, a bend between six martlets or.* The MOUNTENEYS: *Azure, a bend between six martlets or.* The WADSLEYS, and WORTLEYS respectively, charged the *bend gules* of the FURNIVALS, with *three escallops or,* and *three bezants.* The TEMPESTS (*temp.* RICHARD II.) carried: *Argent, a bend between six martlets sable.*

The Counts of SOLMS bear : *Or, a lion rampant azure*, which is said to indicate community of descent with the house of NASSAU, of which the original coat was : *Azure, a lion rampant or*. (*See* TRIER'S *Einleitung zu der Wapen-Kunst*, p. 601, note, Leipzig, 1744.) The Counts of SCHWALENBERG bore, *Gules, a star or;* those of STERNBERG the reverse ; those of WALDECK, *Or, a star sable*. All claimed the same progenitor ; WITEKIND, Count of SCHWALENBERG d. 1190. (*See* LUCÆ, *Grafen Saal*, pp. 648–662.)

In GLOVER'S *Roll* (*temp.* HENRY III.) RICHARD DE HARCOURT uses : *d'Or, à deux barres de goules* (note these are not the French *barres*, but the English *bars*), and in the reign of EDWARD II. this coat is borne by a Sir JOHN HARCOURT ; and by another Sir JOHN, probably a cousin, who carried the coat with the tinctures reversed. Similarly in the reign of EDWARD I. (*First Nobility Roll*, 1297) THOMAS MOULTON, Baron of EGREMONT, bears : *Argent, three bars gules*. In the *Roll* of EDWARD III. this coat is ascribed to Lord MOULTON of Gillesland, while Lord MOULTON of Frankton, bears "*le revers*" (COTGRAVE'S *Roll*). (See the BALLIOL differences in the next section, p. 407.) In France HUCHARS bore : *Argent, a hand within an orle of martlets gules*. The DE LA PLANQUE of the same origin tinctured the charges *sable* (*Armorial de Berry*).

The four sons of GILLES DE MAILLY, who bore : *Or, three mallets vert* (*v. ante*, p. 393), differenced by change of tincture ; the second, third, and fourth sons respectively made the charges, *gules, azure*, and *sable*. The family of DE GROLÉE bore : *Gyronny, or and sable*, but the cadets in Dauphiny changed the metal to *argent*. This mode of difference was frequent in the Low Countries. ARNOLD, Count of ARSCHOT, *circa* 1120, who bore : *Or, three fleurs-de-lis sable*, had five sons ; the eldest inherited the paternal arms ; the second, GERARD of WESEMALE, took : *Gules, three fleurs-de-lis argent* (in this line another differenced coat was : *Or, three fleurs-de-lis gules*). The third, GEOFFREY DE ROTZELAER, bore : *Argent, three fleurs-de-lis gules ;* the fourth, HENRY DE RIVIÈRE : *Argent, three fleurs-de-lis sable ;* the fifth, JEAN DE SCHOONHOVEN : *Gules, three fleurs-de-lis or.* The Dukes of BRABANT carried : *Sable, a lion rampant or,* but GODFREY, brother of Duke HENRY, differenced by bearing the lion *argent.* GAULTIER BERTAUT, Seigneur de MECHLIN, bore : *Or, three pales gules ;* his brother GILLES, Seigneur de BERLAER, changed the field to *argent.* (SPENER, *Opus Heraldicum,* pars. gen., p. 347. MENÊTRIER, *Véritable Art du Blason,* c. 19., p. 352.)

In Holland a very large number of families who bear three *zuilen* (chess-rooks ; *vide ante,* p. 388) are distinguished solely by the change of tincture in field and charges.

In Germany similar mutations are abundant. Two families of BOYNEBURG bear : *Quarterly,* the one *argent and sable ;* the other *argent and azure.* Two families of the Counts of SPANHEIM use : *Chequy,* the one *argent and gules,* the other *azure and or.* The Counts of STERNBERG, and HAYMSBERG, in Carinthia, who bear respectively *Azure,* and *gules, three estoiles or,* had a common ancestor in the Baron von SAANECK. See also LEUCHTENBERG in the next chapter, p. 472.—J. W.]

[As an early Scottish instance of altering the tincture may be cited the family of HUME, originally a cadet of the Earls of MARCH, or DUNBAR, who placed the lion of the Earls of MARCH in a field *vert* instead of *gules.* The BOYDS, whose progenitor is understood to have been a younger brother of the first High Steward of Scotland, bore the STEWART coat with a change of tincture— *Azure, a fess checquy argent and gules.* The *argent* field of the DOUGLAS coat is in some branches converted into *ermine* as early as 1373 ; and the descendants of the DOUGLASES of Dalkeith adopted a further change by making the chief *gules* instead of *azure*. A similar mode of differencing occurs in the earlier Lyon Register in other families. The MURRAYS of Culbin in the north, changed the *azure* field of their family into *sable ;* and there seems reason to believe that the southern FRASERS had originally the field *sable*, the change to *azure* being adopted by the branches who migrated northwards. The engrailed cross of SINCLAIR was borne *azure*, instead of *sable*, by the Herdmanston line ; and several variations of tincture are found among branches of the HAY family ; Boyne, reversing the tinctures, having the field *gules*, and the shields *argent ;* Leys having the field *ermine ;* and Broxmouth retaining the *argent* field, but making the charges *vert*. While the alternate gyronal compartments of the Argyle CAMPBELLS are *or* and *sable*, those of the Loudoun CAMPBELLS are *ermine* and *gules*, these tinctures being taken from the bearings of the family of CRAWFORD, a marriage with whose heiress gave them their Ayrshire lands. A change of tincture of the field frequently occurs in the Lyon Register in case of families bearing the same surname who are not asserted or certainly known to be descended from the same ancestor.—G. B.]

II. BY THE ADDITION OF SMALL CHARGES TO THE FIELD.—Strewing the field with small charges, called in the *Boke of St. Alban's* gerating ; or substituting for a plain field what would now be called a field *semé*,—was a very ancient mode of differencing. Dame JULIANA BERNERS enumerates nine figures as used for that purpose,—the crosslet, the crosslet-flory, the fleur-de-lis, the primrose, cinquefoil, escallop, chaplet, mullet, and crescent. The shield of WILLIAM DE ROMARE, Earl of LINCOLN, who died in 1198, is adduced by Mr PLANCHÉ as an early example of differing by crosses-crosslet ; the principal charges are seven mascles conjoined, three, three, one ; the tinctures are unknown. We find in the *Rolls of Arms* of the thirteenth, and early part of the fourteenth, century many instances of coats crusily, billetty, bezanty, and "pleyn d'escallops," fleuretté, and "à les trefoilles d'or." With these last Sir EDMOND DACRE of Westmoreland powdered the coat borne by the head of his family: *Gules, three escallops or* (*Roll* of EDWARD II.).

We find in the *Roll* of HENRY III. that JOHN BALLIOL, and in the *Roll of the Thirteenth Century* that EUSTACE DE BALLIOL both bore: "*Gulez, à un faux escocheon* (that is an *orle*) *d'argent*," which is also attributed to ALEXANDER DE BALLIOL in ST. GEORGE'S *Roll*; and the first *Roll* of EDWARD III. This is differenced by the inversion of the tinctures for another ALEXANDER DE BALLIOL. A WILLIAM DE BALLIOL bears: *Or, an orle vair* (or *azure*) *with a label gules.* An INGRAM DE BALLIOL uses: *Gules, an orle ermine, with a label azure.* But besides these is another differenced coat: *Azure, crusily an orle or.* This is attributed to EUSTACE DE BALLIOL in the *Roll* of HENRY III. (GLOVER'S *Roll*, No. 40).

In fact most of the coats which we find *semé* of small charges are, in their origin, coats differenced by gerating. The coat borne by the ACTONS of Aldenham, *Gules, crusily or, two lions passant argent*, is evidently a gerated coat of LESTRANGE; for EDWARD DE ACTON married the co-heiress of LESTRANGE (living 1387) who bore simply: *Gules, two lions passant argent.* (*Herald and Genealogist*, ii., p. 43.)

The English BEAUMONTS bore: *Azure, flory, and a lion rampant or*, while those who remained in France, at Brienne in Champagne, had the field *semé* of billets. The original coat of the house of BERKELEY in England (BARCLAY in Scotland) appears to have been: *Gules, a chevron or* (or *argent*). The seals of ROBERT DE BERKELEY, who died 4, HENRY III.; of THOMAS DE BERKELEY, 20, HENRY III.; and MAURICE DE BERKELEY, who died 1281; all show the shield charged with a chevron only. MORIS DE BARKELE, in the *Roll*, temp. HENRY III., bears "*goules, a cheveron argent.*" (In two of the windows at Bristol, the chevron is tinctured *or.*) But THOMAS, son of MAURICE, who died 15, EDWARD II., has the present coat: *Gules, a chevron between ten crosses patée argent*, while in the *Roll* of EDWARD II., "*de Goules od les rosettes de argent et un chevron de argent*" is attributed to Sir THOMAS DE BERKELEY. (*See* my paper on "The Heraldry of Bristol Cathedral" in the *Herald and Genealogist*, vol. iv., p. 289.) In Leicestershire the BERKELEYS gerated with cinquefoils, an ancient and favourite bearing in that county. (*See* p. 322.) In Scotland, the BARCLAYS differenced by change of tincture, and bore: *Azure, a chevron argent between* (or *in chief*) *three crosses patée of the same*. In the *Roll*, temp. HENRY III. (GLOVER'S *Roll*, No. 108), GEOFFREY DE LUCY bears "*de Goules à trois lucies d'or.*" In the first *Roll* of EDWARD I., this is first differenced by the field being made *crusily or*, for GEOFFREY DE LUCY; and then by a change of the tincture of the field, AMAURI DE LUCY bearing: *Azure, crusily three lucies or*. The fess between six crosslets of the Earls of WARWICK originated in the old coat of BEAUCHAMP, *Gules, a fess or*, gerated with crosslets which were afterwards reduced to six, and for which martlets were substituted by the BEAUCHAMPS of Powick. The arms of the HOWARDS, now Dukes of NORFOLK, are in all probability only a differenced coat of BEAUCHAMP, whose dependants they originally were. LA ROQUE says: "La maison de Houvard ou Havart . . . . de France, a le champ de son escu et la bande comme (celle d'Angleterre) accompagnée de six coquilles d'argent." (*Traité de l'Origine des Noms*, p. 203.)

The Counts of SALM in the Ardennes bear: *Argent, two salmon addorsed gules;* but this coat is borne *crusily* by the Counts of UPPER SALM in Lothringen, for difference, and not, as used to be asserted, in memory of a crusading ancestor. The Counts DERNBACH ZU DERN-BACH used : *Or, three hearts in pairle sable,* but another family of Barons of the same name, *dit* GRAUL, differenced by a change of tincture and the addition of smaller charges : *Azure, billetty argent, three hearts in pairle or.*

It is curious to find, on the other hand, a new difference made by the omission of the differencing small charges. The original arms of the Counts of GUELDRES appear to have been three cinquefoils ; but GERARD IV. (1229) married RICHARDE DE NASSAU, and assumed her arms : *Azure, billetty and a lion rampant or.* Count RENAUD, afterwards first Duke of GUELDRES, omitted the billets. (*See* PLANCHE'S *Roll;* and Mr WATSON'S remarks on it in the *Genealogist,* New Series, vol. vi., p. 158.)

These examples might be increased almost indefinitely. Nearly akin to this mode of gerating was that by which small charges were placed *in orle.* One of the numerous ways in which the coat of the LUSIGNAN, or DE VALENCE, families was differenced, was by the addition of *an orle of martlets gules* to the original coat : *Barruly argent and azure;* as shown in *champlevé* enamel on the monument of WILLIAM DE VALENCE, Earl of PEM-BROKE (d. 1296), in Westminster Abbey ; a reduced copy of which (affording also a pretty example of diaper), forms the frontispiece to BOUTELL'S *Heraldry, Historical and Popular.* This coat is also attributed to the Earl's son in the *Caerlaverock Roll* of 1300. Similar to this was the coat of CHAWORTH : *Barruly argent and gules,* which was differenced by an *orle of martlets sable.* In the *Roll* of EDWARD II. Sir PATRICK CHAWORTH bears this coat, but the bars are *or and azure.* On the original coat the martlets were eventually reduced to three, and so became principal charges. In England, in the Low Countries, and in northern France there are abundant instances in which the difference was effected by the addition of a single charge. One of the earliest examples, perhaps, is afforded by the coat of DE VERE, borne *ante* 1221, by ROBERT DE VERE, Earl of OXFORD, who was a younger brother of AUBREY, the second Earl. *Quarterly gules and or, in the first a star of five points argent* (*vide ante*, p. 308). The star is made *ermine* in the *Roll* of RICHARD II. for AUBREY DE VERE. BOUTELL gives, p. 203, an interesting series of the arms of NEVILLE of Raby: *Gules, a saltire argent*, differenced thus by a crescent *sable;* a martlet *gules;* a mullet *sable;* a *fleur-de-lis;* a rose *gules;* a pellet, or annulet, *sable;* and two interlaced annulets *azure*, all borne on the centre point of the saltire. The BEAUCHAMP shield (*Gules, a fess between six martlets or*) is similarly differenced by the additions of a pierced mullet, or a crescent, both of *sable*. The RADCLYFFES, of Winmarleigh, still difference their ancestral coat (*Argent, a bend sable*) *with an escallop gules in the sinister chief.*

In MAURICE, *Les Chevaliers de la Toison d'Or*, we find many like instances; *e.g.* p. 90, the coat of the great family of BORSELE (*Sable, a fess argent*) is differenced by adding a star of six points *argent* in the dexter chief. The Counts of CHÂLONS bore, *Gules, a bend or;* at p. 32, this is differenced by a pierced mullet *sable* upon the bend in dexter chief. (This is also the difference for HUGUES DE CHÂLONS in *l'Armorial de Gueldre*.) In the arms of LOUIS DE CHÂLONS (Knight of the Order, No. lxiv.), the bend is similarly charged with a crescent *azure*. The coat of PHILIPPE DE CRÈVECŒUR (Knight of the Order, No. lxix.), *Gules, three chevrons or*, has a crescent *azure* on the uppermost chevron. CHARLES DE LANNOY (Knight of the Order, No. cxxxvi.) lays aside the ancestral difference of a *bordure engrailed gules* (to which allusion is made on p. 450), and places a crescent *gules* in the centre of his coat: *Argent, three lions rampant vert, crowned or.* PIERRE DE LA

TRÉMOUILLE, Seigneur de DOURS, differenced the main coat of his line, *Or, a chevron gules between three eagles displayed azure*, by the addition of a *fleur-de-lis argent* on the point of the chevron (p. 76). The LALAINS (of which family there were several *Chevaliers de la Toison d'Or*), who bore, *Gules, ten lozenges conjoined 3, 3, 3, 1, argent*, charged the first lozenge with a *lion rampant gules*, from the coat of BARBENÇON. JACQUES DE BRIMEU (Chevalier, No. xviii.) bore, *Argent, three eagles displayed gules, and in the centre point a demi-lion rampant of the last*.

The great family of CHÂTILLON (of the Counts de BLOIS), who bore: *Gules, three pallets vair a chief or*, used, among other differences, a martlet *sable* in dexter chief (*Armorial de Berry*, No. 811). In the *Armorial de Gueldre*, this coat is borne by "LE SIRE DE LA FÈRE" with the difference of a lion rampant *gules*, in the dexter chief. In the same MS., "LE SIRE DE MELUN" bears the plain coat: *Azure, seven bezants 3, 3, 1, and a chief or* (*v.* p. 341), but HUGUES DE MELUN places a martlet *sable* in dexter chief. (The bezants are also nine in number.) The most curious of these differences are perhaps the arms of DE DAMPIERRE (*Armorial de Gueldre*), where the CHÂTILLON chief is charged with *two lions passant affrontés sable*. On the seal of MARIE, Countess of BLOIS, *c.* 1230, the chief is charged with *eight pallets gules* (VRÉE, *Généalogie des Comtes de Flandre*, plate v.). SPENER (*Opus Heraldicum*, p. gen., p. 356) shows that many German coats remain which bear similar charges, evidently originally assumed as differences, the reason of which has faded out of remembrance. In SIEBMACHER'S *Wappenbuch*, plates cxxiv., cxxv. contain four such instances among Rhenish families. HUND VON SALHEIM places a *star of six points sable* in the middle of the coat: *Gules, three crescents argent;* DIE KNOBEL who bear: *Argent, an escucheon gules*, have in sinister chief an annulet *sable*; DIE GROSCHLAG, who bore: *Azure, three bends counter componé argent and gules*, have between the two upper bends an *open crown or*; and the VON LINDAU, whose coat is *Gules, a bend argent*, add in chief a *fleur-de-lis azure*. (In the two last instances the bends are drawn as bends-sinister according to the German practice of reversing the charges for the sake of symmetrical arrangement. The student should bear this in mind in consulting SIEBMACHER, and other engraved armorials of Germany.) This mode of differencing by additional charges was often carried much further than by the insertion of a single one as in the preceding examples. In England the original coat of DE GREY was *Barry of six argent and azure*. JOHAN DE GREY so bears it in the *Roll* of EDWARD I. In the *Roll* of EDWARD II., as borne by GREY, Duke of SUFFOLK, it is differenced by the addition of *three torteaux in chief*. These were converted into annulets by the DE GREYS, Lords WALSINGHAM. (Plate IX., fig. 3.)

At Caerlaverock the two brothers BASSETT difference the family coat: *Ermine, a chief indented gules*, by adding in the one case three mullets, in the other as many escallops, *or*.

The seal (*c.* 1298) of PHILIP, Governor of Flanders, fifth son of Count GUY, has the arms of FLANDERS differenced by a bendlet charged with two escallops, one in chief the other in base. (VRÉE, *Généalogie des Comtes de Flandre*, p. 75.)

One of the best known English examples is that of the coat of the COBHAMS: *Gules, a chevron or*, in which the Ordinary was charged by the cadets with three pierced estoiles, three lions, three crossed-crosslets, three *fleurs-de-lis*, three crescents, and three martlets, all of *sable*. The DESPENCER coat was: *Quarterly, argent and gules a fret or, over all a bend sable*. This coat Sir HUGH LE DESPENCER, in the reign of EDWARD II., differences by charging the bend with three mullets *argent;* for which, in 1476, HENRY SPENCER substitutes three escallops *argent;* and this coat is that now used by the Duke of MARLBOROUGH, and by Earl SPENCER. The homage seal of REGINALD CHEYNE of Inverugie bears in 1292 : *Crusily fitchée, a bend ;* and one of his sons charges the bend with three escallops. Another REGINALD CHEYNE who signs the letter of the Barons of Scotland to the Pope in 1320, substitutes eagles displayed for the escallops.

A number of the descendants of Sir JOHN STEWART of Bonkyl charge the bend which was his difference with the three buckles of BONKYL.

The cadency of the DAUBENYS, which is given pretty fully by BOUTELL, contains some interesting examples which he has not recorded. In the *Roll* of EDWARD II. they bear a *fess engrailed or* (a bearing which was really synonymous in early times with a fess of conjoined fusils, in which latter form the coat appears in 1300, in the *Roll of Caerlaverock*). It is, later, blazoned with in chief two martlets *argent;* three martlets *argent;* three escallops *or;* four lozenges *or.* Again, the fusils (three in number) are depicted *ermine* for difference, with the subsidiary *brisure* of three mullets *or* in chief. Again, the three fusils *argent* conjoined in fess, are each charged a mullet pierced *sable*, or with a *fleur-de-lis sable*, with in chief three martlets *or.* Again, the fess is of four fusils conjoined *argent*, with in chief three martlets *argent*, or three estoiles *or.* (*See* also Fig. 92, p. 600.)

On the other side of the Channel we find from MORICE (*Histoire de Bretagne*, lxv. and ccxliv.), RAOUL D'AUBIGNÉ bearing : *Gules, four lozenges conjoined in fess argent ;* and, in 1200, GUILLAUME D'AUBIGNÉ bears the same between six plates.

III.—The next mode of Difference is by the introduction into the upper part of the shield of the figure known as the LABEL (from *lambeau*, a strip, or shred). In the earliest times it was called a *file*, a name which PLANCHÉ connects with *filiation*. The Label is a narrow horizontal bar, or strip, placed across the upper part of the shield, and having dependent from it at right angles other strips, usually three or five, but sometimes four in mumber. This label is in England considered to be the *brisure* of the *eldest son* (except in the case of Royal Princes), but in olden times its use was not so limited ; nor does it appear that any particular meaning was attached to the number of points, or to its tincture, the former varying even for the same individual, and the latter being only such as to make it conspicuous upon the shield. At Caerlaverock in 1300, the silver label of EDWARD, Prince of WALES, has five points, but in modern practice only three points are used. It seems early to have been the rule in England that the heir, and perhaps also the heir presumptive, should bear his family coat differenced by a label. Abroad, as will be shown later, instances are numerous in which the label was borne by the second son, and I doubt the existence at any time of a regular system by which the degree of filiation could be indicated. In the *Roll of Caerlaverock* the label is repeatedly referred to. Of Sir MAURICE DE BERKELEY (whose banner borne in the siege of that castle is represented on a later page) it is expressly declared that

". . . . un label de asur avoit,
Porce qe ces peres vivoit."

Sir PATRICK DUNBAR, son of the Earl of LOTHIAN (*i.e.* of MARCH), then bore arms similar to his father, with the addition of a label *azure*. On the other hand, Sir JOHN DE SEGRAVE is said to bear his deceased father's arms undifferenced, while his younger brother NICHOLAS carries them with a label *gules;* and in the case of EDMUND of HASTINGS the label is also assigned to a younger brother. Further proof of its being thus borne by cadets is furnished by the evidence in the GRAY and HASTINGS controversy in the reign of HENRY IV., from which it appeared that the younger line of the HASTINGS family had for generations differenced the paternal coat by a label of three points; and, as various knights and esquires had deposed to this label being the cognisance of the nearest heir, it was argued that the defendant's ancestors would not have borne their arms in this way, had they not been the reputed next heirs to the family of the Earl of PEMBROKE. Other instances are well known in which the label became hereditary, and an integral part of the family bearings, as in the case of the English house of COURTENAY (who improperly laid it aside in modern times): and it is still borne thus by the families of BABINGTON of Rothley; RADCLYFFE of Foxdenton; COLVILE of Duffield, etc.

JEAN DE LUXEMBURG, one of the original Knights of the Golden Fleece (No. xiii.), was Count de LIGNEY, and younger brother of PIERRE DE LUXEMBURG, Count de ST. PAUL. He died in 1440, and his arms, as given in MAURICE, p. 15 (*Argent, a lion rampant double queué gules crowned or*), are differenced by *a label azure*. Similarly JACQUES DE LUXEMBURG, Seigneur de RICHEBOURG, younger brother of LOUIS, Comte de ST. PAUL, has the same arms and difference. He was Knight of the Golden Fleece (No. lxvii.), and died 1471. CLAUDE DE NEUFCHÂTEL (*Chevalier de la Toison d'Or*, No. c.), who was second son of THIEBAUT, Seigneur de NEUFCHÂTEL, bore in his brother HENRY'S lifetime (though it may be noted that the latter had no heirs of his body) the arms of NEUFCHÂTEL (*Gules, a bend argent*), *with a label azure.*

The seals of GEOFFREY DE BRABANT, third son of Duke HENRY, are given in VRÉE (*Généalogie des Comtes de Flandres*, plates xxxiii. and xxxiv.). On the one the lion of BRABANT is debruised by a label of *three* points;

on the other the shield borne by his mounted figure, the caparisons of his charger, his *ailette*, and the shield of his counter-seal, are all consistent in bearing the label of *four* points.

In course of time the capacity of the label for differencing was extended by its points being drawn wider and charged; the charges being made to have a genealogical significance. Thus ROBERT, Comte d'ARTOIS, brother of S. LOUIS of FRANCE, bore FRANCE-ANCIENT; and, as *brisure, a label of* CASTILE; that is, of *Gules, each point charged with three castles or*, indicating his maternal descent. (*See* his seal in VRÉE, *Généalogie des Comtes de Flandre*, p. 48, where the label on his seal is of three points; on his counter-seal it is of five. See also Plate I., fig. 5.)

The Dukes of ANJOU used a label *gules, v.* p. 537. The arms of the PLANTAGENET Princes afford us many examples of this extended use of the label as indicative of descent. In the *Calais Roll* (1347) the arms of HENRY PLANTAGENET, first Duke of LANCASTER, are ENGLAND, *a label* (three, or five, points were used) of FRANCE (*See* his seal on Plate XXXVI., fig. 4). He bore the same label after his creation as Duke, upon: *Quarterly*, FRANCE-ANCIENT and ENGLAND. LIONEL, Duke of CLARENCE, third son of EDWARD III., and Earl of ULSTER in right of his wife ELIZABETH DE BURGH, bore a label of five points, charged with crosses (probably ULSTER: *Or, a cross gules*). EDMUND " *Crouchback*," after his marriage with BLANCHE D'ARTOIS, bore ENGLAND, *with a label of* FRANCE.

EDWARD, Earl of RUTLAND, eldest son of EDMUND of LANGLEY, Duke of YORK, bore: FRANCE and ENGLAND *quarterly, with a label of* CASTILE, as above described;— a label *per pale of* CASTILE *and of* LEON (that is of *Argent, charged with lions gules*, or *purpure*), is also attributed to him. His mother was ISABELLA of CASTILLE and LEON. On his seal the sail of the ship borne

SEALS. PLATE XXXV.

EXPLANATION OF FIGURES.

1. Thomas Plantagenet, K.G., Duke of Gloucester, 1395 (*Boutell*). 2. Jean, Duc de Berri, *circa* 1408 (*Demay*). 3. Jeanne de France, Duchess of Burgundy, 1316 (*Vrée*). 4. Henry of Lancaster, Earl of Derby, Hereford, etc.

as Lord High Admiral is charged with an Augmentation derived from the arms of EDWARD the CONFESSOR, impaled with his own (*see* Plate XXXIV., fig. 4, and page 474; the two labels in conjunction have an unusual appearance). This fashion had a great number of imitators among the high nobility of England. In the *Calais Roll* of 1348 occurs the shield of Sir EDWARD DE MONTAGU; *Ermine, three fusils conjoined in fess gules, with a label of three points or each bearing an eagle vert* (engraved in BOUTELL, *Heraldry, Historical and Popular*, p. 225). On the stained glass at Shrewsbury the coat of CHARLETON of POWYS bears the POWYS arms (*Or, a lion rampant gules*), with *a label vert, on each point an eagle or;* CHARLETON having originally borne *Vert, three eagles or* (*Herald and Genealogist*, vi., p. 119). The label on the first and fourth quarters of Sir JOHN BOURCHIER, K.G., Lord BERNERS in 1475, is of *gules, each point charged with three lions of* ENGLAND, his mother having been ANNE PLANTAGENET, granddaughter of EDWARD III. His brother WILLIAM, Lord FITZWARREN, similarly bears a *label of* FRANCE. The eldest brother, HENRY BOURCHIER, Earl of ESSEX, bore his paternal arms undifferenced (*Argent, a cross engrailed sable between four water budgets gules*).

ROBERT DE COURTENAY, second son of HUGH, first Earl of DEVON, by AGNES ST. JOHN, charged his *azure* label with nine of the golden mullets which appear on the chief of his mother's coat:—*Argent, on a chief gules two mullets pierced or.*

Sir JAMES AUDELE, whose mother was a daughter of WILLIAM DE LONGESPEE, bore: *Gules, fretty or, with a label azure charged on each point with a lion rampant or* for his maternal descent (*cf.* Plate XXI., fig. 12). Sir WILLIAM LOVEL whose coat was: *Barry nebuly or and gules*, differenced with a label of VALENCE: *barry of six azure and argent on each of the exterior points two martlets gules* (*vide ante*, p. 409). Sir ROBERT DE LA VACHE differenced his coat: *Gules, three lions rampant argent, with a label of* WAREEN, *chequy or and azure.* The two brothers, WILLIAM and THOMAS LATIMER, who bore: *Gules, a cross patonce or*, difference in the *Roll* of EDWARD II.—the one with a *label sable on each point three plates ;* the label of the other is *azure, each point charged with three fleurs-de-lis or.*

Perhaps the most singular label of which we have any record is that said by Mr BOUTELL, p. 229, on the authority of ASHMOLE, to have been borne both by GASTON DE FOIX, K.G., Count de LONGUEVILLE, Captal de BUCH; and by JOHN DE GRAILLY, K.G., Viscount de CHÂTILLON, Captal de BUCH (created Earl of KENDAL about 1449, though there is some doubt of the regularity of the creation). It is of *sable* with three points, each in the form of a cross, and charged with five escallops *argent.* The arms of DE GRAILLY are: *Argent, on a cross sable five escallops of the field ;* these appear in the *Salle des Croisés* at Versailles for the year 1270. Now BELTZ, in his *Memorials of the Order of the Garter*, has shown that only one Captal de BUCH belonged to the Order of the Garter, and he gives the arms of JOHN DE GRAILLY, K.G., from the *Stall Plates*, as above, without a label, and with the field *or.* BLANCHE DE FOIX, whose arms were: *Quarterly*, 1 and 4. *Or, three pallets gules* (FOIX); 2 and 3. *Or, two cows gules, belled azure* (BÉARN) married JEAN DE GRAILLY, Captal de BUCH in 1328; and if he assumed his wife's arms, he *may* have differenced by a label of GRAILLY as above; but I am not aware of there being any evidence to that effect, and humbly conclude that ASHMOLE *may* have been mistaken on this point, as he certainly is in making the arms of BÉARN: *Azure, three garbs or.*—J. W.]

[Scottish seals of the thirteenth and fourteenth centuries afford many examples of the label, the points being generally three in number, though in some exceptional instances four or five. It is borne in the great majority of cases by the eldest son in his father's lifetime, *e.g.*, on the homage seals of GEOFFREY DE MOWBRAY; and of WILLIAM, eldest son of Sir MALCOLM MURRAY, on the seal of Sir ALEXANDER, eldest son of SAER DE SETON in 1260; by Sir THOMAS ERSKINE, eldest son of Sir ROBERT in 1364, PATRICK, son and heir of Sir DAVID GRAHAM of Dundaff in 1377, JAMES, afterwards second Earl of DOUGLAS, in 1378; DAVID FLEMING, eldest son of THOMAS FLEMING of Biggar, in 1392; MATTHEW STEWART, eldest son of JOHN (recognised as) Earl of LENNOX in 1470; ALEXANDER, Lord GORDON, in lifetime of his father the Earl of HUNTLY, etc. WILLIAM RUTHVEN, Provost of PERTH, eldest son of the Master of RUTHVEN, bore a label of four points in 1503. Two instances occur of a label borne by a powerful and ambitious younger brother. One is WALTER STEWART, Earl of MENTEITH, by marriage, and younger brother of ALEXANDER, the fourth High Steward, in 1292; and we find the label again on the seal of his son ALEXANDER STEWART, Earl of MEN-TEITH. (Query—Has the latter not an additional *brisure*, effected by giving an engrailed or invecked outline to the STEWART fess chequy; or is this an attempt to combine the unknown coat of the former Earls of MENTEITH with the STEWART fess?) The other instance is ROBERT, Duke of ALBANY, younger brother of King ROBERT III., who virtually wielded the supreme power in Scotland during part of his father's and the whole of his brother's reign, and down to his own death in 1420. Before 1403 he had substituted a label for the star, or mullet, which was his original difference. JANET FENTOUN, daughter and heir-apparent of WALTER FENTOUN of Baikie, bore a label in 1448, and dropped it after her father's death. MAR-

GARET STEWART, Countess of ANGUS in her own right, bore a label, it is difficult to say on what ground, in 1366. The most unique label in the Heraldry of Scotland, is to be seen on the homage seal of WILLIAM FRASER, "son of the late Master ALEXANDER FRASER," in which there is no shield, and each point of the label is the recipient of two of the fraises belonging to his paternal coat. Of the arms of the CONGALTONS of that Ilk, the label seems always to have formed an integral part. They are: *Or, a bend gules surmounted by a label of three points azure* (sometimes placed in fess)—a coat which seems to point to their having been descendants or vassals of the VAUS family. In the late Heraldry of Scotland the label fell into general disuse; almost the only instance of its use being by the family of ABERCORN, who, without official sanction, carried a label of three points until, and even after, the extinction of the male line of the ducal house of HAMILTON. In the early Lyon Register Sir JOHN HAY, heir-presumptive to the Earldom of ERROLL (to which he afterwards succeeded) records his arms with a "file of three lambeaux" in chief for difference.— G. B.]

[In modern English usage a label has become *par excellence* the Royal Mark of Cadency. In the lifetime of his brother ARTHUR, HENRY, Duke of YORK (afterwards HENRY VIII.) bore the *label ermine*. So, during the lifetime of HENRY, Prince of WALES, Prince CHARLES STUART (afterwards King as CHARLES I.) was Duke of YORK and ALBANY, and differenced with *a label argent, on each of its points three torteaux in pale*. This label had been previously used by EDMOND of Langley, Duke of YORK (d. 1402), fifth son of EDWARD III. BOUTELL (*Heraldry, Historical and Popular*, p. 240) suggests that this charge of the *torteaux* on the label of YORK came from the arms of the WAKES of Lydel: *Or, two bars gules, in chief three torteaux;* whose heiress married

EDMOND PLANTAGENET, the youngest son of EDWARD I.; and that through his descendants the HOLLANDS it came to EDMOND (of Langley), Duke of YORK. According to HEYLYN, the same difference was used by HENRY, Duke of GLOUCESTER, third son of CHARLES I., but this appears doubtful. JAMES STUART (afterwards King as JAMES II.), followed the precedent of HENRY TUDOR, and as Duke of YORK, bore the label *ermine*.

WILLIAM STUART (called Duke of GLOUCESTER), son of Queen ANNE, bore the silver label charged on the central point with a cross of ST. GEORGE (*gules*).

The family of GEORGE III. bore the following labels of three points, all *argent*:—

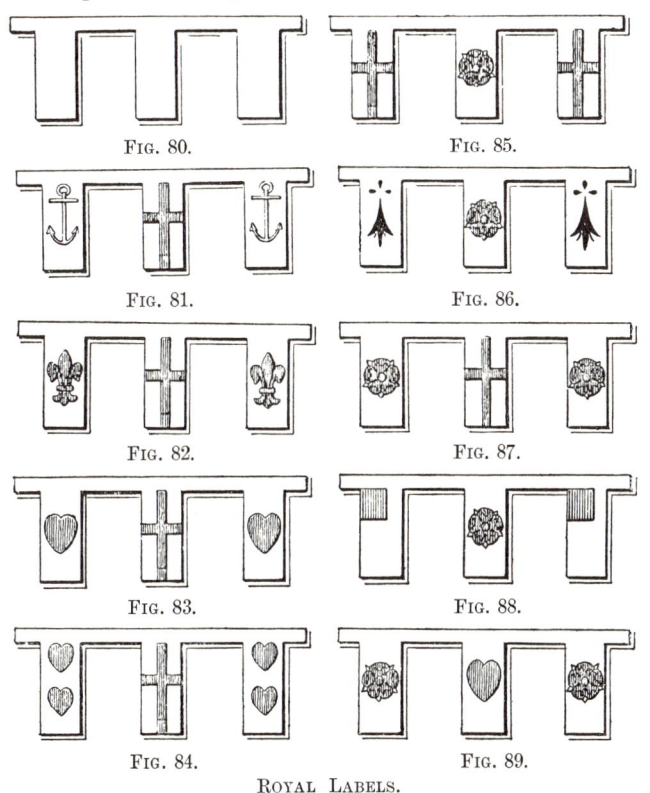

FIG. 80.

FIG. 85.

FIG. 81.

FIG. 86.

FIG. 82.

FIG. 87.

FIG. 83.

FIG. 88.

FIG. 84.

FIG. 89.

ROYAL LABELS.

The Prince of WALES, the plain label *argent* (fig. 80).

FREDERICK, Duke of YORK (as WILLIAM, Duke of GLOUCESTER) a label *argent* with the cross of ST. GEORGE on the centre point.

WILLIAM HENRY, Duke of CLARENCE, the centre point charged with the cross of ST. GEORGE, each of the others with an anchor *azure* (fig. 81).

EDWARD, Duke of KENT, on the central one the cross *gules*, on each of the others a *fleur-de-lis azure* (fig. 82).

ERNEST AUGUSTUS, Duke of CUMBERLAND, on the central point a *fleur-de-lis azure*, on each of the others a cross *gules*.

AUGUSTUS FREDERICK, Duke of SUSSEX, on the central point two hearts in pale *gules*, on each of the others a cross of ST. GEORGE.

ADOLPHUS FREDERICK, Duke of CAMBRIDGE, on the central point the cross of ST. GEORGE, on each of the others two hearts in pale *gules* (fig. 84).

The Princesses also differenced their arms with the same silver label.

CHARLOTTE, Princess Royal, on the centre point a rose of ENGLAND; on each of the others a cross of ST. GEORGE (fig. 85).

The Princess AUGUSTA, on the centre point a rose of ENGLAND; on each of the others an ermine spot *sable* (fig. 86).

The Princess ELIZABETH, on the centre point the cross of ST. GEORGE; on each of the others a rose of ENGLAND (fig. 87).

The Princess MARY, on the centre point a rose of ENGLAND; on each of the others a canton *gules* (fig. 88).

The Princess SOPHIA, on the centre point a heart *gules*; on each of the others a rose of ENGLAND (fig. 89).

The Princess AMELIA, on the centre point a rose of ENGLAND; on each of the others a heart *gules*.

Prince WILLIAM HENRY, Duke of GLOUCESTER, third son of FREDERICK, Prince of WALES, had a label of five points *argent*, on the centre a *fleur-de-lis azure*; on each of the others the cross of ST. GEORGE. This label was also borne by his son WILLIAM FREDERICK, Duke of GLOUCESTER, who during his father's lifetime placed beneath it a second and smaller label of three points *argent*.

The present Princes and Princesses of the Royal Family use for the most part the labels above given thus:—

The Prince of WALES, the silver label (fig. 80).

ALFRED, Duke of EDINBURGH, as the Duke of CLARENCE (fig. 81).

ARTHUR, Duke of CONNAUGHT, as the Duke of KENT (fig. 82).

LEOPOLD, Duke of ALBANY, and his son, on the central point a cross of ST. GEORGE; on each of the others a heart *gules* (fig. 83).

The PRINCESS ROYAL (Empress of GERMANY) (fig. 85).

The late Princess ALICE (Grand-duchess of HESSE) (fig. 86).

The Princess HELENA (of SCHLESWIG-HOLSTEIN) (fig. 87).

The Princess LOUISA (Marchioness of LORNE) (fig. 88).

The Princess BEATRICE (Princess HENRY OF BATTENBERG) (fig. 89).

The Duke of CAMBRIDGE bears his father's label (fig. 84).

On the marriage of Her Majesty the QUEEN to His late Royal Highness the PRINCE CONSORT there was made to him a grant of the Royal Arms of the United

Kingdom with the difference of *a label argent on the central point a cross of* ST. GEORGE; to be borne in the first and fourth quarters, with the arms of SAXONY in the second and third. Her Majesty the QUEEN has told us in her *Life of the Prince Consort* that she herself discovered the precedent for this arrangement (of which the then GARTER was ignorant or unmindful) in the grant made to Prince LEOPOLD of SAXE-COBOURG on the occasion of his marriage with the Princess CHARLOTTE, daughter of GEORGE IV.

In GERMANY, SPENER tells us that the use of the label though occasional, was not frequent: "Sicuti in Gallia vix alius discerniculorum modus frequentior est, ita rariora exempla reperimus in Germania," and he gives a few examples, though he is unable to assign the reason for its assumption as a hereditary bearing. (*Opus Heraldicum*, p. gen., p. 350.) Both houses of the Counts LEININGEN and DAGSBURG, and LEININGEN-WESTERBERG, charged the arms of LEININGEN (which appear in the first and fourth quarters of the shields of both lines as *Azure, three eagles displayed argent*) with a label *gules* in chief. (SPENER'S suggestion as to the possible origin of this label is in *Parte Spec.*, p. 740 of his work. His conjecture as to that which follows, the case of the BLANCKENHEIM quarter, is at p. 243 of the same part.)

In the arms of the Counts of MANDERSCHEID (who bore *Or, a fess dancetty gules;* derived from their initial M), the second quarter contains the arms of the County of BLANCKENHEIM (borne since 1443; but? 1480): *Or, a lion rampant sable over all a label of four points gules.*

In FRANCE the label was the chief recognised mode of difference. The label of ARTOIS has been already mentioned (p. 416). As the arms of the DAUPHIN were sufficiently differenced by the addition of the quarter of DAUPHINY, the silver label became the difference of the

House of ORLEANS, and continued so to be until the death of the Comte de CHAMBORD (HENRI V.) when the House of ORLEANS succeeded to the rights of the main line of FRANCE. But in FRANCE other modes of difference, hereafter to be noticed (p. 439), were adopted for the younger lines of the Royal House, and the only label which needs notice here is the sub-brisure of the Dukes of ANGOULÊME, who charged each point of the ORLEANS label with a crescent *gules*. (The later legitimated Duke of ANGOULÊME used a different brisure. *See* Chapter XVII.) The label borne in the arms of JOHN of BRAGANZA, Constable of PORTUGAL (*Chevalier de la Toison d'Or*, No. 244) is of two points only. (MAURICE, p. 276.) As to the use of this label by the line of BRAGANZA, see the *Nobiliarchia Portugueza*, cap. xxv., p. 217. The labels borne by the Princes of the Royal House were of three points, apparently of *Or*.

It should be noticed that there is no ancient precedent for the modern ugly couped label with dovetail points. The top bar should traverse the whole field.

IV.—The insertion of a CANTON was a not infrequent English and Low-Country mode of differencing. The earliest instance which has come under my notice is found in the seal of PIERRE, called MAUCLERC, son of Count ROBERT of DREUX (*c.* 1215); and husband of ALICE, Duchess of BRITTANY, who added to his paternal coat (*Chequy or and azure, a bordure gules*), *a canton ermine* for BRITTANY. At the siege of Caerlaverock, in 1300, JEAN DE BRETAGNE, Earl of RICHMOND, has this banner, but the bordure has become *a bordure of* ENGLAND, *i.e.* it is *charged with eight lions passant gardant or*, in memory of his mother, BEATRICE, daughter of HENRY III. (The ermine canton is placed *above* the bordure.) BEATRICE was the wife of JEAN DE DREUX, Duke of BRITTANY, grandson of PIERRE, whose arms are described above. It was probably from the use of the ermine canton of BRITTANY by the Earls of RICHMOND, that it came to be employed, as the early *Rolls of Arms* show us that it was, as a frequent mode of differencing in the thirteenth and fourteenth centuries. In a *Roll of Arms* of the time of HENRY III. RALPH BASSETT bears, *Or, three piles gules, a canton ermine;* this also appears in the *Calais Roll* for SIMON BASSETT; and in the Garter Plate of RALPH, Lord BASSETT, K.G. In the *Roll of the Thirteenth Century* RAUFF BASSETT bears: "*Palée d'or et de gulez in un cantele d'argent un crois patée sable;*" and in the *Roll* of RICHARD II. the canton is charged with a *griffon segreant sable.*

These are referred to by WYRLEY, *True Use of Armes*, as proofs "that diuers did adde unto the marke of their owne house, some part of the deuise of that familie from which their mothers descended," or "some parte of the deuise of him who aduanced them . . . which served veri aptlie to distinguish them from their elder house."

The arms of ZOUCHE (*Gules bezanty*); WROTTESLEY, K.G. (*Or, three piles sable*); DESPENCER (*Barry of six or and azure*); TATESHALL (*Chequy argent and gules*); and many others, are all found in our early armorial *Rolls* with the addition of a canton, or quarter, *ermine.*

In the *Calais Roll* the arms of WILLIAM DE WARREN: *Chequy or and azure*, are differenced by the addition of a canton said to be that of FITZALAN (but really that of NERFORD, *see* Chapter on ILLEGITIMACY, p. 556), *Gules, a lion rampant argent.* The use of cantons as augmentations will be spoken of later, but such augmentations were also effective differences. The use by which an heiress transmits to her children her own coat differenced by a canton charged with the arms of her husband, in the case of that husband having already heirs by a previous marriage, is a modern one; but as far back as 1590 the HARFORD arms: *Sable, two bends argent*, were charged with a canton of SCROPE: *Azure, a bend or*, and are so borne at the present day.

A considerable number of coats in Belgium and the Low Countries are at the present day differenced by the addition of a canton, or quarter, charged with another coat; I believe indicative in most cases of maternal descent. An early example is found in the *Armorial de Gueldre* in the arms of the SIRE DE LEEFEDAEL, *Or, three cinquefoils gules, a quarter of the last thereon an eagle displayed argent.* (I must again remind the student that the full coat is first blazoned as it would appear if there were no canton. In the present case although the first is absconded, or hidden by the canton, the coat is nevertheless blazoned as being charged with *three* cinquefoils.) The coat of VAN WESEL in Holland is: *Vert, three cinquefoils argent, a quarter or, thereon three pallets azure within a bordure gules.* DE WILDT of Utrecht bears: *Gules, a bend argent, a quarter azure, thereon three eagles displayed or.* SERAING of Liège, uses: *Gules, fleury or, a quarter of the arms of* BOSSUT (*ante*, p. 181): *Or, a tressure flory-counter-flory vert, over all a saltire gules.* PREUDHOMME of Liège, *Or, a bend gules, on a quarter of the last a lion rampant of the first.*

V.—Akin to this usage is the employment of a SMALL ESCUCHEON in the chief, of which we have an instance in the arms of HUGH DE BALLIOL, in the *Roll* of HENRY III.: *Gules, an orle azure, in the dexter chief a small escucheon* (of GALLOWAY); *Azure, a lion rampant argent crowned or.*

In the *Armorial de Gueldre* the arms of LE SIRE DE VILAIN, who bore: *Sable, a chief argent*, have the chief charged with a small escucheon of VAN GRIMBERGHE: *Or, a fess azure over all a saltire gules*, the composed arms of PERWEYS and AA (*see* MENÊTRIER, *Recherches du Blason*, p. 167). The DE BALYS of Bruges, who use:

Argent, a lion rampant gules, place on the shoulder of the lion a small escucheon of *Or, three crescents gules*. The VAN OUDENHAGEN of Brabant carry: *Or, on a bend sable three mallets argent, and in dexter chief a small escucheon of the arms of* CLUTINCK; *Azure, three fleurs-de-lis argent, au pied coupé*. The VAN RIEUWE of Brussels use: *Or, a chief gules, in the dexter chief a small escucheon; Or, two bars sable*.

The addition of an escucheon *en surtout* containing the maternal arms was carried to a considerable extent in the Low Countries, and several examples will be found later in this chapter (Section XIV., p. 448).

VI.—DIFFERENCING BY THE ADDITION OF AN ORDINARY.—This mode of differencing occurs continually in the early *Rolls of Arms*. At Caerlaverock HENRY of Lancaster, brother and successor of THOMAS, Earl of LANCASTER,

" Portait les armes son frere,
Au beau bastoun sans label,"

i.e., he bore the Royal arms, differenced by a bendlet *azure*. The original GREY coat: *Barry of six argent and azure* is differenced in the *Roll* of EDWARD I. by a bend *gules* for JOHN DE GREY, at Caerlaverock this is engrailed. The GRANDISONS used: *Paly of six argent and azure*, over which is first placed a *bend gules*, and the process of differencing is carried on by charging this bend with escallops, eagles, or buckles, *or* (*see* p. 437).

The SEGRAVE coat: *Sable, a lion rampant argent*, is differenced by the addition of *a bendlet or;* or *a bendlet gules;* and the last is again differenced by engrailing it. The CLIFFORD coat (*Chequy or and azure a bend gules*) is differenced at Caerlaverock by the substitution of a fess for the bend; and later both bend and fess have sub-brisures of cinquefoils, or lions, *argent*. Of this common early mode of difference it is not needful to multiply examples from English Armory.

A bend (*gules*) was the *brisure* of FLANDERS borne by the Counts of NAMUR (*vide* Plate XLIV., fig. 2, from the *Armorial de Gelre*); and other instances of its use are found in VRÉE, *Généalogie des Comtes de Flandre*. It is borne plain by FLORENT of Hainault, and by PHILIP of Flanders (both *circa* 1300). GUILLAUME DE FLANDRE, Seigneur de RICHEBOURG (*c*. 1290) bore the bend *goboné argent and gules*; as did his son JEAN (*c*. 1320). The bend is *raguly* in the case of GUI DE FLANDRE (*c*. 1335). HENRI DE FLANDRE, Comte de LODES, also used the bend *goboné* (*c*. 1320). About the same time ROBERT DE NAMUR makes his bend *wavy* (Plates LXX., LXXI., LXXII., LXXXVI.).

The *brisure* of the Ducs de BOURBON was a bend, or cotice, *gules*. The Ducs de MONTPENSIER differenced this by charging the upper portion with the arms of DAUPHINE (*Or, a dauphin azure*). By the Princes de CONDÉ the bendlet was diminished into *a baton alesé in bend* (the Princes de CONTI added to this a *bordure gules*). The Comtes d'ETAMPES bore: FRANCE-ANCIENT, *a bend componé gules and ermine*; and those of EVREUX had the *bend componé argent and gules*. The BOURBON Princes de la ROCHE SUR YON used: FRANCE-MODERN, *a cotice in bend gules thereon a crescent argent in chief*. The Princes of ACHAIA, of the House of SAVOY, added *a bend azure* to the arms, *Gules, a cross argent*.

With regard to Scottish Differences of this kind the excellent volumes of *Scottish Seals*, published by Mr H. LAING, give us a storehouse of contemporary examples; and much of the following is derived therefrom.

An early instance in Scotland of a bend used for differencing is in the seal of Sir JOHN STEWART, younger son of ALEXANDER, fourth High Steward, and husband of the heiress of Bonkil; who, in 1296, debruises his fess checquy with a bend. ALEXANDER SETON, in his seal appended to the letter by the Scots barons to the Pope in 1320, not only introduces a bend, but places the three crescents of his paternal coat on that bend. EDWARD KEITH, in his seal attached to the same letter, surmounts his paternal coat—*a chief paly of six*—with a bend; the same difference being afterwards used by JOHN, second son of Sir EDWARD KEITH, Marischal. In 1358, WILLIAM RAMSAY, Earl of FIFE by marriage, surmounts his Ramsay eagle with a bendlet engrailed; and a bend charged with three crescents debruises the eagle in the seal of RAMSAY of Dunoon. In 1368 JOHN HAY, of Tillibothil, seals with his paternal coat surmounted by a bend indented. The GORDONS of Lochinvar, in the time of Sir DAVID LINDSAY, and probably earlier, differenced the GORDON coat with a bend *or* placed between the three boar's heads. The seal of JAMES FRASER of Ferendrach, in 1402, shows a bend-sinister indented between three fraises; and in 1499 JOHN OGILVIE, Sheriff-depute of INVERNESS, has also a bend-sinister with the lion passant of his family in base.

MALCOLM SUTHERLAND in 1476 has a fess between his paternal three stars; and JOHN RATTRAY, Bailie of Aberdeen, has his coat similarly differenced in 1504. On the seal of the first ALEXANDER DUNBAR of Westfield, in 1488, a fess is placed between the three cushions, and, contrary to the general usage, surmounts the Royal Tressure. Sir JOHN FOULIS of Ravelston, *c.* 1672, has a fess *vert* charged with a primrose *or* between the three laurel leaves of his paternal coat; a difference allusive to the circumstance that his wife was eldest daughter of Sir ARCHIBALD PRIMROSE, who settled his estate of Dunipace on her sons. Other examples occur about the same time of a fess, sometimes charged, being used in this way, *e.g.*, HAMILTON of Cairnes, who adds to the principal HAMILTON coat a fess *argent* charged with a man's heart *gules*. The coat of the COCKBURNS of

Ormiston has already been alluded to. We find the fess checquy also used as a difference in later times, and with genealogical intent. The GORDONS of Lesmoir have, since 1672, if not earlier, borne *a fess checquy azure and argent between three boar's heads or*, in consequence of the first Laird of Lesmoir having in the sixteenth century married a daughter of STEWART of Laithers; and FORBES of Echt (the older family) bore *a fess checquy argent and gules* between their three bear's heads.

The arms assigned at the same date to Sir JOHN FALCONER of Balmakellie, Master of the Mint to CHARLES II., were those of his brother the first Lord FALCONER (*Or, between three mullets azure, a falcon's head proper issuing from a man's heart gules and crowned*), with the addition of *a chief gules charged with three besants* allusive to his office.

But, with the exception of the bordure, no Ordinary has been so much in use in Scotland for differencing purposes as the chevron. WILLIAM MURRAY, of Gask and Tullibardine, has a chevron between the three stars of his paternal coat in his homage seal of 1292; and this chevron continued to be borne by his descendants until they obtained the royal tressure in the reign of JAMES VI. The shields of JOHN GRAHAM in 1370; THOMAS MONYPENNY of Kinkell, in 1415; and ALEXANDER RATTRAY, in 1628; all have a chevron introduced into their paternal coat. The HAYS of Fudie bore a chevron *sable* between their three escutcheons from an early period; and the Lyon Register is full of more modern instances. Thus FORBES of Monymusk places between his three bear's heads a chevron *argent* charged with a heart *proper* (the heart indicative of a maternal DOUGLAS descent). In like manner OLIPHANT of Bachilton places a chevron *argent* between his three crescents. Another cadet of the OLIPHANT family, OLIPHANT of Prinlis, alters the arrangement of the coat more materially by placing a saltire engrailed *argent* between his three crescents, and arranging them one in chief and two in flank. There are also cases where one Ordinary is substituted for another. The LESLIES of Balquhain differenced the chief coat of their family, *Argent, on a bend azure three buckles or*, by turning the bend into a fess. A very early cadet of the GRAHAM family, GRAHAM of Morphie, adopted an unusually pronounced difference, substituting a chevron for the chief, and at the same time changing the tinctures. The principal GRAHAM coat is : *Or, on a chief sable three escallops of the field;* that of Morphie : *Sable, a chevron between three escallops argent.* Different branches of the PRINGLE family, retaining the escallops which are the principal charge, turn the bend on which they are placed into a chevron and a saltire respectively. (Differencing by the addition of a bordure will be treated separately, p. 437.)

VII.—CHANGING THE BOUNDARY LINE OF AN ORDINARY, by *engrailing, invecking*, or *indenting*, is a frequent expedient in Scotland, both in earlier and in later times. The MACFARLANES, who descend from the LENNOX family, bear the coat of LENNOX, *Argent, a saltire cantoned with four roses gules* (as in Plate XXX., fig. 3), but difference it by making the saltire *wavy;* while the NAPIERS of Merchiston (believed to be LENNOXES by descent) engrail the saltire. In 1370 the seal of Sir NICHOLAS ERSKINE of Kinnoull, second son of Sir ROBERT ERSKINE, shows the pale of his paternal coat engrailed. Allusion has been made above to some of the various ways in which the original PRINGLE coat, *Argent, on a bend sable three escallops or*, has been differenced. The PRINGLES of Smailhome difference it in a less pronounced manner by engrailing the bend. On the seal of PATRICK GRAHAM, Earl of STRATHERN, *jure uxoris* in 1400, the chief is *indented*, and it is either *indented* or *engrailed* on the seal of ROBERT GRAHAM of Kinpunt in 1433, and of ROBERT GRAHAM of Fintry in 1478. At a later date the indentations in the Fintry coat were made deeper, and have been blazoned as piles, and erroneously supposed to have been adopted from the family of LOVEL of Ballumbie, whose heiress the first Sir ROBERT GRAHAM of Fintry married. Doubtless the piles in the coat of DOUGLAS of Lochleven (*Argent, three piles gules, the exterior ones charged with a star of the field*) had the same origin; the seal of Sir HENRY DOUGLAS of Lugton in 1329 has what seems to be an indented chief.—J. W.]

[In the Lyon Register in the time of Sir CHARLES and Sir ALEXANDER ERSKINE the examples of this mode of differencing are very numerous. So far as any general rule of practice can be discovered, the use was to have the Ordinary engrailed for a second son or his descendant, invecked for a third, wavy for a fourth, indented or nebuly for a fifth. But the usage varied a little, and there was a tendency to embattle the Ordinary in the case of a military man, while Sir WILLIAM BRUCE of Balcaskie, known for his skill in navigation, has his chief wavy. As examples of the general rule, the chief engrailed is borne by Sir WILLIAM GRAHAM of Braco, Baronet, "descended of a second son of Montrose;" the chevron engrailed by WALTER RIDDELL, ancestor of the Glenriddell family, and second son of RIDDELL of that Ilk, and by ABERCROMBY of Fetternear, the first of which line was second son of ABERCROMBY of Birkenbog. JAMES DURHAM, second son of the family of DURHAM of Grange, engrails the fess of his family coat, and the bend is carried engrailed by the ELIOTTS of Stobs, "descended from a second son of LAURISTON." The older RUTHERFORDS of Fairnington engrailed their orle. Examples of the chief, chevron, bend, orle, and pile being invecked, wavy, indented, and nebuly for cadets, seem to indicate an attempt to make these differences correspond with third, fourth, fifth, and sixth sons respectively, and their descendants ; though the difficulty of ascertaining the date of the extinction of intermediate lines makes the intention not always so obvious as in the case of the engrailed Ordinary. The engrailed cross of the SINCLAIRS is in one instance differenced by being engrailed on the outer side and invecked on the inner.—G. B.]

[Of the alteration of the boundary line of an Ordinary as a mode of difference we have examples in foreign coats. The French families DE LA FOREST (Marquises d'ARMAILLÉ, and Barons de CRAON) bear: *Argent, a chief sable;* while the line of FOREST-LANDRY in Flanders engrails the chief. (The FORESTEL of Cambray bear *Argent, a chief gules.*) The senior branch of the French house of LA BAUME bore *Or, a bend azure* but the younger line, Comtes de MONTREVEL, bore the bend *dancetty;* while the Marquises de PLUVINEL still further difference the MONTREVEL coat by adding an ermine spot in the sinister chief *sable.*

VIII.—DIMINISHING THE NUMBER OF CHARGES of the same kind is an expedient for differencing seldom if ever practised in Great Britain, but one of which there are examples in Foreign Heraldry. The Counts of BARCELONA bore: *Gules, four pales or;* the house of FOIX which descended from them, diminished the pales, or pallets, to three. While the house of CHOISEUL, Ducs de CHOISEUL, bore *Azure, a cross between twenty billets or,* five in each canton ; the junior line of the Ducs de PRASLIN diminished the number of the billets to eighteen, five in each of the cantons in chief, but only four in those in base. These are exceptions to the old French armorial rule which declares that the elder line is known by the simplicity of the coat: " *Qui porte le moins est le plus.*"—J. W.]

IX. CHANGE OF THE MINOR CHARGES.—[Differencing

by the substitution of one charge for another is more a Scottish than an English usage. In 1476 the seal of THOMAS CUMYN of Altyre has one garb only in place of the three of his family; the two uppermost garbs being replaced by two cushions, and a tressure superadded. The mother of this THOMAS CUMYN was a sister of THOMAS DUNBAR, Earl of Moray: and the arms in fact are much more a DUNBAR, or MORAY, than a CUMYN coat. In 1513 WILLIAM SCOTT, constable-depute of Montrose, replaces the third of the three lion's heads, which formed his family coat, by a rose, suggestive of Montrose, and so with obvious reference to his office. In 1515 we find PATRICK HEPBURN, Earl of BOTHWELL, Great Admiral of Scotland (an infant of four years old, but who entered on possession of his estates and office at once, as did the heirs of all whose ancestors had fallen at Flodden), adding an anchor in base to the HEPBURN coat; and the same was borne by PATRICK HEPBURN, of Bolton, in 1545.

In the early Lyon Register there are about 160 coats in which one or more additional charges have been introduced to difference cadets from their chief. A few examples will suffice. While Lord GRAY bears: *Gules, a lion rampant within a bordure engrailed argent*, GRAY of Ballengarno places an anchor *or*, and GRAY of Haystoun, a writing-pen *proper* in the lion's dexter fore-paw. In a coat consisting of the same charge three times repeated, the difference is usually placed in the centre. Thus GRANT of Ballindalloch, places a boar's head *couped or*, and GRANT of Carron, a dove *argent* holding in her beak an olive branch *vert*, between the three antique crowns which are the arms of their chief. GORDON of Knokespock places a pheon *or*; GORDON of Glasterim a fraise *argent;* GORDON of Earlston a bezant; GORDON of Newark a billet *or;* and GORDON of Tetschie a sheaf of arrows *or*, between the *three boar's heads or, on a field azure*, of the original coat. The SEMPILL coat being: *Argent, a chevron checquy gules and of the field between three hunting-horns sable garnished of the second* (Plate XIII., No. 2), the Beltrees branch (whose founder, a younger son of Lord SEMPILL, married MARY LIVINGSTONE, one of the "Queen's Maries") added three gilliflowers *gules* (from the LIVINGSTONE coat) for difference. The well known coat of DRUMMOND, *Or, three bars wavy gules* (Plate XV., No. 10), is to a certain extent differenced in the same way. The DRUMMONDS of Colquhalzie add three stars in chief; those of BLAIR charge each of the bars with an escallop; and another DRUMMOND, descended from the Kildees branch of the Pitkellony family, has a singular difference, over all a naked man naiant in pale grasping in his dexter hand a sword, and having his sinister hand and feet in action all proper. In the majority of the instances given the difference indicated maternal descent, being often taken from the coat of the family of the wife of the first of the line. When the coat differenced has an Ordinary, a maternal charge of this kind, or an emblem of office or profession, is often found placed on that Ordinary. The chevron on the coat of the Earl of HOPETOUN is charged with a laurel leaf to indicate the descent of his branch of the HOPE family from the heiress of FOULIS of Leadhills. Colonel WALTER WHITEFORD, whose father was a younger son of the house of Miltoun, charges the bend of his paternal coat with three crosses patée "added at his Majestie's speciall command." GEORGE JARDINE has the saltire of his coat charged with three besants, as having been Treasurer of the City of Edinburgh. Sir JOHN AYTOUN of Keppo places his official baton as Usher of the Black Rod on the engrailed cross of his coat. NAPIER of Culcreuch, descended from a third son, charges his saltire with five mullets *argent*. PATERSON of Seafield, second son of the Bishop of ROSS, replaces one of the three mullets in the chief of his paternal coat by a mitre, while the fourth son of the same prelate introduces a mitre *azure* between the three pelicans in the same coat.—G. B.]

[Although before the Reformation it was not compulsory upon ecclesiastics, who were vowed to celibacy, to difference their arms, we yet find that as a matter of fact many did so. Thus Bishop JOHN DE GRANDISON, of EXETER (1327—1369), substitutes a silver mitre for the one of the golden buckles upon the bend in his ancestral coat (*vide ante*, p. 428); WILLIAM COURTENAY, Archbishop of CANTERBURY, 1381—1396, whose arms were *Or, three torteaux and a label azure,* charged each point of his label with a *mitre proper*. (BEDFORD, *Blason of Episcopacy*, p. 44.) Bishop EDMOND STAFFORD of EXETER, 1394—1419, differences his paternal coat *Or, a chevron gules* with a *bordure azure, thereon eight mitres argent;* a still better known example is that of the warlike HENRY LE DESPENSER, Bishop of NORWICH (1370—1406), who differenced the full DESPENSER coat with a *bordure charged with mitres* (eight or fifteen) *or*.

X. DIFFERENCING BY A BORDURE was in former times practised largely in all the western countries; and in Scotland it has always been a prevalent mode of indicating cadency. The simple bordure is, down to the present day, the most usual *difference* for a younger brother or direct cadet. (But *see* pp. 170-174.)

The bordure has great advantages over other modes of differencing since it leaves the original arms intact, and when methodically employed points out as no other difference can do the exact position held in the family by the cadet who bears it. Moreover it admits of being varied for sub-cadets, and of being charged with sub-brisures taken from a maternal coat when there is no right to quarter the entire arms. When a quartered escucheon has to be differenced the bordure added surrounds the entire quartered coat as if it were a simple one. The *Roll of Caerlaverock* shows that this mode of differencing was in operation in England in the reign of EDWARD I. (1300), and we have already noticed one example therefrom in the case of JOHN, Earl of RICHMOND (*ante*, p. 425). HUGH DE VERE, a cadet of the family of the Earl of OXFORD, also differences the coat given on Plate IX., No. 2, p. 410, with *a bordure indented sable*. In GLOVER'S *Roll temp.* HENRY III. the coat of JOHN FITZ-GEOFFREY : *Quarterly or and gules* has a *bordure vair;* and that of WILLIAM DAUBENY DE BEAUVOIR : *Or, two chevrons gules*, has also a bordure of the last ; and so forth.

A number of the PLANTAGENET princes differenced with the bordure. JOHN of ELTHAM, Earl of CORNWALL, second son of EDWARD II., bore the arms of ENGLAND *within a bordure of* FRANCE, derived from his mother ISABEL. THOMAS, of WOODSTOCK, the youngest son of EDWARD III., differenced his father's arms with *a bordure argent* though his elder brothers all used the label. The BEAUFORTS, descendants of JOHN of GAUNT by KATHARINE SWYNFORD, were legitimated in 1397, and from that time bore the quartered arms of FRANCE and ENGLAND within a *bordure compony* of the Lancastrian colours : *Argent and azure*, or of *azure and ermine*. From this circumstance the *bordure gobony* (though borne before this time by legitimate cadets, and not used by the BEAUFORTS until *after* their legitimation) carried with it ever afterwards in England a *soupçon* of illegitimacy, which was confirmed by its later use (*see* p. 443 ; and Chapter XVII.). Abroad it was always a difference of legitimate cadets (*e.g.*, BURGUNDY-MODERN, next page). THOMAS HOLLAND, K.G., Earl of KENT, son of Sir THOMAS HOLLAND by JOAN PLANTAGENET, *the fair maid of Kent* (who afterwards married the Black Prince), was permitted by his half-brother RICHARD II. to bear the arms of ENGLAND *with a bordure argent;* the other brother, JOHN, Duke of EXETER, bore : ENGLAND, *within a bordure of* FRANCE. The TUDOR bordure was of *Azure, charged alternately with fleurs-de-lys and martlets or,* the former derived from the HOLLANDS, the latter from the BEAUCHAMPS of Bletsho. Many English families differenced with the bordure (*e.g.*, the MONTAGUS, and STAFFORDS). One of the points decided in the SCROPE and GROSVENOR case (1390) was that a bordure is not a sufficient difference between strangers in blood, but only between the chief and a cadet of the same family. In modern English practice the bordure as a difference for cadets only continues to be used by those whose ancestors bore it in ancient times. Its other use as a modern mark of illegitimacy is treated in a separate chapter.

In the ROYAL CADENCY OF FRANCE the Dukes of ANJOU bore : FRANCE, within a *bordure gules,* the Dukes of BERRI, FRANCE, with a *bordure engrailed gules ;* the Dukes of ALENÇON, FRANCE, with a *bordure gules charged with eight plates ;* the Dukes of BURGUNDY of the younger line, FRANCE, within a *bordure gobony argent and gules* (Plate XLIV., fig. 6).

The following examples taken from the seals in VRÉE, (*Généalogie des Comtes de Flandres*), show us that the bordure engrailed was frequently used as a difference. MATHIEU DE LORRAINE thus differences in 1323. YOLANTE, Comtesse de NEVERS, bears BURGUNDY-ANCIENT with a *bordure engrailed, circa* 1290 ; BALDWIN, younger son of the Count of FLANDERS, *c.* 1290, FLANDERS *a bordure* (or rather a *filet*) *engrailed ;* ROBERT, younger son of ROBERT DE BETHUNE, Count of FLANDERS, *c.* 1306, the same, etc. The same bordure was used by the LANNOYS, *vide infra.* ANTOINE DE VERGY (Chevalier de la Toison d'Or, No. 5) differences his arms: *Gules, three cinquefoils or with a plain bordure argent.* JEAN DE LA CLITE, Seigneur de COMMINES (Chevalier de la Toison d'Or, No. 8) adds a bordure *or* to the family coat: *Gules, a chevron or between three escallops argent.* (This was the coat borne by PHILIPPE DE COMMINES, the chronicler; therefore correct STODART, *Scottish Arms,* vol. ii., p. 29.)

In Germany of old the use of the bordure as a difference does not appear to have been very frequent. SPENER gives only one example. The families of FLEHINGEN and SICKINGEN both bore: *Sable, five plates in saltire;* and the latter differenced by a *bordure gules* (SIEBMACHER, *Wappenbuch,* i., 118, 122). In the *Wappenrolle von Zürich,* plate ii., 36 shows us the NÜRENBURG coat: *Quarterly argent and sable, with a bordure gules.* SWANDEG (iii., 65), bears: *Argent, an ibex sable, a bordure or;* LOUBGASSEN (v., 97), *Or, six linden leaves vert, a bordure gules;* BONSTETTEN (xvii., 391), *Sable, three lozenges conjoined in fess, a bordure argent;* and about a half dozen other examples are recorded in it.

In the Armory of the Peninsula, although marks of cadency, in our restricted sense of the word, are almost unknown, the bordure, especially as indicating descent from a maternal ancestor, is very largely employed. The most familiar instance is afforded by the Royal Arms of PORTUGAL, in which the arms of PORTUGAL are surrounded by *a bordure of* CASTILE. The arms of the family of CUEVA, Dukes of ALBUQUERQUE, are *Tierced in mantel:* 1 and 2, *Or, a pale gules;* 3, *Vert, a dragon or.* The whole *within a bordure gules charged alternately with seven aspas (i.e.* saltires couped) *and as many escucheons of* MENDOZA (*v. ante,* p. 395; and Plate XXXIII., fig. 12). These last relate to the marriage of MENCIA MENDOZA, daughter of the Duke of INFANTADGO, with BELTRAN, first Duke of ALBUQUERQUE (CHIFFLET, *Arm. Gent. Equit. Aurei Velleris,*

No. 170; and MAURICE, p. 196). The arms of the GIRONS, Dukes of OSSUNA, have been blazoned on page 168, *ante*. In them it is doubtful whether the arms of CASTILE and LEON in chief have been assumed to commemorate an alliance with the Royal House; or whether they are simply Coats of Augmentation; but SPENER (*Op. Her.*, p. spec., p. 130) is decidedly of opinion that the Portuguese escucheons commemorate such an alliance. It will be obvious that these are rather instances of MARSHALLING than of CADENCY proper, and I accordingly refer the reader to the following chapter for other instances of this use. But, besides these bordures charged with entire escucheons, Spanish bordures are frequently found bearing charges derived from those in the coats of maternal progenitors.— J. W.]

[The bordures to be found in the earliest Scottish seals are to so large an extent engrailed as to make it appear that the later·rule to give the plain bordure to immediate cadets was not fully recognised. On the seal of Sir ALEXANDER FRASER appended to the letter of the barons to the Pope (1320) the bordure seems to be engrailed. The seal of ROGER FAUSYDE, in 1326, has—a crane passant within a bordure engrailed. PATRICK HEPBURN, in his seal appended to the Act regarding the succession to the crown, in 1371, has HEPBURN within a bordure engrailed. The bordure engrailed was also borne by DOUGLAS of Drumlanrig, who was of illegitimate descent; by the STEWARTS, Earls of LENNOX (Plate XLII., fig. 1); HAY of Naughton; OLIPHANT of Kelly, etc. WALTER STEWART, son by the second marriage of ROBERT II., bore in 1389 the arms of SCOTLAND within a bordure checquy. HAY of Tillibothil bore his arms in 1370 (according to Sir JAMES BALFOUR) within a bordure checquy: and in 1508 the seal of ROBERT MAXWELL surrounds his MAXWELL coat with a bordure counter-compony, quartering it with DENNISTON.

Bordures-compony were in early times borne by legitimate cadets, as by WALLACE of Ellerslie, and HAMILTON of Preston. Bordures charged appear at a comparatively early date. The seal of Sir ANDREW MURRAY, WALLACE'S companion-in-arms, has a bordure charged with eleven roses, or cinquefoils; and another Sir ANDREW MURRAY, who signs the contract regarding the ransom of DAVID II., has a bordure charged with what seems to be roundles. On the seal of HUGH FRASER in 1377 are three fraises within a bordure charged with nine stars; and HUGH ROSS of Rarichies, second son of HUGH, Earl of ROSS, has on his seal of 1351 a bordure charged with eleven escallops (? ermine spots). The bordure charged with eight roses of the Earls of DUNBAR and MARCH, which occurs as early as 1291, is of course not a difference of filiation (*See* Plate XVII., fig. 3); but in 1452 Sir DAVID DUNBAR of Cockburn, a younger son, differenced his paternal coat by substituting mullets for the roses. The STEWARTS of Rosyth, rejecting the bend borne by most of the descendants of Sir JOHN (husband of the heiress of Bonkyl) placed the Bonkyl buckles on a bordure.

In the Lyon Register differencing by a bordure prevails largely, and is carried out somewhat more systematically than in earlier heraldry. As a general rule a plain bordure, of the tincture of the first charge, indicates that the bearer of it is the first cadet of his house: where a bordure of a different colour occurs, it is equally the rule that the cadet is not so; and the cadets of the original bearer of the bordure are to a great extent differenced by engrailing, invecking, etc., the bordure, as described in the case of other Ordinaries. Sub-cadets are also differenced by charging the bordure with figures, generally from some maternal coat, a sort of cadency especially in use in the case of bordures, which had been already differenced by being engrailed or invecked. Again, the bordure may be quartered, or parted per pale, or per fess; expedients resorted to where there are many prior cadets of former generations. HAMILTON of Presmennan, in the Lyon Register, bears the HAMILTON coat within a bordure quarterly of *vair*, and of counter-compony *argent* and *gules;* and HAMILTON of Neilsland has a bordure quarterly *argent* and *azure*, the first and fourth engrailed, and the second and third invecked. The doubtful legitimacy of the Avondale and Ochiltree STEWARTS, who bore the bordure-compony in Scotland, along with its use by the BEAUFORTS in England, tended latterly to bring that difference into disrepute in the cadency of lawful sons—yet some of the bearers of that bordure during the first twenty years of the Lyon Register were unquestionably legitimate, while others, as SCOTT of Gorrenberry and PATRICK SINCLAIR of Ulbster, were illegitimate, or at best only legitimated. The light in which the bordure-compony had come to be regarded is shown by a *Royal Warrant* granted in 1679 to JOHN LUNDIN of that ILK, allowing him to drop the coat which his family had hitherto carried, and, as descended of a natural son of WILLIAM THE LION, to bear the arms of SCOTLAND within a bordure-compony *argent* and *azure*. The bordure counter-compony is assigned to fifteen persons, none of them, it is believed, of illegitimate descent, and some expressly said to be "lineallie and lawfulie descended" from the ancestor whose arms they bore thus differenced. The idea of this bordure having been at any time a mark of bastardy is a very modern error, arising from a confusion with the bordure-compony. Of the bordure-checquy there are twenty examples during the first twenty years of the Lyon Register.—G. B.]

[The late Mr STODART, Lyon Clerk Depute, who was

an able herald, particularly in matters relating to Scotland, had elaborated a system of differencing by the bordure which would have done much to simplify Scottish cadency. Its weak point was obviously this: that it could only be applied to new matriculations of arms by cadets; and so, if adopted, might have occasioned doubt and misunderstanding in future times with regard to many important Scottish coats now existing, which are differenced with bordures assumed, or granted, without reference to Mr STODART'S system. It is, however, clear from LYON'S remarks that he had adopted the main features of the system; or at least had allowed Mr STODART to act upon it to a considerable extent in new matriculations.

XI. Reference has already been made to the present unsatisfactory use of what are known as the *Marks of Cadency*, which were intended to indicate the order of descent of the different sons of a family. It has been shown (pp. 410-412), that the occasional use of some of these began pretty early both at home and abroad; but it was only in the reigns of the Tudor Sovereigns that they became systematised in English Heraldry. They are practically the only differences employed to denote legitimate cadency by the English College of Arms. They are:—1. A Label for the eldest son; 2. A Crescent for the second; 3. A Mullet for the third; 4. A Martlet for the fourth; 5. An Annulet for the fifth son; 6. A *Fleur-de-lis* for the sixth; 7. A Rose for the seventh; 8. A Cross moline for the eighth; and 9. A Double Quatrefoil for the ninth, which is the *ne plus ultra* of provision. Of these the first six are given in BOSSEWELL'S *Workes of Armorie* (1572), and the author adds: "if there be any more than six brethren the devise or assignment of further difference only appertaineth to the kingis of armes especially when they visite their severall provinces; and not to the father of the children to give them what difference he list, as some without authoritie doe allege."

On Scottish seals of the fourteenth and fifteenth centuries the mullet is more frequently found than any of the other marks of cadency, but it is evidently not regarded as peculiarly appropriated to the third son. Before 1300, Sir DONALD of MAR (son and heir of GRATNEY, Earl of MAR, by the sister of ROBERT BRUCE), bore a mullet of six points in the upper part of the bend upon his seal (LAING, *Scottish Seals*, ii., No. 690). In 1373 it appears in dexter chief on the seal of ROBERT STEWART, Earl of FIFE (afterwards Duke of ALBANY), second son of ROBERT II. (*Ibid.*, i., 786), and from the beginning of the fifteenth century it is fairly common. Similarly there are examples, though fewer, of other marks.—J. W.]

[In 1672, when the Lyon Register was instituted, the import of the English marks of cadency was quite recognised, and during the twenty years following, they are to a limited extent made use of. The crescent is assigned to sixty-eight cadets, who in most instances are specifically described as second sons or descendants of second sons. The mullet in the same way is given thirty-five times to a third son or his representative, the martlet appears eleven times, the annulet six times, the *fleur-de-lis* six times, the rose ten times, and the cross moline twice. There are a very few instances of double marks of cadency, such as a crescent charged with another, or with a mullet.—G. B.]

[As was remarked at the outset of this Chapter the results of this mode of differencing have been far from satisfactory. The main consequence of the practical supersession of all other differences by these minute figures has been that the duty of differencing at all has been much neglected, and remote cadets bear the arms of the head of the house without an idea of impropriety. There are, however, some cases where these differences awarded at a time when they were coming into use, have become permanent in particular branches of the family, and where more than one has been elevated to the peerage we see the differences in use, *e.g.* the crescents in the coats of the Marquess of SALISBURY and Earl STANHOPE; the mullet used by the Earl of CARLISLE, the red rose in the arms of the Earl of ABERGAVENNY. Sir WILLIAM DUGDALE in his *Antient Usage of Bearing Arms* condemns the system strongly; and advises a return to the older and better methods of differencing; and, although in Scotland this usage never superseded these better modes, Sir GEORGE MACKENZIE regrets its partial introduction, and denounces the Marks of Cadency as tending to confound the ancient coats, and to fill the modern with more crescents and mullets than are in the arms of all Europe besides.

XII. DIFFERENCE BY QUARTERING.—MENÊTRIER lays down that the bearing by a cadet of a quartering not borne by the elder line is in itself a sufficient difference; and this rule has been recognised in Scotland. When a younger son of a great house became possessed of a feudal lordship by marriage, or by a grant from the crown he not unfrequently retained the simple coat of his ancestors, and quartered with it the arms of his new possession. Thus ALEXANDER, Duke of ALBANY, son of JAMES II., bore the undifferenced coat of SCOTLAND, quartered with the arms of MARCH, MAN, and ANNANDALE (*see* Plate XXXVI., which is reduced from MICHEL'S *Les Ecossais en France*, etc.). The STEWARTS, Earls of ATHOLE, and of BUCHAN, found the feudal quarterings of these Earldoms a sufficient difference. In later times we find the Lords PITSLIGO bearing the undifferenced coat of FORBES quartered with FRASER; FORBES of Tolquhoun bearing the same coat quartered with PRESTON; and FORBES of Rires bearing WEMYSS in the first and fourth quarters, and the undifferenced coat

PLATE XXXVI.

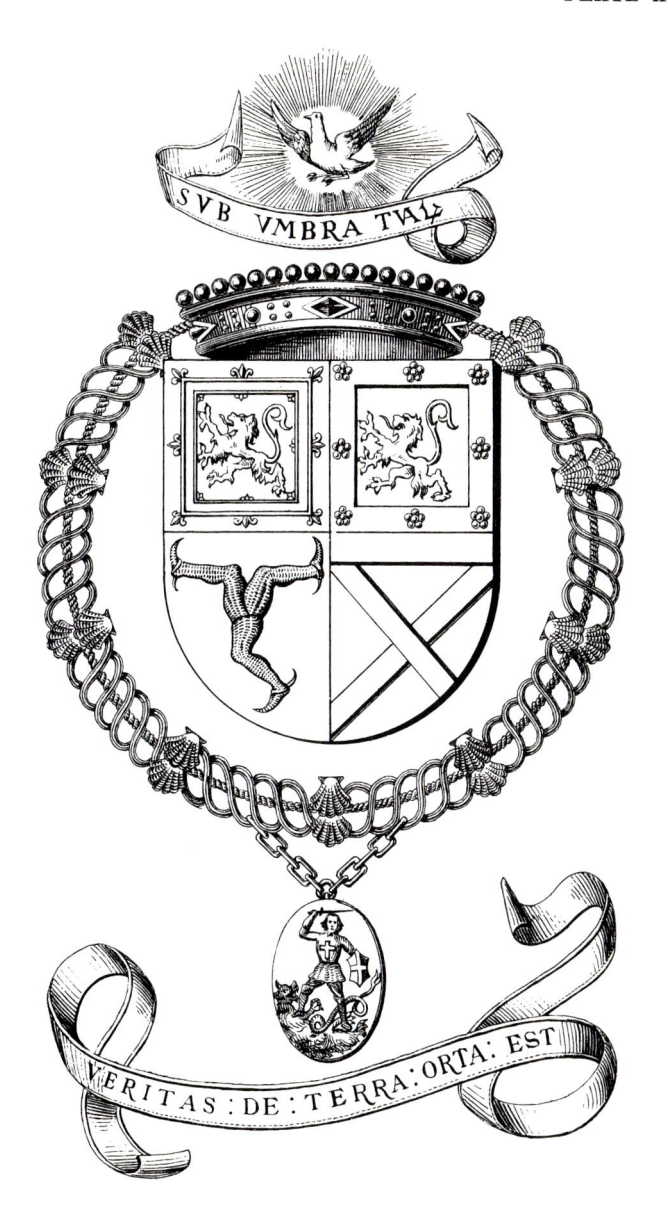

JEAN DUC D'ALBANY.

of FORBES in the second and third. To these cases we may add the well known coat of the BREADALBANE family (the principal cadet line of the CAMPBELLS), as compared with that of the house of ARGYLL. BREADALBANE has, equally with ARGYLL, the undifferenced coat of CAMPBELL in the first and fourth quarters; and each became entitled to use the arms of STEWART of Lorn in virtue of marriage with one of the co-heiresses of JOHN, Lord LORN. In the ARGYLL achievement this alliance is represented by the use of the LORN galley in the second and third quarters; while BREADALBANE has LORN in the second, and the plain coat of STEWART in the third. This is a near approach to what NISBET characterises as a German mode of differencing unknown in Scotland.

It is, however, frequent enough abroad. For instance the Counts of LEININGEN UND DAGSBURG, bore LEININGEN (*v.* p. 424) in the first and fourth quarters, with DAGSBURG in the second and third (*Argent, a lion rampant sable, debruised by an escarbuncle of the field, all within a bordure gules*); and an escucheon *en surtout* for the Lordship of ASPERMONT: *Gules, a cross argent.* The Counts of LEININGEN-WESTERBURG quartered LEININGEN with WESTERBURG (*Gules, a cross between twenty crosslets or*), and placed *en surtout* an escucheon, *Or, a cross azure,* which both SPENER and TRIER profess their inability to explain. (I think it originated in a painter's error.)

The Barons of FRAUENBERG (now FRAUNBERG) in Bavaria, bore: *Quarterly,* 1 and 4. *Gules, a pale argent,* FRAUENBERG; 2 and 3. *Gules, a horse saliant argent bridled sable,* HAAG. The Counts of HAAG, who are of the same descent, difference by transposing the quarters (SPENER, *Op. Her.*, p. spec., pp. 446-7).

The arms of the two lines of LÖWENSTEIN and WERTHEIM, in Virneberg and in Rochefort, were identical as far as eight of the nine quarters were concerned, and only differed in the quartering at the point of the escucheon (SPENER, p. spec., tab. ix.).

XIII. An AUGMENTATION of course serves very effectively as a mode of difference (*See* Chapter XVI.). The use of an official coat does the same.

XIV. DIFFERENCING BY AN ESCUCHEON *en surtout*.—The Escucheon *en surtout* is sometimes used in Germany as a difference. In the family of the Princes of AUERSPERG the eldest line thus bears the arms of GOTTSCHEE (*Argent, a lion rampant gules crowned or*); the VOLKARD line similarly use :—*Argent, a rose gules, seeded or;* and the line of PEILLENSTEIN :—*Azure, a crown or.* It may be interesting if I here append a few of the differenced coats of an English family : the great house of MORTIMER. The main coat has already been given at p. 168 (Plate XVIII., No. 5), and the seal of EDMUND MORTIMER on Plate XXXVII., fig. 2, *Barry or and azure,* etc. (sometimes, as in the *Second Roll* of HENRY III. and the *First Roll* of EDWARD I., *Azure, three bars or,* etc.). RAF DE MORTIMER changes the tincture *Azure* to *Sable* (1, EDWARD II.). HENRY DE MORTIMER (1, EDWARD II.) makes the *argent* escucheon *billetty sable,* possibly *ermine,* which at any rate, was one of the MORTIMER differences, being borne by ROGER MORTIMER (2, HENRY III.). WILLIAM DE MORTIMER bears "*Mortimer's Arms*" with *a bendlet gules;* and GEOFFREY, with *a saltire gules, en surtout* (2, HENRY III.). In the same *Roll* JOAN changes the *azure* bars to *gules.* I close the list with a curious French example : MORTEMER in Poictou bore : *Fascé contré fasce d'or et d'azur, en cœur un écusson d'argent à la bande de gueules* (qui pourrait rappeler une alliance avec les Seigneurs d'Azay le Rideau, qui portaient *d'argent à la bande de gueules*). BOURASSÉ, *La Touraine,* folio, Tours, 1855.

SEALS. PLATE XXXVII.

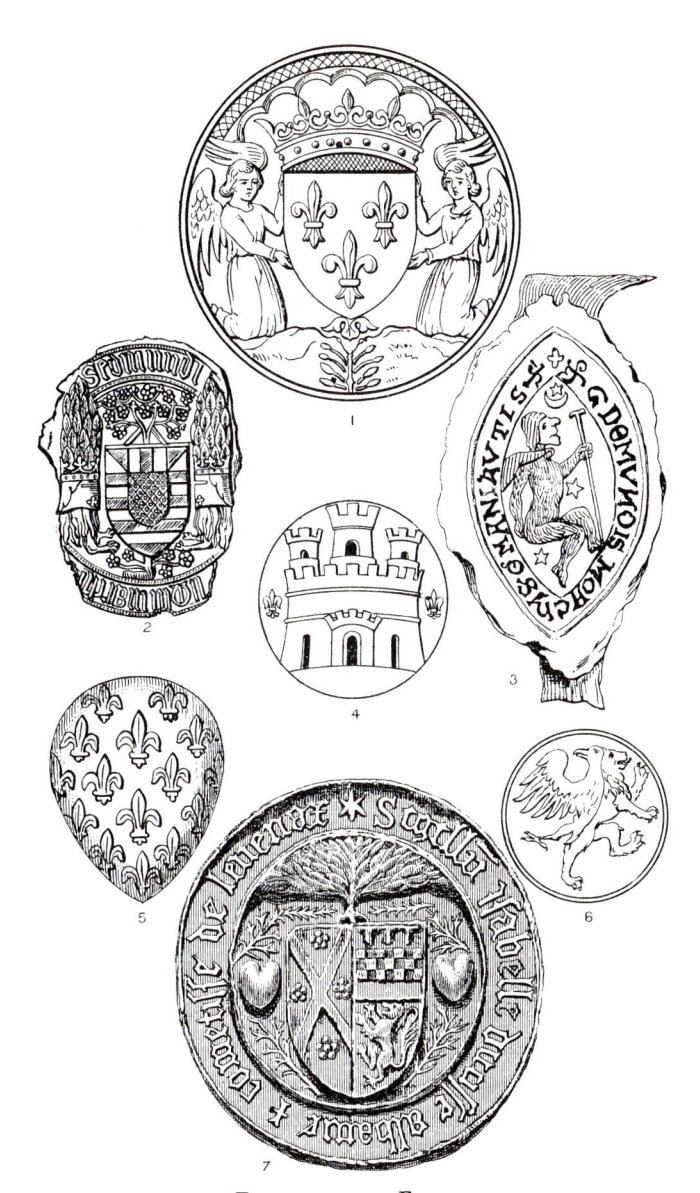

EXPLANATION OF FIGURES.

1. Counter Seal of Louis XII. and Francis I. (*Vrée*). 2. Seal of Edmund Mortimer, 1372. 3. Seal of Guy de Munois, Monk of St. Germain l'Auxerrois (*Eysenbach*). 4. Portion of Seal of Blanche of Castille, Queen of France (d. 1252) (*Vrée*). 5. Seal of Louis, Dauphin of France, 1216. 6. Portion of Seal of Alice of Holland, wife of Jean d'Avesnes, c. 1230 (*Vrée*). 7. Seal of Isabella, Duchess of Albany, Countess of Lennox.

In the case of some of the great families of the Low Countries, of which a number of the members were in succession Knights of the great Order of the Golden Fleece, their arms recorded in the catalogues of CHIFFLET and MAURICE afford interesting information as to the modes of differencing employed in the fifteenth and sixteenth centuries. About the middle of the fourteenth century GUILLAUME DE CROY espoused ISABELLE, heiress of RENTY. Their son JEAN DE CROY accordingly bore, *Quarterly*, 1 and 4. *Argent, three bars gules* (CROY); 2 and 3. *Argent three doloires* (or broad-axes) *those in chief addorsed gules* (RENTY). JEAN DE CROY married MARIE DE CRAON and had two sons. Of these ANTOINE, the elder, on the death of his father at Azincourt in 1415, became Seigneur of CROY and bore the full arms of CROY and RENTY (Chev. No. xv.). The younger son, JEAN (Chev. No. xxii.), bore the same arms but differenced by the addition of an escucheon *en surtout* bearing the arms of his mother MARIE DE CRAON (*Quarterly*, 1 and 4. *Lozengy or and gules*, CRAON; 2 and 3. FLANDERS, *Or, a lion rampant sable*), which continued to form the standing difference of his line. He became the first Count of CHIMAY and founder of that line. Of the line of ANTOINE were several Knights of the Golden Fleece. Of these his grandson (No. cv.) was GUILLAUME, Seigneur de CHIÈVRES, Marquis d'ARSCHOT, and Duke of SORIA, the celebrated tutor of the Emperor CHARLES V. He bore CROY and RENTY, quartered, differenced by an escucheon *en surtout; Quarterly*, 1 and 4. LUXEMBOURG (*Argent, a lion rampant double queué gules*); 2. LORRAINE; 3. BAR. Of these coats LUXEMBURG and BAR were respectively the coats of his maternal grand-parents; LORRAINE was the first coat of his father's mother, MARGUERITE DE LORRAINE-VAUDEMONT, the wife of ANTOINE. MARGUERITE'S full coat (of LORRAINE quartering HARCOURT, and ALENÇON) was similarly borne in an *escucheon en surtout* by her grandson FERRY DE CROY, Seigneur de ROUX (No. cxxiii.), first cousin of GUILLAUME, Duke of SORIA; and by FERRY'S son ADRIAN (No. clxiii.).

Turning now to the line of CHIMAY, we find that both the sons of JOHN were Knights of the Order, and differenced their father's coat, already given, with a *bordure azure platy*. The elder son, PHILIPPE, also had two sons, Knights of the Order, of whom CHARLES, Prince de CHIMAY (No. civ.), the elder, discontinued the bordure, which was retained by the younger, ANTOINE (No. cxxxiv.).

The differences of the knights of the house of LANNOY are even more instructive.

First of their number was HUGH DE LANNOY (No. vii.). His father GILBERT was a younger son, and bore the arms of LANNOY: *Argent, three lions rampant vert crowned or*, differenced by a *filet en bordure engrailed gules;* which was continued by HUGH. His younger brother GILBERT (No. xii.) added to this a *label azure;* while the third brother, BALDWIN (No. xix.), who had as his heritage the lordship of MOLEMBAIS, his mother's portion, relinquished his father's bordure and bore the full arms of LANNOY differenced by an escucheon *en surtout* of MOLEMBAIS: *Argent, four bars azure*. His son BALDWIN (No. lxxxix.), similarly differenced with the arms of *his* mother, ADRIENNE DE BERLAYMONT: *Barry of six vair and gules*. BALDWIN'S son PHILIP (No. clxxxiii.) also differenced with the arms of his mother MICHELE D'ESNE: *Sable, ten lozenges conjoined argent* 3, 3, 1. PHILIP had two wives; by the first, MARGUERITE DE BOURGOGNE (natural daughter of Duke PHILIP by MARIE MANUEL), he had a son JEAN (No. ccviii.) who quartered LANNOY and MANUEL (*v.* p. 507), and placed the full undifferenced quartered coat of BURGUNDY *en surtout*. PHILIP'S second wife was FRANÇOISE

DE BARBENÇON, and her son BALDWIN (No. ccxxxiii.) differenced with an escucheon *en surtout* of her arms: *Argent, three lions rampant gules crowned or.*

In the line of GILBERT, the second son (No. xii.), his son PIERRE (No. xcviii.) bore his father's arms with the bordure, and *in the centre point a star of six points gules.*

Yet another line of LANNOY, descending from HUGH, Seigneur de MINGOVAL, brother of GUILLEBERT, had a succession of three generations of knights. CHARLES (No. cxxxvi.), Viceroy of Naples, laid aside his father's engrailed bordure, and differenced with a crescent *gules* in the centre point. His son PHILIP (No. cxcvii.), Prince of SULMONE, resumed the bordure. He married ISABELLA COLONNA, and their sons CHARLES (ccxxxviii.), and HORACE (cclxix.), both quartered LANNOY and COLONNA (*Gules, a column argent, its capital and base or crowned of the last*).

Illustrations of most of the usages we have described will be found in the list of Montmorency *brisures* with which I conclude this Chapter.

I. *Or, a cross gules between sixteen allerions azure,* is the principal coat of the family in modern times (*see* next page).

The MONTMORENCY DE FOSSEUX added a *star argent in the centre point* (until it became the principal line in 1570), and the lines of COURRIERES and LORESSE did the same.

M— WASTINE: *three plates upon the cross.*

M— BOUTEVILLE; and M— CROISILLES: *a label azure (? argent); and a lozenge or in centre point.*

M— BOURS: in chief *a crescent argent.*

M— ROUPY (ET NOMAING): in chief *a mullet argent (a crescent argent in centre).*

M— DU PLESSIS-CACHELEU: in centre *a mullet sable.*

M— D'AVREMESNIL ET GOUSSAINVILLE: *a label argent.*

M— d'Hubermont: an escucheon *en surtout* of the maternal arms of Oignies: (*Vert, a fess ermine*).

M— de Maffliers: the first canton *argent plain*.

M— S. Leu (et Deuil): the first canton *ermine plain*.

M— Breteuil et Beaussault: the first canton *argent, an estoile sable*.

M— Beausant: an escucheon *en surtout* of Harcourt, *Gules, two bars or*.

II. (Montmorency-Laval: *five escallops argent on the cross*.)

M— L. de Morhem: the same; *a bordure argent*.

M— L. d'Olivet: *the bordure sable with eight plates*.

M— L. St. Aubin, et Bois-Dauphin: *a bordure sable with five lions rampant argent*.

M— L. Châtillon: a canton of Beaumont, *Azure, flory a lion rampant or*.

M— L. de Loue: a canton of Baussay (?).

M— L. de Pacy: a canton, *Gules, three lions rampant argent*.

M— L. de Chalouyau: a canton, *Gules, a lion rampant argent*.

M— L. d'Attichy: a canton, *Argent, a lion (passant sable or) rampant gules*, Erquery.

M— L. de Lezay: *a pheon argent in base of the cross*.

Montmorency de Marly: *Or, a cross gules between four allerions azure* (the original arms of the family), the branch of de Lay made the cross fretty. (Spener, *Opus Heraldicum*, pars. gen., p. 357, corrected.)

M— de Luxe, et de Boutteville: on the cross an escucheon of Bourbon-la-Marche-Préaux: France-ancient, *a bendlet gules charged with three lions rampant argent* (this line became Montmorency-Luxembourg).

M— Hallot: *a label azure*.—J. W.]

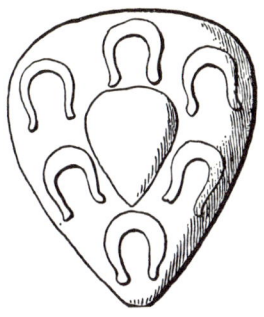

FIG. 90.—ESCUCHEON OF HENRI DE FERRIÈRES, 1205 (*Demay*).

CHAPTER XV.

MARSHALLING. SECTION I.—BY J. W.

IN the earliest days of Heraldry no one was supposed to have a right to more coats of arms than one, nor did more than one coat appear upon a heraldic seal. The hereditary descent of arms was from time to time interrupted by the bearer of a particular coat marrying into a family more powerful, or having larger possessions than his own; in which case it was usual, whether the lady were an heiress or not, that he should adopt her family arms; in so doing he entirely relinquished his paternal ensigns, as it was not thought that he could exhibit both together on the same shield, banner, or seal.

But in the latter half of the thirteenth century, more shields than one began to be exhibited upon the same seal. This is particularly the case in the seals of Queens, and other highly dignified ladies, upon which the owner of the seal was delineated at full length having a shield on either side of her effigy, the one containing her husband's armorial insignia, the other her paternal coat. Thus, in 1263, the seal of AGNES DE FAUCIGNY, wife of Count PETER of SAVOY, bears a female figure holding in the dexter hand the paly shield of FAUCIGNY (*Gules*), *three pallets* (*or*); in her sinister the shield of SAVOY (*Gules*), *a cross* (*argent*). (CIBRARIO, *Sigilli de' Principi di Savoia*, No. 19.) It may be worth while to notice here, that this seal, already bearing the arms now known as those of SAVOY, is one of the many pieces of evidence extant which unite in refuting the fable which declares that these arms (identical with those borne by the great Order of the Hospitallers of St. John the Baptist, the "Knights of St. John" at Rhodes and Malta) were given by the Order to AMADEUS *the Great*, Count of SAVOY (1285-1323), in recognition of assistance said to have been rendered by him to the Knights at a siege of Rhodes, with regard to which historians differ about the date as to whether it was in 1308, 1310, or 1315! (*See* GUICHENON, *Histoire Généalogique de la Maison de Savoye*, i., 126, etc.)

On a seal of MARGARET BRUCE of Skelton, Lady de Ros of Kendal, appended to a document of 1280, is a full length female figure, wearing a mantle lined with ermine, and holding a shield charged with the water-bougets of Ross in her right hand, and one with a lion rampant for BRUCE in the other. (LAING, *Scottish Seals*, ii., No. 142.)

MARGARET, daughter of PHILIP III. of France, second Queen of EDWARD I. of England, had on the obverse of the seal her effigy, habited in a tunic on which are displayed the three lions passant-gardant of ENGLAND; on either side of this effigy is a shield; the dexter bears the *fleurs-de-lis* of FRANCE-ANCIENT; that to the left hand is charged with the coat of her mother MARIE, daughter of HENRY III., Duke of BRABANT (*Sable*), *a lion rampant* (*or*). The reverse of the seal bears the arms of ENGLAND only.

This mode of using arms seems to have been prevalent all over Europe. For instance, the seal of MARGARET of CARINTHIA, wife of FREDERICK IV., Burg-grave of NÜRNBERG in 1307, bears her seated effigy holding two shields: the dexter the arms of ZOLLERN: *Quarterly, Sable and argent;* the other the shield of CARINTHIA; *Per pale* (*Gules*) *a fess* (*argent*) AUSTRIA; and (*Or*) *three lions passant in pale (sable)* CARINTHIA. (*Monumenta Zollerana*, iii., p. 279.) The custom was continued by all the Burg-grafins of the fourteenth century. (*See* Chapter on SUPPORTERS.)

Similar to the seal of Lady de Ros, described above, is the seal in 1378 of MARGARET STUART, Countess of ANGUS by descent, and of MAR by marriage (the mother, by an incestuous intrigue with her brother-in-law, of the DOUGLAS, first Earl of ANGUS); it bears the representation of a lady holding in the dexter hand the shield of MAR, and in the sinister that of STEWART of BONKILL, or STEWART, Earl of ANGUS. (LAING, *Scottish Seals*, i., No. 792.)

There is in the Record Office in London a fine but much defaced seal of MARGARET LOGIE, second Queen of DAVID II. of Scotland, on which, besides the figure of the Queen, are three separate shields. One bears the Royal Arms of SCOTLAND; another, so much injured as to be hardly decipherable, seems to contain the coat of her former husband, Sir JOHN LOGIE; while the third, which had on insufficient grounds been taken for LOGIE, bears the coat of DRUMMOND (*Or*), *three bars wavy* (*gules*). It may be mentioned as indicative of the light which Heraldry so often throws on history, that it was this seal which settled the re-discovery of the long forgotten paternity of DAVID II.'s strong-minded Queen. She was daughter of Sir MALCOLM DRUMMOND of Stobhall; and aunt of the gentler, and more lovable, Queen ANNABELLA. The late Mr RIDDELL (*Scottish Peerage and Consistorial Law*, p. 92) had previously shown that she was not, as generally supposed, daughter of Sir JOHN LOGIE, but his widow. (See *The Exchequer Rolls of Scotland*, vol. ii., pp. lv. and lvi., edited by GEORGE BURNETT, Lyon King of Arms.)

On the more delicately executed seals of the same period without effigies, we have sometimes a regular pattern of ornamental tracery, in which are inserted several separate shields, that containing the principal family coat generally occupying the most prominent position. In a few cases the family badges are introduced as parts of the composition.

The counter-seals of LOUIS X. of France, in 1315, as well as those of his brothers and successors PHILIP V. and CHARLES IV., bear the arms of the kingdom (FRANCE-ANCIENT) on a circular representation of the chains of NAVARRE, their mother's coat. (VRÉE, *Généalogie des Comtes de Flandre*, plates xli., xlii.)

Three seals given in HUEBER'S *Austria Illustrata*, tab. xvi. and xiv., show the aggroupement of several shields in 1348 before quartering had become generally adopted. The first is that of LOUIS, Count PALATINE of the RHINE, and Duke of BAVARIA; on it three shields are arranged *in pairle*, the points meeting in the centre of the escucheon: (1) BAVARIA; (2) the PALATINATE; (3) . . . (?). The second is that of ALBERT, Duke of AUSTRIA, STYRIA, and CARINTHIA. Here the shields of (1) AUSTRIA, (2) STYRIA, and (3) the impaled coat of CARINTHIA, are placed 2 and 1. The two first are *accolés* in chief, and their base points rest on the upper edge of the shield of CARINTHIA. The seal of RUDOLF DE LOSENSTEIN in 1337, has two shields pendant from a tree.

It should be noted that Princes who had several great fiefs, carried their arms separately; one on the shield, another on the banner, and others on the caparisons of their horses. (*See* the seals of the Dukes of AUSTRIA, in HUEBER; those of the SAXON Dukes, in HÖNN, *Des Hauses Sachsen Wappens und Geschlects Untersuchung*, Leipzig, 1704, etc.; and that of JOHN, King of BOHEMIA, in VRÉE.) SIMON DE MONTFORT thus carried a banner of the arms of the honour of Hinckley.

The seal of ELIZABETH DE CLARE, daughter and

heiress of GILBERT DE CLARE, Earl of GLOUCESTER, and niece of EDWARD II., like many other seals of ladies of that date, is without inscription. The central shield bears the arms of ROGER D'AMORI, the lady's third husband, who died *c.* 1322 (*Barry wavy argent and gules a bendlet azure*), with three lions passant-gardant of ENGLAND, surrounding it. A cross of tracery around this central shield contains four circular compartments; that above the shield of AMORI bears the arms of the lady's first husband, JOHN DE BURGH, Earl of ULSTER (*or*) *a cross* (*gules*) *surmounted by a label;* that beneath the shield is charged with the fret of her second husband, THEOBALD DE VERDON (*Or, fretty gules*); while the circles on either side bear her paternal arms of DE CLARE (*Or, three chevrons gules*). In the four angles of the cross are trefoiled compartments; two charged with the castle of CASTILE; two with the arms of LEON, for her grandmother ELEANOR of CASTILE, wife of EDWARD I., whose daughter, JOAN of ACON, was wife of GILBERT DE CLARE.

The seal of ELIZABETH D'AMORI, daughter and heiress of the above named ROGER D'AMORI, and ELIZABETH DE CLARE, affords an equally interesting example of the usage of the time. On it a central compartment of circular shape is filled with octagonal cuspings, on which is placed the shield of the lady's husband, JOHN, Lord BARDOLF (*Azure, three cinquefoils or*). Around it is arranged a series of eight smaller circles charged with arms. In chief and base are the arms of BURGH, but without any label. The dexter and sinister flanks are charged with DE CLARE and D'AMORI, as above. The other four circles bear the lion of LEON or the castle of CASTILE. (*Cf.* the seal of JEANNE DE FRANCE, Plate XXXV., fig. 3.)

A seal of MARGARET of FRANCE (daughter of PHILIP V. by JEANNE, Countess of ARTOIS and BURGUNDY; and wife of LOUIS DE NEVERS, Count of FLANDERS);

bears: FLANDERS, impaling FRANCE-ANCIENT. This central shield is surrounded by a series of four supporters: an angel in chief, a dragon in base, and two eagles in flanks, and by four escucheons alternating with these supporters: of these the 1st and 4th are ARTOIS (FRANCE-ANCIENT, *a label gules*); the 2nd bears the impaled coat repeated; the 3rd is for NEVERS, or the County PALATINE of BURGUNDY: *Azure, billetty, a lion rampant or* (VRÉE, *Gen. Com. Fl.*, plate l.).

Contemporarily with this aggroupement existed another usage for indicating maternal descent, or the possession of a particular fief, by borrowing some bearing from the shield of the wife or mother, or from that of the fief in question, and amalgamating it with the paternal coat.

An English instance of this usage adduced by Mr PLANCHÉ, is that of JOHN DE MOHUN (temp. EDWARD I.), whose family coat, *Gules, a maunch argent*, has been already noticed (p. 376); but in consequence of his marriage with JOANNE D'AGULON, he (or his son) added to the maunch a hand issuing from it, and holding the *fleur-de-lis* which was the bearing of the AGULON family. In the *Roll* of HENRY III., known as GLOVER'S *Roll*, ROBERT DE AGULON bears: *Gules, a fleur-de-lis argent* (No. 63); *see* also ST. GEORGE'S *Roll* (No. 182), *Archæologia*, xxxix.

Many examples of composed coats are to be found in Continental Heraldry, but it is in Scotland that this usage chiefly prevailed.

It is well known that the marriage of Sir JOHN STEWART, younger son of the fourth High Steward of Scotland, with the daughter and eventual heiress of Sir JOHN BONKYL, led the greater number of his descendants in all subsequent times to surmount their fess-chequy with a bend (which was doubtless his difference as a younger son), charged with the three buckles of the shield of BONKYL. We see them on the seal of MARGARET, Countess of ANGUS and MAR, to which reference has been already made (LAING, *Scottish Seals*, i., No. 768).

Immediately on his accession to the throne ROBERT II., in 1371, bestowed on DAVID, his eldest son by his second marriage with EUPHEMIA ROSS, the earldom of STRATHERN which had been forfeited to the Crown. The seal of the prince, in 1374, shows that he amalgamated the fess-chequy of the STEWARTS with the chevrons which had been borne by the former Earls of STRATHERN as their feudal coat (*Or, two chevrons gules*).

JOHN, second son of Sir ALEXANDER COCKBURN, married early in the fourteenth century, JANET, daughter and heiress of Sir ALEXANDER LINDSAY, and thus acquired the estate of Ormiston. He therefore placed the Lindsay fess-checquy between the three cocks of COCKBURN on his armorial shield.

Many other Scottish coats were formed in this way, and allusion has been made to some of them in the chapter on DIFFERENCING.

MARSHALLING, however, consists strictly neither in the aggroupement, nor in the amalgamation, of heraldic bearings, but in the exhibiting of separate coats in one shield which is divided by lines of partition into compartments for their display.

Among the various means adopted for this purpose the most important are—*impalement; quartering;* and the *escucheon en surtout;* each of which, along with a few others belonging chiefly to Continental and Royal Heraldry, will be separately noticed.

IMPALEMENT.

In impalement the shield is *parted per pale, i.e.* is divided by a vertical line into equal portions, a separate coat being placed in each of the divisions.

I. DIMIDIATION.—In the form called *Dimidiation,*

only the half (or a little more than the half) of each of the two coats is seen upon the shield, which is thus occupied by the dexter half of the one coat and the sinister half of the other.

Mr BOUTELL (*English Heraldry*, p. 146) considers that this custom was introduced into England between 1272-1307; there are, however, earlier instances of its use in other countries. The seal of WILLIAM of HAINAULT, younger brother of BALDWIN V., Count of HAINAULT (d. 1194), bears a shield *dimidiated;* the dexter half is *semé* of *fleurs-de-lis;* on the sinister is the chevronny coat of HAINAULT (*Or and sable*), the chevrons being here converted into bends. This seal was in use in 1199 or 1200, and is the earliest instance of dimidiation which occurs to me. (VRÉE, *Généalogie des Comtes de Flandre*, plate iv.) The seal of BEATRICE DE BAUX, in 1258, bears, TOULOUSE dimidiating BAUX. (CIBRARIO, *Sigilli di Savoia*, No. xv.)

The counter-seal of DEVORGILLA, wife of JOHN BALLIOL, daughter of ALAN, Lord of GALLOWAY, by MARGARET, daughter of DAVID, Earl of HUNTINGDON, is appended to the charter of foundation of BALLIOL College, Oxford, 1282. It is of *vesica* shape, and bears three escucheons suspended from a tree; the centre, and by far the largest shield, bears GALLOWAY (*a lion rampant crowned*), dimidiated with BALLIOL (*an orle*, v. p. 407). The smaller escucheons bear the arms of HUNTINGDON and CHESTER for her grandparents. (LAING, ii., 71.)

The seal of ANNETTE DE LAVAL, Dame de COËTMEN, in 1298, bears, MONTMORENCY-LAVAL (*Or, on a cross gules between twenty allerions azure, five escallops argent*) dimidiating COËTMEN (*Gules, seven annulets,* 3, 3, 1, *argent*) (MORICE, *Bretagne*, cxxii.). I am not able, therefore, to give my entire assent to Mr PLANCHÉ'S assertion that "Heraldry had existed as a science at least two hundred years before anything like the present practice of marshalling made its appearance. In our early seals the shield of arms of the husband and wife are displayed separately. Impalement, simply, and by dimidiation, appears in the reign of EDWARD I., and quartering about the same period."—(*Pursuivant of Arms*, p. 164.)

In 1263 the counter-seal of BLANCHE DE NAVARRE bears a shield charged with ALBRET (*Gules plain*), impaling DREUX (*Chequy or and argent, a canton ermine*). (MORICE, *Bretagne*, lxxxi.) It must be remarked here that in early times impaled coats appear as a rule only on the seals of ladies. In opposition to modern ideas we find that it was the wife who impaled her husband's arms with her own, not the husband who impaled the wife's. The shield which appears on the seal of the husband usually contains his own arms only.

"Usually males *quartered* the arms of their wives or ancestresses from whom they acquired their lands; whilst impalements were practically the general bearings of married women who took an immediate interest in their husbands' lands by right of dower. The practice of husbands impaling their wives' arms, whether heiresses or not, probably arose near the close of the 15th century. Even now it is laid down that the arms of a wife should not in general be borne upon the husband's banner, surcoat, or official seal."—("The old Heraldry of the Percies," by Mr DYER LONGSTAFFE in *Archæologia Æliana*, vol. iv.)

There are indeed a few early instances in which a man used an impaled coat; not however, to indicate his own marriage but to denote his parentage.

Thus, about 1290, the counter-seal of GEOFFROI DE BRABANT (son of HENRY, Duke of BRABANT, by his Duchess, ALICE OF BURGUNDY), bears a shield on which are impaled the arms of the two duchies:—*Sable, a lion rampant or*, for BRABANT; and, *Bendy of six or and azure, a bordure gules*, for BURGUNDY-ANCIENT.

(In the last named coat the bordure is not removed at the palar line as in modern usage to be hereafter noticed, p. 474.) So also, about 1300, LOUIS, Count of NEVERS, son of ROBERT DE BÉTHUNE, Count of FLANDERS, by YOLANTE, daughter of EUDES of BURGUNDY, bore on his *secretum* a shield impaling the parental coats viz., BURGUNDY-ANCIENT (the bordure engrailed for difference), and FLANDERS (*Or, a lion rampant sable*). This is a curious arrangement, the place of honour being given to the maternal coat, in which the engrailed bordure for difference is also worthy of remark. It should be noticed that in the present case the bordure is removed at the palar line, unlike the example quoted immediately above. LOUIS (DE CRESSY) Count of NEVERS and RETHEL, and afterwards of FLANDERS (as LOUIS II.), son of the above LOUIS and YOLANTE, married MARGARET of FRANCE, daughter of PHILIP V. Her counter seals bear FLANDERS impaling FRANCE-ANCIENT, but on one of them FRANCE has the precedence. (VRÉE, *Généalogie des Comtes de Flandre*, plate xcviii.)

Sometimes quartered coats are dimidiated, in which case the first and third quarters of the husband's coat are impaled with the second and fourth of the wife's. In these the appearance is that of a plain quartered coat, and may easily mislead the unwary. Thus the seal of MARGARET of BAVARIA, Countess of HOLLAND, and wife of JOHN, Count de NEVERS, in 1385 (afterwards Duke of BURGUNDY), bears a shield *en bannière* which appears a simple instance of quartering, but is really a dimidiated coat. The two coats to the dexter side of the palar line are: In chief BURGUNDY-MODERN (FRANCE-ANCIENT, *a bordure compony argent and gules*), and in base BURGUNDY-ANCIENT, as above. On the sinister side the coat in chief is BAVARIA (*Bendy-lozengy argent and azure*); and the one in base contains the quartered arms of FLANDERS (*Or, a lion rampant sable*);

and HOLLAND (*Or, a lion rampant gules*); the pourfilar line dividing these latter quarters being omitted, as in many like instances. (See *ante;* p. 247, and compare the shield of Queen PHILIPPA of HAINAULT, wife of EDWARD III., in Westminster Abbey.) Similarly, after her first marriage with the Dauphin, the seal of JACQUE-LINE of BAVARIA, Countess of HOLLAND, has on the dexter side the coat of FRANCE in chief, and that of DAUPHINÉ (*Or, a dolphin embowed azure, crested gules*) in base; on the sinister BAVARIA, in chief over the quartered coat of FLANDERS and HOLLAND as above.

The seal of JEANNE, Duchess of BRITTANY, wife of CHARLES of BLOIS, in 1369, bears a lozenge charged with two coats which might be described either as dimidiated, or impaled. The dexter side is *Ermine plain;* the sinister *Ermine, within a border gules* (which of course stops at the palar line).

I recently noticed a somewhat similar instance in a modern window of the Cathedral at Tours, where the arms of GUY DE MONTMORENCY-LAVAL are dimidiated with those of JEANNE DE LAVAL D'OLIVET, his wife, in 1384. (She was widow of the Constable BERTRAND DU GUESCLIN.) The arms are: *Per pale dimidiated*: 1. *Or, on a cross gules between sixteen allerions azure, five escallops argent;* 2. *The same, within a bordure sable charged with fifteen plates.*

In 1298, the seal of ANNETTE DE LAVAL, Dame de COËTMEN, has a shield of MONTMORENCY-LAVAL (as above) dimidiating COËTMEN; *Gules, seven annulets,* 3, 3, 1, *argent*. (MORICE, *Bretagne*, No. cxxii.) In 1306 the seal of PAIEN DE LA ROCHE bears: *Vair,* dimidiating an eagle displayed. (*Ibid.*, No. ccxv.)

It must be noticed that often only one of the coats impaled is affected by *dimidiation*. Thus (*circa* 1310) the counter-seal of MARGARET of HAINAULT, third wife of ROBERT, Comte d'ARTOIS, bears ARTOIS *dimidiated* impaling FLANDERS entire. Here the ARTOIS label appears (probably only on account of the smallness of the coat) to be gobony; and not of *gules* charged with the golden castles of CASTILE as represented on the seal of the Count himself. (VRÉE, *Généalogie des Comtes des Flandre*, plate xlviii.)

On the seal of IOLANTE DE FLANDERS (died 1312), daughter of ROBERT DE BÉTHUNE, Count of FLANDERS, and wife of GAUTIER II., Seigneur d'ENGHIEN, the *dimidiated* coat of ENGHIEN (*Gyronny of ten argent and sable, each piece of the latter charged with three cross-crosslets fitchée of the first*) is impaled with the entire arms of FLANDERS (p. 462). So also on the Great Seal of Queen MARY the dimidiated arms of FRANCE impale the entire arms of SCOTLAND.

The remarkable seals of YOLANTE DE FLANDRE (daughter of ROBERT DE FLANDRES *dit Cassel*, by JEANNE DE BRETAGNE); and wife, first of HENRY IV., Comte de BAR; and next of PHILIP, Comte d'EVREUX, and King of NAVARRE in 1344, show her own arms (FLANDERS *within a bordure engrailed sable*) entire; while those of her husband: *Quarterly*, 1 and 4. NAVARRE; 2 and 3. EVREUX (FRANCE-ANCIENT *over all a bend gobony argent and gules*) are dimidiated; so that the dexter side of the escucheon appears to be party per fess, as only the 1st and 3rd quarters (the dexter half) of the quartered coat appear. On one of her seals this escucheon, supported by eight angels is *en bannière* (*v.* p. 635); it may also be noticed that the engrailed bordure of her own coat runs round the whole of it, and is not removed, as we might have expected, at the palar line. (VRÉE, *Généalogie des Comtes de Flandre*, plate ciii.)

It is curious to note that a century later this same impalement of NAVARRE and EVREUX appears on the seal of JOAN DE NAVARRE, first Queen of HENRY IV. of

PLATE XXXVIII.

MARSHALLING, DIMIDIATION, ETC.

1. Siradia.

2. Breslau.

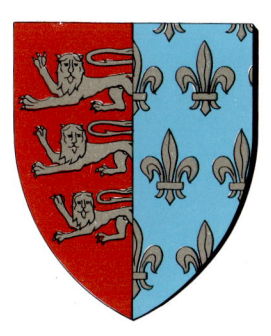

3. England, Dimidiating France.

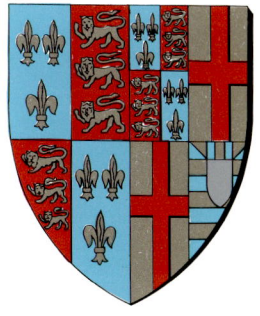

4. Queen Elizabeth of York.

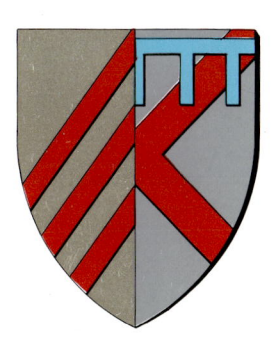

5. Town of Youghal.

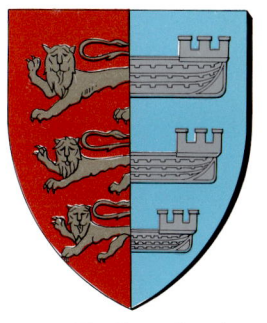

6. The Cinque Ports.

ENGLAND in 1463. This seal contains an impalement, the King's arms (of FRANCE-ANCIENT, and ENGLAND, quarterly) being on the dexter side; and on the sinister side, per fess, in chief NAVARRE, in base EVREUX. (It must be noticed that this would not be a correct *dimidiation* of her arms, in that case EVREUX would be in chief; NAVARRE in base.)

The Royal Armory of England shows much earlier instances of *dimidiation*. The arms of MARGARET of FRANCE, who died in 1319, the second Queen of EDWARD I., remain on her tomb in Westminster Abbey as an exemplification of this mode of Marshalling (Plate XXXVIII., fig. 3). The arms of ENGLAND are upon the dexter side of the escucheon; and this coat undergoes, according to the earlier and more correct fashion, a certain amount of curtailment, though the dimidiation is not complete, only portions of the hindmost parts of the lions being cut off by the palar line; while the coat of FRANCE-ANCIENT appears also dimidiated to the sinister. One of the seals of ISABEL of FRANCE, wife of EDWARD II., bears her standing effigy between two shields, one of ENGLAND, the other of her parental (not personal) arms FRANCE-ANCIENT and NAVARRE both somewhat curtailed by dimidiation.

BOUTELL in his chapter on Marshalling in *Heraldry, Historical and Popular*, gives several early examples of *Impalement by dimidiation*, which should not be overlooked. The seal of EDMOND PLANTAGENET, Earl of CORNWALL (d. 1300), bears his arms (those of RICHARD, Earl of CORNWALL, and King of the Romans, *v. ante*, p. 245) dimidiating those of his wife, MARGARET DE CLARE. Here only the sinister half of his bordure is removed, while the CLARE coat (*Or, three chevrons gules*) is entirely dimidiated and the chevrons become bends, as in the seal of WILLIAM of HAINAULT above given (p. 460). Both coats are dimidiated in BOUTELL'S other examples (WILLIAM DE VALENCE and his wife; and ALIANORE MONTENDRE and her husband GUY FERRE, p. 148). On the seal of MARGARET CAMPBELL, wife of ALEXANDER NAPIER, in 1531, the shield has impaled upon the dexter side the arms of LENOX, on the sinister the dimidiated coat (the sinister half of the quartered arms) of CAMPBELL, and LORN ; thus the galley of LORN appears in the chief, and the CAMPBELL gyrons in base; in agreement with what we have already seen (p. 465) to be a Continental usage. (LAING, *Scottish Seals*, i., No. 158.)

The arms of CHARLOTTE and ISABEL, daughters of WILLIAM, Prince of ORANGE (*d.* 1584), by CHARLOTTE DE BOURBON-MONTPENSIER, were dimidiated by their respective husbands, CLAUDE, Duc de la TRÉMOUILLE, and HENRY DE LA TOUR D'AUVERGNE, Duc de BOUILLON, who retained their own arms entire. These are curious examples because the dimidiation of the arms of the ladies affected the escucheon of pretence, with its escucheon *en surtout*. It will be sufficient if I give the blazon of the arms of ISABEL, Duchess de BOUILLON. Two coats impaled; the dexter entire; the sinister dimidiated :—

A. *Quarterly:* 1. *Azure fleury or, a tower argent* (LA TOUR).

2. *Or, a gonfanon gules fringed vert* (AUVERGNE).

3. *Coticé or and gules* (TURENNE).

4. *Gules, a fess argent* (Duchy of BOUILLON) (SPENER, p. s., p. 364).

Over all: *Or, three torteaux* (County of BOLOGNE).

B. *Quarterly*: 1 and 4. FRANCE, *differenced by a baton péri en bande gules* (the upper portion argent charged with a dolphin embowed azure?) (BOURBON-MONTPENSIER).

2 and 3. *Azure, billetty a lion rampant or* (NASSAU).

On an escucheon, Quarterly: 1 and 4. *Gules, a bend or* (CHALON).

2 and 3. *Or, a hunting-horn azure virolled and stringed gules* (ORANGE). *Sur le tout du tout Chequy of nine or and azure* (GENEVA). The whole escucheon dimidiated.

The seal of ANNE of CYPRUS, wife of LOUIS, Duke of SAVOY, in 1451, bears SAVOY dimidiated, impaling:— *Per fess* (*a*) JERUSALEM (*b*) CYPRUS *Argent, a lion rampant gules crowned or* (CIBRARIO, No. 103).

An early and interesting Irish example of this kind of Marshalling is afforded by a dimidiated coat of CLARE and FITZGERALD. Sir THOMAS DE CLARE, younger son of RICHARD, Earl of HEREFORD, having obtained in 1272 a charter of the territory of Thomond in Connaught, and of whatever lands besides he could win from the Irish by his sword, set sail for Cork with a large retinue, and there fell in with and married JULIANA, daughter and heiress of MAURICE FITZMAURICE FITZGERALD, feudal Lord of INCHIQUIN and YOUGHAL. He became possessor of the town of YOUGHAL; and the official seal of the Provosts of YOUGHAL dimidiated the coats of CLARE and FITZGERALD. (CLARE, *Or, three chevrons gules;* FITZGERALD, *Argent, a saltire gules with a label of five points in chief*) (Plate XXXVIII., fig. 5). (See *Gentleman's Magazine*, 1865.)

Very singular examples of dimidiation are afforded by the arms which appear on the seals of the CINQUE PORTS (Plate XXXVIII., fig. 6), and on those of the Borough of GREAT YARMOUTH. In both the dexter half of the escucheon is occupied by the arms of ENGLAND dimidiated, and the sinister half is occupied by an *azure* field, charged in the case of the CINQUE PORTS with *three ship's hulks argent in pale*, and in that of GREAT YARMOUTH with *three herrings in pale argent*. In both cases only the hinder halves of the charges appear, and they are united at the palar line with the bodies of the three lions of England. An even more curious case of dimidiation is afforded by the arms of the Abbey of St. ETIENNE at CAEN, in which the arms of ENGLAND and those of the Duchy of NORMANDY (*Gules, two lions passant-gardant or*), were dimidiated, so that in the former half three of the fore-quarters of the lions appear, while in the sinister half only two of the hind-quarters are represented.

In German Heraldry some heraldic monsters which appear as charges originated in the practice of dimidiation; and to it Mr PLANCHÉ considers that even the double-headed eagle of GERMANY is due. To this matter attention is paid elsewhere in this book.

The seal of ALICE, sister of WILLIAM of HOLLAND (elected King of the ROMANS), and wife of JEAN D'AVESNES, Count of HAINAULT (d. 1255) bears her effigy standing between an eagle displayed and a lion rampant. On her counter-seal is a monster composed of the eagle and lion conjoined by dimidiation (Plate XXXVII., fig. 6).

An eagle and lion, dimidiated and conjoined under one crown, occur on the seals of LESEK CZARNY, Duke of POLAND (*c.* 1255); of King WLADISLAW LOKIELET (1315); of HEDWIG (1386); of her husband and successor WLADISLAW JAGELLON (LADISLAS V., Duke of LITHUANIA); of WLADISLAW III. (LADISLAS VI.) 1438; and of ALEXANDER of LIVONIA, in 1502.

The arms of several of the provinces of POLAND afford similar examples. The Duchy of SIERADZ, or SIRADIA, bore: *Or, an eagle displayed and a bear sejant sable, conjoined by dimidiation, and surmounted by an open crown.* The Palatinate of SIRADIA bore: *Argent, a bear sejant sable, dimidiated and conjoined with an eagle displayed gules.* The Palatinate of BRESLAU had the same bearings as SIERADZ, but sometimes without the crown. (Plate XXXVIII., figs. 1, 2.) The Palatinate of KIOVIA (KIJOW) had in an azure field the still more curious combination of a mounted knight and a dimidiated bear, beneath an open crown. PODLACHIA had a similar combination of a knight and a dimidiated eagle, in a golden field (v. SPENER, *Opus Heraldicum*, p. spec., p. 696). A considerable number of the noble families of FRISIA bear arms formed by dimidiation. Usually it is the Imperial Eagle displayed which figures in the dexter half of the escucheon. The family of DOUMA bears: *Per pale or and gules, a demi-eagle sable, dimidiating a rose argent.* The Counts of CAMMERSTEIN in Thuringia, bear: *Per pale*, 1. The arms of the EMPIRE, *dimidiated as above;* 2. *Argent, a fess embattled gules.* The Barons of HIMMELBERG in Carinthia bear: *Per pale*, 1. *The Empire dimidiated;* 2. *Gules, a bend argent.* The Imperial Eagle thus dimidiated also forms part of the arms of several German cities. NÜREMBERG impales it with, *Bendy argent and gules;* MEMMINGEN, with *Argent, a cross gules;* KAUFBEVERN, with *Azure, a bend gules* (sic) *between two estoiles or,* etc. The Saxon family VON DRANDORFF dimidiate *Azure, a fess argent,* with *Azure, a fleur-de-lis gules* (sic). (These two would be counted in England *armes-fausses.*) The arms of GENEVA are those of the EMPIRE, dimidiated with *Gules, a key in pale argent, wards in chief.*

The *Wappenrolle von Zürich* contains several dimidiation examples of the fourteenth century. In No. 237, the Suabian family of SCHWABEGG bear: *Gules, an eagle displayed argent; dimidiating, Barry of eight or and gules.* In No. 312, the family of LOCHNOW use: *Or, an eagle displayed gules, armed sable; dimidiating Or, a fess sable.* (Nos. 118, 119, are other examples, but are unnamed.) Lastly, the reigning Dukes of ANHALT still bear *en surtout* above their quartered shield, the arms: *Argent, an eagle displayed gules; dimidiated with the arms of* SAXONY (*Barry sable and or, over all a crançelin vert;* see *Wappenrolle von Zürich,* No. 19).

At Bologna in the Loggia dei Mercanti I noted the arms of GRASSI (1462) in which the arms of the Empire are dimidiated with those of the family: *Gules, an eagle displayed argent, crowned or.* The Angevin *rastrello* (Plate XXXIX., fig. 6, a label of four points *gules*, with three golden *fleurs-de-lis* between the points) surmounts the latter coat. This curious example combines GUELF and GHIBELINE insignia (*see* p. 119). (*See* SCHILLER'S *Wallenstein* for a fanciful account of the dimidiation of the arms of EGRA. Act iii., scene 3.)

II. SIMPLE IMPALEMENT.—The curtailing of the charges which dimidiation involved was found to be practically inconvenient, as rendering the bearings on the coats so dimidiated somewhat uncertain. Chevrons were thus (as in two cases quoted above) converted into bends: and cantons, or quarters, were liable to disappear altogether. Accordingly impalement without dimidiation, though itself not free from inconveniences, was the usage which met with general acceptance in these lands. Instances have been already given which show that this custom had gone on concurrently with dimidiation.

In Britain impalement was practised chiefly by Queens and ladies of Royal Houses, who bore their husband's coat in the dexter, their paternal coat in the sinister, sometimes on a shield, sometimes on a lozenge. In process of time husbands occasionally impaled the coat of the wife with their own, if she were an heiress, though in those times it was more usual to quarter the arms in this case. The present usage of English Heraldry which concedes to a husband, for his life-time, the privilege of impaling his wife's arms with his own though she be not an heiress; and even of arranging the arms of successive wives in the same escucheon is a comparatively modern, and the latter practice is in my opinion not a very commendable one.

Even when it is desirable to indicate a series of

alliances this is better done by shields *accolés* than by impalement, which often cramps the bearings in both the coats thus conjoined. The general modern Continental usage is in this respect much more satisfactory from an artistic point of view than our own. Where impalement is used in Continental Heraldry it usually originated in marriage with an heiress, but it rather takes the place which quartering holds with us, as it assumes a permanent, not a merely temporary significance. Thus the Imperial Arms of AUSTRIA contain three coats impaled: (1) HAPSBURG, *Or, a lion rampant gules;* (2) AUSTRIA, *Gules, a fess argent;* and (3) LORRAINE: *Or, on a bend gules three alerions argent.* So in the arms of the Duchy of CARINTHIA, the arms of AUSTRIA, just described, are impaled with the arms SUABIA (*Or, three lions passant sable*). (They appear on the seal of OTTAKAR, King of BOHEMIA in 1264. See HUEBER, *Austria Illustrata*, tab. iv.; and *post* p. 454 the coat of the Burg-grafin of NÜRNBERG.) The position of the impaled coats is sometimes reversed (*v.* p. 495).

On the Continent impalement was used in a much more general way than among ourselves, as will be readily seen by the inspection of a series of Imperial seals; or by such an exposition of the Imperial quarterings as may be seen, for instance on the splendid *Cheminée* in the Palais de Justice at Bruges. On the Imperial seals AUSTRIA is sometimes impaled with BURGUNDY, sometimes with CASTILLE; JERUSALEM with HUNGARY; ARRAGON with SICILY. In these, and a multitude of other instances, the design was obviously not to commemorate any special matrimonial alliance, but to give to the coats thus impaled a clearer definition than would be obtained in a large shield of many quarters. So the arms of the Counties of FLANDERS and TIROL are very generally conjoined by impalement in a single escucheon, borne upon the great shield of the quarterings of the House of AUSTRIA (*see* fig. 91, p. 497); this is done merely for convenience, and by no means as indicative of a marriage between a Count of FLANDERS and a Countess of TIROL (which as a historic fact never took place), though such an alliance would be denoted, according to our modern British notions, by their impalement.

WILLIAM of WOLFFENBÜTTEL, and his brother MAGNUS II. used, after 1367, the arms of BRUNSWICK : *Gules, two lions passant or, impaled with those of* LÜNE-BURG ; *Or, semé of hearts gules, a lion rampant azure.* In later times these coats were indifferently impaled or quartered (*see* GROTE, *Geschichte der Welfischen Stammwappen*, p. 47 ; Leipzig, 1863), and these impaled coats continued to form "*das Kleine Wappen*" of the Duchy of BRUNSWICK so long as it remained independent.

The Seal of ALBERT, Count PALATINE of the RHINE in 1353, has a shield containing the arms of BAVARIA (*Bendy lozengy Argent and azure*) impaling those of the PALATINATE of the RHINE (*Sable, a lion displayed, double queué or, crowned gules*). (See *Austria ex archivis Mellicensibus illustrata*, plate xviii., fig. 10, fol. Lipsiæ 1722.)

The Dukes of CLEVE often bore CLEVE impaling MARK (*see* MAURICE, *Toison d'Or*, plate l.).

Another very curious and interesting example is afforded by the arms of the Landgraves of LEUCHTENBURG, now extinct. They appear to be : *Per pale Argent and azure a fess counterchanged ;* and are often so blazoned. SPENER, however, points out (*Opus Heraldicum*, pars. spec., lib. i., p. 214) that really we have here two coats united by impalement. The coat of LEUCHTENBURG was simply *Argent, a fess azure ;* but on the extinction of the family of the Counts of HALS, who bore : *Azure, a fess argent*, the Emperor WENCESLAS conferred the fief, which had lapsed to the crown, on the kindred Landgraves of LEUCHTENBERG. (It will be noticed that these two coats are otherwise interesting as an example of differencing by change of tincture, *vide ante*, p. 405). Henceforth the Landgraves of LEUCHTENBERG bore both the coats united by impalement. The original coat of LEUCHTENBERG alone appears in the arms of the present Dukes of LEUCHTENBERG, Princes of EICHSTADT and ROMANOFFSKI in Russia, who are allied to the Imperial House.

In these, and many other cases, impalement was really equivalent to quartering; and in Foreign Armory it continues so to be. There are a multitude of instances in which a *Parti* coat is borne, and has been borne for generations. It very likely at first commemorated a marriage, and the consequent acquirement of possessions; but it now simply has the effect of a quartered coat. (The Counts ZU BRONCHORST for generations continued to impale with their own quartered coat the quartered coat of the County of EBERSTEIN; part of which was acquired by the marriage of Count JOHN II. with SIBYLLA VON EBERSTEIN.) This is especially the case in Spain, where impalements to denote a special marriage are rarely used as they are with us. For instance, the CORDOVAS, Marquises of PRIEGO, bear impaled two of the many coats which appear in the escucheon of the CORDOVAS, Dukes of SESA. Their arms are: *Per pale:* (1) CORDOVA, *Or, three bars gules;* (2) FIGUEROA, *Or, five fig leaves in saltire vert.* The MENDOZAS, Counts of CORUÑA, impale MENDOZA with FIGUEROA as above. The MENDOZAS, Counts de PRIEGO, impaled: (1) CARRILLO (*Gules, a castle triple-towered or*) with MENDOZA (*Vert, on a bend or a bendlet gules*).

The Dukes of GUELDERS early united by impalement their own arms, *Azure, a lion rampant queué, fourchée or*, with those of the County of JULIERS, *Or, a lion rampant sable* (and, according to German fashion, turned their lion to the sinister to face that of JULIERS, so that the lions appear as if combatant).

Originally, even in England, impalement did not invariably imply marriage. On the tomb of THOMAS, second Lord DACRE, K.G., at Lanercost, is a series of impaled and quartered coats containing the arms borne by himself, and his wife, ELIZABETH, heiress of GREYSTOCK. (He quartered MULTON, VAUX, and MORVILLE: she, GREYSTOCK, GRIMTHORPE, FERRERS, and BOTELER.) Of the escucheons one contains BOTELER impaling VAUX (the arms of two heiresses), another includes GREYSTOCK quartering VAUX. According to modern notions these would be absurdities, as there was not direct intermarriage. (See *Archæologia Æliana*, iv., 149.) The coat invented by English Heralds at a much later period, and assigned by them to EDWARD THE CONFESSOR (*Azure, a cross patonce between five martlets or*), was not only assumed and impaled in the place of honour with his own hereditary arms by RICHARD II., but was also assigned by him to be similarly used, either with or without a difference by some of his kinsmen. Thus, THOMAS MOWBRAY, K.G., Duke of NORFOLK, impaled the undifferenced coat; THOMAS, Duke of SURREY, used it with the addition of *a bordure ermine*; JOHN HOLLAND, first DUKE of EXETER; and HENRY BOLINGBROKE (before his accession) both differenced it with *a label argent*, and impaled it with their own arms. (*See* also the seal of EDWARD, Earl of RUTLAND, p. 416, *ante*.)

A remnant of dimidiation has survived in the practice of omitting in impaled coats those portions of the bordures and tressures contained in them, which would naturally be adjacent to the dividing, or palar, line of the shield. This is an early custom of which we have already seen examples, p. 463, but there are many instances in which the bordure, or tressure, is carried right round the coat impaled (*See* also pp. 462, 464). On the brass of

ALIANORE DE BOHUN, Duchess of GLOUCESTER, in Westminster Abbey, 1399, the silver bordure of her husband's difference runs round the quartered coat of FRANCE-ANCIENT and ENGLAND, which is impaled with their arms: *Quarterly:* 1 and 4. *Azure, a bend argent coticed or, between six lions rampant of the last.* 2 and 3. *Gules, two bendlets, the upper or, the lower argent.*

On the seal of THOMAS HOLLAND, Earl of KENT, to whom as already recorded, RICHARD II. assigned the arms of EDWARD THE CONFESSOR, differenced by a *bordure ermine* to be impaled with his paternal coat; the bordure of this augmentation, as well as that of his own arms (which were ENGLAND, *a bordure argent*), remains entire. We have the continuous bordure also on the seal of JOAN BEAUFORT, daughter of JOHN, Earl of SOMERSET, and Queen of JAMES I. of Scotland, to whom she was married in 1424. She bore SCOTLAND, impaling her personal arms: FRANCE and ENGLAND *quartered within a bordure compony argent and azure.* (LAING, *Scottish Seals,* i., 44.) The seal of BEATRICE of Portugal, Countess of ARUNDEL and SURREY, in the reign of HENRY V., bears her arms impaled with those of her husband the Earl, but with her own Castilian bordure unbroken. The arms of CATHARINE of BRAGANZA, Queen of CHARLES II., were also sculptured with the bordure entire. This appears to have been the Portuguese custom. The bordure of CASTILE appears entire on the seal of LEONORA of AUSTRIA, wife of EMMANUEL, King of PORTUGAL, in 1497. So is it also on the seal of ISABELLE of PORTUGAL, third wife of PHILIP LE BON, Duke of BURGUNDY, in 1430. (VRÉE, *Généalogie des Comtes de Flandre,* pp. 134, 125.)

In Spanish coats at the present day the bordure often remains unbroken, even when, as in the example subjoined, *two* bordured coats are impaled. DABANCASA bears:—*Escudo partito, el* 1º *d'Azur y un leon rampante de oro, bordadura de este metal cargada de una cadena de azur; el 2º de Plata y bordadura de gueules y ocho cabezas de águila de oro* (PIFERRER, *Nobiliario de España*, No. 259).

As for the Tressure, it was systematically dimidiated in the Royal Arms during the period in which the coats of ENGLAND and SCOTLAND were borne impaled (*i.e.* from the Union with Scotland in 1707, to the Union with Ireland in 1801), and the incomplete tressure is also to be found on the monument in Westminster Abbey to MARGARET, Countess of LENNOX, grand-daughter of HENRY VII., and mother of HENRY, Duke of ALBANY, and of Lord DARNLEY, second husband of Queen MARY of SCOTLAND. (BOUTELL, *Heraldry Historical and Popular*, plate xxii.)

On the other hand earlier usage prescribes the retention of the Tressure unbroken. It is entire on the seal just referred to of Queen JOAN BEAUFORT; on that of MARY of GUELDERS, Queen of JAMES II.; also on the seal of Trinity Collegiate Church in Edinburgh, founded by the last-named Queen; on her arms sculptured in St. Giles' Church, Edinburgh, impaled with those of her husband (curiously the tressure is incomplete at the top, see *The Story of St. Giles' Cathedral Church, Edinburgh*, by WM. CHAMBERS, LL.D. 1879, p. 9); on the painting at Holyrood of the arms of MARGARET of DENMARK, Queen of JAMES III. in 1485; on the seal of MARY, Queen of Scots in her first widowhood; and in the whole series of impaled coats of the Queens of Scotland in Sir DAVID LINDSAY'S *Armorial MS.* of the reign of JAMES V.

Another armorial MS. in the Lyon Office dimidiates the tressure in a like series of the arms of the Queens of Scotland for all except MARY. In the same MS. the bordure gobony in the personal arms of Queen JOAN BEAUFORT is left entire. In British Heraldry a widow continues to bear her husband's coat impaled with her own, but usually places the combined coats in a lozenge, instead of in a shield.

Before leaving the subject of the combination of arms by dimidiation, it is necessary to point out that this was not only effected by impalement, but, in a few rare instances, by other divisions of the shield. The last coat emblazoned in the most valuable and interesting 14th century MS. the *Wappenrolle von Zürich*, No. 559, affords an example, unfortunately unnamed, in which the dimidiation is not by impalement but per bend. The coat (No. 559) is : *Per bend, in chief, or, a lion rampant gardant dimidiated gules;* in base, *Bendy lozengy argent and azure* (the arms of BAVARIA). It seems to me exceedingly probable that this is the coat of a person of high, but illegitimate, descent.

In the *Herald and Genealogist*, vol. ii., p. 560, is a woodcut of a coat of arms, which appears upon a portrait of the year 1665, and which affords a curious example of the dimidiation of two coats per bend sinister. The coats thus treated are : in chief, *Gules, on a chief argent three mallets penchés sable.* In base, *Argent, on a mound a tree proper, senestré of a stag gules rampant against the trunk, and browsing on its branches.* In the *Genealogist*, new series, vol. v., p. 207 ; nearly a quarter of a century after attention was directed to it, I was able to assign the arms to two families of the name of VAN DER LINDEN ; the one Barons d'HOOG-VOORST ; the other settled at Dordrecht. (Plate XLI., fig. 1.) Another example is afforded by the arms of the Barons von KITTLITZ which is now borne : *Per bend sinister, in chief Or, a bull rampant dimidiated sable ;* in base, *Gules, three bends argent.* This coat is reversed in SIEBMACHER, *Wappenbuch*, i., 29.

One curious use of impalement also remains to be noticed. On the Continent the arms of an unmarried lady of high rank were sometimes represented in the sinister half of a lozenge, the dexter half being left uncharged. These were called *Arms of Expectation* and the dexter half was left to be filled by a future marriage. On the seal of MARGARET of AUSTRIA, Duchess of BURGUNDY in 1495, *fiancée* to CHARLES VIII. of France, her arms are on a lozenge of which the dexter half is left blank, the sinister being disposed thus: *Quarterly*, 1. AUSTRIA (*Gules, a fess argent*); 2. BURGUNDY-MODERN; 3. BURGUNDY-ANCIENT; 4. BRABANT. Over all on an escucheon, FLANDERS, *vide supra* pp. 461, 462. (VRÉE, *Gen. Com. Fl.*, 130.) On the seals of ISABELLA, Infanta of SPAIN, Countess of FLANDERS, daughter of PHILIP II. of SPAIN, in 1598 her arms are thus represented. What is, however, curious is that on the joint seal of herself and her husband, ALBERT, Archduke of AUSTRIA, in 1599, his arms are represented on an escucheon, while hers are still depicted on the sinister side of a lozenge, of which as in the previous instance, the dexter side is left blank. (VRÉE, *de Seghelen der Graven van Vlaendren*, Plates xcv. and xcvii.)

QUARTERING, in its simplest form, is the dividing the shield into four equal sections by a vertical and a horizontal line, intersecting each other in the middle point of the escucheon.

The earliest example known to me of the use of quartered arms is afforded by the seal of JOANNA of PONTHIEU, second wife of FERDINAND III., King of CASTILE and LEON, in 1272. This seal bears on its reverse in a *vesica* the triple-towered castles of CASTILE and the rampant lion of LEON, repeated as in modern quartering. There is no separation of the quarters by a pourfilar line (this is a peculiarity which has already been noticed as existing in the early quartered coats of HAINAULT five-and-twenty years later, *vide ante*, p. 463). The lion in base is *contourné*, a usage which still prevails in many similar cases, particularly in German coats.

HOEPING'S assertion (quoted by NISBET, ii., 86) that the arms of CASTILE and LEON were borne quarterly by FERDINAND of CASTILE, who espoused SANCHA of LEON, *circa* 1065, is unsupported by any evidence. Arms were not used in Spain at so early a date.

The quartered coat of CASTILE and LEON is sculptured in Westminster Abbey on the monument erected to FERDINAND'S daughter, ELEANOR, first Queen of EDWARD I., who died in 1290. Here, according to usual custom, the coat of CASTILE occupies the first and fourth quarters of the shield; that of LEON is placed in the second and third. (Examples are extant in which this order is inverted.)

The earliest seal bearing a quartered coat in the series engraved in HUEBER'S *Austria Illustrata* is that of FRIEDRICH VON AZENPRUK, in 1350.

When three coats have to be marshalled, they ordinarily occupy the first, second, and third quarters, and the first coat is repeated in the fourth. This arrangement is familiar to all in our own Royal Arms, where ENGLAND occupies the first quarter, SCOTLAND the second, IRELAND the third, while ENGLAND is repeated in the fourth quarter. There are, however, examples of a different arrangement. In the escucheon of the arms of ELIZABETH of YORK, Queen of HENRY VII., on his tomb in his chapel at Westminster Abbey, the first quarter is occupied by the quartered arms of FRANCE and ENGLAND, the fourth by that of MORTIMER, while both the second and third are charged with the coat of ULSTER: *Or, a cross gules.* (Plate XXXVIII., fig. 4.)

Should the coats to be thus marshalled be four in number, each naturally occupies a single quarter of the shield. Thus, on the reverse of the seal of ISABELLE of FRANCE, Queen of EDWARD II., each of the four coats of ENGLAND, FRANCE, NAVARRE, and CHAMPAGNE (*Azure, a bend argent coticed potent-counter-potent or*) occupies a single quarter of the shield.

When more coats than four are to be represented, the shield is divided by horizontal and vertical lines into spaces, which are still called *quarters*, how many soever they may be. For five coats the shield would be divided into six portions by two vertical and one horizontal line (or, if preferred, by one vertical and two horizontal lines), and the first coat would usually be repeated in the last quarter to make the number equal—a course which would not be needful if the coats to be quartered amounted to six. In Foreign Heraldry it is usual to specify the number and position of the lines by which the shield is divided. Thus, while an English herald would say simply, *Quarterly of six*, and leave it to the painter's or engraver's taste to arrange the quarterings in three rows of two, or in two rows of three, a French or German herald would ordinarily specify the arrangement to be used in distinct terms, thus: "*Coupé d'un trait, parti de deux autres, qui font six quartiers;*" or "*Das . . . . Wappen besteht aus einem zweimal quer und einmal senkrecht getheilten Schilde.*" Provision would similarly be made for any larger number of quarterings.

In modern British Heraldry the usual reason for quartering is to indicate descent from an heiress, or from more than one, who has married into the family. If there be but one her arms appear in the second and third quarters: if more than three (whose coats could of course be placed in a plain quartered escucheon), the shield is subdivided sufficiently to make room for all; and the arms of the heiresses occupy quarters corresponding in position to their seniority in point of time; though in olden days priority was sometimes given to quarterings indicative of a royal descent, or to the coat of some powerful heiress. If the number of divisions cannot be made conveniently to correspond with the number of coats to be thus accommodated, the difficulty is removed either by the omission of the less important coats, or by the repetition of the first quarter in the last place in the escucheon. Again, it may happen that one of the heiresses whose arms are to be quartered, herself bore a quartered coat, in this case the quarter appropriated to her contains her whole bearings, the shield is then said to be *counter-quartered* (*contré-écartelé*), and the quarter itself is called a *Grand quarter*.

The coat of the Earls of NORTHUMBERLAND as generally borne, and still used by the Dukes (*v.* Plate XXXIX., fig. 3), is an example of the old style of Marshalling. The coat is: *Quarterly of four Grand Quarters*—

I. and IV. *Quarterly*, 1 and 4. *Or, a lion rampant azure*, LOUVAINE(?)

2 and 3. *Gules, three lucies hauriant argent*, LUCY.

II. and III. *Azure, five fusils in fess or*, PERCY-ANCIENT.

The original coat of PERCY (Plate XVIII., fig. 12) was doubtless allusive to the name, but before 1300 it had been abandoned in favour of the blue lion on the golden field which is assigned to HENRY DE PERCY (of Alnwick), first Baron, in the *Roll* of CAERLAVEROCK, and appears on the seal of his letter to the Pope in 1301. In the *Roll* known as GLOVER'S *Roll*, HENRY DE PERCY bears, *d'Azur, à la fesse engrele d'or*, and PIERS PERCY the reverse. (This was the ordinary blazon of a fess fusily at that time, *v.* p. 413.)

HENRY DE PERCI bears: *Azure, five fusils in fess or*, in the *Roll* known as ST. GEORGE'S *Roll*. It appears in the ACRE *Roll* early in the thirteenth century: and with some differences of tincture in other *Rolls*. *Or, five fusils in fess sable* are attributed to ROBERT DE PERCI; and to WALTER DE PERCI, *Azure, five fusils in fess argent*. In the *Second Nobility Roll*, which contains the names and arms of the Barons, etc., summoned to the Parliament held at London, 27 Edward I. (1299), HENRY PERCY, Baron of TOPCLIFFE, bears the coat, *Or, a lion rampant azure*. There can be little doubt that the new coat was adopted on this Baron's marriage to ELEANOR FITZALAN, the daughter of his Lord Paramount, JOHN, Earl of ARUNDEL, whose arms were, *Gules, a lion rampant or*. The assertions in the *Peerages*, and elsewhere, that the change was made in consequence of a marriage of a JOSCELINE DE LOUVAINE to AGNES, a PERCY heiress, is pure fable. Late in the fourteenth century the first Earl of NORTHUMBERLAND married the sister and heiress of Lord LUCY, who settled on him extensive estates on the condition that the LUCY arms should be quartered with those of PERCY. The counter-quartered coat in the I. and IV. of the escucheon described above, represents this alliance; and at a later date the original PERCY coat was resumed and placed in the II. and III. quarters. (See "The Old Heraldry of the Percies" by Mr LONGSTAFFE, in *Archæologia Æliana*, vol. iv.; and *The Pedigrees and early Heraldry of the Lords of Alnwick*, by TATE and LONGSTAFFE, 1866.)

Modern English Heralds have discouraged the use of grand quarterings; and advised that the quartered coat of an heiress should be separated into its component parts, and each of the quarterings be made to follow in turn her paternal coat. There are many cases in which such an arrangement would be quite inappropriate; *e.g.* when there is, as in some Scottish shields, a feudal escucheon borne *en surtout* above the quartered coats; or, when the quarters virtually form one composition by being enclosed within a bordure, assumed as a mark of difference, or cadency.

Very rarely quartering is effected *per saltire*, as in the arms of SICILY (*v.* p. 495), and in some other coats of Spanish origin (*v.* p. 506). The CARDONAS bore two coats impaled:—(A) *Per saltire*, in chief and base, *Or*,

PLATE XXXIX.

MARSHALLING.

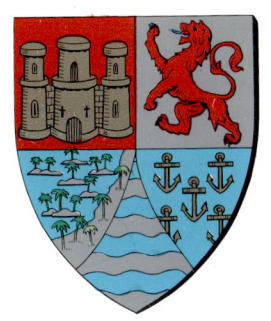

1. Columbus.
2. Seymour. 
3. Percy. 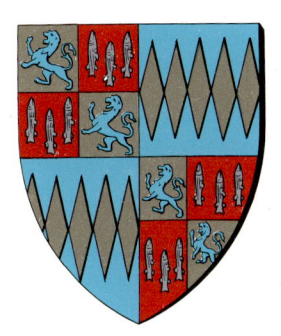
4. Cronberg. 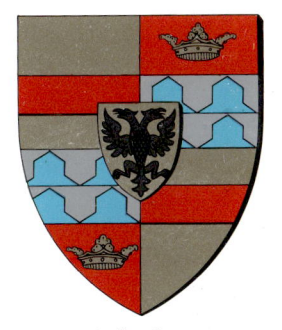
5. Baden. 
6. Angevin-chief.

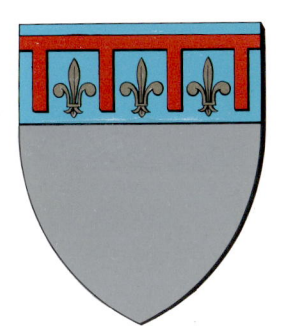

four pallets gules, ARRAGON ; in dexter flank, *Gules, three thistles argent ;* in sinister flank ANJOU. (B) The arms of the Counts of URGEL: *Per saltire* ARRAGON, and *Chequy or and sable* for URGEL (*See* Plate XL. and SALAZAR Y CASTRO, *Casa de Lara*, ii., p. 168).

In Foreign Heraldry the base of the quartered shield is not unfrequently cut off by a horizontal line, forming what is known as a *champagne*, and the space thus made is occupied by one or more coats. At other times a pile with curved sides runs from the base some distance into the quartered shield, which is then said to be *enté en point* (*v.* Plate XVI., fig. 9), and this space is devoted to the display of one or more quarterings.

The main difference between British and Foreign usage with regard to quartering is this, that in England quarterings are usually employed to denote simply descent from an heiress, or representation in blood ; in Scotland they also implied the possession of lands. In Foreign coats the quarterings are often employed to denote the possession of fiefs acquired in other ways than by marriage (*e.g.*, by bequest or purchase), or the *jus expectationis*, the right of succession to such fiefs in accordance with certain agreements. For instance, treaties of *Erb-Verbrüderung* were common in Germany, by which two nobles agreed that on the failure of the line of one, the representatives of the other line should succeed to the possessions of that which had become extinct. (On these *Pacta successionis*, which conveyed the immediate right to the use of the arms as above, consult KNIPSCHILD, *de Nobilitate ejusque Juribus*, 1693, and his other treatise, *de Fidei Commissis.*) It was by such a treaty of *Erb-Verbrüderung* that, in 1632, the Counts of WALDECK came into possession of the County of PYRMONT (*vide post*, p. 490).

THE ESCUCHEON SURTOUT.

Another mode of marshalling came into use some

time after quartering, namely, the placing a small escucheon *en surtout* upon the centre of the quartered coat. In 1404 JOHN, Count of FLANDERS, son and heir of PHILIP *the Bold*, Duke of BURGUNDY, added to his arms the coat of FLANDERS *en surtout*, being the arms of his mother. He thus bore: *Quarterly*, 1 and 4. FRANCE, *within a bordure goboné argent and gules* (BURGUNDY-MODERN); 2 and 3. *Bendy of six or and azure, a bordure gules* (BURGUNDY-ANCIENT); *en surtout, Or, a lion rampant, sable* (FLANDERS). (VRÉE, *de Seghelen der Graven van Vlaendren*, p. 30.)

An earlier seal of MARGARET of BAVARIA, wife of JOHN, Duke of BURGUNDY, *circa* 1385 (VRÉE, *Généalogie des Comtes de Flandres*, p. 60), bears the escucheon impaled by dimidiation, to which reference has been made at p. 462 *ante;* but with the addition of an escucheon *per pale*, on which no charges are now apparent. The shield, which is *en bannière*, is supported by a single full-length angel, who bears it in front of him.

This coat continued to be thus borne up to the time of the marriage of MARY of BURGUNDY with MAXIMILIAN of AUSTRIA, in 1477. But in 1430 PHILIPPE *le Bon* introduced into his main escucheon the arms of the Duchies of BRABANT and LIMBURG, not as separate quarters, but by impaling them respectively in the second and third quarters with the arms of BURGUNDY-ANCIENT (*cf.* Plate XLVII.). The coat then read thus:—*Quarterly*, 1 and 4. BURGUNDY-MODERN (as above); 2. *Per pale*: —(a) BURGUNDY-ANCIENT, (b) *Sable, a lion rampant or*, BRABANT; 3. *Per pale* (a) BURGUNDY-ANCIENT, (b) *Argent, a lion rampant gules crowned or*, LIMBURG. *Over all*, FLANDERS, as above. It will be noticed that this arrangement illustrates what has been already said in the previous section about the Continental use of impaled coats. CHARLES, Count of CHAROLOIS, eldest son of PHILIPPE *le Bon*, before his accession to the Duchy as

CHARLES *le Hardi*, bore his father's arms differenced by a label, but without the escucheon of FLANDERS; a remarkable omission. (*See* MAURICE, *Toison d'Or*, No. 24.) On his seal, *circa* 1430, ADOLPH of CLEVES places the arms of his wife, ANNE of BURGUNDY (a natural daughter of PHILIPPE *le Bon*), in an escucheon upon his quartered coat of CLEVES and MARK. Her arms are: *Quarterly*, 1 and 4. *Azure, a single fleur-de-lis (or)*; 2 and 3. BURGUNDY-ANCIENT ; *over all* FLANDERS. (This is a very noteworthy example, and it is also instructive to notice that their son, PHILIP DE RAVESTEIN, placed a similar escucheon charged with the full Burgundian quarterings, without any mark of bastardy, above his quartered coat of CLEVES and MARK.)

PIERRE DE BEAUFFREMONT, created first Count de CHARNY in 1425, twentieth knight of the Order of the Golden Fleece (one, therefore, of the original members of the Order at its foundation in 1429), bore: *Quarterly*, 1 and 4. *Vairé or and gules*, BEAUFFREMONT ; 2 and 3. *Gules, three cinquefoils or*, VERGY, the latter coat being quartered for his mother, JEANNE DE VERGY ; but upon these coats he placed, *en surtout, Gules, three escucheons argent*, which was the coat of his maternal great-grandmother, GUILLEMETTE DE CHARNY. He married, in 1447, MARIE DE BOURGOGNE, another natural daughter of Duke PHILIPPE *le Bon*. Other Low Country instances of the use of the maternal arms *en surtout* have been noticed in the preceding chapter.

In England, RICHARD, Duke of YORK (d. 1460), father of EDWARD IV., bore *en surtout* upon his seal, the arms of his maternal grandmother (JOAN), daughter, and eventual heiress of THOMAS HOLLAND, Earl of KENT (ENGLAND, *a bordure argent*). His own arms were: FRANCE and ENGLAND *quarterly, differenced by a label argent, on each point three torteaux*. However, two English instances may be pointed out of the same century, in which a husband placed his wife's arms, and not those of an ancestress, *en surtout*. These are afforded by the Garter Plates of Sir JOHN NEVILLE, Lord MONTAGU, afterwards Marquess of MONTAGU (elected K.G., *circa* 1463), and of RICHARD BEAUCHAMP, fifth Earl of WARWICK and ALBEMARLE (elected K.G., *circa* 1400); but it was not until about the beginning of the 17th century that the practice arose by which the husband of an heiress places his wife's arms in an escucheon *en surtout* upon his personal arms, whether his coat be a quartered one or not. Such an escucheon acquired the name of an "escucheon of pretence," and is borne by the husband of the heiress alone; the children who issue from the marriage bear the coats of both parents united, not in this way, but by quartering. GUILLIM, the first edition of whose work, *A Display of Heraldry*, was published in 1611, gives his sanction to the "escucheon of pretence;" but when Sir GEORGE MACKENZIE'S *Treatise on Heraldry* appeared—in 1680—the usage was only beginning to be heard of as a novelty in Scotland, and is alluded to with disapproval. "If a man marry an Heretrix, he himself *impales* only her arms; but his children procreat of that marriage quarters (*sic*) them . . . . Sometimes also (says Guillims) he who marries an Heretrix may carry her arms in an inescutcheon upon his own, because the husband pretends that his heirs shall one day inherit an estate by her; it is therefore called an escutcheon of pretence; but this way of Bearing is not known abroad upon that occasion." (*Science of Heraldry*, chap. xxiv., pp. 80, 81.)

In the Heraldry of the Continent of Europe, it has long been the custom for an elected Sovereign to place his hereditary arms in an escucheon *en surtout* above those of his dominions. This was the invariable custom of the Emperors of GERMANY, and of the Kings of POLAND. Thus JOHN SOBIESKI (JOHN III. of Poland) placed above the arms of that kingdom: (*Quarterly*, 1 and 4. *Gules an eagle displayed argent, crowned or*, POLAND; 2 and 3. *Gules, a knight in full armour proper mounted on a white horse, bearing in his right hand a drawn sword, and on his left arm a shield azure charged with a patriarchal cross argent*, LITHUANIA) an escucheon of his personal arms, *Or, a round buckler purpure*. The Kings of SWEDEN, of the houses of HESSE, VASA, and, in modern times, BERNADOTTE, have done the same (See *Det Svenska Riks Vapnet*, af HANS HILDEBRAND; *Antiquarisk Tidskrift för Sverige*, 1883). The Kings of DENMARK thus bore the arms of OLDENBURG, etc. As having obtained the crown by popular election the Kings of the HELLENES also place *en surtout* upon the arms of the Greek kingdom (*Azure, a Greek cross couped argent*), an escucheon of their personal arms. OTHO, the first king, thus bore the Bavarian arms; the present King GEORGE, a prince of DENMARK, thus uses those of that kingdom. The Royal Arms of our own country furnish us with a similar example in the case of WILLIAM III., who placed the arms of NASSAU (p. 215) *en surtout*, upon the quartered coat of these realms. (*See* Plate LII., figs. 6, 7.) Under the Commonwealth the Great Seals of OLIVER CROMWELL and his son RICHARD as Protectors, bear a shield of arms: *Quarterly*, 1 and 4. *Argent, a cross gules, for* ENGLAND; 2. *Azure, a saltire argent*, for SCOTLAND; 3. *Azure, a harp or stringed argent*, for IRELAND; and upon these quarterings *en surtout* an escucheon of the personal arms of CROMWELL: *Sable, a lion rampant argent*. After 1801 the quartered arms of the family of BRUNSWICK-LÜNEBURG, which from 1714 had formed the fourth quarter of the Royal Arms, were placed *en surtout*. (*See* Plate LII., figs. 9, 10.)

The escucheon *en surtout* has also been used in other Royal Arms as indicative, not of election, but of descent. Thus, on the accession of PHILIP, Duc d'ANJOU, to the throne of SPAIN, his arms (FRANCE, *a bordure gules*) were placed *en surtout* above: Quarterly, 1 and 4. CASTILE; 2 and 3. LEON; *Enté en point of* GRENADA (*Argent, a pomegranate gules leafed and seeded proper*); and these are the present Royal Arms of SPAIN. During the brief reign of King AMADEUS of SAVOY, there was substituted for the escucheon of ANJOU, the arms of SAVOY (*Gules, a cross argent, all within a bordure azure*) with the same intent.

The arms of the princes and princesses of our own Royal House are charged *en surtout* with an escucheon of their paternal arms of SAXONY (Plate XII., fig. 6), and in future reigns this escucheon will form part of the arms of the reigning Sovereign.

Our arrangement of grand quarters in which the same coat is repeated four times, as in the arms of PERCY, Duke of NORTHUMBERLAND (blazoned *ante*, page 481), is almost unknown among the Germans (the coat of the Counts of MANSFELD is an exception), but when quarters are repeated they sometimes adopt a different arrangement, of which an example will be found in the arms of the Prince of WALDECK and PYRMONT at p. 490. In it, and in the shield of the Counts of GIECH, both of which are Quarterly of nine, the quarters 1 and 9, 2 and 8, 3 and 7, 4 and 6 correspond. In the arms of the Counts von HERBERSTEIN (TYROFF, *Wappen des Adels des Königreichs Baiern*, i., 47) which are:—Quarterly of six (in three horizontal rows of two quarters), with an escucheon *en surtout*, the quarters which correspond are 1 and 4, 2 and 5, 3 and 6. In the arms of the Counts of SOLMS we have really two coats impaled, each being quartered: (A) *Quarterly*, 1 and 4. *Or, a lion rampant azure*, SOLMS; 2 and 3. *Per fess gules and or*, MÜNZENBERG. (B) *Quarterly*, 1 and 4. *Or, a rose sable*, WILDENFELS; 2 and 3. *Sable, a lion rampant argent*, SONNEWALDE. If this be regarded as a single coat of eight quarterings, those which correspond are 1 and 6, 2 and 5, 3 and 8, 4 and 7.

To our ideas of Marshalling the coat of the Counts ZU CRONBERG (Plate XXXIX., fig. 4) is strangely arranged, though it is a simple coat of four quarters (with an escucheon of the Empire *en surtout* as an Imperial Augmentation) *Quarterly*, 1 and 4. *Or, a fess gules*, County of HOHEN-GEROLDSECK ; 2. Two rows of *Vair* (Beffroi?) *on a chief gules an open crown or.* 3. Two rows of *Vair, on a champagne gules an open crown or* (both 2 and 3 for CRONBERG). But we find from SPENER, *Opus Heraldicum*, p. spec., 103 (where the Imperial diploma of FERDINAND II., 1663, is given) that the CRONBERG quarters are really a canting coat, " ein quartieter Schild, dessen hinter unter und vorder obertheil roth oder Rubinfarb, der hinterste ober und vorder untertheil aber weisz oder Silberfarb ist. In dem hindern untern und oberen vordern jed-wedern erscheinet eine Königliche goldfarbe CRON. In dem vordern und obern hindern theil aber vier blaue paarweisz neben einander in Glockengestalt gesetzte BERG," etc.

The arms of the Princes of SCHWARZBURG are a curious example of German blazon. It consists, first of all, of two quartered coats impaled :—

(A) *Quarterly*, 1 and 4. *Or, an eagle displayed sable*, ARNSTADT.

2 and 3. *Argent, the attire of a stag gules*, SONDERSHAUSEN.

En surtout, Azure, a lion rampant crowned or, for SCHWARZBURG.

(B) *Quarterly*, 1 and 4. *Chequy gules and argent*, HOHNSTEIN.

2 and 3. *Per fess* (a) *Gules, a lion rampant or* and (b) *Barry of eight or and gules*, LAUTERBURG.

En surtout, Argent, a stag passant sable, KLETTENBERG.

Over these impaled coats is a narrow cross of alternate narrow bends, *Azure, or,* and *sable,* the perpendicular piece divides the quartered coats, and the traverse passes under the two escucheons *en surtout.* On the centre of the cross is a larger escucheon *en surtout* containing as an Imperial augmentation, the Imperial Arms, the crowned double eagle having on its breast a small escucheon, *gules charged with a princely hat.* The base of the whole escucheon is occupied by *a champagne :—Or, thereon a pitchfork, and beneath it a horse comb, both fesseways gules.* These are the official arms of the Office of *Reichs Stallmeister,* held by the Lords of LEUTENBERG.

In the arms of the princely houses, and higher nobility of Germany, the shield is often charged with a number of quarterings and with an escucheon *en surtout.* This is borne for different reasons; and it will be interesting to note the principal of these, and give an example or two of each. The quarterings are usually those of the several fiefs on account of which the bearer had the right to sit and vote in the Diets, or Circles, of the Empire: and often the principal, or original, fief of the family is placed *en surtout.* Thus the Counts of WALDECK (who received the title of Prince in 1682 and 1712) bore: *Quarterly of nine,* 1 and 9. *Argent, a cross moline gules,* County of PYRMONT; 2 and 8. *Argent, three escucheons two and one gules,* County of RAPPOLSTEIN; 3 and 7. *Argent, three raven's heads couped at the neck sable crowned or,* Lordship of HOHENECK; 4 and 6. *Argent, semé of billets couchés azure, a lion rampant gules, crowned or,* Lordship of GEROLDSECK. The fifth or central quarter is concealed by the escucheon *en surtout* of the arms of WALDECK: *Or, an eight-pointed star sable.* (Plate XLI.) So the Margraves of BADEN formerly bore: *Quarterly,* 1. *Argent, a lion rampant gules crowned or* (this lion faces to the sinister, in accordance with the German fashion by which in quartered coats animals are often made to face to the centre of the shield (*vide ante*, p. 420, and *cf.* GUELDERS, *ante* p. 473); Landgravate of the BREISGAU ; 2. *Azure, an eagle's wing in fess argent* (the feathers turned to the base), with a golden *Klee Stengel*, Lordship of USENBERG (otherwise SAUSENBERG); 3. *Gules, on a pale or three chevrons sable*, Lordship of BADENWEILER (*v.* Plate XLVI., fig. 2) ; 4. *Per fess wavy or and azure; the latter charged with two bars argent, and the former with a lion rampant gules issuing from the partition line*, Lordship of RÖTELN (*v.* p. 221). *En surtout* an escucheon for the Margravate of BADEN : *Or, a bend gules.* (See Plate XXXIX., fig. 5.) In later times many other quarterings were added to the shield, and the arms of BADEN were made to occupy its centre quarter without being placed on a distinct escucheon *en surtout*. The great shield of the Grand Dukes of BADEN (who attained that dignity in 1806), contains thirty quarterings ; but generally only the simple coat of BADEN (*Or, a bend gules*) ensigned with a Royal Crown, and supported by a sable griffin, and a golden lion (both regardant and royally crowned) is in use. The arms of SAXONY are often displayed *en surtout* in the quarterings of the several Sovereign Saxon States.

Similarly, while the shield of the Princes of LICHTENSTEIN used to bear the quartered arms of SAXONY, CZERNABOR, and the Duchies of TROPPAU, SILESIA, and JAGERNDORFF (the last being the *enté en point*); the arms of the house of LICHTENSTEIN (*Per fess or and gules*) were placed *en surtout*. (*See* TRIER'S *Einleitung zu der Wapen-kunst*, p. 493.) Later the quarterings of the main shield were: 1. SILESIA ; 2. SAXONY; 3. TROPPAU ; 4. RITTBERG ; *enté* of JAGERNDORFF ; and, as before, LICHTENSTEIN *en surtout*.

So the Counts (afterwards Princes) of METTERNICH formerly bore their family coat : *Argent, three vannets sable, en surtout* above the quartered coats of the Lordships of WINNEBERG and BEILSTEIN (1 and 4. *Gules, between six crosslets or a bend indented azure;* 2 and 3. *Gules, three hunting horns argent* two and one). Other quarterings have been added in modern times, and an Imperial augmentation. (Note the *Armes fausses.*)

Some of the escucheons borne *en surtout* in Germany do indicate possessions acquired by marriage; but usually in times far remote from the present.

Thus the Dukes, now Grand Dukes, of MECKLENBURG, still place the arms of the Lordship of STARGARD (which are: *Per fess gules and or*, and which HENRY the LION, of MECKLENBURG obtained by his marriage with BEATRICE, daughter of ALBERT, Markgrave of BRANDENBURG, in 1220), in an escucheon *en surtout* above their main coat (*Quarterly of six in three rows of two each:* 1. Duchy of MECKLENBURG; 2. Principality of the WENDS; 3. Principality of SCHWERIN; 4. Principality of RATZEBURG; 5. County of SCHWERIN; 6. Lordship of ROSTOCK).

The Princes of ARENBERG, who bear: *Quarterly,* 1 and 4. *Gules, three five-leaved flowers (fleurs de néflier) or,* for the Duchy of ARENBERG; 2 and 3. *Or, a fess chequy of three rows argent and gules* for the County of MARK; place in an escucheon *en surtout* the arms of LIGNE; *Or, a bend gules,* quartered with those of BARBANÇON: *Argent, three lions rampant gules crowned or.* This is a curious example, inasmuch as the arms *en surtout* are those of the husband, not of the wife; for MARGARET, sister and heiress of the last Count of ARENBERG, married JEAN, Baron of LIGNE and BARBANÇON, who obtained the dignity of Prince of the Holy Roman Empire, in 1565.

The Counts of RECKHEIM, who claim descent from the house of ESTE, which bore, *Azure, an eagle displayed argent;* place that coat *en surtout* upon their quartered shield :—1 and 4. *Gules, a cross or* (County of ASPERMONT); 2 and 3. *Or, a lion rampant gules* (County of RECKHEIM).

The Princes of LAMBERG descend from GEORGE SIGISMUND, Baron of LAMBERG, who married at the commencement of the seventeenth century, JOHANNA, daughter and heiress of JOHN SCALIGER (DELLA SCALA) and still bear her arms (*see* Plate XXXII., fig. 9) *en surtout* upon their quartered coat : 1 and 4. *Per pale* (a) *Barry of four argent and azure*, (b) *Gules plain*, LAMBERG ; 2 and 3. *Or, a hound rampant sable collared argent*, for POTTWEIN. In TRIER'S *Einleitung zu der Wapenkunst*, p. 491, the SCALA coat in the LAMBERG arms has also *a mount in base vert*, on which the greyhounds and ladder rest, but this does not appear in the modern blazons.

The Counts of KESSELSTADT place their paternal arms : *Argent, a basilisk passant gules*, in an escucheon *en surtout* upon the simple coat of the family of ORSBECK (now extinct in the male line), from which they descend : *Or, a saltire gules between four nenuphar leaves vert* (TYROFF, *Wappenbuch*, i., Band. Taf. 59).

The foregoing examples will probably be found sufficient to illustrate the German use of Marshalling with regard to coats borne *en surtout ;* on account of the possession of fiefs, by marriage or otherwise.

On the use of this escucheon as a mark of difference, or cadency, *see* p. 448 ; as an indication of the tenure of an official dignity, *see* p. 526; and as containing special grants in augmentation, *see* Chapter XVI.

But before leaving this part of the subject we may here notice that the great German quartered coats sometimes bear several of these escucheons *en surtout.* Thus in the great escucheon of the quarterings of the Royal House of PRUSSIA (*Das grosse Staats-Wappen*), four such separate escucheons appear upon

the palar line, bearing respectively the arms of
PRUSSIA; BRANDENBURG; NÜRNBERG; and HOHEN-
ZOLLERN. Plate XL. represents the achievement of the
Empress MARIA THERESA before her accession to the
Imperial throne when she was Queen of HUNGARY
and BOHEMIA; and, by marriage, Grand Duchess of
TUSCANY. It is a shield of four grand quarters, each
counter-quartered and bearing an escucheon *en surtout*.
Another escucheon crowned is placed on the central point
of the whole shield, so that the five *surtouts* are arranged
in saltire. As there are twenty-nine quarterings, none
of them being repetitions, with a very remarkable variety
of historic interest, the full blazon is here appended.

Quarterly of four Grand Quarters:—

I. Quarterly of six (in two horizontal rows of three quarters each):—
  1. BOHEMIA: *Gules, a lion rampant argent, double queué.*
  2. DALMATIA: *Azure, three leopard's heads affrontés crowned or.*
  3. CROATIA: *Chequy argent and gules.*
  4. ESCLAVONIA:[1] *Gules, issuing from the sinister flank an arm embowed proper, vested gules and holding a sabre argent.*
  5. JERUSALEM: *Argent, a cross potent between four crosslets or.*
  6. INDIA: *Azure, a lion rampant argent holding a cross or.*
     Over all an escucheon per pale. (*a*) *Barry of eight argent and gules,* HUNGARY-ANCIENT. (*b*) *Gules, on a mount in base vert, an open crown or, issuant therefrom a patriarchal cross argent:* HUNGARY-MODERN.

[1] These are now borne as the arms of BOSNIA (a part of ESCLA-VONIA), as will be shown hereafter.

PLATE XL.

Imperial Crown of Austria.

Crown of St. Stephen, Hungary.

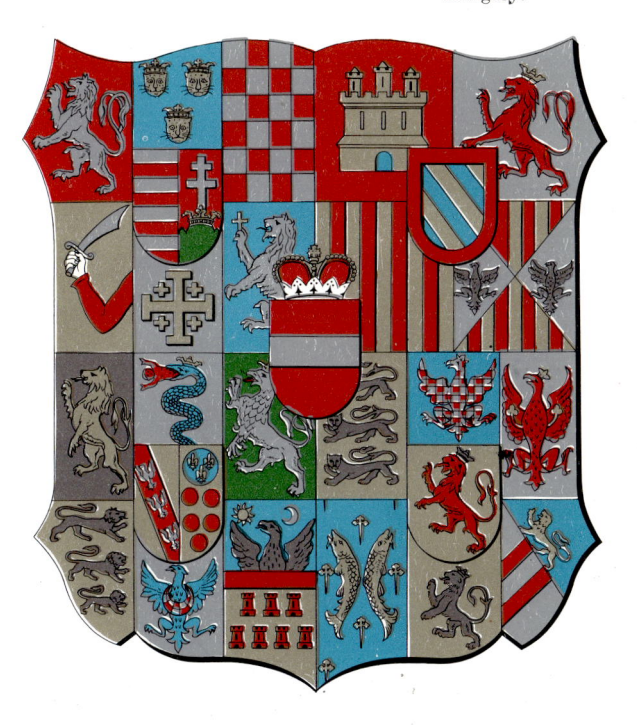

MARIA THERESA.
Queen of Hungary and Bohemia; Archduchess of Austria; and Grand Duchess of Tuscany.

II. Quarterly:—
1. CASTILE: *Gules, a castle triple-towered or.*
2. LEON: *Argent, a lion rampant gules crowned or.*
3. ARRAGON: *Or, four pallets gules.*
4. SICILY: *Per saltire, in chief and base* ARRAGON; *in flanks Argent, an eagle displayed sable.*

Over all the arms of BURGUNDY-ANCIENT; *Bendy of six or and azure, a bordure gules.*

III. Quarterly of six (in two horizontal rows of three each):—
1. BRABANT: *Sable, a lion rampant or.*
2. MILAN: *Argent, a serpent ondoyant in pale azure, crowned or, vorant a child gules.*
3. STYRIA: *Vert, a griffon rampant queué fourchée argent; vomiting flames proper, and crowned or.*
4. CARINTHIA: *Or, three lions passant (contournés) gules* (should be *sable*). (*See* also pp. 454, 471.)
5. CARNIOLA: *Argent, an eagle displayed azure, on its breast a crescent counter-compony of the field and gules.*
6. TRANSYLVANIA (SIEBENBÜRGEN): *Per fess azure and or, over all a bar gules, issuing therefrom a demi-eagle displayed sable, addextré in chief of the sun in splendour, and senestré of a crescent argent. In the base, seven towers, three and four, of the third.*

Over all an escucheon per pale: (*a*) *Or, on a bend gules three allerions argent*, LORRAINE; (*b*) *Or, five balls gules two, two, one, in chief another of larger size, azure, thereon three fleurs-de-lis of the field.* TUSCANY.

IV. Quarterly of six (in three rows of two each):—
1. SWABIA: *Or, three lions passant gardant in pale sable.*

2. (SILESIA:[1]) *Azure, an eagle chequy gules and argent, crowned or.*
3. TYROL: *Argent, an eagle displayed gules; crowned and having "Klee Stengeln" on the wings, or.*
4. BAR: *Azure, semé of crosslets fitchées or, over all two barbel, addorsed of the last.*
5. JULIERS: *Or, a lion rampant sable crowned of the field.*
6. GÖRZ: *Per bend, in chief azure a lion rampant or in base, argent two bends-sinister gules.*

Over all HAPSBURG: *Or, a lion rampant gules, crowned azure.*

On the central point of the whole shield an escucheon, ensigned with the arch-ducal crown, of AUSTRIA— *Gules, a fess argent.*

The plate is enlarged from GATTERER'S *Handbuch der Neuesten Genealogie und Heraldik* (Nürnberg, 1763), but for want of space the supporters (two griffins regardant *or*, their wings and plumage of the neck *sable*) are omitted, as is also the Imperial Crown which in the original is placed on the top edge of the shield; above this two angels hold the Royal Crown of HUNGARY. I have, however, added the crowns (apart from the escucheon) on the same plate (Plate XL.).

This Austrian achievement of MARIA THERESA was selected by the late Dr BURNETT as one of his illustrations, and, on that account, I include it here as having an interest apart from its contents. For it contains some remarkable omissions which lead me to doubt if it ever had official authority. That the arms of FLANDERS and BURGUNDY-MODERN should be omitted, while the far less important coat of BRABANT is included,

[1] I have ventured to make a few important corrections in the blazon. Moreover the coat attributed to SILESIA is really that of MORAVIA.

(497)

is to me almost inconceivable. But there is a still more remarkable omission; it is that of a coat which the house of AUSTRIA held in such estimation that for many generations they gave it the place of honour on their seals. I mean the coat of AUSTRIA-ANCIENT (*see* next page). A comparison of the shield assigned above to the Empress Queen MARIA THERESA, with the ÉCU COMPLET as established by Imperial decree in 1836

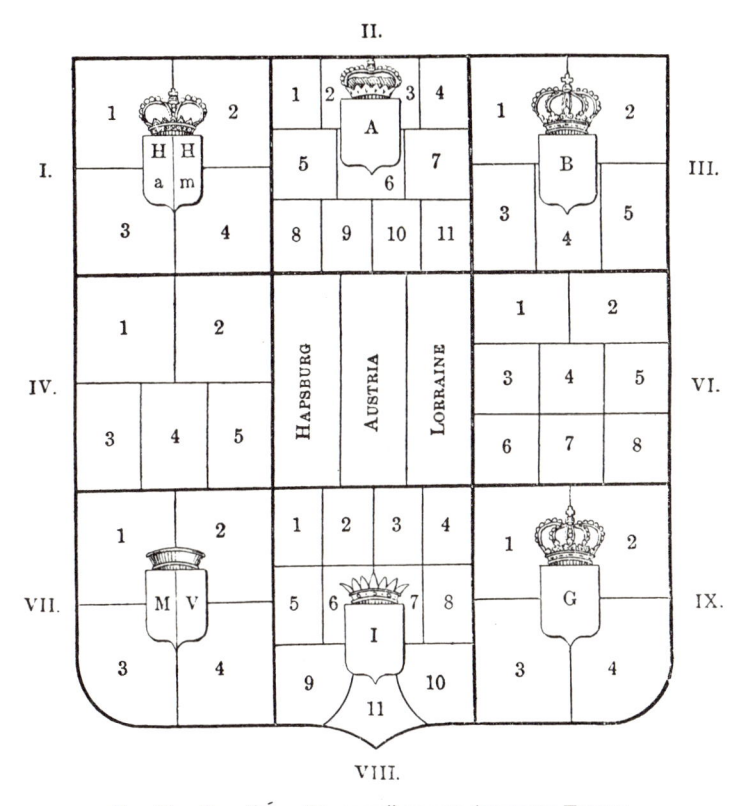

FIG. 91.--THE "ÉCU-COMPLET" OF THE AUSTRIAN EMPIRE.

(which, while it excludes the Burgundian and Netherland coats, contains the arms of all the Austrian possessions, and of those then ruled by members of the Imperial

House), should be of interest to the student of heraldry, which is truly hieroglyphic history. It will avoid unnecessary repetitions of the blazons if I send the reader back by reference to that escucheon, and the woodcut of the *Écu Complet* on page 497 will, I trust, prevent any difficulty arising.

Quarterly of nine Grand Quarters (containing sixty-two quarters) :—

I. *Quarterly* :—

1. DALMATIA, Kingdom (M.T., i. 2). 2. CROATIA, Kingdom (M.T., i. 3).
3. ESCLAVONIA, Kingdom :—*Azure, a river in fess vert, bordered argent, thereon a weasel* (or *marten*), *passant proper, beneath a six-pointed star or.*
4. TRANSYLVANIA (or SIEBENBURGEN) (M.T., iii. 6). On this grand quarter is placed *en surtout* an escucheon, crowned with the *Crown of St. Stephen*, and bearing the impaled coats of the Kingdom of HUNGARY (M.T., i. *surtout*). The coat of HUNGARY-MODERN, if correctly blazoned, always begins with the colour, not with the metal, and is :—*Barry of eight, gules and argent* (or, sometimes, *Gules four bars argent*). The bars are said to represent the four Hungarian rivers — the Danube, Save, Drave, and Theiss ;—just as the triple mount symbolises the three chief peaks of the Carpathians ; but all this mere supposition. The mount in HUNGARY-ANCIENT should be of three *coupeaux;* it is so borne on a separate shield in the Great Seals of RÉNÉ of ANJOU and his successors ; but in them is represented as an isolated mount, and the cross rises without the intervention of the crown, which was a later addition. (*See* VRÉE, *Généalogie*

des Comtes de Flandre, plates cv., cvi.; and compare the seals of the Emperor FERDINAND, plates cxxxiii., cxli.)

II. *Quarterly of eleven quarters* (in three rows of four, three, and four):—
   1. UPPER AUSTRIA:—*Per pale, Or, an eagle displayed sable, dimidiated with: Gules, two pallets argent.*
   2. SALZBURG, Duchy:—*Per pale*:—(a) *Or, a lion rampant sable.* (b) AUSTRIA: *Gules, a fess argent.*
   3. STYRIA, Duchy (M.T., iii. 3):—the "*Stier*" is now blazoned, as a griffin; originally the arms were canting ones, and the "*Stier*" a rampant ox.
   4. THE TEUTONIC ORDER: *Argent, a cross patée sable, bordered of the field, and charged with a cross flory or; over all, an escucheon of the last an eagle displayed of the second.*
   5. TYROL, County: (M.T., iv. 3).
   6. TRIENT, Principality: *Argent, an eagle displayed sable, beaked and membered or, its breast traversed by a pastoral staff in fess of the last.*
   7. BRIXEN, Principality: *Gules, a Paschal Lamb proper, the diadem or.*
   8. HOHEN-EMBS, County: *Azure, a steinbock or, horned sable.*
   9. MONTFORT and FELDKIRCH, County: *Argent, a gonfanon gules, its rings or* (*vide* p. 373).
   10. BREGENZ, County: *Azure, a pale ermine*, or *Fur, a pale ermine.* I have already pointed out (p. 73), how strangely the blazons of this simple coat have varied through the ignorance of the artists and those who employed them.
   11. SONNENBERG, County: *Azure, a hill in base or, surmounted by the sun in its splendour.*

Over all on an escucheon:—AUSTRIA-ANCIENT (the arms of the BABENBURGER line): *Azure, five larks* (or eaglets) *displayed or.* These arms are now assigned specially to *Austria below the Ems.* The BABENBURGER house became extinct in the male line, on the death of Duke FREDERICK of Austria, in 1246. This escucheon *en surtout* is crowned with the Arch-ducal crown of AUSTRIA:—a cap of crimson velvet turned up with a broad band of ermine cut into points which are edged with gold and a row of small pearls. Like the coronet of the Prince of WALES, it is surmounted by a single arch of gold supporting a mound or orb, which is ensigned with a jewelled cross.

III. *Quarterly of five* (in two rows of two quarters in chief and three in base):—

1. MORAVIA, Marquessate: *Azure, an eagle displayed chequy gules and argent, crowned or.*
   This coat is mistakenly attributed to SILESIA in (M.T., iv. 2).
2. SILESIA, Principality: *Or, an eagle displayed sable crowned of the field, on its breast a crescent and crosslet argent.*
3. UPPER LUSATIA, Markgravate: *Azure, in base a wall embattled or, masoned sable.*
4. TESCHEN, Duchy: *Azure, an eagle displayed crowned or.*
5. LOWER LUSATIA, Markgravate: *Argent, an ox passant proper* (*i.e.*, red with white belly and black horns).
   Over all, an escucheon, charged with the arms of the Kingdom of BOHEMIA (to which the above named provinces belonged): *Gules, a lion rampant queue fourchée argent crowned or.*

This escucheon *en surtout* is surmounted by the Royal Crown of BOHEMIA.

IV. *Quarterly of five* (two quarters in chief, and three in base):—

1. CUMANIA: *Argent, a lion rampant gules, in the dexter chief a crescent, in the sinister an estoile, both argent.*
2. BOSNIA: The arms attributed to ESCLAVONIA in (M.T., i. 4).
3. BULGARIA [1]: *Azure, on a bend gules, bordered and coticed argent, a wolf passant gules.*
4. SERVIA [1]: *Gules, a boar's head erect proper pierced by an arrow in pale argent.*
5. RASCIA: *Azure, three horse shoes inverted argent.*

V. *Tierced in pale*:—

1. HAPSBURG, County: *Or, a lion rampant gules, crowned azure.*
2. AUSTRIA: ("*Hauswapen*") *Gules, a fess argent.*
3. LORRAINE, Duchy: *Or, on a bend gules three allerions argent.*

VI. *Quarterly of eight* (in three rows the first of two quarters, the others of three in each):—

1. JERUSALEM, Kingdom: (M.T., i. 5).
2. CASTILE, Kingdom: (M.T., ii. 1).
3. LEON, Kingdom: (M.T., ii. 2).
4. ARRAGON, Kingdom: (M.T., ii. 3).
5. THE INDIES, Kingdom: [2] (M.T., i. 6).
6. SICILY, Kingdom: (M.T., ii. 4).
7. CALABRIA, Duchy: *Sable, a cross argent.* This

[1] As independent states BULGARIA and SERVIA have adopted different arms.

[2] The lion is *crowned or*. It appears here among the arms brought to the House of AUSTRIA on inheriting the Spanish crown, but is not usually seen on the coins or seals of the latter country. It occurs first on the Great Seal of CHARLES VI., among whose titles is "Indiaru: Rex."

coat which is often quartered with ARRAGON is thus given by RIETSTAP (*Armorial Général*) but in the arms of Don FERDINAND D'ARRAGON, Duke of CALABRIA, Viceroy of Valencia, this is thus given : *Quarterly*, 1 and 4. ARRAGON ; 2 and 3. *Argent, a cross potent sable.* (CHIFFLET,*Insignia Gentilitia Equitum Velleris Aurei*, No. 161, and MAURICE, *Toison d'Or*, page 192) so also SPENER says : "Dicitur vero tessera Calabriæ olim fuisse in parma argentea crux patibulata nigra " (*Op. Her.*,p. spec.,p. 237).

8. NAPLES, Kingdom : FRANCE-ANCIENT, *a label gules* (the arms of the Duke of ANJOU).

VII. *Quarterly* :—
1. TUSCANY, Grand-duchy : (M.T., iii. *surtout*).
2. MODENA, Duchy : *Azure, an eagle displayed argent crowned or* (*vide infra*, p. 508).
3. PARMA and PIACENZA, Duchies : *Or, six fleurs-de-lis azure* (the arms of the FARNESE family).
4. GUASTALLA, Duchy : *Argent, a cross patée-throughout gules between four eagles displayed sable* (the arms of the family of GONZAGA, Dukes of MANTUA, etc.).

Over all an escucheon *Per pale* (*a*) MILAN, Duchy (M.T., iii. 3) (*b*) VENICE, *Azure, the winged lion of St. Mark couchant and holding in its paws an open book thereon the words* "PAX TIBI MARCE EVANGELISTA MEUS." These coats together are borne for the Lombardo-Venetian Kingdom and this escucheon *en surtout*, is crowned with the "*Iron Crown*" of LOMBARDY, a plain circlet of gold, enamelled with floral decoration and set with gems (*v.* p. 617).

VIII. *Quarterly of eleven* (arranged in three rows ; the first two each contain four quarters, but the base row has two only and is *enté en point* of a third).

1. CARINTHIA, Duchy : *Per pale (a) Or, three lions passant gardant in pale sable* (as M.T., iii. 4) but with *(b) Gules, a fess argent.* This is the correct form, and the absence of the nearly invariable impalement is one of the causes of my doubts as to the authority of the "Maria Theresa" escucheon.

2. CARNIOLA (KRAIN), Duchy (M.T., iii. 5). The crescent is now usually chequy of three rows.

3. WINDISCHE-MARK : *Argent, a hat sable, turned up, and stringed gules (vide ante,* p. 374).

4. FRIOUL (FRIULI), Duchy : *Azure, an eagle displayed and crowned or.*

5. TRIESTE, *Per fess (a)* in chief, *Or, an eagle displayed sable crowned of the field; (b)* in base, *Gules, a fess argent, thereon an anchor in pale, reversed sable.*

6. ISTRIA, Marquessate : *Azure, a goat passant or, armed gules.*

7. GRADISCA, County : *Per fess or and azure, over all a cross moline argent.*

8. GÖRZ, County : (M.T., iv. 6).

9. RAGUSA, Duchy : *Argent, three bends azure.*

10. CATTARO (or ALBANIA) : *Argent, a lion rampant gules.*

11. ZARA, Duchy (this quarter is the one "in point") : *Argent, a mounted knight in full armour his lance in pale all proper.*

Over all, the arms of ILLYRIA (Kingdom) *Azure, an antique galley or.* This escucheon is surmounted by an antique crown of golden rays (Plate L., fig. 13).

IX. Quarterly:—

1. LODOMIRIA: *Azure, two bars chequy gules and argent.*
2. CRACOW: *Gules, an eagle displayed argent, armed, crowned, and with "Klee stengel" or.*
3. AUSCHWITZ, Duchy: *Argent, an eagle displayed azure.*
4. ZATOR, Duchy: *Azure, an eagle displayed argent.* Over all an escucheon of the Kingdom of GALICIA: *Azure, a fillet in chief* (otherwise a *bar enhanced*) *gules, between a crow sable in chief, and three ancient crowns or in base.* This escucheon is surmounted by a Royal Crown (Plate L., fig. 4.)

This great shield is placed on the breast of the sable double-headed eagle in the golden shield of the Empire. Each of the heads of the eagle is royally crowned; it holds in the dexter claw a drawn sword and a sceptre, and in the sinister the Imperial Orb, all proper.

The shield is supported by two griffins *Or* (their wings and plumage of the head and breast being *sable*), and above it is the closed Imperial Crown.

FRANCE.—In France the varied use of the escucheon *en surtout* does not differ widely from its use in Germany as already described.

We will first give some instances of important coats in which the escucheon *en surtout* contains the arms of the family, while the main shield contains the quarters either of its feudal possessions or its most important ancestors.

The Dukes de la TRÉMOUILLE, who attained the title of "Duc et Pair de France" in 1596, and who were already Princes de Tarente, bear their personal arms: *Or, a chevron gules between three eagles displayed azure, en surtout upon the shield:* Quarterly, 1. FRANCE; 2. SICILY; 3. MONTMORENCY-LAVAL (p. 452); 4. BOURBON-CONDÉ (FRANCE, *a baton alezé in bend gules*). The second and third quarters indicate descent from the marriage of FRANÇOIS DE LA TRÉMOUILLE, Prince de TALMONT (d. 1541) with ANNE, heiress of GUI, Comte de LAVAL, whose wife was CHARLOTTE of ARRAGON, daughter of FREDERICK, King of NAPLES and SICILY. The first and fourth commemorate descent in two lines from the royal house of FRANCE.

The Dukes of ROHAN-CHABOT bear a shield; *Quarterly*, 1. NAVARRE ; 2. SCOTLAND ; 3. BRITTANY; 4. FLANDERS ; and place *en surtout* an escucheon of ROHAN (*Gules, nine mascles conjoined* 3, 3, 3, *or*) quartering CHABOT (*Or, three chabots gules*). In 1461 JOHN, Vicomte de ROHAN, married MARY, second daughter of FRANCIS I., Duke of BRITTANY, by ISABELLA, daughter of JAMES I. of Scotland. FRANCIS died without male issue, as did MARGARET, elder sister of MARY, and the house of ROHAN indicated their supposed rights to the duchy by either quartering its arms, or by placing a coat bearing the arms of ROHAN impaling BRITTANY, *en surtout* above their quarterings. In the case of the Dukes de MONTBASON these were : *Quarterly of eight* (in two rows of four each): 1. FRANCE ; 2. NAVARRE ; 3. ARRAGON ; 4. SCOTLAND ; 5. BRITTANY; 6. MILAN ; 7. LORRAINE ; 8. SAN SEVERINO (*Argent, a fess gules, and a fillet en bordure azure*). The Dukes de ROHAN bore a somewhat different arrangement : *Quarterly*, 1. FRANCE, quartering EVREUX (p. 464); 2. SAN SEVERINO impaling ARRAGON ; 3. MILAN impaling LORRAINE ; 4. SCOTLAND. On the other hand the Ducs de ST. SIMON quartered the personal arms of ROUVROY ST. SIMON (*Sable, on a cross argent five escallops gules*) with those of HAVESQUERQUE (*Or, a fess gules*) and placed *en surtout* an escucheon of VERMANDOIS (*Chequy, azure and or, a chief of* FRANCE-ANCIENT), to denote their claim to a descent from the Counts of VERMANDOIS.

SPANISH.—It is only possible here to give a few examples of Spanish uses of Marshalling, though there are many which are of interest. Quartering is, of course, the mode chiefly employed for indicating descent, but simple impalement is very frequently substituted for it; and in Spanish Heraldry, perhaps more than in any other, the student should be on his guard against assuming that an impaled coat has the meaning which attaches to it among ourselves.

The MENDOZA coat, as borne by the Dukes of INFANTADGO, has already been given (Plate XXXIII., fig. 12, and *see* p. 440). The Counts of CORUÑA impale with this coat the arms of FIGUEROA, *Or, five fig leaves in saltire vert*. The Counts of MIRANDA and Marquises of CAÑETE substitute for the golden flanks, with their motto, other flanks of *Gules, on each ten panelles*, or poplar leaves, *argent*. Two golden chains in saltire pass over the dividing lines, and are united to two other chains fessways in chief and base. This, it will be observed, is an instance of quartering *per saltire*. I am not clear to what family the *panelles* may be traced, but I cannot accept the suggestion of SPENER (*Op. Her.*, p. 254) that they may denote a BOBADILLA alliance.

The Marquises de la BALA SICILIANA, on account of the marriage of PEDRO GONSALEZ DE MENDOZA with ISABELLA DE ALARCON in the 16th century, impale ALARCON (*Gules, a cross fleury argent*) with MENDOZA, curiously giving the precedence to the latter coat. The Counts de PRIEGO impale the arms of CARILLO (*Gules, a castle triple-towered or*) in the second place with MENDOZA in the first, in memory of the marriage of DIEGO HURTADO DE MENDOZA with THERESIA DE CARRILLO (*c.* 1450).

The family of PONCE DE LEON, Duke of ARCOS, impale the coats of LEON and ARRAGON *within a bordure azure, thereon eight escucheons of* BIDAURE (*Or, a fess azure*).

The family of OSORIOS, Counts of VILLALOBOS, bore: *Or, two wolves passant in pale gules;* and after an alliance with the family of MOSCOSO, who bore *Argent,* (SPENER says *or,* but wrongly), *a wolf's head erased sable,* the OSORIOS, Counts of ALTAMIRA, impaled these coats (giving the precedence to MOSCOSO) within a bordure *Or, charged with eight escucheons of the arms of* HENRIQUEZ (*tierced in mantel,* 1 and 2. CASTILE; 3, *in base.* LEON). The OSORIOS, Dukes of AGUIAR, Counts de TRASTAMARA, etc., bore: *Per fess*:—(a) OSORIO; (b) *Argent, three bendlets indented azure,* within the HENRIQUEZ bordure. The present OSORIOS DE MOSCOSO, who have the above titles and many others, being thirteen times Grandees of the first class, bear: *Per fess* [A] *also per fess* (a) OSORIO, (b) *the argent coat with the bendlets;* [B] MOSCOSO, the whole within the HENRIQUEZ bordure given above.

The CORDOVAS, Counts of FIGUEROA, bear: (Plate XLI.) *Tierced in fess*:—

1. *Or, three bars gules,* CORDOVA.
2. *Tierced in pale* (a) FIGUEROA; (b) *Or, three bars vert,* RIBERA; (c) 1 and 4. MANUEL, *Gules, a winged hand holding a sword in pale proper;* 2 and 3. LEON.
3. PONCE DE LEON, as on preceding page.

The CORDOVAS, Counts de FERIA, curiously omit the upper piece (*Or, three bars gules*).

In Spanish Marshalling, as will be seen in the arms of the PONCE DE LEONS, etc., coats impaled or quartered are frequently represented within a bordure, which itself often indicates another alliance. The PIMENTELS of Spain quarter *Or, three bars gules,* with *Vert, five panelles argent,* and surround the whole with *a bordure compony of* CASTILE and LEON. The PIMENTELS of Portugal substitute *escallops* for *panelles,* and their bordure is of *Argent, charged with eight aspas* (saltires coupéd) *gules.*

The LIAÑOS of Castile use: *Per pale*, 1. *Argent, a tower proper;* 2. *Or, four bars azure; all within a bordure gules, charged with eight plates.* The use of the bordure in this manner occasionally causes the bordure and the field to be of the same tincture; thus CARO bears: *Argent, a cross fleur-de-lisée sable, within a* (GUZMAN) *bordure of the first, thereon eight cauldrons of the second.*

ITALY.—In ITALY the modes of marshalling do not differ materially from those already described. The arms of the family are often placed *en surtout*, above a shield of quarterings representing fiefs or alliances. The old Dukes of MODENA used a shield divided per pale into three parts—*Tierced in pale* :—1. *Per fess* (*a*) (*in chief*) *the arms of the* EMPIRE as an augmentation; (*b*) (*in base*) *France, within a bordure indented gules and or,* Duchy of FERRARA. 2. *Gules, the Papal keys in saltire wards in chief the dexter or, the sinister argent, the bows united by a golden cord in base; the keys surmounted in chief by the Papal tiara.* 3. *Per fess* (*a*) *in chief* FERRARA, (*b*) *in base* the EMPIRE as before. *En surtout*, and occupying the whole width of the central pale, an escucheon of the arms of the family of ESTE; *Azure, an eagle displayed argent crowned or.* The Papal pale was an addition to the old quartered coat with its escucheon *en surtout*. The later Dukes of MODENA of the house of HAPSBURG-LORRAINE used a coat: *Per pale* :—(*a*) *Tierced in pale*, 1. HAPSBURG; 2. AUSTRIA; 3. LORRAINE; (*b*) the arms of ESTE, but *with the eagle holding in its dexter claw a sceptre, and in the sinister an orb of gold.*

The Dukes of PARMA similarly tierced their shield in pale:—1. *Per fess* (*a*) *in chief* FARNESE, *Or six fleurs-de-lis*, 3, 2, 1, *azure;* (*b*) *in base,* AUSTRIA *impaling* BURGUNDY-ANCIENT. 2. *Gules, the Papal banner, the lance in pale or surmounted by the Papal keys in saltire*, as in the preceding example. 3. *Per fess* (*a*) *in chief* AUSTRIA *impaling* BURGUNDY-ANCIENT; (*b*) *in base* FARNESE.

En surtout, and occupying the whole width of the central pale, the arms of PORTUGAL. The impalement of AUSTRIA and BURGUNDY denotes the marriage of the Duke OTTAVIO with the celebrated Duchess MARGARET, natural daughter of the Emperor CHARLES V. The escucheon *en surtout* in this case denotes the pretensions of the Dukes of PARMA, on the death of the Cardinal King HENRY in 1580, to the crown of Portugal, arising from the marriage of ALEXANDER, Duke of PARMA, with MARY (d. 1577), daughter of EDWARD, Constable of PORTUGAL, who was younger brother of the Cardinal King and predeceased him.

The Dukes of MIRANDOLA bore a quartered shield with *in chief* the arms of the EMPIRE: *Or, a double-headed eagle displayed sable imperially crowned proper.* The quarterings are, 1 and 4. *Or, an eagle displayed sable, crowned of the field*, for the Duchy of MIRANDOLA; 2 and 3. *Barry of six argent and azure, over all a lion rampant gules crowned or*, for the Duchy of CONCORDIA. The two quarters in chief are separated from those in base by a fess *gules*, and upon it is placed *en surtout* the arms of the family of PICO, to which the Dukes belonged: *Chequy argent and azure.*

Other examples of the separation of the quarters by an Ordinary are to be met with in Foreign Heraldry. The Counts of HÄRD in Sweden bear: *Quarterly*, 1 and 4. *Azure, a lion rampant or, holding in its fore paws a silver buckler charged with the cypher* **XII.** *sable ;* 2 and 3. *Or, a mounted knight proper habited argent.* These quarters are divided by a fess *argent ; charged on the dexter side with a cypher* **F** *sable, royally crowned, and on the sinister with a chapeau gules.* On an escucheon *en surtout* the arms of the family: *Or, a bull's head caboshed gules.*

The Barons of DJURKLOW in Sweden similarly place between their quarterings a *fess patée argent*, and on it *en surtout*, Argent, a bear's paw sable between two lion's gambs proper issuant from a mount in base vert.

A somewhat similar *fess gules masoned sable, arched or voutée in base but embattled in chief* is borne upon their escucheon by the Finnish family of FIEANDT.

The quarters in the Royal Arms of DENMARK have been for many centuries separated by the Cross of the ORDER OF THE DANNEBROG: *Argent, a cross patée-throughout fimbriated gules.* (Sometimes its arms project somewhat beyond the shield.) In imitation of this a considerable number of the principal Scandinavian families use a cross patée-throughout to separate the quarters of their frequently complicated coats. The quarterings in these are often not indicative of descent, but were all included in the original grant of armorial bearings (*v.* p. 546).

On the centre of the cross thus used an escucheon, either of augmentation, or of the family arms, is placed *en surtout*.

As an example I give the arms of the Barons STAEL DE HOLSTEIN: *Quarterly*, 1 and 4. *Gules, two banners in saltire argent enfiled by a coronet or;* 2. *Azure, a lion rampant or holding with all four feet a Danish axe argent, the long curved handle of the second;* 3. *Azure, two cannons in saltire or. The quarters separated by a cross patée-throughout or. En surtout* an escucheon of the arms of STAEL: *Argent, eight balls in orle gules* (Plate XLI., fig. 4).

In the case of the Royal Arms of DENMARK this escucheon is, *Quarterly:* 1. HOLSTEIN; 2. STORMARN; 3. DITMARSHEN; 4. LAUENBURG; and the impaled arms of OLDENBURG and DELMENHORST in an escucheon *sur le tout du tout*.

In other Scandinavian coats a saltire *patée-throughout* is used instead of the cross to divide the quarters. In the arms of the Barons von BERGENSTRÄHLE, the shield is tierced in pairle, and the quarters are divided not by a saltire, but by a pairle *diminuée* and *patée-throughout or*.

PLATE XLI.

MARSHALLING.

1. Van der Linden.

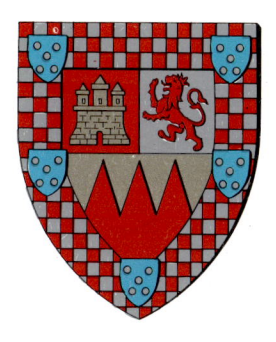

2. Giron, Duc d'Ossuna.

3. Cardona.

4. Stael von Holstein.

5. Cordova, Counts of Figueroa.

6. Waldeck.

A plain cross dividing the quarters, and sometimes charged, is found in the arms of some German families. Thus the Tirolese Counts d'ARCO bear: *Quarterly*, 1 and 4. *Azure, three bows or, fesseways in pale;* 2 and 3. *Or, a bow in pale azure.* These quarters are separated by a *cross argent trellised azure.* The Counts of HOHENWALDECK VON MAXELREIN bear: *Quarterly*, 1 and 4. *Per bend wavy argent and sable a bend counterchanged;* 2 and 3. *Sable, a lion rampant or.* The quarters are separated by a *cross patée-throughout*, on the centre of which is an escucheon *en surtout; Argent, an eagle displayed gules crowned or its feet resting on two batons in saltire of the second.*

Something similar to this is to be found in Scottish Armory. The coat of the SINCLAIR family was, *Argent, a cross engrailed sable.* They inherited the earldoms of ORKNEY and CAITHNESS through female descent from the Norse Jarls of the ORKNEYS. The arms of the Earls of CAITHNESS are thus marshalled: *Quarterly*, 1. *Azure, within a Royal tressure a ship with furled sails all or,* ORKNEY; 2 and 3. *Or, a lion rampant gules,* SPAR (a family in possession of the Earldom of CAITHNESS before the SINCLAIRS); 4. *Azure, a ship in sail or,* CAITHNESS; and over all, dividing the quarters, a cross engrailed *sable* for SINCLAIR. (Plate XLIII., fig. 1.)

It may be of interest here, as illustrative of what has been said in preceding paragraphs, to notice that the Barons SINCLAIR in Sweden (so created 1766, but extinct ten years later), bore the above quartered coats as cadets of CAITHNESS; but separated the quarters, not by the SINCLAIR cross, but by a *cross patée-throughout ermine.* In an escucheon *en surtout* they placed the SINCLAIR arms: *Argent, a cross engrailed sable;* and, as a mark of cadency, they surrounded the main escucheon with *a bordure chequy or and gules.*

The Lords SINCLAIR, on the other hand, adopted the

less unusual arrangement of simply quartering the coats of ORKNEY and CAITHNESS, and placing an escucheon of SINCLAIR *en surtout*. (Plate XLIII., fig. 2).—J. W.]

SECTION II. SCOTLAND—(BY G. B. AND J. W.).

[Systematic Heraldry spread gradually from the Lowlands to the Highlands of Scotland; and figures familiar upon the old sculptured crosses and other monuments became regular heraldic charges. Such are the galley, the eagle displayed, the salmon, a rock, and a hand holding a dagger or a crosslet fitchée. In two armorial seals appended to a document of 1572 (LAING, *Scottish Seals*, ii., 675, 676), those of JOHN MURDOCH M'ALISTER, Captain of CLANRANALD, and his son ALLAN, we have a tree placed in pale between a hand issuing from the dexter flank, and a galley (tied to the tree) on the sinister. (The hand has no dagger or crosslet, and appears to be a sinister hand, unless we are supposed to see its back.) But these figures, and others, soon came to be borne as quarterings by the Highland chiefs in a way which in many cases indicated neither family alliances nor the possession of feudal Lordships. While one branch of the LORDS OF THE ISLES (GLENGARRY) bore the galley and the eagle as in Plate XLIII., fig. 3, several branches, including that of CLANRANALD, adopted a quartered coat of the kind referred to. In an armorial MS. of the date 1603 (said to bear the stamp of authority of Sir DAVID LINDSAY the younger, then LYON), the coat represented in Plate XLIII., fig. 4, is ascribed to "MACKONEIL, laird of Dunnivege and Glennes," *i.e.* the head of the Clan IAN VOR, descending from JOHN, second son of JOHN, LORD OF THE ISLES, and the Princess MARGARET.

The MS. of STACIE, ROSS Herald 1663-1687 gives the coat of MACDONALD of SLATE, the ancestor of the Lords MACDONALD, as: *Quarterly*, 1. *Argent, a lion rampant*

PLATE XLII.

MARSHALLING.

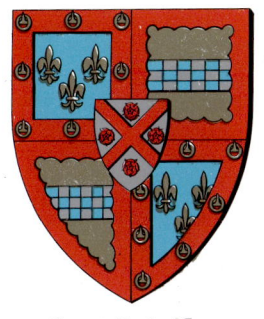

1. Stuart, Earl of Lennox.

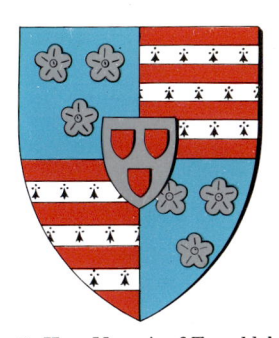

2. Hay, Marquis of Tweeddale.

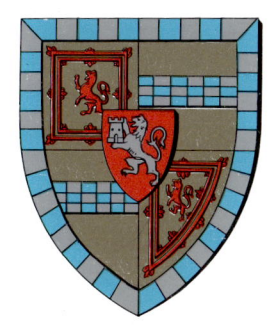

3. Stuart, Lord Methven.

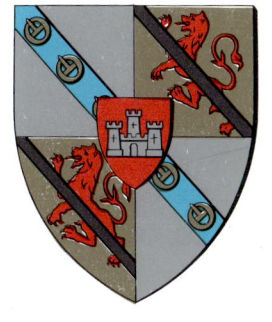

4. Leslie, Lord Lindores.

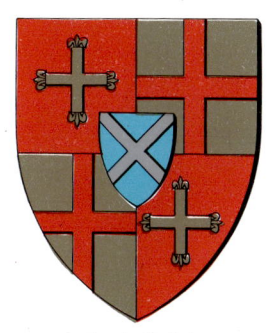

5. Lords Carlyle.

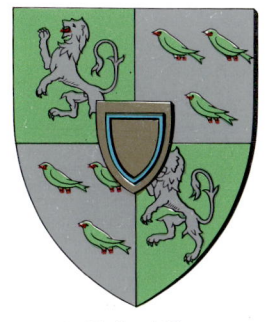

6. Earls of Home.

gules armed or ; 2. *Azure, a hand proper holding a cross of Calvary patée sable ;* 3. *Vert, a ship ermine, her oars in saltire sable on water proper ;* 4. *Parted per fess, wavy vert and argent, a salmon naiant proper* [1] (*cf.* Plate XLIII., fig. 5, the present arms of the Lords MACDONALD).

In the record of the elder Sir DAVID LINDSAY the coat of MACLEAN is: *Azure, a castle triple-towered argent.* In the MS. of the younger Sir DAVID (*circa* 1603) a coat with the same Highland elements as No. 4 is introduced (Plate XLIII., fig. 6).

Quartered coats of the same elements are borne by the MACKINTOSHES, M'NEILLS, M'KINNONS, and FARQUHARSONS, slight differences in the arrangement of the quarters serving to difference the cadets of each.

The higher nobility of Scotland had their arms marshalled somewhat after the Continental fashion ; and as their arrangement has been somewhat misapprehended by those who have studied Heraldry from an exclusively English point of view a few illustrations may advantageously be given here particularly with reference to the bearing of an escucheon *en surtout.* The princely position of the Earls of DOUGLAS in the fifteenth century need hardly be adverted to here, the historical student will need little to be reminded how after the "Red" DOUGLAS supplanted the "Black," the Earls of ANGUS, their virtual successors, notwithstanding their illegitimacy of descent, claimed precedence, not over Earls only, but

[1] [We may compare with this the coat borne by Marshal MACDONALD, created Duke of TARENTO by NAPOLEON I. in 1809 ; *Quarterly,* 1. *Argent, a lion rampant gules ;* 2. *Or, a left hand and arm issuing from the sinister flank habited gules, holding a crosslet fitchée of the last ;* 3. *Argent, on a sea in base vert, in which swims a salmon of the first, a galley sable its pennons gules ;* 4. *Argent, a tree vert surmounted by an eagle displayed sable. On a champagne in base or, a scorpion sable in bend. On the centre point of the quarters a crescent gules for difference.* Above the quarters the chief indicating the dignity of Duke of the French Empire : *Gules, semé of estoiles (mullets) argent.*—J. W.]

over all Peers, with the right of leading the van in battle, and bearing the Royal Crown in Parliament. The seals of both branches of the house of DOUGLAS, which are almost unique in beauty, have a peculiar fitness for exemplifying the subject under consideration.

The seal of WILLIAM, 1st Earl of DOUGLAS, and by marriage, of MAR, appended to a document, *circa* 1378, bears the arms of DOUGLAS (*Argent, a human heart gules, on a chief azure three mullets of the field*) quartered with MAR (*Azure, a bend between six crosslets or*). JAMES, 2nd Earl, who fell at Otterburn in 1388, bore in his father's lifetime the simple coat of DOUGLAS. ARCHIBALD DOUGLAS, Lord of GALLOWAY, on whom the Earldom then devolved, added largely to the family possessions. He acquired Bothwell in Lanarkshire, and other considerable lands in Ross-shire, by marriage with the *widow* (not the daughter as has been represented), of THOMAS MURRAY of Bothwell. His seal, a mutilated example of which is figured on the frontispiece of LAING'S *Supplemental Volume of Scottish Seals*, bears DOUGLAS quartering GALLOWAY (*Azure, a lion rampant crowned or*) and on an escucheon *en surtout*, the coat of MURRAY of Bothwell (*Azure*) three mullets (*Or*). The accident that he thus used the MURRAY coat, while as will be presently shown, his son bore it as a quarter, has misled Mr LAING, and other writers of greater pretensions, into the belief that the seal of the 3rd Earl affords an example in the fourteenth century of the use of an "escucheon of pretence" in the modern acceptation of that term. It may be that the extent and importance of the inheritance which had passed into his possession, led to the prominent place accorded to the arms of the BOTHWELL lordship; or it may only have been a desire for the maintenance of symmetry and a well-balanced escucheon which prompted the arrangement.

His son ARCHIBALD, 4th Earl of DOUGLAS, who

succeeded him in 1401, obtained by charter from the Regent ALBANY in 1409 the Lordship of Annandale. This made a re-arrangement of the quarterings necessary; and the escucheon on his seal is accordingly— *Quarterly:* 1. DOUGLAS; 2. GALLOWAY; 3. MURRAY of Bothwell; 4. ANNANDALE (*Argent, a saltire and chief gules*). In his later years the Earl repaired to France, where he was made Duke of TOURAINE, and Count of LONGUEVILLE and *Pair de* FRANCE, by CHARLES VII., in 1424, and fell at Verneuil in the same year.

His son ARCHIBALD, the fifth Earl of DOUGLAS, and second Duke of TOURAINE, dropped the quarter of Bothwell to make room for a coat indicative of his Duchy (apparently the plain arms of FRANCE :—*Azure, three fleurs-de-lis or* [1]); this is placed in the first quarter, the others being: 2. DOUGLAS; 3. ANNANDALE; 4. GALLOWAY. (Mr LAING, *Scottish Seals,* vol. ii., No. 248, attributes this seal to the fourth Earl.)

WILLIAM, his son, the 6th Earl, during the minority of JAMES II., and when he was in his 17th year, was decoyed into Edinburgh Castle in 1446, and after a mock trial was put to death along with his brother. This caused a re-distribution of the possessions of the house of DOUGLAS. The *Duché pairie* lapsed to the Crown of France, Annandale to that of Scotland, Galloway went to the Earl's sister MARGARET, known as the "Fair Maid of Galloway," who married her cousin WILLIAM (afterwards 8th Earl). JAMES, 7th Earl of DOUGLAS, who succeeded

[1] [This is remarkable, but is paralleled by the plain coat of FRANCE borne for the Duchy of CHÂTELHERAULT by the Earls of ANGUS. CHARLES VII. was the first Sovereign who departed from the principle of conferring the "*pairie*" on princes of the blood alone. Wishing to create for himself allies against the Dukes of BURGUNDY and BRITTANY, who menaced the existence of the monarchy, he conferred on JAMES, King of SCOTLAND, the *pairie* of Saintonge and Rochefort in 1421, and the county and *pairie* of Evreux on JAMES STUART, sire d'Aubigny.—J. W.]

his grand-nephew, was, before his marriage, Earl of AVONDALE. His son WILLIAM, 8th Earl of DOUGLAS, and 2nd of AVONDALE, for a time rose high in the favour of JAMES II., who made him Lieutenant-General of the realm; but entering with the Earl of CRAWFORD into a confederacy against the king in 1446 he was stabbed to death by JAMES in a fit of passion in Stirling Castle. The arms on his seal are the same as those of his father. (*Quarterly:* 1. DOUGLAS; 2. GALLOWAY; 3. MURRAY of Bothwell; 4. *Sable, fretty or* for his lordship of LAUDERDALE.) The 9th, and last Earl, made open war on JAMES as his brother's murderer, but a temporary reconciliation took place, after which the struggle was renewed, and after the flight of DOUGLAS to England, was maintained by his brothers, who were respectively Earls of MORAY and ORMOND; but the battle of Arkenholme in 1455 settled the fate of the Black DOUGLASES. The Earldom, with its vast possessions, was forfeited, and its strongholds of Douglas, Abercorn, Strathaven, and others were dismantled. The Earl lived for many years in England; but in 1484, having invaded Scotland with the exiled Duke of ALBANY, he was taken captive and sent to the religious retirement of Lindores Abbey, where he died.

The seal of the last Earl is one of the most beautiful and interesting of the series. It bears: *Quarterly,* 1. DOUGLAS; 2. LAUDERDALE; 3. MURRAY *of Bothwell;* 4. *Six piles* (? for BRECHIN); *and* GALLOWAY *en surtout.* The arms in the fourth quarter are not easily to be accounted for; if they are for BRECHIN, they are arms of pretension of a remote and far fetched kind. They have been blazoned both as borne by this Earl (and long afterwards by the 6th Earl of ANGUS), as BRECHIN, and sometimes as the coat of "WISHART of Brechin." There never were any "WISHARTS of Brechin." The imagined connection between WISHART and BRECHIN—a fancy of the seventeenth century—arose from the fact that both the ancient family of BRECHIN (descended from a natural son of Prince DAVID,[1] Earl of HUNTINGDON), and the much more modern family of WISHART bore the same charge "*three piles in point gules*" in their arms.—G. B.]

[It must be noticed that the arms of the Lordship of BRECHIN, or Earldom of HUNTINGDON, have the red piles on a golden ground, and they were thus quartered by the MAULES of Panmure. (*See* the *Registrum de Panmure.*) The field of the WISHART coat is *argent*, *vide ante*, pp. 147, 149.—J. W.]

[I at one time thought that an explanation of this quarter might be found in some entries in the *Register of the Great Seal of* 1472, and in the Crown accounts of 1465 and subsequent years, purporting that the rents of certain portions of Brechin were paid to a Countess JONET, wife of WILLIAM, Earl of DOUGLAS, in lieu of her terce. The only possible Countess seemed to be the above-named "Fair Maid of Galloway," widow of the 8th Earl, who though called JONET in the *Great Seal Register*, appeared as MARGARET LINDSAY, Countess of DOUGLAS, in the *Exchequer Rolls*. It seemed as if the "Fair Maid," divorced from her husband, the Earl of ATHOLE, had re-married a LINDSAY. But the discovery of further documentary evidence about this lady, whose name was certainly JONET, led me to abandon this hypothesis for another—namely, that the Countess in question was the widow of WILLIAM, 6th Earl, who, having been beheaded at an early age, had not hitherto been believed to be married. My grounds for this conclusion are stated at length in the Preface to Vol. VII. of the *Exchequer Rolls of Scotland*, and I have not seen reason to alter the views thus expressed. That being

[1] [DAVID had married MAUD, widow of SIMON DE ST. LIZ, Earl of HUNTINGDON; and HENRY I. invested him with the Earldom in 1108.—J. W.]

so, the pretext for assuming the BRECHIN coat is certainly remote. The theory maintained in the *Douglas Book* (vol. i.) that these piles (which reappear in the arms of the 6th Earl of ANGUS) were stakes to represent the Lordship of ETTRICK FOREST deserves consideration, yet difficulties apply to it. Though piles have sometimes been identified with passion nails, I have not found them confounded with stakes. There is a well-known use of stakes as an armorial charge in the coat of YAIR (Plate XXVIII., fig. 12), where they are utterly unlike piles, though they exactly resemble the stakes of the DOUGLAS compartment hereafter to be noticed. Perhaps a slight argument against the piles denoting BRECHIN is, that in some heraldic MSS. in the Advocates' Library and Lyon Office the piles are *vert*. There is also a difficulty arising from the number of the piles being uncertain. On the seal of ARCHIBALD, 6th Earl of DOUGLAS, they are five in number. In the arms of the 1st Marquess of DOUGLAS they are undoubtedly piles, and on the seal of his brother, Sir GEORGE DOUGLAS, are three in number. Is it possible that, though generally attributed to BRECHIN, they may be really borne for the Earldom of AVONDALE? The most remarkable part of the seal is to be found in the two banners which rise behind the shield, each containing two coats quartered. In the dexter banner we have the cushions of MORAY (to which not this lord, but his brother, asserted a claim) quartered with three bars (for . . . . ?) In the sinister banner the stars of BOTHWELL are quartered with (*Gules*) a fess *ermine* — doubtless for the Lordship of CRAWFORD.

To pass now to the Earls of ANGUS, in whose time the connection with France affected to a still greater extent the development of Scottish Armory. The 2nd Earl bore: *Quarterly*, 1 and 4. *Argent, a lion rampant gules for* ANGUS ; 2 and 3. DOUGLAS ; and *en surtout* what appears to be *a bend charged with three estoiles.* This may possibly have been a combination of the arms of DOUGLAS and SANDILANDS for Cavers and Lydel, Jedworth Forest, but it was certainly not the coat of his wife, who was a HAY of Yester. If we had coloured representations of the blazons of all the Earls of ANGUS we should be able to discover when the white lion of ANGUS in the first quarter developed itself, or was metamorphosed, into the GALLOWAY coat. ARCHIBALD, *Bell the Cat*, 5th Earl of ANGUS, bore : 1. ANGUS ; 2. ABERNETHY ; 3. (*Ermine*) *three chevrons* (*Gules*) for LIDDESDALE (the old coat of the SOULIS family, from which, however, there was no descent) ; and 4. (*Sable*) *fretty* (*Or*) LAUDERDALE ; *en surtout* the arms of DOUGLAS. Later Earls, beginning with the 6th, bore : 1. GALLOWAY ; 2. ABERNETHY ; 3. BRECHIN (the piles being five in number); 4. STEWART of Bonkyl; also with DOUGLAS *en surtout*—a coat which has been preserved by succeeding Earls, the sole difference being that the first Marquess of DOUGLAS, who put the crown on the heart, bore also in Continental fashion a *champagne* in base of the arms of AUCHINLECK : *Argent, a cross counter-embattled sable.* (Mr LAING, *Scottish Seals*, ii., 285, thought he could trace a similar base on the seal of the 2nd Earl of ANGUS ; if so, it could not be charged with the AUCHINLECK coat. On an examination of the cast of that seal, I, however, could not detect the existence of the cross in question.) It thus appears that the DOUGLAS quarterings were arranged much more in accordance with Continental ideas of marshalling than in agreement with modern British usage.

A few other Scottish examples, some of them of marshalling which remains unchanged to the present day, will show that the usages referred to were not confined to one great family ; and will also serve to illustrate the use of the escucheon *en surtout* without its modern application of an "escucheon of pretence."

A curious example of Scottish marshalling may be given *in limine* which indicates how little the Scottish lords and heralds of the fifteenth century were trammelled by modern rules. The seal of JOHN STUART, Lord of LORN (LAING, *Scottish Seals*, i., 797), the father of the three co-heiresses, the eldest of whom brought LORN to the house of ARGYLL, bears the following arrangement: *Quarterly*: 1. *Per fess, in chief, a buckle, its pin extending to the dexter; in base counter-compony;* 2 and 3. *A galley in full sail;* 4. *Per fess, the chief counter-compony, and in base a garb.* In this composite coat the buckle marks the paternal descent from STEWART of Bonkyl, while the garb is indicative of the Earldom of BUCHAN, held by ROBERT, Duke of ALBANY, his maternal grandfather. The galley in the second and third quarters, though certainly intended to represent the Lordship of LORN, indicated, notwithstanding, no descent from its ancient Lords. The late learned genealogist, Mr ALEXANDER SINCLAIR, has shown that the supposed descent is a modern blunder. JOHN STEWART, the first Lord of LORN of this house got the Lordship, not by a marriage with the DE ERGADIA heiress, but by exchange with his brother, who was that heiress's husband.

Another interesting specimen of Scottish marshalling is afforded by the seal (LAING, ii., 948) of WILLIAM SUTHERLAND of Duffus, appended to a charter of 1540 which bears a shield *Per fess; the chief per pale (a) three mullets* for SUTHERLAND; (*b*) *three crosslets fitchées* for CHEYNE of Duffus; *in the base a boar's head* for CHISHOLM.

Another interesting seal is that of WALTER STEWART, Earl of ATHOLE and CAITHNESS (*circa* 1420), son of ROBERT II.'s second marriage, and husband of the heiress of BRECHIN, who suffered death in 1437 as an accessory to the murder of his nephew and benefactor, King JAMES I. The blazon is: 1. SCOTLAND, *differenced by a label of three points*. 2. *Paly of six (or) and (sable)* for ATHOLE. 3. *(Or) three piles (gules)* for BRECHIN. 4. *(Azure) a lion rampant (argent) crowned (or)* for GALLOWAY. *En surtout (Azure), a galley under sail (or)* for CAITHNESS. Of course according to modern ideas BRECHIN would have been borne in an escucheon of pretence.

On Plate XLII., fig. 1 is the coat of the STUARTS, Lords of DARNLEY and Earls of LENNOX, who bore (LAING, i., 798, *et seq.*), when they assumed the questionable title of Earl of LENNOX (*i.e.*, circa 1490), *Quarterly*, 1 and 4. FRANCE, *a bordure (gules) thereon eight buckles (or)* for AUBIGNY. 2 and 3. STUART: *(Or)˙ a fess chequy (argent and azure) within a bordure engrailed (gules)*; and, *en surtout (Argent), a saltire between four roses (gules)* for the Earldom of LENNOX.

From about 1500 down to the present day the Lords HAY of Yester, afterwards Earls and Marquesses of TWEEDDALE, have borne their paternal coat (*Argent, three escucheons gules*) *en surtout* on the quartered coats of FRASER of Oliver Castle (*Azure, three cinquefoils argent*), and GIFFORD of Yester (*Gules, three bars ermine*), families through which the HAYS acquired considerable possessions (Plate XLII., fig. 2). The different cadet branches of the house of TWEEDDALE have borne the same arrangement with different bordures.

In like manner the Earls of SUTHERLAND, who descended from the Countess ELIZABETH, wife of ADAM GORDON, were in the habit of placing SUTHERLAND *en surtout* over the quartered coat of GORDON and SETON, a usage which continued until they dropped the surname of GORDON, and bore SUTHERLAND only.

HENRY STUART, Lord METHVEN, who in 1526 became the third husband of MARGARET of England, Queen of

JAMES IV., bore *en surtout* over his quartered coat *Gules, a lion rampant holding between his fore-paws a tower argent* for the Lordship of METHVEN (Plate XLII., fig. 3). Lord LINDORES similarly used the quartered coats of LESLIE and ABERNETHY with, *en surtout: Gules, a castle triple-towered argent* for the lordship of LINDORES (Plate XLII., fig. 4).

The LIVINGSTONES, Earls of LINLITHGOW, bore *en surtout*, over the quartered coat of LIVINGSTONE and CALLENDAR, *Azure, an oak tree or, a bordure argent, thereon eight cinquefoils gules*, for the title of LINLITHGOW. On the seal of DAVID, Earl of CRAWFORD, created Duke of MONTROSE by JAMES III., an escucheon bearing the arms of MONTROSE: *Argent, a rose gules, barbed and seeded proper*, is borne *en surtout* for his Duchy, over his quartered coats of LINDSAY and ABERNETHY.

In the escucheon of the Lords CARLYLE of Torthorwald, from 1473 onwards, a coat probably connected with the title: *Argent, a saltire azure* (sometimes with the addition of a chief charged with mullets) is placed *en surtout* over the quartered arms of CARLYLE and CROSBIE (Plate XLII., fig. 5).

The first Lord HOME, so created in 1473, carried HOME (*Vert, a lion rampant argent*) quartered with PEPDIE (*Argent, three papingoes vert beaked and membered gules*) on the ground of the marriage of HUGH, one of his ancestors, with MARY PEPDIE, heiress of the Barony of DUNGLASS.[1] He acquired considerable possessions by his marriage with the heiress of LANDELL of that Ilk; whose coat, however, did not appear on the escucheon of his grandson and successor, the 2nd Lord HOME, or on that of the immediate descendants of the latter. But it was borne by the Lord HOME of Sir DAVID

[1] [It is curious that the precedence of the 1st and 4th quarters is given to PEPDIE on the seal of PATRICK HOME, Archdeacon of TEVIOTDALE in 1454, LAING, i., 76.—J. W.]

PLATE XLIII.

MARSHALLING.

1. Sinclair, Earl of Caithness.

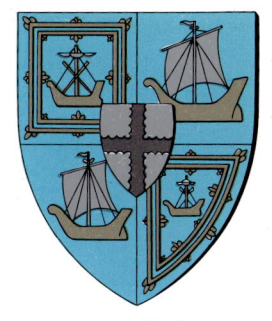

2. Lords Sinclair.

3. M'Donnell of Glengarry.

4. Mackoneil of Dunnivege, etc.

5. Lord Macdonald.

6. Maclean.

LINDSAY'S time, as appears from his register, and is displayed on the seal of the 1st Earl of HOME, by whom it seems to have been adopted in accordance with the then prevailing usage, as the feudal coat of his Earldom (Plate XLII., fig. 6).

In later times it appears not to have been within the prerogative of LYON to authorise the bearing of any feudal coat, or coats, *en surtout* without a special Royal warrant. Two instances, only, occur among later Peers of Scotland of the escucheon *en surtout* being thus granted. Sir PATRICK HUME of Polworth on being created Earl of MARCHMONT in 1690, had in his patent of peerage a Royal warrant permitting him to bear *en surtout* the following coat: *Argent, an orange leaved proper* ensigned with an Imperial Crown *or*. DAVID BOYLE of Kelburne, created Earl of GLASGOW in 1703, also had a Royal warrant to quarter in the principal place of his escucheon a coat of Augmentation: *Or, an eagle displayed gules*, which seems to have been held to warrant the placing of his paternal coat (*Or, three stag's horns fesseways in pale gules*) *en surtout* above this coat quartered with another coat of BOYLE, *Per bend embattled argent and gules*.

In modern grants and matriculations of arms in Scotland it is not the practice to allow the use of any coats *en surtout* except the "escucheon of pretence" when it can be properly claimed.—G. B.]

[The English "use" which began shortly before the Union of 1707 has thus been extended to Scotland.

In both kingdoms the arms of husband and wife may be borne impaled, those of the husband being to the dexter side of the escucheon. But if the wife be an heiress or co-heiress (*i.e.* has no brothers) the husband may place her shield in pretence upon the centre of his plain or quartered coats. Some heralds maintain that the husband is only entitled to do this after he has issue by the heiress.

It must be remembered that the term heiress in British and Scottish Heraldry *now* only means heiress of *blood*, and has no reference at all to possessions. The issue of the marriage are entitled to quarter the arms of the heiress mother in the 2nd and 3rd quarters with those of their paternal line in the 1st and 4th. If the paternal coat be already one containing quarterings, the usual mode adopted now instead of using quarterly quartered coats, is to place the maternal coat with its quarterings (if it has any) after the paternal ones.

In the case of a lady being heiress to her mother, but not to her father (which happens when the mother was an heiress and has no male issue by her marriage, while the father has male issue by another marriage), the modern usage authoritatively sanctioned is that the lady should bear only her maternal arms with the addition of a canton charged with the paternal coat. If she marries, her children (and later descendants) ought to continue to bear this composite coat quartered with their paternal one; but they have no right at all to any other use of the coat in the canton—that of their maternal grandfather (pp. 426, 427). The use thus sanctioned goes back to the time of GERARD LEGH, who assigns to a lady heiress of her mother but not of her father, the maternal arms with the addition of the paternal coat *on a chief, or on a canton*, but the alternative permitted by LEGH is not now in vogue.

To these examples of Marshalling we may fitly join one or two examples of the arms assigned to the issue of a legitimate but morganatic marriage.

The Duke of TECK, issue of the marriage between Duke ALEXANDER of WÜRTTEMBERG and the Countess CLAUDINE VON RHEDAY, Countess of HOHENSTEIN bears: *Per pale:* (a) *Or, three stag's horns fessways in pale sable* (WÜRTTEMBERG); (b) *Or, three lions passant in pale sable the dexter paw raised, gules* (SUABIA). Over all: *Lozengy in bend-sinister sable and or* (Duchy of TECK). I have seen the impaled coats quartered, but do not know if this was done by authority.

The Princes of BATTENBERG, who descend from the marriage of the Prince ALEXANDER of HESSE-DARMSTADT with the Countess JULIA VON HAUCKE, bear:— *Quarterly:* 1 and 4. *Azure, a lion rampant double queué barry of ten gules and argent crowned, and holding in the right paw a sword proper* (HESSE) *within a bordure goboné of sixteen pieces argent and gules;* 2 and 3. *Argent, two pales sable* (BATTENBERG).

An earlier instance is afforded by the arms of the Counts von WARTENBERG, the issue of the morganatic marriage of FERDINAND of BAVARIA (d. 1608). They bore the arms of BAVARIA: *Fusilly-bendy, Argent and azure, charged with the golden lion rampant of the* PALATINATE.

The CHEVALIER DE SAXE (d. 1801), issue of the morganatic marriage of Prince FRANCIS XAVIER of SAXONY, bore the arms of SAXONY, but with the addition of *a fess sable* passing *over* the *crançelin*, and covering the third bar of *sable* and the third bar of *or*.

OFFICIAL ARMS.—Archbishops and Bishops impale the arms of their Sees with their personal arms, the prelate being termed *maritus ecclesiæ*, but in British Armory the dexter side, or place of honour, is given to the official coat. Deans of cathedral and collegiate churches, and certain other dignitaries, Masters of Colleges, the Regius Professors at Cambridge and others, have official arms which might be borne in like manner, but at the present day examples of their use by such personages are very infrequent.

The use of official arms remains, however, constant among the Kings of Arms. GARTER bears: *Argent, St. George's cross, on a chief azure an open crown within the Garter, between a lion of* ENGLAND *and a fleur-de-lis or.* Similarly the official arms of LYON are: *Argent, a lion sejant affrontée gules, holding in its dexter paw a thistle proper, and in the sinister an escucheon of the second; on a chief azure a saltire of the first.* Those of ULSTER are: *Argent, the Cross of St. George, on a chief azure a lion of* ENGLAND,*between the harp of* IRELAND *and a portcullis or.* CLARENCEUX and NORROY have also official coats. CLARENCEUX bears: *Argent, the cross of St. George, on a chief gules a lion of* ENGLAND *crowned or.* (On a seal dated 1598, the lion is uncrowned and a *fleur-de-lis* is placed in the first canton.) That of NORROY is: *Argent, the cross of St. George, on a chief per pale azure and gules, a lion of* ENGLAND *crowned, between a fleur-de-lis and a key erect, all or.* In all cases where an official coat is thus impaled, the bearer may not impale those of his wife in the same escucheon; if he desire to use his wife's arms he may impale them with his own in a separate escucheon, and place the two shields *accolés*.

Foreign ecclesiastics sometimes quarter, sometimes impale, the arms of their See, or other religious foundation, with their personal arms. Sometimes these latter are used in an escucheon *en surtout*. Full information on these subjects, which cannot be dealt with at length here, will be found in my forthcoming treatise on *Ecclesiastical Heraldry*. The lay Electors of the Holy Roman Empire had each an official coat of arms, borne generally *en surtout* above their quarterings. That of the ELECTOR of SAXONY, as Arch-Marshal of the Empire, has already been given at page 346. The ELECTOR PALATINE bore: *Gules, an orb or*, as Arch-Steward. The ELECTOR of BRANDENBURG: *Azure, a sceptre in pale or*, as Arch-Chamberlain (*cf.* p. 380). The ELECTOR of HANNOVER: *Gules, the crown of* CHARLEMAGNE, as Arch-Treasurer (*v.* p. 380). The Counts of LIMPURG place a golden cup in the centre of their quartered arms, as Hereditary Butlers of the Empire (*cf.* BUTLER on p. 381). The insignia of the Hereditary Master of the Horse have been given on p. 490; and those of the Hereditary Standard-Bearer on p. 352. The Grand Masters of the Order of the Hospital of St. John of Jerusalem quartered the arms of the Order (*Gules, a cross argent*) with their personal ones. The Knights of Justice, etc., of the Order bore its arms as above on a chief. By the Statutes of the Grand Priory of the Order of St. John, in England, H.M. the Queen has conferred on the Knights of Justice, etc., the same right; the cross being cantoned alternately with lions gardant, and unicorns, both passant *or*. The Grand Masters of the Teutonic Order quartered its arms with those of their family. The Knights of the Order of St. Stephen in Tuscany bore the arms of that Order in chief, like the Knights of St. John, etc.—J. W.]

CHAPTER XVI.

AUGMENTATIONS.

AUGMENTATIONS are additions made by the Sovereign to the coat of arms of an individual as a recognition of services rendered to the Prince or to the State; or merely as evidence of princely favour. They sometimes take the form of additional quarterings; but more commonly consist of a chief, canton, or an escucheon to be borne thenceforth as an integral part of the hereditary coat. Many of them are exceedingly interesting as historical memorials.

Allusion has been already made (p. 474) to the assumption by RICHARD II. of the mythical arms of EDWARD the CONFESSOR, which he impaled with his own coat, and to the fact that he granted them as marks of special favour to his kinsmen, the HOLLANDS, Dukes of SURREY and KENT; and to THOMAS MOWBRAY, Duke of NORFOLK. We have seen (p. 383) that the same monarch granted to ROBERT DE VERE, K.G., whom he had created Duke of IRELAND, the mythical coat of St. EDMUND; *Azure, three open crowns or, differenced by a bordure argent*, to be quartered with his personal arms: *Quarterly gules and or, a mullet argent*.

We have also had under notice (p. 377) the coat of augmentation granted to, or assumed by, the PELHAMS to perpetuate the memory of the share taken by Sir JOHN PELHAM in the capture of King JOHN of FRANCE at the battle of Poictiers.

HENRY VIII. granted several augmentations: both in commemoration of prowess in the field, and as marks of personal favour.

First among the former class is the augmentation granted to THOMAS HOWARD, Duke of NORFOLK, for his victory at Flodden. To his personal arms: *Gules, a bend between six crosses crosslet fitchy argent*, he was to add an escucheon, to be placed in chief upon the bend, of a portion of the Royal Arms of SCOTLAND: *Or, within the Royal Tressure a demi-lion rampant gules, pierced through the mouth with an arrow, argent.* About the same time an augmentation was granted to Sir JOHN CLERK, who, less than a month before Flodden, had taken captive LOUIS, Duke de LONGUEVILLE, at the battle of Therouenne, known as the *Battle of the Spurs*. The arms of CLERK were: *Argent, on a bend gules between three roundles sable, as many swans of the first.* To this coat he was permitted to add, *a sinister canton azure, charged with a demi-ram salient argent armed or, in chief two fleurs-de-lis gold, and over all a baton of the second.*

GUILLIM considers this the coat of the Duke de LONGUEVILLE, and he has been followed without protest by NISBET, and by many subsequent writers, up to the last edition of FOSTER'S *Baronetage* where the canton is said to be "the arms of LONGUEVILLE." This is of course an entire mistake, though the canton does contain a *composition* from the armorial insignia of the Duke. He was the grandson of the celebrated JEAN, Comte de DUNOIS, bastard son of LOUIS, Duc d'ORLEANS. In 1428, DUNOIS sealed with the arms of ORLEANS (*France, a label argent*), debruised by a *bendlet-sinister argent*, and the shield is supported by a ram. Later he took as supporters the eagles which had been used by his father the Duke, but retained a demy-ram as his crest. As his second wife he married MARIE, daughter of JAMES HARCOURT, Comte de LONGUE-VILLE, and Seigneur de PARTHENAY; and the seal of his son FRANCIS, "Comte de DUNOIS et de LONGUE-VILLE, Seigneur de PARTHENAY" bears the following arms: *Quarterly*, 1 and 4. ORLEANS, *over all a bendlet argent;* 2. (*Azure?*) *an eagle displayed* (*argent?*); 3. *Burele argent and azure a bend gules* (PARTHENAY). The shield has the eagle supporters, and the crest is a ram's head collared. We are thus able to account for the appearance of the ram's head in the coat of augmentation, and the other charges of it need no explanation. (I pointed out the mistake in *Notes and Queries*, 3rd Series, viii., p. 283, so long ago as 1865, and showed that this augmentation was a very different thing from that which the books on Heraldry represented it to be, viz., the assumption of the arms of a vanquished knight as a matter of right by the victor.)

As a mark of personal favour, and in commemoration of his royal descent from ANNE PLANTAGENET, HENRY VIII. augmented the arms of Sir THOMAS MANNERS, K.G., Earl of RUTLAND, with a chief composed from the quartered arms of FRANCE and ENGLAND, and the arms still borne by his descendants, the Dukes of RUTLAND, are: *Or, two bars azure,* a chief of augmentation:—*Quarterly*, 1 and 4. *Azure, two fleurs-de-lis of* FRANCE; 2 and 3. *Gules, a lion of* ENGLAND. (Sir GEORGE MANNERS of BELVOIR, married ANNE, daughter and heiress of Sir THOMAS ST. LEGER, by ANNE PLANTAGENET, sister of EDWARD IV. The title of RUTLAND was one of those borne by the Dukes of YORK.)

HENRY VIII. granted quarterings of augmentation to all his wives except CATHARINE of ARRAGON and ANNE of CLEVES, who both had sufficient of their own. The augmentation of the arms of ANNE BOLEYN

consisted of the first three quarterings. She bore Quarterly of six:
1. LANCASTER: *England with a label of three points argent.*
2. ANGOULÊME: *France-ancient, a label of four points gules.*
3. GUIENNE: *Gules, a lion passant or.*
4. *Quarterly:* 1 and 4. *Or, a chief indented azure,* BUTLER.
2 and 3. *Argent, a lion rampant sable, crowned gules,* ROCHFORT.
5. BROTHERTON: *England, a label argent.*
6. WARREN: *Chequy or and azure.*

These arms are taken from a book once in ANNE'S own possession. It will be noticed that altogether they form an instance of the perversion of the true historical spirit of heraldry of which the reigns of HENRY VIII. and his immediate successors are only too full of examples. ANNE'S own coat, that of BOLEYN: *Argent, a chevron gules between three bull's heads couped sable, armed or,* does not appear at all! BROTHERTON and WARREN were quarterings taken from the coat of ANNE'S mother, ELIZABETH HOWARD, but were borne here against all heraldic rule: while the two paternal coats of BUTLER and ROCHFORT were brought in equally improperly, being the arms of MARGARET BUTLER of ORMOND, mother of ANNE'S father, Sir THOMAS BOLEYN. In one way the whole affair is not inappropriate for it is characteristically false!

To JANE SEYMOUR, HENRY granted a single quarter in augmentation: *Or, on a pile gules between six fleurs-de-lis azure three lions of* ENGLAND, and this coat is still borne in memory of this alliance by the Dukes of SOMERSET in the 1st and 4th quarters of their shield, with those of SEYMOUR (*Gules, two wings conjoined in lure tips downward or*) in the 2nd and 3rd (Plate XXXIX., fig. 2).

To his fifth wife, Lady CATHARINE HOWARD, HENRY granted two coats of augmentation, to be borne in the 1st and 4th quarters:—

1. *Azure, three fleurs-de-lis in pale or, between two flaunches ermine on each a rose gules, barbed and seeded proper.*
2. BROTHERTON (as above).
3. HOWARD (as above).
4. *Azure, two lions passant gardant or, the verge of the escucheon charged with four demi-fleurs-de-lis of the second.*

Only a single coat of augmentation was granted to Queen CATHARINE PARR. It was: *Argent, on a pile gules between six roses of* LANCASTER *three roses of* YORK *all barbed and seeded or.* This coat was quartered with her proper arms (2. PARR; 3. ROSS; 4. MARMION; 5. FITZHUGH; 6. GREEN).

The WHARTON augmentation has been already noticed, p. 376 *ante*.

JAMES I. granted a lion of ENGLAND, to be borne in dexter chief, as an augmentation to the coat of his favourite, ROBERT CARR, Viscount ROCHESTER:—*Gules, on a chevron argent three stars of the first;* and also an additional quartering, to be borne in the 1st and 4th places, viz.: *Quarterly or and gules.*

Several English coats have received augmentation in commemoration of assistance rendered to CHARLES II. after the battle of Worcester. For his distinguished conduct thereat CHARLES granted to Colonel NEWMAN an inescucheon, *Gules, charged with a portcullis imperially crowned or,* to be borne *en surtout* above the paternal coat: *Quarterly sable and argent, in the 1st and 4th quarters three mullets of the second.* JOHN LANE, Esq., of Bentley, for facilitating the King's escape, had a grant of the Arms of ENGLAND, on a canton, upon his paternal coat: *Per fess or and azure, a chevron gules between three mullets counter-changed.* To the WHIT-GREAVE coat (Plate XIV., fig. 3) there was added as an augmentation : *a chief argent, thereon a rose of* ENGLAND *irradiated Or, within a wreath of oak proper.*

The coats granted to Colonel CARLOS and to PENDERELL do not properly come under the head of Augmentations, being new grants of arms, but may be mentioned here ; they only differ in their tinctures. Colonel CARLOS had, in 1658, a grant of *Or, on a mount in base an oak tree vert, over all on a fess gules three Royal Crowns of the first.* PENDERELL had the same, but the field is *argent* and the fess *sable.*

These augmentations and new grants are all conceived in a true heraldic spirit, which was conspicuously absent from the augmentations granted to our naval and military commanders in the 18th and 19th centuries. The DUNCANS of Forfarshire bore : *Gules, a chevron or, between two cinquefoils in chief and a hunting horn in base argent stringed and garnished azure.* The chevron was replaced in the arms of Admiral DUNCAN, the victor of *Camperdown* in 1797 (and who was created Lord CAMPERDOWN and Viscount DUNCAN), by a representation of the gold medal conferred on him by the King, surmounted by a naval crown, and below the medal the word *Camperdown.* Thus, so far as I remember, was created a precedent for two breaches of heraldic good taste, of which there were only too many imitations in later times, viz., the introduction of words into the shield, and of medals, ribbons, and other decorations, which are much more fittingly used as external ornaments than as charges to be perpetuated in a coat of arms. Even these, however, were exceeded in bad taste by augmentations in which the chief was turned into a pictorial representation of a battered fortress, with or without bombarding ships—or of a regular naval engagement. [*See* the arms of FULLER ; Lords EXMOUTH,

GOUGH, and HARRIS; Sir SIDNEY SMITH, CAMPBELL, VYVYAN, and HAMILTON (baronets); VASSALL, etc.] Of these one example will suffice:—Lord Viscount NELSON, who deserved better things even of the heralds of his country, received as an augmentation: *On a chief wavy argent waves of the sea, from which a palm tree issuant between a disabled ship on the dexter and a ruined battery on the sinister, all proper.* (The last word lacks a syllable!) The coat to which this augmentation was made was not itself a very favourable specimen of the heraldic art of the time: *Or, a cross patonce sable, surmounted by a bend gules, thereon another bend engrailed of the field charged with three bombs fired proper.*

Happily the augmentations granted to the great Dukes of MARLBOROUGH and of WELLINGTON are in better taste. To the former was assigned: *Argent, a cross of St. George thereon an escucheon of the arms of* FRANCE; to the latter: *The bearings of the flag of the* UNITED KINGDOM *known as the " Union Jack."* Both these augmentations are borne in escucheons on the honour point of the quartered shield.

It is pleasant to note that the augmentations granted in later years show signs of reversion to a simpler and better heraldic taste.

In Scotland the great armorial augmentation was of course the Royal tressure, examples of the grant of which have been already given. Of other augmentations probably the earliest is that which is said to have been granted to Sir ALEXANDER SETON, Governor of Berwick, *circa* 1320; *a sword paleways azure supporting the Royal Crown proper.* This was placed in the centre of the SETON coat, *Or, three crescents within the Royal Tressure gules.*

JAMES VI. gave special concessions to Sir JOHN RAMSAY of Wyliecleugh, created Viscount HADDINGTON; Sir THOMAS ERSKINE, younger, of Gogar, afterwards Earl of KELLIE; and to Sir HUGH HERRIES of

Cowsland, in memory of the part they took in the frustration of the Gowrie Plot in 1600.

The augmentation which was to be impaled to the dexter of the paternal coat of RAMSAY (*Argent, an eagle displayed sable, armed gules, on its breast a crescent of the first*) was : *Azure, issuant from the sinister flank, a dexter arm holding a sword erect in pale argent, hilted or, piercing a human heart gules, and supporting with its point an Imperial crown proper.*

The ERSKINE augmentation was : *Gules, an Imperial crown within a double tressure flory-counter-flory or*, which was quartered in the 1st and 4th quarters. The grant to Sir HUGH HERRIES resembled that of RAMSAY, being : *Azure, an arm in armour issuing from the dexter side of the shield holding a sword erect supporting on its point the Imperial crown all proper.* An augmentation granted to SANDILANDS, Lord TORPHICHEN was : *Per fess, azure and or, in chief an Imperial crown, in base a thistle vert.*

CHARLES I. granted to Sir JOHN HAY, Earl of KINNOULL, the following augmentation : *Azure, a unicorn salient argent, armed, maned, and unguled or, within a bordure of the last charged with thistles of* SCOTLAND *and roses of* ENGLAND (*gules*) *dimidiated and conjoined.* One such combined rose and thistle was granted, on a canton *argent*, as an augmentation to the arms of Sir NICOLO DE MOLINA, Senator of Venice and Ambassador to King JAMES I. (The grant is given in GUILLIM'S *Display of Heraldry*, p. 389.) MOLINA'S coat was *Azure, a mill wheel or.*

Foreign concessions in augmentation, both in ancient and modern times, are so numerous that a whole volume might be devoted to a record of them and of the circumstances under which they were granted, and we can give only a few specimens in our limited space.

First of all naturally come the IMPERIAL AUGMENTATIONS. A number of these are recorded in DUCANGE, tome vii., p. 106, but the intelligent student will at once perceive that credence cannot be accorded to some of the earlier ones. Those said to be granted by the Emperor FREDERICK I. are probably the earliest which rest on a foundation of truth. In 1162 he is said to have granted to JULIO MARIONI the right to use the Imperial Eagle in his arms, with the title of Count, and a like grant is said to have been made to the family of JOVIO, which some centuries later received from the Emperor CHARLES V. a further augmentation in the shape of the pillars of Hercules (*v.* p. 643).

FREDERICK II. (*c.* 1212) granted CONRAD MALASPINA the ordinary augmentation of a *chief of the* EMPIRE (*Or, an eagle displayed sable*). The MALASPINA arms were: *Per fess gules and or over all, a thorn branch vert with five flowers argent in pale.* To MAFFEO VISCONTI (*vide ante*, p. 274) the Emperor ADOLF granted the right to quarter the Imperial Eagle. This was, however, to all appearance, only an official coat, denoting his tenure of the Vicarate of the Empire in Milan and Lombardy. Mention has already been made of the general use of the Imperial Eagle by officials of the Empire (*vide ante*, pp. 243, 244).

HENRY VII. granted to ALBOINO DELLA SCALA of Verona (who bore *Gules, a ladder of four steps in pale argent*) the right to quarter therewith the eagle of the Empire; while LOUIS, the *Bavarian*, permitted CAN DELLA SCALA to place the eagle in an escucheon above the ladder. The Emperor SIGISMUND granted to LOUIS DEL VERME, in 1433, the title of Count of SANGUINETTO, and the arms of the Empire. (*Quarterly:* 1 and 4. *Gules, three bars argent;* 2 and 3. *Barry of four azure and argent* are the DEL VERME arms.) GIUSTINIANI declares that the four sable eagles which appear in the arms of the GONZAGAS, Dukes of MANTUA (*Argent, between four eagles displayed sable, a cross pateé-throughout gules*), were granted by the Emperor SIGISMUND to GIOVANNI FRANCESCO, first Marquis, in 1433; the ducal title came later, in 1530.

The same Prince had already granted a chief of the Empire to FRANCESCO GIUSTINIANI (*Gules, a castle triple-towered argent, the port sable*) in 1413; and, in 1415, to ELZEAS DE SADE, *an eagle displayed sable, crowned gules*, to be borne in the centre of his arms: *Gules, a star of eight points or.* (These were the arms of LAURA, wife in 1325 of UGO DE SADE,—the muse of PETRARCH.)

The Emperor MAXIMILIAN II. granted to ALBERIC CIBO the principality of MASSA, and as an augmentation, *a chief Or charged with a double-headed eagle sable.* The CIBO arms now are: *Gules, a bend chequy azure and argent, on a chief argent a cross gules;* this chief *abaissé* under another of the EMPIRE: *Or, a double-headed eagle sable, holding in its claws a ribbon charged with the word* "LIBERTAS."

When this prince made Cambray into a Duchy of the Empire in favour of the Bishop JACQUES DE CROY and his successors, he permitted them to add to their arms a chief of the Empire, with the brisure of *a label gules* (the reason of which latter is past finding out).

The Dukes of MIRANDOLA had what appears to be a double Imperial grant (*vide ante*, p. 509).

The Imperial augmentation of the arms of the Dukes of MODENA is also referred to on pp. 508, 509.

The arms of many noble and princely families of the Empire were from time to time honoured with grants of this kind. The Princes of SCHWARTZBURG on elevation to that rank received an augmentation (to be borne *en surtout* above their quarterings) of the arms of the EMPIRE, the eagle having on its breast an escucheon of the AUSTRIAN arms.

Other instances occur in the arms of the Counts von

PAPPENHEIM (a chief of the Empire);—the Counts of CRONBERG; and the Dukes of FRIEDLAND (WALLENSTEIN), already referred to on pp. 220 and 488, both bore an escucheon *en surtout*.

Sometimes the Imperial Eagle in such concessions bears upon its breast the cypher of the Emperor, either in or without a shield; sometimes the grant is of the eagle as a supporter to the arms of the family which are borne on its breast; other grants are of the eagle as an additional crest, or as a mark of distinction between the crests.

All these and others are referred to in SPENER, *Opus Heraldicum*, pars I, cap. 2, p. 56; but probably the instances given will suffice the ordinary reader. It must be noticed that in Italy, during the contests between the Guelphic and Ghibbeline factions, those families which belonged to the latter frequently assumed, without any special Imperial grant, *a chief of the Empire*. On the other hand the Guelphic faction assumed with still greater frequency a chief derived from the arms of the Duke of ANJOU, viz.: *Azure, a label of four points gules, between the points three fleurs-de-lis or.* This is the *rastrello* which meets our eyes at every turn in Florence, Bologna, and other cities of Italy (*vide ante*, p. 469, and Plate XXXIX., fig. 6).

Of French grants of augmentation the most important given by DUCANGE are the following. CHARLES VI., in 1394, permitted GIAN GALEAZZO VISCONTI, Duke of MILAN, who had married ISABEL of FRANCE, to quarter FRANCE-ANCIENT for himself and his heirs. In 1389 he granted the same privilege to his cousin CHARLES D'ALBRET (who bore *Gules plain*).

CHARLES VII. granted to NICOLO D'ESTE, created Duke of FERRARA, the arms of FRANCE-MODERN, *within a plain bordure, indented or and gules.*

The augmentation of the MEDICI arms is referred to on p. 192.

PLATE XLIV.

ARMORIAL DU HERAUT GUELDRE.

1. Bertrand du Guesclin (29).
2. Le Comte de Namur (196).
3. Le Comte de Montbeliard (16).
4. Nicolas de Borssele (216).
5. Le Roy de France (1).
6. Le Duc de Bourgogne.

One of the earliest of French augmentations is that which is said to have been granted by St. LOUIS to GEOFFROI DE CHÂTEAUBRIAND (*vide ante*, p. 331).

In later times the augmentation granted was usually a *chief azure thereon three fleurs-de-lis or*, briefly "a chief of FRANCE." Such a chief was granted by LOUIS XIV. in 1663, with the title of Count, to HANNIBAL DE SCHESTEDT, ambassador from Denmark at the court of France. (This concession seems to be wrongly used nowadays. In RIETSTAP'S *Armorial Général*, it is blazoned as: *d'Azur, à trois fleurs-de-lis d'or, rangées en fasce; à la bordure de gueules chargée en pointe de la device*, " PLUS ESSE QUAM VIDERI.")

An augmentation granted in the present century has historical interest. The family of SÈZE bore: *Azure, three towers in fess between in chief two estoiles and in base a crescent or*, but by a royal decree in 1817, LOUIS XVIII. authorised the Count de SÈZE, defender of King LOUIS XVI., to change these to *Gules, a castle representing the " Temple" argent between in chief two estoiles or, and in base sixteen fleurs-de-lis of the second ranged* 7, 6, 3.

The family of FAUDOAS-BARBAZAN, bearing *Azure, a cross or*, quarter (or sometimes impale with it) the full arms of FRANCE, a concession made by CHARLES VII. in 1434 to the BARBAZAN who had the title of " *Restaurateur du Royaume, et de la Couronne de France*," and was buried among the Kings of FRANCE at St. Denis.

In later times a common augmentation has consisted in a small escucheon to be borne *en surtout*, containing the initial, or cypher, of the Sovereign, sometimes surmounted by the Imperial or Royal, or other Crown; sometimes the escucheon itself is so surmounted. Such an augmentation appears in the arms of the Princes von ESTERHAZY of Hungary: *An escucheon sable charged with the letter* L *or*, and surmounted by a princely crown.

The Bohemian Counts CZERNIN have *en surtout* a crowned escucheon of the arms of AUSTRIA, on the fess the cypher **F III.** *sable*. This is a type of which there are a good many examples. The Bohemian Barons WRAZDA DE KUNWALD bear: *Quarterly*, 1 and 4. *Azure, on a terrace vert a basilisk with wings and tail elevated or;* 2 and 3. *Gules, a bend argent.* Over all a crowned escucheon of the AUSTRIAN Arms the fess charged with the cypher **M T**, between in chief the cypher **F III.** and in base **L I.**

The Barons HOCHBURG bear *en surtout* the arms of HUNGARY-MODERN (*Gules, on a mount in base vert a cross of Lorraine argent rising out of an open crown or*).

Analogous to this is the interesting historical augmentation granted in 1868 to the illustrious Austrian statesman, Count BEUST, the pacificator of HUNGARY : *Per fess* (*a*) *Or, an Imperial eagle issuant sable crowned proper;* (*b*) *Per pale* (1) *Argent an olive branch in bend vert*, (2) the arms of HUNGARY-MODERN ;—over all the arms of BEUST : *Per pale émanché gules and argent; crowned with a ducal coronet of five flowers or.*

The arms granted in 1853 to M. VON ETTENREICH, who saved the life of the Emperor FRANCIS, are: *Quarterly*, 1 and 4. *Or, the Imperial eagle;* 2 and 3 (. . . .). *Two arms united in fess holding a civic crown proper.*

POLISH.—SIGISMUND, King of POLAND, granted in 1512 an augmentation consisting of the arms of that country : *Gules, an eagle displayed argent beaked and membered and having Klee stengeln or*, to be borne in the 1st and 4th quarters ; to the family of STAFILEO of Dalmatia whose personal coat is : *Per fess gules and vert, a vine stalk couped in fess or, bearing in chief two leaves of the second and in base a bunch of grapes gules.*

PLATE XLV.

WAPPENROLLE VON ZÜRICH, I.

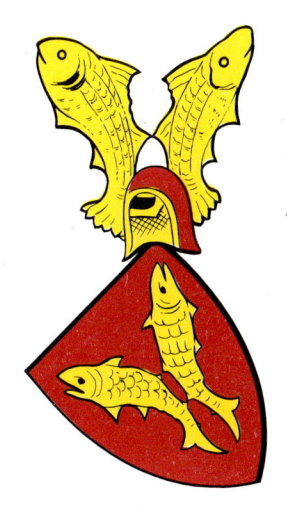

1. Pfirt (30).

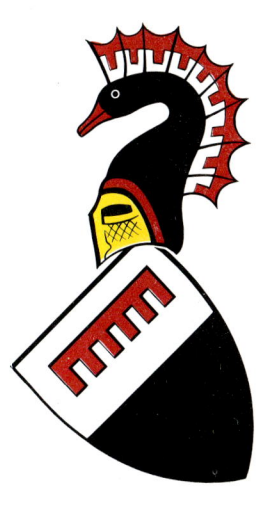

2. Hevtler (222).

3. Chür (131).

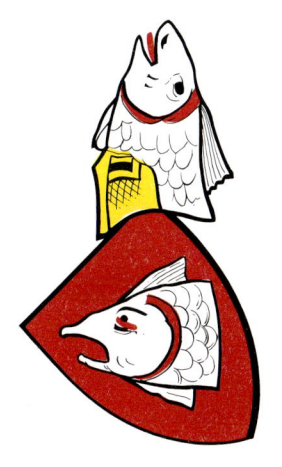

4. Aeschach (218).

CHARLES VII. gave GUILLAUME DE DELMAS DE GRAMMONT a mural crown as an augmentation to his arms (*Argent, a cross moline gules*) as a reward for being the first to mount the breach at the siege of Pontoise in 1444.

The Emperor NAPOLEON III. granted to FIALIN, created Duc de PERSIGNY in 1863, a concession of *Azure, semé of eagles of the* FRENCH EMPIRE to be quartered in the 1st and 4th, with *Argent, on a bend azure three escallops of the field* in the 2nd and 3rd.

The PAPAL CONCESSIONS are among the most interesting; good examples are found in the arms of the Dukes of MODENA, and of PARMA, already given at pp. 508 and 509.

The Neapolitan family of MORRA (Princes of MORRA, Dukes de BELFORTE, etc.) bear in their quartered arms *a pale (gules) charged with two Papal tiaras, each in front of the Papal keys in saltire*. (Their family coat is *Gules, two swords in saltire argent, hilted or, between four mullets of the last.*)

The Marquises of TROTTI-BENVOGLIO bear *Quarterly*: 1 and 4. *Per fess or and azure*, TROTTI; 2 and 3. *Per bend indented or and gules*, BENVOGLIO. The quarters separated by the Papal pale of the GONFALONIERE (as on page 509 above).

The Marquises of GUASTO bear the charges which here appear upon the pale, on an escucheon *en surtout*.

The BARBERINI of Naples place them in chief above their personal arms, *Azure, three bees or*. The SODERINI of Florence, who bear, *Gules, three stag's horns argent*, place in chief the keys in saltire behind the Papal tiara. The Florentine GIROLAMI, who bear, *Argent, a saltire sable*, do the same.

But the Armorials of RUSSIA, SWEDEN, and PRUSSIA contain the greatest number of modern augmentations, some at least of which will be found of interest.

I. RUSSIAN AUGMENTATIONS AND CONCESSIONS.—
The arms granted to OSSIP IVANOVICH, who saved the
life of the Emperor ALEXANDER II. in 1865, and was
raised to nobility by the name of KOMMISSAROV-
KOSTROMSKY, are: *Or, moving from the sinister flank an
arm proper, vested azure, the hand clutching a hydra sable,
winged gules; on a chief of the third a ship fully rigged
bearing the Imperial Standard.*

The augmentation of the Counts RÜDIGER (who bore:
Azure, a saltire argent between four estoiles or) is a chief
*Or, charged with the Imperial eagle issuant and crowned
as in the Imperial arms, on its breast an escucheon gules
bordured or and charged with the crowned Imperial
initial* **H**. That of the Princes and Counts LIEVEN
(who bore: *Azure, a bunch of three stalks of garden lilies
leaved and each bearing three flowers argent*) is the same
but the escucheon is *Azure, bordered and charged with
the letter* **A** *or*, which augmentation is identical with that
of the Counts von der PAHLEN.

The augmentation of SUWOROFF, Prince ITALISKI, is
*a chief of the Imperial arms the eagle issuant, on its breast
the arms of* MOSCOW (*Gules, the mounted knight over-
throwing the dragon proper*).

The Counts and Princes ORLOFF quarter in the 1st,
the Imperial arms, differenced by a chief *azure* on which
is a third Imperial crown.

The Princes MENSCHIKOFF have as an augmentation
an escucheon *Or, charged with the eagles of* RUSSIA, *and
of the Holy Roman Empire, dimidiated and conjoined;*
on the breast an escucheon of the personal arms: *Or, a
heart gules royally crowned proper.*

The OSTENSACKENS, ROSTOPCHINS, MORDWINOFFS,
LEWASCHEFFS, and others have an escucheon *en surtout*
charged with the Imperial eagle.

II. PRUSSIAN AUGMENTATIONS are very numerous
and are of several different kinds. The first consists

generally of a grant of the arms of PRUSSIA to be borne sometimes in the 1st Quarter, as in that granted to the Counts BÜLOW VON DENNEWITZ, who use *Quarterly* 1 and 4. *Argent, the Prussian eagle.*
2 and 3. *Or, a sword argent hilted of the first, enfiled with a laurel crown vert.*
The whole within a bordure gules charged in base with the words "DENNEWITZ, 6 September, 1813," in letters *argent.* The personal arms are quartered on an escucheon *en surtout*, and bear *sur le tout du tout* the BÜLOW coat, *Azure, fourteen balls* 4, 4, 3, 2, 1, *or.*

The Counts of INGENHEIM and BLUMENTHAL, and the Barons CODEVE bear the Prussian eagle in the 1st and 4th quarters. In the arms of the Counts von DYRRHN it occupies the 2nd quarter, and in those of the Comtes SCHLIEBEN both the 2nd and 3rd.

Sometimes it is borne on an escucheon *en surtout*, as in the arms of DOMHARD : Quarterly, 1 and 4. *Sable, a garb or;* 2 and 3. *Azure, a horse saliant argent, all within a bordure or, over all the Royal arms of* PRUSSIA. It is so also in the arms of the Counts GOTTER, and of the Counts GUROWSKI ; the latter bear : *Chequy of* 64 *panes argent and azure, over all an escucheon* of the *Royal Arms of* PRUSSIA.

At times only a portion of the arms is borne, as in the coat of CARLOWITZ : *Per pale:*—(a) *the arms of* PRUSSIA *dimidiated;* (b) *Gules, three roses argent barbed vert, seeded or ;* or in those of ALTROCK : *The Royal Arms of* PRUSSIA *dimidiated, impaling, Gules a greyhound rampant argent, collared or, on a terrace vert, the whole within a bordure of the third.*

Sometimes the shield is divided per fess, and the augmentation is placed in chief, as in the arms of ECKHARDSTEIN ; *Per fess* (1) *in chief the Royal Arms of* PRUSSIA ; (2) *Per bend or and azure over all a fess gules thereon three acorns argent. The whole within a bordure or.*

In modern times the much prized decoration of the Iron Cross has been used as an augmentation of the arms, and some of the most interesting coats are thus treated (the Iron Cross is a cross *patée sable*, with varying dates and cyphers, and bordered *argent*).

To Prince BLÜCHER there was granted the following coat: *Quarterly*, 1 and 4. *Argent, the eagle of* PRUSSIA; 2. *Or, a sword in bend argent, surmounted by the baton of a Field Marshal of* PRUSSIA *in bend sinister, both enfiled by a laurel wreath proper*; 3. *Or, the Iron Cross proper.* Over all the personal arms: *Gules, two keys addorsed paleways argent.* There are four coroneted and crested helms: 1. *The eagle of* PRUSSIA; 2. *Two keys in saltire;* 3. *The sword and baton in saltire;* 4. *A banner of the third quarter.* The supporters are two eagles of PRUSSIA regardant. With this we may place the arms granted to Count von MOLTKE: *Or, the Iron Cross touching the borders of the shield* (it has on the upper arm the initial **W** of silver, surmounted by the Royal crown gold; on the others the dates 1861, 1866, 1870). *On an escucheon, en surtout*, the personal arms: *Argent, three hens sable.* The crest is:—out of an open crown a penache of seven peacock's feathers charged with a disc bearing the Royal Arms of PRUSSIA, with the escucheon of HOHENZOLLERN on the breast of the eagle. The supporters are two eagles of PRUSSIA, each collared with a golden crown and bearing a French "eagle" with the flag all proper. Motto: ERST WÄGEN DANN WAGEN.

We may notice that the Prussian eagles are often given as supporters or crests by way of augmentation; and that these of VON MOLTKE are formed upon those granted to Count von WRANGEL, whose eagles bore the *Dannebrog* (*Gules, a cross argent*), the dexter flag charged with the date 1848; the sinister with 1864; and each having in its dexter canton two swords in saltire proper.

FREDERICK II., King of PRUSSIA, in 1782, granted to the Earl of CLARENDON the right to bear his arms on the breast of the Prussian eagle. In 1791, the Earl of MALMESBURY had an augmentation granted to him of *A chief argent thereon the Prussian eagle*, etc., as in the Royal Arms of PRUSSIA.

In the arms of Count von ROON the quartered shield is *enté en point, Argent, the Iron Cross proper*.

The arms granted to Count HARDENBERG in 1814, resembled those of BLÜCHER: *Quarterly*, 1. PRUSSIA; 2. *Or, a mural crown gules between two laurel branches vert;* 3. *Or, the Iron Cross proper;* 4. *Azure, two keys addorsed paleways or.* Over all the personal arms: *Argent, a boar's head sable, crined or.*

The arms of Prince von BISMARCK have not been augmented; they are *Azure, a stemless trefoil or, in each interval between the leaves an oak leaf argent.*

But to these arms the following supporters have been joined in augmentation; first (on being created Count in 1865), the black eagle of PRUSSIA, and the red eagle of BRANDENBURG (these are ornamented as in the Royal Escucheon, *i.e.*, the Prussian eagle bears on its breast an escucheon of HOHENZOLLERN; the other that borne for the electoral dignity, viz.: *Azure, a sceptre in pale or*). Second (on receiving the rank and title of Prince in 1871), these supporters were made to bear banners, the dexter charged with the arms of LORRAINE (*ante* p. 501), the sinister with the arms of ALSACE: *Gules, a bend between six open crowns in orle or.* The crest is:—Out of an open crown, a Royal crown between two horns per fess alternately *argent* and *azure*. The motto is: IN TRINITATE ROBUR. The achievement is surrounded by a mantle of purple, lined with ermine, and surmounted by the princely crown.

A considerable number of grants have been made to other persons of less importance, who have had their arms augmented with *the Iron Cross proper on a chief argent* (*e.g.* FLÖCKHER, FELDMANN, BAUMEISTER, ESKENS, METTLER, NACHTIGAL, etc.); or have had it granted as a portion of the crest (*e.g.* HAGEN, GÜNDEL, HARTROTT, etc.) Crosses of the Orders of the BLACK EAGLE, ST. JOHN, the RED EAGLE, and that POUR LE MÉRITE have been, but rarely, used in something like the same way. Since the institution of the ORDER OF THE CROWN in 1861, a pretty frequent use has been made of a chief of purplish blue (the colour of its ribbon) charged (not with the Cross of the Order but) with a golden crown, by way of augmentation.

SWEDEN.—GUSTAVUS ADOLPHUS, King of SWEDEN, granted in 1627 to Sir HENRY ST. GEORGE an augmentation as follows: *Argent, a chief azure over all a lion rampant gules crowned or; on a canton of augmentation of the last an escucheon of the Royal Arms of* SWEDEN: —*Azure, three crowns or.*

To many of the Swedish generals, especially in the 18th century, augmentations have been granted consisting of coats of elaborate quarterings, often separated by a cross patée-throughout, and generally lacking in true heraldic taste. These are the coats where one meets cannon, and bombs, and the panoply of modern warfare. A curious mode of augmentation was by the grant of the crowned royal cypher to be placed between the crests. The Barons SCHMIDT thus use the figures **XIV.** between two interlaced **C**'s, beneath a Royal Crown. In the arms of the Barons TAWAST the first quarter is *Azure, the Royal Cypher* **G A** *beneath a crown and having within the* **G** *the figures* **IV.** *all of or.* The Counts of the same name have a like quarter, but the cypher is of interlaced **C**'s, enclosing the figures **XIII**. The Counts UGGLAS, in 1799, have the like quarter but the cypher is **G III**.

PLATE XLVI.

WAPPENROLLE VON ZÜRICH, II.

1. Bretsla (83).

2. Badenweiler (460).

3. Casteln (284).

4. Name unknown (526).

The Barons FLEETWOOD, of English descent, were so created in 1654, and had a grant of the following arms: *Quarterly, separated by a cross patée-throughout argent,* 1 and 4. *Argent, a lion rampant gules;* 2 and 3. *Azure, a royal crown or.* Over all the arms of FLEETWOOD *en surtout: Per pale nebuly azure and or six martlets counter changed* 2, 2, 2.

SPAIN.—The arms granted to COLUMBUS show the mode adopted at that time in conferring heraldic distinctions. His first grant was, *Tierced in mantle:* 1. CASTILE; 2. LEON, *Argent, a lion rampant gules crowned or;* 3. (in base) *Azure, representing the sea, studded with islands argent, bearing trees proper, and the soil strewn with golden grains.* The crest was the Royal Orb with its cross. Later these arms were thus amplified: *Quarterly:*—1. CASTILE; 2. LEON; 3. *Azure, semé of islands and half surrounded by terra firma argent, all bearing tropical trees vert, and semé with golden grains;* 4. *Azure, five anchors in saltire or.* The whole escucheon *Enté en point; Barry wavy argent and azure* (Plate XXXIX., fig. 1).

HERMAN CORTEZ had assigned to him: *Quarterly,* 1. *Or, the Imperial eagle sable;* 2. *Sable, three antique crowns or;* 3. *Gules, a lion rampant or;* 4. *Azure, out of a base wavy argent and of the field the City of* MEXICO *rising proper.* On an escucheon *en surtout* the arms of ARRAGON: *Or, four pallets gules; within a bordure of* CALABRIA (*i.e. Argent, thereon eight crosses potent sable*).

Sometimes grants of augmentation consisted of a bordure of CASTILE; or a bordure componé of CASTILE and LEON.

VASCO DA GAMA, whose arms were: *Chequy of fifteen* (in three perpendicular rows) *Or, and gules on each piece of the last two bars gemels argent,* had an augmentation of the Royal Arms of PORTUGAL to be borne *en surtout.*

CHAPTER XVII.

HERALDIC MARKS OF ILLEGITIMACY.

SEEING that even legitimate cadency is a matter which has been treated very inadequately by most Heraldic writers it is little wonder that the modes of indicating illegitimate descent have been passed over still more lightly. NISBET (from whom SETON'S remarks are, for the most part, condensed) MONTAGU, and PLANCHÉ are the only British heralds who have treated it in anything approaching a satisfactory way, and even in their works four or five pages are all that are devoted to a subject which is both curious and interesting.

According to the correct ideas of former times the possession of coat-armour was the evidence of the *nobility* of the bearer. Now, as a bastard has no legal paternity, being in the eye of the law *filius nullius*, the ancient jurisconsults were disposed to deny the right of any illegitimate child, however princely or noble his actual paternity, to the use of *arma gentilitia*. HÖPING in his treatise *De Jure Insignium* (cap. vii., § 53) confines the right to those who have been formally legitimated by the subsequent marriage of their parents ; or directly by princely authority, and in the latter case only when the right to assume arms has been distinctly conferred in the letters of legitimacy. (BARTOLUS says that though this was the general rule it was not observed in Tuscany.)

As a matter of fact in the Middle Ages, as Mr MONTAGU well remarks in his *Guide to the Study of Heraldry*, " Illegitimacy was really held as being but little derogatory. Opinion and usage were in this respect at variance with the letter of the law. The stern eye of the law looking upon the bastard as belonging to no family nor even to any nation, recognised in him, consequently, no rights either of blood or of inheritance; while the fact appears to have been that in most countries of Europe the natural children of nobles were always reputed noble; they intermarried with the highest families, and in France we find them sharing that invidious privilege of the nobility, exemption from taxes to which the rest of the people were subject."

As long then as public opinion favoured the observance of the law which forbade the use of the arms of their parent to children born out of wedlock, it was their practice to assume, *mero motu*, or by legal grant, new arms for themselves; or else to use the arms of the wives whom they married.

In later times the custom became general that the illegitimate children of a noble (*i.e.* of one who rightfully bore *arma gentilitia*) assumed their father's arms differenced in some striking manner, *e.g.* by the addition of some conspicuous charge to the shield; or in some of the ways hereafter to be indicated. PLANCHÉ is undoubtedly right in thinking that "no positive rule as to the mode of differencing was ever generally laid down, or at any rate attended to." The variety of the differences we shall presently adduce prove the correctness of this assertion, yet there is no doubt that in early times the *brisure* most generally adopted was the bend (or bendlet) sinister. The old French writer DE VARENNES remarks: —"Que tous les Hérauts d'armes par un consentement général ont affecté cette seule pièce des escus d'armes que nous appellons barre" to this purpose (but *see* p. 581).

From the position of this bendlet, drawn diagonally from the upper sinister corner of the escucheon to its dexter base, came the familiar expressions applied to persons of illegitimate birth, "être de côté gauche," and "von der lincken seite."

We have seen (p. 133) that the French name of the bend-sinister is *une barre*, and from this circumstance originated the common, but utterly incorrect, expression "a *bar-sinister*," often used by persons who ought to know better. But the *bar* being a horizontal piece, a diminutive of the Honourable Ordinary the Fess, is not used like the French *barre* as a brisure for illegitimacy, a *bar-sinister* is an absurdity and impossibility. The bend-sinister, usually diminished to the size of a bendlet or baston, was then one of the earliest, and most generally used brisures adopted to denote illegitimacy. In later times, as we shall see, it was further diminished into a still narrower bend called a *filet en barre;* and, later still, this was no longer carried across the whole of the shield but shortened at both ends into the baton-sinister, or the *baton peri in barre*. PLANCHÉ, quoting from the earliest of our English *Rolls of Arms* (that known as GLOVER'S *Roll, circa* 1240-5) gives an instance of the baston being, as he thinks, a mark of illegitimacy. RICHARD LE FITZ MARMADUKE "de goules ung fesce et trois papegayes d'argent a ung baston d'azure surtout." (The arms of MARMADUKE DE TWENG were the same without the baston.) But we must notice that the position of the baston is not specified as *sinister*, and the illegitimacy of the bearer is not clear.

The twelfth article of *Les Coûtumes Générales des trois Bailliages de Lorraine* provides that:—

"Les Bastards advouëz des Gentilshommes seront de la condition des gens anoblis, pourveu qu'ils suivent l'estat de noblesse, et porteront tel nom et titre que leur Pere leur voudra donner. Mais ils barreront leurs surnoms, etc., leurs signatures, et porteront les armes de leur Pere barrées de barres traversantes entierement

l'Ecusson de gauche à droit, et ne leur sera loisible ny à leur descendans d'oster les barres." I have not observed any instance in which a signature was thus "bastardised," though documents may exist to which such signatures were appended. The open way in which the appellation of "Bastard" was used in the Middle Ages upon seals, and in documents written or signed by persons of illegitimate descent, is sufficient to assure us that no feeling of shame would have prevented them from rendering obedience to such ordinances as those quoted.

The *Ordonnances* which were appointed in 1616 by the Archduke ALBERT and his wife for the regulation of the use of arms in the Low Countries (and which form the foundation of CHRISTYN'S *Jurisprudentia Historica*) prescribe :

"Ut spurio sanguine nati, quamvis rescripto Principis legitimati, ipsi Bastardi et naturales, barram insignibus interserant; Eorum autem liberi insignam notam quæ a secundo genitis legitimis rite eos distinguat." Here in the second generation, it will be seen that some striking difference might replace the *barre* or bend-sinister. (*See* ROUCK, *Den Nederlandtschen Herauld*, p. 343; fol. Amst., 1645.)

JEAN DE ST. REMY, Roi d'Armes de l'Ordre de la Toison d'Or in 1463, gives the following among the *Ordonnances* of the Dukes of BURGUNDY relating to marks of illegitimacy. (*See* MENÊTRIER, *Recherches du Blason*, p. 220.) "Un bastard doit porter ses armes comme son Pere, avec un traverse, et prendre son surnom de la Seigneurie dont son dit Pere s'attitule, et point es surnom de son Pere, n'estoit qu'il eust tel titre et surnom que les dites armes. Le Bastard ne peut oster la dite traverse sans le congé et licence du chef des armes, et de ceux du lignage portans les dites armes si ce n'estoit qu'il les voulut mettre en un faux escu." From this note-

worthy statute we find that the *traverse*, or bend-sinister, might be disused, and a less prominent difference substituted for it, under certain circumstances.

SETON in his book on the *Law and Practice of Heraldry in Scotland*, referring apparently to the passage quoted above, says (p. 463), "According to MENÊTRIER a bastard cannot cancel or alter the baton without the consent of the chief of the family, unless he carries his arms in an oval escucheon called a cartouche or false shield." Here SETON is clearly not quoting from MENÊTRIER at first hand, but from NISBET, who appears to have overlooked the important fact that the consent of the other members of the family as well as of its chief was requisite. Moreover MENÊTRIER is speaking of the *traverse*, or bend-sinister, and not of its modern and less obtrusive diminutive the baton. But I refer to this passage of NISBET, repeated in SETON, mainly for the purpose of pointing out that the *faux escu* to which the *Ordonnances* refer is not, as these writers suppose, "*an oval escucheon called a cartouche*," or false shield. (In Vol. II., p. 26, NISBET repeats "'faux escu,' *i.e.*, false shield which we take for a cartouche." By reference to his plate i. in the first volume we find that this cartouche is a simple oval escucheon.) Such oval escucheons, or cartouches, are (see *ante*, p. 56) of frequent use in foreign Armory, especially by ecclesiastics, and certainly have never been in any nation a mark of illegitimacy. But the *faux escu* is simply a shield with a *bordure*. This is clear when we consider the meaning attached by the old heralds to the word *faux*; it is equivalent to *voided*. Thus in GLOVER'S *Roll*, JOHN DE VIPONT bears " de goules à six faux rondlets d'or," the charges being the well-known *annulets*. Again, ROGER BERTRAM bears " de goules et ung faux escucion et croisele d'or," while in the *Roll of Arms of the time of* EDWARD I. the same arms are thus drawn, *Gules, crusilly an orle or*.

There are many examples, but one more will suffice. The familiar coat of BALLIOL: *Gules, an orle argent* is blazoned, "de goules ove ung faux escocheon d'argent." The *faux escu* is clearly therefore a shield with an orle, or bordure, within which the arms of the bastard might be borne. It is, however, right to add that at least one Continental Herald of the first rank applies the term *escu faux*—(*scutum falsum*)—to the plain shields upon which the arms of bastards were borne in a quarter, or large canton, SPENER, *Opus Heraldicum*, p. gen., p. 360. Of this use examples are given below (p. 574).

Another of the Burgundian *Ordonnances*, given by MENÊTRIER from ST. REMY, is as follows:—

"Les fils de Bastards, nez et procreez en loyal mariage, si leur mere est gentil femme, doivent porter leurs armes ecartelées de Pere et de Mere, ayant tousiours la traverse au quartier du Pere, ou si autrement les veulent porter sans traverse les peuvent porter toutes pleines en un faux escu."

We must not imagine that therefore every coat which bears a traverse, or a bendlet-sinister, is necessarily that of a person of illegitimate descent. Marks of bastardy were never brought under strict rules, and in early days there was even less attempt at systematic arrangement than in later times. PLANCHÉ observes that "in the *Roll* of EDWARD II.'s time the legitimate sons bear batons and bends," whilst, to our surprise, we find "Sir JOHAN LOVEL *le bastarde*" bearing the arms of LOVEL:—*Undée or and gules*, differenced with *un label de azure!*" the usual mark of cadency appropriated to legitimate offspring. But I incline to believe that this appropriation of the label to Sir JOHAN LOVEL *le bastarde* is an error. It appears from the *Roll temp.* EDWARD I. that there were two Sir JOHN LOVELS living at the same time. In the *Roll* neither is called "*le bastard;*" but while one differences with a label azure, the other uses the *bendlet sable*. This is obviously a much more likely coat to have been borne by "*le bastard*," and I accordingly think that the chronicler of the *Roll* of EDWARD II. has wronged the legitimate JOHN in this matter.

I have in my cabinet an impression from an early seal, of which the legend is * 𝔖𝔦𝔤𝔦𝔩𝔩𝔲𝔪 𝔧𝔬𝔥𝔦𝔰 𝔟𝔞𝔰𝔱𝔞𝔯𝔡𝔦 𝔡𝔢 ℭ𝔩𝔶𝔣𝔣𝔬𝔯𝔡𝔢 𝔞𝔯𝔪𝔦𝔤: The coat of CLIFFORD: *Chequy or and azure a fess gules*, is debruised by a bendlet (dexter) which, however, passes *under* the fess. Among the knights made by EDWARD III. at the siege of Calais in 1347 was "Sir . . . . GREY, *Le basterd*," who bore the arms of GREY (*Gules, a lion rampant within a bordure engrailed argent*) *debruised by a baston* (dexter) *sable*. In the BOROUGHBRIDGE *Roll* this baston is *goboné argent and gules*.

Sir JOHN DE WARREN, natural son of JOHN, last Earl of the ancient house of WARREN, who died in 1347, bore the arms of WARREN: *Chequy or and azure with a canton of* (the arms of his mother, ALICE DE NERFORD) *Gules, a lion rampant ermine* (*v. ante*, p. 426, see the *Herald and Genealogist*, vii., 193, etc.). Two other illegitimate brothers of Sir JOHN are said by BROOKE to have borne the legitimate differences of, in one case a *chief argent ;* in the other of a *bordure engrailed sable*. (*See* SPENER, *Opus. Her.*, p. g., p. 360).

The earliest instance with which I am acquainted of the use of arms by a royal bastard is the case of FITZROY, natural son of HENRY I., to whom is assigned: *Argent, on a canton gules, a lion of* ENGLAND. The Kentish *Roll of Arms*, probably of the close of the reign of HENRY III., and erroneously called the *Acre Roll*, includes the arms of "RICHARD *fiz le rey*," who appears to be a natural son of King JOHN. He bears the old arms of NORMANDY: *Gules, two lions passant-gardant or ;* in other words, the arms of ENGLAND differenced by the omission of one of the charges. PLANCHÉ engraves the seal of JOHN DE VARENNE, another illegitimate son of King JOHN, which also bears two lions passant-gardant.

One of the ancient modes of indicating illegitimate descent was that by which the father's arms were borne in a bend on an otherwise uncharged shield. Thus the arms of Sir ROGER DE CLARENDON, natural son of EDWARD THE BLACK PRINCE (d. 1376), were: *Or, on a bend sable three ostrich feathers, each having its quill fixed in an escroll argent.* These were derived from the shield which was called by the Prince his "arms for peace":—*Sable, three ostrich feathers, the pen of each passing through an escroll argent bearing the motto* ich diene. This shield, in accordance with the testamentary instructions of the prince, is placed on his tomb in Canterbury Cathedral alternately with his "shield for war":—FRANCE and ENGLAND *quarterly, with a label argent.*

JOHN DE BEAUFORT, eldest natural son of JOHN of GHENT, by KATHARINE SWINFORD, bore: *Per pale argent and azure* (the well known Lancastrian colours) *on a broad bend the arms of* LANCASTER:—ENGLAND, *a label of* FRANCE. (*Cf.* Plates XLVII., fig. 3, and XLVIII., fig. 1.)

This JOHN (created Earl and Marquis of SOMERSET), and the other children of JOHN, Duke of LANCASTER, by KATHARINE SWINFORD were legitimated by Act of Parliament (20 RICHARD II.) and then substituted for the above the Royal Arms within a *bordure componé* of the Lancastrian colours. His brother Cardinal BEAUFORT used the same with a crescent *argent* in the centre point for difference; and the other brother, THOMAS, Duke of EXETER, made his bordure *componé of ermine* (instead of *argent*) and *azure.* After 1417 he changed the bordure to *argent and azure, on each pane of the latter a fleur-de-lis or.*

It will be noticed that these arms were assumed or granted when the BEAUFORTS were *legitimated;* and accordingly that the bordure *goboné* was originally no more a mark of illegitimacy in England than it was in France, where it was a mark of legitimate cadency even for Royal Princes (*v.* p. 439). Indeed, it had been so used in ENGLAND by HUMPHREY, Duke of GLOUCESTER, fourth son of HENRY IV., the tinctures being *argent* and *sable.* (ANTIGONE, natural daughter of Duke HUMPHREY bore these her father's arms with *a baton azure,* and impaled this coat with the arms of her husband, HENRY GRAY, Earl of TANKERVILLE.)

The arms of the legitimated BEAUFORTS are now borne by the SOMERSETS, Dukes of BEAUFORT, who descend from CHARLES SOMERSET, created Earl of WORCESTER, a natural son of HENRY BEAUFORT, third Duke of SOMERSET. CHARLES originally debruised his father's arms with a baton, or bendlet-sinister, which did not pass over the bordure. His crest and badge were subjected to the same *brisure* (*Excerpta Historica,* pp. 328, 329). His eldest son relinquished the baton, and as if in obedience to the *Ordonnance* quoted at p. 552, assumed another *insignem notam* by placing the whole BEAUFORT arms on a broad fess in a golden shield. This, however, was soon discontinued by his descendants who use the BEAUFORT coat without any other *brisure.* We may compare this use of the coat on the fess with the arms borne by JEAN, *bâtard de Bourgogne.* (See Plate XLVII., fig. 4.)

Sir JOHN DE CLARENCE, natural son of THOMAS, Duke of CLARENCE, son of HENRY IV., bore a coat composed from the Royal Arms: *Per chevron gules and azure, in chief two lions counter-rampant-gardant; in base a fleur-de-lis or.*

Mr MONTAGU also gives the following extract from the *Cottonian MS.* Tiberius, E. viii., in the British

Museum. "The base son of a noble woman if he doe geve armes must geve upon the same a surcote .... but unless you doe well marke such coat (you) may take it for a coat flanched." This is illustrated by an example from GLOVER'S MS. (*Lansdowne MSS.* 872), where a certain RADULPHUS DE ARUNDEL bears the coat of the FITZ-ALANS, Earls of ARUNDEL (*Quarterly*, 1 and 4. *Gules, a lion rampant or;* 2 and 3. *Chequy or and azure*) debruised by a "*surcoat*" *argent*, the "surcoat" being the part of the field remaining between the flaunches. MONTAGU reasonably suspects that this RADULPHUS was a son of Cardinal BEAUFORT, by the Lady ALICE FITZALAN, daughter of RICHARD, Earl of ARUNDEL.

An early instance of the *baton péri en barre* (*i.e. the bendlet-sinister couped at both ends*, and this is what NISBET means when he speaks of a baton) is found in the arms of ARTHUR PLANTAGENET, Viscount LISLE, natural son of EDWARD IV. by ELIZABETH LUCY. He bore: *Quarterly*, 1. FRANCE *quartering* ENGLAND; 2 and 3. ULSTER (*Or, a cross gules*); 4. MORTIMER (*cf.* Plate XXXVIII., fig. 4) and over all *a baton peri en barre azure.*

In the "List of Standards and Arms" in *Excerpta Historica*, p. 167, these arms of the House of YORK are debruised, not by the baton, but by *a bendlet-sinister azure.* From the same MS. we learn that crests and badges were also subjected to marks of bastardy. The crest borne by ARTHUR PLANTAGENET :—The silver lion of MARCH, is charged on the breast with *a bendlet-sinister gules;* and his badge, the golden falcon and fetterlock, is similarly debruised. He also used another crest derived from the old PLANTAGENET badges; viz.: On a cap of maintenance *gules,* turned up ermine, and inscribed in front with the letter **A**, a genet gardant, per pale *sable* and *argent* between two broom stalks proper. (*Excerpta Historica*, p. 327.)

HENRY FITZROY, created Duke of RICHMOND and SOMERSET, natural son of HENRY VIII., by ELIZABETH, widow of Sir GILBERT TALBOT, bore: *The Royal Arms within a bordure quarterly of ermine, and of counter goboné or and azure, debruised by a baton sinister argent. Over all on an escucheon of pretence: Quarterly gules, and vairé or and vert, a lion rampant argent, on a chief azure a castle between two buck's heads silver attired or.* (*Excerpta Historica*, p. 337.) The blazon given by HEYLYN, *Help to English History* (Edn. of 1773) is somewhat different. This shield affords a good example of the debased state of Armory in the time of HENRY VIII. We have in it both bordure and baton where one alone was needed, and the complicated escucheon is a mystery unless we count it a further mark of illegitimacy. It was certainly not borne to denote marriage with an heiress, for the Duke's wife was MARY, daughter of THOMAS HOWARD, Duke of NORFOLK; nor can we well suppose the arms to have been those borne by the Duke's mother; indeed if they were their employment by the Duke would be anomalous.

Much better heraldic feeling is evident in the entirely new coat granted in the same reign to " Sir JOHN STANLEY, *bastarde*":—*Or, three eagle's legs erased gules; on a chief azure three buck's heads of the field.* Here, the stag's heads on the *azure* chief, are derived from the same bearings which appear on the azure bend of the STANLEYS, and the eagle's, or griffin's, legs are also taken from a Stanley badge. Six such legs appear on the standard of the Earl of DERBY in the reign of HENRY VIII.

Sir ROGER CHOLMELEY, Chief Baron of the Exchequer (1546-1552), natural son of Sir RICHARD CHOLMELEY, Constable of the Tower, bore: *Gules, the "sword of*

Justice" *in fess between in chief a helmet, and in base two garbs or.* (Compare the CHOLMELEY coat, Plate XXXI., fig. 4).

The illegitimate sons of CHARLES II. usually bore his arms debruised by a baton sinister, but the ill-fated JAMES FITZROY, his son by LUCY WALTERS, created Duke of MONMOUTH, in 1663, had a grant of the following :— *Quarterly*, 1 and 4. *Ermine, on a pile gules three lions of* ENGLAND ; 2 and 3. *Or, a shield of* FRANCE *within the Royal Tressure of Scotland.* For this coat was afterwards substituted the Royal Arms, debruised by a *baton sinister argent*, over all an escucheon of SCOTT of BUCCLEUCH. The batons sinister used by CHARLES FITZCHARLES, Earl of PLYMOUTH, in 1675 ; and by CHARLES, Duke of SOUTHAMPTON, were respectively of *vair*, and of *ermine*. Those of HENRY FITZROY, Duke of GRAFTON ; and of GEORGE FITZROY, Duke of NORTHUMBERLAND, were respectively *goboné* of *argent and azure ;* and of *ermine and azure*. That of CHARLES BEAUCLERC, Duke of ST. ALBANS, was of *Gules, thereon three roses argent barbed and seeded vert*. MARY TUDOR, daughter of King CHARLES II., had a grant of the Royal Arms within a *bordure quarterly of ermine, and of counter-componé argent and gules ;* CHARLES LENNOX, his son by LOUISE DE QUEROUAILLE, Duchess of PORTSMOUTH and of AUBIGNY, bore the Royal arms within a bordure *goboné gules* and *argent*, the silver panes each charged with a red rose of ENGLAND ; over all an escucheon of AUBIGNY, *Gules, three buckles or.*

The arms of JAMES FITZ-JAMES, Duke of BERWICK, son of JAMES II., were those of the king, within a *bordure goboné gules and azure* charged alternately with lions of ENGLAND and *fleurs-de-lis* of FRANCE. HENRY FITZ-JAMES (the *Grand Prior*), and his sister HENRIETTA, bore the Royal arms debruised by a baton sinister of FRANCE.

Lady KATHARINE DARNLEY, daughter of JAMES II. by KATHARINE SEDLEY, bore the Royal arms within a bordure *componé* of ermine, and of FRANCE.

In later times WILLIAM GEORGE FITZ-CLARENCE, Earl of MUNSTER, bore the arms of his father WILLIAM IV. (omitting the crowns) debruised with a baton sinister *azure* thereon three anchors *or*.

This closes the list of the Royal Bastards of ENGLAND who were acknowledged by their parents, or created Peers of the Realm. Space does not permit us to record their crests and supporters here. We may remark that the crests granted to them were *usually* formed out of the Royal Crest, a chapeau being substituted for the crown, the lion being also crowned with a parti-coloured coronet, and gorged with a *componé* collar. The supporters were formed similarly; and a greyhound or horse often replaces the unicorn.

Having seen that the usual differences for Royal bastards were the baton sinister and the bordure *goboné*, we now turn again for instances of the English practice to examples of less illustrious origin. The common difference was certainly the *bendlet sinister* (afterwards shortened into the *baton* sinister, the *baton peri en barre* of the French heralds), thus the MAINWARINGS of Croxton (who descend from the family of that name at Over Peover), in 1546 bore the arms: *Gules, two bars argent*, differenced by a *bendlet or*. There are plenty of similar examples, but other modes of brisure were occasionally employed. CUTHBERT TUNSTALL, Lord Bishop and Palatine of DURHAM, 1530-1559 (who is said to have been an illegitimate offshoot of the old TUNSTALL family who bore: *Sable, three combs argent*), changed the tincture of his coat from *sable* to *azure* (*See* TONGE'S *Visitation of Durham*, p. 26, Surtees Society).

WILLIAM HERBERT, son and heir of Sir RICHARD HERBERT (elder of the two natural sons of WILLIAM, first Earl of PEMBROKE), was created Baron HERBERT of Cardiff, and Earl of PEMBROKE in 1551. He bore the HERBERT arms (*Per pale azure and gules three lions rampant argent*) *within a bordure goboné or and gules, on each pane of the last a bezant*. (See CAMDEN'S *Visitation of Huntingdonshire*, 1613, p. 17.) This bordure was discontinued by the third Earl, and was not replaced by any other "notable mark." It would be curious to inquire if the assumption of the full arms of the family had the sanction of the College of Arms.

In 1603, Sir THOMAS EGERTON was created Baron ELLESMERE, and in 1616, Viscount BRACKLEY. He was a natural son of Sir RALPH EGERTON, Lord High Chancellor, who died in 1616, just as He was about to be created Earl of BRIDGEWATER, and this title was conferred on his son. He bore the EGERTON coat (*Argent, a lion rampant gules between three pheons sable*), with the brisure of *a bordure engrailed of the last*. Here we have the bordure, which is a mark of lawful cadency, improperly used to indicate bastardy; and even it was dropped, apparently in or after 1720, when the EGERTONS had become Dukes of BRIDGEWATER.

In 1627 MONTJOY BLOUNT, natural son of CHARLES, Earl of DEVONSHIRE, was created an English Baron; and in the next year, Earl of NEWPORT. He bore the arms of BLOUNT (*Barry nebuly or and sable*) within *a bordure goboné argent and gules.*

The laxity and venality of some of the old heralds come out in connection with this matter of marks of bastardy. In 1661, HOLME writes to DUGDALE on behalf of a young gentlewoman who was illegitimate . . . . "not to have a Batune across the Coat," but to change the tinctures. The fee offered is five pounds. The postscript to the letter is as follows: "There is an alder-mane's sone in Chester whose great-grandfather was base borne, whom I have been treating with sev'all tymes about the alteration of his coat, telling him for £10 and not under it may be accomplished; five he is willing to give, but not above; if y^w please to accept of that sume y^w may writt me a line or two." (*Herald and Genealogist*, ii., 151.)

The BYRONS, Lords BYRON, originally bore their coat (*Argent, three bendlets enhanced gules*) within a *bordure sable*. The fact is stated in FOSTER'S *Peerage*, but not the reason why. This we find in the most valuable *Complete Peerage* of Mr COKAYNE, "*Norroy*," now in course of publication (vol. ii., p. 98). The family was of illegitimate descent, Sir JOHN BYRON of Newstead, and the next two or three generations, bore the *brisure*, and then quietly allowed it to drop.

The MONTAGUS, Dukes of MANCHESTER; and the Earls of SANDWICH retain the *bordure sable* as the difference of the MONTACUTE coat: *Argent, three fusils conjoined in fess gules*. This, it is said, marks descent from SIMON, a younger brother of John, the third MONTACUTE Earl of SALISBURY. But Sir EGERTON BRYDGES (in his edition of COLLINS's *Peerage*, vol. ii., pp. 42-43), points out that there is not the slightest evidence of the existence of this SIMON; and that the bordure was probably assumed as a mark of illegitimacy to denote the descent of the MONTAGUS from JAMES MONTAGU of Ludsdowne in Kent, natural son of THOMAS, last Earl of SALISBURY.

A *bordure goboné argent and azure* was the *brisure* granted with the arms of SHEFFIELD (*Argent, a chevron between three garbs gules*) to CHARLES HERBERT, or SHEFFIELD, natural son of JOHN, Duke of NORMANBY and BUCKINGHAM.

In 1780 Mr ZACHARY, of Areleykings in the county of Worcester, obtained a patent entitling him to quarter the arms of SACHEVERELL (*Argent, on a saltire azure five water bougets or*) within *a bordure wavy erminois*. His maternal ancestor WILLIAM MUCKELOW had married FRANCES, natural daughter of HENRY SACHEVERELL of Morley who died in 1620. I know of no earlier example than this of the use of the bordure-wavy for the purpose of indicating illegitimate descent, though in modern times it has become the special mark employed by the English Officers of Arms. It is noteworthy that DUGDALE had already granted in 1665 the SACHEVERELL arms within a plain bordure *gules* to GEORGE SACHEVERELL, the son of VALENCE, another illegitimate child of HENRY SACHEVERELL.

In 1781, JOHN INGELBY natural son of Sir JOHN INGELBY of Ripley, was created a baronet, and bore his paternal arms (*Sable, an estoile argent*) with the difference of a *bordure engrailed goboné or and gules*.

The MANNERS arms differenced by a *bordure-wavy gobony argent and sable* were borne by JOHN MANNERS, of Grantham (a natural son of Lord WILLIAM MANNERS), whose son WILLIAM was created a baronet in 1793. In this case the crest was differenced by the addition of a *bendlet-sinister wavy, goboné or and sable*. The sinister bendlet wavy is often used in modern practice to difference the crests of the persons to whom the bordure-wavy has been granted. In the crests of RICH, the WYNDHAM and EUSTACE, and possibly in others, a *saltire wavy or* has been substituted for it, for no apparent reason. In another, that of HARVEY, the crest has no mark of illegitimacy. In other cases, such as PUNSHON, it has been converted into a *pallet wavy azure*, a very small matter indeed on the body of a lamb passant!

No object would be served by giving here a detailed account of the many modern instances in which the present *brisure* of a bordure-wavy has been granted. The curious inquirer will find sufficient examples in the plates of any *Baronetage.* There are one or two instances in which other bordures, *nebulé* or *dovetail*, have been used with similar intent.

The arms of the munificent Sir RICHARD WALLACE, adopted son and testamentary heir of the Marquess of HERTFORD, were a new coat derived from the arms of the family of WALLACE: *Gules, on a pile between two ostrich's heads erased argent, each holding in its beak a horse-shoe or, a lion rampant of the field.* (It is now understood that, though the Baronet was not of legitimate descent, he was not, as at one time reputed, the son of the Marquess himself.)

We may sum up the foregoing as concerning English use thus:—The chief marks of illegitimacy were the bendlet, or baton-sinister; though sometimes the bordure, or *faux escu*, was employed. Instead of the paternal arms thus debruised, an entirely new coat was sometimes granted, the charges of which had some plain reference to the bastard's parentage. Later, the *bordure-goboné*, originally a mark of legitimate cadency, became a recognised mark of illegitimacy. Since the close of last century the bordure-wavy has been the ordinary difference, or *brisure*, employed by the Officers of Arms, in England and Ireland, in grants to persons of illegitimate descent. The crests of persons to whom arms have been granted thus debruised, are differenced, sometimes by the use of wavy lines of partition, sometimes by the addition to them of wavy pallets, saltires, or more generally of bendlets-sinister.

We may remark that the *bordure-wavy*, now so often used, may be quite as fitting a mark of illegitimacy as the old baton, or sinister bendlet, if only its import be generally recognised. But as the knowledge of heraldry becomes more diffused, and the meaning of the *bordure-wavy* more generally understood, we may expect that the complaisance which caused its substitution for the older and better known *brisures* of illegitimacy will again devise some other less known mark, in disregard of the fact that armorial insignia were intended to be plain and clear evidence of descent, and to speak with no ambiguous voice as to the origin of their bearers. It seems to me that in the case of persons whose susceptibilities are too tender to permit them to bear plain and distinct evidence of their descent, the alternative and ancient plan should be adopted, and a new coat composed, as in the instances given of CLARENCE, STANLEY, CHOLMELEY, and WALLACE. This is a course which does wrong to no man; and which seems, to me at least, more honourable and straightforward than that of granting the paternal arms with such obscure differences as (even if they continue to be carried) to confound their bearers with the legitimate cadets of an ancient family.

With regard to this matter, I am obliged to differ from my late friend Mr BOUTELL, who thinks that "this very ambiguity may not be the least satisfactory element of the existing practice" (*English Heraldry*, p. 196). The ambiguity may, I admit, be satisfactory to those who desire it, but it is not so, I think, to the legitimate cadets. A cadet of a great house, bearing his coat-armour properly differenced, will hardly hear with satisfaction that his illegitimate kinsmen, after perhaps a brief use of the *bordure-wavy*, have now dropped it altogether, and in painted glass and sculptured stone set up for themselves the plain arms of the family, and so claim a position superior to that of the lawful cadets.

SCOTLAND.—In Scotland at an early period distinctive marks for bastardy seem to have been rarely if ever employed; families of illegitimate descent bore differences which were also borne by lawful cadets. In his Preface to the *Exchequer Rolls*, vol. i., p. cxxx., Dr BURNETT records one case which may possibly be an exception to the then general rule. MARGARET, wife of

ROBERT GLEN, was a natural daughter of King ROBERT BRUCE. One of the co-heiresses of GLEN married (*temp.* ROBERT III.) Sir JOHN BOSWELL of Balgregie and brought him the estate of Balmuto. Since that time the BOSWELLS have quartered a coat which has no resemblance to that of GLEN, but has been conjectured to be that of ABERNETHY, viz.: *Or, a lion rampant gules, over all a ribbon sable.* No heiress, or co-heiress, of ABERNETHY is known to have married a GLEN ; and, as the ribbon was a general mark of bastardy, it seems probable that this coat may indicate descent from the natural daughter of ROBERT BRUCE.

The third and later Earls of DOUGLAS were illegitimate, and to the DOUGLAS, Earls of ANGUS, the deeper stain attached of incestuous bastardy, yet they all carried the simple DOUGLAS coat; and the families of Drumlanrig and Cavers, sprung from two natural sons of the second Earl of ANGUS, carried, the one a *bordure engrailed gules*, the other a *plain bordure*, for difference. On the other hand Sir WILLIAM DOUGLAS of Nithsdale, natural son of the third Earl of DOUGLAS, carried (according to Sir DAVID LINDSAY) DOUGLAS *debruised by a riband or*, and quartered with EDGAR, for the lordship of Liddesdale.

The majority of Churchmen, whether legitimate or not, used to bear the undifferenced coat of their family. Bastards of the Royal House, however, even when ecclesiastics, had usually, though not always, some difference suggesting their illegitimate birth ; a bend, or bendlet, though also in use for legitimate differencing, being the most frequent. Thus THOMAS STEWART, Archdeacon of St. Andrews, a natural son of ROBERT II., carried SCOTLAND debruised by a bend counter-compony (LAING, ii., 931). ALEXANDER STEWART, Earl of MAR by marriage, a natural son of *the Wolf of Badenoch*, bore no decided mark of bastardy, but quartered *Or, a fess chequy argent and azure between three crowns gules* (a composite coat of STEWART and GARIOCH) with the arms of MAR.

JAMES STEWART, Earl of MORAY, natural son of JAMES IV., bore the feudal coat of MORAY quartered with SCOTLAND *debruised by a bendlet.*

ROBERT STUART, natural son of JAMES V., Abbot, afterwards Commendator, of Holyrood, bore at one time SCOTLAND undifferenced. (It should of course be remembered that the external ornaments of ecclesiastical dignity were in themselves an adequate difference.) His son PATRICK, Earl of ORKNEY, quartered SCOTLAND *debruised by a riband,* with the feudal arms of that Earldom. FRANCIS STUART, afterwards Earl of BOTHWELL, whose father, the Prior of Coldingham, was also a natural son of JAMES V., had in 1665 the Royal coat with a ribbon; and later bore VAUS quartered with HEPBURN, and the undifferenced Royal coat *en surtout.* The Regent MORAY (half brother of ROBERT STUART, Commendator of Holyrood) used SCOTLAND *surmounted by a bendlet;* his descendants in the female line adopted the *bordure componé,* thus: *Quarterly,* 1 and 4. *The Royal Arms within a bordure componé argent and azure;* 2. *Or, a fess chequy argent and azure,* for STUART of DOUNE, husband of ELIZABETH, Countess of MORAY; 3. *Or, three cushions in lozenge within the Royal tressure gules,* for the Earldom of MORAY. This *bordure componé* was borne by the STUARTS of Avandale and Ochiltree, on whose legitimacy doubts had been thrown, but one of the family, JAMES, Earl of ARRAN, to assert his claim to legitimacy, quartered SCOTLAND undifferenced; and STUART with a label of three points. Sir JAMES HAMILTON of Fynnart, the *Bastard of Arran,* sealed at one time with HAMILTON debruised by a bend, but later dropped the *brisure* and even assumed the tressure. Dr BURNETT informed me some years ago that in later times the *bordure - componé* had been adopted as a brisure "by illegitimate branches of other families, and is still to be found in the Lyon Register in modern times, *e.g.* GORDON of Cairnbulg, 1811, and others, even in my time." But it was clearly understood to have no such meaning in the case of families who bore it of old, as the WALLACES of Ellerslie and HAMILTON of Preston and Fingalton. Later, when the *bordure componé* had become used as a mark of illegitimacy, the HAMILTONS took a plain bordure, and the WALLACES a *bordure counter-componé*. In 1742 ARCHIBALD CAMPBELL, heir of Ellerslie through his mother, registered the WALLACE coat with the *bordure componé*, but in 1808, when Sir ILAY CAMPBELL again recorded the coat, the bordure was altered to *counter-componé*. (It is a mistake of SETON that this last bordure (*counter-componé*) was ever a mark of bastardy; it occurs frequently in the Lyon Register as a mark of cadency for families known to be of legitimate descent.)

The late Mr STODART brought to my notice an instance in the Lyon Register of 1763 where a double mark of bastardy is assigned to Colonel WILLIAM CAMPBELL, natural son of ARCHIBALD, Duke of ARGYLE; viz., *a baton sinister gules*, and *a bordure componé argent and azure*.

HAMILTON, Lord BARGENY, who derived from a legitimate son of the first Marquess of HAMILTON, bore HAMILTON quartering ARRAN (*Argent, a ship with furled sail sable*) all within a bordure componé argent and azure, the *argent* panes charged with hearts *gules*, the *azure* with mullets *argent* (in fact a DOUGLAS bordure). The HAMILTONS of Samuelston who descend from Sir JOHN HAMILTON of Clydesdale, natural son of the first Earl of ARRAN, have a singular mark of illegitimacy: *Gules, a roundle chequy argent and azure between three cinquefoils of the second.* The HAMILTONS of Blair, who derived from JOHN, Archbishop of ST. ANDREWS, another natural son of the first Earl of ARRAN, bore: HAMILTON and ARRAN *within a bordure componé argent and gules, charged alternately with saltires and buckles counterchanged.*

According to the present practice of the Lyon Office the *bordure goboné* retains the meaning which, as NISBET says, has only attached to it by "late practices;" and though in some ancient coats—for instance in that of the STEWARTS, Earls of CASTLE STUART in Ireland—it is still retained as a mark of legitimate cadency, it is also the mark which is assigned in the Lyon Office at the present time as the proper difference for the illegitimate child of a person entitled to bear arms.

On the other hand the *bordure-wavy,* which as we have seen is employed for this purpose in England and in Ireland, is in Scotland a mark of legitimate descent. Dr BURNETT could only find for me one instance in which it had been granted in Scotland as a mark of bastardy (SHARP of Kincarrochy, in 1813). (The bordures in the arms of WRIGHT, ERSKINE of Cambo, and OCHTERLONY, I perhaps ought to add are English grants.)

The *bordure-wavy* as a Scottish mark of lawful cadency is borne by GRANT of Rothiemurcus; GORDON of Rusco; CRAUFURD of Cartsburn; GORDON of Hallhead; CAMPBELLS of Inveraw, etc. (*See* NISBET, vol ii., plate ii.). In 1872 it was granted by LYON to a cadet of the English family of ALSTON. In this case the *bordure-wavy or charged with three fleurs-de-lis gules* may not improbably expose the legitimacy of the wearer to unfounded suspicion in England. It ought not to be difficult, I humbly think, for the Heraldic authorities of the three kingdoms to agree to some uniformity of practice in this matter. ULSTER'S present practice is identical with that of the English College, but in 1542 an O'NEILL differenced with a *bendlet-sinister sable.*

A plain bordure gules seems to have been the difference assigned to some illegitimate PLUNKETTS, *c.* 1600, while another PLUNKETT descent is shown in the coat of JOHNSTON : PLUNKETT *within a bordure goboné argent and azure* (BURKE, *General Armory*, 2nd edition, p. 545). In 1705, WILLIAM BUTLER, natural son of JAMES, Duke of ORMONDE, had assigned as his difference a *bend-sinister componé argent and azure*.

We now turn our attention to the practice of other European states.

FRANCE.—One of the earliest instances which have come under my notice is the coat of PIERRE, Bishop of NOYON in 1240, a natural son of PHILIP (AUGUSTUS) II. He bore FRANCE-ANCIENT, *with a bend-sinister argent*. This was also the brisure, borne with FRANCE-MODERN by HENRI, Chevalier D'ANGOULÊME, Grand Prior of the Order of ST. JOHN in France, a natural son of HENRI II. Another son of HENRI II., HENRI DE ST. REMI DE VALOIS bore : *Argent, on a fess the arms of* FRANCE (*Azure, three fleurs-de-lis or*). These arms were retained by his descendants of whom the last were JEANNE, Comtesse de la MOTTE (so notorious in connection with the story of the diamond necklace of Queen MARIE ANTOINETTE), and her sister MARIANNE.

CHARLES DE VALOIS, Duc D'ANGOULÊME, natural son of CHARLES IX. by MARIE TOUCHET, debruised the arms of France by a *bend-sinister or*.

CÆSAR, Duc de VENDÔME (elder of the sons of HENRI IV. by GABRIELLE D'ESTRÉES), bore FRANCE-MODERN *debruised by a baton gules, thereon three lions rampant argent*. This was derived from the brisure of the legitimate house of BOURBON VENDÔME, which bore: FRANCE-ANCIENT, *over all a bend gules, thereon three lions rampant argent;* and this last-named coat was debruised by a *bendlet-sinister argent* by JEAN, *Bâtard de Vendôme,* a natural son of LOUIS, Comte de VEN-

DÔME (d. 1447). The legitimated children of LOUIS XIV. bore: FRANCE-MODERN, *debruised by a baton sinister gules* (*un baton péri en barre*).

The line of the Dukes of BOURBON, descending from the younger son of (ST.) LOUIS IX. affords several interesting instances of illegitimate cadency. JEAN, *bâtard de Bourbon*, Sr. de ROCHEFORT, natural son of Duke PIERRE I. (d. 1356), bore a plain silver shield with BOURBON on a quarter, or large canton (*d'Argent, au franc quartier de* FRANCE *à la bande de gueules*). (Plate XLVIII., fig. 2.) The BOURBON difference of a *bend gules* was diminished to a *baton* (dexter) after the reduction of the number of *fleurs-de-lis* in the Royal Arms to three, and this coat, BOURBON-MODERN, was borne by the Princes de CONDE, etc.

JEAN, *bâtard de Bourbon*, son of Duke JEAN I., who died 1444, bore: BOURBON, *over all a bend-sinister argent*. LOUIS, *bâtard de Bourbon*, Comte de ROUSSILLON, Amiral de FRANCE (d. 1486), son of Duke CHARLES I., bore this *bend-sinister wavy*. (SPENER erroneously gives him a *bend-sinister gules*, *Op. Her.*, p. gen., p. 119.)

MATHIEU, Baron de la ROCHE, *le grand Bâtard de Bourbon* (d. 1505), bore: *Argent, on a bend the Arms of* BOURBON (*d'Argent, à la bande de* FRANCE, *à la cotice de gueules*). His sister MARGUERITE appears to have borne the modern arms of BOURBON, differenced by a *second baton crossing the other in bend-sinister or*.

In the ORLÉANS line we find the following among others:—*Le bâtard d'Orléans* (d. 1380), son of PHILIPPE, Duc d'ORLÉANS, younger brother of King JEAN II., bore: FRANCE-ANCIENT, *a label goboné argent and gules over all a bendlet-sinister argent*. This was borne by his brother LOUIS, Bishop of POITIERS, in 1392.

It has been said that the arms of the house of ORLÉANS were FRANCE, *a label argent*. The celebrated JEAN, Comte de DUNOIS, *bâtard d'Orléans*, b. 1403, had these arms differenced by a *bendlet* (*or cotice*) *sinister sable*. (Plate XLVIII., fig. 5.) CHARLES VII. permitted DUNOIS to change the position of the bendlet to the dexter, as if he had been a legitimate cadet. As we find him bearing the cotice *argent* (*v.* p. 529), the change of tincture was probably made on the same occasion; but his descendants, the Dukes de LONGUEVILLE, bore: ORLÉANS, *a bendlet-sinister gules*. A son of DUNOIS, FRANÇOIS, Grand Chambellan de FRANCE, bore: ORLÉANS, with a *baton coupé in bend argent*.

In the case of the bastards of the house of ANJOU (of which the arms were FRANCE, *a bordure gules*) the bendlet-sinister does not pass over the bordure.

As a curious modern instance I give here the arms of the Duc de MORNY, a notability of the Second Empire, and the moving spirit of the Coup d'État of 2nd December. He was understood to be a natural son of the Comte de FLAHAULT by Queen HORTENSE. His arms were: *Argent, three martlets sable* for FLAHAULT, *within a bordure, componé of the arms of the* FRENCH EMPIRE (*Azure, the eagle and thunderbolt or*), and of DAUPHINY (*Or, a dolphin embowed azure*).

FLANDERS. — BAUDOUIN, *bâtard de Flandre*, and his sister BEATRIX, children of LOUIS DE CRESSY, Comte de FLANDRE (d. 1351), both bore; *Argent, on a canton* (or quarter) the arms of FLANDERS (*Sable, a lion rampant or.*) Their brother ROBERT bore the same but with the field *crusily sable*. Another brother PETERKIN, whose name I do not find in VRÉE's list, bore: *Gules, a swan argent, a canton of* FLANDERS.

LOUIS DE HAEZE, eldest of the illegitimate children of LOUIS LE MALE, Count of FLANDERS (d. 1385), bore: *Vert, on a canton the arms of* FLANDERS (*v. l'Armorial de Gelre*); other sons appear to have used the field *argent*. One of these, LOUIS LE FRISON,

Seigneur de PRAËT et de WOESTINE, married MARIA DE GHISTELLES, and their son JEAN DE FLANDRES, Seigneur de PRAËT, etc.: bore on his seal the arms of his mother, *Gules, a chevron ermine*, placing also the arms of FLANDERS on a quarter, for his father, and adding in the sinister chief point an escucheon, *Argent, a lion rampant gules crowned or* for LIMBURG. (*See* Plate XLVIII., fig. 4.)

The grandson of this JEAN DE FLANDRE was LOUIS, 4th Seigneur de PRAËT, *Chevalier de la Toison d'Or* (No. clxxx.), Governor of Holland, and *Chef des Finances* to CHARLES V. According to CHIFFLET he bore FLANDERS, "*brisé d'une billette d'argent sur la patte droite du lyon.*" But in *Les Recherches des Antiquitez et Noblesse de Flandre* it is said: "Il porta de Flandres plein, sauf que la lyon à la première patte tenoit un anneau d'argent; autres disent qu'il avait une espine au travers de la dicte patte."

BURGUNDY.—The most curious and interesting series of brisures for illegitimate descent is to be found in the following notes on the arms of the principal bastards of Burgundy.

CHRISTYN in his *Jurisprudentia Heroica* gives several brisures besides the *baton ; la pointe coupée, le chef coupé, la pointe trianglée, le chef taillé* or *tranché*, or both; *escloppé à dextre, et à senestre;* and the Burgundian series furnishes us with examples of all.

JEAN, *bâtard de Bourgogne,* son of Duke JEAN, *Sans peur* (who died 1479), bore his father's arms: *Quarterly,* 1 and 4. FRANCE, *a bordure goboné argent and gules,* for BURGUNDY-MODERN ; 2 and 3. *Bendy of six azure and or a bordure gules,* BURGUNDY-ANCIENT; *over all* FLANDERS, *Or, a lion rampant sable;* the whole debruised by a *pointe*, or *champagne or* (this is *la pointe coupée* of CHRISTYN). (Plate XLVII., fig. 1.) Later in life JEAN took Holy Orders, and became Provost of Bruges and

Bishop of Cambray. His fine seal, date 1482, is engraved in VRÉE, *Généalogie des Comtes de Flandre.* On it both chief and point are couped, so that the arms are borne on a very wide fess (Plate XLVII., fig. 4). They are *Quarterly*, 1 and 4. FRANCE-ANCIENT (intended doubtless for BURGUNDY-MODERN, but there is no bordure); 2. BURGUNDY-ANCIENT, impaling BRABANT (*Sable, a lion rampant or*); 3. BURGUNDY-ANCIENT, impaling LIMBURG (*Argent, a lion rampant gules crowned or*). Over all FLANDERS.

On the MS. of the Concordat of Cambray the arms of JEAN as Bishop are blazoned differently: *Quarterly*, 1 and 4. *Or, three lions rampant azure* (See of CAMBRAY); 2 and 3. BURGUNDY-ANCIENT, quartering BURGUNDY-MODERN, over all FLANDERS; the whole is debruised by a bendlet-sinister which (if my memory serves correctly) passes *under* the FLANDERS escucheon.

ANTOINE, Comte de la ROCHE, *le Grand Bâtard de Bourgogne*, Knight of the Golden Fleece, No. liv., one of the many illegitimate children of Duke PHILIPPE *Le Bon*, bore (according to CHIFFLET, and MAURICE) the arms of his father (BURGUNDY-ANCIENT and MODERN, BRABANT, LIMBURG, and FLANDERS as above), *debruised by a bendlet-sinister argent;* but on his seal (in VRÉE, *Généalogie des Comtes de Flandre,* p. 126), these arms without the bendlet are placed on a broad bend (*See* Plate XLVII., fig. 3). An interesting series of papers relating to the tournament held in Smithfield between ANTHONY WOODVILLE, Lord SCALES, brother of the Queen; and his namesake the Bastard of BURGUNDY, will be found in *Excerpta Historica*, pp. 171-222. In conjunction with his brother BAUDOUIN, ANTOINE led the van of the Burgundian army at Granson. The brothers were also present, and made prisoners, at Nancy. LOUIS XI. held ANTOINE in high honour, and gave him considerable grants of

PLATE XLVII.

ILLEGITIMACY.

1. Jean, Bâtard de Bourgogne.

2. Phillipe, le Bâtard, Seigneur de Fontaines.

3. Antoine, Cte. de la Roche, "le grand Bâtard."

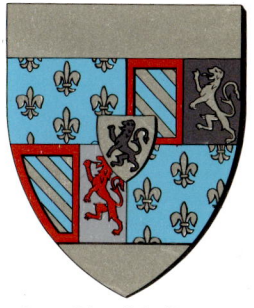

4. Jean, Bâtard de Bourgogne, Evêque de Cambray.

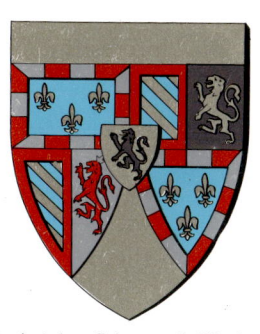

5. Antoine, Seigneur de Wacken.

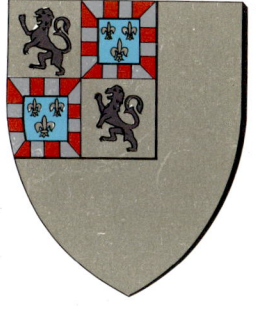

6. Phillipe, Sr. de Crubeque.

land. CHARLES VIII. made him Knight of the Order of ST. MICHAEL.

ANTOINE had an illegitimate son of the same name, who was Seigneur de la CHAPELLE, and is said to have borne the quartered arms of BURGUNDY on a broad fess, or *coupé en chef et en pointe*, "sic duobus discerniculis notatum, sive bis ruptum," says CHRISTYN, quoted by NISBET. There are, however, a sufficient number of instances in which a like arrangement was used by the natural son of a person of legitimate descent, so that I feel exceedingly doubtful about CHRISTYN'S accuracy in calling it a mark of double bastardy. This ANTOINE'S legitimate grandson ANTOINE, fourth of the name, was Seigneur de WACKEN, etc., and Vice-Admiral. His seal bears his arms emblazoned on the sail of the ship which denoted his office; and I have engraved them from it on Plate XLVII., fig. 5. They have the *chef coupé*, and are also *enté en point*.

PHILIPPE, *bâtard de Bourgogne*, Seigneur de FONTAINES, was a natural son of ADOLPH, a legitimate grandson of *le Grand Bâtard*, and was legitimated in 1534, bore the quartered arms of BURGUNDY on a wide chevron in a plain shield. (*See* Plate XLVII., fig. 2.) In this manner were also borne the arms of PHILIPPE, natural son of Duke PHILIPPE *Le Bon*. He was Seigneur de SOMELDYCK, and was elected *Chevalier de la Toison d'Or* in 1500. He was also Admiral by sea. Later in life he took Holy Orders, and, having been legitimated in 1505, he became in 1516 Bishop of UTRECHT. Among the knights who accompanied ANTOINE, *le Grand Bâtard de Bourgogne*, to England was PHILIPPE DE BRABANT, Seigneur de CRUBEQUE, a natural son of Duke PHILIPPE of BRABANT. He bore a plain shield with the quartered arms of BRABANT and BURGUNDY-MODERN on a large canton (Plate XLVII., fig. 6).

PHILIPPE, *bâtard de Nevers*, son of PHILIPPE, Comte de NEVERS (a younger son of Duke PHILIPPE *the Bold*) bore BURGUNDY-MODERN, debruised by *a bend-sinister goboné argent and gules.*

In the painted glass of a window in the south aisle of the great church at Haarlem I observed the arms of a member of the family of SCHAGEN (now known as BEIJEREN-SCHAGEN), which derives its origin illegitimately from one of the Bavarian Counts of HOLLAND. It is, *Bendy or and gules* (HODENPYL, for maternal descent), and on a very large canton are the arms of the Bavarian Counts of HOLLAND: *Quarterly*, 1 and 4. BAVARIA; 2 and 3. HAINAULT *quartering* HOLLAND.

The Counts of WALHEIM descended from JEAN, natural son of JEAN, Duc de BRABANT. Of this family was JEAN DE BERGHES, Seigneur de WALAIN, elected *Chevalier de la Toison d'Or* in 1481. He bore, *Vert, three mascles argent* for his maternal descent from BAUTERSEM, *on a chief Or three pallets gules* for MECHLIN, *and over all a canton of* BRABANT. By other descendants the chief was made *per pale of* FLANDERS and MECHLIN.

SPAIN.—The Armory of Spain furnishes remarkable instances of heraldic brisures for illegitimacy, entirely distinct from those already recorded.

SPENER tells us that TELLIUS, Count of BISCAY, who died in 1370, an illegitimate son of ALFONSO XI., bore, *Per saltire, in chief the arms of* CASTILE, *in flanks* LEON, *in base Argent an eagle displayed sable* for SICILY. Another bore, *Argent, on a lozenge-throughout gules the castle or* for CASTILE, *each division of the argent charged with the lion of* LEON.

The great family of HENRIQUEZ, Dukes of MEDINA DEL RIO SECO, descending from a natural son of ALFONSO XI., bore, like DON PEDRO DE TRASTAMARA, the arms of LEON, *chapé ployé* of CASTILE. Otherwise

PLATE XLVIII.

ILLEGITIMACY.

1. Matthieu, "le grand Bâtard de Bourbon."

2. Jean, Seigneur de Rochefort.

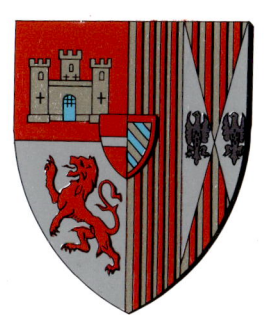

3. Don John of Austria.

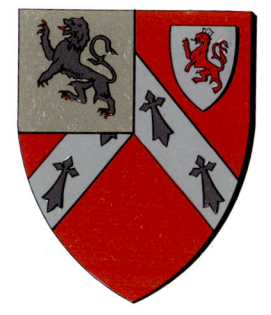

4. Jean, Seigneur de Praet.

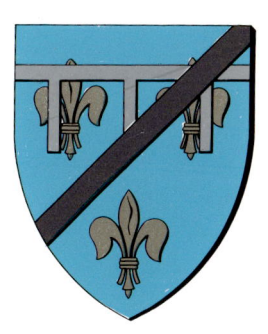

5. Jean, Cte. de Dunois. (*Original arms.*)

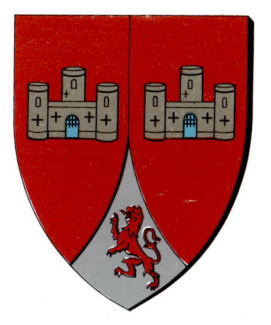

6. Alfonso of Castile.

tierced en mantle, 1 and 2. CASTILE ; 3. LEON, as in Plate XLVIII., fig. 6.

FREDERICK, Duke of BENEVENTO, a natural son of HENRY II. of CASTILE and LEON, bore : *Chequy of nine, five of* CASTILE, *four of* LEON. JAMES of XERICA, son of JAMES I., King of ARRAGON, by THERESIA DE BIDAURE, bore : ARRAGON (*Or, four pallets gules*) *charged with an orle of eight escucheons of* BIDAURE (*Or, a fess azure*).

HENRY, Grand Master of the Order of SANTIAGO, natural son of FERDINAND I., was progenitor of the Dukes of SEGORBIA who bore : *Tierced in pale*, 1. ARRAGON ; 2. *Per fess* CASTILE *and* LEON ; 3. SICILY.

Don JOHN of AUSTRIA, natural son of the Emperor CHARLES V., bore : *Per pale*, 1. *Per fess* CASTILE *and* LEON ; 2. ARRAGON *impaling* ARRAGON-SICILY ; *Over all* AUSTRIA, *impaling* BURGUNDY-ANCIENT. (Plate XLVIII., fig. 3.) His sister MARGARET of PARMA bore the *surtout* only, *see ante*, p. 508.

PORTUGAL.—In Portugal the Dukes of BRAGANZA who descended from AFFONSO, natural son of King JOAÕ I., and who came themselves to the throne in 1640, bore : *Argent, a saltire gules thereon five escucheons azure, on each as many plates in saltire.* AFFONSO'S sister BEATRICE married in 1405, THOMAS FITZALAN, Earl of ARUNDEL. Her seal bears the arms of FITZALAN, quartering WARRENNE, the whole impaling the arms of PORTUGAL as now used without any brisure (the seal is engraved in BOUTELL, *Heraldry, Historical and Popular*, 480).

The NORONHAS descend from AFFONSO, Conde de GIJION, natural son of HENRY II. of CASTILE by ISABELLA, natural daughter of King FERNANDO of PORTUGAL ; they quartered PORTUGAL and NORONHAS *within a bordure componé or and vair*. (Tem por armas o escudo esquartelado ; ao primeiro as armas de Portugal ao segundo as de Castella, mantelado de prata, e dous

Leoens de purpura batalhantes, e huma bordadura composta de ouro e veiros—*Nobiliarchia Portugueza*, p. 311.) The arms of the NORONHAS were therefore the reverse of those of the HENRIQUEZ of Spain, *vide ante*, p. 576.

In Portugal, however, as elsewhere the bendlet-sinister is a recognised mark of bastardy and as such was borne by the ALBUQUERQUES. We find in the *Nobiliarchia Portuguesa* (p. 223) the following:—" Os bastardos haõ de trazer as armas com sua quebra de bastardia . . . . A quebra de bastardia he huma cotica ou risca, que atravessa o escudo em banda, como se vè nas armas da casa de Aveiro, a quem sómente vejo observar esta ley, por descenderem os Duques de D. Jorge, filho bastardo del Rey D. Joaõ II."

The family here referred to bore the title of Conde de LANCASTRO, in remembrance of the descent of the Royal House from JOHN of GHENT, Duke of LANCASTER, whose daughter PHILIPPA was wife of Don JOAÕ I. The connection was, however, remote, as that Prince was only great-grandfather of JOHN II. whose bastard son Don JORGE, had the title DE LANCASTRO.

The SOUSAS, who derive their origin from MARTIN AFFONSO CHICHORRO, and AFFONZO DINIS, natural sons of AFFONSO III. by the two sisters SOUSA, bore the following arms : the first, PORTUGAL quartering LEON ; the second PORTUGAL quartering SOUSA [*Argent, four crescents in cross* (" quadernas de meas Luas ") *gules the points meeting towards the centre*].

The family of MENESEZ, who descend from Don ALONZO SANCHEZ, son of Don DIONIS (King Denis) of PORTUGAL by Doña TERESA MARTINEZ DE MENESEZ, bore : *Argent, a cross componé of nine pieces: five of* CASTILE, *four of* LEON, *between in each canton the five escucheons*—the *Quinas Reales*—from the arms of PORTUGAL.

SAVOY.—In the house of SAVOY the bendlet-sinister was the usual brisure for illegitimacy, but HUMBERT, bâtard de SAVOIE, son of Count AYMON, bore the arms of SAVOY : *Gules, a cross argent debruised with five mufles de lion sable* (SPENER, *Opus Heraldicum*, p. gen., p. 360, quoting from MENÊTRIER, gives these charges as *five crescents azure*, but I think wrongly. *See* GUICHENON, *Hist. Généalogique de la Maison de Savoie*, iii., 271).

In a MS. description of the arms of the Chevaliers who were present at Rome in 1312, on the occasion of the coronation of the Emperor HENRY, we find a somewhat similar coat borne. " M. Guillaume le Bastard, l'Écu de gueules à une croix d'argent à cinq aiglettes de sable." The eagles of course came from the original arms of SAVOY.

The brisure of a bendlet-sinister was used by RÉNÉ, *bâtard de Savoie* (d. 1525) son of Duke PHILIP *Sansterre;* by ANSELMO, Count de COLIGNO, natural son of PHILIP, Prince of ACHAIA and the MOREA ; and by ANTOINE DE BUSQUE, a natural son of JAMES, titular Prince of ACHAIA.

It may here be noted that though the above-named PHILIP, Prince of ACHAIA, was the eldest of the house of SAVOY, yet, as he did not succeed to its possessions, AMADEO made him and his descendants difference by the addition of a *bend azure*, as a mark of the renunciation of the rights of seniority (GUICHENON, *Hist. de la Maison de Savoye*, i., 146). LOUIS DE SAVOIE, *bâtard* D'ACHAIE, Seigneur de RACONIS, living in 1433, was a son of LOUIS, Prince of ACHAIA, and bore as his brisure the azure bendlet, but *sinister.* His descendants, by permission of LOUIS, Duke of SAVOY, turned this into the legitimate brisure of a *bend azure.*

BAVARIA.—In SIEBMACHER'S *Wappenbuch*, vol. ii., are the arms of two Bavarian families which are apparently of illegitimate descent. The family of NUSBERG (or

NUSSBERG), plate lix., bear, *Gules, a fess charged with the arms of* BAVARIA. The family of PÜNTZINGER (plate lxiii.) used BAVARIA *with a chief gules.* The Counts of HOLNSTEIN AUS BAYERN bore *the quartered arms of* BAVARIA *and the* PALATINATE, debruised by a baton sinister gules over all.

HESSE.—The Counts von SCHLOTHEIM in Hesse bear: *Quarterly,* 1 and 4. HESSE (*Azure, a lion rampant barry argent and gules*), *debruised by a bendlet-sinister or;* 2 and 3. *Argent, an escucheon reversed sable* for SCHLOTHEIM. (This is a remarkable difference from the arms of the legitimate Barons von SCHLOTHEIM, who bear: *Argent, an escucheon sable.*) The Barons von SOMMERAU-BECK difference the arms of HESSE with a *bendlet-sinister gules.*

NASSAU-ORANGE. — MAURICE, Prince of NASSAU-ORANGE (d. 1625), had two sons, WILLIAM and LOUIS, Seigneurs of LECK. These had a coat of four of the principal quarterings of their father's shield, NASSAU, KATZENELBOGEN, VIANDEN, and DIETZ, and the only brisure was an escucheon bearing the arms of the Lordship of LECK (*Argent, a lion rampant sable*). The son of LOUIS was HENRY, Count of NASSAU-OUWERKERKE, Master of the Horse to WILLIAM of Orange, who afterwards created his kinsman's son HENRY, Earl of GRANTHAM in 1698.

HENRY FREDERICK, brother of MAURICE, whom he succeeded in the principality, had a natural son FREDERICK, Lord of ZULESTEIN, who bore the same arms as the Seigneurs of LECK, but substituted for its escucheon, that of the Lordship of ZULESTEIN: *Gules, three zuilen argent* (*v.* p. 388), *surmounted by a label of the same.*

In the Museum of Antiquities in the Porte de Hal at Brussels I noticed the interesting brass of WILHELM DE GOICX (*circa* 1555); on it, among the escucheons denoting his descent, is one of NASSAU plain, *enté en point argent*, evidently for one of his ancestors who was a bastard of that house. The Counts of CONROY in Brabant, who were illegitimate descendants of NASSAU, bore NASSAU quartering VIANDEN (*Gules, a fess or*), the whole *enté en point azure.*

NORWAY AND DENMARK.—The Counts of DANESKIOLD-LAURWIGEN and of DANESKIOLD-SAMSOË, who have the family name of GYLDENLÖVE, are illegitimate descendants of the Royal House of DENMARK and NORWAY. The former descend from ULRIC FREDERICK (d. 1704), a natural son of FREDERICK III. They bear: *Quarterly*, 1 and 4. *Azure, a lion rampant argent crowned, holding in its fore-paws and standing on the long-handled Danish axe or* (the arms of NORWAY with a change of tincture). 2. *Per bend-sinister or and sable.* 3. *Per bend-sinister sable and or.* These quarters are separated by a *cross patée-throughout argent.* On the centre point is a *crowned escucheon, Gules, charged with a cross patée and over all two lions passant gardant in pale or. Sur le tout du tout an oval escucheon Gules, crowned, and charged with the cypher* **F. III.**, *also crowned or.* (The foundation of the escucheon is SCHLESWIG, with a change of tincture.) The Counts of DANESKIOLD-SAMSÖE descend from CHRISTIERN GYLDENLÖVE, natural son of CHRISTIERN V. and bear a somewhat similar coat. *Quarterly* 1 and 4. *Gules, a swan argent crowned and gorged with a coronet or* (STORMARN). 2. *Per bend-sinister azure and or.* 3. *Per bend-sinister or and azure.* The remainder as in the preceding coat, but the escucheon *sur le tout du tout* has the cypher **C 5** crowned.

SWEDEN.—The Counts of WASABORG, who descend from a natural son of GUSTAVUS ADOLPHUS, bear: *Quarterly*, 1 and 4. *Argent, two barbel addorsed gules, in chief a crown or.* 2 and 3. *Gules, a griffon rampant crowned or.* Over all an escucheon sable, thereon a "*vase*" (or sheaf) *or, debruised by a bendlet gules.*

Disregarding these Scandinavian examples, which are of modern date and debased style, we find that while the bend-sinister was the usual brisure, yet in the Low Countries the paternal arms were often borne upon a fess, canton, or other honourable Ordinary. In other cases, a point, or a champagne, or a chief was added. In the Peninsula, though the bendlet-sinister was used, a more frequent mode of denoting illegitimacy was by the assumption of a new shield composed from the parental quarterings.

I must, however, remind the student that abroad a bend-sinister, *when not used to debruise other bearings*, is no mark of illegitimacy; and its use carries with it no trace of suspicion. In Germany the custom referred to on pp. 135 and 220 has caused many shields bearing bends to appear as bends-sinister, as in the great armorial — SIEBMACHER'S *Wappenbuch* — where nearly every plate contains examples of bends converted into bends-sinister, and charges turned from the normal position to face the sinister, the helmets and crests being similarly *contournés*, simply for pictorial effect. (All this is, however, so contrary to the pre-conceived ideas of the ordinary British Herald, that I have known amusing instances of a failure to grasp the truth on the part even of highly-placed officials!) In France a considerable number of the coats granted by D'HOZIER, in virtue of the edict of 1696, contain the *Barre*, or bend-sinister, as a principal charge. (See *L'Armorial Général de France*, by HOZIER.)

CHAPTER XVIII.

BADGES.

BEFORE we enter upon the subject of the external ornaments of armorial achievements the less familiar subject of badges claims a little attention.

Family badges may probably have been the earliest form of hereditary insignia, preceding shield, or coat-armory. We have already noted that on the seal of LOUIS VII. of FRANCE (1137-1180) the single *fleur-de-lis* appears simply as a badge or device, not being included in a shield; LOUIS'S successor, PHILIP AUGUSTUS, was the first who bore the *fleur-de-lis* in numbers on a shield (*vide ante*, Chapter XII., p. 328). ODO BURNARD, in the reign of RICHARD I. sealed with a leaf as his badge, and afterwards with three leaves on his shield.

In Scotland JOHN MONTGOMERY sealed with a *fleur-de-lis*, not enclosed in an escucheon, in 1175. (This is noticed as the MONTGOMERY device in a list of English badges in the reign of EDWARD IV.) His descendants bore three *fleurs-de-lis* as arms. ROBERT BRUCE, Earl of CARRICK (the competitor for the Scottish throne, and grandfather of King ROBERT I.), who had on his shield a saltire and chief, the latter charged with a lion passant gardant, also used a seal bearing this charge as his badge, not upon a shield.

WILLIAM DE YNAIS, or INNES, had in his homage seal of 1295 a single six-pointed star not on an escucheon, his descendants bore three stars. (Other examples are given at p. 50, *ante*.) But if badges thus preceded formal hereditary arms they were also in high favour in the days of the purest heraldry. The badge was sometimes, as in the cases referred to above, identical with a charge of the shield, but this became less frequent in later times. Distinct as were crests and badges, the family badge sometimes came to be used as a crest. A badge may be described as a subsidiary family ensign, occasionally accompanied by a motto, borne not by the owner of it himself but by his adherents, dependants, or retainers. The silken hangings of beds, the tapestry of chambers, the caparisons of horses, as well as robes, were often powdered with badges. The badge was largely employed for all decorative purposes. In the fifteenth century, it was used (usually in combination with the crest) as a charge upon the Royal and knightly standards. (*Vide* Chapter XXII.)

At an earlier period it often formed part of the ornamental work of the seals of magnates of the fourteenth century. In this and the following century there was not one of the leading nobility who had not his "*household badge*" (SHAKESPEARE, *Henry VI.*, Act i., s. 1) which, like other heraldic insignia, was often allusive to a name, estate, or office. Some families had more than one badge in general use; for instance, the PERCIES of Northumberland used as their chief badges the silver crescent, and a golden *locket*, or pair of manacles. These are sometimes combined as on the standard of HENRY, 5th Earl, where the manacles are placed within the horns of the crescent. But they also used (as on the standard of HENRY ALGERNON 6th Earl) a key in pale surmounted by an open crown (the badge of their barony of POYNINGS), the falchion of FITZPAYNE, and the bugle-horn of BRYAN. (*See* Mr LONGSTAFFE'S paper on "The Old Heraldry of the Percies," originally published in the *Archæologia Æliana;* and see also the "List of Standards" in *Excerpta Historica*, p. 334, etc.) The bear and ragged staff (originally two separate devices of the BEAUCHAMPS, Earls of WARWICK, the bear being allusive to their remote ancestor URSO), were united by the "King-maker," Earl of WARWICK, and the DUDLEYS who succeeded the NEVILLES, into one badge, "The rampant bear chained to the ragged staff." (A list of the principal badges is printed in Appendix G. Others will be found in the Chapter on STANDARDS already referred to.)

KNOTS of particular form were not infrequently used as badges both in England and elsewhere; *e.g.* the STAFFORD knot, the BOURCHIER knot, the WAKE and ORMOND knot; in all these the silk is twined having some resemblance to the initial letter of the family name. In the BOWEN knot the allusion is double, it is formed of four *bows*, or loops, and each bears a resemblance to one form of the Greek letter B. Knots were also used to unite the badges of two families which had merged into one; or the badge of an office to a personal one. Thus, the badge of the Lords DACRE *of the North*, was a silver escallop united by the DACRE knot *gules* to a ragged staff *argent*. The escallop was one of the charges of their arms (*Gules, three escallops argent*), while the ragged staff was said to commemorate the hereditary forestership of Inglewood, but Lord DACRE of GILSLAND, K.G., who bore this badge on his standard, married ELIZABETH, daughter and heiress of Lord GREYSTOCK, K.G. and this may be the allusion.

The HUNGERFORDS used the badge of a sickle erect, the handles *gules*, the bands *or*. (*See* the seal of Sir ROBERT HUNGERFORD, where the shield is placed between two sickles, the blades each charged with an ermine spot for cadency.) Later (when Lord HUNGERFORD married CATHARINE PEVEREL) this was united by a knot to the golden garb of the PEVERELS, taken from their arms, *Azure, three garbs or* (on the HUNGERFORD and PEVEREL Heraldry, in Cricklade Church, *see* a paper in *Notes and Queries*, 5th Series, viii., 193-194), as appears on a standard of their descendant EDWARD, Lord HASTINGS.

These badges which, as has been said above, were borne generally by the owner's dependants, must when possible be carefully distinguished from the personal devices, temporarily used by exalted persons alone, and not by their households, often with an occult meaning known only to the wearer and his mistress, or special friends, and which was also generally accompanied by an allusive motto. Mr MONTAGU, one of the first English writers who directed attention to the wide subject of badges and devices, gives several instances which he considers to come under the latter category. These include the salamander in flames of FRANÇOIS I., which occurs so frequently at Fontainbleau and Chambord, and of which there is a splendid example above the fireplace of one of the rooms in the Château de Blois. (It was used with varying mottoes—*Nutrisco et extinguo ; Jamais ne estaindra ;* and, as at Azay, *Ung seul desir.*) So also the star of the MONTMORENCYS combined with its Greek motto ΑΠΛΑΝΩΣ ; Lord LATIMER'S human heart with its legend *à Dieu et à ma fiancée ;* and Sir THOMAS HENEAGE'S heart-shaped knot with the motto *Fast tho' untied*, were eventually rather badges than devices. This whole subject has been very fully treated by Mrs PALLISER in her excellent volume *Historic Devices, Badges, and War Cries*, London 1870, and to this work the reader is referred for much amusing and interesting information on the subject, though it will be laid under contribution in the following paragraphs, in which a brief account is given of some of the principal English Royal Badges, including personal devices.

First in order of these is the sprig of Broom, the famous *planta genista* which gave its name of PLANTAGENET to the great house of the Counts of ANJOU,

Kings of ENGLAND; of which it continued to be one of the badges up to the time of HENRY VIII. We have already seen, p. 557, that a *genet cat per pale sable and argent, between two broomcods stalked proper* was the crest granted by EDWARD IV. to his natural son, ARTHUR PLANTAGENET, created Viscount LISLE by HENRY VIII. A sprig of broom appears on each side of the throne in the Great Seal of RICHARD I. (*British Museum Catalogue*, 80). The occasion of the assumption of this badge by the house of ANJOU is entirely unknown. Upon his monumental effigy in Westminster Abbey the robe of RICHARD II. is ornamented with the peascods, or pods of the *planta genista;* the badge does not appear, however, to have been very frequently used in England, although a livery collar of broomcods, with a white hart as the pendant, appears on a portrait of the same prince at Wilton. It does not appear among the Royal badges upon the standards given in *Excerpta Historica* from the MS. in Coll. Arm., i., 2.

A star between the horns of a crescent appears on the Great Seals of RICHARD I., and HENRY III. (*Catalogue of Seals in the British Museum*, Nos. 80 and 100).

EDWARD I. is said to have had as his badge *a rose or, stalked proper* (HARL. MS., 304); and from his time downward roses of gold, white, and red, were used as ornaments on their dress and furniture by many of the House of PLANTAGENET who descended from him.

ELEANOR of Provence was the mother of EDWARD I., and Mr PLANCHÉ very plausibly suggests that from the sunny clime of Provence we have derived, not merely the rose of our gardens, but the famous floral emblems of the rival Royal Houses of YORK and LANCASTER. The tomb of her second son, EDMUND CROUCHBACK, Lord of LANCASTER, was covered with red roses. To his children, THOMAS and HENRY, descended the claim to PROVENCE. HENRY'S eldest son, the 1st Duke of LANCASTER, has on his seal a bunch of roses. JOHN of GAUNT married BLANCHE, his younger daughter and heiress, and claimed PROVENCE accordingly. He bequeathed to St. Paul's Cathedral his bed powdered with roses.

Regarded, probably, as of minor importance to the white swan, the antelope, and other principal cognizances of the Royal House, the use of the rose was retained by the Sovereign, and by the older family of JOHN of GAUNT. Borne white by the House of YORK, the rose is said to have been allusive to the fair ROSAMOND CLIFFORD. It came to the House of YORK by the marriage of RICHARD of CONINGSBURGH, son of EDMOND of LANGLEY with his second wife MAUD, daughter of THOMAS, Lord CLIFFORD. It was tinctured red by the House of LANCASTER, with the BEAUFORT line of which it seems to have been particularly associated; Shakespeare calls it the *Badge of* SOMERSET. Roses of the two colours seem to have corresponded to the livery colours of the PLANTAGENETS, and came, not unnaturally, to be the badge of the contending factions.

Both red and white roses occur on a standard of EDWARD IV., which also bears the Royal Crest of the crowned lion passant gardant. Another standard, of which the principal device is the white rose of YORK *en soleil*, has only smaller charges of the same. A third, bearing the white lion of MARCH, has only white roses. The standard of HENRY V. has the heraldic antelope as its main charge, and the smaller ones are red roses only.

EDWARD III. had as his special badge *rays of the sun descending from a cloud.* (I notice that on the fifth and sixth seal of this Prince (*British Museum Catalogue*, 183, and 186), the legend on the reverse is said to be " preceded by a hand of blessing issuing from a cloud ; " was this the origin of the badge; or is it only a mis-description of the badge usually described as "a cloud and rays"?

This badge appears several times on the standard ascribed to EDWARD III., in the MS. (Coll. Arm.) so often referred to in this chapter. (It is not asserted that these standards were contemporary with the Princes to whom they are assigned.)

The SWAN, *argent*, collared and chained *or*, was a badge of the House of LANCASTER, derived from the BOHUNS, whose co-heiress HENRY IV. had married. According to PLANCHÉ the BOHUNS had inherited this badge through the MANDEVILLES, Earls of ESSEX, from ADAM FITZ SWANNE, who held large estates in the time of the Conqueror. If this conjecture be correct the use of hereditary badges must have long preceded hereditary heraldry.

The WHITE HART lying down (technically *lodged*), ducally collared and chained, was a cognizance of RICHARD II., and has been conjectured to be only a rebus on his name *Rich-hart*. On the other hand it is asserted that the badge was derived from THE FAIR MAID OF KENT, heiress of EDMUND of WOODSTOCK, whose badge was a white hynd ("the Whyte Hynd by the fayre mayden of Kent," HARL. MS., 304, fol. 12), and it is certain that RICHARD'S half-brother, THOMAS HOLLAND, Earl of KENT, used this, his mother's device. RICHARD II. also used the badge of a stock of a tree for Woodstock, and this appears on the banners of HENRY V., etc.

The first distribution of the badge of a white hart as a livery collar was made by RICHARD II. at the jousts held at Smithfield on Sunday, October 12, 1390, in honour of his visitor the Count d'OSTREVANT (son of the Duke of HOLLAND), who was created a Knight of the Garter on the feast of St. EDWARD, the following day. We read that the King distributed his badge of the white hart, gorged with a crown and chain of gold pendent therefrom, to twenty-four Knights of the Garter, in the presence of his stranger guests.

"On the kynges syde were the xxiv. Knyztes of the Garter, and they weren all of sute, here cotes, here armoure, sheldes, hors trappure, and all was whyte hertys with crownes abowte here neckes and chaynes of gold hanginge there uppon, and the crowne hanging lowe before the hertys body, the whyche herte was the kynges livery that he zaf to lordis and ladyes, knyztes and squyers, for to know his household from other people, and at the ferst connynge to here justes xxiv. ladyes ladden those xxiv. lordis of Gartour with chaynes of golde, and all in the same sute of hertys as is aforne sayde, from the toure on horsebacke thorowe the cete of London into Smethfelde, where the justis sholde ben holde." (MS. *Chronicle*, ending with reign of HENRY V., quoted from ANSTIS by BELTZ, *History of the Order of the Garter*, p. 252.) He had in his ninth year mortgaged certain jewels *à la gyse de cerfs blancs* (RYMER).

The Wardrobe Accounts of 1399, show that "*Two jaks volants*," or streamers, were to be prepared for the King's visit to Ireland, of which one was to be worked with white harts. (It is curious that the crest assigned to Ireland (HARL. MS., 1073) was a white hart issuant from a castle. It not improbably dates from this expedition.) JOHN of GAUNT bequeathed to his daughter, the Queen of PORTUGAL, "*mon meilleur cerf d'or*," and the Duchess of YORK in 1392 left to the King "*mon cerf de perle*."

Another cognizance of RICHARD II. was THE SUN IN SPLENDOUR. The second seal of HENRY IV. (*British Museum Catalogue*, 301) has a background composed of quatrefoil spaces charged alternately with suns, and roses *en soleil*. The same badges appear on the first and fourth seals of EDWARD IV. (*British Museum Catalogue*, 300,

313), for the Yorkists always cherished the memory of the unfortunate king who had declared ROGER MORTIMER his heir in preference to the descendants of JOHN of GAUNT. Hence both these devices became in course of time Yorkist badges, the *Sun in Splendour* being familiar to us from the opening lines of SHAKESPEARE'S *Richard III.*

THE FALCON AND FETTERLOCK is generally considered a Yorkist badge. The falcon alone is said to have been used by RICHARD II. With a padlock in its mouth it was a cognizance of JOHN of GAUNT. EDWARD IV., who had the falcon with the lock closed, ordered his son RICHARD to bear it with the lock open, and it is so represented on the gate of HENRY VII.'s chapel at Westminster. *Langelyn* is equivalent to "bind together" (*Promptorium Parvulorum*); and *langele* is still used in the north country with the meaning to hobble, or fetter a horse. Thus the fetterlock may have been assumed as a badge to denote the place Langley. EDMUND of LANGLEY built Fotheringhay Castle on a ground plan of this shape.

OSTRICH FEATHERS.—Of all the English Royal Badges that which is regarded with the most interest is the plume of ostrich feathers associated in legend with the BLACK PRINCE, and in later times appropriated as the special badge of the Princes of WALES.

Its origin has exercised the ingenuity of antiquaries for several centuries. The romantic story which connects the badge with the capture of JOHN of LUXEMBOURG, King of BOHEMIA, at the battle of Cressy in 1346, which first appears in CAMDEN'S *Remains* in 1614, must be dismissed as altogether fabulous. In his first edition that writer says "the tradition is that the Prince won them at the battle of Poictiers," but in the second edition "the truth is that he wonne them at the battle of Cressy, from JOHN, King of BOHEMIA, whom he there slew!" Neither FROISSART nor any contemporary historian can be appealed to in support of this tradition; nor is there any evidence that the ostrich feather was ever the badge or device of King JOHN of BOHEMIA, or that the motto "*Ich Dien*" which has for so long a time been associated with the badge, was ever used by him.

The crest of King JOHN of BOHEMIA, which appears on his seals as engraved in VRÉE (*Généalogie des Comtes de Flandres*, plate lxiii.) was, not an ostrich feather, but the full wings of an eagle (being engraved in profile only one wing is seen on the seals), a favourite Low Country crest of the time. (Plate XLIX., fig. 4.) On his *secretum* the wing has several trefoil, or heart-shaped, charges (possibly linden leaves) which we also find of gold on the eagle wings borne as crests by LOUIS DE NAMUR, and ROBERT DE NAMUR, K.G., as well as by HENRI DE FLANDRES (*see* Plate XLIV., fig. 2, from the contemporary, *Armorial de Gelre*); and this is the crest which surmounts the arms of "*Le roi de Bohême*" in that valuable MS., the leaves being there certainly linden leaves, and, probably so, in the *Wappenrolle von Zürich*, plate i., also of the 14th century. An ostrich feather piercing a scroll was, undoubtedly, the favourite badge of the BLACK PRINCE, but he had no exclusive property in it, as with variations it was similarly used by most of the Plantagenet princes, and is found upon one seal of EDWARD III. himself.

Sir HARRIS NICOLAS in his valuable paper on the Badge (printed in *Archæologia* xxxi., pp. 350-384) informs us that among certain pieces of plate belonging to Queen PHILIPPA of HAINAULT was a large silver gilt dish, enamelled with a black escutcheon with ostrich feathers "*vno scuch nigro cum pennis de ostrich*"; and he suggests that the ostrich feather was probably originally a badge of the Counts of HAINAULT, derived from the County of OSTREVANT, a title which was held by their eldest sons. The sable escucheon with the silver ostrich feathers, not united but borne singly, arranged paleways two and one, the stem of each passing through a little escroll bearing the motto ich diene, is called by the BLACK PRINCE in his will, his shield "for Peace"; and by the provisions of that testament was displayed, and still remains, on his monument in Canterbury Cathedral, alternating with his shield "for War" which bears the Royal Arms (FRANCE and ENGLAND *quarterly*), with a label *argent*, and is surmounted by his other motto: "houmout" (*Hoogh-moed, i.e.,* High-minded, or Magnanimous). The Prince also ordered by his will that the chapel should be ornamented with "*noz bages dez plumes d'ostruce*," and he disposes in it of certain vestments embroidered with the same device. The badge of an ostrich feather borne singly, appears upon several seals of the BLACK PRINCE, but not invariably on those used after CRECY. With the motto *Ich dien* upon the scroll, it is to be seen upon the seal of EDWARD, Duke of YORK, who fell at AGINCOURT. By the other Princes of the Plantagenet line who used the single ostrich feather the little scroll is usually uncharged, but there are differences in the tinctures. We learn from the HARL. MS., 304, folio 12, that the "Feather silver with the pen gold is the KING'S; the ostrich feather, pen and all silver is the PRINCE'S; and the ostrich feather gold, the pen ermine is the Duke of LANCASTER'S." The Seal of HENRY, Duke of LANCASTER, afterwards HENRY IV., bears on either side of his helmed and crested escucheon an ostrich feather erect; a garter, or belt, with its buckle in base, and bearing his favourite motto *Sovereygne*, is twined around the whole feather, and the escroll is omitted. (Plate XXXV., fig. 4.) JOHN of GHENT had before this placed a chain along the quill; and his brother THOMAS, Duke of GLOUCESTER, had used upon his seal the same badge with the substitution of a garter and buckle for the chain. (Plate XXXV., fig. 1.)

The garter-plate of JOHN BEAUFORT, Duke of SOMERSET, bears two ostrich feathers erect with golden escrolls, the "pens" being *compony argent and azure*, the tinctures of the bordure with which the shield is differenced. (*See* Note on p. 598.)

The shield bearing three ostrich feathers is one of those engraved on the obverse of the second seal of HENRY IV. in 1411 (*Brit. Mus. Cat.* No. 259), the others being *a lion rampant within a bordure engrailed*, or *indented*. BOUTELL calls this the shield of the Duchy of CORNWALL; I think it possibly the arms of WALES, as assigned to RHYS AP TUDOR MAWR, Prince of SOUTH WALES; the third shield bears (*Azure*) *three garbs* (*or*) for the Earldom of CHESTER. The Chantry Chapel in Worcester Cathedral, in which lies the body of ARTHUR, Prince of WALES, is ornamented with Royal badges, among which occurs the *single* feather with its escroll; but on a window in St. Dunstan's Church in London, there was, within a wreath of roses, a roundle *per pale sanguine and azure*, charged with the letters **E.P.**, and between them, a plume of ostrich feathers *argent*, their pens *or*, passing through an escroll inscribed with the motto *Ich Dien*, and ensigned with the Prince's coronet. This was for EDWARD (afterwards EDWARD VI.), eldest son of HENRY VIII., but who was never Prince of WALES. EDWARD appears also to have placed the badge on a radiant sun, in which manner it was also used by HENRY, son of JAMES I. Since this reign the plume of feathers has become the peculiar badge of the Princes of WALES.

HENRY V. used a fire-beacon; an antelope lodged, gorged, and chained *or;* and the white swan of BOHUN; all three combined are to be seen in Westminster Abbey, in King HENRY'S Chantry. HENRY VI. retained the antelope, but also used two ostrich feathers in saltire *or* and *argent;* and a panther inflamed. RICHARD III.'s chief badge was the white boar, armed and bristled gold.

His banner bears this device, and is powdered with golden suns (HARL. MS. 4632).

The chief TUDOR badges were the golden portcullis with its motto *Altera securitas*, supposed to be, after the fashion of the time, a rather far-fetched pun on the name TUDOR (Two door, or a second door); (the portcullis, however, seems rather to be a Lancastrian or BEAUFORT badge; and its motto might imply that the BEAUFORT descent was an additional title to the throne); and the crowned rose of YORK and LANCASTER combined. Sometimes this rose is *per pale argent and gules;* sometimes the red rose is placed within the white, or the white within the red; sometimes the flower is *quarterly gules and argent.*

Other TUDOR badges were:—the Royal Crown in, or above, a bush of hawthorn all proper, combined with the Royal Cypher; the red dragon of WALES; and the silver greyhound of LANCASTER (this sometimes has a golden collar charged with the red rose). The crown and bush were allusive to the story that after the battle of BOSWORTH the golden circlet of RICHARD'S helm was found in a hawthorn bush by Sir REGINALD BRAY, and that with it Lord STANLEY crowned HENRY on the battlefield.

One of the standards of HENRY VII. (which were of longitudinal stripes of the TUDOR livery colours—white and green), bears the red dragon *inflamed* as its principal device, and the field is *semé* of flames. Another bears the white greyhound collared *gules*, and the field is charged with red roses. Yet another has the red dragon, but the field bears both red and white roses.

The standard of HENRY VIII. has as its principal device the red dragon passant. The subsidiary badges are the *fleur-de-lis or*, the York and Lancaster rose (that is the white rose inside the red one); and flames of fire. The portcullis continued to be in use as a Royal badge in this reign.

EDWARD VI. bore the same badges, and the radiant sun.

Queen MARY (TUDOR) had for her badge a red rose within a white one, impaled by dimidiation with a sheaf of arrows *or*, tied with a golden knot upon a semi-circular field *argent* and *vert*, the whole surrounded with rays, and ensigned with an open crown *or*. The arrows were a badge of the Queen's mother, KATHARINE of ARRAGON who inherited them from her progenitor, Queen ISABELLA of CASTILE.

ELIZABETH had numerous devices particularly her own, such as a phœnix, and a sieve. She also used her mother's badge of the falcon with crown and sceptre, besides the usual Royal badges of the crowned rose, the *fleur-de-lis*, and a harp *or* stringed *argent*, crowned of the first, used respectively for ENGLAND, FRANCE, and IRELAND.

Under the House of STUART the badges above named were used for the kingdoms; but the roses were sometimes white, sometimes red, sometimes united (the white within the red, or *quartered argent and gules*). Two STUART badges were also in use: a lion rampant *gules*, and the Scottish thistle. The latter was often represented in conjunction with the English rose; both being dimidiated and conjoined on a single stalk, with its proper leaf on either side, and a Royal Crown resting on the conjoined flower.

No trace seems to exist of the thistle as the badge of Scotland, earlier than the time of JAMES III.; but that it was in use during that reign appears from an inventory of the jewels and furniture which at his death came into the possession of his sons. One of the articles named was a "covering of variand .... tartan browdered with thissels and a unicorn." BARBOUR'S poem of "The Thistle and the Rose" shows the former floral emblem to have been in general recognition as a Royal badge at the time of the wedding of JAMES IV. (1523), and the thistle figures prominently on the paper of the ratification by JAMES of his treaty of marriage with MARGARET of ENGLAND.

The present Royal badges, as settled under the Sign Manual in 1801, are:—

1. A white rose within a red one, barbed, seeded, and slipped proper; ensigned with the Imperial Crown, for ENGLAND.
2. A thistle, slipped and leaved proper; ensigned with the Imperial Crown, for SCOTLAND.
3. A harp *or* stringed *argent;* ensigned as before, for IRELAND.
4. On a mount *vert* a dragon *passant*, its wings expanded and endorsed *gules*, for WALES.

LIVERY COLLARS, composed of the badges or devices of a house, and often having the principal badge as a pendant, were much in use in England about the fifteenth century. They were often employed to denote political partisanship, as in the case of the collars of Suns and Yorkist Roses with the pendent White Boar of RICHARD III. The best known of these Livery Collars, the Collar of SS, was originally a Lancastrian decoration. The origin of the device has been the subject of almost interminable discussion, and is still far from clear. The letter S has been variously supposed to be the initial of the word *Souverayne, Seneschal* (JOHN of GAUNT was *Steward, " Seneschalus,"* of ENGLAND) and *Swan*. The last derivation proposed by Mr PLANCHÉ, was suggested by the badge of a swan which appears pendent from the Collar of SS on the effigy of the poet GOWER in Southwark Church. I am not aware that there is any corroboration of this opinion elsewhere. Under HENRY VII. the collar lost its Lancastrian associations, and down to the present day it has been worn as a part of their official costume by certain officers of State, including

Lords Chief Justices, Kings of Arms, and the Lord Mayor of London.

Evidence exists of a limited use of family badges in Scotland. A contemporary list of badges of the principal English nobles, which Mr PLANCHÉ printed from a manuscript in the College of Arms, includes two Scottish examples. The badge of the Earl of DOUGLAS is said to be a heart *gules;* and that of Sir THOMAS MONTGOMERY a *fleur-de-lis.* Figures that may be supposed to be badges, or devices, occur on the Great Seals of Scotland, and on the seals of some of the more considerable nobles. A stag couchant on the reverse of the seal of WALTER STEWART, Earl of ATHOLE, has been considered a personal device.

Often, however, either the crest or some charge taken from the arms, seems, in Scotland as elsewhere, to have done duty as the badge.

A different species of badge, unrecognised by authority, has gradually sprung up among the Highland clans, namely a leaf or sprig of some tree or shrub, usually carried in the bonnet which the chief wears, along with two eagle's feathers.

A list of badges is given in the Appendix.

NOTE.—On the Privy Seals of our Sovereigns the ostrich feather is still employed as a badge. The shield of arms is usually placed between two lions *sejant* (*gardant*) *addorsed*, each holding the feather. On the Privy Seal of HENRY VIII. the feathers are used without the lions; and this was the case on the majority of the seals of the Duchy of LANCASTER. On the reverse of the present seal of the Duchy the feathers appear to be *ermine* (*Brit. Mus. Cat.,* No. 747). On the obverse of this seal, and on that of GEORGE IV., the Royal Supporters hold banners of the arms of ENGLAND, and of the Duchy (ENGLAND, *a label for difference*).

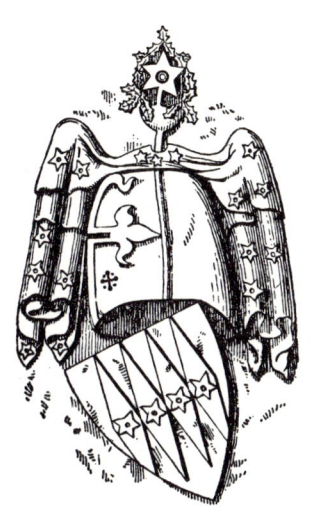

FIG. 92.—DAUBENY ACHIEVEMENT.

CHAPTER XIX.

EXTERNAL ORNAMENTS.

I.—HELM AND CREST, WREATH, CREST-CORONET, LAMBREQUIN.

OF the external ornaments of a shield of arms the most important is the helmet with its crest, to which later was joined the wreath or a crest-coronet, and the lambrequins, or mantlings.

We find from ancient seals that the armorial shield was in use before crests appeared upon the helms. The cylindrical helmet of PHILIPPE D'ALSACE, Count of FLANDERS (c. 1181), bears indeed the figure of a lion similar to that upon his shield, but this is no true crest, it is simply painted on the side of the helm. The earliest crested helm is that of RICHARD I. of England in 1198, it bears a lion-passant in the centre of a fan-shaped crest. No other example is known until we come to the seal of MATTHIEU DE MONTMORENCY in 1224; on it the cylindrical flat-topped helm has the crest of a peacock's head and neck. The similar helm of OTHO, Count of BURGUNDY in 1248, bears three small banners. The helm of ALEXANDER III. of Scotland (*c.* 1307) has a flat top edged with a coronet, and bearing a fan-shaped crest. (Plate XLIX., fig. 8.) The contemporaneous seal of EDWARD I. of England has a similar helm but no crest. The oval-topped helm was soon ornamented with the fan-shaped crest as shown in Plate XLIX., fig. 9, from the seal of CHARLES, Count de VALOIS (*c.* 1295); and this *écran* continues to be used as the crest of many important German families. The earliest crested helm which appears among the seals given in HUEBER'S *Austria*, is that of ULRIC DE CHAPELLE in 1280; the shield is *couché*, and the helm is surmounted by a wing. On the seal of GEOFFREY D'ARSCHOT (*c.* 1295) the helm has the fan-crest, and on either side a tall cock's feather (?) rises from its base, this is a type often repeated, and was perhaps the germ of the use of wings which later became so frequent. A dragon *couchant* between two feathers is the crest of CHARLES, Count de VALOIS, in 1308; and, with the dragon *statant*, is that of PHILIPPE DE VALOIS in 1307; while in 1316, the helm of EDWARD III. of England bears a lion statant without a crown. (Plate XLIX., fig. 2.) The seals of JEAN D'AVESNES, and of FLORENT of HAINAULT (*c.* 1295) show their helms crested with an eagle displayed.

In England the crested helm had not the same importance as in Germany and the Low Countries. The crests are not recorded in the many ancient *Rolls of Arms* which are still extant. This may have arisen from the fact that in early times the crest was considered rather a personal than a hereditary possession; it was subject to change at the caprice of the bearer, and all members of a family did not necessarily use the same crest. In fact the use of a different crest was an early mode of denoting cadency. In SIEBMACHER'S *Wappenbuch*, vol. iii., we find that no less than thirty-one branches of the Alsacian family of ZORN (who bore: *Per fess gules and or, in chief a star argent*) differenced solely in this way.

In German Armory the helmets are of two kinds only: shut, or visored; open, or barred; the former were used by the newly ennobled, and the greatest importance attached to the crested helm; this was fostered by the regulations of the tourneys, which required the shields of the combatants to be exposed before the contest, *penchés* beneath the crested helm (*see* Appendix C).

In France the timbred helm came to be considered the prerogative of the military *noblesse*, and was denied to *nouveaux annoblis*, who were only entitled to use it on becoming in the third generation *bons gentilhommes*. When, in 1372, CHARLES V. conferred on the *bourgeoisie* of Paris the right to use armorial bearings, it was strenuously denied that they could use the timbred helm. In 1568 an edict of CHARLES IX. prohibited the use of *armoiries timbrées* to any who were not noble by birth.

In the Imperial patent of arms in my possession, granted by the Emperor LEOPOLD under his sign manual to Dr F. GHIBELLI, the escucheon is surmounted by two helms coroneted but without crests.

Originally helmets were of the same shape and materials for all ranks; but in later times (when they had ceased to be generally worn) distinctions were made in depicting them, and the rank of the owner was denoted by their matter, shape, and position. MENÊTRIER, in 1680, says the helm should be of gold for sovereigns; of silver for princes and great nobles; and of polished steel for simple nobles or gentlemen.

The old French heralds differ as to the number of the *grilles*, or bars, which should denote the various ranks of nobility, but I do not propose to occupy space with an account of these diversities, being very much of PLANCHÉ'S opinion that, "the various positions of the helmet, and the rules for its being open, closed, or barred, are all of comparatively modern date, and as useless as embarrassing." In modern British Heraldry the helm of the sovereign is of gold, placed full-face, and having golden *grilles ;* the helms of peers are of silver, in profile, with five golden *grilles ;* those of baronets and knights are of steel, full-faced with open vizor; and those of gentlemen are of steel, placed in profile with the vizor closed.

FIG. 93.　　FIG. 94.　　FIG. 95.　　FIG. 96.
MODERN "RANK" HELMETS.

The barred helm only came into general use at the very end of the sixteenth century. An examination of the interesting series of Stall-Plates at Windsor shows that "only one barred or tourney helm . . . . is found on the early plates, viz.: on that of RICHARD PLANTAGENET, Duke of GLOUCESTER (*el.* 1475). The helms on the early plates, though of various fashions, are all of the same class of tilting helms, drawn in profile; and those which are antecedent to 1421 are drawn, in accordance with the general custom, so as to face the High Altar (*v.* p. 134), thus those on the north side are turned to the sinister." (*See* Mr HOPE'S excellent paper on the "Early Stall Plates," in *Archæologia* for 1889.) Lord KNOLLYS, in 1615, is the first baron whose plate shows the barred helm; and it was only about the time of the Restoration that the full-faced helmet became a distinguishing mark for baronets and knights.

The crested helms which are now suspended above the stalls of the Knights of the Garter are *affrontés*, but the crests are all made to range to the dexter. Now, in the days when helmets and crests were really worn, the animal used as a crest looked straight forward from the front of the helm. But when represented on seals, etc., as borne by a knight riding to the right or left; or when arranged above an escucheon, the animal while placed to range with the helm, often had its head turned a little so as to face the spectator. Thus the lion passant, or statant, of the Crest of England became the lion statant-gardant. (*See* Plate XXXV., fig. 4.) So far as the crest was concerned it was really not intended originally to be a variant from the lion passant. Accordingly no knight in ancient times, and no decently well-informed foreign heraldic artist in our own, would think of placing on a full-faced helm a lion or other beast presenting its side to the spectator, with its head over the wearer's right shoulder and its tail over the left! Yet this is how the crests are represented in the Chapel of the "Most Noble" Order of Christian Chivalry, and the *chapeaux* that support many of them are turned round to the side of the helm in a way which would be suggestive of anything but sobriety on the part of the wearer! This is a matter which affords matter for amused amazement to the intelligent foreigner. (*Herald and Genealogist*, viii., 366.)

In Germany and other northern countries, where the crested helmet and crest are of as much importance as the shield of arms, several crested helms are generally placed above a quartered escucheon. Each formerly denoted a noble fief for which the proprietor had a right to vote in the "circles" of the Empire.[1] When the number of the helms is even, they are arranged so that all look inwards towards the centre line of the escucheon,

[1] No less than thirteen were thus arranged above the shield of the Markgraves of *Brandenburg Anspach*.

half being turned to the dexter, half to the sinister. If the number be uneven, the principal helm is placed in the centre *affronté*, the others with their crests being *tournés* towards it; thus some face to the dexter, some to the sinister. (In Scandinavia the centre helm is *affronté*; the others, with their crests, are often turned outwards.) One of the good points of the illustrations in FOSTER'S *Peerage*, was that he had the courage thus to arrange many of his helmets and crests in a common-sense way, without regard to the modern ignorant custom which prescribes that, whether the helm be full-faced or in profile, all crests shall look in the same direction, *i.e.*, to the dexter.

In Germany when several crested helmets are used, two of them are often placed upon the heads of the supporters (as in fig. 98, page 627); not as permanent additions to them but *pro hac vice*. The modern English use by which crests are represented floating about in the air above the shield, without a helm, or any other adequate support, is not one that commends itself to the German herald (who very rarely dissevers the helm from the crest), or, indeed, to any one else who can give the subject intelligent consideration. In France the use of crests is not nearly so general as in England and Germany; in Italy, and especially in Spain and Portugal, it is less frequent still. This has greatly arisen from the unrestricted use of coronets by those who, according to our insular ideas, would have no right to them (*v.* p. 626).

Many writers have denied the right of ecclesiastics (and, of course, of women) to the use of helmet and crest. SPENER, the great German herald, defends their use by ecclesiastics, and says that, in Germany at any rate, universal custom is opposed to the restriction. There, the prelates, abbots, and abbesses, who held princely fiefs by military tenure, naturally retained the full knightly insignia. On the other hand, in the southern kingdoms clerics almost invariably replace the helmet and crest by the ecclesiastical hat.

The early crests were frequently derived from the charges of the escucheon; an examination of any series of ancient seals will show this, and many continue to be borne without material change up to the present day. On the other hand, at least as frequently the crests do not correspond to the charges, and have been repeatedly varied at the caprice of the owners. Sometimes the crest assumed had reference to an office held by the wearer. On the seal of DAVID LINDSAY, Lord CRAWFORD, in 1345, the crest is a key erect, which is said to have been adopted to denote the wardenship of the Castle of Berwick, or of Edinburgh. The Earls of DUNBAR and MARCH, Wardens of the Marches, had as a crest a horse's head bridled; and the JOHNSTONS of Annandale, Wardens of the West Marches, a spur between a pair of wings; in both cases the crest was assumed with reference to their constant readiness to discharge the duties of those offices (NISBET, ii., 19). More frequently the crest referred to descent. Thus, that of the LYONS, Earls of STRATHMORE: a demi-woman holding in her right hand a thistle, and placed within two laurel branches proper, commemorates an alliance with the daughter of ROBERT II. The STUARTS of Traquair, as descendants of the Earls of BUCHAN, used a garb as their crest. SETON of Touch used a boar's head *or*, in memory of a descent from a GORDON heiress; just as in England the demi-monk, the crest of the Lords STOURTON, commemorates a descent from the family of LE MOYNE. The crest of the WOODWARDS—a white greyhound sejant on a golden crest-coronet—was derived from the CLINTONS of Baddesley through the marriage (*c.* 1460) of JOHN WODEWARD with their heiress PETRONILLA. The Lancastrian greyhounds (*v.* p. 595) are still the supporters of the CLINTONS, Dukes of

NEWCASTLE, of the Earls FORTESCUE (once Lords CLINTON), and of the present Lords CLINTON.

Among the earliest crests assumed without reference to the charges of the shield, were buffalo, or ox horns, and wings. These latter if cut square at the top were called *vols bannerets*, and were sometimes charged with the arms. Thus the crest of BERTRAND DU GUESCLIN, on his seal in 1365, was an eagle's head between a *vol banneret*, thereon a bend charged with his arms: *Argent, a double-headed eagle displayed, debruised by a bendlet gules* (*cf.* Plate XLIV., fig. 1). The crest of JOHN DE GRAILLY, K.G., Captal de BUCH, was a man's head in profile with long asses' ears. The SOUDAN DE LA TRAU, K.G., in 1379 used the same crest; both appear on their stall-plates at Windsor, and the seal of the latter is in BELTZ, *Memorials of the Order of the Garter*, p. 269. The ox-horns which appear so frequently in German crests were affixed one on either side of the helm. Originally, as will be seen in the *Zürich Wappenrolle* and in our example (Plate XLIX., fig. 1), the horns were simply curved and pointed. In the more florid heraldry of later times they are recurved, and have a mouth-piece in which are sometimes placed tufts or plumes of feathers (*See* Plate XLIX., figs. 5, 6, 7). This latter form, not being understood by French armorists, received the absurd name of *trompes d'éléphant*, or *proboscides!* These horns are usually of the tinctures of the shield. If this be *barry* the horns will probably be so also; if it be *per pale* the dexter horn will be of the one tincture, the sinister of the other. If the coat is *quarterly* each horn will be divided *per fess*, so that the colours appear alternately (*see* BOYNEBURG below, and Plate XLIX., fig. 6). Sometimes the horns are stringed, as on the seal of MARQUARD DE SCHELTENBERG in 1310 (*see* HUEBER, *Austria Illustrata*, tab. vii., 13, and the *Zürich Wappenrolle*, plates ii., iv., ix., and xxi.).

Sometimes one crest serves for two quartered coats,

CRESTS.   PLATE XLIX.

EXPLANATION OF FIGURES.

1, 5, 6, 7, 10. From Hildebrand's *Heraldisches Musterbuch.* 2. Edward III. of England. 3. Burggrave of Nürnberg. 4. John, King of Bohemia. 8. Alexander III. of Scotland. 9. Charles Comte de Valois.

thus the crest of BAVARIA was the PALATINATE golden lion, sejant between two horns (or as many wings) charged with the *fusilly-bendy* of BAVARIA.

The wings are usually those of eagles; they are nearly as frequently found, are probably as ancient as the horns, and are generally tinctured on the same principle. Thus the crest of the Counts zu TRAUN, who bear: *Per pale argent and sable* is:—out of a crest coronet *or* a pair of wings, the dexter *argent* the sinister *sable*. When a *vol* forms the crest, the whole bearings of the shield are often found upon each of the wings. Such a crest is still borne by the Duke of NORFOLK. Sable eagle's wings are often powdered with linden leaves of gold or silver (*v.* Plate XLIX., fig. 3, and p. 592).

Penaches, plumes, usually of peacock's or ostrich feathers, were very frequently used in mediæval times in England, and are still in great favour abroad. The *eyes* of peacock's feathers are often used to adorn crests, see Plate XLIX., figs. 3 and 10, and Plate XLVI., fig. 1. The crest of AUSTRIA is a *penache* of peacock's feathers rising from a golden coronet (*v.* p. 614).

The human figure, which is a favourite crest in Germany, is usually a half-length, without arms, and is often habited in the bearings of the shield (*v.* Plate XLVI., fig. 2). Its arms are frequently replaced by a pair of horns, which gives the figure a *bizarre* appearance to British eyes. The explanation is easy; the human figure was originally placed *between* the horns, which were attached to the helm. The same explanation suffices for such crests as that of MUMPELGARD, Plate XLIV., fig. 3, where the arms are replaced by fish.

Though the use of the coroneted helm is general, German crests often rise from a cap, or chapeau; and there are numerous examples in which a hat is the sole crest. The usual shape is perhaps a tall conical hat charged with the arms. The crest of SAXONY is a familiar example of this. Out of a coronet rises a tall hat charged with the arms, coroneted at the point, and ending in a small tuft of three peacock's feathers. From ignorance of its meaning this hat is often erroneously blazoned a "Column" (!), a term which is also applied to the *plumail,* or *tuyau,* the tube out of which feathers sometimes rise, an ancient form of which is shown in Plate XLIX., fig. 7. Curious mediæval hats, used with considerable frequency, are represented in Plate XLIV., fig. 4, and Plate XLVI., fig. 3.

The mitre, or a mitred figure, is occasionally found as a crest, and has sometimes given rise to the most absurd explanations. It is usually borne to indicate that the user, or his progenitors, held the office of advocate (*Avoué; Vidame; Vogt*) to a bishopric, or great ecclesiastical foundation. (The curious crest, Plate XLV., fig. 3, is only a mitre in profile, with tufts of feathers at the points.)

According to British ideas there are many anomalies in the German use of crests. Occasionally a shield bearing a single coat is timbred with two or more crested helms; and still more curiously these are sometimes identical. Thus, the Barons von BOYNEBURG, who bear: *Quarterly sable and argent,* have three coroneted helms, each bearing a hat per pale of the colours, and surmounted by two buffalo horns per fess alternately of the same. The Counts of MARCK used as crest an entire buffalo head, enveloping the helm so that the mouth served as the visor. The head was crowned with a coronet of gold fleurons upon a circlet *chequy argent* and *gules,* out of which the horns arose. The crest of the Royal House of France was a double *fleur-de-lis,* so placed that from every point of view a full *fleur-de-lis* was seen.

In Germany, Russia, and Austria the Imperial and Prussian eagles, usually on a coroneted helm, are frequently given as augmentations.

In Great Britain the crest has become the part of the armorial insignia most generally employed. We find it divorced from the helm and coat of arms, doing the duty of a badge on household furniture, on silver plate, on servants' buttons, on the panels of carriages, and the harness of their horses. It need hardly be said that all this is an entire departure from the original idea of the crest as the ornament of a knightly helm; that the use of a crest by ladies (unless they are sovereign princesses) is an indefensible anomaly; and that to speak (as people who ought to be better informed often do) of a whole achievement— arms, helm, crest, and motto—as " our *crest*," is as absurd as it would be to call a suit of clothes a tiara!

In British Armory crests are (theoretically) susceptible of differences; the crests of the Plantagenet princes, for instance, were differenced by the labels used on their coats of arms; and the same custom has been shown to obtain with regard to the labels used by the Princes of the Royal House at the present day. But the use of the modern marks of cadency—the crescent, mullet, etc. —upon their crests by persons of lower station is even more infrequent than their use in the armorial escucheon. In Scotland, where cadets and sub-cadets are very numerous, and the prevalent system of differencing is inapplicable to crests, the custom has long prevailed by which cadet lines are allowed to use a different one from that employed by the chief line of the family. (Compare the Continental use described on p. 601.)

According to modern English practice two crests can only be properly borne, either when a special grant of a crest has been made by the crown as an honourable augmentation, or in virtue of a Royal licence to use an additional family name and the corresponding Armorial Insignia. In Scotland the system of change of name by Royal licence does not obtain, but it may be remarked here that before the year 1809 no instance can be found of more than a single crest being used by an individual north of the Tweed; and it was considerably later that instances of the modern practice began to appear in the Lyon Register in some (though by no means in all) cases in which a double surname had been assumed; and in a very few other instances in which this apology could not be made for the innovation.

The entire lack of true heraldic feeling which characterised the armory of the last century and the first half of the present, is shown nowhere more forcibly than in the tasteless and absurd devices granted to be borne as crests. Objects which it would be impossible to attach to the summit of a helm are frequently found, and of these the Lyon Register contains more than a fair share. Such are the waves of the sea with floating ships, etc., which appear in connection with the achievements of Lords NELSON and CAMPERDOWN; of CALDER and DICK-CUNYNGHAM (barts.); the shipwreck of Lord EXMOUTH; the clouds of BLACKWOOD, EMERSON, KER, and STODART; the rainbows of HOPE, BENSON, and EDWARDS; the coronets floating in the air above the hand of DUNBAR (bart.); the sun shining on a stump of a tree of GRANT (bart.); the bees flying about the hive of Lord LANSDOWNE, etc. Tastes of course differ, but the writer can hardly think that the *épergne* given to Lieutenant-General SMITH by his friends at Bombay was a fitting ornament for a helmet; or that the fact of its presentation was worthy of perpetual commemoration in his armorial achievement (*see* Crests of SMITH-GORDON, Bart.). It is quite clear that many figures now used would never have had official sanction had the origin and design of crests been duly remembered. Something might be done to remove present incongruities by more intelligent drawing, *e.g.*, arms embowed should not be drawn in the unstable position of resting on the elbow; and hands holding wreaths, etc., should issue, not from the heavens above, but from the helm beneath.

LAMBREQUINS AND WREATHS.—Ancient crests were moulded out of *cuir bouilli*, and fixed on the helm by a *calotte* or cap of the same substance. This appears from the old tourney rules printed in MENÊTRIER, *de l'Origine des Armoiries et du Blason*, pp. 79, 80, from a MS. in the library of SEGUIER, Chancellor of France, printed in Appendix C. In the *Zürich Wappenrolle* there are no wreaths, and the *calotte* is usually of a red colour (*see* Plates XLV. and XLVI.). In later times the line of junction was masked by a wreath of silk, the ends of which floated behind. Some have seen in this a reminiscence of the turbans of the Saracens. In a large number of cases crest and calotte are in one piece (*see* Plates XLIV., XLV., XLVI.). In the *Armorial de Gelre*, the calotte no longer fits the helm tightly, though it often forms part of the crest, but it has greater length behind, and its floating edges are scalloped; this was the origin of the *lambrequins*. In other cases the calotte is distinct, and varies in colour, from the crest. It has become a *capuchon* or *capeline*, and the line of junction with the crest is either hidden by a crest-coronet or covered by a hat from which the crest rises. The *tortil* or wreath occurs but seldom in the *Armorial de Gelre*. In many instances the *capeline* was *armoyée* (*v.* Plate XLIV., figs. 5, 6). On the *capeline* of ROBERT II. of Scotland are the arms of BRUCE. Other Scottish examples are found in the cases of the Sire de SANDILANDS, and Sir GAUTHIER HALYBURTON, in both of which the lambrequins are *armoyés*. In the arms of the Duc de BAVIÈRE, shield, *capeline*, and crest are all alike tinctured with the Bavarian fusils. When the crest was formed by the head and neck of a bird its plumage was prolonged to serve as a *capeline*, as in Plate XLIV., fig. 1. There are several instances of these feather lambrequins in the stall-plates at Windsor. (*See* those of Sir HUGH COURTENAY; THOMAS, Earl of WARWICK; Sir THOMAS ERPINGHAM; Sir WILLIAM ARUNDEL, etc.) In Plate XLV., fig. 4, from the *Zürich Wappenrolle*, we see the scaly skin of a salmon similarly used. The mane of the lion, which forms the crest of MERTZ; and the hair and beard of the men in the case of the crests of BOHN, LANDSCHADEN, etc., are similarly prolonged into lambrequins. The *capeline* was not merely ornamental, it discharged the same office as the *puggree* does on a modern helmet, protecting the head and neck of the wearer from the rays of the sun. When the helmet ceased to be worn, the *capeline*, as depicted in painting or sculpture, underwent a double conversion; first into lambrequins of the helmet, and then into a mantling surrounding the arms. The picturesque lambrequins have now degenerated into mere unmeaning flourishes and scrolls, and, whether they envelope the shield or not, are known as mantlings. In Germany the tinctures of the lambrequins of the crested helms correspond with those of the quartering to which they belong. When a single helm is used with a quartered coat the lambrequins vary on either side so as to correspond with the tinctures of the adjacent quarters. According to modern British usage, while the rule for the tinctures of the wreath is that they should be of the principal metal and colour of the arms, the mantlings are of *gules*, or crimson, lined with white. This is so general that, with the usual official tendency to regulate that which needs no regulation, modern grants of arms distinctly prescribe these as the tinctures of the mantlings, instead of permitting the wearer to follow the old custom of using mantlings composed, like the wreath, of the principal tinctures. One of the respects in which we may expect (or at all events may hope for) better things as a result of the spread of a greater knowledge of heraldry combined with better artistic taste is in this matter of the mantlings and lambrequins. We need only look at the early stall-plates of the Knights of the Garter to find precedents for treatment of these which are both heraldic and truly artistic. Thus the mantlings of the arms of GEORGE, Duke of CLARENCE, are *semé* of the white roses of YORK. Those of Sir JOHN BOURCHIER, Lord BERNERS, have their silver lining powdered alternately with water-budgets (the charge of his arms) and with his badge, the Bourchier Knot; while the crimson mantling is *semé* of golden billets from one of his quarterings. The azure mantling of HENRY V. as Prince of WALES is *semé* of the French golden *fleurs-de-lis;* and that of JOHN, Lord BEAUMONT (K.G., 1397) is similarly flory *argent*, as the field of his arms. The BÉTHUNES, Ducs de SULLY, etc., Princes de BÉTHUNES HESDIGNUEL bear exceptionally a golden helm with lambrequins of *azure, fleury or*, their arms being *Argent, a fess gules*. The DAUBENY mantling is *semé* of mullets (*see* Fig. 92, p. 600). On the brass of Sir JOHN WYLCOTE at Tew the lambrequins are chequy; and the WARRENS also used the mantling *chequy or and azure* from their arms. (VINCENT's MSS. in Coll. Arm.) On the seals of Sir JOHN BUSSY in 1391 and 1407 the mantlings are barry, the coat being *Argent, three bars sable*. (*Visitation of Huntingdon*, pp. 67, 68.)

There are many exceptional cases in which the rule that the lambrequins should agree with the tinctures of the arms is not observed; *e.g.*, the Swiss GULDINEN have lambrequins of *or* and *argent;* the Prussian STEINMANS of *purple* only; the GHELDERSONS of *vert* and *azure*.

There is as great variety in the use of the wreath. A knight in the old tournament days on occasion substituted a *contoise* of the colours of his mistress, or a sleeve of her dress, for the armorial wreath of his own colours. COSSO in Dalmatia uses *azure* and *gules;* DOPF, *sable* and *gules*. In more cases the wreath is of three or more tinctures; it is chequy on the seals of ROBERT STEWART, Duke of ALBANY, in 1389, and of his son MURDOCH (LAING, i., 787, 789). Occasionally a wreath of flowers or leaves is substituted for the ordinary *tortil*. The wreath of PATRICK HEPBURN appears to be of roses in *l'Armorial de Gelre*, and several German examples are to be found in SIEBMACHER. The helm of ENGELBERT, Comte de NASSAU, was *couronné d'une haye d'or*, and there are several examples of the use of a crown of thorns. The wreath of the TROUTBECKS is formed of trouts in an example in MOULE'S *Heraldry of Fish;* that of JEAN DE GUEVARA, Comte d'ARIANO, was of peacock's feathers. I have collected very many other curious examples for which my present limits afford no space. Among us the modern wreath is usually very badly drawn; it is disproportionately large, and like a straight twisted bar, balanced on the top of the helm! (*See* the funny examples at Windsor.)

The CREST-CORONET.—The use of this was developed from the wreath. It is an open crown, usually of gold, and having (but not invariably) four foliations like those of a ducal coronet, by which name it still is vulgarly designated, though there is in it no reference to ducal or any other titular rank. It was much employed in the Low Countries and in Germany, where, however, it is properly considered an adjunct to the helm rather than a portion of the crest, but there are few examples of its use in the *Zürich Wappenrolle;* one of these is that of the Dukes of AUSTRIA (*ante*, p. 608), but there is no coronet on the seals of LEOPOLD in 1216, of ALBERT in 1286, or of FREDERICK in 1311. The coronet is used by RODOLPH in 1305, and FREDERICK in 1313 (*see* HUEBER, *Austria Illustrata*). Sometimes the coronet was tinctured of other colours than gold. In the *Armorial de Gelre*, that used by "*le Roi de Navarre*," is actually of *ermine!* The use of a coroneted helm is said by some writers to be peculiar to those who are of tourney nobility—whose ancestors had taken part in those conflicts. BRYDSON (*Summary View*, p. 189), thought it a distinction of a banneret (but this it certainly was not in England), and he quotes OLIVIER DE LA MARCHE, "that none ought to adorn the tymbres of their armorial ensigns with a golden crown but gentlemen of name, arms, and cry."

By the regulations of the English College of Arms no new grants of crests arising from crest-coronets, or chapeaux, are made to ordinary applicants. But mural, naval, and Eastern, crowns form part of the grant in the case of persons who have respectively served with great distinction as military or naval officers, or in the public service of our Asiatic possessions. These coronets are figured on Plate L. Other forms of the crest-coronet are rarely found, that used by the Marquess of RIPON is of *fleurs-de-lis;* and that of the RIDDELLS of Ardnamurchan is said to be "the coronet of a French count."

MANTLES AND PAVILIONS.—The mantles which are frequently drawn around the arms of sovereigns and great nobles must be distinguished from the mantlings or lambrequins of the helm; though, as has been said, both were simply enlargements of the capeline, and like it were often *armoyées*. In later times the arms of Sovereigns; the German Electors, etc., were mantled, usually with crimson velvet fringed with gold, lined with ermine, and crowned; but the mantling *armoyé* was one of the marks of dignity used by the *Pairs de France*, and by cardinals resident in France; it was also employed by some great nobles in other countries. An early example is afforded by the arms of the Duke of LORRAINE (MOULE, *Heraldry of Fish*, p. 71). In NISBET the arms appended to the dedications of the work to the Duke of HAMILTON and the Earl of MORTON are thus *armoyées*. The mantling of the Princes and Dukes of MIRANDOLA was *Chequy argent and azure*, lined with ermine. Other families used a mantling which, though not strictly *armoyée*, was *semé* with one or other of the charges of their arms. In France the mantling of the *Chancellier* was of cloth of gold; that of *Présidents*, of scarlet, lined with alternate strips of ermine and *petit gris*.

Some Sclavonic families have mantlings of fur only; that of the Hungarian CHORINSKI is a bear skin. In Sweden the mantlings are specified in the patent, and are often curiously varied. In England the suggestion that the arms of peers should be mantled with their Parliament robes was never generally adopted. In France, NAPOLEON I., who used a mantling of purple *semé* of golden bees, decreed that the Princes and Grand-Dignitaries should use an *azure* mantling thus *semé*; those of dukes were to be plain, and lined with vair instead of ermine. In 1817, a mantling of *azure*, fringed with gold and lined with ermine, was appropriated to the dignity of *Pair de France*.

From the use of the large mantling was developed the crowned canopy known as the *pavilion*, of which we see traces on the Great Seals of the Kings of FRANCE since LOUIS XI. (*See* VRÉE; and LECOY DE LA MARCHE, *Les Sceaux*, pp. 135-148, Paris 1890.) This pavilion of the King of FRANCE was of *azure semé de fleurs-de-lis d'or*. The King of PRUSSIA assumed a pavilion of crimson, *semé* of golden crowns and Prussian eagles; and bearing aloft the banner of the Prussian Arms.

FIG. 97.—THE CROWN OF CHARLEMAGNE.

CHAPTER XX.

EXTERNAL ORNAMENTS.

II.—CROWNS AND CORONETS.

THE earliest form of the crowns and coronets in use in western Europe is a circlet of gold, plain or jewelled, or ornamented with enamels. Of these the first which is of heraldic interest is the celebrated IRON CROWN OF LOMBARDY, gifted by Queen THEODOLINDA (died 616) to the Basilica of Monza where it is still preserved. It is a jointed circlet of gold about three inches in width. It derives its name from the iron band which runs round its interior, and is said to have been forged out of *Il Sacro Chiodo,* one of the nails used at the Crucifixion. With it the Kings of ITALY are crowned. It is used as a heraldic ornament in the *Écu Complet* of the Austrian Empire. (*See* p. 502.)

The crown of CHARLEMAGNE is preserved in the Imperial Treasury at Vienna. (*See* the engraving above, fig. 97.) This is the model on which has been formed the present Imperial crown of the German Empire. The circlet resembles that of the crown of

CHARLEMAGNE, but is set alternately with crosses and eagles-displayed in gems, and it has four ogee arches terminating in the orb and cross. (*See* Plate LV., fig. 1.) When the crown of CHARLEMAGNE appears as a heraldic charge, as in the arms of HANNOVER (Plate LII., figs. 9, 10), it is drawn in profile.

The circlet of gold worn by our English kings was early ornamented with points, or floriations. The seal of EDWARD THE CONFESSOR shows the king wearing a crown with four rays. That of WILLIAM THE CONQUEROR is a circlet which has four trefoils, or strawberry leaves, of which three are visible. Cuspings supporting a pearl, or a smaller foliation, were soon introduced, and this open and foliated crown is that which appears on the head of the sovereign in the early Great Seals of ENGLAND, FRANCE, etc. The crown of HENRY IV. has smaller *fleurs-de-lis* introduced between the (six ?) conventional strawberry leaves; small groups of pearls separate all the foliations.

HENRY V. was the first English king who added the arches (with their orb and cross) to the circlet, and converted the open coronet into that which is technically known as a close crown. The arches of the crowns used by later sovereigns (though the open circlet occasionally appears up to the reign of HENRY VIII.) were generally four in number, but HENRY VI. and CHARLES I. used the crown with eight arches. The rim of the crown of England has been heightened with alternate *fleurs-de-lis* and crosses *patée* (four of each) since the time of HENRY VI. The cap within the crown, worn by RICHARD III., and perhaps by earlier sovereigns, is distinctly shown in the crown of the Great Seal of HENRY VIII. The ogee curves of the golden arches, set with pearls, which appear in the crowns of CHARLES II. and all succeeding sovereigns, have disappeared from use during the later part of the reign of Queen VICTORIA, and the arches have now the simple curve which is found in the early examples. The actual crown worn at the coronation of Her Majesty (Plate L., fig. 2) differs in shape from the Imperial crown as represented on the coinage, etc. (Plate L., fig. 1). The bands, which have nearly the shape of a right angle, are formed of wreaths of oak leaves in brilliants, with acorns of pearls in brilliant cups. (Correct BOUTELL, p. 320.)

The crown of the Prince of WALES resembles the Imperial crown except that it has but a single arch supporting a small orb and cross. The coronet used by the other sons of the Sovereign is like that of the Prince of WALES — a circlet heightened with four crosses *patée* alternating with as many *fleurs-de-lis*— but it is not arched-in (Plate L., fig. 3). In the coronets used by the princesses two conventional strawberry leaves are substituted for two of the crosses *patée*. (Plate L., fig. 6.) Their coronet, therefore, bears two crosses *patée*, four *fleurs-de-lis*, and two strawberry leaves (the cross *patée* occupies the central place in all the British princely coronets). The grand-children of the Sovereign use a coronet in which four crosses *patée* alternate with as many strawberry leaves. (Plate L., fig. 7.)

The Royal crown of SCOTLAND is a circle of gold set with stones and pearls, and heightened with ten (entire) golden *fleurs-de-lis*, alternating with as many floriations resembling crosses *fleury* set with gems. Four rather small arches support a mound of blue enamel on which rests a cross slightly *patée*, set with an amethyst and pearls. (The Regalia of SCOTLAND have been very fully and accurately described by Messrs REID and BROOK, in most interesting papers printed in the *Proceedings of the Society of Antiquaries of Scotland*, 1890, pp. 18-141.)

The Royal crowns used by most foreign sovereigns, whatever be their titular rank, though they differ slightly in details, are (with exceptions hereafter noted) of one general type—a circlet of gold heightened with eight floriations between which are low cuspings supporting a pearl. The crown is closed in by eight pearled arches, surmounted by an orb and cross. (Plate L., fig. 4.)

The use of the closed crown by foreign sovereigns (the Emperor being excepted) dates only from the sixteenth century. The arms of Queen LEONORA of PORTUGAL, in 1498, have only the open circlet. I think the Spanish crown was not generally closed in before the times of the Emperor CHARLES. ERIK XIV. (1560-1568) was the first of the Swedish kings to bear the closed crown. Among the Danish regalia in the castle of Rosenborg, near Copenhagen, is still preserved the elegant open crown, probably made about the year 1600, worn by CHRISTIAN IV. The closed crown appears to have been adopted by CHRISTIAN V. (*c.* 1670).

FRANCE.—CHARLES VIII. is said to have assumed the closed crown in 1495, after the conquest of Naples, but it does not appear upon his Great Seal, or on that of his successors until the reign of HENRY II., 1547. FRANCIS I. (1515) is also said to have used the closed crown, and it certainly appears on the seal of his queen, LEONORA of PORTUGAL. The crown borne later by himself and his successors is a circlet of gold heightened with eight *fleurs-de-lis* (more accurately by eight *demi-fleurs-de-lis*), closed by eight pearled bands which unite in a *fleur-de-lis*. (Plate L., fig. 17.) The crown of the Dauphin was similar, but was arched in by four dolphins embowed supporting with their tails the crowning *fleur-de-lis*. (Plate L., fig. 18.) The coronet of the other children of the king (*les fils de France*) was a circlet adorned with eight (*demi-*) *fleurs-de-lis*. (Plate L., fig. 19.) That used by the princes, their children, was set alternately with four (*demi-*) *fleurs-de-lis* and as many conventional strawberry leaves. (Plate L., fig. 20.)

The crown adopted by NAPOLEON, and used under both Empires, was a gemmed circlet of gold supporting, and completely closed in by, eight Imperial eagles, whose elevated wings united with alternate conventional palm branches, rising from Greek honeysuckle floriations, to support the orb and cross.

The crown of the HOLY ROMAN EMPIRE, the crown worn by the GERMAN Emperors, appears to have been completely closed, not merely arched, at an early date, probably in imitation of the diadems used by the Byzantine Emperors from the time of BASIL I. The seal of HENRY I. (1002-1024) is closed in, and has also four rays or spikes surmounted by balls. That of his successor CONRAD I. has an open crown of four foliations; but CONRAD's son, the Emperor HENRY II., reverted to the previous type, and, with variations in detail, this was maintained by most of his successors. (The exceptions known to me are LOUIS IV., CHARLES IV., and RUPERT, who are represented with open crowns. *See* ROEMER-BÜCHNER, *Die Siegel der Deutschen Kaiser;* and GLAFEY, *Specimen Decadem Sigillorum.*) The *vittæ*, or fillets, are clearly indicated on the seals of CONRAD, 1143; FREDERICK, 1165; and PHILIP, 1203.

The crown of WLADISLAS, King of BOHEMIA, 1160, is shown by his Great Seal to have been of the same type as that worn by the Emperor at the same period (GLAFEY, tab. x., fig. 39). The type used by the later Emperors of GERMANY, and by the Emperors of AUSTRIA, is shown on Plate XL., as is also the celebrated crown of HUNGARY, the *Szent Korona*, or crown of St. STEPHEN.

RUSSIA.—The present Imperial crown of RUSSIA does not differ very materially from that used by the later German Emperors. A gemmed band rises from the floriated circlet and crosses the head from back to front, supporting on its summit the orb and cross; the side pieces of the cap are sections of a sphere, as in the old German and Austrian Imperial crowns.

The treasury of the Kremlin at Moscow contains among the regalia several most curious and ancient Russian crowns. Of these one of the most interesting is the crown of VLADIMIR (*Monomachus*), which is a dome-shaped cap of six sections, of gold filigree adorned with gems. It is truncated, and the opening is covered by a hemisphere of like workmanship supporting large gems and a tall cross of Latin shape. The circlet is covered by a broad band of sable fur. This is said to have been sent to St. VLADIMIR in the tenth century, but is certainly of later workmanship. The crown of PETER ALEXIEVITCH is similar in general character, but has a circlet from which rise small pliant rods of gold topped with large uncut gems. The crowns of SIBERIA, KAZAN, etc., are all of the general tiara, or pagoda shape, but are not easily described without reference to coloured engravings; such will be found in the splendid work, *The Antiquities of the Russian Empire*, 4to., 1849-52, of which there is a copy in the Art Library at South Kensington.

The PRUSSIAN Royal crown (distinct from the Imperial crown of GERMANY) is of gold, the circlet set with large diamonds, and heightened with diamond rosettes or foliations; it is arched-in with eight bands set with diamonds, and is surmounted by the orb and a brilliant cross.

The other European Royal crowns need no special mention; generally they are used not only by the sovereign and his consort, but as a heraldic ornament by the princes of the Royal House. Thus the crown of the late Prince ALBERT of SAXE-COBURG-GOTHA, the lamented Prince Consort of Queen VICTORIA (a younger brother of the reigning Duke of SAXE-

(623)

COBURG), was in all respects of the Royal type, differing only in minor details from that given in Plate L., fig. 4.

The archducal crown of AUSTRIA is at present a circlet of gold set with strawberry leaves, and having a single arch, as in the crown of the Prince of WALES. It also shows the cap of crimson velvet which rarely appears in the present day in foreign Royal crowns. The crown of the Electors of the Holy Roman (or Germanic) Empire was, like the old archducal crown of AUSTRIA, provided with a circlet of ermine cut into points ; in the archducal crown these points were edged with gold and pearls (see page 500).

The crown used by many German Princes (*Fürsten*) resembles the old electoral crown, having a scalloped circlet of ermine, a crimson velvet cap, and four golden arches with the orb and cross (Plate L., fig. 29). Other bearers of princely titles in Italy, etc., use a crown practically identical with a Royal one.

The Grand Dukes of TUSCANY used a circlet of gold set in front with a large *fleur-de-lis florençée*, the rest of the rim being ornamented with blades of iris leaves, and intermediate buds of the same flower.

The coronet of the Doges of VENICE is represented in Plate L., fig. 10 ; the plain coronet of gold enclosed a cap of cloth of gold, or silk damask, of peculiar shape.

CORONETS.—When we come to the consideration of the coronets borne by the European nobility, we must remark at the outset that great licence prevails, and that it is only in our own land that we can be certain that the coronet which is used as a heraldic adornment is a clear indication of the rank of the user.

Even the ducal coronet (Plate L., fig. 21), which is common to that rank in all European countries, is sometimes employed on the Continent by nobles of an inferior title, without exposing them, as such an assumption would do among us, to comment or derision. The ducal coronet, it appears from RIETSTAP, is generally borne by Marquises in Belgium and the Netherlands. It was also borne by the Marshals of France and their wives. I may remark also that all Grandees of the first class in Spain have the right to use the ducal coronet, though they may choose to be known by an inferior title; a Spanish grandee will frequently prefer to be known as the possessor of a great historical Marquessate or County than as the owner of a more modern Dukedom. All Spanish Dukes are grandees. Sometimes the titles of two ranks are there borne together. The well-read student of history will at once remember that OLIVAREZ, the Minister of State of PHILIP IV., was known as the "*Conde-Duque.*"

The coronet of a Marquess among us is a circlet of gold heightened with four strawberry leaves, and as many large pearls set alternately (Plate L., fig. 33). In other countries the number of strawberry leaves remains the same, but our single pearl is often replaced by a group of two or three smaller ones, separate or conjoined. (Plate L., figs. 22, 27, 32.) Fig. 27 is that which is most frequently used by French Marquises at the present day, but under LOUIS XIV. the form in fig. 22 (but with three pearls instead of two) was just as frequent.

The coronet of an Earl (Plate L., fig. 34) has the usual circlet of gold, heightened with eight strawberry leaves, and as many large pearls raised on high points, or rays. The coronet of a Count abroad is usually ornamented with sixteen pearls, of which nine are visible. In Germany these are usually placed on high points; in the old French coronets they are raised very very little above the circlet (*see* Plate L., figs. 23 and 30). Another French coronet used by Counts has the circlet set with four groups, each of three pearls in a

PLATE I.

CROWNS AND CORONETS.

1. Imperial.
2. Royal.
3. Prince of Wales.
4. Royal.
5. Sons of Sovereign.
6. Princesses.
7. Grandsons of Sovereign.
8. Viscounts. (*Netherlands.*)
9. Baron. (*Belgium.*)
10. Doge of Venice.
11. Vidame.
12. Nobles.
13. Eastern.
14. Vallary.
15. Naval.
16. Mural.
17. King of France.
18. Dauphin.
19. Fils de France.
20. Prince. (*France.*)
21. Ducal.
22. Marquis. (*France.*)
23. Count. (*France.*)
24. Viscount. (*France.*)
25. Baron. (*France.*)
26. President.
27. Marquis.
28. Noble. (*Germany.*)
29. Prince. (*Holy Roman Empire.*)
30. Count. (*Germany.*)
31. Baron. (*Germany.*)
32. Marquis.
33. Marquess.
34. Earl.
35. Viscount.
36. Baron.

trefoil, and with smaller pearls on the rim in the intermediate spaces. The Counts of the NETHERLANDS use a coronet very closely resembling that which is now known among us as the "crest-coronet;" but the intermediate cusping of our crest-coronet has not (or ought not to have) the small alternating pearl which appears in the coronet of the Dutch Counts; in other words, their coronet much resembles that of a Marquess (fig. 33), but has much smaller pearls.

The Viscount's coronet is with us a golden circlet with twelve pearls, of which seven are visible, set close to the rim. (Plate L., fig. 35.) In France it had at first only four pearls, of which three were visible; but later these were a little raised and four smaller pearls were placed in the intervals. (Plate L., fig. 24.) The Viscounts of the Netherlands have attributed to them by RIETSTAP a coronet set with four pearls on points, of which three are visible; and the intermediate spaces are occupied by strawberry leaves. (Plate L., fig. 8.)

The Baron's coronet with us has the circlet set with six large pearls, of which four are visible. In Germany, and in Italy, the coronet resembles that of a Count, but has only twelve pearls, of which seven are visible. (Plate L., fig. 31.) In France, the baronial coronet is a circle of gold wreathed with strings of small pearls. (Plate L., fig. 25.) A curious coronet is used by the Barons of the Low Countries created under Austrian rule; it is represented in Plate L., fig. 9, and is a circlet of gold with a cap ornamented with gold and pearls.

The coronet of a Vidame (*Vogt, Avoué,*) was a circlet of gold ornamented with four crosses *patée*, of which three are visible. (Plate L., fig. 11.)

The Chancellor of France, and the *Premiers Présidents* used, instead of a coronet, a *mortier*, or cap edged with gold (Plate L., fig. 26).

The Admirals of the United Provinces of the Netherlands adorned their escucheons with a naval crown composed of prows of ships. (*See* the monuments of DE RUYTER, VAN GALEN, and KINSBERGEN, in the Nieuwe Kerk, and those of SWEERS, HULST, etc., in the Oude Kerk, at Amsterdam.)

Plate L. contains two figures, Nos. 12 and 28, which have not yet been described. They are the coronets often used abroad by Jonkheers, hereditary knights, and nobles generally, who have not the right to the titles of Baron and upwards. These coronets when they appear on carriages or visiting-cards are often supposed by the unlearned to mean something much more than they really indicate. They are on all fours with the crest-coronet, or with the circlets which appear in early times upon the basinets of knights, and out of which no doubt the crest-coronet was evolved. But by the average Englishman, whose idea is that there is no nobility apart from the Peerage, the foreign coronet is assumed to be the index of high noble and titled rank, and the *ignotum* is taken only too often *pro magnifico* with very little reason indeed.

NAPOLEON, who had no objection to assume an Imperial crown for himself, endeavoured to substitute for the helmets and coronets of his nobles a series of velvet *toques*, or hats turned up with various colours, and ornamented with ostrich feathers. Those who are curious on the subject will find these all set out in SIMON, *L'Armorial Général de l'Empire Français*, tome i., but they were tasteless in design, and the new *noblesse* were not likely willingly to use insignia which marked them out as *nouveaux annoblis;* they had consequently but a very brief existence. The title of Marquess was not conferred by NAPOLEON; and is unknown in Poland and Scandinavia.

Fig. 98.—Arms, Etc., of Prince Putbus.

CHAPTER XXI.

EXTERNAL ORNAMENTS.

III.—SUPPORTERS.

SUPPORTERS are figures of living creatures placed at the side, or sides, of an armorial shield, and appearing to support it. French writers make a distinction, giving the name of *Supports* to animals, real or imaginary, thus employed; while human figures or angels similarly used are called *Tenants*. Trees, and other inanimate objects which are sometimes used, are called *Soutiens*.

MENÊTRIER and other old writers trace the origin of supporters to the usages of the tournaments, where the shields of the combatants were exposed for inspection, and guarded by their servants or pages disguised in fanciful attire,—"C'est des Tournois qu'est venu cet usage parce que les chevaliers y faisoient porter leurs lances, et leurs écus, par des pages, et des valets de pied, déguisez en ours, en lions, en mores, et en sauvages."

—*Usage des Armoiries*, p. 119. The old romances give us evidence that this custom prevailed; but I think only after the use of supporters had already arisen from another source.

There is really little doubt now that ANSTIS was quite correct when in his *Aspilogia* he attributed the origin of supporters to the invention of the engraver, who filled up the spaces at the top and sides of the triangular shield upon a circular seal with foliage, or with fanciful animals. Any good collection of mediæval seals will strengthen this conviction. For instance, the two volumes of LAING'S *Scottish Seals* afford numerous examples in which the shields used in the 13th and 14th centuries were placed between two creatures resembling lizards or dragons. (*See* the seal of ALEXANDER DE BALLIOL, 1295. LAING, ii., 74.) In CIBRARIO, *Sigilli de' Principi de Savoia, etc.*, Torino, 1834, the shield of BEATRICE of Savoy, Dauphine de VIENNOIS in 1279, is placed between the *lacs d'amour*, which were a badge of her house and still appear in the collar of the ORDER OF THE ANNUNCIADA. On the seal of AMADEUS V., Count of Savoy, in 1309, the shield has on either side a lion's head; and on the counter-seal the spaces above and around the shield are each charged with the same. The seals of EDWARD, Count of Savoy, in 1311, 1322, etc., are similarly arranged. (*See* also VRÉE, *Gen. Com. Fl.*, plate lxxviii.) On the counter-seal of MAGNUS (LADISLAS) of Sweden, in 1275, the shield (. . . . *semé* of small hearts, three bends-sinister, over all a lion rampant, crowned for the first time) is surmounted by an open crown and placed between two others in flanks. (*See* HILDEBRAND, *Det Svenska Riks-Vapnet*, fig. 14, p. 23, and SCHEFFER, Tab. F, fig. 24.) The seal of JOHN SEGRAVE has a garb on either side of the shield. On the counter-seal of CHARLES of ANJOU, in 1308, the shield of COUCY is placed between four lions rampant, within a quatrefoil. The seal of JOHN, Duke of NORMANDY, eldest son of the King of FRANCE, before 1316 bears his arms (FRANCE-ANCIENT, a *bordure gules*) between two lions rampant away from the shield, and an eagle with expanded wings standing above it. The *secretum* of ISABELLE de FLANDRES (*c.* 1308) has her shield placed between three lions, each charged with a bend (VRÉE, *Gen. Com. Flandr.*, plates xliii., xliv., xcii.). In 1332 AYMON of SAVOY places his arms (SAVOY, *with a label*) between a winged lion in chief and a lion without wings at either side. Later, on the seal of AMADEUS VI., a lion's head between wings became the crest of SAVOY. In 1332 AMADEUS bears SAVOY on a lozenge (*v.* p. 58) between in chief two eagles, in base two lions. (CIBRARIO, Nos. 61, 64; and GUICHENON, tome i., No. 130.) In Scotland the shield of REGINALD CRAWFORD in 1292 is placed between two dogs, and surmounted by a fox; in the same year the paly shield of REGINALD, Earl of ATHOLE, appears between two lions in chief and as many griffins in flanks (LAING, i., 210, 761).

The seal of HUMBERT II., Dauphin de VIENNOIS, in 1349, is an excellent example of the fashion. The shield of DAUPHINY is in the centre of a quatrefoil. Two savages mounted on griffins support its flanks; on the upper edge an armed knight sits on a couchant lion, and the space in base is filled by a human face between two wingless dragons. The spaces are sometimes filled with the Evangelistic symbols, as on the seal of YOLANTE de FLANDRES, Countess of BAR (*c.* 1340). The seal of JEANNE, Dame de PLASNES in 1376 bears her arms *en bannière* (p. 57) in a quatrefoil supported by two kneeling angels, a demi-angel in chief, and a lion couchant gardant in base.

But though in this abhorrence of a vacuum originated the use of animals, etc., as quasi supporters, other causes certainly co-operated. Allusion has been made to the usage by which on vesica-shaped seals ladies of high rank are represented as supporting with either hand shields of arms (*vide ante*, p. 454). From this probably arose the use of a single supporter. MARGUERITE DE COURCELLES in 1284, and ALIX DE VERDUN in 1311, bear in one hand a shield of the husband's arms, in the other one of their own. The curious seal of MURIEL, Countess of STRATHERNE, in 1284, may be considered akin to these. In it the shield is supported partly by a falcon, and partly by a human arm issuing from the sinister side of the *vesica*, and holding the falcon by the jesses (LAING, i., 764). The early seal of BOLESLAS III., King of POLAND, in 1255, bears a knight holding a shield charged with the Polish eagle (VOSSBERG, *Die Siegel des Mittelalters*). In 1283 the seal of FLORENT of HAINAULT bears a warrior in chain mail supporting a shield charged with a lion impaling an eagle dimidiated. Probably that which contributed most to the general adoption of a single supporter was the use by the German Emperor of the eagle displayed, bearing on its breast his personal arms, a fashion early adopted by his kinsmen and feudatories. Thus FLORENT, Count of HOLLAND, brother of the Emperor WILHELM, bore (*c.* 1260) the shield of HOLLAND on the breast of an eagle displayed, a usage maintained by later Counts, *e.g.*, by WILLIAM III. and his sister MARGARET, wife of the Emperor LOUIS, as well as by their sons, WILLIAM, Count of OSTREVANT, Duke of BAVARIA (*d.* 1377), and ALBERT, Count Palatine of the RHINE; these two used the double-headed eagle. We have seen the use of the eagle in this way by RICHARD of CORNWALL, elected King of the Romans in 1256 (*ante*, p. 245), and by his son EDMUND, Duke of CORNWALL. In Scotland about the same date the Earl of MENTEITH placed his shield on the breast of an eagle, as does ALEXANDER, Earl of ROSS, in 1338; in 1345 the shield of Sir DAVID LINDSAY is thus supported; and on the seal of EUPHEMIA, Countess of ROSS, in 1394, the shield of ROSS is borne on the breast of an eagle, while the arms of LESLIE and COMYN appear on its displayed wings. [*Cf.* the imperfect seal of MARGARET STEWART, Countess of ANGUS, in 1366; the shields remaining on the wings are ANGUS (*a lion rampant*), and STEWART (*a fess chequy and label*).] In 1370 the seal of LOUIS, Duc d'ANJOU, bears his shield on the breast of a crowned eagle displayed, whose feet rest on couchant lions (DEMAY, fig. 260).

On the seal of HUMPHREY DE BOHUN in 1322 the *guige* is held by a swan, the badge of the Earls of HEREFORD; and in 1356 the shield of the first Earl of DOUGLAS is supported by a lion whose head is covered by the crested helm, a fashion of which there are many examples. A helmed lion holds the shield of MAGNUS I., Duke of BRUNSWICK, in 1326. (That of a successor, Duke HENRY, in 1373 is supported by a single angel.) On the seal of JEAN, Duc de BERRI, in 1393 the supporter is a helmed swan (compare the armorial slab of HENRY of LANCASTER, in BOUTELL, plate lxxix.). JEAN IV., Comte d'ALENÇON (1408) has a helmed lion sejant as supporter. In 1359 a signet of LOUIS *van Male*, Count of FLANDERS, bears a lion sejant, helmed and crested, and mantled with the arms of FLANDERS between two small escucheons of NEVERS, or the county of Burgundy (*Azure, billetty a lion rampant or*), and RETHEL (*Gules, two heads of rakes fessways in pale or*). His seal in 1382 has a similar lion between four escucheons of ARTOIS, NEVERS, BRABANT, and RETHEL. I have engraved this seal (fig. 99, p. 648) from VRÉE, *de Seghelen der Graven van Vlaendren*, plate xxvi. A single lion sejant, helmed and crested, bearing on its breast the quartered arms of BURGUNDY between two or three other escucheons, was used by the Dukes up to the death of

CHARLES *the Bold* in 1475. In LITTA'S splendid work, *Famiglie celebri Italiane*, the BUONAROTTI arms are supported by a brown dog sejant, helmed, and crested with a pair of dragon's wings issuing from a crest-coronet. On the seal of THOMAS HOLLAND, Earl of KENT in 1380, the shield is buckled round the neck of the white hind lodged, the badge of his half-brother RICHARD II. Single supporters were very much in favour in the 13th and 14th centuries and the examples are numerous. CHARLES, Dauphin de VIENNOIS (*c.* 1355), has his shield held by a single dolphin. (In 1294 the seal of the Dauphin JEAN, son of HUMBERT I., bears the arms of DAUPHINÉ pendent from the neck of a griffon.) The shields of arms of BERTRAND DE BRICQUEBEC, in 1325; PIERRE DE TOURNEBU, in 1339; of CHARLES, Count of ALENÇON, in 1356; and of OLIVIER DE CLISSON, in 1397, are all supported by a warrior who stands behind the shield. In England the seals of HENRY PERCY, first Earl, in 1346, and another in 1345, have similar representations.

The earliest appearance of the unicorn as a supporter of the Royal Arms of SCOTLAND is on a gold coin of JAMES III. The unicorn is single. Other Scottish examples of single supporters are found on the seals of ALEXANDER ROXBURGH, 1367; NICOLAS DOUGLAS, 1392; ADAM FORRESTER, 1400; ARCHIBALD, Earl of DOUGLAS, in 1418, as Duke of TOURAINE in 1421 (his wife, MARGARET, in 1425 has an angel as the supporter of her shield); of WILLIAM, Earl of DOUGLAS, in 1446. The arms of the city of PERTH: *Gules, a paschal lamb argent, the banner azure, a saltire and royal tressure of the second*, are borne on the breast of a double-headed eagle displayed. (*See* LAING, *Scottish Seals;* and SETON, *Scottish Heraldry*, pp. 269, 270.)

The seals of MARY, Duchess of BURGUNDY, show her use of an angel, or of a lion, as a single supporter, and her husband, the Archduke MAXIMILIAN, similarly used a single lion sejant, crested and helmed. On the *secretum* of CHARLES V. and later Kings of FRANCE, a single angel appears behind the shield as a single supporter bearing the sceptre and the *main de justice*.

FERDINAND and ISABELLA, out of devotion to St. JOHN, placed the shield of the Royal Arms (*Quarterly:* 1 and 4. CASTILE *quartering* LEON; 2 and 3. ARRAGON), on the breast of the single-headed Apostolic eagle displayed, of which use there are many examples on the *reja*, and walls of the *Capilla de los Reyes* at Granada, and, if I remember aright, at Seville also.

In England there are a few examples of the use of a single supporter in later times. CHARLES I. is said to have granted to the lord of the Manor of Stoke Lyne the right to bear his arms on the breast of a displayed hawk.

The use of DOUBLE SUPPORTERS, as at present, arose contemporaneously with that of the single one. In the majority of cases both supporters were alike, but even at an early date this was by no means invariably the case. In Brittany the supporters were usually different, and there is a frequent combination of the lion and the griffon, as on the seals of ALAIN DE BEAUMONT, 1298; GUI DE BLOIS, 1367; BERTRAND DU GUESCLIN, 1373; CLÉMENT, Vicomte de THOUARS, 1378; ROBIN DE GUITÉ, 1379; and CHARLES, Comte de DAMMARTIN, in 1394. Even after the use of double supporters had become general a third figure is often placed behind the shield, and forms a connecting link with the old practice of filling the void spaces on seals to which we have already referred. On the seal of WILLIAM STERLING in 1292, two lions rampant support the shield in front of a tree. The shield on the seal of OLIVIER ROUILLON in 1376 is supported by an angel, and by two demi-lions couchant-gardant in base. That of PIERRE AVOIR, in

1378, is held by a demi-eagle above the shield, and by two mermaids. On many ancient seals the supporters hold the crested helm above a *couché* shield.

Instances have been given in which a single supporter has a mantling *armoyée*. Double supporters are similarly treated, as are the eagles of JEAN D'HARCOURT in 1410, the lions of HUGH DE GRAMMONT in 1341. On the seal of PERRONELLE, Vicomtesse de THOUARS, in 1378 the mantling is of DREUX (*Chequy or and azure, a bordure gules*, see DEMAY, fig. 259). On that of ALAIN DU PERRIER in 1387 the lions sejant hold banners, and have *volets* apparently of vair (MORICE, *Bretagne*, tome ii.).

The counter-seals of RUDOLF IV., Archduke of AUSTRIA, in 1359 and 1362, afford instances in which a second set of supporters is used to hold up the crested helm. The shield of AUSTRIA is supported by two lions on whose *volets* are the arms of HAPSBURG and PFIRT; the crested helm (coroneted, and having a penache of ostrich feathers) is also held by two lions whose *volets* are charged with the arms of STIRIA, and of CARINTHIA. (HUEBER, *Austria Illustrata*, tab. xviii.)

In 1372 the seal of EDMUND MORTIMER represents his shield hanging from a rose-tree, and supported by two lions couchant (of MARCH), whose heads are covered by coroneted helmets with a *penache* (*azure*) as crest. (*See* Plate XXXVII., fig. 2.) BOUTELL directs attention to the fact that the shield of EDMUND DE ARUNDEL (1301-1326) is placed between similar helms and *penaches* without the supporting beasts (*Heraldry, Historical and Popular*, pp. 271-418).

Crested supporters have sometimes been misunderstood, and quoted as instances of double supporters—for instance, by LOWER, *Curiosities of Heraldry*, who gives (p. 144) a cut from the achievement of the French D'ALBRETS as "the most singular supporters, perhaps, in the whole circle of Heraldry." These supporters are two lions couchant (*or*), each helmed, and crested with an eagle *au vol levé*. These eagles certainly assist in holding the shield, but the lions are its true supporters; nor is this arrangement by any means unique. The swans which were used as supporters by JEAN, Duc de BERRI, in 1386, are each mounted upon a bear. Two wild men, each *à cheval* on a lion, support the escucheons of GERARD D'HARCHIES (1476) and of NICOLE DE GIRESME in 1464. Two lions sejant, helmed and crested (the crest is a human head with the ears of an ass), were the supporters of ARNAUD D'ALBRET in 1368 (DEMAY, p. 214).

Really curious supporters are those of the Roman CESARINI, Dukes de CITTANOVA. They are two eagles; the head of the dexter bears the hind-quarters of a bear passant (away from the shield!), the sinister the fore-quarters of the same animal.

On the secretum of JAMES I. the Royal Arms of SCOTLAND are supported by two lions rampant-gardant; but JAMES V. changed them to two unicorns royally gorged and chained. Queen MARY used the unicorns, but her privy seal has the lions.

Several instances of TRIPLE SUPPORTERS have been already given. The shield of JACQUELINE DE BÉTHUNE, in 1422, is supported by four angels; that of YOLANTE DE FLANDRES, Countess of BAR, etc. (bearing *en bannière* NAVARRE quartering EVREUX, dimidiated, and impaled with FLANDERS *a bordure engrailed*) is supported by no less than eight demi-angels.

The escucheon of JEAN, Duc de BERRI, *circa* 1408, has six bears as its supporters. I have engraved this pretty and spirited design on Plate XXXV., fig. 2, from DEMAY, p. 216.

The supporters of the Royal Arms in France in modern times were two angels habited in albs, over which were dalmatics charged with the Royal Arms, and holding banners of the same. When the shields of FRANCE and NAVARRE were borne *accolées*, as by LOUIS XIV., the dexter supporter was habited of FRANCE; the sinister of NAVARRE.

The FRENCH ROYAL SUPPORTERS were the following:—PHILIP AUGUSTUS used two lions; LOUIS VIII., two wild boars (the supporters of the Dukes of BRITTANY); ST. LOUIS (IX.), two dragons; PHILIP III., two eagles; PHILIP V., two lions; CHARLES IV., two lions; PHILIP VI., two greyhounds; JOHN, two swans (chained to the shield); CHARLES V., two greyhounds (*azure, blessés de gueules*) or two dolphins; Charles VI., CHARLES VII. and LOUIS XI., two winged stags; CHARLES VIII., two unicorns; LOUIS XII., two porcupines; FRANCIS I., two salamanders; HENRY II., two greyhounds; FRANCIS II., two lions of SCOTLAND; HENRY III., two white eagles (of POLAND); HENRI IV., two "*vaches de Béarn de gueules;*" LOUIS XIII., two figures of HERCULES. These were not borne to the exclusion of the angels, which were common to all the Kings after CHARLES VII. LOUIS XIV. and his successors used no others. (The above list is mainly from LA ROQUE, *Traité Singulier du Blason*, Paris, 1673.)

The arms of the DAUPHIN were supported by angels in dalmatics, that of the dexter is charged with the arms of FRANCE, that of the sinister with the arms of DAUPHINY. The other princes of the blood used angels in albs without dalmatics. The use of angel supporters was *not*, as is sometimes asserted, a prerogative of the Royal House in France.

In France, and indeed on the Continent generally, the use of supporters is not nearly so restricted as with us. A noble has the right to all the insignia of nobility, even though he be an untitled gentleman. If, as in Italy and Spain, he does not generally use supporters, it is only because fashion has made their use infrequent, not because he considers them the peculiar property of great nobles—they, in fact, use them as little as he does. Nor would it be thought that he needed the Royal, or any other, licence to assume or to change them, any more than to leave off their use. No doubt, in some great families the supporters have become practically hereditary, and the present representatives probably use what their ancestors used three or four centuries ago. Where, as is often the case in Germany, an armorial augmentation has taken the form of a special grant of supporters (*v.* pp. 544, 545), no doubt these will continue to be used without change. What is meant is simply that there is and has been practical liberty with regard to these matters; not only where (as in France) there is no longer a College of Arms, but in other countries where armorial insignia were under regular supervision.

An attempt was indeed made by the Archduke ALBERT to restrict the too general use of supporters, as of coronets and titles, in the Low Countries, by the *Ordonnances* to which reference has already been made in these pages (p. 551). One of these prescribed:—
"Vt nemo sibi aut alteri tribuat titulum Baronis aut majorem, aut secus insignia sua delatores, aut sustentatores ponat, coronasve indebite assumptas, nisi hæc sibi per litteras Principum nostrorum probet attributa, seu perditis per bella litteris notorié possessa, quo casu aliæ dabuntur litteræ actis Heraldorum inscribendæ. (ZYPŒUS. *Notitia Iuris Belgici,* i., xii., and MENÊ-TRIER, *Usage des Armoiries,* p. 215.) These *Ordonnances* had little practical result; and I only quote them here lest it should be supposed that what I have said above was written in ignorance of their existence. In early times there is no doubt whatever that supporters, like crests, had not a hereditary character, nor was their use even in England confined to peers, or other great nobles. Even now a good many untitled families

bear them by prescription; such are the HILTONS of Hilton, TREVANIONS of Cornwall, the FULFORDS, LUTTRELS, etc. As their assumption was unrestricted, so was their use. A noble family, for instance, which had become accustomed to use golden lions as supporters would have them drawn or engraved with a variety of attitude which would shock the pedantic notions of many people now-a-days who think they know all about Heraldry. At one time the lions would look towards the shield; at another would be *affrontés;* at another *regardant;* at another they might even be *en barroque;* so that the supporters were two golden lions, that was enough. Nor was it required that they should be absolutely unlike those borne by any other family. It is only in modern times that the over-regulation of what really did not need restriction has checked artistic fancy, and under the pretence of forbidding licence has limited lawful liberty.

Now-a-days, it would appear that every minute detail must be specified in the blazon, down to the colour of a sailor's neck-tie, the number of buttons on his jacket, or the fact of his shoes being either buckled or tied. Learned gentlemen (with and without tabards) warmly debate such highly important matters as whether a leopard supporter must show one ear or two! It may somewhat appease any who, after having read this, are inclined to denounce me either as an ignoramus or as a radical innovator, if I remind them that I only express the views of one who certainly was neither the one nor the other — my late learned friend, JOHN GOUGH NICHOLS. He quotes with approval, from so old and usually pedantic an authority as BOSSEWELL, a passage declaring the needlessness of specifying such *minutiæ*, and says, " It is agreeable . . . . to come across instructions so rational as these, which we venture to regard as more in correspondence with the simple and homogeneous blazon of still earlier days than with the minute technicalities of our own, which the irreverent are sometimes bold enough to stigmatise as the 'jargon of Heraldry.'" (*Herald and Genealogist*, ii., 109.)

In the Netherlands, and especially in Belgium, the use of supporters which also hold erect armorial banners is not infrequent. The possession of lands which were once *fiefs en bannière* may sometimes be thus denoted; but I think that where, as is often the case, the arms on the banners do not coincide with those on the shield, their use may be a kind of Marshalling, and the banners may commemorate an important line of descent.

In Spain the infrequency of the use of supporters by the high nobility is probably due to the fact that the Regulations of the ORDER OF THE GOLDEN FLEECE permitted no supporters, and only one crested helm, to a shield surrounded by the collar of the Order. The finely carved achievements of the VELASCOS, which are supported by savages, in the glorious *Capilla del Condestable* in the Cathedral at Burgos, are exceptional.

In Italy the use of supporters was very infrequent in late mediæval times, and is still very far from general. In Germany their use is somewhat more in accordance with our own, but the fashion of placing the arms of princes, and counts of the Empire, on the breast of an eagle displayed is still not unfrequently seen. (*Cf.* Arms of Earl of CLARENDON at p. 545; though the eagle is there the Prussian one.) Instances are met with, chiefly in German and Slavonic Heraldry, in which the shield is encircled by a serpent, or dragon. Of this fashion I have a dozen or more instances, but one will suffice. The Barons von WARTENBERG, who bear *Per pale or and sable*, have the shield encircled by a dragon which holds its tail in its teeth. In the *Grünenberg* Armorial the shield of the Count of COSSENTANIA has around it a serpent with a female head. Single supporters are occasionally met with in modern Continental use, but, like the preceding examples, belong rather to the curiosities of Heraldry. SIEBMACHER'S *Wappenbuch* contains several examples. The Counts VON HOCHENEGG in Austria (who bore *Chequy argent and sable, a quarter gules*) have the shield supported by a man-at-arms in profile, turned to the dexter, holding in his right hand a halberd, and having on his head a helm crested (out of a coronet two wings as the arms). *Wappenbuch,* i., 35. The arms and crest borne by the modern Counts are entirely different, but a man-at-arms is still used as the supporter. The Barons NEU use a single knight; the Barons van de MOER, in Holland, a single bear; the Prussian STERNEMANNS, a Roman warrior. The Counts von BOINEBURG, whose arms are *Quarterly sable and argent,* bear them on the breast of a double-headed eagle displayed *Quarterly argent and sable,* the heads crowned proper.

The Arms of the SWISS Cantons are frequently represented with a single supporter; thus the Arms of the Canton of BERNE (*Gules, on a bend or, a bear passant sable*), are as often supported by one bear as by two; and those of ZÜRICH (*Per bend-sinister argent and azure*) by one lion rampant brandishing a sword as by two.

A still better known example is afforded by the Arms of the UNITED STATES OF AMERICA: *Paly of ten* (sometimes of thirteen) *gules and argent, on a chief azure as many stars* (of five points) *argent* as there are States in the Union. These are supported by an eagle displayed proper, holding in the dexter claw a laurel wreath, in the other three silver arrows. The motto (generally held in the eagle's beak) is *E Pluribus Unum.* (Plate LIV., fig. 2.)

The Lombard Counts da MULA use two supporters but place them both on the sinister side of the shield. They are; a sea griffin per fess *or* and *vert,* supporting on its head a naked woman with extended arms, her sinister hand holds the shield; the dexter, a laurel wreath all proper.

On some early seals the arms are represented not on a shield but on a banner, usually held by a "beast," or single supporter. Thus on the seal of HENRY PERCY, eldest son of the Earl of NORTHUMBERLAND in 1445, the arms (of PERCY quartering LUCY) differenced by a label, are displayed on a banner supported by a lion sejant-gardant. (*Archæologia Æliana*, vol. iv., p. 185.) In the hall of Naworth Castle the arms of DACRE, MULTON, GRIMTHORP, and GREYSTOCK are thus depicted on banners held by "beasts." The seal of WALTER, Lord HUNGERFORD, K.G., has in 1432 the arms (*Sable, two bars argent, in chief three plates*) differenced by a label, placed between the HEYTESBURY sickles, while on either side of the crested helm rises a banner: the dexter of HEYTESBURY (*Per pale indented gules and vert, a chevron or*); the sinister of HUSSEY (*Barry of six ermine and gules*), both are differenced by a label.

The Lombard family of MILLESIMO, Marquises de SAVONA, who bear *Bendy or and gules*, place the escucheon on the breast of the Imperial Eagle, which rests its claws on a triumphal car drawn by two lions passant *argent* crowned *or*. This very curious arrangement brings us naturally to the consideration of what are known as COMPARTMENTS. This term is one peculiar to Scottish heraldry and denotes the architectural panel, a figure of no definite form, on which the shield and supporters are often made to rest. It is also applied to the ground or terrace, upon which these supporters stand in ancient seals, and in modern continental practice. Our own custom by which supporters are represented balancing themselves with unstable footing upon a thing resembling the scroll of a gas burner; or with even less comfort upon the edge of the motto ribbon, is one which is almost peculiar to ourselves, and is ludicrous in the highest degree.

Abroad, the supporters are much more reasonably represented as standing usually on a piece of solid ground (*see* fig. 98, p. 627) (though in the case of angels, or fish, clouds, or waves of the sea are occasionally employed). Many of the escucheons in FOSTER'S PEERAGE have the supporters thus sensibly supported.

Our own departure from the common sense practice of ancient times has led to the compartment, when retained in use, being supposed to be a peculiar mark of high dignity or royal favour. The seals of the Earls of DOUGLAS from 1434, have in the base a "pale of wood wreathed," supposed to represent the forest of Jedburgh. The same device appears on the seal of GUILLAUME DE BAVIÈRE, Comte D'OSTREVANT in 1412, on which the shield of arms (*v.* pp. 462, 463) is held by a single lion sejant on a mound enclosed by wattled pales with a gate, said to represent the palisade with which he blockaded the citadel of Hagenstein and the chateau of Everstein. (VRÉE, *Gen. Com. Fl.*, i., 368). His daughter JACQUELINE DE BAVIÈRE (wife successively of the DAUPHIN, the Dukes of BRABANT, and GLOUCESTER, and of FRANCIS DE BORSELE) used this same device of the hedge. The compartment used by the DRUMMONDS, Earls of PERTH, is a green mount, *semé* of caltraps. The appropriate motto is *Gang Warily*. The MACFARLANES have a wavy compartment with the words, *Loch Sloy*.

The arms of OGILVY, baronets of Inverquharity, are supported by two savages who stand on as many serpents nowed and spouting fire, the whole being arranged upon a mount, or compartment. The arms of the Barons von LÖBENSTEIN (*Or, three bars gules*) are supported by two golden lions regardant, who tread under foot a serpent bent into an oval, proper.

The term compartment is often improperly applied to other bearings which would be more fitly described either as devices, or supporters. Such are the salamander of DOUGLAS, the star of SETON, the chained savage of ROBERTSON of Struan ; all placed beneath the respective shields of arms.

On the seals of JOHN LANDEL (*c.* 1224), and the counter-seal of MALCOLM, Earl of LENNOX in 1292, the shield is placed between the attires of a stag's head caboshed ; as it was also by the DENHAMS.

INANIMATE OBJECTS are sometimes used to fill the office of supporters. Of these the best known example is afforded by the "Pillars of Hercules," assumed as supporters with the motto, *Ne plus ultra* by CHARLES V. After the discovery of America the *ne* was omitted. The PIOSASCO family of Savoy, who bear : *Argent, nine martlets sable*, use as supporters "due torni o cilindri, col motto, *Qui, Qui,*" (*See* the *Teatro Araldico* of TETTONI E SÁLADINI ; 8 vols. 4to, *Milan*, 1841. RIETSTAP oddly misreads the blazon, and gives the supporters as bulls !) Akin to these are the military trophies, the banners, weapons, etc., which are not unfrequently found in use in Continental Armory as adjuncts to the shield. The ACHARDS of Poitou have the shield thus accosted by four halberts. The DALZELLS of Bins had in 1685 the grant of a pair of tent-poles to be placed one on either side of the shield. The shield of the Marquises ALBERTI is accosted, or embraced, by two lighted flambeaux. The Breton family of BASTARD have the shield accosted by two swords, points in base. The SCHEPERS of Holland, and the BILLES of Denmark, place two anchors in saltire behind the shield. I have collected a considerable number of examples of the use of banners in this way : *e.g.* the TOLEDOS, dukes of ALVA, surround the shield with twelve Moorish Standards ; the BAZANS have twenty-eight; the CORDOVAS sixty-four. Several German families have a trophy of arms, similar to that used as a background for his achievement by the Earl of BANTRY. The BRANDOLINI of Italy had the right to crown their arms, and to place on either side of them a naked sword. The motto was *Pour loyauté maintenir*, and the whole was a concession of a King of Cyprus.

With this class of External Ornaments we may group the collars, crosses, ribbons, and badges of Orders of Knighthood, the latter of which are not only suspended beneath the shield but in many cases the shield is placed upon the cross or star; as by the Members of the ORDERS OF S. JOHN, AVIZ, the TEUTONIC ORDER, etc. We may also refer, though we can do so but briefly, to some of the marks of office which accompany the shields of great Officers of State. The Lord Chancellor of England places two maces in saltire (or one in pale) behind the shield, and the purse of the Great Seal beneath. The Earl Marshal uses in like manner two golden rods tipped with black enamel. The Lord High Chamberlain might use two golden keys in saltire (MORGAN, *Sphere of Gentry*, iv., p. 82) and the Lord Chamberlain of the Household a golden key in pale, etc. In Scotland the Lord High Chamberlain used the two golden keys; the Great Master of the Household, two batons gules, *semé* of thistles and surmounted by the Crest of Scotland; the Justice General, two naked swords. The Duke of ARGYLL as possessing these two dignities places a baton and a naked sword in saltire behind his arms; the Earl Marshal, two batons *gules, semé of thistles or*.

In the Museum at Brussels is the portrait of FERDINAND DE BOISSCHOT, Comte D'ERPS, Chancellor of BRABANT (*d.* 1649). His arms (*Or, three fers de moulin azure*) are placed upon the cross of SANTIAGO, two golden maces are in saltire behind the shield, and the whole is surmounted by his coronet.

In France, the *Admiral* placed two anchors in saltire (and the *Vice-Admiral* one in pale) behind the shield; the beams are *Azure, fleury or.* The *Marshals* used two similar batons; the *Chancellor*, as many maces; the *Grand Esquire*, two sheathed and belted swords (*azure, fleury or*) in pale; the *Grand Master of Artillery*, two mounted cannon; the *Grand Constable* (like the *Grand Master* of the ORDER OF S. JOHN), two arms in armour issuing from clouds at the base of the shield holding a naked sword paleways on either side. Under the Empire, the *Vice Connétable* similarly used the swords, but sheathed, and *semés* of golden bees. The *Grand Chamberlain* had two golden keys in saltire (the imperial eagle in the bows); and the batons of the *Maréchaux de France* were *semés* of bees instead of *fleurs-de-lis*.

In Italy the Duca de SAVELLI, as *Marshal of the Conclave*, hangs on either side of his shield a key, the cords of which are knotted beneath his coronet.

In Holland Admirals used the naval crown (*ante*, p. 626), and added two anchors in saltire behind the shield, as on the monument of VAN TROMP in the Oude Kerk at Delft.

In Spain the Admirals of Castile and of the Indies placed an anchor in bend behind the shield.

The *Cordelière*, or *Lacs d'Amour*, a knotted cord with tassels, was often placed around the lozenge, or shield of arms, by widows and abbesses in France; while the use of garlands, or palm branches, about the escucheon was never thought to need the intervention of any heraldic authorities. On Plate XXXVI., the arms of the Duke of ALBANY are represented ornamented with the Collar and Badge of the ORDER OF S. MICHAEL.

Occasionally arms are found improperly surrounded by a motto band after the fashion of the ORDER OF THE GARTER; more usually the motto is placed in a riband below the shield, or in a listel above the crest.

By the understood English use supporters are at present borne by all temporal peers, including those who have life peerages, but not by bishops as such. (This is a modern restriction without ancient precedent or authority, or rather in defiance of it, but as to this I refer the reader to my forthcoming work on *Ecclesiastical Heraldry*.) They are also borne as personal distinctions by Knights Grand Crosses of the Several Orders, and it is considered that there is precedent for their use by certain great officers of the Royal Household. (As a matter of fact the precedents have to be sought in times when the use of supporters was not so strictly limited by custom as it is now.) The right to use supporters has been occasionally conceded by Royal Warrant, and a modern example is recorded in Appendix D. A few of the persons to whom these warrants have been granted are baronets, but baronets as such have no right to use them. These eldest sons of peers above the rank of viscount, and the younger sons of dukes and marquesses, generally use the supporters of the family, but this modern return to a less restricted use of them has not the approval of the English College of Arms. The use of supporters by prescription in the case of some old English families has been already alluded to.

In Scotland the use of supporters is less restricted. By custom they are employed by the chiefs of the more important clans, and the representatives of all minor barons who had full baronial rights prior to 1507. The baronial status implied, in theory at least, the right to sit in Parliament until that year when parliamentary representation was finally established. There is no foundation for the oft-repeated assertion that Scottish baronets are, as such, entitled to supporters. In some cases they bear them by virtue of the baronial qualification ; or as being chiefs of important families; but in various cases when application has been made for them they have been refused. It has often been laid down that LYON has the power of conferring supporters *ex gratia* on persons who would not be considered as having a claim to them by the strict heraldic rule of modern times. Mr SETON expresses considerable doubt as to the existence of any such power; and though I do not take quite the same strong view as is held by him upon the subject, I must admit that, except at one not very glorious period in the history of the Lyon office (1763-1820), the power has been sparingly used, and usually on fairly satisfactory grounds. But any further remarks on this subject may be deferred until the time when I may be able to print Dr BURNETT'S chapter on the Lyon office, for which I cannot find space in these volumes. In Ireland, according to Sir BERNARD BURKE, the heads of the different septs assert their right to use supporters; but there is no instance of their registration in Ulster's office, by an Irish chieftain in right of his chieftaincy alone, and without the possession of a peerage dignity. In Wales, the Barons of EDEIRNION in Merioneth, who enjoyed baronial rights in their domains, and who had these rights specially confirmed after the subjugation of the country, have always used them without question.

In the selection of the supporters for new peers a little better taste might well be exercised. Where the new peer is a descendant from a family which bore supporters, one or both of these may fairly be assumed, with or without difference as may appear desirable. But a fashion has sprung up of clogging modern supporters with escucheons pendent from the neck, which would make free motion difficult, if not impossible, to the living beast. This fashion is now in great favour; and the supporters granted to nearly all peers of new creation afford instances of it. (*See* those of Lords ARDILAUN, BELPER, GRANTLEY, HATHERTON, LAMINGTON, LATHOM, etc., etc.) These escucheons are often charged with bearings indicative of descent; but the Low Country use, to which reference has been made, of supporters holding banners, is a much more suitable and truly heraldic way of denoting this. Supporters are often, not improperly, charged with a mark of cadency; but to affix to the shoulders of Lord ROMILLY'S greyhounds a "lily slipped proper" (?), or to charge the bodies of Lord EVERSLEY'S talbots with the mace of the Speaker of the House of Commons, are incongruities which in my judgment are as faulty artistically as they are heraldically.

Other supporters, in which this lack of artistic taste and of true heraldic feeling is conspicuous, are what we may call "chintz supporters," in which the body of the beast is covered with a pattern (!) (*See* the supporters of the Earls of ILCHESTER, CLANCARTY, DARTMOUTH, etc.).

FIG. 99.—SEAL OF LOUIS, COUNT OF FLANDERS.

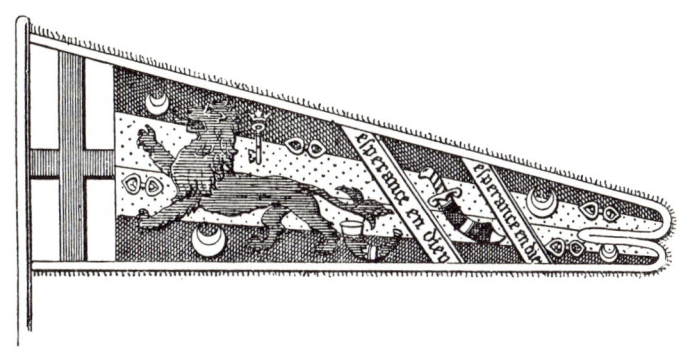

FIG. 100.—BANNER OF PERCY.

CHAPTER XXII.

FLAGS, BANNERS, STANDARDS, ETC.

THE earliest banners with which we are concerned are those which appear on the Bayeux tapestry, examples of which are figured here and in Plate XXXV.

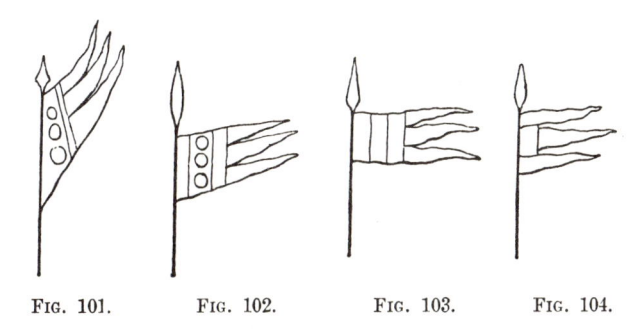

FIG. 101.   FIG. 102.   FIG. 103.   FIG. 104.

Of the thirty-seven pennons borne on their lances by the Norman soldiers, twenty-eight are represented as terminating in triple points, or streamers, and we may therefore conclude that this was the usual form at the period. In the *British Museum Catalogue of Seals*, the lances borne by the effigies of WILLIAM THE CONQUEROR, and WILLIAM RUFUS, are said to have triple streamers

(Nos. 15 and 22). The number of points was, however, by no means constant, nor were the streamers always pointed. In both these respects there was considerable variation in later times, and the pennon which fluttered at the end of the lance was as often triangular, or swallow-tailed. A Saxon banner in the Bayeux tapestry is triangular, with four streamers issuing from the lower edge. (FRENCH, *Banners of the Bayeux Tapestry*, xvi., 5.)

If we turn to the other contemporary source of information, we find that on early seals the owner was frequently represented bearing a lance, to the head of which was attached a flag, often of considerable size. The lance of RAOUL, Comte de VERMANDOIS, in 1116, has a square banner, charged probably with the chequers of VERMANDOIS, and having attached to its edge three attenuated streamers. (DEMAY, p. 158.) The seal of WILLIAM, Count of FLANDERS, in 1122, shows a long banner split throughout nearly its whole length, and pointed at the ends (WREE, *de Seghelen*, plate vii.). That of BALDWIN V., Count of HAINAULT (d. 1194), is of similar character; neither of these have any distinguishable device. The seal of LEOPOLD, Duke of AUSTRIA, *circa* 1199, is swallow-tailed. His seal three or four years later has the flag simply divided towards the extremity into two unpointed but fringed tails. Other seals in 1216 and 1231 have three such tails; in 1217 the banner is charged with the *stier* of STYRIA (*v. ante*, p. 499). This arrangement alternates with the banner proper for a long time after the general adoption of the latter. (HUEBER, *Austria Illustrata*.) The lance of JEAN DE CHALONS, Comte de BOURGOGNE, in 1239, has at its head a small square banner *armoyée* (*Azure, a bend or*), and having four narrow tails, or bannerols. The well-known brass of Sir JOHN DAUBERNOUN (1277) at Stoke d'Abernon, in Surrey, represents him with his lance, to the head of which is attached a small pennon with a single point, bearing his arms, *Azure, a chevron or.*

The BANNER which was used eventually by knights-bannerets, barons, and all persons of higher rank, was a rectangular flag, usually square, but often oblong in

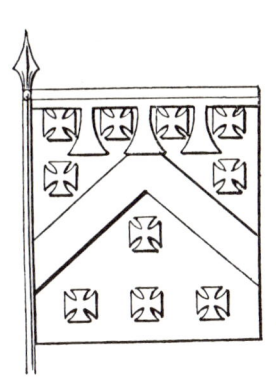

FIG. 105.—BANNER OF MAURICE DE BERKELEY.

shape, and attached to the staff by one of the longer sides. This was emblazoned over its whole surface with the arms of the wearer. (*See* fig. 105, the banner of MAURICE DE BERKELEY, from the *Roll of Caerlaverock.*) DEMAY gives as an example the banner of MATHIEU DE MONTMORENCY in 1230. In VRÉE, the earliest seals with the banner-proper are those of HENRY I. and III., Dukes of BRABANT (*c.* 1230 and 1260). OTTAKAR, Duke of AUSTRIA, is represented on his seal in 1264, bearing a shield with the Austrian fess, and having a lance with a banner of STYRIA (HUEBER, tab. iv., No. 4). By a later fashion a long bannerol, pointed or cleft, was attached to the upper portion of the external part of the "fly." But in earlier times, when a knight was to be raised to the rank of banneret on the field or battle, the ceremonial consisted in the cutting off of the points of the pennon, so that it was made to assume the square shape of a banner, exactly or approximately.

Under the feudal system knights were of two classes :— Bachelors and Bannerets. A *bachelerie* was a noble fief inferior in importance to that held by a knight. Sometimes two or three *bacheleries* sent only a single man at arms to the army between them. The chevaliers-bacheliers bore the lance with a pennon, and fought under the command of a knight-banneret. A knight-banneret was one who held a *fief en bannière*, investiture of which was given by the delivery of a banner by the prince, or superior; he was obliged not only to give personal military service, but also to provide as many knights as his fief contained knightly fees, and these fought under his banner. Until he had received the rank of knighthood, though his banner was displayed and knights followed it, he was styled *un Écuyer-Banneret*, and received only the pay of a chevalier, instead of the double pay to which a chevalier-banneret was entitled. MENÊTRIER gives the following from an old MS.: " Quand un Bachelier a grandement servy et suivy la guerre, et que il a terre assez, et qu'il puisse avoir Gentilshommes ses hommes et pour compagner sa Banniere, il peut licitement lever Banniere et non autrement. Car nul homme ne peut, ne doit porter ne lever Banniere en bataille, s'il n'a du moins cinquante hommes d'armes tous ses hommes, et les Archers, ou Arbalestriers qui luy appartiennent ; et s'il les a, il doit à la premiere bataille où il se trouvera apporter un Pennon des ses armes, et doit venir au Connestable, ou aux Mareschaux, ou à celui qui sera Lieutenant de l'Ost pour le Prince, requerir qu'il porte Banniere, et si luy octroyent, doit sommer les Heraux pour témoignage, et doivent decouper la queue du Pennon, et alors le doit porter, et lever avant les autres Bannieres au dessons des autres Barons. (*Recherches du Blason*, pp. 15, 16.)

In Flanders the required number of men at arms seems to have been only twenty-five. At the siege of Caerlaverock in 1300 this also seems to have been about the proportion; there was a banner to every twenty-five or thirty men. MENÊTRIER gives, from OLIVIER DE LA MARCHE, an account of the way in which LOUIS, a cadet of the family of VIEUILLE, and himself holding the lands of Sains, a *terre en bannière,* was raised to the rank of banneret. "Si bailla le Roy d'Armes un coûteau au Duc et prit le Pennon en ses mains, et le bon Duc sans oster le gantelet de sa main senestre fit un tour au tour de sa main de la queue du Pennon, et de l'autre main coupa le dit Pennon : et demeura quarré : et la banniere faite le Roy d'Armes bailla la banniere audit Messire Louys et luy du : Noble Chevalier, recevez l'honneur que vous fait au jour d'huy vostre Seigneur et Prince, et soyez au jour d'huy bon Chevalier, et conduisez vostre banniere à l'honneur de vostre lignage."

The banner was the sign of a command, and all persons who would now be called general officers had the right to its use whatever their civil rank might be.

On the tomb of Sir LEWIS ROBSART, K.G., Lord BOURCHIER, d. 1431 ; in the Chapel of St. Paul in Westminster Abbey, a banner *armoyée* is placed at each corner of the slab, those at the bottom are supported the one by a lion, the other by a falcon. Compare with this the use of a banner *armoyée,* held by the lion sejant gardant on the seal of Sir HENRY PERCY, *ante* p. 641.

The use of banners held by the supporters used in Belgium has been already noticed, p. 641. Somewhat akin to the use of the banner was the custom of displaying the arms upon the large square sail of the mediæval ship by the Lords High Admirals. Instances of this are found not only in the pictorial illustrations which remain of battles, etc., but on the seals of these high personages. As an example we give on Plate XXX., fig. 4, the sail of the Earl of RUTLAND from his seal.

STANDARDS.—In and after the reign of EDWARD III.,

a large flag known as the Standard came into use, it varied in size according to the rank of the person using it, but does not appear to have been allowed to any who were not knights. The HARLEIAN MS., No. 2358, written about the time of HENRY VIII., gives the length of these standards; the king's eight or nine yards, a duke's seven, an earl's six, a baron's five, a banneret's four-and-a-half, and a knight's four yards long. The LANSDOWNE MS. 255, makes the standard of a Marquis six-and-a-half yards in length, and that of a viscount five-and-a-half.

These standards all contained in the nearly square compartment close to the staff, the red Cross of St. GEORGE on a silver field, the rest of the standard, which tapered gradually, was generally divided into two or four longitudinal stripes usually of the owner's livery colours. On these stripes were placed the various badges or devices, separated from each other by slanting slips containing the motto of the bearer. The standard was split a little way from the end, and the divided pieces were rounded into a semi-circular shape. Fig. 100, at the head of this chapter is the standard of HENRY PERCY, sixth Earl of NORTHUMBERLAND (1527-1537). It is divided into four horizontal bands, the upper being russet, the two central ones yellow, and the lowest tawny. The whole is powdered with silver crescents and "lockets," or manacles, and also contains the PERCY blue lion passant; a silver key crowned, the badge of POYNINGS; a blue bugle-horn unstringed garnished gold, that of BRYAN; and a falchion, hilted *or* and sheathed *sable*, for FITZPAYNE. (*Heraldry of the Percies*, p. 211.)

Several of the Royal standards of the same type have already been described in a previous chapter.

Besides these, *pennoncelles*, or "pencils," were also used in considerable numbers; they were of smaller size than the standard but somewhat similar in shape, though shorter and unsplit, they also contained the Cross of ST.

GEORGE, and usually only a single badge without motto bands (eleven of these as used by the PERCYS are engraved in the article already referred to, and one is represented on Plate XXXV., fig. 3).

The *ancient* guidon is said to have been a smaller standard with a swallow tail. It was charged with a cognizance or badge.

NATIONAL FLAGS.—Besides the banners and standards referred to above, which were peculiar to individuals, a separate flag was used as the National Emblem. This was often of large size, so large as to require to be transported upon a carriage. This usage seems to have been derived from the Saracens "in the midst of whom was a wagon drawn by eight oxen upon which was raised their red banner" (*see* TURPIN'S *Life of Charlemagne* in DUCANGE, *Glossarium ; sub voce* "*Carrocium*"). The battle fought between the English and Scotch in 1138 at Northallerton, was called *The Battle of the Standard* from a consecrated standard thus brought on the field in its carriage. The pole was surmounted by a pyx bearing the Sacred Host; and from the shaft floated the banners of ST. CUTHBERT, ST. WILFRED, ST. JOHN, and ST. PETER. At the Battle of Bouvines in 1214, the Imperial Standard was thus borne :—" Aquilam deauratam super draconem pendentem in pertica longa erecta in quadriga."

Frequent allusion is made by the Italian historians and poets to the Carroccio, on which the standard of the republics of Florence, Milan, or Pisa, etc., was borne, *e.g.*, TASSONI says,

" Ecco il carroccio uscir fuor della porta
Tutto coperto d'oro."
—*La Secchia Rapita.*

Two of the poles of the Carroccio of Florence, taken at the Battle of Monte-aperto in 1260, are still fastened to the columns of the cupola of the Cathedral of Siena.

The national banners borne in the English army at Caerlaverock in 1300 were; first, that of ST. GEORGE, given above; next, that known as the banner of ST. EDMUND: *Azure, three crowns or;* and lastly, that which has been more than once noticed as containing the arms of EDWARD THE CONFESSOR (these two are mentioned in the Wardrobe Accounts of 1299). To these later was added a banner containing the well-known device of the Trinity; and the four, with another of the Royal Arms, were those borne at Agincourt. (*See* paper "On the Banners used in the English Army."—*Retrospective Review*, 2nd series, i., p. 90.)

The banner of ST. GEORGE in combination with the banner of ST. ANDREW of Scotland formed the first flag known as the "*Union Jack*." The latter was *Azure, a saltire* (or cross of ST. ANDREW) *argent;* and on the union of the crowns the red cross of ST. GEORGE—fimbriated *argent*, both as a reminiscence of its original field, and in order to prevent a breach of the rule which forbade colour to be used on colour—was placed upon the Scottish flag. This Union Jack was declared to be the national ensign of Great Britain in 1606, and it continued so to be until the Union with Ireland in 1801. At that time the charge of the flag which was supposed to represent the last-named kingdom: *Argent, a saltire gules*, was added in such a way that the "Union Jack" now consists of a blue field on which are conjoined the silver saltire of ST. ANDREW, and the red saltire of ST. PATRICK (the latter fimbriated or bordered *argent* where it touches the *azure* field), and, over the whole, the red cross of ST. GEORGE with its white fimbriation.

The banner of ST. GEORGE, with the "Union" placed in the first canton is known as the "White Ensign," and is the flag of the Royal Navy, and of a few privileged yacht clubs. A blue flag with the "Union" in the upper corner is known as the "Blue Ensign," and is flown by the ships connected with the Naval Reserve, and by some yacht clubs. A like flag, but of red, is the "Red Ensign"—the flag of the British Mercantile Marine. These three flags were up to 1864 the distinguishing ensigns of the three squadrons of the British Navy, but these divisions no longer exist.

The celebrated ORIFLAMME of France is said to have originated in the *Chape de S. Martin*, which was the banner of the Abbey of Marmoutiers. The vulgar tradition was that this was part of the actual blue cloak of the Saint which he divided with the beggar of Amiens, as in the well-known story. But the word "*capa*" or "*capsa sancti Martini*" rather denoted the reliquary in which certain remains of the saint were enclosed. This was the *vexillum*, which the Counts of ANJOU had the right of taking to battle with them in the belief of thus obtaining the assistance of the saint in the conflict. A MS. of the Church of S. Martin, treating of the prerogatives of the Counts of ANJOU in respect of the abbey, says:—"Ipse habet vexillum beati Martini quoties vadet in bello." Dr REEVES has shown that "the Irish *vexilla* were boxes,"—reliquaries, or portable shrines — and, following in his steps, Dr JOSEPH ANDERSON, in the sixth of his Rhind Lectures for 1879, on *Scotland in Early Christian Times*, has given us excellent reasons for believing that the celebrated *vexillum* of the Brecbennoch, of which the custody was confirmed by WILLIAM THE LION in 1211-1214, to the newly founded monastery of Arbroath (Aberbrothock), was a similar reliquary containing relics of S. Columba, and is in all probability the casket now known as the Monymusk reliquary. Its identification was long delayed by the common, but entirely erroneous, idea that *vexillum* necessarily denoted a banner. There seems to have been a similar confusion of ideas in France ; and at any rate the unlearned transferred to the *Chape de S. Martin*, which had become a banner bearing his image, the same reverence which had formerly been paid to the *vexillum* in the forme of a *chasse,* or reliquary, which had once been the chief treasure of the church of S. Martin of Tours. The *vexillum* was borne by CLOVIS in 507 against ALARIC at the battle of Vouillé; and three centuries later was the *palladium* of CHARLEMAGNE at the battle of Narbonne.

It seems probable that the precious relic having thus come into the royal keeping was not restored to the abbey but preserved in the royal palace, while the abbey had to content itself with the embroidered coverings which had enclosed the shrine, and from which possibly the *oriflamme* as a standard was first manufactured. The Counts of ANJOU, who were governors of Touraine, claimed for themselves the office of hereditary standard bearers of *la Chape de S. Martin ;* but the Kings of FRANCE having fixed their residence at Paris their devotion to S. Martin was insensibly transferred to S. Denis, who thus became the patron saint of the realm ; and the *Chape de S. Martin* ceased to be the *oriflamme* of FRANCE. It is difficult to determine at what period the Church banner, or gonfanon, of the Abbey of S. Denis, became in its turn the chief of those under which the French kings fought. The Counts of the Vexin, as chief feudatories of the Abbey, bore by hereditary right the banner of S. Denis, but PHILIP I. appears to have transferred to the crown the rights of these turbulent vassals on the death of SIMON, last Count of the Vexin, without issue in 1088. It is not easy to say whether the celebrity of the *Enseigne de Saint Denis* is anterior to this reunion or not, but it was already known as the *oriflamme.* PHILIPPE MOUSKES in his rhyming chronicle of France, says :—

"Si a fait bailler esraument
L'oriflambe de Saint Denise."

As to its form and colour there is no doubt that it resembled the banners already described under the title *gonfanon*, having three points : and that it was composed of crimson silk with green fringe and tassels. "Oriflamme .... d'un vermeil samit à guise de gonfanon à trois queues, et avoit entour houppes de soye verte." (*Chronique de Flandre.*) It was not charged, and the common idea that it was *semé* of *fleurs-de-lis* is as entirely erroneous as the other one that it derived its name from golden flames similarly used. It was preserved in the Treasury of S. Denis, apart from the lance and cross beam, and in time of war was taken from the altar by the King himself after a solemn service. Its presence in the army denoted that of the sovereign also; the battle of Agincourt in 1415 is said to be the only instance in which the oriflamme was raised in the absence of the King ; in that case its bearer was made prisoner and died of his wounds, and the after history of the oriflamme is quite unknown. M. REY, in his *Histoire du Drapeau de la Monarchie Française*, to which I am indebted for a great part of the above notice, patriotically insists that as Père ANSELME declares LOUIS XI. to have received the oriflamme at S. Denis in 1465, it *must* have been preserved and restored. We may, however, be quite sure that if the old oriflamme were not forthcoming a substitute would be provided.

The royal flag of France was white,—"*le drapeau blanc.*" The origin of the Tricolor of France, with its vertical division into blue, white, and red, is found in the union of the *drapeau blanc* with the colours of the City of Paris (*v.* p. 369). In 1789, July 14, it was determined that a *garde civique* of 40,000 men, should be raised, to be called the Parisian militia ; that its colours should be those of the city, blue and red, to which on the proposal of M. DE LA FAYETTE the white from *le drapeau blanc* was added; together an ensign which, in LA FAYETTE'S own words, "devait faire le tour du monde" (*Memoires de La Fayette*, ii., p. 286). On the 17th, Louis XVI. returning to Paris, was presented by the *Maire* with a tri-coloured cockade, and placed it in his hat as having become, as BAILLY said, "the distinguishing symbol of Frenchmen." Under the Empire the staff of the flag as used in the army was surmounted by the Imperial Eagle.

The Imperial Standard was the tricolor, *semé* of golden bees, and bearing the Imperial Eagle crowned in the central compartment, *i.e.* on the white portion of the flag.

The IMPERIAL STANDARD OF GERMANY is of yellow silk fringed with gold. It bears the German single-headed eagle, displayed, on its breast an escucheon of the arms of PRUSSIA (*v.* p. 543) with the inescucheon of HOHENZOLLERN (*Quarterly argent and sable*). The main escucheon is surrounded by the collar of the ORDER OF THE BLACK EAGLE. The German Eagle is of *sable, beaked and membered gules*, and is surmounted by the Imperial Crown as described at p. 621.

PLATE LI.

THE ROYAL ARMS OF ENGLAND, ETC., I.

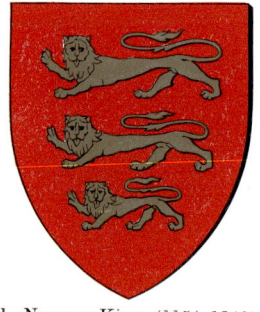

1. Norman Kings (1154–1340).

2. Plantagenets (1340–1405).

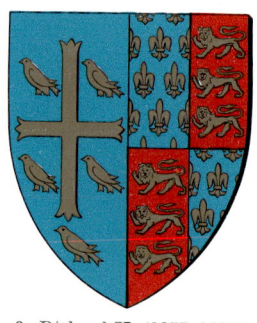

3. Richard II. (1377–1399).

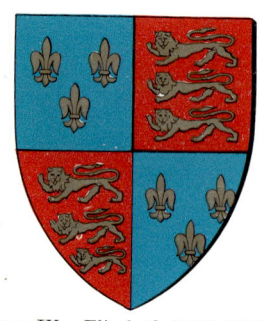

4. Henry IV.—Elizabeth (1405–1603).

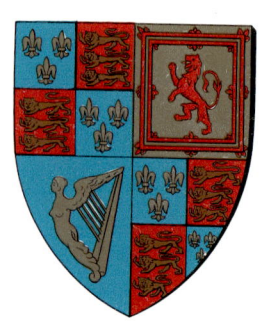

5. House of Stuart (1603–1688).

CHAPTER XXIII.

MISCELLANEOUS.

THIS concluding chapter contains some matters which, had our limits permitted it, would have been treated much more fully. They are :—
    I. The Royal Arms and Supporters of England.
    II. National Arms of the chief European Countries.
    III. Curious Partitions, and a few remarkable Coats.
    IV. *Armes Parlantes*, or Canting Coats.
    V. Conclusion.

I. ROYAL ARMS AND SUPPORTERS.—On Plates LI. and LII. are arranged the Royal arms of ENGLAND, and of the United Kingdom of GREAT BRITAIN and IRELAND.

The Norman kings who bore arms used only the present arms of ENGLAND (Plate LI., fig. 1). With these the PLANTAGENET kings after 1340 quartered the arms of FRANCE-ANCIENT in the first and fourth places (Plate LI., fig. 2). With this quartered coat RICHARD II. combined by impalement the mythical arms of EDWARD THE CONFESSOR, as in Plate LI., fig. 3. From 1405 to the close of the reign of ELIZABETH in 1603, the coat of the English sovereigns was: FRANCE-MODERN, quartering ENGLAND; as in Plate LI., fig. 4. (There are a few examples, as on the south porch of Gloucester Cathedral, in which ENGLAND has the precedence.)

The supporters used were as follows (the early ones are doubtful) :—
    EDWARD III. A golden lion and silver falcon (*Harl. MS.*, 1073, Brit. Mus.).

RICHARD II. Two white harts (?) (*Vincent's MS.*, Coll. Arm.).

HENRY IV. A golden lion, the white antelope of BOHUN (before his accession he used two swans holding ostrich feathers in beak); the antelope and swan.

HENRY V. The lion and antelope as above. (?)

HENRY VI. Two antelopes (of BOHUN); the lion and antelope; the lion and heraldic tiger.

EDWARD IV. The lion of ENGLAND, and black bull (of CLARE); two silver lions (of MARCH).

EDWARD V. The white lion and white hart.

RICHARD III. Two silver boars, armed *or*. The lion of ENGLAND, and a boar.

HENRY VII. The dragon (*gules*) of WALES. A silver greyhound (of BEAUFORT). The lion of ENGLAND, and the dragon of WALES. Two greyhounds *argent*.

HENRY VIII. The dragon and greyhound (as above). Two greyhounds. The lion and dragon. The antelope and stag (*Exchequer Seal*).

EDWARD VI. The lion and dragon. The lion and greyhound.

MARY. The lion and greyhound. The lion and dragon (*or*).

ELIZABETH (as her sister). The dragon and greyhound. On *Exchequer Seal*, the heraldic antelope and stag, gorged and chained. [The antelope appears like a goat on *Exchequer Seals* of JAMES II. and GEORGE I. (*Brit. Mus. Cat.*).]

On the accession of JAMES VI. of Scotland to the throne of England the arms became: *Quarterly* 1 and 4. FRANCE and ENGLAND quarterly. 2. SCOTLAND. 3. IRELAND. This coat was borne by all the STUART Sovereigns. (Plate LI., fig. 5.) WILLIAM of ORANGE, as an elected Sovereign, placed upon it *en surtout* his

PLATE LII.

THE ROYAL ARMS OF GREAT BRITAIN, ETC., II.

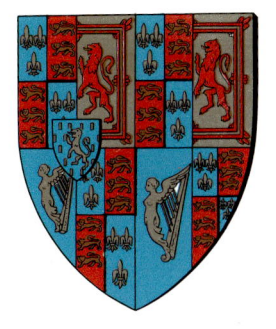

6. William III. and Mary II. (1689–1694).

7. William III. (1694–1702).

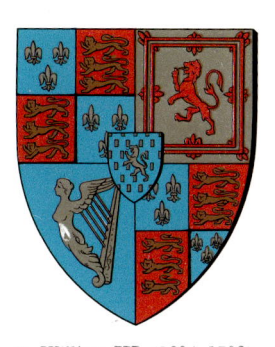

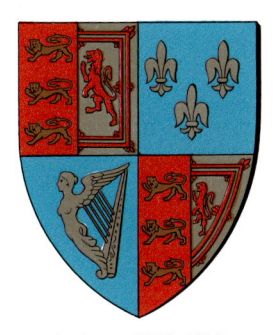

8. Anne (1702–1714).

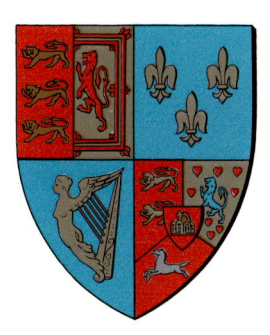

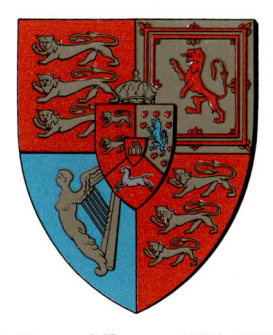

9. House of Hanover (1714–1801).

10. House of Hanover (1801–1837).

arms of NASSAU : *Azure, billetty and a lion rampant or.* (Plate LII., fig. 7.) The supporters were the lion of ENGLAND, and the unicorn of SCOTLAND. Instances of other supporters are to be met with. On the *Exchequer Seal* of CHARLES I. they are an antelope and a stag both ducally gorged and chained ; and on his seal used at the Session in S. Wales, the supporters are a dragon and heraldic antelope. On the *Privy Seal* of JAMES II., and on that for the Duchy of LANCASTER, the arms of the Duchy are supported by two greyhounds sejant addorsed, each holding an ostrich feather. On the *Seal of Common Pleas* of JAMES I., CHARLES II., and GEORGE I., the supporters are a griffin and a greyhound. ANNE used the lion and greyhound.

After the union with Scotland in 1707, the arms are :— *Quarterly*, 1 and 4. ENGLAND, impaling SCOTLAND ; 2. FRANCE-MODERN ; 3. IRELAND. (Plate LII., fig. 8.)

On the succession of GEORGE I. in 1714, his arms as Elector of HANNOVER were introduced into the Royal shield. These were :—*Tierced in pairle reversed ;* 1. BRUNSWICK : *Gules, two lions passant gardant in pale or.* 2. LUNEBURG : *Or, semé of hearts gules a lion rampant azure.* 3. (In point) WESTPHALIA : *Gules, a horse courant argent ;* and over all, for the electoral dignity, *Gules, the crown of* CHARLEMAGNE *or* (*v.* p. 617, fig. 97), and the Royal arms consequently were (Plate LII., fig. 9) *Quarterly*, 1. ENGLAND impaling SCOTLAND ; 2. FRANCE ; 3. IRELAND ; 4. *The Hannoverian quartered coat* (as above).

After the union with Ireland, in 1801, the arms of FRANCE ceased to be employed, and the Royal arms up to the death of WILLIAM IV., in 1837, were : *Quarterly*, 1 and 4. ENGLAND ; 2. SCOTLAND ; 3. IRELAND. *Over all the Hannoverian escucheon.* (Plate LII., fig. 10.)

On the accession of Queen VICTORIA, in 1837, the Hannoverian escucheon was removed, and the Royal arms assumed their present form.

The supporters since the time of JAMES I. are thus blazoned: *Dexter*, a lion rampant gardant *or*, crowned with the Imperial crown. *Sinister*, a unicorn *argent*, armed, unguled and maned *or*, gorged with an open crown of crosses *patée* and *fleurs-de-lis*, and chained of the last. These supporters are sometimes represented holding banners. On the Great Seal of JAMES I. the dexter banner is charged with a cross patonce, the sinister with the arms of EDWARD THE CONFESSOR. On later Great Seals the banners bear respectively the crosses of ST. GEORGE and ST. ANDREW (*see* also p. 598).

The Royal crest is, on the Imperial crown a lion statant gardant, also crowned with the Imperial crown.

The motto, *Dieu et mon droit*, said to have been assumed by EDWARD III., appears to have been first used by EDWARD IV. On the Great Seal of MARY I. the motto is *Temporis filia veritas ;* on that of ELIZABETH the motto is *Pulchrum pro patria pati ;* but that which seems to have been most in favour with her was *Semper eadem*, afterwards used by JAMES I. and by Queens ANNE and MARY II. JAMES I. is said to have used *Beati pacifici*. Under the Commonwealth the motto was *Pax quæritur bello*. WILLIAM III. sometimes used the NASSAU motto—*Je maintiendrai*.

The arms of Queens Consort were supported on the dexter side by the lion of ENGLAND; on the sinister by one of the supporters of their personal arms. It will be remembered that the Royal arms have always been borne within the Garter with its motto *Honi soit qui mal y pense* since the foundation of that Order by EDWARD III.

II. NATIONAL ARMS.—The Arms of the AUSTRIAN EMPIRE are given on Plate LIII., fig. 1. The double-headed eagle with golden beak and claws, holds in its right claw a golden sceptre and a drawn sword; in the left, the Imperial Orb. Each head is royally crowned. On the breast is the escucheon: *Tierced in pale:* 1.

NATIONAL ARMS.   PLATE LIII.

1. Arms of Austrian Empire.

2. Arms of Russian Empire.

HAPSBURG ; 2. AUSTRIA ; 3. LORRAINE. Around it are the Collar of the ORDER OF THE GOLDEN FLEECE ; and the Grand Cordon of the ORDER OF MARIA THERESA. On the wings and tail of the Imperial Eagle are eleven crowned escucheons :—1. HUNGARY (Ancient and Modern impaled) ; 2. ESCLAVONIA ; 3. AUSTRIA *above the Enns*, impaling AUSTRIA *below the Enns ;* 4. SALZBURG ; 5. STYRIA ; 6. TYROL ; 7. (at top of sinister wing) BOHEMIA ; 8. ILLYRIA ; 9. ESCLAVONIA ; 10. MORAVIA, impaling SILESIA ; 11. CARINTHIA, impaling CARNIOLA. (These are all blazoned on pages 494, 495.) The Imperial Crown is placed above the crowned heads of the double eagle.

When supporters are used they are :—Two griffons *Or*, the plumage and the breast and wings *sable*.

The Arms of the GERMAN EMPIRE are already described at page 543, and are shown on Plate LIV., fig. 1.

The Arms of RUSSIA (Plate LIII., fig. 2) are borne on the breast of the crowned Imperial double-headed eagle (with red beaks and claws) the right claw holds the Imperial sceptre, the left the Orb. The central shield contains the shield known as the Arms of MOSCOW : *Gules, the mounted effigy of St. George slaying the dragon all proper.* Around it hangs the collar and badge of the ORDER OF ST. ANDREW. On the dexter wing are four escucheons : 1. KAZAN : *Argent, a dragon sable winged gules crowned or ;* 2. POLAND (*v.* p. 254) ; 3. TAURIA, *Or, a double-headed eagle displayed sable* on its breast a shield : *Azure, thereon a cross triple-traversed, within a bordure or ;* 4. *Tierced in pairle*, KIEV, NOVGOROD, and VLADIMIR. On the sinister wing are :—1. ASTRAKAN : *Azure, a royal crown, surmounting a scimitar fessways proper ;* 2. SIBERIA : *Ermine, two martins* (or sables) *counter-rampant, supporting a royal crown ; behind them two arrows in saltire, and a bow in fess gules ;* 3. Quarterly : KABARDA, IBERIA, KARTALINIA, and ARMENIA; *enté en point of* CIRCASSIA, *over all* GEORGIA[1]; 4. FINLAND: *Gules, semé of roses argent, over all a lion rampant crowned or, brandishing a sword and holding in its sinister paw the scabbard proper.*

The Imperial Crown is placed above the crowned heads of the eagles.

BADEN: (*v.* p. 491) *Or, a bend gules.* Supporters, *two griffins regardant sable, crowned or.*

BAVARIA: (*v.* p. 525) Supporters, *two lions rampant regardant queue fourchée proper, crowned or.*

BELGIUM: *Sable, a lion rampant or.* Supporters, *two crowned lions rampant or, each holding a banner tierced in pale sable, or, and gules.* Motto, *L'Union fait la force.*

BULGARIA: *Gules, a lion rampant or.*

DENMARK: *Or, semé of hearts gules, three lions passant gardant in pale azure.* Supporters, *two savages with clubs, wreathed proper.* Motto, *Dominus mihi adjutor.* Generally the full shield is used: *Quarterly*, separated by the Cross of the DANNEBROG, *argent bordered gules* (*v.* p. 510); 1. DENMARK; 2. ICELAND (*v.* p. 271); 3. *Gules, a dragon crowned or*, VANDALIA; 4. *Or, two lions passant gardant in pale azure*, SLESVIG. Over all an escucheon, *Quarterly* 1. HOLSTEIN: *Gules, an escucheon per fess argent and of the field, between three demi-nettle leaves and as many passion nails in pairle of the second*; 2. STORMARN, *Gules, a swan argent royally gorged or*; 3. DITMARSCHEN, *Gules, a mounted knight proper*; 4. LAUENBURG, *Gules, a horse's head argent.* Sur le tout du tout OLDENBURG (*Or, two bars gules*), impaling DELMENHORST (*Azure, a cross patée alesée or*).

GREECE: *Azure, a Greek cross couped argent.* Supporters, *two savages* (of DENMARK).

[1] In the plate GEORGIA alone appears (this is often the case when the arms are depicted on a small scale). *Or, S. George proper, mounted on a horse sable, slaying a dragon of the third winged vert.*

NATIONAL ARMS.   PLATE LIV.

ARMS OF GERMAN EMPIRE.

ARMS OF UNITED STATES OF AMERICA.

HESSE (*v. ante*, p. 525). Supporters, *two lions queue fourchée or.*

ITALY: *Gules, a cross argent.*

LUXEMBURGH: *Barry of ten azure and argent over all a lion rampant gules crowned or.*

NETHERLANDS: *Azure, semé of billets, a lion rampant crowned or, holding in its dexter paw a naked sword, and in the sinister a bundle of arrows proper.* Supporters, *two lions crowned or.* Motto, *Je maintiendrai.*

PORTUGAL: *Argent, five escucheons in cross azure on each as many plates in saltire, all within a bordure gules thereon seven castles or.* Supporters, *two dragons proper holding banners of the Arms.*

ROUMANIA: *Quarterly* 1. *Azure, an eagle displayed holding a sceptre, sword, and cross, in dexter chief a sun or* (WALLACHIA). 2. *Gules, a bull's head caboshed, between its horns a star, and in sinister chief a crescent or* (MOLDAVIA). 3. *Gules, on an open crown a lion rampant crowned and holding a star or.* 4. *Azure, two dolphins affrontés, heads in base, tails in chief.* Over all HOHENZOLLERN: *Quarterly, Argent and sable.*

SAXONY (*v.* Plate XII.): Supporters, *two lions regardant, crowned proper.*

SPAIN: *Quarterly*, CASTILE and LEON, *enté en point of* GRENADA. Over all an escucheon of FRANCE-MODERN. Supporters are seldom used, but are *two golden lions holding banners of the Arms.*

SWEDEN AND NORWAY. The shield is divided into three parts by a golden pairle *patée-throughout;* 1. (in chief) SWEDEN, *Azure, three open crowns or.* 2. NORWAY, *Gules, a lion rampant crowned or, holding a long-handled Danish axe argent.* 3. GOTHLAND, *Azure, three bends-sinister wavy or, over all a lion rampant gules.* Over all the personal Arms of the King; VASA, *impaling* PONTÉCORVO:—1. VASA, *Tierced in bend azure, argent, and gules, over all a sheaf or.* 2. PONTÉCORVO,

Azure, in chief the eagle of the French Empire Or; in base a bridge of three arches towered, and passing over a river all argent.

SERVIA: *Gules, a cross argent between four fusils proper.*

MONACO: *Fusilly argent and gules.*

MONTENEGRO: *Gules, a double-headed eagle displayed argent crowned or, and holding sceptre and orb; on its breast an escucheon Azure, in base a mount vert, thereon a lion passant or.*

SWITZERLAND: *Gules, a cross couped argent.*

TURKEY: *Gules, a crescent decrescent, and an estoile within its horns argent.*

WÜRTTEMBERG: *Or, three stag's attires fessways in pale sable,* impaling *Or, three lions passant in pale sable, their right paws écorchés gules* (SWABIA). Supporters, *a lion of the arms crowned or, and a stag proper.*

III. CURIOUS PARTITIONS, ETC.— Foreign and especially German Heraldry contains many curious coats formed by partition lines unknown to British Armory. Of these some examples have been already given in Plates V., VI., VIII., and XXIX., but a few more are added in Plates LIII. and LIV., and I here append a French or a German blazon of these coats. These, it is hoped, will not only be interesting and instructive to a student, but may be made useful as exercises. It will tax all his powers to describe them succinctly in the terms of English blazon.

PLATE LV.

1. LANG VON LANGENAU: Von Silber und roth in vier Reyhen geweckt, oben mit einem Lincks angestückten güldenen Winckel.
2. ROSDORFF: Losangé d'argent et de gueules à une enchaussure senestre de gueules.

PLATE LV.

PARTITIONS, ETC.

1. Lang *v.* Langenau.
2. Rosdorff. 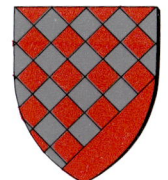
3. Eyfèlsberg. 
4. Stauffeneck. 
5. Marschalck. 
6. Polman. 
7. Goldegger. 
8. Schrot. 
9. Kirmreitter. 
10. Altorf. 
11. Helckner. 
12. Leuberstorf.

3. Eyfelsberg zum Weyr : Fascé de quatre pièces, de gueules, d'azur, d'argent, et d'or, un lion d'or brochant sur le tout.
4. Stauffeneck : De gueules, à trois fasces d'argent, le champ chaperonné du second.
5. Marschalck von Stuntsberg : In rothen schild einen nach der lincken Seiten gelegten silbernen Sparren (*chevron couché*).
6. Polman : D'or, au sautoir échiqueté de deux tires d'argent et de gueules, auquel manque le bras supérieur à dextre.
7. Goldegger : Ein Rechts-getheilter silberner Schild, hinten mit funf nach der Lincken aufsteigenden rothen Spitzen.
8. Schrot : De sable, à une fleur-de-lis d'or posée en bande, mouvante d'une enchaussure senestre du même émail.
9. Kirmreitter : De sable à une équerre d'or.
10. Altorf : Coupé en chef, faillé en taillant, recoupé, retaillé, et encore recoupé, de sable sur argent.
11. Helckner : Ein roth und silberne Schild mit zweyen offnen und ineinander gefügten Nachen in zwei Theil getheilt. (Taillé de deux côtés en forme de gueule de lion de gueules et d'argent.)
12. Leuberstorf : Mi-tranché, failli en taillant, et retranché vers senestre, d'argent sur gueules.

Plate LVI.

1. Orzon : D'Argent, à deux cantons de sable en chef, et une pointe du second émail mouvante de la base de l'écu.
2. Tappe : Durchgeschnitten :—Die lincke Helffte von einem ablangs durchgeschnitten doppelten schwarzen Adler, im güldnen Schild.

3. RUESDORFF : De sable au pal retrait en chef d'argent.
4. LÖWENSTEIN : Ein mit schwarz und gold viermal ablangs gegenstreiffter Schild, mit einem übergelegten schwartzen Quer-Streiff.
5. EGGENBERG : In silbernem felde drei schwarze Adler, welche mit den schnäbeln eine güldene Crone in der Vertieffung halten, und in Form eines Schächer-Creutzes schweben.
6. SQUARCIAFICHI : De gueules à la croix potencée, repotencée en bande à l'extrémité senestre du bout supérieur, en barre au bras dextre de la croix, et en bande et en barre aux deux côtés du pied de la croix, le tout d'or.
7. OBERNBURG : Einen silbernen und schwartz sechsmal lincks-gestreifften Schild, wovon der obere aufsteigende schwartze und untere absteigende silberne Streiff abgekürtst sind.
8. PILAWA : D'Azur, à une croix alésée de trois traverses d'argent, à laquelle manque le bras inférieur à dextre.
9. LINDECK : Im blauen Schild eine aus dem untern rechten Winckel aufsteigende, und unter sich gekrümmte güldene Spitze.
10. KAUFFUNGEN : Mi-tranché au dessus du canton dextre de la pointe, failli en remontant vers le canton dextre du chef, et retranché vers le flanc senestre de l'écu un peu au dessous du chef, d'or sur gueules.
11. HEYERLING ZU WINKHL : Coupe, au 1, d'Or à deux pointes accostées de sable ; au 2, d'Or à une pile de sable.
12. DOLENGA : D'Azur au fer de cheval versé d'argent, sommé d'une croix patée d'or, et accompagné entre ses branches d'une flèche tombante et empennée du deuxième émail.

PLATE LVI.

PARTITIONS, ETC.

1. Orzon.
2. Tappe. 
3. Ruesdorf. 
4. Löwenstein. 
5. Eggenberg. 
6. Squarciafichi. 
7. Obernburg. 
8. Pilawa. 
9. Lindeck. 
10. Kauffungen. 
11. Heyerling. 
12. Dolenga.

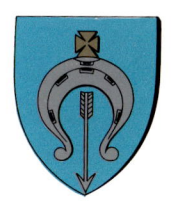

IV. ARMES PARLANTES.—Nothing is more certain than that by far the larger number of the arms assumed in early times were phonetic in character— *armes parlantes*—allusive to the name, title, or office of the bearer.

The notion at one time current in this country that such arms belonged to the degenerate days of heraldry, and were a sign of debasement, is thoroughly refuted by an examination of our own *Rolls of Arms*, and a reference to the *Wappenrolle von Zürich*, and other early foreign authorities. In them the canting element is preponderant; and proves to be so more and more as we investigate the changes which have taken place in the French and other languages within the last six centuries, and the varying names of animals and other charges in provincial dialects. Many armorial allusions which in early times were obvious are now entirely lost, or require much research for their discovery. Heraldry was in its beginnings intended more for use than for show; it was addressed as much to the unlearned as to the learned, since its primary object was to enable soldiers to readily recognise their leaders at a time when, as has been shown in the early chapters of this work, the defensive armour worn caused a difficulty in distinguishing them. The examples selected from the *Rolls of Arms*, etc., in illustration of the earlier portion of this book will show how very largely the bearings selected played upon the names of the wearers. Mr ELLIS's view was that in the case of many families it is impossible to say whether they took their names from their arms, or *vice versa;* an opinion in which he stands almost alone among critical investigators of the subject. It is in Scandinavia only —where the adoption of surnames under GUSTAVUS ADOLPHUS was long posterior to the use of armorial bearings—that we find any warrant for the idea that the name was derived from the bearings of the shield.

In Scandinavia a large number of family names were thus derived; not only where the name is that of an animal, but there are very many instances of such appellations as LEJONHUFVUD (lion's head), HJORTS-HORN (stag's horn), SPARRE (chevron), STIERNA, CRON-HJELM, GYLLENSKJOLD, GYLLENSPARRE, GYLLEN-STJERNA, OXENSTJERNA, SILFWERHJELM, etc., all derived from the bearings of the shield.

But in the southern kingdoms the reverse was the case, and the examples I have selected from the Armory of all the Continental nations abundantly prove this position. Some of the allusions may seem to us very far-fetched, but a pun was dear to the mediæval mind. "Tout ce qui, dans la nature ou dans les arts, pouvait donner naissance à une équivoque était mis à contribution." I have engraved on Plate XXXVII., fig. 3, from EYSENBACH, a seal which, though not armorial, is an excellent instance of the taste of the time. It is that of GUI DE MUNOIS, monk of St. Germain l'Auxerrois. The cowled ape in the sky, scratching its back with its hand, was a hieroglyphic in which all might read: *Singe-air-main-dos-serre*,—Saint Germain d'Auxerre!

I have now to bring to a conclusion a work which has been to me a labour of love; and which I trust may be found of some interest and value to the increasing number of students of Heraldry. It has been a matter of regret to me that I have had of necessity to leave out much valuable and interesting matter, and to deal somewhat superficially with subjects which I have ample materials for treating more fully and systematically. But, as it stands, the work embodies the collections of many years; and I trust that, apart from the absence of literary graces, to which it makes no pretension, its faults—of which no critic can be better aware than the writer—may be found rather those of omission than of commission. I have not, as my abundant references will show, been slow to acknowledge the sources of my information, and it would have been a valuable addition to the book if (as I had purposed) it had been possible to include in it a full catalogue of the multitude of works which have been put under contribution in the course of its compilation. I shall count myself no mean benefactor to my brethren if I increase their interest in a very important branch of archæology. To myself for many years it has afforded a great deal of that rest which is produced by a change of labour; it has given increased enjoyment to foreign travel, it has acted as an incentive to the study of history, and has led me to some knowledge of many out of the way but most interesting collateral subjects.

The value of heraldry is becoming more and more generally recognised, not only in respect of its poetic associations, and of its decorative capacities, but as a link between the present and the past. In the past it has been a faithful chronicler of the history, alike of Royal dynasties and of private families. It, in fact, constituted a thorough system for distinguishing not only family from family, but one branch of a family from another. Every change in the hereditary succession of a kingdom; every fresh accession of territory; every union of houses by marriage, occasioned a corresponding change in the coat of arms, so that it became a record whose nice distinctions asserted, briefly but clearly to those who understood its language, a number of facts regarding its owner.

And in the present, though the crested helm and the emblazoned shield have no longer all the significance which they once possessed when they were in actual use, they have still strong hereditary claims upon our recognition. Although it be the boast of our gentry, or lesser nobility (as well as of our greater nobility or Peers), that they receive into their ranks with open arms the eminent and the meritorious, whatever be their origin and lineage, the possession of *insignia gentilitia* is still the legal test of gentility, and one of the duties still delegated in our country by the Sovereign to the Kings of Arms is that of assigning appropriate bearings to those who have acquired a social importance that entitles them to take a place among the gentlemen of their country, and which may serve as a bond of union to their family and hand down their name and memory to their descendants.

Fig. 106.—Tabard, or Coat of Arms.

REFERENCE MATERIALS

ENGLISH GLOSSARY.

(N.B.—*The Reader is advised also to consult the Index.*)

A

ABASED—Applied to an Ordinary, or other charge, which occupies a lower position than usual in the shield.

ABATEMENTS—Certain marks of disgrace invented by the old heralds, but which naturally never came into use. MÉNÉTRIER justly calls them "*sottises Anglaises.*" The marks of illegitimacy are the only *abatements* in use (*see* Chapter XVII.).

ACCOSTED—Placed side by side. When used of animals the F. equivalent is *accosté;* but when of shields *accolé.*

ADDORSED (F. *adossé*)—Placed back to back.

AFFRONTÉ—A synonym for *gardant;* also *see Combatant.*

AILE, or AISLÉ—Winged.

AILETTES—Small square wings attached to the shoulders of knights in armour (*v.* Plate XXXIV., fig. 1).

ALANT—A mastiff with short ears.

ALLERION (F. *alérion*)—A young eagle without beak or feet (p. 258).

AMETHYST—The gem employed to designate the tincture *purpure.*

AMPHISBŒNA—A serpent having a head at each end of its body.

ANCRED, or ANCHORED (F. *ancré*)—Having extremities ending in figures resembling the flukes of an anchor (p. 158).

ANGENNE—A flower of six petals.

ANGLED (F. *anglé*)—Having figures in the angles.

ANNULET (F. *annelet, see* also *Vires*)—A plain ring; one of the modern marks of cadency, used for a fifth son (p. 444).

ANTELOPE (Heraldic)—A beast with nearly straight and tapering horns; it has a long lashed tail, and a goat's beard (*v.* p. 236).

APPAUMÉ—Describes the open hand showing the palm.

ARCHED—Curved, usually a synonym for *embowed* (but *see* Plate X., fig. 5).
ARGENT—Silver.
ARMED (F. *armé*)—The term applied to the horns, hoofs, beaks, and talons, of beasts or birds of prey when they differ from the rest of the body.
ARMOYÉ—Applied to *lambrequins*, *ailettes*, *mantlings*, and caparisons charged with armorial devices (*v.* pp. 611 and 615).
ARRACHÉ—A synonym for *erased*, which see.
ARRONDIE—Rounded.
ASPERSED (F. *semé*)—Sprinkled, or strewed.
ASSIS—Seated; a synonym for *sejant*.
ATTIRED (*cf.* F. *sommé*, or *ramé*)—Used, instead of *armed*, for the horns of deer, etc., when differing from the rest of the body.
ATTIRES—The horns of stags, etc. (F. *ramure*, a single horn *demi-ramure*).
AVELLANE—Applied to a cross whose arms resemble a filbert in its husk (*v. ante*, p. 162).
AYLETS—Cornish-choughs (*v.* p. 264).
AZURE (F. *azur*)—The colour *blue*, probably from *lapis lazuli*, is usually of a darker tint in British than in Foreign Armory.

B

BAILLONNÉ—Applied to a beast which holds a staff in its teeth.
BALLS (F. *boules* de . . .)—The colour must be specified.
BANDED (F. *bandé*, *lié*)—Encircled with a band, applied to garbs when tied of another colour (*v.* p. 342); (*see* also *Cintré*, and *Sanglé*).
BAR—A diminutive of the fess (*v.* p. 125).
BARBED—Said of flowers, showing a leaf between the petals.
BARNACLES—A twitch for compressing the nostrils of a horse (*v. Brey*).
BARRULET (F. *burelé*)—A diminutive of the bar (*v.* p. 128). *Cf.* the French Glossary, *Fasce en divise*.
BARRULY (F. *burelé*)—Covered with ten or more barrulets.
BARRY (F. *fascé*)—Covered with bars (*v.* p. 92). BARRY-PILY (p. 101).
BARRY-BENDY—Divided into lozenge-shaped pieces by horizontal and diagonal lines intersecting.
BARS-GEMELS (F. *jumelles*)—Barrulets borne in pairs.

Bar-wise—Placed in a horizontal direction.
Base—The lower part of the shield.
Basilisk—(*V.* p. 293).
Baton—(*See* Chapter on Illegitimacy).
Battlements (F. *creneaux*)—See *Embattled.*
Beacon (F. *fanal*)—A fire grate set on a pole against which a ladder leans. It is generally shown lighted, or *inflamed* (*v.* p. 352).
Beaked (F. *becqué*)—Having the beak of a different tincture from that of the body.
Belled—Said of cows (F. *clariné*), hawks (*grilleté*), or other creatures to which bells are attached.
Bend (F. *bande*)—One of the Ordinaries (*see* Chapter III., p. 129).
Bendlet—A diminutive of the bend (*v.* p. 131).
Bendwise (F. *penché*)—Said of mallets, helmets, etc.
Bendy (F. *bandé*)—Covered with bends (*v.* p. 94).
Bevily (F. *mortaisé*)—Dovetailed (*v.* p. 77), a partition line.
Bezant—A gold plate, or flat piece of gold without impression (*cf.* Figured and *v.* p. 189, and Plate XIX., fig. 2).
Bezanty, or Bezantée—*Semé*, or strewed, with bezants.
Bi-corporate—Having two bodies.
Billet (F. *billette*)—An oblong rectangular charge; a *Sub-Ordinary* (*v.* Chapter V., p. 186, Plate XIX., fig. 1).
Billetty (F. *billeté*)—*Semé*, or strewn, with billets (*v.* p. 112).
Bird-bolt—A short arrow with blunted head (*v.* p. 350).
Bladed—Having leaves differing in tincture from the rest of the plant.
Bordered (F. *bordé, liseré*)—Edged of a different tincture (*v.* p. 353).
Bordure (F. *bordure*)—A border applied to the shields; one of the *Sub-Ordinaries* (*see* Chapter V.).
Boterol—The metal end of a sheath or scabbard (*v.* p. 321).
Botonny (F. *treflé*)—Applied to crosses, crosslets, etc., whose arms end in a trefoil shape (*v.* p. 160, Plate XIV., fig. 11).
Bouget (F. *bouse*)—(*See Water-bouget, v.* p. 355).
Bourdon—A pilgrim's staff (*v.* p. 375).
Braced—Interlacing; usually applied to chevronels (*v.* p. 140 and Plate XIII., fig. 12).
Branched (F. *tigé*).
Bretessé (F. *brétessé*)—Having embattlements on both sides opposed to one another.
Breys (F. *broyes,* and *morailles*)—(*See Barnacles* above, and p. 357).

(679)

BRIGANTINE—A coat of mail.
BRISURE—A mark of cadency (*v.* Chapter XIV., etc.).
BROAD ARROW—The head of an arrow having two smooth barbs detached from the shaft (*v.* PHEON, from which it differs, *see* p. 350).
BROGUE, or SHAMBROGUE—A kind of shoe (*v.* p. 392).
BUDDING (F. *boutonné*).
BURGONET—A steel cap.

C

CABOSHED, or CABOSSED (F. *cabossé*)—Is the term applied to the head of an animal (*cf.* F. *massacre*) borne *affronté* and showing no part of the neck.
CABRÉ—A term applied to a horse saliant (*cf. Rampant*).
CADENCY, MARKS OF (F. *brisures*)—Figures introduced into the shield to distinguish the cadets of a family from its head, and from one another (*v.* Chapter XIV., p. 396).
CALTRAP (F. *chausse-trape*)—A ball of iron with projecting spikes (*v.* p. 352).
CALVARY-CROSS—A "long" cross, mounted on steps (*v.* p. 152).
CANTING-ARMS—(F. *armes parlantes*)—Are those which have a punning reference to the name of the bearer (*v.* p. 671).
CANTON—One of the SUB-ORDINARIES (*v.* p. 165).
CANTONED (F. *cantonné*)—Said of a cross placed between objects which occupy the corner spaces of the field.
CAPARISONED (F. *bardé, houssé*).
CARBUNCLE (F. *rais des carbuncles*)—(*V. Escarbuncle*).
CARTOUCHE—An oval shield (*v.* p. 56).
CAT-A-MOUNT—A wild cat (always *gardant*).
CATHARINE-WHEEL—The instrument of the martyrdom of Saint Catharine, a wheel having sharp curved teeth on the rim.
CENTAUR—A mythological animal having the bust and arms of a man conjoined with the body of a horse (*v.* p. 298).
CERCELÉE—(*V. Resercelée*). Applied to a cross denotes that its ends are curled on each side into circular figures (*v.* p. 160).
CHAMBER—A short piece of ordnance.
CHAMFRONT—The armour-plate for the head of a horse.
CHAMPAGNE—A narrow piece cut off the base of a shield (*v.* p. 311).
CHAMPAINE—NISBET'S term for *Urdy*.
CHAPEAU—A "cap of maintenance," *v. infra*.

CHAPLET (F. *chapelet*)—A garland of leaves and flowers.
CHARGE—A figure borne on the field in a coat of arms.
CHARGED (F. *chargé*)—Is said of a field, ordinary, or other bearing, upon which a charge is placed.
CHEQUY (F. *échiqueté, cf. équipollé*)—Divided into rectangular pieces, usually squares, of alternate tinctures (*v.* p. 99, Plate XVII., fig. 6).
CHESS-ROOK (F. *roc d'échiquier*)—The "castle" used in the game of chess (p. 387, *ante*).
CHEVAL-TRAP (F. *chausse-trape*)—(*See* Caltrap).
CHEVRON—One of the ORDINARIES, or principal charges of Armory (*vide* Chapter IV., p. 135).
CHEVRON, PER (F. *divisé en chevron*)—(*V.* pp. 77 and 88).
CHEVRONEL—A diminutive of the chevron (*v. ante*, p. 139).
CHEVRONNY (F. *chevronné*)—Divided into pieces shaped like a chevron.
CHIEF (F. *chef*)—One of the ORDINARIES, or principal pieces, in Heraldry (*v. ante*, Chapter IV., p. 116).
CHIMÆRA (F. *chimère*)—A mythological figure (*v.* p. 294).
CHOUGH (F. *choucas*)—(*See* Cornish chough).
CINQUE-FOIL (F. *Quintefeuille*)—A herb of five leaves (*v.* p. 322).
CIRCULAR-BORDURE—(*V.* p. 173).
CIVIC-CROWN—A wreath of oak leaves and acorns.
CLARICHORD, or CLARION—(*See* Chapter XIII., p. 386).
CLOSE (F. *clos*)—Said of a bird whose wings are not expanded.
CLOSET—A diminutive of the bar (*v.* p. 126).
COCKATRICE—(*See* Basilisk, p. 293).
COLLARED—1. (F. *colleté*) Having a collar round the neck; 2. (*accolé*) Said of the shield, when ornamented with the collar or ribbon of an Order of Knighthood.
COMBATANT (F. *affronté*)—Fighting; said of two lions or other beasts rampant face to face (*v.* p. 220 and Plate XXII., fig. 1).
COMPARTMENT—A term applied to the ground or other object on which the shield and its supporters rest, as distinct from the scroll or "gas bracket" ornament applied by herald-painters to this purpose in the days of debased heraldry.
COMPLEMENT, IN HER—A term applied to the full moon (*v.* F. LUNE, *pleine*).
COMPONÉ, COMPONY (F. *componé*)—Formed by a single row of rectangular pieces of alternating tinctures.

(681)

CONJOINED—United (*v.* Plate XX., fig. 5).
CONJOINED-IN-LURE—Is said of two wings united (F. *vol*), the tips being downwards (*v.* Plate XXV., fig. 5).
CONTOURNÉ—Is applied to animals which face the sinister side of the shield (*v.* p. 220).
CORDED—Said of a cross, or saltire, of which the parts are bound together by cords.
CORNISH CHOUGH (F. *choucas*)—A crow with red beak and legs.
COTICE—A diminutive of the bend (*v.* p. 131).
COTICED (F. *coticé, cotoyé; cf. accompagné*)—Placed between two cotices. This term is also applied to the fess, chevron, etc. Thus, a fess between two barrulets, or a chevron between two chevronels, is said to be coticed (Plates XII., fig. 10 ; and XIII., fig. 6).
COUCHANT (F. *couchant, gisant*)—Lying down, but with uplifted head.
COUCHÉ—A shield is said to be *couché* when it is suspended with the sinister angle uppermost, as in many ancient seals and armorials (*see* Plates XLIV., XLV., and XLVI.).
COUNTER-CHANGED (F. *de l'un à l'autre; de l'un en l'autre*)—Having an interchange of tinctures (*v.* Plate XIX., fig. 4).
COUNTER-COMPONY—Formed by a double row of small squares of alternating tinctures (*see* Plate XVII., fig. 5). *N.B.*—*See contre componé*, for which this is not always the equivalent.
COUNTER-EMBATTLED (F. *bretessé*)—Embattled on both sides, so that the battlement, or merlon, on the one side is opposed to the embrasure on the other.
COUNTER-EMBOWED—Bent in the reverse direction.
COUNTER-FLORY—When an Ordinary, an orle or tressure, is flory on both sides (*cf.* Plate XVII., figs. 10 and 12).
COUNTER-PASSANT—Proceeding in opposite directions (*v.* Plate XXII., fig. 2).
COUNTER-SALIANT—Leaping in opposite directions.
COUNTER-TRIPPANT, or COUNTER-TRIPPING—Is said of beasts of chase passing each other.
COUNTER-VAIR (F. *contre vair*)—Is an arrangement of *vair* by which the bells of the same colour are arranged base to base and point to point (*v.* Plate IV., fig. 8).
COUPED (F. *coupé*)—Cut clean off by a straight line, as distinct from *erased* in which the line is jagged.

(682)

COUPLE-CLOSE—The diminutive of a chevronel (*v.* p. 140).
COURANT (F. *courant*)—Running.
COWARD (F. *couard*)—A term applied to an animal which has its tail between its legs.
CRAMPETTE—(*See Boterol*).
CRAMPONS—Hooks used in building, usually borne singly abroad, in pairs in British Armory.
CRANCELIN—A wreath of peculiar shape (*v.* p. 131, and Plate XII., fig. 6).
CRENELLÉ—Embattled (*cf. Bretessé*).
CREST-CORONET—The little crown out of which some crests rise (*cf. Ducal Coronet, infra*).
CRESTED (F. *crêté*)—Is said when the crest or comb of a cock, cockatrice, etc., is of a different tincture to the rest of the body.
CRINED (F. *chevelé*, said of a human being ; *criné*, of an animal)— when the colour of the hair or mane is to be described.
CRONEL, or CORONEL (F. *roc*)—The blunted head of a lance used in tournaments (*cf.* CHESS-ROOK and p. 387).
CROSS (F. *croix*)—One of the ORDINARIES (*see* Chapter IV.).
CROSSLET (F. *croisette*)—A diminutive of the cross (*see* Chapter IV.).
CROWNED (F. *couronné, cf. diademé*, and distinguish).
CROZIER (F. *crosse*)—A pastoral staff, with a crook or curved head, used by Archbishops, Bishops, Abbots, and Abbesses. The later use, which would confine the word to the cross borne (not *by*, but) *before* an Archbishop as a sign of dignity, is inexact (*see Pastoral-Staff*).
CRUSSILY, or CRUSILY (F. *crusilé*)—*Semé* of small crosses, usually cross-crosslets ; if not, the shape of the crosslet requires to be named (*e.g.*, Crusily-fitchy, Plate XXVI., fig. 9).
CUBIT-ARM (F. *avant-bras*)—The hand and the arm cut off at the elbow.
CURVED (*v.* F. *anché, vouté, affaissé, courbé*, in *French Glossary*).

D

DANCETTÉ, or DANCETTY (F. *danché, cf. Vivré*)—The larger form of indentation, of which the points do not exceed three in number (*see* partition lines of the shield, Chapter III., pp. 75, 76).

DANSE, or DANCETTE—The term used in old writers for *a bar indented*, or *dancetty*.

DEBRUISED—Is the term employed when a bend, fess, or other Ordinary is placed across an animal or other charge.

DECKED—Ornamented.

DECRESCENT (F. *contourné*)—The term applied to a moon when in its last quarter, having its horns turned to the sinister side of the escucheon (*v.* p. 307).

DEFAMED (F. *diffamé*)—Said of an animal deprived of its tail.

DEGRADED—Said of a cross of which the arms end in steps.

DEGREES (F. *grices*)—Steps (of a cross-calvary, etc.).

DEJECTED—Thrown down.

DELVE—A square turf or clod of earth (*v.* p. 187).

DEMEMBERED, or DISMEMBERED (F. *démembré, cf. morné*)—Is said of an animal or charge, from which portions are severed, and removed slightly from the main body of the charge, but so as to preserve the general shape of the figure (*see* Arms of MAITLAND, Plate XXI., fig. 8).

DEMI—The half. In Armory the upper or foremost half is the one used (unless the reverse be specified), except in the case of coats united by dimidiation, when the division of the dimidiated charge is made by a perpendicular line. In this case a demi-eagle or demi-fleur-de-lis would be the dexter or sinister half of the bird or flower, applied to the line of partition.

DETRIMENT—A term applied to the full moon when borne of a sable, or red, colour as if eclipsed.

DEVELOPED—Displayed. Said of a flag or banner unfurled.

DEXTER—The right hand side.

DIAMOND—The jewel used to indicate *sable* in the fanciful way of blazoning by precious stones.

DIAPERED (F. *diapré*)—Covered with fretwork or floral enrichment of a colour slightly differing from the rest of the bearing (p. 114).

DIFFERENCED—(*See Brisures*, or Marks of CADENCY, Chapter XIV.)

DIMIDIATED—Divided into halves.

DISCLOSED—With wings expanded ; the equivalent for *displayed* in the case of birds which are domestic, or not birds of prey.

DISMEMBERED—(*See Demembered*).
DISPLAYED (F. *éployé*)—The expanded wings of a bird of prey are described by this term.
DISTILLING (F. *dégouttant*)—Letting fall drops (*cf.* Plate XVII., fig. 9).
DISTINCTION (F. *différence*)—(*See Brisure*).
DORMANT—Sleeping; it differs from *couchant*, as the head of the animal is not raised, but rests on its fore-paws.
DOUBLE QUATREFOIL—The brisure for a ninth son in the modern system of *Differences*.
DOUBLE QUEUÉ—Having two tails (*see Queue fourchée*).
DOUBLE TRESSURE (F. *double trécheur*)—One tressure within another (*v.* SUB-ORDINARIES, Chapter V.).
DOUBLED (F. *doublé*)—The term applied to mantles and lambrequins, lined of a different tincture, or with fur.
DOVETAIL (F. *mortaisé*)—One of the lines of partition (*vide* p. 77), seldom used as the bounding line of an Ordinary except in very modern coats. In the Arms of COWELL and of PICKFORD the chief is dovetailed. (NISBET calls this partition *patée*.) The Coat of LUCAS, Baronet, is: *Per bend argent and gules, a bend dovetailed between six annulets all counter-changed.*
DRAGON—An imaginary monster; in British Heraldry it is a quadruped (*see* Chapter X.).
DRAGON'S HEAD, and TAIL—Were the terms respectively applied to *tenné* (orange) and *sanguine* (murrey) in the mode of blazoning by the planets (*v. ante*, p. 65).
DUCAL CORONET—The term applied by custom, but quite erroneously, to the small coronet out of which many crests are represented as rising. *Crest-coronet*, first suggested by Mr BOUTELL, is a term as easily understood and much more correct (*v. ante* in the Chapter on EXTERNAL ORNAMENTS, *s.v.* CREST, p. 614).
DUCIPER—An old name for a cap of dignity.

E

EASTERN CROWN—A band of gold from which arise pointed rays (*v.* page 615, and Plate L., fig. 13).
ECLIPSED (F. *ombre de soleil*)—The sun is said to be eclipsed if represented of a red, or sable, tincture (*v.* p. 306).
EIGHTFOIL—The same as the double quatrefoil, *q.v.*

ELECTORAL CROWN—(*V.* Chapter XX., p. 623).

ELEVATED—(F. *levé*)—The term applied to wings raised above the head.

EMBATTLED—(F. *crenellé, brétessé, bastillé,* which see, pp. 75, 76)—Having battlements like the wall of a fortress; the pieces projecting upwards are called *merlons,* the intervening spaces *embrasures.*

EMBOWED (F. *courbé*)—Bent. When applied to arms and legs the elbow or knee is to the dexter.

EMBRASURE—(*Vide supra, Embattled*).

EMBRUED—Stained with blood (*cf.* F. *ensanglanté*).

EMERALD—The stone used to indicate the tincture *vert.*

ENALURON—A fanciful old term applied to a bordure charged with eight birds; now obsolete.

ENDORSE—A diminutive of the *Pale* (*v.* Chapter IV.).

ENDORSED—(*V. Addorsed*).

ENFIELD—An imaginary animal of very rare occurrence, having the head of a fox, maned; the fore-legs are those of an eagle, the body and hind-legs those of a greyhound, and the tail that of a lion; (the crest of O'KELLY).

ENFILED (F. *enfilé*)—The term applied to a sceptre, sword, or lance, which passes through a ring, wreath, or coronet; also to a weapon which pierces a head, heart, or portion of a body.

ENGOULÉ—(*See Glossary of French Terms*). Is applied to the extremities of Ordinaries, etc., which enter the mouth of an animal (Plate XII., fig. 5).

ENGRAILED (F. *engrêle, cf. échancré,* and distinguish)—A form of the partition line (*v. ante*, pp. 75, and 77).

ENHANCED (F. *haussé*)—The term applied when an Ordinary, or other charge, is raised above its usual position. (The converse of *abaissé.*)

ENSIGNED—Adorned.

ENTÉ—Grafted.

ENTÉ EN POINTE—(*V. ante,* Chapter IV.). A division of the shield (Plate XVI., p. 9).

ENTOYRÉ—An obsolete term for a bordure charged with eight inanimate charges.

ENURNEY—An old fanciful term, now obsolete, formerly applied to a bordure charged with eight animals.

ENVIRONED—Surrounded, enveloped.

EQUIPPED (F. *équipé*)—Fully armed and caparisoned ; rigged.
ERADICATED (F. *arraché*)—Torn up by the roots; applied to trees and plants (Plate XXIX., figs. 2 and 3).
ERASED (F. *arraché*)—Forcibly torn off, so as to leave the severed part jagged, as distinguished from *couped*.
ERECT (F. *haut*)—Set in a vertical position.
ERMINE, ERMINES, ERMINOIS—(*See* FURS, Chapter III., and Plate IV.).
ESCALLOP-SHELL (F. *coquille, cf. vannet*)—A common charge of blazon showing the outside, as distinguished from *Vannet*, which see.
ESCARBUNCLE—The term applied to a bearing which originated in the iron bands radiating from the centre of an ancient shield, and serving to strengthen it (*v. ante*, p. 45, and Plate I.). *Per saltire argent and gules, two gryphon's heads erased in fess, and as many escarbuncles in pale all counter-changed*, is the coat of LAMPSON, Baronet.
ESCUCHEON—Points of, are described at p. 59.
ESCUCHEON OF PRETENCE—The small shield borne upon the centre of his own achievement by a man who marries an heiress, or co-heiress, and containing her Arms (*v.* Chapter XV. on MARSHALLING, p. 486).
ESQUIRE (F. *giron*)—A term applied to a gyron (*see* Chapter V., and Arms of MORTIMER, Plate XVIII., fig. 5).
ESTOILE—A star ; its mode of delineation, as distinguished from a mullet, is discussed *ante*, p. 307.
EXPANDED (F. *éployé* of wings, *épanoui* of flowers, *ouvert* of fruits) —Opened or displayed.
EYES—Express tincture by F. *allumé; animé* for birds, etc.

F

FALSE (F. *faux, fausse*)—A term applied to things *voided* (*v.* p. 552).
FAN—In British Armory is a winnowing fan for blowing away chaff.
FAULCHION (F. *badelaire*)—A sword with a broad blade.
FEATHERED (F. *empenné*)—The term used to describe the fact that the wings of an arrow differ in tincture from the shaft. (A synonym of *Flighted*.)
FER-DE-FOURCHETTE — The term used (but rarely found) for crosses, etc., which end in a forked iron.

FER-DE MOLINE—The *mill-rind*, or iron in the centre of a millstone, through which the shaft passes.
FERMAIL—A buckle.
FESS—One of the *Honourable Ordinaries*, or principal charges, of Armory (*v. ante*, Chapter IV.).
FESS, PER (F. *coupé*)—(*V.* p. 79).
FESS POINT—The central point of the escucheon (*v.* p. 59).
FESSWAYS (F. *en abime* .... *en cœur*)—In the direction pertaining to a fess.
FETTERED—(*V. Spancelled*).
FETTER-LOCK—A shackle with a lock (*v.* p. 591).
FIELD (F. *champ*)—The surface of the shield upon which the charges are depicted.
FIGURED (F. *figuré*)—A term applied to the sun, crescents, coins, etc., when they contain a human face; and to bezants or plates stamped like a coin.
FILE (F. *lambel*)—An old term for the label.
FILLET—A diminutive of the chief. A fillet *en bordure* is a diminutive of the bordure.
FIMBRIATED (F. *bordé*)—Having a narrow bordure.
FIRE-BALL—A grenade.
FIRMÉ—A term applied to a *cross-patée-throughout*, *i.e.*, reaching the edges of the escucheon (*v.* p. 153).
FINNED (F. *lorré*, *cf. Fierté* in *French Glossary*).
FITCHÉ, or FITCHED (F. *fiché*)—Applied to crosses, etc., which have a point whereby they can be fixed in the ground.
FLANCHES, or FLAUNCHES (F. *flanqué en rond*)—Sub-Ordinaries (*see* Chapter V., p. 185). This bearing has been granted pretty frequently in recent times, *e.g.*, see the coats of BAGGE, LAWES, and SAVORY, Baronets.
FLANKS (F. *flancs*)—The sides of the escucheon.
FLASQUES—Diminutives of *Flaunches* (*v.* p. 185).
FLEURETTY, FLEURY (FLORY) (F. *fleur-de-lisé*)—A term applied to a surface *semé* of *fleurs-de-lis*.
FLEURY (F. *fleuré*, *fleurettée*)—Ornamented with *fleurs-de-lis* (*v. cross-fleury*, p. 117).
FLEXED—Bent or bowed (*cf. vouté*, *affaissé*).
FLIGHTED (F. *empenné*)—(*See Feathered*).
FLORY, FLORETTY—(*See Fleury*).
FLOTANT—Floating; said of banners, etc.
FLOWERED (F. *fleuri*)—Said of plants.
FOLIATED—Leaved.

FORMY, or FORMÉE—(*See Patty*, or *Patée*).
FOUNTAIN—Conventionally represented by a roundle *wavy argent and azure* (Plate XIX., fig. 5).
FOURCHÉ (F. *fourché, fourchetté*) — Forked (*see Cross-fourchée*, p. 161).
FRACTED (F. *brisé*, and *cf. failli*)—Broken.
FRAISE, or FRASER—A cinquefoil in Scotland (*v.* p. 323, Plate XXX.).
FRET (F. *frette*) — A *Sub-Ordinary* (*v.* Chapter V., p. 181) (*v. Treillis*, in *French Glossary*, and Plate XIX., fig. 11).
FRETTED (F. *fretté*)—Interlaced (*cf.* Plate XIX., fig. 11).
FRETTY—Covered with fretwork or interlacings (*v. Treillissé*).
FRUCTED (F. *fruité*, and *cf. Englanté*)—Bearing fruit.
FURCHY—(*See Fourché*).
FURNISHED (F. *équipé*)—Equipped, or provided with sails, ropes, etc.
FUSIL (F. *fusée*)—A narrow lozenge (a SUB-ORDINARY, *v.* pp. 116, 182).
FUSILLY (F. *fuselé*)—Covered with fusils (*v.* Chapter III., p. 100).
FYLFOT—The Gammadion, an ancient symbol composed of four Gammas (Γ) united in cross.

G

GALLEY (F. *navire* and *galère*)—A ship propelled by sails and oars (*see Lymphad*).
GAL-TRAPS (F. *chausse-trape*)—(*See Caltrap*).
GAMB (F. *membre de lion*)—The whole fore-leg of a beast, as distinct from a paw.
GARB (F. *gerbe*)—A wheat-sheaf (if composed of any other grain the fact must be specified) (*v.* p. 340).
GARDANT—Full-faced (*v. Lion*).
GARLAND—A wreath of flowers and leaves.
GARNISHED—Ornamented (*cf. liséré*).
GARTER—An old term for a diminutive of a bendlet.
GAUNTLET (F. *gantelet*)—A glove of steel plates.
GAZE, AT (F. *affronté*, or *gardant*)—Used of a beast of chase.
GEMELLS (BARS-GEMELS) (F. *jumelles*)—Small barrulets borne in pairs (*v. ante*, p. 128).
GEM-RING—An annulet set with a precious stone.
GENET—A small animal like a weasel.
GERATED—Differenced by small charges (*v.* p. 406).
GIMMEL-RING—Two annulets interlaced.

(689)

GIRON, or GYRON— A SUB-ORDINARY (*v.* p. 167).
GIRONNY, or GYRONNY (F. *gironné*)—A division of the field (*v. ante*, p. 83).
GLIDING (F. *ondoyante*)—Applied to reptiles or fishes moving forward with undulations of the body.
GOBONY, or GOBONÉ—(*See Compony*).
GOLPES—The obsolete name applied to roundles of *purpure* (*v.* p. 190, Chapter V.).
GONFANON—An ecclesiastical banner described at p. 372 (*see also Oriflamme*, Chapter XXII.).
GORE, or GUSSET—One of the old fanciful Abatements.
GORGE (F. *bouse*)—A water bouget, *q.v.*, p. 355.
GORGED (F. *colleté*)—Wearing a collar.
GORGES, or GURGES (F. *gouffre*)—A whirlpool represented conventionally (Plate XIX., fig. 6, and *see* p. 193).
GOUTTE, a drop.
GOUTTÉE, GUTTY, GUTTÉE—*Semé* with drops (*see* Chapter III.).
GRADED—Having steps (A CROSS-GRADED, F. *croix perronnée*).
GRADIENT—Applied to a tortoise walking.
GRAFTED—A term sometimes used for ENTÉ, *q.v.*
GREAVES—Armour for the legs.
GRICES—Steps ; (also the appellation of the young of the wild boar).
GRIECES (F. *marcassins, cf. sangiier*)—(*V. Grices*).
GRIFFON—A chimerical animal, the fore part that of an eagle, the hinder that of a lion ; the " male griffon " has no wings.
GRINGOLY, or GRINGOLÉE—The term applied to crosses, etc., whose extremities end in the heads of serpents (*v.* Plate XV., fig. 6).
GUARDANT—(*V. Gardant*).
GUIDON—A kind of banner with a semi-circular end.
GUIVRÉ—(*V. Gringoly*).
GULES (F. *gueules*)—The colour red.
GUN-STONE—The old name for a pellet or sable roundle (*v.* p. 190).
GURGES—(*V. s. Gorges*).
GUSSET (F. *gousset*)—A pairle without the top opening.
GUTTY, or GUTTÉE—*Semé* of drops.
GUZES—The obsolete name given by the old armorists to roundles of *sanguine* or blood colour (*v.* p. 190).
GYRON—A *Sub-Ordinary* (*v.* F. *Giron*).
GYRONNY (F. *gironné*)—(*See Gironny*). Very occasionally Ordinaries are *gyroned*—*e.g.*, Vair on a chevron gules three

bezants; *a chief gyronny Or and sable*, is the coat of HOZIER, Baronet.

H

HABERGEON—A coat of mail.
HABITED (F. *habillé*)—Clothed, vested.
HACKLE (F. *broie*)—A hemp-break.
HAIE—A hedge.
HALBERT—A pole-axe.
HAMES—Part of the equipment of a horse.
HANDLED (F. *futé*)—Said of spears, etc.
HARPY—A mythological creature (*v.* Chapter X.).
HART—A stag in its sixth year.
HARVEST-FLY—A kind of butterfly.
HATCHMENT—A term for Atchievement; the representation of the full armorial bearings of a deceased person, fixed upon his house, or in a church.
HAUBERK—A coat of chain-mail.
HAURIANT—Applied to fish in a perpendicular attitude, or pale-ways (*v.* p. 268).
HAUSSÉ—Said of a charge placed higher in the escucheon than its usual position.
HAWK'S BELLS and JESSES (bells, F. *grelots* or *grillets*)—The bells are globular in form and are affixed to the hawk's legs by small leather straps called jesses.
HAWK'S LURE—A decoy used by falconers to recover the hawk. It is composed of two wings conjoined with the tips downward (hence wings so represented are said to be *in lure*, or *conjoined in lure*); they have also a line attached, ending in a ring, by which the falconer waved the lure in the air.
HAY-FORK—A name for the *pall* or *pairle* in Scotland.
HEADS—Of men, beasts, etc., are drawn in profile unless the blazon specify that they are *affrontés*, or *gardant*.
HEMP-BRAKE (F. *broie*)—*See* Hackle or Heckle.
HILL, HILLOCK (F. *mont*)—The latter term is used if more than one appear in a coat, unless the charges are separated by an Ordinary.
HILTED (F. *garni*)—Is used to describe the tincture of the hilt of a sword if it differ from that of the blade.
HIND—The female stag, usually tripping.

HOODED (F. *chaperonné*)—Wearing a hood, applied both to human figures and to hawks.

HOOFED—Having the hoofs of a particular tincture (distinguish from *unguled* which applies only to beasts with cloven feet).

HOOPED (F. *cerclé*).

HORN, HUNTING (F. *cor de chasse, grelier, huchet;* See French Glossary).

HORN, OF A STAG (F. *demi-ramure*).

HORNED (F. *armé*)—Having horns of a special tincture but compare *attired*.

HUIT-FOIL—An eight foil (*q.v.*), or double quatre foil.

HUMMETTY—Couped at the ends, said of an Ordinary which does not touch the edge of the shield.

HURST (F. *bois, forêt*)—A clump of trees.

HURT—A roundle of an azure colour (*v.* p. 190).

HYDRA—A mythological monster (*v.* Chapter X., p. 296).

I

IBEX—An antelope with straight horns in British Armory, the horns project from the forehead and are serrated. In Foreign Armory the charge is drawn *au naturel*.

ICICLES—Are *gouttes* reversed.

IMBRUED—(*See Embrued;* F. *ensanglanté*).

IMPALED—Coats conjoined paleways, that is by the shield being divided into two parts by a perpendicular or palar line and having one coat placed on each side thereof, are said to be impaled (*see* Chapter on MARSHALLING).

IMPERIAL CROWN—Differs not from a Royal Crown in general. The crowns of specific empires however differ from one another (*see* Plate L., and Chapter XX. on CORONETS AND CROWNS).

IN LURE—(*See Lure*).

IN PRIDE (F. *rouant*)—Said of a peacock with expanded tail.

IN SPLENDOUR—Said of the sun irradiated (Plate XXVIII., fig. 1).

INCENSED—Is the same as *inflamed*. Said of animals which have flames issuing from mouth and ears.

INCRESCENT (F. *croissant-tourné*) — Said of a crescent whose horns are turned to the dexter side of the shield.

INDENTED (F. *danché, dentelé, endenté*)—A partition line with small indentations (*v.* p. 75).

INDORSED—(*V. Endorsed, cf.* F. *Adossé*).

INESCUCHEON—A small shield borne *en surtout*, usually containing the arms of an heiress or some feudal charge in British Heraldry, but used with different meanings in Foreign Armory (*see* Chapter on MARSHALLING).
INFLAMED (F. *ardent, flambant*)—(*See Incensed* and *Allumé*).
INK-MOLINE—(*V. Fer de Moline*)—A mill-rind.
INTERLACED (F. *entrelacé*)—Linked together. Said of annulets, the bows of keys, crescents, etc.
INVECKED, or INVECTED (F. *cannelé*)—One of the partition lines, the reverse of *engrailed* (*v.* pp. 75, 76) than which it is much less frequently employed.
INVERTED (F. *versé*)—Reversed.
IRRADIATED (F. *rayonné, cf. herissé*).
ISSUANT, or ISSUING (F. *issant*). (For the distinction between this and *naissant v. ante*, p. 221, and Plate XXII., figs. 4, 5.)

J

JELLOPED—Said of the comb of a cock or cockatrice. (Wattled.)
JESSANT—Shooting forth.
JESSANT DE LIS—Said of a leopard's face with a *fleur-de-lis* passing through the mouth (*v.* p. 225 and Plate XXII., fig. 11).
JESSED—Having straps or thongs.
JESSES—The straps of hawk's bells (*v.* p. 261).
JOWLOPPED—(*V. Jelloped*).
JUPITER—The planet signifying *azure* in the old blazon by heavenly bodies (*v.* p. 65).

K

KNOTTED—Of trees, F. *noueux*; of a cord, or a snake, *noué*.

L

LABEL (F. *lambel*)—A mark of cadency, also in occasional use as a charge (*v.* pp. 188 and 414).
LADDER (SCALING) (F. *échelle d'escalade*)—A ladder with hooks; occasionally of a single piece with short traverses (*v. ante*, p. 364).
LAMB, THE PASCHAL (F. *agneau pascal*, or *Agnus Dei*)—Is described *ante*, p. 236.
LAMBREQUIN—The mantling of a helm (*v.* p. 610).
LANGUED (F. *lampassé*)—The term used to denote that the tongue

of a beast or bird is of a different tincture from the rest of the charge, or from that usually employed. All birds and beasts are langued *gules* unless they are themselves of that tincture, in that case they are langued *azure*, unless the blazon distinctly express that the tongue is to be of some other tincture. If the general rule given above is followed there is no need to mention that the animal is langued at all.

LARMES—Gouttes of blue tincture, tears.

LATTICE—(*See Trellis*, p. 97).

LEASH (F. *longe*)—The line by which falcons are tied to the hand, or by which hounds are retained.

LEASHED (F. *longé*).

LEAVED (F. *feuillé, cf. pampré*).

LEG OF AN EAGLE (F. *main d'aigle*).

LEGGED (Membered) (F. *membré*)—Is said when the legs of a bird differ in tincture from the rest of the body.

LEOPARD—The lion passant-gardant in French Heraldry.

LEOPARD-LIONNÉ—(*See* French Glossary) a lion rampant-gardant.

LEOPARD'S FACE—Is used when the head is represented *affronté* or *gardant*, no part of the neck being visible.

LEOPARD'S HEAD—Is used either when the head is in profile, or *affronté* if part of the neck, either couped or erased, is visible.

LEVER—The name given to the bird (really the eagle, the evangelistic symbol of St. John) in the arms of the city of Liverpool; now drawn as a cormorant.

LIGHTED, or INFLAMED (F. *allumé*).

LINED—Attached to a line or cord; is also said of mantles, caps, etc.

"LINES OF PARTITION"—Are described in Chapter III.

LIONCEL—A young lion; sometimes used by pedantic heralds to denote the beasts when several (more than three) are borne in the same field.

LOCHABER-AXE—A pole-axe whose top has a hook.

LODGED (F. *couché*)—Is said of a hart, and other beasts of chase, when lying on the ground; distinguish from *couchant* applied to beasts of prey.

LOZENGE (F. *losange*) — One of the SUB-ORDINARIES (*v.* Chapter V.); also one of the forms of the escucheon (*v.* pp. 58, 631, and add that English examples of this use occur on early seals of FURNIVAL and PAYNELL).

LOZENGY (F. *losangé*)—Covered with lozenges (*v.* p. 100).

Lucy—An old name for the pike fish.

Lure—(*See Hawk's Lure*).

Lymphad (F. *galère*)—A galley propelled by oars but also having a mast and square sail (*v.* p. 367).

M

Maintenance, Cap of—A cap of dignity; usually of crimson or azure velvet "turned up" or lined with ermine or other fur, or stuff of a different tincture. Often used to support crests in mediæval times.

Manche, or Maunche (F. *manche-mal taillée*)—The old-fashioned sleeve of a lady's garment; its full form is *maunche mal taillée* (*v.* p. 376 and Plate XXXIII., fig. 1).

Maned—Having a mane of a different tincture from the rest of the body.

Mantel (Tierced in)—A division of the shield (*v.* Chapter III., p. 88).

Mantelé—(*See above*).

Manticora, or Man-tiger—A fabulous beast.

Mantle, Mantling—The cloak or robe placed around a shield of arms (*see* the Chapter on External Ornaments).

Mantlings (F. *lambrequins*)—The coverings of helmets cut into foliage shape.

Mars—In blazoning by planets represents *gules*.

Martlet (F. *merlette*)—A martin or swallow, without legs, but with the tufts of feathers at their junction with the body (*v. ante*, p. 266); the mark of cadency for the fourth son.

Mascle (F. *mâcle*)—A voided lozenge (*see* Chapter V., page 184).

Masculy (F. *maclé*)—Covered with mascles.

Masoned (F. *maçonné*)—Divided by lines, usually of sable, to represent the mortar between the stones of castles, bridges, and other buildings.

Maunche—(*V. Manche*).

Membered (F. *membré*)—The term used to describe the legs of a bird if of a different tincture from the rest of the body. Some armorial writers think the term includes the beak, which is certainly not the case in French Armory.

Mercury—The planet used to denote *purpure*.

Merlion (F. *merlette*)—A synonym for the martlet.

MERLONS — The pieces of an embattlement between the embrasures.

METALS—*Or* and *Argent*.

MILL-PICK—A tool with sharp head and short handle, used to dress mill-stones.

MILL-RIND—(*See Fer de Moline*, and *Anille*).

MINIVER—A fur ; a corruption of *menu-vair* (*v. ante*, p. 69).

MITRE—The cap of an abbot, bishop, or archbishop.

MOLINÉ, CROSS—A cross with arms, like the ends of a mill-rind. It resembles a cross *ancree*, but the hooks at the end of the arms not so acute. It is used among the modern marks of cadency as the difference for an eighth son.

MORION—A steel cap.

MORSE—A sea-lion.

MORT—A death's head, or skull.

MORTAR—A piece of ordnance ; a druggist's bowl.

MORTNÉ, or MORNÉ—A French term for a lion without tongue, teeth, or claws.

MOTTO — A short sentence, accompanying armorial bearings, usually borne on a separate listel or ribbon, sometimes in the coat itself (*v.* p. 395, and Plate XXXIII., fig. 12).

MOUND (*monde*)—An orb or globe of sovereignty, usually ensigned with a cross.

MOUNT—A hill in base of the shield. In Foreign Heraldry is often drawn conventionally with three *coupeaux* or domes (*cf.* Plate XXVIII., figs. 8, 9).

MOUNTED—Applied to a horse bearing a rider.

MOUNTING—Rising ; (F. *montant*, of a crescent).

MOURNÉ—Blunted (*morné*), applied to spears.

MULLET—A star usually of five straight points ; if of more the fact must be specified. It is taken for the rowel of a spur, and is then pierced. (On the distinction between *mullets* and *estoiles*, *v. ante*, p. 307.)

MURAL-CROWN—A coronet of gold, with battlements along its upper edge (Plate L., fig. 16).

MURREY—The colour *Sanguine*.

MUSCHETOURS (F. *mouchetures*)—The tail of the ermine without the three hairy spots usually drawn at its top.

MUSIMON—A fabulous beast, ram and goat combined.

MUSION—A mouser, a domestic cat (*v. ante*, p. 97).

MUZZLED (F. *emmuselé*)—Applied to bears and other beasts which have the mouth tied with bands.

N

NAIANT (F. *nageant*)—Swimming ; applied to fish borne fesseways, or horizontally (distinguish from *hauriant*).

NAILED (F. *cloué*)—(*V. Treillis*, and p. 97).

NAISSANT—Rising out of the middle of a fess or other Ordinary. The distinction between this term and *issuant* is explained *ante*, p. 221.

NARCISSUS—A sex-foil.

NAVAL CROWN—A coronet of gold, ornamented on its upper edge with alternate sterns and sails of ships (*see* Plate L., fig. 15, and pp. 615 and 646).

NEBULÉE, or NEBULY (F. *nebulé*)—A line of partition (*v. ante*, pp. 75, 76). This line is infrequent in ancient coats either as a partition line, or as the bounding line of an Ordinary ; but in modern times it has been pretty frequently employed as a difference, and in some cases not inappropriately, to indicate a possible but doubtful descent from a family bearing arms.

NERVED (F. *nervé*)—Said of the leaves of trees on which the fibres are drawn of a different tincture from the rest of the leaf.

NILLÉ—Formed by slender traces or narrow lines.

NOMBRIL—One of the points of the escucheon (*v. ante*, p. 59).

NOWED (F. *noué*)—Knotted, also said of the tails of reptiles.

NUAGÉ—(*See Nebulée*).

O

OGRESS—An old name for a gun-stone, pellet, or roundle of *sable* (*v.* p. 190).

OMBRÉ—Shaded.

ONDY, or ONDÉE (*Undy, undée*)—Wavy (*v.* p. 75).

OPINICUS—A fabulous animal of rare occurrence, resembling a gryphon winged, and with a lion's legs, and short tail.

OPPRESSED—(*See Debruised*).

OR—The metal gold.

ORB (F. *monde*)—(*See Mound*).

ORDINARIES—Certain heraldic charges of most frequent occurrence (*see* Chapter IV.).

ORDINARIES, SUB- —Heraldic charges also of frequent use, but not so important as the preceding (*see* Chapter V.).

(697)

OREILLER—A cushion, or pillow (*v. ante*, p. 377).
ORGAN-REST — A "clarion" or rest (*v. ante*, p. 386, and Plate XXXIII., fig. 11).
ORLE—A narrow border within the shield but removed from its edge ; one of the SUB-ORDINARIES, Chapter V., p. 175.
ORLE, IN—Charges arranged in a circular form, or following the outline of the shield.
ORLÉ—An old term for *bordered*.
OVER-ALL—The term used when a charge or an Ordinary or an escucheon is placed upon others. The French equivalent is *en surtout* (*v.* pp. 483, etc.).
OVERT (F. *ouvert*)—Open ; applied to gates, and to the wings of birds expanding for flight.
OWL (F. *hibou, cf. Oiseau-duc*)—This bird is always drawn full-faced.

P

PALE—One of the Ordinaries (*see* Chapter IV.).
PALISADO, CROWN, or VALLARY—A coronet of gold ornamented on the upper edge of the rim with golden palisades (*v.* Plate L., fig. 14).
PALL—(1.) An Archiepiscopal vestment of white wool, shaped like the letter Y, and bearing five crosses *patées fitchées sable* (originally the pins fastening it to the chasuble). (2.) One of the Ordinaries (*v.* pp. 150, 375 ; Plate XVI.).
PALLET—A diminutive of the *Pale*.
PALMER'S STAFF (F. *bourdon*) — A pilgrim's walking-stick (*v.* p. 375).
PALY—Divided into perpendicular divisions like pales.
PALY-BENDY—Divided into lozenge-shaped pieces by lines paleways and bendways (*v.* p. 100).
PANTHER (F. *panthière*)—In heraldry is drawn conventionally, and with fire issuing from mouth and ears (*v.* p. 226).
PAPILONNÉ—A form of *vair* (*v.* pp. 71-73 and Plate VIII., fig. 6), covered with scales like butterfly's wings.
PARTITION LINES (*V.* p. 77).
PARTY (per *bend, pale, fess*, etc.)—Are the phrases used to denote that the field or charge is divided by a line drawn in the direction of the Ordinary named.
PASCHAL LAMB (F. *agneau-pascal; Agnus Dei*)—(Is described at p. 236).

PASSANT—The heraldic term for a beast walking and looking straight before it (of the lion, F. *lion leopardé*).

PASSANT-COUNTER-PASSANT (F. *passant-contre-passant*)—Is said of two or more animals walking alternately in opposite directions—the first to the dexter, the second to the sinister, the third as the first, etc. (*v.* Plate XXII., fig. 2).

PASSANT-GARDANT—Denotes that the beast is walking forward but that its head is *affronté*, or full-faced (*cf. lion*).

PASSANT-REGARDANT—Walking forward but with the head looking backward (Plate XXI., fig. 6.)

PASSANT-REPASSANT—The same as the preceding.

PASSION CROSS—A name for the *long* cross (*see* fig. 47, p. 164). It differs from the Calvary Cross in not having steps.

PASSION NAIL (F. *clous de la passion*)—A long spike with a quadrangular head. The Ordinary known as the Pile is sometimes, but erroneously, called by this name.

PATONCE—A floriated form of the cross (*see* p. 157, and fig. 56, p. 164).

PATRIARCHAL CROSS—(*See* p. 152 and fig. 50, p. 164).

PATTY, PATÉE (FORMY, FORMÉE)—A form of the cross, each arm expanding from the centre and terminated by a straight line (*v.* p. 154).

PATTY-THROUGHOUT—Means that the bearing is carried right out to the edge of the shield (Plate XIV., fig. 5).

PAVILION—A tent. It is also the name given to the canopy under which the arms of sovereigns are sometimes represented (*v.* Chapter XIX., p. 615).

PAW (F. *patte*)—The foot of an animal, couped, or erased at the first joint; distinguish from *Gamb*.

PEACOCK (F. *paon*)—Is drawn passant unless it is blazoned a

PEACOCK IN ITS PRIDE (F. *paon rouant*)—It is then drawn with tail expanded in a circle.

PEAN—A form of ermine, a fur with a sable ground and golden spots.

PEARL—The precious gem used to denote silver or white.

PEARLED (F. *grêlé*)—Adorned with pearls.

PEEL (F. *pelle*)—A baker's instrument.

PEGASUS—The winged horse of mythology (*v. ante*, Chapter X., p. 298).

PELICAN—In Armory is drawn conventionally; usually with

expanded wings, with neck embowed vulning its breast whence drops of blood distil for the nourishment of her young ones which are placed beneath her in the nest; she is then said to be a

PELICAN IN HER PIETY—(*See* above).
PELLET—A *sable* roundle (see OGRESS, GUNSTONE, and p. 190).
PENDENT—Hanging down.
PENON, or PENNON—A small oblong flag.
PENONCELLE, or PENCIL—A diminutive of the pennon.
PENNY-YARD-PENNY—A silver penny.
PER—Through, or by means of (*see* PARTY, above).
PERCLOSE—The half of a buckled garter.
PERFORATE (F. *percé, cf. ajouré*)—Pierced.
PETRONEL—An early form of the pistol.
PHEON—The broad head of a dart or javelin (*see* p. 350). In English Armory it is borne with the point towards the base, in French coats the reverse is usually the case (*v.* Plate XXXI., fig. 7).
PHŒNIX—A mythological bird represented like an eagle in the midst of flames.
PIERCED (F. *percé, ajouré*)—Is the term when a cross, mullet, or other charge has a perforation through which the field is visible.

The form of the piercing should be expressed except in the case of mullets where it is always circular (*v.* p. 307).

PILE—One of the ORDINARIES (*see* Chapter IV. and Plate XVI.).
PILGRIM'S SCRIP—A wallet or bag (*v.* p. 375).
PILGRIM'S STAVES—Bourdons (p. 375).
PLATE—A flat roundle of silver (*v.* p. 189).
PLATY, or PLATÉE—*Semé* of plates.
PLAYING TABLES—A backgammon-board.
PLOYÉ—Curved, or bent (*v.* p. 137).
POINT, IN—Is said when piles, swords, etc., are arranged in the form of a pile that is approaching each other in the base of the shield.
POINTED (F. *aiguisé; cf. Fiché*).
POINTS—The pendants of the label.
POINTS OF THE ESCUCHEON—(*See* p. 59, figs. 15 and 16).
POMEIS—Green spherical roundles resembling apples (p. 190).
POMELLED—Describes the knob, or pomel, at the end of a sword hilt.

OMMELLY, or POMMETTY (F. *pommetté*)—Is said of a cross whose arms end in balls.

POPINJAY (F. *papegaye*)—An old name for a parrot.

PORTCULLIS (F. *herse sarasine*)—A strong grating let down to close the passage through a castle gate; it usually has spikes in its base, and chains attached to its upper beam (*v.* p. 365).

POSÉ—The same position as *statant*.

POTENT—An old name for a crutch. The name given to a fur composed of crutch-like or T-shaped pieces (really only a form of vair, *vide* pp. 70, 71, and Plate IV., figs. 11 and 12). It is sometimes termed

POTENT-COUNTER-POTENT—(*V.* p. 71).

POTENT, CROSS—(*See* page 156).

POTENTÉ, or POTENCY—A partition or dividing line of the field seldom used (*v.* p. 177).

POWDERED—The old phrase for *semé*.

PRETENCE, ESCUCHEON of (F. *écusson sur le tout*)—(*See* Escucheon, p. 486).

PRIDE, IN (F. *rouant*)—*See Peacock*, also applied to a Turkey cock with tail expanded.

PROPER—Borne of its natural colours (F. *au naturel;* of flesh, *carnation, v.* p. 102).

PURFLED—Bordered (*bordé*).

PURPURE—The heraldic name of the colour purple.

PYOT—A magpie.

Q

QUADRATE—In the form of a square. When a cross-potent has a square projection in the centre it is said to be a *cross-potent-quadrate*, as in the arms of LICHFIELD (Plate XIV., fig. 7).

QUARTER (F. *franc-quartier*)—A SUB-ORDINARY (*v.* Chapter V., p. 166).

QUARTERED (F. *écartelé*) — Divided into quarters or quarterings.

QUARTERINGS, or QUARTERS (F. *écartelures*)—Different coats, not necessarily only four in number, combined in one escucheon to denote descent, etc. (*see* Chapter XV. on MARSHALLING).

QUARTERLY (F. *écartelé*)—The division of the shield by a perpendicular and a horizontal line into four nearly equal parts called *quarters*.

QUARTER-PIERCED—(*V.* Plate XIV., fig. 3).

QUATREFOIL—A herb with four leaves.

QUEUE—The tail of a beast.

QUEUE FOURCHÉE—Having a double tail (Plate XXI., fig. 9).

QUISE, À LA (for *à la cuisse*)—Said of the leg of a bird erased at the thigh.

R

RADIANT (F. *rayonné*)—Shining with rays.

RAGULED, or RAGULY (F. *ragulé, cf. Ebranché* and *Ecoté*)—Like the stem of a tree from which the branches have been lopped. It is also, but very infrequently, used as a line of partition, and is drawn with regular projections, as in p. 75, fig. 24. Ordinaries are not often formed by this line, except the cross and the saltire. But exceptionally the coat of KNOTSHULL is, *Azure gutty d'eau, a chevron raguly between three crescents argent*. In a few modern grants the fess is *raguly; e.g.*, JESSEL, Baronet, bears : *Azure, a fess raguly ermine, between three eagle's heads erased argent; in the centre chief point a torch inflamed paleways proper*. There is a modern use of the *raguly* line as a partition in the coat of Sir FREDERICK LEIGHTON, Baronet, P.R.A., which is : *Quarterly, per fess raguly or and gules, in the second and third quarters a wyvern of the first*.

RAINBOW—Conventional (*v.* Plate XIX., fig. 7).

RAMPANT—Standing upright on the hind legs (*cf.* F. *acculé*, of a rearing horse). In Foreign Heraldry this is the normal position of the lion, and does not need to be expressed. *D'Azur, au lion d'or* is *Azure, a lion rampant or*. A bull rampant is said to be *furieux;* a horse, *effaré*, or *cabré* (*cf.* F. *Grimpant*, applied to a stag).

RAMPANT-GARDANT—Standing up on the hind-legs, but with the face *affrontée* (of the lion F. *leopard-lionné*) (*v.* Plate XXI.).

RAMPANT-REGARDANT—Standing up upon the hind-legs, but with the head looking backwards (*v.* Plate XXI.).

RAMPANT-SEJANT—Sitting in profile, but pawing the air.

Ravissant (*see French Glossary*)—Is the term applied to a beast of prey carrying off an animal in its jaws.

Rayonnant (F. *rayonné*)—Adorned with beams of light (*v.* Plate X., fig. 8).

Rays—Of the sun, in number are sixteen.

Rebated (*cf.* F. *en retrait*)—Having a portion of the end removed.

Recercelée—Having the ends curled back in circular form (applied to the cross, *v.* p. 160).

Reflected, or Reflexed—Bent back; usually said of the line or chain attached to the collar of an animal, and bent over the back of it.

Regardant—Looking backward (*v.* Plate XXI., fig. 3).

Reindeer—In Heraldry, is a stag with two sets of attires.

Rere-mouse—A bat.

Rest (F. *claricorde*)—(*See Clarion*).

Retorted—Bent, or twisted back.

Retranché—(*V. French Glossary*).

Riband—A diminutive of the bendlet.

Rigged (F. *equippé, habillé*).

Rising (F. *essorant*)—Preparing for flight; said of birds only (*v.* p. XXV., fig. 7).

Rompu—Fracted or broken (*v.* p. 139).

Rose—In modern cadency is the difference used by the seventh son (*see* p. 444).

Rounded—(F. *arrondi*).

Roundles—Sub-Ordinaries (*see* Chapter V., p. 189).

Rousant—Said of swans with wings endorsed and preparing for flight.

Ruby—The gem used to denote *gules* in the system of blazoning by precious stones.

Rustre (F. *ruste*)—A lozenge with a circular piercing (*v.* p. 185).

S

Sable—The tincture black.

Sagittary—A centaur, armed with bow and arrow (*v.* p. 299).

Saliant (F. *cabré*, or *effaré*, *cf. Rampant*)—Leaping; of a horse on its haunches.

Saltire (F. *sautoir*)—The Ordinary shaped like an X.

Saltireways (F. *en sautoir*)—Arranged in the form of a saltire.

Saltorels (F. *flanchis*, Spanish *aspas*)—Small saltires

Sans-nombre—Synonym for *Semé*.

SAPPHIRE—The precious stone used for *azure* in the system of blazoning by gems.
SARACEN'S HEAD—The head of a Moor, usually borne wreathed of two colours. (Plate XX., fig. 4.)
SARCELLÉ (*Recercelée*)—(*V.* p. 160).
SARDONYX—The gem representing *Sanguine* in the blazon of arms by gems.
SATYR—A mythological figure, half man, half goat, horned.
SCALED (F. *écaillé*).
SCALLOP (F. *coquille, vannet*)—(*V. Escallop*).
SCARPE—A diminutive of the bend-sinister, very seldom used.
SCINTILLANT (F. *étincellant*)—Sparkling, or emitting sparks.
SCRIP—A pilgrim's purse.
SCROLL—A ribbon charged with a motto (*v. Escroll*).
SCRUTTLE—A winnowing fan.
SEA-DOG (F. *chien-de-mer*)—A seal, drawn conventionally with a beaver's tail, a finned crest along the whole back, with web feet and a scaly body and legs (*v.* p. 300).
SEA-HORSE (F. *cheval-mariné*)—A monstrous animal; the head and forebody of a horse, with webbed feet joined to a fish-like tail.
SEA-LION (F. *lion-mariné*)—As the preceding, with the substitution of the head and mane of a lion.
SEEDED—Applied to roses, indicating the colour of the seed-vessels.
SEGREANT—Applied to wyverns and gryphons when represented rampant with endorsed or expanded wings (*v.* Plate XXVII., fig. 5).
SEJANT (F. *assis, accroupi*)—Sitting.
SEJANT-ADDORSED—Said of two beasts sitting back to back.
SEMÉ—Strewn, or powdered regularly, with small charges (*v.* Plate VIII., figs. 8, 9, 10, and p. 112).
SENGREEN—A house-leek.
SERAPH (F. *séraphin*)—A child's head between three pairs of wings, the two uppermost and the two lowest crossed.
SHACK-BOLT (F. *ceps*)—A fetter.
SHAFTED—Handled; said of a spear or pike.
SHAKE-FORK—A *pall*, or *pairle*, with chevron-pointed ends.
SHAMBROUGHS—A kind of slipper.
SHEEP—(Grazing, F. *brebis;* passant, F. *mouton*).
SHIVERED (F. *éclaté*)—Broken irregularly.
SINISTER—The left-hand side. (BEND-SINISTER, pp. 133, 582.)

SINOPLE—The French term for *vert*, or green.
SIREN—A mermaid.
SKENE—A Scottish knife.
SLASHED—Ornamented with slashings; apertures cut in a vestment to allow the lining or under garment to be seen.
SLIPPED—Having a slip or stalk torn off from the stem; applied to leaves and flowers. (Plate XXX., figs. 4, 8, 10, 11.)
SPANCELLED—Is said of a horse whose fore and hind legs are hobbled together.
SPHYNX—A mythological creature, described under MONSTERS (Chapter X., p. 295).
SPLENDOUR, IN—A term applied to the sun irradiated and having a human face. (Plate XXVIII., fig. 1.)
SPOTTED (F. *moucheté;* of insects, *miraillé, bigarré, marqué*).
SPRINGING — Equivalent of rampant for stags and smaller beasts.
STAFF—(Of a bishop F. *crosse;* of a pilgrim F. *bourdon*).
STANDARD—(*See* Chapter XXII.).
STAPLE—An iron fastening.
STAR—(*See Mullet*, and *Estoile*, and Plate XXVIII., figs. 5, 6, 7.)
STARVED (F. *effeuillé*)—Denuded of leaves.
STATANT (F. *posé, statant, arreté*)—Standing.
STOCK (F. *chicot, estoc*).—Of a tree.
STELLION—An old name for a lizard or snake.
STRINGED (F. *cordé*)—Said of a musical instrument with cords or strings; also of the cord or belt of a bugle-horn, or of a bow.
SUFFLUE—An old name for a *Rest*, or *Clarion, q.v.*
SURCOAT—The portion of the field of an escucheon lying between a pair of *flaunches*, or *flasques* (*v.* p. 557).
SURMOUNTED (F. *surmonte*)—A charge upon which another is placed is sometimes said to be surmounted by it.
SURTOUT, SUR LE TOUT—*Over all*, said of an escucheon of pretence.
SUSTAINED—An English phrase for *soutenu*, for which *see* the Glossary of French Terms.
SWEPE—A synonym for the balista or mangonel (*v.* p. 365).
SWIVEL—A name for a handcuff, or locket; two rings connected by a bolt (*see* under BADGES, p. 584).
SYKES—A fountain drawn conventionally (*v.* p. 193 *ante*, and Plate XIX., fig. 5).

T

TABARD—A surcoat, embroidered or painted with armorial bearings, now used by officers of arms (fig. 106, p. 674).

TAILED — (Of comets, etc., F. *caudé*, and *cometé;* of animals, *queué*).

TALBOT—An old English hunting dog.

TARGET—A circular shield.

TAU—A cross in the shape of a T (fig. 61, p. 164).

TAWNY, TENNÉ—The tincture of *Orange*.

TERRACE (F. *terrasse*)—A "*champagne*" (or narrow mount in base bounded by a straight line).

THOYE—An old name for a lynx.

THUNDERBOLT (F. *foudre*)—Conventionally represented as a twisted bar inflamed at the ends ; winged, and having issuing from its centre four forked and barbed darts in saltire.

TIARA—The *triregno*, or Papal mitre. A white cap of oval shape, rising from an open crown ; encircled by two other coronets, and surmounted by a small orb with its cross. The tiara has *infulæ*, or pendants, embroidered with gold, and fringed.

TIERCED (F. *tiercé*)—Divided into three approximately equal areas ; applied to the field. (For the different modes of tiercing *see* pp. 86, 87 and Plate VI.)

TILTING-SPEAR—A blunted lance (*v. cronel*).

TIMBRE—A French term for the helmet with its wreath, lambrequins, and crest.

TINCTURE—Heraldic colour.

TIRRET, or TURRET—A manacle or swivel.

TOISON D'OR—The badge of the Order of the Golden Fleece.

TOPAZ—The precious stone used to denote *or*, or gold, in the fanciful system of blazoning by gems.

TORQUED (F. *tortillé*)—Wreathed or twisted (Plate XI., fig. 6).

TORSE—An old term for the crest-wreath.

TORTEAU—A flat cake ; in English Heraldry tinctured *gules* (*v. ante*, p. 190).

TORTOILY—An old word for *semé* of torteaux.

TOUCHING (At the points)—(*Cf.* F. *appointé, abouté*).

TOURNÉ—Regardant.

TOWERED (F. *donjonné*)—Having turrets.

TRANSFIXED—Pierced through.

TRANSFLUENT—The term applied to a stream passing through the arches of a bridge.

TRANSPOSED—Removed from its ordinary position.

TREFOILED (F. *treflé*)—As applied to a cross, denotes that its arms terminate in trefoils; as applied to another Ordinary, it denotes that it is edged with trefoils; as applied to the field, it is an abbreviated expression for *semé* of trefoils.

TREILLÉ (F. *treillisé, or trellised*)—Latticed, as distinguished from *fretty* (*v.* p. 97).

TRESSURE (F. *trécheur*)—A diminutive of the orle (*v.* p. 175).

TRESSURE-FLORY (F. *trécheur-fleur-de-lisé*)—A small single orle ornamented with *fleurs-de-lis*, all the heads of which point outwards, and the stalks inward.

TRESSURE-FLORY-COUNTER-FLORY—The same as the above, but with the difference that the heads (and stalks) point alternately outwards and inwards.

TRESSURE-FLORY-COUNTER-FLORY (Double)—The Royal Tressure of Scotland (*v.* p. 176).

TRICORPORATE—Having three bodies united in a single head (*v.* Plate XXI., fig. 10).

TRIDENT—A long handled fish-spear with three prongs, or teeth.

TRIPARTED—Divided into three.

TRIPPANT, TRIPPING—The term applied to animals of the chase in the *passant*, or walking, attitude.

TRONONNÉ (F. *tronçonné*)—Dismembered; divided but preserving the general outline.

TRUNCATED, TRUNKED—Said of trees cut smoothly off at top and bottom.

TRUNKED (F. *affuté*)—Having the trunk of a specified colour.

TRUSSING (F. *empiétant*)—The term applied to a bird of prey that has seized with claws and beak another animal (*v.* p. 262).

TURNED-UP (F. *rebrassé*)—Said of a cap of which the edging or lining of a different colour is shown.

TURRETED (F. *donjonné*)—Having small towers.

TUSKED (F. *armé*)—Having teeth or tusks (F. of tusks, *defendu*); used when these differ from the ordinary colour, or from that of the body.

U

UMBRATED (F. *ombré*)—Shadowed.

UNDÉE, UNDY (F. *ondé*)—Wavy (*v.* p. 77).

UNGULED (F. *onglé*)—Having hoofs; applied to stags, unicorns, bulls, etc., whose cloven feet are of a different tincture from the rest of the body.

UNICORN—A fabulous animal, having the general form of a horse, but with a twisted horn proceeding from its forehead, the beard of a goat, cloven feet, and a lion's tail.

URCHIN (F. *hérisson*)—An old name for the hedgehog.

URDÉE, URDY—(*See* partition lines, p. 77).

URINANT—The term for a fish paleways but with its head in base; the reverse of *hauriant*.

V

VAIR—One of the heraldic furs (*see* p. 69, and Plate IV.).

VAIRÉ—Vair of other tinctures than the usual blue and white (*see* Plate IV., fig. 13, and page 71).

VALLARY CROWN—The crown of palisades (*v.* Plate L., fig. 14).

VAMBRACE—Armour for the arm.

VAMBRACED—Wearing a vambrace.

VAMPLATE (F. *arret de lance*)—The circular plate of steel fixed on a tilting lance to protect the hand.

VANNET—An escallop shell without ears, and showing the inside of the shell.

VENUS—The colour *vert* in blazoning by planets.

VERDOY—An old term for a bordure charged with flowers, fruit, or leaves.

VERT (F. *sinople*)—The tincture *green*.

VERVELS, VERRULES, VERRELS—Small rings, or ferules.

VESTED—Habited.

VIGILANCE—The stone held by a stork or crane in its uplifted foot is thus called (*v.* p. 263).

VIGILANT—In an attitude of watchfulness.

VIRES—Annulets (*v.* Plate XIX., fig. 10).

VIROLED (F. *virolé*)—Ornamented with rings or verrels (Plate XXXIII., fig 10).

VIZOR—The movable part of a basinet (the "*garde-visure*").

VOIDED (F. *vidé*)—Is said of an Ordinary of which the interior is removed leaving the field visible within the narrow outlines (*v.* Plate XIV., figs. 4 and 8).

VOIDER—A diminutive of the SUB-ORDINARY the *Flaunches*, rarely used in practice (*v.* p. 186).

Vol—A pair of wings conjoined (Plate XXV., fig. 5).
Volant—Flying.
Vorant (F. *engoulant*)—Devouring, or swallowing whole (Plate XXVII., fig. 4, *cf. Empiétant*, and distinguish).
Vulnant, Vulning—Wounding ; said of a pelican (p. 264).
Vulned—Wounded.

W

Water Bags, or Water Budgets—(*See* Chapter XIII., p. 355).
Wattled (F. *barbé*)—A term used for the gills of a cock, or cockatrice, when the colour has to be expressed (*cf.* Plate XXVII., fig. 9). (*See Jelloped.*)
Wavy—(*V. Undy*). A line of partition (p. 75); when said of a rough sea (F. *mer agité*).
Weel—A fish-pot of ozier work.
Weir, Wear—A dam of wattles interwoven.
Wervels—*V. Vervels.*
Whirlpool—*V. Gurges.*
Winged (F. *ailé*)—Having wings.
Woodman (F. *sauvage*)—A savage.
Wreath (F. *tortil; bourlet*)—The twisted bands of silk round the base of the crest. Also any chaplet or garland.
Wreathed (F. *cablé; tortillé*)—Having, or wearing, a wreath ; sometimes said of an Ordinary (*v.* Plate XI., fig. 6).
Wyvern—A monstrous animal (*v.* Chapter X., p. 292). The wyvern of British Heraldry, a dragon with only two legs, and resting on a nowed tail, does not differ from the dragon as generally depicted in Foreign Heraldry (*v.* Plate XXVII., fig. 8).

GLOSSARY OF THE FRENCH TERMS OF BLAZON.

(N.B.—*The Reader is advised to consult the Index for further references.*)

A

ABAISSÉ — This term is applied — (1.) To an Ordinary or other charge occupying a lower place in the shield than that which is usually assigned to it. Thus, a chief is said to be *abaissé* when it does not reach to the top edge of the shield; or again, when two chiefs appear in the same coat (*v.* Plate X., fig. 4, and p. 119) the lower is said to be *abaissé* beneath the upper. The fess and the chevron are sometimes found *abaissés*.—(2.) To the wings of an eagle, or other bird (*au vol abaissé*), when their points are directed to the base of the shield.—(3.) To a sword, or other weapon, held with its point downward.

ABIME (*v. Cœur*)—Is the name given to the centre point (p. 59, fig. 16) of the shield. A charge occupying this position is said to be *en abime;* but if it be the sole charge its position is not expressed. DE CLISSON : *d'Azur, à trois molettes d'argent et un croissant du même en abime.* (*Azure, a crescent between three mullets argent.*)

ABOUTÉ—Is the term applied to lozenges, and other like charges, which touch each other by their acute points. When the points of piles, etc., have a charge (as a rose) at the end the same term is used. The ermine spots in the arms of HURLESTON of England : *Argent, four ermine spots in cross sable,* are thus blazoned : *d'Argent, à quatre queues d'hermine en croix et aboutées en cœur,* because the upper points of the spots touch each other in the centre of the shield.

ACCOLÉ—This term is used—(1.) Of two escucheons placed side by side so as to touch each other, as in the case of the arms of husband and wife when borne in separate escucheons. LOUIS XIV. bore the Arms of FRANCE and NAVARRE thus *accolés* (*see* Chapter on MARSHALLING). —(2.) Of mascles, lozenges, and other charges, which are conjoined or touch each other. Thus in the arms of ROHAN (p. 185) the mascles are *accolées* (*de Gueules, à neuf macles d'or accolées et aboutées de gueules*).—(3.) Of shields, surrounded by the collar, or ribbon, of an Order of Knighthood.—(4.) It is also used erroneously for *colleté, q.v.*

ACCOMPAGNÉ DE—This term is employed when an Ordinary, or other principal charge occupying the middle of the shield, has other charges accompanying it (distinguish from *Accosté*). ESPARBEZ: *d'Argent, à la fasce de gueules accompagnée de trois merlettes de sable* (*Argent, a fess between three martlets sable*).

ACCORNÉ—This is said of animals whose horns are of a different tincture from that of their bodies; (ST. BELIN: *d'Azur, à trois rencontres de belier d'argent, accornées d'or*).

ACCOSTÉ—This term is used—(1.) Of charges placed side by side.—(2.) Instead of *Accompagné* (*see* above) when the charges run in the same direction as the piece which they accompany. Thus the sword in the arms granted to her brothers in memory of JEANNE D'ARC is *accosté* by the *fleurs-de-lis*. *Argent, a pale between six annulets gules*, would be blazoned: *d'Argent, au pal de gueules accosté de six annulets du même*, if the annulets were placed paleways. (This is one of the niceties of French blazon.)

ACCROUPI—This is the equivalent of our *sejant*, as applied to lions and other animals. Our wyvern is thus drawn (Plate XXVII., fig. 8). (PASCAL-COLOMBIER: *d'Argent, à un singe accroupi de gueules.*)

ACCULÉ—Is the phrase employed—(1.) When a horse, or other animal, is represented rampant, but thrown back on its haunches. (It is sometimes used for *Accroupi.*) —(2.) When two cannons are represented in the same line, with their breeches opposed to each other.— (3.) When two crescents are represented, the one with its horns upwards, the lower with its horns towards the base of the shield. (RONCHAUX: *d'Azur, à deux croissans acculés d'argent, accompagnés de quatre bezans en croix.*)

ADEXTRÉ (*cf. Senestré*)—This is said of—(1.) A charge which is accompanied by another charge placed upon its right side. (Note, that the position of this secondary charge may also be in chief, or in base, which fact must then be noted.)—(2.) A shield which is charged with a pale united to the dexter flank is said to be *adextré*. (This is really a partition.)

ADOSSÉ—The equivalent of our *addorsed;* is used of animals, birds, fishes, wings, axes, keys, and other objects placed back to back. (CLUNY: *d'Azur, à deux cles d'or adossés en pal, les anneaux entrelacés.*) (*Cf. Affronté*, and *see* Plate XXIX., fig. 9.)

AFFAISSÉ—Is the term applied to a fess, or bend, curved in the direction of the base of the shield. (It is the opposite of *Vouté, q.v.*)

AFFRONTÉ—Is the reverse of *Adossé*, being used of charges which face each other. (CHIAVARO: *de Gueules, à deux clés d'or affrontées en pal.*) (*See* also Plate XXII., fig. 1.)

AFFUTÉ—This term is applied—(1.) To the carriage of a piece of ordnance when it differs from the tincture of the cannon.—(2.) It is also applied to the trunks of trees.

AGITÉ—Is said of a sea with curling waves.

AGNEAU-PASCAL — This is a lamb, usually passant, having a nimbus around its head, and bearing a banner or bannerol of *argent* charged with a red cross (Plate XXIV., fig. 4).

AIGLE—When the eagle is borne in profile, and in its natural form, it is termed *une aigle de profil;* otherwise the *aigle* of Heraldry is always represented in the form known as *displayed*, and this fact does not therefore need to be specified. In French blazon *aigle* is always of the feminine gender. In early German examples the eagle is always represented *au vol abaissé* (*v.* HILDEBRANDT, *Heraldisches Musterbuch*, 4to, Berlin, 1872), and not, as in more recent times, with the tips of the wings raised above the head of the bird. The development of the eagle is well marked in HILDEBRANDT'S plates. Though in the 15th century the wings reach the level of the head, it is only at the close of the 16th, or early in the 17th, that they begin to rise distinctly above it.

AIGLE, MAIN D'—This is the technical term for an eagle's leg in French blazon.

AIGLONS, AIGLETTES (AIGLIAUX, *obsolete*) — These are terms employed by heraldic purists for eagles when more than one appear in a shield, unless they are separated from each other by a fess, bend, or other Ordinary.

AIGUIÉRE—A water-vessel used in religious ceremonies.

AIGUISÉ (*cf. Fiché*)—When a pale, or cross, etc., has one of its ends (usually the lowest) sharpened, this is the phrase used to denote the fact. (BOUTON, *Nouveau Traité de Blason*, pp. 196-7, distinguishes between a *pal fiché* and a *pal aiguisé*, considering that in the latter case both ends are pointed. This is a mistake.)

AILÉ—Birds with plumage, or insects with wings, or windmills with sails, of a different colour from the body, are said to be *ailés* of that tincture. So also, hearts, hands, swords, animals, and other charges which have not naturally wings, are said to be *ailés* of such and such a tincture.

AIRE—This is the technical name of the nest in which a pelican and her young are represented.

AJOURÉ (Pierced)—Is the term applied—(1.) When the windows of a tower or other building are of a colour differing from that of the charge. (Note, that the gate is not said to be *ajourée*, but *ouverte*.)—(2.) It is said of openings, usually square, in the field ; *e.g.*, VON UBERACKER in Bavaria bears : *de Gueules, ajouré en chef d'une seule pièce d'or*. (The opening commences at the edge of the shield.)—(3.) A cross with an opening in the centre is also said to be *ajouré*, the shape of the opening being specified (*v. Percé*). (VIRY : *de Sable, à la croix ancrée d'argent ajourée en carre—Sable, a cross moline square pierced argent ;* and *cf.* Plate XIV., fig. 6.)

AJOUTÉ—This word is used in the rare cases in which the battlements of a chief *crénelé* differ in tincture from the rest of the Ordinary.

AJUSTÉ—Is said of an arrow placed on the string of a bent bow.

ALAISÉ, ALÉSÉ, ALEZÉ—These words are used to express the fact that the Ordinary to which they are applied does not touch the edge of the shield with one (or more) of its extremities. The term is the synonym of *raccourci* (see also *retrait*). (Plate LVI., fig. 8.)

ALCYON—A chimerical bird represented of a swan-like form, sitting on its nest, which floats on the waves of the sea.

ALÉRION—This is the name given to eaglets, when represented without beaks or legs. They are not borne singly.

ALLUMÉ—Is the term indicating—(1.) The flame of a torch, candle, grenade, or other burning matter, when it differs in tincture from the rest of the charge.—(2.) It is also used to indicate the colour of the eyes of birds and other animals. (LA FARE : *d'Azur, à troix flambeaux d'or allumé de gueules.*)

AMPHIPTÈRE (*Amphistère*, BOUTON, *Nouveau Traité de Blason*) —A winged serpent (*v.* p. 294).

AMPHISBÈNE—(*Cf.* Amphisbœna in *English Glossary*).

ANCHÉ—A term applied to the curving of a scimitar ; the horn of a stag, a bend, etc. (VON MOLSBACH : *d'Azur, à une demi-ramure de cerf anchée et chevillée de six cors d'argent.*)

ANCOLIE—An imaginary flower of three petals, its slipped stalk is always upwards.

ANCRÉ—Said of crosses and saltires whose arms divide into pieces like the flukes of a grapnel (*v.* Plate XV., fig. 11).

ANGEMME, ou ANGENNE—A flower of heraldry very rarely met with, and with regard to which heralds differ as to whether it be a quatre- or a cinque-foil. BOUTON makes them of five thin separate petals with a small round piece in the centre. The Counts of TANCARVILLE bear : *de Gueules, à l'écusson d'argent, à l'orle d'angemmes d'or* (*Nouveau Traité de Blason*, p. 391. As used by the English TANKERVILLES, *temp.* EDWARD I., they did not differ from the ordinary cinquefoils).

ANGLÉ—Said of a cross, or saltire, which has rays or other figures in its angles. The Florentine MACHIAVELLI bore : *Argent, a cross azure anglé with four nails of the same.* (Note that this differs from *between* four nails, the latter are in saltire in the MACHIAVELLI coat.)

ANILLE—A French form of the mill-rind, or *fer de moulin;* it is formed by two semi-circles addorsed and connected by two horizontal bands which thus leave a nearly square aperture.

ANILLÉE (Croix) (*cf. Nillée*)—A cross *anillée* has the appearance of being formed out of two *anilles*, one in pale the other in fess.

ANIMÉ (*cf. Allumé*)—A term applied to describe the tincture of the eyes of animals.

ANNELET—The equivalent of our *annulet*, a ring of metal of equal width all round.

ANTIQUE, À LA—A term used to denote a fashion no longer in general use; a *couronne à l'antique* is the rayed, or Eastern, crown (Plate L., fig. 13).

APPAUMÉ—Said of a hand extended and showing the palm. WAROQUIER: *d'Azur, à une main dextre d'argent appaumée et posée en pal.*

APPOINTÉ—Is said of chevrons, lozenges, swords, and other charges which touch each other at the point (*v.* p. 148. AQUIN, and Plate XVI., fig. 3).

AQUILON (*cf. Borée*, etc.)—A conventional representation of the north wind, as the head of an infant with inflated cheeks (*v.* p. 311).

ARC EN CIEL—The conventional colours by which this is represented in Foreign Armory are: *or, gules, vert, argent.* Any others require specification (*see* Plate XIX., fig. 7).

ARCHE DE NOË—Is drawn like the toy of our infancy, but in some Polish coats has a high prow and stern ending in lion's heads (*v.* p. 371).

ARCHIÈRES—These are the slits, or apertures, usually cruciform, made in the battlements, or walls, of a fortress to admit of the passage of arrows.

ARCTÉ—Curved in an arc, an old phrase of PETRA SANCTA.

ARDENT—Said of a glowing coal. The coat of CARBONNIÈRES is: *d'Azur, à quatre bandes d'argent chargées de charbons de sable, ardentes de gueules.*—*Azure, four bendlets argent charged with coals sable inflamed gules.* (*Inflamed* scarcely conveys the correct idea.)

ARGENT—Silver.

ARGUS, TÊTE D'—Is represented in the form of a human head *semé* of eyes. It is the charge of the arms of SANTEUIL (*v.* p. 201).

ARMÉ—Is said—(1.) Of the talons of animals;—(2.) Of the heads of arrows, spears, etc., when these differ in tincture from the rest of the bearing. It is also used of a man wearing armour.

ARMES-PLEINES—The term for the undifferenced coat of arms

which, in theory, belongs to the head of a family alone.

ARRACHÉ—A term equivalent both for our *eradicated* and *erased* (DE LAUNAY : *d'Argent, à un arbre de sinople arraché;* GROIN : *d'Argent, à trois têtes de lion arrachées de gueules couronnées d'or*).

ARRETÉ (POSÉ)—Standing still, equivalent to *statant.*

ARRETS-DE-LANCE—Vamplates, to protect the hand holding a lance in the tourney.

ARRIÈRE-MAIN—(*V. Contre-appaummée*).

ARRONDI—Curved into a circular form.

ASSIS—The term equivalent to *sejant,* applied to dogs, cats, squirrels, etc.

AVANT-BRAS—The arm from below the elbow.

AVANT-MUR—A small piece of wall attached to a castle, or tower, in some coats (*v.* p. 362). ORIOL : *d'Azur, à une tour senestrée d'un avant mur d'argent.*

AZUR—The colour *azure*, or blue.

B

BADELAIRE—A faulchion.

BAILLONNÉ—Is said of any animal represented holding a baton, or stick, between its jaws.

BANDE—The Ordinary known as a bend.

BANDE, EN—Is said of a charge or charges placed bendways, or in the direction taken by the bend.

BANDÉ — (1.) Divided into bends (of equal number). — (2.) Banded.

BANDÉ-CONTRE-BANDÉ — Bendy, counterchanged per bend-sinister.

BANNERET (VOL)—(*V. Vol-banneret*).

BANNIÈRE—A flag of a square shape, the distinctive ensign of a chevalier banneret (*v.* pp. 57, 640, 652).

BANNIÈRE, EN—A form of the escucheon (*v.* p. 57).

BAR—The fish known as *barbel*, generally borne in pairs, addorsed paleways (Plate XXVI., fig. 9).

BARBÉ—Bearded, of animals ; wattled, of cocks, dolphins, etc.

BARDÉ—Caparisoned in armour ; said of a horse. RIPERDA : *de Sable, au chevalier d'or le cheval bardé d'argent.*

BARRE—A *bend-sinister* (Plate XII., fig. 12). Hence comes the common mistake as to a "bastard bar." A "bar-sinister" is an absurdity, the bar being a horizontal piece, and as much dexter as sinister (*v.* pp. 126 and 582).

BARRÉ—Covered with bends-sinister in equal numbers.

BARROQUE, EN—A term applied to supporters, when they are drawn as if emerging from behind the shield.

BASILIC—The basilisk (*v.* p. 293, *ante*).

BASTILLÉ—Embattled on the lower edge. BELOT : *d'Argent, à trois lozenges d'azur, au chef cousu bastillé d'or.*—Argent, three lozenges azure, a chief embattled (*cousu*) or.

BATAILLÉ—When the clapper of a bell is, as often, of a different colour from the rest of the charge, it is said to be *bataillé*. BELLEGARDE : *d'Azur, à une cloche d'argent bataillé de sable* (*Azure, a bell argent the clapper sable*).

BÂTON—(1.) A stick.—(2.) A cotice couped at the ends. In the coats of the later French princes it was used as a mark of difference in the case of those who had been legitimated (*see* Chapter XVII., p. 572).

BÂTON D'ESCULAPE—A rod and a serpent intertwined.

BÂTON FLEUR-DE-LISÉ—A rod ending in a *fleur-de-lis*, often *arraché*, having roots at the end as in the coat of DELBENE : *Azure, two batons fleur-de-lisée and eradicated in saltire argent.*

BECQUÉ—Indicates the colour of the beak of a bird. COLIGNI : *de Gueules, à l'aigle d'argent, couronné, becqué, et membré, d'azur.*

BEFFROI—Vair of the largest size (*v.* p. 69).

BÉLIER-MILITAIRE—A battering ram.

BÉQUILLE DE ST. ANTHOINE—A term for the cross-tau (*q.v.*).

BESANT—Coin of gold or silver, usually without stamp. If the head be depicted it is *figuré*.

BESANTÉ—*Semé* of bezants.

BESANT-TOURTEAU—A roundle partly of metal, partly of colour, is always placed on a field of *colour* (*v. Tourteau-besant*).

BIGARRÉ—Said of a butterfly's wings of divers colours.

BILLETÉ—*Semé* of *billettes*.

BILLETTE—A rectangular figure with elongated sides ; always borne perpendicularly unless otherwise specified ; when placed horizontally it is said to be *couchée*.

BISSE—Name of a serpent when twined into knots (*cf. Guivre*).

BOCQUET—A lance, or pike-head.

BŒUF—The ox has a pendent tail ; distinguish from *taureau*.
BONNET-ALBANAIS—A pointed hat bent in the form of a semi-circle.
BORDÉ—Edged ; said of Ordinaries having a bordure of a different colour ; also of the shield if it has a very narrow bordure (*cf. Filet en bordure*).
BORDURE—One of the SUB-ORDINARIES (*v.* Chapter V.).
BORÉE—(*V. Aquilon*).
BOUCLÉ—(1.) Buckled.—(2.) Said of the ring in the nostrils of an animal (*v.* p. 235, *cf. Buffle*).
BOULES—In German Armory nearly all the roundles are thus globular, and are shaded accordingly (*v.* p. 190).
BOURDON (DE PÉLERIN)—A pilgrim's staff, usually balled at the top.
BOURDONNÉ (*cf. Pommetty*)—Said of a cross whose arms terminate, like a bourdon, in balls. ROCHAS : *d'Or, à la croix bourdonnée de gueules au chef d'azur chargé d'une étoile d'or.*
BOURLET—The wreath of a crested helm.
BOUSE—The water-bouget.
BOUTEROLLE—The end of a scabbard, somewhat in the form of a linden or nenuphar leaf.
BOUTOIR—The snout of a boar ; used in describing the position of the head when exceptionally it is placed paleways, or in bend, *le boutoir vers le chef, ou vers l'angle droit, de l'écu.*
BOUTONNÉ—(1.) Having buds.—(2.) Buttoned.
BRANCHÉ—Branched (*v. Tigé*).
BRÉBIS—A sheep *grazing* (distinguish from *Mouton*).
BRÉTESSÉ—Is said of Ordinaries embattled on both sides, so that the merlon on one side corresponds to the merlon on the other (*v.* arms of SCARRON, p. 130).
BRÉTESSÉ (*contré*)—Embattled on both sides, but with the merlon on the one side corresponding to the embrasure on the other.
BRIS D'HUIS—The long hinge of a door (*v. Vertenelle*).
BRISÉ—(1.) Broken ; said of lances, chevrons, etc., VIOLLE : *d'Or, à trois chevrons brisés de sable.*—See *rompu* and *écimé*, and distinguish.—(2.) Differenced by a brisure.
BROCHANT—Is said of charges which are placed upon other charges so as to pass over them (*see* Arms of TORSAY on next page ; and Plate XIII., figs. 5 and 9).

BROYES (*cf. Morailles*)—(1.) A twitch for horses.—(2.) A hemp brake.

BUFFLE—An ox-head with a ring in the nostrils is blazoned as a *tête de buffle*, as in the arms of MECKLENBURG.

BURÈLE—A diminutive of a bar—a barrulet.

BURELÉ—Barry of ten or more pieces, equal in number. TORSAY: *Burelé d'argent et d'azur, à la bande de gueules brochante sur le tout.*

C

CABLÉ—Wreathed (*v. Tortillé*), is said of Ordinaries wreathed like a cable.

CABOCHÉ—Caboshed (*v.* p. 233).

CABRÉ—(*Cf. Effaré*). Is said of a horse thrown back on its haunches.

CADUCÉE—The rod of Mercury, winged at the end, and having two serpents entwined around it.

CALATRAVE, CROIX DE—(*V.* p. 158).

CALVAIRE, CROIX—(*V.* p. 152).

CANETTE—A duck without beak or feet like a *merlette*. (Some writers, however, make the distinction that *canettes* have beaks and feet while *merlettes* have not.)

CANNELÉ—Invecked (*v.* p. 76).

CANTON—A diminutive of the *franc-quartier*.

CANTONNÉ—Said of a cross, or other charge, along with which one or more charges are borne in the cantons of the shield. Thus BRUNSVELT in Holland bears: *Azure, a cross couped argent,* cantonnée of *four roses of the same.* We should simply say "between."—It is also used of four charges placed 2 and 2.

CAPUCHON—(*V. Chaperon*). A hood.

CARNATION—The "proper" colour of flesh.

CARREAUX—Cushions, usually *en lozenge*.

CAUDÉ—Said of a star or comet's tail.

CEINTRÉ—A synonym for *voute*.

CEINTRÉ—Said of an orb of sovereignty, banded.

CEP DE VIGNE—A vine shoot.

CEPS—A handcuff.

CERCLÉ—Hooped.

CHABOTS—Chubs, borne hauriant.

CHAMP—The field of the shield.

CHAMPAGNE, or PLAINE—The base of the shield cut off by a

(719)

straight line ; distinguish from a mound which is made by a curved line (fig. 36, p. 77, and *see* p. 311).

CHANDELIERS DE L'EGLISE—Have three branches.

CHANTANT—Crowing.

CHAPÉ—A division of the shield by two straight lines issuing from the middle of the top line of the shield to the dexter and sinister base (Plate VI., fig. 8, and p. 88).

CHAPÉ-CHAUSSÉ—The combination of *chapé* with *chaussé* (*see* the latter term below).

CHAPÉ-PLOYÉ — The same formed by curved, or concave lines (Plate VI., fig. 10).

CHAPELET—(1.) A rosary.—(2.) A wreath.

CHAPERON—(1.) A hood.—(2.) The hood of a falcon.

CHAPERONNÉ—(1.) Wearing a hood.—(2.) A diminutive of *chapé* (p. 89). (*See* Plate LV., fig. 4.)

CHARGÉ—Charged.

CHÂTEAU—A castle, flanqued with towers (distinguish from *tower*, *v.* p. 359).

CHÂTELÉ—*Semé* of castles (*cf.* Plate VIII., fig. 10).

CHAUDIÈRE—The cauldron ; a frequent Spanish charge.

CHAUSSÉ—The reverse of *chapé*, that is, the lines start from the middle of the base and end in the extremities of the top line of the shield. When the shield is both *chapé* and *chaussé* both forms undergo some diminution, and the *field* takes a lozenge shape, *chapé-chaussé* thus becomes the same as *vêtu*, *see* p. 89. (For even a greater diminution *see* p. 89, Arms of SANTAPAU.)

CHAUSSÉ-PLOYÉ—*Chaussé*, but with curved lines (*see* p. 88).

CHAUSSETRAPES—Caltraps.

CHAUVE-SOURIS—The bat ; it is borne displayed like an eagle.

CHEF—The Chief.

CHEF DE FRANCE—A chief *azure* charged with three *fleurs-de-lis or* (in early coats *semé de fleurs-de-lis*), (*v.* p. 539).

CHEF DE L'EMPIRE (*Germanique*)—*Un chef d'or à une aigle eployée de sable* (*v.* p. 536-538).

Variations not known in British Armory are these :—

CHEF-CHEVRON—The union of the chief with the chevron without any dividing line.

CHEF-DEXTRE—A chief formed by a line proceeding from the sinister end of the top line of the shield, and crossing the shield to the point where the line forming the chief begins, thus making a long giron, or triangular bearing, with its base on the dexter flank.

CHEF-PAL—The union of the chief with the pale (*v.* p. 120).

CHEF-SENESTRE—The reverse of CHEF-DEXTRE; the partition line starts from the dexter end of the top line and crosses to the sinister flank (Plate LV., fig. 1).

CHEF-TRIANGULAIRE—Is formed by two lines starting from the extremities of the top line of the shield, and uniting in the honour point.

CHEF-VOUTÉ—Is a chief formed by an arched line instead of by a straight one (Plate X., fig. 5).

CHÉRUBINS—Angel's heads with two or six wings (*v.* p. 201).

CHEVELÉ—Is said of human heads which have the hair of a special tincture named.

CHEVILLÉ—Is used when it is desired to give the number of "points" (*cors*) on a stag's attire (*cf.* Arms of MOLSBACH on p. 713).

CHEVRON—The Ordinary so called may be *abaissé, alaisé, brisé, coupé, couché, écimé, ployé, versé, vuidé, tourné,* etc.

CHEVRON, DIVISÉ EN—Parti per chevron (*v.* p. 81).

CHEVRON, EN—Is said of objects arranged in the form taken by the Ordinary.

CHEVRONNÉ—Covered with chevrons (Plate VII., fig. 5).

CHICOT—(*V. Écot*). A thick knotted stick.

CHIMÈRE—(*V. Chimæra*, p. 294).

CHOUCAS—The Cornish chough.

CHOUETTE—The great owl, always borne *affrontée*.

CIMIER—The crest.

CINTRÉ—Banded; said of the *Monde* (*q.v.*), or *Orb*.

CLAIREVOIES—The lozenge-shaped spaces within a fret or trellis.

CLARICORDE—The name for the English charge known as a *rest, sufflue, clarion,* etc. (*v.* p. 386).

CLARINÉ—This term is used when it is desired to describe the colour of the bells of cows or sheep.

CLECHÉE—Said of a cross the arms of which are shaped like the handle of an ancient key. The Cross of Toulouse is a *cross-clechée* (*v.* Plate XV., fig. 7, and p. 161).

CLOUÉ—Is said when the heads of nails appear on trellises (*v.* p. 97), horse-shoes, etc.

CLOUS-DE-LA-PASSION — Passion nails, having a triangular or

square head. (CHAUSNES : *d'Azur, au chevron d'or accompagné de trois clous de la passion du même.*)

CŒUR, EN (*en abîme*)—In the centre point of the shield.

COLLETÉ—Collared ; said—(1.) Of a dog or other animal.—(2.) Of a spur attached to the collet or collar.—(3.) Of a wild animal seized by the neck or ears by a hound (vulgarly "collared").

COLONNES—(1.) Architectural charges.—(2.) The name sometimes given to the *zules* (*zuylen*) or chess-rooks, in Dutch charges.

COMBLE—A diminutive of the chief, and half its width.

COMÈTE—The comet is represented in Foreign Armory as an estoile of six or eight rays, one of which is prolonged into a wavy tail, usually in bend but not always ; the position must therefore be specified. *Caudé* is the term applied to the tail.

COMETÉ—Having a tail or termination like a comet.

COMPON — One of the rectangular pieces of which compony is made up.

COMPONÉ—Is said of a bordure or other Ordinary, divided into one row of rectangular pieces alternating in colour (Plate XVII., fig. 4).

CONQUE-MARINE—The conch shell borne by a triton.

CONTOURNÉ—Turned to face the sinister side of the shield. In the case of a crescent both horns are towards the sinister (*v.* p. 307).

CONTRÉ-APPAUMÉ—Said of a human hand placed so as to show its back (rarely employed).

CONTRE-BANDÉ, CONTRE-BARRÉ, CONTRE-CHEVRONNÉ, CONTRE-FASCÉ, CONTRE-PALÉ — All these are terms which indicate that the field is covered with bends, bends-sinister, chevrons, fesses, or pales, and that it is also divided by a line on the two sides of which the metal and colour are alternately placed. Thus the coat of HORBLER is : *Parti, et contre bandé d'or et de gueules.* Here the coat *bendy or and gules* is also divided by the palar line, so that the bend which is *or* on the dexter side becomes *gules* on the sinister, and so on alternately throughout. MEIRANS : *Contre palé d'argent et d'azur à la fasce d'or.* Here the pallets are counter-changed on each side of the fess (*see* also p. 96).

CONTRE-COMPONNÉ (Counter-compony) — Made up of compons

arranged alternately. The Counts SEVA : *Fasce d'or et de sable à la bordure contre-componnée de même.* (Here the compons of *or* are at the ends of the *sable* bars, and *vice versa.*)

CONTRE-ÉCARTELÉ (Counter-quartered) — Is said of quarterings which are themselves quartered (*see* Plate XXXIX., fig. 3).

CONTRE-FLAMBANT—Flaming on opposite sides.

CONTRE-HERMINE (Ermines).—A fur of which the field is *sable* and the spots white (Plate IV.).

CONTRE-PASSANT (Counter-passant)—Said of two or more animals, arranged paleways, and proceeding in opposite directions (*v.* Plate XXII., fig. 2).

CONTRE-VAIR—Vair so arranged that in any two rows the panes of the same tincture are conjoined by their bases, or by their points, as in Plate IV., fig. 8.

CONTRE-VAIRÉ—The same arrangement as in counter-vair, but with tinctures other than *argent* and *azure*.

COQUERELLES—A group of three filberts in their cups arranged one in pale and two fesseways.

COQUILLAGE—(*V. Conque-marine*).

COQUILLE—An escallop shell, placed to show the convex side of the shell (*cf. Vannet*).

COR-DE-CHASSE—A hunting horn ; in French Armory is always stringed (*cf. Grelier* and *Huchet*), and the lip piece, as in English (but not in Scottish) Heraldry, is to the sinister side of the shield.

CORDÉ—Said of bows ; or of hunting horns or harps whose strings require specification. (ARPAIOU : *d'Azur, à une harpe cordée d'or.*)

CORDELIÈRE — A knotted cord placed in a circular form round the escucheon or lozenge of widows.

CORMORAN—A cormorant, usually drawn *proper*.

CORNES—The horns used in crests, especially in Germany.

CORNIÈRE—The handle of a cauldron.

CORS—The *points* of a stag's attire (*v.* MOLSBACH, p. 713).

COTICE—A diminutive of a *bande*, or bend, of which it is only the third part.

COTICE-EN-BARRE—The like diminutive of the bend-sinister.

COTICÉ—(1.) Is said of a field divided into bendlets of at least the number of ten.—(2.) Cotised ; said of an Ordinary (fess, pale, bend) placed between its diminutives, as in Plates X. (fig. 11) and XI. (fig. 12) (*cf. Cotoyé, infra*).

COTICÉ-EN-BARRE—Bendy-sinister of ten or more pieces.
COTOYÉ—Is said of a bend or bend-sinister placed between two charges which take the same direction as the Ordinary. (*Cf. Accosté* and *Accompagné*, and note the difference.)
COUARD—Coward; said of a lion or other beast drawn with its tail between its legs.
COUCHÉ—Couchant; said—(1.) Of an animal lying down, but not asleep, with the head in the air (distinguish from *Dormant*).—(2.) Of billets placed horizontally (*v.* p. 490)—(3.) Of a chevron (*v.* p. 137, and Plate LV., fig. 5).
COULEUVRE—A serpent, usually drawn in pale and with undulating body.
COULISSÉ—Said of a castle whose gateway shows the portcullis.
COUPÉ—(1.) Parti per fess (Plate V., fig. 3).—(2.) *Couped;* said of parts of animals cut smoothly off, as distinct from erased. —(3.) Of a *fleur-de-lis* divided horizontally.
COUPÉ ALTERNATIVEMENT—(*V.* CRESTS, p. 606).
COUPEAU—Name for the summits of the conventional hill; usually drawn *de trois coupeaux*—that is, with three rounded summits like inverted cups (*v.* p. 311).
COUPLE-DE-CHIENS—An instrument of the chase serving to couple two hounds in one leash.
COUPLÉS—Is said—(1.) Of hounds thus united.—(2.) Of other things tied together.
COURANT—Courant, running.
COURBÉ—Curved. (1.) Said of the dolphin, etc.—(2.) Equivalent of *vouté*, as applied to a fess, etc.
COURONNÉ—Surmounted by a crown or coronet.
COURTINE—(1.) A curtain of masonry uniting two towers.—(2.) The side pieces of a pavilion or mantling.
COUSU—Is the term used to indicate that the law forbidding the use of metal on metal, or colour on colour, has been intentionally disregarded. This frequently happens in the case of the chief; less frequently in that of other Ordinaries (*v. ante, Bastillé*, arms of BELOT). The violation of the rule occurs but seldom in the coats of the old French *noblesse;* frequently in those of towns and corporations secular and religious.
COUVERT—Said—(1.) Of a cup or chalice having a cover.—(2.) Of a tower, or building, with a pointed roof.
CRAMPON—A cramp or hook of iron used in building. It is a

perpendicular piece, with a hook at each end on the opposite sides.

CRAMPONNÉ—Is said of the cross (and other figures) of which an arm, or *traverse*, ends in a *crampon*, or hook.

CRANCELIN—A figure derived from German Heraldry; a bend curved and ornamented on the upper edge with leaves and pearls like a coronet. The arms of SAXONY (*see* Plate XII.).

CRÉMAILLIÈRE—The ratchet hook of a cauldron; a charge frequent in the Armory of some parts of Germany (*v.* p. 390).

CRÉNEAUX—Is the French term for the *merlons*, or portions projecting upwards, of an embattlement. In Italy the form of the battlement indicated the political party of the owner of the building. The Guelphic battlement is the ordinary rectangular one; the Ghibbeline has an angular or swallow-tail notch in the upper line.

CRÉNELÉ—Embattled on the upper side (Plate XI., fig. 4). LA LANDE : *d'Argent, à la fasce crénelée de gueules.*

CRÉQUIER—A wild cherry tree, drawn conventionally, as in Plate XXIX., fig. 4; and, better, at p. 344, fig. 72.

CRÊTE—The crest of a cock, dolphin, or other animal. (N.B. *Not* of a helmet, which is *cimier.*)

CRÊTÉ—Having the crest of a special tincture.

CRI-DE-GUERRE—A motto placed in a listel above the crest.

CRINÉ—Word used in indicating the colour of the hair.

CROC, or CROCHET—A hook.

CROISÉ—Charged, or ornamented, with a cross.

CROISSANT—A half moon, drawn conventionally *montant*, or with its horns upwards. (Note that any other position requires specification; and *see tourné, versé, contourné, figuré,* and *lunels.*)

CROISSETTES—Small crosses.

CROIX, EN—Arranged in the form of a cross.

CROIX, PASSÉ EN—Is said of two lances, or other charges, placed the one in pale, the other crossing it fessways.

CYCLAMOR—An orle.

D

DAIM—A deer; it has broader and wider antlers than the *cerf.*

DALMATIQUE—Is the name of the tunicle with short sleeves, often *armoyée*, worn by angels over their long flowing robes (*see* French Supporters, pp. 636-7).

DAUPHIN — This animal is usually drawn *embowed*, or *courbé en pal* — *i.e.*, with its head in chief, and its body curved towards the sinister side of the shield, and its tail beneath the head; in fact, like a ꓳ, ꓛ reversed (Plate XXVI., fig. 7). When drawn *naiant* (fessways in pale), the body is not so much curved (Plate XXVI., fig. 8). When drawn *hauriant* the curvature is still less.

DE L'UN À L'AUTRE — DE L'UN EN L'AUTRE — Counter-changed. The coat of RODES is : *Per pale sable and argent, thirteen estoiles in three palar rows*, 4, 5, 4, *counter-changed*. The French blazon shows the difference of the two phrases :— *Parti de sable et d'argent, à treize étoiles rangées en trois pals, les cinque du milieu de l'un à l'autre, et les quatre de chaque flanc de l'un en l'autre.* A nicety of French blazon.

DÉCAPITÉ — Having the head removed.

DÉFAILLANT — Is said when a cross or other charge is deficient in some portion. The blazon must indicate the position of the deficiency; thus a cross deprived of its right arm would be said to be *défaillant à dextre*, etc.

DÉFENDU — Tusked; is said of an elephant, or wild boar.

DÉFENSES — Are the tusks of a wild boar or elephant (a porcupine in a ball is styled *en défence*).

DÉGOUTTANT (*De sang*) — Distilling drops of blood.

DEJOINT — Is said of an Ordinary severed in the middle and displaced.

DÉMANCHÉ — Without a handle.

DÉMEMBRÉ — Without members; said of birds.

DEMI-RAMURE — Is a single horn of a stag (*cf. ramure*).

DEMI-VOL — A single wing, as *vol* means both wings.

DENCHÉ — Indented (*cf. Dentelé*).

DENCHURE — A filet in chief indented.

DENTÉ — Toothed, same as

DENTELÉ — Indented, but with more and smaller indentations than *Denché, q.v.*

DÉPOUILLE — The name of the skin of a lion or other animal.

DÉSARMÉ — Disarmed, without claws or talons.

DEVISE — A motto.

DEXTRE — The right side of the shield, opposite to the beholder's *left* hand.

DEXTROCHÈRE—The whole right hand and arm (*cf. avant-bras*, which distinguish ; and *Senestrochère*).
DIADEMÉ—Is said of Imperial eagles whose heads are surrounded by annulets, or glories.
DIAPRÉ—Diapered (*v.* p. 114).
DIFFAMÉ—Deprived of its tail.
DIMINUÉ—Is said of charges, or Ordinaries, borne of a smaller size than usual.
DIVISE (*v. Fasce en divise*)—(*See* Plate X., fig. 6). A barrulet borne in the chief of the shield. (POISIEU : *de Gueules, à deux chevrons d'argent, sommés d'une divise de même.*)
DIVISÉ EN CHEVRON—Parti per chevron.
DOLCE—A kind of fox ; an animal found in Italian coats.
DOLOIRE—A broad axe (*v.* p. 449, arms of RENTY, and p. 348).
DONJONNÉ—Equivalent to "towered with a single tower" (*cf. Sommé*). PRUNIER : *de Gueules, à une tour donjonnée d'argent.*
DOUBLETS—Gnats drawn in profile.
DRAGON—The French dragon has usually only two legs, and is like our British wyvern (*v.* Chapter X., p. 292).
DRAGON-MONSTREUX—Is a dragon with a human head, bearded with serpents (*v.* p. 293).
DRAGONNÉ—An epithet applied to animals which are drawn as monsters with a dragon's tail. BRETIGNY : *d'Or, au lion dragonné de gueules, armé, lampassé, et couronné d'or.*
DUC—*Le hibou-duc*, a small kind of owl, always drawn *affronté;* found in Low Country crests.

E

EBRANCHÉ—Is said of a trunk of a tree deprived of its branches.
ECAILLÉE—Scaled. Said—(1.) Of a fish.—(2.) Of an Ordinary covered with scales like those of a fish, as in the arms of the Counts TATTENBACH of Bavaria : *d'Argent, à une bande écaillée de gules* (*cf. Papelonné*, which is probably the same bearing, and *v.* p. 72).
ECARTELÉ—(1.) Divided into four approximately equal parts by the palar and the fess line.—(2.) Is said of a shield divided into four or more quarterings.
ECARTELÉ EN ÉQUERRE is described at p. 82 (*see* also Plate V., fig. 11).

ECARTELÉ EN SAUTOIR—Parti per saltire (Plate V., fig. 12).
ECARTELURES—Quarterings.
ECHANCRÉ—Is like *engrailed*, but has much wider and deeper indentations (*cf. canelé*).
ECHÉLLES D'ESCALADE—Scaling-ladders—(1.) Of two side pieces, each having a hook at the top. (2.) A single pole, hooked, and having short traverses, or steps.
ECHIQUETÉ—Chequy; in Foreign Modern Armory, is of thirty-six panes, when the whole field is chequy.
ECIMÉ—Is said of a chevron whose top is cut straight off (*v.* p. 138, Plate XIII., fig. 9). Distinguish from *Brisé* and *Rompu* (Plate XIII., figs. 10 and 11).
ECLATÉ—Splintered; is said of spears and lances.
ECORCHÉ—Is said of animals whose paws are tinctured gules (*cf.* the lions in arms of WURTEMBERG).
ECOT—Is equivalent of *Chicot*, a piece of the branch of a tree.
ECOTÉ—Is the old style of *raguly*, having projections as if boughs had been cut off. LECHERAINE in Savoy: *d'Azur, à la bande écotée de gueules.*
ECOTÉ, CONTRE—*Counter-raguly;* said of a field so divided.
ECRAN—Is the French name for the fan-shaped crest so frequently found in German Heraldry. Usually it is octagonal, but sometimes of fewer sides, having a plane surface often charged with the arms of the shield, the edge *echancré*, and the points ornamented with little balls, or tufts of feathers (*v.* p. 600, Plate XLVI., fig. 1).
ECREVISSE—Usually drawn in pale, head in chief.
ÉCU, DE L'—A term used in blazoning crests and mantlings in which the charges of the shield are represented just as they are on the shield.
ÉCU EN BANNIÈRE—Said of the square shield used by bannerets, and by some families descending from ancient bannerets (*v. ante*, p. 57).
ÉCUSSON EN ABIME—An escucheon in the centre of the shield; sometimes has arisen from an undue enlargement of the bordure. *Gules, an escucheon en abîme argent* was quite probably originally: *Argent, a bordure gules.*
ÉCUSSON, FAUX—Name for an orle, or an inescucheon having a bordure (*v.* p. 553).
ÉCUSSON SUR LE TOUT—(*V. En surtout*, p. 448).
EFFARÉ—Is said of a horse (*v. Cabré*, and *Forcené*).

EFFAROUCHÉ—A useless term of blazon, used for *rampant* by some authors for cats, unicorns, etc. (*v. Furieux*).

EFFEUILLÉ—Deprived of its leaves.

ELANCÉ—Is a term applied to a stag saliant, or springing forward.

EMAIL—(1.) Colour (plural *Emaux*).—(2.) Was used for the small enamelled escucheons of their master's arms, worn upon the breast by the ancient heralds.

EMANCHE—A figure formed of two or more pile-like pieces conjoined, and issuing from the point or flanks of the shield (Plate XVI., fig. 8, and Plate LV., fig. 9).

EMANCHÉ—Is said when these piles are of greater length in proportion to their breadth, reaching nearly across the shield (Plate VIII., fig. 2). *Parti-emanché d'argent et de gueules* is the coat of HOTMAN. This may also be formed in the other ways—*coupé*, *tranché*, or *taillé*.

EMANCHURE—Is the name of one of the small triangular sections when the field is *chapé*.

EMBOUCHÉ—Is said of horns, etc., whose mouthpiece is of a different tincture from the rest of the charge.

EMBOUTÉ—Is said of batons, etc., which have a piece at the end differing in tincture from the rest.

EMBRASSÉ—Is the equivalent for *parti per chevron* when the lines forming it rise not from the base points, but from the extremities of a flank. It may, therefore be *embrassé à dextre*, or *à senestre*, and this particular needs to be specified (*cf.* Plate VI., fig. 12, which is *embrassé vivré*).

EMMANCHÉ—The term applied to denote that a charge has a handle of a different tincture.

EMMUSELÉ—Is said of an animal wearing a muzzle differing in tincture from the rest of the beast.

EMOUSSÉ—Is said of the point of a spear, or other weapon, blunted at the end.

EMPENNÉ—*Flighted;* is said of the feathers of arrows, etc.

EMPIÉTANT—Is said of a bird of prey holding in its beak and talons another creature (*cf. Ravissant*).

EMPOIGNANT—Holding in a closed fist.

EMPOIGNÉE—Is said of a bunch of arrows, spears, etc., held in the fist, and spreading in various directions.

EN FORME—Said of a hare couchant.

ENCHAINÉ—Chained.

ENCHAUSSÉ—(*V. Chaussé*).

ENCHAUSSURE—The name of one of the angular sections, two of which make the partition *chaussé* (Plate LV., figs. 2 and 8).

ENCLAVÉ—Is said when, in a coat divided per pale per fess per bend, a piece (usually square in form) intrudes into the opposite colour.

ENCLOS—Enclosed ; is said of a charge within an orle, or tressure.

ENCLUME—A mallet.

ENCOCHÉ (*v. Ajusté*)—Said of an arrow and string adjusted to a bent bow.

ENDENTÉ—Indented (*cf. Denché*).

ENFILÉ—Enfiled ; said of a sword, lance, or other long-shaped charge, around which coronets, wreaths, annulets, etc., are placed.

ENGLANTÉ—Said of an oak bearing acorns (Plate XXIX., 1).

ENGLOUTISSANT, or ENGOULANT — Swallowing whole (Plate XXVII., fig. 4).

ENGOULÉ—Is said of the arms of a cross, or saltire, or the extremities of a bend, etc., which, as in many Spanish blazons, enter the mouth of a dragon, or lion, (*v.* Plate XII., fig. 5).

ENGRÊLÉ—Engrailed.

ENGRÊLURE—A very narrow bordure engrailed.

ENGUICHÉ—When horns, etc., have the mouthpiece and bell environed with rims of metal, etc., this term is used (*v.* Plate XXXIII., fig. 10).

ENQUERRE, À, or À ENQUÉRIR — Is said of certain *armes fausses* to which a legend is attached.

ENSANGLANTÉ—Said of an animal stained with blood.

ENTÉ—A partition line, resembling *undy*, or the old form of *nebuly* (but *see Pointe infra*).

ENTRAVAILLÉ—Interlaced (*cf. Entrelacé*). VERTAMY : *d'Azur, à trois fasces d'argent, et un chevron d'or entravaillé* (the chevron is sometimes *argent* like the bars). Is also said of fish and other animals, fretted or interlaced with bars, bends, etc. *Gules, two bars wavy azure with two barbel addorsed or, entravaillés in the bars*, is the coat of RIVIÈRE DE ST. DENIS DES MONTS (*v.* MOULE'S *Heraldry of Fish*, p. 76).

ENTRELACÉS—Interlaced (Plate XIII., fig. 12) said of annulets, chevrons, crescents, etc.

ENTRETENUS—Is said of the bows of keys, etc., interlaced.

Eole—Like Boreas, the conventional symbol of the wind.

Epanoui—Opened, or expanded ; said of flowers, and especially of the Florentine lily, *florençée*.

Eployé—Displayed ; said of the eagle.

Equerre—A mason's or carpenter's square.

Equerre, Ecartelé en (*v.* Plate V., fig. 11, and p. 82).

Equipé—Is said of boats, ships, etc., rigged.

Equipollé—Is said of a large form of chequy (Plate VII., fig. 8). *Chequy of nine pieces azure and argent* would be blazoned : *Cinq points d'azur équipollés à quatre points d'argent*, the coat of St. Gelais.

Escarre—Is the name of a small filet, sometimes placed on the edge of a *franc-quartier*, or canton, which is of the same tincture as the field, in order to prevent the arms becoming *armes fausses*.

Essonier—A synonym for tressure.

Essorant—Soaring, or taking flight (Plate XXV., fig. 7, *v.* p. 262).

Essoré—Is said of the pointed roofs of castles, etc., when differing in tincture from the rest of the charge.

Estacade—A palisade.

Estoc—(*V. Chicot*).

Etai (Estaye)—A chevronel.

Etêté—(*V. Décapité*).

Etincelant—Sparkling, or shooting out sparks, like the flints in the collar of the Order of the Golden Fleece.

Etoile—(On this charge, *v. ante*, p. 307).

Evasée, Evidé—Voided. Hülsen bears : *Or, a pile reversed in bend-sinister, voided gules*.

Eviré—Without the attributes of sex.

F

Failli—Is said of a chevron one of whose sides is fractured (specify which) ; or of a pale which does not quite reach the border of the shield (specify whether in chief or in base). It is also said of those partition lines which in some German parted coats are only carried a portion of their distance (*see* Plate LV., figs. 10 and 12).

Falot—A torch, or fire-grate.

Fanal—A beacon.

Fasce—A fess.

Fasce, En—Placed in the direction of a fess.

FASCÉ—Barry of six pieces usually, if of four or eight specify the number (Plate VII., fig. 2).

FASCÉ-CONTRE-FASCÉ—Is said of a shield per pale, and barry counterchanged.

FAUX-ÉCU—A shield charged with an escucheon which has a bordure (*v.* p. 553).

FER-DE-LANCE—Sometimes pointed, sometimes blunt (*emoussé*) or a *cronel* (*v.* p. 387).

FER-DE-MOULIN—(*V. Anille*).

FERMAIL—A buckle; its form requires to be specified.

FEUILLÉ—Leaved.

FEUILLÉ DE SCIE—A term sometimes applied to bars indented on the bottom edge only. COSSÉ, Duc et Pair de BRISSAC, bore: *de Sable, à trois feuilles de scie d'or;* otherwise, *de Sable, à trois fasces d'or denchées par le bas.*

FICHÉ, FITCHY—Having a point to fix in the ground.

FIERTÉ—Is a French term applied to the whale, when its teeth, tail, and fins are tinctured *gules*.

FIGURÉ—Is said of the sun, crescents, moons, and besants which have on them the delineation of a human face.

FIL—A file, or label.

FILET—A narrow band, a diminutive of the bend, or bend-sinister.

FILET EN BORDURE—(*V. Filière.*)

FILET EN CROIX—A cross formed of very narrow pieces.

FILIÈRE—A diminutive of the bordure.

FLAMBANT—Inflamed.

FLAMBANT, CONTRE—Inflamed on both sides.

FLANCHIS—The name given to *saltorels*, or diminutive saltires (Plate XV., fig. 12).

FLANCS—The flanks, or sides, of the shield.

FLANQUÉ-EN-ROND—(Plate XVIII., fig. 6). The French blazon of our *Flaunches, e.g., d'Azur, à trois fleurs-de-lis d'or en pal, flanqueés en rond d'argent* (*Azure, three fleurs-de-lis in pale or, between two flaunches argent*), the coat of BOUDRIC.

FLEUR-DE-LISÉ (*flory*)—Said of a cross, etc., whose extremities end in *fleurs-de-lis* (*v.* p. 117).

FLEURÉ, CONTRE—Having *fleurs-de-lis* arranged alternately on both sides.

FLEURÉ, FLEURETÉ, FLEURONNÉ (*flory*)—Terms applied to Ordinaries bordered flory.

FLEURI—Flowered, applied to plants.

FLORENCÉE—A term applied (1.) To the *fleur-de-lis* as borne in the arms of FLORENCE (*v.* Plate XXX., fig. 7), and budding forth *fleurs-de-lis.*—(2.) As applied to a cross, etc., it is the equivalent of *fleur-de-lisé, q.v.*

FOI—The name for two arms issuing from the flanks, clenching the hands in the centre of the shield (*v.* p. 205).

FORCENÉ—Equivalent for *Effaré,* and *Cabré, q.v.*

FORCES (*forces à tondeur*)—Shears with square ends.

FOUDRE—A thunderbolt (masculine gender in blazon).

FOURCHÉ—Said (1.) Of a lion's tail—(2.) Of anything else forked at the end, *e.g.,* the arms of a cross.

FOURCHETÉ—Same as *Fourché.*

FOURRURE—Fur *au naturel* (*v.* p. 73).

FRANC-QUARTIER—The QUARTER or CANTON, *v.* p. 165. In Foreign Armory it is usually charged.

FRETTE—The *fret* is almost peculiar to English Heraldry (*v.* p. 181, Plate XIX., fig. 11).

FRETTÉ, FRETTY—(*V. Treillis,* etc.) French heralds make fretty of six pieces only, three in each direction.

FRUITÉ—Said of trees the colour of whose fruit is to be specified.

FURIEUX—Synonym for *Effarouché,* is said of bulls, etc., rampant.

FUSÉE—A fusil (Plate XVIII., fig. 11).

FUSELÉE, FUSILLY—(Plate VII., fig. 10).

FUSIL—A steel for striking fire, as in the Collar of the ORDER OF THE GOLDEN FLEECE.

FUTÉ—Is said—(1.) Of the trunk of a tree when of a colour different from the rest of the charge. It is used also—(2.) of the staves of pikes, lances, etc.

G

GAI—Is said of a horse without harness or trappings.

GALÈRE—A lymphad or galley (*v.* Plate XXXII., figs. 11 and 12).

GARNI—Is said of swords and other arms, equivalent for our *hilted and pommelled.*

GÉRION, TÊTE DE—A head formed of three human faces, *cf.* Arms of MORRISON (Plate XX., fig. 5).

GIRON—A *gyron* (*v.* Plate XVIII., fig. 4).

GIRONNANTS—Is said of gyrons curved in the form of a scroll or volute (*v.* Plate VIII., fig. 4).

GIRONNÉ—Divided regularly into girons (Plate VI.).

GIRONNÉ EN CROIX—Is said when the lines forming it are not

those of regular gyronny, but two issue from each edge or border of the shield.

GIRONNE, MAL—When the girons are fewer in number than eight (*v.* Plate VI., fig. 3).

GIROUETTÉ—Adorned with *girouettes*, attribute of castles, etc. (*v.* pp. 358, 359).

GISANT—A synonym for *Couché*.

GONFALON, or GONFANON—A church banner (*v.* p. 372).

GORGÉ—(*V. Colleté*).

GOUFFRE—A *gurges*, or whirlpool (*v.* Plate XIX., fig. 6 and p. 193).

GOUSSET—A *pairle* not opened in chief.

GOUTTES—Drops, synonym for LARMES; modern heralds make this distinction, the GOUTTE has a straight tail the LARME a wavy one.

GRAPPIN—Is a grapnel, drawn with four flukes.

GRÊLÉ—Adorned with pearls set close, and not raised on points.

GRÊLIER—A hooped or circular hunting-horn of large size, without cords or attachments.

GRELOTS, GRILLETS—Hawk's bells (Plate XXV., fig. 8).

GRENADES—Pomegranates, usually drawn slipped with a couple of leaves and having a little crown of leaves on the top; when they show the seed they are *ouverts*.

GRENADES DE GUERRE—A modern bearing usually drawn inflamed.

GRIFFON—The gryphon, or griffin (*v.* Chapter X., p. 286).

GRILLES—The bars of a helmet.

GRILLET—(*V. Grelot*).

GRILLETÉ—Having *grelots*, or bells, attached to it.

GRIMPANT—Equivalent of *rampant* as applied to a stag.

GRINGOLÉ—Applied to a cross, the extremities of the arms of which end in heads of serpents (*v.* Plate XV., fig. 6).

GRUE—The crane is represented with uplifted foot holding a stone —its *vigilance* (*v.* p. 263).

GUEULES (*Gules*)—The heraldic name for the colour red.

GUIDON—A split bannerol (Chapter XXII., p. 655).

GUIVRE—A large snake *engloutissant*, or *vorant*, a child (Plate XXVII., fig. 4).

GUMÈNE—The cable of an anchor.

H

HABILLÉ—(1.) Habited.—(2.) Rigged and fitted with sails.

HACHE-DANOISE—Has a long curved handle (*v.* p. 510).

HACHEMENS—Lambrequins.
HALISANT—(*V. Engloutissant*, and *Vorant*).
HAMEYDE—The name given to three bars *coupés* arranged in pale.
HARDI—Said of a cock with uplifted head and right foot.
HAUSSÉ—The term applied to Ordinaries, etc., placed higher in the shield than their natural position (reverse of *Abaissé*).
HÉRISSÉ—Is said of *étoiles* which have little rays between the larger ones.
HÉRISSONNÉ—Or the preceding is said of a hedgehog, or of a cat, whose quills, or hairs, stand erect.
HERMINÉ, CROIX D'—Cross formed of four ermine tails, the spots in the centre of the shield (*cf. Abouté*).
HERSÉ—(*V. Coulissé*).
HERSE-SARASINE—A portcullis.
HIE—A rare charge, a paving rammer.
HOMME-MARIN—A Triton.
HONNEUR, POINT D'—The honour point of the shield.
HOUSSÉ—Caparisoned.
HUCHET—A hunting horn without bands (*v. Cor de Chasse*).
HURE—The head of a wild boar or fish.

I

IMMORTALITÉ—The name for the fire out of which the phœnix rises.
ISOLÉ—Said of a mount or hill separated from the base of the shield.
ISSANT—(*Issuant, cf. Naissant*), and see Plates XXII., 3, 4, and XXIV., fig. 8).

J

JANUS, TÊTE DE—A man's head with a double face.
JUMELLES—*Bars-gemels* (Plates IX., fig. 6, and XI., fig. 11). CAETANI : *d'Argent, à une jumelle ondée d'azur, en bande*.

L

LAMBEL—A label (*v*. pp. 188 and 414).
LAMBREQUINS—The mantling of a helm, usually in floriations as distinct from the *capeline*, or hood.
LAMPASSÉ—Langued ; applied to the eagle and to quadrupeds ; but

LANGUÉ—Is said of other creatures, whose tongues require specification.
LARMES—(*V. Gouttes*).
LÉGENDE—A motto.
LÉOPARD—A lion passant-gardant.
LÉOPARD, TÊTE DE—Is always *affrontée*.
LÉOPARD-LIONNÉ—A lion rampant-gardant.
LEVÉ—(1.) Said of a bear rampant (upright).—(2.) Of wings with their points upwards.
LEVRIER—A greyhound, usually collared.
LEVRON—A greyhound without a collar.
LICORNE—The unicorn.
LIÉ—Tied, or banded. GONDI : *d'Or, à deux masses d'armes en sautoir de sable, liées de gueules.*
LIMAÇON—The snail; always drawn out of its shell and showing its horns.
LION—Usually drawn *rampant;* this is understood unless the contrary be expressed (Plate XXI., fig. 1).
LION DE S. MARC—The evangelistic symbol (*v.* p. 219).
LION, OMBRE DE—(*V. ante*, p. 223).
LION-LÉOPARDÉ—A lion passant (Plate XXI., fig. 4).
LIS-DE-JARDIN—The lily as distinct from the *fleur-de-lis*.
LISÉRÉ—Bordered.
LISTEL—The ribbon of a motto.
LONGE—The line by which hawks were held.
LONGÉ—Having a line attached.
LORRÉ—Term used to indicate the colour of the fins of fish.
LOSANGE—A lozenge.
LOSANGÉ—Covered with lozenges.
LOSANGÉ EN BANDE—Is said of lozenges arranged in bend.
LOSANGÉ EN BARRE—Is the same in bend-sinister.
LOUP—The wolf, is distinguished from the fox by having its tail in the air.
LOUP-CERVIER—An imaginary animal.
LUNE—The full moon with a human face.
LUNELS—A bearing found in Southern Heraldry, consisting of four crescents arranged in cross, all the horns being directed towards the centre of the shield (*v.* p. 579).

M

MÂCLE—A mascle.
MÂCLÉ—Masculy.

MAÇONNÉ—Having the divisions of the stones (or mortar lines) indicated in a different tincture.

MAILLET—A mallet of a peculiar shape, having a broad head and short handle. Often it is placed bendways on a chief or other Ordinary, and is then said to be *penché*.

MAIN D'AIGLE—The whole leg of an eagle, including the tufts of the thigh. These have developed into a wing attached to the leg, in the arms of MANUEL (*v*. p. 507).

MAIN-BÉNISSANTE—A right hand of which the thumb and first two fingers are erect, the others bent into the palm.

MAL-GIRONNE—(*V. Gironné*).

MAL-ORDONNÉ—Said of charges placed one and two.

MAL-TAILLÉ—A term applied to a manche.

MANCHE-MAL-TAILLÉE—(*V. ante*, p. 376).

MANIPULE—An ecclesiastical vestment which appears attached to some examples of the *dextrochère*.

MANTELÉ—(1.) Mantled.—(2.) A division of the shield, a small point in base.

MARCASSINS—The young of the wild boar.

MARINÉ—Said of animals converted into monsters by the addition of a fish's tail.

MARMITE—A cooking-pot with a handle on each side, and three feet.

MARQUÉ—Spotted, said of dice.

MARQUETÉ—Said of the body of a butterfly (*cf. Miraillé*).

MARTINET—A martlet.

MASQUÉ—Hooded.

MASSACRE—The horns or attire of a stag united by the scalp.

MASSES D'ARMES—Maces (*v*. Arms of GONDI, p. 735).

MASURÉ—Said of a castle, etc., in ruins.

MÉDUSE, TÊTE DE—Head of the Gorgon.

MELUSINE—A mermaid in a tub has this name (*v*. p. 303).

MEMBRE D'AIGLE—The leg of an eagle, claws uppermost.

MEMBRE DE LION—A lion's leg.

MEMBRÉ—The term applied when the legs of a bird are of a distinct tincture.

MENUVAIR, MINIVER—The smaller size of vair (*v*. p. 69).

MENUVAIRÉ—Said of a field of *menuvair* when other tinctures than *argent* and *azure* are employed.

MERLETTE—The martlet, borne without beak or feet (*cf. Canette* and *Martinet*).

MÉTAUX—*Or* and *argent*.

MEUBLES—The designation of all charges.

MEZAIL—The front, or middle, of a helm.

MIDAS, TÊTE DE—The head of a man with an ass's ears. HERDA, in Saxony, bears : *Gules, the head of* MIDAS *sable*. It appears also in some of the crests of the Low Countries (*see* Chap. XIX., p. 606).

MI-PARTI—Said of dimidiated arms, and of an Ordinary *parti per pale*. SALIGNON : *d'Azur, au chevron mi-parti d'or et d'argent* (*cf.* MI-TRANCHÉ). (Plate LV., fig. 12).

MIRAILLÉ—The term used to indicate the markings on the wings of butterflies (*cf. Marqueté*).

MOLETTE—The wheel of a spur, abroad usually of six rays. It is said to be *colletée* when it is attached to the iron of the spur.

MONDE—The Orb of Sovereignty, *cintré et croisé*.

MONSTRUEUX—Is said of an animal with a human head.

MONTANT—Said of a crescent in its proper position (*e.g.*, with horns upwards), when borne with others which have not that position.

MORAILLES—A twitch (*v. Broyes*, and Plate XXXII., fig. 1).

MORNÉ — Said of a lion *disarmed* and *diffamed; i.e.*, without claws, tongue, or tail ; also of an eagle without beak or claws.

MORTAISÉ—Dovetailed.

MORTIER—The cap worn by French judges (Plate L., fig. 26).

MOUCHETÉ—Spotted.

MOUCHETURES—The tails in *ermine*, and *ermines*, etc.

MOUTON—A sheep. (Compare *Brebis*, and note difference ; the *Mouton* has its head erect.)

MOUTON À PILOTER—A pile driver.

MOUVANT—Said of animals, or other charges, which seem to proceed from the borders of the shield, or the edge of an Ordinary (Plate XXII., fig. 4).

MUR—A wall (*v. Avant-mur*). If *crénelé* it should be specified.

N

NACELLE—A small boat, flat bottomed, is the charge in the arms of the Polish *herba* of LODZIA (*v. ante*, p. 370).

NAGEANT—*Naiant*.

NAISSANT—Is said of the upper part of an animal rising out of the midst of an Ordinary, etc. (distinguish from *Issant*, and *see ante*, p. 221, and Plate XXII., figs. 3, 4, and 5).

NATUREL, AU—*Proper;* of the natural colour.

NAVIRE—A ship; specify the number of masts (*cf. Vaisseau*).

NEBULÉ—Nebuly (*v.* Plate VII., fig. 3).

NENUPHAR, FEUILLES DE—The leaves of an aquatic plant, sometimes blazoned as hearts, scarabœi (*v. ante*, p. 321).

NERVÉ—Nerved, said of the leaves of plants which have the lines in a different colour.

NOMBRIL—(*V.* points of the escucheon, *ante*, p. 59).

NOUÉ—Knotted; said (1.) Of the tail of a lion.—(2.) Of cords.—(3.) Of a fess which has one or more enlargements.

NOUEUX—Knotted, as applied to branches, staves, trunks of trees, etc. (*cf. Ragulé*).

NOURRI—Is said of *fleurs-de-lis* "*au pied coupé,*" *i.e.*, of which the lower piece is removed.

NUAGÉ—A synonym for *Nebulé*.

NUÉES—In early blazon the clouds are usually indicated by nebuly lines. In later instances they are drawn less conventionally. The puffings at the shoulder of the arms which appear as charges in some Foreign coats were ignorantly turned into clouds, and are at present so drawn and blazoned (*v.* p. 205, arms of MECKLENBURG).

O

OMBELLE—A pavilion, or umbrella, which replaces the standard in certain Papal augmentations (*cf.* p. 508).

OMBRE DE LION—*V. Lion*.

OMBRE DU SOLEIL—*V. Soleil*.

OMBRÉ—Shaded.

ONDOYANT—Is said of a serpent whose body undulates.

ONDY—Undy or Wavy (*v.* p. 77).

ONGLÉ—Having talons of a specified tincture.

OR—Gold.

ORANGE—The colour *Tenné*.

OREILLÉ—Is said—(1.) of *Vannets*, which have *oreilles*, the small projections at the hinge of a scallop shell.—(2.) Of animals, having their ears of a specified tincture.

OREILLERS—Pillows, or Cushions.

ORLE—A small bordure detached from the edge of the shield.

ORLE, EN—Said of figures arranged around the escucheon near the edge within the space which would be occupied by the bordure (*cf.* Plate XVII., fig. 9).

ORLÉ—Bordured (obsolete).

OTELLES—(*V. ante*, p. 154).

OUVERT—Open, is said—(1.) Of a pomegranate showing its seeds. —(2.) Of a castle gate.—(3.) Of the wings of birds.

P

PAIRLE—A *pall*, or *pairle* (*v.* Plate XVI., fig. 10).

PAIRLE, EN—In *pairle* (*i.e.*, occupying the position taken by a *pairle*).

PAISSANT—Feeding (*v. Brebis*).

PAL—A pale.

PAL, EN—Said of charges arranged vertically.

PALÉ, PALY—Covered with an equal number of pales, usually six ; if not, specify the number (*v.* Plate VII., fig. 1).

PALÉ, CONTRE—(*V. Contre, ante*, p. 721).

PALISSÉ—Is a division of the shield by sharpened pallets counter-changed. It is also the term used to denote an enclosure of pales, as in the coat of the town of DERBY.

PALME—A palm branch.

PALMIER—A palm tree.

PÂMÉ—Is said of a dolphin with its mouth wide open.

PAMPRÉ—Is the term used when it is desired to express the tincture of the leaves of a vine shoot, or bunch of grapes.

PANACHÉ—Plumed.

PAN-DE-MUR—A piece of wall attached to a tower (*cf. Avant-mur*).

PANELLES—Is the name given to poplar leaves.

PANNES—Furs.

PANNETON, or PENNETON—The blade, or head, of a key.

PANTHÈRE AU NATUREL—Only occurs as a supporter.

PANTHÈRE-HÉRALDIQUE—In some Styrian coats has the form of a Griffon, inflamed at the mouth and ears. The original coat of STYRIA was, however, a *Stier*, and the ignorance of the artists has been the sole cause of the conversion of the horns of the harmless ox into flames, as of equally ridiculous transmutations in other coats.

PAON—The Peacock, is said to be *rouant* when it shows its tail in a circular form.

PAPEGAY—A popinjay, or parrot.

PAPELONNÉ (Plate VIII., fig. 6) — On this bearing *see* Chapter III., pp. 71-73, and *cf. Ecaillé*, p. 44.
PARÉ—Vested (*cf. Habillé*).
PARTI—Divided per pale (Plate V., fig. 1).
PASSANT—Walking with the fore-foot raised (one of the hinder ones is often slightly raised).
PASSÉ (EN CROIX, EN SAUTOIR)—Is said of *lances* and other long charges arranged in cross, or in saltire.
PATÉE—Patty (*v. ante*, p. 153).
PATÊNÔTRE (*Croix*)—A cross of small beads.
PAVILLION—(1.) The opening of a horn opposite to the mouthpiece.—(2.) The tent-like mantling or *baldachino* which is often drawn surmounting the arms of sovereign princes (*v.* p. 615).
PEAUTRÉ—Indicates the colour of the tails of mermaids and fishes, if that requires to be specified.
PENCHÉ—Said of Mallets or Helmets, placed bendways.
PENNON—A small flag, triangular in French Armory; applied also to a large *banner* (or shield) containing quarterings.
PERCÉ—Pierced, or *voided*.
PERCHÉ—Perched, said of birds.
PÉRI EN BANDE—Is said of a baton placed bendways.
PÉRI EN BARRE—Is said of a baton in bend-sinister (Plate XII., fig. 12).
PERRONÉ, CROIX—One whose four arms end in steps.
PHÉON—A pheon, drawn point upward in French coats (*v.* p. 350).
PHŒNIX—(*V.* p. 298).
PIÈCES HÉRALDIQUES—The Ordinaries in Armory.
PIÉTÉ—(*V. Pelican*, in *English Glossary*, and p. 264).
PIGNATES—Small jugs.
PIGNON—A pyramidal heap of stones, or steps, in the base of shield.
PIGNONNÉ—(*Tranché-crénele*) is *per bend embattled*, so that the *créneaux* take the form of small steps.
PILE—A *pile*, an Ordinary descending from the chief to the base: the reverse of the *pointe*.
PLAINE—A diminutive of the CHAMPAGNE, and only half its size, occupying the base of the shield (*v.* p. 311).
PLEIN—Said of a field of one tincture when uncharged (*v.* pp. 66, 67).
PLIÉ—Folded.—(1.) Said of bird's wings *close*.—(2.) Of Ordinaries, or other charges, slightly bent out of a straight line (*cf. Voutée, Affaissée, Ployé*, etc.).

PLIÉ EN ROND—Said of reptiles bent in a circle, the head biting the tail.

PLOMB, À—Is said when the lines of the *merlons* in an embattled bend or saltire are drawn in pale, and not at right angles to the line of the Ordinary. (*V.* Plate V., fig. 5.)

PLOYÉ—(*V. Chapé*, etc., *v.* Plates V., fig. 5, and XIII., fig. 4).

PLUMETÉ—(Plate VIII., fig. 7, *v. ante*, p. 72, Chapter III.).

POINT DU CHEF—The central point in the chief (*see* B, Fig. 16).

POINT D'HONNEUR—The point K in Fig. 15.

POINTE—(1.) The point, or lower part of the shield.—(2.) The converse of the pile (pile reversed) issuing from the base, and diminishing towards the chief (*see* Plate LVI., fig. 1). (For a *pointe entée*, *v.* Plate XVI., fig. 9.)

POINTS-ÉQUIPOLLES—(*V. Equipollés*).

POMMES-DE-PIN—Have the stalk upwards.

POMMETTÉE—Pommelly or pometty (Plates XIV., fig. 12, and XV. fig. 7).

PORTILLÉ—A term used to specify the colour of the gate of a house, etc.

POSÉ—(1.) Statant.—(2.) Placed in a certain position.

POTENCE—A figure shaped like a T.

POTENCÉ—(1.) Charged with *potences*.—(2.) Said of a cross with the arms like potences (*see* Plate LVI., fig. 6).

POURPRE—The colour *purpure*.

PROBOSCIDES—The *horns* in German crests are erroneously termed *proboscides* in French blazon (*v.* Chapter XIX., CRESTS).

Q

QUARTEFEUILLE—A quatre-foil.

QUARTIERS—Divisions of the shield containing different coats of arms.

QUEUE-FOURCHÉE—Having a forked tail (Plate XXI., fig. 9).

QUINTEFEUILLE—A cinque-foil (*feuille de pervanche*).

R

RABAT—The turn-back of a collar, or cuff (*cf. Rebrassé*).

RACCOURCI—Synonym of *Alaisé*.

RAIS—The rays of estoiles, or escarbuncles.

RAMÉ—Branched, said of a stag's horn.

RAMPANT—The distinctive attitude of a lion erect on one foot.

Ranchier—A term uncertainly applied to—(1.) Rams (Bouton, *Nouveau Traité de Blason*, p. 349). — (2.) A deer (Gourdon de Genouillac, p. 270) (*cf. Renchier*).
Rangé—Arranged in a certain form, or direction, *e.g., rangé en chef, en croix*, etc.
Rangier—A reaping hook without a handle.
Ravissant—Carrying off its prey (*v.* p. 228, and *cf. Empiétant*).
Rayonnant—Irradiated (Plate X., fig. 8).
Rebattements—An obsolete term for parted coats.
Rebrassé — Said of cuffs, etc., turned back (*cf. Rabats* and *Bordé*).
Recercelé—Said of a *cross-ancrée* with larger circles and more convolutions (*v.* p. 160).
Recoupé—When in a shield divided per fess a piece is again divided per fess. (*V.* Plate LV., fig. 12.)
Redorte—A branch of a tree bent into a double saltire circular or oval shape (Plate XXIX., fig. 6).
Refente—The space between the petals of a trefoil, quatrefoil, etc. (*cf.* Arms of Bismarck, p. 545).
Regardant—Said of animals (1.) Looking backwards (2.) Gazing at a star in chief.
Rempli—Is said of an Ordinary voided, and filled up with another tincture, thus Montfort : *d'Argent, à trois rustres de sable remplis d'or.*
Renard—A fox drawn like a wolf but with a pendent tail.
Renchier—A deer (Menêtrier, *Méthode du Blason*, p. 631.)
Renchier—(*V. Ranchier*).
Rencontre—The head of a lion placed *affronté* (*cf. Caboshed*).
Renversé—Is said of the chevron, and other charges, borne in a reversed position (*cf.* Plate XIII., fig. 5).
Repotencé—Is said of any piece *potencée*, which has another potence at the extremity of the potences (*see* Plate LVI., fig. 6).
Resarcelé—Is said of a cross, or other Ordinary, which is coticed ; also of a cross which has a bordure running round it at a little distance from the edge. The figures are practically identical.
Retrait—Is said of an Ordinary which only touches one edge of the shield, and does not proceed very far towards the other. *Un chef retrait* is one about half its proper width (*v. Raccourci*, and *Alaisé*). (Plate LVI., fig. 3.)
Re-tranché—Again divided in bend (*cf. Recoupé*).

(743)

RETROUSSÉ—Turned up, or bordered.
ROC—A cronel of a lance (*v.* p. 387).
ROC D'ÉCHIQUIER—The rook or castle at chess.
ROMPU—Broken. Said of a chevron of which one or other of the pieces has a break in it (Plate XIII., fig. 11), *cf. Brisé* which refers to a chevron when the break is at the point, (Plate XIII., fig. 10).
ROUANT—Said of a peacock in its pride.
ROUE DE ST. CATHERINE—A wheel having blades upon its rim.
RUSTE, RUSTRE—A rustre (*v.* Arms of MONTFORT, p. 185).

S

SABLE—The colour black.
SAFFRE—A sea eagle, or osprey.
SAILLANT—Said of animals of the chase, horses, etc., in the attitude of leaping forward.
SANGLÉ—Is said of an animal girt with a band whose colour is to be specified. GLAUBITZER : *d'Azur, au poisson d'argent en fasce, sanglé de gueules.*
SANGLIER—A wild-boar (*cf. Marcassin*).
SAUTOIR—A saltire.
SAUTOIR, EN—Is said of charges arranged in the directions taken by the Ordinary.
SAUTOIR, PASSÉS EN—Is said of swords, or other charges arranged saltireways.
SEMÉ — Powdered ; covered with small charges of indefinite number, but arranged with regularity according to modern usage. On old seals (*e.g.*, those of SWEDEN where the field is *semée* of hearts) the small charges point irregularly in all directions.
SEMÉ DE FRANCE—*Semé* of golden *fleurs-de-lis.*
SENESTRE—The left hand side of the shield, opposite to the right hand of the beholder.
SENESTRÉ—Is said of an Ordinary or charge, which has one or more subordinate charges to the left of it. It is also a partition of the shield in which the sinister side of a pale touches the sinister edge of the shield (*cf. Adextré*).
SENESTROCHÈRE—The whole left arm issuing from the side of the escucheon (*cf. Dextrochère*, and distinguish from *Avant-bras*, pp. 204, 205).

Sinople—The colour green.

Sirène—A mermaid (*v.* p. 301).

Soc de Charrue—A plough-share.

Soleil—The sun (with a human face, and irradiated with sixteen rays alternately wavy and straight).

Soleil, Ombre de—The sun eclipsed ; tinctured *gules*, or *sable*.

Sommé—(1.) Said of a castle towered ; Castillo : *d'Or, à une tour sommée de trois tourelles de gueules* (*v.* Donjonné).
—(2.) Said of a charge which supports another (*v.* p. 43, Arms of Poisieu).

Soutenu—Said of an Ordinary or charge which is supported by another, as a *chief* by a *divise*, etc.

Sphinx—A fabulous animal (*v.* p. 300).

Stangue—The stem of an anchor (*cf. Trabe*).

Supports—Animals used as supporters (distinguish from *tenants*).

Sur le Tout du Tout—Is said often of an escucheon placed *en surtout* upon another which is itself *en surtout*.

Surchargé—Is said of a charge which is itself charged.

Surmonté—Is said of a charge above which another is placed without touching it (distinguish from *sommé* where the pieces touch—a refinement not always observed).

Surtout, or Sur le Tout—Over all, *en surtout*.

T

Tacheté—Spotted.

Taf—A synonym for *Tau*, *q.v.*

Taillé—Divided per bend-sinister.

Taré—Describes the position of a helmet, *e.g.*, *taré de front*, *de profile*, etc. ; equivalent of *Posé*.

Tau—The Cross of St. Anthony (*v.* p. 161).

Tenants—Human beings, monkeys, or angels, acting as supporters (distinguish from *supports*). When the shield is supported both by a *tenant* and by a *support*, both are known by the latter name. (*See* Chapter XXI.)

Terrasse—A terrace ; diminutive of the *champagne* (*v.* p. 311).

Terrasse-isolée—The terrace is so named when it is detached from the borders of the escucheon.

Terrassé—Placed on, or growing out of, a *terrasse*.

Tertre—A small mount, usually of three coupeaux in the base of the shield (*v.* p. 311).

Tiercé—Tierced. A partition of the shield into three equal or approximately equal portions, *e.g.*, TIERCÉ EN PAL, TIERCÉ EN FASCE, TIERCÉ EN BANDE, TIERCÉ EN MANTEL, etc.

TIERCE-FEUILLES—Trefoils without the tail or stem.

TIERCES—Barrulets borne in threes, as *gemelles* are in pairs.

TIGE—The stem of a plant.

TIGÉ—Is said when the stem differs in colour from the rest of a plant.

TIGRE-HÉRALDIQUE—The conventional tiger (*v.* p. 208).

TIMBRE—The crested helm, with its wreath and lambrequins.

TIMBRÉ—Ornamented with helm, etc.

TIRE—A row of panes, or points, in chequy.

TOISON—The fleece and head of a sheep, as in the badge of the ORDER OF THE GOLDEN FLEECE.

TORTIL—A wreath of silk of two or more colours.

TORTILLÉ—Wreathed with a twisted band; said of Moor's heads, also of the bands of a sling (*cf. Wreathed, English Glossary*).

TOUR—A tower; distinguish from the castle, which has two or more towers connected by a wall, or curtain.

TOURNÉ—Is said of a crescent whose points are turned to the dexter side of the escucheon (*cf. Contourné*, where they are turned to the sinister).

TOURTEAUX (E. *torteaux*)—Discs of colour on a field of metal, or fur.

TOURTEAUX-BESANTS—Discs composed partly of colour, partly of metal, and placed as charges on a field of metal or fur (*v. Besants-tourteaux*).

TOURTELÉ—An obsolete term for *semé of tourteaux*.

TRABE—The traverse, or beam, of an anchor (*v. Stangue*).

TRAIT—Equivalent for *Tire* (*q.v.*).

TRANCHÉ—A division of the shield, *Parti per bend* (*cf. Taillé*).

TRANGLES—A synonym for *Tierces*.

TRÊCHEUR—The diminutive of an orle. The tressure is often borne flory, but more frequently is double, and flory-counter-flory (*v. ante*, p. 175).

TRÈFLE—A trefoil, three leaves and a wavy stem; distinguish from *Tierce-feuille* (*q.v.*).

TRÈFLÉ—Ornamented with trefoils (Plate XIV., fig. 11, and *see* also Plate XXIX., fig. 11).

TREILLIS—A trellis (*v. ante*, p. 97).

TREILLISSE—Trelliced. (RIETSTAP thinks it a fretty of thinner pieces, and more than six in number; but this is not the distinction, which is pointed out on p. 97.) As a curiosity I add the arms of NARISCHKIN of Russia : *Gules, a fess of the same trellised or.*

TRIANGLE—A triangle, sometimes pierced, or *voided.*

TRIANGLÉ—Covered with triangles ; that is, the field is divided by horizontal and diagonal lines (both bends and bends-sinister).

TROMPES—The horns used as crests.

TRONÇONNÉ—Cut, or broken into fragments, but preserving the general outline of the charge (*cf.* Plate XXI., fig. 8).

V

VACHE—Has its tail along the flank as one of its distinguishing features.

VAIR—One of the furs.

VAIR-ANTIQUE—The old form of *vair* (*see* Plate IV.).

VAIR-EN-PAL—(*V.* Plate IV.).

VAIR-ONDÉ—(*V.* Plate IV.).

VAIRÉ—Term employed when the vair is of other tinctures than the usual *argent* and *azure.*

VAISSEAU—A ship with three masts (*cf. Navire*).

VANNETS—Escallops turned to show the inside, and usually without *oreilles* (*cf. Coquille*).

VERGETTE—A pallet ; a diminutive of the pale.

VERGETTÉ—Covered with pallets.

VERSÉ—Inverted ; synonym of *renversé,* and used of a crescent whose horns point to the base of the shield.

VERTENELLE—The hinge of a gate.

VÊTU—A field *chapé-chaussé* (*v. ante,* p. 719, and *see* Plate VI., fig. 11).

VÊTU EN OVALE—Having a bordure which leaves the field of an oval shape.

VÊTU EN RONDE—Having a circular bordure.

VIDÉ—Voided.

VIGILANCE—The stone carried by a stork or crane.

VILENÉ—Having the virile parts of a specified tincture.

VIRES—Concentric annulets, usually three in number.

VIROLÉ—Is said of the bands of metal encircling a hunting-horn.

VIVRÉ—*Dancetty.*

VOGUANT—Sailing ; equivalent for *Flottant.* CASTELLI : *d'Azur, à un vaisseau voguant sur un mer, le tout au naturel, accompagné en chef d'une étoile d'or.*

VOL—The two wings of a bird.

VOLANT—Flying with expanded wings.

VOL-BANNERET—The term for the wings of a bird used as a crest, when they are represented as cut off square at the upper ends (*v.* Plate XLIV., fig. 1, and p. 606).

VOLET — A small mantling, or *capeline*, attached to a helmet (*v.* Plate XLIV., figs. 5, 6).

VOÛTE—Arched (*v.* Plate XI., fig. 7); contrary of *Affaisé*.

APPENDIX A.

ORDONNANCE of CHARLES III., Duke de Lorraine, respecting the Assumption of "*the Particle*," 1585.

"De par le Duc de Calabre, Lorraine, Bar, Gueldre, etc. . . . Nous avons été dûment averti que plusieurs de nos sujets, tant natifs de nos pays que venus d'ailleurs, se sont de tant avancés par subtilité, connivence, tolérance de nos Officiers et autres moyens illicites, qu'ils ont tâché d'usurper et s'attribuer les titres et qualités de Noblesse ; . . . et, qui plus est, les dits anoblis, pour se déguiser, ou faire égarer la connaissance de leur race et basse condition dont ils sont nouvellement descendus, changent et altèrent les surnoms de leurs aieux et famille, des quels ils ont pris la source et origine de leur Noblesse, par adjonction à leurs surnoms de cette vocale : *la, de, le, du,* ou de quelque Seigneurie forgée à leur fantaisie ; en sorte qu'aujourd'hui il est forte difficile, voire presque impossible, de reconnaître ceux qui sont extraits d'ancienne famille de Noblesse, ou par Nous et nos prédécesseurs décorés d'icelle entre tels ; . . . à quoi pour remédier et obvier à de tels abus, avons inhibé et défendu, inhibons et défendons à toutes personnes, quelles elles soient, qu'ils n'aient à se qualifier ni de titres, ni de qualités de Noblesse, ni d'autres plus grands titres et qualités, si donc ils ne sont extraits de Noblesse et qualité ou prérogative qu'ils s'attribuent, et si défendons aux anoblis et issus de Nobles qu'ils n'aient à soi par adjonction vocale *le, la, du,* ou *de,* et semblables mots qui ne servent que pour obscurcir la famille dont ils sont sortis, à changer ou à altérer en façon que ce soit leurs surnoms, ains se contenir ou arrêter à celui de leurs aïeux, grand-père ou père, qui aura obtenu de Nous ou de nos Prédécesseurs titre de Noblesse, et aux quels par cette concession leur Noblesse et qualité aura pris source et origine, et sans qu'il leur soit loisible ajouter et prendre plus grande qualité qu'il ne leur appartient, si donc ils n'en ont concession et privilége particulier de Nous et de nos prédécesseurs, et ce à peine d'amende arbitraire. . . . Mandons à notre procureur général, et à ses substituts qu'ils y tiennent tellement le main et fassent rayer, tant des registres des causes judiciaires comme ailleurs, ceux qui se sont ingérés et voudront ingérer de prendre et usurper les dits qualités de Noble adjonction de ces vocales : *le*, *la*, *de*, ou *du*, et attribution d'autres plus grandes qualités qui ne leur appartiennent, dont ils ne seront seigneurs."

APPENDIX B.

PORTUGUESE REGULATIONS AS TO THE BEARING ON DIFFERENCES OF ARMS (*v.* p. 396).

" O CHEFE de linhagem he obrigado a trazer as armas direitas, sem differença, ou mistura de outras algumas armas. E sendo chefe de mais que huma linagem, será obrigado a trazer as armas direitas de todas aquellas linhagens de que sor chefe, e sem mistura, em seus quarteis. Os otros Irmãos, e todos os otros da linhagem, as haõ de trazer com differença. E assim poderaõ trazer ate quatro Armas, se quizerem, daquelles, de quem descenderem, esquartelados, e mais naõ. E se quizerem trazer sómente as armas da parte de suas mãys, podelo haõ fazer. E os bastardos haõ de trazer as armas com sua quebra de bastardia. A differença que haõ de trazer os filhos segundos, lhe ha de ordenar o Rey de Armas, a quem pertence ; costuma assentarse no canto do escudo, e ha de ser huma flor, huma estrella, ou hum passaro, ou outra cousa semelhante. E aqulle espaço, em que se poem a differença, se chamã *Brica*."—(*Nobiliarchia Portugueza*, p. 223).

APPENDIX C.

TOURNEY REGULATIONS FOR THE EXPOSURE OF ARMS AND CREST, DRAWN UP BY RÉNÉ, DUC D'ANJOU, ROI DE SICILÉ ET JERUSALEM.

"VOUS tous Princes, Seigneurs, Barons, Cheualiers, et Escuyers, qui auez intention de tournoyer, vous estes tenus vous rendre és heberges le quatrième jour deuan le jour du Tournoy, pour faire de vos Blasons fenestres, sur payne de non estre receus audit Tournoy. Les armes seront celles-cy. Le tymbre doit estre sur vne piece de cuir boüilly, la quelle doit estre bien faultrée d'vn doigt d'espez, ou plus, par le dedans : et doit contenir la dite piece de cuir tout le sommet du heaulme, et sera couuerte la dite piece du lambrequin armoyé des armes de celuy qui le portera, et sur le dit lambrequin au plus haut du sommet, sera assis le dit Tymbre, et autour d'iceluy aura vn tortil des couleurs que voudra le Tournoyeur.

" Item, et quand tous les heaulmes seront ainsi mis et ordonnez pour les departir, viendront toutes Dames et Damoiselles, et tous Seigneurs, Cheualiers, et Escuyers, en les visitant d'vn bout à autre, la present les Juges, qui meneront trois ou quatre tours les Dames pour bien voir et visiter les Tymbres, et y aura vu Heraut ou poursuiuant, qui dira aux Dames selon l'endroit où elles seront, le nom de ceux à qui sont les Tymbres, afin que s'il y en a qui ait des Dames médit, et elles touchent son Tymbre, qu'il soit le lendemain pour recommandé."—(MENÊTRIER, *L'Origine des Armoiries*, pp. 79-81.)

APPENDIX D.

GRANT OF AUGMENTATION OF ARMS AND SUPPORTERS TO THE FATHER OF CAPTAIN SPEKE, THE DISCOVERER OF THE SOURCES OF THE NILE.

"VICTORIA R.—Whereas we, taking into our Royal consideration the services of the late JOHN HANNING SPEKE, Esquire, Captain in our Indian Military Forces, in connection with the discovery of the sources of the Nile, and who was, by a deplorable accident, suddenly deprived of his life before he had received any mark of our Royal favour ; and being desirous of preserving in his family the remembrance of these services by the grant of certain honourable armorial distinctions to his family arms :—Know ye that we, of our princely grace and special favour have given and granted, and by these presents do give and grant unto WILLIAM SPEKE, of Jordans, in the parish of Ashill, in the county of Somerset, Esquire, the father of the said JOHN HANNEN SPEKE, our Royal Licence and Authority that he and his descendants may bear to his and their armorial ensigns the honourable augmentation following : that is to say,—On a chief a representation of flowing water superinscribed with the word NILE ; and for a crest of honourable augmentation a crocodile ; also the Supporters following : that is to say—on the dexter side a Crocodile, and on the sinister side a Hippopotamus, provided that the same be first duly exemplified according to the Law of Arms, and recorded in our College of Arms, etc.

"Given at our Court of St. James's, the 26th day of July 1867, in the thirty-first year of our Reign.

" By Her Majesty's Command,

" GATHORNE HARDY."

The arms to be augmented were : *Barry of eight azure and argent, over all an eagle displayed with two heads gules* (Plate XXV., fig. 2). The crest, *a porcupine.* It is worthy of notice that *per incuriam,* the grant is to *all the descendants of* WILLIAM SPEKE.

APPENDIX E.

DOCUMENT RECORDING THE CONCESSION OF A CREST BY JOHN, COMTE DE SAAREBRUCK, TO HIS NEPHEW, HAMAN (OR HANNEMANN), COMTE DE DEUX-PONTS (ZWEI-BRÜCKEN) BITSCHE.

"NOUS, Haman, Comte de Deux-Ponts et Sire de Bitche, à tous ceux qui ces présentes lira ou entendront lire savoir faisons : que *le vol coupé d'argent et de sable* que nous portons en cimier nous a été octroyé et concédé en fief pour notre vie durante par notre cher oncle le Comte Jean de Sarrebruck. En témoignage de quoi, nous, sus dit Haman, Comte de Deux Ponts, Sire de Bitche, avons appendu notre scel aux présentes qui ont éte données le premier mardi qui suit le jour de Quasimodo de l'an, depuis la naissance de Dieu, mil trois cent soixante et cinq" (*i.e.,* April 22, 1365)—*Le Héraut d'Armes,* p. 208.

APPENDIX F.

LES ARMES FAUSSES.

It is only possible to give here, in fulfilment of the promise made at p. 67, a few of the multitudinous instances in which the law requiring colour on metal and metal on colour is disregarded. The following are from SIEBMACHER'S *Wappenbuch:*—GRUNBERG: *Gules, a fess vert* (i., 57)—VON BREITENBUCH : *Azure, two chevrons gules* (i., 94)—VON WALDAU : *Azure, three crescents, those in chief addorsed, the third reversed gules* (i., 54)—VON GÖRLITZ : *Per pale argent and or, two hatchets addorsed in pale counterchanged* (i., 156)—GRASSE : *Azure, ten stars gules,* 1, 2, 3, 4 (iv., 69) —GREFEN : *Argent, a saltire couped or* (i., 153)—VON FRIDUNG : *Argent, a pallet between two wings affrontés paleways or* (iii., 105) —BERGER : *Azure, two bars sable, over all a chevron countercompone argent and gules* (iii., 149) -- HILTPRANDT : *Bendy (sinister) sable and azure, over all a lion rampant or* (ii., 50).

The others are from various sources :—BUBENHAUSER : *Per fess gules and azure, a fleur-de-lis counter-changed*—The Counts LEONBERG : *Gules, a bend azure*—ULF : *Azure, a fess gules*—DORO : *Argent, a lion or*—DOTTENSTEIN : *Azure, an eagle displayed gules.* The very earliest coat of the MONTMORENCYS was : *Or, a cross argent*—ADELSBACH bore : *Per fess gules and azure, a lion counterchanged*—HENEMA : *Or, a boar rampant argent*—KROGEDANTZ : *Purpure, two reindeer horns gules*—MERKMAN : *Argent, three fleurs-de-lis or*— CABOGA : *Azure, a bend gules* — CAMPLIONCH : *Gules, a pale azure*—EGILSBERG : *Sable, on a cross gules a sun or* BORDOLO : *Gules, a cross vert*—CIMANI : *Azure, three bends gules* —ALBACHSEN : *Gules, on a bend azure three crescents or*—SANDBERG : *Or, a chevron argent between three trefoils vert.*

Here are a couple of dozen instances, taken at random from the Armory of Germany, Denmark, Italy, and Spain, and out of a very considerable number which I have recorded. It is quite possible that one or other might be suspected of being erroneously blazoned, but this will not get rid of the multitude that remain. I therefore humbly think I have proved my case, and that future compilers of books on Heraldry should "gang warily" if they are to avoid the imputation of ignorance when they talk of the arms of JERUSALEM, etc., as "the only instance" of the violation of rule.

APPENDIX G.

BADGES.

Acorn (slipped)—ARUNDEL.
Anchor (*or*)—LORD HIGH ADMIRAL.
Annulet—CLIFFORD ; NEVILLE.
Barnacles, or Breys—ST. LEGER.
Bear, and Ragged Staff—Earl of LEICESTER ; the bear *sable*, the staff *argent*, Earl of WARWICK ; the Earl of KENT the reverse (*v.* pp. 584, 585).
Bear's Head (muzzled)—Lord MORLEY.
Boar (*white*)—Lord WINDSOR ; COURTENEY, Earl of DEVON ; *blue*, VERE, Earl of OXFORD.
Bouget (*silver*)—BOURCHIER ; ROOS ; TRUSBUTT.
Buck—Lord MONTACUTE.
Bucket—Lord WELLES.
Buckle—PELHAM (*v.* p. 377) ; WILLOUGHBY.
Bull (*black*, horned *or*)—CLARENCE ; dun, NEVILLE.
Bull's Head (*argent*)—WHARTON ; *gules*, OGLE ; *sable*, gorged with golden crown, HASTINGS.
Cinquefoil—ASTLEY.
Crampet—DELAWARR.
Dragon (*red*)—CUMBERLAND ; *black*, CLIFFORD, BURGH ; *green*, PEMBROKE.
Eagle—CAMBRIDGE ; with child in nest. STANLEY.
Eagle's Claw—STANLEY (*v.* p. 558).
Elephant—BEAUMONT ; SANDYS.
Escallop—SCALES ; DACRE (*v.* p. 585).
Faggot—COURTENEY.
Falcon—ST. JOHN ; LA ZOUCHE.
Fetterlock—SUFFOLK.
Fire Beacon—COMPTON.
Fish-hook—NEVILLE.
Galley (*sable*)—NEVILLE.
Greyhound—MAULEVERER ; CLINTON ; RICH.
Griffin—Lord WENTWORTH ; head only, FIENNES, Lord DACRE.
Hedge-hog—SYDNEY.
Helmet—CHOLMONDELEY.
Horns (*silver*)—CHENEY.

Horse (*white*)—FITZALAN.
Horse-collar—ST. JOHN.
Horse-shoe—FERRERS.
Lion (*gold*)—SUFFOLK ; *white*, HOWARD ; crowned and gardant, GREY.
Lion's Head (erased)—BRANDON.
Maiden's Head—BUCKINGHAM.
Maunch—HASTINGS.
Mermaid—BERKELEY.
Mill-sail—WILLOUGHBY.
Mulberry (leaf and fruit)—MOWBRAY.
Ostrich—DIGBY.
Pelican—CROMWELL.
Pepper-sheaf—PEVERELL (*v.* p. 342).
Raven—CUMBERLAND.
Rudder—WILLOUGHBY DE BROKE
Saracen's Head—COBHAM.
Ship—NEVILLE.
Ship's Buoy—NEVILLE.
Sickle—HUNGERFORD (*see* PEVERELL, *v.* p. 585).
Spear-head—PEMBROKE.
Staples—NEVILLE ; STAPLETON.
Star—SUSSEX ; FITZWALTER ; VERE.
Stump of Tree—WOODSTOCK ; BEDFORD.
Swan—BOHUN ; GLOUCESTER ; BUCKS ; STAFFORD ; HUNSDON.
Talbot—SHREWSBURY ; MONTACUTE.
Unicorn—WINDSOR.
Wheat-sheaf—BURLEIGH ; CECIL ; EXETER.
Wings (of bat)—DAUBENY.
Wolf (*argent*)—MORTIMER.

APPENDIX H.

TRANSFERENCE OF RIGHT IN ARMS.

"To all them wch shall see or heare this present lettre, Thomas Grendall of Fenton, cousin and heyre to John Beaumeys, sometime of Sawtre, greeting. As the armes of the ancestors of the said

John, since the day of his death, by lawe and right of inheritance, are escheted unto me as to the next heyre of his linage, know yee that I, the aforesaid Thomas, have given and granted by these presents the whole armes aforesaid, with theyr appurtenances, unto Sir William Moigne, Knight, which armes are Argent, a cross azure, five garbes or, to have and to hould the said armes, with theyr appurtenances, to the said Sr William and his heyres and assignes for ever. In witnesse whereof, I have to these present letters set my seale. Given at Sawtre the 22 day of Novembr. in the 15 yeare of King Richard the Second."—(*Visitation of Huntingdon*, p. 16.)

Another curious armorial transaction, as late as 1777, is recorded in STODART, *Scottish Arms*, ii., 306 ; in which Neil Grant (who claimed to be representative "of the family of Grant of Auchernack, chieftain or head of the Clan Allan") professed to divest himself of his "coat of arms and ensign armorill," and transfer them to his "near and beloved cousine, Doctor Gregory Grant, physician in Edinburgh."

INDEX.

A la cuisse, 701.
AA, VANDER, *arms*, 94 ; 143, 427.
AACHEN, *arms*, 283.
AAVAILLE, *arms*, 185.
Abaissé, 119 ; 709.
ABARCA, *arms*, 392.
ABARIA, *arms*, 89.
Abased, 676.
Abatements, 676.
ABBATI, *arms*, 121.
ABBENBROEKS, *arms*, 392.
ABBEVILLE DALENONCOURT, *arms*, 170.
ABEL, *arms*, 196.
,, ,, ascribed to, 23.
ABERBROTHOCK, Monastery of, 657.
ABERBURY, *arms*, 124 ; Pl. XI., fig. 4, p. 124.
ABERCORN, Family, *label*, 420.
,, Stronghold of, 516.
ABERCROMBY of Birkenbog, 433.
,, of Fetternear, *brisure*, 433.
ABERDEEN, City of, *arms*, 179 ; Pl. XXXII., fig. 5, p. 361 ; seal of, 179.
,, Earl of, *arms*, 180.
ABERDEENSHIRE, Names, 400.
ABERGAVENNY, Earl of, *rose*, 446.
ABERNETHY, *arms*, 106, 133, 519, 522, 566 ; Pl. IX., fig. 6, p. 108.
ABERNONS, d', *arms*, 136.
ABICI, *arms*, 394.
ABILLON, Earl of, *arms*, 186.
Abime, 709.
ABINGDON, Earl of, *arms*, 352.
ABLEIGES, Comtes d', *arms*, 239.
Abouté, 705, 709.
ABOYNE, CHARLES, Earl of, *arms*, 180.
,, Earl of, *arms*, Pl. XVII., fig. 12, p. 172.
ABRY, Ducs d', *arms*, 113.
ABSPERG, *arms*, 89 ; Pl. VI., fig. 10, p. 84.
Accolé, 636, €76, 680, 710.
Accompagné, 109, 681, 710.
ACCORAMBONI, *arms*, 289.
Accorné, 710.
Accosté, 109, 676, 710.
Accosted, 676.
Accroupi, 703, 710.
Acculé, 701, 710.
ACHAIA, JAMES, Titular Prince of, 579.
,, LOUIS, Prince of, 579.
,, PHILIP, Prince of, 579.
,, Princes of, *brisure* of, 429.
ACHAIUS, fictitious King of the Dalriadic SCOTS, 176, 335.
ACHARD, *supporters*, 643.

ACHEY DE THORAISE, Marquises, *arms*, 348.
ACHTOW, Abbot of, 371.
ACON, JOAN of, 457.
Acorn (slipped), as a *badge*, 753.
Acorns, 340.
ACQUAVIVA, *arms*, 214.
ACRE *Roll*, 481, 554.
ACTIUM, Battle of, 277.
ACTON, EDWARD DE, *arms*, 407.
ADALBERT, *arms*, 173.
ADAM, *arms*, 195.
,, ,, ascribed to, 23.
,, as a charge, 195.
ADAMOLI, *arms*, 195.
Adder nowed, Pl. XXVII., fig. 1, p. 288.
ADDERBURY, *arms*, 124.
Adders, 273.
Addorsed, 290, 676.
Addossés, 220.
ADELSBACH, *arms*, 752.
Adextré, 711.
ADLERSTJERNA, *arms*, 309.
Admiral, Castile, mark of office, 645.
,, French, mark of office, 645.
,, Holland, mark of office, 645.
,, Lord High, *badge*, 753.
,, of the Indies, mark of office, 645.
ADOLF, Emperor, *augmentation*, granted by, 536.
,, of NASSAU, *coins of*, 246.
Adossé, 270, 676, 711.
ADRIANI, *arms*, 235.
Advocates' Library, Heraldic MSS. in, 518.
AELST, VAN, *arms*, 341.
Æolus, Head of, 201.
ÆSCHACH, *arms*, Pl. XLV., fig. 4, p. 540.
ÆSCHYLUS, Description of devices on shields, 29.
Affaissé, 125, 682, 687, 711, 740.
AFFAITATI, *arms*, 289.
Affenartig, 198.
AFFENSTEIN, *arms*, 240.
AFFLECK, *arms*, 127.
AFFONSO III., King of PORTUGAL, 578.
,, son of JOAÕ I., King of PORTUGAL, 577.
Affronté, 603, 604, 676, 680, 688, 698, 701, 711.
Affûté, 706, 711.
AGINCOURT, Battle of, 593, 659.
Agité, 711.
Agneau pascal, 692, 697, 711.
AGNELLI, Marquis, *arms*, 235.
Agnus Dei, 692, 697.
AGOULT, Marquises d', *arms*, 228.
AGRAIN, EUSTACHE d', Prince of Sidon and Cæsarea, *arms*, 118.

(757)

Agricultural implements as charges, 393.
AGUIAR, Dukes of, *arms*, 507.
AGULON, *arms*, 458.
„ JOANNE d', 458.
„ ROBERT, *arms*, 331.
AHEIM, *arms*, 669.
AHLEFELD, *supporters*, 231.
Aigle, 711.
„ *Main d'*, 712.
Aiglettes, 712.
Aigliaux, 712.
Aiglons, 712.
Aiguiére, 712.
Aiguisé, 123, 699, 712.
Aiguisee, Cross, fig. 60, p. 164.
AIKENHEAD, *arms*, 340.
Aile, 676.
Ailé, 708, 712.
Ailettes, 676.
AILSA, Marquises of, *arms*, 163.
Aire, 712.
AIRLY, Earl of, *arms*, 216.
Aislé or *Aile*, 676.
Ajouré, 158, 699, 712.
Ajouté, 712.
Ajusté, 712, 729.
Alaisé, 712, 742.
ALAMANI, *arms*, 95.
Alant, 676.
ALARCON, *arms*, 506.
„ ISABELLA DE, 506.
ALARIC, 658.
ALBACHSEN, *arms*, 752.
ALBANIA, *arms*, 503.
ALBANY, ALEXANDER, Duke of, *arms*, 446.
„ Duke of, 516.
„ „ *arms*, 645.
„ Dukes of, *wreath*, 614.
„ HENRY, Duke of, 476.
„ ISABELLA, Duchess of, *seal*, Pl. XXXVII., fig. 7, p. 448.
„ JEAN, Duc d', *arms*, Pl. XXXVI., p. 446.
„ JOHN, Duke of, 180.
„ LEOPOLD, Duke of, *label*, 423 ; Fig, 83, p. 421.
„ Regent, 515.
„ ROBERT, Duke of, 178, 520 ; *brisure*, 445 ; *label*, 419.
ALBASTER, *arms*, 349.
ALBEMARLE, Earl of, *arms*, 273 ; *Garter Plate*, 486.
ALBERGHI, *arms*, 73.
ALBERICI, *arms*, 73.
ALBERT, Archduke, 246 ; *Ordonnances of*, 551, 637.
„ Count PALATINE of the RHINE, *seal of*, 251.
„ Emperor, *arms*, 247.
„ PIERRE D', 10.
ALBERTAS, Marquis d', *arms*, 228.
ALBERTI, *arms*, 355.
„ Marquises, *supporters*, 643.
ALBRET, *arms*, 66, 461.
„ ARNAUD D', *supporter*, 635.
„ CHARLES D', *augmentation*, 538.
„ *supporters*, 634.
ALBUQUERQUE, *arms*, 440, 578.
„ BELTRAN, First Duke of, 440.
ALCHERIUS ADALONIS, 10.
Alcyon, 713.

ALDAM, *arms*, 130, 146.
ALDENBURG, VON, *arms*, 86.
ALEGRE, Marquis de TOURZEL, *arms*, 112.
ALENCON, *arms*, 449.
„ CHARLES, Count of, *supporters*, 632.
„ Comte d', *arms*, 140.
„ Dukes of, *arms*, 439.
„ JEAN IV., Comte d', *supporter*, 631.
Alérion, 258, 676, 713.
Alésé, 712.
ALESSANDRI, Counts, *arms*, 236.
ALESSO, Marquis d'ERAQUY, *arms*, 279.
ALEXANDER II., Emperor of RUSSIA, 542.
„ II., King of SCOTLAND, 92 ; *seal* of, 177.
„ III., King of SCOTLAND, 209 ; *crest*, 600 ; Pl. XLIX., fig. 8, p. 606 ; *seal* of, 177.
„ III., Pope, 40, 66.
„ IV., Pope, *arms*, 256.
„ VII., Pope, *arms*, 319.
„ *arms*, 21.
„ *arms*, Pl. IX., fig. 11, p. 108.
„ Earl of STIRLING, *arms*, 109.
„ JOHN of Kinglassie,*arms*, 139.
„ Lord of the ISLES, *seal of*, 367.
ALEXANDROWICZ, Counts, *arms*, 351.
ALEXIUS I., Biography of the Greek Emperor by his daughter, 26.
Alezé, 712.
ALF, *arms*, 350.
ALFONSO XI., King of SPAIN, 576.
ALICE, Princess, Grand Duchess of HESSE, *label*, 423 ; Fig. 86, p. 421.
ALIGHIERI, DANTE, *arms*, 126.
ALINGTON, Lords, *arms*, 180.
ALKEVEDERS, *arms*, 240.
ALKMAAR, VAN, *arms*, 140.
ALLAIRE, *arms*, 280.
ALLAN, Chief of Clan, 755.
ALLEMAN, AYMAR, *arms*, 52.
„ EUDES, Seigneur des CHAMPS, *arms*, 51.
„ GUI, *arms*, 52.
„ ODO, *arms*, 52.
„ of Arbent, *arms*, 52.
„ of Uriage, *arms*, 52.
„ of Vaubonnois, *arms*, 52.
„ SIBOUD, Bishop of GRENOBLE, *arms*, 52.
ALLEMANDS, *arms*, 370.
ALLEN, *arms*, 124, 294.
„ J. ROMILLY, *Christian Symbolism in Great Britain and Ireland*, 300.
Allerion, 258, 676.
ALLEYN, *arms*, 156.
Alligator, The, 277.
ALLOIS, *arms*, 181.
Allumé, 693, 686, 713, 714.
ALM, VON DER, *arms*, 121.
ALMOND, *arms*, 145.
ALOST, Seigneur d', *arms*, 118.
Alphabet, Letters of the, as charges, 394.
ALPHONSO VI., 168.

(758)

ALPHONSO of Castile, *seal* of, 244.
ALQUERIA DE BOIGUES, *arms*, 284.
ALSACE, *arms*, 545.
,, PHILIPPE, d', Comte de FLAN-DERS, *seal*, 36, 48 ; *helmet*, 599.
ALSTON, *bordure*, 569.
ALTAMIRA, Counts of, *arms*, 507.
ALTDORF, Counts von, *arms*, 213.
ALTENBURG, Burg-gravate of, *arms*, 324.
ALTHANN, Barons, *arms*, 394.
ALTORF. *arms*, 669 ; Pl. LV., fig. 10, p. 668.
ALTROCK, *arms* and *augmentation*, 543.
ALTSTETEN, *arms*, 93.
ALVA, Duke of, 99.
,, ,, *arms*, 100.
,, ,, *supporters*, 643.
ALZON, *arms*, 97.
Amaranth or *Columbine* colour, 61.
AMBESACE, *arms*, 387.
AMBLISE, Princes d', *arms*, 113.
AMBOISE, *arms*, 91.
AMBOIX, *arms*, 317.
AMELIA, Princess, *label*, 423.
AMELIN, *see* VRANX.
AMELOT, 12.
AMERICA, Discovery of, 643.
,, UNITED STATES OF, *arms*, *supporter*, and *motto*, 640.
AMERONGEN, BARONS TAETS D', *arms*, 124.
Amethyst, 65, 676.
AMHERST, Earls AMHERST, *arms*, 347.
AMICI, *arms*, 87 ; Pl. VI., fig. 5, p. 84.
AMIRATO, *arms*, 93.
AMORI, D', *arms*, 93, 457.
,, ELIZABETH D', *seal*, 457.
,, ROGER D', *arms*, 457.
Amphiptère, The, 294, 713.
Amphisbène, 713.
Amphisbœna, 676, 713.
Amphistère, 713.
AMPURIAS, *arms*, 93.
AMSTERDAM, City of, *arms*, 146, 283.
,, Nieuwe and Oude Kerk in, 626.
AMUNDEVILLE, *arms*, 122.
Amusement, *Instruments of*, as charges, 387.
Ananas, 341.
ANAUT, *arms*, 318.
ANCASTER, Duke of, *arms*, 352.
ANCE, Comte d', et de MAGUSAC, supposed *arms* of, 46.
ANCEZUNE, Ducs de CADEROUSSE, *arms*, 293.
ANCHÉ, 682, 713.
Anchor as a *badge*, 753 ; as a charge, 370.
Anchored or *Ancred*, 676.
Anchors as *supporters*, 643.
Ancolie, 713.
ANCRAM, *arms*, 371.
Ancré, 676, 713.
Ancred, 676.
Ancrée, *Cross*, 158.
ANDELOT, Marquesses d', *arms*, 257.
ANDERSEN, *arms*, 120.
ANDERSON, *arms*, 232.
,, Dr JOSEPH, *Scotland in Early Christian Times*, 657.
ANDERTON, *arms*, 354.
ANDLAU, Barons, *arms*, 141.

ANDRÉ, D', Seigneurs de MONTFORT, 10.
ANDRÉE, Duc d', *arms*, 308.
ANDRONICUS PALÆOLOGUS, *coins* of, 250.
ANDUSE, Seigneur d', 12.
ANFREVILLE, *see* GUYOT, 344.
Angel supporter, 631, 632, 633, 635, 636.
,, *Demi*, as *supporters*, 635.
Angemme, 713.
Angenne, 676, 713.
ANGERS, Cloister of ST. AUBIN at, 299.
,, DU PLESSIS, *arms*, 71.
ANGERVILLE, D', 17.
Angevin *rastrello*, 470.
Anglé, 676, 713.
Angled, 676.
ANGLERIA, Lordship, 274.
ANGLURE, Counts de BOURLEMONT and ESTOGES, *arms*, 113.
,, *Les Saladins d'*, 113.
ANGOULÊME, *arms*, 531.
,, Duc d', *arms*, 570.
,, Dukes of, *label*, 425.
,, HENRI, Chevalier d', *arms*, 570.
ANGRIA, Duchy of, *arms*, 321.
ANGUILLARA, *arms*, 120, 272.
ANGUIVARIA, Lordship, 274.
ANGUS, ARCHIBALD, *Bell the Cat*, 5th Earl of, *arms*, 519.
,, *arms*, 519, 631.
,, Countess of, *label*, 420.
,, ,, *seal*, 455, 631.
,, 2nd Earl of, *arms*, 518.
,, ,, *seal*, 519.
,, 6th Earl of, *arms*, 516, 518, 519.
,, Earls of, *arms*, 179, 322, 455, 513, 515, 518, 519, 566.
,, ,, *crest*, 294.
,, Margaret, Countess of, *seal*, 459.
,, of the ISLES, *seal* of, 367.
,, *White lion* of, 519.
ANHALT, *arms*, 67.
,, Dukes of, *arms*, 321, 469.
Anille, 731.
Anillée (croix), 713.
Animate charges, 194, 208, 242.
Animé, 686, 714.
ANJORRANT, Marquises of, *arms*, 334.
ANJOU, *arms*, 483 ; Pl. XXXIX., fig. 6, p. 482.
,, CHARLES, Comte d', *seals* of, 329, 628.
,, Comtes d', *arms*, 261, 657, 658.
,, ,, *badge*, 586.
,, Ducs d', *arms*, 104, 439, 502, 538, 572.
,, Dukes of, *label*, 416, 470.
,, LOUIS, Duc d', arms on Eagle, 631.
,, NAPLES, *arms*, 258.
,, PHILIP, Duc d', and King of SPAIN, *arms*, 487.
,, RENÉ, Duc d', Tourney Regulations, 749.
,, ,, of, *seal*, 498.
,, *seal* of MARIE D', 57.
,, *tomb* of GEOFFROI PLANTAGENET, Count d', 43.
ANNANDALE, *arms*, 144, 378, 446, 515.
ANNANDS, Lords of ANNANDALE, *arms*, 144.

(759)

ANNE, Queen of England, *arms*, Pl. LII.,
fig. 8, p. 662; *motto* of, 421, 664; *supporters* on *seal*, 663.
Annelet, 676, 714.
ANNESLEY, *arms*, 91.
Annille, 713.
ANNS, *arms*, 306.
Annulet, 676, Pl. XIX., fig. 8, p. 192.
,, as a *badge*, 753.
,, for fifth son, 444.
,, *Stoned*, Pl. XIX., fig. 9, p. 192.
ANNUNCIADA, ORDER OF THE, 628.
ANREP, *arms*, 391.
ANREP-ELMPT, Counts, *arms*, 392.
ANSELME, Père, 659.
ANSOLDUS ROGERII, 10.
ANSTIS, *Aspilogia*, 628.
,, quoted by BELTZ, 590.
ANSTRUTHER, *arms*, 147, 149; Pl. XVI.,
fig. 2, p. 146.
ANTELMI, *arms*, 349.
Antelope, The, 236, 676; Pl. XXIV.,
fig. 5, p. 236.
,, as a *badge*, 588, 594.
ANTIOCH, Principality of, *arms*, 141.
Antiquarian Society, Roll of Arms of,
376.
*Antiquaries of Scotland, Proceedings of
Society of*, 619.
Antiquaries, Society of, London, 63.
Antique, à l', 713.
Antiqvarisk Tidskrift för Sverige, 52, 487.
ANTOING, *arms*, 213.
ANTONELLI, *arms*, 197.
Ants, 284.
ANTWERP, *arms*, 283, 361.
ANVERS, D', 17.
ANVIN, *arms*, 186.
ANWICKE, *arms*, 152.
AOSTA, Duchy of, *arms*, 214.
APCHIER, Marquises d', *arms*, 360.
Ape, The, 240.
APELVOISIN, *arms*, 366.
APFALTRER, Barons, *arms*, 317.
Apollo, Winged horse of, 298.
Apparel, Wearing, as charges, 392.
Appaumé, 204, 676, 714.
APPELBOOM, *arms*, 317.
Appendix A, 748.
,, B, 749.
,, C, 749.
,, D, 750.
,, E, 751.
,, F, 752.
,, G, 753.
,, H, 754.
APPLEGARTH, *arms*, 340.
APPLEGH, *arms*, 240.
Apples, 340.
APPLETON, *arms*, 340, 341.
Appointé, 705, 714.
APREECE, *arms*, 348.
Aquilon, 714, 717.
AQUIN, *arms*, 148, 714.
AQUINO, Ducs de CASOLI, *arms*, 95.
ARBALESTES, Vicomtes de MELUN,
arms, 349.
ARBALESTIER, 349.
ARBOUVILLE, Marquis d', *arms*, 93.
ARBROATH, Monastery of, 657.
ARC, Brothers of JEANNE D', *arms*,
331, 710.
Arc en ciel, 714.
Archæologia, 63, 70, 252, 458, 592, 602.

Archæologia Æliana, 461, 474, 482, 584,
641; Pl. XXXIV., fig. 3.
,, *Cantiana*, 73.
*Archæological Association, Journal of the
British*, 291, 386.
Archæology, Heraldry important branch
of, 672.
ARCHAMBAULTS, *arms*, 57.
Archbishops, *arms*, 525.
Arche de Noë, 714.
Arched, 677.
ARCHEL, L', *arms*, 371.
ARCHER, *arms*, 363.
ARCHERS, *arms*, 350.
Arches, 363.
ARCHIAC, Marquis d', *arms*, 260.
Archières, 714.
ARCO, Counts d', *arms*, 349, 511.
ARCOS, Duke of, *arms*, 506.
Arcté, 714.
ARCY D', *arms*, 174.
Ardent, 692, 714.
ARDILAUN, Lord, *supporters*, 647.
ARENBERG, Duchy of, *arms*, 492.
,, MARGARET, sister and
heiress of the last Count
of, 492.
,, Princes of, *arms*, 492.
ARENSBERG, County of, *arms*, 256.
ARESEN, *arms*, 229.
ARFETTI, *arms*, 198.
ARGELO, D', *arms*, 318.
ARGENCON, D', *see* BOFFIN.
ARGENSOLA, *arms*, 341.
Argent or Silver, 60, 65, 677, 714; Pl. III.,
fig. 2, p. 60.
,, *plein*, D', 66.
ARGENTEUIL, Comte, *arms*, 184.
ARGENTINE, D', *arms*, 381.
ARGOTE DE MOLINA *Nobleza del Andaluzia*, 353.
Argus, Head of, 201.
,, *Tête d'*, 714.
ARGYLE, ARCHIBALD, Duke of, 568.
,, *arms*, 83, 84, 368, 447, 644.
,, House of, 520.
ARGYLLSHIRE names, 400.
ARIANO, Comte d', *wreath*, 614.
,, ,, *arms*, 213.
ARIGONIO, *arms*, 313, 364; Pl. XXXII.,
fig. 8, p. 358.
Arithmetical figures as charges, 394.
ARKEL, *arms*, 99, 124, 127; Pl. XI.,
fig. 9, p. 124.
ARKENHOLME, Battle of, 516..
ARLOTT, *arms*, 225.
Arm, Human, 204.
Arma inquirenda, 103, 729.
ARMAGH, *arms* of See, 375.
ARMAGNAC, Counts of, *arms*, 213.
,, *seal* of JEAN, Comte d',
58.
ARMAILLÉ, Marquises d', *arms*, 434.
ARMANES, Marquises of BLACON,
arms, 93.
Armé, 677, 691, 706, 714.
Armed, 211, 227, 257, 677.
ARMELLINI, *arms*, 140.
ARMENIA, *arms*, 666.
Armes fausses, Les, 752.
,, *parlantes*, 661, 670, 679.
,, *-pleines*, 65, 66, 714.
,, *pour enquérir*, 103, 729.
Armi dei Municipj Toscani, Le, 359.

(760)

Armorial bearings, Object for adoption of, 45.
,, ,, on coins, 44.
,, ,, on monuments, 43.
,, ,, on shields, 45.
,, ,, playing upon names of wearers, 671.
,, combats, 33.
,, de Berry, 169, 393, 394, 404, 411.
,, de Gelre, or de Geldre, 34, 55, 165, 169, 223, 254, 331, 332, 357, 362, 373, 393, 410, 411, 427, 429, 572, 593, 611, 614, 615; Pl. XLIV., p. 538.
,, Insignia, Origin of, 19.
Armorists, Ignorance of old, 62.
Armory, Sources of information regarding, 36.
Armour, Norman, 53.
Armoyé, 611, 615, 634, 650, 653, 654, 677, 725.
Arms, Pl. XX., fig. 10, p. 198.
,, and Crest, Tourney regulations for the exposure of, 749.
,, Earliest period to which use of can be traced, 32.
,, Gifts and assignations of, 35.
,, Kings of, collar, 598.
,, of expectation, 478.
,, of Kings of Arms, 525, 526.
,, Official, 525.
,, on a banner, 641.
,, Pictorial, 312.
,, Portuguese regulations as to the bearing of differences of arms, 749.
,, Rolls of, 357, 600.
,, Transference of right in, 754.
ARMSTRONG, arms, 206.
ARNAUD, GARCIA, Comte d'ANCE et de MAGUSAC, supposed arms of, 46.
ARNEEL, arms, 272.
ARNIM, Counts, arms, 126.
ARNOLET DE LOCHFONTAINE, Marquises de BUSSY d'AMBOISE, arms, 153.
ARNSTADT, arms, 489.
ARNSTEIN, Counts von, arms, 93.
AROUET DE VOLTAIRE, arms, 314.
ARPAIOU, arms, 722.
ARPAJON, Duc d', arms, 384.
ARQUINVILLIERS, arms, 72.
Arraché, 677, 686, 715.
ARRAGON, arms, 122, 156, 471, 483, 495, 501, 502, 505, 506, 547, 577, 633; Pl. X., fig. 9, p. 118.
,, CATHARINE of, 530.
,, CHARLOTTE of, 258, 505.
,, Don FERDINAND D', Duke of CALABRIA, arms, 502.
,, KATHARINE of, badge, 596.
ARRAGON-SICILY, arms, 577.
ARRAN, arms, 368, 568, 570.
,, Earl of, arms, 163, 567, 568, 569.
ARRAS, arms, 372.
,, See of, arms, 240.
ARREAU, arms, 350.
Arret de lance, 707, 715.
Arreté, 704, 715.
Arrière Main, 715.
ARRIPE, D', arms, 337.
Arrondi, 677, 702, 715.
Arrow, Pl. XXXI., fig. 6, p. 346.
,, Broad, 350.
Arrows, 349.

Arrows in bundles, 350.
,, Sheaf of, as a badge, 596.
ARSCHOT, ARNOLD, Count of, arms 404.
,, GEOFFREY D', crest, 600.
,, Marquises d', arms, 127, 449.
ARTENSAC, see CALMELS.
ARTEVELDE, PHILIP VAN, 278.
,, VAN, arms, 337.
ARTHUR, King, arms (?), 21.
,, Prince of WALES, 420.
Artichokes, 344.
Artillery, Grand Master, French, mark of office, 645.
ARTOIS, arms, 458, 463, 631.
,, BLANCHE D', 416.
,, JEANNE, Countess of, 457.
,, label, 424, 464.
,, ROBERT, Comte d', 463.
,, ,, ,, arms and label, 416.
,, ,, D', Pl. II., fig. 5, p. 44.
ARUNDEL, arms, 266.
,, badge, 753.
,, BEATRICE, Countess of, seal, 475.
,, Earl of, 577.
,, ,, arms, 557.
,, EDMUND DE, shield, 634.
,, JOHN, Earl of, arms, 482.
,, RADULPHUS DE, arms, 557.
,, RICHARD, Earl of, 557.
,, Sir WILLIAM, lambrequin, 612.
ASBACH, arms, 136.
ASCHAU, arms, 61.
ASGILL, crest, 295.
Ash colour or Cendrée, 61.
ASHLEY, crest, 295.
ASHMOLE, quoted, 418.
ASHWEED, arms, 240.
ASLOWSKI, arms, 93.
Aspas, 702.
ASPENELL, arms, 276.
ASPERG, arms, 373.
ASPERMONT, County of, arms, 493.
,, Lordship of, arms, 447.
Aspersed, 677.
ASPINALL, arms, 320.
ASPREMONT, GUILLAUME D', seal of, 189.
,, Lordship of, arms, 141.
Ass, The, 237.
Assis, 677, 703, 715.
Aster, The, 336.
ASTI, Dukes of, arms, 214.
ASTLEY, Earls of SHAFTESBURY, 234.
,, Lord, arms, 322.
ASTON, arms, 81; Pl. V., fig. 8, p. 80.
ASTRAKAN, arms, 665.
Astronomical charges, 305.
ATAIDES, arms, 95.
ATH, D', 17.
ATHLONE, Earls of, arms, 127.
ATHOLE, arms, 521; Pl. VII., fig. 1, p. 90.
,, Dukes of, arms, 207.
,, Earl of, 517.
,, ,, badge, 598.
,, ,, seal and arms, 520.
,, Earldom of, arms, 90.
,, Earls of, arms, 368, 446.

(761)

ATHOLE, REGINALD, Earl of, *supporters*, 629.
ATTICHY, MONTMORENCY - LAVAL D', *brisure*, 452.
Attired, 232, 677.
Attires, 232, 677.
ATTLEY, *badge*, 753.
ATTON, *arms*, 153.
Au naturel, 700, 732.
Au pied coupé, 738.
AUBAS, *see* FORESTIE.
AUBER, *arms*, 173.
AUBERD, *arms*, 67.
AUBIGNÉ, GUILLAUME D', *arms*, 413.
,, RAOUL D', *arms*, 413.
AUBIGNY, *arms*, 124, 521, 559.
,, Duchess of, 559.
,, Sire d', 515.
AUBRAIS, DES, *arms*, 371.
AUBUSSONS, Comte de la FEUILLADE, etc., *arms*, 159.
,, Duc de la ROANNAIS, *arms*, 159.
AUCHENLECK, *arms*, 127, 142, 519.
AUCHMUTY, *arms*, 347.
AUDELE, Sir JAMES, *arms*, 417.
AUDELEY, *arms*, 96.
,, Lord, grants *arms*, 35.
,, Lords, *arms*, 136.
AUERSPERG, Princes of, *arms*, 234, 448.
AUFFRECK, *arms*, 207.
Augmentation, Chief, used as an, 119.
,, *Difference by an*, 448.
Augmentations, 528, 655.
,, Imperial, 535.
AUGUSTA, Princess, *label*, 422; Fig. 86, p. 421.
AUGUSTINS, *arms*, 137.
AUNOY, GUILLAUME D', *arms*, 118.
AURBERG, *arms*, 88; Pl. VIII., fig. 3, p. 100.
AURELLE DE LA FREDIÈRE, *arms*, 188.
AUSCHWITZ, Duchy, *arms*, 504.
AUSSONNE, Marquises d', *arms*, 316.
AUSTIN, *arms*, 152.
Austria ex archivis Mellicensibus illustrata, 472 (*see* HUEBER for other references to this book).
AUSTRIA, *achievements* of Empress MARIA THERESA of, 494.
,, ALBERT, Archduke of, *seal*, 478.
,, ,, Duke of, *seal*, 456.
,, ,, of, 246.
,, ANCIENT, *arms*, 497, 500.
,, Arch-ducal *crown*, 500, 623.
,, *arms*, 247, 253, 454, 456, 471, 478, 499, 508, 509, 537, 540, 577, 664, 665.
,, *crest*, 607.
,, *crest* as augmentation, 608.
,, *crown* of Emperors of, 621.
,, Don JOHN of, *arms*, 577; Pl. XLVIII., fig. 3, p. 576.
,, Duke FREDERICK of, 500.
,, Dukes of, *arms*, 456.
,, Emperors of, *arms*, 258.
,, "*Hauswapen*," *arms*, 123, 472, 501.
,, *Imperial arms*, 471.
,, *Imperial seals*, 471.
,, LEONORA of, *seal*, 475.

AUSTRIA, LEOPOLD, ALBERT, and FREDERICK, Dukes of, 614.
,, LEOPOLD, Duke of, *banner*, 650.
,, MARGARET of, Duchess of BURGUNDY, *seal*, 478.
,, MAXIMILIAN of, 484.
,, -MODERN, *arms*, 253.
,, Old Imperial *crowns* of, 622.
,, Original *arms* of Emperors of, 212.
,, OTTAKAR, Duke of, *seal* and *banner*, 651.
,, RODOLPH and FREDERICK, Dukes of, *crest-coronet*, 614.
,, RUDOLF IV., Archduke of, two sets of *supporters*, 634.
,, *seal* of LEOPOLD of, 243.
,, *supporters of arms*, 288, 634.
,, The "Ecu Complet" of, Fig. 91, p. 497.
,, UPPER, *arms*, 499.
AUSTRIAN EMPIRE, *arms*, 497, 664; Pl. LIII., fig. 1, p. 664.
,, ,, *supporters* of, 665.
AUTENRIED, Barons von, *arms*, 94.
AUTHIER, 12.
AUTROCHE, *arms*, 277.
AUVERGNE, *arms*, 466.
,, Comtes d', *arms*, 360, 373.
,, Dauphin, d', 269.
,, HENRY DE LA TOUR D', Duc de BOUILLON, *arms*, 466.
,, ROBERT V., Count of, 373.
AUX, Marquis d', *arms*, 388.
Avant-bras, 682, 715, 726.
Avant-mur, 715, 737.
AVAUGOUR, D', *arms*, 118.
AVAZZI, *arms*, 280.
AVELAND, Lord, *arms*, 192.
Avellane, 677.
,, *Cross*, 162.
AVESNES, D', *seal* of ALICE, wife of JEAN, 245; Pl. XXXVII., fig. 6, p. 448.
,, JEAN D', Count of HAINAULT, 468.
,, *crest*, 600.
AVILLIERS, D', *arms*, 170.
AVOGLI, Counts, *arms*, 231.
AVOIR, PIERRE, *supporters*, 633.
AVONDALE, Earldom of, *arms*, 518.
,, JAMES and WILLIAM, Earls of, 516.
Aroué, 625.
AVREMESNIL, MONTMORENCY D', *brisure*, 451.
Axe, 348.
,, *Battle*, 348.
,, *Lochaber*, 348.
AYDIE, Marquises de RIBERAC, *arms*, 238.
AYLESFORD, Earls of, *arms*, 289.
Aylets, 677.
AYLMER, Lords, *arms*, 265.
AYLOFFE, Sir JOSEPH, 24.
AYSCOUGH, *arms*, 237.
AYTOUN of Keppo, Sir JOHN, *brisure*, 436.
AZENPRUK, FRIEDRICH VON, *arms*, 479.

AZINCOURT, Battle of, 449.
Azur, 677, 715.
,, *plein, d'*, 66.
Azure or Blue, 60, 62, 65, 677 ; Pl. III.,
   fig. 4, p. 60.
,, Shield, plain, 66.

BAAD, *arms*, 370.
BABENBURGER, *arms*, 500.
BABINGTON, *arms*, 108 ; Pl. IX., fig. 9,
   p. 108.
,, of Rothley, *label*, 415.
Bachelerie, 652.
Backgammon-boards as charges, 387.
BACON, *arms*, 227.
BACQUERE, *arms*, 228.
BACQUEVILLE, DE, *arms*, 393.
Badelaire, 686, 715.
BADEN, *arms*, 129, 491, 666 ; Pl. XXXIX.,
   fig. 5, p. 482.
,, Grand Dukes of, *arms*, 212, 221.
,, ,, *Great Shield* of, 491.
,, Margravate of, *arms*, 490.
Badenoch, Wolf of, 566.
BADENWEILER, Lordship of, *arms*, 491 ;
   Pl. XLVI., fig. 2, p. 546.
BADGER, *arms*, 239.
,, The, 239.
Badges, 583, 753.
BADLESMERE, *arms*, 128.
BAEZA, Capture of, 143.
BAGGE, *arms*, 687.
BAGOT, *arms*, 139.
,, family, 399.
,, Dukes of BUCKINGHAM, 399.
BAGRATION, Princes, *arms*, 384.
BAIBEL, *arms*, 302.
BAIGNEAU, *arms*, 176.
BAIGNI, *arms*, 82.
BAILLETS, DES, *arms*, 133.
BAILLEUL, *arms*, 78.
BAILLIE of Lamington, *arms*, 308.
Baillonné, 677, 715.
BAILLY quoted, 660.
BAIRD, *arms*, Pl. XXIII., fig. 1, p. 228.
,, of Auchmedden, *arms*, 227.
BAISNE, *arms*, 364.
BAKER, *arms*, 263.
BALA SICILIANA, Marquises de la,
   arms, 506.
BALBI, *arms*, 230.
,, Family, 16.
,, -PORTO, *arms*, 125 ; Pl. XI.,
   fig. 7, p. 124.
BALCKENSTADT, Counts von, *arms*, 94.
BALFOUR, *arms*, 238.
,, Sir JAMES, 441.
BALINCOURT, Marquis de, *arms*, 220.
BALIOL, *arms*, Pl. XVII., fig. 8, p. 172.
Balista as a charge, 365.
BALISTE, *arms*, 349.
BALLENSTEDT, Counts von, *arms*, 94.
BALLIOL, ALEXANDER DE, *arms*, 407.
,, ,, *seal*, 628.
,, *arms*, 460, 553.
,, COLLEGE, OXFORD, 460.
,, EUSTACE DE, *arms*, 407.
,, HUGH DE, *arms*, 427.
,, INGRAM DE, *arms*, 407.
,, JOHN, 460.
,, ,, *arms*, 407.
,, ,, King of SCOTLAND,
   arms, 174.
,, WILLIAM DE, *arms*, 407.

Balls, 677.
BALMANNO, *arms*, 142.
BALNEO, *arms*, 82.
BALYS, DE, *arms*, 427.
BALZAC, Marquis d'ENTRAGUES, *arms*,
   146.
,, BANASTRE, *arms*, 153.
BANBURY, Earl of, *arms*, 160.
BAND, Sir WALTER, *arms*, 260.
Bandé, 94, 677, 678, 715.
Bande, 129, 678, 715.
Bandé-contre-bandé, 715.
Bande, En, 715.
Banded, 350, 677.
BANDEIRA, *arms*, 352.
BANDINELLI, *arms*, 66.
BANDINI, *arms*, 192.
BANDON, Earl of, *arms*, 273.
BANESTER, *arms*, 140, 157.
BANESTRE, *arms*, 157.
BANGOR, Viscounts, *arms*, 157.
Bannatyne Club Miscellany, 233.
Banner, 651.
,, *armoyée*, 653, 654.
,, *Church* as a charge, 372.
,, from Bayeux Tapestry, Pl
   XXXIV., fig. 2.
Banneret (vol), 715.
Banneret's *banner*, 651.
,, *standard*, Length of, 654.
BANNERMAN, *arms*, 351.
Bannerol, 651.
Banners, 649.
,, as *supporters*, 643.
,, *Military*, 351.
,, National, of English Army at
   CAERLAVEROCK, 656.
,, of the *Bayeux Tapestry*, 650.
,, used in the *English Army*, 656.
,, Marquis de PUYGIRON, *arms*,
   307.
Bannière, 715.
,, *En*, 715.
BANTRY, Earl of, *arms*, 644.
BANVILLE DE TRUTEMNE, *arms*, 69.
Bar, 677, 715.
,, and *Canton*, joined, 167.
,, -*sinister*, a misnomer, 126.
,, The, 125, 270.
,, Varieties of, 127.
,, -*wise*, 678.
BAR and MONTBELIARD, seal of
   THIERRY II., Count of, 47.
,, *arms*, 270, 309, 449, 496 ; Pl. XXVI.,
   fig. 9, p. 266.
,, Countess of, *seal*, 629.
,, ,, *supporters*, 635.
,, HENRY IV., Comte de, 464.
BARA, *Le Grand Blason d'Armoiries*, 2.
BARBANÇOIS, Marquis de, *arms*, 225.
BARBANÇON, *arms*, 223, 492.
BARBANI, *arms*, 203.
BARBARANI, Counts, 213.
BARBAROSSA, FREDERICK, 210.
BARBAZAN, *Restaurateur du Royaume
   et de la Couronne de France*, 539.
Barbé, 708, 715.
Barbel, 325, 349, 677.
Barbel, The, Pl. XXVI., fig. 9, p. 266 ; 270.
BARBENÇON, *arms*, 411.
,, FRANÇOISE DE, *arms*,
   450.
BARBENTANE, Marquises de, *arms*,
   234.

(763)

BARBERINI, *arms* and *augmentation*, 541.
BARBIER, LE, Marquises de KERJAN, *arms*, 126.
BARBONIANI, *arms*, 203.
BARBOTTE, *arms*, 67.
BARBOUR, *The Thistle and the Rose*, 596.
BARBU, LE, *arms*, 145.
BARBY, Counts of, 270.
BARCELONA, Counts of, *arms*, 122, 434.
BARCLAY, *arms*, 154, 407, 408.
,, of Touch, *arms*, 172 ; Pl. XVII., fig. 6, p. 172.
Bardé, 679, 715.
BARDOLF, *arms*, 322.
,, JOHN, Lord, *arms*, 457.
BARENSTEIN, *arms*, 229.
BARESTIJNS, *arms*, 188.
BAREY, *see* BARRÉ.
BARGE DE VILLE, DE LA, *arms*, 66.
BARGENY, Lord, *arms*, 568.
BARIN, *arms*, 280.
BARING, Earl of Northbrook, *arms*, 230.
BARISONI, *arms*, 72.
BARKELE, MORIS DE, *arms*, 408.
BARKER, Sir CHRISTOPHER, *Heraldic Collections*, 386.
Barley, Ears of, 341.
BARLOT, *arms*, 57, 155.
Barnacles, 357, 677 ; Pl. XXXII., fig. 1, p. 358.
,, as a *badge*, 753.
BARNAKE, *arms*, 357.
BARNARD, *arms*, 229.
BARNEWALL, Lord TRIMLESTOWN, *arms*, 170, 171.
Baron Chrétien, Premier, 11.
BARONCELLI, *arms*, 93.
Baronets, *helm* of, 602.
Baron's *banner*, 651.
,, *coronet*, 625.
,, *standard*, Length of, 654.
BAROZZI, *arms*, 123.
BARR, *arms*, 339.
,, WILLIAM DE, 210.
Barre, 133, 715.
Barré, 716.
BARRE, *arms*, 134.
BARRÉ DE BAREY, Barons, *arms*, 95.
BARRINGTON, Viscounts, *supporters*, 288.
Barroque, En, 716.
BARRUEL DE ST. VINCENT, *arms*, 95.
Barrulet, 126, 128, 677.
Barruly, 677.
Barry, 92, 677 ; Pl. VII., fig. 2, p. 90.
,, *-bendy*, 100, 677.
,, *-nebuly*, 93 ; Pl. VII., fig. 3, p. 90.
,, *-pily*, 101, 677 ; Pl. VIII., fig. 2, p. 100.
,, *wavy*, 93.
BARRY, DE, *arms*, 231.
BARRYMORE, Earls of, *arms*, 93.
BARRYS, Earls of BARRYMORE, *arms*, 93.
Bars, Pl. XI., fig. 8, p. 124.
,, *counter-embattled*, Pl. XI., fig. 9, p. 124.
,, *-gemels (gemells)*, 128, 677, 687 ; Pl. XI., fig. 11, p. 124.
,, *wavy*, Pl. XI., fig. 10, p. 124.
BART, DE, *arms*, 94.
BARTELLE LA MOIGNON, *arms*, 68.

BARTHÉLEMY, DE, 10.
BARTOLUS, 548.
BARTON, *arms*, 227.
BAS, *arms*, 294.
BASCLE, LE, *arms*, 184.
Base, 678.
,, *Dexter*, 59.
,, *Middle*, 59.
,, *Sinister*, 59.
BASFORD, *arms*, 301.
BASIL I., BYZANTINE Emperor, *crown*, 621.
Basilic, 716.
Basilicus, 294.
Basilisk, 293, 678.
BASING, *arms*, 160, 169.
BASKERVILLE, *arms*, 192.
BASSET, *arms*, 93, 128.
BASSETT, *arms*, 93, 147, 412.
,, RALPH, Lord, *arms*, 426.
,, RAUFF, *arms*, 426.
,, SIMON, *arms*, 426.
BASSEWITZ, Counts von, *arms*, 227.
BASSINGBOURNE, *arms*, Pl. VI., fig. 2, p. 84.
BASSINGBURNE, *arms*, 86.
BASSINGFORD, *arms*, 191.
BASSOMPIERRE, Marquis de, *arms*, 140.
BASTARD *supporters*, 643.
Bastillé, 685, 716.
Bataillé, 374, 716.
BATH, Earl of, *arms*, 386.
,, Marquess of, *arms*, 94.
Bâton, 135, 678, 716.
,, *d'Esculape*, 716.
,, *fleur-de-lisé*, 716.
,, *peri en barre*, 560.
Baton, sinister, 560 ; Pl. XII., fig. 12, p. 130.
BATTENBERG, *arms*, 525.
,, Princes of, *arms*, 525.
,, Princess BEATRICE, Princess HENRY of, *label*, 423.
Battering ram, 352 ; Pl. XXXI., fig. 8, p. 346.
Battle-axe, Pl. XXXI., fig. 3, p. 346.
Battlements, 678.
BATTUTI, *arms*, 374.
BATURLE DU CASTEL, *arms*, 130.
BAUDRAC, *arms*, 296.
BAULANDE, *arms*, 181.
BAUME, LA, *arms*, 434.
,, Counts de ST. AMOUR, *arms*, 129.
BAUMEISTER, *augmentation*, 546.
BAUSSAY, *Canton* of, 452.
BAUTERSEM, *arms*, 576.
BAUX, *arms*, 99, 460.
,, BEATRICE DE, *seal*, 460.
,, Duc d'ANDREE, *arms*, 308.
BAVARIA, *arms*, 57, 67, 100, 251, 456, 462, 463, 472, 477, 525, 576, 580, 611, 666 ; Pl. VII., fig. 11, p. 90.
,, ALBERT of, Count of HAINAULT, HOLLAND, etc., 57.
,, *crest* and *arms*, 607.
,, FERDINAND of, 525.
,, JACQUELINE of, Countess of HOLLAND, *seal*, 463, 642.
,, LOUIS, Duke of, *seal*, 456.

BAVARIA, MARGARET of, Countess of HOLLAND, seal, 58, 462, 484.
,, ,, seal and arms, 57.
,, Marks of illegitimacy in, 579.
,, seal of Duke WILLIAM of, 251.
,, WILLIAM, Duke of, arms on eagle, 630.
,, ,, of, Comte d' OSTREVANT, seal, supporter, and compartment, 642.
BAVARIAN, coins of the Emperor LOUIS THE, 251.
BAYERN, see HOLNSTEIN.
Bayeux Tapestry, 29, 53, 54, 291, 367, 649.
,, ,, banner from Pl. XXXIV., fig. 2.
,, ,, Description of, 30.
,, ,, pennons from, Figs. 101-104, p. 649.
BAYNARD, arms, 137.
BAYSSE, arms, 68.
BAZAN, supporters, 643.
BAZENTIN, arms, 331.
BAZIN, arms, 169.
Beacon, 678.
Beacons, 352.
BEACONSFIELD, Viscountess, arms, 339.
Beaked, 678.
,, as applied to birds, 257.
Bean cods, 343.
Beans, 343.
Bear, 229 ; Pl. XXIII., fig. 4, p. 228.
,, and ragged staff as a badge, 584, 753.
,, as a supporter, 640.
,, Polar, 229.
Beard, The, 203.
BÉARN, arms, 418.
,, Counts of, arms, 122, 234.
,, seals of Counts of, 56.
BEARN, Viscount of, seals to contract of marriage of GUILLELMINE, dtr. of CENTULUS GASTON II., 46.
Bear's head as a badge, 753.
Bears' heads, 229 ; Pl. XXIII., fig. 5, p. 228.
Beasts, 208.
Beati pacifici, 664.
BEATON, arms, 185.
,, Cardinal, 185.
BEATRICE, daughter of JOAÕ I., King of PORTUGAL, 577.
,, Princess, Princess HENRY of BATTENBERG, label, 423 ; Fig. 89, p. 421.
BEAUCHAMP, arms, 123, 408, 410 ; Pl. XI., fig. 1, p. 124 ; Pl. XV., fig. 4, p. 144.
,, Earls of WARWICK, arms, 163.
,, ,, ,, badge, 585.
,, of Bletsho, 439.
,, of Powick, arms, 408.
,, RICHARD, Earl of WARWICK and ALBEMARLE, Garter Plate, 486.
BEAUCLERC, CHARLES, Duke of ST. ALBANS, arms, 559.
BEAUFFREMONT, DE, arms, 71, 485.
,, Ducs de, arms, 70.

BEAUFFREMONT, PIERRE DE, Count de CHARNY, arms, 485.
BEAUFORT, arms, 438, 556.
,, badge, 595.
,, bordure, 443.
,, Cardinal, 557.
,, ,, arms, 555.
,, Duke of, arms, 556 ; supporters, 226.
,, Greyhound of, 662.
,, HENRY, 3rd Duke of SOMERSET, 556.
,, JOAN, seal, 475.
,, JOHN DE, arms, 555.
,, ,, Marquis of SOMERSET, arms, 555.
,, ,, Duke of SOMERSET, Garter Plate of, 594.
,, line, badge, 588.
,, Queen JOAN, seal, 476.
,, THOMAS, Duke of EXETER, arms, 555.
BEAUGENCY, RAOUL DE, seal of, 47.
BEAUHARNAIS, Marquises de, arms, 266.
BEAUMANOIR, Marquis de LAVARDIN, arms, 57, 186.
BEAUMEYS, JOHN, arms transferred, 754.
,, ,, of Sautray, arms, 35.
BEAUMONT, ALAIN DE, supporters, 633.
,, arms, 91, 127, 139, 145, 215, 407, 452 ; Pl. XIII., fig. 11, p. 136.
,, badge, 753.
,, JOHN, Lord, mantling, 613.
,, ROBERT DE, Earl of LEICESTER, arms, 322.
BEAUMOUNT SUR OISE, seal of MATHIEU II. Count of, 48.
,, SUR OISE, seal of MATHIEU III., Count of, 48.
BEAUPOIL, 12.
BEAUREGARD, 338.
BEAUREPAIRE, arms, 136.
BEAUSAINT, see ROCHE.
BEAUSANT, MONTMORENCY DE, brisure, 452.
BEAUSSAULT, MONTMORENCY DE, brisure, 452.
BEAUVAU, DE, arms, 219.
BEAUVOIR, GUILLAUME DE, 51.
,, ,, Seigneur de, arms, 51.
,, see DAGUET.
,, see DAUBENY, 438.
Beaver, The, 239.
BEC, arms, 159, 160, 303.
,, CRÉPIN, DU, arms, 100.
,, DU, Marquises de Vardes, arms and supporters, 303.
BÈCHE, DE LA, 17.
BECHE, Syr EDMUND OF THE, 17.
BECKET, THOMAS À, Archbishop of CANTERBURY, arms, 264.
Becqué, 257, 678, 716.
BEDFORD, badge, 754.
,, Blason of Episcopacy, 437.
,, Duke of, arms, 107.

(765)

BÉDOYERE, DE LA, *arms*, 187.
BEE, *arms*, 281.
BEEBEE, *arms*, 281.
Beehives, 284.
BEERVELT, VAN, *arms*, 127.
Bees, 281.
,, *Golden*, 281.
BEESTON, *arms*, 281.
BEETHOVEN, LUDWIG VAN, 15.
Beetroot, The, 343.
Beffroi, 716.
,, (*vair*), 69.
BEHR, *arms*, 229.
BEIJEREN-SCHAGEN family, 576.
BEILSTEIN, Lordship of, *arms*, 492.
BEJARANO, *arms*, 276.
BEKE, *arms*, 159, 160.
BELASYSE, *arms*, Pl. X., fig. 11, p. 118.
,, Earls of FAUCONBERG, *arms*, 123.
BELCHER, *arms*, 70.
BELESME, *arms*, 139.
,, PHILIPPE DE, *arms*, 140.
BELFILE, *arms*, 189.
BELFORTE, Dukes of, *arms* and *augmentation*, 541.
BELGIUM, *arms*, 666.
,, *coronet* of Marquises in, 624.
,, *motto* of, 666.
,, Use of *canton* in, 427.
,, ,, *supporters* in, 639.
Bélier-militaire, 716.
BELIN, *arms*, 236.
BELL, *arms*, 374.
BELLAFILLA, *arms*, 123.
BELLARMINE on origin of double-headed eagle, 249.
BELLCHAMBER, *arms*, Pl. XXV., fig. 8, p. 260.
Belled, 235, 678.
,, applied to Falcon, 261.
BELLEGARDE, *arms*, 716.
BELLEGARSE, Comtes de, *arms*, 374.
BELLENDEN, quoted, 233.
BELLERO, *arms*, 277.
BELLEVILLE, DE, *arms*, 85.
BELLEVOIRS, *arms*, 202.
BELLEW, *arms*, 96.
BELLINCIONI, *arms*, 173.
BELLOMONTE, ROBERT DE, Earl of LEICESTER, *arms*, 322.
Bells as charges, 373.
BELLUOMI, *arms*, 213.
BELLY, *arms*, 191.
BELOT, *arms*, 716, 723.
BELPER, Lord, *supporters*, 647.
BELS, *arms*, 374.
BELSCHES, *arms*, 70.
BELSUNCE, Marquises de, *arms*, 296.
BELTZ, *Memorials of the Order of the Garter*, 324, 418, 590, 606.
Bend, 78, 678 ; Fig. 39, p. 116 ; 129 ; Pl. XII., fig. 1, p. 130.
,, *Charges on a*, Pl. XII., fig. 3, p. 130 ; Pl. XII., fig. 4, p. 130.
,, *cotised*, Pl. XII., fig. 10, p. 130.
,, *embattled à plomb*, Per, Pl. V., fig. 5, p. 80.
,, *embattled*, Per, Pl. V., fig. 4, p. 80.
,, *engoulée*, 131 ; Pl. XII., fig. 5, p. 130.
,, *ermine*, Pl. XII., fig. 2, p. 130.
,, *Parted per*, 80 ; Fig. 31, p. 77.
,, *sinister*, Pl. XII., fig. 11, p. 130.

Bend - sinister - fitchée, Per, Pl. V., fig. 7, p. 80.
,, ,, *Parted per*, 80 ; Fig. 32, p. 77.
,, ,, Per, Pl. V. fig. 6, p. 80.
,, ,, The, Fig. 40, p. 116, 133.
,, Varieties of, 130.
BENDERS, *arms*, 302.
Benalet, sinister, 560.
,, The, 131, 135, 678.
Bendlets enhanced, Pl. XII., fig. 8, p. 130.
,, *wavy*, Pl. XII., fig. 7, p. 130.
Bendways, 108 ; Pl. XII., fig. 9, p. 130.
Bendwise, 678.
Bendy, 94, 678.
,, *per pale counter-changed*, 96.
,, *wavy*, Pl. VII., fig. 4, p. 90.
BENE, DEL, *arms*, 332.
BENEVENTO, FREDERICK, Duke of, *arms*, 577.
BENEWITZ, *arms*, 176.
BENIGNI, *arms*, 133.
BENNERAYE, DE LA, *arms*, 240.
BENNET, Earl of TANKERVILLE, *arms*, 222.
BENNS, *arms*, 238.
BENOIT, *arms*, 204, 371.
BENSON, *crest*, 610.
BENSTEDT, *arms*, 82.
BENTHEM, *arms*, 143.
BENTINCK, Dukes of PORTLAND, *arms*, 159.
BENTOUX, *arms*, 183.
BENVOGLIO, *arms*, 541.
BENZONI, *arms*, 72.
Béquille de St. Anthoine, 716.
BÉRANGER, *arms*, 86.
,, PIERRE JEAN DE, 14.
BERBERICH, *arms*, 302.
BERBISSY, *arms* and *supporter*, 302.
BERCHOLTSHOFEN, VON, *arms*, 91.
BERENGUER, *arms*, 188.
BERESFORD, *arms*, 229.
BERG, Counts von SCHELKLINGEN, *arms*, 95.
,, see RUMLINGEN.
BERGEN OP ZOOM, *arms*, 332.
BERGENSTRÅHLE, Barons von, *arms*, 510.
BERGER, *arms*, 752.
BERGHES, JEAN DE, Seigneur de WALAIN, *arms*, 576.
BERINGTON, *arms*, 66.
BERKELEY, *arms*, 136, 407.
,, *badge*, 754.
,, Earls of, *arms*, 154.
,, *seal* of MAURICE DE, 407 ; *banner*, Fig. 105, p. 651.
,, *seal* of ROBERT DE, 407.
,, *seal* of THOMAS DE, 407.
,, Sir MAURICE DE, *label of*, 414.
,, Sir THOMAS DE, *arms*, 408.
,, *supporters* and *badge*, 303.
,, THOMAS, son of MAURICE, DE, *arms*, 408.
BERLAER, Seigneur de, *arms*, 405.
BERLAYMONT, ADRIENNE DE, *arms*, 450.
BERLO, Counts of, *arms*, 126.
BERMINGHAM, *arms*, 130.
BERMOND, 12.
BERMUDEZ, *arms*, 353.

BERN, *arms*, 134.
BERNADOTTE, House of, *arms*, 487.
BERNALEZ, *arms*, 372.
BERNARD, *arms*, 229.
,, DE FAUCONVAL, Barons, *arms*, 156.
,, Earl of BANDON, *arms*, 273.
BERNARDUS ANFREDI, 10.
BERNBACH, *arms*, 271.
BERNE, Canton of, *arms* and *supporters*, 229, 640.
BERNERS, *arms*, 81.
,, Dame JULIANA, *Boke of St. Albans*, 19, 35, 151, 406.
,, Lord, *arms*, 417.
,, ,, *mantling*, 613.
BERNSTEIN, *arms*, 288.
BERRI, Dukes of, *arms*, 439.
,, JEAN, Duc de, *seal*, Pl. XXXV., fig. 2, p. 416 ; *supporters*, 631, 635.
,, *seal* of, 57.
BERRY, *Encyclopædia Heraldica*, 151.
,, *Roi d'Armes, Armorials of*, 113, 161, 402.
BERSTETT, Barons, *arms*, 213.
BERTAUT, GAULTIER, Seigneur de MECHLIN, *arms*, 405.
BERTHELAY QUESQUERTIN, *arms*, 222.
BERTIE, *arms*, Pl. XXXI., fig. 8, p. 346.
,, Earl of Abingdon, etc., *arms*, 352.
BERTRAM, ROGER, *arms*, 552.
BERTRAND, *arms*, 91.
BERWICK, Castle of, 605.
,, Duke of, *arms*, 559.
Besant, 190, 716.
Besanté, 716.
Besants-tourteaux, 716, 745.
Besom, as a charge, 390.
BESOYEN, *arms*, 145.
BESSBOROUGH, Earl of, *arms*, 391.
BESSON, *arms*, 198.
BESYNGBURGH, *arms*, 167.
BETHUNE, *arms*, 185.
BÉTHUNE, Ducs de SULLY, *arms*, 123.
,, JACQUELINE DE, *supporters*, 635.
,, ROBERT DE, Count of FLANDERS, 462, 464.
,, ROBERT, Son of ROBERT DE, Count of FLANDERS, *brisure*, 439.
BÉTHUNES, Ducs de SULLY, *lambrequin*, 613.
,, HESDIGNUEL, Princes de, *lambrequins*, 613.
BEUCHLINGEN, Counts von, *arms*, 93.
BEUST, *arms*, 540.
,, Count, *augmentation*, 540.
BEUVILLE, *arms*, 68.
BEVERWIJCK, *arms*, 145.
BEVILACQUA, Princes of, *arms*, 260.
BEVILL, *arms*, Pl. XXIV., fig. 1, p. 236.
,, of Gwarnack, *arms*, 234.
Bevily, 678.
BEYER, DE, *arms*, 374.
Bezant, 189, 678.
Bezantée, 678.
Bezants, Pl. XIX., fig. 2, p. 192.
Bezanty, 678.
BIANCHETTI, *arms*, 95.
BIBER, *arms*, 239.

BIBERSTEIN, *see* MARCHALCK.
BIBRA, Barons, *arms*, 239.
BICCHIERI, *arms*, 382.
BICHI, *arms*, 275.
Bi-corporate, 678.
BIDAURE, *arms*, 506, 577.
,, THERESIA DE, 577.
BIEDMA, *arms*, 121.
BIEDERMANN, Baron, *arms*, 322.
BIEL, Barons, *arms*, 348.
BIELSKI, Counts, *arms*, 347.
Bigarré, 704, 716.
BIGOT, *arms*, 141.
,, Counts of ST. QUINTIN, *arms*, 284.
,, DE LA CHAUMIÈRE, *arms*, 284.
BILLES, *supporters*, 643.
Billet, 117, 165, 186, 678 ; Pl. XIX., fig. 1, p. 192.
Billeté, 678, 716.
Billette, 678, 716.
Billetty, 112, 678 ; Pl. VIII., fig. 11, p. 100.
BILLICHS, *arms*, 240.
BILLY, *arms*, 186.
BILQUES DE ORCION, *arms*, 306.
BIORN, *arms*, 229.
BIÖRNSEN, *arms*, 141.
BISCHOFF, *arms*, 371.
BISCIA, *arms*, 364.
Bird-bolt, 678.
,, -*bolts*, 350.
,, *of Paradise*, 267.
BIRON, *arms*, 129, 132.
,, Duc do, *arms*, 81.
BISCAY, TELLIUS, Count of, *arms*, 576.
BISE, *arms*, 66.
BISHOPS, *arms*, 525.
BISMARCK, Counts von, *arms*, 320, 742.
,, Prince, 320.
,, ,, von, *arms* and *supporters*, 545.
Bisse, 716.
BISSET, *arms*, 133, 191.
BISSI, *arms*, 275.
BISSY, Marquis de, *arms*, 273.
BITSCH, Lordship of, *arms*, 169.
BLACHE, FALCOZ DE LA, Comtes d'ANJOU, *arms*, 261.
BLACK EAGLE, Cross of the Order of the, 546.
,, or *Sable*, 60, 65.
,, Prince, 439, 591.
,, ,, *badge* of the, 592, 593.
,, Prince's *shield* for peace, 593.
,, ,, *shield* for war, 593.
BLACKADDER, *arms*, 325.
BLACKSTOCK, *arms*, 318.
BLACKSTONE'S definition of Esquire, 7, 8.
BLACKWOOD, *crest*, 610.
BLACON, Marquises of, *arms*, 93.
Bladed, 678.
BLAKET, *arms*, 137.
BLANCHAERT, *arms*, 136.
BLANCHE of CASTILE, *seal* of Queen, 329 ; Pl. XXXVII., fig. 4, p. 448.
BLANCKENHEIM, County of, *arms* and *label*, 424.
BLANDIN, *arms*, 187.
BLANKENBERG, *arms*, 234.
BLANKFRONT, *arms*, 169.
BLARU, Marquise de, *arms*, 331.
BLASERE, DE, *arms*, 387.

Blazon, French, 109.
,, J. Gough Nichols's Rules of, 110.
,, Rules of, 101, 105.
BLEDDYN, EDNOWAIN AP, arms, 333.
BLENCOWE, arms, 165.
,, ADAM OF, arms granted to, 35.
Blessing hand, A, 204.
Bleu-céleste, or light blue, 61.
,, du ciel, or light blue, 61.
BLIX, arms, 311.
BLOIS, CHARLES DE, 58, 463.
,, Château de, 586.
,, Counts de, arms, 411.
,, GUI DE, supporters, 633.
,, MARIE, Countess of, seal, 411.
BLOM, arms, 338.
BLOME, Counts, arms, 241.
BLOMMESTEIN, VAN, arms, 338.
Blood colour or Sanguine, 60, 65.
BLOSSEVILLE, Marquis de, arms, 340.
BLOT, Comtes de, arms, 214.
BLOUNT, arms, 93, 359, 561; Pl. VII., fig. 3, p. 90.
,, Earl of DEVON, arms, 93.
,, MOUNTJOY, Earl of NEWPORT, arms, 561.
BLÜCHER, Prince, arms and augmentation, 544.
Blue-bottles, 337.
,, Light, or Bleu-céleste, 61.
,, or Azure, 60, 62, 65.
BLUMENTHAL, Counts of, augmentation, 543.
BLUMERT, arms, 337.
BLUNDEVILLE, RANULF, Earl of CHESTER, arms, 341.
BLUNT, arms, 359.
Boar, Pl. XXIII., fig. 1, p. 228.
,, as a badge, 753.
,, The Wild, 227.
,, White, as a badge, 594.
Boars as supporters, 636.
Boar's head, 227.
,, ,, as a crest, 605.
Boars' heads, Pl. XXIII., fig. 2, p. 228.
Boats as charges, 369.
BOBADILLA alliance, 506.
BOCK, Die Kleinodien des Heil. Römischen Reiches, 244, 245, 248.
BOCQUET or BOQUET, arms, 66, 716.
BODENHAM, arms, 388.
Bœuf, 717.
BEUVRES, arms, 68.
BOFFIN D'ARGENÇON, arms, 161.
BOGAERT, VAN DEN, arms, 316.
BOGUSLAWSKI, arms, 371.
BOHEMIA, arms, 218, 252, 494, 665.
,, CHARLES IV., King of, 252.
,, JOHN, King of, seal, 456.
,, King of, 591.
,, ,, counter-seal of, 252.
,, Kingdom, arms, 500.
,, OTTAKAR, King of, seal, 471.
,, Queen of, achievement, 494.
,, Royal Crown of, 501.
BOHN, crest, 612.
BOHUN, ALIANORE DE, Duchess of GLOUCESTER, arms, 475.
,, arms, 262.
,, badge, 589, 594, 754.

BOHUN, HUMPHREY DE, supporter, 631.
,, White antelope of, 662.
BOIGUES, see ALQUERIA.
BOINEBURG, Counts VON, arms, 640.
Bois, 691.
BOIS, arms, 68.
,, DAUPHIN MONTMORENCYLAVAL DE, brisure, 452.
,, DU, arms, 240.
,, -GEFFROY, Marquis of arms, 280.
,, YVON, arms, 140.
BOISSCHOT, FERDINAND DE, Comte D'ERPS, arms, 644.
BOISSIEU, arms, 223.
BOJANOWSKI, Barons, arms, 236.
BOKINGHAM, JOHN, Bishop of LINCOLN, arms, 160.
BOLEBEC, Barons, arms, 214.
BOLESLAS III., King of POLAND, seal of, 630.
,, seal of, King, 254.
BOLEYN, ANNE, arms and augmentation, 530.
,, arms, 531.
,, Sir THOMAS, 531.
BOLINGBROKE, HENRY, arms, 474.
BOLLORD, arms, 280.
BOLOGNA, Loggia dei Mercanti in, 470.
BOLOGNE, Count of, 373.
,, County of, arms, 466.
BOLTON, arms, 350.
,, Elements of Armorie, 2.
BON, arms, 370.
BONACOLSI, arms, 128.
BONAR of Kimmerghame, arms, 346.
BONELLI, Marquises, arms, 95.
BONES COMBES, arms, 207.
BONI, arms, 78.
BONIFACE VIII., Pope, arms, 132.
BONKYL, arms, 458.
,, buckles, 413.
,, Sir JOHN, 458.
BONNEFOUX, Barons, arms, 388.
Bonnet-Albanais, 717.
BONNEUIL, Marquis of, arms, 306.
BONNIÈRES, Ducs de GUINES, arms, 71.
BONO, arms, 371.
BONSTETTEN, arms, 440.
BONVICINI, arms, 119.
BONVILLE, arms, 79.
BONVINO, arms, 66.
BOOTH, arms, 227.
Boots as charges, 392.
BOQUET or BOCQUET, arms, 66.
Bordé, 678, 687, 700, 717, 742.
BORDEAUX, arms, 66.
Bordered, 678.
BORDOLO, arms, 752.
Bordure, 116, 165, 170, 678, 717; Pl. XVII., fig. 1, p. 172; Pl. XVII., fig. 2, p. 172; Pl. XVII. fig. 3, p. 172.
,, checquy, Pl. XVII., fig. 6, p. 172.
,, circular, 173.
,, componé, 555; Pl. XVII. fig. 4, p. 172; 564, 569.
,, ,, and counter-componé, 568.
,, counter-compony, 443; Pl. XVII., fig. 5, p. 172.
,, Difference by a, 437.
,, Double, 173.

Bordure of CASTILE, 172; Pl. XVII., fig. 7, p. 172.
,, of ENGLAND, 172.
,, of FRANCE, 172.
,, Treatment of, in *impaled coat*, 474.
,, Use of, in Scotland, 170.
,, Varieties of, 171.
,, *wavy*, 564, 569.
Bordures-compony, 442.
BOREAS, *Head of*, 201, 311, 730.
Borée, 714, 717.
BORGHARTS, *arms*, 143.
BORGHESE, *arms*, 292.
,, Princes, 16.
BORGHOLOET, *see* DILFT.
BORGO, *see* POZZO.
BORIAS, *arms*, 311.
BORLUUT DE HOOGSTRATEN, Counts, *arms*, 232.
BORMANS, DE, *arms*, 374.
BOROLLA, *arms*, 93.
BOROUGHBRIDGE *Roll*, 554.
BORSAN, *arms*, 96.
BORSELE, *arms*, 410; Pl. XLIV., fig. 4, p. 538.
,, FRANCIS DE, 642.
BORTHWICK, Lord, *arms*, 323.
BOSCAWEN, Admiral, *supporters*, 300.
,, Earls of FALMOUTH, *arms*, 324.
BOSE, Counts of, *arms*, 61.
BOSELYNGTHORPE, Sir RICHARD DE, *arms*, 44.
BOSNIA, *arms*, 501.
,, and SERVIA, Czar of, 251.
BOSSENSTEIN, *arms*, 66.
BOSSEWELL, *Armorie of Honor*, 2, 444, 638.
BOSSU, Comte de, *arms*, 129.
BOSSUT, *arms*, 181, 427.
BOSTAQUET, *see* DUMONT.
BOSWELL, *arms*, 566.
,, of Balgregie, Sir JOHN, 566.
BOSWORTH, Battle of, 595.
BOTELER, *arms*, 125, 163, 474.
BOTELERS, Lords SUDELEY, *arms*, 155.
Boterol, 678.
BOTH, *arms*, 370.
BOTHELIER, *arms*, 337.
BOTHELL, *arms*, 337.
BOTHMAR, Counts, *arms*, 370.
BOTHMER, *arms*, 370.
BOTHWELL, Earl of, *arms*, 567.
,, ,, *brisure*, 435.
,, *seal* of AGNES, Countess of, 369.
,, *stars* of, 518.
BOTILHER, *arms*, 381.
BOTON, *arms*, 121.
Botonnée, 160.
Botonny, 678.
,, *Cross*, 160.
BOTREAUX, *arms*, 278.
BOTVILLE, *arms*, 94.
BOUCHAGE, *arms*, 71.
,, Count de, *arms*, 289.
BOUCHARD, 11.
,, Lord of MONTMORENCY, 11.
BOUCHOUT, VAN, *arms*, 141.
BOUCIQUAUT, Marechal de, *arms*, 254.
Bouclé, 717.

BOUDOYER, *arms*, 93.
BOUDRIC, *arms*, 731.
Bouget, 678.
,, as a *badge*, 753.
BOUILLON, Count of, 373.
,, Duc de, *arms*, 123, 185, 360, 466.
,, Duchy of, *arms*, 466.
,, GODFREY DE, 47, 243, 373.
,, ISABEL, Duchess de, *arms*, 466.
BOULA DE MAREUIL, *arms*, 191.
BOULAINVILLIERS, *arms*, 93.
,, Counts, *arms*, 127.
BOULBON, *see* RAOUSSET.
BOULENGER, *arms*, 191.
Boules, 677, 717.
BOULOGNE, Counts of, *arms*, 192, 373.
,, MATHILDE DE, 373.
Bouquet, A, 339.
Bouquetins, 232.
BOURASSÉ, *La Touraine*, 189, 448.
BOURBON, *arms*, 571.
,, -CONDÉ, 258.
,, ,, *arms*, 504.
,, Ducs de, *bend*, 429.
,, Duke CHARLES I. of, 571.
,, Duke Jean I. of, 571.
,, Dukes of, 571.
,, House of, 57.
,, JEAN, *bâtard de*, *arms*, 571.
,, -LA - MARCHE - PRÉAUX, *arms*, 452.
,, LOUIS, *bâtard de*, *arms*, 571.
,, MATHIEU, *le grand Bâtard de* and his sister MARGUERITE, *arms*, 571; Pl. XLVIII., fig. 1, p. 576.
,, -MODERN, *arms*, 571.
,, MONTPENSIER, *arms*, 466.
,, ,, CHARLOTTE DE, 466.
,. PIERRE I., Duke of, 571.
,, ,, ,, *supporters*, 303.
,, VENDÔME, *arms*, 570.
BOURCHIER, *badge*, 753.
,, HENRY, Earl of ESSEX, *arms*, 417.
,, *knot*, 585, 613.
,, Lord, *tomb* of, 653.
,, Sir JOHN, Lord BERNERS, *arms*, 417.
,, Sir JOHN, Lord BERNERS, *mantling*, 613.
Bourdon, as a charge, 375, 678, 697, 704.
,, (*de Pélerin*), 717.
BOURDON, *arms*, 375.
,, DU PLESSIS, *arms*, 375.
Bourdonné, 717.
Bourdons, 717.
BOURG, LE, *arms*, 272.
BOURGHIELLES, *arms*, 68.
BOURGOGNE, ADOLPH, grandson of *le Grand Bâtard de*, 575.
,, ANTOINE, *le Grand Bâtard de*, *arms*, 574, 575.
,, BAUDOUIN, *bâtard de*, 574.
,, Comte de, *banner*, 650.
,, Duke PHILIP DE, 450.
,, JEAN, *bâtard de*, 556.
,, ,, ,, *arms*, 573; Pl. XLVII., fig. 1, p. 574.

(769)

BOURGOGNE, MARGUERITE DE, 450.
,, MARIE DE, 485.
,, PHILIPPE, *bâtard de*, *arms*, 575.
BOURKE, 17.
BOURLEMONT, Counts de, *arms*, 113.
Bourlet, 708, 717.
BOURNAZEL, Marquises de, *arms*, 316.
BOURS, MOMTMORENCY DE, *brisure*, 451.
Bouse, 355, 678, 689, 717.
BOUTEILLER DE SENLIS, Le, *arms*, 81.
BOUTELL, *Christian Monuments*, 44, 57.
,, *English Heraldry*, 460, 565.
,, *Heraldry, Historical and Popular*, 76, 114, 187, 401, 409, 410, 413, 417, 418, 420, 465, 476, 577, 594, 619, 631, 634; Pl. XXXV., fig. 1, p. 416.
Bouterolle, 717.
BOUTEVILLE, MONTMORENCY DE, *brisure*, 451.
Boutoir, 717.
BOUTON, *Nouveau Traité de Blason*, 233, 712, 713, 742.
Boutonné, 717.
BOUTTEVILLE, MONTMORENCY DE, *brisure*, 452.
BOUVIER, GILLES LE, *Armorial of*, 113, 161, 402.
BOUVINES, Battle of, 245, 655.
BOVILE, *arms*, 81.
Bow, Pl. XXXI., fig. 5, p. 346.
BOWEN, *knot*, 585.
BOWES, *arms*, Pl. XXXI., fig. 5, p. 346.
,, of Streatham, *arms*, 349.
,, Lords, *arms*, 349.
Bows, 349.
,, *Cross*, 349.
BOYD, *arms*, 405.
BOYLE, *arms*, 80, 523; Pl. V., fig. 4, p. 80; Pl. XXIII., fig. 12, p. 228.
,, of Kelburne, *arms*, 234.
,, ,, DAVID, *arms*, 523.
BOYNE, Viscounts, *supporters*, 302.
BOYNEBURG, *arms*, 405.
,, Barons Von, *arms* and *crest*, 608.
BOYSLEVÉ, Marquis d'HAROUÉ, *arms*, 145.
BOZON, RALPH DE, *arms*, 350.
BRABANT, ALICE, daughter of HENRY I., Duke of, 373.
,, *arms*, 461, 478, 484, 495, 496, 574, 575, 576, 631.
,, Chancellor of, mark of office, 644.
,, Duchy of, *arms*, 214, 484.
,, Duke PHILIPPE of, 575.
,, Dukes of, *arms*, 405, 642.
,, GODFREY, brother of Duke HENRY, *arms*, 405.
,, GEOFFREY DE, *arms*, 461; *seal* and *label*, 415.
,, HENRY I. and III., Dukes of, *seals* and *banners*, 651.
,, HENRY, Duke of, 415, 461.
,, JEAN, natural son of JEAN, Duc de, 576.
,, *Lion of*, 415.
,, MARIE, daughter of HENRY III., Duke of, *arms*, 454.

BRABANT, PHILIPPE DE, Seigneur de CRUBEQUE, *arms*, 575.
BRACCHE, *supporters*, 294.
Braced, 140, 678.
BRACHET, 12.
BRACKENBURY, *arms*, 96, 140.
BRACKLEY, Viscount, *arms*, 561.
BRADBURY, *arms*, 224.
BRADSHAW, *arms*, 131.
BRAGANZA, CATHARINE of, *arms*, 475.
,, Dukes of, *arms*, 577.
,, House of, *label*, 425.
,, JOHN of, *label*, 425.
BRAHE, *arms*, 120.
BRAITEAU, Vicomtes de, *arms*, 280.
Branch, Linden, 318.
,, *Olive*, 317.
,, *Palm*, 319.
Branché, 717.
Branched, 678.
BRANCHELEY, *arms*, 156.
BRANDAY, see GAZET.
BRANDENBURG ANSPACH, MARGRAVES of, *helms*, 603.
,, *arms*, 344, 494.
,, BEATRICE, daughter of ALBERT, MARKGRAVE of, 492.
,, Death of JOHN, MARKGRAVE of, 40.
,, Elector of, *arms*, 526.
,, MARKGRAVATE of, *arms*, 255.
,, (Prussia), *arms*, 67.
,, *Red eagle of*, 545.
BRANDIS, *arms*, 314.
BRANDOLINI, *arms* and *motto*, 644.
BRANDON, *badge*, 754.
BRANDT, Barons, *arms*, 314.
,, Counts de MARCONNÉ, *arms*, 314.
BRANT I., Polish Clan of, *arms*, 314.
BRAOSE, *arms*, 213, 215.
BRASCHI, Dukes of NEMI, *arms*, 311.
BRAUN VON WARTENBERG, Counts, *arms*, 183.
BRAUNBERG, Barons VON, *arms*, 126.
Braunschweiger Chronicle, 41.
BRAUNSDORF, see STEIN.
BRAY, Sir REGINALD, 595.
BREADALBANE, *arms*, 368.
,, Earls of, *arms*, 84, 447.
Bream naiant, Pl. XXVI., fig. 5, p. 266.
,, The, 268.
BREAME, *arms*, 268; Pl. XXVI., fig. 5, p. 266.
Brebis, 703, 717, 737, 739.
BRECBENNOCH, *Vexillum* of the, 657.
BRECHANE of *Auld*, Lord of, *arms*, 149.
BRECHIN, *arms*, 149, 516, 517, 518, 519, 521; Pl. XVI., fig. 3, p. 146.
,, City of, *arms*, 147.
,, Heiress of, 521.
,, Lordship of, 147, 517.
,, See of, *arms*, 147.
BRECKNOCK, Baron of, *arms*, 71.
BREDA, Lordship of, *arms*, 146.
BREDOW, Counts, *arms*, 365.

(770)

Breeches as charges, 392.
BREGENZ, *arms*, 73.
,, County, *arms*, 499.
BREHNA, County of, *arms*, 321.
BREISGAU, Landgravate of, *arms*, 491.
BREITENBACH, *arms*, 139.
BREITENBUCH, VON, *arms*, 752.
BREMEN, *arms*, 283.
BRENT, *arms*, 289.
BRESLAU, Palatinate of, *arms*, 468 ; Pl. XXXVIII., fig. 2, p. 464.
BRET, LE, *arms*, 68.
BRETAGNE, ALICE, Duchess of, 55.
,, *arms*, 91, 342.
,, CONAN, Count of, 30.
,, JEAN DE, Earl of Richmond, *arms*, 425.
,, JEANNE DE, 464.
,, *seal* of JEANNE DE, 58.
BRETESCHE, Marquis de la, *arms*, 155.
Bretessé, 124, 678, 681, 682, 685, 717.
,, *line*, 76.
BRETEUIL, Comtes de, *arms*, 262.
,, MONTMORENCY DE, *brisure*, 452.
BRETIGNY, *arms*, 726.
BRETSLA, *arms*, Pl. XLVI., fig. 1, p. 546.
BREUBERG, *arms*, 308.
,, Lordship of, *arms*, 126.
BREUS, *arms*, 215.
BREWES, *arms*, 215.
BREWSE, *arms*, 214.
BREWYS, *arms*, 213.
Breys, 357, 678.
,, as a *badge*, 758.
BRÉZÉ, Comtes de MAULEVRIER, *arms*, 164.
,, Duc de, 164.
BRIAN BOROIHME, *Harp of*, 384.
BRICQUEBEC, BERTRAND DE, *supporter*, 632.
BRIDGE, *arms*, 362.
Bridges, 362.
BRIDGEWATER, Duke and Earl of, 561.
BRIERLEY, *arms*, 162.
BRIESEN, *arms*, Pl. VI., fig. 6, p. 84.
,, VON, *arms*, 88.
BRIEY, *arms*, Pl. X., fig. 12, p. 118.
,, Counts de, *arms*, 123.
Brigantine, 679.
BRIMEN, JACQUES DE, *arms*, 411.
BRIORDE, GERARD DE, *arms*, 130.
BRIQUEVILLE, *arms*, 91.
BRIS DE HOUARÉE, LA, *arms*, 27.
Bris d'huis, 717.
Brisé, 138, 688, 717, 743.
BRISSAC, Duc de, *arms*, 731.
BRISTOL, BUTLER, Bishop of, *arms*, 381.
,, City of, *arms*, 312.
,, Earl of, *arms*, 331.
,, Marquess of, *arms*, 320.
,, See of, *arms*, 379.
Brisure, 396, 679.
BRITAIN, *coronet* of a Marquess in, 624.
,, *coronets* of children and grandchildren of the Sovereign of, 619.
,, Form of *shield* in, 56.
,, GREAT, *arms*, 56, 237 ; Pl. LII., p. 662.
,, *helmets* for different ranks, 602.
,, *Impalement* in, 470.

BRITAIN, Kings of GREAT, using *escucheon en surtout*, 487.
,, Royal *arms*, 479.
,, Tincture of mantling in, 612.
,, ,, wreath in, 612.
,, WILLIAM III., King of, *arms*, 487.
British Museum Catalogue of Seals, 37, 210.
330, 384, 587, 588, 590, 594, 598, 662, 649.
BRITTANY, ALICE, Duchess of, 425.
,, *arms*, 425, 505.
,, *canton* of, 426.
,, Death of GEOFFREY PLANTAGENET, Duke of, 40.
,, Duke of, 515.
,, Dukes of, *arms*, 68.
,, ,, *supporters*, 636.
,, *Furs* common in *armory* of, 74.
,, JEANNE, Duchess of, *seal*, 463.
,, MARGARET, daughter of FRANCIS I., Duke of, 505.
,, MARY, daughter of FRANCIS I., Duke of, 505.
BRIXEN, Principality, *arms*, 499.
Broad arrow, 679.
BROADHURST, *arms*, 97.
Brochant, 717.
,, *sur le tout*, 109.
BROCK, *arms*, 239.
BROCKE, *arms*, 182.
Brog as a charge, 363.
BROGLIE, *arms*, Pl. XV., fig. 11, p. 144.
,, Ducs de, *arms*, 145.
Brogue, 679.
Broi, 690.
BROME, *arms*, 79.
BROMFIELD, *arms*, 131.
,, EDMUND, Bishop of LLANDAFF, *arms*, 217.
BROMLEY, Barons MONTFORD, *arms*, 82.
BRONCHORST, Count JOHN ZU, 473.
,, Counts ZU, *arms*, 473.
BRONCKHORST, Counts of, *arms*, 192.
BRONKHORST, VAN, *arms*, 127.
BROOK and REID, Description of Scottish Regalia, 619.
BROOKE, 554.
Broom as a *badge*, 586.
BROSSE, Vicomtes de, *arms*, 342.
BROTHERTON, *arms*, 531, 532.
BROTIN, *arms*, 71.
BROUCHIER, *arms*, 359.
BROUILLART, *arms*, 136.
BROUILLI, DE, Marquises de PIÉNNE, *supporters*, 298.
BROUN, *arms*, 333.
Brown colour, or *Brûnatre*, 61.
BROWN, *arms*, 333.
,, of Colstoun, *arms*, 331.
BROWNING, *arms*, 93.
Broyes, 678, 718, 737.
BROYES, Seigneurs de, *arms*, 357.
,, SIMON DE, *seal* of, 47.
BRUCE, *arms*, 212, 611.
,, CHRISTIAN, 178.
,, ISOBEL, 177.
,, *Lion rampant* for, 454.

(771)

BRUCE, Lord of ANNANDALE, *arms,* 144.
,, MARGARET, of Skelton, *seal,* 454.
,, of Annandale, *arms,* Pl. XV., fig. 10, p. 144.
,, of Balcaskie, *arms,* 144.
,, ,, Sir WILLIAM, *brisure,* 433.
,, of Kinross, *arms,* 144.
,, ROBERT, 144.
,, ,, Earl of CARRICK, *badge,* 583.
,, ,, King of SCOTLAND, 33, 34, 177, 178, 378.
,, sister of ROBERT, 445.
BRÜCKNERS, *arms,* 362.
BRUDENELL, Earl of CARDIGAN, *arms,* 392.
BRUERE, Sir WILLIAM, *seal,* 301.
BRUGES, Palais de Justice at, 471.
BRÜHL, *arms,* 136.
BRUININGK, Barons de, *supporters,* 297.
BRUIS, ROBERT DE, Baron of BRECKNOCK, *arms,* 71.
BRULART, 12.
BRÜMMER, *arms,* 374.
Brunâtre, or Brown colour, 61.
BRUNNER, *Annales Boici,* 40.
BRUNSVELT, *arms,* 718.
BRUNSWICK, *arms,* 214, 472, 663.
,, Dukes of, *arms,* 234.
,, -LÜNEBURG, *arms,* 487.
,, MAGNUS I. and HENRY, Dukes of, *supporter,* 631.
BRUSSELS, City of, *arms,* 196, 283.
,, Museum of Antiquities at, 580, 644.
BRUUN, *arms,* 200.
BRUWERE, Sir WILLIAM, *seal,* 301.
BRUYN, LE, *arms,* 170.
BRYAN, *arms,* 147.
,, *badge,* 654.
,, *Bugle-horn* of, 584.
BRYDGE'S, Sir EGERTON, "COLLINS'S *Peerage,*" 562.
BRYDSON, *Summary View,* 615.
BRYRERLEGH, *arms,* 160.
BRZOSTOWSKI, Counts, *arms,* 357.
BUBENHAUSER, *arms,* 752.
BUBNA, *arms,* 383.
BUCCAFOCO, *arms,* 201.
BUCH, Capital de, *crest,* 606.
,, ,, *label,* 418.
BUCHAN, *arms,* 367.
,, Earl of, *arms,* 342.
,, Earldom of, 520.
,, Earls of, 605.
,, ,, *arms,* 446.
BUCHANAN, *arms,* 179.
BUCHEG, *arms,* 325.
BÜCHHEIM, County of, *arms,* 342.
BÜCHNER, Dr ROEMER, *Die Seigel der Deutschen Kaiser,* 243, 244, 247, 248, 252, 253.
Buck as a *badge,* 753.
BUCK, *arms,* 101; Pl. VII., fig. 12, p. 90.
Bucket as a *badge,* 753.
Buckle as a *badge,* 753.
BUCKINGHAM and NORMANBY, JOHN, Duke of, 562.
,, *badge,* 754.
,, Duke of, *arms,* 135, 343.

BUCKINGHAM, Dukes of, 399.
BUCKINGHAMSHIRE, Earl of, 185.
,, Earls of, *arms* 259.
Buckles, Pl. XXXIII., fig. 2, p. 376.
,, as charges, 377.
,, *Lozenge-shaped,* Pl. XXXIII., fig. 3, p. 376.
Bucks, 231.
BUCKS, *badge,* 754.
BUCQUOY, Princes de, *arms,* 95.
Budding, 679.
Budget, Water, 355.
Buffle, 718.
BUGGE, *arms,* 151.
Bugle-horn as a *badge,* 584.
,, as a charge, 385.
BUISSONS, DE, *arms,* 316.
,, Marquises d'AUSSONNE, *arms,* 316.
BULGARIA, *arms,* 501, 666.
BULGARINI, *arms,* Pl. XIII., fig. 5, p. 136.
,, Counts, *arms,* 138.
Bull, Pl. XXIV. fig. 1, p. 236.
,, as a *badge,* 753.
Bulls, 234.
Bull's head, Pl. XXIV., fig. 2, p. 236; 235.
,, as a *badge,* 753.
BULING, *arms,* 350.
BÜLOW, *arms,* 121, 543.
,, VON DENNEWITZ, Counts, *arms* and *augmentation,* 543.
BUNBURY, *arms,* 130; Pl. XII., fig. 3, p. 130.
BUOCAFOCO, *arms,* 201.
BUONACORSI, *arms,* 189.
BUONAROTTI, *arms,* 632.
BUONCOMPAGNI, Princes, *arms,* 293.
BURDON, *arms,* 375.
Burelé, 94, 677, 718.
Burèle, 718.
BURGH, *arms,* 457.
,, *badge,* 753.
,, DE, 17.
,, ,, Earl of ULSTER, *arms,* 141.
,, ELIZABETH DE, 416.
,, JOHN DE, Earl of ULSTER, *arms,* 457.
Burgonet, 679.
BURGOS, Cathedral at, 639.
BURGUNDY, ALICE of, 461.
,, -ancient, *arms,* 57, 253, 439, 462, 478, 484, 485, 495, 461, 462, 508, 573, 574, 577.
,, ANNE of, *arms,* 485.
,, *arms,* 450, 471, 509, 575, 631.
,, County of, *arms,* 631.
,, ,, PALATINE of, *arms,* 458.
,, Duchess of, *seal,* 478.
,, Duke CHARLES, *the bold,* 632.
,, Duke JEAN of, 573.
,, Duke of, 515.
,, ,, *arms,* 253; Pl. XLIV., fig. 6, p. 538.
,, Duke PHILIPPE, *Le Bon* of, 574.
,, ,, ,, the bold of 576.
,, Dukes of, *arms,* 439.

(772)

BURGUNDY, Dukes of, *Ordonnances*, 551.
,, JEANNE, Countess of, 457.
,, ,, Duchess of, *seal*, Pl. XXXV., fig. 3, p. 416.
,, JOHN, Duke of, 462, 484.
,, Marks of illegitimacy in, 573.
,, MARY, Duchess of, *supporter*, 632.
,, ,, of, 484.
,, modern, *arms*, 57, 462, 478, 484, 496, 573, 574, 575, 576.
,, OTHO, Count of, *crest*, 600.
,, PHILIP LE BON, Duke of, 475.
,, ,, the Bold, Duke of, 484.
,, PHILIPPE, natural son of Duke PHILIPPE LE BON, *arms*, 575.
,, *saltire* in, 143.
,, *seal* of HUGH II., Duke of, 47.
,, YOLANTE, daughter of EUDES of, 462.
BURKE, *General Armory*, 360, 401, 570.
,, Sir BERNARD, 647.
,, ,, *The Rise of Great Families*, 399.
BURLAY, *arms*, 191.
BURLEIGH, *badge*, 754.
BURNABY, *arms*, 270.
BURNARD, ODO, *badge*, 583.
,, ,, *seal* and *arms*, 50.
,, of Faringdon, *seal* and *arms*, RICHARD, 50.
BURNETT, *arms*, 319.
,, Dr GEORGE, Lyon King of Arms, 51, 158, 400, 496, 565, 567, 569, 647.
,, ,, Lyon King of Arms, *arms*, 51.
,, ,, Lyon King of Arms, edits part of *Exchequer Rolls of Scotland*, 455, 565.
,, of Kemnay, *arms*, 51.
,, of Leys, *arms*, 50.
BUROSSE, *arms*, 337.
BUSC, *arms*, 261.
BUSCH, *arms*, 313, 316, 391; Pl. XXIX., fig. 5, p. 318.
Bush and Crown as a *badge*, 595.
BUSH, *arms*, 315.
BUSQUE, ANTOINE DE, *arms*, 579.
BUSSNANG, Barons von, *arms*, 98.
BUSSY, D'AMBOISE, Marquises de, *arms*, 153.
,, Sir JOHN, *mantling* and *arms*, 613.
BUTEN, VAN, *arms*, 235.
BUTERA, Princes de, *arms*, 89.
BUTKENS, System of lines representing colour, 64.
,, *Trophies de Brabant*, 51.
BUTLER, *arms*, 118, 163, 531.

BUTLER, Bishop of DURHAM and BRISTOL, *arms*, 381.
,, Earls of LANESBOROUGH, *arms*, 381.
,, of Ormond, Margaret, *arms*, 531.
,, WILLIAM, *bend sinister*, 570.
BUTLERS of Ormonde, *arms*, 381.
Butterflies, 280.
BYDANT, *arms*, 272.
BYE, *arms*, 281.
BYRES, *arms*, 283.
BYRON, *arms*, Pl. XII., fig. 8, p. 130.
,, Lord, *arms*, 132.
,, Lords, *arms*, 562.
,, of Newstead, Sir JOHN, *arms*, 562.
BYSANTIUM, 189.
BYSSHE, Sir EDWARD, Notes on, *De Studio Militari*, 19, 33.
BYSTRZONOWSKI, Counts, *arms*, 237.

CAARTEN, *arms*, 387.
Cabbage, The, 343.
CABELLIC, *arms*, 156.
Caberfae, 233.
Cablé, 125, 708, 718.
Caboché, 718.
CABOGU, *arms*, 752.
Caboshed, 233, 679.
Cabossé, 679.
Cabossed or *Caboshed*, 233, 679.
Cabré, 679, 701, 702, 718, 727.
CABRERA, *arms*, 235.
CADE, JACK, 346.
CADENAT, *arms*, Pl. XXXI., fig. 11, p. 346.
Cadency, Marks of, 444, 679.
,, or *Differencing*, 396.
,, Principal modes of, 402.
,, Royal mark of, 420.
CADENETS, *arms*, 354.
CADEROUSSE, Ducs de, *arms*, 214, 293.
CADIFOR VAWR, IVAN AP, *arms*, 288.
CADRODHARD, *arms*, 230.
Caducée, 718.
CAEN, ABBEY of ST. ETIENNE at, *arms*, 468.
CAERLAVEROCK, National banners of English Army at siege of, 425, 656.
,, *Roll*, 409, 413, 414, 438, 481, 651.
CÆSAREA, Prince of, *arms*, 118.
CAETANI, *arms*, 132, 734.
CAITHNESS, *arms*, 369, 511, 512, 521.
,, Earl of, *arms*, 142; Pl. XXXII., fig. 12, p. 358; Pl. XLIII., fig. 1, p. 522.
,, Earl of, *seal* and *arms*, 520.
,, Earldom of, 511.
,, ,, *arms*, 368.
,, Earls of, *arms*, 369, 511.
,, ,, *supporters*, 288.
,, *seal* of JOHN, Earl of, 368.
,, *seal* of THOMAS MURRAY, Bishop of, 369.
CAIXAL, *arms*, 203.
CALABRIA, Duchy, *arms*, 156, 501, 547.
,, Duke of, *arms*, 502.

(773)

Calais Roll, 416, 417, 426.
,, Second, 166.
CALAIS, Siege of, 167, 554.
Calatrava, Cross of, 158, 718.
Calatrave, Croix de, 158, 718.
CALDER, achievement, 610.
CALDORA, arms, 81.
Caldron, The, 275.
Caldrons, Pl. XXXIII., fig. 8, p. 376.
CALERGI, Princes of, arms, 95.
CALL, arms, 386.
CALLENDAR, arms, 186, 522 ; Pl. XIX., fig. 1, p. 192.
CALMELS D'ARTENSAC, arms, 231.
Calotte, 611.
Caltrap, 352, 679 ; Pl. XXXI., fig. 9, p. 346.
CALVADOS, Church of St. Pierre de Dive in, 254.
Calvaire, Croix, 718.
Calvary-Cross 152, 679 ; Fig. 49, p. 164.
Calves, 234.
CAMARA, arms, 361.
CAMBACÉRES, le Duc, 15.
CAMBI, arms, 73.
CAMBRAY, Duke of, augmentation, 537.
,, MS. of the Concordat of, 574.
,, seal and arms of JEAN, Bishop of, 574 ; Pl. XLVII., fig. 4, p. 574.
CAMBRIDGE, ADOLPHUS FREDERICK, Duke of, label, 422 ; Fig. 84, p. 421.
,, badge, 753.
,, badge of RICHARD, Earl of, 324.
,, Duke of, label, 423.
,, KING'S COLLEGE, arms, 325.
CAMDEN, 35.
,, Marquis, arms, 231.
,, on Nobility, 4, 7, 8.
,, Remains, 591.
,, Visitation of Huntingdonshire, 206, 363, 561.
,, WILLIAM, arms, 163.
Camel, The, 231.
CAMEL, arms, 231.
CAMERINO, Dukes of, arms, 71.
CAMERON, arms, 127.
CAMIN, Principality of, arms, 159.
CAMMERSTEIN, Counts of, arms, 469.
CAMOENS, arms, 294.
CAMPBELL, ARCHIBALD, of Ellerslie, arms, 568.
,, arms, 78, 447, 466 ; Pl. VI., fig. 1, p. 84.
,, arms in Lyon Office Register, 400, 401.
,, Bart., arms, 534.
,, Col. WILLIAM, arms, 568.
,, Duke of ARGYLL, arms, 83, 84, 406.
,, Earl of BREADALBANE, arms, 84.
,, Earls of CAWDOR, arms, 84.
,, Earls of LOUDOUN, arms, 85.
,, Lords STRATHEDEN, arms, 84.
,, MARGARET, seal, 466.
., of Ardkinlas, supporters, 303.

CAMPBELL of Argyle, arms, 406.
,, of Glenorchy, arms, 84.
,, of Inveraw, bordure, 569.
,, of Loudoun, arms, 406.
,, of Strachur, arms, 84.
,, Sir ILAY, arms, 568.
CAMPBELLS in ARGYLL, 400.
CAMPERDOWN, achievement of Lord, 610.
,, Lord, arms and augmentation, 533, 610.
CAMPLIONCH, arms, 752.
CAMPORELLS, arms, 93.
CAMPOS, see MONTEIRO, 381.
CANABRI, arms, 121.
CANALI, arms, 121.
,, Counts, arms, 136.
CANDAVÈNE, arms, 49.
Candles as charges, 372.
CANDOLLE, Marquises de, arms, 81.
Canelé, 727.
CANETE, Marquises of, arms, 506.
Canette, The, 266, 718, 736.
CANIVET, NICOLAS, arms, 180.
CANIZARES, arms, 174.
CANNEGIETER, arms, 382.
Cannelé, 138, 692, 718.
,, line, 76.
CANNING, arms, 200.
Cannon as charges, 366.
CANO, Barons de MEGHEM, arms, 360.
CANTACUZENE, arms, 318.
CANTALUPO, Princes de, arms, 128.
CANTELOWE, WILLIAM DE, arms, 331.
CANTELU, MICHAEL DE, arms, 73.
CANTELUPE, arms, 225, 333.
,, THOMAS DE, Bishop of HEREFORD, 225.
,, WILLIAM DE, arms, 331.
CANTERBURY, arms of See, 150, 375 ; Pl. XVI., fig. 11, p. 146.
,, Cathedral, 593.
,, JOHN D'UFFORD, Archbishop of, 142.
,, RALPH TURBINE, Archbishop of, arms, 152.
,, THOMAS A BECKET, Archbishop of, arms, 264.
,, WILLIAM COURTENAY, Archbishop of, arms, 437.
Canting-arms, 679.
Canton, 116, 165, 166, 167, 679, 718 ; Pl. XVIII., fig. 1, p. 190 ; Pl. XVIII., fig. 2, p. 190.
,, and Fess, Pl. XVIII., fig. 3, p. 190.
,, or Bar, joined, 167.
,, Difference by the insertion of a, 425.
Cantoned, 679.
Cantonné, 679, 718.
Cap or Mortier, 625.
Caparisoned, 679.
CAPECI, arms, 214.
Capeline, 611, 612, 615.
CAPELLO, arms, 374, 392.
CAPET, HUGH, Duke of FRANCE, etc., 11.
,, Line of, 283.
CAPLENDORF, Counts von, arms, 90.
CAPPELLI, arms, 374, 392.
CAPPERS, arms, 392.
CAPPONI, arms, 80.

(774)

CAPRINI, *arms*, 277.
Caps as charges, 392.
,, *of maintenance* as charges, 392.
Capuchon, 611, 718.
CARBONNIÈRES, *arms*, 714.
Carbuncle, 679.
CARDEN, *arms*, 365.
CARDIGAN, Earl of, *arms*, 392.
,, Prince of, *arms*, 212.
Cardinals in France, *mantling armoyé*, 615.
CARDON, *arms*, 335.
CARDONAS, *arms*, 335, 482; Pl. XLI., fig. 3, p. 510.
CARDOZO, *arms*, 339.
Cards as charges, 387.
CARENCY, Princes de, *arms*, 121, 319.
CAREW, *arms*, 223.
CARILLO, *arms*, 506.
CARINTHIA, ALBERT, Duke of, *seal*, 456.
,, Duchy, *arms*, 454, 455, 456, 471, 495, 503, 634, 665.
,, MARGARET of, *seal*, 454.
CARLAVEROCK, Siege of, 273.
CARLINGFORD, Lord, *supporter*, 232.
CARLISLE, Earl of, *mullet*, 446.
CARLOS, Colonel, *arms*, 533.
CARLOWITZ, *arms* and *augmentation*, 543.
CARLSSON, *arms*, 101.
CARLYLE, *arms*, 157, 522; Pl. XLII., fig. 5, p. 512.
,, Lord TORTHORWALD, *arms*, 142, 522.
CARMICHAEL, *arms*, 125, 127; Pl. XI., fig. 6, p. 124.
Carnation, 700, 718.
,, or naked flesh colour, 62.
Carnations, 337.
CARNEGIE, Earls of SOUTHESK, *arms*, 258.
CARNIOLA, Duchy, *arms*, 247, 256, 495, 503, 665.
CARO, *arms*, 508.
CAROLATH-BEUTHEN, Princes, *arms*, 337.
CAROUGES, JEANNE, Dame de, *seal* of, 86.
CARR, ROBERT, Viscount ROCHESTER, *arms* and *augmentation*, 532.
Carreaux, 378, 718.
CARRICK, Earl of, *badge*, 583.
CARRILLO, *arms*, 473.
,, THERESIA DE, 506.
CARRO, *arms*, 378.
CARROCCIO, 655.
CARROLL, *arms*, 162.
Carrots, 344.
CARR'S MS., 366.
CARS, Ducs des, *arms*, 121.
CARTIER D'YVES, Barons, *arms*, 183.
Cartouche, 679.
Cartulary of St. Père de Chartres, 10.
CARTWRIGHT, *arms*, 310.
CASANOVA, 16.
,, *arms*, 363.
CASOLI, Ducs de, *arms*, 95.
CASSAGNAC, *see* GRANIER, 339.
CASSAGNET, Marquis de FIMARCON, *arms*, 129.
CASSANTS, *arms*, 284.
CASSILIS, Earls of, *arms*, 163.
CASTANEDA, *arms*, 93.

CASTEL, *see* BATURLE.
CASTELAIN, *arms*, 289.
CASTELLANE, DE, *arms*, 358.
CASTELLETS, *arms*, 360.
CASTELLI, *arms*, 746.
CASTELN, *arms*, 222; Pl. XLVI., fig. 3, p. 546.
CASTILE, ALFONSO of, *arms*, Pl. XLVIII., fig. 6, p. 576.
,, *arms*, 168, 253, 306, 329, 358, 391, 416, 441, 457, 464, 471, 478, 479, 488, 495, 501, 507, 547, 576, 577, 578, 633, 667.
,, BLANCHE, dtr. of ALFONSO VIII., King of, 329; *seal*, Pl. XXXVII., fig. 4, p. 448.
,, *bordure* of, 172, 329, 440, 475, 507; Pl. XVII., fig. 7, p. 172.
,, ELEANOR of, 457.
,, ,, *monument*, 479.
,, FERDINAND of, 479.
,, ,, III., King of, 478.
,, *label* of, 416.
,, Queen ISABELLA of, *badge*, 596.
,, *seal* of ALPHONSO of, 244.
CASTILLE and LEON, ISABELLA of, 416.
,, *arms*, 471; Pl. XXXII., fig. 3, p. 358.
,, DE, Marquis de CHENOISE, *supporters*, 303.
,, Marquises de CHENOISE, *arms*, 358.
,, SANCHO, Infant of, *seals* to contract of marriage of, 46.
CASTILLO, *arms*, 744.
,, *see* FERNANDES.
CASTILLON, Marquises of, *arms*, 358.
Castle, 357; Pl. XXXII., figs. 3 and 6, p. 358.
,, *with other buildings*, 362.
CASTLE STUART, Earl of, *arms*, 569.
CASTRIES, Duc de, *arms*, 141.
CASTRO DE, *arms*, 192.
Cat, 97, 226.
,, *Genet*, as a *badge*, 557, 587.
Cut-a-mount, 226, 679.
CATANEI, *arms*, 72.
Catapult as a charge, 365.
CATENAS, *arms*, 360.
Catharine-wheel, 679.
CATHCART, *arms*, 307; Pl. XXVIII., fig. 4, p. 308.
CATTARO, *arms*, 503.
Caudé, 705, 718.
CAUDRELIER, LE, *arms*, 266.
Cauldron as a charge, 389.
CAUMONT, DE, 12.
,, *Abécédaire d'Archéologie*, 287, 293, 299, 301.
CAVALLI, *arms*, 237.
CAVAN, Earl of, *arms*, 323.
CAVE, *arms*, 96.
CAVENDISH, Dukes of DEVONSHIRE, *arms*, 233.
CAVILL, *arms*, 124.
CAWDOR, Earls of, *arms*, 84.
CEBA, *arms*, 72.
CECIL, *badge*, 754.
,, Lord ROOS, 17.

Ceintré, 718.
Celery, 344.
CELLES, *arms*, 133.
Cendrée or ash colour, 61.
CENNINO, *arms*, 294.
Censers as charges, 372.
Centaur, 298, 679.
,, Female, 298.
,, -sagittaire, 299.
CENTELLES, *arms*, 100.
Centre, le (abîme); "en cœur," 59.
Cep de Vigne, 718.
CEPEDES, *arms*, 379.
Ceps, 703, 718.
CERAMI, Princes of, *arms*, 310.
Cerberus, 304.
Cercelée, 679.
Cerclé, 691, 718.
CESARINI, Dukes de CITTANOVA, supporters, 635.
CETRACINI, *arms*, 99.
CETTNER, Counts, *arms*, 352.
CEVA, Barons, *arms*, 93.
CHABAN, Comte de, *arms*, 281.
CHABOT, 12.
,, *arms*, 505.
Chabots, 718.
CHADWICK, *arms*, 175.
CHAI, *arms*, 68.
CHAILLU, DU, *Viking Age*, 367.
CHAILONS, *arms*, 202.
Chains, 353; Pl. XXXI., fig. 10, p. 346; Pl. XXXI., fig. 11, p. 346.
CHALANDRAS, *see* FAYDIDE.
CHALANGE, *arms*, 306.
Chalice as a charge, 372.
CHALMERS, *arms*, Pl. XXII., fig. 4, p. 222.
,, of Balnacraig, *arms*, 221.
CHALON, *arms*, 129, 466.
CHALONS, Counts of, *arms*, 410.
,, HUGUES DE, *arms*, 410.
,, JEAN DE, Comte de BOURGOGNE, *banner*, 650.
,, LOUIS DE, *arms*, 410.
CHALOUYAU, MONTMORENCY-LAVAL DE, *brisure*, 452.
Chamber, 679.
Chamberlain, Grand, French, mark of office, 645.
,, Lord High, of England, mark of office, 644.
,, Lord High, of Scotland, mark of office, 644.
,, of the Household, Lord, mark of office, 644.
CHAMBERS, WM., *The Story of St. Giles' Cathedral Church, Edinburgh*, 476.
CHAMBON, Marquis d'ARBOUVILLE, *arms*, 93.
CHAMBORD, Comte de, 425.
Chameleon, 277.
Chamfront, 679.
Chamois, 232.
Champ, 687, 718.
Champagne, 311, 483, 679, 705, 718.
,, Parted per, fig. 36, p. 77.
CHAMPAGNE, *arms*, 479.
,, Grand Capitulaire of, 10.
,, seal of Counts of, 48.
CHAMPERNONS, *arms*, 136.
CHAMPNEY, *arms*, 184; Pl. XVIII., fig. 11, p. 190.
CHAMPREDONDE, *arms*, 337.

CHAMPS, EUDES ALLEMAN, Seigneur de, *arms*, 51.
CHAMPSDIVERS, *arms*, 136.
CHANAC, *arms*, 79.
Chancellor, French, mark of office, 645.
Chandeliers de l'Eglise, 719.
CHANDOS, *arms*, 146, 403; Pl. XVI., fig. 1, p. 146.
,, Sir JOHN, K.G., 403.
Chantant, 719.
CHANTRELL, *arms*, 264; Pl. XXV., fig. 12, p. 260.
Chapé, 81, 88, 719, 741; Pl. VI., fig. 8, p. 84.
,, -chaussé, 89, 719, 746.
,, ployé, 719; Pl. VI., fig. 10, p. 84.
Chapeau, 679.
Chapel, 363.
Chapelet, 680, 719.
CHAPELLE, ANTOINE, Seigneur de, *arms*, 575.
,, DE LA, *arms*, 97, 363.
,, ULRIC DE, *crest*, 600.
Chaperon, 718, 719.
Chaperonné, 89, 691, 719.
Chaplet, 680; Pl. XXX., fig. 9, p. 332.
Chaplets of leaves or flowers, 336.
CHAPPELL, *arms*, 370.
CHARBONNEAU, *arms*, 365.
CHARDOIGNE, *arms*, 187.
CHARDON DU HAVET, *arms*, 336.
Chargé, 680, 719.
Charged, 680.
Charges, Animate, 194, 208, 242.
,, Astronomical, 305.
,, Common, 102.
,, Difference by addition of small, 406.
,, ,, change of the minor, 434.
,, ,, diminishing the number of, 434.
,, Different kinds of, 101.
,, Inanimate, 305.
,, Military, 345.
,, Miscellaneous, 345.
CHARLEMAGNE, 176, 658.
,, adopts the *Eagle* as his ensign, 242.
,, *arms*, 21.
,, *crown* of, 254, 526, 617, 618, 663; Fig. 97, p. 617.
,, ,, as a charge, 380.
CHARLES I., King of BRITAIN, 420, 421, 535, 633; *arms*, Pl. LI., fig. 5, p. 661; *crown*, 618.
,, ,, supporters on Exchequer Seal of, 663.
,, II., King of BRITAIN, 146, 181, 316, 431, 475, 532, 559; *arms*, Pl. LI., fig. 5, p. 661.
,, ,, King of BRITAIN, *crown*, 618.
,, ,, supporters on Seal of Common Pleas of, 663.
,, IV., Emperor HOLY ROMAN EMPIRE, *crown*, 621.
,, ,, King of FRANCE, supporters, 636.

(776)

CHARLES IV., King of FRANCE, seal, 354, 456.
,, ,, HUNGARY and BOHEMIA, 252.
,, ,, seal of the Emperor, 248.
,, V., Duchess MARGARET, daughter of Emperor, 509, 577.
,, ,, Emperor, 449, 573, 577, 620.
,, ,, ,, augmentations granted by, 536.
,, ,, Great Seal of the Emperor, 253.
,, ,, King of FRANCE, 601.
,, ,, ,, ,, Edict of, 329.
,, ,, ,, ,, supporter, 633, 636.
,, ,, ,, ,, supporters and motto, 643.
,, VI., Aurea Bulla of the Emperor, 253.
,, ,, King of FRANCE, augmentation granted by, 538.
,, ,, King of FRANCE, supporters, 636.
,, ,, of SPAIN, Great Seal of, 501.
,, VII., augmentation granted by, 538, 541.
,, ,, King of FRANCE, 57, 113, 250, 331, 515, 539, 572.
,, ,, King of FRANCE, supporters, 636.
,, ,, seal of the Emperor, 253.
,, VIII., 575.
,, ,, King of FRANCE, 478.
,, ,, ,, ,, crown, 620.
,, ,, ,, ,, supporters, 636.
,, IX., ,, FRANCE, 570, 601.
,, arms, 317.
,, EMANUEL, King of SARDINIA, supporter of, 244.
,, Emperor, as King of SPAIN, crown, 620.
,, Roll, 350, 357, 377, 378, 379.
,, THE BOLD, Duke of BURGUNDY, 39, 485.
CHARLETON, arms, 212, 417.
,, of POWYS, arms, 417.
CHARLOTTE, Princess, daughter of King GEORGE IV. of ENGLAND, 424.
,, Princess Royal, label, 422; Fig. 85, p. 421.
CHARNY, Count de, arms, 485.
,, GUILLEMETTE DE, arms, 485.
CHAROLOIS, CHARLES, Count of, arms, 484.
CHARPENTIER, LE, 16.
CHARTERIS of Kinfauns, arms, 179.
CHARTERS, arms, 123.
Chasse or Reliquary, 658.
CHASTELLUX, Marquises de, arms, 186.
CHASTRE, DE LA, arms, 351.
Château, 719.
CHÂTEAU-GONTIER, arms, 140.

CHÂTEAU MELIAND, arms, 127.
CHATEAUBRIAND, arms, 112, 330, 341.
,, GEOFFREY DE, 330.
,, GEOFFROI DE, augmentation, 539.
,, motto, 331.
CHÂTEAUNEUF, DE, 14.
CHÂTELAIN, arms, Pl. XXXII., fig. 6, p. 358.
CHATELAINS, arms, 359.
Chatelé, 719.
CHÂTELHERAULT, Duchy of, arms, 515.
CHÂTILLON, Ducs de, arms, 257.
CHÂTILLON, arms, 411.
,, EUSTACIA DE, secretum of, 54.
,, MONTMORENCY-LAVAL DE, brisure, 452.
,, Viscount de, label, 418.
CHATON DE MORANDAIS, Marquises, arms, 317.
CHATTERTON, arms, 156.
Chaudière, 719.
CHAUMELLS, arms, 314.
CHAUMIÈRE, see BIGOT.
CHAUMONT, arms, 118, 314.
CHAUSNES, arms, 721.
Chaussé, 88, 719.
,, -ployé, 88, 719; Pl. VI., fig. 9, p. 84.
,, -trape, 352, 679, 680, 688.
,, -trapes, 719.
CHAUTONS, arms, 278.
Chauve-souris, 719.
CHAUVIGNY, arms, 214.
CHAWORTH, arms, 139, 409.
,, Sir PATRICK, arms, 409.
CHAYLAU, arms, 202.
CHAYTOR, arms, 322.
Checquy, Pl. VII., fig. 6, p. 90; Pl. VII., fig. 7, p. 90.
Chef, 117, 680, 719.
,, -chevron, 719.
,, cousu, 104.
,, de France, 719.
,, de l'Empire (Germanique), 719.
,, -dextre, 719.
,, le canton dextre du, 59.
,, ,, sénestre du, 59.
,, le point du, 59.
,, -pal, 720.
,, -senestre, 720.
,, -triangulaire, 720.
,, -routé, 720.
CHEMILLÉ, arms, 72.
CHENEY, badge, 753.
CHENOISE, Marquises de, arms, 358.
,, ,, supporters, 303.
CHEPSTOW, arms, 364.
CHEPY, Marquises of, arms, 128.
Chequy, 99, 680.
CHÉRINS, arms, 201.
Cherries, 341.
Cherub, 201.
Cherubims, 720.
CHÉRUEL, Dictionnaire Historique des Institutions, etc., de la France, 269.
CHESNE, DU, arms, 340.
CHESNEAU, DU, arms, 136.
Chess pieces as charges, 387.
,, -rook, 680.
CHESTER, arms, 460.

(777)

CHESTER, Earl of, *arms*, 341, 342.
,, Earldom of, *arms*, 594.
CHESTERFIELD, Earls of, *arms*, 81.
CHETTLES, *arms*, 281.
CHETWODE, *arms*, 109 ; Pl. IX., fig. 12, p. 108.
Cheval-mariné, 703.
,, *trap*, 352, 680.
CHEVALERIE, *arms*, 237.
Chevaliers-bacheliers, 652.
Chevaliers-banneret, 57, 652.
Cherelé, 682, 720.
CHEVERELL, *arms*, 223.
Cheveron, The, 135.
Chevillé, 720.
Chevron, 78 ; Fig. 41, p. 116 ; 135, 680, 720 ; Pl. XIII., fig. 1, p. 136.
,, *braced* or *interlaced*, 140.
,, *broken* or *fracted*, 138.
,, *Charges on a*, Pl. XIII., fig. 3, p. 136.
,, *checquy*, Pl. XIII., fig. 2, p. 136.
,, *coticed*, 140 ; Pl. XIII., fig. 8, p. 136.
,, *Divisé en*, 720.
,, *écimé*, 138 ; Pl. XIII., fig. 9, p. 136.
,, *En*, 720.
,, *failli*, 139.
,, *fracted*, Pl. XIII., fig. 10, p. 136.
,, *Parted per*, 81 ; Fig. 34, p. 77.
,, *Per*, 680 ; Pl. V., fig. 8, p. 80.
,, *ployé*, Pl. XIII., fig. 4, p. 136.
,, *reversed*, Pl. XIII., fig. 5, p. 136.
,, *rompu*, 139 ; Pl. XIII., fig. 11, p. 136.
,, Varieties of, 137.
Chevronel, 139, 680 ; Pl. XIII., fig. 7, p. 136.
Chevronné, 98, 680, 720.
Chevronny, 98, 680 ; Pl. VII., fig. 5, p. 90.
Chevrons interlaced, Pl. XIII., fig. 12, p. 136.
CHEYNE, *arms*, 163.
,, of Duffus, *arms*, 520.
,, REGINALD, *arms*, 413.
CHIAVARO, *arms*, 711.
CHICHESTER, Earls of, *badge*, 377.
,, See of, *arms*, 194.
,, SEFFRID TURBINE, Bishop of, *arms*, 152.
CHICHORRO, MARTIN AFFONSO, 578.
Chicot, 704, 720, 727, 730.
CHIDIOK, Sir JOHN, *arms*, 176.
Chief, 116, 117, 680 ; Pl. X., fig. 1, p. 118.
,, *arched*, Pl. X., fig. 5, p. 118.
,, *Dexter*, 59.
,, *Ghibbeline*, 119.
,, *Guelphic*, 119.
,, *indented*, Pl. X., fig. 2, p. 118.
,, *Middle*, 59.
,, *Napoleonic Ducal*, Pl. X., fig. 3, p. 118.
,, *pale*, 120.
,, *sinister*, 59.
,, used as an *augmentation*, 119.
Chien-de-mer, 703.
CHIÈVRES, Seigneur de, *arms*, 449.
CHIFFLET, JEAN JACQUES, *Insignia Gentilitia Equitum Ordinis Velleris Aurei*, 282, 440, 449, 502, 573, 574.
CHILDERIC, supposed tomb of, 281.
Chimæra, 294, 680, 720.
CHIMAY, ANTOINE DE, *arms*, 450.

CHIMAY, CHARLES, Prince of, *arms*, 450.
,, Counts and Princes of, *arms*, 127, 348, 449.
,, PHILIPPE DE, *arms*, 450.
Chimère, 680, 720.
CHINA, Imperial Dragon of, 292.
Chiodo, Il Sacro, 617.
CHIPPENDALE, *arms*, 222.
CHISHOLM, *arms*, 520.
CHIVALETS, *arms*, 237.
CHIVERS, *arms*, 167.
CHOISEUL, Ducs de, *arms*, 434.
,, ,, PRASLIN, *arms*, 434.
CHOLMELEY, *arms*, 559, 565.
,, Sir RICHARD, 558.
,, Sir ROGER, *arms*, 558.
CHOLMONDELEY, *arms*, 342, 349 ; Pl. XXXI., fig. 4, p. 346.
,, *badge*, 753.
,, Marquises, 342.
CHORINSKI, *mantling*, 616.
Choucas, 680, 720.
Chouette, 720.
Chough, Cornish, 264, 680 ; Pl. XXVI., fig. 1, p. 266.
CHRIST, *arms* ascribed to, 20.
Christian Names, 9.
CHRISTIAN IV., King of DENMARK, *crown*, 620.
,, V., King of DENMARK, *crown*, 620.
,, definition of Esquire, 8.
,, *Notes to Blackstone*, 8.
CHRISTIERN V., King of DENMARK and NORWAY, CHRISTIERN GYLDENLOVE, natural son of, 581.
CHRISTYN, 575.
,, *Jurisprudentia Heroica*, 551, 573.
Chronicon Turonense, 39, 40.
Chronicum Belgicum Magnum, 41.
CHRYSOSTOM, ST., Homily XIII., *Ep. to Cor.*, 9.
CHÜR, *arms*, 373 ; Pl. XLV., fig. 3, p. 539.
Church banner, 658.
,, *candlestick* as a charge, 372.
CHUTE, *arms*, 347.
CIBO, ALBERIC, *arms* and *augmentation*, 537.
,, *arms*, 537.
CIBRARIO, *Sigilli de' Principi de Savoia*, 453, 460, 467, 628, 629.
CIMANI, *arms*, 752.
Cimier, 720, 724.
CINI or CINTI, *arms*, 61.
CINQUE PORTS, *arms*, 467 ; Pl. XXXVIII., fig. 6, p. 464.
Cinque-foil, 680, 322.
,, as a *badge*, 753.
Cinquefoils, Pl. XXX., fig. 1, p. 332.
CINTI, or CINI, *arms*, 61.
Cintré, 720.
CIOLEK, *arms*, 234.
CIOLI, *arms*, 136.
CIPRIANI, *arms*, 275.
CIRCASSIA, *arms*, 666.
Circular-bordure, 680.
CISNEROS, RODRIQUE GONSALEZ DE, *arms*, 167.
CISTERNA, Princes DELLA, *arms*, 293.

(778)

Cities as charges, 363.
CITTANOVA, Dukes de, *supporters*, 635.
Civic-crown, 680.
CLAIRAMBAULT, Marquis de VENDEUIL, *arms*, 221.
CLAIRAUNAY, *arms*, 297.
Claire voies, 97, 720.
CLAIRON, DE, Comtes de HAUSSONVILLE, *arms*, 160.
CLANCARTY, Earl of, *supporters*, 648.
CLANRANALD, Captain of, *arms*, 512.
CLANRICARDE, Lord, 17.
CLAPS, *arms*, 311.
CLARE, *arms*, 146, 457, 465, 467; Pl. XIII., fig. 7, p. 136.
,, *Black bull* of, 662.
,, Earl of GLOUCESTER, *badge*, 386.
,, Earls of GLOUCESTER, 139, 457.
,, ELIZABETH DE, *seal*, 456.
,, GILBERT DE, Earl of GLOUCESTER, 457.
,, Lords of GLAMORGAN, 386.
,, MARGARET DE, *arms*, 465.
,, Sir THOMAS DE, 467.
CLARENCE, *arms*, 565.
,, *badge*, 753.
,, Duke of, *arms* and *label*, 416.
,, GEORGE, Duke of, *mantling*, 613.
,, Sir JOHN DE, illegitimate, *arms*, 556.
,, THOMAS, Duke of, 556.
,, WILLIAM HENRY, Duke of, *label*, 422; Fig. 81, p. 421.
CLARENCEUX, King of Arms, *arms*, 526.
CLARENDON, Earl of, *arms*, 183, 639.
,, ,, *augmentation*, 545.
,, Sir ROGER DE, illegitimate, *arms*, 555.
Clarichord, 680.
Claricorde, 702, 720.
Clariné, 235, 678, 720.
Clarion, as a charge, 386.
,, or *Clarichord*, 680; Pl. XXXIII., fig. 11, p. 376.
CLARKE, *arms*, 122.
CLAVER, *arms*, 113.
CLAYHILLS of Invergowrie, *arms*, 61.
Clechée, 720.
CLELAND, *arms*, 237; Pl. XXIV., fig. 7, p. 236.
CLEMENT IV., Pope, *arms*, 43.
CLÉMENT, Maréchal de France, *arms*, 129.
CLÉRAMBAULT, *arms*, 94.
CLERK, *arms*, 529.
,, Sir JOHN, *augmentation*, 529.
CLERMONT, Lord, *supporter*, 232.
,, NESLE, *arms*, 270.
CLEVÉ, Dukes of, *arms*, 472.
CLEVELAND, Dukes of, *supporters*, 288.
CLEVES, ADOLPH of, *seal*, 485.
,, ANNE of, 530.
,, *arms*, 485.
,, Dukes of, *arms*, 354.
CLIFFORD, 17.
,, *arms*, 428, 554.
,, *badge*, 753.
,, *Fair Rosamond*, 324, 588.
,, MAUD, daughter of Lord, 324.

CLIFFORD, MAUD, daughter of THOMAS, Lord, 588.
CLIFFORDS, DE, 17.
CLINTON, *badge*, 753.
,, Duke of NEWCASTLE, *arms*, 163.
,, ,, ,, *supporters*, 605.
,, Lord, *supporters*, 606.
,, of Baddesley, *arms*, 333.
,, ,, PETRONILLA, heiress of, 605.
CLISSON, DE, *arms*, 709.
,, OLIVIER DE, *seal* and *shield* of, 56.
,, ,, *supporter*, 632.
CLITE, JEAN DE LA, Seigneur de COMMINES, *arms*, 440.
CLOCK, *arms*, 374.
CLOEPS DE HEERNESSE, Barons, *arms*, 341.
CLOOS, NICHOLAS, Grant of Nobility to, 5.
CLOOT, *arms*, 191.
Clos, 680.
Close, 680.
,, applied to Falcon, 261.
,, *Roll* 1252, 209.
Closet, The, 126, 680.
Clouds, 310.
Cloué, 696, 720.
Cloués, 97.
Clous de la passion, 698, 720.
CLOVIS, King of the Franks, 281, 326, 658.
,, the same as LOUIS, 327.
CLUN, *arms*, 118.
CLUNY, *arms*, 711.
CLUSEAU, DE, *arms*, 167; Pl. XVIII., fig. 4, p. 190.
CLUTINCK, *arms*, 428.
CLUTTON, *arms*, Pl. XIII., fig. 8, p. 136.
CLYFFORDE, JOHIS BASTARDI DE, *seal*, 554.
Coats, *Parted*, 74.
COBHAM, *arms*, 136, 412.
,, Viscount, *arms*, 273.
Cockatrice, 293, 680; Pl. XXVII., fig. 9, p. 288.
COCKBURN, *arms*, 265.
,, JOHN, second son of Sir ALEXANDER, *arms*, 459.
,, of Ormiston, *fess*, 430.
Cock-fish, The, 299.
Cocks, 265; Pl. XXVI., fig. 3, p. 266.
COCKS, Earl SOMERS, *arms*, 234.
COCQ, LE, Counts de HUMBEKE, *arms*, 265.
CODEVE, Barons, *augmentation*, 543.
COELEN, *arms*, 343.
COELHO, NICOLAO, *arms*, 238.
COERNEY, *see* CONDE.
COËTIVY, Princes de MORTAGNE, *arms*, 93.
COËTMEN, *arms*, 460, 463.
,, Dame de, *seal*, 460, 463.
COËTQUEN, Marquises de, *arms*, 95.
Cœur, En, 721.
CŒURET, Marquis de NESLE, *arms*, 202.
CŒURVERT, *arms*, 202.
Cohort Ensigns, Figs. 5 and 6, p. 19.
COIGNE, *arms*, 68.

(779)

COING, arms, 222.
Coins, Heraldic Devices on, 24, 44.
COISLIN, Ducs de, arms, 128.
COISPEL, arms, 279.
COKAYNE, arms, 265 ; Pl. XXVI., fig. 3, p. 266.
,, Complete Peerage, 562.
COKE, Sir EDWARD, on Nobility, 4.
COKER, arms, 392.
COLBERT-CHABANNAIS, Marquises de, arms, 275.
,, Marquis de SEIGNELAY, arms, 275.
,, supporter, 297.
COLE, arms, 277.
COLIGNI, arms, 716.
COLIGNO, ANSELMO, Count de, arms, 579.
COLIGNY, Ducs de CHÂTILLION, etc., arms, 257.
COLLALTO, Princes of, arms, 81.
Collar of SS, 597.
,, of Suns and Roses, 597.
Collared, 680.
Collars, Livery, 597.
College of Arms, 287, 646.
,, ,, MS., 589, 598.
COLLEONI, Counts, arms, 203.
COLLET, arms, 150.
Colleté, 680, 689, 721, 733, 737.
COLLINS'S Peerage, 562.
COLLONGUE, arms, 68.
COLOGNE, arms, 283.
,, Prince-Archbishops, Electors of, arms, 141.
COLOMBIER, arms, 136.
COLOMBIÈRE, DE LA, arms, 88.
,, ,, La Science Héroïque, 2, 23, 190.
Colonia Nemausensis, 277.
COLONNA, arms, 302, 451 ; Pl. XXXII., fig. 7, p. 358.
,, ISABELLA, 451.
,, Princes, 16.
,, ,, of PALESTRINA, etc., arms, 363.
Colonnes, 721.
Colour on Colour, etc., 102.
Colours represented by lines, etc., 64.
,, ,, planets and precious stones, 65.
,, used in Heraldry, 60.
COLQUHOUN, arms, 143.
COLSTON, arms, 270.
COLT, arms, 237.
Colt, The, 237.
Columbine or Amaranth colour, 61.
COLUMBUS, arms and augmentation, 312, 547 ; Pl. XXXIX., fig. 1, p. 482.
Column, Pl. XXXII., fig. 7, p. 358.
Columns, 363 ; Pl. XXXII., fig. 8, p. 358.
COLVILE, arms, Pl. XIV., fig. 6, p. 140.
,, of Duffield, label, 415.
COLVILLE, arms, 157, 159.
,, of Ochiltree, arms, 159.
Combatant, 220, 680.
Combats, Armorial, 33.
COMBAUT, DE, Ducs de COISLIN, arms, 128.
Comble, 721.
COMBOURG, Counts, arms 95.

Combs as charges, 391.
Comet, The, 310.
Cometé, 705, 721.
Comète, 728.
COMINS, arms, 342.
COMMENGES, Counts of, arms, 154.
,, seal of, Count BERNARD V., 154.
COMMINES, PHILIPPE DE, arms, 440.
Commonwealth, motto of, 664.
COMNENA, ANNA, biography of her father, 26.
COMNENI, arms, 374.
COMPAGNI, arms, 130.
Compartment, 680.
Compartments, 641.
Complement, 680.
Compon, 721.
Componé, 680, 721.
Compony, 680.
COMPTON, badge, 753.
,, of Catton, arms, 226.
COMYN, arms, 631.
,, Earl of BUCHAN, arms, 342.
CONAN, Count of BRETAGNE, 30.
Conclave, Master of the, Italy, mark of office, 645.
CONCORDIA, Duchy of, arms, 509.
CONDÉ DE COERNEY, arms, 376.
,, Princes de, arms, 571.
,, ,, bend, 429.
CONGALTON, arms and label, 420.
CONGREVE, arms, 348 ; Pl. XXXI., fig. 3, p. 346.
CONIGAN, Barons de ROZ, arms, 151.
CONINGSBURGH, RICHARD of, 588.
,, Earl of CAMBRIDGE, badge of, 324.
Conjoined, 681.
,, in lure, 260, 681.
CONNAUGHT, 384.
,, ARTHUR, Duke of, label, 423 ; Fig. 82, p. 421.
CONNISBURGH, seals and arms of GILBERT and WILLIAM, 50.
Conque-marine, 721, 722.
CONRAD I., Emperor, HOLY ROMAN EMPIRE, crown, 621.
,, II., seal of the Emperor, 328.
CONROY, Counts of, arms, 581.
CONSIDINE, arms, 175.
Constable, Grand, French, mark of office, 645.
CONSTABLE, arms, 93.
CONSTANTINE XIV., Emperor of BYZANTIUM, 251.
Constellations, 309.
CONTARINI, arms, 122.
CONTI, Princes de, bend, 429.
Contoise, 613.
Contourné, 220, 681, 683, 721, 745.
Contré, 717.
Contre, 739.
,, -appaumé, 721.
,, -bandé, 721.
,, -barré, 721.
,, -chevronné, 721.
,, -componné, 721.
,, -écartelé, 722.
,, -fasce, 722.
,, -flambant, 722.
,, -hermine, 722.
,, -palé, 721.

Contre-passant, 722.
„ *-vair*, 681, 722.
„ *-vairé*, 722.
CONTRIZAKIS, *arms*, 66.
CONYERS, *arms*, 376.
Cooking-pot as a charge, 275, 389.
COOLE, *arms*, 343.
„ DE, *arms*, 342.
COOLMAN, *arms*, 343.
COPE, *arms*, Pl. XXX., fig. 4, p. 332.
„ WILLIAM, *arms*, 325.
Coped, 88.
Coquerelles, 722.
Coquillage, 722.
Coquille, 686, 703, 722.
Cor de chasse, 691, 722.
CORBET, *seals* and *arms* of ROBERT, PATRICK, and WALTER, 50.
„ THOMAS, *arms*, 264.
CORBOLI, *arms*, 264.
Cordé, 704, 722.
Corded, 681.
Cordelière, 645, 722.
CORDOVA, *arms*, 128, 473, 507.
„ Dukes of SESA, *arms*, 473.
„ Marquises of PRIEGO, *arms*, 473.
„ Counts de FERIA, *arms*, 507.
„ Counts of FIGUEROA, *arms*, 507; Pl. XLI., fig. 5, p. 510.
„ *supporters*, 644.
CORKE, *arms*, 222; Pl. XXII., fig. 9, p. 222.
Cormoran, 722.
CORNAIS, DES, *arms*, 181.
CORNEILLAN, Counts de, *arms*, 264.
CORNEILLE, *arms*, 106, 264.
Cornes, 722.
CORNET, *arms*, 386.
Cornflowers, 337.
Cornhill Magazine, 246.
Cornière, 722.
Cornish chough, 681.
CORNUT DE ST. LÉONARD, LE, *arms*, 187.
CORNWALL, Earl of, *arms*, 257; Pl. XVII., fig. 1, p. 172.
„ „ *seal*, 465.
„ EDMUND, Duke of, *arms* on Eagle, 630.
„ JOHN of Eltham, Earl of, *brisure*, 438.
„ RICHARD, Earl of, *arms*, 172, 465; *arms* on Eagle, 630; *seal* of, 245.
„ *shield* of the Duchy of, 594.
CORNWALLIS, *arms*, 264; Pl. VIII., fig. 12, p. 100.
„ Marquesses of, *arms*, 114.
Coronel or *Cronel*, 682.
Coronet, Ducal, Pl. L., fig. 21, p. 624.
Coronet of Baron, Pl. L., fig. 36, p. 624.
„ *Baron of Belgium*, Pl. L., fig. 9, p. 624.
„ *Baron of France*, Pl. L., fig. 25, p. 624.
„ *Baron of Germany*, Pl. L., fig. 31, p. 624.
„ *Count of France*, Pl. L., fig. 23, p. 624.

Coronet of Count of Germany, Pl. L., fig. 30, p. 624.
„ *Doge of Venice*, Pl. L., fig. 10, p. 624.
„ *Earl*, Pl. L., fig. 34, p. 623.
„ *Fils de France*, Pl. L., fig. 19, p. 624.
„ *Grandsons of Sovereigns*, Pl. L., fig. 7, p. 624.
„ *Marquis*, Pl. L., figs. 27, 32, and 33, p. 624.
„ *Marquis of France*, Pl. L., fig. 22, p. 624.
„ *Noble of Germany*, Pl. L., fig. 28, p. 624.
„ *Nobles*, Pl. L., fig. 12, p. 624.
„ *President*, Pl. L., fig. 26, p. 624.
„ *Prince of France*, Pl. L., fig. 20, p. 624.
„ *Princesses*, Pl. L., fig. 6, p. 624.
„ *Sons of Sovereigns*, Pl. L., fig. 5, p. 624.
„ *Vidame*, Pl. L., fig. 11, p. 624.
„ *Viscount*, Pl. L., fig. 35, p. 624.
„ *Viscount of France*, Pl. L., fig. 24, p. 624.
„ *Viscounts of Netherlands*, Pl. L., fig. 8, p. 624.
Coronets, 617, 623; Pl. L., p. 624.
„ as charges, 379.
„ attempt to restrict use of, 637.
Corpus Christi College, Oxford, *arms*, 264.
CORRARO, *arms*, 89, 182.
CORRER, *arms*, 182.
Cors, 232, 722.
CORSANT, *arms*, 163.
CORSBY, *arms*, 141.
CORSICA, *arms*, 200.
CORTEZ, HERMAN, *arms* and *augmentation*, 312, 363, 547.
CORTI, *arms*, 202.
CORUÑA, Counts of, *arms*, 506.
COSSÉ, Duc de BRISSAC, *arms*, 731.
COSSENTANIA, Count of, *arms*, 639.
COSSINGTON, *arms*, 324.
COSSO, *wreath*, 614.
COSTA, DA, *arms*, 206.
COSTANZO, *arms*, 206.
COSTE, DE LA, *arms*, 376.
„ DU VIVIER, DE LA, *arms*, 206.
COTGRAVE'S *Roll*, 404.
Cotice, 131, 132, 681.
„ *en barre*, 722.
„ Varieties of, 133.
Coticé, 96, 681, 722.
„ *en barre*, 723.
Coticed, 128, 681.
COTONER, *arms*, 338.
„ RAFAEL and NICOLAS, 338.
Cotoyé, 681, 723.
COTTEBLANCHE, *arms*, 392.
COTTERS, *arms*, 277.
Cottes as charges, 392.
Cotton plant, 338.
Cottonian MS., 556.
Couard, 682, 723.
Couchant, 217, 232, 681.
Couché, 138, 600, 634, 681, 693, 723, 733.
COUCI, *arms*, Pl. VII., fig. 2, p. 90.

(781)

COUCY, *arms*, 48, 70, 92.
,, ENGUERRAN, DE, *seal* and *shield* of, 56.
,, ENGUERRAND IV. de, 70.
,, INGELRAM DE, 92.
,, *motto*, 92.
,, Queen MARIE DE, 92.
,, *seal*, 48.
,, *supporters*, 628.
COÜDENBERG, *arms*, 361.
COUE, *arms*, 133.
Couleuvre, Une, 275, 723.
Coulissé, 723, 734.
Count, *coronet* of a, 624.
,, Senator of the French Empire, *badge*, 276.
Counter-changed, 109, 681.
,, *-compony*, 681.
,, *-embattled*, 681.
,, *-embowed*, 681.
,, *-flory*, 681.
,, *-passant*, 220, 681; Pl. XXII., fig. 2, p. 222.
,, *-rampant*, 220.
,, *-saliant*, 681.
,, *-trippant*, 681.
,, *-tripping*, 681.
Counterpotent, Pl. IV., fig. 12, p. 62.
Countervair, 681; Pl. IV., fig. 8, p. 62.
Coupé, 79, 123, 681, 687, 723, 728.
,, *alternativement*, 723.
Coupeau, 723.
Coupeaux, 311.
Couped, 681.
COUPER, Lord, *supporters*, 298.
Couple-close, 140, 682.
,, *-de-chiens*, 723.
Couplés, 723.
Courant, 232, 682, 723.
Courbé, 682, 685, 723.
COURCELLES, *arms*, 81.
,, MARGUERITE DE, as a *supporter*, 630.
COURCY, DE, 17.
,, ,, Barons of Kingsale, *arms*, 258.
COURLAND, Duke of, *arms*, 215, 390.
Couronné, 682, 723.
COURRAN, *arms*, 185.
COURRIERES, MONTMORENCY DE, *brisure*, 451.
COURTENAY, *arms*, Pl. XIX., fig. 3, p. 192.
,, *label*, 415.
,, ROBERT DE, *label*, 417.
,, Sir HUGH, *lambrequin*, 612.
,, WILLIAM, Archbishop of CANTERBURY, *arms*, 437.
COURTENEY, *arms*, 192.
,, *badge*, 753.
,, Earl of DEVON, *badge*, 753.
Courtine, 723.
COURVOL, Marquises de, *arms*, 159.
COUSIN DE LA TOUR - FONDUE, Counts, *arms*, 205.
COUSTIN, 12.
Cousu, 723.
Couvert, 723.
COVERDALE, *arms*, 81.
Coward, 682.
COWDREY, *arms*, 112.
COWE, *arms*, 133.

COWELL, *arms*, 684.
Cows, 234.
,, as *supporters*, 636.
CRAB of Robslaw, *arms*, 273.
Crabs, 273.
CRACOW, *arms*, 359, 504.
CRAIGMYLE, *arms*, 51.
Crampet as a *badge*, 753.
Crampette, 682.
Crampon, 723.
Cramponné, 724.
Crampons, 682.
Crancelin, 131, 682, 724.
Crane, The, 263.
CRANE, *arms*, 80.
CRANSTOUN, Lords, *arms*, 263.
CRAON, *arms*, 100, 434, 449.
,, MARIE DE, *arms*, 449.
CRAUFURD of Cartsburn, *bordure*, 569.
CRAUFURD'S *Peerage*, 83.
Craupaud," Sobriquet of "*Johnnie*, 278.
CRAVEN, Earls of, *arms*, 163.
CRAWFORD and ERCILDOUN, *seal* of WILLIAM LINDSAY, Lord of, 51.
,, *arms*, 406.
,, DAVID, Earl of, *seal*, 522.
,, Earls of, *arms*, 179, 257, 516.
,, Lord, *crest*, 605.
,, Lordship of, *arms*, 518.
,, REGINALD, *supporters*, 629.
,, *seal* and *arms* of Sir DAVID LINDSAY, Lord of, 51.
,, Sir GREGAN, 233.
CRAWFURD, *arms*, 124, 232.
CRAYEN, *arms*, 264.
Crayfish, 273.
CRAYN, Duchy of, *arms*, 256.
CRECY, Battle of, 593.
Crémaillière as a charge, 390, 724.
Créneaux, 678, 724.
Crénelé, 124, 724.
,, *line*, 76.
Crenellé, 682, 685.
Créquier, 318, 724; Pl. XXIX., fig. 4, p. 318.
CRÉQUY, *arms*, 318; Pl. XXIX., fig. 4, p. 318.
,, Ducs de, *arms*, 318.
Crescent and Star as a *badge*, 587.
,, as a *badge*, 584.
,, *Cross* and, Pl. XXVIII., fig. 4, p. 308.
,, *-decrescent*, 307.
,, for second son, 444.
,, *-increscent*, 306.
Crescents, Pl. XXVIII., fig. 2, p. 308.
CRESPIN, *arms*, 206.
CRESSY, *arms*, 337.
,, Battle of, 591.
,, LOUIS DE, Comte de FLANDRE, 752.
,, ,, Count of NEVERS, 462.
Crest, 599.
,, *-coronet*, 599, 614, 682.
Crested, 682.
CRESTIENNOT, *arms*, 340.
Crests, Pl. XLIX., p. 606.
,, Derivation of early, 605.
,, German use of, 608.

(782)

Crests, Materials of which they were made, 611.
,, Right of ecclesiastics to use, 604.
,, Right of women to use, 604.
Crêté, 682, 724.
Crête, 724.
CRÉTIENTÉ, First four Barons of the, 11.
CREVANT, Marquis d'HUMIÈRES, *arms*, 81.
CRÈVECŒUR, *arms*, 139.
,, PHILIPPE DE, *arms*, 410.
CREWES, *arms*, 213.
Cri-de-guerre, 724.
CRICHTON of Frendraught, *arms*, 212.
Crickets, 284.
Cricklade Church, 585.
Criné, 682, 724.
Crined, 682.
CRISPIN, *arms*, 206.
CROATIA, Kingdom, *arms*, 494, 498.
Croc, 724.
Crochet, 724.
Crocodile, The, 273, 277.
CROELS, *arms*, 370.
CROESEN, *arms*, 382.
,, Vicomtes, *arms*, 382.
CROFTS, JAMES, *arms*, 146.
Croisades, *Salle des*, 10, 12, 71, 117, 163, 170, 212, 213, 221, 337, 342, 346, 373, 393, 418.
Croisé, 724.
Croisette, 682.
CROISILLES, MONTMORENCY DE, *brisure*, 451.
Croissant, 306, 724.
,, *contourné*, 307.
,, *-tourné*, 306, 691.
,, *-versé*, 307.
Croissettes, 724.
Croix, 682.
,, *bourdonnée*, 160.
,, *En*, 724.
,, *Passé en*, 724.
,, *perronée*, 689.
CROIX, LA, Duc de, CASTRIES, *arms*, 141.
CROMWELL, *arms*, 214, 487.
,, *badge*, 754.
,, OLIVER, *Great Seal*, 487.
,, RICHARD, *Great Seal*, 487.
CRONBERG, *arms*, 489 ; Pl. XXXIX., fig. 4, p. 482.
,, Counts of, *augmentation*, 538.
,, Counts ZU, *arms*, 489.
Cronel, 682, 705, 731.
Cronels, 347.
CRONENBURG, Barons de, *arms*, 137.
CRONHJELM, 672.
CRONSFELD, County of, *arms*, 192.
CROSBIE, *arms*, 522.
Cross, 682 ; Pl. XIV., fig. 1, p. 140.
,, *aiguisée*, 162 ; Fig. 60, p. 164.
,, *ancrée*, 158 ; Pl. XV., fig. 2, p. 144.
,, and *Crescent*, Pl. XXVIII., fig. 4, p. 308.
,, *avellane*, 162.
,, *botonnée*, Pl. XIV., fig. 11, p. 140.
,, *botonny*, 160.
,, ,, *fitchy*, 160.
,, *-Calvary*, 152 ; Fig. 49, p. 164.
,, *clechée*, 161.

Cross, couped, 153.
,, *crosslet-fitchy*, 162.
,, *crosslets*, Pl. XV., fig. 4, p. 144.
,, ,, *fitchée*, Pl. XV., fig. 5, p. 144.
,, *fleur-de-lisée*, 158 ; Fig. 57, p. 164 ; Pl. XIV., fig. 10, p. 140.
,, *fleuretté*, 158.
,, *flory*, Pl. XIV., fig. 9, p. 140 ; Fig. 58, p. 164.
,, ,, or *Fleury*, 157.
,, *flurty*, 158.
,, *formy*, 153.
,, *fourchée*, 161.
,, *fourchetté*, 161.
,, *fourchy*, Fig. 59, p. 164.
,, *Greek*, 153 ; Fig. 48, p. 164.
,, *gringolee*, 161, 276 ; Pl. XV., fig. 6, p. 144.
,, *guivre*, 161.
,, *hummetty*, 153.
,, *Latin*, 152.
,, *long*, 152.
,, *Maltese*, 155 ; Fig. 55, p. 164.
,, *moline*, 158 ; Pl. XV., fig. 1, p. 144.
,, ,, for eighth son, 444.
,, ,, *square pierced*, Pl. XIV., fig. 6, p. 140.
,, ,, *voided*, Pl. XV., fig. 3, p. 144.
,, of *Calatrava*, 158.
,, ,, *Jerusalem*, 156.
,, ,, *Lorraine*, 152 ; Fig. 52, p. 164.
,, ,, the *Passion*, 151, 152 ; Fig. 47, p. 164.
,, ,, *Toulouse*, 161 ; Pl. XV., fig. 7, p. 144.
,, or *crossed crosslet*, 162.
,, *patée checquy*, Pl. XIV., fig. 5, p. 140.
,, ,, *formée*, 153.
,, *patonce*, 157 ; Fig. 56, p. 164.
,, ,, *voided*, Pl. XIV., fig. 8, p. 140.
,, *patriarchal*, 152 ; Fig. 50, p. 164.
,, *patty*, 153 ; Fig. 53, p. 164.
,, ,, *fitchy*, 155 ; Fig. 54, p. 164.
,, *pommelly*, 160.
,, *pommetty*, 160.
,, *potent*, 156 ; fig. 51, p. 164.
,, ,, *fitchy*, 156.
,, ,, *-quadrate*, 700 ; Pl. XIV., fig. 7, p. 140.
,, *quarter pierced*, Pl. XIV., fig. 3, p. 140.
,, *raguly*, Pl. XIV., fig. 2, p. 140.
,, *recercellée*, 160.
,, *retranchée*, 162.
,, ,, *and pommettée*, Pl. XIV., fig. 12, p. 140.
,, *sarcelly*, 160.
,, *tau*, 161, Fig. 61, p. 164.
,, The, 116, 141, 151.
,, *urdée*, 162.
,, Varieties of, 142.
,, *Victoria*, 155.
,, *wavy voided*, Pl. XIV., fig. 4, p. 140.
Crosse, 682, 704.
Crosslet, 682.
Crosslets, 162.
CROSSLEY, *arms*, 162.
CROUSNILHON, *arms*, 156.
CROVILLE, *arms*, 142.
Crow, The, 264.
Crown and Bush as a *badge*, 595.
,, closed, 620.

Crown, Dauphin's, Pl. L., fig. 18, p. 624.
,, *Eastern*, Pl. L., fig. 13, p. 624.
,, *Eastern* or *antique* as a charge, 379.
,, *Imperial*, Pl. L., fig. 1, p. 624.
,, *King of France's*, Pl. L., fig. 17, p. 624.
,, *Mural*, Pl. L., fig. 16, p. 624.
,, *Naval*, Pl. L., fig. 15, p. 624.
,, of CHARLEMAGNE, as a charge, 380.
,, of Italy, Cross of the Order of, 244.
,, Order of the, in Prussia, 546.
,, *Prince of Holy Roman Empire's*, Pl. L., fig. 29, p. 624.
,, *Prince of Wales'*, Pl. L., fig. 3, p. 624.
,, *Royal*, Pl. L., figs. 2 and 4, p. 624.
,, *Royal*, as a charge, 380.
,, *Vallary*, Pl. L., fig. 14, p. 624.
Crowned, 682.
Crowns, 617; Pl. L., p. 624.
,, *Antique*, Pl. XXXIII., fig. 5, p. 376.
,, as charges, 379.
,, *Ducal*, Pl. XXXIII., fig. 4, p. 376.
,, *of Thorns*, 337.
,, Type of Foreign Royal, 619.
CROY, ADRIAN DE, *arms*, 450.
,, ANTOINE DE, *arms*, 449.
,, Bishop JACQUES DE, *augmentation*, 537.
,, Comtes de CHIMAY, *arms*, 127.
,, FERRY DE, Seigneur de ROUX, *arms*, 450.
,, GUILLAUME DE, 449.
,, Duke of SORIA, etc., *arms*, 449.
,, JEAN DE, *arms* of, 11, 449.
,, Marquises d'ARSCHOT, *arms*, 127.
,, Princes de, *arms*, 127.
,, ,, de CHIMAY, *arms*, 127, 348.
Crozier as a charge, 371, 682.
CRUBEQUE, PHILIPPE, Seigneur de, *arms*, 575; Pl. XLVII., fig. 6, p. 574.
CRULLS, *arms*, 276.
Crusade, Second, 31.
,, Third, 32, 36.
Crusilé, 682.
Crusily or *Crussily*, 112, 682.
CRUSSOL, Duc d'USEZ, *arms*, 94.
CRUYCKENBERG, Counts de, *arms*, 136.
Cubit arm, 204, 682.
Cucumbers, 344.
CUEVA, Dukes of ALBUQUERQUE, *arms*, 440.
Culverin as charges, 366.
CUMANIA, *arms*, 501.
CUMBERLAND, *badge*, 753, 754.
,, ERNEST AUGUSTUS, Duke of, *label*, 422.
CUMYN of Altyre, THOMAS, *seal*, 435.
CUNNINGHAM, *arms*, 150; Pl. XVI., fig. 12, p. 146.
,, *arms in Lyon Office Register*, 400.
Cups as charges, 381.
,, *covered*, Pl. XXXIII., fig. 7, p. 376.
Curved, 682.
CUSA, Cardinal NICOLAS DE, *arms*, 273.
Cushions as charges, 377; Pl. XXXIII., fig. 9, p. 376.

CUSTANCE, *arms*, 185.
CUSTINE, Marquises de, *arms*, 132.
Cyclamor, 724.
Cymbals as charges, 383.
CYNAN, MERGETH AP, *arms*, 199.
CYPRUS, ANNE of, *seal*, 467.
,, *arms*, 467.
,, King of, 644.
CZARNY, LESEK, Duke of POLAND, *seal*, 468.
CZERNABOR, *arms*, 491.
CZERNIN, Counts, *augmentation*, 540.
CZERWNIA, *arms*, 66.

DABANCASA, *arms*, 475.
DACHAU, *see* HOFREITER.
DACHS, *arms*, 239.
DACHSBERG, Counts von, *arms*, 239.
DACRE, *arms*, 273, 641; Pl. XXVI., fig. 12, p. 266.
,, *knot*, 585.
,, Lord, *badge*, 753.
,, of GILSLAND, *badge* of Lord, 585.
,, *of the North*, badge and *arms* of, Lord, 585.
,, Sir EDMOND, *arms*, 407.
,, THOMAS, second Lord, *tomb*, 474.
DADVISARDS, Marquises de TALAIRAN, *arms*, 338.
DAGSBURG, Counts, *arms*, 744.
,, ,, *label*, 424.
DAGUET DE BEAUVOIR, *arms*, 122.
Daim, 724.
DAISIE, *arms*, 336.
Daisy, The, 336.
DALBIAC, *arms*, 277.
DALENONCOURT, ABBEVILLE, *arms*, 170.
DALHOUSIE, Earls of, *arms*, 123, 147.
DALINGRIDGE, *arms*, 142.
DALLAWAY, Rev. JAMES, *Inquiry into the Origin and Progress of Heraldry in England*, 24.
DALLINGTON, *arms*, 217.
DALMATIA, *arms*, 498.
,, Kingdom, *arms*, 498.
Dalmatique, 724.
DALRYMPLE, *arms*; Pl. XV., fig. 9. p. 144.
DALZELL, Pl. XX., fig. 1, p. 198.
,, of Bins, *supporters*, 643.
DALZIEL, *arms*, 197.
DAM, Vicomtes von, *arms*, 362.
DAMAS, 12.
DAMIGLIA, *arms*, 95.
DAMMARTIN, CHARLES, Comte de, *supporters*, 633.
DAMPIERRE, DE, *arms*, 411.
DANBY, *arms*, 347.
Dancetté, 682.
Dancetty line, 76; Fig. 23, p. 75.
,, or *Dancetté*, 682.
Danché, 682, 691.
,, *line*, 76.
DANE, *arms*, 155.
DANESKIOLD-LAURWIGEN, Counts of, *arms*, 581.
,, -SAMSOE, Counts of, *arms*, 581.
,, *supporters*, 231.
DANGERFIELD, 17.
DANIEL, Book of, 196.

(784)

DANIEL in Heraldry, 196.
DANIELI, *arms*, 196.
DANIELS, *arms*, 196.
Danish Regalia, 620.
DANNEBROG, 545.
,, Cross of the Order of the, 510, 666.
Danse, 683.
DANTE ALIGHIERI, *arms*, 126.
,, *Divina Commedia; l'Inferno*, 299.
,, quoted, 275.
Danube River, 498.
DANVERS, 17.
D'ARCY, *arms*, 323.
DARNLEY, Lady KATHARINE, *arms*, 560.
,, Lord of, *arms*, 476, 521.
DARTMOUTH, EARL of, *arms*, 233.
,, ,, *supporters*, 648.
DARWIN, *arms*, 273.
DASBOURG, *arms*, 165.
DAUBENEY, *arms*, 124.
DAUBENY, *achierement*, Fig. 92, p. 600.
,, *arms*, 349, 413, 438.
,, *badge*, 754.
,, DE BEAUVOIR, WILLIAM, *arms*, 438.
,, *mantling*, 613.
DAUBERNOUN, Sir JOHN, *arms* and *pennon*, 650.
DAUBIGNY, *arms*, 124.
DAUN, Counts of, *arms*, 96.
DAUNEY, *arms*, 292; Pl. XXVII. fig. 7, p. 288.
DAUNT, *arms*, 352.
DAUPHIN, *arms* of the, 424.
,, *coronet* of the, 269.
,, *crown* of the, 620.
,, The, 269, 725.
,, ,, *supporters*, 636.
DAUPHINÉ, *arms*, 424, 429, 463, 572, 632, 636.
,, *shield* of, 629.
DAVID, 12.
,, *arms*, 21, 384.
,, I., King of Scotland, 233.
,, II., ,, ,, 34, 442, 455.
DAWRE, *arms*, 281.
DAWSON, *arms*, 155.
DAWTREY, *arms*, 133.
DE CAUMONT, *Abécédaire d'Archéologie*, 254.
De, definition of term, 8.
,, Use of term, 10, 11, 12, 13, 14, 15, 16, 17, 18.
De l'un à l'autre, 681, 725.
,, *en l'autre*, 681, 725.
DEATH, 17.
Debruised, 683.
DEBSCHÜTZ DE SCHADEWALDE, Barons, *arms*, 320.
Décapité, 725, 730.
DECAUMONT, 12.
Decked, 683.
DECKEN, Counts van der, *arms*, 390.
Decrescent, 683.
,, and *Increscent*, Pl. XXVIII., fig. 3, p. 308.
DEDNAM, *arms*, 167.
DEEGHBROODT, *arms*, 314.
Défaillant, 725.
Defamed, 683.
Défendu, 227, 706, 725.

Défenses, 227, 725.
Dégouttant, 684, 725.
Degraded, 683.
Degrees, 683.
DEHANTCHOUMAKER, 16.
DEICHSLERS, *arms*, 150.
DEISIE, *arms*, 336.
Dejected, 683.
Dejoint, 725.
DELAFIELD, *arms*, 342.
DELAHAY, *arms*, 146.
DELAMERE, 17.
,, *arms*, 132.
,, Barons, *arms*, 342.
,, Lords, *supporters*, 288.
DELAWARE, 17.
DELAWARR, *badge*, 753.
,, Earls of, *arms*, 124.
,, ,, *supporters*, 294.
,, Lords, 17.
DELBENE, *arms*, 332, 716.
DELFT, Oude Kerk at, 645.
DELLA ROVERE, Dukes of URBINO, *arms*, 319.
DELMAS DE GRAMMONT, GUILLAUME, *arms* and *augmentation*, 541.
DELMENHORST, *arms*, 510, 666.
Delve, The, 186, 187, 683.
Démanché, 725.
DEMAY, 631, 634, 650, 651; Pl. XXXIV., fig. 1, p. 388; Pl. XXXV., fig. 2, p. 416.
,, *Le Costume, d'après les Sceaux*, 37, 47, 48, 49, 50, 54, 56, 57, 58, 208, 254, 303, 328, 356, 369, 402, 635.
Demembered, 683.
Démembré, 683, 725.
DEMETRIUS PALÆOLOGUS, *seal* of, 250.
DEMEULENAER, 16.
Demi, 683.
,, *-lion*, 220.
,, *-ramure*, 677, 691, 725.
,, *-vol*, 260, 725.
DEMMIN, *Weapons of War*, 46.
Denché, 725, 729.
,, *line*, 76.
Denchure, 725.
DENHAM, *arms*, 191.
,, *shield*, 643.
DENIS, *arms*, 202.
DENMARK, 379.
,, *arms*, 113, 272, 666; Pl. VIII., fig. 9, p. 100.
,, Ensign of Prince of, 208.
,, Kings of, using *escucheon en surtout*, 487.
,, MARGARET of, *arms*, 476.
,, Marks of illegitimacy in, 581.
,, motto of, 666.
,, Royal *Arms* of, 510.
,, Royal House of, 581.
,, Portrait of MARGARET of, 334.
,, *supporters* of, 666.
DENNEWITZ, *see* BÜLOW.
DENNIS, *arms*, 226.
DENNISTON, *arms*, 442.
DENNISTOUN, *arms*, 130.
Denté, 725.
Dentelé, 691, 725.
,, *line*, 76.
DENYS, *arms*, 226.

(785)

Depaulis Collection, 333.
Dépouille, 725.
DERBY, *arms* of town, 739.
„ CHARLOTTE DE LA TRÉ-MOILLE, Countess of, 258.
„ Earl of, 324.
„ Earls of, *arms*, 71, 207, 356.
„ FERRERS, Earls of, 52.
„ HENRY, Earl of, *seal*, Pl. XXXV., fig. 4, p. 416.
„ *standard* of Earl of, 558.
DERING, *Essay* by Sir EDWARD, 397.
DERNBACH, Counts of, *arms*, 202.
„ ZU DERNBACH, Counts, *arms*, 409.
DERVAL, Barons, *arms*, 126.
DERX, *arms*, 231.
Désarmé, 725.
DESENBERG, *see* SPIEGEL.
DESGABETS D'OMBALE, *arms*, 67.
DESPALAU, *arms*, 363.
DESPENCER, *arms*, 412, 426.
„ Sir HUGH LE, *arms*, 412.
DESPENSER, HENRY LE, Bishop of NORWICH, *brisure*, 437.
DETIMMERMAN, 16.
Detriment, 683.
DEUIL, MONTMORENCY DE, *brisure*, 452.
DEUX PONTS (Zwei-Brücken Bitsche), concession of a crest to HAMAN (or HANNEMANN), Comte de, 751.
Developed, 683.
DEVEREUX, 17.
Devils, 303.
Dévise, 725.
DEVON, Earls of, *arms*, 93, 214.
„ „ *badge*, 753.
„ HUGH, Earl of, 417.
DEVONSHIRE, CHARLES, Earl of, 561.
„ Dukes of, *arms*, 233.
DEVORGILLA, wife of JOHN BALLIOL, *seal*, 460.
Dexter, 683.
„ side of *shield*, 59.
Dextre, 725.
Dextro-chère, 205, 726, 736, 743.
DEYBROOT, *arms*, 314.
DEYN, *arms*, 160.
Diademé, 682, 726.
Diamond, 65, 683.
Diapered, 683.
Diapering, 114.
Diapré, 683, 726.
DIAZ, *arms*, 133, 214, 310.
DIBBITS, *arms*, 336.
Dice as charges, 387.
DICK-CUNYNGHAM, *achievement*, 610.
DICKSON, *arms*, 309.
DIDIER DE MORTAL, *arms*, 203.
DIDRON, *Annales Archæologiques*, 294.
DIEDEN, *see* DIETRICH.
DIEK, *arms*, 231.
DIENHEIM, *arms*, 120.
„ VON, *arms*, Pl. X., fig. 5, p. 118.
DIETRICH, *arms*, 156.
„ DE DIEDEN, Barons, *arms*, 305.
DIETZ, *arms*, 580.
Dieu et mon droit, 664.
Diffamé, 683, 726.
Diffamed, 219.
Difference, 684.

Difference by a *bordure*, 437.
„ by an augmentation, 448.
„ by an escucheon en surtout, 448.
„ by addition of a label, 413.
„ „ an Ordinary, 428.
„ „ Mark of Cadency, 444.
„ „ small charges, 406.
„ „ „ escucheon in chief, 427.
„ by change of the minor charges, 434.
„ „ tincture, 403.
„ „ the boundary line of an ordinary, 432.
„ by diminishing the number of charges, 434.
„ by quartering, 446.
„ by the insertion of a Canton, 425.
Differenced, 683.
Differencing or *Cadency*, 396.
„ Principal modes of 402.
DIGBY, *badge*, 754.
„ Earl of Bristol, *arms*, 331.
DIGHTON, *arms*, 237; Pl. XXIV., fig. 5, p. 236.
DIJON, *arms*, 283.
„ Stained glass of Notre Dame at, 302.
DILFT DE BORGHVLOET, Counts van der, *arms*, 145.
DILLINGTON, *arms*, Pl. XXI., fig. 7, p. 212.
Dimidiated, 683.
Dimidiation, 459 ; Pl. XXXVIII., p. 464.
„ *per bend*, 477.
Diminué, 726.
DINIS, AFFONZO, 578.
DIONIS, King of PORTUGAL, 578.
Disclosed, 683.
Dismembered or *Demembered*, 217, 683.
Displayed, 259, 684.
DISRAELI, BENJAMIN, 339.
Distilling, 684.
Distinction, 684.
DITMARSHEN, *arms*, 510, 666.
Divise, 119, 126, 726 ; Pl. X., fig. 6, p. 118.
Divisé en chevron, 81, 680, 726.
DJURKLOW, Barons of, *arms*, 509.
DOBRZENSKY, Barons, *arms*, 263.
DOES, 231.
Dog, The, 240, 632.
„ „ *Sea*, 300.
DOGGE, *arms*, 268.
DOIGNON, Marquesses GUIOT DE, *arms*, 265.
Dolce, 726.
DOLENGA, *arms*, 670 ; Pl. LVI., fig. 12, p. 670.
„ Counts, *arms*, 356.
DOLFINI, *arms*, 270 ; Pl. XXVI., fig. 8, p. 266.
DOLKS, *arms*, 272.
DOLL, *arms*, 272.
Doloire, 726.
DOLOMIEU, Marquis de, *arms*, 289.
Dolphin, 268 ; Pl. XXVI., fig. 7, p. 266.
„ as *supporter*, 632.
Dolphins, Pl. XXVI., fig. 8, p. 266.
„ as *supporters*, 636.
DOMAIGNE, *arms*, 96.
Domesday Book, 399.
Domestic Charges, 389.

(786)

DOMEYERS, *arms*, 391.
DOMHARD, *arms* and *augmentation*, 543.
Dominus mihi adjutor, 666.
DONATI, *arms*, 79.
DONATO family, 16.
Donjonné, 705, 706, 726, 744.
DONNERSPERG, *arms*, 311.
DONODEI, *arms*, 336.
DONOP, Barons von, *arms*, 365.
DONZÉ, *arms*, 72.
DONZEL, *arms*, 72.
DOORE, *arms*, 281.
DOPF, *wreath*, 614.
DORAND, *arms*, 124.
DORE, *arms*, 281.
DORGELO, *arms*, 318.
DORIA, *arms*, 256.
,, family, 16.
Dormant, 217, 684.
DORNBERG, Barons von, *arms*, 87.
,, DE HERTZBERG, Barons, *arms*, 78.
DORNHEIM, *arms*, 271.
DORO, *arms*, 752.
DOTTENSTEIN, *arms*, 752.
Doublé, 684.
Double-quatrefoil, 684.
,, *queué*, 684.
,, *trécheur*, 684.
,, *tressure*, 684.
Doubled, 684.
DOUBLET, *arms*, 138.
Doublets, 726.
Douglas Book, 518.
DOUGLAS, 1st Earl of, 202.
,, ,, *supporter*, 631.
,, 1st Marquess of, *arms*, 518, 519.
,, and MAR, WILLIAM, 1st Earl of, *seal*, 514.
,, JAMES, 2nd Earl of, *arms*, 514.
,, ,, ,, ,, *label*, 419.
,, ARCHIBALD, 3rd Earl of, *seal* and *arms*, 514.
,, ,, 4th Earl of, *seal* and *arms*, 514.
,, ,, 5th Earl of, *arms*, 515.
,, ,, 6th Earl of, *seal*, 518.
,, ,, Duke of TOURAINE, 515.
,, ,, Earl of, *seal*, 632.
,, ,, Lord of GALLOWAY, *seal* and *arms*, 514.
,, *arms*, 178, 202, 405, 514, 515, 516, 518, 519, 566; Pl. XX., fig. 12, p. 198.
,, *arms in Lyon Office Register*, 400.
,, *bordure*, 568.
,, Countess JONET, wife of WILLIAM, Earl of, 517.
,, Earl of Angus, 455, 566.
,, ,, ,, *crest*, 294.
,, ,, *badge*, 598.
,, ,, MORAY, 516.

DOUGLAS, Earls of ORMOND, 516.
,, ,, ANGUS, 455, 566.
,, ,, *arms*, 178, 515.
,, ,, MORTON, *arms*, 179.
,, ,, *seals* and *compartment*, 642.
,, JAMES, 7th Earl of, 515.
,, ,, 9th Earl of, *seal* and *arms*, 515.
,, ,, Earl of AVONDALE, 515.
,, MARGARET, Countess of, *supporter*, 632.
,, ,, "Fair Maid of Galloway," 515.
,, NICOLAS, *seal*, 632.
,, of Cavers, *arms*, 566.
,, ,, Dalkeith, *arms*, 405.
,, ,, Drumlanrig, *arms*, 566.
,, ,, ,, *bordure*, 441.
,, ,, Lochleven, *arms*, 433.
,, ,, Lugton, Sir HENRY, *seal*, 433.
,, ,, Nithsdale, Sir WILLIAM, *arms*, 566.
,, *Salamander* of, 643.
,, Sir GEORGE, *arms*, 518.
,, Sir JAMES, 202.
,, Stronghold of, 516.
,, WILLIAM, 6th Earl of, 515, 517.
,, ,, 8th Earl of, 515, 517.
,, ,, ,, *seal* and *arms*, 516.
,, ,, ,, Earl of, *seal*, 632.
DOUGLASES, "Red" and "Black," 513, 516.
DOULLÉ, *arms*, 279.
DOUMA, *arms*, 469.
DOURS, Seigneur de, *arms*, 411.
Dove cots, 363.
Doves, 267.
Dovetail, 683.
Dovetailed line, Fig. 26, p. 75, 77.
DOWNE, Earl of, *arms*, 290.
DOWNES, *arms*, 232 ; Pl. XXIII., fig. 10, p. 228.
DOWNSHIRE, Marquis of, *supporter*, 232.
DRACHENFELS, Barons von, *arms*, 292.
Draco, 291.
Dracones, 291.
DRAECK, Barons de, *arms*, 292.
DRAGE, *arms*, 292.
DRAGHO, *arms*, 292.
,, DE, *arms*, 292.
DRAGOMANNI, *arms*, 292.
Dragon, 290, 684, 726 ; Pl. XXVII., fig. 7, p. 288.
,, as a *badge*, 753.
,, as a *crest*, 600.
,, *monstreux*, 293, 726.
,, Red, as a *badge*, 595.
,, *shield* encircled by a, 639.
DRAGON DE RAMILLIES, DE, *arms*, 292.
Dragonné, 726.
Dragons as *supporters*, 636.
Dragon's head, 65.
,, ,, and *tail*, 65, 684.

(787)

DRAKE, *arms*, 292; Pl. XXVII., fig. 8, p. 288.
DRAKELOWS, *arms*, 290.
DRANDORFF, VON, *arms*, 469.
Drave River, 498.
DRAYTON, *arms*, 142.
,, MICHAEL, *arms*, 298.
Dresden China, Red *swords* on, 347.
Dress, Articles of, as charges, 375.
DREUX, *arms*, 461, 634.
,, BEATRICE, Wife of JEAN DE, Duke of BRITTANY, 425.
,, Counts de, *arms*, 170.
,, PIERRE DE, *seal* and *secretum* of, 55.
,, ,, called MAUCLERC, son of Count ROBERT of, *arms*, 425.
,, *seal* and *secretum* of ROBERT II., Comte de, 55.
DREYSE, JOHAN NICOLAS, *arms*, 366.
DRIESCHE, VAN, *arms*, 136.
Drinking glasses as charges, 382.
DROGOMIR, *arms*, 207.
Dromedary, The, 231.
DROUALLEN, *arms*, 280.
DRUAYS, *arms*, 68.
DRUMMOND, *arms*, 128, 436, 455; *arms in Lyon Office Register*, 400; Pl. XI., fig. 10, p. 124.
,, Earl of PERTH, *Compartment* and *motto*, 642.
,, JAMES, *Sculptured Monuments of Iona and the West Highlands*, 367.
,, of Blair, *brisure*, 436.
,, ,, Colquhalzie, *brisure*, 436.
,, ,, Concraig, *arms*, 79.
,, ,, Kildies, *arms*, 199.
,, ,, ,, *brisure*, 436.
,, ,, Pitkellony, *brisure*, 436.
,, Queen Annabella, 455.
,, Sir MALCOLM of Stobhall, 455.
Drums as charges, 383.
DRYLAND, *arms*, 124.
DU CANGE, 39, 250, 535, 538.
,, *Dissertatio de Inferioris Ævi Numismatibus*, 248.
,, *Dissertation sur l'histoire de St. Louis, par de Joinville*, 40.
,, *Glossarium*, 655.
DUBLIN, *arms* of See, 375.
,, City, *arms*, 361.
,, Marquess of, *arms*, 383.
DUBOIS, *arms*, 315.
DUBUISSON, *arms*, 165.
Duc, 726.
DUC, *see* VIOLLET.
Ducal coronet, 684.
DUCAS, *arms*, 141.
Duciper, 684.
DUCKINFIELD, *arms*, Pl. XIV, fig. 4, p. 140.
Duckling, The, 266.
Ducks, 267.
DUCKWORTH, *crest*, 300.
DUCLAU, Barons, *arms*, 277.
DUDLEY, Earl of WARWICK, *badge*, 585.
,, Lord, *arms*, 218.
DUDZEELE, Van, *arms*, 142.

DUFF, Earls and Duke of FIFE, *arms*, 212.
DUGDALE, Sir WILLIAM, *Antient Usage of Bearing Arms*, 446, 561, 563.
DUGUID, *arms*, 155.
DUINEN, *arms*, 136.
DUIVEN, *arms*, 136.
Duke's *standard*, Length of, 654.
DUMONT DE BOSTAQUET, *arms*, 238.
DUNBAR, ALEXANDER, of Westfield, *fess*, 430.
,, *arms*, Pl. XVII., fig. 3, p. 172.
,, *crest*, 610.
,, Earls of, *arms*, 171, 405.
,, ,, *bordure*, 442.
,, ,, *crest*, 605, 610.
,, Earls of MORAY, *arms*, 378.
,, of Westfield, *arms*, 378.
,, Sir DAVID, of Cockburn, *brisure*, 442.
,, Sir PATRICK, *label* of, 414.
,, THOMAS, Earl of MORAY, 435.
DUNCAN, Admiral (Viscount), *arms* and *augmentation*, 533.
DUNDEE, City of, *arms*, 334.
,, Earl of, 149.
DUNGLASS, Barony of, 522.
DUNKELD, See of, *arms*, 152.
DUNNING, *arms*, 162.
DUNOIS, FRANCIS, Comte de, *seal*, 530.
,, JEAN, Comte de, *arms*, 571; Pl. XLVIII., fig. 5, p. 576.
,, ,, ,, *seal*, 529.
DURANT, *arms*, 162.
DURFORT, *arms*, 129.
Durham, Visitation of, 366.
DURHAM, BUTLER, Bishop of, *arms*, 381.
,, CUTHBERT TUNSTALL, Bishop of, *arms*, 560.
,, Earl of, *arms*, 235.
,, HUGH PUDSEY, Bishop of, *arms*, 154.
,, JAMES, *brisure*, 433.
,, of Grange, 433.
DUROY, Barons, *arms*, 68.
DURRANT, *arms*, 162.
DUSSEAUX, *arms*, 124.
DUYSENTDAELDERS, *arms*, 389.
DYMOCK, *arms*, 345.
DYRRHN, Counts von, *augmentation*, 543.
DYSON, *arms*, 306.
DZIULI, *arms*, 276.

Eagle, 242.
,, Apostolic, 633.
,, *arms* on breast of an, 630, 639.
,, as a *badge*, 753.
,, as a *crest*, 600.
,, as a *supporter*, 640.
,, *-demi*, as *supporter*, 634.
,, *displayed*, Pl. XXV., fig. 1, p. 260.
,, *Double headed*, 248.
,, German, 660.
,, *Imperial*, Pl. XXV., fig. 3, p. 260.
,, of the HOLY ROMAN EMPIRE, 242.
,, ORDER OF THE BLACK, 660.
,, *Two-headed*, Pl. XXV., fig. 2, p. 260.
Eagles as *supporters*, 635, 636.

Eagles, Imperial and Prussian, as *crests*, 608.
,, Parts of, 259.
Eagle's claw as a *badge*, 753.
,, *head*, Pl. XXV., fig. 4, p. 260.
,, ,, as a *crest*, 606.
,, *legs*, 260.
,, *wings*, 259.
Eaglet, 259.
EAM, Sir HENRY, *arms*, 221.
Earl Marshal of ENGLAND, mark of office, 644.
,, ,, SCOTLAND, mark of office, 644.
Earl's *coronet*, 624.
,, *standard*, Length of, 654.
Earth worm, 279.
East, *arms* of Emperors of the, 249.
Eastern crown, 684.
Eatables as charges, 391.
EBERSPERG, Barons Von, *arms*, 227.
EBERSTEIN, Counts of, *arms*, 214.
,, County of, *arms*, 473.
,, SIBYLLA VON, 473.
Ebranché, 701, 726.
Écaillé, 703, 726.
Écartelé, 700.
Ecartele, 81, 726.
,, *en équerre*, 82, 726.
,, *en sautoir*, 82, 727.
Écartelures, 700, 727.
ECCLES of Kildonan, *arms*, 348.
ECCLESHALL, *arms*, 403.
Ecclesiastical things as charges, 371.
Echancré, 685, 727.
,, *line*, 76.
Échelle d'escalade, 692, 727.
Echiqueté, 99, 680, 727.
Écimé, 138, 727.
ECKFOORD, *arms*, 299.
ECKHARDSTEIN, *arms* and *augmentation*, 543.
Éclaté, 703, 727.
Eclipsed, 684.
Ecorché, 727.
Écot, 720, 727.
Ecoté, 701, 727.
,, *contre*, 727.
Écoté line, 76.
Écran, 600.
Ecran, 727.
Ecrevisse, 727.
Écu, De l', 727.
,, *en bannière*, 727.
,, *la pointe de l'*, 59.
,, *le nombril de*, 59.
Écusson, 169.
,, *en abime*, 727.
,, *Faux*, 727.
,, *sur le tout*, 700, 727.
Écuyer-Banneret, Un, 652.
EDEIRNION, Barons of, *supporters*, 647.
EDGAR, *arms*, 566.
,, ATHELING, *arms* assigned to, 157.
EDINBURGH, ALFRED, Duke of, *label*, 423; Fig. 81, p. 421.
,, *arms* in St. Giles' Church in, 476.
,, Castle of, 605.
,, City, *arms*, 360.
,, Trinity Collegiate Church in, *seal*, 476.

EDMONDSON, *Complete Body of Heraldry*, 24.
EDMONSTON, *arms*, 307.
EDMONSTONE, *arms*, 178.
EDMUND (Crouchback), Earl of LANCASTER, monument of, 114.
,, son of RICHARD, Earl of CORNWALL, etc., *arms*, 245.
EDNOUAIN, *arms*, Pl. XXVII., fig. 2, p. 288.
EDNOWAIN AP BLEDDYN, *arms*, 333.
,, Lord of LLYS BRADWEN, *arms*, 274.
EDWARD, *arms*, 364.
,, I., King of ENGLAND, 34, 50, 70, 128, 170, 322, 377, 387, 404, 421, 438, 454, 457, 458, 465, 479, 482, 713; *arms*, Pl. LI., fig. 1, p. 661; *badge*, 323, 587; *helm*, 600; *Roll*, 408, 412, 428, 448, 552, 553; *seal* of, 330.
,, II., King of ENGLAND, 128. 257, 404, 408, 412, 448, 457, 465, 479; and his Queen ISABEL, 438; *arms*, Pl., LI., fig. 1, p. 661; *Roll* of, 260, 403, 407, 408, 409, 412, 413, 418, 553, 554; *seal* of, 330.
,, III. King of ENGLAND, 221, 324, 357, 416, 417, 420, 438, 463, 554, 592, 653; *arms*, Pl. LI., fig. 2, p. 661; *badge*, 588, 593; *crest*, 600; Pl. XLIX., fig. 2, p. 606; foundation of ORDER of the GARTER by, 664; *motto* of, 664; PHILIPPA, Queen, of, 257; *Roll of*, 287, 289, 404, 407; *seal* of, 324, 330; *standard* ascribed to, 589; *supporters* of, 661.
,, IV., King of ENGLAND, 167, 308, 485, 530, 557, 583, 587; *arms*, Pl. LI., fig. 4, p. 661; *badge*, 591; *motto* of, 664; *Restoration of*, 17; first and fourth *seals* of, 590; *standard* of, 588; *supporters* of, 662.
,, V., King of ENGLAND, *arms*, Pl. LI., fig. 4, p. 661; *supporters* of, 662.
,, VI., King of ENGLAND, 384; *arms*, Pl. LI., fig. 4, p. 661; *badge*, 594, 596; *supporters* of, 662.
,, THE BLACK, PRINCE, 555.
,, CONFESSOR, King of ENGLAND, 30; *arms*, 44, 369, 417, 474, 475, 528, 656, 661, 664; *crown*, 618.
EDWARDS, *crest*, 610.
EE, VAN DER, *arms*, 394.
EECKHOUT, VAN DEN, *arms*, 143.
Eel, The, 272.
Eel-spears as charges, 393.
EESE, VAN DER, *arms*, 237.
EESEN, *arms*, 153.
Effaré, 701, 702, 718, 727, 732.
Effarouché, 728, 732.
EFFEREN VON STOLBERG, *arms*, 189.
Effeuillé, 704, 728.

EGLESFELD, ROBERT DE, *arms*, 257.
EGBRET, *arms*, 94.
EGERTON, *arms*, 561.
,, Sir RALPH, Lord High Chancellor, 561.
,, Sir THOMAS, Viscount BRACKLEY, *arms*, 561.
EGGENBERG, 261.
,, *arms*, 670 ; Pl. LVI., fig. 5, p. 670.
EGGER, Counts von, *arms*, 184.
Eggs as charges, 391.
EGILSBERG, *arms*, 752.
EGLINTON, Earls of, *arms*, 180 ; Pl. XIX., fig. 9, p. 192.
,, ,, *supporters*, 293.
,, HUGH, Earl of, *seal* of, 180.
EGLOF DE SCHÖNAU, *arms*, 279.
EGMOND, *arms*, Pl. VII., fig. 5, p. 90.
,, Counts, *arms*, 98, 99.
EGMONT, *arms*, 125.
,, Counts, *arms*, 98, 99.
EGRA, *Dimidiatian of arms of*, 470.
EGREMONT, Baron of, *arms*, 404.
EICHSTADT, Princes of, *arms*, 473.
EIDEN, Sir JACOB VAN, *arms*, 180.
Eightfoil, 684.
Eisen-farbe, 62.
Elancé, 728.
Elderberries, 341.
Electoral-crown, 685.
Elephant, as a *badge*, 753.
,, The, 230.
Elephant's head, 231.
,, *tusks*, 231.
Elevated, 685.
ELIOT, Earl of ST. GERMAN'S, *arms*, 128.
ELIOTT of Stobs, *brisure*, 433.
ELIZABETH, Princess, *label*, 422 ; Fig. 87, p. 421.
,, Queen of ENGLAND, 661 ; *arms*, Pl. LI., fig. 4, p. 661 ; *badge*, 384, 596 ; *device*, 298 ; Funeral of, 384 ; Great Seal of, 664 ; *motto* of, 664 ; *supporters* of, 662.
ELLESMERE, Baron, *arms*, 561.
ELLEY, *arms*, 270.
ELLIOT, *arms*, 387.
ELLIOTS in south Scotland, 400.
ELLIOTT, Earl of MINTO, *arms*, 200.
ELLIS, *arms*, 301.
,, W. G., *Antiquities of Heraldry*, 26, 27, 28, 43, 44, 73, 86, 99, 125, 672.
ELPHINSTONE, *arms*, 227, 230 ; Pl. XXIII., fig. 2, p. 228.
,, JAMES, Lord COUPER, *supporters*, 298.
ELST, VAN DER, *arms*, 200.
ELTERSHOFEN, *arms*, 82, 87.
ELY, Bishop of, *arms*, 90.
,, GEOFFREY RIDEL, Bishop of, *arms*, 167.
,, JOHN DE FONTIBUS, Bishop of, *arms*, 309.
,, See of, *arms*, 379 ; Pl. XXXIII., fig. 4, p. 376.
Email, 728.
Émanche, 148.
Emanché, 728.
Emanche, 728 ; Pl. XVI., fig. 8, p. 146.
Émanché en pal, 101.

Emanchure, 728.
Emaux, 728.
Embattled, 685.
,, *line*, Fig. 18, p. 75, 76.
Embouché, 728.
Embouté, 728.
Embowed, 204, 269, 685.
Embrassé, 90, 728 ; Pl. VI., fig. 12, p. 84.
,, *à dextre*, etc., 728.
,, *vivré*, 728.
Embrasure, 685.
Embrued, 685.
EMBRUN, *arms* of See, 375.
EMELIE, *arms*, 198.
Emerald, 65, 685.
EMERSON, *crest*, 610.
EMLAY, *arms*, 198.
EMLINE, *arms*, 198.
EMLYN, *arms*, Pl. XX., fig. 2, p. 198.
Emmanché, 728.
Emmuselé, 695, 728.
EMO, *arms*, 94.
Emoussé, 728, 731.
Empenné, 686, 687, 728.
Emperors of the East, *arms*, 249.
Empiétant, 262, 706, 728, 742.
EMPIRE, *arms* of the, 469, 508, 509, 537.
,, *chief of the*, 536, 537, 538.
Empoignant, 728.
Empoignée, 728.
En abîme, 687, 721.
,, *cœur*, 687.
,, *forme*, 728.
,, *retrait*, 702.
,, *sautoir*, 702.
,, *surtout*, 697, 727.
Enaluron, 685.
Enchaîné, 728.
Enchaussé, 728.
Enchaussure, 729.
,, single, 89.
Enclavé, 729.
Enclos, 729.
Enclume, 729.
Encoché, 729.
Encyclopædia Britannica, 190.
END, *arms*, 222.
Endenté, 691, 729.
,, *line*, 729.
Endorse, The, 123, 685.
Endorsed, 685.
Enfield, 685.
Enfilé, 729.
Enfiled, 685.
ENGERN, Duchy of, *arms*, 321.
ENGHIEN, D', *arms*, 86, 464.
,, GAUTIER II., Seigneur d', 464.
ENGLAND, *arms*, 108, 171, 416, 417, 438, 439, 465, 468, 475, 476, 479, 485, 530, 532, 555, 557, 559, 593, 598, 662, 663 ; Pl. LI., p. 661.
,, *arms*, during Commonwealth, 487.
,, *badge*, 596, 597.
,, *banner* of, 141.
,, *bordure* of, 172, 425.
,, *crest* of, 603.
,, *crested helm* in, 600.
,, *crowns*, 618.
,, *De* in, 16.
,, *Differencing* in, 397.

ENGLAND dimidiating FRANCE, arms, Pl. XXXVIII., fig. 3, p. 464.
,, Dimidiation in, 465.
,, Earl Marshal of, mark of office, 644.
,, Early Great Seals of, 618.
,, ensign of Princes of, 208.
,, escucheon en surtout in, 485.
,, furs common in armory of, 74.
,, Historical Heraldry of, 218.
,, Impalement in, 474.
,, Kings of, badges, 587.
,, Large number of names in, 400.
,, Lions of, 146, 216, 454, 457, 531, 532, 554, 559, 662.
,, Lord Chancellor of, mark of office, 644.
,, Lord High Chamberlain of, mark of office, 644.
,, MARGARET of, Queen of JAMES IV. of SCOTLAND, 521.
,, MARGARET, Queen of EDWARD I., seal of, 454.
,, Mode of representing crests in, 602, 603, 604.
,, Princess MARGARET of, 597.
,, Rose of, 421, 533, 559.
,, Royal arms and supporters of, 661.
,, Royal lions of, 216.
, single supporter in, 633.
,, steward of, 597.
,, supporters in, 646.
,, The label in, 414.
Englanté, 688, 729.
ENGLISH arms, 224.
,, College of Arms, regulations on crest-coronets, 615.
,, families who use the de, 17.
,, Glossary, 676.
,, marks of illegitimacy, 564.
Engloutissant, 729, 734.
Engoulant, 708, 729.
Engoulé, 131, 685, 729.
Engrailed line, 685 ; Fig. 17, p. 75.
Engrêle, 685.
Engrêlé, 729.
,, line, 75.
Engrêlure, 729.
Enguiché, 384, 729.
Enhanced, 132, 685.
Enquérir, à, 729.
Enquerre, à, 729.
Ensanglanté, 685, 729.
Ensign, Blue, 657.
,, Red, 657.
,, White, 656.
Ensigned, 685.
Enté, 685, 729.
,, en point, 483, 685.
,, ,, ,, Parted per, Fig. 35, p. 77.
,, ,, pointe, 148.
,, line, 76.
Entoyré, 685.
ENTRAGUES, Marquis d', arms, 146.
Entravaillé, 729.
Entrelacé, 692, 729.
Entretenus, 729.
Enurney, 685.

Environed, 685.
Eole, 730.
Épanoui, 686, 730.
Éployé, 684, 686, 730.
EPPSTEIN, Counts of, arms, 98.
EPTINGEN, arms, 261.
Equerre, 730.
,, Ecartelé en, 730.
Equipé, 686, 688, 730.
Equipollé, 680, 730, 741 ; Pl. VII., fig. 8, p. 90.
Equippé, 702.
Equipped, 686.
Eradicated, 315, 686.
ERAQUY, Marquis d', arms, 280.
Erased, 686.
ERATH, Barons, arms, 221.
Erb-Verbrüderung, Treaties of, 483.
ERBACH, Counts of, arms, 126.
ERCILDOUN and CRAWFORD, seal of WILLIAM LINDSAY, Lord of, 51.
Erect, 274, 686.
,, -wavy, 274.
ERGADIA heiress, DE, 520.
ERIK XIV., King of SWEDEN, crown, 620.
ERIKSENS, arms, 136.
Ermine, 63, 67, 68, 686 ; Pl. IV., fig. 2, p. 62.
,, (ancient), Pl. IV., fig. 1, p. 62.
,, shield, plain, 68.
,, spots, Pl. XXIV., fig. 12, p. 236.
Ermines, 63, 686 ; Pl. IV., fig. 3, p. 62.
,, shield, plain, 68.
Erminois, 63, 686 ; Pl. IV., fig. 4, p. 62.
,, shield, plain, 68.
ERPACH, Counts of, arms, 308.
ERPINGHAM, arms, 174.
,, Sir THOMAS, lambrequin, 612.
ERPS, Comte d', arms, 644.
ERQUERRER, arms, 91.
ERQUERY, arms, 452.
ERROLL, Earldom of, 420.
ERSKINE, arms, 346 ; Pl. X., fig. 7, p. 118.
,, Earls of MAR, arms, 120.
,, of Cambo, arms, 569.
,, ,, Dun, arms, 346.
,, ,, Gogar, Sir THOMAS, Earl of KELLIE, augmentation, 534, 535.
,, ,, Kinnoull, Sir NICHOLAS, brisure, 432.
,, Sir ALEXANDER and Sir CHARLES, 433.
,, ,, CHARLES, Lyon King of Arms, 361.
,, ,, ROBERT, 432.
,, ,, THOMAS, son of Sir ROBERT, label, 419.
ERSKYN, Lord of BRECHINE, arms, 149.
ERTHAL, Barons von, arms, 126.
Escallop as a badge, 585, 753.
,, shell, 272, 686 ; Pl. XXVI., fig. 12, p. 266.
Escarbuncle, 686.
Escarre, 730.
ESCHAVANNES', JOUFFROY D', Traité Complet du Blason, 388.
ESCHELBACH, arms, 95.
ESCLAVONIA, Kingdom, arms, 494, 498, 501, 665.

(791)

ESCLIGNAC, D', *arms*, 213.
ESCOBARS, *arms*, 390.
ESCOCE, LE ROY D', *arms*, 177.
ESCORNA, *arms*, 174.
ESCORNAIX, *arms*, 181.
Escucheon, 169, 686; Pl. XIX., fig. 12, p. 192.
,, *en surtout*, 459.
,, ,, *Difference by an*, 448.
,, English and French, *Points of*, Figs. 15, 16, p. 59.
,, *in chief, Difference by addition of small*, 427.
,, *of pretence*, 686.
,, or *Inescucheon*, 169.
,, *surtout*, The, 483.
ESEL, *arms*, 237.
ESENDORF, VON, *arms*, 82.
ESKENS, *augmentation*, 546.
ESME, *arms*, Pl. XXII., fig. 5, p. 222.
,, Sir HENRY, *arms*, 221.
ESNE, MICHELE D', *arms*, 450.
ESPAGNET, Marquises d', *arms*, 338.
ESPARBEZ, *arms*, 710.
Esquire, 686.
,, definitions of term, 7.
ESQUIROU DE PARIEU, *arms*, 120.
ESSARTS, Seigneur des, 12.
ESSCHEDE, *arms*, 379.
ESSENAU, *see* SOUMERET.
ESSEX, Earl of, *arms*, 417.
,, ,, supposed effigy of, 45, 115.
,, Earls of, 589.
,, ,, *arms*, 81.
Essonier, 730.
Essorant, 259, 702, 730.
Essoré, 730.
Estacade, 730.
ESTAMPES, *arms*, Pl. X., fig. 4, p. 118.
,, Chevalier d', Bailli de VALENCE, *arms*, 119.
,, D', *arms*, 146.
Estaye, 730.
ESTCOURT, *arms*, 118; Pl. X., fig. 2, p. 118.
ESTE, House of, 492.
,, ,, *arms*, 256, 508.
,, NICOLO D', Duke of FERRARA, *arms* and *augmentation*, 538.
ESTERHAZY-GALANTHA, *arms*, 288.
,, Princes Von, *augmentation*, 539.
ESTISSAC, *arms*, 91.
Estoc, 704, 730.
ESTOGES, Counts de, *arms*, 113.
Estoile, 308, 686; Pl. XXVIII., fig. 6, p. 308.
ESTON, *arms*, 299.
ESTOUBLON, Marquises d', *arms*, 284.
ESTOUTEVILLE, *arms*, 94.
ESTRÉES, GABRIELLE D', 570.
ESTUER, D', *see* ROQUE.
Etai, 730.
ETAMPES, Comtes d', *arms*, 429.
,, Ducs d', *arms*, 342.
ETCHINGHAM, *arms*, 96, 182.
Etété, 730.
ETHELRED, King of WESSEX, *arms* assigned to, 156.
Étincellant, 703, 730.
Etoile, 730.
ETON, COLLEGE OF ST. MARY at, *arms*, 334.

Etruscan Vases, Figures on, Figs. 1, 2, 3, 4, p. 18.
ETTENREICH, M. von, *arms* and *augmentation*, 540.
ETTRICK FOREST, Lordship of, *arms*, 518.
EU, *tomb* of Comtes d', 332.
EUBING, *arms*, 89, 182.
Eucalyptus branch, 339.
EUGÉNIE, Empress of FRANCE, 390.
EUGENIUS III., Pope, 40.
EURIPIDES, description of devices on shields, 29.
European countries, *national arms* of chief, 661.
EUSTACE, *crest*, 563.
EVA, *arms*, 196.
EVANS, *arms*, 333, 339.
EVANS' tour *Through Bosnia and the Herzegovina*, 251.
Evasée, 730.
EVE, *arms* ascribed to, 23.
,, in Heraldry, 195.
EVEREUX, D', 17.
EVERSLEY, Lord, *supporters*, 648.
EVERSTEIN, château of, 642.
Evidé, 730.
Eviré, 219, 730.
EVREUX, AMAURI D', Earl of GLOUCESTER, *arms*, 79.
,, *arms*, 464, 465, 505, 635.
,, Comtes d', *bend*, 429.
,, County and *Pairie* of, 515.
,, PHILIP, Comte d', 464.
EWIG, *arms*, 320.
Excerpta Historica, 5, 291, 292, 556, 557, 558, 574, 584, 587.
Exchequer Rolls of Scotland, 455, 517.
EXETER, *badge*, 754.
,, Duke of, *arms*, 439, 474, 555.
,, EDMOND STAFFORD, Bishop of, *arms*, 437.
,, JOHN DE GRANDISON, Bishop of, *brisure*, 437.
,, See of, *arms*, 371; Pl. XXXIII., fig. 6, p. 376.
EXMOUTH, *crest* of Lord, 610.
,, Lord, *arms*, 533.
Expanded, 686.
Expectation, Arms of, 478.
External ornaments, 599, 617, 627.
EYCK, VAN, *arms*, 123, 143, 340.
Eye, Pl. XX., fig. 11, p. 198.
,, *Human*, 201.
Eyes, 686.
EYFELSBERG ZUM WEYR, *arms*, 668; Pl. LV., fig. 3, p. 668.
EYRE, SIMON, *arms*, 239.
EYSENBACH, *Histoire du Blason*, etc., 38, 46, 673; Pl. XXXVII., fig. 3, p. 448.
,, on hereditary arms, 37.
EYTZENRIET, *arms*, 166.
EZE, VANDER, *arms*, 68.
EZEKIEL, Book of, 253.
EZEL, *arms*, 364.

FABERT, *arms*, 141.
FABYAN'S *Chronicle*, 17.
FACCHINETTI, *arms*, 318.
FADA, *arms*, 294.
Faggot as a *badge*, 753.
FAGNANI, *arms*, 256.

FAHRBECK, *arms*, 120.
Failli, 139, 688, 730.
FAIRFAX, *arms*, 107 ; Pl. IX., fig. 7, p. 108.
FALAISE, *seal* of, 333.
Falchion as a *badge*, 584.
Falcon and Fetterlock as a *badge*, 591.
,, as a *badge*, 753.
,, *rising*, Pl. XXV., fig. 7, p. 260.
,, The, 261.
,, with crown and sceptre as a *badge*, 596.
FALCONBRIDGE, *arms*, 212.
FALCONER, Lord, *arms*, 431.
,, of Balmakellie, Sir JOHN, *arms*, 431.
,, of Hawkerston, RICHARD, *seal* and *arms* of, 50.
FALCOZ DE LA BLACHE, Comtes d'ANJOU, *arms*, 261.
FALEBOWSKI, *arms*, 371.
Falkirk Roll, 175.
FALLOWES, *arms*, 231.
FALMOUTH, Earls of, *arms*, 324.
,, Viscounts, *supporters*, 300.
Falot, 730.
False, 686.
Families, List of eminent, who never use particule, 12.
Fan, 686.
Fan-shaped *crest*, 599.
Fanal, 678, 730.
FANCHON, *arms*, 131.
FARE, LA, *arms*, 713.
FAREMOUTIERS, *seal* of Abbey of, 329.
FARNESE *arms*, 502, 508.
FARQUHARSON, *arms*, 212, 513.
Fascé, 92, 677, 731.
,, *-contre-fascé*, 731.
Fasce, 123, 730.
,, *En*, 730.
,, *en divise*, 126, 677, 726.
,, *voutée*, 125.
FAUCHE, PIERRE DE LA, *seal* of, 58.
FAUCIGNY, AGNES DE, *seal*, 453.
,, *arms*, 453.
,, Princes de LUCINGE, *arms*, 91, 122.
FAUCONBERG, *arms*, 212.
,, Earls of, *arms*, 123.
FAUCONVAL, *see* BERNARD.
FAUDOAS-BARBAZAN, *arms* and *augmentation*, 539.
Faulchion, 584, 686.
FAULQUEZ, Marquis of, *arms*, 136.
Faun, 304.
FAURE, DU, *arms*, 197, 379.
,, ,, *Abrégé Méthodique de la Science Héraldique*, 2.
Fausse, 686.
Fausses, Les armes, 752.
FAUSYDE, ROGER, *seal*, 441.
Faux, 686.
,, *-écu*, 564, 731.
FAVELETTE, *arms*, 145.
FAVERGES, *arms*, 140.
FAVIÉRES, *arms*, 344.
FAVYN, *Théâtre d'Honneur et de Chevalerie*, 134.
FAWKES, *arms*, 184 ; Pl. XVIII., fig. 8, p. 190.
FAYDIDE DE CHALANDRAS, *arms*, 239.
FAYDIT, 12.

FAYETTE, M. DE LA, 659.
,, *Memoires de la*, 660.
Feathered, 349, 686.
Feathers, Ostrich, as *crests*, 592, 607.
,, *Peacock*, as *crests*, 607.
FEATHERSTONE, *arms*, 222.
FECHENBACH, Barons von, *arms*, 279.
Feet, Human, 206.
FEILLÉE, *see* ORANGE, 340.
FELBRIDGE, *arms*, 217.
FELDKIRCH, County, *arms*, 373, 499.
FELDMANN, *augmentation*, 546.
FEND, *arms*, 302.
Fennel, 344.
FENTOUN, JANET, daughter of WALTER, *label*, 419.
FENWICK, *arms*, 266 ; Pl. XXVI., fig. 4, p. 266.
Fer-de-fourchette, 686.
,, *-lance*, 731.
,, *-moline*, 687, 692.
,, *-moulin*, 731.
FERDINAND I., King of Spain, 577.
,, II., Imperial diploma of, 489.
,, and ISABELLA of Spain, *arms* on eagle, 633.
,, Emperor, *seal*, 499.
FÈRE, LE SIRE DE LA, *arms*, 411.
FERIA, Counts de, *arms*, 507.
Fermail, 687, 721.
Fermaux as charges, 377.
FERNANDES DE CASTILLO, *arms*, 359.
FERNANDEZ, *arms*, 353.
FERNANDO of PORTUGAL, ISABELLA, natural daughter of King, 577.
FERNE, Sir JOHN, *Blazon of Gentrie*, 19, 22, 97.
FERNLAND, *arms*, 112.
FERON, JEAN LE, *Le Grand Blazon d'Armoiries*, 2.
FERRAGUT, *arms*, 356.
FERRARA, Duchy of, *arms*, 508 ; *arms* and *augmentation*, 538.
FERRE, GUY, 466.
FERRERA, *arms*, 128.
FERRERS, *arms*, 184, 355, 356, 474.
,, *badge*, 754.
,, Earl, *arms*, 165.
,, Earls of DERBY, 52.
,, ,, ,, *arms*, 71, 356.
FERRET, *arms*, 354.
FERRETTE, Counts of, *arms*, 271.
FERRI, *arms*, 346.
FERRIER, *arms*, 356.
FERRIÉRE DE TESSÉ, *arms*, 173.
FERRIÉRE, LA, *arms*, 356.
FERRIÉRES, HENRI DE, *arms*, 356.
,, ,, *escucheon* of, Fig. 90, p. 453.
,, ,, *seal* and *shield* of, 54.
FERRONAY, *arms*, 257.
Fess, 78, 123, 687 ; Fig. 38, p. 116 ; Pl. XI., fig. 1, p. 124.
,, and *canton* joined, 167.
,, *arched*, Pl. XI., fig. 7, p. 124.
,, *betweeen chevrons*, Pl. XIII., fig. 6, p. 136.
,, *checquy*, Pl. XI., fig. 5, p. 124.

(793)

Fess, cotised, Pl. XI., fig. 12, p. 124.
,, *dancettée,* Pl. XI., fig. 2, p. 124 ; Pl. XI., fig. 3, p. 124.
,, *embattled,* Pl. XI., fig. 4, p. 124.
,, *Parted per,* 79 ; Fig. 29, p. 77.
,, *Per,* 687 ; Pl. V., fig. 3, p. 80.
,, *point,* 59, 687.
,, *tortillé,* Pl. XI., fig. 6, p. 124.
,, Varieties of, 124.
Fessways, 108, 687.
FETTERCAIRN, Thanes of, 313.
Fettered, 687.
Fetter-lock, 687.
,, as a *badge,* 753.
FETZER, *arms,* 134.
FEUILLADE, Comte de la, *arms,* 159.
Feuillé, 693, 731.
Feuille de pervanche, 741.
Feuille de scie, 731.
FEUQUERAY, *arms,* 142.
FEVERE DE MANEGHEM, LE, *arms,* 344.
FEZENSAC, *arms,* 213.
,, Marquis de, *arms,* 191.
FIALIN, Duc de PERSIGNY, *arms* and *augmentation,* 541.
FIASCHI, Marquises, *arms,* 382.
Fiché, 687, 699, 712, 731.
FICHTERS, *arms,* 226.
FIDELER, *arms,* 182.
FIEANDT, *arms,* 510.
Fief-en bannière, 652, 639.
FIEFVET, *arms,* 128.
Field, 686.
Fields of a single metal, tincture, or fur, 65.
FIENNES, *arms,* 99, 213.
,, Lord DACRE, *badge,* 752.
FIERAMOSCA, *arms,* 280.
Fierté, 272, 687, 731.
FIESCHI, 16.
,, *arms,* 95.
FIESQUE, DE, 16.
FIFE, Earl of, *bend,* 430.
,, ,, *brisure,* 445.
,, Earls and Dukes of, *arms,* 212.
FIGLIAMBUCHI, *arms,* 73.
FIGUEIREDOS, *arms,* 320.
FIGUEROA, *arms,* 473, 506, 507.
,, Counts of, *arms,* 507 ; Pl. XLI., fig. 5, p. 510.
FIGUEROAS, *arms,* 320.
Figuré, 687, 731.
Figured, 687.
Fil, 731.
File, 187, 414, 687.
Filet, 731.
,, *en bordure,* 731.
,, *en croix,* 731.
Filière, 731.
FILIOLA, Princes de, *arms,* 140.
Fillet, 119, 133, 687.
Filum, 187.
FIMARCON, Ducs de, *arms,* 213.
,, Marquis de, *arms,* 129.
Fimbriated, 687.
FINCH, Earls of AYLESFORD, *arms,* 289.
Finches, 267.
FINCHFIELD, *arms,* 128.
FINCKENAUGEN, 267.
FINDERNE, *arms,* 156.
FINIELS, *arms,* 201.
FINLAND, *arms,* 666.

Finned, 687.
FIOLO, *arms,* 145.
Fir cones, 341.
,, *tree,* 315, 317.
Fire, 314.
,, *-ball,* 687.
,, *-beacon* as a *badge,* 594, 753.
,, *-pans* as charges, 393.
FIRENZUOLA, *arms,* 224.
FIRMAS, *arms,* 68.
Firmé, 687.
First Nobility Roll, 70, 404.
FISCHL, *arms,* 239.
Fish, 268.
,, *heads,* 272.
,, *-hook* as a *badge,* 753.
,, ,, as charges, 393.
,, *jaws,* 272.
,, The *Cock-,* 299.
Fishes in pairle, 271.
Fitché, 123, 687.
Fitched, 687.
Fitchy, 731.
FITZ-ALAN, *arms,* 94, 118, 213, 577.
,, ,, *badge,* 754.
,, ,, *canton,* 426.
,, ,, Earl of ARUNDEL, *arms,* 557.
,, ,, CHRISTIAN, granddaughter of WALTER, 125.
,, ,, ELEANOR, 482.
,, ,, Lady ALICE, 557.
,, ,, THOMAS, Earl of ARUNDEL, 577.
,, -ALURED, *arms,* 128.
,, -CLARENCE, WILLIAM GEORGE, Earl of MUNSTER, *arms,* 560.
,, -GEOFFREY, JOHN, *arms,* 438.
,, -HENRY, *arms,* 142.
,, -HUGH, *arms,* 140.
,, -ROGER, *arms,* 213.
,, -SIMON, JOHN, *arms,* 170.
,, -SIMONS, *arms,* 188.
,, -SWANNE, ADAM, 589.
,, -URSE, *arms,* 229.
,, -WARINE, *arms,* 82.
FITZCHARLES, CHARLES, Earl of PLYMOUTH, *arms,* 559.
FITZGERALD, *arms,* 467.
,, Duke of LEINSTER, *supporter,* 240.
,, Lady HENRY, 17.
,, MAURICE FITZMAURICE, JULIANA, dtr. of, 467.
FITZGERALDS, Dukes of LEINSTER, etc., *arms,* 143.
FITZHUGH, *arms,* 532.
FITZJAMES, HENRIETTA, *arms,* 559.
,, HENRY, the Grand Prior, *arms,* 559.
,, JAMES, Duke of BERWICK, *arms,* 559.
FITZPAYNE, *badge,* 654.
,, *Falchion* of, 584.
FITZROY, GEORGE, Duke of NORTHUMBERLAND, *arms,* 559.
,, HENRY, Duke of GRAFTON, *arms,* 559.
,, ,, Duke of RICHMOND and SOMERSET, *arms,* 558.
,, JAMES, Duke of MONMOUTH, *arms,* 559.

FITZROY, natural son of King HENRY I., *arms*, 554.
FITZSYMON, *arms*, 387.
FITZWALTER, *arms*, Pl. XIII., fig. 6, p. 136.
,, *badge*, 754.
FITZWARREN, WILLIAM, Lord, *label*, 417.
FITZWILLIAM, *arms*, 336; Pl. VII., fig. 9, p. 90.
FITZWILLIAMS, Earls of SOUTHAMPTON and FITZWILLIAM, *arms*, 100.
FIZE, DE, *arms*, 394.
FIZEAUX, *arms*, 66.
Flags, 649.
,, *National*, 655.
FLAHAULT, *arms*, 572.
,, Comte de, 572.
Flambant, 692, 731.
,, *contre*, 731.
Flambeaux as *supporters*, 643.
Flanc dextre, le, 59.
,, *sénestre, le*, 59.
Flanches, 687; Pl. XVIII., fig. 6, p. 190.
Flanchis, 702, 731.
Flancs, 687, 731.
FLANDERS, *arms*, 58, 212, 247, 251, 449, 458, 462, 463, 464, 471, 478, 484, 485, 496, 505, 572, 573, 574, 576, 631, 635.
,, BALDWIN, son of Count of, *brisure*, 439.
,, *brisure* of, 429.
,, Count GUY of, 412; *helmet*, 599.
,, Counts of, *seals*, 45.
,, County of, *arms*, 471.
,, *De* in, 16.
,, Effigy of WILLIAM, Count of, 43.
,, IOLANTE DE, *seal*, 464.
,, ISABELLA, Countess of, *seal*, 478, 629.
,, JOHN, Count of, *arms*, 484.
,, LOUIS II., Count of, 462, 572.
,, ,, van Male, Count of, *signet* of, 681.
,, Marks of illegitimacy in, 572.
,, PHILIP I., Count of, *seal*, 26, 32, 36, 47, 208.
,, ,, Governor of, *arms*, 412.
,, ,, of, *bend*, 429.
,, ROBERT DE, 464.
,, *seal* of Count ROBERT of, 47.
,, WILLIAM, Count of, *banner*, 650.
Flandre, Chronique de, 659.
,, *Les Recherches des Antiquitez et Noblesse de*, 573.
FLANDRE, BAUDOUIN, *bâtard de*, and his sister BEATRIX, *arms*, 572.
,, GUI DE, *bend*, 429.
,, GUILLAUME DE, *bend*, 429.
,, HENRI DE, *crest*, 592.
,, ,, ,, Comte de LODES, *bend*, 429.

FLANDRE, JEAN DE, *bend*, 429.
,, ,, ,, Seigneur de PRAET, *arms*, 573.
,, JEANNE DE, *seal* of, 70.
,, LOUIS, Comte de, 572; *seal*, Fig. 99, p. 648.
,, PETERKIN, *bâtard de, arms*, 572.
,, ROBERT, *bâtard de, arms*, 572.
,, YOLANTE DE, Countess of BAR, *seal*, 464, 629.
,, YOLANTE DE, Countess of BAR, *supporters*, 635.
Flank, dexter, 59.
,, *sinister*, 59.
Flanks, 687.
Flanqué en rond, 687, 731.
Flasque, The, 117, 165, 185, 687.
Flaunch, The, 117, 165, 184, 687.
Flax plant, 338.
Fleas, 285.
FLÉCHIN, Marquis de WAMIN, *arms*, 94.
FLEECE, ORDER OF THE GOLDEN, *badge* of the, 665, 745; *collar* of the, 665, 730, 732; regulations of the, 639.
FLEETWOOD, Barons, *arms* and *augmentation*, 547.
FLEHINGEN, *arms*, 440.
FLEMAL, *arms*, 143.
FLEMING, *arms*, Pl. XVII., fig. 10, p. 172.
,, DAVID, son of THOMAS, *label*, 419.
,, MALCOLM, *arms*, 178.
,, of Biggar, *arms*, 178.
,, Sir MALCOLM, 178.
Flesh colour or *Carnation*, 62.
FLETCHER of Saltoun, *arms*, 158.
Fleur-de-lis, 326, Pl. XXX., fig. 5, p. 332.
,, and *leopard's face*, 333.
,, as a *badge*, 583, 595, 596, 598.
,, *florencée*, Pl. XXX. fig. 7, p. 332.
,, for sixth son, 444.
,, supposed origin of, 326.
Fleur-de-lisé, 687, 731; Pl. XXX., fig. 6, p. 332.
,, *cross*, 158; Fig. 57, p. 164.
Fleuré, 687, 731.
,, *contre*, 731.
Fleureté, 731.
Fleuretté, Cross, 158.
Fleurettée, 687.
Fleuretty, 687.
Fleuri, 687, 731.
Fleuronné, 731.
Fleury, 112, 687.
,, *Cross*, 157.
Flexed, 687.
Flies, 280.
Flighted, 349, 687.
FLOCKHER, *augmentation*, 546.
FLODDEN, Battle of 435, 529.
FLORENCE, *arms*, 283, 330, 732; Pl. XXX., fig. 7, p. 332.
,, Carroccio of, 655.
,, Church of San Lorenzo in, 192.
,, *coins* of, 327.
,, *standard* of, 655.
Florencée, 730, 731.

(795)

FLORENT V., Count of HOLLAND, *secretum* of, 245.
Floretty or *Flory*, 687.
Florin, The, 327.
Flory, 112, 687, 731.
,, *Cross*, 157 ; Fig. 58, p. 164.
Flotant, 687.
Flowered, 687.
Flowers, 315.
Flurty, *Cross*, 158.
Flute as a charge, 387.
Foi, 205, 732.
FOI DE ST. MAURICE, *arms*, 206.
FOIX, BLANCHE DE, *arms*, 418.
,, Counts of, *arms*, 122, 418, 434.
,, GASTON DE, *label*, 418.
,, Prince de, *arms*, 129.
,, *seals* of Counts of, 56.
Foliated, 687.
FONTAINE, DE, *arms*, 170.
FONTAINES, PHILIPPE, Seigneur de, *arms*, 575 ; Pl. XLVII., fig. 2, p. 574.
FONTENAI, *arms*, 91.
FONTENAY, Marquises de, *arms*, 262.
FONTIBUS, JOHN DE, Bishop of ELY, *arms*, 309.
FORABOSCHI, *arms*, 113.
FORBES, *arms*, 229, 446, 447 ; Pl. XXIII., fig. 5, p. 228.
,, *arms in Lyon Office Register*, 400.
,, of Echt, *fess*, 431.
,, ,, Monymusk, *chevron*, 431.
,, ,, Rires, *arms*, 446.
,, ,, Tolquhoun, *arms*, 446.
FORBESES in Aberdeen, 400.
FORCE, Ducs de la, 12.
Forcené, 727, 732.
Forces, 732.
,, *à tondeur*, 732.
Forest, 316 ; Pl. XXIX., fig. 5, p. 318.
FOREST, DE LA, *arms*, 316.
,, ,, Marquises d'AR-MAILLÉ, *arms*, 434.
,, -LANDRY, *brisure*, 434.
FORESTEL, *arms*, 434.
FORESTIE DES AUBAS, DE LA, *arms*, 316.
Forêt, 691.
FOREZ, Counts of, *arms*, 212.
FORMANOIRS, *arms*, 202.
Formée or *Formy*, 688.
Formy, 688.
,, *Cross*, 153.
FORNARA, *arms*, 98.
FORREST, *arms*, 315.
FORRESTER, ADAM, *seal*, 632.
,, Lord, of Corstorphine, *arms*, 385.
,, of Carden, *arms*, 385.
FORSYTH, *arms*, 289.
FORT, Baron le, *arms*, 231.
FORTESCUE, Earl, *arms*, 133.
,, ,, *supporters*, 606.
FORTIGUIERRE, *arms*, 79.
FORTUNATI, *arms*, 66.
Fortune, Personification of, in Heraldry, 197.
FOSCARI, *arms*, 166.
FOSSEUX, MONTMORENCY DE, *brisure*, 451.
FOSTER'S *Baronetage*, 83, 84, 529.
,, *Peerage*, 83, 84, 194, 562, 604, 642.

Fotheringhay Castle, 591.
FOUCAUD, 12.
FOUCAULD, *arms*, 212.
,, Seigneur de la ROCHE, 11.
Foudre, 705, 732.
FOULIS, *arms*, 319 ; Pl. XXIX., fig. 8, p. 318.
,, of Leadhills, 436.
,, Sir JOHN, of Ravelston, *fess*, 430.
Fountain, 193, 688 ; Pl. XIX., fig. 5, p. 192.
FOUQUET, 12.
,, *arms*, 240.
Fourché, 214, 688, 732.
,, *Cross*, 161.
Fourcheté, 732.
Fourchetté, 688.
,, *Cross*, 161.
Fourchy, *Cross*, Fig. 59, p. 164.
FOURNILLON, *arms*, 336.
Fourrure, 732.
FOUSKARNAKI, *arms*, 195.
Fox, The, 230.
FOX, Bishop, *arms*, 264.
Foxes countersalient, Pl. XXIII., fig. 6, p. 228.
FOY, DE LA, *arms*, 206.
Fracted, 688.
Fraise, 323, 688.
Fraises, Pl. XXX., fig. 2, p. 332.
Franc-canton, 166.
,, *quartier*, 165, 700, 732.
FRANCE-ANCIENT, *arms*, 112, 329, 354, 369, 416, 429, 452, 456, 458, 462, 464, 465, 475, 502, 505, 538, 570, 571, 574, 629, 661 ; Pl. VIII., fig. 8, p. 100 ; *arms*, Pl. XLIV., fig. 5, p. 537.
,, ,, *fleurs-de-lis* of, 454.
,, *arms*, 104, 146, 171, 330, 439, 463, 464, 466, 479, 484, 485, 488, 504, 505, 515, 521, 529, 530, 534, 539, 555, 557, 559, 570, 572, 573, 593, 635, 636, 662, 663, 710 ; Pl. XXV., fig. 3, p. 260 ; Pl. XXX., fig. 5, p. 332.
,, *augmentations* in, 538.
,, *badge*, 596.
,, *bordure* of, 172, 438, 439, 560.
,, *cap* of Chancellor of, 625.
,, *cap* of *Premiers Présidents* in, 625.
,, *chief* of, 539.
,, *coronet* of a baron in, 625.
,, ,, of a count in, 624.
,, ,, of a viscount in, 625.
,, ,, of marquis in, 624.
,, *coronets* of "*les fils de*", 620.
,, *crests* in, 604.
,, *crowns* of, 620.
,, DAUPHIN of, 642.
,, ,, *arms*, Pl. XXVI., fig. 7, p. 266 ; 269.
,, Duke of, 11.
,, Early *Great Seals* of, 618.
,, Form of *shield* in, 56.
,, FRANÇOIS, Grand Chambellan de, *arms*, 572.

FRANCE, *Great Seals* of Kings of, 616.
,, Imperial Standard of, 660.
,, ISABEL of, *seal*, 465, 479.
,, Isle de, 11.
,, JEANNE DE, *seal* of, 457; Pl. XXXV., fig. 3, p. 416.
,, King JOHN of, 528.
,, *label* of, 416, 417.
,, *"Le drapeau blanc"* of, 659.
,, LOUIS, Dauphin of, *seal*, Pl. XXXVII., fig. 5, p. 448.
,, *mantling* for princes, dukes, etc., in, 616.
,, ,, of the *Chancellier*, 616.
,, ,, of the *Présidents*, 616.
,, MARÉCHAUX DE, *coronet*, 624.
,, MARGARET, dtr. of PHILIP III. of, *seal*, 454.
,, ,, of, *arms*, 465.
,, ,, ,, *seal*, 457, 462.
,, Marks of illegitimacy in, 570.
,, ,, office in, 645.
,, -MODERN, *arms*, 429, 538, 570, 571, 661, 663, 667.
,, *Oriflamme* of, 658.
,, Origin of Tricolor of, 659.
,, *Pairs de, mantling armoyé*, 615.
,, *Pavilion* of Kings of, 616.
,, Residence of Kings of, 658.
,, Rhyming Chronicle of, 658.
,, *Royal arms*, 112.
,, ,, *cadency* of, 439.
,, ,, flags of, 659.
,, ,, House of, 505.
,, ,, ,, *crest*, 608.
,, ,, *supporters*, 635, 636.
,, *Toques* denoting different ranks in, 626.
,, Use of *escucheon en surtout* in, 504.
,, ,, *label* in, 424.
,, ,, *supporters* in, 636.
FRANCHI, *arms*, 79, 86; Pl. VI., fig. 4, p. 84.
FRANCIOTI, *arms*, 288.
FRANCIS I., King of FRANCE, *crown*, 620; *device* of, 294; *seal* of, 329, 334; Pl. XXXVII., fig. 1, p. 448; *supporters*, 636.
,, II., King of FRANCE, *supporters*, 636.
,, Emperor, 540.
FRANÇOIS I., *badge*, 586.
FRANCONI, *arms*, 72.
FRANCQUART, in Belgium, system of lines representing colour, 64.
FRANGIPANI, *arms*, 391.
FRANKFURT. City of, *arms*, 255.
FRANKS, CLOVIS, King of the, 326.
Fraser or *Fraise*, 688.
FRASER, *arms*, 323, 406, 446; Pl. XXX., fig. 2, p. 332.
,, *arms* in *Lyon Office Register*, 400.
,, HUGH, *bordure*, 442.
,, JAMES of Ferendrach, *bend*, 430.
,, of Oliver Castle, *arms*, 521.
,, Sir ALEXANDER, *seal*, 441.

FRASER, WILLIAM, son of ALEXANDER, *label*, 420.
FRAUENBERG, Barons of, *arms*, 447.
FRAUNBERG, Baron, *arms*, 121, 447.
FRAUNHOFEN, Baron, *arms*, 121.
FREDERICK I., BARBAROSSA, Duke of SWABIA, 244.
,, I., Emperor, *augmentations* granted by, 536.
,, II., Emperor, 208.
,, ,, *augmentations* granted by, 536.
,, ,, *banners* of, 245.
,, III., King of DENMARK and NORWAY, ULRIC FREDERICK, nat. son of, 581.
,, IV., Burg-grave of NÜRNBERG, 454.
,, Emperor, HOLY ROMAN EMPIRE, *crown*, 621.
,, Prince of WALES, 423.
FREDIÈRE, see AURELLE.
FRENCH Armory, *helmet* in, 601.
,, *blazon*, 109.
,, EMPIRE, *arms*, 572.
,, ,, *Eagles* of, 541
,, ,, Staff of flag, 660.
,, G. J., *On the Banners of the Bayeux Tapestry*, 149, 291, 650.
,, Glossary, 709.
,, Revolution, effect of, on Heraldry, 25.
FREPPELS, *arms*, 284.
FRERE, *arms*, 186.
FRESNAY, *arms*, 71.
FRESTEL, *arms*, 96.
Fret, 116, 165, 181, 688; Pl. XIX., fig. 11, p. 192.
FRETEL, *arms*, 96.
Frette, 688, 732.
Fretté, 688, 732.
Fretted, 688.
Fretty, 96, 688, 732; Pl. VIII., fig. 5, p. 100.
FREVILLE, *arms*, 157.
FRIBERG, *arms*, 184.
FRIDUNG, VON, *arms*, 752.
FRIEDLAND, Duke of, *arms*, 220.
,, ,, *augmentation*, 538.
FRIES, *arms*, 295.
FRIOUL, Duchy, *arms*, 503.
FRISIA, *Dimidiation* in, 469.
FRIULI, Duchy, *arms*, 503.
Frogs, 274, 278.
FROHBERG, Counts von, *supporters*, 304.
FROISSART, 35, 378, 592.
,, *arms*, 127.
FROSCH, *arms*, 279.
FROSCHAMMER, *arms*, 279.
FROSCHAUER, *arms*, 279.
FRÖSCHL, *arms*, 279.
Fructed, 688.
Fruité, 688, 732.
Fruits, 315, 339.
FRUMBESEL, *arms*, 237.
Frying pans as charges, 390.
FUCHSS, Counts, *arms*, 230.
FUENSALDA, *arms*, 193.
FUGGER, *arms*, 331.

(797)

FUGGER, *Spiegel der Ehren des Hauses Oesterreich*, 247.
FULFORD, *supporters*, 638.
FULLER, *arms*, 533.
FULLERTON, *arms*, 239.
FUMEZ, Marques de, *arms*, 148.
Furchy, 688.
Furieux, 701, 728, 732.
Furnished, 688.
FURNIVAL, *arms*, 403.
,, GERARD DE, *arms*, 403.
,, THOMAS, *arms*, 403.
,, WALTER DE, *arms*, 403.
Furs, 63 ; Pl. IV., p. 62.
,, in Heraldry, supposed origin of, 22.
,, Use of in different countries, 74.
FÜRSTENBURG, Counts of, *arms*, 126.
FÜRSTENHAUER, *arms*, 153.
FÜRSTENWARTER, Barons von, *arms*, 360.
Fuseau, 184.
Fusee, 184.
Fusée, 688, 732.
FUSÉE DE VOISENON, *arms*, 184.
Fuselé, 100, 688, 732.
FUSELIER, LE, *arms*, 184.
Fusil, 182, 183, 688, 732 ; Pl. XVIII., fig. 11, p. 190 ; Fig. 46, p. 116.
Fusilly, 100, 185, 688, 732 ; Pl. VII., fig. 10, p. 90.
,, *in bend*, 100 ; Pl. VII., fig. 11, p. 90.
Fusils conjoined, Pl. XVIII., fig. 12, p. 190.
Futé, 690, 732.
Fylfot, 82, 688.
FYNDERNE, *arms*, 156.

GABRIELI, Princes, 16.
GAETANI, *arms*, 132.
Gai, 732.
GAINSBOROUGH, Earls of, *arms*, 96.
GAL, LE, *arms*, 93.
GALBA, *medal* of, 328.
GALEN, VAN, *monument* of, 626.
GALEOTTI, *arms*, 128.
Galère, 688, 694, 732.
GALICIA, *arms* of kingdom of, 372, 504.
GALISSONIÈRE, Marquis de la, *arms*, 280.
Galley, 688.
,, as a *badge*, 753.
,, as a charge, 367.
GALLOT, *arms*, 140.
GALLOWAY, ALAN, Lord of, 460.
,, *arms*, 427, 460, 514, 515, 516, 519, 521.
,, Fair Maid of, 515, 517.
,, Lordship of, *arms*, 214.
Gal-traps, 688.
GAM, Sir DAVID, *arms*, 348.
GAMA, VASCO DA, *arms*, 100.
,, ,, *arms* and *augmentation*, 547.
GAMACHES, Marquises of, *arms*, 118.
GAMARAGE, Comte de, *arms*, 319.
Gamb, 222, 688.
GAMIN, *arms*, 191.
Gammadion, 82.
GAND, BAUDOIN DE, Seigneur d' ALOST, *arms*, 118.
GANGALANDI, *arms*, 82.
GANGES, Seigneurs de, 10.
GANNAY, *arms*, 140.

Gantelet, 688.
GANTIER, LE, 16.
Garb, 688 ; Pl. XXX., fig. 12, p. 332.
,, as a *badge*, 585.
,, as a *crest*, 605.
GARBETT, *arms*, 352.
Garbs, 341.
GARCIAS, *arms*, 263.
GARCIN, *arms*, 276.
GARCINI, *arms*, 276.
Gardant, 688.
GARDNER, *arms*, 133.
GARIOCH, *arms*, 567.
Garland, 688.
GARLAND, *arms*, 336.
,, GUI DE, *seal* of, 48.
Garni, 690, 732.
GARNIER, Comte de GRAY, *arms*, 118.
Garnished, 384, 688.
GARRAULT, *arms*, 296.
Garter, 688.
GARTER, *arms* of ORDER OF THE, 141.
,, *crested helms* above the stalls of the Knights of the, 603.
,, King of Arms, *arms*, 424, 525.
,, *motto*, 664.
,, *shields* of Knights of the, 63.
,, *Stall Plates* of the Knights of the, 63, 134, 602, 612.
GARVINE, *arms*, 268.
GASCELIN, *arms*, 112.
GASCQ, 12.
GASTINELS, *arms*, 364.
Gates as charges, 393.
GATTERER, *Handbuch der Neuesten Genealogie und Heraldik*, 496.
GAUNT, JOHN of, 438, 555, 578, 588, 590, 597.
,, ,, *badge*, 591, 593.
Gauntlet, 688.
GAUTHIER DE GOURAVEL, *arms*, 183.
GAVENOR, *arms*, 230.
GAVESTON, PIERS, Earl of CORNWALL, *arms*, 257.
GAWDEY, *arms*, 277.
Gaze, At, 232, 688.
GAZET DE BRANDAY, *arms*, 279.
GAZZARI, *arms*, 293.
Ged, The, 271.
GEDDES, *arms*, 271.
,, W. D., and P. DUGUID, *Heraldic Ceiling of Aberdeen Cathedral*, 84.
GEESDORP, VAN, *arms*, 183.
Geese, 267.
GELENIUS, system of lines representing colour, 64.
GELIOT, *La Vraie et Perfect Science des Armoiries*, 2.
GELLHEIM, Battle of, 246.
Gem-ring, 688.
GEMELL, Barons, *arms*, 198.
GEMELLI, *arms*, 198.
Gemells, 688.
GENDRON, *arms*, 165, 200.
Geneologist, The, 62, 131, 409, 477.
GENESTET, *arms*, 202.
Genet, 688.
GENEVA, *arms*, 467, 469.
,, Counts of, *arms*, 99.
GENEVILLE, Lords, *arms*, 357.
GENEVILL, GEOFFREY DE, *arms*, 357.
GENEVILLE, DE, *arms*, 47.

(798)

GENEVILLE, DE, Seigneurs de BROYES, *arms*, 357.
  ,, SIMON DE, *arms*, 357.
GENICEI, *arms*, 98.
GENNEP, VAN, *arms*, 337.
GENOA, *arms*, 283.
  ,, Republic of, *arms*, 141.
GENOUILLAC, *see* GOURDON.
GENT, VAN, *arms*, 161.
Gentlemen, *helm* of, 601, 602.
  ,, Use of term, 6.
Gentleman's Magazine, 20, 246, 467.
GEORGE I., Elector of HANNOVER, *arms*, 663.
  ,, ,, King of BRITAIN, *arms*, Pl. LII., fig. 9, p. 662; *Exchequer Seal* of, 662; *supporters* on *Seal of Common Pleas* of, 663.
  ,, II., King of BRITAIN, *arms*, Pl. LII., fig. 9, p. 662.
  ,, III., King of BRITAIN, *arms*, Pl. LII., figs. 9 and 10, p. 662; *labels* of his family, 421.
  ,, IV., *arms*, Pl. LII., fig. 10, p. 662; *seal* of, 598.
GEORGES, Four, Kings of BRITAIN, *arms*, 237.
GEORGIA, *arms*, 666.
GERARD, *arms*, 143.
Gerated, 688.
Gerbe, 688.
Gérion, Téte de, 200, 732.
GERLINGTON, *arms*, 283.
GERMAN Armory, *helmets* in, 601.
  ,, *eagle*, 660.
  ,, Electors, *arms*, 615.
  ,, Emperor's *crown*, 617, 621.
  ,, EMPIRE, *arms*, 254, 665; Pl. LIV., fig. 1, p. 666.
  ,, Princes (*Fürsten*), *crown*, 623.
GERMANY, *arms* of Emperor on Eagle, 630.
  ,, *coronet* of a Baron in, 625.
  ,, ,, Count in, 624.
  ,, *crest* as augmentation, 608.
  ,, *crested helm* in, 600, 603, 604.
  ,, *crown*, Emperors of, 621.
  ,, double-headed eagle of, 468.
  ,, Emperor of, *arms*, 252.
  ,, Emperors of, using *escucheon en surtout*, 486.
  ,, Imperial *crown* of, 622.
  ,, ,, *standard* of 660.
  ,, mode of differencing, 405.
  ,, old Imperial *crowns* of, 622.
  ,, Princess Royal, Empress of, *label*, 423.
  ,, *standard* of the Empress of, 660.
  ,, Tinctures of *lambrequins* in, 612.
  ,, Use of *bordure* in, 440.
  ,, ,, *label* in, 424.
  ,, ,, *supporters* in, 637, 639.
GEROLDSECK, Counts of, *arms*, 215.
  ,, Lordship of, *arms*, 490.
GERVIS, *arms*, 352.
GÈVRES, Duc de, 12.
  ,, *supporters*, 294.
GEYER, *arms*, 261.
GEYSS, *arms*, 299.

GHELDERSON, *lambrequin*, 613.
GHENT, *arms*, 283.
  ,, JOHN of, Duke of LANCASTER (*see* GAUNT).
GHERARDINI, *arms*, 128.
GHIBELINE, *chief*, 119, 470, 538.
GHIBELLI, Dr, Patent of arms granted to, 601.
GHIGI, *arms*, 319.
GHISELIN, *arms*, 280.
GHISI, *arms*, 88.
GHISNES, INGELRAM DE, *arms*, 71.
GHISTELLES, *arms*, 136.
  ,, MARIA DE, 573.
GIACINTO, *arms*, 338.
GIBBON, 157.
GIBELLINI, *supporters*, 303.
GIECH, Counts of, *arms*, 488.
GIEDE, *arms*, 271.
GIELIS, *arms*, 393.
GIFFARD, *arms*, 97, 183, 216.
GIFFORD, *arms*, 357; Pl. XXI., fig. 4, p. 212.
  ,, of Yester, *arms*, 521.
GIJION, AFFONSO, Conde de, 577.
GILLART, *arms*, 295.
GILLES, Seigneur de BERLAER, *arms*, 405.
Gillyflowers, 337.
Gimmel-ring, 688.
GINKELS, Earls of, ATHLONE, *arms*, 127.
GIOLFINI, *arms*, 72.
GIOVANELLI, Princes, *arms*, 370.
GIRAULD, GUILLAUME DE, 10.
GIRESME, NICOLE DE, *supporters*, 635.
GIROLAMI, *arms* and *augmentation*, 541.
Giron, 167, 686, 689, 732.
GIRON, *arms*, 168.
  ,, Duke of OSSUNA, etc., *arms*, 167, 441; Pl. XLI., fig. 2, p. 510.
Gironnants, 732.
Gironné, 83, 689, 732, 736.
  ,, *en Croix*, 732.
  ,, *Mal*, 733.
Gironny, 689.
Girouette, 358, 733.
Gisant, 681, 733.
GISE, *arms*, 101; Pl. VIII., fig. 1, p. 100.
GISSEY, *arms*, 372.
GIUDICI, *arms*, 87.
GIUSTI, *arms*, 79.
GIUSTINIANI, 536.
  ,, FRANCESCO, *arms* and *augmentation*, 537.
GIUSTO, *arms*, Pl. V., fig. 3, p. 80.
GLADSTONE, *arms*, 175.
GLAFEY, *Specimen decadem Sigillorum*, 243, 328, 621.
GLAMORGAN, Lords of, 386.
GLANNES, Barons de VILLERS FARLAY, *arms*, 343.
GLANVILLE, *arms*, 145; Pl. XV., fig. 12, p. 144.
GLASGOW, City and See of, *arms*, 316.
  ,, City of, *arms* and *supporters*, 271.
  ,, Earl of, *arms*, 234, 523.
GLAUBITZER, *arms*, 743.
GLAVENAS, *arms*, 153.
GLEDSTANES, *arms*, 175, 199; Pl. XVII., fig. 9, p. 172.
GLEGG, *arms*, 220; Pl. XXII., fig. 2, p. 222.

(799)

GLEICHEN, Counts of, *arms*, 214.
GLEN, *arms*, 586.
,, MARGARET, wife of ROBERT, 565.
Gliding, 274, 689.
GLOGAU, Dukes of, *arms*, 255.
Glossary, English, 676.
,, French, 709.
GLOUCESTER, ANTIGONE, natural daughter of Duke HUMPHREY of, *arms*, 556.
,, *badge*, 754.
,, Duchess of, *arms*, 475.
,, Duke of, 642.
,, ,, *arms*, Pl. XVII., fig. 4, p. 172.
,, ,, *helm*, 602.
,, Earl of, 457.
,, ,, *arms*, 79, 257.
,, ,, *badge*, 386.
,, Earls of, *arms*, 139.
,, HENRY, Duke of, *label*, 421.
,, HUMPHREY, Duke of, *arms*, 171.
,, ,, Duke of, *bordure*, 556.
,, THOMAS, Duke of, *badge*, 593; *seal*, Pl. XXXV., fig. 1, p. 416.
,, WILLIAM, Duke of, *label*, 422.
,, ,, FREDERICK, Duke of, *label*, 423.
,, ,, HENRY, Duke of, *label*, 423.
,, ,, STUART, Duke of, *label*, 421.
GLOVER'S *Ordinary of Arms*, 133, 148, 169, 557.
,, *Roll of Arms*, 193, 208, 264, 265, 331, 376, 357, 379, 404, 407, 408, 438, 458, 481, 550, 552.
Gloves as charges, 392.
GOATLEY, *crest*, 295.
Goats, Pl. XXIV., fig. 3, p. 236.
,, and *Goat's heads*, 235.
GOBBI, *arms*, 231.
Goblets as charges, 382.
Goboné or *Gobony*, 689, 721.
GODEFROI, *arms*, 113.
GOESHEN, *arms*, 202.
GOETHE, *arms*, 308.
GOFFE, *arms*, 188.
GOGH, VAN, *arms*, 374.
GOHAING, *arms*, 143.
GOICX, WILHELM DE, brass of, 580.
Gold or *Or*, 60, 65.
,, shield, plain, 66.
GOLDEGGER, *arms*, 669; Pl. LV., fig. 7, p. 668.
GOLDINGTON, *arms*, 130.
GOLDISBURGH, *arms*, 160.
Golpes, 190, 689.
GONDI, *arms*, 736.
GONDRECOURT, Counts of, *arms*, 214.

GONDY, *arms*, 735.
Gonfalon, 733.
GONFALONIERE, Papal pale of the, 541.
Gonfanon, 658, 659, 689, 733.
,, as a charge, 372.
GONNELIEU, *arms*, 130.
GONTAUT, Duc de BIRON, *arms*, 81.
GONZAGA, Dukes of MANTUA, *arms*, 94, 259, 502, 536.
,, GIOVANNI FRANCESCO, 1st Marquis of MANTUA, *augmentation*, 537.
GONZALES, *arms*, 361.
GORCKEN, *arms*, 290.
GORCUM, VAN, *arms*, 203.
GORDON, *arms*, 227, 435, 436, 521.
,, ADAM, 521.
,, ALEXANDER, Lord, *label*, 419.
,, family, *arms*, 180.
,, heiress of, 605.
,, of Cairnbulg, *arms*, 568.
,, ,, Earlston, *brisure*, 435.
,, ,, Glasterim, *brisure*, 435.
,, ,, Hallhead, *bordure*, 569.
,, ,, Knokespock, *brisure*, 435.
,, ,, Lesmoir, *fess*, 431.
,, ,, Lochinvar, *bend*, 430.
,, ,, Newark, *brisure*, 435.
,, ,, Rusco, *bordure*, 569.
,, ,, Tetschie, *brisure*, 435.
GORDONS in Aberdeen, 400.
Gore, 689.
GORE, Earl of ARRAN, *arms*, 163.
Gorge, 193, 689.
Gorgé, 733.
Gorged, 689.
Gorges, 689.
GORGES, *arms*, 193; Pl. XIX., fig. 6, p. 192.
GORKE, *arms*, 290.
GÖRLITZ, VON, *arms*, 752.
GORREVOD, Ducs de PONT DE VAUX, *arms*, 136.
,, Princes of the HOLY ROMAN EMPIRE, *arms*, 136.
GORTERE DE, *arms*, 140.
GORZ, County, *arms*, 496, 503.
GÖSCHEN, *arms*, 92, 202.
Goshawk, Pl. XXV., fig. 6, p. 260.
GOSNOLD, *arms*, 80.
GOSPATRIC, *arms*, 191.
GOTHLAND, *arms*, 667.
GOTSCHEN, VON, *arms*, 92.
GÖTTER, Counts, *arms*, 136.
,, ,, *augmentation*, 543.
GOTTSCHEE, *arms*, 448.
GOTTSTEIN, Counts von, *supporters*, 231.
GOUDELIN, Vicomtes de PLÉHÉDEL, *arms*, 346.
GOUDIE, *arms*, 278.
Gouffre, 689, 733.
GOUGH, Lord, *arms*, 534.
,, *monuments*, 57.
,, Viscount, *supporter*, 292.
GOUJON, *monument* by, 164.
GOURAVAL, *see* GAUTHIER.
GOURDON DE GENOUILLAC, *arms*, 741; *L'Art Héraldique*, 329.
GOURNAY, *arms*, 67.
GOURNEY, *arms*, 142.

GOUSSAINVILLE, MONTMORENCY DE, *brisure*, 451.
GOUSSANCOURT, *Martyrologe des Chevaliers de l'Ordre de S. Jean de Jerusalem*, 365, 402.
Gousset, 689, 733.
Goutté, 114, 689.
Gouttes, 113, 689, 733, 735.
GOUVIS, *arms*, 71.
GOVAERTS, *arms*, 184.
GOWER, *arms*, 157.
,, poet, 597.
Gowrie Plot, 535.
GOYER, DE, *arms*, 184.
GOYON, 12.
,, Ducs of VALENTINOIS, *arms*, 215.
,, Vicomtes de, *arms*, 214.
GRAÇAY, *arms*, 213.
Graded, 689.
GRADENIGHI, *arms*, 365.
GRADENIGO, Counts, *arms*, 365; Pl. XXXII., fig. 10, p. 358.
Gradient, 689.
GRADISCA, Counts of, *arms*, 159, 503.
GRAFENEGG, Counts von, *arms*, 182.
Grafted, 689.
GRAFTON, Duke of, *arms*, 559; Pl. XII., fig. 12, p. 130.
GRAHAM, *arms*, 432.
,, *arms in Lyon Office Register*, 400.
,, Duke of MONTROSE, *arms*, 273.
,, JOHN, *chevron*, 431.
,, of Braco, Sir WILLIAM, *brisure*, 433.
,, ,, Dundaff, PATRICK, son of Sir DAVID, *label*, 419.
,, ,, Fintry, Sir ROBERT, 433.
,, ,, ,, *brisure*, 433.
,, ,, Garvock, *arms*, 178.
,, ,, Inchbrackie, *arms*, 363.
,, ,, Kinpunt, ROBERT, *brisure*, 432.
,, ,, Morphie, *arms*, 432.
,, PATRICK, Earl of STRATHERN, *brisure*, 432.
GRAILLY, DE, *arms*, 418.
,, JOHN DE, Captal de BUCH, *crest*, 606.
,, ,, ,, *label*, 418.
GRAMMONT, DE, 14.
,, HUGH DE, *lions armoyé*, 634.
,, *see* DELMAS, 541.
,, Ducs de, *arms*, 214.
GRANADA, *arms*, Pl. XXX., fig. 10, p. 332.
,, *Capilla de los Reyes*, 633.
GRANATA, *arms*, 339.
Grand Capitulaire of Champagne, 10.
,, *Escuyer*, French, mark of office, 645.
GRAND PRÉ, Comtes de, *arms*, 94.
GRANDE GUERCHE, Marquis of LA, *arms*, 280.
GRANDIN, *arms*, 339.
GRANDISON, *arms*, 428.
,, JOHN DE, Bishop of EXETER, *brisure*, 437.
GRANDORGE, *arms*, 341.
GRANGE, *arms*, 339.
GRANGER, *arms*, 339.
GRANIER, *arms*, 339.

GRANIER DE CASSAGNAC, *arms*, 339.
GRANOLLACHS, *arms*, 279.
Grant of Augmentation, etc., to WILLIAM SPEKE, 750.
GRANT, *arms*, 380; Pl. XXXIII., fig. 5, p. 376.
,, *arms in Lyon Office Register*, 400.
,, *crest*, 610.
,, Dr GREGORY, *arms* transferred to 755.
,, NEIL, transfers *arms*, 755.
,, of Auchernack, 755.
,, ,, Ballindalloch, *arms*, 351.
,, ,, ,, *brisure*, 435.
,, ,, Carron, *brisure*, 435.
,, ,, Rothiemurcus, *bordure*, 569.
GRANTHAM, HENRY, Earl of, 580.
GRANTLEY, Lord, *supporters*, 647.
GRANTMESNIL, *arms*, 121.
Grants of Nobility, 5.
GRANTZ, *arms*, 336.
GRANULLAS, *arms*, 201.
GRANVILLE, *arms*; Pl. XXXIII., fig. 11, p. 376.
,, Earls of BATH, *arms*, 386.
,, Lords of NEATH, 386.
Grapes, Bunch of, as a charge, 391, 339.
Grappin, 733.
GRASSE, *arms*, 212, 752.
Grasshoppers, 284.
GRASSI, *arms*, 470.
GRATET, *arms*, 289.
GRAUL, 409.
GRAVENECK, Counts von, *arms*, 182.
GRAY and HASTINGS Controversy, 415.
,, Comte de, *arms*, 118.
,, HENRY, Earl of TANKERVILLE, *arms*, 556.
,, Lord, *arms*, 174, 435.
,, of Ballengarno, *brisure*, 435.
,, ,, Haystoun, *brisure*, 435.
,, ,, Howick, *arms*, 215.
GREAT BRITAIN, *crests* in, 609.
,, ,, Royal *arms* of, 661.
,, YARMOUTH, *arms*, 467.
Greares, 689.
GREECE, *arms*, 153, 487, 666.
,, GEOPGE, King of, *arms*, 487.
,, OTHO, King of, *arms*, 487.
,, *supporters*, 666.
Greek Cross, 153; Fig. 48, p. 164.
Green or *Vert*, 60, 65.
GREEN, *arms*, 532.
GREENE, *arms*, 232.
GREFEN, *arms*, 752.
GREGORY IX., Pope, *arms*, 256.
,, XII., Pope, *arms*, 293.
,, ST., THE GREAT, 9.
GREIFFENSTEIN, Barons von, *arms*, 289.
GREIFFN, *arms*, 289.
GREILLY, DE, Lords of MANCHESTER, *arms*, 132.
GREINDL, Barons von, *arms*, 341.
Grêlé, 698, 733.
Grêlier, 691, 733.
Grelot, 733.
Grelots as charges, 373, 690, 733.
GRENADA, *arms*, 488, 667 (*see* GRANADA).
,, Kingdom of, *arms*, 339.
Grenades, 733.
,, de Guerre, 733.
GRENDALL, THOMAS, of Fentoun, grants *arms*, 35.

(801)

GRENDALL, THOMAS, transfers *arms*, 755.
GRENÉE, LA, *arms*, 140.
GRENIER, *arms*, 339.
GRENOBLE, SIBOUD ALLEMAN, Bishop of, *arms*, 52.
GRESHAM, *crest*, 285.
GRESLEY, *arms*, 71.
GREY, 17.
,, and HASTINGS Controversy, 320.
,, *badge*, 754.
,, DE, *arms*, 192, 412, 428, 554 ; Pl. IX., fig. 3, p. 108.
,, ,, Lord WALSINGHAM, *arms*, 412.
,, Duke of SUFFOLK, *arms*, 412.
,, Lady JANE, *arms*, 192.
,, JOHAN DE, *arms*, 412.
,, JOHN DE, *arms*, 428.
,, Sir ——, *Le Bastard*, *arms*, 554.
Greyhound as a *badge*, 753.
,, *White*, as a *badge*, 595.
,, ,, as a *crest*, 605.
,, The, 241.
Greyhounds as *supporters*, 636.
GREYS, Earls of STAMFORD, *arms*, 92.
GREYSPACH, *arms*, 93.
GREYSTOCK, *arms*, 183, 474, 641.
,, Baron of, *arms*, 336, 378.
,, ELIZABETH, dtr. of Lord, 585.
,, ,, heiress of, *arms*, 474.
,, JOHN, Baron of, *arms*, 44.
,, RANULPH DE, 378.
,, WILLIAM, Baron of, grants *arms*, 35.
GRIB, *arms*, 287.
GRIBAUVAL, Marquises of, *arms*, 128.
Grices, 683, 689.
Grieces, 689.
GRIENENSTEIN, *arms*, 93.
GRIESENBERG, *arms*, 98.
GRIFFA, *arms*, 288.
GRIFFENSTEIN, *arms*, 289.
Griffin as a *badge*, 753.
,, or *Griffon*, or *Gryphon*, The, 286.
,, *Sea*, 290.
,, ,, as a *supporter*, 640.
,, *Segreant*, Pl. XXVII., fig. 5, p. 288.
GRIFFIN, Monsire de, *arms*, 287.
Griffin's claws, 286.
,, *egg*, 287.
,, *head*, 289 ; Pl. XXVII., fig. 6, p. 288.
GRIFFITH, Princes of CARDIGAN, etc., *arms*, 212.
GRIFFITHS, *arms*, 333.
Griffon, see *Griffin*, 689, 733.
,, as *supporter*, 632, 633.
GRIFFONI, *arms*, 80.
GRIFONI, *arms*, 99.
GRIGNAN, Comte de, *arms*, 132.
,, Comtesse de, 132.
GRIGNON, Marquis de, 12.
GRIGNY, Marquis de, *arms*, 165.
Grillage, 98.
Grilles, 601, 602, 733.
Grilleté, 678, 733.
Grillets, 690, 733.
GRILLO, Marquises d'ESTOUBLON, *arms*, 284.
GRIMALDI, *arms*, Pl. VII., fig. 10, p. 90.

GRIMALDI, Princes of MONACO, *arms*, 100.
GRIMBERGHE, VAN, *arms*, 427.
GRIMMINCK, *arms*, 241.
Grimpant, 701, 733.
GRIMTHORP, *arms*, 641.
GRIMTHORPE, *arms*, 474.
GRINDALL, *arms*, 157.
Gringolé, 689, 733.
,, *cross*, 161, 276.
Gringoly, 689.
GRIONI, *arms*, 285.
GROBBENDONCK, *arms*, 187.
GROENENDYK, *arms*, 338.
GROIN, *arms*, 715.
GROLEE, DE, *arms*, 404.
GROONENDYCK, *arms*, 370.
GROSCHLAG, DIE, *arms*, 412.
GROSVENOR, 129.
,, and SCROPE Case, 341, 439.
,, *arms*, Pl. XXX., fig. 12, p. 332.
,, Dukes of Westminster, *arms*, 342.
GROTE, *Geschichte der Welfischen Stammwappen*, 472.
GROUCHES, Marquises of CHEPY and GRIBAUVAL, *arms*, 128.
GRUBEN, *arms*, 390.
GRUDNA-GRUDZINSKI, DE, *arms* 359.
Grue, 733.
GRUNBERG, *arms*, 752.
Grünenberg Armorial, 639.
GRUTEL, *arms*, 71.
GRYF, *herba* of, *arms*, 289.
GRYNS, *arms*, 201.
Gryphon-mariné, 290.
,, The (see *Griffin*), 286.
Grypishey, 287.
GRZYMALA, Counts, *arms*, 359.
,, *herba* of, *arms*, 359.
GUALTERI, *arms*, 132.
Guardant, 689.
GUASCHI, *arms*, 80.
GUASTALLA, Duchy, 502.
GUASTO, Marquises of, *augmentation*, 541.
GUÉ, DU, Vicomtes de MÉJUSSUAUME, 142.
GUELDERS, Duchy of, *arms*, 99, 491.
,, Dukes of, *arms*, 409, 473.
,, MARY of, *seal*, 476.
"GUELDRE," *Armorials of the Herald*, 402.
GUELDRES, Counts of, *arms*, 409.
,, GERARD IV., Count of, *arms*, 409.
,, RENAUD, Duke of, *arms* 409.
GUELF, 470.
Guelphic *chief*, 119, 538.
GUÉNONVILLE, *see* GUETTEVILLE.
GUESCLIN, BERTRAND DU, 463.
,, ,, ,, *arms*, 254 ; Pl. XLIV., fig. 1, p. 538.
,, ,, ,, *crest*, 606.
,, ,, ,, *supporters*, 633.
GUESPEREAU, *arms*, 284.

GUÉTTEVILLE DE GUENONVILLE, *arms*, 72, 353.
Gueules, 689, 733.
,, *plein*, 66.
GUÉVARA, *arms*, 132.
,, JEAN DE, Comte d'ARIANO, *wreath*, 614.
GUI DE MUNOIS, monk of St. Germain l'Auxerrois, *arms*, 672.
GUIBERT, *arms*, 349.
GUICCIARDINI, *arms*, 386.
GUICHE, Ducs de, *arms*, 214.
,, LA, *arms*, 143.
GUICHENON, *Histoire Généalogique de la Maison de Savoye*, 454, 579.
,, quoted, 629.
Guidon, 655, 689, 733.
GUIENNE, *arms*, 531.
GUILDFORD, JOHN of, 209.
GUILLAND, *arms*, 68.
GUILLAUME, DE, Seigneurs de MONTPELLIER, 10.
,, Duke of SORIA, 450.
,, le Bastard de SAVOIE, *arms*, 579.
GUILLIM, *Display of Heraldry*, 2, 22, 23, 64, 188, 225, 486, 529, 535.
GUILLOU DE LA LARDAIS, *arms*, 113.
GUINANDS, *arms*, 277.
GUINES, Counts and Dukes of, *arms*, 71.
GUIOT DE DOIGNON, Marquesses, *arms*, 265.
,, ,, PONTEIL, Counts, *arms*, 265.
GUIPUSCOA, *arms* of Province, 566.
GUISCARD, 12.
GUITÉ, ROBIN DE, *supporters*, 633.
GUITON, Vicomtes de, *arms*, 388.
GUITTARDI, *arms*, 383.
GUITTON, *arms*, 383.
Guivre, 733.
Guivré, 689.
,, *cross*, 161.
GUIZOT, M., *arms*, 126.
GUJANS, *arms*, 202.
GULDINEN, *lambrequin*, 613.
Gules or Red, 60, 62, 65, 689 ; Pl. III., fig. 3, p. 60.
,, shield, plain, 66.
GULIELMUS GIRAUDI, 10.
,, RAIMUNDI, 10.
Gumène, 733.
GÜNDEL, *augmented crest*, 546.
GUNDRICHING, *arms*, 91.
GUNNING, *arms*, 366.
Gun-stone, 190, 689.
GUNTHER VON SCHWARZBURG, *seal* of the Emperor, 248.
GUNTHERUS, quoted by DUCANGE, 244.
Gurges, 193, 708 ; Pl. XIX., fig. 6, p. 192.
,, or *Gorges*, 689.
GURNEY, *arms*, 142.
GUROWSKI, Counts, *arms* and *augmentation*, 543.
GURWOOD, *arms*, 136.
Gusset or *Gore*, 689.
GUSTAVUS ADOLPHUS, King of SWEDEN, 546, 581.
GUTAKOWSKI, Counts, *arms*, 356.
GUTHRIE of Halkerstoun, *arms*, 216.
GÜTINGEN, *arms*, 325.
Gutté d'eau, Pl. VIII., fig. 12, p. 100.
Guttée or *Gouttée*, 689.

Gutty or *Goutée*, 114, 689.
GUYOT D'ANFREVILLE, *arms*, 344.
Guzes, 190, 689.
GUZMAN, *arms*, 275, 390, 508 ; Pl. XXXIII., fig. 8, p. 376.
,, Counts of TEBA, *arms*, 390.
,, Dukes of MEDINA-SIDONIA, *arms*, 390.
GWENT, Princes of, *arms*, 212.
GWRGANT, JESTYN AP, *arms*, 140.
GWYN, *arms*, 169.
GYLDENHOFF, Barons, 314.
GYLDENLÖVE, Counts of DANESKIOLD-LAURWIGLEN, *arms*, 581.
,, Counts of DANESKIOLD-SAMSOË, *arms*, 581.
GYLLENSKJOLD, 672.
GYLLENSPARRE, 672.
GYLLENSTJERNA, 672.
GYNES, INGELRAM DE, *arms*, 71.
Gyron or *Giron*, 165, 167, 689 ; Fig. 44, p. 116 ; Pl. XVIII., fig. 4, p. 190.
Gyronny of eight, Pl. VI., fig. 1, p. 84.
,, *six*, Pl. VI., fig. 3, p. 84.
,, *twelve*, Pl. VI., fig. 2, p. 84.
,, or *Gironny*, 83, 689.
Gyrons, Pl. XVIII., fig. 5, p. 190.

HAAG, Counts, *arms*, 121, 447.
HAARLEM, stalls in the Cathedral of, 134.
HAAS, *arms*, 238.
Habergeon, 690.
HABERSTOCK, *arms*, 298.
Habillé, 690, 702, 733, 740.
Habited, 690.
Hache Danoise, 733.
HACHE, DE LA, *arms*, 142.
Hachemens, 734.
HACKE, *arms*, Pl. XIX., fig. 7, p. 192.
,, Baron, *arms*, 310.
Hackle, 690.
HADDINGTON, Viscount, *augmentation*, 534, 535.
HADELN, Barons, *arms*, 390.
HADRIAN, *coin of*, 328.
HAEFTEN, Barons von, *arms*, 119.
HAEHNEL, *arms*, 306.
HAERSOLTE, Barons van, *arms*, 140.
HAEZE, LOUIS DE, *arms*, 572.
HAGEN, *arms*, 162.
,, *augmented crest*, 546.
HAGENSTEIN, citadel of, 642.
HAHN, Counts, *arms*, 265.
Haie, 690.
HAIG, *arms*, Pl. IX., fig. 5, p. 108.
,, of Bemersyde, *arms*, 106.
HAINAULT, ALBERT DE BAVIÈRE, Count of, 57.
,, ALICE, Countess of, 468.
,, *arms*, 58, 460, 576.
,, ,, of Queen PHILIPPA of, 247.
,, BALDWIN V., Count of, 460.
,, ,, ,, of, *banner*, 650.
,, Counts of, *arms*, 98.
,, ,, *budge*, 592.
,, early quartered *coats* of, 478.

HAINAULT, FLORENT of, *bend*, 429.
,, ,, *crest*, 600.
,, MARGARET of, *seal*, 463.
,, PHILIPPA, of, 592.
,, Queen PHILIPPA of, *shield* of, 463.
,, *seal* and *arms* of BALDWIN THE BRAVE, Count of, 48.
,, *seal* and *arms* of MARGARET, Countess of, 58.
,, *seal* of FLORENT of, 630.
,, WILLIAM of, *seal*, 460, 465.
HALBERSTADT, Principality of, *arms*, 78.
Halberts, 348, 690.
,, as *supporters*, 643.
HALDERMANSTETEN, VON, *arms*, 88; Pl. VI., fig. 7, p. 84.
HALES, *arms*, 349, 350; Pl. XXXI., fig. 6, p. 346.
HALEWIJN, *arms*, 223.
Halisant, 734.
HALKETT, *arms*, 147.
HALLOFTE, *arms*, 183.
HALLOT, MONTMORENCY DE, *brisure*, 452.
HALPENY, *arms*, 278.
HALS, Counts of, *arms*, 472.
HALYBURTON, Sir GAUTHIER, *lambrequin*, 611.
Ham, 228.
HAM, *arms*, 228.
HAMBROEK, VAN, *arms*, 123.
HAMBURG, *arms*, 283, 361.
HAMELINAYE, Viscounts JAN DE LA, *arms*, 271.
HAMELYN, *arms*, 97.
HAMERE-ROLLAINCOURT, D', *arms*, 393.
Hames, 690.
Hameyde, 734.
HAMILTON, *arms*, 323, 368, 567, 568, 570; Pl. XXX., fig. 1, p. 332.
,, *arms in Lyon Office Register*, 400.
,, Bart., *arms*, 434.
,, Duke of, *mantling armoyé*, 616.
,, fámily, 420.
,, Lord BARGENY, *arms*, 568.
,, Marquess of, 568.
,, of Blair, *arms*, 568.
,, ,, Cairnes, *fess*, 430.
,, ,, Clydesdale, Sir JOHN, 568.
,, ,, Colquot, *arms*, 186.
,, ,, Fynnart, Sir JAMES, *arms*, 567.
,, ,, Neilsland, *arms*, 171.
,, ,, ,, *bordure*, 443.
,, ,, Presmennan, *bordure*, 443.
,, ,, Preston and Fingalton, *arms*, 568.
,, ,, ,, *bordure*, 442.
,, ,, Samuelston, *arms*, 568.
HAMING, *arms*, 374
Hammers as charges, 393.
HAMNER, *arms*, 270.

HANAU, Counts of, *arms*, 139, 169.
Hand, A Blessing, 204.
,, human, 204.
,, sinister, Pl. XX., fig. 7, p. 198.
Handled, 690.
HANE DE STEENHUYSE, Counts d', *arms*, 290.
HANNET, Barons, *arms*, 161.
HANNOVER, *arms*, 618.
,, Elector of, *arms*, 237, 380, 526.
,, House of, *arms*, Pl. LII., figs. 9 and 10, p. 662.
HANNOVERIAN *quartered coat*, 663.
HAPSBURG, *arms*, 247, 471, 496, 508, 634, 664.
,, Counts of, *arms*, 212.
,, County, *arms*, 501.
,, -LORRAINE, House of, 508.
HARCHIES, GERARD D', *supporters*, 635.
HARCOURT, *arms*, 126, 449; Pl. XI., fig. 8, p. 124.
,, JEAN D', eagles *armoyée*, 634.
,, MARIE, dtr. of JAMES, Comte de LONGUEVILLE, 529.
,, RICHARD DE, *arms*, 404.
,, Sir JOHN, *arms*, 404.
HARD, Counts of, *arms*, 509.
HARDBEANE, *arms*, 343.
HARDENBERG, Count, *arms* and *augmentation*, 545.
Hardi, 734.
HARDING, HUGH, Grant of *arms* to, 33, 34.
HARDY, GATHORNE, 751.
Hare, 237; Pl. XXIV., fig. 7, p. 236.
HARELBEKE, *arms*, 137.
HAREWOOD, Earls of, *arms*, 157.
HARFORD, *arms*, 427.
HARGENVILLERS, *arms*, 72.
HARLAND, Sir ROBERT, *arms*, 299.
HARLEIAN MSS., 66, 148, 167, 188, 375, 386, 387, 587, 589, 590, 593, 595, 654, 661.
HARLESTON, *arms*, 128; Pl. XI., fig. 12, p. 124.
HARLEWIN, *arms*, 112.
HARLEY, *arms*, 122; Pl. XII., fig. 10, p. 130.
,, Earl of OXFORD, *arms*, 132.
HAROLD of England, 30.
HAROUÉ, Marquis d', *arms*, 145.
Harp as a *badge*, 596.
HARPE, LA, *arms*, 384.
HARPEN, *arms*, 384.
HARPENY, *arms*, 278.
HARPHAM, *arms*, 384.
Harps as charges, 383.
HARPSFIELD, *arms*, 384.
Harpy, 690.
,, The, 295.
HARRINGTON, *arms*, 181; Pl. XIX., fig. 11, p. 192.
HARRIS, Lord, *arms*, 534.
HARSDORF, Barons, *arms*, 360.
HARSICK, *arms*, 118.
Hart, 690.
,, *White*, as a *badge*, 589.
HARTROTT, *augmented crest*, 546.
Harts, 231.

HARTZHEIM, VON, *arms*, 82 ; Pl. V., fig. 12, p. 80.
Harvest-fly, 690.
HARVEY, *crest*, 563.
HASENBERG, Barons, *arms*, 133.
HASTINGS and GRAY Controversy, 415, 320.
,, *arms*, 376 ; Pl. XXXIII., fig. 1, p. 376.
,, *badge*, 753, 754.
,, Battle of, 30.
,, DE, 16.
,, Earls of HUNTINGDON, *arms*, 376.
,, Earls of PEMBROKE, *arms*, 376.
,, EDMUND of, *label* of, 414.
,, EDWARD, Lord, *standard* of, 586.
,, HENRY DE, *arms*, 376.
,, *label*, 415.
Hat as a crest, 608.
,, *Cardinal's* as a charge, 374.
Hatchets as charges, 394.
Hatchment, 690.
Hatfield Broad Oak, Essex, 308.
HATHERTON, Lord, *supporters*, 647.
Hats as charges, 392.
HATTON, Earl of WINCHELSEA, *arms*, 343.
Hauberk, 690.
HAUCKE, Countess JULIA VON, 525.
HAUDION, Count de WYNEGHEM, *arms*, 183.
HAULTEPENNE, Baron d', *arms*, 331.
Hauriant, 268, 690.
Haut, 686.
Haussé, 120, 132, 685, 690, 734.
HAUSSONVILLE, Comtes de, *arms*, 160.
HAUTEN DE, *arms*, 88.
HAUTIN, *arms*, Pl. VI., fig. 8, p. 84.
HAUTOTS, *arms*, 227.
HAUTPENNE, Barons de, *arms*, 112.
HAVERING, *arms*, 214.
HAVESQUERQUE, *arms*, 505.
HAVET, *see* CHARDON.
Hawk as *supporter*, 633.
HAWKER, *arms*, 262.
Hawk's bells and *jesses*, 690.
,, ,, Pl. XXV., fig. 8, p. 260.
,, *lure*, 690.
HAWLE, *arms*, 80.
HAWLEY, *arms*, 80.
Hay-fork, 690.
HAY, *arms*, 170, 406 ; Pl. XIX., fig. 12, p. 192.
,, *arms in Lyon Office Register*, 400.
,, JOHN, of Tillibothil, *bend*, 430.
,, Marquis of TWEEDDALE, *arms*, Pl. XLII., fig. 2, p. 512.
,, of Boyne, *arms*, 406.
,, ,, Broxmouth, *arms*, 406.
,, ,, Fudie, *chevron*, 431.
,, ,, Leys, *arms*, 406.
,, ,, Naughton, *bordure*, 441.
,, ,, Tillibothil, *bordure*, 441.
,, ,, Yester, 519.
,, ,, ,, Lord, *arms*, 521.
,, Sir JOHN, Earl of KINNOULL, *augmentation*, 535.
,, ,, *label*, 420.
HAYA, EVA, wife of WILLIAM DE, 170.
HAYE, JEAN DE LA, *arms*, 305.

HAYMSBERG, Counts of, *arms*, 405.
HAYNIN, *arms*, 142.
HAZELRIGG, *arms*, 319 ; Pl. XXIX., fig. 7, p. 318.
Head, Human, 199.
,, *Moor's*, 200.
,, *Saracen's*, 199.
,, *Savage's*, 199.
,, *of Æolus*, 201.
,, ,, *Argus*, 201.
,, ,, *Boreas*, 201.
,, ,, *Janus*, 201.
,, ,, *Midas*, 201.
,, ,, *St. Denis*, 201.
,, ,, *St. John the Baptist*, 201.
Heads, 690.
,, *conjoined*, Pl. XX., fig. 5, p. 198.
HEARNE, *arms*, 336.
Heart, Pl. XX., fig. 12, p. 198.
,, as a *badge*, 598.
,, *Human*, 202.
HEATHCOTE, Lord AVELAND, *arms*, 192.
HECKE, VAN DEN, *arms*, 99 ; Pl. VII., fig. 8, p. 90.
HECTOR, *arms*, 21.
Hedge, Pl. XXVIII., fig. 12, p. 308.
Hedge-hog as a *badge*, 753.
,, The, 239.
HEDWIG, *seal*, 468.
HEDWORTH, *arms*, 140.
HEECKEREN, Barons, *arms*, 141.
HEERDT, Counts, *arms*, 130.
HEERNESSE, *see* CLOEPS, 341.
HEIDEGK, *arms*, 265.
Heiligenscheine, 244, 253.
HEIM, VON DER, *arms*, 230.
HEIN, *arms*, 217.
HEINBURG, Barons, *arms*, 128.
HELCK, VAN DER, *arms*, 277.
HELCKNER, *arms*, 669 ; Pl. LV., fig. 11, p. 668.
HELENA, Princess of SCHLESWIG-HOLSTEIN, *label*, 423 ; Fig. 87, p. 421.
HELFENSTEIN, Counts von, *arms*, 230.
HELLEMMES, *arms*, 71.
HELLEN, VAN DER, *arms*, 372.
HELLENES, Kings of, using *escucheon en surtout*, 487.
Helm or *Helmet*, 599 ; Pl. XXXI., fig. 4, p. 346.
,, as a *badge*, 753.
,, in French Armory, 601
,, of Baronets, 602 ; Fig. 95, p. 602.
,, ,, Gentlemen, 601, 602 ; Fig. 96, p. 602.
,, ,, Knights, 602.
,, ,, Nobles, 601.
,, ,, Peers, 602 ; Fig. 94, p. 602.
,, ,, Princes, 601.
,, ,, Sovereign, 601, 602 ; Fig. 93, p. 602.
,, ,, Right of ecclesiastics to use, 604.
,, ,, ,, women to use, 604.
,, ,, timbred, 601.
Helmets, 36, 349.
,, in German Armory, 601.
,, for different ranks, 601, 602 ; Figs. 93–96, p. 602.
Hemp-brake, 690.
HEMPTINES, Barons d', *arms*, 357.
Hen, The, 265.

(805)

HENDERSON, *arms*, Pl. XVI., fig. 5, p. 146; Pl. XXIV., fig. 12, p. 236.
„ of Fordel, *arms*, 148.
HENEAGE, Sir THOMAS, *badge*, 586.
HENEMA, *arms*, 752.
HENLINGTON, *arms*, 188.
HENNEBERG, Counts of, *arms*, 265.
HENNIN, Comte de BOSSU, *arms*, 129.
„ Counts, *arms*, 370.
HENRI I., King of FRANCE, *crown* and *sceptre* of, 328.
„ II., King of FRANCE, 164, 570; *crown*, 620; Death of, 40; *seal* of, 49; *supporters*, 636.
„ III., King of FRANCE, *supporters*, 636.
„ IV., King of FRANCE, 13, 570; *supporters*, 636.
„ V., King of FRANCE, 425.
HENRION, Baron de PANSEY, *arms*, 278.
HENRIQUEZ, *arms*, 507, 578.
„ Dukes of MEDINA DEL RIO SECO, *arms*, 576.
HENRY I., Emperor HOLY ROMAN EMPIRE, *crown*, 621.
„ „ King of ENGLAND, 121, 517, 554.
„ „ *seal* of the Emperor, 328.
„ II., Emperor HOLY ROMAN
„ „ EMPIRE, *crown*, 621.
„ „ King of CASTILE and LEON, 577.
„ „ „ ENGLAND, 40, 44; *arms*, Pl. LI., fig. 1, p. 661.
„ III., Duke of BRABANT, *arms*, 454.
„ „ Emperor, *seal* of, 243.
„ „ King of ENGLAND, 29, 79, 122, 193, 208, 245, 291, 331, 345, 403, 404, 407, 425, 438, 448, 554; *arms*, Pl. LI., fig. 1, p. 661; *Great Seal* of, 587; *Rolls of Arms* of, 170, 407, 408, 426, 427, 448, 458.
„ IV., King of ENGLAND, 171, 415, 464, 556, 589, 593; *arms*, Pl. LI., fig. 4, p. 661; *crown*, 618; Gifts, etc., of *arms* during reign, 35; *seal* of, 330; second *seal* of, 590, 594; *supporters* of, 662.
„ V., King of ENGLAND, 209, 383, 475; *arms*, Pl. LI., fig. 4, p. 661; *badge*, 594; *banner* of, 589; *crown*, 618; *mantling*, 613; proclamation about *arms*, 36; *standard* of, 588; *supporters* of, 662.
„ VI., King of ENGLAND, 5, 325, 334; *arms*, Pl. LI., fig. 4, p. 661; *badge*, 594; *crown*, 618; Gifts, etc., of *arms* during reign, 35; *supporters* of, 662.
„ VII., Emperor, *augmentations* granted by, 536.
„ „ King of ENGLAND, 107, 325, 476, 597; *arms*, Pl. LI., fig. 4, p. 661; *badge* and *standard*, 292, 595; *supporters* of, 662; *tomb*, 479.

HENRY VIII., King of ENGLAND, 285, 376, 384, 420, 529, 530, 531, 558, 594, 654; *arms*, Pl. LI., fig. 4, p. 661; *badge*, 587, 595; *coins* of, 44; *crown*, 618; *Pricy Seal* of, 598; *standard* of, 292, 595; *supporters* of, 662.
„ Cardinal King, 509.
„ Coronation of the Emperor in 1312, 579.
„ DE RIVIÈRE, *arms*, 405.
„ Prince of Wales, 420.
„ THE FOWLER, 41, 42.
HEPBURN, *arms*, 137, 567.
„ PATRICK, Earl of BOTHWELL, *brisure*, 435.
„ „ of BOLTON, *brisure*, 435.
„ „ *seal*, 441.
„ „ *wreath*, 614.
Herald, Duties of, 1.
Herald and Genealogist, 5, 407, 408, 417, 477, 555, 562, 603, 639.
Heraldry, Designations of, used by various authorities, 2.
„ Imperfection of many treatises on, 67.
„ Primary object of, 671.
„ Reviving interest in, 25.
„ Value of, 673.
Heraldry of the Percys, 654.
HERAUT, *arms*, 136.
Herba or *Clan*, in Poland, 289.
HERBERSTEIN, Counts von, *arms*, 136, 488.
HERBERT, *arms*, 561.
„ Earl of PEMBROKE, etc., *arms*, 224.
„ of Cardiff, Baron, *arms*, 561.
„ or SHEFFIELD, CHARLES, *arms*, 562.
„ Sir RICHARD, 561.
„ WILLIAM, Earl of PEMBROKE, *arms*, 561.
HERBESTEIN, Counts of, *arms*, 136.
HERCULES as *supporter*, 636.
„ in Heraldry, 197.
„ Pillars of, as *supporters*, 643.
HERDA, *arms*, 133, 737.
HEREFORD, ADAM, d', *shield*, 46; Pl. II., fig. 2, p. 44.
„ *badge* of Earls of, 631.
„ HENRY, Earl of, *seal*, Pl. XXXV., fig. 4, p. 416.
„ PUREFOY, Bishop of, *arms*, 206.
„ RICHARD, Earl of, 467.
„ See of, *arms*, 333; Pl. XXII., fig. 11, p. 222.
„ THOMAS DE CANTELUPE, Bishop of, 225.
„ Viscount, *supporter*, 232.
HERGOTT, *Monumenta Austriæ*, 243.
HERINGAUD, *arms*, 268.
HÉRIPONT, *arms*, 129.
Hérissé, 692, 734.
HÉRISSE, LE, *arms*, 239.
Hérisson, 707.
HÉRISSON, *arms*, 239.
Hérissonné, 734.
HERKLOTS, *arms*, 197.
Hermine, Contre, 63, 68.

Hermine, d', 68.
Herminé, Croix d', 734.
HERODOTUS, Tale of POLYCRATES related by, 271.
Heron, The, 263.
HERON, *arms*, 263.
HERONDON, *arms*, 263.
HERRENBERG, *arms* of Counts of, 373.
HERRERA, *arms*, 390.
HERRIES, *arms*, 239; Pl. XXIV., fig. 10, p. 236.
,, of Cowsland, Sir HUGH, *augmentation*, 534, 535.
Herring, The, 268.
Herrison, Pl. XXIV., fig. 10, p. 236.
HERSCHEL, Sir JOHN, *arms*, 310.
Hersé, 734.
Herse as a charge, 365.
,, *sarasine*, 365, 700, 734.
HERSTRATEN, *arms*, 82.
HERTENSTEIN, Counts von, *arms*, 66.
HERTFORD, Marquess of, 564.
HERTZBERG, *see* DORNBERG, *arms*, 78.
HERVEY, *arms*, Pl. XXIX., fig. 10, p. 318.
,, JOHN, *arms*, 320.
,, Marquess of BRISTOL, *arms*, 320.
HERVILLY DE MALAPERT, *arms*, 112.
HERWEGH, *arms*, 134.
HERZEELE, Marquis of FAULQUEZ, *arms*, 136.
,, Marquis of NETTANCOURT, *arms*, 136.
HESDIGNUEL, *see* BÉTHUNES.
HESHUYSENS, *arms*, 201; Pl. XX., fig. 11, p. 198.
HESME, *arms*, 152.
HESSE, ALICE, Grand Duchess of, *label*, 423.
,, -DARMSTADT, Prince ALEXANDER of, 525.
,, ,, *supporters*, 666.
,, Grand Dukes of, *arms*, 219, 487, 525, 580.
,, Marks of illegitimacy in, 580.
HEUSCH, DE, *arms*, 350.
HEUVEL, VAN DEN, *arms*, 145.
HEVTLER, *arms*, Pl. XLV., fig. 2, p. 540.
HEYERLING ZU WINKHL, 670; Pl. LVI., fig. 11, p. 670.
HEYLBROUCK, VAN, *arms*, 138.
HEYLYN, *Help to English History*, 421, 558.
HEYTESBURY, *sickle* and *arms*, 641.
HEYTON, *arms*, 155.
Hibou, 697.
HICKMAN, *arms*, Pl. V., fig. 2, p. 80.
,, Earls of PLYMOUTH, *arms*, 79.
HICKS, *arms*, 360.
Hie, 734.
Highland *badges*, 598.
,, chiefs, *arms*, 314.
HILDEBRAND, HANS, *Det Svenska Riks Vapnet*, 52, 379, 388, 487, 628.
HILDEBRANDT, *Heraldisches Musterbuch*, 344, 711; Pl. XLIX., p. 606.
HILDESHEIM, Principality of, *arms*, 78.
HILINGER, *arms*, 321; Pl. XXIX., fig. 11, p. 318.

Hill, 689; Pl. XXVIII., fig. 9, p. 308.
HILL, *arms*, 306.
Hillock, 690.
Hilted, 690.
HILTON, *arms*, 336.
,, of Hilton, *supporters*, 638.
HILTPRANDT, *arms*, 752.
HIMMELBERG, Barons of, *arms*, 469.
Hind, 690.
,, *arms* on white, 632.
HINDER, DIE, *arms*, 271.
Hinds, 231.
HINSBERG, *arms*, Pl. XXVIII., fig. 9, p. 308.
Hirondelle, 266.
HIRSCHBERG, Barons von, *arms*, 232.
HIRSCHMANN, *arms*, 232.
Historical MSS. Commission, Report of, 287.
HITCHCOCK, *arms*, 277.
HITROF, *arms*, 346.
HJORTSHORN, 672.
HOBART, *arms*, Pl. XVIII., fig. 6, p. 190.
,, Earl of BUCKINGHAMSHIRE, *arms*, 185, 259.
HOBILLIONS, *arms*, 319.
HOCHART, *arms*, 226.
HOCHBURG, Barons, *augmentation*, 540.
HOCHENEGG, Counts VON, *arms*, 640.
HOCHREUTERS, *arms*, 298.
HODENPYL, *arms*, 576.
HOEDE, *arms*, 336.
HOEGHOLM, Barons of, *arms*, 304.
HOEGKS, Barons of HOEGHOLM, *arms*, 304.
HOENS, Barons, *arms*, 188.
HOEPING, 479.
HOETIMA, *arms*, 113.
HOFREITER DE DACHAU, *arms*, 192.
HOHENECK, Lordship of, *arms*, 490.
HOHEN-EMBS, County, *arms*, 499.
,, -GEROLDSECK, County of, *arms*, 489.
HOHENHAUSER, *arms*, 217.
HOHENSTEIN, Countess of, 524.
HOHENWALDECK VON MAXELREIN, Counts of, *arms*, 511.
HOHENZOLLERN, *arms*, 81, 254, 380, 494, 660, 667.
,, *escucheon* of, 544, 545.
,, FREDERICK of, BURG-GRAVE of NÜRNBERG, 255.
HOHNSTEIN, *arms*, 489.
,, *see* THUN.
HOLAND, Earls of KENT, etc., *arms*, 216. (*See* HOLLAND.)
HOLBEACH, *arms*, 136.
HOLBERG, *arms*, 295.
HOLLAND, ALBERT DE BAVIÈRE, Count of, 57.
,, ALICE, sister of WILLIAM of, *seal*, 468: Pl. XXXVII., fig. 6, p. 448.
,, *arms*, 58, 101, 212, 215, 216, 247, 251, 463, 576; Pl. VIII., fig. 2, p. 100.
,, Bavarian Counts of, *arms*, 576.
,, Countess of, *seal*, 462, 463.
,, Duke of, 589.
,, *ensign* of Counts of, 208.
,, family, 421.

HOLLAND, FLORENT. Count of, *arms* on Eagle, 630.
,, JOAN, dtr. of THOMAS, *arms*, 485.
,, JOHN, Duke of EXETER, *arms*, 439, 474.
,, *Lion* of, 245.
,, Marks of office in, 645.
,, mode of differencing, 405.
,, *seal* and *arms* of MARGARET, Countess of, 58.
,, *secretum* of FLORENT V., Count of, 245.
,, ,, MARGARET, Countess of, 247.
,, Sir THOMAS, 438.
,, THOMAS, Earl of KENT, *arms*, 438, 439, 632.
,, ,, Earl of KENT, *badge*, 589.
,, ,, Earl of KENT, *seal*, 475.
,, WILLIAM III., Count of, 245; *arms* on Eagle, 630.
HOLLANDS, Dukes of SURREY and KENT, *augmentation*, 528.
HOLLIS, Earl of CLARE, *arms*, 146, 147.
HOLLOFTE, *arms*, 183.
HOLME, 561.
,, RANDLE, 191.
HOLNSTEIN AUS BAYERN, Counts of, *arms*, 580.
HOLSTEIN, *arms*, 510, 666.
,, *see* STAEL.
HÖLTSLER, *arms*, 374.
HOLY ROMAN EMPIRE, *arms* of the Arch-Marshalship of the, 346.
,, ,, ,, *crown* of Electors of, 621, 623.
,, ,, ,, *eagle* of, 242.
,, ,, ,, *Ensign* of Arch-Chamberlain of the, 380.
,, ,, ,, Lay Electors of, *arms*, 526.
HOLYROOD HOUSE, *altarpiece at*, 334; *seal* of ABBEY of, 233.
HOMBURG, Lordship of, *arms*, 358.
HOME, 1st Earl of, *seal*, 523.
,, ,, Lord, *arms*, 522.
,, 2nd Lord, 522.
,, *arms*, 214, 265, 522.
,, Earls of, *arms*, 175; Pl. XLII., fig. 6, p. 512.
,, HUGH, 522.
,, PATRICK, Archdeacon of TEVIOTDALE, *seal*, 522.
HOMER, *Odyssey*, 300.
Homme-marin, 734.
HONDT, DE, *arms*, 241.
Honi soit qui mal y pense, 664.
HONORIUS, Pope, 245.
HÖNN, *Des Hauses Sachsen Wappens und Geschlechts Untersuchung*, 456.
Honneur, Point d', 734.
HOO, Lords, *arms*, 81.
,, ,, *supporters*, 295.
,, Viscount, *supporters*, 302.
Hooded, 691.
Hoofed, 691.
HOOGSTRATEN, *see* BORLUUT.

HOOGVOORST, Barons d', *arms*, 393 477.
HOOLA, *arms*, 183.
HOOP, Barons van der, *arms*, 370.
Hooped, 691.
HOPE, *arms*, 191.
,, *crest*, 610.
,, Early Stall Plates, 63, 602.
,, *Emblem* of, 370.
,, family, 436.
HOPETOUN, Earl of, *brisure*, 436.
HOPING, *De Jure Insignium*, 548.
HÔPITAL DE VITRY, Marquises de l', *arms*, 265.
HORACE, *de Arte Poetica*, 300.
HORBLER, *arms*, 721.
HORBURY, Sir JOHN, *arms*, 128.
HORENBERG, *arms*, 385.
Horn, Hunting, 691.
,, *of a stag*, 691.
HORN, Count of, 99.
,, Princes of, *arms*, 386.
HORNBERG, *see* HORNECK.
HORNECK DE HORNBERG, Barons, *arms*, 385.
Horned, 691.
Horns as a *badge*, 753.
,, as charges, 384.
,, *Buffalo*, as *crests*, 606.
,, *Ox*, as *crests*, 606, 607.
HORNUNG, *arms*, 336.
Horse, 237; Pl. XXIV., fig. 6, p. 236.
,, as a *badge*, 754.
,, *-collar* as a *badge*, 754.
,, *-shoe* as a *badge*, 754.
,, The *Sea-*, 299.
Horseman, Pl. XX., fig. 3, p. 198.
HORSEMAN, *arms*, 353.
Horse's head as a *crest*, 605.
Horseshoe, 355.
HORTENSE, Queen, 572.
HOSPITALLERS OF ST. JOHN, *arms*, 454.
HOTMAN, *arms*, 148, 728.
HOUARÉE, *see* BRIS.
HOUBLONS, *arms*, 319.
HOUCHIN, Marquis de LONGASTRE, *arms*, 183.
HOUDETOT, Marquises de, *arms*, 227.
HOUGHTON, *arms*, 127.
Household, Great Master of the, Scotland, mark of office, 644.
Houses, 363.
Houssé, 679, 734.
HOUTHEM, Barons van, *arms*, 69.
HOUVEN, Baron von der, *arms*, 382.
HOVEN, VAN DER, *arms*, 356.
HOWARD, *arms*, 532; Pl. XVII., fig. 11, p. 172.
,, *badge*, 754.
,, Duke of NORFOLK, *arms*, 408.
,, ELIZABETH. *arms*, 531.
,, Lady CATHARINE, *arms* and *augmentation*, 532.
,, MARY, dtr. of THOMAS, Duke of NORFOLK, 558.
,, THOMAS, Duke of NORFOLK, *augmentation*, 529.
HOWTH, Earl of, *supporter*, 302.
,, Earls of, *crest* and *supporter*, 300.
HOZIER, 14.
,, *arms*, 690.
,, D', *coats* granted by, 582.
HRZISTIC, *see* SKRBENSKY.

(808)

HUBERMONT, MONTMORENCY D', *brisure*, 452.
HUCHARS, *arms*, 404.
Huchet, 691, 734.
HUCHTENBROEK, VAN, *arms*, 145.
HUEBER, *Austria Illustrata*, 456, 471, 472, 479, 600, 606, 611, 612, 614, 634, 650, 651.
HUGHES, *arms*, 213.
Huit-foil, 691.
HULLES, *arms*, 146.
HULSE, *arms*, 147 ; Pl. XVI., fig. 7, p. 146.
HÜLSEN, *arms*, 730.
HULST, *monument of*, 626.
,, VAN, *arms*, 320.
,, VAN DER, *arms*, 319.
Human arm, The, 204.
,, *body*, Parts of, in Heraldry, 199.
,, *eye*, The, 201.
,, *feet*, 206, 207.
,, *figure* as a *crest*, 637.
,, ,, The, 194.
,, *hand*, The, 204.
,, *head*, 199.
,, ,, with ass's ears as a *crest*, 635.
,, *heart*, 202.
,, *legs*, 206.
,, *rib bones*, 206.
HUMBEKE, Counts de, *arms*, 265.
HUMBERT I., 632.
,, III., Dauphin de VIENNOIS, 209.
HUME, *arms*, 214, 265, 405.
,, of Polworth, Sir PATRICK, *arms*, 523.
HUMIÈRES, *arms*, 96, 129.
,, Marquis d', *arms*, 81.
HUMMELS, *arms*, 283.
Hummetty, 123, 691.
HUND VON SALHEIM, *arms*, 411.
HUNDESCOTE, *arms*, 170.
HUNDT, Barons, *arms*, 241.
HUNGARY-ANCIENT, 471, 494, 498, 665.
,, CHARLES IV., King of, 252.
,, *crown* of, 621.
,, -MODERN, *arms*, 494, 498, 540, 665.
,, Queen of, *achievement*, 494.
HUNGERFORD, *badge*, 585, 754.
,, Lord, 585.
,, Sir ROBERT, *seal* of, 585.
,, WALTER, Lord, *seal* and *arms*, 641.
HUNNENWEILER, *arms*, 134.
HUNSDON, *badge*, 754.
HUNTER, *arms*, Pl. XXXIII., fig. 10, p. 376.
,, of Hunterston, *arms*, 385.
HUNTERCOMBE, *arms*, 128 ; Pl. XI., fig. 11, p. 124.
Huntingdon, Visitation of, 363, 613, 755.
HUNTINGDON, *arms*, 460.
,, DAVID, Earl of, *arms*, 147.
,, Earldom of, *arms*, 517.
,, Earls of, *arms*, 376.
,, MARGARET, dtr. of DAVID, Earl of, 460.
,, MAUD, widow of SIMON, Earl of, 517.
,, Prince DAVID, Earl of, 517.

Hunting-horn, Pl. XXXIII., fig. 10, p. 376.
,, as a charge, 384.
HUNTLY, Earl of, 419.
,, Marquess of, 180.
Hure, 227, 272, 734.
HURLESTON, *arms*, 709.
Hurst, 316, 691.
HURSTHELVE, WILLIAM DE, *arms*, 394.
Hurt, 190, 691.
HURTLE, *arms*, 191.
HURUS, *arms*, 267.
HUSSEY, *arms*, 93, 142, 392, 641.
Hyacinth, 338.
HYDE, *arms*, Pl. XVIII., fig. 7, p. 190.
,, Earl of CLARENDON, *arms*, 183.
Hydra, The, 296, 691.

IAN VOR, Chief of Clan, 512.
IBANEZ DE SEGOVIA, *arms*, 141.
IBERIA, *arms*, 665.
Ibex, 691.
ICELAND, *arms*, 271, 666 ; Pl. XXVI., fig. 11, p. 266.
ICHINGHAM, *arms*, 96.
Icicles, 691.
IDDESLEIGH, Earl of, *arms*, 108.
IFIELD, *arms*, 341.
IGELSTRÖM, *arms*, 279.
ILCHESTER, Earl of, *supporters*, 648.
ILE ADAM, le Sire de L', 11.
Illegitimacy, Pl. XLVII., p. 574 ; Pl. XLVIII., p. 576.
,, Heraldic marks of, 548.
,, in Bavaria, marks of, 579.
,, ,, Burgundy, marks of, 573.
,, ,, England, marks of, 564.
,, ,, Flanders, marks of, 572.
,, ,, France, marks of, 570.
,, ,, Germany, marks of, 580.
,, ,, Holland, marks of, 576.
,, ,, Ireland, marks of, 569.
,, ,, Portugal, marks of, 577.
,, ,, Savoy, marks of, 579.
,, ,, Scandinavia, marks of, 581.
,, ,, Scotland, marks of, 569.
,, ,, Spain, marks of, 576.
ILLYRIA, Kingdom, *arms*, 503, 665.
Imbrued, 691.
Immortalité, 734.
Impaled, 691.
Impalement, 459, 470.
,, of *quartered shields*, 462.
Imperial crown, 691.
In Lure, 691.
In Pride, 691.
In Splendour, 691.
Inanimate charges, 305.
,, objects in place of *supporters*, 643.
INAYS, *seal* of WILLIAM DE, 50.
Incensed, 691.
INCHIQUIN, Lord of, 467.
Increscent, 691.
,, *Decrescent*, Pl. XXVIII., fig. 3, p. 308.
Indented, 691.
,, *line*, 76 ; Fig. 19, p. 75.
INDIA, *arms*, 494.
INDIES, Kingdom, The, *arms*, 501.
Indorsed, 691.

(809)

Industrial Implements as charges, 393.
Inescucheon, The, 116, 165, 169, 692.
INFANTADGO, Duke of, 440.
,, ,, arms, 395, 506.
Inflamed or Lighted, 692, 693.
Infulæ, 705.
INGELBY, JOHN, arms, 563.
,, of Ripley, Sir JOHN, arms, 563.
INGENHEIM, Counts of, augmentation, 543.
INGHAM, arms, 157.
INGLEBY, arms, 309; Pl. XXVIII., fig. 6, p. 308.
INGLETHORPE, arms, 142.
Ink-moline, 692.
INNES, arms, 50.
,, Ane Account of the Familie of, 50.
,, WILLIAM DE, badge, 583.
INNOCENT II., Pope, 40.
,, III., ,, 40.
,, ,, ,, arms, 256.
,, IX., ,, arms, 318.
,, XII., ,, 381.
Insects, 280.
Insignia gentilitia, Possession of, legal test of gentility, 673.
Interlaced, 692.
Invecked, 692.
,, line, 76 ; Fig. 20, p. 75.
Invected or Invecked, 692.
INVERNESS-SHIRE Names, 400.
Inverted, 692.
IRELAND, arms, 383, 479, 662, 663.
,, ,, during commonwealth, 487.
,, badge, 596, 597.
,, Dimidiation in, 467.
,, Duke of, arms, 383.
,, ,, augmentation, 528.
,, supporters in, 647.
IRIARTE, arms, 353.
Iris, The, 333.
Irish marks of illegitimacy, 569.
IRON CROSS, The, 544.
IRON CROWN OF LOMBARDY, 617.
Irradiated, 692.
IRRIBERI, arms, 171.
IRVINE, arms, 319.
,, of Drum, arms, 319.
ISABEL of France, 538.
ISABELLE, heiress of RENTY, 449.
ISENBURG, Lordship of, arms, 126.
ISHAM, arms, 148 ; Pl. XVI., fig. 4, p. 146.
ISLE, ADAM, see VILLIERS.
,, JOURDAIN, L', arms, 161.
ISLES, ALEXANDER, Lord of the, seal of, 367.
,, ANGUS OF THE, seal of, 367.
,, JOHN, son of JOHN, Lord of the, 512.
,, Lords of the, 368.
,, ,, ,, arms, 178.
,, ,, ,, (Glengarry branch). arms, 512.
,, Lordship of, arms, 367.
,, seal of JOHN, Lord of the, 367.
ISNARD, arms, 337.
Isolé, 734.
Issant, 692, 734.
ISSOUDUN, Town of, arms, 150.
Issuant, 221, 692, 734 ; Pl. XXII., fig. 3, p. 222; Pl. XXII., fig. 4, p. 222.

Issuing or Issuant, 692.
ISTRIA, Marquessate, arms, 503.
ITALISKY, see SUWAROFF.
ITALY, arms, 666.
,, coronet of a Baron in, 625.
,, crests in, 604.
,, de in, 16.
,, Form of shield in, 56.
,, Furs common in Armory of, 74.
,, Introduction of Hereditary Arms into, 52.
,, Marks of office in, 645.
,, Marshalling in, 508.
,, Use of supporters in, 636, 639.
IVAN AP CADIFOR VAWR, arms, 288.
,, BASILOVITZ of MOSCOW, arms of Grand Duke, 250.
IVANOVICH, OSSIP, arms, 542.

JABLONOWSKI, Counts, arms, 359.
Jacinth, 65.
JACQUEMINOT, Counts, arms, 338.
JAGENSDORFF, arms, 379.
JAGERNDORFF, Duchy of, arms, 491.
JAGOU, arms, 280.
JAMES I., King of ARRAGON, 577.
,, ,, ,, BRITAIN, 384, 532, 535, 594 ; arms, Pl. LI., fig. 5, p. 661 ; Great Seal of, 664 ; motto of, 664 ; supporters on Seal of Common Pleas of, 663.
,, ,, King of SCOTLAND, 233, 475, 521 ; supporters, 635.
,, II., King of BRITAIN, 421, 559, 566 ; arms, Pl. LI., fig. 5, p. 661 ; Exchequer Seal of, 662 ; supporters on Privy Seal of, 663.
,, ,, King of SCOTLAND, 446, 476, 515, 516.
,, III., King of SCOTLAND, 179, 476, 522, 632 ; badge, 596 ; coins, coverlet, and portrait of, 334.
,, IV., King of SCOTLAND, 522, 567 ; badge, 597.
,, V., King of SCOTLAND, 179, 180, 335, 476, 567 ; supporters, 635.
,, VI., King of SCOTLAND, 180, 431, 534, 662 ; arms, Pl. LI., fig. 5, p. 661.
JAMIESON, arms, 371.
JANER, arms, 201.
JANINA, herba of, arms, 351.
JANISZEWSKI, arms, 357.
JANSDAM, arms, 183.
Janus, Head of, 201.
,, Tête de, 734.
JARDINE, arms, 144, 145.
,, DE LA, arms, 71.
,, GEORGE, brisure, 436.
JARSDORFF, arms, 74.
JASTREZEMBIEC, arms, 356.
JATSKOW, arms, 226.
Jaw bone, The, 203.
JAWORSKI, arms, 391.
Je maintiendrai, 664, 667.
JEAN II., King of FRANCE, 571.
,, DE, 10.
,, ,, SCHOONHOVEN, arms, 405.
,, Sans-Peur, Duc de BOURGOGNE, 57.

(810)

JEANNE D'ARC, *arms* of brothers of, 710.
,, Dame de PLASNES, *arms*, 57.
JEDBURGH, Forest of, 642.
,, Lords of, *arms*, 305.
JELITA, *arms*, 347.
Jelloped, 265, 692.
JENYN'S Collection, 375.
JERMYN, Earl of ST. ALBANS, *arms*, 307.
JERNINGHAM, *arms*, 377; Pl. XXXIII.; fig. 3, p. 376.
JERUSALEM, *arms*, 467, 471, 494; Pl. IX., fig. 1, p. 108.
,, *cross of*, 156.
,, First Christian King of, 243.
,, Kingdom, *arms*, 103, 501.
,, Order of ST. JOHN, *arms*, 119, 141, 527.
,, RÉNÉ, Roi de, Tourney regulations, 749.
Jessant, 692.
,, *de lis*, 225, 692; Pl. XXII., fig. 11, p. 222.
Jessed, applied to Falcon, 261, 692.
JESSEL, *arms*, 701.
JESSES, 692.
JESTYN AP GWRGANT, *arms*, 140.
JEZ, *arms*, 239.
JEZIERSKI, Counts, *arms*, 351.
JOAŌ I., King of PORTUGAL, 577.
JOERG, *arms*, 195.
JOGHEMS, *arms*, 348.
JOHN II., King of PORTUGAL, 578.
,, King of BOHEMIA, *badge* and *crest*, 592; Pl. XLIX., fig. 4, p. 606; *seal*, 456.
,, King of ENGLAND, 173, 303, 554, 555; *arms*, 32; Pl. LI., fig. 1, p. 661; *seal*, 37.
,, King of FRANCE, Capture of, 377; *supporters*, 636.
,, Lord of the ISLES, etc., *seal* of, 367.
,, *seal* of, Prince of ENGLAND, 210.
JOHNSON, Origin of name, 10.
JOHNSTON, *arms*, 144, 145, 378, 570.
,, *crest*, 605.
JOHNSTONES in south Scotland, 400.
JOINVILLE, *arms*, 47.
,, Seigneurs de BROYES, *arms*, 357.
JONES, *arms*, 348.
JONG, DE, *arms*, 322.
Jonkheers, *coronet* of, 626.
JÖRGER, *arms*, 195.
JOSEPH, *arms* ascribed to, 23.
JOSEPHINE, Empress of the French, 266, 283.
JOSUA, Duke, *arms* (?), 21.
JOURDAIN, L'ISLE, *arms*, 161.
JOUSSEAUME, Marquis de la BRETESCHE, *arms*, 155.
JOVE, *arms*, 395.
JOVIO, *augmentation*, 536.
JOWETT, *arms*, 369.
Jowlopped, 265, 692.
JOYEUSE, Comtes de, *arms*, 296.
JUDAS MACHABEUS, *arms* (?), 21.
JULBACH, Counts VON, *arms*, 78.
JULIERS, *arms*, 496.
,, County of, *arms*, 99, 473.
,, Duchy of, *arms*, 212.
JULIUS CÆSAR, *arms* (?), 21.

Jumelles, 128, 677, 688, 734.
JUNGINGENS, *arms*, 392.
Jupiter, 65, 692.
Jus expectationis, 483.
JUSTICE GENERAL, SCOTLAND, mark of office, 644.
,, LORD CHIEF, *collar*, 598.
JUTPHAAS, VAN, *arms*, 143.
JUYÀ, *arms*, 91.

KABARDA, *arms*, 665.
KAISER, *arms*, 380.
KALF, *arms*, 296.
KALFF, *arms*, 235.
KALITSCH, Barons von, *arms*, 228.
KAMAROWSKI, Counts, *arms*, 342.
KARA HISAR, Fort of, 250.
KARTALINIA, *arms*, 665.
KATCHENEVSKI, *arms*, 343.
KATZENELBOGEN, *arms*, 580.
KAUFBEVERN, *arms*, 469.
KAUFFUNGEN, *arms*, 670; Pl. LVI., fig. 10, p. 670.
KAUNITZ, Princes von, *arms*, 321.
KAZAN, *arms*, 665.
,, *crown*, 622.
KEATE, *arms*, 226.
KEATS, *arms*, 226.
KECK, *arms*, 133.
KEITH, *arms*, 179; Pl. X., fig. 10, p. 118.
,, Earls MARISCHAL, *arms*, 122.
,, EDWARD, *bend*, 430.
,, JOHN, second son of Sir EDWARD, *bend*, 430.
KEKITMORE, *arms*, 394.
KELDON, *arms*, 150.
KELK, *arms*, 133.
KELLIE, Earl of, *augmentation*, 534, 535.
KELVERDON, *arms*, 150.
KEMELS, *arms*, 231.
KEMP, *arms*, 183, 206.
KENDAL, Earl of, *label*, 418.
KENDENICH, *arms*, 139.
KENNEDY, *arms*, 178.
,, Earls of CASSILIS, etc., *arms*, 163.
KENNETH III., King of Scotland, 197.
KENSINGTON, Lord, *supporter*, 232.
KENT, Dukes of, *augmentation*, 528.
,, Earl of, *arms*, 216, 438, 439, 632.
,, ,, *badge*, 589, 753.
,, ,, *seal*, 475.
,, EDWARD, Duke of, *label*, 422; Fig. 82, p. 421.
,, Fair Maid of, 438, 589.
,, JOAN, daughter of THOMAS HOLLAND, Earl of, *arms*, 485.
KENTIGERN, 271.
KENTISH *Roll of Arms*, 554.
KENTY, *arms*, 297.
KEPPEL, Earl of ALBEMARLE, *arms*, 273.
KER, *crest*, 610.
,, Lords of JEDBURGH, *arms*, 305.
KÉRANGUEN, *arms*, 219.
KERBESCAT, *arms*, 219.
KERBOURIOU, *arms*, 218.
KERCKEM, *arms*, 112.
,, Baron de WYER, *arms*, 331.
KERFORD, *arms*, 280.
KERGROAS, *arms*, 155.
KERJAN, Marquises de, *arms*, 126.
KERLECH, *arms*, 93.

(811)

KERLEORET, see VIEUXCHÂTEL.
KEROULLÉ, arms, 341.
KERS in south Scotland, 400.
KERSBEKE, DE, arms, 187.
KESSELSTADT, Counts of, arms, 493.
KESTEVEN, Duke of, arms, 352.
KETELHODT, Baron, arms, 349.
KETHEL, arms, 121.
KETTENHEIM, VON, arms, 120.
KETTLER, Duke of COURLAND, arms, 390.
Key as a badge, 584.
,, ,, crest, 605.
Keys, Pl. XXXIII., fig. 6, p. 376.
KEYS, ROGER and THOMAS, Grant of Nobility to, 5.
KEYSER, arms, 380.
KFELLER DE SACHSENGRÜN, Barons, arms, 150.
KIES, arms, 203.
KIEV, arms, 665.
KIJOW, Palatinate of, arms, 468.
KILDARE, Earls of, arms, 143.
KILGOUR, arms, 173.
KILLINGWORTH, arms, 364.
KILPEC, arms, 345; Pl. XXXI., fig. 1, p. 346.
KILSYTH, Viscount, arms, 337.
King (Chess) as a charge, 388.
KINGDOM, arms, 352.
Kings of Arms, arms, 525, 526.
King's standard, Length of, 654.
KINGSALE, Barons of, arms, 258.
,, ,, supporters, 297.
KINGSCOTE, arms, 166; Pl. XVIII., fig. 2, p. 190.
KINGSLEY, arms, 385.
KINNAIRD, Estate of, 258.
KINNOULL, Earl of, augmentation, 535.
KINSBERGEN, monument of, 626.
KIOVIA, Palatinate of, arms, 468.
KIP, arms, 266.
KIPPENHEIM, arms, 271.
KIRCHNER, arms, 363.
KIRKE, arms, 182.
KIRKPATRICK, arms, 144.
KIRMREITTER, arms, Pl. LV., fig. 9, p. 668.
KIRTON, arms, 138.
KITTLITZ, Barons von, arms, 477.
Klee-Stengeln, The, 344, 491.
KLETTENBERG, arms, 489.
KLINGSPOR, Baltisches Wappenbuch, 267, 297, 392.
KLÖCKEL, arms, 374.
KNATCHBULL, arms, 132, Pl. XII., fig. 9, p. 130.
Knight as a supporter, 640.
,, Banneret, Creating of a, 651.
,, ,, Duties of a, 652.
Knight (Chess) as a charge, 388.
KNIGHT, arms, 170, 171.
Knights, helm of, 602.
,, Hereditary, coronet of, 626.
,, under feudal system, 652.
KNIGHTS HOSPITALLERS, arms, 141.
KNIPSCHILD, de Fidei Commissis, 483.
,, de Nobilitate ejusque Juribus, 483.
KNOB, arms, 296.
KNOBEL, DIE, arms, 411.
KNOLLYS, Earls of BANBURY, arms, 160.

KNOLLYS, Lord, helm, 602.
Knots as badges, 585.
KNOTSHULL, arms, 701.
Knotted, 692.
KNOWLES, arms, 160; Pl. XV., fig. 3, p. 144.
KNOX, Earl of RANFURLAY, arms, 175.
KOEHNE, Notice sur les Sceaux et Armoiries de la Russie, 251.
KOHARY, Princes of, arms, 218.
KOMMISSAROV-KOSTROMSKY, arms, 542.
KOMOROWSKI, Counts, arms, 234.
KONARSKI, Counts, arms, 289.
KÖNIG, arms, 380.
,, Barons, arms, 380.
,, von, arms, 260.
KÖNIGSTEIN, Lords of, arms, 212.
KONINCK, arms, 379.
KONING, arms, 388.
KORAB, arms, 371.
Koran, reference to, 271.
KORBLER, arms, 96.
KORESSIOS, arms, 251.
KORNKOOPERS, arms, 318.
KOSKÜLL, Barons, arms, 321.
KRAIN, Duchy, arms, 503.
KRANZ, arms, 336.
Kränzlein, 131.
KRAUTERS, arms, 298.
KRECHWITZ, arms, 271.
KREYTSEN, Counts, arms, 120.
KROCHER, arms, 231.
KROGEDANTZ, arms, 752.
KRZYWDA, arms, 356.
KUGLER, arms, 304.
KULENTHAL, see TRUCHSESS.
KUMPSTHOFF, arms, 343.
KÜNIGL, arms, Pl. V., fig. 7, p. 80.
,, Counts von, arms, 81.
KUNWALD, see WRAZDA.
KYLE, arms, 372.
KYNASTON, arms, 136.
KYNDER, arms, 364.
KYRKE, arms, 182.

LA CROIX et SERÉ, Histoire de l'Orfévrerie-joaillerie, 282.
LABARTE, Handbook of the Arts of the Middle Ages, 243.
Label, 117, 165, 187, 414, 687, 692, 734; Figs. 80–89, p. 421.
,, a Royal mark of cadency, 420.
,, Difference by the addition of a, 413.
,, for eldest son, 444.
,, Varieties of, 189.
Lacs d'amour, 628, 645.
LADBROOKE, arms, 136.
Ladder, Pl. XXXII., fig. 9, p. 358.
,, -scaling, 692.
Ladders, 364.
LADISLAS VI., seal, 468.
LAHER, Barons von, arms, 93.
LAHR, VON, arms, 66.
LAINCEL, Counts, arms, 348.
LAINÉ, M., 12.
LAING, Dr, Historical Description of the Altarpiece at Holyrood, 334.
,, H., Scottish Seals, 49, 50, 51, 177, 178, 179, 298, 322, 330, 335, 367, 368, 369, 378, 401, 429, 445, 454, 455, 459, 460, 466, 475, 512, 514, 515, 519, 520, 521, 522, 566, 614, 628, 630, 632.
LAITERBERG, arms, 365.

LALAIN, *arms*, 411.
LALANDE, *arms*, 188.
Lamb, Paschal, 236, 692; Pl. XXIV., fig. 4, p. 236.
LAMB, *arms*, 236.
LAMBART, Earl of CAVAN, *arms*, 323.
Lambeau, 414.
Lambel, 187, 687, 692, 734.
LAMBERG, *arms*, 493.
  ,,   GEORGE SIGISMUND, Baron of, 493.
  ,,   Princes of, *arms*, 493.
LAMBERT, *arms*, 235.
  ,,   *crest*, 295.
LAMBERVILLE, *see* PIGACHE.
LAMBRECHT, *arms*, 235.
Lambrequin, 599, 611, 612, 692, 694, 734.
Lambs, 235.
LAMBTON, Earl of DURHAM, *arms*, 235.
LAMI, *arms*, 296.
LAMINGTON, Lord, *supporters*, 647.
LAMMENS, *arms*, 235, 236.
LAMOIGNON, President, *arms*, 165.
LAMONT, *arms*, 213.
LAMORAL, Count EGMOND, *arms*, 98, 99.
Lampassé, 692, 734.
LAMPLOWE, *arms*, 158; Pl. XIV., fig. 9, p. 140.
LAMPLUGH, *arms*, 158.
LAMPOINS, *arms*, 236.
LAMPSON, *arms*, 686.
LANARIO, *arms*, 317.
LANCASTER and YORK, combined *rose* of, 595.
  ,,   *armorial slab* of HENRY of, 631.
  ,,   *arms*, 531.
  ,,   ,, and *colours*, 555.
  ,,   *badge* of Royal House of, 324, 587, 588, 589.
  ,,   BLANCHE, daughter of HENRY, Duke of, 588.
  ,,   Duchy, *seals* of, 598, 663.
  ,,   Duke of, *arms* and *label*, 416.
  ,,   ,, *badge*, 591, 593.
  ,,   Earl of, *monument*, 114.
  ,,   EDMUND CROUCH-BACK, Lord of, *tomb*, 587.
  ,,   HENRY of, *arms*, 428; *seal*, Pl. XXXV., fig. 4, p. 416.
  ,,   JOHN, Duke of, 438, 555, 588, 590, 593, 597.
  ,,   PHILIPPA, daughter of Duke of, 578.
  ,,   *Roses* of, 532.
  ,,   *seal* of HENRY, 1st Duke of, 587, 593.
  ,,   *Silver greyhound* of, 595.
  ,,   THOMAS, Earl of, *arms*, 428.
LANCASTRO, CONDE DE, 578.
  ,,   DON JORGE DE, 578.
Lance head, 348.
Lances, 347.
LANCY, *arms*, 142.
Land tenure, 3.
LANDALE, *arms*, 175.
LANDAU, Counts von, *arms*, 95.
LANDE, LA, *arms*, 724.

LANDEL, *arms*, 175.
LANDELL of that Ilk, 522.
LANDELLS, *arms*, 176.
LANDESCRON, *arms*, 380.
LANDSCHADEN, *crest*, 612.
LANE of Bentley, JOHN, *arms* and *augmentation*, 532.
LANESBOROUGH, Earls of, *arms*, 381.
LANFRANCHI, *arms*, 79.
LANG VON LANGENAU, *arms*, 668; Pl. LV., fig. 1, p. 668.
Langele, 591.
Langelyn, 591.
LANGEN, *arms*, 82.
LANGLEY, *arms*, 293; Pl. XXVII., fig. 9, p. 288.
  ,,   EDMUND of, 588, 591.
LANGLOIS, *arms*, 370.
Langué, 735.
Langued, 211, 227, 692.
LANNES, Maréchal, Duc de MONTEBELLO, *arms*, 346.
LANNOY, *arms*, 450.
  ,,   BALDWIN DE, *arms*, 450, 451.
  ,,   CHARLES DE, *arms*, 410, 451.
  ,,   ,, Viceroy of Naples, *arms*, 451.
  ,,   GILBERT DE, *arms*, 450, 451.
  ,,   GUILLEBERT DE, 451.
  ,,   HORACE DE, *arms*, 451.
  ,,   HUGH DE, *arms*, 450.
  ,,   ,, Seigneur de MINGOVAL, 451.
  ,,   PHILIP DE, *arms*, 450.
  ,,   ,, Prince of SULMONE, *arms*, 451.
  ,,   PIERRE DE, *arms*, 451.
  ,,   *bordure*, 439.
LANSAC, *see* VIVIER.
LANSDOWNE, Lord, *crest*, 610.
  ,,   MS., 557, 654.
LANSER, *arms*, 370.
LANVAON, *arms*, 93.
LAPLACE, *arms*, 309.
LAPOUKHIN, Princes, *arms*, 288.
LARDAIS, *see* GUILLOU.
LARDIER, *arms*, 187.
Larmes, 693, 733, 735.
LASCARIS, *arms*, 251.
LASCELLES, *arms*, 157, 336; Pl. XXX., fig. 9, p. 332.
LASSO, ORLANDO DI, *arms*, 387.
LASTEYRIE, 12.
LATHOM, Lord, *supporters*, 647.
LATIMER, *arms*, 153, 157.
  ,,   Lord, *badge*, 586.
  ,,   WILLIAM and THOMAS, *arms* and *labels*, 418.
Latin cross, 152.
LATRI, *arms*, 100.
Lattice, 693.
LATTRE, ROLAND DE, *arms*, 387.
LAUDEL, JOHN, *seal*, 643.
LAUDERDALE, *arms*, 516, 519.
  ,,   Lordship of, 516.
LAUENBURG, *arms*, 510, 666.
LAUNAY, DE, *arms*, 715.
  ,,   DU VALAY, *arms*, 344.
LAURENCE, *arms*, Pl. XIV., fig. 2, p. 140.
LAURES, *arms*, 317.
LAURIE, *arms*, 381.
LAURISTON, 433.

(813)

LAUTERBACH, arms, 313 ; Pl. XXVIII., fig. 11, p. 308.
LAUTERBURG, arms, 489.
LAUTREC, arms, 161, 214.
LAUTZ, arms, 383.
LAUZON, arms, 274.
LAVAL (see MONTMORENCY).
,, ANNE, heiress of GUI, Comte de, 505.
,, ANNETTE DE, Dame de COËT-MEN, seal, 460, 463.
,, arms, 68, 258.
,, GUY, Comte de, 258.
LAVARDIN, Marquises de, arms, 57, 186.
LAVAULX-VRÉCOURT, Counts, arms, 270.
LAWES, arms, 687.
LAWLEY, arms, 154 ; Pl. XIV., fig. 5, p. 140.
LAWRENCE, arms, 142.
,, SIR JAMES, Nobility of British Gentry, 4.
LAY, MONTMORENCY DE, arms, 452.
LAYFORTH, arms, 133.
Le Héraut d'Armes, 7.
Le hibou-duc, 726.
Leaf as a badge, 583.
LEAKE, Garter King of Arms, 384.
Leash, 693.
Leashed, 693.
Leaved, 693.
Leaves, Aspen, 320.
,, adossés, Lime, Pl. XXIX., fig. 9, p. 318.
,, Fig, 320.
,, Hazel, 319 ; Pl. XXIX., fig. 7, p. 318.
,, Holly, 319.
,, Laurel, 319 ; Pl. XXIX., fig. 8, p. 318.
,, Linden, 320.
,, Nenuphar, 321.
,, Oak, 320.
,, of plants, 319.
,, Rue, 321.
LÉCHERAINE, arms, 727.
LECK, Lordship of, arms, 580.
,, WILLIAM and LOUIS, Seigneurs of, arms, 580.
LECOY DE LA MARCHE, Les Sceaux, 616.
LEDEBUR, Barons, arms, 136.
Leeches, 279.
LEEFDAEL, Sire de, arms, 165, 427.
LEEFVELT, VAN, arms, 68.
LEESON, Earl of MILTOWN, arms, 311.
Leg, Pl. XX., fig. 8, p. 198.
,, of an eagle, 693.
LEGAT, arms, 152.
Légende, 735.
Leges Hastiludiales, 41.
LEGGE, Earl of DARTMOUTH, arms, 233.
Legged, 693.
LEGH, GERALD, Accidence of Armory, 2, 19, 21, 190, 524.
Legs, Pl. XX., fig. 9, p. 198.
,, Human, 206.
LEIBENSTEIN, see STEIN.
LEICESTER, Earl of, arms, 218, 219, 322, 323, 350; Pl. XXI., fig. 9, p. 212.
,, ,, badge, 753.

LEICESTER, Lord DE TABLEY, 18.
LEICHNAM, arms, 204.
LEIGH, arms, 366.
LEIGHTON, Sir FREDERICK, arms, 701.
LEININGEN, Counts of, arms, 424, 447.
,, ,, label, 424.
,, -WESTERBERG, Counts, label, 424.
LEINSTER, 384.
,, Duke of, arms, 143.
,, ,, supporter, 240.
,, King of, arms, 342.
LEITÖENS, arms, 127.
LEJONHUFVUD, 672.
Lemons, 340.
LENFANT-DIEU, arms, 195.
LENNOX, arms, 144, 432 ; Pl. XXX., fig. 3, p. 332.
,, CHARLES, arms, 559.
,, Earl of, arms, 325, 521 ; Pl. XLII., fig. 1, p. 512.
,, ,, bordure, 441.
,, ISABELLA, Countess of, seal, Pl. XXXVII., fig. 7, p. 448.
,, MALCOLM, Earl of, seal, 643.
,, MARGARET, Countess of, monument, 476.
,, MATTHEW, son of JOHN, Earl of, label, 419.
LENONCOURT, Cardinal de, arms, 142.
LENOX, arms, 466.
LENTILHAC, arms, 129.
LEO, arms, 173.
,, XIII., Pope, arms, 310.
LÉON, arms, 62, 104, 168, 212, 253, 306, 390, 416, 441, 457, 479, 488, 495, 501, 506, 507, 547, 576, 577, 578, 633, 667.
,, bordure of, 507.
,, FERDINAND III., King of, 478.
,, PONCE DE, Duke of ARCOS, arms, 506.
,, Princes de, arms, 185.
,, SANCHA of, 479.
LEONBERG, Counts, arms, 752.
Leopard, 209, 210, 225, 693.
,, Herald, 209.
Léopard, 735.
,, lionné, 209, 210, 211, 693, 701, 735.
,, Tête de, 735.
Leopard's face, 693 ; Pl. XXII., fig. 12, p. 222.
,, ,, and Fleur-de-lis, 333.
,, head, 225, 693.
LEOPOLD, Archduke, 282.
,, Emperor, Patent of arms granted by, 601.
LERMA, Dukes of, arms, 309.
LERNOUT, arms, 148 ; Pl. XVI., fig. 9, p. 146.
Les Coûtumes Générales de trois Bailliages de Lorraine, 550.
LESLIE, arms, 367, 377, 522, 631 ; Pl. XXXIII., fig. 2, p. 376.
,, Lord LINDORES, arms, Pl. XLII., fig. 4, p. 512.
,, of Balquhain, arms, 432.
LESSEPS, Count de, arms, 344.
LESTRANGE, arms, 216, 407.

LESVAL, *arms*, 360.
LESZCZYC, *arms*, 363.
„ DE RADOLIN-RADOLINSKI, Counts, *arms*, 363.
Letters of the Alphabet as charges, 394.
Lettuce, 344.
LEUBERSTORF, *arms*, 669 ; Pl. LV., fig. 12, p. 668.
LEUCHTENBERG, Dukes and Landgraves of, *arms*, 123, 473.
LEUTENBERG, Lords of, 490.
LEUZE, Barons de, *arms*, 338.
Levé, 685, 735.
LEVEN, Earl of, *arms*, 335 ; Pl. XXX., fig. 8, p. 332.
Lever. 693.
LEVERSAGE, *arms*, 366.
LEVESON, *arms*, 319.
LEVIS, Ducs de MIREPOIX, and de VENTADOUR, *arms*, 140.
Levrier, 735.
Levron, 735.
LEWASCHEFF, *augmentation*, 542.
LEWEN, ROBERT, Sheriff of Newcastle, *arms*, 366.
LEWENTHAL, *see* TOD.
LEXINGTON, Lord, *arms*, 165.
LEYBURNE, *arms*, 224.
LEYDEN, Burg-gravate of, *arms*, 307.
LEYEN, Counts and Princes of, *arms*, 121.
LEZAY, MONTMORENCY-LAVAL DE, *brisure*, 452.
LEZERGUE, *arms*, 156.
LIAÑOS, *arms*, 508.
LIBOTTON, *arms*, 156.
LICHFIELD, See of, *arms*, 156, 700 ; Pl. XIV., fig. 7, p. 140.
LICHNOWSKI, Princes, *arms*, 319, 339.
LICHTENSTEIN, Princes of, *arms*, 491.
Licorne, 735.
LIDDESDALE, *arms*, 519.
„ Lordship of, 566.
Lié, 385, 677, 735.
LIEVEN, Princes and Counts, *arms* and *augmentation*, 542.
Lighted, 693.
LIGHTFORD, *arms*, 121.
Lightning, 310.
LIGNE and BARBANÇON, JEAN, Baron of, 492.
„ Principality of, *arms*, 129.
LIGNEY, Count de, *arms* and *label*, 415.
LIGNIÈRES, *arms*, 160.
LIHONS, *arms*, 334.
LILLIE, *arms*, 334.
Lily, The, 333.
LIMA, *arms*, 91.
Limaçon, 735.
LIMBURG, *arms*, 484, 573, 574.
„ Duchy of, *arms*, 484.
Lime branch, Pl. XXIX., fig. 6, p. 318.
„ *leaves addossés*, Pl. XXIX., fig. 9, p. 318.
LIMÉROU, *see* ORENGES, 340.
LIMESAY, DE, *arms*, 51, 256.
LIMOJON, *arms*, 340.
LIMOS, *arms*, 340.
LIMPURG, Counts of, *arms*, 526.
LINAGE, Counts de, *arms*, 138.
„ *see* ROZIER.
LINCOLN, JOHN BOKINGHAM, Bishop of, *arms*, 160.
„ shield of Earl of, 406.

LINDAU, VON, *arms*, 412.
LINDECK, *arms*, 670 ; Pl. LVI., fig. 9, p. 670.
LINDEN, VAN DER, *arms*, 477 ; Pl. XLI., fig. 1, p. 510.
LINDENBERG, *arms*, 299.
LINDENPALM, *arms*, 139.
LINDENS, VAN DER, *arms*, 393.
LINDORES Abbey, 516.
„ Lord, *arms*, 522 ; Pl. XLII., fig. 4, p. 512.
„ Lordship of, *arms*, 358, 522.
LINDSAY, *arms*, 358, 522.
„ II., MS., 84.
„ DAVID, Duke of MONTROSE, *arms*, 522.
„ „ Lord CRAWFORD, *crest*, 605.
„ Earl of CRAWFORD, *arms*, 179.
„ JANET, daughter and heiress of Sir ALEXANDER, 459.
„ MARGARET, Countess of DOUGLAS, 517.
„ SIMON, *seal* and *arms* of, 51.
„ Sir DAVID, 430, 566.
„ „ *arms* on eagle, 631.
„ „ Lord of CRAWFORD, *seal* and *arms* of, 51.
„ „ Lyon King of Arms, *Register* of, 523.
„ „ (the elder), Lyon King of Arms, *Record* of, 513.
„ „ (the younger), Lyon King of Arms, *Armorial MS.* of, *illuminated*, 84, 149, 171, 402, 476, 512, 513.
„ WILLIAM, Lord of ERCILDOUN and CRAWFORD, *seal* of, 51.
LINDSAYS, *Lives of the*, 51.
LINDSEY, Earl of, *arms*, 352.
LINDT, DE, *arms*, 183.
Lined, 693.
Lines of Partition, 693.
LINGUET, *arms*, 203.
LINIÈRES DE MOTTEROUGE, *arms*, 96.
LINLITHGOW, Earl of, *arms*, 522.
„ Earldom of, *arms*, 522.
LINTRÉ, Sire de, *arms*, 332.
Lion, 208, 735.
„ *arms* on a, 631.
„ as a *badge*, 754.
„ as a *supporter*, 632, 633.
„ *bicorporate*, 219.
„ *contournés*, 220.
„ *couchant*, 217.
„ *de S. Marc*, 735.
„ *Demi-*, 220.
„ „ *naissant*, 221.
„ „ *issuant*, 221.
„ *diffamed*, 219.
„ *dismembered*, 217 ; Pl. XXI., fig. 8, p. 212.
„ *dormant*, 217.
„ *eriré*, 219.
„ *léopardé*, 209, 211, 698, 735.
„ *mariné*, 703.
„ *morné*, 218.

(815)

Lion, *Ombre de*, 735.
,, Palatinate, as a *crest*, 607.
,, Parts of, 222.
,, *passant*, 216.
,, ,, as a *crest*, 599, 603.
,, *queue fourchée*, 218 ; Pl. XXI., fig. 9, p. 212.
,, *rampant*, 212 ; Pl. XXI., fig. 1, p. 212.
,, ,, as a *badge*, 596.
,, ,, as a *supporter*, 640.
,, ,, *gardant*, 215 ; Pl. XXI., fig. 2, p. 212.
,, ,, *regardant*, 216 ; Pl. XXI., fig. 3, p. 212.
,, *salient*, 217 ; Pl. XXI., fig. 7, p. 212.
,, *sejant*, 217.
,, ,, *affronté*, 217.
,, ,, as a *supporter*, 642.
,, ,, *gardant*, 217, 641.
,, ,, *rampant*, 217.
,, *statant*, 217.
,, ,, as a *crest*, 600, 603.
,, ,, *gardant*, 217.
,, ,, ,, as a *crest*, 603.
,, *The Sea-*, 299.
,, *Tricorporate*, 219 ; Pl. XXI., fig. 10, p. 212.
,, *Two-headed*, 219.
,, *Winged*, 219 ; Pl. XXI., fig. 11, p. 212.
,, with helm as *supporter*, 631.
Lioncel, 693.
Lioncels, 219 ; Pl. XXI., fig. 12, p. 212.
Lioness, 222.
Lions addorsed, 220.
,, as *supporters*, 634, 636.
,, *combatant*, 220 ; Pl. XXII., fig. 1, p. 222.
,, *couchant*, and *helmed* and *crested*, as *supporters*, 635.
,, *counter-passant*, 220.
,, ,, *-rampant*, 220.
,, *demi-*, as *supporters*, 633.
,, *passant*, Pl. XXI., fig. 4, p. 212.
,, ,, *gardant*, Pl. XXI., fig. 5, p. 212.
,, ,, *-regardant*, Pl. XXI., fig. 6, p. 212.
,, *rampant* as *supporters*, 633.
,, ,, *-gardant* as *supporters*, 635.
,, *sejant* as *supporters*, 634.
,, ,, *helmed* and *crested* as *supporters*, 635.
Lion's *gambs*, Pl. XXII., fig. 7, p. 222.
,, *head* as a *badge*, 754.
,, *heads*, 222 ; Pl. XXII., fig. 6, p. 222.
,, ,, *reversed* and *jessant de lis*, Pl. XXII., fig. 11, p. 222.
,, *paws*, Pl. XXII., fig. 8, p. 222.
,, *tails*, Pl. XXII., fig. 9, p. 222.
LIPPE, *arms*, 203.
,, Barons VON DER, *arms*, 188.
,, Princes of, *arms*, 324.
Lips, The, 203.
LIRONI, *arms*, 383.
Lis-de-jardin, 735.
LISBURNE, Earl of, *arms*, 333.
Liséré, 678, 688, 735.
LISLE, Viscount, *arms*, 557.
,, ,, *badge*, 587.
LISLES, DE, *supporter*, 239.
LISSAU, *see* SPANOFFSKY.

Listel, 735.
LITHUANIA, *arms*, 199, 255, 487.
,, LADISLAS V., Duke of, *seal*, 468.
LITTA, *Celebri Famiglie Italiane*, 281, 632.
LITTLETON, Viscount COBHAM, *arms*, 273.
Livery Collars, 597.
LIVINGSTON, WILLIAM, *arms*, 178.
LIVINGSTONE, *arms*, 522.
,, Earl of LINLITHGOW, *arms*, 522.
,, MARY, 436.
,, Viscount TEVIOT, *arms*, 340.
,, ,, KILSYTH, *arms*, 337.
LIVONIA, Alexander of, *seal*, 468.
Lizards, 274, 277.
LLANDAFF, EDMUND BROMFIELD, Bishop of, *arms*, 217.
LLEWELLYN AP GRIFFITH, Prince, *arms*, 224.
LLOYD, *arms*, 213 ; Pl. XX., fig. 4, p. 198.
,, Lord MOSTYN, *arms*, 200.
LLYS BRADWEN, EDNOWAIN, Lord of, *arms*, 274.
Loaves as charges, 391.
LÖBENSTEIN, Barons, *arms*, 128.
,, ,, von, *arms*, *supporters*, and *compartment*, 642.
LOBKOWITZ, Princes of, *arms*, 256.
,, System of lines representing colour, 64.
LOBLEY, *arms*, 240.
Lobsters, 273.
Lochaber-axe, 693.
LOCHFONTAINE, *see* ARNOLET.
LOCHNOW, *arms*, 469.
Locket as a *badge*, 584.
LOCKHART'S *Spanish Ballads*, 202.
LODBROKE, *arms*, 136.
LODES, Comte de, *bend*, 429.
Lodged, 232, 589, 693.
LODOMIRIA, *arms*, 504.
LODZIA, *arms*, 737.
,, Counts, 370.
,, *herba* of, *arms*, 370.
LOEN, *arms*, 223.
LOFFREDO, *arms*, 71.
LOGAN, *arms*, 147.
LOGIE, MARGARET, *seal*, 455.
,, Sir JOHN, *arms*, 455.
LOHÉAC, *arms*, 71.
,, DE TRÉVOASEC, *arms*, 184.
LOIR, JEAN, 13.
LOKE, *arms*, 337.
LOMBARDI, *arms*, 256.
LOMBARDO - VENETIAN Kingdom, *arms*, 502.
LOMBARDY, *Iron Crown* of, 502, 617.
,, Queen THEODOLINDA of, 617.
LOMELLINI, *arms*, 79.
London, Visitation of, 353.
LONDON, Art Library at South Kensington, 622.
,, City of, *arms*, 346.
,, ,, *supporters*, 291.
,, Lord Mayor of, *collar*, 598.
,, Record Office of, 455.
,, See of, *arms*, 346, 371.
,, St. Dunstan's Church, 594.

LONDON, Vane of Royal Exchange of, 285.
Long Cross, 152.
LONGASTRE, Marquis de, *arms*, 183.
LONGCHAMP, WILLIAM DE, Bishop of ELY, *arms*, 90.
Longe, 693, 735.
Longé, 693, 735.
LONGESPEÉ, WILLIAM, Earl of SALISBURY, *arms*, 219, 224, 417 ; Pl. XXI., fig. 12, p. 212.
LONGSHARE, *arms*, 274.
LONGSTAFFE, DYER, *The Old Heraldry of the Percies*, 461, 482, 584.
„ TATE and, *The Pedigrees and early Heraldry of the Lords of Alnwick*, 482.
LONGUEVAL, Princes de BUCQUOY, *arms*, 95.
LONGUEVILLE, *arms*, 163.
„ Comte de, 515, 530.
„ Dukes de, *arms*, 572.
„ FRANCIS, Comte de, *seal*, 530.
„ LOUIS, Duke of, *arms*, 529.
LOOS-CORSWAREN, Princes of, *arms*, 93.
LOPPIN, *arms*, 228.
LORAINE, anagram of the name, 258.
Lord Chancellor of ENGLAND, mark of office, 644.
LOREDAN, *arms*, 213.
LORENZ, Barons, *arms*, 126.
Lorenzo, Church of San, in Florence, 192.
LORESSE, MONTMORENCY DE, *brisure*, 451.
LORETTE, *arms*, 195.
LOREYN, *arms*, 133 ; Pl. XII., fig. 11, p. 130.
LORN, *arms*, 368, 447, 466 ; Pl. XXXII., fig. 11, p. 358.
„ *galley* of, 368.
„ JOHN, Lord, 447.
„ 1st Lord of, 520.
„ Lord of, *seal*, 520.
„ Lords of, 368.
„ Lordship of, 520.
LORNE, Princess Louise, Marchioness of, *label*, 423.
Lorraine, Cross of, 152 ; Fig. 52, p. 164.
„ *Les Coûtumes Générales de*, 550.
LORRAINE, *arms*, 258, 449, 471, 495, 505, 508, 545, 664.
„ *badge* of Dukes of, 153.
„ CHARLES III., Duke of, 13.
„ Duchy, *arms*, 501.
„ Duke of, *mantling armoyé*, 616.
„ MATHIEU DE, *brisure*, 439.
„ Ordonnance of CHARLES III., Duke of, 748.
„ supposed *arms* of ADELBERT of, 46.
„ VAUDEMONT, MARGUERITE DE, *arms*, 449.
Lorré, 687, 735.
Losange, 693, 735.
Losangé, 100, 694, 735.
„ *en bande*, 735.
„ „ *barre*, 735.

LOSENSTEIN, RUDOLF DE, *seal*, 456.
LOSS, *arms*, 279.
LOTEREL, *arms*, 403.
„ Sir GEOFFREY, *arms*, 403.
LOTHAIR, Emperor, 40, 41.
LOTHIAN, Earl of, 414.
„ Marquessate of, *arms*, 305.
LOUBGASSEN, *arms*, 440.
LOUDOUN, Earls of, *arms*, 85.
LOUE, MONTMORENCY-LAVAL DE, *brisure*, 452.
LOUIS II., the German, 39.
„ IV., Emperor HOLY ROMAN EMPIRE, 57, 58, 247, 630 ; *augmentations* granted by, 536 ; *coins* of, 251 ; *crown* of, 621 ; *Great Seal* of, 247.
„ V., King of FRANCE, *seal* of, 354.
„ VI., King of FRANCE, *coins* of, 327 ; *crown* and *sceptre* of, 328.
„ VII., King of FRANCE, 329 ; *badge*, 583 ; called FLORUS, 327 ; *signet* of, 328.
„ VIII., King of FRANCE, *seal* of, 329 ; *supporters*, 636.
„ IX., (ST.), King of FRANCE, 330, 571 ; *seal* of, 329 ; *supporters*, 636.
„ X., King of FRANCE, *seal*, 456.
„ XI., King of FRANCE, 12, 192, 574, 659 ; *Great Seal*, 616 ; *supporters*, 636.
„ XII., King of FRANCE, *seal* of, 329, 334 ; Pl. XXXVII., fig. 1, p. 448 ; *supporters*, 636.
„ XIII., King of FRANCE, 327 ; *supporters*, 636.
„ XIV., King of FRANCE, 13, 14, 240, 275, 282, 297, 354, 571, 624 ; *arms*, 636, 710 ; *augmentation* granted by, 539 ; *supporters*, 636.
„ XVI., King of FRANCE, 539, 660.
„ XVIII., King of FRANCE, 14 ; *augmentation* granted by, 539.
„ or LOIS, or LOYS, 327.
„ the same as CLOVIS, 327.
LOUISE, Princess, Marchioness of LORNE, *label*, 423 ; Fig. 88, p. 421.
Loup, 735.
„ -*cervier*, 735.
LOUVAIN, *arms*, 214, 215, 481 ; Pl. XXI., fig. 1, p. 212.
„ JOSCELINE DE, 482.
„ Seven patrician families of, 184.
LOUVILLE, *arms*, 93.
LOUVOIS, Marquis de, *arms*, 277.
LOVARI, *arms*, 237.
LOVEL of Ballumbie, supposed *arms*, 433.
„ Sir JOHAN, *arms*, 553.
„ Sir WILLIAM, *arms*, 417.
LOVELL, *arms*, 215, 240.
LOVENICH, *arms*, 127.
LÖVENSCHILD, *arms*, 213.
LOW COUNTRIES, *coronet* of Baron in the, 625.
„ „ Introduction of Hereditary arms into, 51.
„ „ Use of *canton* in the, 427.

(817)

LOWE, *arms*, 228.
LOWEL, *arms*, 80 ; Pl. V., fig. 6, p. 80.
LÖWENSTEIN, *arms*, 447, 669 ; Pl. LVI., fig. 4, p. 670.
,, Counts of, *arms*, 126.
LOWER, M. A., *Curiosities of Heraldry*, 20, 22, 23, 25, 31, 98, 117, 397, 634.
LOWTHER, *arms*, Pl. XIX., fig. 8, p. 192.
Lozenge, 165, 182, 693 ; Fig., 45, p. 116 ; Pl. XVIII., fig. 7, p. 190.
Lozenges conjoined, Pl. XVIII., fig. 9, p. 190.
Lozengy, 100, 185, 693 ; Pl. VII., fig. 9, p. 90.
,, *couped*, Pl. VIII., fig. 1, p. 100.
,, *in bend*, 100.
LUCA, *Grafen Saal*, 404.
LUCAS, *arms*, 684.
LUCCA, *arms* of city, 394.
Luce, The, 268.
LUCHTENBURG, VAN, *arms*, 128.
LUCIANO, *arms*, 82.
LUCINGE, Princes de, *arms*, 91, 122.
Lucy, 271, 694.
LUCY, AMAURI DE, *arms*, 408.
,, *arms*, 268, 306, 481, 482, 641.
,, ELIZABETH, 557.
,, GEOFFREY DE, 408.
LUDERITZ, Barons von, *arms*, 370.
LUETTE, *arms*, 382.
Luna, 65.
LUNA, *arms*, 307.
LUNDIN, JOHN, of that ILK, *bordure*, 443.
Lune, 735.
LÜNEBURG, Duchy of, *arms*, 113, 472, 663.
Lunels, 735.
LUNELS, *arms*, 307.
LUPARELLA, *arms*, 228.
LUPIA, *arms*, 161.
Lure, 694.
,, *Conjoined in*, 260.
LUSATIA, LOWER, Markgravate, *arms*, 500.
,, UPPER, Markgravate, *arms*, 500.
LUSIGNAN, *arms*, 94, 409.
,, *crest* and *supporters*, 303.
,, HUGH DE, Count de la MARCHE, 303.
Lute as a charge, 382.
LUTTEREL (*see* LOTEREL), *arms*, 403.
,, *supporters*, 638.
LUTWYCHE, *arms*, 224 ; Pl. XXII., fig. 10, p. 222.
LÜTZOW, Barons von, *arms*, 365.
LUXE, MONTMORENCY DE, *brisure*, 452.
LUXEMBOURG or LUXEMBURG, *arms*, 449, 667.
,, ,, JOHN of, King of BOHEMIA, 591.
LUXEMBURG, JACQUES DE, *arms* and *label*, 415.
,, JEAN DE, *arms* and *label*, 415.
,, PIERRE DE, Count de ST. PAUL, 415.
LUYTENBURG, VAN, *arms*, 128.
LUZYANSKI, *arms*, 272.
Lymphad, 367, 694.

Lymphad under sail, Pl. XXXII., fig. 12, p. 358.
,, *with fire*, Pl. XXXII., fig. 11, p. 358.
LYNDE, DE LA, *arms*, 142.
Lynx, The, 226.
Lyon Office, Heraldic MSS. in, 476, 518.
,, ,, Official *Register of Arms*, Entries in, 400, 568, 610.
,, Register, Institution of, 445.
LYON, *arms*, 178, 283.
,, Earl of STRATHMORE, *arms*, 215.
,, ,, ,, *crest*, 605.
,, KING OF ARMS, 179, 523, 569, 649.
,, ,, ,, *arms*, 526.
,, ,, ,, duties, 401.
LYONNAIS ET FOREZ, Counts of, *arms*, 212.
Lyre as a charge, 383.

MABILLON, 47, 287.
MABUSE the painter, 334.
M'ADAM, *arms*, 350.
M'ALISTER, ALLAN, *arms*, 512.
,, JOHN MURDOCH, Captain of CLANRANALD, *arms*, 512.
M'DONALD of CLANRANALD, *arms*, 512.
M'DONELL of GLENGARRY, *arms*, 512 ; Pl. XLIII., fig. 3, p. 521.
M'DOUGALL, *arms*, 213.
M'GREGOR, *arms*, 317 ; Pl. XXIX., fig. 2, p. 318.
M'KINNON, *arms*, 513.
M'LAREN, *arms*, 139.
M'LAURIN, *arms*, 371.
M'LEOD, *arms*, 207, 358 ; Pl. XXVIII., fig. 10, p. 308.
,, of LEWIS, *arms*, 314.
M'MAHON, Pl. XXI., fig. 6, p. 212.
M'MURROUGH, King of LEINSTER, *arms*, 342.
M'NEILL, *arms*, 213, 513.
MACDONALD, *arms*, 212.
,, Lord, *arms*, 512, 513 ; Pl. XLIII., fig. 5, p. 522.
,, Marshal, *arms*, 513.
,, of Slate, *arms*, 512.
MACDONALDS in INVERNESS, 400.
MACFARLANE, *arms*, 144, 325.
,, *brisure*, 432.
,, *compartment*, 642.
MACHIAVELLI, *arms*, 713.
,, family, 16.
MACIAS, *arms*, 387.
MACINTOSH, *arms*, 212.
MACKENZIE, *arms*, 233 ; Pl. XXIII., fig. 11, p. 228.
,, *arms in Lyon Office Register*, 400.
,, Sir GEORGE, *Science of Heraldry*, etc., 2, 349, 446, 486.
MACKINTOSH, *arms*, 513.
MACKONEIL, of Dunnivege and Glennes, *arms*, 512 ; Pl. XLIII., fig. 4, p. 522.
MACLEAN, *arms*, 513 ; Pl. XLIII., fig. 6, p. 522.
Mâcle, 694, 735.
Mâclé, 694, 735.
MACMAHON, *arms*, 216, 263.
,, Le Maréchal MARIE EDMÉ PATRICE, Duc de MAGENTA, *arms*, 216.

MACMAHON, Marquises of, *arms*, 216.
MAÇON, *arms*, 285.
Maçonné, 694, 736.
MADAN, *arms*, 262.
MADDEN, *arms*, 262.
MADOETS, *arms*, 184.
MADRID, City of, *arms*, 313.
MAES, *arms*, 184.
MAFFLIERS, MONTMORENCY DE, *brisure*, 452.
MAGALHAENS, *arms*, 99.
MAGALOTTI, *arms*, 394.
MAGDEBURG, Duchy of, *arms*, 79.
MAGENTA, Duc de, *arms*, 216.
MAGNALL, *arms*, 365.
MAGNAVILLE, GEOFFREY DE, Earl of ESSEX, 115.
,, ,, ,, Earl of ESSEX, supposed effigy of, 45.
MAGNE, 204.
MAGNENEY, *Recueil des Armes*, 64.
MAGNUS (LADISLAS) of Sweden, *counter-seal* of, 628.
MAGUIRE, *arms*, 199 ; Pl. XX., fig. 3, p. 198.
MAGUSAC, Comte de, supposed *arms* of, 46.
MAHLBERG, Lords of, *arms*, 212.
MAHREN, Markgravate of, *arms*, 256.
Maiden's head as a *badge*, 754.
MAIENTHAL, *arms*, 66.
MAIGRET or MEGRET, *arms*, 66.
MAILLANE, Marquises de, *arms*, 227.
MAILLART, *arms*, 128.
MAILLEN D'OHEY, Marquises, *arms*, 391.
Maillet, 736.
MAILLY, *arms*, 393.
,, GILLES DE, *arms*, 404.
Main-bénissante, 736.
,, *d'aigle*, 693, 736.
MAINGOT, 12.
,, *arms*, 96.
Maintenance, Cap of, 694.
MAINWARING of Croxton, *arms*, 560.
MAIR, *arms*, 200.
MAISONNEUVE, DE, 16.
MAISTRE, Counts de, *arms*, 338.
,, XAVIER DE, 338.
MAITLAND, *arms*, 179, 217 ; Pl. XXI., fig. 8, p. 212.
Maize, 344.
MAJOR, *arms*, 364.
Mal-gironné, 85, 736.
,, *-ordonné*, 150, 736.
,, *-taillé*, 736.
MALAGAMBAS, *arms*, 207.
MALAPERT, Baron de NEUFVILLE, *arms*, 112, 331.
,, *see* HERVILLY.
MALASPINA, *arms*, 536.
,, CONRAD, *arms* and *augmentation*, 536.
MALATESTA, *arms*, 201.
MALCHUS, Counts of MARIENRODE, *arms*, 380.
MALDEGHEM, PHILIPPE DE, *secretum* of, 54.
MALEMORT, *arms*, 93.
MALGOL, *arms*, 138.
MALHERBE, *arms*, 320.
MALLERBY, *arms*, 320.
Mallets as charges, 393.

MALMAYNS, *arms*, 204.
MALMESBURY, Earl of, *augmentation*, 545.
MALMONT, *arms*, 136.
MALOLACU, DE, *arms*, 130.
MALPAS, Barons of, *arms*, 157.
MALTA, Knights of, *see* HOSPITALLERS.
Maltese Cross, 155 ; Fig. 55, p. 164.
MALTRAVERS, *arms*, 96, 181.
MALVOISIN, 12.
Man, Pl. XX., fig. 1, p. 198.
,, *-at-arms* as *supporter*, 640.
,, *-tiger*, 694.
MAN, ISLE OF, *arms*, 206, 446 ; Pl. XX., fig. 9, p. 198.
Manacles as a *badge*, 584.
Manche, 694.
,, *mal taillée*, 694, 736.
MANCHESTER, Dukes of, *arms*, 562.
,, ,, *supporters*, 287, 288.
,, Lords of, and City of, *arms*, 132.
MANCICOURT, *arms*, 140.
MANDELSLOH, Counts of, *arms*, 385.
MANDERSCHEID, Counts of, *arms* and *label*, 424.
MANDEVILLE, Earls of ESSEX, 589.
,, ,, ,, *arms*, 81.
Mandoline as a charge, 383.
Maned, 694.
MANEGHEM, *see* FEVERE, 344.
MANFREDI, *arms*, 81, 162 ; Pl. XIV., fig. 12, p. 140.
MANIAGO, Count, *arms*, 92.
Manipule, 736.
MANNERS, *arms*, 563.
,, Lord ROOS, 17.
,, ,, WILLIAM, 563.
,, of Belvoir, Sir GEORGE, 530.
,, ,, Grantham, JOHN, *arms*, 563.
,, Sir JOHN, Earl of RUTLAND, *augmentation*, 530.
,, Sir WILLIAM, 563.
MANNY, Sir WALTER DE, *arms*, 140.
Man's head with ass's ears as a *crest*, 606.
MANSEL, *arms*, 376.
MANSFELD, Counts of, *arms*, 488.
MANSOURAH, Battle of, 331.
Mantel, Tierced in, 694.
Mantelé, 88, 694, 736.
MANTELLI, *arms*, 213.
MANTEUFFEL, Counts von, *arms*, 123.
Manticora, 694.
Mantle, 694.
Mantled, 88.
Mantles or *Mantlings*, 615, 694.
MANTUA, Dukes of, *arms*, 94, 250, 259, 502, 536.
,, 1st Marquis of, *augmentation*, 537.
MANUEL, *arms*, 450, 507, 736.
,, King, 238.
,, MARIE, 450.
MANVOISIN, 12.
MAR, *arms*, 163, 455, 514, 567.
,, Countess of, *seal*, 455, 459.
,, Earls of, *arms*, 120, 178, 566.
,, ,, *supporters*, 288.
,, GRATNEY, Earl of, 445.

MAR, MARGARET, Countess of, *seal*, 459.
,, Sir DONALD of, *brisure*, 445.
MARANS, *arms*, 169.
Marcassin, 689, 736, 743.
MARCELS, *arms*, 153.
MARCH, Earl of, 414.
,, ,, *arms*, 168, 171, 405, 446.
,, ,, *bordure*, 442.
,, ,, *crest*, 605.
,, *Lions* of, 634.
,, *Silver lions* of, 557, 588, 662.
MARCHAL DE SAINCY, *arms*, 366.
MARCHALCK VON BIBERSTEIN, *arms*, 96 ; Pl. LV., fig. 5, p. 668
MARCHAND, *arms*, 66.
MARCHE, Count de la, 303.
,, OLIVIER DE LA, 615, 653.
,, (*see* LECOY).
MARCHMONT, Earl of, *arms*, 523.
MARCHYDD AP CYNAN, *arms*, 199.
MARCK, Counts de la, *arms*, 125 (*see* MARK).
,, ,, *crest*, 608.
MARCONNÉ, Counts de, *arms*, 314.
Maréchaux de France, mark of office, 645.
MAREUIL, *see* BOULA.
MARGARET, Countess of HOLLAND, *secretum* of, 247.
,, dtr. of PHILIP III. of France, *seal*, 454.
,, Queen of EDWARD I. of ENGLAND, 11 ; *seal*, 454.
MARGENS, *arms*, 69.
MARGUERIE, Marquises de, *arms*, 336.
MARGUERIT, *arms*, 336.
Marguerite, The, 336.
MARIA THERESA, *arms*, 104 ; Pl. XL., p. 494.
,, ,, Empress, *arms*, 494.
,, ,, *Grand Cordon* of the ORDER of, 665.
MARIE ANTOINETTE, Queen, 570.
,, dtr. of HENRY III., Duke of BRABANT, *arms*, 454.
MARIENRODE, Counts of, *arms*, 380.
Marigold, 338.
Mariné, 736.
MARIONI, JULIO, *augmentation*, 536.
MARISCHAL, Earls, *arms*, 122.
MARK, County of, *arms*, 125, 472, 485, 492.
MARKHAM, *arms*, 221 ; Pl. XXII., fig. 3, p. 222.
MARKINGTON, *arms*, 80.
Marks of Cadency, 397.
MARLBOROUGH, Duke of, *arms*, 413.
,, ,, *augmentation*, 534.
,, ,, *supporters*, 293.
MARLY, MONTMORENCY DE, *arms*, 452.
MARMADUKE, RICHARD LE FITZ, *arms*, 550.
MARMION, *arms*, 345, 532.
,, PHILIP, Baron of SCRIVELSBY, 345.
Marmite, 736.
MARMOUTIERS, Abbey of, 657.
MARMYON, *arms*, 345.
MARNEY, *arms*, 216.
Marqué, 704, 736.
Marquess's *coronet*, 624.
Marqueté, 736.

Marquis's *standard*, Length of, 654.
Mars, 65, 694.
,, *Symbol for*, 309.
MARSCHALCK, *arms*, 669.
MARSEILLES, Figure from Abbey of ST. VICTOR, Pl. II., fig. 4, p. 44.
MARSHALL, *arms*, 90.
,, *badge*, 355.
,, Earl of PEMBROKE, *arms*, 215.
Marshalling, 453 ; Pl. XXXVIII., p. 464 ; Pl. XXXIX., p. 482 ; Pl. XLI., p. 510 ; Pl. XLII., p. 512 ; Pl. XLIII., p. 522.
,, in Britain, Modern, 523.
,, *Modes of*, 459.
Marshals, French, mark of office, 645.
MARSI, Counts, de, *arms*, 124.
MARSIGNY, *see* SERGEANT, 343.
MARSTON, *arms*, 235.
MARTDORF, *arms*, 222.
MARTELL, JOHN, RICHARD, and WILLIAM, *arms*, 393.
MARTIAN, LE SEIGNEUR DE, *arms*, 394.
Martin, The, 266.
MARTIN, *arms*, 126.
Martinet, 736.
,, *arms*, 185.
MARTINI, *Capa* or *Capsa Sancti*, 657.
Martlet for fourth son, 444.
Martlets, 266, 694 ; Pl. XXVI., fig. 4, p. 266.
MARY I., Queen of ENGLAND, *arms*, Pl. LI., fig. 4, p. 661 ; *badge*, 596; *Great Seal* of, 664 ; *motto* of, 664.
,, II., Queen of BRITAIN, 113 ; *arms*, Pl. LII., fig. 6, p. 662 ; *motto* of, 664.
,, Princess, *label*, 422 ; Fig. 88, p. 421.
,, Queen of SCOTLAND, 476 ; *device* of, 298 ; *Great Seal of*, 464 ; *seal* of, 330, 335, 476 ; *supporters* of, 635, 662.
Mascally, 185.
MASCARENHAS, *arms*, 127.
Mascle, 117, 182, 184, 694 ; Pl. XVIII., fig. 8, p. 190.
Mascles conjoined, Pl. XVIII., fig. 10, p. 190.
Masculy, 694.
Masoned, 694.
Masqué, 736.
MASSA, Principality of, 537.
Massacre, 234, 679, 736.
Masses d'Armes, 736.
MASSON, *arms*, 187.
,, LE, *arms*, 319.
MASSOW, Barons, *arms*, 126.
MASSY, *arms*, 284.
MASTON, *arms*, 130.
Masuré, 736.
Matchlock as a charge, 366.
MATELIEFS, *arms*, 336.
MATHEWS, *arms*, 212.
MATHIAS, *arms*, 387.
MATILDA, Queen of WILLIAM of Normandy, 29.
MATOS, *arms*, 317.
MATTHEWS, *arms*, 263.
MAUBLANC, *arms*, 68.
MAUD, Empress, 29.

(820)

MAUGIRON, *arms*, 85 ; Pl. VI., fig. 3, p. 84.
MAULE, *arms*, 517 ; Pl. XVII., fig. 2, p. 172.
,, Earls of PANMURE, *arms*, 171.
,, Lords PANMURE, and Earls of DALHOUSIE, *arms*, 123, 147.
,, Sir DAVID, *arms*, 171.
MAULÉON, *arms*, 214.
MAULEVERER, *badge*, 753.
MAULEVRIER, *arms*, 241.
,, Comtes de, *arms*, 164.
,, Marquises, de, *arms*, 275.
Maunch, Maunche, or *Manche*, 694 ; Pl. XXXIII., fig. 1, p. 376.
,, ,, ,, as a *badge*, 754.
,, ,, ,, as a charge, 376.
MAUNDEVILLE, Sir JOHN, *Travels*, 286.
MAUPEOU, Marquises de, *arms*, 239.
MAURICE, *Blazon des Armoiries de tous les Chevaliers de l'Ordre de la Toison d'Or*, 89, 181, 348, 402, 410, 415, 425, 441, 449, 472, 485, 502, 574.
MAUVOISIN, *arms*, 127.
MAWLEY, *arms*, 130.
MAXELREIN, *see* HOHENWALDECK.
MAXIMILIAN II., Emperor, 387.
,, ,, ,, *augmentation* granted by, 537.
,, Archduke, *supporter*, 633.
,, King of the Romans, *counter-seal* of, 253.
MAXWELL, *arms*, 143.
,, ROBERT, *seal* and *bordure*, 441.
MAXWELLS in south Scotland, 400.
MAYA, *arms*, 365.
MAYER'S, C. VON, *Heraldisches A b c-Buch*, 388.
MAYNARD, *arms*, Pl. XX., fig. 7, p. 198.
,, ST. MICHEL, Counts, *arms*, 204.
,, Lords, *arms*, 204.
MAYNIER, Barons d'OPPEDE, *arms*, 139.
MAZINGEN, *arms*, 348.
MAZINGHEM, *arms*, 86.
MEARES, *arms*, 369.
MEAUX, le Vicomte de, 11.
,, Vicomtes de, *arms*, 337.
MECHLIN, *arms*, 576.
,, Seigneur de, *arms*, 405.
MECKLENBURG, *arms*, 159, 288, 718.
,, Duchy of, *arms*, 492.
,, HENRY the LION of, 492.
,, Princes and Grand Dukes of, *arms*, 79, 205, 492.
MEDCALFE, *arms*, 235.
MEDICI, *arms* and *augmentation*, 538.
,, Grand Dukes of TUSCANY, *arms*, 192.
MEDICO DAL SALE, *arms*, 304.
MEDINA DEL RIO SECO, Dukes of, *arms*, 576.
,, -SIDONIA, Dukes of, *arms*, 390.
Méduse, Tête de, 736.
MEER, VAN DER, *arms*, 322.

MEERMAN, Barons, 303.
MEGENZER, *arms*, Pl. VIII., fig. 4, p. 100.
,, VON, *arms*, 87.
MEGHEM, Barons de, *arms*, 360.
MEGRET or MAIGRET, *arms*, 66.
MEHRENBERG, *arms*, 163.
MÉJUSSUAUME, Vicomtes de, *arms*, 142.
MEIRANS, *arms*, 721.
MELDRUM, *arms*, 238 ; Pl. XXIV., fig. 8, p. 236.
MELGUEIL, Comte de, *arms*, 118.
MELIORATI, *arms*, 310.
Melons, 341.
MELUN, *arms*, 340.
,, HUGUES DE, *arms*, 411.
,, le Vicomte de, 11.
,, *le sire de, arms*, 411.
,, Vicomtes de, *arms*, 349.
Melusine, 303, 736.
Membered, 694.
,, as applied to birds, 257.
Membré, 257, 693, 694, 736.
Membre d'Aigle, 736.
,, *de lion*, 688, 736.
MEMMI, *arms*, 340.
MEMMINGEN, *arms*, 469.
Men on lions as *supporters*, 635.
MENDEL, *arms*, 87.
MENDEZ, *arms*, 219.
MENDOSA, *arms*, Pl. XXXIII., fig. 12, p. 376.
MENDOZA, *arms*, 353, 440, 473, 506.
,, Counts de PRIEGO, *arms*, 473.
,, ,, of CORUÑA, *arms*, 473.
,, DIEGO HURTADO DE, 506.
,, Duke of INFANTADGO, *arms*, 395, 506.
,, MENCIA, 440.
,, PEDRO GONSALEZ DE, 506.
MENESEZ, *arms*, 66, 353, 578.
,, Doña TERESA MARTINEZ DE, 578.
MENESTRIER or MENÊTRIER, *Abrégé Méthodique des Principes Héraldiques*, 2, 24, 44, 51, 61, 353, 388, 446, 552, 553, 579, 601, 653, 676.
,, ,, *l'Art du Blason Justifié*, 154.
,, ,, *La Nouvelle Méthode du Blason*, 169.
,, ,, *La Pratique des Armoiries*, 3.
,, ,, *Méthode du Blason*, 148, 154, 181, 742.
,, ,, on origin of double-headed eagle, 250.
,, ,, on origin of *supporters*, 627.
,, ,, *Recherches du Blazon*, 396, 427, 551, 652.

(821)

MENESTRIER or MENÊTRIER, *Traité de l'Origine des Armoiries et du Blason*, 24, 43, 52, 168, 275, 611.
,, ,, Treatises of, 402.
,, ,, *Usage des Armoiries*, 628, 637.
,, ,, *Véritable Art du Blason*, 405.
MENSCHIKOFF, Princes, *arms* and *augmentation*, 542.
MENSDORFF-POUILLY, Counts, *arms*, 212.
MENTEITH, *arms*, 130.
,, Earl of, *arms* on Eagle, 630.
,, ,, *label*, 419.
MENTZ, Archbishop of, 282.
Menu-vair, 69, 736.
Menuvairé, 736.
MENZIES, *arms*, 118.
MEPPEN, *arms*, 90.
Mer agité, 708.
MERAVIGLIA, Counts of, *arms*, 139.
Mercantile Marine, *flag* of British, 657.
MERCKELSBACH, *arms*, 162.
MERCŒUR, *arms*, 128.
Mercury, 65, 694.
MEREDITH, *arms*, 213.
MERGETH AP CYNAN, *arms*, 199.
MERKMAN, *arms*, 752.
Merlette, 266, 694, 736.
Merlion, 694.
Merlons, 685, 695, 724.
Mermaid, 300; Pl. XXVII., fig. 12, p. 288.
,, as a *badge*, 754.
Mermaids as *supporters*, 634.
Merman, The, 302.
MERSEMAN, *arms*, 184.
MERTON, *arms*, 343.
MERTZ, *crest*, 612.
MESLAY, Comte de, *arms*, 280.
MESNIL, LE RÉVÉREND DU, *arms*, 68.
MESTICH, *arms*, 290.
Metal on Metal, etc., 102.
Metals, 695.
,, represented by dots, etc., 64.
,, ,, ,, planets and precious stones, 65.
,, *used in Heraldry*, 60.
Métaux, 736.
METCALFE, *arms*, 235.
METHVEN, Lord of, *arms*, 521; Pl. XLII., fig. 3, p. 512.
,, Lordship of, *arms*, 522.
METSCH, *arms*, 136.
METTERNICH, Counts of, *arms*, 491.
METTLER, *augmentation*, 546.
Meubles, 737.
MEULAN, *seal* and *arms* of JEAN DE 49.
,, ,, ,, ROGER DE, 49.
MEULLENT, Counts of, *arms*, 214.
MEUNIER, LE, 16.
MEUX, JOHN DE, *arms*, 289.
MEXBOROUGH, Earl of, *arms*, 130.
MEXICO, City of, 547.
,, ,, as a charge, 363.
MEYNELL, *arms*, 71.
MEYRICK, Sir CHARLES, 47.

Mezail, 737.
MEZERAY, *l'Abrégé Chronologique de l'Histoire de France*, 38.
Mi-parti, 737.
MICHAEL, *coins of*, 250.
MICHELI, *arms*, 93, 389.
,, Doge DOMENICO, *arms*, 389.
MICHELL, *arms*, 185.
MICHEL'S *Les Ecossais en France*, 446.
Midas, *Head of*, 201, 606, 737.
,, *Tête de*, 201, 606, 737.
MIEROSZEWSKY, in Silesia, *arms*, 61.
MIGNIANELLI, *arms*, 70. 71.
MILAN, Duchy of, *arms*, 274, 275, 495, 502, 505.
,, Duke of, *augmentation*, 538.
,, *standard* of, 655.
Military charges, 345.
Mill-pick, 695.
,, -*rind*, 695.
,, -*sail* as a *badge*, 754.
,, -*sails* as *charges*, 393.
MILLAR, *crest*, 204.
MILLESIMO, Counts, *arms*, 95.
,, Marquises DE SAVONA, *arms*, 641.
MILLY, *arms*, 337.
MILON, 12.
MILTOWN, Earl of, *arms*, 311.
MINGOVAL, Seigneur de, 451.
MINIBERTI, *arms*, 347.
Miniver, 695, 736.
MINSHULL, *arms*, 307.
MINTO, Earl of, *arms*, 200.
MINUTOLI, *arms*, 223.
MIOLANS, *arms*, 95.
Miraillé, 704, 737.
MIRAMOMELIN, Commander of the Moors, 353.
MIRANDA, Counts of, *arms*, 506.
MIRANDOLA, Dukes of, *arms*, 509.
,, ,, *augmentation*, 537.
,, *mantling*, 616.
MIREPOIX, Duc de, *arms*, 140.
MIRON, 12.
Mirrors as charges, 391.
Mit einer lincken stufe, 87; Pl. VIII., fig. 3, p. 100.
,, *rechten stufe*, 87.
MITCHELL, *arms*, 185.
MITFORD, *arms*, Pl. XXIV., fig. 11, p. 236.
,, Lord REDESDALE, *arms*, 239.
Mitre, 695.
,, as a *charge*, 371.
,, as a *crest*, 608.
Mitred figure as a *crest*, 608.
MITTROWSKI, *arms*, 121.
MIZOU, *arms*, 93.
MOCENIGO, *arms*, 322.
MODENA, Dukes of, 256.
,, ,, *arms*, 502, 508.
,, ,, *augmentation*, 537, 541.
MOER, Barons VAN DE, *supporter*, 640.
MOFFAT, *arms*, 144, 145.
MOHR DE TARANTSBERG, Counts, *arms*, 200.
MOHUN, *arms*, 142, 205.
,, JOHN DE, *arms*, 458.
,, WILLIAM DE, *arms*, 376.

(822)

MOIGNE, Sir WILLIAM, *arms* transferred to, 755.
,, ,, *arms* granted to, 35.
MOIGNON, *see* BARTELLE.
MOLAY, DE, *arms*, 129.
MOLDAVIA, *arms*, 667.
Mole, 239; Pl. XXIV., fig. 11, p. 236.
MOLEMBAIS, *arms*, 128, 450.
,, BALDWIN DE, *arms*, 450.
MOLEN, Marquis DE ST. PONCY, *arms*, 145.
MOLESWORTH, Viscounts, *supporters*, 298.
Molette, 308, 737.
MOLEYNS, DE, 17.
MOLINA, Sir NICOLO DE, *arms* and *augmentation*, 535.
Moline, Cross, 158, 695.
MOLINEUX, *arms*, 159.
MOLL, *arms*, 239; Pl. XIII., fig. 4, p. 136.
,, VON, *arms*, 137.
MOLLE, *arms*, 239.
MOLSBACH, VON, *arms*, 713.
MOLSEN, Battle of, 243.
MOLYNEUX, *arms*, Pl. XV., fig. 1, p. 144.
,, Earls of SEFTON, *arms*, 159.
MOLTKE, *arms*, 266.
,, Count VON, *arms* and *augmentation*, 544.
MONACO, Princes of, *arms*, 100, 668.
MONCADA, *arms*, 391.
MONCHY, DE, *arms*, 303.
Monde, 695, 696, 737.
MONESTAY, *arms*, 128.
Money as a charge, 389.
MONFRAIN, *arms*, 187.
Monk, demi-, as a *crest*, 605.
MONMOUTH, Duke of, *arms*, 146, 559.
MONNET, Sires de, *arms*, 389.
MONRO of Foulis, *arms*, 259.
Monsters, 286.
Monstrance as a charge, 372.
Monstrueux, 737.
Mont, 690.
MONTACUTE, *arms*, 183, 257, 287, 562; Pl. XVIII., fig. 9, p. 190.
,, *badge*, 754.
,, Earls of SALISBURY, 562.
,, Lord, *badge*, 753.
,, SIMON, 562.
,, DE, *arms*, 287.
MONTAGU, 548, 557, 586.
,, Dukes of MANCHESTER and Earls of SANDWICH, *arms*, 562.
,, Earls of SALISBURY, *arms*, 183.
,, Family, 459.
,, *Guide to the Study of Heraldry*, 25, 548, 556.
,, Marquess of, *Garter Plate*, 486.
,, of Ludsdowne, JAMES, 562.
,, Sir EDWARD DE, *arms*, 417.
MONTALEMBERT, *arms*, Pl. XV., fig. 2, p. 144.
,, Marquises de, *arms*, 159.

MONTALT, *arms*, 213.
MONTANGON, *arms*, 85.
Montant, 306, 695, 724, 737.
MONTAUBAN, *arms*, 112, 137.
,, Princes de, *arms*, 185.
MONTAUSIER, Ducs de, *arms*, 124.
MONTBAR, DE, *arms*, 88.
MONTBAZON, *arms*, 214.
,, Ducs de, *arms*, 185, 505.
MONTBEILLARD, Counts of, *arms*, 270; Pl. XLIV., fig. 3, p. 537.
MONTBELIARD, *seal* of THIERRY II., Count of, 47 (*see* MUMPELGARD).
MONTCHAL, *arms*, 193.
MONTCHENSY, *arms*, 169.
MONTCLAR, *arms*, 136.
MONTCONIS, *arms*, 127.
MONTE-APERTO, Battle of, 655.
MONTEBELLO, Duc de, *arms*, 346.
MONTEIL, ADHÉMAR DE, Comte de GRIGNAN, *arms*, 132.
MONTEIRO DE CAMPOS, M. A., *La Nobiliarchia Portugueza*, 381, 425, 578.
MONTENDRE, ALIANORE, 466.
MONTENEGRO, *arms*, 668.
MONTEPULCIANO, *arms*, 288.
MONTESQUIOU, DE, *arms*, 108.
,, Marquis de FEZENSAC, *arms*, 191.
MONTFAUCON, *Les Monumens de la Monarchie Française*, 31, 282, 328.
MONTFERRAT, Duchy of, *arms*, 118.
,, Marquesses of, *arms*, 250.
MONTFORD, Barons, *arms*, 82.
MONTFORT, *arms*, 96, 162, 742, 743; Pl. XV., fig. 6, p. 144.
,, *arms* of Counts of, 373, 499.
,, Seigneurs de, 10.
,, SIMON DE, Earl of LEICESTER, *arms*, 218; Pl. XXI., fig. 9, p. 212; *banner of*, 456.
MONTGOMERY, *arms*, 50, 219, 331.
,, Earl of, *arms*, 224.
,, JOHN, *badge*, 583.
,, Sir THOMAS, *badge*, 598.
MONTGOMMERY, *arms*, 219.
MONTHERMER, *arms*, Pl. XXV., fig. 1, p. 260.
,, RALPH DE, Earl of GLOUCESTER, *arms*, 257.
MONTI, *arms*, 72, 73; Pl. VIII., fig. 6, p. 100.
MONTJEAN, *arms*, 96.
MONTJOY, *arms*, 112.
MONTLEART, *arms*, 191.
MONTLEON, *arms*, 214.
MONTMORENCY, DE, *arms*, 258, 451, 752.
,, ,, *badge*, 586.
,, ,, *brisures*, 451.
,, ,, kills HENRY II. of France, 40.
,, ,, MATHIEU, *banner*, 651.
,, ,, ,, I., *seal* of, 48.
,, ,, ,, II., *seal* of 37, 48.
,, ,, MATTHIEU, *crested helm*, 599.
,, -LAVAL, *arms*, 258, 452, 460, 463, 504.

(823)

MONTMORENCY-LAVAL, GUY DE, arms, 463.
,, Lord of, 11.
,, -LUXEMBOURG, 452.
,, see BOUCHARD.
MONTPELLIER; Seigneurs de, 10.
MONTPENSIER, Ducs de, bend, 429.
MONTRAVEL, Comte de, arms, 317.
MONTREVEL, Comtes de, arms, 81; brisure, 434.
MONTROSE, Burgh of, arms, 324, 522.
,, Duke of, arms, 273.
,, ,, seal, 522.
MONTS, see RIVIÈRE, 729.
Monumenta Zollerana, 455.
Monuments, Armorial bearings on, 43.
Monymusk reliquary, 657.
MONYPENNY, arms, 270.
,, THOMAS, of Kinkell, chevron, 431.
Monza, Basilica of, 617.
Moon, The, 306.
Moor-jord, 267.
Moor's Head, 200; Pl. XX., fig. 6, p. 198.
Moose-deer, The, 232.
Morailles, 678, 718, 737.
MORANDAIS, see CHATON.
MORAVIA, arms, 496, 500, 665.
,, Markgravate of, arms, 256.
MORAY, cushions of, 518.
,, Earl of, arms, 177, 378, 435, 516, 567.
,, ELIZABETH, Countess of, 567.
,, Regent, arms, 567.
,, THOMAS, Earl of, arms, 378.
MORDWINOFF, augmentation, 542.
MOREA, PHILIP, Prince of the, 579.
MORETON, 12.
,, arms, 241.
MOREUIL, arms, 221.
MORGAN, arms, 213, 288.
,, SYLVANUS, Sphere of Gentry and Armilogia, 23, 59, 644.
MORHEM, MONTMORENCY - LAVAL DE, brisure, 452.
MORICE, Mémoires pour servir de Preuves à l'Histoire Ecclésiastique et Civile de Bretagne, 46, 413, 460, 461, 463, 634.
MORIEN, arms, 188.
Morion, 695.
Morions as charges, 392.
MORISON, arms, Pl. XX., fig. 5, p. 198.
,, of Dairsie, arms, 200.
MORLEY, arms, 226.
,, Earls of, arms, 186.
,, Lord, badge, 753.
MORNAY, DE, arms, 218.
Morné or Mortné, 218, 683, 695, 737.
MORNY, Duc de, arms, 266, 572.
MOROSINI, arms, 129.
MORRA, Dukes of BELFORTE, arms and augmentation, 541.
,, Princes of MORRA, etc., arms and augmentation, 541.
MORRISON, arms, 732.
MORSAN, Marquises de, arms, 372.
Morse, 695.
MORSKI, Counts, arms, 348.
MORSLEDE, VAN, arms, 132.
Mort, 695.
MORTAGNE, Princes de, arms, 94.
Mortaisé line, 77, 678, 684, 737.
MORTAL, see DIDIER.

Mortar, 695.
MORTE, arms, 203.
MORTEMAR, Ducs de, arms, 93.
MORTEMER, arms, 448.
Mortier, 625, 737.
MORTIMER, arms, 112, 331, 448, 479, 557; Pl. XVIII., fig. 5, p. 190.
,, badge, 754.
,, Earl of MARCH, arms, 168, 169.
,, EDMUND, seal of, 168, 448; Pl. XXXVII., fig. 2, p. 448; supporters, 634.
,, GEOFFREY DE, arms, 448.
,, HENRY DE, arms, 448.
,, JOAN DE, arms, 448.
,, RAF DE, arms, 448.
,, ROGER, 591.
,, ,, arms, 448.
,, WILLIAM DE, arms, 448.
Mortné, 695.
MORTON, Earl of, arms, 179.
,, ,, mantling armoyé, 616.
MORVILLE, arms, 474.
MOSCOSO, arms, 507.
,, OSORIOS DE, arms, 507.
MOSCOW, arms, 542, 665.
,, arms of Grand Duke IVAN BASILOWITZ of, 250.
,, Kremlin at, 622.
MOST, arms, 89.
MOSTYN, Lord, arms, 200.
MOTTE-FOUQUÉ, Barons de la, arms, 333.
,, JEANNE, Comtesse de la, and her sister MARIANNE, arms, 570.
,, LA, arms, 170.
MOTTEROUGE, see LINIÈRES.
Motto, 695.
Mottoes, Royal, 664.
MOUCHARD, Comte de CHABAN, arms, 281.
Moucheté, 704, 737.
Mouchetures, 695, 737.
MOUCHY, Ducs de, arms, 129.
MOULE, THOMAS, The Heraldry of Fish, 268, 271, 299, 300, 301, 302, 614, 615, 729.
MOULINS, arms, 91.
MOULTON of Frankton, Lord, arms, 404.
,, ,, Gillesland, Lord, arms, 404.
,, THOMAS, Baron of EGREMONT, arms, 404.
Mound, 695.
Mount, A, 311, 695; Pl. XXVIII, fig. 8, p. 308.
,, Burning, 314; Pl. XXVIII., fig. 10, p. 308.
MOUNT-TEMPLE, Lord, supporter, 298.
Mounted, 695.
MOUNTENEY, arms, 403.
MOUNTFORD, arms, 96, 214.
Mounting, 695.
Mourné, 695.
Mouser, A, 97.
MOUSKES, PHILIPPE, rhyming chronicle of France, 245, 658.
MOUSSAYE, LA, Vicomte de ST. DENOUAL, arms, 96.
Mouton, 703, 737.
,, à piloter, 737.

Mouvant, 737.
MOWBRAY, *arms*, 213.
,, *badge*, 754.
,, GEOFFREY DE, *label*, 419.
,, Lord, *supporter*, 300.
,, THOMAS, Duke of NOR-FOLK, *arms*, 474.
,, ,, Duke of NORFOLK, *augmentation*, 528.
MOYLE, *arms*, 237.
MOYNE, LE, family, 605.
MOZZI, *arms*, 161; Pl. XV., fig. 7, p. 144.
MUCHAMPS, *arms*, 280.
MUCKELOW, WILLIAM, 563.
MUDERSBACH, *arms*, 85.
MÜHL, Barons, *arms*, 318.
MÜHLINGEN, County of, *arms*, 256.
MULA, Counts DA, *supporters*, 640.
Mulberry as a *badge*, 754.
Mule, The, 237.
MULERT, *arms*, 140.
MÜLLER, Baron, *arms*, 339.
Mullet, The, 308, 695; Pl. XXVIII., fig. 7, p. 308.
,, for third son, 444.
MULLINS, 17.
MULTON, *arms*, 127, 474, 641.
MUMPELGARD, Counts of, *arms*, 270.
,, ,, *crest*, 607.
MUN, Marquises de, *arms*, 381.
MUNDEGUMBRI, of Eagleshame, JOHN DE, *seal* and *arms* of, 50.
MUNGO, ST., 271.
MUNOIS, GUI DE, Monk of St. Germain l'Auxerrois, *seal* of, 672; Pl. XXXVII., fig. 3, p. 448.
MUÑOZ, *arms*, 353.
MUNRO, *arms*, Pl. XXV., fig. 4, p. 260.
MUNSTER, 384.
,, Earl of, *arms*, 560.
MUNSTERBERG, Dukes of, *arms*, 234.
MUNTZENBERG, Counts of, *arms*, 79.
MÜNZENBERG, *arms*, 488.
Mur, 737.
Mural-crown, 695.
MURAT, 206.
MURRAY, *arms*, 308.
,, *arms in Lyon Office Register*, 400.
,, of Bothwell, *arms*, 514, 515, 516.
,, ,, ,, THOMAS, 514.
,, ,, Culbin, *arms*, 406.
,, ,, Touchadam, *arms*, 179.
,, ,, Tullibardine, *arms*, 179.
,, Sir ANDREW, *bordure*, 442.
,, THOMAS, Bishop of CAITHNESS, *seal* of, 369.
,, WILLIAM of Gask, *chevron*, 431.
,, ,, son of Sir MALCOLM, *label*, 419.
Murrey, 695.
MUSCHAMP, *arms*, 128, 281.
Muschetours, 695.
Mushroom, 344.
Musical instruments as charges, 382.
Musimon, 695.
Musion, 97, 226, 695.
MUSY, *arms*, 213.
Muzzled, 695.
MYNTER, *arms*, 364.
MYPONT, *arms*, 136.

Nacelle, 737.
NACHTIGAL, *augmentation*, 546.
Nageant, 696, 737.
Naiant, 268, 696.
Nailed, 696.
NAIMER, *arms*, 374.
Naissant, 221, 696, 734, 737; Pl. XXII., fig. 5, p. 222.
NAMANS, Barons, *arms*, 126.
NAMUR, Counts of, *arms*, 429; Pl. XLIV., fig. 2, p. 538.
,, LOUIS DE, *crest*, 592.
,, ROBERT DE, *bend*, 429.
,, ,, *crest*, 592.
NANI, *arms*, 78, 80.
NAPIER, ALEXANDER, 466.
,, *arms*, 144, 325.
,, of Culcreuch, *brisure*, 436.
,, ,, Merchiston, *brisure*, 432.
,, PATRICK, Lord, *arms*, 179.
NAPIER'S *Partition of the Lennox*, 180.
NAPLES, Conquest of, 620.
,, FREDERICK, King of, 505.
,, Kingdom, *arms*, 502.
NAPOLEON I., Emperor of the FRENCH, 309, 513; *mantling*, 616.
,, III., Emperor of the FRENCH, 390; *augmentation* granted by, 541.
,, *crown* of, 621.
,, never conferred title of Marquess, 626.
,, substitutes *toques* for *coronets*, 626.
NAPOLEON'S *golden bees*, 281, 282.
NARBONNE, Battle of, 658.
,, Ducs de, *arms*, 66.
Narcissus, 696.
NARISCHKIN, *arms*, 746.
NASH, *arms*, 219.
NASHE, *arms*, Pl. XXI., fig. 10, p. 212.
NASSAU, *arms*, 163, 212, 215, 256, 385, 404, 466, 487, 580, 581, 602; Pl. VIII., fig. 11, p. 100.
,, coins of ADOLF of, 246.
,, ENGELBERT, Comte de, *wreath*, 614.
,, *motto*, 664.
,, -ORANGE, HENRY FREDERICK, Prince of, 580.
,, ,, Marks of illegitimacy in, 580.
,, ,, MAURICE, Prince of, 580.
,, OUWERKERKE, HENRY, Count of, 580.
,, Princes of ORANGE, *arms*, 113.
,, RICHARDE DE, *arms*, 409.
NATHELEY, *arms*, 274; Pl. XXVII., fig. 1, p. 288.
National arms, 664.
,, *flags*, 655.
Naturel, Au, 738.
Naval Reserve, *flag* of, 657.
Naval crown, 696.
NAVARRE, *arms*, 66, 235, 353, 354, 464, 465, 479, 505, 635, 636, 710; Pl. XXXI., fig. 10, p. 346.
,, BLANCHE DE, *seal*, 461.
,, *chains of*, 354, 456.
,, JOAN DE, *seal*, 464.

(825)

NAVARRE, King of, *crest coronet*, 615.
„ PHILIP, King of, 464.
Navire, 688, 738, 746.
Navy, *flag* of Royal, 656.
Naworth Castle, 641.
NAYE, DE LA, *arms*, 74.
NEATH, Lordship of, 386.
Nebulé, 696, 738.
„ *line*, 76; Fig. 22, p. 75.
Nebuly or *Nebulée*, 696.
Needle-gun as a charge, 366.
NEILSON, *arms*, 109.
NELSON, Lord Viscount, *arms* and *augmentation*, 534, 610.
NEMAUSUS, *medal* of, 277.
NEMI, Dukes of, *arms*, 311.
Nenuphar leaf, 321, 738.
„ *Feuilles de*, 738.
NEPTUNE as a charge, 196.
NERFORD, ALICE DE, *arms*, 554.
„ *arms*, 426.
Nervé, 696, 738.
Nerved, 696.
NESLE, Marquis de, *arms*, 202.
NESSELRODE, Counts von, *arms*, 124.
NETHERLANDS, Admirals of, mark of office, 626.
„ *arms*, 667.
„ *coronet* of a Count in the, 625.
„ „ a Viscount in, 625.
„ „ Marquises in, 624.
„ *motto*, 667.
„ *Royal supporters*, 667.
„ Use of *supporters* in the, 639.
NETTANCOURT, Marquis of, *arms*, 137.
Nettle, The, 320.
NEU, Barons, *supporter*, 640.
NEUENHOF, Barons von, *arms*, 355.
NEUFCHÂTEL, *arms*, 415.
„ CLAUDE DE, *arms* and *label*, 415.
„ HENRY DE, 415.
„ THIEBAUT, Seigneur de, 415.
NEUFVILLE, *arms*, 96.
„ Baron de, *arms*, 331.
„ *see* MALAPERT.
NEUHOFF, Barons von, *arms*, 355.
NEUMAYER, *arms*, 374.
NEVERS, *arms*, 458, 631.
„ JOHN, Count de, 462.
„ LOUIS, Count of, *seal*, 462.
„ „ DE, Count of FLANDERS, 457.
„ PHILIPPE, *bâtard de, arms*, 576.
„ „ Comte de, 576.
„ YOLANTE, Comtesse de, *brisure*, 439.
NEVILE, *arms*, 213.
NEVILLE, *badge*, 753, 754.
„ Earl of WARWICK, *badge*, 585.
„ „ „ etc., *arms*, 143.
„ of Raby, *arms*, 410.
„ Sir JOHN, Marquess of MONTAGU, *Garter Plate*, 486.
NEWCASTLE, Duke of, *arms*, 163.
„ Duke of, *supporters*, 605.

NEWDEGATE, *arms*, 222; Pl. XXII. fig. 7, p. 222.
NEWMAN, Colonel, *arms* and *augmentation*, 532.
NEWPORT, Earl of, *arms*, 561.
NEYDECK, Barons von, *arms*, 137.
NICEY, *supporters*, 198.
NICHOLS, J. GOUGH, *Herald and Genealogist*, 46, 110, 111, 638.
„ „ *Rules of Blazon*, 110.
NICOLAS, Sir HARRIS, on the *badge* of Ostrich Feathers, 592.
NICOLAY, Counts, *arms*, 241.
NICOLSON, *arms*, 262.
NIEDER LAUSITZ, Margravate of, *arms*, 234.
NIEMPTSCHER, DIE, *arms*, 297.
NIESIECKI, *Korona Polska*, 359.
NIGHTINGALE, *arms*, 324.
Nillé, 696, 713.
N MES, City of, *arms*, 277.
NISBET, Scottish Herald, *An Essay on the Ancient and Modern Use of Armory*, 2.
„ *Marks of Cadency*, 401.
„ on origin of *double-headed eagle*, 248.
„ *System of Heraldry*, 2, 23, 83, 84, 157, 158, 159, 227, 248, 401, 447, 479, 529, 548, 552, 557, 569, 575, 605, 615, 684.
NITHARD, 39.
Noah's Ark as a charge, 371.
NOAILLES, Ducs de NOAILLES, *arms*, 129.
„ „ MOUCHY, *arms*, 129.
„ Prince de FOIX, *arms*, 129.
NOBELAER, *arms*, 262.
Nobiliarchia Portuguesa, 381, 425, 578.
Nobility, Definitions of, 37.
Noble, Use of term, 6.
Nobles, *coronet* of, 626.
„ *helm* of, 601.
NOCERA, JOVIUS, Bishop of, 52.
NOÉ, LA, *arms*, 213.
NOEL, *arms*, Pl. XVIII., fig. 1, p. 190.
„ Earls of GAINSBOROUGH, *arms*, 96.
NOGARET, *arms*, 318.
NOLTHENIUS, *arms*, 196.
NOMAING, MONTMORENCY DE, *brisure*, 451.
Nombril, 696, 738.
NOMPAR, *arms*, 87.
„ Ducs de la FORCE, 12.
NOORDEN, VAN, *arms*, 213.
NOORT, VAN, *arms*, 238.
NOOTEN, VAN, *arms*, 387.
NORFOLK, Duke of, *arms*, 408, 474.
„ „ *augmentation*, 528, 629.
„ „ *crest*, 607.
„ Dukes of, *arms*, 99, 213.
„ THOMAS, Duke of, 558.
NORIE, *arms*, 175.
NORMAN *flags*, 649.
„ kings, *arms* of, 661; Pl. LI., fig. 1, p. 661.
„ *shield*, 54.
NORMANBY and BUCKINGHAM, JOHN, Duke of, 562.

(826)

NORMANDY, Duchy of, *arms*, 468 ; 554.
,, *furs* common in *armory* of, 74.
,, *seal* and *arms* of JOHN, Duke of, 629.
,, WILLIAM, Duke of, 29, 30.
NORONHAS, *arms*, 577, 578.
NORROY, King of Arms, *arms*, 526.
NORTH, Baroness, *supporters*, 292.
NORTHALLERTON, Battle of, 655.
NORTHBROOK, Earl of, *arms*, 230.
NORTHCOTE, *arms*, 132 ; Pl. IX., fig. 10, p. 108.
,, Lord IDDESLEIGH, *arms*, 108.
NORTHUMBERLAND, Duke of, *arms*, 488, 559.
,, Dukes and Earls of, *arms*, 184, 214, 481.
,, Earl of, 482, 641.
,, ,, *standard* of, 654.
NORTON, *arms*, 147.
NORWAY, 379.
,, and SWEDEN, personal *arms* of King of, 667.
,, *arms*, 208, 581, 667.
,, Marks of illegitimacy in, 581.
,, Royal House of, 581.
NORWICH, HENRY LE DESPENCER, Bishop of, *brisure*, 437.
Notes and Queries, 62, 134, 167, 335, 530, 586.
Noué, 696, 738.
Noueux, 692, 738.
Nourri, 738.
NOUST, *arms*, 283.
NOVGOROD, *arms*, 665.
NOVION, Seigneur de, 12.
Nowed, 274, 696.
NOYCE, *arms*, 337.
NOYON, PIERRE, Bishop of, *arms*, 570.
NOZIER, *arms*, 318.
Nuagé, 696, 738.
,, *line*, 76.
Nuées, 738.
NUGENT, Marquises of WESTMEATH, *arms*, 126.
NÜREMBERG, or NÜRNBERG, *arms*, 440, 469, 494.
,, Burg-grave of, 255, 454.
,, *crest*. Pl. XLIX., fig. 3, p. 606.
,, Burg-grafin of, *arms*, 471.
,, City of, *arms*, 296.
,, FREDERICK of HOHENZOLLERN, Burg-grave of, 255.
NUSBERG, *arms*, 579, 580.
NUSSBERG, *arms*, 580.
NUTSHALL, *arms*, 240.
NUVOLONI, *arms*, 72.
NYDEGGEN, Marquesses of, *arms*, 214.

Oak, The, 315, 316.
OBER-LAUSITZ, Markgravate of, *arms*, 362.
OBERNBURG, *arms*, 670 ; Pl. LVI., fig. 7, p. 670.
OBERREIDERN, *arms*, 370.
O'CALLAGHAN, Viscounts, *arms*, 316.
OCHSENSTEIN, Baron von, *arms*, 126.
OCHTERLONY, *arms*, 569.

O'CONOR-DON, *arms*, 317.
ODENKIRCHEN, *arms*, 93.
ODET, *arms*, 347.
ODC, Bishop of BAYEUX, 29.
,, *filius* ISAMBARDI, 10.
ODORSKI, *arms*, 289.
OELPER, *arms*, 229.
OETTER, *Wappenbelustigung*, 244.
OFFER, *arms*, 370.
Official arms, 525.
OFFORD, D', *arms*, 142.
OGILVIE, JOHN, Sheriff-depute of Inverness, *bend*, 430.
OGILVY, Earl of AIRLY, *arms*, 216.
,, of Inverquharity, *supporters* and *compartment*, 642.
OGLANDER, *arms*, 263 ; Pl. XXV., fig. 11, p. 260.
OGLE, *badge*, 753.
Ogress, 190, 696.
OHA DE ROCOURT, *arms*, 188.
O'HARA, *arms*, Pl. X., fig. 8, p. 118.
,, Lords, TYRAWLEY, *arms*, 121.
OHEY, D', *see* MAILLEN.
Oiseau-duc, 697.
OISI, Comtes d', *arms*, 221.
OKE, *arms*, 341.
OKEDEN, *arms*, 341.
O'KELLY, *arms*, 361.
OKSZA-GRABOWSKI, Counts, 348.
OKULICZ, *arms*, 348.
OLDENBURG, Princes of, *arms*, 127, 487, 510, 666.
OLDHAM, Bishop, *arms*, 264.
OLDMIXON, *arms*, 348.
OLIPHANT, *arms*, 307 ; Pl. XXVIII., fig. 2, p. 308.
,, of Bachilton, *chevron*, 431.
,, of Condie, *arms*, 172 ; Pl. XVII., fig. 5, p. 172.
,, of Kelly, *bordure*, 441.
,, of Prinlis, *chevron*, 431.
OLIVAREZ, "*Conde-Duque*," 624.
OLIVER, *arms*, 317.
OLIVET, MONTMORENCY-LAVAL D', *brisure*, 452.
,, MONTMORENCY-LAVAL D', JEANNE, *arms*, 463.
OLIVIERA, *arms*, 317.
OLIVIERS, *arms*, 317.
OLUJA, *arms*, 141.
OMBALE, D', *see* DESGABETS.
Ombelle, 738.
Ombré, 696, 706, 738.
Ombre de lion, 738.
,, ,, *soleil*, 305, 684, 738.
OMODEI, *arms*, 81.
OMPHAL, D', *arms*, 146.
Ondé, 76, 706.
Ondée or *Ondy*, 696.
Ondoyant, 272, 689, 738.
,, in *pal*, 275.
Ondoyants en pal, 274.
Ondy, 696, 738.
O'NEILL, *difference*, 569.
,, Earl of TYRONE, *arms*, 204.
O'NEYLANS, *arms*, 292.
Onglé, 232, 707, 738.
ONSLOW, *arms*, 264 ; Pl. XXVI., fig. 1, p. 266.
OOSTDIJK, *arms*, 143.
OOSTENWOLDE, VAN, *arms*, 187.
Opinicus, 696.
OPPEDE, Barons d', *arms*, 139.

(827)

Oppressed, 696.
Or or Gold, 60, 65, 696, 738 ; Pl. III., fig. 1, p. 60.
,, *plein d'*, 66.
Orange, 738.
,, *branch*, 338.
,, or *Tenny*, 60, 65.
ORANGE, *arms*, 461.
,, CHARLOTTE and ISABEL, daughters of WILLIAM, Count of, *arms*, 466.
,, CHARLOTTE, daughter of WILLIAM, Prince of, 258.
,, DE LA FEILLÉE, D', *arms*, 340.
,, Princes of, *arms*, 113, 129, 146, 385.
,, WILLIAM of, 580.
Oranges, 190, 340.
Orb, 696.
,, *of Sovereignty* as a charge, 380.
ORCION, *see* BILQUES.
Ordinaries, 78, 102, 116, 696.
,, *Honourable*, 116.
,, Origin of, 117.
,, *Subordinate*, 116, 165, 696.
Ordinary, Difference by addition of an, 428.
,, ,, *changing the boundary line of an*, 432.
Ordonnance of CHARLES III., Duke of LORRAINE, 748.
Ordonnances, regulating use of *de*, 12, 13.
Oreillé, 738.
Oreillers, 378, 697, 738.
Oreilles, 273.
ORENGES DE LIMÉROU, *arms*, 340.
Organ-pipes as charges, 386.
,, *-rest*, 697.
,, *-rests* as charges, 386.
Oriflamme, of FRANCE, 657, 658.
Origen de las dignidades seglares de Castilla y Leon, 390.
ORIGO, *arms*, 86.
ORIOL, *arms*, 715.
ORKNEY, Earldom of, 511 ; *arms*, 368, 369, 511, 512, 567.
,, *seal* of Earl of, 369.
ORKNEYS, Norse Jarls of the, 511.
Orlé, 697, 739.
Orle, En, 739.
,, *In*, 697.
,, *of martlets*, Pl. XVII., fig. 9, p. 172.
,, The, 116, 165, 174, 697, 738 ; Pl. XVII., fig. 8, p. 172.
ORLÉANS, Dukes of, *arms*, 530, 571, 572.
,, House of, *label*, 424, 425.
,, JEAN, *bâtard d'*, *arms*, 571.
,, *Le bâtard d'*, *arms*, 571.
,, LOUIS, Duc d', *arms*, 529.
,, PHILIPPE, Duc d', 571.
ORLÖFF, Counts and Princes, *augmentation*, 542.
ORMOND, Earl of, 516.
,, *knot*, 585.
ORMONDE, JAMES, Duke of, 570.
,, BUTLERS of, *arms*, 381.
Ornaments, External, 599, 617, 627.
ORSBECK, *arms*, 493.
ORSENIGHI, *arms*, 394.
ORSINI, *arms*, 120 ; Pl. X., fig. 6, p. 118.
ORTELART, *arms*, 93.
ORTENBURG, Counts von, *arms*, 260.
ORTINS, *arms*, 173.

ORTLIEB, *arms*, 320, 321 ; Pl. XXIX., fig. 9, p. 318.
ORY, *arms*, 277.
ORZON, *arms*, 669 ; Pl. LVI., fig. 1, p. 670.
O'SHEA, *arms*, 347.
OSMOND, 12.
OSORIO, *arms*, 507.
,, Count of ALTAMIRA, *arms*, 507.
,, ,, ,, TRASTAMARA, *arms*, 507.
,, ,, ,, VILLALOBOS, *arms*, 507.
,, DE MOSCOSO, *arms*, 507.
,, Dukes of AGUIAR, etc., *arms*, 507.
OSSOLIN-OSSOLINSKI, Counts, *arms*, 348.
OSSUNA, Duke of, *arms*, 167, 168, 441 ; Pl. XLI., fig. 2, p. 510.
OST-FRIESLAND, Princes of, *arms*, 295.
OSTEN, *see* PROKESCH.
OSTENSACKEN, *augmentation*, 542.
OSTERBECH, *arms*, 295.
OSTERHAMMER, *arms*, 236.
OSTERHAUSEN, *arms*, 236.
OSTERRIETH, *arms*, 236.
OSTERTAG, *arms*, 236.
OSTICHE, Barons d', *arms*, 122.
OSTREVANT, Comte d', 589, *seal, supporter*, and *compartment*, 642.
,, County of, 592.
,, *seal* of Count of, 251.
,, WILLIAM, Count of, *arms* on eagle, 630.
Ostrich as a *badge*, 754.
,, *feathers*, 263.
,, ,, as a *badge*, 591, 598.
,, The, 263.
OSTROWSKI, *arms*, 289, 371.
OSWALD, *arms*, 198.
Otelle, 154.
Otelles, 739.
OTHÉGRAVEN, *arms*, 162.
OTTACAR VON STEYERMARCK, poem by, 246.
OTTAVIO, Duke, 509.
Otter, Pl. XXIV., fig. 8, p. 236.
Otters and *Otter's heads*, 238.
OTTO IV., Emperor, *coins* of, 244, 245.
OUDENHAGEN, VAN, *arms*, 428.
OULTRE, *arms*, 143.
OUPEY, *arms*, 112, 331.
OUTRAM, *supporters*, 224.
Ouvert, 686, 697, 739.
Over all, 697.
Overt, 697.
OVID, *Metamorphoses*, 300.
Owl, The, 262, 697 ; Pl. XXV., fig. 9, p. 260.
OWSTINS, *arms*, 137.
Oxen, 234.
OXENSTJERNA, 673.
OXFORD, City of, *arms*, 312.
,, Earl of, 438.
,, ,, *arms*, 132, 410.
,, ,, *badge*, 753.
OYLY, D', *arms*, 132.
OYRY, *arms*, 182.

PABST, *arms*, 372.
Pacta successionis, 483.

PACY, MONTMORERCY-LAVAL DE, *brisure*, 452.
PADILLAS, *arms*, 390.
PADUA, City of, *arms*, 141.
PAERNON, *arms*, 66.
PAEUW, DE, *arms*, 267.
PAHLEN, Counts von der, *augmentation*, 542.
PAIN ET VIN, *arms*, 391.
Pairle, en, 739.
„ The, 116, 150, 739.
Paissant, 739.
Pal, 120, 739.
„ *en*, 739.
Palace, 363.
PALACIO, *arms*, 199.
PALÆOLOGUS, coins of ANDRONICUS, 250.
„ *seal* of DEMETRIUS, 250.
PALATINATE, *arms*, 580.
„ *lion rampant* of the, 525.
PALATINE, FREDERICK, II., Count, 40.
„ Elector, *arms*, 526.
PALAU, *arms*, 363.
Pale, cotised, Pl. X., fig. 11, p. 118.
„ *indented*, Per, Plate V., fig. 2, p. 80.
„ *Parted per*, 78 ; Fig. 28, p. 77 ; Pl. V., fig. 1, p. 80.
„ *rayonné*, Pl. X., fig. 8, p. 118.
„ *retrait*, 121.
„ The, 78, 120, 697 ; Fig. 37, p. 116 ; Pl. X., fig. 7, p. 118.
„ Varieties of, 121.
Palé, 739.
„ *contre*, 739.
PALEOLOGUS, SOPHIA, daughter of THOMAS, 250.
PALESTRINA, Princes of, *arms*, 363.
Paleways, 108.
PALIANO, Dukes of, *arms*, 363.
Palisado crown, 697.
Palissé, 739.
„ *line*, 77.
Pall, The, 116, 150, 697 ; Pl. XVI., fig. 10, p. 146 ; Pl. XVI., fig. 11, p. 146.
„ as a charge, 374.
PALLANDT, *arms*, 93.
Palle, 192.
Pallé or *Palé*, 90.
Pallets, 122, 697 ; Pl. X., fig. 9, p. 118 ; Pl. X., fig. 10, p. 118.
„ *hummetty* and *pitché*, Pl. X., fig. 12, p. 118.
PALLIOT, French Armorist, 76.
PALLISER, Mrs, *Historic Devices, Badges, and War Cries*, 192, 586.
Pallium, as a charge, 150, 371, 374.
PALM, *arms*, 317.
Palme, 739.
PALMER, *arms*, 375.
Palmer's staff, 697.
Palmier, 739.
PALMIERI, *arms*, 319.
Pals retraits, 123.
PALVERT, *arms*, 91.
Paly, 90, 697, 739 ; Pl. VII., fig. 1, p. 90.
„ *-bendy*, 100, 697 ; Pl. VII., fig. 12, p. 90.
„ *per bend*, 92.
„ *per fess*, 92.
„ *wavy*, 91.
Pamé, 269.

Pâmé, 739.
Pampré, 693, 739.
Panaché, 739.
Pan-de-Mur, 739.
Panelles, 739.
PANHUYS, *arms*, 184.
PANMURE, Earls of, *arms*, 171.
„ Lords, *arms*, 147.
Pannes, 739.
Panneton, 739.
Pan's pipe as a charge, 386.
PANSEY, Baron de, *arms*, 278.
Pansy, The, 337.
Panther, Demi-, 226.
„ The, 226, 697.
„ „ Heraldic, 226.
Panthère au naturel, 736.
„ *héraldique*, 697, 739.
PANTOJAS, *arms*, 158.
Paon, 739.
„ *rouant*, 698.
PAPACODA, *arms*, 223.
PAPAL *augmentations*, 541.
„ *tiara* as a charge, 372.
Papegay, or *Papegai*, 700, 739.
Papelonné, 71, 72, 73, 74, 726, 740 ; Pl. VIII., fig. 6, p. 100.
PAPENBROEK, *arms*, 146.
Papilonné, 697, *v. Papelonné*.
PAPILLON, Vicomtes de BRAITEAU, *arms*, 280.
Papingoes, 265 ; Pl. XXVI., fig. 2, p. 266.
PAPPENHEIM, Counts von, *augmentation*, 538.
PARADIS DE PAULHAC, *arms*, 267.
Paradise, Bird of, 267.
PARAVICINI, Counts, 262.
PARCHWITZ, Barons von, *arms*, 297.
PARDAILLAN, *arms*, 128.
Paré, 740.
PARIEU, *see* ESQUIROU.
PARIS, *arms*, 283.
„ Bibliothéque Royale at, 282.
„ Bourgeoisie of, 601.
„ City of, *arms*, 369.
„ „ colours, 659.
„ Count of, 11.
„ MATTHEW, 40.
„ „ MS. of, 251.
„ *seal* of Châtelet of, 333.
„ „ Nôtre Dame at, 329.
„ University of, *arms*, 205.
PARIZOT, *arms*, 265.
PARKER, Earls of MORLEY, *arms*, 185.
„ *Glossary of Heraldry*, 309.
PARMA, ALEXANDER, Duke of, 509.
„ Dukes of, *arms*, 283, 502, 508.
„ „ *augmentation*, 541.
„ Margaret of, *arms*, 577.
PARR, *arms*, 532.
„ Queen CATHARINE, *arms* and *augmentation*, 532.
Parrot, The, 265.
Parted coats, 74.
„ *per bend*, 80.
„ „ „ *sinister*, 80.
„ „ *chevron*, 81.
„ „ *fess*, 79.
„ „ *pale*, 78.
PARTHENAY, *arms*, 530.
„ FRANCIS, Seigneur de, *seal*, 530.
Parti, 78, 740.

(829)

Parti et contre-bandé, 96.
„ *per chevron*, 728.
Particle, The *Ordonnance* respecting the assumption of, 748.
Particule Nobiliaire, Origin of, 8, 9.
Partition, *arms* showing *Modes of*, Pl. V., p. 80 ; Pl. LV., p. 668 ; Pl. LVI., p. 670.
„ *lines*, 74, 75, 697.
„ *Mode of*, 74, 77.
Partitions, 668.
„ Curious, and remarkable coats, 661.
Party, 697.
PASCAL, *arms*, 236 ; Pl. XXIV., fig. 4, p. 236.
Paschal Lamb, 236, 697.
PASCHAL-COLOMBIER, *arms*, 240, 710.
PASQUIER, le Duc, 15.
Passant, 216, 698, 740.
„ *contre-passant*, 698.
„ *counter-passant*, 698.
„ *gardant*, 698.
„ *regardant*, 698.
„ *repassant*, 698.
Passé (*en Croix*, *en Sautoir*) 740.
Passion Cross, 698 ; Fig. 47, p. 164.
„ „ of the, 1.
„ *nails*, 147, 698.
Pastoral-staff as a charge, 371.
PASTUREAU, *arms*, 236.
Patée, 153.
„ *fichée*, 155.
„ *Formée*, *cross*, 153.
„ or *Patty*, 698, 740.
Patênôtre (croix), 740.
PATERSON of Seafield, *brisure*, 436, 437.
Patonce, 698.
„ *Cross*, 157 ; Fig. 56, p. 164.
Patriarchal, *Cross*, 152, 698 ; Fig. 50, p. 164.
Patte, 698.
PATTERSON, *arms*, 264.
Patty, 698.
„ *cross*, 153 ; Fig. 53, p. 164.
„ *fitchy*, *cross*, 155 ; Fig. 54, p. 164.
„ *throughout*, 698.
PATYNS, *arms*, 392.
PAUL V., Pope, *arms*, 292.
PAULET, Marquess of WINCHESTER, *arms*, 347.
PAULHAC, PARADIS DE, *arms*, 267.
PAULI, VON, *arms*, 195.
PAULSDORF, *arms*, 290.
„ VON, *arms*, 82.
PAVIA, Certosa at, 274.
Pavilions, 615, 698, 740.
Paw, 222, 698.
PAWNE, *arms*, 267.
Pax quæritur bello, 664.
Peacock, 266, 698.
„ *in its pride*, 698.
PEACOCK, *arms*, 267.
Peacock's head as a *crest*, 600.
Pean, 63, 698 ; Pl. IV., fig. 5, p. 62.
Pearl, 65, 698.
Pearled, 698.
Pears, 340.
Peas, 344.
Peautré, 740.
PECCI, Counts, *arms*, 310.
PECHA, *arms*, 283.
Peel, 698.
PEEL, Sir ROBERT, *arms*, 283.

Peers, *helm* of, 602.
Pegasus, The, 298, 698.
PEGRIZ, *arms*, 387.
PEILLENSTEIN, Line of, *arms*, 448.
PELETS, *arms*, 203.
Peletta, 190.
PELHAM, *arms*, 264, 377.
„ *augmentation*, 528.
„ *badge*, 753.
„ Earls of CHICHESTER, *badge*, 377.
„ Sir JOHN, 528.
„ „ DE, *arms*, 377.
Pelican,|264, 698 ; Pl. XXV., fig. 12, p. 260.
„ as a *badge*, 754.
„ *in her piety*, 699.
Pelle, 698.
Pellet, 190, 699.
PELLEZAY, *arms*, 66.
Pelorus, Cape, 300.
PEMBRIDGE, *arms*, 93.
PEMBROKE, *badge*, 753, 754.
„ Earl of, 415.
„ „ *arms*, 215, 224, 376, 409, 561.
„ „ enamelled *shield* of, 114.
„ WILLIAM, first Earl of, 561.
Penache, 634.
Penaches as *crests*, 607.
PENAFIEL, Marquis of, *arms*, 167.
Penché, 601, 678, 736, 740.
Pencil or *Penoncelle*, 699.
Pencils, 654.
Pendent, 699.
PENDERELL, *arms*, 316, 533.
PEÑERANDAS, *arms*, 361.
PENICUIK, *arms*, 385.
Penneton, 739.
Pennon or *Penon*, 699, 740.
Pennoncelle of PERCY, Pl. XXXIV., fig. 3, p. 388.
Pennoncelles, 654, 699.
PENNYCOOK, *arms*, 385.
Penny-yard-penny, 699.
Penon, 699, 740.
PENTHIÈVRE, Comtes de, *arms*, 342.
PEPDIE, *arms*, 265, 522 ; Pl. XXVI., fig. 2, p. 266.
„ MARY, 522.
PÉPIN, *arms*, 150 ; Pl. XVI., fig. 10, p. 146.
PEPPENBERG, *arms*, 131.
Pepper-pods, 341.
„ *-sheaf* as a *badge*, 754.
Per, 699.
PERALTA, *arms*, 288, 353.
Percé, 699, 740.
PERCEVAL, Dr, 70.
Perché, 740.
PERCHE, Counts de, *arms*, 139.
„ *seal* and *arms* of GEOFFROI, Count of, 49.
„ *seal* of ROTROU, III., Count of, 49.
PERCI, HENRY DE, *arms*, 481.
„ ROBERT DE, *arms*, 481.
„ WALTER DE, *arms*, 481.
Perclose, 699.
PERCY, AGNES, 482.
„ *arms*, 215, 481, 482, 641 ; Pl. XVIII., fig 12, p. 190 ; Pl. XXXIX., fig. 3, p. 482.

(830)

PERCY, *badges*, 584, 654.
,, Duke of NORTHUMBERLAND, *arms*, 184, 488.
,, Earl of NORTHUMBERLAND, *arms*, 214.
,, HENRY 5th Earl, *badge*, 584.
,, ,, ALGERNON, 6th Earl, *badge*, 584.
,, ,, Baron of TOPCLIFFE, *arms*, 482.
,, ,, Earl of NORTHUMBERLAND, *standard* of, 654; Fig. 100, p. 649.
,, ,, Earl, *supporter*, 632.
,, ,, *seal*, 641.
,, *Pennoncelle* of, Pl. XXXIV., fig. 3, p. 388.
,, PIERS, *arms*, 481.
,, Sir HENRY, *seal*, 653.
PEREIRA, *arms*, 158; Pl. XIV., fig. 10, p. 140.
PEREZ, *arms*, 358.
Perforate, 699.
Pergola, 150.
Pergula, 150.
Péri en bande, 740.
,, ,, *barre*, 740.
PERRIER, ALAIN DU, *supporters*, 634.
Perroné, Croix, 740.
PERROTT, *arms*, 340.
PERSIGNY, Duc de, *arms* and *augmentation*, 541.
PERTH, City *arms* and *supporter*, 179, 632.
,, Earl of, *compartment* and *motto*, 642.
PERWEYS, *arms*, 427.
PERY, *arms*, 185.
PESC, *arms*, 394.
PESHALL, *arms*, 155.
PETER ALEXIEVITCH of Russia, *crown*, 622.
PETIT, *arms*, 236.
PETMORE, *arms*, 112.
PETRA SANCTA, 714.
,, ,, System of lines representing colour, 64.
,, ,, *Tesseræ Gentilitiæ*, 64.
PETRARCH, Muse of, 537.
Petronel, 699.
PETRUS *filius* ALBERTI, 10.
PEVEREL, *badge* and *arms*, 585.
,, CATHARINE, 585.
PEVERELL, *arms*, 342.
,, *badge*, 754.
PFIRDT or PFIRT, Counts of, *arms*, 271, 634; Pl. XLV., fig. 1, p. 540.
PFUHLINGEN, *arms*, 86.
PFULL, Baron, *arms*, 310.
PHARAMOND (?), *arms*, 278.
Pheasants, 267.
Pheon, 350, 699; Pl. XXXI., fig. 7, p. 346.
Phéon, 740.
PHILIP I., King of FRANCE, 11; *crown* and *sceptre* of, 328, 658.
,, ,, of FLANDERS, *seal* of, 26, 32.
,, III., King of FRANCE, 454; *supporters*, 636.
,, IV., (*le Bel*), King of FRANCE, 40, 282; JEANNE, wife of, 354.
,, ,, King of SPAIN, 624.

PHILIP V., King of FRANCE, 40, 457, 462; *seal* of, 354, 456; *supporters*, 636.
,, VI., King of FRANCE, *supporter*, 636.
,, (A U G U S T U S), King of FRANCE, 269; *arms*, 583; *seal* of, 328; *supporters*, 636.
,, (A U G U S T U S) II., King of FRANCE, 570.
,, Emperor HOLY ROMAN EMPIRE, *crown*, 621.
,, son of LOUIS VII., King of FRANCE, 329.
PHILIPPA of HAINAULT, Queen of EDWARD III., *arms*, 247, 257.
PHILIPPE DE VALOIS, King of FRANCE, *coins* of, 44.
,, *le Bon*, Duke of BURGUNDY, 484, 485.
PHILIPPEAUX, 12.
Phœnix, 267, 298, 699, 740.
,, as a *badge*, 596.
PHOUSKARNAKI, *arms*, 195.
PIACENZA, Duchy, *arms*, 502.
PICCOLOMINI, Princes, *arms*, 307.
PICHON, *arms*, 70.
Pickaxes as charges, 393.
PICKFORD, *arms*, 684.
PICO, *arms*, 509.
Pièces héraldiques, 102, 740.
PIEDEFER, *arms*, 213.
PIENNE, Marquises de, *supporters*, 298.
Pierced, 322, 699.
PIERRE, DE, Seigneurs de GANGES, 10.
PIERREFEU, *arms*, 160.
PIERREFORT, *arms*, 68.
PIERREPONT, *arms*, 362.
Piété, 740.
Piety, Pelican in her, 264.
PIFERRER, *Nobiliario de los Reinos y Señorios de España*, 207, 235, 284, 387, 390, 395, 476.
Pig, The *domestic*, 227.
PIGACHE DE LAMBERVILLE, *arms*, 310.
PIGNATELLI, Princes, *arms*, 381.
Pignates, 740.
,, as charges, 382.
Pignon, 740.
Pignonné, 740.
Pike head, 348.
,, The, 268, 271.
PILAWA, *arms*, 670; Pl. LVI., fig. 8, p. 670.
Pile, 146, 699, 740; Figs. 43, p. 116; Pl. XVI., fig. 1, p. 146.
,, *reversed*, Pl. XVI., fig. 7, p. 146.
,, Varieties of, 146.
Piles from sinister, Pl. XVI., fig. 5, p. 146.
,, ,, *base*, Pl. XVI., fig. 6, p. 146.
,, *in chief*, Pl. XVI., fig. 4, p. 146.
,, *in point*, Pl. XVI., fig. 3, p. 146.
,, *Three*, Pl. XVI., fig. 2, p. 146.
PILGRIM, *arms*, 375.
Pilgrim's scrip, 699.
,, *scrips* as charges, 375.
,, *staves*, 699.
,, ,, as charges, 375.
PILKINGTON, *arms*, 157; Pl. XIV., fig. 8, p. 140.
Pillars, 363.
PILLERA, *arms*, 350.

(831)

PIMENTELS, *arms*, 507.
PIN, LA TOUR DU, *arms*, 269.
Pine Apples, 341.
Pinks, 337.
PINOS, *arms*, 341.
PINS, Marquises de, *arms*, 341.
PIOSASCO, *arms*, *supporters*, and *motto*, 643.
PIOT, *arms*, 370.
PIPER, *arms*, 387.
PIRCH, *arms*, 197.
PISA, *standard* of, 655.
PITSLIGO, Lord, *arms*, 446.
PITTI, *arms*, 121.
PIUS II., Pope, *arms*, 307.
,, III., Pope, *arms*, 307.
,, VI., Pope, *arms*, 311.
PIZARRO, *arms*, 363.
PLACIDIA, *crown* of the Empress, 328.
Plain shields, 65.
Plaine, 718, 740.
PLANCHÉ, Mr, *Lancaster Herald*, 308.
,, *Pursuivant of Arms*, 25, 47, 117, 170, 207, 209, 210, 225, 258, 287, 327, 333, 355, 376, 378, 386, 394, 406, 414, 458, 459, 461, 548, 549, 550, 553, 555, 587, 589, 598, 599, 602.
,, *Roll of Arms*, 104, 357, 409.
PLANCKENBERG, see STORCK.
Planets, 309.
PLANQUE, DE LA, *arms*, 404.
Planta genista as a *badge*, 586.
PLANTAGENET, ANNE, 417, 530.
,, ARTHUR, Viscount LISLE, *arms*, 557 ; *badges*, 557, 586, 587.
,, *champlevé enamel* of GEOFFREY, Pl. I., fig. 3, p. 44.
,, EDMOND, 421.
,, ,, Earl of CORNWALL, *seal*, 465.
,, ,, of LANGELEY, 588.
,, EDMUND CROUCHBACK, Earl of LEICESTER, *arms* and *label*, 219, 416 ; *tomb* of, 587.
,, ,, Duke of YORK, 416.
,, ,, of WOODSTOCK, 589.
,, EDWARD, Earl of RUTLAND, *arms* and *label*, 416 ; *seal* of, 369.
,, GEOFFREY, Duke of BRITTANY, death of, 40 ; *shield* of, 45.
,, GEOFFROI, Count D'ANJOU, *tomb* of, 43.
,, HENRY, Duke of LANCASTER, *arms* and *label*, 416.
,, JOAN, 438.
,, JOHN, of ELTHAM, Earl of CORNWALL, *brisure*, 438.

PLANTAGENET kings, *arms* of, 661 ; Pl. LI., fig. 2, p. 661.
,, *labels*, 416.
,, LIONEL, Duke of CLARENCE, *arms* and *label*, 416.
,, RICHARD, *badge*, 591.
,, ,, Duke of GLOUCESTER, *helm*, 602.
,, ,, of CONINGSBURGH, 588.
,, THOMAS and HENRY, 587.
,, ,, Duke of GLOUCESTER, *seal*, Pl. XXXV., fig. 1, p. 416.
,, ,, of WOODSTOCK, *brisure*, 438.
PLANTAGENETS, livery colours of the, 588.
PLASNES, JEANNE, Dame de, *arms*, 57.
,, ,, ,, ,, and *supporters*, 629.
Plata, 190.
Plate, 189, 699.
Platée or *Platy*, 699.
PLATT, *arms*, 97.
Platy, 699.
Playing tables, 699.
,, *tops* as charges, 388.
PLAYTER, *arms*, 95 ; Pl. VII., fig. 4, p. 90.
PLÉDRAN, Vicomte de, *arms*, 185.
PLÉHÉDEL, Vicomtes de, *arms*, 346.
Plein, 740.
PLESSEN, Barons, *arms*, 234.
PLESSIS-CACHELEU, MONTMORENCY DU, *brisure*, 451.
,, RICHELIEU, DU, *arms*, 140.
,, *see* ANGERS.
,, ,, BOURDON.
Plié, 740.
,, *en rond*, 741.
Plomb, à, 741.
Ploughshares as charges, 393.
Plovers, 267.
PLOWDEN, *arms*, 124 ; Pl. XI., fig. 3, p. 124.
,, EDMUND, 124.
Ployé, 88, 137, 699, 741.
Plumail, 608.
Plumes as *crest*, 607.
Plumeté, 71, 72, 741 ; Pl. VIII., fig. 7, p. 100.
PLUNKETT, *bordure*, 570.
PLUTARCH, Description of devices on shields, 29.
PLUVINEL, Marquises de, *brisure*, 434.
PLYMOUTH, Earl of, *arms*, 79, 559.
POBOG, *arms*, 356.
PODENAS, Princes de CANTALUPO, *arms*, 128.
,, SIX, *arms*, 128.
PODLACHIA, *arms*, 469.
POER, LE, *arms*, 118.
POERDS, DE LA, 17.
POGORSKI, *arms*, 299.
POICTIERS, Battle of, 528, 591.
POICTOU and CORNWALL, *seal* of RICHARD, Earl of, 245.
,, Counts of, *arms*, 215.

POIGNET, *arms*, 204.
Point d'honneur le, 59, 741.
,, *du chef*, 741.
,, *Honour*, 59.
,, *In*, 699.
,, *Nombril*, 59.
Pointe, 148, 741.
,, *entée*, Pl. XVI., fig. 9, p. 146.
,, *le canton dextre de la*, 59.
,, ,, *sénestre de la*, 59.
POINTE, DE LA, *Chevaliers de l'Ordre du St. Esprit*, 297, 299, 303, 354.
Pointed, 699.
Points, 699.
,, *équipolles*, 741.
,, *of the escucheon*, 699.
POIRIER, *arms*, 240.
POISIEU, DE, *arms*, 120, 726, 744.
POISSONIER, *arms*, 302.
POITIERS, Battle of, 377.
,, LOUIS, Bishop of, *arms*, 571.
,, Church of St. Hilaire at, 332.
,, DIANE DE, 164.
POLAND, *Dimidiation* in 468.
,, Duke of, *seal*, 468.
,, *Furs* unknown in *Armory* of, 74.
,, JOHN III., King of, *arms*, 486.
,, Kingdom of, *arms*, 199, 254, 255, 487, 665.
,, Kings of, using *escucheon en surtout*, 486.
,, Title of Marquess unknown in, 626.
,, *White eagles* of, as *supporters*, 636.
POLANEN, *arms*, 370.
POLANI, *arms*, 86.
POLASTRON, *arms*, 213.
POLE, Duke of SUFFOLK, *arms*, 225 ; Pl. XXII., fig. 12, p. 222.
POLIGNAC, Princes of, *arms*, 93.
POLISH *augmentations*, 540.
POLLIA, *arms*, 298.
POLLNITZ, Barons von, *arms*, 136.
POLMAN, *arms*, 669 ; Pl. LV., fig. 6, p. 668.
POLWARTH, Lord, *supporter*, 303.
POLYCRATES, tale of, related by HERODOTUS, 271.
Pomegranate, 339 ; Pl. XXX. fig. 10, p. 332.
Pomeis, 190, 699.
Pomelled, 699.
POMERANIA, *arms*, 288.
POMEREU, Marquis de RICEYS, *arms*, 340.
Pomeys, 190.
Pommelly, 700.
,, *cross*, 160.
Pommes-de-pin, 741.
Pommetté, 160, 700, 741.
Pommetty, 717.
,, *cross*, 160.
,, or *Pommelly*, 700.
POMPADOUR, Marquise de, 361.
Pompey, 190.
PONANGE, Marquises de ST., *arms*, 275.
PONCE DE LEON, *arms*, 507.
,, ,, Duke of ARCOS, *arms*, 506.
PONDORFFER, VON, *arms*, 122.

PONIATOWSKI, Princes, *arms*, 234.
PONIN-PONINSKI, Princes, 370.
PONNAT, *arms*, 267.
PONSONBY, Earl of BESSBOROUGH, *arms*, 391.
PONT DE VAUX, Ducs de, *arms*, 136.
,, DU, *arms*, 187.
PONTAUT, *arms*, 362.
PONTBRIANT, *arms*, 362.
PONTCHASTEAU, EON DE, *seal* of, 46.
PONTE, Counts da, *arms*, 362.
PONTECORVO, *arms*, 667.
PONTECROIX, Marquis de, *arms*, 185.
PONTEIL, Counts GUIOT DE, *arms*, 265.
PONTEVÈS, Marquises of, *arms*, 362.
PONTEVEZ, Ducs de SABRAN, *arms*, 213.
PONTHIEU, Count of, 30.
,, JOANNA of, *seal*, 478.
PONTOISE, siege of, 541.
PONTON, *arms*, 96.
PONT'S MS., 145, 175, 198, 349, 381.
POPE, Earl of DOWNE, *arms*, 290.
POPEL, *arms*, 79.
Popinjay, 265, 700.
POPOLESCHI, *arms*, 141.
PORCELLETS, DES, Marquises de MAULLANE, *arms*, 227.
Porcupine, The, 239.
Porcupines as *supporters*, 636.
PORET, Marquis de BLOSSEVILLE, *arms*, 340.
Portal, 363.
Portcullis, 700.
,, as a *badge*, 595.
,, as a charge, 365.
PORTE, LA, *arms*, 136, 363.
PORTEOUS, 381.
PORTER, *arms*, 374.
PORTIA, Princes of, *arms*, 332.
Portillé, 741.
PORTLAND, Dukes of, *arms*, 159.
PORTMAN, *arms*, 331.
PORTOCARRERO, *arms*, 100 ; Pl. VII., fig. 7, p. 90.
PORTSMOUTH, Duchess of, 559.
PORTUGAL, *arms*, 100, 168, 172, 440, 509, 547, 577, 578, 667 ; Pl. XVII., fig. 7, p. 172.
,, BEATRICE of, *seal*, 475.
,, Constable of, *label*, 425.
,, *crests* in, 604.
,, EMMANUEL, King of, 475.
,, ISABELLE of, *seal*, 475.
,, Marks of illegitimacy in, 577.
,, MARY, dtr. of EDWARD, Constable of, 509.
,, Queen LEONORA of, *crown*, 620.
,, of, 590.
,, "Quinas" of, 238.
,, *supporters*, 667.
,, Use of *bordure* in, 440.
Portuguese Regulations as to the bearing on Differences of *arms*, 749.
Posé, 217, 700, 704, 715, 741, 743.
,, *en pal*, 109.
,, *en sautoir*, 109.
Pot as a charge, 389.
,, -*hook* as a charge, 390.
POT, 12.
POTEMKIN, Princes, *arms*, 205.

(833)

Potence, 741.
Potencé, 741.
„ line, 77, 156.
Potency or Potenté, 700.
Potent, 70, 71, 700 ; Pl. IV., fig. 11, p. 62.
„ counter, 70, 71.
„ „ potent, 70, 700.
„ cross, 156, 700 ; Fig. 51, p. 164.
„ fitchy, cross, 156.
Potenté line, 77, 700 ; Fig. 25, p. 75.
POTIER, arms and supporters, 294.
„ Duc de GÈVRES, 11.
„ Marquis de GRIGNON, 12.
„ Seigneur de NOVION, 12.
Pots as charges, 381.
POTTWEIN, arms, 493.
POTULITZ-POTULICKI, Count, arms, 359.
POULAIN, arms, 237.
POUR LE MÉRITE, Cross of the Order, 546.
Pourpre, 741.
Powdered, 700.
POWELL, arms, 333.
POWER, 17.
POWIS, Earl of, supporter, 231.
POWLETT, Marquess of WINCHESTER, arms, 347.
POWYS, arms, 417.
„ Princes of, 212.
POYLE, arms, 357.
POYNINGS, Barony of, badge, 584, 654.
POYNTZ, arms, 94.
POZZO DI BORGO, Prince, arms, 360.
„ Princes, DELLA CISTERNA, arms, 293.
PRAËT, JEAN, Seigneur de, arms, 573 ; Pl. XLVIII., fig. 4, p. 576.
„ LOUIS LE FRISON, Seigneur de, 572, 573.
PRAGUE, arms, 359.
PRASLIN, Ducs de, arms, 434.
PRAUN, Dr MICHAEL, Von dem Adelichen Europa, und denen Heerschilden des Teutschen Adels, 41.
Prawns, 273.
PREEDE, arms, 279.
PREISSAC, arms, 213.
Premier Baron Chrétien, 11.
PRESCOTT, arms, 262 ; Pl. XXV., fig. 9, p. 260.
PRESSIGNY, arms, 168.
„ RENAUD DE, Maréchal de FRANCE, arms, 168.
PRESTER JOHN, A, 194.
PRESTON, arms, 296, 446 ; Pl. XXVII., fig. 10, p. 288.
PRESTWICK, arms, 301 ; Pl. XXVII., fig. 12, p. 288.
Pretence, escucheon of, 700.
PREUDHOMME, arms, 427.
PREUILLY, GEOFFREY DE, death of, 39, 40.
PREYSING, VON, arms, 79.
PRICE, arms, 200, 261, 348 ; Pl. XXV., fig. 7, p. 260.
Pride, In, 700.
„ Peacock in its, 267.
PRIDEAUX, arms, 136.
PRIEGO, Counts de, arms, 473, 506.
„ Marquises of, arms, 473.
PRIGNANI, arms, 257.
PRIME, arms, 206 ; Pl. XX., fig. 8, p. 198.

PRIMROSE, arms, 337.
„ ARCHIBALD, Viscount, arms, 180.
„ of Dalmenie, Sir ARCHIBALD, arms, 181.
„ Sir ARCHIBALD, 430.
Primroses, 337.
PRINCE CONSORT, arms, 131, 423, 424.
„ OF WALES, arms, 131.
Princes-Grands-Dignitaires of France, arms, 283.
„ helm of, 601.
Princess Royal, Empress of GERMANY, label, 423 ; Fig. 85, p. 421.
PRINGLE, arms, 137, 273, 432 ; Pl. XIII., fig. 3, p. 136.
„ of Smailhome, brisure, 432.
Proboscides, 606, 741.
PROKESCH D'OSTEN, Counts, arms, 295.
Promptorium Parvulorum, 591.
Proper, 212, 700.
„ or natural colour, 62.
PROVENCE, ELEANOR of, 322, 587.
„ „ arms, 122.
„ Rose of, 32.
PRUNELÉ, 12.
PRUNIER, arms, 726.
PRUSS II., herba of, arms, 351.
PRUSSIA, armorials of, 541.
„ arms, 125, 140, 159, 212, 265, 288, 321, 344, 494, 543, 544, 545, 660.
„ baton of Field Marshal of, 544.
„ Black eagle of, 544, 545.
„ FREDERICK II., King of, augmentations granted by, 545.
„ great escucheon of Royal House, 493.
„ pavilion of King of, 616.
„ Royal crown, 140, 254, 622.
PRUSSIAN augmentations, 542.
PRYSE, arms, Pl. XXI., fig. 3, p. 212.
„ of Goggergin, arms, 216.
PRZEROWA, arms, 352.
PRZICHOWITZ, Counts, arms, 263.
PUCCI, arms, 200.
PUCELLE, Brothers of LA, arms, 331.
PUCHBERG, arms, 307 ; Pl. XXVIII., fig. 3, p. 308.
PUDSEY, HUGH, Bishop of DURHAM, arms, 154.
PUGET, Marquises de BARBENTANE, arms, 234.
Puggree, 612.
Pulchrum pro patria pati, 664.
PULLICI, arms, 285.
PUNCHYON, arms, 193 ; Pl. XIX., fig. 4, p. 192.
Punning arms, 672.
PUNSHON, crest, 563.
PÜNTZINGER, arms, 580.
PUPELLIN, arms, 67.
PUREFOY, Bishop of HEREFORD, arms, 206.
Purfled, 700.
Purple or Purpure, 60, 62, 65.
Purpure or Purple, 60, 62, 65, 700 ; Pl. III., fig. 7, p. 60.
„ shield plain, 67.
PUTBUS, Prince, arms, etc., of, Fig. 98, p. 627.
PUTTKAMMER, Barons von, arms, 290.

PUY, DU, *arms*, 212.
,, -PAULIN, DE, *arms*, 66.
PUYGIRON, Marquis de, *arms*, 307.
Pyot, 700.
PYPE, *arms*, 386.
PYRMONT, County of, 483.
,, ,, *arms*, 490.
,, Prince of, *arms*, 488.
Quadrate, 700.
QUAEDBACH, *arms*, 381.
QUARANTA, *arms*, 394.
QUAREBBE, *arms*, 393.
Quarrels, 350.
Quartefeuille, 741.
Quarter, The, 116, 165, 167, 700.
,, *-pierced*, 701.
Quartered, 700.
Quarterfoil, 322, 701, 741.
Quartering, 459, 478.
,, British usage in regard to, 483.
,, *Difference by*, 446.
,, Foreign usage in regard to, 483.
,, *per saltire*, 482.
Quarterings, 700.
,, Modern English Heralds against grand, 482.
Quarterly, 81, 700; Fig. 30, p. 77; Pl. V., fig. 9, p. 80.
,, *en équerre*, 82; Pl. V., fig. 11, p. 80.
,, of four coats, 479.
,, of more than four coats, 480.
,, of three coats, 479.
,, *per fess indented*, Pl. V., fig. 10, p. 80.
,, *per saltire*, 82.
Quarters or *Quarterings*, 700.
Quartiers, 741.
QUATERMAINE, *arms*, 205.
QUATREBARBES, 12.
Quatrefoil, Double, for ninth son, 444.
,, The, 322, 701; Pl. XXIX., fig. 12, p. 318.
QUEEN, Marriage of the, 423.
,, VICTORIA, *Life of the Prince Consort*, 424.
QUEEN'S COLLEGE, OXFORD, *arms*, 257.
Queens-Consort, *supporters* of, 664.
QUEENSBERRY, Marquess of, *arms*, 180.
QUÉLEN, Barons de, *arms*, 185.
,, Ducs DE LA VAUGUYON, *arms*, 319.
QUERNFURTH, Barons of, *arms*, 214.
QUEROUAILLE, LOUISE DE, Duchess of PORTSMOUTH, 559.
QUESADA, *arms*, 122.
QUESQUERTIN, BERTHELAY, *arms*, 222.
Queue, 214, 701.
,, *fourchée*, 218, 701, 741.
Queué, 705.
QUEXADA, *arms*, 203.
QUIJADA, *arms*, 203.
QUINCI, DE, *arms*, Pl. XVIII., fig. 10, p. 190.
QUINCY, DE, Earls of WINCHESTER, *arms*, 184.
QUINSON, *arms*, 68.
QUINTANA, *arms*, 387.

Quintefeuille, 680, 741.
Quise, à la, 701.

RAAPHORST, *arms*, 93.
Rabats, 741, 742.
Rabbit, The, 238.
RABENSTEIN, Counts of, *arms*, 170.
RABENSTEINER, *arms*, 207.
Raccourci, 741, 742.
RACONIS, LOUIS, Seigneur de, *arms*, 579.
RADA, *arms*, 158.
RADCLYFFE, *arms*, 131.
,, of Foxdenton, *label*, 415.
,, ,, Winmarleigh, *arms*, 410.
Radiant, 701.
RADOLIN-RADOLINSKI, *see* LESZCZYC.
RADZIWILL, Princes, *arms*, 386.
RAE, *arms*, Pl. XXIII., fig. 9, p. 228.
,, of Pitsindie, *arms*, 232.
RAEPSAET, *arms*, 343.
RAET, Barons de, *arms*, 392.
RAGNINA, *arms*, 281.
Ragulé, 701, 281.
Raguled, 701.
Raguly, 727.
,, *line*, 76; Fig. 24, p. 75.
,, or *Raguled*, 701.
RAGUSA, Duchy, *arms*, 395, 503.
RAIMBERT, *arms*, 139.
RAIMOND, GUILLAUME DE, 10.
Rainbow, 310, 701; Pl. XIX., fig. 7, p. 192.
RAINIER, *arms*, 122.
Rais, 741.
,, *d'escarbuncles*, 679.
Rakes as charges, 393.
Ram, Battering, 352.
Ramé, 232, 677, 741.
RAMEFORT, DE, *arms*, 189.
RAMENSPERG, *arms*, 236.
RAMÉRA, *arms*, 339.
RAMILLIES, *see* DRAGON.
Rampant, 212, 701, 702, 733, 741.
,, *-gardant*, 215, 701.
,, *-regardant*, 216, 701.
,, *-sejant*, 701.
Rams, 235.
RAMSAY, *arms*, 258, 535.
,, of Dunoon, *bend*, 430.
,, ,, Wyliecleugh, Sir JOHN, Viscount HADDINGTON, *augmentation*, 534, 535.
,, WILLIAM, Earl of FIFE, *bend*, 430.
RAMSEY, *arms*, 236.
Ramure, 677.
Ranchier, 742.
RANDOLPH, *arms*, Pl. XXXIII., fig. 9, p. 376.
,, Earls of MORAY, *arms*, 378.
,, THOMAS, Earl of MORAY, *arms*, 177.
RANFURLY, Earl of, *arms*, 175.
Rangé, 742.
,, *en chef*, 742.
,, ,, *croix*, 742.
Rangés en pal, 109.
,, ,, *sautoir*, 109.
Rangier, 742.
RANGONI, Marquises, *arms*, 119.

(835)

RANKEN, *arms*, 348.
RANTZAU, Counts, *arms*, 78.
RANULF, Earls of MORAY, *arms*, 378.
,, *seal*, 378.
RAOUSSET DE BOULBON, Counts, *arms*, 154.
RAPACCIOLI, *arms*, 343.
RAPE, *arms*, 343.
RAPPACH, *arms*, 134.
RAPPOLSTEIN, County of, *arms*, 170, 490.
RASCIA, *arms*, 501.
RASPÉ, *arms*, 343.
Rastrello, 470.
Rat, The, 240.
RATISBON, Sepulchral Monument at, *arms* on, 24.
RATTRAY, *arms*, 163; Pl. XV., fig. 5, p. 144.
,, ALEXANDER, *chevron*, 431.
,, JOHN, Bailie of ABERDEEN, *fess*, 430.
RATZEBURG, Principality of, *arms*, 159, 492.
RAUCH, *arms*, 134.
Rauten Kranz, 131; Pl. XII., fig. 6, p. 130.
RAVANI, *arms*, 343.
Raven as a *badge*, 754.
,, The, 264.
RAVEN, *arms*, 264.
RAVENSBERG, Count of, *arms*, 140.
RAVENTHORPE, *arms*, 264.
RAVESCHOOT, *arms*, 264.
RAVESTEIN, PHILIP DE, *arms*, 485.
Ravishing, 228.
Ravissant, 228, 702, 728, 742.
RAWSON, *arms*, 358.
RAYMOND II., Comte de SUBSTANTION, et de MELGUEIL, *arms*, 118.
RAYNOR, *arms*, 292.
Rayonnant, 308, 702, 742.
Rayonné, 692, 701, 702.
Rays, 702.
Rebated, 702.
Rebattements, 90, 742.
Rebrassé, 706, 741, 742.
Recercelé, 679, 702, 703, 742.
Recercellée, cross, 160.
RECHTEREN, Counts of, *arms*, 141.
RECHTHALER, *arms*, 87.
RECKHEIM, *arms*, 212.
,, County of, *arms*, 492, 493.
Recoupé, 742.
Red or *Gules*, 60, 62, 65.
,, *shield*, special use of, 67.
RED EAGLE, Cross of the Order of the, 546.
REDESDALE, Lord, *arms*, 239.
REDINGHURST, *arms*, 82.
REDMAIN, *arms*, 379.
Redorte, 742.
REEDE, Counts, *arms*, 127.
,, -GINKELS, Earls of ATHLONE, *arms*, 127.
REES, *arms*, 348.
REEVES, Dr, quoted, 657.
Refente, 742.
Reflected, 702.
Reflexed or *Reflected*, 702.
REFUGE, DU, *arms*, 275.
Regardant, 702, 742.
REGENSTEIN, County of, *arms*, 234.

Register of the Great Seal, 180, 517.
Registrum de Panmure, 171, 517.
REGROLTZWILE, *arms*, 320.
REICHBROD, *arms*, 391.
REICHENSTEIN, Counts von, *arms*, 348.
Reichs Stallmeister, arms of the office of, 490.
REID and BROOK, Description of Scottish Regalia, 619.
REIDER, *arms*, 195.
REIGSDORP, *arms*, 296.
REILLE, Counts, *arms*, 299.
REINACH, Counts, *arms*, 223.
Reindeer, The, 232, 702.
REINECK, Barons von, *arms*, 230.
,, Counts of, *arms*, 94.
REINFELDEN, *arms*, 93.
Rempli, 742.
Renard, 742.
RENARD, *arms*, 230.
RENAUD I., of BAR, *seal* of, 270.
,, *arms*, 230.
Renchier, 742.
Rencontre, Un, 234, 742.
RENNEBURG, *arms*, 139.
RENNER, *arms*, 237.
RENNES, City of, *arms*, 91.
RENTY, *arms*, 348, 449, 726.
,, ISABELLE, heiress of, 449.
Renversé, 308, 742, 746.
Repotencé, 742.
Reptiles, 273.
Rere-mouse, 702.
Resarcelé, 742.
Rest, 702.
Rests as charges, 386.
RETHEL, *arms*, 631.
,, Count of, 462.
Retorted, 702.
Retrait, 742.
Retranché, 702, 742.
Retranchée, cross, 162.
Retrospective Review, 656.
Retroussé, 743.
REVALDOS, *arms*, 289.
REVELATION, Book of, 194, 203.
REVENTLOW, Counts, *arms*, 362.
RÉVÉRONI. *arms*, 279.
REVEST, DE, *arms*, 92.
REY, M., *Histoire du Drapeau, des Couleurs, et des Insignes de la Monarchie Française*, 279, 282, 326, 327, 328, 332, 333, 659.
REYNELL, *arms*, 362.
REYNOLDS, *arms*, 365.
REYNOLDSWYLE, *arms*, 320.
RHAIN, *see* SCHEUCHENSTUEL.
RHEDAY, Countess CLAUDINE VON, 524.
RHEINAU, *arms*, 173.
RHINE, ALBERT, Count PALATINE of the, *arms* on Eagle, 630.
,, ,, Count PALATINE of the, *seal*, 251, 472.
,, Counts PALATINE of the, *arms*, 212.
,, LOUIS, Count PALATINE of the, *seal*, 456.
,, PALATINATE of the, *arms*, 456, 472.
,, ,, ,, Electoral *badge*, 380.
RHODES, siege of, 454.
RHODIUS, *arms*, 202.

RHYS AP TUDOR MAWR, Prince of SOUTH WALES, *arms*, 594.
Rib bones, Human, 206.
Riband, The, 131, 133, 702.
RIBAUMONT, DE, *arms*, 165.
RIBEAUPIERRE, Counts de, *arms*, 170.
RIBERA, *arms*, 507.
RIBERAC, Marquises de, *arms*, 238.
RICEYS, Marquis de, *arms*, 340.
RICH, *badge*, 753.
,, *crest*, 563.
RICHARD I., CŒUR DE LION, King of ENGLAND, *arms*, Pl. LI., fig. 1, p. 661; *badge*, 587; *crested helm*, 599; *Great Seal* of, 587; *seal* of, 32, 37, 54, 208, 210, 301, 583; *shield* of, 54.
,, II., King of ENGLAND, 324, 383, 403, 439, 475, 555; *arms*, 474, 528, 661; Pl. LI., fig. 3, p. 661; *badge*, 587, 589, 590, 591, 632; *Roll of*, 410, 426; *supporters* of, 662.
,, III., King of ENGLAND, 595; *arms*, Pl. LI., fig. 4, p. 661; *badge*, 594; *crown*, 618; *supporters* of, 662; *white boar* of, 597.
,, Earl of CORNWALL and King of the ROMANS, *arms*, 173, 245; *seal* of, 245.
,, *fiz le rey*, natural son of King JOHN, *arms*, 554.
RICHARDOT, *arms*, 319.
RICHEBOURG, Seigneur de, *arms* and *label*, 415.
,, ,, ,, *bend*, 429.
RICHELET, *Dictionnaire*, 14.
RICHELIEU, Cardinal Duc de, *arms*, 140.
RICHMOND and SOMERSET, Duke of, *arms*, 558.
,, *arms*, 128.
,, *badge* of the honour of, 324.
,, Duke of, *supporter*, 297.
,, Earls of, *arms*, 170, 425, 426.
,, JOHN, Earl of, 438.
RICHTERSWYL, *arms*, 120.
RIDDELL, *arms*, 341; Pl. XXX., fig. 11, p. 332.
,, Mr, 179.
,, of Ardnamurchan, *crest-coronet*, 615.
,, of that Ilk, 433.
,, *Scottish Peerage and Consistorial Law*, 455.
,, WALTER, *brisure*, 433.
,, *Additional Remarks on the Lennox Representation*, 180.
RIDEL, GEOFFREY, Bishop of ELY, *arms*, 167.
RIENECK, *see* VOIGT.
RIETBERG, Princes of OST-FRIES-LAND, *arms*, 295.
RIETSTAP, *Armorial Général*, 88, 101, 169, 205, 502, 539, 624, 625, 643, 745.
RIETTER, DIE, *arms*, 302.
RIEUWE, VAN, *arms*, 428.
RIGEL, VON, *arms*, 148; Pl. XVI., fig. 8, p. 146.
Rigged, 702.

RIGSTRUP, *arms*, 296.
RILEY, *arms*, 155.
RINACH, *arms*, 223.
RINALDI, *arms*, 94.
RIPERDA, *arms*, 715.
RIPON, Marquess of, *crest-coronet*, 615.
Rising, 259, 702.
RITTBERG, *arms*, 295, 491.
RIVARI, *arms*, 289.
River, A, 313; Pl. XXVIII., fig. 11, p. 308.
RIVERS, Earls of DEVON, *arms*, 214.
RIVIÈRE DE ST. DENIS DES MONTS, *arms*, 729.
,, HENRY DE, *arms*, 405.
RIZZOLETTI, *arms*, 172.
RJEVSKI, *arms*, 267.
ROANNAIS, Duc de la, *arms*, 159.
ROBALOS, *arms*, 289.
ROBERT I. (BRUCE), King of SCOTLAND, 33, 34, 177, 178, 566, 583.
,, II., King of SCOTLAND, 178, 441, 445, 459, 520, 566, 605; *capeline*, 611.
,, III. King of SCOTLAND, 178, 419, 566.
ROBERTOUN, *arms*, 349.
ROBERTSON, *arms*, Pl. XXIII., fig. 3, p. 228.
,, of Strowan or Struan, *arms*, 229.
,, ,, ,, *chained savage* of, 643.
,, Origin of name, 10.
ROBSART, Sir LEWIS, Lord BOURCHIER, *tomb* of, 653.
Roc, 388, 682, 743.
,, *d'échiquier*, 387, 680, 743.
ROCA, *arms*, 388.
ROCABERTI, *arms*, 388.
ROCABRUNA, *arms*, 388.
ROCCHI, *arms*, 388.
ROCELINE, *arms*, 377.
ROCHAS, *arms*, 717.
ROCHAUSEN, *arms*, 86.
ROCHE, ANTOINE, Comte de la, *arms*, 574; Pl. XLVII., fig. 3, p. 574.
,, DE BEAUSAINT, DE LA, *arms*, 188.
,, MATHIEU, Baron de la, *arms*, 571.
,, PAIEN DE LA, *seal*, 463.
,, Seigneur de la, 11.
,, SUR YON, Princes de la, *bend*, 429.
ROCHECHOUART, Ducs de MORTEMAR, *arms*, 93.
ROCHEFORT, *arms*, 71.
,, JEAN, Sr. de, *arms*, 571; Pl. XLVIII., fig. 2, p. 576.
,, *Pairie* of, 515.
ROCHEFOUCAULD, LA, *arms*, Pl. XIII., fig. 9, p. 136, 138.
,, Le Duc de la, 11.
ROCHESTER, Bishop of, 142, 152.
,, Earl of, *arms*, 106.
,, JOHN TURBINE, Bishop of, *arms*, 152.
,, Viscount, *arms* and *augmentation*, 532.
ROCHFORT, *arms*, 531.

(837)

ROCHOW, *arms*, 229.
ROCKENHAUS, Counts, *arms*, 78.
ROCOURT, *see* OHA.
ROCQUENGHIEN, *arms*, 181.
RODE, LA, *arms*, 129.
RODEMACHER, *arms*, 93.
RODENBERG, *arms*, 230.
RODENEGGS, Counts WOLKENSTEIN, *arms*, 137.
RODES, *arms*, 725.
RODOLPH, Emperor, 246.
Roebuck, 232.
ROECK, DE, *arms*, 264.
ROEMER-BÜCHNER, *Die Siegel der Deutschen Kaiser*, 243, 244, 247, 248, 252, 253, 328, 621.
ROGERS, *arms*, 220.
ROGIER, ANSOLDE DE, 10.
„ *arms*, 123.
ROHAN, *arms*, 185, 505, 710.
„ -CHABOT, Dukes of, *arms*, 505.
„ Dukes de, *arms*, 505.
„ JOHN, Vicomte de, 505.
ROHRMANN, *arms*, 388.
ROISIN, Marquises de, *arms*, 95.
ROJAS, *arms*, 309.
ROKEWOOD, *arms*, 388.
ROLA, *herba* of, *arms*, 351.
„ -WOLSKI, Counts, *arms*, 351.
Rolls of Arms (*See* VINCENT, CALAIS, PLANCHÉ, GLOVER, CARLAVEROCK, etc.), 36, 69, 96, 268, 355, 401, 671.
„ „ 13*th Century*, 177, 252, 357, 393, 403, 407, 426.
„ „ „ and 14*th Centuries*, 407.
Roman warrior as a *supporter*, 640.
ROMANES, *arms*, 335.
ROMANOFFSKI, Princes of, *arms*, 473.
ROMANS, RICHARD, King of the, 245, 465.
„ „ „ *arms* on eagle, 630.
„ WILLIAM, King of the, 468.
ROMARE, WILLIAM DE, Earl of LINCOLN, *shield* of, 406.
ROMBERG, Barons, *arms*, 322.
ROME, *arms* of City, 395.
ROMIEU, *arms*, 375.
ROMILLY, Lord, *supporters*, 648.
Rompu, 139, 702, 743.
ROMRÉE, Counts of, *supporter*, 231.
ROMUL, *arms*, 228.
RONCHAUX, *arms*, 710.
RONCHIVECCHI, *arms*, 134.
RONQUEROLLES, *arms*, 73.
Rook (chess) as a charge, 387.
ROON, Count von, *augmentation*, 545.
ROORDA, *arms*, 188.
ROOS, DE, *arms*, 355 ; *badge*, 753.
„ „ Barony, 17, 18.
ROQUE D'ESTUER, DE LA, *arms*, 388.
„ DE LA, *arms*, 388.
„ „ „ *Traité de l'Origine des Noms*, 408.
„ „ „ *Traité singulier du Blason*, 327, 636.
„ „ „ Treatises of, 402.
„ LE, *Traité de Noblesse*, 5.
ROQUELAURE, Ducs de, *arms*, 388.
ROQUEMAUREL, *arms*, 388.
ROQUES, *arms*, 388.

Roquet, 388.
ROQUETTE, *arms*, 388.
RORDORF, *arms*, 182.
ROS, DE, *arms*, 355 ; Pl. XXXI., fig. 12, p. 346.
„ „ Barony of, 17, 18 (*see* ROOS).
„ EVERARD DE, 355.
„ Lady DE, of KENDAL, *seal*, 454.
ROSAMOND, Fair, 324.
ROSDORFF, VON, *arms*, 89, 668 ; Pl. LV., fig. 2, p. 668.
Rose, 323, 702.
„ as a *badge*, 587.
„ *crowned*, as a *badge*, 596.
„ for seventh son, 444.
„ *Red* and *white*, as a *badge*, 595.
ROSE, *arms*, 355.
„ of Kilravock, *arms*, 355.
ROSEBERY, ARCHIBALD, Earl of, *arms*, 180.
„ Earls of, *arms*, 337.
ROSENBERG, Princes of, *arms*, 92, 323, 324.
ROSENBORG, Castle of, 620.
ROSENECK, *arms*, 325.
Roses, Pl. XX., fig. 3, p. 332.
„ *slipped*, Pl. XXX., fig. 4, p. 332.
„ Wars of the, 324, 398.
ROSMADEC, Marquises of, *arms*, 91.
ROSNY, *arms*, 127.
ROSOY, *seal* and *arms* of JULIENNE, Dame de, 49.
„ *seal* and *arms* of ROGER DE, 49.
ROSS, ALEXANDER, Earl of, *arms* on Eagle, 630.
„ *arms*, 532, 631.
„ Bishop of, 437.
„ Earldom of, *arms*, 367, 368.
„ EUPHEMIA, 459.
„ „ Countess of, *arms* on Eagle, 631.
„ HUGH, Earl of, 442.
„ Lords, *arms*, 355.
„ of Rarichies, HUGH, *bordure*, 442.
„ *seal* of ALEXANDER, Earl of 367.
„ „ JOHN, Earl of, 367.
„ *water-bougets* of, 454.
ROSSEL, *arms*, 278.
ROSSELYN, *arms*, 377.
ROSSI, *arms*, 66, 213.
„ Princes of CERAMI, *arms*, 310.
RÖSSLER, *arms*, 237.
ROSSLYN, Earl of, *arms*, 142.
ROST, Counts von, *arms*, 78.
ROSTAING, *arms*, 214.
ROSTOCK, Lordship of, *arms*, 288, 492.
ROSTOPCHIN, *augmentation*, 542.
ROSVERN, *arms*, 277.
RÖTELEN, County of, *arms*, 221, 491.
ROTENBURG, Counts von, *arms*, 126.
ROTHALL, Counts von, *arms*, 161.
ROTHE, JOHANNES, of Eisenach, treatise by, 19.
ROTHSCHILD, *arms*, 351.
ROTZELAER, GEOFFREY DE, *arms*, 405.
Rouant, 691, 700, 739, 743.
ROUCK, DE, System of lines representing colour, 64.
„ *Den Nederlandtschen Herauld*, 551.
ROUCY, *arms*, 212.

Roue de St. Catherine, 743.
ROUILLON, OLIVER, *supporters,* 633.
ROUMANIA, *arms,* 667.
Rounded, 702.
Roundles, 165, 189, 702 ; Pl. XIX., fig. 4, p. 192.
,, Names of, on Continent, 191.
ROUPY, MONTMORENCY DE, *brisure,* 451.
Rousant, 702.
ROUSE, *arms,* 127.
ROUSSELET, *arms,* 68.
ROUSSET, *arms,* 161, 162.
ROUSSILLON, GERARD DE, romance of, 269.
,, LOUIS, Comte de, *arms,* 571.
ROUVILLE, DE, *arms,* 270.
ROUX, *arms,* 68.
,, Seigneur de, *arms,* 450.
ROVERE, DELLA, Dukes of URBINO, *arms,* 318.
ROXBURGH, ALEXANDER, *seal,* 632.
Royal *arms* and *supporters,* 661.
,, Family, *labels,* 423.
,, ,, using *escucheon en surtout,* 488.
ROZ, Barons de, *arms,* 151.
ROZEN, DU, *arms,* 187.
ROZIER DE LINAGE, *arms,* Pl. XIII., fig. 10, p. 136.
RUBEI, *arms,* 66.
Ruby, 65, 702.
RUCHSTEIN, VON, *arms,* 90 ; Pl. VI., fig. 12, p. 84.
RUDBERG, *arms,* 93.
Rudder as a *badge,* 754.
RUDICKHEIM, *arms,* 131.
RÜDIGER, Counts, *arms* and *augmentation,* 542.
RUDOLPHUS, *Heraldica Curiosa,* 3, 42.
RUELLE, DE LA, *arms,* 279.
RUESDORF, *arms,* Pl. LVI., fig. 3, p. 670.
RUFFELAERT, *arms,* 93.
RUKOFF, *arms,* 281.
Rules of Blazon, 101, 105, 110.
RUMLINGEN DE BERG, Barons, *arms,* 138.
RUPERT, Emperor, HOLY ROMAN EMPIRE, *crown,* 621.
RÜPPELIN, Barons von, *arms,* 150.
RUSÉ, 12.
RUSKIN'S *Modern Painters,* 211.
RUSPOLI, Princes, *arms,* 319.
RUSSELL, *arms,* 278 ; Pl. IX., fig. 8, p. 108.
,, Duke of BEDFORD, *arms,* 107.
RUSSIA, *Armorials* of, 541.
,, *arms,* 250, 665 ; Pl. LIII., fig. 2, p. 664.
,, *crest* as *augmentation,* 608.
,, *eagles* of, 542.
,, Imperial *crown* of, 621.
Russian Empire, The Antiquities of the, 622.
RUSSIAN *augmentations,* 542.
Ruste, 185, 702, 743.
Rustre, The, 117, 182, 185, 702, 743.
RUTHERFORD of Fairnington, *brisure,* 433.
RUTHVEN, Master of, 419.
,, WILLIAM, Provost of PERTH, *label,* 419.

RUTLAND, Duke of, *supporter,* 297.
,, Dukes of, *arms,* 530.
,, Earl of, *arms* and *label,* 416.
,, ,, *augmentation,* 530.
,, ,, *seal,* 369.
,, ,, ,, sail with *arms* from, Pl. XXXIV., fig. 4, p. 388.
,, EDWARD, Earl of, *arms,* 474.
RÜXNER'S *Thurnier Buch,* 41.
RUYSBROEK, Counts de, *arms,* 122.
RUYTER, Admiral de, *arms,* 127.
,, *monument* of, 626.
RYCKEVORSEL, VAN, *arms,* 279.
Rye, Pl. XXX., fig. 11, p. 332.
,, *Ears* of, 341.
RYE, *arms,* 257, 341.
RYMER, quoted, 590.
RYTS, VAN DER, *arms,* 139.
RYTWIANY-ZBOROWSKI, Counts de, *arms,* 356.

SAANECK, Baron von, 405.
SAAREBRUCK, concession of a crest by JOHN, Comte de, 751.
SAARWERDEN, Counts of, *arms,* 256.
SABBEN, *arms,* 188.
SABBINGEN, VAN, *arms,* 128.
SABCOTT, *arms,* 351.
Sable, 702, 743.
,, or Black, 60, 65 ; Pl. III., fig. 5, p. 60.
,, *plein, de,* 67.
,, *shield,* plain, 67.
SABLÉ, Marquises de, *arms,* 275.
SABLONNIERE, DE LA, *arms,* 204.
SABRAN, *arms,* 214.
,, Ducs de, *arms,* 213.
SACHEVERELL, *arms,* 563.
,, GEORGE, *arms,* 563.
,, of Morley, FRANCES, daughter of HENRY, 563.
,, VALENCE, daughter of HENRY, 563.
SACHSENGRUN, *see* KFELLER.
SACQUEVILLE, *arms,* 260.
SACQUINVILLE, *arms,* 260.
SADE, ELZEAS DE, *arms* and *augmentation,* 537.
,, LAURA, wife of UGO DE, 537.
Saffre, 743.
SAFFRES, *arms,* 259.
Sage, 344.
Sagittary, 702.
Saillant, 743.
SAILLY, *arms,* 96.
SAINCY, *see* MARCHAL, 366.
Saint Denis, Enseigne de, 658.
SAINT PRIEST, *arms,* 99.
,, VRAIN, ISABELLA DE, *arms,* 58.
SAINTONGE, *Pairie* of, 515.
Salamander as a *badge,* 586.
,, The, 294.
Salamanders as *supporters,* 636.
SALAMONI, *arms,* 100.
SALAZAR Y CASTRO, *Casa de Lara,* 483.
SALHEIM, *see* HUND.
Saliant, 217, 702.
SALIGNON, *arms,* 136, 737.
SALINS, DE, *arms,* 129.
,, Vicomtes de, *arms,* 389.
SALIS, Counts de, *arms,* 318.

(839)

SALISBURY, Earl of, *arms*, 183, 219, 224, 257 ; Pl. XXI., fig. 12, p. 212.
,, Earls of, 562.
,, Marquess of, *crescent*, 446.
,, See of, *arms*, 195.
,, THOMAS, Earl of, 562.
SALM, Counts and Princes of, *arms*, 271, 408.
Salmon hauriant, Pl. XXVI., fig. 6, p. 266.
,, The, 268, 271.
SALMON, *arms*, 268.
SALONISI, *arms*, 95.
SALPERWICK, Marquis de GRIGNY, *arms*, 165.
Saltire, 702 ; Fig. 42, p. 116, 142 ; Pl. XV., fig. 8, p. 144 ; Pl. XV., fig. 9, p. 144.
,, *ancrée*, Pl. XV., fig. 11, p. 144.
,, *and chief*, Pl. XV., fig. 10, p. 144.
,, *Charges on*, 144.
,, *couped*, Pl. XV., fig. 12, p. 144.
,, ,, and *flory*, 145.
,, *echanchré*, 145.
,, *Parted per*, Fig. 33, p. 77.
,, *Per*, Pl. V., fig. 12, p. 80.
,, *pommetty*, 145.
,, *Quarterly per*, 82.
,, Varieties of, 145.
Saltireways, 702.
Saltorels, 702.
SALUCES, Marquessate of, *arms*, 118.
SALVERT, Marquises de, *arms*, 159.
SALVIAC, *arms*, 358.
SALZBURG, Duchy, *arms*, 499, 665.
SAMSON, *arms*, 196.
,, in Heraldry, 196.
SAMUELSON, *arms*, 298.
SAN SEVERINO, *arms*, 505.
,, Ducs de, *arms*, 124.
SANCHEZ, *arms*, 131 ; Pl. XII., fig. 5, p. 130.
,, DON ALONZO, 578.
SANCHO, *the Strong*, of NAVARRE, 353.
SANCOURT, *arms*, 96.
SANDBERG, *arms*, 752.
SANDFORD, *arms*, 82, 93 ; Pl. V., fig. 10, p. 80.
SANDILANDS, *arms*, 519.
,, Lord TORPHICHEN, *augmentation*, 535.
,, Sire de, *lambrequin*, 611.
SANDON, *arms*, 82.
SANDOVAL, *arms*, 130.
SANDWICH, Earl of, *supporter*, 302.
,, Earls of, *arms*, 562.
SANDWYK, VAN, *arms*, 213.
SANDYS, *arms*, 142, 163.
,, *badge*, 753.
Sanglé, 743.
Sanglier, 227, 689, 743.
Sanguine or Blood colour, 60, 65, 703 ; Pl. III., fig. 9, p. 60.
SANGUINETTO, Count of, *arms* and *augmentation*, 536.
Sans-nombre, 702.
SANTAPAU, Princes de BUTERA, *arms*, 89.
SANTEUIL, *arms*, 201, 714.
SANTHEUVEL, VAN DEN, *arms*, 238.
SANTIAGO, Cross of, 644.
,, HENRY, Grand Master of the Order of, 577.
SAPCOTE, *arms*, 363.

Sapphire, 65, 703.
Saracen *banner*, 655.
Saracen's Head, 199, 703 ; Pl. XX., fig. 4, p. 198.
,, ,, as a *badge*, 754.
Sarcellé, 703.
Sarcelly, *Cross*, 160.
SARDINIA, *arms*, 200 ; Pl. XX., fig. 6, p. 198.
,, King of, *supporter* of, 244.
Sardonyx, 65, 703.
SARRANTE, *arms*, 66.
SART, Counts de, *arms*, 136.
SARTIGES, *arms*, 139.
SASSENAGE, AYMER DE, *arms*, 51.
,, GUILLAUME DE, *arms*, 51.
SASSOFERRATO, BARTOLO DI, *De Armis et Insignis*, 19.
SATTELBOGEN, *arms*, 87.
Saturn, 65.
SATURNINI, *arms*, 299.
Satyr, 703.
SAULX, *arms*, 213.
SAUSENBERG, Lordship of, *arms*, 491.
Sautoir, 142, 702, 743.
,, *En*, 743.
,, *Passés en*, 743.
Sauvage, 708.
SAUVAGEOT collection, 332.
SAVA, Barons, *arms*, 172.
Savage, Pl. XX., fig. 2, p. 198.
,, or Wild Man in Heraldry, 198.
Savage's head, 199.
SAVALLETTE, *arms*, 295.
Save River, 498.
SAVELLI, Duca de, *arms*, 645.
SAVEUSE, Marquises de, *arms*, 186.
SAVILE, *arms*, Pl. XII., fig. 4, p. 130.
,, Earl of MEXBOROUGH, *arms*, 130.
SAVIOUR, THE BLESSED, in Heraldry, 194.
SAVOIE, *see* SAVOY.
SAVONA, Marquises DE, *arms*, 641.
SAVORY, *arms*, 687.
SAVOY, AMADEUS VI. of, *seal*, 629.
,, ,, of, King of SPAIN, *arms*, 488.
,, ,, *the Great*, Count of, 454, 579.
,, *arms*, 57, 453, 467, 488, 579, 629.
,, AYMON of, *arms* and *supporters*, 579, 629.
,, Count PETER of, 453.
,, Counts of, *arms*, 244.
,, *crest*, 629.
,, Duke PHILIP, *sans terre*, 579.
,, Dukes of, *arms*, 141.
,, HUMBERT, *bâtard de*, *arms*, 579.
,, LOUIS DE, *bâtard* D'ACHAIE, *arms*, 579.
,, ,, Duke of, 467, 579.
,, Marks of illegitimacy in, 579.
,, *original arms*, 579.
,, RENÉ, *bâtard de*, *arms*, 579.
,, *seal* of AMADEUS, V. Count of, 628.
,, ,, EDWARD, Count of, 628.
SAXE, Chevalier de, *arms*, 525.
,, COBOURG, Prince LEOPOLD of, *arms*, 424.
,, -COBURG, Duke of, 622.

(840)

SAXE - COBURG - GOTHA, *crown* of Prince ALBERT of, 622.
SAXON Duchies, *arms*, 67, 265, 321, 362.
,, *flags*, 650.
SAXONY, *arms*, 131, 469, 488, 491, 525, 724; Pl. XII., fig. 6, p. 130.
,, *crest*, 607.
,, Dukes of, *arms*, 456.
,, Elector of, *arms*, 526.
,, Kings of, *arms*, 346.
,, Palatinate of, *arms*, 256,
,, Prince FRANCIS XAVIER of, 525.
,, *supporters*, 667.
SAY, Lords, *arms*, 81.
SAYN, Counts of, *arms*, 358.
,, Princes of, *arms*, 216.
SCALA, ALBOINO DELLA, *arms* and *augmentation*, 536.
,, *arms*, 364, 493; Pl. XXXII., fig. 9, p. 358.
,, CAN DELLA, *augmentation*, 536.
,, JOHANNA, daughter and heiress of JOHN DELLA, *arms*, 493.
,, Princes, 364.
,, DELLA, *arms*, 364.
Scaled, 703.
,, *badge*, 753.
SCALES, Lord, 574.
,, ROBERT DE, *arms*, 273.
SCALI, *arms*, 364.
SCALIGER, *arms*, 364, 493.
,, JOHANNA, daughter and heiress of JOHN, *arms*, 493.
Scallop, 703.
,, *shell*, 272.
SCALTENIGHI, *arms*, 72.
SCANDINAVIA, *crested helms* in, 604.
,, Title of Marquess unknown in, 626.
Scarpe, 703.
SCARRON, *arms*, 130.
Sceptres as charges, 380.
SCHAD, *arms*, 260.
SCHADEWALDE, *see* DEBSCHÜTZ.
SCHAEP, *arms*, 235.
SCHAGEN family, 576.
SCHATZ, *arms*, 166.
SCHAUMANN, *arms*, 383.
SCHAW, *arms*, Pl. XXXIII., fig. 7, p. 376.
,, of Sauchie, *arms*, 381 (*see* SHAW).
SCHAWENBURG, Barons von, *arms*, 176.
SCHEFFER, *de Antiquis verisque Regni Sueciæ Insignibus*, 379, 628.
SCHELDORFER, VON, *arms*, Pl. V., fig. 5, p. 80.
SCHELKLINGEN, Counts von, *arms*, 95.
SCHELTENBERG, MARQUARD DE, *seal* of, 606.
SCHEPERS, *supporters*, 643.
SCHESNAYE, *arms*, 185.
SCHESTEDT, Count HANNIBAL DE, *augmentation*, 539.
SCHEUCHENSTUEL DE RHAIN, *arms*, 198.
SCHEURLER, *arms*, 74.
SCHIECK, *arms*, 336.
SCHILLER, *Wallenstein*, 470.
SCHILLING, Counts von, *arms*, 389.

SCHINDEL, DIE, *arms*, 186.
SCHIO, Counts DA, 302.
SCHIPSTOW, *arms*, 364.
SCHIVES, *arms*, 226.
SCHLEGEL, *arms*, 94.
SCHLEICH, *arms*, Pl. VI., fig. 9, p. 84.
,, VON, *arms*, 88.
SCHLEIDEN, *arms*, 68.
SCHLESWIG, *arms*, 581, 666.
,, -HOLSTEIN, Princess HELENA of, *label*, 423.
SCHLIEBEN, Comtes, *augmentation*, 543.
SCHLOTHEIM, Barons, and Counts von, *arms*, 580.
SCHMID, *arms*, 191.
SCHMIDBURG, Baron von, *arms*, 377.
SCHMIDT, Barons, *augmentation*, 546.
,, *Die Wappen aller Fürsten und Staaten*, 73.
Schneckenweise, Pl. VIII., fig. 4, p. 100.
SCHNEIDER, VON, 15.
SCHONAICH, Barony of, *arms*, 337.
SCHÖNAU, *see* EGLOF.
SCHÖNBORN, Counts von, *arms*, 342.
SCHÖNBURG, Princes of, *arms*, 94.
SCHÖNEN, *arms*, 256.
SCHÖNFELD, Counts von, *arms*, 318.
SCHÖNSTEIN, *arms*, 121.
SCHOONHOVEN, JEAN DE, *arms*, 405.
,, VAN, *arms*, 203, 405.
SCHOONVELT, VAN, *arms*, 127.
SCHOREL, VAN, *arms*, 196.
SCHORISSE, VAN, *arms*, 181.
SCHRECK, *arms*, 276.
SCHROT, *arms*, 669; Pl. LV., fig. 8, p. 668.
Schröterhörner, 321.
SCHROTT, VON, *arms*, 89.
SCHWABEGG, *arms*, 469.
SCHWALENBERG, Counts of, *arms*, 404.
,, WITEKIND, Count of, 404.
SCHWARTZBURG, Princes of, *augmentation*, 537.
SCHWARZBURG, *arms*, 489.
,, Princes of, *arms*, 489.
,, *seal* of the Emperor GUNTHER VON, 248.
SCHWARZENBERG, Princes of, *arms*, 91, 200.
SCHWEIDNITZ, Counts von, *arms*, 817.
SCHWEREN, *arms*, 89.
SCHWERIN, *arms*, Pl. VI., fig. 11, p. 84.
,, County of, *arms*, 79, 182, 205, 492.
,, Principality of, *arms*, 492.
Scintillant, 703.
Scissors as charges, 392.
SCLAVONIA, *arms*, 374.
Sclavonic families, *mantling*, 616.
SCLEROS, *arms*, 284.
SCOPULI, *arms*, 390.
SCORPIONE, *arms*, 277.
Scorpions, 274, 277.
SCOT, JOHN, of Thirlstane, *arms*, 179.
,, of Harden, *supporters*, 302.
SCOTLAND, *arms*, 330, 441, 443, 446, 455, 464, 475, 476, 479, 505, 521, 529, 566, 567, 662, 663.
,, *arms*, during Commonwealth, 487.
,, *augmentation* in, 534.

SCOTLAND, *badge*, 596, 597.
,, Change of name in, 609.
,, *coins* of, 334.
,, *crest* of, 644.
,, Differencing in, 397.
,, Earl Marshal, mark of office, 644.
,, *ensign* of Princes of, 208.
,, Family *badges* in, 598.
,, Feudalism in, 399.
,, Great Master of the Household, mark of office, 644.
,, *Great Seals* of, 598.
,, Heraldic marks of illegitimacy in, 565.
,, ISABELLA, dtr. of King JAMES I. of, 505.
,, JAMES, King of, 515.
,, Justice General, mark of office, 644.
,, *Lions* of, as *supporters*, 636.
,, Lord High Chamberlain, mark of office, 644.
,, Marshalling in, 512.
,, Mode of differencing, 405.
,, Names in southern counties of, 400.
,, *National emblem* of, 334.
,, Princess MARGARET of, 512.
,, Queen MARY of, 476.
,, *Royal crest* of, 217.
,, ,, *crown* of, 619.
,, Regalia of, 619.
,, *saltire* in, 143.
,, Small number of names in, 400.
,, *supporters* in, 296, 632, 635, 646.
,, The *double tressure* in, 146, 176.
,, *unicorn* of, 663.
,, Use of *bordure* in, 441.
,, ,, *chevron* in, 431.
,, ,, *label* in, 419.
SCOTS, ACHAIUS, Mythical King of the Dalriadic, 176.
SCOTT, *arms*, 162; Pl. XXII., fig. 6, p. 222.
,, *arms in Lyon Office Register*, 400.
,, of Balweary, *arms*, 222.
,, ,, Buccleuch, *arms*, 559.
,, ,, Gorrenberry, *bordure*, 443.
,, Sir WALTER, *Quentin Durward*, 97.
,, ,, *supporter*, 303.
,, WILLIAM, *brisure*, 435.
Scottish marks of illegitimacy, 569.
SCOTTS in south Scotland, 400.
Scourges as charges, 374.
Scrip, 703.
SCRIVELSBY, Baron of, 345.
Scroll, 703.
SCROPE, *arms*, 111, 129, 341, 427; Pl. XII., fig 1, p. 130.
,, and GROSVENOR Controversy, 341, 439.
Scruttle, 703.
SCRYMGEOUR, *arms*, 149.
,, Earl of DUNDEE, 149.
,, MARGARET, 149.
SCUDAMORE, *arms*, 155, 357; Pl. XXXII., fig. 2, p. 358.
,, Viscounts, *arms*, 357.

SCYLITZES, *arms*, 241.
Scythes and *Scythe blades*, 350.
Sea-dog, The, 300, 703.
,, *-griffin*, 290.
,, *-horse*, The, 299, 703; Pl. XXVII., fig. 11, p. 288.
,, *-lion*, The, 299, 703.
,, *-stag*, The, 299.
,, *-unicorn*, 297.
SEA, Sir MARTYN OF THE, 17.
SEAFIELD, Earl of, *arms*, 380.
Seal, Earliest instance of armorial, 26.
Seals, 55, 56, 238; Pl. XXXV., p. 416; Pl. XXXVII., p. 448.
,, Armorial Bearings on, 44.
,, *Devices* on Burgh, 313.
,, Various, 36, 37.
SECCANO, *arms*, 256.
SECKENDORF, *arms*, Pl. XXIX., fig. 6, p. 318.
SECKENDORFF, Counts von, *arms*, 318.
Second Nobility Roll, 71, 357, 481.
SEDAN, Princes of, *arms*, 360.
SEDLEY, KATHARINE, 560.
SEEBACH, *arms*, 298.
Seeded, 325, 703.
SEEVES, *arms*, 226.
SEFTON, Earls of, *arms*, 159.
SEGALAS, *arms*, 285.
SEGOING, *Armorial Universel*, 260.
,, *Le Trésor Héraldique*, 2.
,, *Mercure Armorial*, 2.
SEGORBIA, Dukes of, *arms*, 577.
SEGOVIA, *see* IBANEZ.
SEGRAVE, *arms*, 214, 342, 428.
,, JOHN, *seal*, 628.
,, NICHOLAS DE, *label* of, 414.
,, Sir JOHN DE, *arms*, 414.
Segreant, 287, 703.
SEGUIER, 12.
,, Library of, 611.
SÉGUR, *arms*, 228.
SEIGNELAY, Marquis de, *arms*, 275.
SEINSHEIM, *arms*, 200.
SEINTELOWE (?) WILLIAM DE, 33, 34.
Sejant, 217, 703.
,, *-addorsed*, 703.
,, *-affronté*, 217.
,, *-gardant*, 217.
,, *-rampant*, 217.
Semé, 112, 677, 702, 703, 743; Pl. VIII., fig. 10, p. 100.
,, *de France*, 743.
,, *of hearts*, Pl. VIII., fig. 9, p. 100.
,, *of fleurs-de-lis*, Pl. VIII., fig. 8, p. 100.
Semper eadem, 664.
SEMPILL, *arms*, 436; Pl. XIII., fig. 2, p. 136.
,, Lords, *arms*, 137.
,, of Beltrees, *brisure*, 436.
SÉNÉCHAL, LE, *arms*, 185.
Senestre, 743.
Senestré, 711, 743.
Senestrochère, 205, 726, 743.
Sengreen, 703.
SENLIS, *see* BOUTEILLER.
SENS, LE, Marquises de MORSAN, *arms*, 372.
Sepulchral Monument, *arms* on, at RATISBON, 24.
SERAING, *arms*, 427.
Seraph, 703.
Séraphin, 703.
SERBY, NICOLAS, *Leopard Herald*, 209.

(842)

SERENELLI, *arms,* 303.
SERGEANT DE MARSIGNY, Le, *arms,* 343.
SERLE, *arms,* 78.
Serpent, Shield encircled by a, 639.
,, *vorant,* Pl. XXVII., fig. 4, p. 288.
,, with a female head, 640.
Serpents, 273.
Serpent's heads, 276.
Serra, 299.
SERVATI, *arms,* 126.
SERVIA and BOSNIA, Czar of, 251.
,, *arms,* 501, 668.
SESA, Dukes of, *arms,* 473.
SETON, ALEXANDER, *bend,* 429.
,, *arms,* 307, 521, 534.
,, G., *The Law and Practice of Heraldry in Scotland,* 44, 84, 548, 552, 553, 568, 632, 647.
,, of Touch, *crest,* 605.
,, Sir ALEXANDER, *arms,* 178.
,, ,, ,, Governor of Berwick, *augmentation,* 534.
,, Sir ALEXANDER, son of SAER DE, *label,* 419.
,, Sir CHRISTOPHER, 178.
,, *Star* of, 643.
SETTIMO, Princes de FILIOLA, *arms,* 140.
SEUBERSDORFF, VON, *arms,* 95.
SEUSENEGG, Barons von, *arms,* 183.
SEVA, Counts, *arms,* 722.
SEVASTOS, *arms,* 333.
SÉVIGNÉ, Letters of, Mme. De, 132.
,, Marquises de, *arms,* 82.
SEWELL, *arms,* 283.
SEYMOUR, *arms,* 531; Pl. XXV., fig. 5, p. 260; Pl. XXXIX., fig. 2, p. 482.
,, Duke of SOMERSET, *arms,* 260.
,, ,, ,, *crest,* 298.
,, JANE, Queen, *augmentation,* 531.
SÈZE, *arms,* 539.
,, Count de, *augmentation,* 539.
SFORZA, *arms,* 218.
Shack-bolt, 703.
Shafted, 703.
SHAFTESBURY, Earls of, *arms,* 234.
Shake-fork, 151, 703; Pl. XVI., fig. 12, p. 146.
SHAKESPEARE, WILLIAM, *arms,* 347.
,, *arms,* Pl. XXXI., fig. 2, p. 346.
,, *Henry VI.,* 584.
,, *Richard III.,* 591.
Shambrogue or *Brogue,* 679.
Shambrogues as charges, 392.
Shambroughs, 703.
Shamrock, The, 320.
SHARP of Kincarroch, *arms,* 569.
Shawms as charges, 383.
SHAWS of Sauchie, *arms,* 381.
Sheaves, 350.
Sheep, 235, 703.
SHEFFIELD, *arms,* 562.
,, Duke of BUCKINGHAM, *arms,* 343.
,, or HERBERT, CHARLES, *arms,* 562.
Shell-fish, 272.
Shepherd's pipe as a charge, 387.

SHERBURN, *arms,* Pl. XXI., fig. 2, p. 212.
SHERBURNE of Stonyhurst, *arms,* 216.
Shield, 11th Century, Pl. I., fig. 6, p. 54.
,, between the attires of a stag's head, 643.
,, Different forms of, Figs. 7, 8, 9, 10, 11, 12, 13, 14, p. 53.
,, English and French, *Points of,* Figs. 15, 16, p. 59.
,, Form of, in BRITAIN, 56.
,, ,, ,, FRANCE, 56.
,, ,, ,, ITALY, 56.
,, ,, ,, SPAIN, 55, 56.
,, lozenge shape, supposed derivation of, 58, 59.
,, Red, special use of, 67.
,, Square, 57.
,, used by unmarried lady or widow, 58.
Shields, 351.
,, 12th century chessmen, Pl. I., figs. 8, 9, 10, p. 54.
,, Different forms of, 53, 56, 57.
,, from Bayeux Tapestry, Pl. I., figs. 1, 2, 3, p. 54.
,, of a single metal, tincture, or fur, 66.
,, on cross or star of an Order, 644.
,, Oval and Circular, 56, 57.
,, suspended at Tournaments, 55.
Ship, as a *badge,* 754.
,, as a charge, 369.
SHIPBROKE, RICHARD, Baron of, descendants, 399.
Ships as charges, 367.
Ship's buoy as a *badge,* 754.
SHIRLEY, Earl FERRERS, *arms,* 165.
Shivered, 703.
Shod, 88.
Shoe, Horse, 355.
Shoes as charges, 392.
Shovels as charges, 393.
SHREWSBURY, *badge,* 754.
,, Earl of, *arms,* 174.
Shrimps, 273.
SIBELL, *arms,* 225.
SIBERIA, *arms,* 665.
,, *crown,* 622.
SICHTERMANN, *arms,* 240.
SICILE, RENÉ, Roi de, Tourney Regulations, 749.
SICILY, *arms,* 258, 471, 482, 495, 501, 504, 576, 577.
,, FREDERICK, King of, 505.
,, *seal* of CHARLES, King of, 329.
SICKINGEN, *arms,* 440.
Sickle as a *badge,* 585, 754.
SIDON, Prince of, *arms,* 118.
SIEBENBÜRGEN, *arms,* 495, 498.
SIEBMACHER, *Wappenbuch,* 64, 66, 73, 90, 92, 95, 98, 114, 134, 161, 166, 182, 191, 263, 289, 290, 297, 336, 373, 402, 411, 412, 440, 477, 579, 582, 601, 614, 640, 752.
SIENA, Cathedral of, 656.
SIERADZ, Duchy of, *arms,* 468.
Sieve as a *badge,* 596.
SIGINOLFI, *arms,* 92.
SIGISMUND, *arms* of Emperor, 249.
,, Emperor, 251, 252, 255.
,, ,, *augmentation* granted by, 536, 537.
,, King of POLAND, *augmentation* granted by, 540.

(843)

SIGNIA, Family of, *arms* of, 256.
SILESIA, Duchy of, *arms*, 255, 491, 496.
,, Principality, *arms*, 500, 665.
SILFWERHJELM, 672.
Silk-worms, 280.
Silver or *argent*, 60, 65.
,, Shield, plain, 66.
SIMIANE, *arms*, Pl. VIII., fig. 10, p. 100.
,, GUIRAND DE, *seal* of, 47.
,, Marquises de, *arms*, 113.
SIMON, *L'Armorial Général de l'Empire Français*, 259, 283, 626.
SINCLAIR, *arms*, 368, 369, 406, 511, 512.
,, Barons, *arms*, 511; Pl. XLIII., fig. 2, p. 522.
,, *brisure*, 434.
,, *cross*, 511.
,, Earl of CAITHNESS, *arms*, Pl. XLIII., fig. 1, p. 522.
,, Earl of ROSSLYN, *arms*, 142.
,, HENRY, Earl of ORKNEY, *seal*, 369.
,, ,, Lord, 369.
,, Lord, *arms*, 511.
,, Mr ALEXANDER, 520.
,, of HERDMANSTON, *arms*, 406.
,, of HERDMANSTOUN, *arms*, 34.
,, of ROSLIN, *arms*, 34.
,, of ULBSTER, PATRICK, *bordure*, 443.
Sinister, 703.
,, side of *shield*, 59.
Sinople, 704, 707, 744.
,, *Plein-de-*, 67.
SIRADIA, Duchy of, *arms*, 468; Pl. XXXVIII., fig. 1, p. 464.
,, Palatinate of, *arms*, 468.
Siren, 704.
Sirène, 300, 744.
SISSINK, *arms*, 304.
SIX, *arms*, 128.
SIXTUS IV., Pope, *arms*, 318.
Skates as charges, 392.
Skeleton, The, 203.
SKENE, 704.
,, *Celtic Scotland*, 371.
SKRBENSKY DE HRZISTIC, Barons, *arms*, 120.
Skull, The, 203.
Slashed, 704.
SLAWATA, Counts of, *arms*, 93.
Sleeve, Hanging, as a charge, 376.
SLEICH, *arms*, 166.
SLESVIG, *arms*, 581, 666.
Sling, The, as a charge, 365.
Slipped, 320, 325, 704.
Slippers as charges, 392.
SMITH, *crests*, 610.
,, GORDON, *crest*, 610.
,, Sir SIDNEY, *arms*, 534.
Smithfield, Jousts held at, 589.
Snails, 280.
Snake entwined, Pl. XXVII., fig. 3, p. 288.
Snakes, 274; Pl. XXVII., fig. 2, p. 288.
SNEEVOET, *arms*, 207.
SO, *arms*, 130.
SOBIESKI, *arms*, 351.
,, JOHN, King of POLAND, *arms*, 486.
Soc de charrue, 744.
SODERINI, *arms* and *augmentation*, 541.
SOISSONS, *arms*, 214.

SOISSONS, 13th century Maire de, Pl. I., fig. 1, p. 44.
,, *seal* of CONON, Count of, 48.
Sol, 65.
SOLAGES, *arms*, 305.
SOLDANIERI, *arms*, 71.
SOLDATI, *arms*, 347.
SOLDONIERI, *arms*, 72.
Soleil, 744.
,, *Ombre de*, 744.
SOLIGNAC, *arms*, 118.
SOLMS, Counts and Princes of, *arms*, 214, 325, 404, 488.
SOLVI, *arms*, 153.
SOMBEKE, *arms*, 140.
SOMELDYCK, PHILIPPE, Seigneur de, *arms*, 575.
SOMERFORD, *arms*, 232; Pl. XXIII., fig. 8, p. 228.
SOMERLED, 368.
SOMERS, Earl, *arms*, 234.
SOMERSET and RICHMOND, Duke of, *arms*, 559.
,, *badge* of, 588.
,, CHARLES, Earl of WORCESTER, 556.
,, Duke of, 556.
,, ,, *crest*, 298.
,, ,, *supporter*, 297.
,, ,, BEAUFORT, *arms*, 556.
,, Dukes of, *arms*, 260, 531.
,, Garter Plate of Duke of, 594.
,, JOHN, Earl of, 475.
,, Marquis of, *arms*, 555.
SOMERVILLE, *arms*, 123.
,, Lord, *supporters*, 279.
SOMERY, *arms*, 131.
Sommé, 677, 726, 744.
SOMMERAU-BECK, Barons von, *arms*, 580.
SON, VAN, *arms*, 305, 306.
SONDERNDORFF, Barons von, *arms*, 380.
SONDERSHAUSEN, *arms*, 487.
SONNBERG, Counts de, *arms*, 305.
SONNEBERG, Count von, *arms*, 306.
SONNEMAER, *arms*, 306.
SONNENBERG, *arms*, Pl. XXVIII., fig. 1, p. 308.
,, County, *arms*, 499.
SONNEWALDE, *arms*, 488.
SOPHIA, Princess, *label*, 422; Fig. 89, p. 421.
SORIA, Duke of, *arms*, 449.
,, GUILLAUME, Duke of, 450.
SORIN, *arms*, 265.
SOTO, *arms*, 353.
SOUBISE, Princes de, *arms*, 185.
SOUEFF, *arms*, 280.
SOULIS, *arms*, 519.
SOULT, *arms*, Pl. X., fig. 3, p. 118.
SOUMERET D'ESSENAU, *arms*, 185.
SOUSA, *arms*, 578.
,, sisters, 578.
Soutenu, 704, 744.
SOUTHAMPTON, CHARLES, Duke of, *arms*, 559.
,, Earls of, *arms*, 100.
SOUTHESK, Earls of, *arms*, 258.
Southwark Church, 597.
Soutiens, 627.
Sovereign, *helm* of, 601, 602.
Sovereigns, *Privy Seals* of our, 598.

SPADA, *arms*, 346, 347.
SPAIN, *arms*, 667.
,, *augmentations* in, 547.
,, *coronet* of Grandees of the first class in, 624.
,, *crests* in, 604.
,, *De* in, 16.
,, Dukes in, 624.
,, Form of *shield* in, 55, 56.
,, *furs* common in *Armory* of, 74.
,, Introduction of Hereditary *arms* into, 52.
,, ISABELLA, Infanta of, *seal*, 478.
,, King AMADEUS of, *arms*, 488.
,, Marks of illegitimacy in, 576.
,, ,, office in, 645.
,, *marshalling* in, 506.
,, PHILIP II., King of, 478.
,, ,, King of, *arms*, 488.
,, Royal *arms*, 488.
,, *seals* of ALFONZO of, 58.
,, *supporters*, 667.
,, Use of *bordure* in, 440.
,, ,, *supporters* in, 636, 639.
SPALDING, *arms*, 163, 345.
Spancelled, 687, 704.
SPANHEIM, Counts of, *arms*, 405.
SPANOFFSKY DE LISSAU, *arms*, 120.
SPAR, *arms*, 369, 511.
SPARNECK, VON, *arms*, 98.
SPARRE, 672.
,, *arms*, 136.
,, Barons de CRONENBURG, *arms*, 137.
Spear, Pl. XXXI., fig. 2, p. 346.
,, *head*, 348.
,, ,, as a *badge*, 754.
Spears, 347.
SPEKE, *arms*, 254, 750; Pl. XXV., fig. 2, p. 260.
,, Captain JOHN HANNEN, 750.
,, *crest* and *supporter* of, 277.
,, Grant of *augmentation* to WILLIAM, 750.
SPELMAN'S, Sir HENRY, definition of Esquire, 7; *Aspilogia*, 210.
SPENCER, Earl, *arms*, 413.
,, HENRY, *arms*, 413.
SPENER, *Opus Heraldicum*, 3, 247, 321, 402, 405, 411, 424, 440, 441, 447, 448, 452, 466, 469, 472, 489, 502, 506, 507, 538, 554, 555, 571, 576, 579, 604.
Sphinx, 744.
,, The, 295, 704.
Spiders, 281.
SPIEGEL, *arms*, 391.
,, BARONS, *arms*, 127.
,, ZUM DESENBERG, Counts, *arms*, 391.
SPITZENBERG, Counts von, *arms*, 92.
Splendour, *In*, 305, 704.
SPOLETO, Dukes of, *arms*, 170.
SPOLVERINI, Marquises, *arms*, 132.
Spotted, 704.
SPRINGHOSE, *arms*, 138.
Springing, 232, 704.
SPROTTIE, *arms*, 271.
SPRÜNER, *arms*, 336.
Spur, *Winged*, as a *crest*, 605.
Spurs, Battle of the, 529.
SQUARCIAFICHI, *arms*, 670; Pl. LVI., fig. 6, p. 671.
SQUIRE, *arms*, 239, 240.

Squirrel, The, 239.
ST. ALBAN'S, Duke of, *arms*, 559.
,, ,, Earl of, *arms*, 307.
,, AMAND, *arms*, 127.
,, ,, TRISTAN DE, *Traité du Lis*, 282.
,, AMOUR, Counts de, *arms*, 129.
,, ANDREW, *arms*, 195.
,, ,, *badge* of ORDER of, 665.
,, ,, *banner* of, 656.
,, ,, *collar* of ORDER of, 665.
,, ANDREW'S *cross*, 143, 664; Pl. XV., fig. 8, p. 144.
,, ,, JOHN, Archbishop of, 568.
,, ANTHONY, Order of, *arms*, 161.
,, *Anthony's fire*, 368.
,, AUBERT, GÉRARD DE, *arms*, 48.
,, AUBIN, MONTMORENCY-LAVAL *brisure*, 452.
,, BELIN, *arms*, 710.
,, BERNARD, 287.
,, BRICE, *arms*, 91.
,, COLUMBA, Relics of, 657.
,, CRICQ, Comtes de, *arms*, 370.
,, CUTHBERT, *banner* of, 655.
,, DENIS, 658.
,, ,, Abbey of, 31, 658, 659.
,, ,, Burial place of the Kings of FRANCE at, 559.
,, ,, *head of*, 201.
,, ,, *oriflamme* at, 659.
,, ,, Treasury of, 659.
,, ,, windows of Abbey of, 31.
,, DENOUAL, Vicomtes de, *arms*, 96.
,, DIDIER, *arms*, 96.
,, EDMUND, *arms*, 528.
,, ,, *banner* of, 656.
,, ,, of Wessex, *arms* assigned to, 383.
,, EDWARD, Feast of, 589.
,, ETHELREDA, mythical *arms*, 379.
,, GALL, *arms*, 229; Pl. XXIII., fig. 4, p. 228.
,, GELAIS, *arms*, 730.
,, ,, Marquises of, *arms*, 153.
,, GEORGE, *arms*, 195; Pl. XIV., fig. 1, p. 140.
,, ,, *banner* of, 656.
,, ,, Chapel of, at WINDSOR, 134 (*see Stall Plates*).
,, ,, *cross* of, 141, 421, 422, 423, 654, 655, 656, 664.
,, ,, Sir HENRY, *arms* and *augmentation*, 546.
,, GEORGES, Marquises de VÉRAC, *arms*, 141.
,, ,, ,, VÉRAC, *supporters*, 303.
,, ,, Roll, 305, 376, 403, 407, 458, 481.
,, GERMAN'S, Earl of, *arms*, 128.
,, GILLES, *arms*, 161.
,, ,, Charter of RAYMOND DE, bearing *seal*, 46.
,, HILAIRE, *arms*, 202.
,, JOHN, 633.
,, ,, AGNES, *arms*, 417.
,, ,, *badge*, 753, 754.
,, ,, *banner* of, 655.
,, ,, Cross of the Order of, 546.
,, ,, Grand Master of the Order of, mark of office, 645.
,, ,, Knight of, Pl. X., fig. 4, p. 118.

(845)

ST. JOHN, KNIGHTS HOSPITALLERS of, *arms*, 141.
„ „ of JERUSALEM, Grand Master of Order, *arms*, 527.
„ „ of JERUSALEM, Order of, *arms*, 119.
„ „ the Baptist, head of, 201.
„ KENTIGERN'S *bell*, 316.
„ LAWRENCE, Earls of HOWTH, *supporter*, 300.
„ LEGER, ANNE, daughter and heiress of Sir THOMAS, 530.
„ „ *badge*, 753.
„ LEONARD, see CORNUT.
„ LEU, MONTMORENCY DE, *brisure*, 452.
„ LIZ, MAUD, widow of SIMON DE, 517.
„ „ SIMON DE, Earl of HUNTINGDON, 517.
„ *Louis, La Vie de*, 11.
„ LOUIS, King of FRANCE, *augmentations* granted by, 539.
„ „ of FRANCE, 416.
„ MACHAR'S, ABERDEEN, Heraldic ceiling of, 84.
„ MARK, *symbol* of, 219.
„ MARTIN and the beggar, 657.
„ „ *arms*, 68.
„ „ *chape de*, 657, 658.
„ „ in Heraldry, 195.
„ MATTHIAS, 387.
„ MAUR, Ducs de MONTAUSIER, *arms*, 124.
„ MAURICE, see FOI.
„ MICHAEL, *arms*, 195.
„ „ in Heraldry, 196.
„ „ Order of, 645.
„ MICHEL, see MAYNARD.
„ MUNGO'S *bell*, 316.
„ PATRICK, *Cross of*, 143.
„ „ Order of, 143.
„ „ *saltire* of, 656.
„ PAUL, Count de, 415.
„ „ Counts of, *arms*, 214, 342.
„ „ *emblem* of, 346.
„ „ LOUIS, Comte de, 415.
„ Paul's Cathedral, 588.
„ PAUL'S *sword* as a charge, 371.
„ PERN, Marquis de, *arms*, 186.
„ PETER, *banner* of, 655.
„ PETER'S *keys* as charges, 371.
„ PHILIBERT, *arms*, 95.
„ POL, *seal* of ENGUERRAN, Count de, 49.
„ PONCY, Marquis de, *arms*, 145.
„ QUINTIN, Counts of, *arms*, 284.
„ REMI DE VALOIS, HENRI DE, *arms*, 570.
„ REMY, JEAN DE, *Roi d'Armes de l'Ordre du Toison d'Or*, 551.
„ SIMON, Duc de, *Mémoires*, 14.
„ „ Ducs de, *arms*, 505.
„ „ JEAN DE, *arms*, 118.
„ „ ROUVROY, *arms*, 505.
„ STEFANO, Order of, 119.
„ STEPHEN, *crown* of, 621.
„ „ Knights of Order of, *arms*, 527.
„ VINCENT, see BARRUEL.
„ VLADIMIR, 622.
„ VRAIN, *seal* of ISABEL DE, 254.
„ WILFRED, *banner* of, 655.
STACIE, ROSS Herald, MS. of, 512.

STADNICKI, Counts of, *arms*, 172.
STAEL, *arms*, 356, 510.
„ DE HOLSTEIN, Barons, *arms*, 510 ; Pl. XLI., fig. 4, p. 510.
Staff, 704.
„ *Ragged*, as a *badge*, 585.
STAFFORD, *arms*, 111 ; Pl. XIII., fig. 1, p. 136.
„ *badge*, 754.
„ Duke of BUCKINGHAM, *arms*, 135.
„ Dukes of BUCKINGHAM, 399.
„ EDMOND, Bishop of EXETER, *arms*, 437.
„ family, 439.
„ *knot*, 585.
STAFILEO, *arms* and *augmentation*, 540.
Stag at gaze, Pl. XXIII., fig. 8, p. 228.
„ *couchant* as a *badge*, 598.
„ *lodged*, Pl. XXIII., fig. 10, p. 228.
„ The *sea*, 299.
„ *trippant*, Pl. XXIII., fig. 7, p. 228.
Stags, 231.
„ *courant*, Pl. XXIII., fig. 9, p. 228.
„ *Winged*, as *supporters*, 636.
Stag's head cabossed, Pl. XXIII., fig. 11, 228.
„ *horns*, Pl. XXIII., fig. 12, p. 228.
STAHLIN VON STORKSBURG, *arms*, 260.
STAIN, Baron, *arms*, 130.
„ VON, *arms*, 383.
Stair, Pl. XXXII., fig. 10, p. 358.
„ as a charge, 365.
STALTON, *arms*, 259.
Stall Plates at Windsor, 602, 612, 613.
STAMFORD, Earls of, *arms*, 92.
„ „ *supporter*, 297.
STANDAERTS, *arms*, 352.
Standard, 704.
„ Battle of the, 655.
Standards, 649, 653.
„ Moorish, as *supporters*, 643.
„ *Royal*, 654.
STANGATE, *arms*, 136.
Stangue, 744.
STANHOPE, *arms*, Pl. V., fig. 9, p. 80.
„ Earl, *crescent*, 446.
„ „ of CHESTERFIELD, *arms*, 81.
STANLEY, *arms*, 233, 558, 565.
„ *badge*, 753.
„ Lord, 595.
„ Sir JOHN, *bastarde*, *arms*, 588.
STANSFELD, *arms*, 235.
STANSFIELD, *arms*, 235.
Staple, 704.
Staples as a *badge*, 754.
STAPLETON, *arms*, 131, 213, 218.
„ *badge*, 754.
Star, 704.
„ and *crescent* as a *badge*, 587.
„ as a *badge*, 583, 754.
STARCKENBERG, *arms*, 90.
STARCKENS, *arms*, 196.
STARGARD, Lordship of, *arms*, 492.
STARHEMBERG, Princes of, 226.
Stars, 307 ; Pl. XXVIII., fig. 5, p. 308.
Starved, 704.
Statant, 217, 704.
„ *gardant*, 217.
STAUFFENECK, *arms*, 669 ; Pl. LV., fig. 4, p. 668.

STAUNTON, Sir WILLIAM DE, *arms*, 44.
Staves as charges, 381.
STAYLTON, *arms*, 259.
STEAD, *arms*, 296.
STECKBORN, *arms*, 78.
STEEN, Counts von, *arms*, 393.
STEENHUYSE, *see* HANE.
STEENHUYSEN, Prince de, *arms*, 319.
STEIN, Baron, *arms*, 130.
,, DE BRAUNSDORF, Barons, *arms*, 220.
,, ZU LEIBENSTEIN, Barons, *arms*, 131.
STEINFURT, Counts von, *arms*, 262.
STEINMAN, *lambrequin*, 613.
Stellion, 704.
STEPHEN NEMANJA, Czar of SERVIA and BOSNIA, 251.
STEPS, *arms*, 375.
STERCK, *arms*, 231.
STERLING, WILLIAM, *supporters*, 633.
STERNBERG, Counts of, *arms*, 404, 405.
STERNEMANNS, *supporter*, 640.
STERNENBERG, Counts von, *arms*, 308.
STETTIN, Duchy of, *arms*, 288.
Steward, ALEXANDER, fourth, 429.
,, ,, ,, High, 419, 458.
STEWART (*see* STUART), ALEXANDER, Earl of MAR, *arms*, 566.
,, ALEXANDER, Earl of MENTEITH, *label*, 419.
,, *arms*, 125, 405, 419, 447, 459, 567, 631; Pl. XI., fig. 5, p. 124.
,, *arms in Lyon Office Register*, 400.
,, Earl of ANGUS, *arms*, 455.
,, ,, CASTLE STUART, *arms*, 569.
,, ,, LENNOX, *bordure*, 441.
,, JAMES, Earl of MORAY, *arms*, 567.
,, JOHN, 1st Lord of LORN, 520.
,, MARGARET, Countess of ANGUS, *label*, 420.
,, ,, Countess of ANGUS, *seal*, 631.
,, MATTHEW, *label*, 419.
,, of Avondale, *bordure*, 443.
,, ,, Bonkill, *arms*, 455.
,, ,, Bonkyl, 520.
,, ,, ,, *arms*, 519.
,, ,, Laithers, *fess*, 431.
,, ,, Lorn, *arms*, 447.
,, ,, Ochiltree, *bordure*, 443.
,, ,, Rosyth, *bordure*, 442.
,, ROBERT and MURDOCH, Dukes of ALBANY, *wreath*, 614.
,, ,, Earl of FIFE, *brisure*, 445.
,, *seal* and *arms* of ALAN, 49.
,, Sir JOHN, 458.
,, ,, ,, of Bonkyl, *arms*, 413.
,, ,, ,, of Bonkil, *bend*, 429, 442.
,, THOMAS, Archdeacon of St. Andrews, *arms*, 566.
,, WALTER, *bordure*, 441.
,, ,, ,, Earl of ATHOLE and CAITHNESS, *seal* and *arms*, 520.

STEWART, WALTER, Earl of ATHOLE, *badge*, 598.
,, ,, ,, MENTEITH, *label*, 419.
STEWARTS, Earls of ATHOLE, *arms*, 446.
,, ,, BUCHAN, *arms*, 446.
STEYERMARCK, OTTACAR VON, poem by, 246.
STIERNA, 672.
STIRIA, *arms*, 654.
STIRLING, *arms*, 377.
,, Earl of, *arms*, 109.
Stirlings of Keir, The, 377.
Stirrups, 357; Pl. XXXII., fig. 2, p. 358.
STIXEN, *arms*, 260.
Stock, 704.
STOCKAU, Counts of, *arms*, 79.
Stockfish, The, 271; Pl. XXVI., fig. 11, p. 266.
STOCKTONS, *arms*, 318.
STODART, *crest*, 610.
,, Mr, *Lyon Clerk Depute*, 360, 443, 568.
,, Scottish *Arms*, 50, 84, 85, 148, 150, 173, 181, 258, 279, 283, 302, 352, 377, 378, 381, 402, 440, 755.
,, System *of differencing*, 444.
STOFFELLA, *arms*, 309.
Stoke Lyne, Lord of Manor of, *arms* on Hawk, 633.
STOKE D'ABERNON, 650.
STOLBERG, Counts zu, *arms*, 98.
,, *see* EFFEREN.
STÖRCK VON PLANCKENBERG, *arms*, 74.
Stork, The, 263; Pl. XXV., fig. 11, p. 260.
STORKSBURG, STAHLIN VON, *arms*, 260.
STORMARN, *arms*, 262, 510, 666.
STOTHARD, C., drawing of Bayeux tapestry, 30.
STOURTON, *arms*, 193; Pl. XIX., fig. 5, p. 192.
,, Lord, *crest*, 605.
,, ,, *supporter*, 300.
STRACHAN, *arms*, Pl. XXIII., fig. 7. p. 228.
,, of Glenkindy, *arms*, 232.
STRANGE, LE, *arms*, Pl. XXI., fig. 5, p. 212.
STRANSHAM, *arms*, 121.
STRATHAVEN, Stronghold of, 516.
STRATHEDEN, Lords, *arms*, 84.
STRATHERN, ancient, *arms*, 138.
,, DAVID, Earl of, *seal*, 459.
,, Earl of, *brisure*, 432.
,, Earls of, *arms*, 138, 459.
,, *seal* of MURIEL, Countess of, 630.
STRATHMORE, Earls of, *arms*, 215, 349; *crest*, 605.
STRAUSS, *arms*, 263.
Strawberries, 341.
Strawberry flower, The, 323.
STRAYNSHAM, *arms*, 121.
STRELLS, *arms*, 138.
Stringed, 704.
STRODE, *arms*, 238.
STROZZI, DE, 16.
,, *tomb* of ANTONIO, 281.

(847)

STRUENSEE, Counts, *arms*, 370.
STRYVELIN, Sir JOHN DE, *arms*, 377.
STRZEMIE, *herba* of, *arms*, 357.
STUART (*see* STEWART), *arms*, 125, 138, 521, 567; Pl. LI., fig. 5, p. 661.
,, *badges*, 596.
,, Dr JOHN, *Sculptured Stones of Scotland*, 29.
,, ,, *Registrum de Panmure*, 171, 517.
,, Exhibition in London, 334.
,, FRANCIS, Earl of BOTHWELL, *arms*, 567.
,, HENRY, Lord of METHVEN, *arms*, 521; Pl. XLII., fig. 3, p. 512.
,, JAMES, Duke of YORK, *label*, 421.
,, ,, Earl of ARRAN, *arms*, 567.
,, ,, Sire d'AUBIGNY, 515.
,, JOHN, Lord of LORN, *seal*, 520.
,, Lord of DARNLEY and Earl of LENNOX, *arms*, 521; Pl. XLII., fig. 1, p. 512.
,, MARGARET, Countess of ANGUS and MAR, *seal*, 455.
,, of Avondale, *arms*, 567.
,, ,, Doune, *arms*, 567.
,, ,, Ochiltree, *arms*, 567.
,, ,, Traquair, *crest*, 605.
,, PATRICK, Earl of ORKNEY, *arms*, 567.
,, Prince CHARLES, Duke of YORK and ALBANY, *label*, 420.
,, ROBERT, Commendator of Holyrood, *arms*, 567.
,, Sovereigns, *coat* of, 662.
,, WILLIAM, Duke of GLOUCESTER, *label*, 421.
STÜBNER, *arms*, 90.
Stump of a tree as a *badge*, 754.
STUMPF, *arms*, 240.
STURMY, *arms*, 221.
STUTEVILLE, *arms*, 94.
STYRIA, ALBERT, Duke of, *seal*, 456.
,, *banner* of, 651.
,, Duchy, *arms*, 247, 456, 495, 499, 665, 739.
,, *Stier* of, 650.
SUABIA, *arms*, 471, 525.
Sub-ordinaries, 78, 102, 116, 165.
SUBSTANTION, Comte de, *arms*, 118.
SUDELEY, Lords, *arms*, 155.
Sufflue, 704.
Sufflues as charges, 386.
SUFFOLK, *badge*, 753, 754.
,, Duke of, *arms*, 225, 412; Pl. XXII., fig. 12, p. 222.
SULBY, Sir JOHN, *arms*, 128.
SULLY, Ducs de, *arms*, 123.
,, ,, *lambrequin*, 613.
,, Sir JOHN, *arms*, 128.
SULMETINGEN, *arms*, 134.
SULMONE, Prince of, *arms*, 451.
SUMIN-SUMINSKI, Counts, *arms*, 363.
Sun in splendour, as a *badge*, 590.
,, *Rays of the*, as a *badge*, 588.
,, The, 305; Pl. XXVIII., fig. 1, p. 308.

Sunflower, 338.
Supporter, Single, 630.
Supporters, 627.
,, Attempt to restrict use of, 637.
,, charged with Mark of Cadency, 648.
,, Double, 633.
,, Eight, 635.
,, Four, 635.
,, Mode of representing, 641.
,, Origin of, 627, 628.
,, Right to use, 638.
,, Six, 635.
,, Triple, 635.
Supports, 627, 744.
Sur le Tout, 744.
,, ,, ,, *du Tout*, 744.
Surchargé, 744.
Surcoat, 704.
,, ensigns on, 82.
SURGÈRES, *arms*, 96.
Surmonté, 704, 744.
Surmounted, 704.
Surnames, 10.
,, adoption of, posterior to use of armorial bearings, 671.
,, derived from armorial bearings, 672.
SURREY, BEATRICE, Countess of, *seal*, 475.
,, Dukes of, *arms*, 216, 474.
,, ,, *augmentation*, 528.
,, Earls of, *arms*, 99.
,, THOMAS, Duke of, *arms*, 474.
SURTEES, *arms*, 167.
,, Society, 366, 560.
Surtout, 744.
,, *Sur le Tout*, 704.
SUSENBERG, Counts of, *arms*, 215.
SUSSEX, AUGUSTUS FREDERICK, Duke of, *label*, 422.
,, *badge*, 754.
Sustained, 704.
SUTHERLAND, *arms*, 308, 520, 521; Pl. XXVIII., fig. 5, p. 308.
,, Duke of, *arms*, 157, 319.
,, Earls of, *arms*, 521.
,, ELIZABETH, Countess of, 521.
,, MALCOLM, *fess*, 430.
,, of Duffus, WILLIAM, *seal*, 520.
SUTTIE, *arms*, 382.
SUTTON, Lord DUDLEY, *arms*, 218.
,, Lord LEXINGTON, *arms*, 165.
SUWAROFF, Marshal, *arms*, 311.
SUWOROFF, Prince ITALISKI, *augmentation*, 542.
SWABIA, *arms*, 495, 668.
,, Duke of, 244.
,, *seal* of RODOLPH of, 243.
Swallow, The, 266.
Swan as *supporter*, 631.
,, The, 262; Pl. XXV., fig. 10, p. 260.
,, *White*, as a *badge*, 588, 589, 594, 754.
SWANDEG, *arms*, 440.
Swans as *supporters*, 636.
,, on bears as *supporters*, 635.
SWART, *arms*, 137.
SWEDEN, 379.
,, and NORWAY, *arms*, 667.
,, *Armorials* of, 541.
,, *arms*, 379, 546, 667.

(848)

SWEDEN, *augmentations* in, 546.
" Earliest known *shield* in, 333.
" GUSTAVUS ADOLPHUS, King of, *augmentations* granted by, 546.
" Introduction of Hereditary *arms* into, 52.
" Kings of, using *escucheon en surtout*, 487.
" Marks of illegitimacy in, 581.
SWEERS, *monument* of, 626.
SWEERTS, *supporter*, 304.
SWEETING, *arms*, 382.
Swepe, 365, 704.
SWIENEZIC, *arms*, 153.
SWIETEN, Barons von, *arms*, 382.
Swift, The, 266.
SWILLINGTON, *arms*, 289.
SWINFORD, KATHARINE, 555.
SWINNERTON, *arms*, 158.
SWISS Cantons, *supporter*, 640.
SWITZERLAND, *arms*, 153, 668.
Swivel, 704.
Sword, The, 345 ; Pl. XXXI., fig. 1, p. 346.
Swords as *supporters*, 643.
SWYNEHOWE, *arms*, 227.
SWYNETHWAYTE, *arms*, 228.
SWYNFORD, KATHARINE, 438.
SYDNEY, *arms*, Pl. XXXI., fig. 7, p. 346.
" *badge*, 753.
" Earl of LEICESTER, *arms*, 350.
Sykes, 193, 704.
SYKES, *arms*, 193.
SYMENS, *arms*, 159.
Syren, The, 300.
SZCEPANOWSKI, *arms*, 289.
SZOLDRSKI, Counts, 370.

Tabard, 705 ; Fig. 106, p. 674.
TABLEY, Lord DE, 18.
TABOUROT, *arms*, 383.
Tacheté, 744.
TACITUS, description of devices on shields, 29.
TAETS D'AMERONGEN, Barons, *arms*, 124.
Taf, 744.
TAFFIN, *arms*, 150.
TAGLIAVIA, *arms*, 317 ; Pl. XXIX., fig. 3, p. 318.
Tailed, 705.
Taillé, 80, 728, 744, 745.
TALAIRAN, Marquises de, *arms*, 338.
Talbot, 241, 705 ; Pl., XXIV., fig. 9, p. 236.
" as a *badge*, 754.
TALBOT, *arms*, 215, 241.
" Earl of SHREWSBURY, *arms*, 174.
" ELIZABETH, widow of Sir GILBERT, 558.
TALE, VON, *arms*, 82 ; Pl. V., fig. 11, p. 80.
TALLYRAND-PÉRIGORD, Prince, *arms*, 223.
TALMONT, CLAUDE, Prince de, 258, 505.
" Princes de, *arms*, 257.
TANCARVILLE, Counts of, *arms*, 713.
TANIERE, LA, *arms*, 134.
TANKERVILLE, *arms*, 713.
" Earl of, *arms*, 222, 556.
TANNENVELS, *arms*, 223.
TAPPE, *arms*, 669 ; Pl. LVI., fig. 2, p. 671.

TARANTSBERG, *see* MOHR.
TARDY, Comte de MONTRAVEL, *arms*, 317.
Taré, 744.
" *de front*, 744.
" *de profile*, 744.
TARENTE, or TARENTO, Princes de, *arms*, 257, 504, 513.
Target, 705.
TARLET, *arms*, 262.
TARLO, Counts, *arms*, 348.
TARRAGONE, *arms*, 69.
TASSONI, *La Secchia Rapita*, 655.
TATE and LONGSTAFFE, *The Pedigrees and early Heraldry of the Lords of Alnwick*, 482.
TATESHALL, *arms*, 426.
TATTENBACH, Counts, *arms*, 726.
Tau, 705, 744.
" *Cross*, 161 ; Fig. 61, p. 164.
TAURIA, *arms*, 665.
TAVANNES, Duc et Pair de, *arms*, 213.
TAWAST, Barons and Counts, *augmentation*, 546.
Tawny, 705.
TAYLARD, *arms*, 222.
TEBA, Counts of, *arms*, 390.
TECK, Duke of, *arms*, 524, 525.
Teeth, The, 203.
TEIXEIRA, *arms*, 141.
TELLEZ, *arms*, 353.
TELLIER, LE, Marquis de LOUVOIS, *arms*, 277.
TEMPEST, *arms*, 403.
TEMPESTA, *arms*, 311.
TEMPLETOWN, Viscounts, *arms*, 160.
Temporis filia veritas, 664.
Tenants, 627, 744.
Tenné or Orange, 60, 65.
" " *Tawny*, 705.
TENNENT, *arms*, 145.
Tenny or Orange, 60, 65 ; Pl. III., fig. 8, p. 60.
TENNYSON, *arms*, 226.
" Lord, *arms*, 226.
TENREMONDE, *arms*, 72 ; Pl. VIII., fig. 7, p. 100.
TENTENIER, *arms*, 351.
TENTON, *arms*, 351.
Tent-poles as *supporters*, 643.
Tents, 351.
TERBRUGGEN, *arms*, 319.
Terrace, A, 311, 705.
Terrasse, 705, 744.
" *-isolée*, 744.
Terrassé, 744.
Tertre, 312, 744.
TESCHEN, Duchy, *arms*, 500.
TESSE, *see* FERRIÈRE.
TESSON, JOURDAIN DE, *shield*, Pl. I., fig. 4, p. 54.
TESTU, Marquis de BALINCOURT, *arms*, 220.
Tête de Gérion, 200.
TETNANG, *arms*, 373.
TETTONI E SALDINI, *Teatro Araldico*, 643.
TEUFEL, *arms*, 304.
" VON, *arms*, 87.
TEUTONIC ORDER, Grand Masters, *arms*, 527.
" " THE, *arms*, 499.
TEVIOT, Viscount, *arms*, 340.
TEYES, *arms*, 135.

(849)

TEYEYES, *arms*, 135.
TEZART JACQUES, Baron de TOURNEBU, 12.
„   „   Seigneur des ESSARTS, 12.
Thalers as charges, 389.
THANET, Earls of, *crest*, 300.
The Book of Arms of the Nobility of Bosnia, or Illyria, and Servia, 251 (*see* EVANS).
Theiss River, 498.
THEODORE, King of CORSICA, *arms*, 355.
THEODORUS LASCARIS, *coins* of, 250.
THEODOSIUS THE GREAT, 328.
THEROUENNE, Battle of, 529.
THIARD, Marquis de BISSY, *arms*, 273.
THIBAULT IV., 324.
THIERMES, Counts de, *arms*, 173.
THIERRY, II. of BAR, *seal* of, 270.
„   French historian, 29.
„   WILLIAM, Abbot of, 287.
THIMUS, *arms*, 383.
Thistle, 596; Pl. XXX., fig. 8, p. 332.
„   as *badge* of Scotland, supposed origin of, 335, 596.
„   The, 334.
THISTLE, ORDER OF THE, 334.
THOLOSANI, *arms, supporters* and *crest*, 303.
THOMAS PALEOLOGUS, SOPHIA, daughter of, 250.
THONEY RAUF, *arms*, 376.
THORAISE, *see* ACHEY.
Thorns, Crowns of, 337.
THOROLD, *arms*, 235; Pl. XXIV., fig. 3, p. 236.
THOU, DE, Comte de MESLAY, *arms*, 280.
THOUARS, CLÉMENT, Vicomte de, *supporters*, 633.
„   PERRONELLE, Vicomtesse de *mantling*, 634.
„   Vicomtes and Ducs de, *arms*, 257.
Thoye, 705.
THOYTS, *arms*, 310.
THUMERY, *arms*, 337.
THUN DE HOHNSTEIN, Counts, *arms*, 129.
Thunderbolt, 311, 705.
THURN and TAXIS, Princes of, *arms*, 360, 380.
Thurnier-Ordnung, 41.
THWENG or TWENGE, MARMADUKE DE, *arms*, 265.
THYNNE, Marquess of BATH, *arms*, 94.
Tiara, 705.
TICHBORNE, *arms*, 118; Pl. X., fig. 1, p. 118.
Tiercé, 86, 129, 705, 744.
„   *en bande*, 745.
„   „ *fasce*, 745.
„   „ *mantel*, 745.
„   „ *pairle*, 88.
„   „ „ *renverseé*, 88.
„   „ *pal*, 745.
„   „ *feuille*, 745.
Tierced, 705.
„   *in bend*, 87; Pl. VI., fig. 5, p. 84.
„   „ *sinister*, 87.
„   „ *fess*, 86; Pl. VI., fig. 4, p. 84.
„   „ *gyron gyronnant*, 87.
„   „ *pairle*, Pl. VI., fig. 6, p. 84.

Tierced in pairle reversed, Pl. VI., fig. 7, p. 84.
„   „ *pale gironnant*, 87.
„   or *tripartite shield*, 86.
„   *per fess*, 129.
Tierces, 745.
Tigé, 678, 745.
Tige, 745.
Tiger, passant, 224.
„   *rampant*, 224.
„   The, 224; Pl. XXII., fig. 10, p. 222.
TIGNIVILLE, *arms*, 185.
Tigre-héraldique, 745.
TILLY, Marquis de BLARU, *arms*, 331.
Tilting-spear, 705.
Timbre, 705, 745.
Timbré, 745.
Tinctures, 60, 705; Pl. III., p. 60.
„   *Difference by change of*, 403.
„   represented by letters and abbreviations, 64.
„   „   by lines and dots 64.
„   „   „ planets and precious stones, 64.
TIPTOT, *arms*, 142.
Tire, 745.
TIROL, Countess of, 472 (*see* TYROL).
„   County of, *arms*, 255, 471.
Tirret, 705.
Titles, Attempt to restrict use of, 637.
TITUS, Arch of, 291.
Toads, 274, 278.
Tobacco plant, 338.
TOD VON LEWENTHAL, *arms*, 203.
TOFTE, *arms*, 394.
TOGORES, *arms*, 306.
Toison d'Or, 705, 745.
„   Chapel of the CHEVALIERS DE LA, 134.
TOKE, *arms*, 290; Pl. XXVII., fig. 6, p. 288.
TOLEDO, ALVAREZ DE, Duke of ALVA, *arms*, 100.
„   Duke of ALVA, *supporters*, 643.
„   Kingdom of, *arms*, 128, 380.
TOLLEMACHE, *arms*, 96, 182.
TOLLENAER, *arms*, 389.
TOLLENS, *arms*, 139.
TÖLNZ, VON, *arms*, 101.
TOMASI, *arms*, 94.
TOMKOWITZ, *arms*, 189.
TOMLIN, *arms*, 193.
TONGE'S *Visitation of Durham*, 366, 560.
Tongue, The, 203.
TONNELIER, LE, Comtes de BRETEUIL, etc., *arms*, 262.
TONNERRE, *arms*, 129.
Topaz, 65, 705.
TOPCLIFFE, *arms*, 388.
„   Baron of, *arms*, 482.
TOPOR, *herba* of, *arms*, 348.
Tops, as charges, 388.
Toques, denoting different ranks in France, 626.
TORA, *arms*, 234.
TORCY, Marquises de, *arms*, 275.
TORELLES, *arms*, 361.
TORPHICHEN, Lord, *augmentation*, 535.
Torqued, 705.
TORSAY, *arms*, 717, 718.
Torse, 705.
Torteau, 190, 705; Pl. XIX., fig. 3, p. 192.

(850)

TORTHORWALD, Lord, *arms*, 142.
Tortil, 708, 745.
Tortillée, 125, 705, 708, 718, 745.
Tortoily, 705.
Tortoise, The, 277.
Tortoises, 274.
TORTOX, *arms*, 191.
TOUCHE, LA, *arms*, 191.
,, *see* VACHE.
TOUCHET, Lords AUDLEY, *arms*, 136.
,, MARIE, 570.
Touching, 705.
TOULOUSE, *arms*, 460.
,, Counts of, *arms*, 46, 161.
,, *cross* of, 161.
,, *seal* of RAYMOND VII., Count of, 161.
,, *seals* of Counts of, 56.
Tour, 745.
TOUR D'AUVERGNE LA, Vicomtes de TURENNE, etc., *arms*, 360.
,, DE VINAY, LA, *arms*, 362.
,, DU PIN, LA, *arms*, 269.
,, FONDUE, *see* COUSIN.
,, LA, *arms*, 466.
TOURAINE, ARCHIBALD, Duke of, *seal*, 632.
,, Duke of, 515.
,, Governors of, 658.
TOURNAI, Comtes D'OISI, *arms*, 221.
Tournament, earliest regular, 40.
Tournaments, 39, 40.
,, Attempts to stop, 40.
,, *shields* suspended at, 55.
TOURNAY, City of, *arms*, 141.
Tourné, 705, 745.
TOURNEBU, Baron de, 12.
,, PIERRE DE, *supporter*, 632.
Tournés, 604.
Tourney Regulations for the exposure of *arms* and *crest*, 749.
TOURS, Cathedral at, 463.
,, Church of ST. MARTIN, 658.
Tourteaux, 190, 745.
,, *-besants*, 745.
Tourtelé, 745.
TOURZEL, Marquis de, *arms*, 112.
Tower, Pl. XXXII., fig. 4, p. 358.
,, *triple towered*, Pl. XXXII., fig. 5, p. 358.
,, with other buildings, 362.
Towered, 705.
Towers, 359.
TOWERS, *arms*, 359; Pl. XXXII., fig. 4, p. 358.
Towns as charges, 363.
Trabe, 745.
TRAFFORD, 17.
,, *arms*, 288; Pl. XXVII., fig. 5, p. 288.
TRAFFORDS, DE, 17.
TRAINEL, Marquises of, *arms*, 120.
Trait, 745.
TRAJAN'S Column, 291.
,, ,, Cohort ensigns on, 27.
Tranché, 80, 728, 745.
,, *-crénelé*, 740.
Trangles, 745.
Transfixed, 705.
Transfluent, 706.
Transposed, 706.
TRANSYLVANIA, *arms*, 495, 498.
TRAPPE, *arms*, 352.

TRAPPEQUIERS, *arms*, 294.
TRAPPER, *arms*, Pl. XXXI., fig. 9, p. 346.
TRASTAMARA, Counts de, *arms*, 507.
,, DON PEDRO DE, *arms*, 576.
TRAU, The SOUDAN DE LA, *crest*, 606.
TRAUN, Counts of, *arms*, 78.
,, ,, zu, *arms* and *crest*, 607.
TRAUTSON, Princes von, *arms*, 356.
Traverse, 151.
TRAZEGNIES, *arms*, 223.
TRÉANNA, *arms*, 184.
Trécheur, 706, 745.
,, *-fleur-de-lisé*, 706.
TRÉDERN, *arms*, 167.
Tree, *Apple*, 317.
,, *Dry*, 318.
,, *Fir*, Pl. XXIX., fig. 2, p. 318.
,, *Nut*, 318.
,, *Oak*, Pl. XXIX., fig. 1. p. 318.
,, *Olive*, 317.
,, *Palm*, 317 ; Pl. XXIX., fig. 3, p. 318.
,, *Pine*, 317.
,, *Stock* of a, as a *badge*, 589.
,, *Wild Cherry*, 318.
,, *Willow*, 318.
Trees, 315.
Treflé, 160, 678, 706; Pl. XXIX., fig. 11, p. 318.
Trèfle, 745.
Trèflé, 745.
Trefoil, The, 320; Pl. XXIX., fig. 10, p. 318.
Trefoiled, 706.
TREGENT, *arms*, 284.
TREGOZ, *arms*, 230.
Treillé, 706.
Treillis, 97, 732, 745.
Treillisé, 706.
Treillisse, 745.
Trellis, 97, 693.
Trellised, 706.
TREMAYNE, *arms*, 206; Pl. XX., fig. 10, p. 198.
TREMENHEERE, *arms*, 364.
TRÉMOILLE, or TRÉMOUILLE, CHARLOTTE DE LA, Countess of DERBY, 258.
,, or TRÉMOUILLE, DE LA, *arms*, 257, 504.
,, or TRÉMOUILLE, CLAUDE, Duc DE LA, *arms*, 466.
,, or TRÉMOUILLE, FRANÇOIS DE LA, Prince de TALMONT, 505.
,, PIERRE DE LA, Seigneur de DOURS, *arms*, 411.
TRÉSÉOLS, *arms*, 306.
TRESMES, Ducs de, *supporters*, 294.
Tressure, 116, 165, 176, 706; Pl. XVII., fig. 11, p. 172; Pl. XVII., fig. 12, p. 172.
,, *double*, in SCOTLAND, 176.
,, *-flory*, 706.
,, ,, *-counter-flory*, 706 ; Pl. XVII., fig. 10, p. 172.
,, ,, *-counter-flory* (Double), 706.
,, Treatment of, in impaled coats, 476.
TREVANION, *supporters*, 638.

TREVELYAN, arms, 237, 270.
TREVES, Prince-Archbishops, Electors of, arms, 141 (see TRIER).
TRÉVOASEC, see LOHÉAC.
TRIANGI, Counts, arms, 201.
Triangle, 746.
Trianglé, 101, 746.
TRIBLE, arms, 67.
TRICARDS, arms, 336.
TRICORNET, Barons, 386.
Tricorporate, 706.
Trident, 706.
TRIE, GUILLAUME DE, arms, 129.
TRIENT, Principality, arms, 499.
TRIER, Einleitung zu der Wapen-kunst, 404, 447, 491, 493.
,, Prince-Archbishops, Electors of, arms, 141 (see TREVES).
TRIESTE, arms, 503.
TRIMLESTOWN, Lord, arms, 170.
TRIMNELL, crest, 295.
TRINACRIA, symbol of, 206.
Triparted, 706.
Tripartite shield, 86.
Trippant, 232, 706.
Tripping or Trippant, 706.
Triregno, 704.
TRIVULZI, arms, 91, 201.
TROGOFF, arms, 187.
TROISDORFF, arms, 183.
TROLLES, arms, 304.
TROMBY I., herba of, arms, 386.
TROMENEC, arms, 181.
TROMP, VAN, monument, 645.
Trompes, 746.
,, d'éléphant, 606.
Tronçonné, 706, 746.
TRONCOSO, arms, 318.
Trononné, 706.
TROPPAU, Duchy of, arms, 491.
TROTTI, arms, 79, 541.
,, -BENVOGLIO, Marquises of, arms and augmentation, 541.
TROTTIER, arms, 375.
Trout, The, 271 ; Pl. XXVI., fig. 10, p. 266.
TROUTBECK, arms, 271 ; Pl. XXVI., fig. 10, p. 266.
,, wreath, 614.
TROWBRIDGE, arms, 362.
TROY, Siege of, 21.
TRUCHSESS DE KULENTHAL, arms, 161.
Truffels, 344.
TRUHENDIN, Counts von, arms, 92.
Trumpets, as charges, 384, 386.
TRUMPINGTON, arms, 385.
Truncated, 706.
Trunked or Truncated, 706.
TRUSBUTS, Barons of Wartre, arms, 355 ; badge, 753.
,, ROSA, heiress of the, 355.
TRUSSELL, arms, 97.
Trussing, 262, 706.
TRUTEMNE, see BANVILLE, 69.
TRYE, arms, 129.
TRZYKRETI, arms, 239.
TUCKER, arms, 299 ; Pl. XXVII., fig. 11, p. 288.
TUDOR, badges, 595.
,, bordure, 439.
,, HENRY, Duke of YORK, label, 421.
,, MARY, arms, 559.

TUDOR sovereigns, supporters, 292.
TUFEL, arms, 191.
Tulips, 337.
TUNSTALL, arms, 391, 560.
,, CUTHBERT, Lord Bishop and Palatine of Durham, arms, 560.
TURBINE, arms, 152.
,, JOHN, Bishop of ROCHESTER, arms, 152.
,, RALPH, Archbishop of CANTERBURY, arms, 152.
,, SEFFRID, Bishop of CHICHESTER, arms, 152.
TURENNE, arms, 466.
,, Vicomtes de, arms, 96, 360.
TURKEY, arms, 668.
TURLING, arms, 87.
TURNBULL, arms, 235 ; Pl. XXIV., fig. 2, p. 236.
Turned-up, 706.
Turnip, The, 343.
TURPIN DE VINAY, arms, 362.
TURPIN'S Life of Charlemagne, 655.
Turret or Turret, 705.
Turreted, 706.
TURRETINI, arms, 93.
TUSCANY, Grand Duchess of, achievement, 494.
,, ,, Dukes of, arms, 192, 495, 502.
,, ,, ,, crowns, 623.
Tusked, 706.
Tuyau, 608.
TWEEDDALE, Marquess of, arms, 521.
TWEEDIE, arms, 145.
TWENG, MARMADUKE DE, arms, 550.
Tynes, 232.
TYRAWLEY, Lords, arms, 121.
TYRCONNEL, Earls of, arms, 143.
TYRE, WILLIAM OF, Historia Belli Sacri, 243.
TYROFF, Wappenbuch des Adels des Königreichs Baiern, 304, 349, 488, 493.
TYROL, County, arms, 496, 499, 665 (see TIROL).
TYRONE, Earl of, arms, 204.
TYRREL, arms, 139.

UBERACKER, VON, arms, 712.
UCKERMAN, arms, 87.
UFFELE, Barons von, arms, 162.
UFFORD, D', arms, 142.
UGGLAS, Counts, augmentation, 546.
UITENHAGE, arms, 160.
ULF, arms, 752.
ULMES, Counts des, supporters, 198.
ULSTER, arms, 479, 557.
,, badge of, 204.
,, Earl of, arms, 141, 457.
,, ,, label, 416.
,, King of Arms, 569.
,, ,, arms, 526.
,, ,, ,, created, 384.
ULSTER'S Register, 175.
ULYSSES, 300.
Umbrated, 706.
UMFRAVILL, GILBERT DE, Earl of ANGUS, arms, 322.
Undée, 696, 706.
Undy or Undée, 696, 706, 708.
,, line, Fig. 21, p. 75, 76.
Unguled, 232, 707.
Unicorn, 296, 707.
,, as a badge, 754.

(852)

Unicorn, as *supporters*, 632.
„ *Sea*, 297.
Unicorns as *supporters*, 635, 636.
Unicorns' *heads*, Pl. XXVII., fig. 10, p. 288.
Union fait la force, L', 666.
„ *Jack*, 656.
UNITED KINGDOM, *flag* of, 534, 656.
„ STATES OF AMERICA, *arms*, *supporter*, and *motto*, 640; Pl. LIV., fig. 2, p. 666.
UNIVERSITY COLLEGE, OXFORD, *arms*, 157.
UNRUH, Counts, *arms*, 212.
UPTON, *arms*, 160.
„ NICHOLAS, De Studio Militari, 19, 33, 209.
„ Viscount TEMPLETOWN, *arms*, 160.
Uranus, *Symbol for*, 310.
URBACH, Barons von, *arms*, 78.
URBAN VI., Pope, *arms*, 257.
URBINA, *arms*, 353.
URBINO, Dukes of, *arms*, 318.
Urchin, The, 239, 707.
Urdée, 707.
„ *cross*, 162.
Urdy line, 77; Fig. 27, p. 75.
„ or Urdée, 707.
UREDIUS, 47 (see VRÉE).
URGEL, Counts of, *arms*, 483.
Urinant, 707.
Urkundenbuch der Abtei Sanct Gallen, 9.
URQUHART, *arms*, 227.
URSINS, *arms*, Pl. X., fig. 6, p. 118.
„ DES, *arms*, 120.
URSO, 585.
USENBERG, 260.
„ Lordship of, *arms*, 491.
USEZ, Duc d', *arms*, 94.
USHER, *arms*, 381; Pl. XXII., fig. 8, p. 222.
„ Ulster King of Arms, 381.
UTRECHT, PHILIPPE, Bishop of, *arms*, 575.
UYTREDER, *arms*, 339.
UZEL, Counts d', *arms*, 95.

Vache, 746.
VACHE DE LA TOUCHE, LA, *arms*, 234.
„ Sir ROBERT DE LA, *arms*, 418.
VACHER, *arms*, 234.
Vair, 63, 67, 68, 69, 707, 746; Pl. IV., fig. 7, p. 62.
„ *ancient*, 96; Pl. IV., fig. 6, p. 62.
„ *-antique*, 746.
„ *appointé*, 70.
„ *contre*, 70.
„ *counter*, 70, 71.
„ *en pal*, 70, 746.
„ *in bend*, 70.
„ *in pale*, 70; Pl. IV., fig. 9, p. 62.
„ *-ondé*, 746.
„ *undy*, Pl. IV., fig. 10, p. 62.
Vairé, 707, 746.
„ *en pal*, 70.
VAIRE, *arms*, 71.
VAIRIÈRE, *arms*, 71.
Vairy or Vairé, 71; Pl. IV., fig. 13, p. 62.
Vaisseau, 738, 746.
VALAY, see LAUNAY, 344.
VALENCE, Bailli de, *arms*, 119.
„ DE, *arms*, 94, 409, 466.
„ ETHELMAR DE, Bishop of Winchester, *arms*, 44.

VALENCE, *label* of, 417.
„ WILLIAM DE, Earl of PEMBROKE, 466; *arms*, 409; enamelled *shield* of, 114.
VALENCIA, *arms* of Kingdom of, 363.
„ Viceroy of, *arms*, 502.
VALENTINOIS, Dukes of, *arms*, 100, 215.
VALETTE, THOMAS DE LA, *arms*, 160.
VALKENBURG, *arms*, 214.
Vallary Crown, or Palisado, 697, 707.
VALLET (DE VIRIVILLE), M., 113.
„ Armorial de Berry, 362.
VALLGORNERA, *arms*, 127.
VALLOINES, *arms*, 91, 123.
VALOIS, CHARLES, Count de, *crest*, 600; Pl. XLIX., fig. 9, p. 606.
„ CHARLES DE, Duc d'ANGOULÊME, *arms*, 570.
„ Figure from *seal* of PHILIPPE, Comte de, Pl. XXXIV., fig. 1, p. 388.
„ see ST. REMI.
VALONIIS, DE, *arms*, 91, 123.
VALOYNES, *arms*, 97, 123.
Vambrace, 707.
Vambraced, 204, 707.
Vamplate, 707.
Van or Vander, Definition of terms, 16.
VANDALIA, *arms*, 666.
VANDEPUT, *arms*, 270.
VANNELAT, *arms*, 273.
Vannet, 273, 686, 703, 707, 746.
VANNS, *arms*, 203.
VAQUER, *arms*, 235.
VARAMBON, Marquess de, *arms*, 257.
VARANO, Dukes of CAMERINO, *arms*, 71.
VARDES, Marquises de, *arms* and *supporters*, 303.
VARELA, *arms*, 354.
VARENCHON, *arms*, 71.
VARENNE, JOHN DE, natural son of King JOHN, *arms*, 555.
VARENNES, DE, 549.
VARGAS, BARNABÉ, MORENO DE, 167.
VAROQUIER, *arms*, 204.
VARROUX, *arms*, 69.
VASA, House of, *arms*, 487, 667.
VATATZES, *arms*, 251.
VAUDEMONT, *arms*, 94.
VAUDETAR, *arms*, 93.
VAUGHAN, *arms*, 224; Pl. XXVII., fig. 1, p. 288.
„ Earl of LISBURNE, *arms*, 333.
„ of Talgarth, *arms*, 274.
VAUGUYON, Ducs de la, *arms*, 319.
VAULTIER, *arms*, 338.
VAUS, *arms*, 567.
„ *family*, 420.
VAUX, *arms*, 474.
VAVASSEUR, *seal* of MALGERUS or MAUGER, LE, 394.
VAVASSOUR, *arms*, 394.
VEALE, *arms*, 235.
VEEN, Van, *arms*, 137, 186.
Vegetable kingdom, 315.
Vegetables, 343.
VEGNUDINI, *arms*, 197.
VELASCO, *achievements*, 639.
VELEN, Counts of, *arms*, 266.
VELKIERCH, *arms*, 373.
VELORT, RENAUD DE, *supporters*, 240.

(853)

VENASQUE, arms, 161.
VENDELINI, arms, 136.
VENDEUIL, Marquis de, arms, 221.
VEND ME, CÆSAR, Duc de, arms, 570.
,, Counts de, 39.
,, ,, of, arms, 104.
,, ,, JEAN, Bâtard de, 570.
,, LOUIS, Comte de, 570.
VENDRAMINI, arms, 86.
VENICE, arms, 502 ; Pl., XXI., fig. 11, p. 212.
,, coronet of Doges of, 623.
,, Republic of, arms, 219.
VENNINGEN, arms, Pl. XXX., fig. 6, p. 332.
,, Barons, arms, 332.
VENTADOUR, Duc DE, arms, 140.
Venus, 65, 707.
VERA, DE, arms, 71.
VÉRAC, Marquises de, arms, 141.
,, ,, supporter, 303.
VERDON, arms, 96, 97, 181, 214.
,, THEOBALD DE, arms, 457.
Verdoy, 707.
VERDUN, ALIX DE, as a supporter, 630.
VERDUZAN, arms, 191.
VERE, AUBREY DE, arms, 410.
,, badge, 754.
,, DE, arms, 308, 410 ; Pl. IX., fig. 2, p. 108.
,, Earl of OXFORD, badge, 753.
,, HUGH DE, brisure, 438.
,, ROBERT DE, Duke of IRELAND, arms, 383.
,, ,, ,, ,, IRELAND, augmentation, 528.
,, ,, ,, ,, Earl of OXFORD, arms, 410.
VERET, arms, 71.
Vergette, 123, 746.
Vergetté, 746.
VERGEYLL, arms, 272.
VERGNE, DE LA, arms, 188.
VERGNIES, arms, 338.
VERGY, ANTOINE DE, arms, 439.
,, arms, 485.
,, JEANNE DE, 485.
VERHAMME, arms, 228.
VERMANDOIS, arms, 125, 505.
,, chequers of, 650.
,, Counts of, 505.
,, RAOUL, Comte de, banner, 650.
VERME, DEL, arms, 536.
,, LOUIS DEL, Count of SAN-GUINETTO, arms and augmentation, 536.
VERNEUIL, Battle of, 515.
VERNEY, DU, arms, 279.
VERNON, arms, 306.
,, Descent of, 399.
,, RICHARD DE, seal and shield of, 54.
VERONA, City of, arms, 141.
Verrels or Vervels, 707.
VERREYCHEN, arms, 136.
VERREYCKEN, arms, 341.
Verrules or Vervels, 707.
VERRUSALEM, arms, 184.
Verry, 71.
VERSCHOW, arms, 381.
Versé, 692, 746.
Vert, or Green, 60, 65, 707 ; Pl. III., fig. 6, p. 60.

Vert shield, plain, 67.
VERTAMY, arms, 729.
Vertenelle, 746.
VERTHAMONT, arms, 214.
Vervels, 707, 708.
VESCI, Viscount de, arms, 152.
VESENTINA, arms, 196.
VESEY, 17.
,, Viscount de VESCI, arms, 152.
VESPUCCI, arms, 281.
Vested, 707.
Vêtu, 89, 746 ; Pl. VI., fig. 11, p. 84.
,, en ovale, 173, 746.
,, ,, ronde, 173, 746.
Vetusa Monumenta, 30.
Vexillum, 657.
VEXIN, Counts of the, 658.
,, SIMON, last Count of the, 658.
VIALART, arms, 156.
VIAN, LOUIS, La Particule Nobiliaire, 10, 13.
VIANDEN, arms, 580, 581.
,, Counts of, arms, 123.
VIARO, arms, 121.
Vice-Admiral, French, mark of office, 645.
,, Connétable, French, mark of office, 645.
VICENZA, City of, arms, 141.
Victoria cross, 155.
VICTORIA, Queen, 399 ; accession of, 663 ; crown of, 618 ; crown of the Prince Consort of, 622.
Vidame, coronet of a, 625.
Vidé, 707, 746.
VIEDMA, arms, 317.
VIENNA, Imperial Treasury of, 617.
VIENNE, arms, 257.
VIENNOIS, BEATRICE of Savoy, Dauphine de, shield of, 628.
,, CHARLES, Dauphin de, supporter, 632.
,, Dauphin de, arms, 269.
,, HUMBERT II., Dauphin de, supporters, 629.
,, JEAN, Dauphin de, supporter, 632.
VIERACKER, VAN, arms, 161.
VIEUILLE, LOUIS, raising of, to rank of banneret, 653.
VIEUXCHÂTEL DE KERLEORET, DU, arms, 359.
Vigilance, 263, 707, 746.
Vigilant, 707.
VIGNACOURT, ADRIAN, and ALOF DE, arms, 332.
VIGNAY, arms, 362.
VILAIN, LE SIRE DE, arms, 427.
Vilené, 746.
VILLA, arms, 96.
VILLAGOMEZ, arms, 158.
VILLALOBOS, Counts of, arms, 507.
VILLE, see BARGE.
VILLEHARDOUIN, arms, 160.
VILLENEUVE, arms, 346.
VILLEPROUVÉE, arms, 133.
VILLEQUIER, arms, 158.
VILLERS, arms, 339.
,, FARLAY, Barons de, arms, 343.
VILLIERS, arms, 93.
,, DE L'ISLE ADAM, arms, 205.

VILLIERS, Lord ROOS, 17.
VILLY, *arms*, 338.
VINAY, see Tour.
„ *see* TURPIN.
VINCENT, *arms*, 322 ; Pl. XXIX., fig. 12, p. 318.
VINCENT'S MSS. in College of Arms, 613, 662.
Vine, The, 319.
VINESAUF, GEOFFREY, 210.
VINEY, *arms*, 339.
VIOLA, 382.
Violet, The, 337.
Violins as charges, 382.
VIOLLE, *arms*, 717.
VIOLLET LE DUC, *Dictionnaire raisonné du Mobilier*, 388.
Violoncello as a charge, 383.
VIPONT, JOHN DE, *arms*, 552.
Vires, 707, 746 ; Pl. XIX., fig. 10, p. 192.
VIRGIL, *Æneid*, 27, 39.
VIRGIN, BLESSED in Heraldry, 195.
„ *Effigy* of the BLESSED, 328.
„ *Symbol* of the BLESSED, 326.
VIRIEU, *arms*, Pl. XIX., fig. 10, p. 192.
Virolé, 707, 746.
Viroled, 707.
Virollé, 385.
VIRY, *arms*, 712.
VISCONTI, *arms*, 274 ; Pl. XXVII., fig. 4, p. 288.
„ GIAN GALEAZZO, Duke of MILAN, *augmentation*, 538.
„ MAFFEO, *augmentation*, 536.
„ *tomb* of JEAN GALEAZZO, 274.
Viscount's *coronet*, 625.
„ *standard*, Length of, 654.
VISDELOU, 12.
Visitation of Devonshire, 1620, 621.
VITRÉ (*Morice*) *shield*, Pl. I., fig. 5, p. 54.
„ ROBERT DE, *shield* of, 46.
VITRY, Marquises de l'HÔPITAL DE, *arms*, 265.
VIVIER DE LANSAC, DU, *arms*, 66.
„ *see* COSTE.
Vivré, 682, 746.
„ *line*, 76.
Vizor, 707.
VLADIMIR, *arms*, 665.
„ (*Monomachus*) of Russia, *crown*, 622.
VLASBLOM, *arms*, 338.
VLIEGE, *arms*, 280.
VLIET, VAN, 183.
VOERST, Barons, *arms*, 139.
VOET, *arms*, 207.
Vogt, 625.
Voguant, 746.
VOGUÉ, Marquises de, *arms*, 265.
Voided, 184, 707.
Voider, The, 185, 707.
VOIGT DE RIENECK, Counts, *arms*, 236.
VOISENON, *see* FUSÉE.
VOIT, *arms*, 90.
Vol, 260, 708, 747.
„ *abaissé*, *Un*, 260.
„ -*banneret*, 606, 747.
Volant, 259, 707, 746.
Volcano, A, 314.
VÖLCKER, VON, *arms*, 60.
Volet, 634, 747.
VOLKARD, line of, *arms*, 448.
VÖLKEL, 128.

Vols bannerets, 606, 747.
VOLTAIRE, *see* AROUET.
VOLZ, *arms*, 152, 154.
Von, Definition of term, 8.
VOORST, Barons, *arms*, 139.
Vorant, 708, 734.
VOS, Counts VAN, *arms*, 230.
VOSSBERG, *Die Siegel des Mittelalters* 630.
VOUILLÉ, Battle of, 658.
Vouté, 125, 681, 686, 739, 747.
VRANX D'AMELIN, *supporters*, 295.
VRÉE or WREE, *Die Seghelen der Graven ran Vlaendren*, 37, 43, 45, 47, 245, 253, 478, 484, 631, 650, 651 ; Pl. XXXV., fig. 3, p. 416 ; Pl. XXXVII., figs. 1, 4, 6, p. 448.
„ „ *Généalogie des Comtes de Flandre*, 20, 54, 55, 57, 58, 70, 93, 94, 96, 118, 129, 177, 244, 247, 251, 329, 354, 411, 412, 415, 416, 429, 439, 456, 458, 460, 462, 464, 475, 478, 484, 498, 572, 574, 592, 616, 628, 629, 642.
VROOMBAUTS, *arms*, 161.
Vulnant, 708.
Vulned, 708.
Vulning, 708.
„ (Pelican), 264.
Vulture, The, 261.
VYVYAN, Baronet, *arms*, 534.

WACHTER, *arms*, 263.
WACKEN, ANTOINE, Seigneur de, *arms*, 575 ; Pl. XLVII., fig. 5, p. 574.
WADE, *arms*, 160.
WADSLEY, *arms*, 403.
WAELSCAPPEL, *arms*, 127.
WAES, *arms*, 184.
WAHLEN, *arms*, 272.
WAIDER, *arms*, 234.
WAKE, *knot*, 585.
„ of Lydel, *arms*, 420.
WALAIN, JEAN, Seigneur de, *arms*, 576.
WALDAU, VON, *arms*, 752.
WALDBURG, Princes von, *arms*, 341.
WALDECK, Counts of, 483 ; *arms*, 404, 490 ; Pl. XLI., fig. 6, p. 510.
„ Princes of, *arms*, 308, 488.
WALDEGRAVE, *arms*, 78 ; Pl. V., fig. 1, p. 80.
WALDENFELS, Barons von, *arms*, 297.
WALDERSEE, Counts, *arms*, 81.
WALES, ARTHUR, Prince of, 594.
„ *badge*, 597.
„ „ of Prince of, 264, 292, 591, 594.
„ *coronet* of Prince of, 500.
„ *crown* of Prince of, 619, 623.
„ EDWARD, Prince of, *label* of, 414.
„ FREDERICK, Prince of, 423.
„ HENRY, Prince of, 420.
„ „ „ *badge*, 594.
„ Prince of, 342.
„ „ *arms*, 131.
„ „ *label*, 414, 422, 423 ; Fig. 80, p. 421.
„ „ *mantling*, 613.
„ „ NORTH, *arms*, 224.
„ „ SOUTH, *arms*, 594.
„ Principality of, *arms*, 224.
„ *Red Dragon* of, 595, 662.

(855)

WALES, *supporters* in, 647.
WALEWSKI, Counts, *arms*, 363.
WALHEIM, Counts of, 576.
WALKINSHAW, *arms*, 315.
WALLACE, *arms*, 213, 565.
,, of Ellerslie, *arms*, 568.
,, ,, ,, *bordure*, 442.
,, Sir RICHARD, *arms*, 564.
WALLACHIA, *arms*, 667.
WALLENRODT, Counts, *arms*, 377.
WALLENSTEIN, *arms*, 92, 220.
,, *augmentation*, 538.
,, Duke of FRIEDLAND, *arms*, 92, 220.
WALLONCAPELLE, *arms*, 127.
WALLOP, *crest*, 302.
Walls, 362.
WALMODEN, Counts of, *arms*, 232.
Walnuts, 341.
WALSH, Counts, *arms*, 350.
WALSINGHAM, Lord, *arms*, 412.
,, Sir EDWARD, *arms*, 387.
WALTERS, LUCY, 559.
WALWORTH, Sir WILLIAM, 346.
WAMBRECHIES, *arms*, 142.
WAMIN, Marquis de, *arms*, 94.
WANCY, *arms*, 392.
WANGELIN, *arms*, 78.
Wappenrolle von Zürich, 55, 69, 73, 93, 94, 98, 120, 131, 138, 170, 184, 191, 213, 218, 222, 230, 236, 239, 240, 252, 256, 260, 265, 267, 288, 289, 320, 323, 325, 348, 361, 365, 370, 373, 382, 385, 392, 440, 469, 477, 593, 606, 614, 671; Pl. XLV., p. 540; Pl. XLVI., p. 546.
WARCOING, *arms*, 142.
WARD, *arms*, 153; Pl. XII., fig. 2, p. 130.
,, of Bexley, *arms*, 130.
,, Viscount BANGOR, *arms*, 157.
WARDEN, *arms*, 340.
Wardrobe Accounts, The, 590.
WARNBACH, *arms*, 94.
WAROQUIER, *arms*, 204, 714.
WARR, LA, 17.
WARREN, *arms*, 125, 531, 554; Pl. VII., fig. 6, p. 90.
,, JOHN DE, last Earl of SURREY, 554.
,, *label*, 418.
,, *mantling*, 613.
,, Sir JOHN DE (illegitimate), *arms*, 554.
,, WILLIAM DE, *arms*, 426.
WARRENNE, *arms*, 577.
WARRENS, Earls of SURREY, *arms*, 99.
Warrior as *supporter*, 632.
Wars of the Roses, 398.
WARTENBERG, Barons of, *arms*, 213.
,, ,, von, *arms*, 639.
,, Counts von, *arms*, 525.
,, *see* BRAUN.
WARTRE, Barons of, *arms*, 355.
WARWICK, Earl of, *arms*, 143, 163, 257, 408.
,, ,, *badge*, 585, 753.
,, ,, *Garter Plate*, 486.
,, THOMAS, Earl of, *lambrequin*, 612.
WARWIKE, Sir GUY, Earl of, *arms*, 21.
WASABORG, Counts of, *arms*, 581.
WASSELEY, *arms*, 161.
WASSENAER, VAN, *arms*, 307.
WASSERBURG, Count von, *arms*, 24.

WASTERLEY, *arms*, 161.
WASTINE, MONTMORENCY DE, *brisure*, 451.
Water, 312.
,, *bags*, 708.
,, *budget*, 355, 708; Pl. XXXI., fig. 12, p. 346.
WATERHOUSE, *arms*, 146.
WATKINS, *arms*, 348.
WATSON, *arms*, 316; Pl. XXVIII., fig. 8, p. 308.
,, of Saughton, *arms*, 313.
,, on PLANCHÉ'S *Roll*, 409.
Wattled, 708.
WATZDORFF, *arms*, 78.
WAUCHOPE of Niddry, *arms*, 342.
WAUNCY, *arms*, 392.
WAVRIN, Counts of, *arms*, 169.
,, *seal* and *arms* of HELLIN DE, 49.
,, ,, ,, ROBERT DE, 49.
Wavy, 708.
,, *line*, 76; Fig. 21, p. 75.
WAY, *arms*, 268; Pl. XXVI., fig. 6, p. 266.
WAYE, *arms*, 127.
Wear, 708.
Wearing apparel as charges, 392.
WEDDERBURN, *arms*, 325.
Weel, 708.
WEELE, *arms*, 261; Pl. XXV., fig. 6, p. 260.
WEERDE, VAN DE, *arms*, 118.
WEERT, DE, *arms*, 262.
WEILER, *arms*, 263.
Weir, 708.
WEISSENWOLFF, Counts of, *arms*, 228.
WELLES, *arms*, 212.
,, Lord, *badge*, 753.
WELLINGTON, Duke of, *augmentation*, 534.
WELLS, *arms*, 193.
WEMYSS, *arms*, 446.
WENCESLAS, Emperor, 252, 472.
WENDEN, Duchy of, *arms*, 288, 492.
WENDS, Principality of the, *arms*, 492.
WENTWORTH, Lord, *badge*, 753.
WENZESLAUS, Emperor, *counter-seal* of, 252.
WERDENBERG, *arms*, 373.
WERDENSTEIN, VON, *arms*, 98.
WERF, VAN DE, *arms*, 124.
WERIANT, *arms*, 365.
WERNIGERODE, Counts von, *arms*, 271.
WERTHEIM, *arms*, 447.
Wervels, 708.
WESEL, VAN, *arms*, 427.
WESEMAEL, Sire de, *arms*, 332, 405.
WESEMALE, GERARD of, *arms*, 405.
WESSEX, King of, *arms* assigned to, 156.
WEST, *arms*, Pl. XI., fig. 2, p. 124.
WESTCAPPEL, *arms*, 127.
WESTERBURG, *arms*, 447.
WESTERREICH, Counts von, *arms*, 87.
WESTHOFEN, *arms*, 380.
WESTLEY, *arms*, 161.
WESTMEATH, Marquises of, *arms*, 126.
WESTMINSTER ABBEY, 409, 479, 591, 594.
,, ,, Chapel of St. Paul in, 653.
,, Church of St. Peter, 291.

WESTMINSTER, Dukes of, *arms*, 342.
„ HENRY VII.'s chapel, 591.
WESTMORELAND, Earls of, *arms*, 143.
WESTON, Bishop, *arms*, 152.
WESTPHALIA, *arms*, 237, 663; Pl. XXIV., fig. 6, p. 236.
„ Duchy of, *arms*, 256.
WESTS, Earls DELAWARR, *arms*, 124.
Whale, The, 272.
WHALLEY ABBEY, *arms*, 272.
„ *arms*, 272.
WHARTON, *augmentation*, 532.
„ *badge*, 753.
„ THOMAS, Lord, *arms*, 376.
Wheat ear as a charge, 391.
„ -*sheaf* as a *badge*, 754.
„ *Sheaves*, 341.
Whirlpool, 193, 708.
WHISTLEFORD, *arms*, 80.
WHITEFORD of Miltoun, 436.
„ WALTER, *brisure*, 436.
WHITGREAVE, *arms*, Pl. XIV., fig. 3, p. 140.
„ *augmentation*, 533.
WHITHORSE, *arms*, 98.
WIASEMSKI, *arms*, 267.
WICHERS, *arms*, 340.
WIDVILLE, *arms*, 167.
„ Queen ELIZABETH, *arms*, 308.
WIED, Princes of, *arms*, 267.
„ „ von, *arms*, 126.
WIEDERHOLD, Barons von, *arms*, 236.
WIGMUR, *arms*, 131.
WIJER, Barons de, *arms*, 112.
WILBRAHAM, *arms*, 132; Pl. XII., fig. 7, p. 130.
WILDENBERG, *arms*, 289.
WILDENFELS, Lordship of, *arms*, 325, 488.
WILDENFINGEN, *arms*, 382.
WILDENVELS, *arms*, 223.
WILDT, DE, *arms*, 427.
WILHELM, Emperor of GERMANY, 630.
WILKIE, *arms*, 125.
WILKINSON, *arms*, 297.
WILL, *arms*, 197, 361.
WILLIAM I., THE CONQUEROR, King of ENGLAND, 29, 30; *crown* 618; Effigy of, 649.
„ II., RUFUS, King of ENGLAND, Effigy of, 649.
„ III., King of BRITAIN, 113; *arms*, Pl. LII., figs. 6 and 7, p. 662; *motto* of, 664.
„ IV., King of BRITAIN, 560, 663; *arms*, 237; Pl. LII., fig. 10, p. 662.
„ Count of HOLLAND, 245.
„ of BAVARIA, *seal* of Duke, 251.
„ of ORANGE, *coat* of, 662.
„ THE LION, King of SCOTLAND, 147, 443, 657.
WILLIAMS, *arms*, 333, 348; Pl. XXIII., fig. 6, p. 228.
„ of Thame, Lord, *arms*, 386.
„ -WYNNE, *arms*, 230.
WILLOUGHBY, *arms*, 96; Pl. VIII., fig. 5, p. 100.
„ *badge*, 753, 754.

WILLOUGHBY DE BROKE, *badge*, 754.
WILMOT, *arms*, Pl. IX., fig. 4, p. 108.
„ Earl of ROCHESTER, *arms*, 106, 107.
WINCHELSEA, Earls of, *arms*, 343.
WINCHESTER COLLEGE, *arms*, 334.
„ Earls of, *arms*, 184.
„ Marquess of, *arms*, 347.
„ See of, *arms*, 264.
WINDISCHE-MARK, 374.
„ „ *arms*, 503.
WINDSOR, *arms*, 143.
„ *badge*, 754.
„ Lord, *badge*, 753.
„ Stall Plates at, 602, 612, 613.
WINDYGATE (?), *arms*, 365.
Wing as a *crest*, 600.
Winged, 708.
Wings, Pl. XXV., fig. 5, p. 260.
„ as *crests*, 606, 607.
„ (of bat) as a *badge*, 754.
WINNEBERG, Lordship of, *arms*, 492.
WINTON, DE, 16.
WINWOOD, *arms*, 160; Pl. XIV., fig. 11, p. 140.
WISE, *arms*, 285.
WISEMAN, *arms*, 348.
WISHART, *arms*, 147, 517.
WISHARTS, erroneously styled Lords of BRECHIN, 147.
„ of Brechin (?), *arms*, 516.
WITH, DE, *arms*, 289, 297.
„ OLIVER DE, *arms*, 289.
WITTGENSTEIN, Counts von, *arms*, 122.
WITZLEBEN, Barons von, *arms*, 98.
WLADISLAS, King of BOHEMIA, *crown*, 621.
WLADISLAW III., *seal*, 468.
„ JAGELLON, *seal*, 468.
„ LOKIELET, King, *seal*, 468.
WODEWARD, JOHN, 605.
WOERDEN, *arms*, 183.
WOESTINE, LOUIS LE FRISON, Seigneur de, 572, 573.
WOESTWYNCKELE, *arms*, 186.
WOHNSFLETH, *arms*, 229.
Wolf as a *badge*, 754.
„ The, 228.
WOLF, DE, *arms*, 228.
WOLFFENBÜTTEL, MAGNUS II. of, *arms*, 472.
„ WILLIAM of, *arms*, 472.
WOLFFSTHAL, Counts of, 228.
WOLKENSTEIN, Counts, *arms*, 137.
WOLLASTON, *arms*, 309; Pl. XXVIII., fig. 7, p. 308.
WOLLSTONECROFT, *arms*, 301.
WOLRYCHE, *arms*, 262; Pl. XXV., fig. 10, p. 260.
WOLSELEY, *arms*, Pl. XXIV., fig. 9, p. 236.
„ Viscount, *arms*, 241.
WOLTHERS, *arms*, 236.
Wolves' heads, Pl. XXIII., fig. 3, p. 228.
Woman, demi-, as a *crest*, 605.
WONZ, *arms*, 275.
WOOD, *arms*, Pl. XXIX., fig. 1, p. 318.
„ of Balbegno, *arms*, 313, 316.
„ „ Hareston, *arms*, 316.
WOODFORD, *arms*, 226.
Woodlouse, 285.
Woodman, 708.

(857)

WOODSTOCK, *badge*, 754.
,, EDMUND of, 589.
WOODVILLE, ANTHONY, Lord SCALES, 574 ; Pl. XVIII., fig. 3, p. 190.
,, ELIZABETH, *arms*, 167.
WOODWARD, *arms*, 187, 233, 259, 285, 319.
,, *crest*, 605.
,, J., *Ecclesiastical Heraldry*, 526, 646.
,, ,, *Heraldry of Bristol, Cathedral*, 303, 408.
,, ,, *Heraldry of Spain and Portugal*, 62, 131, 135, 143, 174, 275, 317, 353.
WORACZICSKY-BISINGEN, Counts, *arms*, 82.
WORCESTER, Battle of, 316, 532.
,, Cathedral, Chantry Chapel in, 594.
,, Earl of, 556.
Words, Pl. XXXIII., fig. 12, p. 376.
,, as charges, 394.
WORDSWORTH, *arms*, 373.
WORKMAN'S MS., 84, 148, 365, 402.
Worms, 279.
WORSLEY, *arms*, 118.
WORTLEY, *arms*, 403.
WOUTERS, *arms*, 132.
WRANGEL, Count von, *eagles* of, 544.
WRATISLAW, Counts VON, *arms*, 79.
WRAZDA DE KUNWALD, Barons, *arms* and augmentation, 540.
Wreath, 599, 708.
,, Variety of use of, 613.
Wreathed, 708.
Wreaths, 536, 611.
WREDE, Count, *arms*, 33
WREE (*see* VREE).
WRIGHT, *arms*, 569.
WROTON, *arms*, 147 ; Pl. XVI., fig. 6, p. 146.
WROTTESLEY, *arms*, 426.
,, Descent of Lord, 399.
WULF, DE, *arms*, 238.
WULFER, *arms*, 236.
WUNHALE, *arms*, 379.
WURMBRAND, Counts von, *arms*, 292.
WURSTER, *arms*, 228.
WÜRTTEMBERG, *arms*, 524, 668, 727.
,, Duke ALEXANDER of, 524.
,, Dukes of, *arms*, 352.
WYATT, *arms*, 357 ; Pl. XXXII., fig. 1, p. 358.
WYCOMBE, *arms*, 220 ; Pl. XXII., fig. 1, p. 222.
WYER, Baron de, *arms*, 331.
WYL, VAN, *arms*, 94.
WYLCOTE, Sir JOHN, *lambrequin*, 613.
WYNDHAM, *crest*, 563.
WYNEGHAM, Count de, *arms*, 183.
WYNN, *arms*, 200, 213, 333.
WYNNE, WILLIAMS, *arms*, 230.
WYNTWORTH, *arms*, 152.
WYOT, *arms*, 357.
WYRLEY, *True Use of Armorie*, 2, 426.
WYSS, *arms*, 298.
WYTHE, *arms*, 289.
Wyvern, The, 292, 708 ; Pl. XXVII., fig. 8, p. 288.
WYVILL, *arms*, 140 ; Pl. XIII., fig. 12, p. 136.

XAINTRAILLES, *arms*, 153.
XERICA, JAMES of, *arms*, 577.
XIMENEZ, *arms*, 66.

YAIR, *arms*, 518.
YARDLEY, *arms*, 241.
YARE, *arms*, Pl. XXVIII., fig. 12, p. 308.
YEROPKIN, *arms*, 267.
YNAIS, WILLIAM DE, *badge*, 583.
YOENS, *arms*, 93.
YON, *see* ROCHE.
YORK and ALBANY, CHARLES, Duke of, *label*, 420.
,, ,, LANCASTER, combined rose of, 595.
,, *arms* of See, 375.
,, *badge* of Royal House of, 324, 587, 588, 591.
,, Duchess of, 590.
,, Dukes of, 416, 530.
,, EDMOND of Langley, Duke of, *label*, 420, 421.
,, FREDERICK, Duke of, *label*, 422.
,, HENRY, Duke of, *label*, 420.
,, ,, TUDOR, Duke of, *label*, 421.
,, House of, *arms*, 557.
,, JAMES STUART, Duke of, *label*, 421.
,, Queen ELIZABETH of, *arms*, 479 ; Pl. XXXVIII., fig. 4, p. 464.
,, RICHARD, Duke of, *arms*, 485.
,, *Roses* of, 532.
,, *seal* of EDWARD, Duke of, 593.
,, *White rose* of, 588, 613.
YORKIST *badge*, 591.
YOUGHAL, *arms*, Pl. XXXVIII., fig. 5, p. 464.
,, Lord of, 467.
,, Town and Provosts of, 467.
YOUNG, Sir JOHN, *arms*, 149.
,, WILLIAM, *arms*, 150.
YRUSTA, *arms*, 353.
YSARN, 12.
YSEMBART, *supporter*, 304.
YSSOUDUN, Town of, *arms*, 150.
YVE, *arms*, 122.
YVES, *see* CARTIER.
YVOR, *arms*, 153.

ZABIELLO, Counts, *arms*, 348.
ZACHARY of Areleykings, *arms*, 562.
ZACHREISS, *arms*, 394.
ZAHRINGEN, BERCHTOLD IV. VON, *shield*, Pl. I., fig. 7, p. 54.
,, Dukes of, *arms*, 214.
ZALEWSKI, Counts, *arms*, 234.
ZALLONI, *arms*, 371.
ZAMOISKY, *arms*, 347.
ZANCHINI, *arms*, 354.
ZANGIACOMI, Barons, *arms*, 317.
ZANI, *arms*, 230.
ZAPATA, *arms*, 392.
ZAPOL-ZAPOLSKI, Counts, *arms*, 356.
ZARA, Duchy, *arms*, 503.
ZATOR, Duchy, *arms*, 504.
ZAVALA, *arms*, 122.
ZEDLITZ, Barons and Counts, *arms*, 377.
ZEDWITZ, Counts von, *arms*, 87.
ZENO, *arms*, 95.
ZEROTIN, House of, *arms*, 256.

ZERRES, *arms*, 133.
ZGRAIA, *arms*, 66.
ZMODSKI, *arms*, 349.
ZOLLERN, *arms*, 454.
ZON, *arms*, 305.
ZORN, *arms* and *crests*, 601.
ZOTRA, *arms*, 129.
ZOUCHE, *arms*, 192, 426 ; Pl. XIX., fig. 2, p. 192.
,, LA, *badge*, 753.
,, Sir WILLIAM DE LA, *arms*, 167.
ZUG, Canton of, *arms*, 123.
Zules, 721.

ZULESTEIN, FREDERICK, Lord of, *arms*, 580.
,, Lordship of, *arms*, 580.
ZUÑIGA, *arms*, 353.
ZUYLEN, 721.
ZUR SUNNEN, *arms*, 138.
ZÜRICH, *arms* and *supporter*, 640.
,, Canton of, *arms*, 80.
ZUSTO, *arms*, Pl. V., fig. 3, p. 80.
ZUTPHEN, Counts of, *arms*, 214.
ZUYLEN, *arms*, 388.
,, as charges, 388.
ZYPŒUS, *de Notitia juris Belgici*, 396, 637.

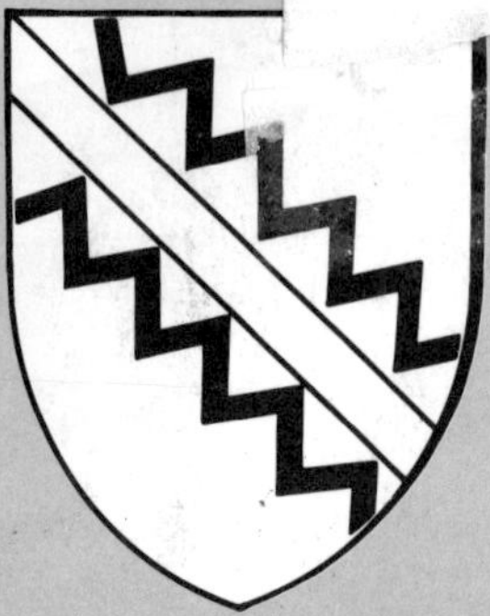

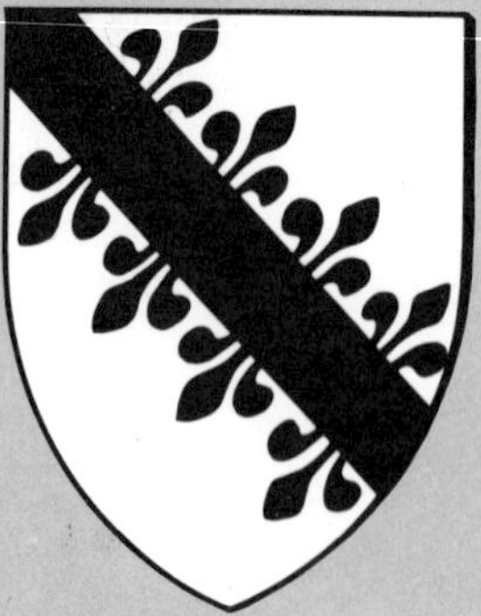

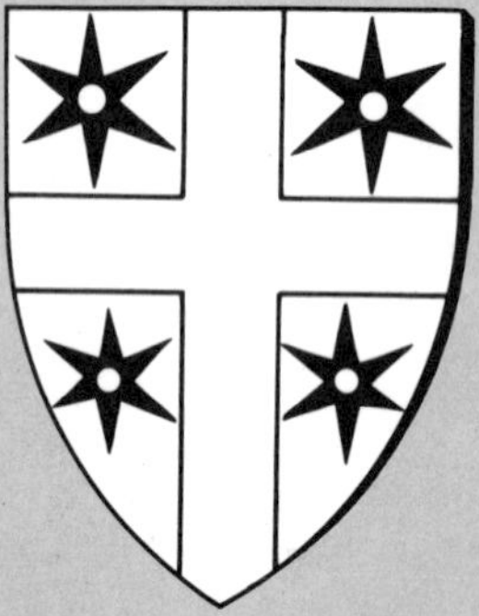

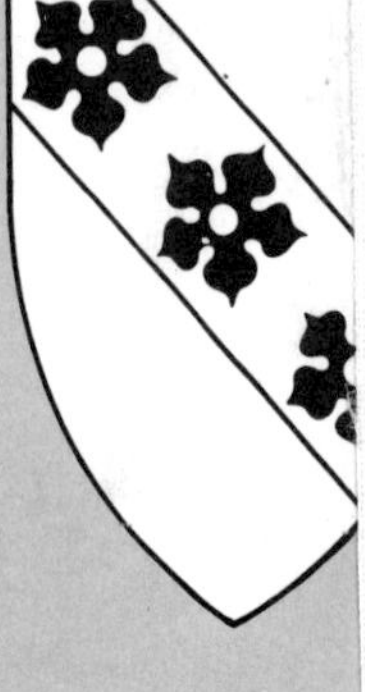